SO-BCN-951

Rick Steves'

MEDITERRANEAN CRUISE PORTS

Rick Steves with Cameron Hewitt

CONTENTS

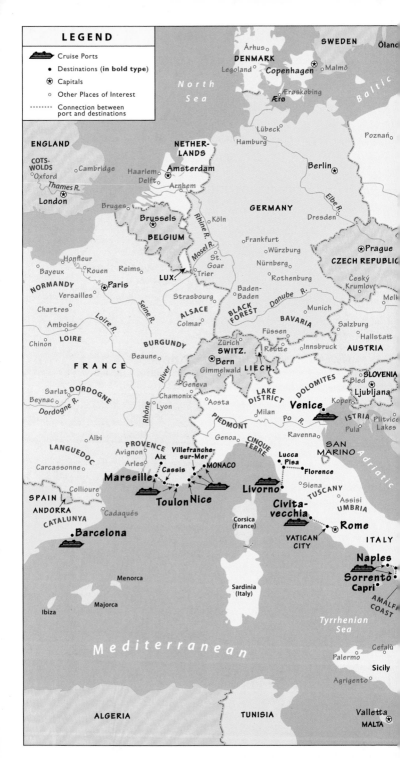

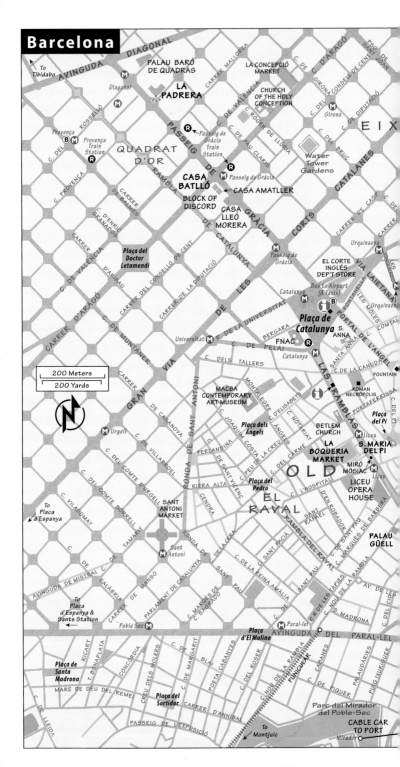

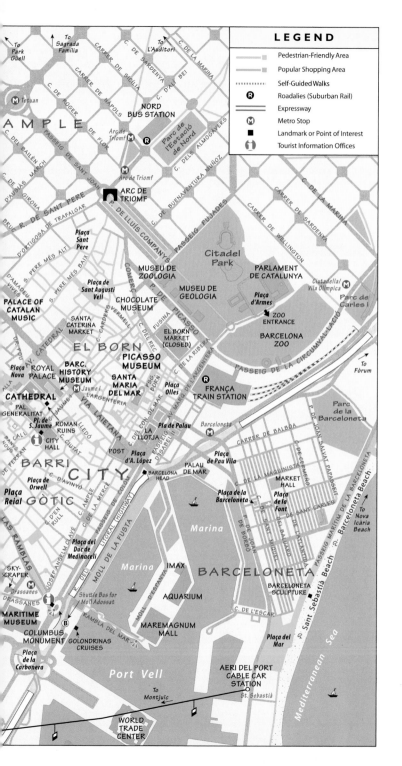

LEGEND

	Pedestrian-Friendly Area
	Popular Shopping Area
··········	Self-Guided Walks
Ⓡ	Roadalies (Suburban Rail)
	Expressway
Ⓜ	Metro Stop
■	Landmark or Point of Interest
🛈	Tourist Information Offices

To Park Güell

To Sagrada Familia

To L'Auditori

C. DE SARDENYA

C. DE SICILIA

CARRER DE NÁPOLS

C. DE ROGER DE FLOR

C. DALI BEI

C. DE LA MARINA

Ⓜ Tetuan

A M P L E

C. DEL BAILEN

PASSEIG DE SANT JOAN

C. DE NÁPOLS

NORD BUS STATION

Arc de Triomf Ⓜ Ⓡ

Parc de l'Estació de Nord

C. DELS ALMOGÀVERS

CARRER DE LA MARINA

C. DE LES MÉS MARCH

D'AVINYÓ GIRONA

PASSEIG DE SANT PERE

Arc de Triomf Ⓜ

■ ARC DE TRIOMF

PG. DE LLUIS COMPANYS

C. DE BUENAVENTURA MUÑOZ

CARRER DE SARDENYA

BRUC R. DE SANT PERE

D'ORTIGOSA DE TRAFALGAR

Plaça Sant Pere

PASSEIG PUJADES

CARRER DE WELLINGTON

S. PERE MÉS ALT

S. PERE MÉS BAIX

Plaça de Sant Augustí Vell

COMERÇ

MUSEU DE ZOOLOGIA

Citadel Park

PARLAMENT DE CATALUNYA

Ciutadella/ Vila Olímpica Ⓜ

D'AMADEU VIVES

CHOCOLATE MUSEUM

P. DE PICASSO

MUSEU DE GEOLOGIA

Plaça d'Armes

Parc de Carles I

PALACE OF CATALAN MUSIC

CARDERS VERMELL

C. DEL REC

FUSINA

ZOO ENTRANCE

SANTA CATERINA MARKET

EL BORN MARKET (CLOSED)

BARCELONA ZOO

V. CATEDRAL

EL BORN

PSG. BORN

C. DE LA RIBERA

PASSEIG DE LA CIRCUMVAL·LACIÓ

To Fòrum

Plaça Nova

ROYAL PALACE

BARC. HISTORY MUSEUM

PICASSO MUSEUM

SANTA MARIA DEL MAR

AV. MARQUÉS DE L'ARGENTERA

CATHEDRAL

L'ARGENTERA

Plaça Olles

Ⓡ

PAL. GENERALITAT

Ⓜ Jaume I

VIA LAIETANA

FRANÇA TRAIN STATION

Pl. de S. Jaume

CALL

ROMAN RUINS

C. DEL CONSOLAT DE MAR

Parc de la Barceloneta

🛈 CITY HALL

LLEDO

Pla de Palau

Barceloneta Ⓜ

DE FERRAN

POST

Plaça d'A. López

CARRER DE BALBOA

B A R R I

LA LLOTJA

PALAU DE MAR

Plaça de Pau Vila

P. DE JOAN SALVAT PAPASSEIT

C I T Y

D'AVINYÓ

BARCELONA HEAD

PASSEIG D'ISABEL II

DE LA MAQUINISTA

R. DE LA BARCELONETA

Plaça de Orwell

Plaça Reial

G Ò T I C

C. D'EN RULL

C. AMPLE

C. DE LA MERCÈ

Plaça de la Barceloneta

MARKET HALL

Plaça de la Font

LAS RAMBLAS

JOSEP ANGLÍ M CLAVÉ

Plaça del Duc de Medinaceli

LITORAL (HIGHWAY)

Marina

DE SANT CARLES

DEL BALUARD

DE SANT MIQUEL

To Nova Icària Beach

SKY-SCRAPER

Ⓜ Drassanes

IMAX

BARCELONA

DE BORBÓ

P. DE JOAN

DE L'ATLANTIDA

DE LA BARCELONETA

Sant Sebastià Beach

Barceloneta Beach

MARITIME MUSEUM

DRASSANES

🛈

Ⓑ

Marina

AQUARIUM

BARCELONETA SCULPTURE

R. DE LA BARCELONETA

PASSEIG MARITIM

DE LA BARCELONETA

Mediterranean Sea

COLUMBUS MONUMENT

GOLONDRINAS CRUISES

Shuttle Bus for Moll Adossat

RAMBLA DEL MAR

MAREMAGNUM MALL

MOLL D'ESPANYA

C. DE L'ESCAR

Plaça del Mar

Plaça de la Carbonera

Port Vell

AERI DEL PORT CABLE CAR STATION

To Montjuïc

St. Sebastià

WORLD TRADE CENTER

Florence

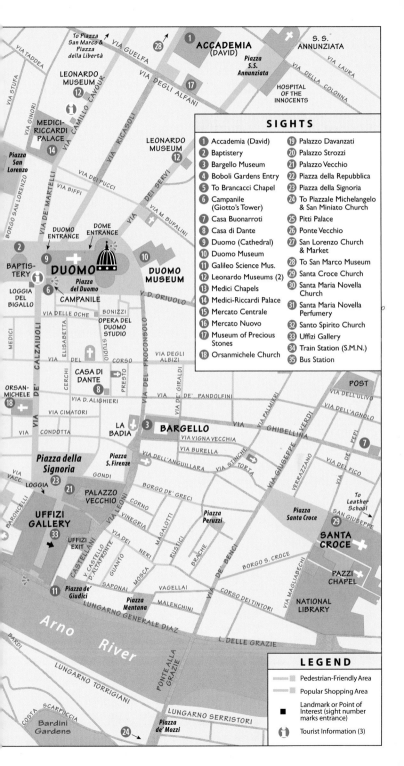

SIGHTS

1 Accademia (David)	19 Palazzo Davanzati
2 Baptistery	20 Palazzo Strozzi
3 Bargello Museum	21 Palazzo Vecchio
4 Boboli Gardens Entry	22 Piazza della Repubblica
5 To Brancacci Chapel	23 Piazza della Signoria
6 Campanile (Giotto's Tower)	24 To Piazzale Michelangelo & San Miniato Church
7 Casa Buonarroti	25 Pitti Palace
8 Casa di Dante	26 Ponte Vecchio
9 Duomo (Cathedral)	27 San Lorenzo Church & Market
10 Duomo Museum	28 To San Marco Museum
11 Galileo Science Mus.	29 Santa Croce Church
12 Leonardo Museums (2)	30 Santa Maria Novella Church
13 Medici Chapels	31 Santa Maria Novella Perfumery
14 Medici-Riccardi Palace	32 Santo Spirito Church
15 Mercato Centrale	33 Uffizi Gallery
16 Mercato Nuovo	34 Train Station (S.M.N.)
17 Museum of Precious Stones	35 Bus Station
18 Orsanmichele Church	

LEGEND

- Pedestrian-Friendly Area
- Popular Shopping Area
- ■ Landmark or Point of Interest (sight number marks entrance)
- Tourist Information (3)

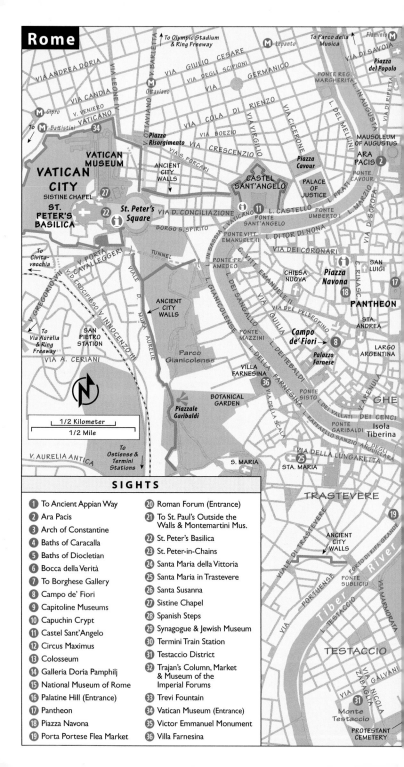

Rome

SIGHTS

1. To Ancient Appian Way
2. Ara Pacis
3. Arch of Constantine
4. Baths of Caracalla
5. Baths of Diocletian
6. Bocca della Verità
7. To Borghese Gallery
8. Campo de' Fiori
9. Capitoline Museums
10. Capuchin Crypt
11. Castel Sant'Angelo
12. Circus Maximus
13. Colosseum
14. Galleria Doria Pamphilj
15. National Museum of Rome
16. Palatine Hill (Entrance)
17. Pantheon
18. Piazza Navona
19. Porta Portese Flea Market
20. Roman Forum (Entrance)
21. To St. Paul's Outside the Walls & Montemartini Mus.
22. St. Peter's Basilica
23. St. Peter-in-Chains
24. Santa Maria della Vittoria
25. Santa Maria in Trastevere
26. Santa Susanna
27. Sistine Chapel
28. Spanish Steps
29. Synagogue & Jewish Museum
30. Termini Train Station
31. Testaccio District
32. Trajan's Column, Market & Museum of the Imperial Forums
33. Trevi Fountain
34. Vatican Museum (Entrance)
35. Victor Emmanuel Monument
36. Villa Farnesina

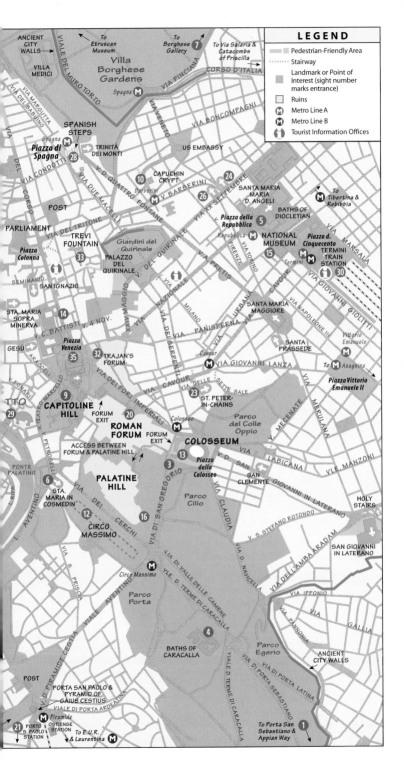

Pedestrian-Friendly Area

Stairway

Landmark or Point of Interest (sight number marks entrance)

Ruins

Ⓜ Metro Line A

Ⓜ Metro Line B

Tourist Information Offices

ANCIENT CITY WALLS

VILLA MEDICI

To Etruscan Museum

Villa Borghese Gardens

To Borghese Gallery ➆

To Via Salaria & Catacombs of Priscilla

CORSO D'ITALIA

VIALE DEL MURO TORTO

VIA DI MEL BABUINO

VIA MARGUTTA

Spagna Ⓜ

VIA PINCIANA

VIA VENETO

VIA BONCOMPAGNI

SPANISH STEPS

Spagna

Piazza di Spagna ㉘

TRINITÀ DEI MONTI

US EMBASSY

VIA CONDOTTI

VIA DUE MACELLI

VIA D. QUATTRO FONTANE

CAPUCHIN CRYPT ⑩

Barberini V. BARBERINI ㉖

㉔ SANTA MARIA MARIA D. ANGELI

VIA XX SETTEMBRE

BATHS OF DIOCLETIAN

To Ⓜ Tibertina & Rebibbia

POST

PARLIAMENT

VIA DEL TRITONE

Piazza Colonna

TREVI FOUNTAIN ㉝

Giardini del Quirinale

PALAZZO DEL QUIRINALE

V. DEL QUIRINALE

Piazza della Repubblica ⑤

Repubblica Ⓜ

NATIONAL MUSEUM ⑮

Termini Ⓜ

Piazza d. Cinquecento

TERMINI TRAIN STATION

VIA MARSALA

㉚

VIA GIOVANNI GIOLITTI

SEMINARIO

SAN IGNAZIO

VIA NAZIONALE

VIA A. PRETIS

FIRENZE

VIA TORINO

VIA GIOVANNI GIOLITTI

STA. MARIA SOPRA MINERVA ⑭

V. C. BATTISTI V. 4 NOV.

GESÙ

VIA C. BATTISTI

VIA DEI SERPENTI

MILANO

VIA PANISPERNA

VIA URBANA

SANTA MARIA MAGGIORE

VIA CAVOUR

VIA NAPOLEONE III

Vittorio Emanuele Ⓜ

Piazza Venezia ㉟

㉜ TRAJAN'S FORUM

ARACOELI

V. TEATRO MARCELLO

VIA DEI FORI IMPERIALI

Cavour Ⓜ

VIA GIOVANNI LANZA

SANTA PRASSEDE

To Ⓜ Anagnina

Piazza Vittorio Emanuele II

V. FUNARI

TTO

㉙

⑨ CAPITOLINE HILL

FORUM EXIT

ROMAN FORUM

FORUM EXIT ⑳

VIA CAVOUR

VIA DELLE SETTE SALE

ST. PETER-IN-CHAINS ㉓

V. MECENATE

MERULANA

V. PETROSELLI

⑥ STA. MARIA IN COSMEDIN

ACCESS BETWEEN FORUM & PALATINE HILL

③ Colosseo Ⓜ

COLOSSEUM ⑬

Piazza della Colosseo

V. D. SAN

VIA LABICANA

HOLY STAIRS

PONTE PALATINO

L. AVENTINO

PALATINE HILL

VIA DI SAN GREGORIO

VIA DEI CERCHI

⑫

⑯

CIRCO MASSIMO

Parco del Colle Oppio

SAN CLEMENTE

SAN GIOVANNI IN LATERANO

VIA CLAUDIA

VYLE MANZONI

VIA S. STEFANO ROTONDO

SAN GIOVANNI IN LATERANO

VIA PRISCA

VIA S. AVENTINO

Circo Massimo Ⓜ

Parco Cilio

VIA DI VALLE DELLE CAMENE

VYLE D. TERME DI CARACALLA

Parco Porta

VIA DELL'AMBA ARADAM

VIA IPPONIO

VIA PANNONIA

VIA GALLIA

BATHS OF CARACALLA ④

Parco Egerio

ANCIENT CITY WALLS

POST

PORTA SAN PAOLO & PYRAMID OF GAIUS CESTIUS

VIALE DI PORTA ARDEATINA

Piramide

OSTIENSE STATION

PORTO S. PAOLO STATION ㉑

To E.U.R. & Laurentina Ⓜ

VIA D. PIRAMIDE CESTIA VIALE AVENTINO

VIALE D. TERME DI CARACALLA

VIALE DI PORTA LATINA

VIA DI PORTA LATINA

VIA DI PORTA SEBASTIANO

To Porta San Sebastiano & Appian Way ①

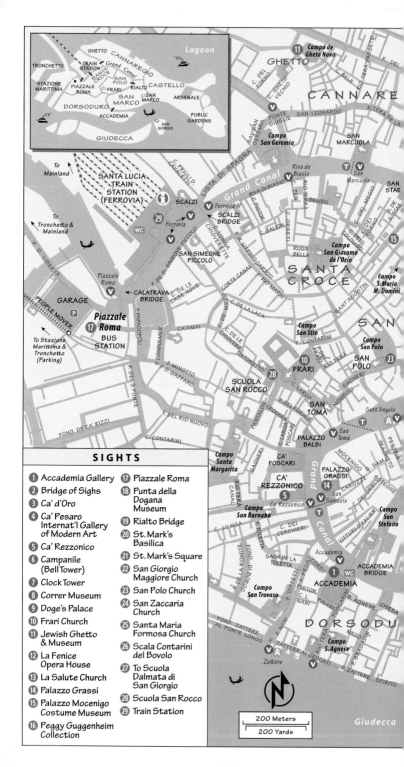

Inset map labels:
GHETTO · CANNAREGIO · Lagoon · TRONCHETTO · Train Station · Grand Canal · RIALTO · CASTELLO · STAZIONE MARITTIMA · PIAZZALE ROMA · SANTA CROCE · SAN POLO · FRARI · DORSODURO · SAN MARCO · SAN MARCO · ACCADEMIA · ARSENALE · SAN GIORGIO · PUBLIC GARDENS · GIUDECCA

Main map labels:
To Mainland · SANTA LUCIA TRAIN STATION (FERROVIA) · SCALZI · Ferrovia W · SCALZI BRIDGE · Grand Canal · Riva de Biasio · SAN · Marcuola · SAN STAE · To Tronchetto & Mainland · Ferrovia · SAN SIMEONE PICCOLO · LISTA DI SPAGNA · GHETTO · Campo de Gheto Novo · CANNARE · SAN LEONARDO · Campo San Geremia · SAN MARCUOLA · Campo San Giacomo de l'Orio · SANTA CROCE · Campo S.Maria M. Domini · SAN · P. D. LIBERTÀ · PEOPLE MOVER · GARAGE · To Stazione Marittima & Tronchetto (Parking) · Piazzale Roma · CALATRAVA BRIDGE · BUS STATION · Campo San Stin · Campo San Polo · FRARI · SAN POLO · SCUOLA SAN ROCCO · Campo Santa Margarita · CA' FOSCARI · CA' REZZONICO · Campo San Barnaba · SAN TOMÀ · PALAZZO BALBI · PALAZZO GRASSI · PALAZZO MOCENIGO · Campo San Stefano · Campo San Trovaso · ACCADEMIA · ACCADEMIA BRIDGE · DORSODU · Campo S.Agnese · Zattere · Giudecca

200 Meters
200 Yards

N

SIGHTS

1. Accademia Gallery
2. Bridge of Sighs
3. Ca' d'Oro
4. Ca' Pesaro Internat'l Gallery of Modern Art
5. Ca' Rezzonico
6. Campanile (Bell Tower)
7. Clock Tower
8. Correr Museum
9. Doge's Palace
10. Frari Church
11. Jewish Ghetto & Museum
12. La Fenice Opera House
13. La Salute Church
14. Palazzo Grassi
15. Palazzo Mocenigo Costume Museum
16. Peggy Guggenheim Collection
17. Piazzale Roma
18. Punta della Dogana Museum
19. Rialto Bridge
20. St. Mark's Basilica
21. St. Mark's Square
22. San Giorgio Maggiore Church
23. San Polo Church
24. San Zaccaria Church
25. Santa Maria Formosa Church
26. Scala Contarini del Bovolo
27. To Scuola Dalmata di San Giorgio
28. Scuola San Rocco
29. Train Station

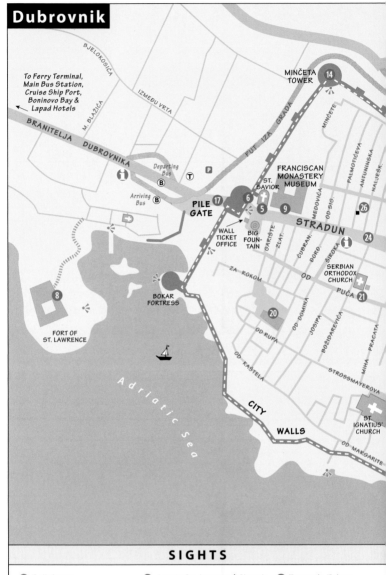

Dubrovnik

To Ferry Terminal,
Main Bus Station,
Cruise Ship Port,
Boninovo Bay &
Lapad Hotels

BJELOKOSIĆA

IZMEĐU VRTA

BRANITELJA DUBROVNIKA

M. BLAŽIĆA

PUT IZA GRADA

MINČETA
TOWER

MINČETE

Departing
Bus

Arriving
Bus

PILE
GATE

WALL
TICKET
OFFICE

BIG
FOUN-
TAIN

FRANCISCAN
MONASTERY
MUSEUM

ST.
SAVIOR

STRADUN

GARIŠTE

ZLAT.

ČUBRAN.

MEDOVIĆA

OD SIG.

PALMOTIĆEVA

ANTUNINSKA

NALJEŠK.

BOKAR
FORTRESS

ZA ROKOM

OD

SIROKA

ĐORĐ.

PUČA

SERBIAN
ORTHODOX
CHURCH

FORT OF
ST. LAWRENCE

OD DOMINA

OD RUPA

OD KAŠTELA

JOSIPA

BOŽIDAREVIĆA

STROSSMAYEROVA

MIHA

PRACATA

Adriatic Sea

CITY

WALLS

OD MARGARITE

ST.
IGNATIUS'
CHURCH

SIGHTS

1. Bell Tower
2. Buža Gate
3. Cable Car
4. Cathedral
5. Church of St. Savior
6. City Wall Entrances (3)
7. Dominican Monastery
   Museum & Church
8. Fort of St. Lawrence
9. Franciscan Monastery
   Museum & Church

10. Jesuit St. Ignatius' Church
11. Lazareti (Old
    Quarantine Building)
12. Luža Square &
    Orlando's Column
13. Maritime Museum &
    Aquarium
14. Minčeta Tower
15. To Museum of Modern Art
16. Old Port
17. Pile Gate
18. Ploče Gate

19. Rector's Palace
20. Rupe Granary &
    Ethnographic Museum
21. Serbian Orthodox
    Church & Icon Museum
22. Sponza Palace &
    Memorial Room of
    Dubrovnik Defenders
23. St. Blaise's Church
24. Stradun (a.k.a. Placa)
25. Synagogue Museum
26. War Photo Limited

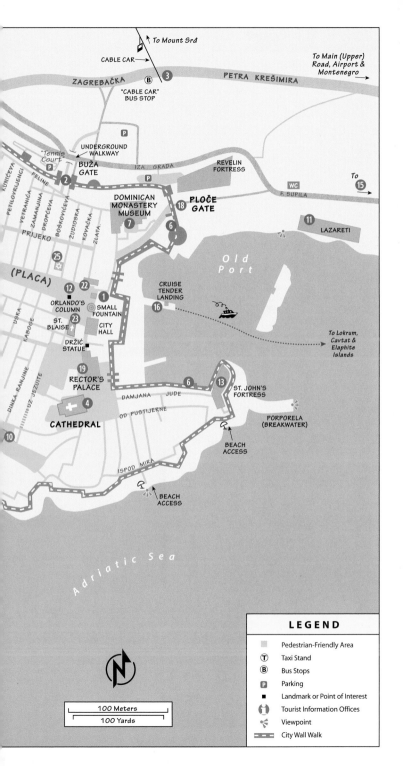

To Mount Srđ

CABLE CAR

ZAGREBAČKA

B **3**

"CABLE CAR" BUS STOP

PETRA KREŠIMIRA

To Main (Upper) Road, Airport & Montenegro

P

UNDERGROUND WALKWAY

"Tennis Court"

P

KUNIĆEVA
PETILOVRIJENCI
VETRANIĆA
ZAMANJINA
DROPČEVA
PELINE

2

BUŽA GATE

IZA GRADA

REVELIN FORTRESS

P

WC

To **15**

F. SUPILA

BOŠKOVIĆEVA
ŽUDIOSKA
KOVAČKA
ZLATA

PRIJEKO

DOMINICAN MONASTERY MUSEUM

7

18

PLOČE GATE

6

11

LAZARETI

Old Port

25

(PLAČA)

12 **22**

ORLANDO'S COLUMN

1

SMALL FOUNTAIN

CITY HALL

CRUISE TENDER LANDING

16

USKA
KABOGE

ST. BLAISE

23

DRŽIĆ STATUE

To Lokrum, Cavtat & Elaphite Islands

DINKA RANJINE
UZ JEZUITE

19

RECTOR'S PALACE

4

CATHEDRAL

DAMJANA JUDE

6

13

ST. JOHN'S FORTRESS

10

OD PUSTIJERNE

PORPORELA (BREAKWATER)

BEACH ACCESS

ISPOD MIRA

BEACH ACCESS

Adriatic Sea

N

100 Meters

100 Yards

LEGEND

Pedestrian-Friendly Area

T Taxi Stand

B Bus Stops

P Parking

■ Landmark or Point of Interest

Tourist Information Offices

Viewpoint

City Wall Walk

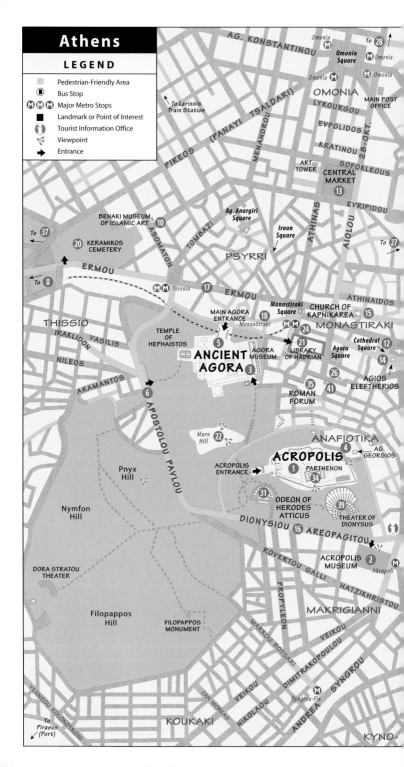

SIGHTS

1. Acropolis
2. Acropolis Museum
3. Agora Museum
4. Anafiotika Neighborhood
5. Ancient Agora
6. Apostolou Pavlou Street
7. Arch of Hadrian
8. To Benaki Cultural Center
9. Benaki Museum of Greek History & Culture
10. Benaki Mus. of Islamic Art
11. Byzantine & Christian Mus.
12. Cathedral (Mitropolis)
13. Central Market
14. Church of Agios Eleftherios
15. Church of Kapnikarea
16. Dionysiou Areopagitou St.
17. Ermou Street
18. Flea Market
19. Jewish Museum
20. Keramikos Cemetery
21. Library of Hadrian
22. Mars Hill (Areopagus)
23. Museum of Cycladic Art
24. Museum of Greek Folk Art (Ceramics)
25. Museum of Greek Folk Art (Main)
26. Museum of Greek Popular Instruments
27. To Mus. of the City of Athens
28. To National Archaeological Museum & Exarchia District
29. National Garden
30. National War Museum
31. Odeon of Herodes Atticus
32. Panathenaic (Olympic) Stadium
33. Parliament
34. Parthenon
35. Roman Forum
36. Syntagma Square
37. To Technopolis & Gazi District
38. Temple of Olympian Zeus
39. Theater of Dionysus
40. Tomb of the Unknown Soldier & Evzone Guards
41. Tower of the Winds
42. Zappeion

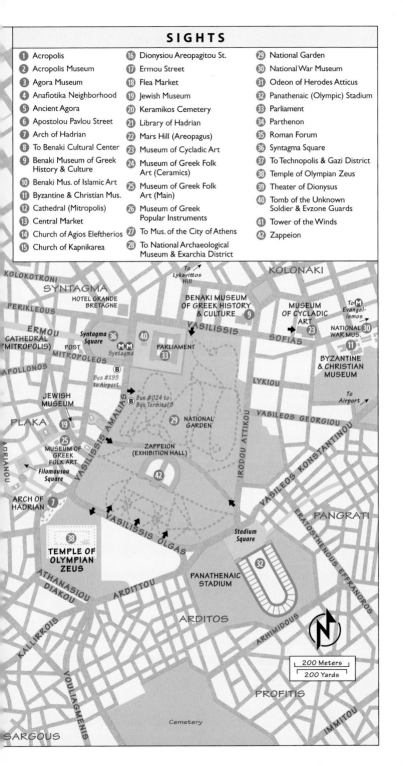

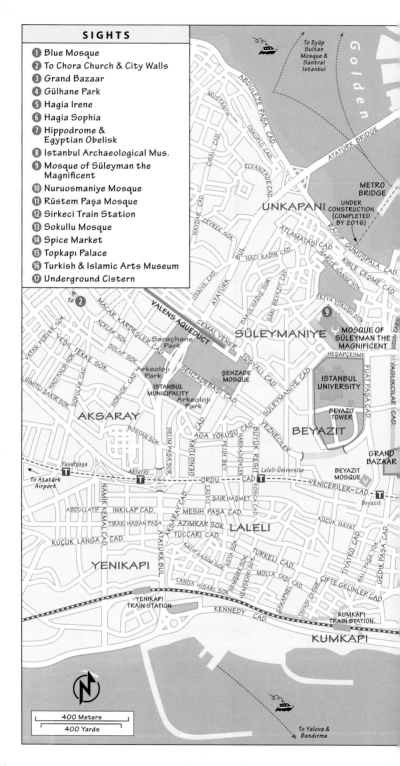

SIGHTS

1. Blue Mosque
2. To Chora Church & City Walls
3. Grand Bazaar
4. Gülhane Park
5. Hagia Irene
6. Hagia Sophia
7. Hippodrome & Egyptian Obelisk
8. Istanbul Archaeological Mus.
9. Mosque of Süleyman the Magnificent
10. Nuruosmaniye Mosque
11. Rüstem Paşa Mosque
12. Sirkeci Train Station
13. Sokullu Mosque
14. Spice Market
15. Topkapı Palace
16. Turkish & Islamic Arts Museum
17. Underground Cistern

400 Meters
400 Yards

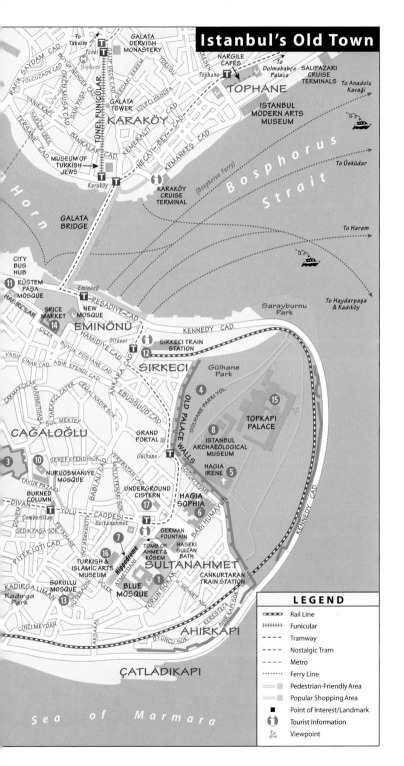

Istanbul's Old Town

To Taksim
GALATA DERVISH MONASTERY
NARGILE CAFÉS
To Dolmabahçe Palace
SALIPAZARI CRUISE TERMINALS
To Anadolu Kavaği
TOPHANE
ISTANBUL MODERN ARTS MUSEUM

RAFIK SAYDAM CAD.
YOLCUZADE CAD.
BÜYÜK HENDEK CAD.
TÜNEL FUNICULAR
OKÇUMUSA CAD.
ŞAIR ZIYA PAŞA CAD.
SERDAR-I EKREM
YÜKSEK
YANIK KAPI
SAZLI BEK
BANKALAR CAD.
GALATA TOWER
KARAKÖY
EMERALTI
LÜLECI HENDEK CAD.
NECATI-BEY CAD.
KEMANKEŞ CAD.

MUSEUM OF TURKISH JEWS
Karaköy
KARAKÖY CRUISE TERMINAL

Horn
(Bosphorus Ferry)
Bosphorus Strait
To Üsküdar

GALATA BRIDGE
To Harem

CITY BUS HUB
RÜSTEM PAŞA MOSQUE
HACIRCILAR
Eminönü
SPICE MARKET
NEW MOSQUE
EMINÖNÜ
ÇİÇEK
REŞADIYE CAD.
HAMIDIYE CAD.
Sirkeci
KENNEDY CAD.
SIRKECI TRAIN STATION
SIRKECI

Sarayburnu Park
To Haydarpaşa & Kadıköy

VASIF ÇINAR CAD.
ÇAKMAKÇILAR
MAHMUTPAŞA
BÜYÜK POSTANE CAD.
AŞIR EFENDI CAD.
ANKARA CAD.
EBUSSUUD CAD.

Gülhane Park
OLD PALACE WALLS
GÜLHANE PARKI YOL.
TOPKAPI PALACE

CAĞALOĞLU
ŞEREF EFENDI SOK.
CEMAL NADIR SOK.
SUL. MEKTEP
TARAKÇI CAFER
GRAND PORTAL
YEREBATAN CAD.
Gülhane
ISTANBUL ARCHAEOLOGICAL MUSEUM
SOĞUKÇEŞME
HAGIA IRENE

NURUOSMANIYE MOSQUE
TAVUK PAZARI
BURNED COLUMN
DIVAN
Çemberlitaş
YOLU
MOLLAFENARI SOK.
BABIALI CAD.
UNDERGROUND CISTERN
Sultanahmet
HAGIA SOPHIA

DÖNEM
GEDIK PAŞA SOK.
PEYKHANE
PIYER LOTI CAD.
CADDESI
GERMAN FOUNTAIN
Hippodrome
TOMB OF AHMET & KÖSEM
HASEKI SULTAN BATH
BABI HUMAYUN

TURKISH & ISLAMIC ARTS MUSEUM
ÜÇLER
AT MEYDANI
SULTANAHMET
BLUE MOSQUE
CANKURTARAN TRAIN STATION

KADIRGA LIMAN CAD.
SOKULLU MOSQUE
Kadırga Park
CINCI MEYDANI
SÜTERAZI
TORUN SOKAK
AKSAKAL
KERESTE
M. MEHMET AĞA
OYUNCU SOK.
AKBIYIK KAPI SOK.
KENNEDY CAD.

AHIRKAPI

ÇATLADIKAPI

Sea   of   Marmara

LEGEND

▭▭▭	Rail Line
┼┼┼┼┼	Funicular
- - -	Tramway
– – –	Nostalgic Tram
— — —	Metro
··········	Ferry Line
▨	Pedestrian-Friendly Area
▨	Popular Shopping Area
■	Point of Interest/Landmark
ⓘ	Tourist Information
⚲	Viewpoint

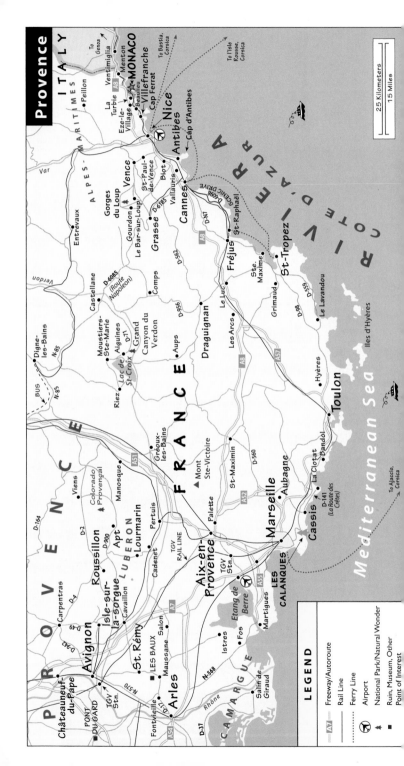

More for your trip?
Maximize the experience with Rick Steves as your guide

Guidebooks
Titles covering every country in Europe

Phrase Books
French, Italian, Spanish and more

DVDs and Blu-rays
100 episodes from public television's *Rick Steves' Europe*

Free Audio Tours and Rick's Audio Europe™ App
Covering the big sights in Venice, Florence, Rome, Athens and more

Small-Group Tours
40 itineraries on terra firma from Portugal to Turkey

For all the details, visit ricksteves.com

Avalon Travel
a member of the Perseus Books Group
1700 Fourth Street
Berkeley, CA 94710

Printed in Canada by Friesens.
First printing October 2014

ISBN 978-1-61238-768-0
ISSN 2160-6471
Third Edition

For the latest on Rick's lectures, guidebooks, tours, public radio show, and public television series, contact Rick Steves' Europe, 130 Fourth Avenue North, Edmonds, WA 98020-3114, tel. 425/771-8303, www.ricksteves.com, rick@ricksteves.com.

Rick Steves' Europe
Managing Editor: Risa Laib
Editorial & Production Manager: Jennifer Madison Davis
ETBD Editors: Glenn Eriksen, Tom Griffin, Cameron Hewitt, Suzanne Kotz, Cathy Lu, Carrie Shepherd
Writing and Research: Cameron Hewitt
Editorial Intern: Kimberly Downing
Maps & Graphics: David C. Hoerlein, Sandra Hundacker, Lauren Mills, Mary Rostad

Avalon Travel
Senior Editor and Series Manager: Madhu Prasher
Editor: Jamie Andrade
Assistant Editor: Maggie Ryan
Copy Editor: Patrick Collins
Proofreader: Suzie Nasol
Indexer: Stephen Callahan
Cover Design: Kimberly Glyder Design
Maps & Graphics: Kat Bennett, Mike Morgenfeld
Front Cover Photo: Emerald Princess in Santori, Greece © Courtesy of Princess Cruises
Additional Photography: Tankut Aran, Dominic Bonuccelli, Ben Cameron, Mary Ann Cameron, Rich Earl, Trish Feaster, Tom Griffin, Jennifer Hauseman, Cameron Hewitt, David C. Hoerlein, Anne Jenkins, Gene Openshaw, Rhonda Pelikan, Michael Potter, Carol Ries, Steve Smith, Robyn Stencil, Rick Steves, Gretchen Strauch, Bruce VanDeventer, Laura VanDeventer, Les Wahlstrom, David Willet, Dorian Yates

Rick Steves'®

MEDITERRANEAN CRUISE PORTS

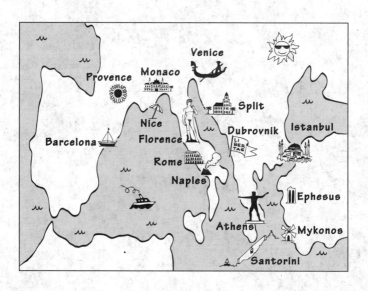

INTRODUCTION

Imagine yourself lazing on the deck of a floating city as you glide past the rooftops of Monaco, Venice, Mykonos, or Istanbul. Stepping off the gangway, you're immersed in the vivid life of a different European city each day. Tour some of the world's top museums, explore the ruins of an ancient metropolis, nurse a *caffè latte* while you people-watch from a prime sidewalk café, or take a dip in the Aegean at a pebbly beach. After a busy day in port, you can head back to the same cozy bedroom each night, without ever having to pack a suitcase or catch a train. As the sun sets and the ship pulls out of port, you have your choice of dining options—from a tuxedos-and-evening-gowns affair to a poolside burger after a swim—followed by a world of nightlife. Plying the calm Mediterranean waters through the night, you wake up refreshed in a whole new city—ready to do it all again.

Cruising in Europe is more popular today than ever before. And for good reason. Taking a cruise can be a fun, affordable way

to experience Europe—*if* you choose the right cruise, keep your extra expenses to a minimum...and use this book to make the absolute most of your time in port.

Unlike most cruising guidebooks, which dote on details about this ship's restaurants or that ship's staterooms, *Rick Steves' Mediterranean Cruise Ports* focuses on the main attraction: some of the grandest cities in Europe. Even if you have just eight hours in port, you can still ramble the colorful Ramblas of Barcelona, kick the pebbles that stuck in Julius Caesar's sandals at the Roman Forum, hike to the top of Athens' Acropolis, and

Map Legend

⚐ Viewpoint	⛴ Cruise Port/Dock	) (Tunnel
✦ Entrance	✈ Airport	Pedestrian Zone
❶ Tourist Info	Ⓣ Taxi Stand	------- Railway
WC Restroom	**T** Tram Stop	·········· Ferry/Boat Route
⛪ Castle	**M** Metro Stop	├─┼─┤ Tram
▪ Statue/Point of Interest	**V** Vaporetto Stop (Venice)	‖‖‖‖‖ Stairs
▨ Building	**T** Traghetto Crossing (Venice)	- - - - Walk/Tour Route
⬆ Church	**G** Gondola Station (Venice)	- - - - - Trail
⬇ Mosque	**A** Alilaguna Stop (Venice)	o⊦⊦⊦⊦⊦o Funicular
◈ Synagogue	Ⓑ Bus Stop	⌁⌁⌁ Park
◎ Fountain	**P** Parking	

Use this legend to help you navigate the maps in this book.

hear the Muslim call to prayer warble across the rooftops from an Istanbul minaret.

Yes, you could spend a lifetime in Florence. But you've got a few hours...and I have a plan for you. Each of this book's destination chapters is designed as a mini-vacation of its own, with advice about what to do and detailed sightseeing information for each port. And, to enable you to do it all on your own, I've included step-by-step instructions for getting into town from the cruise terminal.

For each major destination, this book offers a balanced, comfortable mix of the predictable biggies and a healthy dose of "Back Door" intimacy. Along with marveling at the Parthenon, Michelangelo's *David*, and Picasso's canvases, you'll perch on a bench alongside fisherfolk gazing out at the whitewashed harbor of a Greek island village.

In each port, you'll get all the specifics and opinions necessary to wring the maximum value out of your limited time and money. The best options in each port are, of course, only my opinion. But after spending half my adult life researching Europe, I've developed a sixth sense for what travelers enjoy.

About This Book

The book is divided into three parts: First, I'll suggest strategies for choosing which cruise to take, including a rundown of the major cruise lines, and explain the procedure for booking a cruise. Next, I'll give you a "Cruising 101"-type travel-skills briefing, with advice about what you should know before you go, and strategies for mak-

Please Tear Up This Book!

There's no point in hauling around 60 pages on Barcelona for a day in Santorini. That's why I've designed this book to be ripped apart. Before your cruise, attack this book with a

utility knife to create an army of pocket-sized mini-guidebooks—one for each port of call.

I love the ritual of trimming down the size of guidebooks I'll be using: Fold the pages back until you break the spine, neatly slice apart the sections you want with a utility knife, then pull them out with the gummy edge intact. If you want, finish each one off with some clear, heavy-duty packing tape to smooth and reinforce the spine, or use a heavy-duty stapler along the edge to prevent the first and last pages from coming loose.

To make things even easier, I've created a line of laminated covers with slide-on binders. Every evening, you can make a ritual of swapping out today's pages for tomorrow's. (For more on these binders, see www.ricksteves.com.)

As I travel in Europe, I meet lots of people with even more clever book treatments. This couple was proud of the job they

did in the name of packing light: cutting out only the pages they'd be using and putting them into a spiral binding.

While you may be tempted to keep this book intact as a souvenir of your travels, you'll appreciate even more the footloose freedom of traveling light while you're in port.

ing the most of your time both on and off the ship. And finally, the vast majority of this book is dedicated to the European ports you'll visit, with complete plans for packing each day full of unforgettable experiences.

I haven't skimped on my coverage of the sights in this book—which is why it's a bricklike tome. To get the most out of the book, please don't hesitate to tear out just the pages that you need for each day in port (see sidebar).

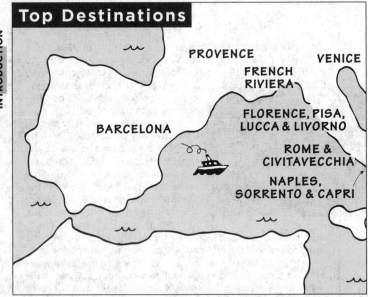

Top Destinations

PROVENCE

VENICE

FRENCH RIVIERA

FLORENCE, PISA, LUCCA & LIVORNO

BARCELONA

ROME & CIVITAVECCHIA

NAPLES, SORRENTO & CAPRI

Is a European Cruise Right for You?

I'm not going to try to convince you to cruise or not to cruise. If you're holding this book, I assume you've already made that decision. But if you're a cruise skeptic—or even a cruise cynic—and you're trying to decide whether cruising suits your approach to experiencing Europe, I'll let you in on my own process for weighing the pros and cons of cruising.

I believe this is the first and only cruising guidebook written by someone with a healthy skepticism about cruises. When I was growing up, cruising was a rich person's hobby. I used to joke that for many American cruisers, the goal was not travel but hedonism: See if you can eat five meals a day and still snorkel when you get into port.

Experiencing Europe's culture, people, and natural wonders economically and hassle-free has been my goal for three decades of traveling, tour guiding, and writing. And after all that time, I haven't found a more affordable way to see certain parts of Europe than cruising (short of sleeping on a park bench). For a weeklong European cruise that includes room, board, transportation, tips, and port fees, a couple can pay as little as $100 per night—that's as

SPLIT

DUBROVNIK

ISTANBUL

EPHESUS & KUŞADASI

ATHENS &
PIRAEUS

MYKONOS

SANTORINI

MORE PORTS
IN GREECE

much as a budget hotel room in many cities. To link all the places on an exciting one-week European cruise on your own, the hotels, railpasses, boat tickets, taxi transfers, restaurants, and so on would add up fast. The per-day base cost for mainstream cruises beats independent travel by a mile. And there's no denying the efficiency of sleeping while you travel to your next destination—touring six dynamically different destinations in a single week without wasting valuable daylight hours packing, hauling your bags to the station, and sitting on a train.

And yet, I still have reservations. Just as someone trying to learn a language will do better by immersing themselves in that culture than by sitting in a classroom for a few hours, I believe that travelers in search of engaging, broadening experiences should eat, sleep, and live Europe. Good or bad, cruising insulates you from Europe. If the carpet merchants of Kuşadası are getting a little too pushy, you can simply retreat to the comfort of 24-hour room service, tall glasses of ice water, American sports on the TV, and a boatload of people who speak English as a first language (except, perhaps, your crew). It's fun—but is it Europe?

For many, it's "Europe enough." For travelers who prefer to tiptoe into Europe—rather than dive right in—this bite-sized approach can be a good way to get your feet wet. Cruising works well as an enticing sampler for Europe, to help you decide where you'd like to return and really get to know.

People take cruises for different reasons. Some travelers cruise as a means to an end: experiencing the ports of call. They appreciate the convenience of traveling while they sleep, waking up in an interesting new destination each morning, and making the most out of every second they're in port. This is the "first off, last on" crowd that attacks each port like a footrace. You can practically hear their mental starter's pistol go off when the gangway opens.

Other cruisers are there to enjoy the cruise experience itself. They enjoy lying by the pool, taking advantage of onboard activities, dropping some cash at the casino, ringing up a huge bar tab, napping, reading, and watching ESPN on their stateroom TVs. If the *Mona Lisa* floated past, they might crane their necks, but wouldn't strain to get out of their deck chairs.

With all due respect to the latter group, I've written this book primarily for the former. But if you really want to be on vacation, aim for somewhere in the middle: Be sure to experience the ports that really tickle your wanderlust, but give yourself a "day off" every now and again in the less-enticing ports to sleep in or hit the beach.

Another advantage of cruising is that it can accommodate a family or group of people with vastly different travel philosophies. It's possible for Mom to go to the museum, Dad to lie by the pool, Sally to go snorkeling, and Bobby to go shopping...and then all of them can have dinner together and swap stories about their perfect days. (Or, if they're really getting on each other's nerves, there's plenty of room on a big ship to spread out.)

Cruising is especially popular among retirees, particularly those with limited mobility. Cruising rescues you from packing up your bags and huffing to the train station every other day. Once on land, accessibility for wheelchairs and walkers can vary dramatically—though some cruise lines offer excursions specifically designed for those who don't walk well. A cruise aficionado who had done the math once told me that, if you know how to find the deals,

it's theoretically cheaper to cruise indefinitely than to pay for a retirement home.

On the other hand, the independent, free-spirited traveler may not appreciate the constraints of cruising. For some, seven or eight hours in port is a tantalizing tease of a place where they'd love to linger for the evening—and the obligation to return to the ship every night is frustrating. Cruisers visiting Rome will never experience the Eternal City after dark. If you're antsy, energetic, and want to stroll the cobbles of Europe at all hours, cruising may not be for you. However, even some seasoned globetrotters find that cruising is a good way to travel in Europe on a shoestring budget, yet still in comfort.

One cruise-activities coordinator told me that cruisers can be divided into two groups: Those who stay in their rooms, refuse to try to enjoy the dozens of activities offered to them each day, and complain about everything; and those who get out and try to get to know their fellow passengers, make the most of being at sea, and have the time of their lives. Guess which type (according to him) enjoys the experience more?

Let's face it: Americans take the shortest vacations in the rich world. Some people choose to dedicate their valuable time off to an all-inclusive, resort-style vacation in Florida, Hawaii, or Mexico: swimming pools, song-and-dance shows, shopping, and all-you-can-eat buffets. Cruising gives you much the same hedonistic experience, all while you learn a lot about Europe—provided you use your time on shore constructively. It can be the best of both worlds.

Understanding the Cruise Industry

Cruising is a $30 billion-a-year business. Approximately one out of every five Americans has taken a cruise, and each year about 15 million people take one. In adjusted dollars, cruise prices haven't risen in decades. This, partly, has sparked a huge growth in the cruise industry in recent years. The aging baby boomer population has also boosted sales, as older travelers discover that a cruise is an easy way to see the world. While the biggest growth has come from the North American market, cruise lines have also started marketing more internationally.

The industry has changed dramatically over the last generation. For decades, cruise lines catered exclusively to the upper crust—people who expected top-tier luxury. But with the popularity of *The Love Boat* television series in the 1970s and 1980s, then the one-upmanship of increasingly bigger megaships in the early 1990s, cruising went mainstream. Somebody had to fill all the berths on those gargantuan vessels, and cruise lines lowered their prices to attract middle-class customers. The "newlyweds and nearly deads" stereotype about cruise clientele is now outmoded. The industry has made bold efforts to appeal to an ever-broader customer base, representing a wide spectrum of ages, interests, and income levels.

In order to compete for passengers and fill megaships, cruise lines offer fares that can be astonishingly low. In fact, they make little or no money on ticket sales—and some "loss-leader" sailings actually lose money on the initial fare. Instead, the cruise lines' main income comes from three sources: alcohol sales, gambling (onboard casinos), and excursions. So while cruise lines are in the business of creating an

unforgettable vacation for you, they're also in the business of separating you from your money (once on the ship) to make up for their underpriced fares.

Just as airlines have attempted to bolster their bottom lines by "unbundling" their fares and charging more "pay as you go" fees (for food, checking a bag, extra legroom, and so on), cruise lines are now charging for things they used to include (such as "specialty restaurants"). The cruise industry is constantly experimenting with the balance between all-inclusive luxury and nickel-and-dime, à la carte, mass-market travel. (For tips on maximizing your experience while minimizing your expenses, see the sidebar on page 80.)

It's also worth noting that cruise lines are able to remain profitable largely on the backs of their low-paid crew, who mostly hail from the developing world. Working 10 to 14 hours a day, seven days a week—almost entirely for tips—the tireless crew are the gears that keep cruises spinning. (For more, see page 73.)

Understanding how the cruise industry works can help you take advantage of your cruise experience...and not the other way around. Equipped with knowledge, you can be the smart consumer who has a fantastic time on board and in port without paying a premium. That's what this book is all about.

Traveling as a Temporary Local

Most travelers tramp through Europe as if they're visiting the cultural zoo. "Oooh, that Greek fisherman is mending his nets! Excuse me, could you do that in the sunshine with my wife next to you so I can take a snapshot?" This is fun. It's a part of travel. But a camera bouncing on your belly tells locals you're hunting cultural peacocks. When I'm in Europe, I try to be the best Greek or Spaniard or Italian I can be.

Europeans generally like Americans. But if there is a negative aspect to their image of Americans, it's that we are loud, wasteful, ethnocentric, too informal (which can seem disrespectful), and a bit naive.

Even if you believe American ways are best, your trip will go more smoothly if you don't compare. Enjoy doing things the European way, and you'll experience a more welcoming Europe.

We travel all the way to Europe to enjoy differences—to become temporary locals. You'll experience frustrations. Certain truths that we find "God-given" or "self-evident," such as cold beer, ice in drinks, bottomless cups of coffee, and bigger being better, are suddenly not so true. One of the benefits of travel is the eye-opening realization that there are logical, civil, and even better alternatives. A willingness to go local ensures that you'll enjoy a full dose of European hospitality.

While Europeans look bemusedly at some of our Yankee excesses—and worriedly at others—they nearly always afford us individual travelers all the warmth we deserve.

Judging from all the happy feedback I receive from travelers who have used my books, it's safe to assume you'll enjoy a great, affordable vacation—with the finesse of an independent, experienced traveler.

Thanks, and bon voyage!

Back Door Travel Philosophy

From *Rick Steves' Europe Through the Back Door*

Travel is intensified living—maximum thrills per minute and one of the last great sources of legal adventure. Travel is freedom. It's recess, and we need it.

Experiencing the real Europe requires catching it by surprise, going casual..."through the Back Door."

In many ways, spending a lot of money on sightseeing and excursions only builds a thicker wall between you and what you came to see. Europe is a cultural carnival, and, time after time, you'll find that its best acts are free and the best seats are the cheap ones.

A tight budget forces you to travel close to the ground, meeting and communicating with the people, not relying on service with a purchased smile.

Connecting with people carbonates your experience. Extroverts have more fun. If your trip is low on magic moments, kick yourself and make things happen. If you don't enjoy a place, maybe you don't know enough about it. Seek the truth. Recognize tourist traps. Give a culture the benefit of your open mind. See things as different but not better or worse. Any culture has much to share.

Of course, travel, like the world, is a series of hills and valleys. Be fanatically positive and militantly optimistic. If something's not to your liking, change your liking.

Travel can make you a happier American as well as a citizen of the world. Our Earth is home to seven billion equally precious people. It's humbling to travel and find that people don't have the "American Dream"—they have their own dreams. Europeans like us, but, with all due respect, they wouldn't trade passports.

Thoughtful travel—even from the comfortable springboard of a cruise ship—engages us with the world. In tough economic times, it reminds us what is truly important. By broadening perspectives, travel teaches new ways to measure quality of life.

Globe-trotting destroys ethnocentricity, helping you understand and appreciate different cultures. Rather than fear the diversity on this planet, celebrate it. Among your prized souvenirs will be the strands of different cultures you choose to knit into your own character. The world is a cultural yarn shop, and Back Door travelers are weaving the ultimate tapestry. Join in!

PART 1: CHOOSING AND BOOKING A CRUISE

CHOOSING A CRUISE

Each cruise line has its own distinct personality, quirks, strengths, and weaknesses. Selecting a cruise that matches your travel style and philosophy can be critical for the enjoyment of your trip. On the other hand, some cruisers care only about the price, go on any line that offers a deal, and have a great time.

Still, the more your idea of "good travel" meshes with your cruise line's, the more likely you are to enjoy both your trip and your fellow passengers. For information on booking a cruise, see the next chapter.

Gathering Information

Comparison-shopping can be a fun part of the cruise experience. Read the cruise-line descriptions in this chapter, then browse the websites of the ones that interest you. Ask your friends who've cruised, and who share your interests, about the lines they've used, and what they thought of each one. Examine the cruise lines' glossy brochures (view online, request them, or get them from your local travel agent)—how the line markets itself says a lot about what sort of clientele it attracts. Tune into the ubiquitous TV commercials for cruise lines. Photos of individual ships' staterooms and amenities—which you'll also find on the cruise lines' websites—can be worth a thousand words in getting a sense of the vibe of each vessel.

Once you've narrowed down the choices, read some impartial online reviews. The most popular site, www.cruisecritic.com, has reviews of cruise lines, specific ships, tips for visiting each port, and more. Other well-respected websites are www.cruisediva.com, www.cruisemates.com, and www.avidcruiser.com. If you feel that cruising is all about the ship, check www.shipparade.com, which delves into details about each vessel.

Many travel agencies that sell cruises have surprisingly infor-

Cruising the Internet

While there are many cruise-related websites, Cruise Critic (www.cruisecritic.com) dominates cyberspace. Not only are its forums crammed with reviews about ships, excursions, local guides, and ports of call, but it's also a nifty networking tool. By signing up on its Roll Call page for your cruise, you can introduce yourself to others on the same ship and look for partners to share taxis or local guides. Some cruise lines—such as Azamara, Celebrity, Crystal, and Royal Caribbean—even sponsor a social gathering of Cruise Critic members early in the cruise, often with complimentary food and drinks.

mative websites. One of the best, www.vacationstogo.com, not only sorts different cruise options by price and destination, but also has useful facts, figures, and photos for each ship and port.

Most cruising guidebooks devote more coverage to detailed reviews of specific ships and their amenities than to the destinations—which make them the perfect complement to this book. Look for *The Unofficial Guide to Cruises, Frommer's European Cruises and Ports of Call, Fodor's Complete Guide to European Cruises,* and others. (For destination-specific guidebooks, see the list on page 1249.)

As you compare cruises, decide which of the factors in the following section matter the most to you, then find a cruise line that best matches what you're looking for.

Cruise Considerations

In the next few pages you'll find a wide range of issues, big and small, to take into account when selecting your cruise. Of these, the three main factors—which should be weighted about equally—are **price, itinerary** (length, destinations, and time spent in each port), and **cruise line** (personality and amenities).

If you've cruised in the Caribbean but not Europe, be aware that there are some subtle but important differences. In general, European cruises are more focused on the destinations, while Caribbean cruises tend to be more focused on the ship (passengers spend more time on the ship, and therefore the shipboard amenities are more important). People choosing among European cruises usually base their decision on the places they'll be visiting: Big cities or island villages? Ancient ruins or modern museums? Beach time or urban strolling? In contrast, on a Caribbean cruise the priority is simply hedonistic fun in the sun.

Cruise Line

This chapter will give you a quick overview of some of the major lines to help you find a good match. For example, some cruise lines embrace cruising's nautical heritage, with decor and crew uniforms that really let you know you're on a ship. Others are more like Las Vegas casinos at sea. An armchair historian will be disappointed on a hedonistic pleasure boat, and a young person who's in a mood to party will be miserable on the *S.S. Septuagenarian*. Do you want a wide range of dining options on the ship, or do you view mealtime as a pragmatic way to fill the tank? After dinner, do you want to get to bed early, or dance in a disco until dawn?

American vs. European: While most US travelers opt for an American cruise line, doing so definitely Americanizes your travel experience. When you're on board, it feels almost as if you'd never left the good old U. S. of A.—with American shows on the TV, Heinz ketchup in the buffet line, and fellow Yanks all around you. If you'd rather leave North America behind, going with a European-flavored cruise line can be an interesting cultural experience in itself. While Europeans are likely to be among the passengers on any cruise line, they represent a larger proportion on European-owned or -operated boats. Surrounded by Germans who enthusiastically burp after a good meal, Italians who nudge ahead of you in line, and French people who enjoy sunbathing topless—and listening to every announcement translated into six different languages—you'll definitely know you're in Europe. I recently cruised for a week in Norway as one of just 13 Americans on a budget ship with more than 2,000 passengers. I never saw another Yank, spent my time on board and in port with working-class Italians and Spaniards from towns no tourist has ever heard of, and had what was quite possibly the most truly "European" experience of my life.

Environmental Impact: Most forms of travel come with a toll on the environment. And cruise ships are no exception—they gulp fuel as they ply scenic seas, struggling to find waste-disposal methods that are as convenient as possible while still being legal. Some cruise lines are more conscientious about these issues than others. If environmental impact is a major concern of yours, you can compare the record for all the major cruise lines at www.foe.org/cruise-report-card.

Length

European cruises can range in length from a few days to a few weeks. The typical cruiser sails for seven days, but some travelers enjoy taking a 10-, 12-, or 14-day cruise, then adding a few days on land at either end to stretch their trip to two weeks or more. A cruise seven days or shorter tends to focus on one "zone" of the Mediterranean (Spain; Italy and France; Greek Isles); a longer cruise is more likely to provide you with a sampler of the whole area.

When to Go

Most Mediterranean cruises take place during a seven-month period of relatively warm weather, roughly between April and October. While July and August are popular times to cruise—with kids (and their teachers) on summer vacation—that also makes them the most crowded months, and the oppressive heat can make exploring the ports miserable. Shoulder season (May-June and Sept-Oct) usually has fewer crowds and more comfortable weather. Popular cruise ports are never really uncrowded, but they may be a little less jammed in shoulder season. And the weather, while potentially a bit chilly in May or October, is usually quite pleasant at the Mediterranean's southern latitudes. For a month-by-month climate chart that includes various ports, see page 1251.

Price

If you're on a tight budget and aren't fussy, look for the best deals. From the Mass-Market to the Ultra-Luxury categories, the per-person price can range from $100 to $700+ per day. Sales can lower those prices. (For more on cruise pricing, see page 37.)

While going with the cheapest option is tempting, it may be worth paying a little extra for an experience that better matches your idea of a dream cruise. If you're hoping for glitzy public spaces and sparkling nightly revues, you'll kick yourself later if you saved $40 a day—but ended up on a musty ship with stale shows. If you want to maximize time exploring European destinations, it can be worth paying an extra $20 a day for an itinerary with two more hours at each port—that translates to just 10 bucks an hour, a veritable steal compared to the extra experiences it'll allow you to cram in. Don't be penny-wise and pound-foolish in this regard.

On the other hand, in my (admittedly limited) cruise experience, I've noticed a trend: The more people pay for the cruise, the higher their expectations—and, therefore, the more prone they are to disappointment. I've cruised on lines ranging from bargain-basement to top-end, and I've noticed an almost perfect correlation between how much someone pays and how much they enjoy complaining. In my experience, folks who pay less are simply more fun to cruise with. When considering the people I'll wind up dining and going on shore excursions with, price tag aside, I'd rather go with a mid-range cruise line than a top-end one.

When evaluating prices and making a budget, remember to take into account all of the "extras" you might wind up buying from the cruise line: alcoholic drinks, meals at specialty restaurants, the semi-mandatory "auto-tip" (about $10-12 per day per person), shore excursions, and your gambling tab from the casino, just to name a few. (For more details on these hidden costs, see page 38.)

Ship Size and Amenities

When it comes to cruise ships, bigger is not necessarily better... although it can be, depending on your interests.

The biggest ships offer a wide variety of restaurants, activities, entertainment, and other amenities (such as resources for kids). The main disadvantage of a big ship is the feeling that you're being herded along with thousands of other passengers—3,000 tourists piling off a ship into a small port town definitely changes the character of the place.

Smaller ships enjoy fewer crowds, access to out-of-the-way ports, and less hassle when disembarking (especially when tendering—see page 118). If you're focusing your time and energy on the destinations anyway, a smaller ship can be more relaxing to "come home" to. On the other hand, for all of the above reasons, cruises on the smallest ships are typically much more expensive. Small ships also physically can't offer the wide range of eateries and activities as the big vessels; intimate, yacht-like vessels have no room for a climbing wall or an ice rink. And finally, on a small ship, you may feel the motion of the sea more than on a big ship (though because of the stabilizers used by small ships, this difference isn't that dramatic).

Think carefully about which specific amenities are important to you, and find a cruise line that offers those things. Considerations include:

Food, both in terms of quality and variety (some cruise lines offer a wide range of specialty restaurants—explained on page 100; generally speaking, the bigger the ship, the more options are available);

Entertainment, such as a wide range of performers (musicians, dancers, and so on) in venues both big and small;

Athletic facilities, ranging from a running track around the deck, to a gym with equipment and classes, to swimming pools and hot tubs, to a simulated surf pool and bowling alley, to a spa with massage and other treatments;

Children's resources, including activities and spaces designed for teens and younger kids, and a babysitting service (for more on cruising with kids, see page 95);

Other features, including a good library, lecturers, special events, a large casino, wheelchair accessibility, and so on.

Some first-time cruisers worry they'll get bored while they're on board. Don't count on it. You'll be bombarded with entertainment options and a wide range of activities—particularly on a big ship.

Destinations

If you have a wish list of ports, use it as a starting point when shopping for a cruise. It's unlikely you'll find a cruise that visits every one of your desired destinations, but you can usually find one that comes close.

Most itineraries of a week or more include a day "at sea": no stops at ports—just you and the open sea. These are usually included for practical reasons. Most often a day at sea is needed to connect far-flung destinations with no worthwhile stop in between... but cruise lines also don't mind keeping passengers on board, hoping they'll spend more money. Because cruise ships generally travel at around 20 knots—that's only about 23 land miles per hour—they take a long time to cover big distances. For some cruise aficionados, days at sea are the highlight of the trip; for other passengers, they're a boring waste of time. If you enjoy time on the ship, try to maximize days at sea; if you're cruising mainly to sightsee on land, try to minimize them.

Time Spent in Port

If exploring European destinations is your priority, look carefully at how much time the ship spends in each port. Specific itinerary rundowns on cruise-line websites usually show the scheduled times of arrival and departure. Typical stops can range anywhere from 6 to 12 hours, with an average of around 8 or 9 hours. At the same port—or even on the same cruise line—the difference in port time from one cruise ship to another can vary by hours.

Most cruise lines want you on the ship as long as possible—the longer you're aboard, the more likely you are to spend money there (and for legal reasons, they can't open their lucrative casinos and duty-free shops until they're at sea).

In general, the more expensive Luxury- and Ultra-Luxury-class lines offer longer stays in port. However, even if you compare cheaper lines that are similar in price, times can vary. For example, Norwegian, Costa, and MSC tend to have shorter times in port, while Carnival and Royal Caribbean linger longer.

Repositioning Cruises

Ships that cruise in Europe are usually based in the Caribbean during the winter, so they need to cross the Atlantic Ocean each spring and fall. This journey, called a "repositioning cruise," includes a lengthy (5-7 days) stretch where the ship is entirely at sea. Also called a "crossing" or a "transatlantic crossing," these are most common in early April (to Europe), or late October and November (from Europe).

If you really want to escape from it all, and just can't get enough of all the shipboard activities, these long trips can be a dream come true; if you're a fidgety manic sightseer, they're a nightmare. Before committing to a repositioning cruise, consider taking a cruise with a day or two at sea just to be sure you really, really enjoy being on a ship that much. Several notes of warning: The seas can be rougher on transatlantic crossings than in the relatively protected waters closer to land; the weather will probably be cooler; and there are a couple of days in the middle of the voyage where most ships lose all satellite communication—no shipboard phones, Wi-Fi, or cable channels. While the officers are in touch with land in the event of emergencies, your own day-to-day contact with the outside world will disappear.

If you're considering a repositioning cruise, don't be misled by the sometimes astonishingly low sticker price. (These typically don't sell as well as the more destination-oriented cruises, so they're perennially on the push list.) You'll only need a one-way plane ticket between the US and Europe—but that may exceed the cost of a round-trip ticket (don't expect to simply pay half the round-trip price).

Cruise Lines

I don't pretend to be an expert on all the different cruise lines—the focus of this book is on the destinations rather than the ships. But this section is designed to give you an overview of options to get you started. (To dig deeper, consider some of the sources listed under "Gathering Information," at the beginning of this chapter.)

While nobody in the cruise industry formally recognizes different "classes" of companies, just about everybody acknowledges that cruise lines fall into four basic categories, loosely based on the price range (estimated per-person prices given here are based on double occupancy in the cheapest cabin, and don't include taxes, port fees, or additional expenses): **Mass-Market** ($100-200/day), **Premium** ($200-350/day), **Luxury** (sometimes called "**Upper Premium**"; $350-700/day), and **Ultra-Luxury** ($700 or more/day). Of course, a few exceptions straddle these classifications and buck the trends, and some cruise lines are highly specialized—such as Disney Cruise Line (very kid-friendly and experience-focused) and Star Clippers (an authentic tall-ship experience with a mainsail that passengers can help hoist).

Most cruise lines are owned by the same handful of companies. For example, Carnival Corporation owns Carnival, Costa, Cunard, Holland America, Princess, Seabourn, and five other lines (representing about half of the worldwide cruise market). Royal Caribbean owns Celebrity and Azamara Club Cruises. Within these groups, each individual line may be, to varying degrees, operated by a different leadership, but they do fall under the same umbrella and tend to have similar philosophies and policies.

In assembling the following information, I've focused exclusively on European itineraries. The average hours in port are based on a selection of each line's sailings; your cruise could be different, so check carefully.

Mass-Market Lines

The cheapest cruise lines, these huge ships have a "resort-hotel-at-sea" ambience. Prices are enticingly low, but operators try to make up the difference with a lot of upselling on board (specialty restaurants, borderline-aggressive photographers, constant pressure to shop, and so on). The clientele is wildly diverse (including lots of families and young people) and, generally speaking, not particularly well-traveled; they tend to be more interested in being on vacation and enjoying the ship than in sightseeing. Mass-Market lines provide an affordable way to sample cruising.

Carnival

Contact Information: www.carnival.com, tel. 888-CARNIVAL

Number and Capacity of Ships: *Carnival Legend* carries 2,124 passengers; *Carnival Sunshine* carries 3,002.

Average Hours in Port: 11-12 hours

Description: Although Carnival isn't planning to run any Mediterranean cruises in 2014, it may be back in future years. Carnival has long had a reputation for a floating-frat-party "Fun Ship" ambience; the company is trying to tone down this image, though it's kept the discos and flashy decor. The line's European offerings usually are limited; it makes most of its money on short vacations to Alaska and the Caribbean. It tries to entice Europe-bound travelers with low prices and huge new ships—a great value, but for some, it's a "lowest common denominator" cruise experience.

Overall, expect a younger demographic with mostly Americans on board. There are plenty of youth programs, and lots of activities aimed at singles and young couples, such as a Caribbean-themed pub, an outdoor fitness area, and mini golf. The main dining room tends to serve American cuisine, but there are also plenty of specialty restaurants. Because these ships are so big, they are an attractive low-cost option, but that also means huge crowds—especially when tendering. However, the long times in port help make up for any time lost waiting in line.

Costa

Contact Information: www.costacruise.com, tel. 800-GO-COSTA

Number and Capacity of Ships: 16 ships, ranging from 800 to 3,780 passengers

Average Hours in Port: 6-7 hours

Description: With frequent sales that can drive its prices lower, Costa is one of the cheapest lines for European cruises. It also has

the largest fleet and the most seven-day cruises in the region. Although owned by Carnival, Costa proudly retains its Italian identity. Most of your fellow passengers will be Europeans, with large contingents of Italians, French, Spanish, and Germans. (Only a small fraction of Costa passengers are from the US or Canada.) North American cruisers find both pros and cons about traveling with a mostly European crowd: While some relish the fact that it's truly European, others grow weary of the time-consuming multilingual announcements, and have reported "rude" behavior from some fellow passengers (some Europeans are not always polite about waiting in line). The ships' over-the-top, wildly colorful decor borders on gaudy—it can be either appealing or appalling, depending on your perspective. Onboard activities also have an Italian pizzazz, such as singing waiters or heated international bocce-ball tournaments. Outrageous ambience aside, the cruising experience itself is quite traditional (there's no open seating in the dining room, and formal nights are taken seriously). Dining options are limited to the main dining room (serving reliably well-executed, if not refined, Italian fare), huge buffets serving disappointing cafeteria fare, and sparse, overpriced, and underwhelming specialty restaurants.

Costa attracts a wide demographic—from twentysomethings to retirees—and you can expect families during the summer and school breaks. While Costa boasts about its Italian cuisine, some American cruisers have found the food disappointing. In addition to visiting the predictable big ports, Costa is more likely to venture to some lesser-known stops, such as Malta, Morocco, and secondary ports on Sicily. The short hours in port draw criticism—and Costa's shore excursion packages are relatively expensive.

The January 2012 *Costa Concordia* disaster took more than 30 lives and cast a pall over the cruise-ship industry. Costa's parent company, Carnival, promised a complete investigation and increased focus on safety.

MSC Cruises

Contact Information: www.msccruises.com, tel. 877-655-4655
Number and Capacity of Ships: 12 ships, each carrying 1,000-3,275 passengers
Average Hours in Port: 6 hours
Description: "Beautiful. Passionate. Italian." MSC's slogan sums it up. Even more so than the similar Costa (described earlier), this

low-priced, Italian-owned company caters mostly to Europeans—only about 5 percent of the passengers on their European cruises are from the US or Canada. This is a plus if you want to escape America entirely on your vacation, but can come with some language-barrier and culture-shock issues. Since children ride free, summer and school breaks tend to be dominated by families, while at other times passengers are mostly retirees.

The basic price is often a borderline-outrageous bargain (deep discounts are common), but MSC charges for amenities that

are free on many other cruise lines—such as basic drinks, room service, and snacks. In the dining room, you even have to pay for tap water. MSC has shorter hours in port than most cruise lines, and their shore excursions have a heightened emphasis on shopping. The food and entertainment are average; your choices at the breakfast and lunch buffets are the same for the entire cruise. Keep your expectations low—as one passenger noted, "It's not really a cruise—just a bus tour that happens on a nice boat."

Norwegian Cruise Line (NCL)

Contact Information: www.ncl.com, tel. 866-234-7350

Number and Capacity of Ships: 13 ships, ranging from 2,000 to 4,100 passengers

Average Hours in Port: 8-9 hours

Description: Norwegian was an industry leader in the now-widespread trend toward flexibility, and is known for its "Free-style Cruising" approach. "Whatever" is the big word here (as in, "You're free to do...whatever"). For example, their ships typically have no assigned seatings for meals (though reservations are encouraged), and offer the widest range of specialty restaurants, which can include French, Italian, Mexican, sushi, steakhouse, Japanese teppanyaki, and more. Norwegian also has a particularly wide range of cabin categories, from very basic inside cabins to top-of-the-line, sprawling suites that rival the Luxury lines' offerings.

Norwegian has a Las Vegas-style glitz. On the newer ships, such as the gigantic, 4,100-passenger, much-publicized *Norwegian Epic*, the entertainment is ramped up, with world-class shows—such as Blue Man Group and Cirque du Soleil—requiring advance ticket purchase. Their vessels tend to be brightly decorated—bold murals curl across the prows of their ships, and the public areas are colorful (some might say garish or even tacky). This approach, coupled with relatively low prices, draws a wide range of passengers: singles and families, young and old, American and European, middle-class and wealthy.

Onboard amenities cater to this passenger diversity; along with all of the usual services, some ships have climbing walls and bowling alleys. The crew is also demographically diverse, and the service is acceptable, but not as doting as on some cruise lines, making some passengers feel anonymous. Education and enrichment activities are a low priority—most lectures are designed to sell you something (excursions, artwork, and so on), rather than prepare you for the port.

Royal Caribbean International
Contact Information: www.royalcaribbean.com, tel. 866-562-7625
Number and Capacity of Ships: 21 ships, ranging from 1,800 to 5,400 passengers
Average Hours in Port: 10 hours
Description: Royal Caribbean is the world's second-largest cruise line (after Carnival). Similar to Carnival and Norwegian, but a step up in both cost and (in their mind, at least) amenities, Royal Caribbean edges toward the Premium category.

Offering an all-around quintessential cruising experience, Royal Caribbean attracts first-time cruisers. The majority are from the US and Canada. The line likes to think of itself as catering to a more youthful demographic: couples and singles in their 30s to 50s on shorter cruises; 50 and up on cruises longer than seven nights. With longer hours in port and onboard fitness facilities (every ship has a rock-climbing wall, some have water parks and mini golf), they try to serve more active travelers.

The food on board is American cuisine, and its entertainment style matches other cruise lines in this category—expect Vegas-style shows and passenger-participation games. Even though some of its ships are positively gigantic, Royal Caribbean, which prides itself on service, delivers; most of its passengers feel well-treated.

Premium Lines
A step up from the Mass-Market lines both in price and in elegance, most Premium lines evoke the "luxury cruises" of yore. The ships can be nearly as big as the Mass-Market options, but are designed to feel more intimate. The upselling is still there, but it's

more restrained, and the clientele tends to be generally older, better-traveled, and more interested in sightseeing. While the Mass-Market lines can sometimes feel like a cattle call, Premium lines ratchet up the focus on service, going out of their way to pamper their guests.

Celebrity

Contact Information: www.celebritycruises.com, tel. 800-647-2251

Number and Capacity of Ships: 11 ships, ranging from 1,800 to 2,850 passengers

Average Hours in Port: 10-11 hours

Description: Originally a Greek company, Celebrity was bought by Royal Caribbean in 1997 and operates as its upscale sister cruise line. (The "X" on the smokestack is the Greek letter "chi," which stands for Chandris—the founder's family name.) Celebrity distinguishes itself from the other Premium category lines with bigger ships and a slightly younger demographic. Celebrity likes to point out that its larger ships have more activities and restaurants than the smaller Premium (or even Luxury category) ships. Most of its passengers are from the US or Canada, and it's reportedly popular with baby boomers, seniors, gay cruisers, and honeymooners. Among the Premium lines, Celebrity offers some of the best amenities for kids (aside from Disney, of course).

Celebrity's smallest stateroom is quite spacious compared with those on other lines in this category. On its European cruises, the main dining room cuisine seems more European than American (with some high-end options—a plus for many travelers), but there are plenty of specialty restaurants, ranging from Asian-fusion to a steakhouse. Most ships are decorated with a mod touch—with all the bright lights and offbeat art, you might feel like you're in Miami Beach. Adding to the whimsy, some ships even come with a real grass lawn on the top deck. Celebrity's service consistently gets high marks, and the onboard diversions include the usual spas, enrichment lectures, Broadway revues, cabarets, discos, theme parties, and casinos.

Cunard Line

Contact Information: www.cunard.com, tel. 800-728-6273

Number and Capacity of Ships: *Queen Elizabeth* carries 2,092 passengers, *Queen Mary 2* carries 2,620, and *Queen Victoria* carries 2,014.

Average Hours in Port: 10 hours

Description: Cunard Line plays to its long, historic tradition and caters to an old-fashioned, well-traveled, and well-to-do clientele in their 50s and older. Passengers on their European itineraries tend to be mostly British, along with some Americans and other Europeans. Although the line is suitable for families (kids' programs are staffed by trained British nannies), it's not seriously family-friendly. This line features large ships and offers a pleasantly elegant experience with a British bent—you can even have afternoon tea or enjoy bangers and mash in a pub.

About a sixth of the passengers book suites and have access to specialty restaurants—a remnant of the traditional class distinctions in jolly olde England. The entertainment and lecture programs tend to be more "distinguished"; there's a good library; and activities include ballroom dancing, croquet, tennis, fencing, and lawn bowling. Each ship has a viewable collection of historic Cunard artifacts. The famously refined Cunard dress code seems to be more of a suggestion these days, as many show up in relatively casual dress at formal dining events. Passengers report mixed reviews—some feel that the experience doesn't quite live up to the line's legacy.

Disney Cruise Line

Contact Information: www.disneycruise.com, tel. 800-951-3532
Number and Capacity of Ships: 4 ships, ranging from 2,700 to 4,000 passengers
Average Hours in Port: 10-11 hours
Description: Although Disney doesn't run European cruises every year, it does occasionally dip into this market (check their website). Disney is the gold standard for family cruise vacations. The majority of the passengers are families and multigenerational—expect at least one-third of the passengers to be kids. There'll be plenty of Disney flicks, G-rated floor shows, and mouse ears wherever you turn. Like its amusement parks, Disney's ships have high standards for service and cleanliness. The food is kid-friendly, but the ships also have a high-end Italian restaurant for a break for parents. While your kids will never be bored, there are a few adult diversions as well (including an adults-only swimming pool)—but no casino. Disney doesn't do a lot of cruising in this region, but it may be the best option if you're taking along your kids or grandkids. Be warned: Parents who think a little Disney goes a long way might overdose on this line.

Holland America Line (HAL)

Contact Information: www.hollandamerica.com, tel. 877-932-4259
Number and Capacity of Ships: 15 ships, ranging from 835 to 2,100 passengers
Average Hours in Port: 9-10 hours
Description: Holland America, with a history dating back to 1873 (it once carried immigrants to the New World), prides itself on

tradition. Generally, this line has one of the most elderly clienteles in the business, though they're trying to promote their cruises to a wider demographic (with some success). Cruisers appreciate the line's delicate balance between a luxury and a casual vacation—it's formal, but not *too* formal.

Ship decor emphasizes a connection to the line's nautical past, with lots of wood trim and white railings; you might feel like you're on an oversized yacht at times. That's intentional: When building their biggest ships, Holland America designers planned public spaces to create the illusion that passengers are on a smaller vessel (for example, hallways bend every so often so you can't see all the way to the far end). This line also has high service standards; they operate training academies in Indonesia and the Philippines, where virtually all of their crew hails from. These stewards are trained to be good-natured and to make their guests feel special. Dining options on board tend to be limited; there isn't a wide range of specialty restaurants.

Holland America takes seriously the task of educating their passengers about the ports; most ships have a "Travel Guide" who lectures on each destination and is available for questions, and some excursions—designated "Cruise with Purpose"—are designed to promote a more meaningful, participatory connection with the destinations (though these are relatively rare in Europe).

Princess

Contact Information: www.princess.com, tel. 800-774-6237
Number and Capacity of Ships: 18 ships, ranging from 680 to 3,080 passengers
Average Hours in Port: 9-10 hours
Description: Princess appeals to everyone from solo travelers to families, with most passengers over 50. Because their market reach is so huge, expect many repeat cruisers enjoying their mainstream cruise experience. While Princess has long been considered a Premium-category line, many cruise insiders suggest that the line has been lowering its prices—and, many say, its standards—so these days it effectively straddles the Premium and Mass-Market categories. Still, Princess passengers tend to be very loyal.

Princess got a big boost when the 1970s *Love Boat* TV series featured two Princess ships. Those "love boats" have now been retired, and the Princess fleet is one of the most modern in the industry—half of its ships have been launched in the last 10 years. It's known for introducing innovative features such as a giant video screen above the main swimming pool showing movies and

sports all day...and into the night. Still, while the ships are new, the overall experience is traditional compared with some of the bold and brash Mass-Market lines. The line has the usual activities, such as trivia contests, galley tours, art auctions, and middle-of-the-road musical revues—though some passengers report that they found fewer activities and diversions on Princess ships than they expected for vessels of this size. While its service gets raves and the food is fine, there is some repetition in the main dining room—expect the same dessert choices each night.

Luxury Lines

While some purists (who reserve the "Luxury" label for something really top-class) prefer to call this category "Upper Premium," it's certainly a notch above the lines listed previously. Luxury lines typically use smaller ships, offer better food and service, command higher prices, and have a more exclusive clientele. You get what you pay for—this is a more dignified experience, with longer days in port and less emphasis on selling you extras. In general, while Luxury ships are very comfortable, the cruise is more focused on the destinations than the ship.

Once you're in this price range, you'll find that the various lines are variations on a theme (though there are a few notable exceptions, such as the unique casual-sailboat ambience of Windstar, or the opportunity to actually rig the sails on Star Clippers). It can be hard to distinguish among the lines; within the Luxury category, passengers tend to go with a cruise line recommended to them by a friend.

Note: Luxury and Ultra-Luxury lines (described later) generally run smaller ships, which can visit out-of-the-way ports that larger cruise ships can't. However, remember the drawbacks of smaller ships: fewer onboard activities, a narrower range of restaurants, and—for some travelers prone to seasickness—a slightly rougher ride.

Azamara Club Cruises

Contact Information: www.azamaraclubcruises.com, tel. 877-999-9553

Number and Capacity of Ships: *Journey* and *Quest* each carry 694 passengers.

Average Hours in Port: 11-12 hours

Description: Azamara Club Cruises attracts a moderately affluent, educated, and active middle-age to retirement-age traveler.

This relatively new line (revamped and rebranded in 2010) is still finding its way in the Luxury cruise market. Some passengers call Azamara a "work in progress," but it seems to be developing a successful formula. Their stated aim is to allow their customers to immerse themselves in each destination. Azamara passengers want value and are interested in more unusual destinations and longer port stays—their itineraries include more frequent overnight stops. The clientele is mainly American and British, along with a few Germans and other nationalities. There are no programs or facilities for children.

The atmosphere is casual, with open seating at meals and a focus on good food and wine; the cuisine is Mediterranean-influenced with other international dishes and healthy options. With a high crew-to-passenger ratio, the service is attentive. Live entertainment is more limited than on larger ships; the types of programs encourage meeting other guests, which contributes to a cozier, more social experience. Cabins and bathrooms can be small, but are well laid-out. The company's good-value, all-inclusive pricing covers many amenities you'd pay extra for on other lines, such as good house wine, specialty coffees, bottled water and sodas, basic gratuities (for cabin stewards, bar, and dining), self-service laundry, and shuttle buses in some ports.

Oceania Cruises

Contact Information: www.oceaniacruises.com, tel. 800-531-5619
Number and Capacity of Ships: *Marina* and *Riviera* each carry 1,250 passengers; *Insignia, Nautica,* and *Regatta* each carry 684.
Average Hours in Port: 9-10 hours
Description: Oceania Cruises appeals to well-traveled, well-heeled baby boomers and older retirees who want fine cuisine, excellent service, and a destination-oriented experience—toeing the fine line between upscale and snooty. The atmosphere is casually sophisticated—tastefully understated elegance. Although the line does not discourage children, kids' amenities (and young passengers) are sparse. Oceania's itineraries tend to be on the longer side; European sailings under 10 days are rare.

Staterooms are particularly well-equipped, reminiscent of stylish boutique hotels, with a cozy and intimate atmosphere. On the smaller ships, the staterooms and bathrooms are smaller than on most Luxury ships—but with great beds and fine linens. Oceania touts its cuisine; some of their menus were designed by celebrity chef Jacques Pépin, and their ships have a variety of specialty restaurants—French, Italian, steakhouse, and so on—for no extra charge (but reserve ahead). The larger ships have a culinary arts center with hands-on workshops (for a fee).

Oceania is noted for courting experienced crew members and for low crew turnover. The ships offer extensive onboard libraries, but relatively few organized activities, making these cruises best for those who can entertain themselves (or who make the most of time in port). While a few extras (such as specialty coffee drinks) are included, others are still à la carte; these, and Oceania's excursions, are a bit pricier than average.

Star Clippers

Contact Information: www.starclippers.com, tel. 800-442-0551

Number and Capacity of Ships: *Royal Clipper* carries 227 passengers; *Star Clipper* and *Star Flyer* each carry 170.

Average Hours in Port: 8-9 hours

Description: Star Clippers takes its sailing heritage very seriously, and its three ships are among the world's largest and tallest sailing vessels (actual "tall ships," with diesel engines for backup power). While the Windstar ships (described next) also have sails, those are mostly for show—Star Clippers' square-riggers are real sailboats. Passengers with nautical know-how are invited to pitch in when sails are hoisted or lowered. If the weather is right during the trip, you can even climb the main mast up to the crow's nest (wearing a safety harness, of course). There's a goose-bump-inducing ceremony every time you leave port: The crew raises the sails while haunting music plays over the loudspeakers.

With its sailing focus, Star Clippers draws more active, adventurous customers, ranging in age from 30s to 70s, who don't need to be pampered. Passengers are primarily Europeans (one recent sailing had passengers from 38 countries), and almost 60 percent are repeat customers. People who choose Star Clippers love the simple life on board a sailboat; enjoy a casual, easygoing cruise experience; and don't want the nightclubs and casinos offered by mainstream cruise lines. Kids are welcome, but there are no children's programs, counselors, or video-game parlors. Given the constraints of a small vessel, the cabins are not as big or luxurious as you might expect at this price range (for example, none have verandas).

The food, while adequate, comes in modest (European-size) portions. There's open seating in the dining room, the dress code is casual, and there are no rigid schedules. Activities include beach barbecues, crab races, scavenger hunts, talent nights, fashion shows, and performances by local musicians. You'll also have access to complimentary water activities, including snorkeling, kayaking, and sailing.

Windstar Cruises

Contact Information: www.windstarcruises.com, tel. 888-258-7245
Number and Capacity of Ships: *Wind Surf* carries 312 passengers, *Wind Star* and *Wind Spirit* each carry 148, and *Star Pride* carries 212. Two 208-passenger ships (Seabourn's *Spirit* and *Legend*) are scheduled to join the fleet in the spring of 2015.
Average Hours in Port: 10 hours
Description: Windstar's gimmick is its sails—each of its ships has four big, functional sails that unfurl dramatically each time the ship leaves port. (While the sails are capable of powering the ship in strong winds, they're more decorative than practical—although they do reduce the amount of fuel used by the engines.) This line provides an enticing bridge between the more rough-around-the-edges sailboat experience of Star Clippers (described above) and the comforts of mainstream lines. For many, it's an ideal combination—the romance of sails plus the pampering of a Luxury cruise. For this price range, it has a relatively casual atmosphere, with no formal nights.

Windstar passengers are professionals and experienced independent-minded travelers who range in age from 40s to 70s. First-time cruisers, honeymooners, and anniversary celebrants are enticed by Windstar's unique approach. The smaller ships favor more-focused itineraries and smaller ports, with generous time ashore. Passengers are more "travelers" than "cruisers"—they're here to spend as much time as possible exploring the port towns.

The small vessels also mean fewer on-ship activities. The casino and swimming pool are minuscule, the smaller ships have only one specialty restaurant, and nightlife is virtually nonexistent. However, the lounge hosts talented musicians, and each stateroom has a DVD player (there's a free DVD library). On some days when the ship is tendered, they lower a platform from the stern, allowing passengers to enjoy water-sports activities right off the back of the vessel. The food is high-quality, and there's a barbecue night on the open deck. Windstar also touts its green-ness (thanks to those sails) and its rare open-bridge policy, whereby passengers can visit the bridge during certain times to see the instruments and chat with the captain and officers.

Ultra-Luxury

You'll pay top dollar for these cruises, but get an elite experience in return. The basic features of the previously described Luxury cruises apply to this category as well: small ships (with the exception of Crystal), upscale clientele, a classier atmosphere, less emphasis on onboard activities, and a more destination-focused experience. There's less focus on selling you extras—at these prices, you can expect more and more extras to be included (ranging from alcoholic drinks to shore excursions).

Crystal Cruises

Contact Information: www.crystalcruises.com, tel. 888-722-0021
Number and Capacity of Ships: *Serenity* carries 1,070 passengers; *Symphony* carries 922 passengers.
Average Hours in Port: 10 hours
Description: While most Luxury and Ultra-Luxury lines have smaller ships, Crystal Cruises distinguishes itself by operating larger ships, closer in size to the less-expensive categories. This allows it to offer more big-ship activities and amenities, while still fostering a genteel, upper-crust ambience (which some may consider "stuffy"). Crystal attracts a retired, well-traveled, well-heeled crowd (although there are also a fair number of people under 50). Approximately 75 percent of the travelers are from the US and Canada, and the rest are mainly British. There are basic programs for children (most kids seem to come with multigenerational family groups) that are better than those on most Ultra-Luxury lines.

The food and the service are both well-regarded (and their seafood comes from sustainable and fair-trade sources). Their acclaimed enrichment programs are noted for having a wide range of minicourses in everything from foreign languages to computer skills, and excursions include opportunities for passengers to participate in a local volunteering effort.

Note: Crystal Cruises are sold exclusively through travel agents.

Regent Seven Seas Cruises (RSSC)

Contact Information: www.rssc.com, tel. 877-505-5370
Number and Capacity of Ships: *Voyager* and *Mariner* each carry 700 passengers; *Navigator* carries 490.
Average Hours in Port: 10-11 hours
Description: Regent Seven Seas Cruises appeal to well-educated, sophisticated, and affluent travelers—generally from mid-40s to retirees—looking for a destination-oriented experience. Their exclusive, clubby, understatedly elegant atmosphere attracts many repeat cruisers (the *Voyager* seems especially popular). Most passengers are from North America, with the rest from Great Britain, New Zealand, and Australia. The line welcomes families during

summer and school breaks, when it offers a children's program; the rest of the year, there's little to occupy kids.

Their "ultra-inclusive" prices are, indeed, among the most inclusive in the industry, covering premium soft drinks, house wines, tips, ground transfers, round-trip airfare from the US, one night's pre-cruise hotel stay, and unlimited excursions. The ships are known for their spacious, elegantly appointed suites (all with verandas). This line has some of the industry's highest space-per-guest and crew member-per-guest ratios, and customers report outstanding service. The French-based cuisine has an international flair, and also attempts to mix in local fare from the ships' ports of call. Passengers tend to be independent-minded and enjoy making their own plans, rather than wanting to be entertained by the cruise line (the entertainment is low-key, and notably, there is no onboard photography service). The crew tries to incorporate the ship's destinations into the entertainment, events, and lectures. Excursions include private tours, strenuous walking tours, and some soft-adventure offerings such as kayaking.

Seabourn Cruise Line

Contact Information: www.seabourn.com, tel. 866-755-5619

Number and Capacity of Ships: *Odyssey, Sojourn,* and *Quest* each carry 450 passengers; *Spirit* and *Legend* each carry 208 (but will be sold to Windstar in spring of 2015).

Average Hours in Port: 10 hours

Description: Seabourn Cruise Line attracts affluent, well-traveled couples in their late 40s to late 60s and older, who are not necessarily cruise aficionados but are accustomed to the "best of the best." Deep down, Seabourn passengers want to be on a yacht, but don't mind sharing it with other upper-class travelers—who, as the line brags, are "both interesting and interested." The focus is on exploring more exotic destinations rather than just relaxing on the ship. Most passengers are American, and the onboard atmosphere is classically elegant. Kids are present in summer and during school vacations, usually with multigenerational groups.

These ships feel like private clubs, with pampering as a priority. The extremely high crew member-to-guest ratio is about 1:1, and the crew addresses guests by name. Activities are designed for socializing with other passengers. Most of the ships offer a stern platform for swimming and kayaking right off the back of the ship. The line's all-inclusive

pricing includes freebies like a welcome bottle of champagne, an in-suite bar (with full bottles of your preselected booze), and nearly all drinks, including decent wines at mealtime (you pay extra only for premium brands). Also included are tips, some excursions, poolside mini-massages, and activities such as exercise classes and wine-tasting seminars.

SeaDream Yacht Club

Contact Information: www.seadream.com, tel. 800-707-4911
Number and Capacity of Ships: *SeaDream I* and *SeaDream II* each carry 110 passengers.
Average Hours in Port: 12+ hours
Description: SeaDream's tiny, intimate ships—the smallest of all those described here—are essentially chic, Ultra-Luxury megayachts. This line appeals to active travelers who are well-heeled and well-traveled, ranging in age from 40s to 70s (the shorter itineraries appeal to those still working). Passengers are primarily from North America and Europe, the atmosphere is laid-back, and the dress code is country-club casual (with no formal nights). There are no kids' facilities or services on board.

The attentive crew anticipates guests' needs without fawning. The unstructured environment is best for independent-minded passengers, as you're pretty much on your own for entertainment. The line is perfect for those who want to relax on deck and be outdoors as much as possible. In fact, a unique—and extremely popular—activity is sleeping out under the stars on double loungers. Itineraries include overnight stays in port (allowing guests the option to experience local nightlife) and are somewhat flexible, allowing the captain to linger longer in a port or depart early. Rather than hiring local guides for all their shore excursions, some trips are led by the ship's officers or other crew members. (Note that organized excursions may be canceled if the quota isn't reached, which can happen, given the small number of passengers.) The ships have a sports platform off the stern with water-sports toys such as kayaks and water skis, and there's a fleet of mountain bikes for exploring the destinations. Prices include decent house wines, cocktails, tips, water-sports equipment, DVDs, and shore excursions.

Silversea Cruises

Contact Information: www.silversea.com, tel. 877-276-6816
Number and Capacity of Ships: *Silver Spirit* carries 540 passengers, *Silver Whisper* carries 382, *Silver Wind* and *Silver Cloud* each carry 296, and *Silver Shadow* carries 382.
Average Hours in Port: 11 hours
Description: The Italian-owned, Monaco-based Silversea Cruises is popular with well-educated, well-traveled, upper-crust cruisers,

generally ranging in age from late 40s to 80s (with many in their 70s). Most passengers are accustomed to the finest and are very discriminating. The ships' Art Deco design lends an elegant 1930s ambience, and the atmosphere on board is clubby. Half of their clientele is from North America, with the other half predominantly from the UK, Europe, and Australia. There are no organized children's programs, and you'll see few children on board.

The cuisine is considered very good, and the service excellent; the spacious suites even have an assigned butler. Partly as a function of the ships' small size and fewer passengers, the events and entertainment are low-key.

BOOKING A CRUISE

Once you've narrowed down your cruise-line options, it's time to get serious about booking. This chapter covers where, when, and how to book your cruise, including pointers on cruise pricing, cabin assignments, trip insurance, pre- and post-cruise plans, and other considerations.

Where to Book a Cruise

While plane tickets, rental cars, hotels, and most other aspects of travel have gradually migrated to do-it-yourself, cruises are the one form of travel that is still booked predominantly through a travel agent. In fact, 85 percent of cruises are booked through travel agencies.

While it's possible to book a cruise directly with the cruise line, most lines actually prefer that you go through an intermediary. That's because their customers are rarely just booking a cruise—while they're at it, they want to look into airfares, trip insurance, maybe some hotels at either end of the cruise, and so on. That's beyond the scope of what cruise lines want to sell—their booking offices mainly take orders, they don't advise—so they reduce their overhead by letting travel agents do all that hard work (and hand-holding).

It can also be cheaper to book through a travel agent. Some cruise lines discount fares that are sold through their preferred agents; because they've built up relationships with these agents over the years, they don't want to undersell them. In other cases, the travel agency reserves a block of cabins to secure the lowest possible price, and then passes the savings on to their customers.

There are, generally speaking, two different types of cruise-sales agencies: your neighborhood travel agent, where you can get in-person advice; or a giant company that sells most of its inventory online or by phone. Because cruise prices vary based on volume, a big agency can usually undersell a small one. Big agencies are also more likely to offer incentives (such as onboard credit or cabin upgrades) to sweeten the pot. However, some small agencies belong to a consortium that gives them as much collective clout as a big agency. And some travelers figure the intangible value of personal service they get at a small agency is worth the possibility of paying a little extra. (Although most travel agents don't charge a fee, their commission is built into the cruise price.)

The big cruise agencies often have websites where you can easily shop around for the best price. These include www.vacationstogo.com, www.cruisecompete.com, and www.crucon.com. One site, www.cayole.com, tries to predict when prices for a particular departure may be lowest—giving you advice about how soon you should book.

I use the big websites to do some comparison-shopping. But—call me old-fashioned—when it comes time to book, I prefer to sit down with a travel agent to make my plans in person. Ideally, find a well-regarded travel agent in your community who knows cruising and will give you the personal attention you need to sort through your options. Tell them the deals you've seen online, and ask if they can match or beat them. A good travel agent knows how to look at your whole travel picture (airfare, hotels, and so on), not just the cruise component. And they can advise you about "insider" information, such as how to select the right cabin. Keep in mind that if you do solicit the advice of a travel agent, you should book the cruise through them—that's the only way they'll get their hard-earned commission. Once you've booked your cruise, you can arrange airfare through your travel agent, or you may choose to do that part on your own; for hotels, I always book direct.

When to Book a Cruise

Most cruise lines post their schedules a year or more in advance. A specific departure is called a "sailing." If you want to cruise in the summertime, and your plans are very specific (for example, you have your heart set on a certain sailing, or a particular cabin setup, such as adjoining staterooms), it's best to begin looking the preceding November. (For cruises in shoulder season—spring and fall—you may have a little more time to shop around.) Because the cruise lines want to fill up their ships as fast as possible, they typically offer early-booking discounts if you buy your cruise well in advance (at least 6-12 months, depending on the company).

Meanwhile, the most popular time of year to book a cruise is during the first few weeks of January. Dubbed "wave season" by

Sample Pretrip Timeline

While this can vary, here's a general timeline for what to do and when—but be sure to carefully confirm with your specific cruise line.

What to Do	Time Before Departure
Book cruise and pay initial deposit	8-10 months (for best selection)
Buy trip insurance, if desired	At time of booking (if through cruise line); within about 2 weeks of booking (if through a third party)
Full payment due	45-60 days
Online check-in	Between booking and full payment (check with cruise line)
Fly to meet your cruise	1-2 days ahead (remember you lose one day when flying from the US to Europe)

industry insiders, this is when a third of all cruises are booked. If you wait until this time, you'll be competing with other travelers for the deals. The sooner you book, the more likely you are to have your choice of sailing and cabin type—and potentially an even better price.

If a cruise still has several cabins available 90 days before departure, they're likely to put them on sale—but don't count on it. People tend to think the longer they wait, the more likely it is they'll find a sale. But this isn't always the case. Last-minute sales aren't as likely for Europe as they are for some other destinations, such as the Caribbean. Unlike the Caribbean market, the European market has a much shorter season and fewer ships, which means fewer beds to fill...and fewer deals to fill them. And even if you do find a last-minute deal, keep in mind that last-minute airfares to Europe can be that much more expensive.

If you're unsure of when to book, consult your travel agent.

How to Book a Cruise

Once you find the cruise you want, your travel agent may be able to hold it for you for a day or two while you think it over. When you've decided, you'll secure your passage on the cruise by paying a deposit. While this varies by cruise line, it averages about $500 per person (this becomes nonrefundable after a specified date, sometimes immediately—ask when you book). No matter how far ahead you book, you generally won't have to pay the balance until

45-60 days before departure. After this point, cancellation comes at a heftier price; as the departure date approaches, your cruise becomes effectively nonrefundable. In general, read the fine print of your cruise ticket carefully.

Cruise Pricing

Like cars or plane tickets, cruises are priced very flexibly. Some cruise lines don't even bother listing prices in their brochures—they just send customers to the Web. In general, for a Mass-Market cruise, you'll rarely pay the list price. Higher-end cruises are less likely to be discounted.

The main factor that determines the actual cost of a cruise is demand (that is, the popularity of the date, destination, and specific ship), but other factors also play a role.

Cruise lines and travel agencies use **sales and incentives** to entice new customers. With the recent proliferation of megaships, there are plenty of cabins to fill, and cruise industry insiders rigidly follow the mantra, "Empty beds are not tolerated!" The obvious approach to filling up a slow-selling cruise is to reduce prices. But they may also offer "onboard credit," which can be applied to your expenses on the ship (such as tips, alcoholic drinks, or excursions). In other cases, they may automatically upgrade your stateroom ("Pay for Category C, and get a Category B cabin for no extra charge!"). To further entice you, they might even throw in a special cocktail reception with the captain, or a night or two at a hotel at either end of your cruise. Your travel agent should be aware of these sales; you can also look online, or—if you're a fan of a particular cruise line—sign up to get their email offers.

Some cruise lines offer **discounts** for seniors (including AARP members), AAA members, firefighters, military, union workers, teachers, those in the travel industry, employees of certain corporations, and so on. It never hurts to ask.

Keep in mind that you'll pay a premium for **novelty.** It usually costs more to go on the cruise line's newest, most loudly advertised vessel. If you go on a ship that's just a few years older—with most of the same amenities—you'll likely pay less.

If you are a **repeat cruiser**—or think you may become one—sign up for the cruise line's "frequent cruiser" program. Like the airlines' mileage-rewards programs, these offer incentives, upgrades, and access to special deals.

No matter who you book your cruise through, use a **credit card** to give yourself a measure of consumer protection. A credit-card company can be a strong ally in resolving disputes.

If the **price drops after you book** your cruise, try asking for a new price. A good time to ask is just before or when you make the final payment. They don't have all your money yet and tend to be more eager to look for specials that will reduce your bottom line. You'll often be given a discount, or possibly an upgrade.

Taxes, Port Fees, and Other Hidden Charges

The advertised price for your cruise isn't all you'll have to pay. All the miscellaneous taxes, fees, and other expenses that the ship incurs in port are divvied up and passed on to passengers, under the category **"taxes and port fees."** While this can vary dramatically from port to port, it'll run you a few hundred dollars per person. These amounts are not locked in at the time you book; if a port increases its fees, you'll pay the difference.

Like airlines, cruise lines reserve the right to tack on a **"fuel surcharge"** in the event that the price of oil goes over a certain amount per barrel. This can be added onto your bill even after you book the cruise.

Once you're on the cruise, most lines automatically levy an **"auto-tip"** of around $10-12/day per person (which you can adjust upward or downward once on board). While this won't be included in your up-front cruise cost, you should budget for it. Many cruisers also choose to give excellent crew members an additional cash tip. For more details on tipping, see page 79.

Special Considerations

Families, singles, groups, people celebrating milestones, and those with limited mobility are all special in my book.

If you're traveling with a family, note that fares for **kids** tend to be more expensive during spring break and summertime, when they're out of school and demand is high; it can be cheaper to bring them off-season. Adjoining staterooms (also called "connecting" rooms) that share an inside door tend to book up early, particularly in the summertime. If those are sold out, consider an inside cabin across from an outside cabin. Some rooms have fold-down bunk beds (or "upper berths"), so a family of three or four can cram into one room (each passenger after the second pays a reduced fare)—but the tight quarters, already cramped for two people, can be challenging for the whole clan. Like connecting staterooms, these triple or quad cabins sell out early. Note that women who are more than six months **pregnant**—and **babies** who are younger than six months—are typically not allowed on a cruise.

Single cabins are rare on cruise ships; almost all staterooms are designed with couples in mind. Therefore, cruise rates are quoted per person, based on double occupancy. If you're traveling solo, you'll usually have to pay a "single supplement." This can range from reasonable (an additional 10 percent of the per-person double rate) to exorbitant ("100 percent" of the double rate—in other words, paying as much as two people would). On average, figure paying about 50 percent above the per-person double rate for your own single cabin. Sometimes it's possible to avoid the single supplement by volunteering to be assigned a random roommate by the cruise line, but this option is increasingly rare.

Groups taking eight or more cabins may be eligible for discounts if they're booked together—ask. The discounts often don't add up to much, but you may wrangle a shipboard credit or a private cocktail party.

If you'll be celebrating a **special occasion**—such as a birthday or anniversary—on board, mention it when you book. You may get a special bonus, such as a fancy dessert or cocktails with the captain.

If you have **limited mobility,** cruising can be a good way to go—but not all cruise lines are created equal. Some ships are wheelchair-accessible, including fully adapted cabins; others (especially small vessels) may not even have an elevator. When shopping for your cruise, ask the cruise line about the features you'll need, and be very specific. Unfortunately, once you reach port, all bets are off. While some cities are impressively accessible, others (especially smaller towns) may have fewer elevators than the ship you arrived on. The creaky and cobbled Old World doesn't accommodate wheelchairs or walkers very well. Taking a shore excursion can be a good way to see a place with minimum effort; cruise lines can typically inform you of the specific amount of walking and stairs you'll need to tackle for each excursion.

Cabin Classes

Each cruise ship has a variety of staterooms. In some cases, it can be a pretty narrow distinction ("Category A" and the marginally smaller "Category B"). On other ships, it can be the difference between a "Class 1" suite with a private balcony and a "Class 10" windowless bunk-bed closet below the waterline. On its website, each cruise line explains the specific breakdown of its various categories, along with the amenities in each one. In general, the highest demand is for the top-end and bottom-end cabins. Also, as verandas are increasingly popular, the most affordable rooms with verandas are often the first fares to sell out.

You'll see these terms:

Inside/Interior: An inside cabin has no external windows (though there's often a faux porthole to at least create the illusion of outside light). While these terrify claustrophobes, inside cabins offer a great value that tempts budget travelers. And many cruisers figure that with a giant ship to explore—not to mention Europe at your doorstep each morning—there's not much point hanging out in your room anyway.

Outside: With a window to the sea, an outside cabin costs

more—but for some travelers, it's worth the splurge to be able to see the world go by. But be aware that you're rarely able to open those windows (for that, you need a veranda—see next). If your view is blocked (by a lifeboat, for example), it should be classified as "obstructed."

Veranda: Going one better than an outside cabin, a "veranda" is cruise jargon for a small outdoor balcony attached to your room.

Because windows can't be opened, one big advantage of a veranda is that you can slide open the door to get some fresh air. The size and openness of verandas can vary wildly; for wind-shear reasons, some verandas can be almost entirely enclosed, with only a big picture window-sized opening to the sea. Sitting on the veranda while you cruise sounds appealing, but keep in mind that most of the time you're sailing, it'll be dark outside.

Suite: A multi-room suite represents the top end of cruise accommodations. These are particularly handy for families, but if you can't spring for a suite, ask about adjoining staterooms (see earlier).

Location Within Ship: In general, the upper decks (with better views, and typically bigger windows and more light) are more desirable—and more expensive—than the lower decks. Cabins in the middle of the ship (where the "motion of the ocean" is less noticeable) are considered better than those at either end. And cabins close to the engines (low and to the rear of the ship) can come with extra noise and vibrations.

Look for the **deck plan** on your cruise line's website. If you have a chance to select your own cabin (see next section), study the deck plan carefully to choose a good location. You'd want to avoid a cabin directly below a deck that has a lot of noisy foot traffic (such as the late-night disco or stewards dragging pool chairs across the deck).

Cabin Assignments and Upgrades

Cruise lines handle specific cabin assignments in different ways. While some cruise lines let you request a specific stateroom when you book, others don't offer that option; they'll assign your stateroom number at a future date. In other cases, you can request a "guarantee"—you pay for a particular class and are guaranteed that class of cabin (or better), but are not yet assigned a specific stateroom. As time passes and the cruise line gets a better sense of the occupancy on your sailing, there's a possibility that they will upgrade you to a better cabin for no extra charge. There's no way of predicting when you'll find out your specific cabin assignment—it can be months before departure, or days before. (Cabin assignments seem to favor repeat cruisers, rewarding customers for their loyalty.)

If you need a specific type of stateroom—for instance, you have limited mobility and need to be close to the elevator, or you're traveling with a large family and want to be as close together as possible—opt for a specific cabin assignment as early as you can.

If you don't have special needs, you might as well take your chances with a "guarantee"; you're assured of getting the class of cabin that you paid for...and you could wind up with a bonus veranda.

Assigned Dining: Traditionally, cruisers reserved not only their stateroom, but also which table and at what time they'd like to have dinner each night. Called a "seating," this tradition is fading. It's still mandatory on a few lines, but most lines either make it optional or have done away with it entirely. If your cruise line requires (or you prefer) a specific seating, reserve it when you book your cruise or cabin. (For more on assigned dining, see page 98.)

Travel Insurance

Travel insurance can minimize the considerable financial risks of traveling: accidents, illness, cruise cancellations due to bad weather, missed flights, lost baggage, medical expenses, and emergency evacuation. If you anticipate any hiccups that may prevent you from taking your trip, travel insurance can protect your investment.

Trip-cancellation insurance lets you bail out without losing all of the money you paid for the cruise, provided you cancel for an acceptable reason, such as illness or a death in the family. This insurance also covers trip interruptions—if you begin a journey but have to cut it short for a covered reason, you'll be reimbursed for the portion of the trip that you didn't complete.

Travel insurance is also handy in the unlikely event that your ship breaks down mid-trip. Though the cruise line should reimburse you for the cruise itself, travel insurance provides more sure-fire protection and can cover unexpected expenses, such as hotels or additional transportation you might need once you've gotten off the ship.

Travel insurance also includes basic medical coverage—up to a certain amount. If you have an accident or come down with a case of the "cruise-ship virus," your policy will cover doctor visits, treatment, and medication (though you'll generally have to pay a deductible). This usually includes medical evacuation—in the event that you become seriously ill and need to be taken to the nearest adequate medical care (that is, a big, modern hospital).

Baggage insurance, included in most comprehensive policies (and in some homeowner or renter insurance policies), reimburses you for luggage that's lost, stolen, or damaged. However, some items aren't covered (ask for details when you buy). When you check a bag on a plane, it's covered by the airline (though, again, there are limits—ask).

Insurance prices vary dramatically, but most packages cost between 5 and 12 percent of the price of your trip. Two factors affect the price: the trip cost and your age at the time of purchase (rates go up dramatically for every decade over 50). For instance, to insure a 70-year-old traveler for a $3,000 cruise, the prices can range from about $150 to $430, depending on the level of coverage. To insure a 40-year-old for that same cruise, the cost can be about $90-215. Coverage is generally inexpensive or even free for children 17 and under. To ensure maximum coverage, it's smart to buy your insurance policy within a week of the date you make the first payment on your trip. Research policies carefully; if you wait too long to purchase insurance, you may be denied certain kinds of coverage, such as for pre-existing medical conditions.

Cruise lines offer their own travel insurance, but these policies generally aren't as comprehensive as those from third-party insurance companies. For example, a cruise-line policy only covers the cruise itself; if you book your airfare and pre- and post-cruise hotels separately, they will not be covered. And if your cruise line ceases operations, their insurance likely won't cover it. On the other hand, many cruise-line policies are not tied to age—potentially making them attractive to older passengers who find third-party policies prohibitively expensive.

Reputable independent providers include Betins (www.betins. com, tel. 866-552-8834 or 253/238-6374), Allianz (www.allianztravelinsurance.com, tel. 866-884-3556), Travelex (www.travelexinsurance.com, tel. 800-228-9792), Travel Guard (www.travelguard.com, tel. 800-826-4919), and Travel Insured International (www.travelinsured.com, tel. 800-243-3174). Insuremytrip.com allows you to compare insurance policies and costs among various providers (they also sell insurance; www.insuremytrip.com, tel. 800-487-4722).

Some credit-card companies may offer limited trip-cancellation or interruption coverage for cruises purchased with the card—it's worth checking before you buy a policy. Also, check whether your existing insurance (health, homeowners, or renters) covers you and your possessions overseas. For more tips, see www.ricksteves.com/insurance.

Airfare and Pre- and Post-Cruise Travel

When booking your airfare, think carefully about how much time you want before and after your cruise. Remember that most Europe-bound flights from the US travel overnight and arrive the following day. The nearest airport is often far from the cruise port; allow plenty of time to get to your ship. You'll need to check in at least two hours before your cruise departs (confirm with your cruise line; most passengers show up several hours earlier).

If your travel plans are flexible, consider arriving a few days before your cruise and/or departing a few days after it ends—particularly if the embarkation and disembarkation points are places you'd like to explore. Remember, if you arrive just hours before (or depart just hours after) your cruise, you won't actually have any time to see the beginning and ending ports at all. Common starting and ending points include Barcelona, Rome, Venice, Athens, and Istanbul—all of which merit plenty of time (and are covered a little more thoroughly in this book for that reason).

Arriving at least a day early makes it less likely that you'll miss the start of your cruise if your flight is delayed. If you miss the ship, you're on your own to catch up with it at its next port. In talking with fellow cruisers, while I've rarely heard of people missing the boat at a port of call, I've heard many horror stories about flight delays causing passengers to miss the first day of the cruise—and often incurring a time-consuming, stressful, and costly overland trip to meet their ship at the next stop.

In the past, most cruises included what they called "free air" (or "air/sea"), but these days your airfare to and from Europe costs extra—and you're usually best off booking it yourself. (Relatively few cruise passengers book airfare through their cruise line.) If you book your airfare through the cruise line, you'll typically pay more, but in case of a flight delay, the cruise line will help you meet the cruise at a later point. However, booking your airfare this way has its disadvantages—the cruise line chooses which airline and routing to send you on. They'll select an airline they have a contract with, regardless of whether it's one you want to fly (though it's sometimes possible to pay a "deviation fee" to switch to an airline and routing of your choice).

If you decide to add some days on either end of your trip, it's best to make your own arrangements for hotels and transfers. While most cruise lines offer pre- and post-tour packages (that include the hotel, plus transfers to and from the airport and the cruise port), they tend to be overpriced. For each of the arrival and departure cities in this book, I've recommended a few hotels for you to consider.

Some embarkation ports are quite distant from town (for example, Civitavecchia is nearly 50 miles from Rome). For these ports, a cruise-line airport transfer—which saves you a complicated journey through a big city's downtown—may be worth considering. You can often book a transfer even if you're booking your pre- or post-tour hotel on your own—ask.

In some rare circumstances, it's convenient for a cruise passenger to leave the ship before the cruise is completed—for example, you want to get off to have some extra time in Rome, rather than spend a day at sea to return to your starting point in Barcelona. Cruise lines usually permit this, but you'll pay for the full cost of the cruise (including the portion you're not using), and you'll need to get permission in advance.

Online Check-in

At some point between when you book and when your final payment is due, you'll be invited to check in online for your cruise. This takes only a few minutes. You'll register your basic information and sometimes a credit-card number (for onboard purchases—or you can do this in person when you arrive at the ship). Once registered, you'll be able to print out e-documents (such as your receipt and boarding pass), access information about shipboard life, and learn about and prebook shore excursions.

PART II: TRAVEL SKILLS FOR CRUISING

BEFORE YOUR CRUISE

As any sailor knows, prepare well and you'll enjoy a smoother voyage. This chapter covers what you should know before you go (including red tape, money matters, and other practicalities), as well as pointers for packing.

Know Before You Go

Red Tape

You need a **passport** to travel to the countries covered in this book. You may be denied entry into certain European countries if your passport is due to expire within three months of your ticketed date of return. Get it renewed if you'll be cutting it close. It can take up to six weeks to get or renew a passport (for more on passports, see www.travel.state.gov).

For entrance into Turkey, you may also need a **visa before you arrive**; this is most likely if your journey originates or ends in Turkey, or if you are making multiple stops there. If your cruise begins in Turkey, you must buy a visa prior to your arrival (easiest to do online at www.evisa.gov.tr, see page 1086). You can make day trips into Turkish ports without a visa, but you can't spend the night on shore without one. If you do need a visa on a cruise-sponsored excursion, your cruise line should notify you.

If you're traveling with **kids,** each minor must possess a passport. Grandparents or guardians can bring kids on board sans parents only if they have a signed, notarized document from the parent(s) to prove to authorities that they have permission to take the child on a trip. Even a single parent traveling with children has to demonstrate that the other parent has given approval. Specifically, the letter should grant permission for the accompanying adult to travel internationally with the child. Include your name,

Before-You-Go Checklist

Here are a few things to consider as you prepare for your cruise:

- Contact your **credit- and debit-card companies** to tell them you're going abroad and to ask about fees, limits, and more; see next page.
- Ask your **health insurance** provider about overseas medical coverage, both on the ship and on shore. For more on health care, see page 81.
- Consider buying **trip insurance.** For details, see page 41.
- For cruises with **assigned dining,** request your preference for seating time and table size when you reserve. See page 98.
- Vegetarians, those with food allergies, or anyone with a **special diet** should notify their cruise line at least 30 days before departure. See page 97.
- Your US **mobile phone** may work in Europe; if you want the option to use it while traveling, contact your mobile phone service provider for details. See page 87.
- Some major sights in Italy and Spain accept **reservations,** which can help you avoid long lines. For a list of sights to book in advance, see page 50.
- Be sure that you **know the PIN** for your credit and/or debit cards. You will likely encounter the chip-and-PIN payment system, which is widely used in Europe. For details on this system, see page 131.
- **Smokers**, or those determined to avoid smoke, can ask about their ship's smoking policy. See page 86.
- If you're prone to **seasickness,** ask your doctor for advice; certain medication requires a prescription. For a rundown of seasickness treatments, see page 82.
- If you're starting your cruise in Turkey or spending the night on shore in Turkey before or after your cruise, you will need **a visa** before you go. See facing page.
- If you're taking a **child** on a cruise without both parents, you'll need a signed, notarized document from the parent(s). See facing page.

the name of your child, the dates of your trip, destination countries, and the name, address, and phone number of the parent(s) at home. If you have a different last name from your child, it's smart to bring a copy of the birth certificate (with your name on it). For parents of adopted children, it's a good idea to bring their adoption decree as well.

Before you leave on your trip, make two sets of **photocopies** of your passport, tickets, and other valuable documents (front and back). Pack a copy and leave a copy with someone at home—to fax or email to you in case of an emergency. It's easier to replace a lost or stolen passport if you have a photocopy proving that you really had what you lost. A couple of passport-type pictures brought from home can expedite the replacement process.

Money

At the start of your cruise, you must register your credit card (either at check-in or on board the ship). All purchases are made using your room number, and you'll be billed for onboard purchases when you disembark. Be aware that the cruise line may put a hold on your credit card during your trip to cover anticipated shipboard expenses; if you have a relatively low limit, you might come uncomfortably close to it. If you're concerned, ask the cruise line what the amount of the hold will be.

For your time on **land,** bring both a credit card and a debit card. You'll use the debit card at cash machines (ATMs) to withdraw local cash for most purchases, and the credit card to pay for larger items. Some travelers carry a third card as a backup, in case one gets demagnetized or eaten by a temperamental machine. As an emergency reserve, I also bring a few hundred dollars in hard cash (in easy-to-exchange $20 bills).

Cash

Most cruise ships are essentially cashless (though you may want to bring some US cash for tipping at casinos). But on land, cash is just as desirable as it is at home. Don't bother changing money before you leave home—ATMs in Europe are easy to find and use (for details, see page 130). And skip traveler's checks—they're not worth the fees or waits in line at slow banks.

Credit and Debit Cards

For maximum usability, bring cards with a Visa or MasterCard logo. You'll also need to know the PIN code for each card in numbers, as there are no letters on European keypads. Before your trip, contact the company that issued your debit or credit cards and ask them a few questions.

• Confirm your card will work overseas, and alert them that you'll be using it in Europe; otherwise, they may deny transactions if they perceive unusual spending patterns.

• Ask for the specifics on transaction **fees.** When you use your credit or debit card—either for purchases or ATM withdrawals— you'll typically be charged additional "international transaction" fees of up to 3 percent (1 percent is normal) plus $5 per transaction. If your card's fees seem high, consider getting a different card just for your trip: Capital One (www.capitalone.com) and most credit unions have low-to-no international fees.

• If you plan to withdraw cash from ATMs, confirm your daily

withdrawal limit, and if necessary, ask your bank to adjust it. Some travelers prefer a high limit that allows them to take out more cash at each ATM stop (saving on bank fees), while others prefer to set a lower limit in case their card is stolen. Note that foreign banks also set maximum withdrawal amounts for their ATMs. Also, remember that you're withdrawing euros, not dollars—so if your daily limit is $300, withdraw just €200. Many frustrated travelers have walked away from ATMs thinking their cards were rejected, when actually they were asking for more cash in euros than their daily limit allowed.

• Find out your card's **credit limit.** Some cruise lines put a hold on your credit card to cover anticipated onboard expenses; if this or your on-shore spending is likely to crowd your limit, ask for a higher amount or bring a second credit card.

• Get your bank's emergency **phone number** in the US (but not its 800 number, which isn't accessible from overseas) to call collect if you have a problem.

• Ask for your credit card's **PIN** in case you need to make an emergency cash withdrawal or encounter Europe's "chip-and-PIN" system (for details, see page 131). The bank won't tell you your PIN over the phone, so allow time for it to be mailed to you.

Practicalities

Time Zones: Spain, France, Italy, Croatia, and most of the rest of continental Europe are generally six/nine hours ahead of the East/ West Coasts of the US. Greece and Turkey are one hour ahead of most of Europe, and seven/ten hours ahead of the East/West Coasts of the US. (If you cross a time zone on your ship, your cabin steward will leave a reminder on your bed the evening before to set your watch.)

The exceptions are the beginning and end of Daylight Saving Time: Europe "springs forward" the last Sunday in March (two weeks after most of North America), and "falls back" the last Sunday in October (one week before North America). For a handy online time converter, see www.timeanddate.com/worldclock.

Watt's Up? Virtually all cruise ships have American-style outlets, so you don't need an adapter or converter to charge your phone or blow-dry your hair. (If you're cruising with a European line, you may want to confirm the outlet type.)

But if you're staying at a hotel before or after the cruise, you'll need to adapt to Europe's electrical system, which is 220 volts, instead of North America's 110 volts. Most newer electronics (such as hair dryers, laptops, and battery chargers) convert automatically, so you won't need a converter, but you will need an adapter plug with two round prongs for continental Europe (sold inexpensively at travel stores in the US). Avoid bringing older appliances that

Rick Steves Audio Europe

If you're bringing a mobile device, be sure to check out **Rick Steves Audio Europe,** where you can download free audio tours and hours of travel interviews (via the Rick Steves Audio Europe smartphone app, www.ricksteves.com/audioeurope, iTunes, or Google Play).

My self-guided **audio tours** are user-friendly, easy to follow, fun, and informative, covering the major sights and neighborhoods in Rome, Florence, Venice, Athens, and Ephesus. Compared to live tours, my audio tours are hard to beat: Nobody will stand you up, the quality is reliable, you can take the tour exactly when you like, and they're free.

Rick Steves Audio Europe also offers a far-reaching library of intriguing **travel interviews** with experts from around the globe.

don't automatically convert voltage; instead, buy a cheap replacement appliance in Europe.

Driving in Europe: If you're planning on renting a car, bring your driver's license. An International Driving Permit—an official translation of your driver's license—is recommended in France and technically required in some countries, such as Greece, Spain, Turkey, and Italy (sold at your local AAA office for $15 plus the cost of two passport-type photos; see www.aaa.com). While that's the letter of the law, I've often rented cars in these countries without having this permit. If all goes well, you'll likely never be asked to show the permit—but it's a must if you end up dealing with the police.

Reservations at Major Sights: Some popular sights take reservations, allowing you to skip their long, boring, ticket-buying lines. Making reservations to visit the following sights in Italy and Spain isn't mandatory, but it is smart:

For **Florence's** Uffizi Gallery (Renaissance paintings), book well in advance; for the Accademia (Michelangelo's *David*), a minimum of a few days is enough (see page 396).

If you want to climb **Pisa's** Leaning Tower, you can book online (see page 467).

In **Rome,** the Vatican Museum (Sistine Chapel) takes online reservations (see page 577).

In **Barcelona,** you can make online reservations for the Picasso Museum (see page 206), Parc Güell (see page 206), and Antoni Gaudí's over-the-top Sagrada Família (see page 212).

Discounts: While this book does not list discounts for sights and museums, seniors (age 60 and over), students with International Student Identification Cards, teachers with proper identification, and youths under 18 often get discounts—but you have to ask. To get a teacher or student ID card, visit www.statravel.com or www.isic.org.

Online Translation Tip: You can use Google's Chrome browser (available free at www.google.com/chrome) to instantly translate websites. With one click, the page appears in (very rough) English translation. You can also paste the URL of the site into the translation window at www.google.com/translate.

Packing

One of the advantages of cruising is unpacking just once—in your stateroom. But don't underestimate the importance of packing light. Cruise-ship cabins are cramped, and large suitcases consume precious living space. Plus, you'll still need to get to the airport, on and off the plane, and between the airport and the cruise port. The lighter your luggage is, the easier your transitions will be. And when you carry your own luggage, it's less likely to get lost, broken, or stolen.

Consider packing just one carry-on-size bag (9" by 22" by 14"). I know—realistically, you'll be tempted to bring more. But cruising with one bag can be done without adversely impacting your trip (I've done it, and was happy I did). No matter how much you'd like to bring along that warm jacket or extra pair of shoes, be strong and do your best to pack just what you need.

Here's another reason to favor carry-on bags: If the airline loses your checked luggage and doesn't get it to your embarkation port by the time your ship sets sail, the bags are unlikely to catch up to you. If you booked air travel through the cruise line, the company will do what it can to reunite you with your lost bags. But if you arranged your own flights, the airline decides whether and how to help you—and rarely will it fly your bags to your next port of call. (If you purchase travel insurance, it may cover lost luggage—ask when you buy; for details on insurance, see page 41.) For this reason, even if you check a bag, be sure you pack essentials (medications, change of clothes, travel documents) in your carry-on.

If you're traveling as part of a couple, and the one-piece-per-person idea seems impossible, consider this compromise: Pack one bag each, as if traveling alone, then share a third bag for bulky cruise extras (such as formal wear). If traveling before or after the cruise, you can leave that third, nonessential bag at a friendly hotel or in a train-station luggage locker, then be footloose and fancy-free for your independent travel time.

Remember, packing light isn't just about the trip over and back—it's about your traveling lifestyle. Too much luggage marks you as a typical tourist. With only one bag, you're mobile and in control. You'll never meet a traveler who, after five trips, brags: "Every year I pack heavier."

Baggage Restrictions

Baggage restrictions provide a built-in incentive for packing light. Some cruise lines limit you to two bags of up to 50 pounds apiece; others don't enforce limits (or request only that you bring "a reasonable amount" of luggage). But all airlines have restrictions on the number, size, and weight of both checked and carry-on bags. These days, except on intercontinental flights, you'll most likely pay for each piece of luggage you check—and if your bag is overweight, you'll pay even more. Check the specifics on your airline's website (or read the fine print on your airline eticket).

Knives, lighters, and other potentially dangerous items are not allowed in airplane carry-ons or on board your cruise. Large quantities of liquids or gels must be packed away in checked baggage. Because restrictions are always changing, visit the Transportation Security Administration's website (www.tsa.gov) for an up-to-date list of what you can bring on the plane with you...and what you must check.

If you plan to check your bag for your flight, mark it inside and out with your name, address, and emergency phone number. If you have a lock on your bag, you may be asked to remove it to accommodate increased security checks, or it may be cut off so the bag can be inspected (to avoid this, consider a TSA-approved lock). I've never locked my bag, and I haven't had a problem. Still, just in case, I wouldn't pack anything valuable (such as cash or a camera) in my checked luggage.

As baggage fees increase, more people are carrying on their luggage. Arrive early for aircraft boarding to increase the odds that you'll snare coveted storage space in the passenger cabin.

What to Bring

How do you fit a whole trip's worth of luggage into one bag? The answer is simple: Bring very little. You don't need to pack for the worst-case scenario. Pack for the best-case scenario and simply buy yourself out of any jams. Bring layers rather than pack a heavy coat. Think in terms of what you can do without—not what might be handy on your trip. When in doubt, leave it out. The shops on your cruise ship (or on shore) are sure to have any personal items you forgot or have run out of.

Use the "Packing Checklist" on page 58 to organize and make your packing decisions.

Clothing

Most cruisers will want two to three changes of clothes each day:

comfortable, casual clothes for sightseeing in port; more formal evening wear for dinners on the ship; and sportswear, whether it's a swimsuit for basking by the pool or athletic gear for hitting the gym or running track. But that doesn't mean you have to bring along 21 separate outfits for a seven-day cruise. Think versatile. Some port wear can double as evening wear. Two pairs of dressy dinner slacks can be worn on alternating nights, indefinitely. As you choose clothes for your trip, a good rule of thumb is: If you're not going to wear an item more than three times, don't pack it. Every piece of clothing you bring should complement every other item or have at least two uses (for example, a scarf doubles as a shoulder wrap; a sweater provides warmth and dresses up a short-sleeve shirt). Accessories, such as a tie or scarf, can break the monotony and make you look snazzy.

First-time cruisers may worry about "formal nights." While most cruises do have a few formal nights with a dress code, they're not as stuffy as you might think. And those formal nights are optional—you can always eat somewhere other than the formal dining room. So dress up only as much as you want to (but keep in mind that if you plan to eat every meal in the dining room, you must adhere to its dress code—most cruise lines forbid shorts or jeans there at dinnertime). For a general idea of what people typically wear on board, read the sidebar on the next page, then find out what your ship's dress code is.

When choosing clothes for days in port, keep a couple of factors in mind: First, the Mediterranean can be very hot in the summer, so it's smart to bring breathable, light-colored clothes and a hat. Also, some European churches (particularly in Italy) enforce a strict "no shorts or bare shoulders" dress code. Pants with zip-off/zip-on legs can be handy in these situations.

Laundry options vary from ship to ship. Most provide 24-hour laundry service (at per-piece prices), enabling those without a lot of clothing to manage fine. But self-service launderettes are rare on board—ask your cruise line in advance about available options. Remember that you can still bring fewer clothes and wash as needed in your stateroom sink. It helps to pack items that don't wrinkle, or look good wrinkled. You should have no trouble drying clothing overnight in your cabin (though it might take longer in humid climates).

It can be worth splurging a little to get just the right clothes for your trip. For durable, lightweight travel clothes, consider ExOfficio (www.exofficio.com), TravelSmith (www.travelsmith.com), Tilley Endurables (www.tilley.com), Eddie Bauer (www.eddie-bauer.com), and REI (www.rei.com).

Ultimately—as long as you don't wear something that's outrageous or offensive—it's important to dress in a way that makes you

Cruise Ship Dress Code

First-time cruisers sometimes worry about the need to dress up on their vacation. Relax. Cruise ships aren't as dressy as they used to be. And, while on certain nights you may see your fellow cruisers in tuxes and formal gowns, there's usually a place to go casual as well. (In general, the more upscale a cruise is, the more formal the overall vibe—though some luxury lines, such as Windstar, have a reputation for relaxed dress codes.)

During the day, the dress code is casual. People wear shorts, T-shirts, swimsuits with cover-ups, flip-flops, or whatever they're most comfortable in. (On pricier cruises, you may see more passengers in khakis or dressy shorts and polo shirts.)

But in the evenings, a stricter dress code emerges. On most nights, dinner is usually "smart casual" in the main dining room and at some (or all) specialty restaurants. People are on vacation, so they generally aren't too dressed up—though jeans, shorts, and T-shirts are no-nos. For men, slacks and a button-down or polo shirt is the norm; most women wear dresses, or pants or skirts with a nice top. Plan to wear something a little nicer on the first evening; after you get the lay of the land, you can adjust your wardrobe for the rest of the meals.

Most cruises host one or two "formal" nights per week. On these evenings, men are expected to put on jackets (and sometimes ties), while women generally wear cocktail dresses—or pair a dressy skirt or pants with something silky or sparkly on top. Basically, dress as you would for a nice church wedding or a night at the theater. A few overachievers show up wearing tuxedos or floor-length dresses. Note that formal nights will sometimes extend beyond the dining room into the ship's main theater venue.

Some cruises also have "semiformal" nights, which fall be-

comfortable. No matter how carefully you dress, your clothes probably will mark you as an American. And so what? To fit in and be culturally sensitive, I watch my manners, not the cut of my clothes.

Here are a few specific considerations:

Shirts/blouses. Bring short-sleeved or long-sleeved shirts or blouses in a cotton/polyester blend. A sweater or lightweight fleece is good for layering (handy for chilly evenings). Dark colors don't show wrinkles or stains, though light colors can be more comfortable on sunny days in port. Indoor areas on the cruise ship can be heavily air-conditioned, so you may need a long-sleeved top, a sweater, or a wrap even in the height of summer.

Pants/skirts and shorts. Bring lightweight pants or skirts for hot and muggy big cities and churches with modest dress codes. Jeans can be too hot for summer travel—and most cruise lines don't consider jeans appropriate "smart casual" wear. Button-down wal-

tween the standard "smart casual" dress code and the formal nights—for example, men might wear slacks and a jacket, but no tie.

Cruise passengers are evenly split on the "formal night" phenomenon: Some look forward to dressing up and do so with gusto; others just want to be as casual as possible while on vacation. For those who don't want to dress up at all, most cruise ships have dining venues that are completely informal—the buffet, the poolside grill, and so on. Here you'll see people wearing shorts, swimsuits, cover-ups, and flip-flops. If you never want to put on a collared shirt, you can simply eat at these restaurants for the entire cruise. But be aware that you'll be passing gussied-up passengers in the hallways on formal nights—so you might feel a bit out of place if you go totally casual. Bring along a presentable top and pair of pants or skirt for the nights you want to spiff up a bit.

To pack light for your cruise, bring multifunctional clothing that allows you to go minimally formal and also feel chic in port. Men can get by with slacks and a sports coat—which are more versatile than a suit. (I got a lot of good use out of my summery sports coat.) Women can wear a casual dress and jazz it up with accessories, such as nice jewelry or a wrap. A scarf, wrap, or jacket makes a regular outfit (such as black pants and a tank top) more formal.

If you want to get decked out without lugging excess clothing on board, ask if your cruise line has a tuxedo-rental program (some cruise lines also offer a rental program for women's formal wear). You may be able to borrow a loaner jacket or rent a tux on the spot, but selection can be limited—so it's better to order in advance. Simply provide your measurements beforehand, and a tux will be waiting in your cabin when you board.

let pockets are safest (though still not as thief-proof as a money belt, described later). Shorts are perfectly acceptable aboard your ship, but on land in Europe they're considered beachwear, mostly worn in coastal or lakeside resort towns. No one will be offended if you wear shorts, but you may be on the receiving end of some second glances.

Shoes. Bring one pair of comfortable walking shoes with good traction. Comfort is essential even on board, where you'll sometimes be walking considerable distances just to get to dinner. And getting on and off tenders can involve a short hop to a pier—practical shoes are a must for port days. Sandals or flip-flops are good for poolside use or in case your shoes get wet. And don't forget appropriate footwear to go with your dinner clothes (though again, think versatile—for women, a nice, stylish pair of sandals is nearly as good as heels).

Jacket. Bring a light and water-resistant windbreaker with a hood. Gore-Tex is good if you expect rain. For summer travel, I wing it without rain gear.

Swimsuit and cover-up. If you plan on doing a lot of swimming, consider bringing a second swimsuit so that you always have a dry one to put on. Most cruise lines forbid swimsuits anywhere beyond the pool area, so cover-ups are a necessity.

Packing Essentials

Money belt. This flat, hidden, zippered pouch—strapped around your waist and tucked under your clothes—is smart for the peace of mind it brings. You could lose everything except your money belt, and the trip could still go on. Lightweight and low-profile beige is best. Whenever you're in port, keep your **cash, credit cards, driver's license,** and **passport** secure in your money belt, and carry only a day's spending money in your front pocket.

Toiletries kit. Sinks in staterooms come with meager countertop space. You'll have an easier time if you bring a toiletries kit that can hang on a hook or a towel bar. Cruise ships provide small bottles of shampoo and itsy-bitsy bars of soap, so you may prefer to bring along your own supplies. Put all squeeze bottles in sealable plastic baggies, since pressure changes in flight can cause even good bottles to leak.

Bring any **medication** and vitamins you need (keep medicine in original containers, if possible, with legible prescriptions), along with a basic **first-aid kit.** If you're prone to motion sickness, consider some sort of **seasickness remedy.** For various options, see page 82. There are different schools of thought on **hand sanitizers** in preventing the spread of germs. Some cruise lines embrace them, others shun them (see page 83)—but they can come in handy when soap and water aren't readily available.

If you wear **eyeglasses** or **contact lenses,** bring a photocopy of your prescription—just in case. A strap for your glasses/sunglasses is handy for water activities or for peering over the edge of the ship in a strong breeze.

Sunscreen and sunglasses. Bring protection for your skin and your eyes. Many passengers underestimate the power of the Mediterranean sun, get a massive sunburn the first day, and spend the rest of the cruise recovering.

Laundry supplies (soap and clothesline). If you plan to wash your own clothes, bring a small squeeze bottle of detergent. Some cruise-ship bathrooms have built-in clotheslines, but you can bring your own just in case (the twisted-rubber type needs no clothespins).

Packing aides. Packing cubes, clothes-compressor bags, and shirt-folding boards can help keep your clothes tightly packed and looking good.

Sealable plastic baggies. Bring a variety of sizes. In addition to holding your carry-on liquids, they're ideal for packing a picnic lunch, storing damp items, and bagging potential leaks before they happen. Some cruisers use baggies to organize their materials (cruise-line handouts, maps, ripped-out guidebook chapters, receipts) for each port of call. If you bring them, you'll use them.

Small daypack. A lightweight pack is great for carrying your sweater, camera, literature, and picnic goodies when you visit sights on shore. Fanny packs (small bags with thief-friendly zippers on a belt) are an alternative, but they're magnets for pickpockets (never use one as a money belt).

Small extra bag. A collapsible tote bag can come in handy for bringing purchases home from your trip. It's also useful for the first and last days of your cruise, if you check your larger bags to be carried on or off the ship for you. During these times, you'll want to keep a change of clothes, any medications, and valuables with you.

Water bottle. If you bring one from home, make sure it's empty before you go through airport security (fill it at a fountain once you're through). The plastic half-liter mineral water bottles sold throughout Europe are reusable and work great.

Travel information. This book will likely be all you need. But if you want more in-depth coverage of the destinations or information on a place not covered in this book, consider collecting some other sources. (For suggestions, see page 1249.) I like to rip out appropriate chapters from guidebooks and staple them together. When I'm done, I give them away.

Address list. If you plan to send postcards, consider printing your mailing list onto a sheet of adhesive address labels before you leave.

Postcards from home and photos of your family. A small collection of show-and-tell pictures (either printed or digital) is a fun, colorful conversation piece with fellow cruisers, your crew, and Europeans you meet.

Small notepad and pen. A tiny notepad in your back pocket or daypack is a great organizer, reminder, and communication aid.

Journal. An empty book to be filled with the experiences of your trip will be your most treasured souvenir. Attach a photo-copied calendar page of your itinerary. Use a hardbound type designed to last a lifetime, rather than a spiral notebook.

Packing Checklist

*Indicates items you can purchase online at www.ricksteves.com.

- ❑ Shirts/blouses: long- and short-sleeve
- ❑ Sweater or lightweight fleece
- ❑ Pants/skirts
- ❑ Formal night clothes: Dress pants/skirt with nice shirt/top or cocktail dress
- ❑ Formal wear (optional): Sports coat or tux for men, evening gown for women
- ❑ Shorts
- ❑ Swimsuit and cover-up
- ❑ Underwear and socks
- ❑ Shoes: walking/sandals/dress-up
- ❑ Rainproof jacket with hood
- ❑ Tie or scarf
- ❑ Pajamas/nightgown
- ❑ *Money belt
- ❑ Money—your mix of:
  - ❑ Debit card (for ATM withdrawals)
  - ❑ Credit card
  - ❑ Hard cash (in easy-to-exchange $20 bills)
- ❑ Documents plus photocopies:
  - ❑ Passport
  - ❑ Printout of airline and cruise etickets
  - ❑ Driver's license
  - ❑ Student or teacher ID card
  - ❑ Insurance details
- ❑ *Daypack
- ❑ *Extra, collapsible tote bag
- ❑ Sealable plastic baggies

Electronics and Entertainment

Go light with your electronic gear: You want to experience Europe, not interface with it. Of course, some mobile devices are great tools for making your trip easier or better. Note that many of these things are big-ticket items; guard them carefully or consider insuring them (see page 41). Note that Wi-Fi aboard cruise ships can be slow and expensive—see page 86.

Consider bringing the following gadgets: **digital camera** (and associated gear); **mobile phone/smartphone** (for details on using a US phone in Europe—or on a cruise ship—see page 87); **other mobile devices** (laptop, tablet, portable media player, ereader); and **headphones/earbuds** (travel partners can bring a Y-jack for two sets of earphones). A small **auxiliary speaker** for your mobile device turns it into a better entertainment center. For each item, remember to bring the **charger** and/or extra **batteries** (you can buy batteries on cruise ships and in Europe, but at a higher price).

- ❑ Electronics—your choice of:
    - ❑ Camera (and related gear)
    - ❑ Mobile phone or smartphone
    - ❑ iPod/MP3 player/portable DVD player
    - ❑ Laptop/netbook/tablet
    - ❑ Ebook reader
    - ❑ Chargers for each of the above
- ❑ Leisure reading
- ❑ *Empty water bottle
- ❑ Wristwatch and *alarm clock
- ❑ *Toiletries kit
    - ❑ Toiletries (soap, shampoo, toothbrush, toothpaste, floss, deodorant)
    - ❑ Medicines (including seasickness remedies if needed)
    - ❑ First-aid kit
    - ❑ Hand sanitizer
    - ❑ Glasses/contacts (with prescriptions)
- ❑ Sunscreen and sunglasses
- ❑ *Laundry soap and *clothesline
- ❑ *Earplugs/*neck pillow
- ❑ *Travel information (guidebooks and maps)
- ❑ Address list (for sending postcards)
- ❑ Postcards and photos from home
- ❑ *Notepad/journal and pen
- ❑ Miscellaneous supplies (list on following page)

If you plan to carry on your luggage, note that all liquids must be in 3.4-ounce or smaller containers and fit within a single quart-size sealable bag. For details, see www.tsa.gov.

Most cruises have limited TV offerings and charge a premium for pay-per-view movies (though you'll find DVD players in some staterooms). If you crave digital distraction, preload your mobile device with a selection of movies or TV shows. Cruise lines generally disable your stateroom TV's input jack, so you can't run a movie from your device on the TV.

For long days at sea, bring some leisure reading, whether on an ereader or just a good old paperback. Most ships also have free lending libraries and sell US paperbacks at reasonable prices.

Some travelers use **digital recorders** to capture pipe organs, tours, or journal entries. Having a portable **radio** can be fun if you want to tune in to European stations as you travel.

Note: Most ships use North American electrical outlets, but if you're staying at a European hotel, you'll need an **adapter** to plug in electronics (for details, see "Watt's Up?" on page 49).

Many staterooms have a limited number of outlets, so a lightweight **power strip** can be helpful if you have a lot of gadgets to charge at one time.

Miscellaneous Supplies

The following items are not necessities, but they generally take up little room and can come in handy in a pinch.

Basic **picnic supplies,** such as a Swiss Army-type knife and plastic cutlery, enable you to shop for a very European lunch at a market or neighborhood grocery store. Munch in port or in your stateroom (but remember not to pack a knife in your carry-on bag when flying).

Sticky notes (such as Post-Its) are great for keeping your place in your guidebook. **Duct tape** cures a thousand problems. A **tiny lock** will keep the zippers on your checked baggage shut.

A small **flashlight** is handy for reading under the sheets while your partner snoozes, or for finding your way through an unlit passage (tiny-but-powerful LED flashlights—about the size of your little finger—are extremely bright and compact).

Not every stateroom comes with an **alarm clock,** so bring a small portable one just in case (or you can use the alarm on your mobile phone). A **wristwatch** is handy for keeping track of important sailing and dinner times.

If night noises bother you, you'll love a good set of expandable foam **earplugs;** if you're sensitive to light, bring an **eye mask.** For snoozing on planes, trains, and automobiles, consider an inflatable **neck pillow.**

Spot remover (such as Shout wipes) or a dab of Goop grease remover in a small plastic container can rescue stained clothes. A small **sewing kit** can help you mend tears and restore lost buttons. Because European restrooms are often not fully equipped, carry some toilet paper or **tissue packets** (sold at all newsstands in Europe).

What Not to Pack

Don't bother packing **beach towels,** as these are provided by the cruise line.

Candles, incense, or anything else that burns is prohibited on a cruise ship—leave them at home. The same goes for clothes irons, coffee makers, and hot plates.

Virtually every cruise-ship bathroom comes equipped with a **hair dryer** (though if you need one for before or after your cruise, you may want to check with your hotels). The use of **flat irons, curlers,** or other hair-care appliances that heat up (and present a potential fire hazard) is discouraged, though most cruise lines tolerate their use.

   Walkie-talkies can be handy for families who want to keep in touch when they split up to explore a giant ship, but because they transmit on European emergency channels, US models are illegal in Europe. Texting between mobile phones can be an affordable alternative, depending on your plan.

ON THE SHIP

Now that you've booked your cruise and packed your bags, it's time to set sail. This chapter focuses on helping you get to know your ship and adjust to the seafaring lifestyle.

Initial Embarkation

You've flown across the Atlantic, made your way to the port, and now finally you see your cruise ship along the pier, looming like a skyscraper turned on its side. The anticipation is palpable. But unfortunately, getting checked in and boarding the ship can be the most taxing and tiring part of the entire cruise experience. Instead of waltzing up a gangway, you'll spend hours waiting around as hundreds or even thousands of your fellow passengers are also processed. Add the fact that ports are generally in ugly and complicated, expensive-to-reach parts of town (not to mention that you're probably jet-lagged), and your trip can begin on a stressful note. Just go with the flow and be patient; once you're on the ship, you're in the clear.

Arrival at the Airport

Cruise lines offer hassle-free airport transfers directly to the ship. While expensive, these are convenient and much appreciated if you're jet-lagged or packing heavy. Taxis are always an option for easy door-to-door service but can be needlessly expensive (in many cities, taxis levy additional surcharges for both the airport and the cruise port). Public transportation can be a bit more complicated, and may be a drag with bags, but usually saves you plenty of money. For cities where cruises are likely to begin or end, I've included details on connecting to the airport on your own—either by taxi or by public transit—so you can easily compare the cost and hassle with the transfer options offered by your cruise line. I've also included hotel recommendations.

Don't schedule your arrival in Europe too close to the departure of your cruise, as flights are prone to delays. Arriving on the same day your cruise departs—even with hours to spare—can be risky. And keep in mind that flights departing from the US to Europe generally get in the next calendar day. For more on these topics, see page 43.

Remember: Arriving in Europe a day or more before your cruise gives you the chance to get over jet lag, see your departure city, and avoid the potential stress of missing your cruise.

Checking in at the Port

Before you leave home, be clear on the exact location of the port for your ship (some cities have more than one port, and large embarkation ports typically have multiple terminals), as well as the schedule for checking in and setting sail. On their initial sailing, most ships depart around 17:00, but cruise lines usually request that passengers be checked in and on board by 15:30 or 16:00. (Like Europe, this book uses the 24-hour clock.) Better yet, arrive at the port at least an hour or two before that to allow ample time to find your way to the ship and get settled in. Most ships are open for check-in around 13:00. You might be able to drop off your bags even earlier—allowing you to explore your embarkation port (or your ship) baggage-free until your stateroom is available. Early check-in also helps you avoid the longest check-in lines of the day, which are typically in the midafternoon.

When you arrive at the terminal, cruise-line representatives will direct you to the right place. There are basically three steps to getting on the ship, each of which might involve some waiting: 1) dropping off bags; 2) check-in; and 3) embarkation (security checkpoint, boarding the ship, and finding your stateroom).

First, you have the option to **drop off your bags**—usually at a separate location from check-in. From here, your bags will be transported to your stateroom. If you're packing light, I recommend skipping the drop-off and carrying your own bags to the cabin, which allows you to dispense with formalities and potential delays (waiting to check the bags, and later, waiting for them to arrive in your cabin). But if you're packing heavy—or just want to be rid of your bags to do a little last-minute sightseeing before boarding—checking your bags typically works fine. Your cruise materials (mailed to you prior to your trip) likely included luggage tags marked with your cabin number; to save time, affix these to your bags before dropping them off (if you don't have these tags, baggage stewards can give you some on the spot). From here, the crew will deliver your bags to your stateroom. On a big ship, this can

Cruising Terms Glossary

To avoid sounding like a naive landlubber, learn a few nautical terms: It's a "line," not a "rope." It's a "ship," not a "boat."

aft/stern: back of ship

all aboard: time that all passengers must be on board the ship (typically 30 minutes before departure)

astern: ahead of the stern (that is, in front of the ship)

beam: width of the ship at its widest point

bearing/course: direction the ship is heading (on a compass, usually presented as a degree)

berth: bed (in a cabin) or dock (at a port)

bridge: command center, where the ship is steered from

bulkhead: wall between cabins or compartments

colors: ship's flag (usually the country of registration)

deck: level or "floor" of the ship

deck plan: map of the ship

disembark: leave the ship

draft: distance from the waterline to the deepest point of the ship's keel

embark: board the ship

even keel: the ship is level (keel/mast at 90 degrees)

fathom: unit of nautical depth; 1 fathom = 6 feet

flag: ensign of the country in which a ship is officially registered (and whose laws apply on board)

fore/bow: front of the ship

funnel/stack: ship's smokestack

galley: kitchen

gangway: stairway between the ship and shore

gross registered tonnage: unit of a ship's volume; 1 gross registered ton = 100 cubic feet of enclosed space

hatch: covering for a hold

helm: steering device for the ship; place where steering device is located

HMS: His/Her Majesty's Ship (before the vessel name); British-flagged ships only

hold: storage area below decks

hotel manager: officer in charge of accommodations and food operations

hull: the body of the ship

keel: the "fin" of the ship that extends below the hull

knot: unit of nautical speed; 1 knot = 1 nautical mile/ hour = 1.15 land miles/hour

league: unit of nautical distance; 1 league = 3 nautical miles = 3.45 land miles

leeward: direction against the wind (that is, into the wind); downwind

lido (lido deck): deck with outdoor swimming pools, athletic area, and other amenities

line: rope

list/listing: tilt to one side

ON THE SHIP

maître d': host who seats diners and manages dining room

manifest: list of the ship's passengers, crew, and cargo

midship/amidships: a spot halfway between the bow and the stern

MS/MSY: motor ship/motorized sailing yacht (used before the vessel name)

muster station: where you go if there's an emergency and you have to board the lifeboats

nautical mile: unit of nautical distance; 1 nautical mile = 1.15 land miles

pilot: local captain who advises the ship's captain, or even steers the ship, on approach to a port

pitch/pitching: rise and fall of the ship's bow as it maneuvers through waves

port: left side of the ship (here's a mnemonic device: both "left" and "port" have four letters)

prow: angled front part of the ship

purser/bursar: officer in charge of finances, sometimes also with managerial responsibilities

quay: dock or pier (pron. "key")

rigging: cables, chains, and lines

roll/rolling: side-to-side movement of a ship

seating: assigned seat and time for dinner in the dining room (often optional)

stabilizer: fin that extends at an angle from the hull of the ship into the water to create a smoother ride

staff (or "cruise staff"): crew members who work in the entertainment and activities division

starboard: right side of the ship

stateroom/cabin: "hotel room" on the ship

stem: very front of the prow

steward: serving crew, including the cabin steward (housekeeping), dining steward (waiter), or wine steward (sommelier)

superstructure: parts of the ship above the main deck

swell: wave in the open sea

technical call: when the ship docks or anchors, but passengers are not allowed off (except, in some cases, when those passengers have bought an excursion)

tender: small boat that carries passengers between an anchored ship and the shore

tendered: when a ship is anchored (in the open water) rather than docked (at a pier); passengers reach land by riding tender boats

upper berth: fold-down bed located above another bed

veranda: private balcony off a stateroom

wake: trail of disturbed water that a ship leaves behind it

weigh: raise (for example, "weigh anchor")

windward: in the direction the wind is blowing (with the wind); upwind

take hours; if you'll need anything from your luggage soon after departure—such as a swimsuit, a jacket for dinner, or medication—keep it with you. Don't leave anything fragile in your bags. And be aware that your bags might be sitting in the hallway outside your room for quite some time, where passersby have access to them; while theft is rare, you shouldn't leave irreplaceable documents or other valuables in them. Pack as you would for bags being checked on an airline.

At **check-in,** you'll be photographed (for security purposes) and given a credit-card-like room key that you'll need to show whenever you leave and reboard the ship. Crew members will inspect your passport. They also may ask for your credit-card number to cover any onboard expenses (though some cruise lines ask you to do this after boarding, at the front desk). Remember that they may place a hold on your credit card to cover anticipated charges. If you're accompanying a child on board, see page 46 for the documentation you may need.

As part of check-in, you'll fill out a form asking whether you've had any flu-like symptoms (gastrointestinal or nose/throat) over the last several days. If you have, the ship's doctor will evaluate you free of charge before you are allowed to board. This is a necessary public-health measure, considering that contagious diseases spread like wildfire on a cruise ship (see page 83).

After check-in, you'll be issued a boarding number and asked to wait in a large holding area until your number is called. It could take minutes...or hours.

When your number comes up, you'll have to clear immigration control/customs (usually just a formality—you may not even have to flash your passport) and go through a **security check** to make sure you have no forbidden items, ranging from firearms to alcohol (many cruise lines won't let you BYOB on board, and others limit how much you can bring; for details, see page 103).

Your First Few Hours on Board

Once you're on the ship, head to your **stateroom** and unpack. (For more on your stateroom, see "Settling In," later.) During this time, your cabin steward will likely stop by to greet you. The cabin steward—who is invariably jolly and super-personable—is responsible for cleaning your room (generally twice a day, after breakfast and during dinner) and taking care of any needs you might have.

As soon as you step on board, you'll be very aware that you're on a seaborne vessel. You'll quickly remember the old truism about landlubbers having to find their **"sea legs."** At first, you may stagger around like you've had one too many. Hang onto handrails (on stairways and, if it's really rough, in the hallways) and step carefully. You'll eventually get used to it, and you might even discover when you return to shore that you'll need to find your "land legs" all over again. While you may worry that the motion of the ocean will interfere with sleep, many cruisers report exactly the opposite. There's just something soothing about being rocked gently to sleep at night, with the white noise of the engines as your lullaby.

Just before departure, the crew holds an **emergency drill** (or **muster drill**) to brief you on the location of your lifejacket, how to put it on, and where to assemble in the event that the ship is evacuated (called a muster station). After being given a lifeboat number, you must gather at your muster station, along with others assigned to the same lifeboat (though sometimes this drill is held elsewhere on the ship). This is serious business, and all are required to participate. For more on safety on board—and how to prepare for the worst-case scenario—see the "Cruise-Ship Safety Concerns" sidebar.

It's traditional—and fun—for passengers to assemble on the deck while the ship **sets sail,** waving to people on shore and on other ships. On some lines, the ship's loudspeakers play melodramatic music as the ship glides away from land. Sometimes the initial departure comes with live musicians, costumed crew members, and a festive cocktail-party atmosphere.

You'll also get acquainted with the ship's **dining room** or other restaurants. If your ship has traditional "seatings"—an assigned time and seat for dinner each night—this first evening is an important opportunity to get to know the people you'll be dining with. If you have any special requests, you can drop by the dining room a bit before dinnertime to chat with the maître d'.

Memorize your **stateroom number**—you'll be asked for it constantly (when arriving at meals, disembarking, making onboard purchases, and so on). And be aware of not only your cruise line, but the name of your specific ship (e.g., Norwegian *Gem*, Royal Caribbean *Splendour of the Seas*, Celebrity *Constellation*, Holland America *Noordam*)—people in the cruise industry (including those in port) refer to the ship name, not the company.

Various **orientation activities** are scheduled for your first evening; these may include a ship tour or a presentation about the various shore excursions that will be offered during the cruise. While this presentation is shamelessly promotional, it can be a good use of time to find out your options.

Life on Board

Your cruise ship is your home away from home for the duration of your trip. This section provides an overview of your ship and covers many of the services and amenities that are offered on board.

Settling In

From tiny staterooms to confusing corridors, it might take a couple of days to adjust to life on board a ship. But before long, you will be an expert at everything from getting to the dining room in the shortest amount of time to showering in tight spaces.

Your Stateroom

While smaller than most hotel rooms, your cabin is plenty big enough if you use it primarily as a place to sleep, spending the majority of your time in port and in the ship's public areas. As you unpack, you'll discover that storage space can be minimal. But—as sailors have done for centuries—cruise-ship designers are experts at cramming little pockets of storage into every nook and cranny. Remember where you tuck things so you can find them when it's time to pack up at the end of your trip.

Unpack thoroughly and thoughtfully right away. Clutter makes a small cabin even smaller. I pack heavier when cruising than when traveling on land, so I make a point to unpack completely, establishing a smart system for keeping my tight little cabin shipshape. Deep-store items you won't need in your suitcase, which you can stow under your bed (or ask your steward to show you any hidden storage areas). Survey all storage areas and make a plan to use them smartly. For example, use one drawer for all things electronic, establish a pantry for all food items, and use the safe for some things even if you don't bother locking it. Unclutter the room by clearing out items the cruise line leaves for you (such as promotional materials). I have a ritual of toggling from shore mode to ship mode by putting my pocket change and money belt (neither of which are of any value on board) in a drawer or the safe when I return to the ship.

Staterooms usually have a safe, coffee maker, minifridge, phone for calling the front desk or other cabins, and television. TV channels include information about the ship, sales pitches for shore excursions and other cruises, various American programming (such as ESPN or CNN), and pay-per-view movies. Some lines even broadcast my TV shows. The beds are usually convertible—if you've got a double bed but prefer twins, your cabin steward can pull them apart and remake them for you (or vice versa). Inside the cabin is a lifejacket for each passenger. Make note of where these are stored, and the best route to your muster station, just as you would the locations of emergency exits on an airplane.

Cabin **bathrooms** are generally tight but big enough to take

care of business. Bathrooms come equipped with hair dryers. First-time cruisers are sometimes surprised at the high water pressure and dramatic suction that powers each flush. Read and heed the warnings not to put any foreign objects down the toilet: Clogged toilets are not uncommon, and on a cruise ship, this can jam up the system for your whole hallway...not a good way to make friends.

Getting to Know Your Ship

After you're settled in your stateroom, start exploring. As you wander, begin to fill in your mental map of the ship with the things you may want to find later: front desk, restaurants, theater, and so on. Many cruises offer a tour of the ship early on, which can help you get your bearings on a huge, mazelike vessel. Deck plans (maps of the ship) are posted throughout the hallways, and you can pick up a pocket-size plan to carry with you. If your ship has touchscreen activity schedules and deck plans on each floor, use them.

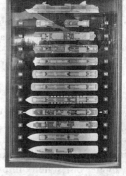

On my first day, I physically hike the entire ship, deck by deck, inside and out, to see what's where. Ships have peaceful outdoor decks that are rarely visited (perfect for sunsets). They have plenty of bars, cafés, and lounges, some of which may fit your style to a T. Crew members know about their ship's special little places, but many passengers never find them. Discover these on your first day rather than your last. Pop into each of the specialty restaurants for a chat with the maître d' and to survey the menu, cover charge, and seating.

As you walk down long hallways, it's easy to get turned around and lose track of whether you're headed for the front (fore) or the back (aft) of the ship. For the first couple of days, I carry around my ship deck plan and try to learn landmarks: For example, the restaurants (and my cabin) are near the back of the ship, while entertainment venues (casino, big theater) are at the front. Several banks of elevators are usually spread evenly throughout the ship. Before long, you'll figure out the most direct way between your stateroom and the places you want to go. It can also be tricky to find your room in a very long, anonymous hall with identical doors. Consider marking yours in a low-profile way (for example, tape a small picture below your room number) to help you find it in a hurry.

The double-decker main artery running through the middle of the ship, often called the **promenade deck,** connects several key amenities: theater, main dining room and other eateries, shopping area, library, Internet café, art gallery, photography sales point, and so on. Wrapping around the outside of the promenade deck is the namesake outdoor (but covered) deck, where you can go for a stroll.

At the center of the promenade deck is the main **lobby** (often called the atrium). This area, usually done up with over-the-top decor, has bars, a big screen for occasional presentations, tables of stuff to buy, and not enough seating. If you get lost exploring the ship, just find your way to the lobby and reorient yourself.

The lobby is also where the **guest services desk** is located. Like the reception desk of a hotel, this is your point of contact if you have concerns about your stateroom or other questions. Nearby you'll usually find the excursions desk (where you can get information about and book seats on shore excursions), a "cruise consultant" (selling seats on the line's future sailings), and the financial services desk (which handles any monetary issues that the guest services desk can't).

If the lobby is the hub of information, then the **lido deck** is the hub of recreation. Generally the ship's sunny top deck, the lido has

swimming areas, other outdoor activities, and usually the buffet restaurant. With a variety of swimming pools (some adults-only, others for kids) and hot tubs; a casual poolside "grill" serving up burgers and hot dogs; ice-cream machines; long rows of sunbathing chairs; and "Margaritaville"-type live music at all hours, the lido deck screams, "Be on vacation!"

Information

Each evening, the **daily program** for the next day is placed inside your cabin or tucked under your door. These information-packed leaflets offer an hour-by-hour schedule for the day's events, from arrival and all-aboard times to dinner seatings, bingo games, and AA meetings. (They're also peppered with ads touting various spa specials, duty-free sales, and drink discounts.) With a staggering number of options each day, this list is crucial for keeping track of where you want to be and when. I tuck this in my back pocket and refer to it constantly. Bring it with you in port to avoid that moment of terror when you suddenly realize you don't remember what time you have to be back on the ship.

Most cruise lines also give you an **information sheet** about each port of call. These usually include a map and some basic historical and sightseeing information. But the dominant feature is a list of the cruise line's "recommended" shops in that port and discounts offered at each one. Essentially, these are the shops that pay the cruise line a commission. These stores can be good places to shop, but they aren't necessarily the best options. (For more details on shopping in port, see page 134.)

The daily program and/or information sheet usually lists your vessel's **port agent** for that day's stop. This is where you'd turn in the unlikely event that you miss your departing ship (for details, see page 140).

Most cruise lines offer **"port talks"**—lectures about upcoming destinations. The quality of these can vary dramatically, from educational seminars that will immeasurably deepen your appreciation for the destination, to thinly veiled sales pitches for shore excursions.

Better cruises have a **destination expert** standing by when you get off the ship to answer your questions about that port (usually near the gangway or in the lobby). Again, beware: While some are legitimate experts, and others work for the local tourist board, most are employees of local shops. They can give you some good sightseeing advice, but any shopping pointers they offer should be taken with a grain of salt.

English is generally the first **language** on the ship, though—especially on bigger ships—announcements are repeated in other languages as well (often French, German, Italian, and/or Spanish, depending on the clientele). Most crew members who interact with passengers speak English well—though usually it's their second language.

When passing important landmarks, especially on days at sea, the **captain** may periodically come over the loudspeaker to offer commentary. Or, if the seas are rough, the captain may try

Cruise-Ship Safety Concerns

The tragic grounding of the *Costa Concordia* in January of 2012 off the coast of Italy had some cruisers asking, "How safe is my cruise ship?"

Like any form of travel, cruising comes with risks. But statistically, even taking into account the *Concordia* disaster, cruising remains remarkably safe. Since 2005, more than 100 million people have taken cruises worldwide; during that time, there have been an estimated 50 deaths—nearly two-thirds of them occurring on the *Concordia*. In the US, your odds of being killed in a given year in a car accident are one in 7,000; the odds of dying in a cruise ship-related accident are one in 6 million.

A set of laws called Safety of Life at Sea (SOLAS) has regulated maritime safety since the *Titanic* sank a century ago. After the *Concordia* disaster, regulations now require that a safety briefing and muster drill take place before departure. Still, the *Concordia* disaster underscores that cruisers should take responsibility for their own safety. Know where lifejackets are stowed (they're usually in your stateroom, but on very large ships, they may be kept at the muster station). If you are traveling with kids, ask the cruise line for child-size lifejackets to have on hand. Be clear on the location of your muster station, and know how to get there—not only from your stateroom, but from other parts of the ship. Pack a small flashlight, and keep it handy.

Legally, ships are required to have one lifeboat seat per person on board, plus an additional 25 percent. Aside from the primary lifeboats, large white canisters on the ship's deck contain smaller inflatable lifeboats, which can be launched if the normal lifeboats are disabled. In the event of an evacuation, crew members are responsible for providing instructions and for loading and operating the lifeboats. In theory, a cruise ship's evacuation procedure is designed to safely remove everyone on board within 30 minutes. However, actual full-ship evacuation is almost never practiced. The "women and children first" rule is nautical tradition, but not legally binding. The captain, however, is legally obligated to stay with the ship to oversee the evacuation.

Ultimately, the *Costa Concordia* disaster is a glaring exception to the otherwise sterling safety record of the cruise industry. But it is a cautionary tale that should encourage cruisers to take the initiative to protect themselves, in case the worst-case scenario becomes a reality.

to soothe rattled nerves (and stomachs) with an explanation of the weather that's causing the turbulence.

Speaking of **announcements,** cruise lines have varying philosophies about these: Some lines barrage you with announcements every hour or so. On other lines, they're rare. On most ships, in-cabin speakers are only used for emergency announcements. If you can't make out a routine announcement from inside your cabin, crack the door to hear the hallway loudspeakers, or tune your TV to the ship-information channel, which also broadcasts announcements.

Your Crew

Your hardworking crew toils for long hours and low pay to make sure you have a great vacation. Whether it's the head waiter who remembers how you like your coffee; the cabin steward who cleans your room with a smile and shows you pictures of his kids back in Indonesia; or the unseen but equally conscientious workers who prepare your meals, wash your laundry, scrub the deck, or drive the tender boats, the crew is an essential and often unheralded part of your cruise experience.

The all-purpose term for crew members is "steward"— cabin steward (housekeeping), wine steward (sommelier), dining steward (waiter), and so on. Your cabin steward can be very helpful if you have a basic question or request; for something more  complicated, ask the front-desk staff or the concierge. In the dining room, the maître d' assigns tables and manages the dining room, the head waiter takes your order, and the assistant waiters bring your food and bus your dishes.

The ship's cruise director (sometimes called a host or hostess) is a tireless cheerleader, keeping you informed about the various activities and other happenings on board, usually via perky announcements over the ship's loudspeaker several times a day. The cruise director manages a (mostly American) "cruise staff" that leads activities throughout the ship. I have a lot of sympathy for these folks, partly because of my own background as a tour guide—I can't imagine the responsibility of keeping thousands of people informed and entertained 24/7. Experienced cruisers report that the more enthusiastic and energetic the cruise director and staff are, the more likely you are to enjoy your cruise. Gradually you'll come to feel respect, appreciation, and even affection for these people who really, really want you to have a great time on your vacation.

A great bonus for me is to make friends with members of the crew. They are generally hardworking, industrious, young, and fun-loving people from the developing world who, in spite of their required smiles, genuinely enjoy people. Many are avid travelers, and you'll see them enjoying time on shore (when they are given a break) just like you. While there are strict limits to how crew members can mingle with passengers, you are more than welcome to have real and instructive conversations with them about cruise life, their world back home, or whatever.

Befriending a crew member can also come with a bonus drink. If you see a crew member nursing a drink on their own at a shipboard bar, strike up a conversation. There's a good chance they'll offer to buy you a drink. That's because when drinking alone, they have to pay for their own drinks; but if they're "entertaining" a passenger, both their drink and yours are on the cruise line. It's a win-win.

Crew Wages

Other than the officers and cruise staff, a ship's crew is primarily composed of people from the developing world. With rare exceptions, these crew members are efficient, patient, and friendly (or, at least, always smiling).

It's clear that crew members work hard. But most passengers would be surprised to learn just how long they work—and for how little. Because US labor laws don't apply to sailing vessels, cruise lines can pay astonishingly low wages for very long hours of work. Crew members who receive tips are paid an average base salary (before tips) of about $1 each day. This makes tips an essential part of the crew's income (see "Tipping" on page 79). After tips, the English-speaking service crew who interact with passengers make about $2,000-3,000 per month, while the anonymous workers toiling at entry-level jobs below decks can make less than $1,000 per month. While clear industry-wide numbers are hard to come by, the following monthly wages (after tips) are typical:

Cabin steward	$2,000
Waiter	$3,000
Bartender	$1,800
Cook	$1,500-2,100
Dishwasher	$600
Seaman (maintenance)	$1,500
Cruise staff	$2,000
Cruise director	$5,800
Captain	$10,000

These earnings don't seem unreasonable...until you factor in the long hours. Most crew members sign a nine- to ten-month contract, then get two or three months off. While they are under contract, they work seven days a week, at least 10 hours a day; the international legal maximum is 14 hours a day, but according to insiders, some crew members put in up to 16 hours. The hours worked are rarely consecutive—for example, a crew member might work 6 hours, have 2 or 3 hours off, then work 7 more hours. They rarely if ever get a full day off during their entire months-long contract, though they get enough sporadic time off during the day to be able to rest and occasionally enjoy the ports of call. Do the math: If most crew members work an average of 12 hours a day, 30 days a month, that's 360 hours a month—more than double the 160 hours of a 9-to-5 worker.

Cruise lines do cover their crew's accommodations, food, medical care, and transportation (including a flight home once their contract is completed). This means the crew can pocket or send home most of their earnings. While income-tax laws do not apply on the ship, crew members are required to pay taxes in their home country.

The Secret Lives of Crew Members

Most cruise lines have somewhere between 1.5 and 2 passengers per crew member. So a 3,000-passenger ship has around 2,000 crew members, who need to be housed and fed—in some ways, they are a vast second set of passengers. The crew's staterooms—the lowest (below the waterline, close to the rumbling engine noise)

and smallest on the ship—are far more humble than your own, and usually shared by two to six people. Some cruise staff may have nicer cabins in the passenger areas, but only officers get outside cabins.

While you may see officers eating in the passenger dining room or buffet, most of the crew dines in mess halls with menus that reflect the cuisine of their native lands. Working long hours and far from home, the crew expects to eat familiar comfort food—Southeast Asians want fish and rice; Italians get pasta; and so on. A well-fed crew is a happy crew, which leads to happy passengers—so substantial effort and resources go toward feeding the crew.

The more diverse the crew, the more complicated and expensive it can be to keep everyone satisfied. On some ships, each nationality has its own mess hall and menu that changes day to day. Some cruise lines have found it more efficient to hire employees predominantly from one or two countries. For example, on Holland America, the cabin crew is entirely Indonesian, while the kitchen and dining room crew is Filipino (to recruit employees, the cruise line operates training academies in those two countries).

Running a Cruise Ship

The business of running a ship is divided into three branches, which work together to create a smooth experience: the engine room; the hotel (rooms and food service); and the deck. This last branch includes the physical decks and railings as well as the bridge (the area from which the ship is navigated) and tendering (shore transport). Each department has its leader (chief engineer, hotel manager, and chief officer, respectively), with the captain overseeing the entire operation.

Of course, these days the captain doesn't actually steer the ship while standing at a big wooden wheel. Modern cruise

ships are mostly computerized. The "watch"—responsibility for guiding the ship and dealing with any emergencies—rotates among the officers, who usually work four hours on, then eight hours off. The watch continues when the ship is at anchor or docked, when officers must keep an eye on moorings, make sure the ship is in the correct position, and so on.

The ship is dry-docked (taken out of the water) every two years or so to clean algae, barnacles, and other buildup from the hull and to polish the propeller. A very smooth propeller is crucial for a fluid ride—a dented or porous one can lead to lots of noise and bubbles. Sometimes a crew engineer will put on a wetsuit and dive down to polish the rudder underwater.

As you approach a port (or a challenging-to-navigate passage), a little boat zips out to your cruise ship, and a

"pilot"—a local captain who's knowledgeable about that port—hops off. The pilot advises your ship's captain about the best approach to the dock and sometimes even takes the helm. Once the job is done, another boat might zip out to pick up the pilot.

If you're intrigued by the inner workings of your ship, ask about a behind-the-scenes tour. Many ships offer the opportunity to see the galley (kitchen), food stores, crew areas, and other normally off-limits parts of the ship (usually for a fee).

Many crew members have spouses back home who are raising their children; in port, they buy cheap phone cards or use Skype to keep in touch. In fact, most portside Internet cafés and calling shops target the crew rather than the passengers ("Cheap rates to the Philippines!"). If a café near the port offers free Wi-Fi for customers, you'll invariably see a dozen of your crew huddled over their laptops, deep in conversation.

While many crew members have families to feed, others are living the single life. The crew tends to party together (the crew bar is even more rollicking than the passenger bars), and inter-crew romances are commonplace—though fraternization between crew members and passengers is strictly forbidden.

Is It Exploitation?

The national and racial stratification of the entire crew evokes the exploitation and indentured servitude of colonial times: The officers and cruise staff are often Americans, Brits, or Europeans, while those in menial roles (kitchen, waitstaff, cleaning crew, engineers) are Indonesian, Filipino, or another developing-world nationality. It's a mark of a socially conscious company when Southeast Asian employees are given opportunities to rise through the ranks and take on roles with greater responsibility.

The cruise lines argue that their employees are making far more money at sea in glamorous locations—where they get occasional time off to leave the ship and explore the ports—than they would at menial jobs back home. What some see as exploitation, others see as empowerment. Another way to look at it is as "insourcing"—importing cheap labor from the lowest bidder. For better or worse, the natural gregariousness of the crew gives cruisers the impression that they can't be so terribly unhappy with their lives. And the remarkable loyalty of many crew members (working many, many years for the same cruise line)—especially on certain lines—is a testament to the success of the arrangement.

Is it wrong to employ Third World people at low wages to wait on First World, mostly white, generally wealthy vacationers? I don't know. But I do know that your crew members are some of the friendliest people on board. Get to know them. Ask about their families back home. And make sure they know how much you appreciate everything they're doing to make your trip more comfortable.

Money Matters

Most cruise ships are essentially cashless. Your stateroom key card doubles as a credit card. When buying anything on board, you'll simply provide your cabin number, then sign a receipt for the expense. You'll likely need cash on board only for tipping (explained later), paying a crew member to babysit, or playing the casino (most slot machines and table games take cash; you can use your onboard account to finance your gambling, but you'll pay a fee for the privilege). To avoid exorbitant cash-advance fees at the front desk, bring along some US cash for these purposes.

Most cruise lines price everything on board (from drinks to tips to souvenirs) in US dollars, regardless of the countries visited during the trip.

Onboard Expenses

First-time cruisers thinking they've paid up front for an "all-inclusive" trip are sometimes surprised by how many add-ons they are offered on board. Your cruise ticket covers accommodations, all the meals you can eat in the ship's main dining room and buffet (with some beverages included), and transportation from port to port. You can have an enjoyable voyage and not spend a penny more (except for expenses in port). But the cruise industry is adept at enticing you with extras that add up quickly. These include shore excursions, casino games, premium drinks (alcohol, name-brand soft drinks, and lattes), specialty restaurant surcharges (explained later, under "Eating"), duty-free shopping, fitness classes, spa treatments, photos, and many other goods and services.

It's very easy to get carried away—a round of drinks here, a night of blackjack there, a scuba dive, a castle tour, and more. First-timers—even those who think they're keeping a close eye on their bottom line—can be astonished when they get their final onboard bill, which can easily exceed the original cost of the trip (or so hope the cruise lines).

With a little self-control, you can easily limit your extra expenditures, making your seemingly "cheap" cruise actually cheap. It's a good idea to occasionally check your current balance (and look for mistaken charges) at the front desk or via your cabin TV. You don't have to avoid extras entirely. After all, you're on vacation—go ahead and have that "daily special" cocktail to unwind after a busy day of sightseeing, or stick a $20 bill into a slot machine. But you always have the right to say, "No, thanks." As long as you're aware of these additional expenses and keep your spending under control, a cruise can still be a great value.

Getting Local Cash on Board

While you don't need much cash on board the ship, you will need local money for your time in port, as many European vendors will not accept credit cards or dollars. It's possible to get local cash on board the ship—but it's expensive. At the front desk, you can exchange cash or traveler's checks into the local currency (at bad rates and often with high commissions), or you can get a cash advance on your credit card (at a decent exchange rate but typically with exorbitant fees).

You'll save money if you plan ahead and make use of ATMs near the cruise port. For each destination, I've noted the location of the nearest ATM, which can often be found inside the cruise terminal or close to it (for more on withdrawing money in port, see page 130).

Most ports of call in this book are in the euro zone and use the same currency. For places that don't use the euro (Croatia and Turkey), it can be worth the added expense to change a small amount of cash on board the ship to finance your trip into town.

Tipping

Tipping procedures aboard cruise ships have changed dramatically over the last two decades. Through the late 1980s, cruising was a pastime of the wealthy, and passengers enjoyed tipping the crew royally as part of the experience. Each crew member—cabin steward, maître d', head waiter, assistant waiter, and so on—expected to be tipped a specific amount per day. After the final passenger disembarked, the crew would meet and dump all their tip money into a communal pot, to be divided equally among themselves. But as cruising went mass-market, more frugal middle-class passengers began signing up. Having already paid for their trip, many resented the expectation to tip...so they simply didn't. The crew's take-home pay plummeted, and many workers quit, leaving the cruise lines in dire straits.

These days, cruise lines use a standard "auto-tip" system, in which a set gratuity (generally about $10-12/person per day) is automatically billed to each passenger's account and then divided among the crew (this system, started around 2000, effectively formalizes the process that had been going on for decades). About a third of this tip goes to your cabin steward, a third to the restaurant stewards, and a third to others, including people who worked for you behind the scenes (such as the laundry crew). While overall tips are still not what they were 20 years ago, auto-tipping has proven to be a suitable compromise for both passengers and crew.

Cruise lines explain that, with auto-tipping, additional tipping is "not expected." But it is still most certainly appreciated by the crew. This can cause stress for passengers who are unsure whom, how much, and when to tip; conscientious tippers miss the "good old days" when there was a clearly prescribed amount earmarked for each crew member. Even more confusing, with all the new alternative dining options, you likely won't be served by the same waiter every night—in fact, you might never eat at the same

Money-Saving Tips

Many people choose cruising because it's extremely affordable. When you consider that you're getting accommodations, food, and transportation for one low price, it's simply a steal. But reckless spending on a cruise can rip through a tight budget like a grenade in a dollhouse. If you're really watching your money, consider these strategies:

Buy as little on board as possible. Everything—drinks, Internet access, knickknacks—is priced at a premium for a captive audience. For most items, you're paying far more than you would off the ship. If you're shopping for jewelry, find a local boutique in port rather than patronize your ship's shop.

Skip the excursions. While cruise-line excursions are easy and efficient, you may be charged $80-100/person for a transfer into town and a walking tour of the old center. But for the cost of a $2 bus ticket, you can get downtown yourself and join a $15 walking tour that covers most of the same sights. This book's destination chapters are designed to help you understand your options.

Stick with the main dining room. If your ship has specialty restaurants that levy a surcharge, skip them in favor of the "free" (included) meals in the main dining room—which are typically good quality.

Save some breakfast for lunch. If you're heading out for a long day in port, help yourself to a big breakfast and bag up the leftovers to keep you going until dinnertime. Some cruise lines will sell you a packed lunch for about $10.

Minimize premium beverage purchases. Because alcohol,

restaurant twice. In general, the rule of thumb is to give a cash tip at the end of the cruise to those crew members who have provided exceptional service (for specific guidelines, see page 104).

At any point, you can increase or decrease your auto-tip amount to reflect your satisfaction with the service you've received. So, if you don't have cash for your final tip, you can simply go to the front desk and increase the auto-tip amount instead (but try to do so before the final night, when accounts are being finalized).

Some passengers prefer to zero out their auto-tip, then pay their favorite crew members in cash to make sure the money winds up with the "right" person. But this can backfire in two ways: First, many crew members adhere to the old system of pooling and dividing tips, including those received in cash—so your cash tip might be split after all. Second, your preferred crew member may choose not to split the cash tip at all—so somebody who worked hard for you, unseen, misses out on much-needed income. The fairest option is to let the auto-tip do what it's designed to do, and then add a cash bonus for the people you wish to reward.

soda, and specialty coffee drinks all cost extra, drink tabs can add up fast. Since many cruise lines prohibit or limit bringing your own alcohol on board, you'll pay dearly for wetting your whistle.

Stay out of the casino. With a casino and slots on board, it's easy to fall into a gambling habit. Most cruise lines allow you to use your key card to get cash from your room account for gambling. But read the fine print carefully—you're paying a percentage for this convenience. Also, keep in mind that your odds of winning may be even less than at land-based casinos (see page 93).

Don't buy onboard photos. Come to think of it, don't even let them take your photo—so you won't be tempted to buy it later.

Don't use the shipboard mobile phone network or Wi-Fi. Shipboard Internet access and phone rates are very high. To check your email, visit an Internet café in port rather than on board. For phone options, see page 88.

Take advantage of free services on board. Rather than buy a book, check one out from the ship's library. Instead of ordering a pricey pay-per-view movie in your cabin, enjoy the cruise's free musical performances, classes, and activities. Read your daily program: There's something free going on, somewhere on the ship, virtually every minute of every day.

Don't cheap out at the expense of fun. If you're having a nice dinner, spring for a glass of wine—but keep a mental tally of all these little charges so you're not shocked by the final bill.

ON THE SHIP

In addition to a monetary tip, crew members appreciate it when you pass along positive feedback. Most cruise lines provide guests with comment cards for this purpose, and they can be taken very seriously when determining promotions. If someone has really gone above and beyond for you, fill out a comment card on their behalf.

Health

Health problems can strike anywhere—even when you're relaxing on a cruise ship in the middle of the Mediterranean. Every ship has an onboard doctor (though he or she may not be licensed in the US). If you have to visit the shipboard physician, you will be charged. Before you leave home, ask your health insurance company if the cost is covered or reimbursable; if you buy travel insurance, investigate how it covers onboard medical care.

Fortunately, some of the most common health concerns on cruise ships, while miserable, are temporary and relatively easy to treat.

Seasickness

Naturally, one concern novice cruisers have is whether the motion of the ship will cause them to spend their time at sea with their head in the toilet. And, in fact, a small percentage of people discover (quickly and violently) that they have zero tolerance for life at sea. But the vast majority of cruisers do just fine.

Fortunately, the Mediterranean is an almost entirely enclosed sea with very little tide or turbulence, compared to the open ocean. Remember that you're on a gigantic floating city—it takes a lot of agitation to really get the ship moving. Cruise ships are also equipped with stabilizers—wing-like panels that extend below the water's surface and automatically tilt to counteract rolling (side-to-side movement) caused by big swells.

But rough seas can occur, and when they do, waves and winds may toss your ship around quite noticeably. (As one captain told me, "If you're in a storm in the middle of the Atlantic, no ship is big enough.") When this happens, chandeliers and other fixtures begin to jiggle and clink, motion sickness bags discreetly appear in the hallways, and the captain comes over the loudspeaker to comfortingly explain what's being done to smooth out the ride. Lying in bed, being rocked to sleep like a baby, you hear the hangers banging the sides of your closet. Some cruisers actually enjoy this experience; for others, it's pure misery.

If you're prone to motion sickness, visit your doctor before your cruise, and be prepared with a remedy (or several) in case you're laid low. Below are several options that veteran cruisers swear by.

Dramamine (generic name: Dimenhydrinate) is easy to get over the counter but is highly sedating—not ideal unless you are desperate. Some cruisers prefer the less-drowsy formula, which is actually a different drug (called Meclozine, sometimes marketed as **Bonine**). **Marezine** (generic name: Cyclizine) has similar properties and side effects to Dramamine.

Scopolamine patches (sometimes called by the brand name Transderm) are small (dime-sized) and self-adhesive; just stick one on a hairless area behind your ear. They work well for many travelers (the only major side effect is dry mouth), but require a prescription and are expensive (figure $15 for a three-day dose). Some cruisers apply them prophylactically just before first boarding the ship (especially if rough weather is forecast). After removing one of these patches, wash your hands carefully—getting the residue in your eyes can cause dilated pupils and blurry vision.

Elasticized **Sea-Bands** have little buds that press on the pressure points on your wrist associated with nausea. You can buy them in any drugstore. They are easy to wear (if a bit goofy-looking—they look like exercise wristbands), and many people prefer them as a cheap and nonmedicinal remedy.

The similar but more sophisticated **Reletex** resembles (and is worn like) a wristwatch. It operates on the same principle as Sea-Bands but is designed to be less constricting (direct pressure delivered to exactly the right spot). But it's quite expensive ($100-200) and best for those who have a big problem with seasickness.

Every cruise aficionado has a favorite homegrown seasickness remedy. Some say that eating green apples or candied ginger can help settle a queasy stomach. Others suggest holding a peeled orange under the nose. Old sea dogs say that if you stay above deck, as close to the middle of the ship as possible, and keep your eyes on the horizon, it will reduce the effects of the motion.

Illness

Like a college dorm or a day-care center, a cruise ship is a veritable incubator for communicable disease. Think about everything that you (and several thousand other passengers) are touching: elevator buttons, railings, serving spoons in the buffet, and on and on. If one person gets sick, it's just a matter of time before others do, too.

The common cold is a risk. But perhaps even more likely are basic gastrointestinal upsets, most often caused by the norovirus (a.k.a. the Norwalk virus)—tellingly nicknamed the "cruise-ship virus." Most often spread through fecally contaminated food or person-to-person contact, the norovirus is your basic nasty stomach bug, resulting in nausea, diarrhea, vomiting, and sometimes fever or cramps. It usually goes away on its own after a day or two.

Because contagious maladies are a huge concern aboard a ship, the cruise industry is compulsive about keeping things clean. Between cruises, ships are thoroughly disinfected with a powerful cleaning agent. When you check in, you'll be quizzed about recent symptoms to be sure you aren't bringing any nasty bugs on board. Some cruise lines won't allow passengers to handle the serving spoons at the buffet for the first two days—the crew serves instead. And, if you develop certain symptoms, the cruise line reserves the right to expel you from the ship at the next port of call (though, in practice, this is rare—more likely, they'll ask you to stay in your stateroom until you're no longer contagious).

Many cruise lines douse their passengers with waterless hand sanitizers at every opportunity. Dispensers are stationed around the ship, and smiling stewards might squirt your hands from a spray bottle at the entrance to restaurants or as you reboard the ship after a day in port. Whether this works is up for debate. Several studies have demon-

strated that using these sanitizers can actually be counterproductive. The US Centers for Disease Control (CDC) recommend them only as an adjunct to, rather than a replacement for, hand washing with soap and warm water. The gels work great against bacteria, but not viruses (such as the norovirus). Following the CDC's lead, some cruise lines have discontinued the use of waterless sanitizers—and have seen an immediate *decrease* in their rate of outbreaks. The logic is that hand sanitizers actually discourage proper hand-washing behavior. When people apply sanitizers, they assume their hands are clean—and don't bother to wash with soap and water. All the while, that spunky norovirus survives on their hands, gets transferred to the serving spoon at the buffet, and winds up on other people's hands while they're eating dinner.

On your stateroom TV, you might find a channel with instructions on how to wash your hands. Patronizing, yes. But not undeservedly. In a recent international study, Americans were found to be less diligent than other nationalities when it comes to washing their hands after using the bathroom. They then go straight to the buffet, and...you know the rest. It's disgusting but true. If you're a total germophobe, you have two options: Avoid the buffet entirely—or just get over it.

Staying Fit on Board

While it's tempting to head back to the buffet for a second dessert (or even a second dinner) at 11:00 p.m., file away this factoid: A typical cruise passenger gains about a pound a day. After two weeks at sea, you've put on the "Seafaring 15."

Whether you're a fitness buff or simply want to stave off weight gain, cruise ships offer plenty of opportunities to get your body moving. Most ships have fitness centers with exercise equipment, such as bikes, treadmills, elliptical trainers, and weight machines. Some offer the services of personal trainers, plus classes like boot camp, spinning, Pilates, and yoga (newbies and yoga-heads alike will find it an interesting challenge to hold tree pose on a moving ship). These services usually cost extra, though some classes can be free (usually things like stretching or ab work).

If you're not the gym type, there are other ways to burn calories. Besides swimming pools, many ships have outdoor running tracks that wrap around the deck, complete with fresh air and views. And some ships have more extreme-type sports, such as rock-climbing walls and surfing simulators.

Even if you don't take advantage of sports-related amenities,

Water, Trash, and Poo: The Inside Scoop

Wondering how cruise ships deal with passengers' basic functions? Here are the answers to some often-asked questions:

Is the water clean and drinkable? Drinking water is usually pumped into the ship at the point of embarkation. Throughout the duration of the cruise, this supply is what comes out of your bathroom tap and is used in restaurant drinks.

Larger ships also have the capacity to desalinize (remove salt from) seawater for use aboard. While perfectly safe to drink, this water doesn't taste good, so it's reserved primarily for cleaning. The water in your stateroom's toilet or shower might be desalinated.

Waste water from the ship is purified on board. While theoretically safe to drink, it's usually deposited into the sea.

Where does the trash go? Trash from shipboard restaurants is carefully sorted into garbage, recyclables, and food waste. Garbage is removed along with other solid waste in port. Cruise lines pay recycling companies to take the recyclables (interestingly, in the US it's the other way around; the companies pay the ship for their recyclables). Food waste is put through a powerful grinder that turns it into a biodegradable puree. This "fish food" is quietly piped out the end of the ship as it sails through the night.

What happens to poo? You may wonder whether shipboard waste is deposited into the sea as you cruise. These things are dictated by local and international law as well as by the policies of individual cruise lines. Most mainstream cruise lines do not dump solid waste into the sea. Instead it is collected, stored, and removed from the ship for proper disposal in port.

ON THE SHIP

simply staying active throughout your cruise will help keep those multicourse dinners from going straight to your hips. With multiple levels, your cruise ship is one giant StairMaster. Take the stairs instead of the elevator (which often saves time, too), or run down to the bottom floor and hike back up to the top a couple of times a day. Opt for a walking tour instead of a bus tour when you're in port. Hit the dance floor at night. But just in case, bring along your roomy "Thanksgiving pants."

Smoking

Smoking presents both a public health issue and a fire hazard for cruise lines. While policies are evolving, these days most cruise lines prohibit smoking in nearly all enclosed public spaces as well as in many outdoor areas. You may be able to smoke in certain bars or lounges and in dedicated outdoor spots. Most cruise lines allow passengers to light up in their staterooms or on their verandas but do not have designated "smoking" cabins—they simply clean the cabin thoroughly after a smoker has stayed there (generally with impressive success). If you're a dedicated smoker or an adamant nonsmoker, research the various cruise lines' policies when choosing your vacation.

Communicating

Because phoning and Internet access are prohibitively expensive on board—and because the times you'll be in port are likely to coincide with late-night or early-morning hours back home (8:00-17:00 in most of Europe is 2:00-11:00 a.m. on the East Coast and 23:00-8:00 a.m. on the West Coast)—keeping in touch affordably can be tricky. Let the folks back home know not to expect too many calls, or figure out if there are any late evenings in ports when it might be convenient to call home.

Consider asking any crew members you befriend about the cheapest, easiest places in each port to get online or to make cheap phone calls. They spend many months away from home and are experts at staying in touch. (But keep in mind some of the options at the ports are "seamen's clubs"—open only to crew members, not the general public.)

Getting Online

It's useful to get online periodically as you travel—to confirm trip plans, get weather forecasts, catch up on email, or post status up-dates and photos from your trip. But with high prices and slow speeds, shipboard Internet is not the best option.

Most cruise ships have an Internet café with computer terminals, and many also have Wi-Fi (some offer it in select areas of the ship, others provide it in staterooms). Either way, onboard Internet access is very expensive—figure $0.50-1/minute (the more minutes you buy, the cheaper they are, and special deals can lower the cost substantially). Before you pay for access, be warned that—since it's satellite-based rather than hardwired—onboard Internet is tortoise-slow compared to high-speed broadband (remember dial-up?). And while using VoIP (Skype or Google Talk) to make voice or video calls over a Wi-Fi connection is an excellent budget option on land, it's impractical on the ship. Onboard Internet access has such limited bandwidth that these services often don't work well, or at all.

In short, shipboard Internet access is practical only for quick tasks, such as downloading email. Limit the time you need to spend online by reading and composing emails or social media posts offline, then going online periodically just to download/upload. You can also set up certain smartphone apps to do this; for example, some news apps let you download all of the day's top stories at once, rather than clicking to read them one at a time. When you're done, be sure that you properly log out of the shipboard network to avoid unwittingly running up Internet fees.

Ideally, wait until you're in port to get online. If you have a mobile device, find a café on shore where you can sit and download your email or log into Facebook over Wi-Fi while enjoying a cup of coffee—at a fraction of the shipboard cost. Or hop on a computer at an Internet café to quickly go online. For more pointers on getting online in port, see page 128.

Phoning

If you want to make calls during your trip, you can do it either from land or at sea. It's much cheaper to call home from a pay phone on shore (explained on page 128) or from a mobile phone on a land-based network (explained later). Calling from the middle of the sea is pricey, but if you're in a pinch, you can dial direct from your stateroom telephone or use a mobile phone while roaming on the costly onboard network. For details on how to dial European phone numbers, see page 1242.

Stateroom Telephones: Calling **within the ship** (such as to the front desk or another cabin) is free on your stateroom telephone, or from phones hanging at strategic locations around the ship. Some ships provide certain crew members with an on-ship mobile phone and a four-digit phone number. If there's a crew member or service desk you want to contact, just remember their number and dial it toll-free.

Calling **to shore** (over a satellite connection) is usually possible, but expensive—anywhere from $6 to $15 a minute (if you prepay for a large block of calling time, it can be cheaper—for example, $25 for 12 minutes; ask for specifics at the front desk). Note: Similar charges apply if someone calls from shore to your stateroom.

Mobile Phones: Using a mobile phone while traveling is con-

Mobile Phone Options

Traveling with a mobile phone is handy and practical. There are two basic options: roaming with your own phone (expensive but easy) or buying and using SIM cards with an unlocked phone (a bit more hassle, but potentially much cheaper).

Roaming with Your US Mobile Phone

This pricier option can be worthwhile if you won't be making or receiving many calls, don't want to bother with SIM cards, or want to stay reachable at your US number. Start by calling your mobile-phone service provider to ask whether your phone works in Europe and what the rates are (likely $1.29-1.99 per minute to make or receive calls, and 20–50 cents to send or receive text messages). Tell them to enable international calling on your account, and ask your carrier about any global calling deals to lower the per-minute costs. When you land in Europe, turn on your phone and—bingo!—you have service. Because you'll pay for receiving calls and texts, be sure your family knows to call only in an emergency.

Buying and Using SIM Cards in Europe

If you're comfortable with mobile-phone technology, will be making lots of calls, and want to save some serious money, consider this very affordable alternative: Carry an unlocked mobile phone, and use it with a European SIM card to get much cheaper rates.

Getting an **unlocked phone** may be easier than you think. You may already have an old, unused mobile phone in a drawer. When you got the phone, it was probably "locked" to work only with one company—but if your contract is now up, your provider may be willing to send you a code to unlock it. Otherwise, you can simply buy an unlocked phone: Search your favorite online shopping site for an "unlocked quad-band phone" before you go, or wait until you get to Europe and buy one at a mobile-phone shop there. Either way, a basic model costs less than $50.

Once in Europe, buy a **SIM card**—the little chip that inserts into your phone (either under the battery, or in a slot on the side)—to equip the phone with a European number. SIM cards are sold at mobile-phone shops, department-store electronics counters, and some newsstand kiosks for $5–10, and usually include about that much prepaid calling credit (making the card itself virtually free). Because SIM cards are prepaid, there's no contract (in fact, they expire after just a few months of disuse).

When using a SIM card in its home country, it's free to receive calls and texts, and it's cheap to make calls—domestic calls average 20-30 cents per minute (toll lines can be substantially more). Rates are higher if you're roaming in another country, but as long as you stay within the European Union, these fees are capped (about 30 cents/minute for making calls or 10 cents per minute for receiving calls). Texting is cheap even if roaming.

When buying a SIM card, ask about fees for domestic and international calls, roaming charges, and how to check your credit balance and buy more time. If text or voice prompts are in another language, ask whether they can be switched to English.

Smartphones and Data Roaming

You can take your smartphone to Europe, using it to make phone calls (sparingly) and send texts, but also to check email, listen to audio tours, and browse the Internet. You may have heard horror stories about people running up outrageous data roaming bills on their smartphones. But if you understand the options, it's easy to avoid these fees and still stay connected. Here's how.

For voice calls and text messaging, smartphones work like any mobile phone (as described under "Roaming with Your US Mobile Phone," earlier).

To get online with your phone, you have two options: Wi-Fi and mobile data. Because free Wi-Fi hotspots are generally easy to find in Europe (at most hotels, many cafés, and even some public spaces), the cheap solution is to use Wi-Fi anytime you find it on land. (Wi-Fi networks on board are much more expensive.)

But what if you can't get to a hotspot? Most providers offer an affordable, basic data-roaming package for Europe: $25 or $30 buys you about 100 megabytes—enough to view 100 websites or send/receive 1,000 text emails. If you don't buy a data-roaming plan in advance, but use data in Europe anyway, you'll pay very high rates—about $20 per megabyte, or about 80 times what you'd pay with a plan. As long as you can reach the mobile-phone network on land, you can also access the data roaming network—allowing you to go online while your ship cruises close to land.

While a data-roaming package is handy, your allotted megabytes can go quickly. To keep a cap on usage and avoid incurring overage charges, manually turn off data roaming on your phone whenever you're not actively using it. (To turn off data and voice roaming, look in your phone's menu—try checking under "Cellular" or "Network," or ask your mobile-phone provider how to do it.) As you travel through Europe, jump from Wi-Fi hotspot to Wi-Fi hotspot. If you need to get online when you can't easily access Wi-Fi, you can turn on data roaming just long enough for that task, then turn it off again. You can also limit how much data your phone uses by switching your email settings from "push" to "fetch" (you choose when to download messages rather than having them automatically "pushed" to your device). By carefully budgeting data this way, 100 megabytes can last a long time.

If you want to use your smartphone exclusively on Wi-Fi—and not worry about either voice or data charges—simply turn off both voice and data roaming (or put your phone in "Airplane Mode" and then turn your Wi-Fi back on). If you're on a long trip, are positive you won't be using your phone for voice or data roaming, and want to save some money, ask your provider about suspending those services altogether.

By sticking with Wi-Fi wherever possible and budgeting your use of data, you can easily and affordably stay connected.

venient. Even if you don't expect to make many voice calls, texting can be particularly handy for people cruising together who want to split up occasionally and still be in touch. Before you go too far, though, read the "Mobile Phone Options" sidebar to understand what types of mobile phones can be used in Europe, and how to use them cost-effectively.

If you're comfortable using an unlocked mobile phone with European SIM cards (explained in the sidebar), here's a good plan for enjoying phone service throughout your cruise: Buy a SIM card in the city where your cruise starts, and load it with enough credit to last your entire trip (since SIM cards generally can't be topped up in other countries, if you run out, you'll need to buy another SIM card in the new country). Then use your credit sparingly all along the coast. Because it's much more expensive to make calls outside of the SIM card's home country, limit yourself to extremely brief calls and text messages. If you buy your SIM card within the European Union, roaming fees in other EU countries (including Spain, France, Italy, Croatia, and Greece) are capped, allowing you to make affordable calls for most destinations in this book—but be careful when crossing into non-EU territories, such as Turkey, where rates can skyrocket.

Important: If you are using a mobile phone, it's essential to distinguish between land and sea networks. Because many European cruise itineraries stay fairly close to land, you can often roam on the cheaper **land-based networks,** even when you're at sea. Your phone will automatically find land-based networks if you're within several miles of shore. The **onboard network,** which doesn't even turn on until the ship is about 10 miles out, is far more expensive— about $2.50-5/minute (ask your mobile service provider for details about your ship).

Before placing a call or accessing a data-roaming network from your ship, carefully note which network you're on (this is displayed on your phone's readout, generally next to the signal bars). You might not recognize the various land-based network names; to be safe, learn the name of the cruise-line network (it's usually something obvious, such as "Phone at Sea")—then avoid making any calls or using data if that name pops up. To prevent accidentally roaming on the sea-based network, simply disable roaming (or put your phone in "Airplane Mode") as soon as you board the ship. And be warned that receiving a call—even if you don't answer it—costs the same as making a call.

Here's a case study: On a recent one-week cruise to the Greek islands, at my first stop I paid $10 for a SIM card that allowed affordable calls within Europe—and cheap calls to the US. Because that cruise's itinerary rarely ventured far from land-based networks, I was able (with only a few, brief exceptions) to call home for pennies a minute, without ever needing to resort to the pricey onboard network.

Satellite Phones: If you want the freedom to make calls anywhere, anytime, at a fixed rate, consider renting a satellite phone. For example, www.bluecosmo.com rents phones for $40/week, with calling rates of $1.35-1.89/minute (depending on how many minutes you purchase), plus $10-55 for shipping. Once you add up all those costs, this option isn't cheap—but it's versatile.

Onboard Activities

Large cruise ships are like resorts at sea. In the hours spent cruising between ports, there's no shortage of diversions: swimming pools, hot tubs, and water slides; sports courts, exercise rooms, shuffleboard courts, giant chessboards, and rock-climbing walls; casinos with slots and table games; shopping malls; art galleries with works for sale; children's areas with playground

equipment and babysitting services; and spas where you can get a facial, massage, or other treatments. Many activities have an extra charge associated—always ask before you participate.

To avoid crowds, take advantage of shipboard activities and amenities at off times. The gym is quieter late in the evenings, when many cruisers are already in bed. Onboard restaurants are typically less crowded for the later seatings. If you're dying to try out that rock-climbing wall, drop by as soon as you get back on the ship in the afternoon; if you wait an hour or two, the line could get longer.

Days at sea are a good time to try all the things you haven't gotten around to on busy port days, but be warned that everyone else on the ship has the same idea. Services such as massages are particularly popular on sea days—book ahead and be prepared to pay full price (if you get a massage on a port day, you might get a discount). Premium restaurants and other activities also tend to fill up far earlier for days at sea, so don't wait around too long to book anything you have your heart set on.

Remember, the schedule and locations for all of these options—classes, social activities, entertainment, and more—are listed in your daily program.

Social Activities

Many ships offer a wide array of activities, ranging from seminars on art history to wine- and beer-tastings to classes on how to fold towels in the shape of animals (a skill, you'll soon learn, that your cabin steward has mastered). Quite a few of these are sales pitches in disguise, but others are just for fun and a great way to make friends. Bingo, trivia contests, dancing lessons, cooking classes, goofy poolside games, newlywed games, talent shows, nightly mixers for singles, scrapbooking sessions, high tea—there's something

for everyone. Note that a few offerings might use code words or abbreviations: "Friends of Bill W" refers to a meeting of Alcoholics Anonymous; "Friends of Dorothy" or "LGBT" refers to a meeting of gay people. Ships have a community bulletin board where these and other meetings are posted. You can even post your own.

Entertainment and Nightlife

Most cruise ships have big (up to 1,000-seat) theaters with nightly shows. An in-house troupe of singers and dancers generally puts on

two or three schmaltzy revue-type shows a week (belting out crowd-pleasing hits). On other nights, the stage is taken up by guest performers (comedy acts, Beatles tribute bands, jugglers, hypnotists, and so on). While not necessarily Broadway-quality, these performances are a fun diversion; since they're typi-

cally free and have open seating, it's easy to drop by for just a few minutes (or even stand in the back) to see if you like the show before you commit. On some of the biggest new megaships, the cruise lines are experimenting with charging a fee and assigning seats for more elaborate shows.

Smaller lounges scattered around the ship offer more intimate entertainment with just-as-talented performers—pianists, singers, duos, or groups who attract a faithful following night after night. Some cruisers enjoy relaxing in their favorite lounge to cap their day.

Cruises often screen second-run or classic movies for passengers to watch. Sometimes there's a dedicated cinema room; otherwise, films play in the main theater at off times.

Eating, always a popular pastime, is encouraged all hours of the day and night. While the main shipboard eateries tend to close by about midnight, large ships have one or two places that remain open 24 hours a day.

And if you enjoy dancing, you have plenty of options ranging from classy ballroom-dance venues to hopping nightclubs that pump dance music until the wee hours.

Shopping

In addition to touting shopping opportunities in port, cruise ships have their own shops on board, selling T-shirts, jewelry, trinkets,

and all manner of gear emblazoned with their logo. At busy times, they might even set up tables in the lobby to lure in even more shoppers. In accordance with international maritime law, the ship's casino and duty-free shops can open only once the ship is seven miles offshore.

While shopping on board is convenient and saves on taxes, most of the items sold on the ship can be found at home or online—for less. If you like to shop, have fun doing it in port, seeking out locally made mementos in European shops. (If you enjoy both sightseeing and shopping, balancing your port time can be a challenge; I'd suggest doing a quick surgical shopping strike in destinations where you have something in particular you'd like to buy, so you won't miss out on the great sights.) You'll find more information on shopping in port on page 134. In the destination chapters, I've given some suggestions about specific local goods to shop for.

Casino

Cruise ships offer Vegas-style casinos with all the classic games, including slots, blackjack, poker, roulette, and craps. But unlike Vegas—where casinos clamor for your business with promises of

the "loosest slots in town"— cruise ships know they have a captive audience. And that means your odds of winning are even worse than they are in Vegas. Onboard casinos also offer various trumped-up activities to drum up excitement. Sure, a poker

tournament can be exciting and competitive—but I can't for the life of me figure out the appeal of a slot tournament (no joking). If you want to test your luck—but you're not clear on the rules of blackjack, craps, or other casino games—take advantage of the free gambling classes that many cruise lines offer early in the trip.

Art Gallery

Many ships have an art gallery, and some even display a few genuinely impressive pieces from their own collection (minor works by

major artists). But more often the focus is on selling new works by lesser-known artists. Your ship might offer lectures about the art, but beware: These often turn out to be sales pitches for "up-and-coming" artists whose works are being auctioned on board. While the artists may be talented, the "valuation" prices are dramatically inflated. Art auctions ply bidders with free champagne to drive up the prices...but no serious art collector buys paintings on a cruise ship.

Photography

Once upon a time, photographers snapped a free commemorative portrait of you and your travel partner as you boarded the ship. But when the cruise lines figured out that people were willing to shell out $8-15 for one of these pictures, they turned it into big business. Roving photographers snap photos of you at dinner, and makeshift studios with gauzy backgrounds suddenly appear in the lobby on formal night. As you disembark at each port, photographers ask you to pose with models

in tacky costumes (flamenco dancers in Spain, toga-clad "ancients" in Greece, and—inexplicably—parrots in Croatia). Later that day, all those photos appear along one of the ship's hallways for everyone to see (perusing my fellow passengers' deer-in-the-headlights mug shots is one of my favorite onboard activities). While it's hard to justify spending 10 bucks on a cheesy snapshot, you might be able to bargain the price down toward the end of the trip. Repeat cruisers report that if you swing by the photography area on the last evening, the salespeople—eager to unload their inventory—may cut a deal if you pay cash.

Spa/Beauty Salon

Most cruise ships have spa facilities, where you can get a massage, facial, manicure, pedicure, and so on. There may also be a beauty salon where you can get your hair done. While convenient, these services are obviously priced at a premium—though specials are often available. These treatments often come with a sales pitch for related products. Tip as you would back home (either in cash or by adding a tip when you sign the receipt).

Library

The onboard library has an assortment of free loaner books, ranging from nautical topics to travel guidebooks to beach reading. Usually outfitted with comfortable chairs and tables, this can also be a good place to stretch out and relax while

you read. If the ship's staterooms are equipped with DVD players, the library may have DVDs for loan or rent.

Chapel

Many ships have a nondenominational chapel for prayer or silent reflection. If you're cruising during a religious holiday, the cruise line may invite a clergy member on board to lead a service.

Cruising with Kids

Cruises can be a great way to vacation with a family. But do your homework: Cruise lines cater to kids to varying degrees. For example, Disney, Celebrity, and Royal Caribbean are extremely kid-friendly, while other lines (especially the higher-end luxury ones) offer virtually nothing extra for children—a hint that they prefer you to leave the kiddos at home.

Kids' Programs and Activities

Family-friendly cruise lines have "kids clubs" that are open for most of the day. It's a win-win situation for both parents and children. Kids get to hang out with their peers and fill their time with games, story time,

ON THE SHIP

arts and crafts, and other fun stuff, while parents get to relax and enjoy the amenities of the ship.

Most kids clubs are for children ages three and older, and require your tots to be potty-trained. Kids are separated by age so that tweens don't have to be subjected to younger children. For older kids, there are teen-only hangouts. If you have kids under three, options are limited: You might find parent/baby classes (no drop-and-go) and, in rare cases, onboard day care.

Rules for kids clubs differ across cruise lines. Some charge for the service, others include it. While kids clubs are generally open throughout the day (about 9:00-22:00), some close at mealtimes, so you'll have to collect your kids for lunch and dinner. Port-day policies vary—some kids clubs require a parent or guardian to stay on board (in case they need to reach you); others are fine with letting you off your parental leash.

There are also plenty of activities outside the kids club. All ships have pools, and some take it to the next level with rock-climbing walls, bowling alleys, and in-line skating. Arcades and movies provide hours of entertainment, and shows are almost always appropriate for all ages. Many scheduled activities are fun for the whole family, such as art classes, ice-carving contests, or afternoon tea.

Babysitting

Because cruise lines want you to explore the ship and have fun (and, of course, spend money at bars and the casino), many have babysitting services. On some ships, you can arrange for a babysitter to come to your stateroom, while others offer late-night group babysitting for a small fee.

To line up babysitting, ask at the front desk or the kids club. Or, if you and your child hit it off with one of the youth counselors at the kids club, you could consider asking her or him for some private babysitting. Oftentimes, crew members have flexible hours and are looking to earn extra money. Some have been separated from their families and even relish the opportunity to play with your kids—let them!

When hiring a babysitter, ask up front about rates; otherwise, offer the standard amount you pay at home. And remember to have cash on hand so you can compensate the babysitter at the end of the evening.

Food

Pizza parlors, hamburger grills, ice cream stands...thanks to the diverse dining options on ships, even the pickiest of eaters should be satisfied. Here are some tips for dining with children:

If you prefer to eat with your kids each night, choose the first dinner seating, which has more families and suits kids' earlier eating schedules. If your kids are too squirmy to sit through a five-course formal dinner every night, choose the buffet or a casual poolside restaurant (described later, under "Eating").

Don't forget about room service. This can be a nice option for breakfast, so you don't have to rush around in the morning. It's also an easy solution if you're cabin-bound with a napping child in the afternoon.

If your kids have convinced you to let them drink soda (which costs extra on a cruise), buy a soft drink card for the week to save over ordering à la carte.

In Port

If you plan to take your kids off the ship and into town, remember that a lot of Europe's streets and sidewalks are old, cobbled, and uneven—not ideal for a stroller. If your kids can't walk the whole way themselves, consider bringing a backpack carrier rather than a stroller for more mobility.

While excursions are often not worth the expense, they make sense for some ports and activities, especially when you have kids in tow. You don't have to deal with transportation, nor do you have to worry about missing the boat. (For more on excursions, see page 107).

If you do take your kids into port, consider draping a lanyard around their necks with emergency contact information in case you get separated. Include your name and mobile phone number, your ship's name, the cruise line, the itinerary, a copy of the child's passport, and some emergency cash.

Eating

While shipboard dining used to be open-and-shut (one restaurant, same table, same companions, same waitstaff, same time every night), these days you have choices ranging from self-service buffets to truly inspired specialty restaurants. On bigger ships, you could spend a week on board and never eat at the same place twice.

Note that if you have food allergies or a special diet—such as vegetarian, vegan, or kosher—most cruise lines will do their best to accommodate you. Notify them as far ahead as possible (when you book your cruise or 30 days before you depart).

Types of Dining

Most cruise ships have a main dining room, a more casual buffet, a variety of specialty restaurants, and room service.

Main Dining Room

The main restaurant venue on your ship is the old-fashioned dining room. With genteel decor, formal waiters, and a rotating menu  of upscale cuisine, dining here is an integral part of the classic cruise experience.

Traditionally, each passenger was assigned a particular seating time and table for all dinners in the dining room. But over the last decade or so, this **"assigned dining"** policy has been in flux, with various cruise lines taking different approaches. Some lines (including Royal Caribbean, Costa, MSC, Celebrity, and Disney) still have assigned dining. Others (such as Holland America, Princess, and Cunard) make it optional: You can choose whether you want an assigned seating (if you don't, just show up, and you'll be seated at whichever table is available next). Norwegian Cruise Line, along with several of the smaller luxury lines (Oceania, Silversea, Azamara, Windstar, Star Clippers, Seabourn, Regent Seven Seas), have no assigned dining—it's first-come, first-served, in any dining venue.

If you choose assigned dining, you'll eat with the same people every night (unless you opt to dine elsewhere on some evenings). Tables for two are rare, so couples will likely wind up seated with others. You'll really get to know your tablemates...whether you like it or not. Some cruisers prefer to be at a table that's as large as possible—if you are seated with just one other couple, you risk running out of conversation topics sooner than at a table with 10 or 12 people.

Diners are assigned either to an early seating (typically around 18:30) or a late seating (around 20:45). Avid sightseers might prefer the second seating, so they can fully enjoy the port without rushing back to the ship in time to change for dinner (on the other hand, the first seating lets you turn in early to rest up for the next day's port). In general, families and older passengers seem to opt for the first seating, while younger passengers tend to prefer the later one.

If your cruise line has assigned dining (whether mandatory or optional), you can request your seating preferences (time and table size) when you book your cruise. These assignments are first-come, first-served, so the earlier you book and make your request, the better. If you don't get your choice, you can ask to be put on a waiting list.

Formal Nights

Many cruises have one or two designated formal nights each week in the main dining room, when passengers get decked out for dinner in suits and cocktail dresses—or even tuxes and floor-length gowns (for tips on how to pack for formal night, see the sidebar on page 54). In general, on formal nights the whole ambience of the ship is upscale, with people hanging out in the bars, casinos, and other public areas dressed to the nines. And cruises like formal nights because passengers behave better and spend more money (for example, ordering a nicer bottle of wine or buying the posed photos).

Ships may also have semiformal nights (also one or two per week), which are scaled-down versions of the formal nights—for example, men wear slacks and a tie, but no jacket.

Some passengers relish the opportunity to dress up on formal nights. But if you don't feel like it, it's fine to dress however you like—as long as you stay out of the dining room. Skip the formal dinners and eat at another restaurant or the buffet, or order room service.

If you're not happy with your assignment, try dropping by the dining room early on the first night to see if the maître d', who's in charge of assigning tables, can help you. He'll do his best to accommodate you (you won't be the only person requesting a change—there's always some shuffling around). If the maître d' is able to make a switch, it's appropriate to thank him with a tip.

Some people really enjoy assigned dining. It encourages you to socialize with fellow passengers and make friends. Tablemates sometimes team up and hang out in port together as well. And some cruisers form lasting friendships with people they were, once upon a time, randomly assigned to dine with. If, on the other hand, you're miserable with your dinner companions, ask the maître d' to reseat you. Be aware that the longer you wait to request a change, the more difficult (and potentially awkward) it becomes.

If you get tired of assigned dining, you can always find variety by eating at the buffet or a specialty restaurant, or by ordering room service. And if you have an early seating but decide to skip dinner one night to stay late in port, you can still dine at the other onboard restaurants. Since the various onboard eateries are all included (except for specialty-restaurant surcharges), money is no object. While I enjoy the range of people at my assigned dinner table, I usually end up dining there only about half the nights on a given cruise.

Note that the main dining room is typically also open for breakfast and lunch. At these times, it's generally open seating (no preassigned tables), but you'll likely be seated with others. The majority of travelers prefer to have a quick breakfast and lunch at the buffet (or in port). But some cruisers enjoy eating these meals in the dining room (especially on leisurely sea days) as a more civilized alternative to the mob scene at the buffet; it's also an opportunity to meet fellow passengers who normally sit elsewhere at dinner.

Dress Code: In the main dining room, most cruise lines institute a "smart casual" dress code. This means no jeans, shorts, or T-shirts. Men wear slacks and button-down or polo shirts; women wear dresses or nice separates. "Formal night" dress codes apply in the dining room (see sidebar, previous page).

Casual Dining: Buffet and Poolside Restaurants

Besides the main dining room, most ships have at least one additional restaurant, generally a casual buffet. This has much longer

hours than the dining room, and the food is not necessarily a big step down: The buffet often has some of the same options as in the dining room, and it may even have some more unusual items, often themed (Greek, Indian, sushi, and so on). Most ships also have an even more

casual "grill" restaurant, usually near the pool, where you can grab a quick burger or hot dog and other snacks. These options are handy if you're in a hurry, or just want a break from the dining room.

When eating at the buffet, keep in mind that this situation—with hundreds of people handling the same serving spoons and tongs, licking their fingers, then handling more spoons and tongs—is nirvana for communicable diseases. Compound that with the fact that some diners don't wash their hands (incorrectly believing that hand sanitizer is protecting them from all illness), and you've got a perfect storm. At the risk of sounding like a germophobe, wash your hands before, during, and after your meal. For more on this cheerful topic, see page 83.

Dress Code: The buffet and "grill" restaurants have a casual dress code. You'll see plenty of swimsuits and flip-flops, though most cruise lines require a shirt or cover-up in the buffet.

Specialty Restaurants

Most ships (even small ones) have at least one specialty eatery, but some have a dozen or more. If there's just one specialty restaurant on board, it serves food (such as steak or seafood) that's a notch above what's available in the dining room. If there are several, they specialize in different foods or cuisines: steakhouse, French, sushi, Italian, Mexican, and so on.

Because specialty restaurants are more in demand than the

ON THE SHIP

traditional dining room, it's smart to make reservations if you have your heart set on a particular one. At the beginning of your cruise, scope out the dining room's menu for the week; if one night seems less enticing to you, consider booking a specialty restaurant for that evening. Days at sea are also popular nights in specialty restaurants. I enjoy using the specialty restaurants when I want to dine with people I've met on the ship outside of my usual tablemates. Remember that if you want a window seat with a view, eat early. When darkness settles, the window becomes a pitch-black pane of glass, and that romantic view is entirely gone.

Occasionally these restaurants are included in your cruise price, but more often they require a special cover charge (typically $10-30). In addition to the cover charge, certain entrées incur a supplement ($10-20). A couple ordering specialty items and a bottle of wine can quickly ring up a $100 dinner bill. If you're on a tight budget, remember: Specialty restaurants are optional. You can eat every meal at the included dining room and buffet if you'd rather not spend the extra money. (By the way, if you order a bottle of wine and don't finish it, they can put your name on it and bring it to you in the main dining hall the next night.)

Some routine cruisers allege that the cruise lines are making the food in their dining room intentionally worse in order to steer passengers to the specialty restaurants that charge a cover. But from a dollars-and-cents perspective, this simply doesn't add up. The generally higher-quality ingredients used in specialty restaurants typically cost far more than the cover charge; for example, you might pay $20 to eat a steak that's worth $30. The cover charge is designed not to be a moneymaker, but to limit the number of people who try to dine at the specialty restaurants. It's just expensive enough to keep the place busy every night, but not cheap enough that it's swamped. So if cruise food is getting worse, it's not on purpose.

Dress Code: Specialty restaurants usually follow the same dress code as the main dining room (including on formal nights), though it depends on how upscale the menu is. The steakhouse might be more formal than the main dining room; the sushi bar could be less formal. If you're unsure, ask.

Room Service
Room service is temptingly easy and is generally included in the cruise price (no extra charge). Its menu appears to be much more limited than what you'd get in any of the restaurants, but you can often request items from the dining room menu as well. (If you don't want to dress up on formal night—but still want to enjoy the generally fancier fare on those evenings—ask in advance whether you can get those same meals as room service.) Either way, it's very

convenient, especially on mornings when the ship arrives in port early. By eating breakfast in your room (place your order the night before), you can get ready at a more leisurely pace and avoid the crowd at the buffet. You can also arrange for room service to be waiting when you get back on the ship from exploring a port.

It's polite to thank the person who delivers your food with about a $2 tip; sometimes you can put this on your tab and sign for it, but not always, so it's smart to have cash ready.

Dress Code: From tuxes and gowns to your birthday suit, when you order room service, it's up to you.

Cruise Cuisine

Reviews of the food on cruise ships range wildly, from raves to pans. It's all relative: While food snobs who love locally sourced

bistros may turn up their noses at cruise cuisine, fans of chain restaurants are perfectly satisfied on board. True foodies should lower their expectations. High-seas cuisine is not exactly high cuisine.

Cruise food is as good as it can be, considering that thousands of people are fed at each meal. Most cruise lines replenish their food stores about every two weeks, so everything you eat—including meat, seafood, and produce—may be less than fresh. Except on some of the top-end lines, the shipboard chefs are afforded virtually no room for creativity: The head office creates the recipes, then trains all kitchen crews to prepare each dish. To ensure cooks get it just right, cruise lines hang a photo in the galley (kitchen) of what each dish should look like. This is especially important since most of the cooks and servers come from countries where the cuisine is quite different.

Cruise-ship food is not local cuisine. Today's menu, dreamed up months ago by some executive chef in Miami, bears no resemblance to the food you saw this afternoon in port. It can be frustrat-

ing to wander through a Greek village, passing tavernas with luscious tomato salads and succulent seafood, only to go back to your ship and be served Caesar salad and prime rib.

On the other hand, cruise menus often feature famous but unusual dishes that would cost a pretty penny in a top-end restaurant back home. It can be fun to sample a variety of oddball items (such as frog legs, escargot, or foie gras) and higher-end meats (filet mignon, guinea fowl, lobster, crab)...with no expense and no commitment. (If you don't like it, don't finish it. Waiters are happy to bring you something else.)

Whether cruise food is good or bad, one thing's for sure: There's plenty of it. A ship with 2,500 passengers and 1,500 crew members might brag that they prepare "17,000 meals a day." Do the math: Someone's going back for seconds. A lot of someones, in fact. (If you're one of them, see "Staying Fit on Board" on page 84.)

All things considered, cruise lines do an impressive job of providing variety and quality. But cruise food still pales in comparison to the meals you can get in port, lovingly prepared with fresh ingredients and local recipes. Some travelers figure there's no point paying for food in port when you can just eat for free on the ship. But after a few days of cruise cuisine, I can't wait to sit down at a real European restaurant or grab some authentic street food...and I can really taste the difference.

Drinks

In general, tap water, milk, iced tea, coffee and tea, and fruit juices are included. Other drinks cost extra: alcohol of any kind, name-brand soft drinks, fresh-squeezed fruit juices, and premium espresso drinks (lattes and cappuccinos). You'll also pay for any drinks you take from your stateroom's minibar (generally the same price as in the restaurants). Beverages are priced approximately the same as in a restaurant on land.

Early in your cruise, ask about special offers for reduced drink prices, such as discount cards or six-for-the-price-of-five beer offers. This also goes for soft drinks—if you guzzle Diet Coke, you can buy an "unlimited drink card" at the start of the cruise and order as many soft drinks as you want without paying more.

Cruise lines want to encourage alcohol sales on board, but without alienating customers. Before you set sail, find out your cruise line's policy on taking alcohol aboard so you can BYOB to save money. Some cruise lines ban it outright; others prohibit only hard liquor but allow wine and sometimes beer. On some ships, you may be able to bring one or two bottles of wine when you first board the ship. Keep in mind that if you bring aboard your own bottle of wine to enjoy with dinner on the ship, you'll most likely face a corkage fee (around $10-20).

To monitor the alcohol situation, cruise lines require you to go through a security checkpoint every time you board the ship. It's OK to purchase a souvenir bottle of booze in port, but you may have to check it for the duration of the cruise. Your purchases will be returned to you on the final night or the morning of your last disembarkation.

If you're a scofflaw who enjoys a nip every now and again, note that various cruising websites abound with strategies for getting around the "no alcohol" rules.

Eating on Port Days

For some travelers, port days present a tasty opportunity to sample the local cuisine. Others prioritize their port time for sightseeing or shopping rather than sitting at a restaurant waiting for their food to arrive. And still others economize by returning to the ship for lunch (which, to me, seems like a waste of valuable port time). For more tips on eating while in port, see page 137.

To save money, some cruise passengers suggest tucking a few items from the breakfast buffet into a day bag for a light lunch on the go. While this is, to varying degrees, frowned upon by cruise lines, they recognize that many people do it—and, after all, you are paying for the food. If you do this, do so discreetly. Some experienced cruisers suggest ordering room service for breakfast, with enough extra for lunch. Or you can get a room-service sandwich the evening before and tuck it into your minifridge until morning. To make it easier to pack your lunch, bring along sealable plastic baggies from home.

Final Disembarkation

When your cruise comes to an end, you'll need to jump through a few hoops before you actually get off the ship. The crew will give you written instructions, and you'll often be able to watch a presentation about the process on your stateroom TV. Many ships even have a "disembarkation talk" on the final day to explain the procedure. I keep it very simple: I review my bill for extra charges, accept the auto-tip, and carry my own bags off the ship any time after breakfast. While the specifics vary from cruise to cruise, most include the following considerations.

On your last full day on the ship, you'll receive an itemized copy of your **bill**. This includes the auto-tip for the crew (explained on page 79), drinks, excursions, shopping, restaurant surcharges, and any other expenses you've incurred. This amount will automatically be charged to the credit card you registered with the cruise line. If there are any mistaken charges, contest them as soon as you discover them (to avoid long lines just as everyone is disembarking).

If you'd like to give an additional cash **tip** to any crew members (especially those with whom you've personally interacted or who have given you exceptional service), it's best to do so on the final night in case you can't find the tippee in the morning. It's most common to tip cabin stewards and maybe a favorite waiter or two, particularly if they served you several times over the course of your cruise. There is no conventional amount or way to calculate tips; simply give what you like, but keep in mind that the crew has extremely low base wages (about $1/day). Traditionally, the cruise lines provide envelopes (either at the front desk or sometimes left in your stateroom on the final evening) for you to tuck a cash tip inside and hand it to the crew member.

The night before disembarking, leave any **bags** you don't want to carry off the ship (with luggage tags attached) in the hall outside your room. The stewards will collect these bags during the night, and they'll be waiting for you when you step off the ship. Be sure *not* to pack any items you may need before disembarking the next morning (such as medications, a jacket, or a change of clothes). I prefer to carry off my own bags—that way, I don't have to pack the night before and go without my personal items the last morning. Also, I can leave anytime I want, and I don't have to spend time claiming my bags after I've disembarked.

Before leaving your cabin, check all the drawers, other hidden stowage areas, and the safe—after a week or more at sea, it's easy to forget where you tucked away items when you first unpacked.

In the morning, you'll be assigned a **disembarkation time.** At that time, you'll need to vacate your cabin (so the crew can clean it for the passengers arriving in a few hours) and gather in a desig-nated public area for further instructions on where to leave the ship and claim your luggage.

It's possible to get an **early disembarkation time**—particu-larly if you're in a hurry to catch a plane or train, or if you just want to get started on your sightseeing. Request early disembarkation near the start of your cruise, as there is a set number of slots, and they can fill up. Another option is to walk off with all your luggage (rather than leaving it in the hall overnight and reclaiming it once off the ship)—as this opportunity may be limited to a designated number of passengers, ask about it near the start of your cruise.

If you're hungry, you can have breakfast—your last "free" meal before re-entering the real world. Once you do leave the ship at the appointed time, the bags you left outside your room the night before will be waiting for you in the terminal building.

If you're sightseeing around town and need to **store your bags,** there is often a bag-storage service at or near the cruise terminal (I've listed specifics for certain ports in this book). If you're stay-ing at a hotel after the cruise, you can take your bags straight there when you leave the ship; even if your room is not ready, the hotelier is usually happy to hold your bags until check-in time.

Most cruise lines offer a **transfer** service to take you to your hotel or the airport. Typically you'll do better arranging this on your own (taxis wait at the cruise terminal, and this book's destina-tion chapters include detailed instructions for getting into town or to the airport). But if you book it through the cruise line, they may offer the option to let you pay a little extra to keep your stateroom and enjoy the pool until catching the airport shuttle for your afternoon flight. Some cruise lines also offer excursions at the end of the journey that swing by the city's top sights before ending at your hotel or the airport. This can be a good way to combine a sightseeing excursion with a transfer.

For **customs** regulations on returning to the US, see page 136.

ON THE SHIP

IN PORT

While some people care more about shipboard amenities than the actual destinations, most travelers who take a European cruise see it mainly as a fun way to get to the ports. This is your chance to explore some of Europe's most fascinating cities, characteristic seaside villages, and engaging regions.

Prior to reaching each destination, you'll need to decide whether you want to go on an excursion (booked on board through your cruise line) or see it on your own. This chapter explains the pros and cons of excursions and provides a rundown of which destinations are best by excursion—and which are easy to do independently (see the sidebar on page 114). It also fills you in on the procedure for getting off and back on the ship, and provides tips on how to make the most of your time on land.

Excursions

In each port, your cruise line offers a variety of shore excursions. While the majority involve bus tours, town walks (led by a local guide hired for the day by the cruise line), and guided visits to museums and archaeological sites, others are more active (biking, kayaking, hiking), and some are more passive (a trip to a beach, spa, or even a luxury-hotel swimming pool for the day). Most also include a shopping component (such as a visit to a glassmaker's studio in Venice, a jewelry shop in Santorini, or a carpet-weaving demonstration in Turkey). When shopping is involved, kickbacks are common. Local merchants may pay the cruise line or guide to bring the group to their shops, give them a cut of whatever's bought, or both. In extreme cases, shops even provide buses and drivers for excursions, so there's no risk the shopping stop will be missed. The prices you're charged are likely inflated to cover these payouts.

Excursions aren't cheap. On European cruises, a basic two- to three-hour town walking tour runs about $40-60/person; a half-day bus tour to a nearby sight can be $70-100; and a full-day bus-plus-walking-tour itinerary can be $100-150 or more. Extras (such as a boat ride or a lunch) add to the cost. There seems to be little difference in excursion costs or quality between a mass-market and a luxury line (in fact, excursions can be more expensive on a cheap cruise than on a pricey one).

On the day of your excursion, you'll gather in a large space (often the ship's theater, sometimes with hundreds of others), waiting for your excursion group to be called. You're given a sticker to wear with a number that corresponds to your specific group/bus number. Popular excursion itineraries can have several different busloads. Once called, head down the gangway—or to the tenders—to meet your awaiting tour bus and local guide.

Excursion Options

The types of excursions you can book vary greatly, depending on the port. In a typical midsized port city, there might be two different themed walking tours of the city itself (for example, one focusing on the Old Town and art museum, and another on the New Town and architecture); a panoramic drive into the countryside for scenery, sometimes with stops (such as a wine-tasting, a restaurant lunch, or a folk-dancing show); and trips to outlying destinations, such as a neighboring village or an archaeological site.

Some ports have an even wider range of options. For example, if you dock at either Marseille or Toulon in southern France, you'll be offered various Provençal itineraries that combine appealing towns and sights, such as Avignon, Arles, Aix-en-Provence, the ruined castle at Les Baux, the Roman aqueduct of Pont du Gard, and countryside wineries. In these regions, excursions feature destinations bundled in different ways—look for an itinerary that covers just what you're interested in (see the "Excursions" sidebars in each destination chapter to help you sort through your options).

In some cases, there's only one worthy destination, but it takes some effort to reach it. For example, from the port of Civitavecchia, it's nearly 50 miles into Rome, with little else to see or do nearby. It's possible—using this book—to get to these places by public transportation. But the cruise line hopes you'll pay them to take you instead.

Most excursions include a guided tour of town, but for those who want more freedom, cruise lines also offer "On Your Own" (a.k.a. "transfer-only" or "transportation-only") excursions: A bus will meet you as you disembark, and you might have a guide who narrates your ride into town. But once you reach the main destination, you're set free and given a time to report back to the bus. While more expensive than public transportation, these transfers cost less than fully guided excursions and are generally cheaper than hiring a taxi to take you into town (although you can split the cost of a taxi with other travelers).

Most cruise lines can also arrange a private driver or guide for you. While this is billed as an "excursion," you're simply paying the cruise line to act as a middleman. It's much more cost-effective to make these arrangements yourself (you can use one of the guides or drivers I recommend in this book).

Booking an Excursion

The cruise lines make it easy to sign up for excursions. There's generally a presentation on excursions in the theater sometime during the first few days of your cruise (or during a day at sea), and a commercial for the different itineraries runs 24/7 on your stateroom TV. You can sign up at the excursions desk, through the concierge, or (on some ships) through the interactive menu on your TV. You can generally cancel from 24 to 48 hours before the excursion leaves (ask when you book); if you cancel with less notice—for any reason—you will probably have to pay for it.

You can also book shore excursions on the cruise line's website prior to your trip. But be warned: It's common to sign up in advance, then realize once on board that your interests have changed. Some cruise lines levy a cancellation fee; most waive that fee if you cancel the first day you're on board, while others will waive it if you upgrade to a more expensive excursion.

If you have to cancel because of illness, some cruise lines' excursions desks may be willing to try to sell your tickets to another passenger (and refund your money); if not, they can write you a note to help you recoup the money from your travel insurance.

Cruise lines use the words "limited space" to prod passengers to hurry up and book various extra services—especially excursions. (They're technically correct—if there's not room for every single passenger on board to join the excursion, then space is, strictly speaking, "limited," even if the excursion never sells out.) Sometimes excursions truly do fill up quickly; other times, you can sign up moments before departure. This creates a Chicken Little situation: Since they *always* claim "limited space," it's hard to know whether an excursion truly is filling up fast. If you have your heart set on a particular excursion, book it as far ahead as you can. But if you're on the fence, ask at the excursions desk how many seats are left and how soon they anticipate it filling up. If your choice is already booked when you ask, request to be added to the wait list—it's not unusual for the cruise line to have last-minute cancellations or to add more departures for popular excursions.

Take an Excursion, or Do It on My Own?

Excursions are (along with alcohol sales and gambling) the cruise lines' bread and butter. To sell you on them, they like to convey the "insurance" aspect of joining their excursion. They'll tell you that you can rest easy, knowing that you're getting a vetted local tour guide on a tried-and-true itinerary that will pack the best experience into your limited time—and you'll be guaranteed not to miss your ship when it leaves that evening.

Some excursions are a great value, whisking you to top-tier and otherwise-hard-to-reach sights with an eloquent guide on a well-planned itinerary. But others can be disappointing time- and money-wasters, carting passengers to meager "sights" that are actually shopping experiences in disguise.

This book is designed not necessarily to discourage you from taking the cruise lines' excursions, but to help you make an informed decision, on a case-by-case basis, about whether a particular excursion is a good value for your interests and budget. In some situations (such as the Ephesus excursion from Kuşadası), I would happily pay a premium for a no-sweat transfer with a hand-picked, top-notch local guide. In other cases (such as a trip from Barcelona's port to its bustling, sights-packed city center—an easy bus ride on your own), the information in this book will allow you to have at least as good an experience, with more flexibility and freedom for a fraction of the price.

Pros and Cons of Excursions

Here are some of the benefits of taking an excursion, as touted by the cruise lines. Evaluate how these selling points fit the way you travel—and whether they are actually perks, or might cramp your style.

Returning to the Ship on Time: Cruise lines try to intimidate you into signing up for excursions by gravely reminding you that if you're on your own and fail to make it back to the ship on time, it could leave without you. If, however, a cruise-line excursion runs late for some reason, the ship will wait. In most places, provided that you budget your time conservatively (and barring an unforeseen strike or other crisis), there's no reason you can't have a great day in port and easily make it back on board in time. But if you don't feel confident about your ability to navigate back to the ship on time, or you have a chronic issue with lateness, an excursion may be a good option.

Getting Off First: Those going on excursions have priority for getting off the ship. This is especially useful when tendering, as tender lines can be long soon after arrival. But if you're organized and get a tender ticket as early as possible, you can make it off the ship almost as fast as the excursion passengers. (For more on tendering, see page 118.)

Optimizing Time in Port: Most excursions are well-planned by the cruise line to efficiently use your limited time in port. Rather

than waiting around for a bus or train to your destination, you're whisked dockside-to-destination by the excursion bus. However, when weighing the "time savings" of an excursion, remember to account for how long it takes 50 people (compared to two people) to do everyday tasks: boarding a bus, walking through a castle, even making bathroom stops. If you're on your own and want to check out a particular shop, you can stay as long as you like—or just dip in and out; with a cruise excursion, you're committed to a half-hour, an hour, or however long the shopkeeper is paying your guide to keep you there. Every time your group moves somewhere, you're moving with dozens of other people, which always takes time. In many ports, you may actually reach the city center faster on your own than with an excursion, provided you are ready to hop off the ship as soon as you can, don't waste time getting to the terminal building, and know how, when, and where to grab public transport.

Many cruise lines schedule both morning and afternoon excursions. If you're a 30-minute bus ride from a major destination and select a morning excursion, your guide is instructed to bring you back to the ship (hoping that you'll join an afternoon excursion as well). If you prefer to spend your afternoon in town, it's perfectly acceptable to skip the return bus trip and make your way back to the ship, later, on your own (just be sure your guide knows you're splitting off).

Accessing Out-of-the-Way Sights: In most destinations, there's a relatively straightforward, affordable public-transportation option for getting from the cruise port to the major city or sight. But in a few cases, minor sights (or even the occasional major sight) are challenging, if not impossible, to reach without paying for a pricey taxi or rental car. For example, if your cruise is coming in to Toulon, and you've always wanted to see the Pont du Gard aqueduct, you'll find it next to impossible to get there by public transportation—so the most reasonable choice is an excursion. This book is designed to help you determine how easy—or difficult—it is to reach the places you're interested in seeing.

Touring with Quality Guides: Most excursions are led by local guides contracted through the cruise line. While all guides

have been vetted by the cruise line and are generally high-quality, a few oddball exceptions occasionally sneak through. The guide is the biggest wildcard in the success of your tour, but it's also something you have very little control over. You won't know which guide is leading your excursion until he or she shows up to collect you.

An alternative can be to hire a good local guide to show you around on a private tour. For two people, this can cost about as much as buying the excursion, but you get a much more personalized experience, tailored to your interests. And if you can enlist other passengers to join you to split the cost, it's even more of a bargain. I've recommended my favorite guides for most destinations; many of them are the same ones who are hired by the cruise lines to lead their excursions. Because local guides tend to book up when a big cruise ship is in town, it's smart to plan ahead and email these guides well before your trip.

Cruise lines keep track of which guides get good reviews, and do their best to use those guides in the future. If you do go on an excursion, take the time to give the cruise line feedback, good or bad, about the quality of your guide. They really want to know.

IN PORT

Beware of Crew Members' Advice

While most cruise lines understand that their passengers won't book an excursion at every port, there is some pressure to get you to take them. And if you ask crew members for advice on sightseeing (independent of an excursion), they may be less than forthcoming. Take crew members' destination advice with a grain of salt.

Philosophically, most cruise lines don't consider it their responsibility to help you enjoy your port experience—unless you pay them for an excursion. The longer you spend on the ship, the more likely you are to spend more money on board, so there's actually a financial disincentive for crew members to help you get off the ship and find your own way in the port. You're lucky if the best they offer is, "Take a taxi. I have no idea what it costs."

I have actually overheard excursion staff dispense misinformation about the time, expense, and difficulty involved in reaching downtown from a port ("The taxi takes 25-30 minutes, and I've never seen a bus at the terminal"—when in fact, the taxi takes 10 minutes and there's an easy bus connection from the terminal). Was the crew being deceptive, or just ignorant? Either way, it was still misinformation.

The best plan is to get sightseeing information on your own. That's why detailed instructions for getting into town from the port are a major feature of this book. The local tourist office often sets up a desk or info tent right on the pier, in the terminal, or where shuttle buses drop you. Otherwise, you can usually find a tourist information office (abbreviated **TI** in this book) in the town center.

The Bottom Line on Excursions

Some passengers are on a cruise because they simply don't want to invest the time and energy needed to be independent...they want to be on vacation. Time is money, and you spend 50 weeks a year figuring things out back home; on vacation, you want someone else to do the thinking for you. If that's you, excursions can be a good way to see a place.

But in many destinations, it honestly doesn't take that much additional effort or preparation to have a good experience without paying a premium for an excursion. And cost savings aside, if you have even a middling spirit of adventure, doing it on your own can be a fun experience in itself.

Planning Your Time

Whether you're taking an excursion, sightseeing on your own, or doing a combination of the two, it's important to plan your day on land carefully. Be sure to read this book's sightseeing information and walking tours the night before to make the most of your time, even if you're taking an excursion—many include free time at a sight or neighborhood, or leave you with extra time in port.

First, keep in mind that the advertised amount of time in port can be deceptive. If the itinerary says that the ship is in town from 8:00 to 17:00, mentally subtract an hour or two from that time. It can take a good half-hour to get off a big ship and to the terminal building (or even longer, if you're tendering), and from the terminal, you still have to reach the town center. At the end of the day, the all-aboard time is generally a half-hour before the ship departs. Not only do you have to be back on board by 16:30, but you must also build in the time it takes to get from downtown to the ship. Your nine-hour visit in port just shrank to seven hours...still plenty of time to really enjoy a place, but not quite as much time as you expected.

It's essential to realize that if you are late returning to the ship, you cannot expect them to wait for you (unless you're on one of the

Excursion Cheat Sheet

This (admittedly oversimplified) roundup shows which major ports are best by excursion and which are doable on your own (with this book in hand). For the full story, read the arrival information in each chapter.

Destination (Port)	Excursion?
BARCELONA	**NO**

Ride the shuttle bus right into the heart of town, within easy walking distance (or Metro ride) of most sights

PROVENCE (Marseille/Toulon)	**YES**

Various great destinations within reach of the underwhelming port towns; an excursion can efficiently combine several.
From Marseille's Port: Shuttle bus to Old Port, walk or ride Métro to train station, then take a train to Aix-en-Provence (45 minutes) or Cassis (25 minutes).
From Toulon's Main Port: 30-minute walk (or short bus ride) to train station, then take a train to Marseille (45-60 minutes) or Cassis (35 minutes).

FRENCH RIVIERA (Nice/Villefranche/Monaco)	**NO**

All three ports—and more—are connected by frequent, fast, and easy trains and buses (10-20 minutes between each one by train, longer but more scenic by bus). Train stations are an easy walk, public-transit ride, or taxi trip from each port.

FLORENCE, PISA, LUCCA (Livorno)	**MAYBE**

Shuttle bus into downtown Livorno; take public bus to train station; then take a train to Pisa (20 minutes), Lucca (1-1.25 hours), or Florence (1.5 hours). Excursions offer a no-hassle connection that also includes tours of the major sights.

ROME (Civitavecchia)	**MAYBE**

Short walk to train station, then 45-80-minute train into Rome. Doable on your own, but an excursion helps you sightsee efficiently in this big city.

NAPLES, POMPEII (Naples/Sorrento)	**NO**

From Naples' Port: Take local buses or taxis (or, if it's running, the subway) to most sights in the city; Pompeii is an easy 40-minute train ride away.
From Sorrento's Port: Easy train ride to Pompeii (30 minutes) or Naples (70 minutes).

IN PORT

Destination (Port)	Excursion?
AMALFI COAST, CAPRI (Naples/Sorrento)	**YES**

Both are doable on your own from either port (especially Capri by boat—50 minutes from Naples, 20-25 minutes from Sorrento), but crowded and unreliable public transit risks not making it back in time. An excursion buys you peace of mind that the ship won't leave without you.

VENICE	**NO**

It's an easy 5-minute monorail ride to the Grand Canal for a slow vaporetto cruise through town, or a speedy 30-minute express boat directly to St. Mark's Square. Even walking (about 45 minutes to St. Mark's Square) is delightful in this unique city.

SPLIT	**NO**

The port is just a few steps from the easy-to-tour Old Town.

DUBROVNIK	**NO**

Cruisers are either tendered directly to the heart of the Old Town, or docked at the port (15-minute bus or taxi ride from Old Town). Once in the Old Town, everything worth seeing is walkable.

ATHENS (Piraeus)	**MAYBE**

Downtown is 20-60 minutes by public bus, Metro, or taxi (depending on traffic). But the important ancient sites benefit from a good guide, and an excursion offers easy connections.

MOST GREEK ISLANDS (Mykonos, Santorini, Corfu, Rhodes, Heraklion, and Katakolo/Olympia)	**NO**

Usually easy and fast to get into town or beaches. Just relax and be on vacation. Exceptions: Katakolo port (an excursion makes seeing Olympia easier) and Heraklion (an excursion allows you to connect both in-town sights and out-of-town palace).

ISTANBUL	**NO**

Cruise ship drops you off near the Golden Horn, an easy walk or tram or taxi ride from virtually every major sight in town.

EPHESUS (Kuşadası)	**YES**

Reaching Ephesus requires a complicated ride in shared minibus taxis (30-40 minutes) plus a 15-minute walk; or a pricey taxi. An excursion makes transport easy, and the magnificent site warrants a good guide.

cruise line's excursions, and it's running late). The cruise line has the right to depart without you...and they will. While this seems harsh, cruise lines must pay port fees for every *minute* they are docked, so your half-hour delay could cost them more than your cruise ticket. Also, they have a tight schedule to keep and can't be waiting around for stragglers (for tips on what to do if this happens to you, see the end of this chapter).

To avoid missing the boat, work backward from the time you have to be back on board. Be very conservative, especially if you're going far—for example, riding a train or bus to a neighboring town. Public transportation can be delayed, and traffic can be snarled at rush hour—just when you're heading back to the ship. One strategy is to do the farthest-flung sights first, then gradually work your way back to the ship. Once you know you're within walking distance of the ship, you can dawdle to your heart's content, confident you can make it back on time.

If you're extremely concerned about missing the ship, just pretend it departs an hour earlier than it actually does. You'll still have several hours to enjoy that destination and be left with an hour to kill back at the cruise port (or on board).

Note that transportation strikes can be a problem in Europe (particularly in France, Italy, and Greece). These can hit at any time, although they are usually publicized in advance. If you're going beyond the immediate area of the port, ask the local TI, "Are there any strikes planned for today that could make it difficult for me to return to my ship?" Even when there is a planned strike, a few trains and buses will still run—ask for the schedule.

If you're an early riser, you'll notice that your ship typically arrives at the port some time before the official disembarkation time. That's because local officials need an hour or more to "clear" the ship (process paperwork, passports, and so on) before passengers are allowed off. Even if you wake up early and find the ship docked, you'll most likely have to wait for the official disembarkation time to get off.

While you have to plan your time smartly, don't let anxiety paralyze you: Some travelers—even adventurous ones—get so nervous about missing the boat that they spend all day within view of the cruise port, just in case. Anyone who does that is missing out: In very few cities is the best sightseeing actually concentrated near the port. Cruise excursion directors have told me that entire months go by when they don't leave anyone behind. You have to be pretty sloppy—or incredibly unlucky—to miss your ship.

Managing Crowds

Unless you're on a luxury line, you can't go on a cruise and expect to avoid crowds. It's simply a fact of life. So be prepared to visit sights

at the busiest possible time—just as your cruise ship funnels a few thousand time-pressed tourists into town (or, worse, when three or four ships simultaneously disgorge).

Keep in mind that my instructions for getting into town might sound easy—but when you're jostling with several hundred others to cram onto a public bus that comes once every 20 minutes, the reality check can be brutal. Be patient...and most important, be prepared. You'll be amazed at how many of your fellow cruisers will step off the ship knowing nothing about their options for seeing the place. By buying and reading this book, and doing just a bit of homework before each destination, you're already way ahead of the game.

Make a point of being the first person down the gangway (or in line for tender tickets) each day, and make a beeline for what you most want to see. While your fellow passengers are lingering over that second cup of coffee or puzzling over the bus schedule, you can be the first person on top of the city wall or on the early train to your destination. Yes, you're on vacation, so if you want to take it easy, that's your prerogative. But you can't be lazy and also avoid the crowds. Choose one.

Getting Off the Ship

Your ship has arrived at its destination, and it's time to disembark and enjoy Europe. This section explains the procedure for getting off the ship and also provides a rundown of the services you'll find at the port.

Docking Versus Tendering

There are two basic ways to disembark from the ship: docking or tendering. On most European cruise itineraries, docking is far more common than tendering.

Docking

When your ship docks, it means that the vessel actually ties up to a pier, and you can simply walk off onto dry land. However, cruise piers (like cruise ships) can be massive, so you may have to walk 10-15 minutes from the ship to the terminal

building. Sometimes the port area is so vast, the cruise line will offer a shuttle bus between the ship and the terminal building.

Tendering

If your ship is too big or there's not enough room at the pier, the ship will anchor offshore and send passengers ashore using small boats called tenders. Passengers who have paid for excursions usually go first; then it goes in order of tender ticket (or tender number).

Tender tickets are generally distributed the night before or on the morning of arrival. Show up as early as you can to get your tender ticket (you may have to wait in line even before the official start time); the sooner you get your ticket, the earlier you can board your tender. Even then, you'll likely have to wait. (Sometimes passengers in more expensive staterooms are given a "VIP tender ticket," allowing them to skip the line whenever they want.)

The tenders themselves are usually the ship's lifeboats, but in some destinations, the port authority requires the cruise line to hire local tenders. Because tenders are small vessels prone to turbulence, transferring from the ship to the tender and from the tender to shore can be rough. Take your time, be sure of your footing, and let the tender attendants give you a hand—it's their job to prevent you from going for an unplanned swim.

Tendering is, to many passengers, the scourge of cruising, as it can waste a lot of time. Obviously, not everyone on your big ship can fit on those little tenders all at once. Do the math: Your ship carries some 2,000 passengers. There are three or four tenders, which can carry anywhere from 30 to 150 people apiece, and it takes at least 20 minutes round-trip. This can all translate into a lot of waiting around.

There are various strategies for navigating the tender line: Some cruisers report that if you show up at the gangway, ready to go, before your tender ticket number is called, you might be able to slip on early. A crush of people will often jam the main stairwells and elevators to the gangway. Some of these folks might block your passage despite having later tender tickets than yours. If you use a different set of stairs or elevators, then walk through an alternate hallway, you might be able to pop out near the gangway rather than get stuck in the logjam on the main stairwell. If you anticipate crowd issues while tendering, scope out the ship's layout in advance, when it's not busy.

Another strategy to avoid the crush of people trying to get off

What Should I Bring to Shore?

- Your room **key card.** No matter how you leave the ship—tendering or docking, with an excursion or on your own—the crew must account for your absence. Any time you come or go, a security guard will swipe your room key. Your photo will flash onscreen to ensure it's really you. With this punch-in-and-out system, the crew knows exactly who's on board and who's on shore at all times.

- **Local cash.** After living on a cashless cruise ship, this is easy to forget. If you plan to withdraw local currency at an ATM, be sure to bring your debit card (and a credit card if you plan to make purchases).

- **Passport.** It's smart to carry your passport at all times (safely tucked away in a money belt—explained on page 56). While you typically won't have to show a passport when embarking or disembarking at each port (except the first and possibly the last), you may need it as a deposit for renting something (such as an audioguide or a scooter), or as ID when making a credit-card purchase or requesting a VAT refund. And you'll certainly want it in case you miss the boat and have to make your way to the next port. Some ships actually keep your passport until the end of the cruise. In that case, you'll go on shore without it; if you're one of the rare few who misses the ship, you'll find your passport with the port agent at the terminal office.

- **Hot-weather gear,** including sunscreen, a hat, sunglasses, lightweight and light-colored clothing, and a water bottle (or buy one in port). Mediterranean climates can be scorchingly hot in the summertime.

- **Long pants,** if you plan to visit major churches in Spain, France, and Italy. These places may enforce a strict "no shorts, no bare shoulders" dress code for everyone (even kids).

- Your cruise's **destination information sheet** (daily program). At a minimum, jot down the all-aboard time and—if applicable—the time of the last tender or shuttle bus to the ship, along with contact details for the port agent (see page 121).

- This **guidebook,** or—better yet—tear out just the pages you need for today's port (see sidebar on page 3).

the ship upon arrival is to simply wait an hour or two, when you can waltz onto a tender at will. While you'll miss out on some valuable sightseeing time on shore, some cruisers figure that's a fair trade-off for avoiding the stress of tendering at a prime time.

If there's an advantage to tendering, it's that you're more likely to be taken to an arrival point that's close to the town's main points of interest (for example, in Dubrovnik, tenders bring cruise passengers right to the super-central Old Port, while anchored ships put in at a dock a bus ride away from the Old Town). When you figure in the time it would take to get from the main cruise port to the city center, tendering might actually save you some time—provided you get an early tender ticket. In fact,

on smaller ships, it can even be an advantage to tender—there's little to no waiting, and you're deposited in the heart of town.

Strangely, crowds are rare on tenders returning to the ship; apparently passengers trickle back all through the day, so even the last tenders of the day are rarely jam-packed. (And if they are, the ship won't leave without you, provided you're waiting in the tender line.)

The Port Area

In most destinations, the port is not in the city center; in some cases (such as Livorno for Florence, Civitavecchia for Rome, or Piraeus for Athens), the port is actually in a separate town or city a lengthy train or bus ride away. In this book's destination chapters, I describe how near (or far) the port is from the town center. Be warned that the port area is, almost as a rule, the ugliest part of town—often an industrial and/or maritime area that had its historic charm bombed to bits in World War II. But once you're in the heart of town, none of that will matter.

Many ports have a terminal building, where you'll find passport check/customs control, and usually also ATMs, some duty-

free shops, sometimes a travel agency and/or car-rental office, and (out front) a taxi stand and bus stop into town. Better terminals also have a TI that's staffed at times when cruise ships arrive.

Most ports have lines painted on the pavement (often blue) that lead you from where you step off the ship or exit the port gate to services (such as TIs or terminal buildings) or transportation options (such as bus stops).

Note: Your passport will rarely be checked on a European cruise. Most of the destinations covered in this book belong to the open-borders Schengen Agreement, so you don't need to show a passport when crossing the border. Even in other countries, it likely won't be checked—they know you're on a cruise ship, that you'll be returning to the ship that evening, and that you're likely to spend a lot of money in port, so they want to make things easy for you. Of the destination countries in this book, only Turkey requires a visa, although it's generally not necessary for cruise-ship passengers (explained on page 46). So, while it's wise to carry your passport for identification purposes, don't be surprised if you never actually need it.

Port Agents

In every port, your cruise line has an official port agent—a local representative who's designated to watch out for their passengers while they're in port. This person's name and contact information is listed on the port-of-call information sheet distributed by your cruise line and usually also in the daily program. Be sure to have this information with you when you go on shore; if you have an emergency and can't contact anyone from your ship, call the port agent for help. Likewise, if you're running late and realize that you won't make it back to the ship by the departure time, get in touch with your port agent, who will relay the information to the ship so they know you aren't coming. If you do miss the ship, sometimes the port agent can point you in the right direction for making your way to the next port of call on your own (for details, see "What If I Miss My Boat?" at the end of this chapter).

Sightseeing on Your Own

If you're planning to strike out on your own, you need to figure out in advance where you're going, how to get there, and what you want to do once you're there.

Getting into Town

When it's a long distance from the ship to the cruise terminal, cruise lines usually offer a free shuttle bus to the terminal; if it's a short distance, you can walk. Either way, once you're at the terminal, you'll need to find your own way into town.

By Taxi

Exiting the terminal, you'll usually run into a busy taxi stand, with gregarious, English-speaking cabbies offering to take you for a tour around the area's main sights. While taxis are efficient, be aware that most cabbies' rates are ridiculously inflated to take advantage of cruisers. You may be able to persuade them to just take you into town (generally at a hiked-up rate), though they usually prefer to find passengers willing to hire them for several hours. Sometimes just walking a block or two and hailing a cab on the street can save you half the rate.

To keep the fare reasonable, consider taking the taxi only as far as you need to (for example, to the nearest subway station to hop a speedy train into the city, rather than pay to drive all the way across town in congested traffic). Also keep in mind that there must be somebody on your ship who's going to the same place you are—strike up a conversation at breakfast or on the gangway to find someone to team up with and split the fare.

Remember: Taxis aren't just for getting from the port to town; they can also be wonderful time-savers for connecting sights within a big city. For more taxi tips, see the sidebar.

By Bus

Near the terminal, often just beyond the taxi stand, you'll usually find a **public bus** stop for getting into town. This is significantly cheaper than a taxi, and often not much slower. Even with an entire cruise ship emptying all at once, waiting in a long line for the bus is relatively rare. These buses usually take local cash only and sometimes require exact change. If you see a kiosk or ticket vending machine near the bus stop, try to purchase a bus ticket there, or at least buy something small to break big bills and get the correct change.

Occasionally, there's a **shuttle bus** into town; while handy, this happens mostly in ports that lack a good public-transit connection (such as Barcelona, Marseille, and La Seyne for Toulon). If there is a shuttle, it's often your best option. The shuttle bus typically costs about $4-10 round-trip (buses run frequently when the ship arrives, then about every 15-20 minutes; pay attention to where the bus drops you downtown, as you'll need to find that stop later to return to the ship).

The shuttle bus can get very crowded when the ship first unloads—do your best to get off the ship and onto the bus quickly. At slower times, you might have to wait a little while for the bus to fill up before it departs. Note that the port shuttle sometimes doesn't start running until sometime after your ship actually docks (for example, you disembark at 7:00, but the bus doesn't start running until 8:30). This is a case when it can be worth springing for a taxi to avoid waiting around.

By Excursion

Cruise lines sometimes offer "On Your Own" excursions that include unguided transportation into town, then free time on your own. This may be worthwhile in places where the port is far from the main point of interest (such as the port of Livorno for Florence or the port of Civitavecchia for Rome). While more expensive than public transportation—and sometimes even more expensive than a shared cab—this is a low-stress option that still allows you freedom to see the sights at your own pace. For details, see page 108.

Seeing the Town

If you're touring a port on your own, you have several options for getting around town and visiting the sights (see the destination chapters for specifics).

On a Tour

It's easy to get a guided tour without having to pay excessively for an excursion. And there are plenty of choices, from walking to bus tours. Cruise Critic (www.cruisecritic.com) is a great resource for exploring these options.

At or near the terminal, you'll generally find travel agencies offering **package tours.** These tours are similar to the cruise-ship excursions but usually cost far less (half or even a third as much). How-ever, what's offered can change from day to day, so they're not as reliable as the cruise line's offerings. It's possible to reserve these in advance, typically through a third party (such as a travel agency).

A great budget alternative is to join a regularly scheduled **local walking tour** (in English, departing at a specified time every day). Again, these are very similar to the cruise lines' walking tours and often use the same guides. Look for my walking tour listings in the destination chapters or ask at the local TI.

In a large city where sights are spread out, it can be conve-nient to join a **hop-on, hop-off bus tour.** These buses make a circle through town every 30 minutes or so, stopping at key points where passengers can hop on or off at will. While relatively expensive (figure around €25-30 for an all-day ticket), these tours are easier than figuring out public transportation, come with commentary (either recorded or from a live guide), and generally have a stop at or near the cruise port.

Some cruisers hire a **private guide** to meet them at the ship and take them around town (see page 110). Book directly with the guide, using the contact informa-tion in this book; if you arrange the guide through a third party—such as a local travel agent or the cruise line—you'll pay a premium.

Taxi Tips

There's no denying that taxis are the fastest way to get from your ship to what you want to see. But you'll pay for that convenience. Regular fares tend to be high, and many cabbies are adept at overcharging tourists—especially cruise passengers—in shameless and creative ways. Here are some tips to avoid getting ripped off by a cabbie.

Finding a Cab: In most cruise-port towns, it's generally easy to flag down a cab. A taxi stand is usually right at the cruise terminal. If not (or if you're already in town), ask a local to direct you to the nearest taxi stand. Taxi stands are often listed prominently on city maps; look for the little Ts.

Fly-by-night cabbies with a makeshift "Taxi" sign on the rooftop and no company logo or phone number on the door are less likely to be honest. In Italy these unofficial taxis are illegal.

Establishing a Price: To figure the fare, you can either use the taxi meter or agree on a set price up front. In either case, it's important to know the going rate (the destination chapters include the prevailing rates for the most likely journeys from each port). Even if I'm using the taxi meter, I still ask for a rough estimate up front, so I know generally what to expect.

In most cities, it's best to use the **taxi meter**—and cabbies are legally required to do so if the passenger requests it. So insist. Cabbies who get feisty and refuse are probably up to no good. If you don't feel comfortable about a situation, just get out and find another taxi.

Even with the meter, cabbies can still find ways to scam you. For instance, they may try to set it to the pricier weekend tariff,

On Your Own

If you prefer to sightsee independently and are going to Florence, Rome, Venice, or Athens, take advantage of my free **audio tours,** which guide you through the most interesting neighborhoods and most famous sights in each of those cities. Audio tours allow your eyes to enjoy the wonders of the place while your ears learn its story. Before your trip, download the tours to your mobile device via the Rick Steves Audio Europe smartphone app, www.ricksteves.com/audioeurope, iTunes, or Google Play. These give all the information you'll want, while saving you lots of time and money—perfect for the thoughtful, independent cruiser.

It's possible to **rent a car** to see the sights. While this makes sense for covering a wide rural area (such as the far-flung beaches

even if it's a weekday (since trips on nights and weekends generally cost more). Check the list of different meter rates (posted somewhere in the cab, often in English) to make sure your driver has set the meter to the correct tariff. If you're confused about the tariff your cabbie has selected, ask for an explanation.

It's also possible (though obviously illegal) for cabbies to tinker with a taxi meter to make it spin like a pinwheel. If you glance away from the meter, then look back and see that it's mysteriously doubled, you've likely been duped. However, some extra fees are on the level (for instance, in most cities, there's a legitimate surcharge for picking you up at the cruise port). Again, these should be listed clearly on the tariff sheet. If you suspect foul play, following the route on your map or conspicuously writing down the cabbie's license information can shame him into being honest.

Agreeing to a **set price** for the ride is another option. While this is usually higher than the fair metered rate would be, sometimes it's the easiest way to go. Just be sure that the rate you agree to is more or less in the ballpark of the rate I've listed in this book. Consider asking a couple of cabbies within a block or two of each other for estimates. You may be surprised at the variation.

Many cabbies hire out for an hourly rate; if you want the taxi to take you to a variety of outlying sights and wait for you, this can be a good value. You can also arrange in advance to hire a driver for a few hours or the whole day (for some destinations, I've listed my favorite local drivers).

Settling Up: It's best to pay in small bills. If you use a large bill, state the denomination out loud as you hand it to the cabbie. They can be experts at dropping a €50 note and picking up a €20. Count your change. To tip a good cabbie, round up about 5-10 percent (to pay a €4.50 fare, give €5; for a €28 fare, give €30). But if you feel like you're being driven in circles or otherwise ripped off, skip the tip.

on a Greek isle or charming villages in Provence), I would never rent a car to tour a big city—public transportation is not only vastly cheaper, but it avoids the headaches of parking, unfamiliar traffic patterns, and other problems. In general, given the relatively short time you'll have in port and the high expense of renting a car for the day (figure €40-100/day, depending on the port), this option doesn't make much sense. However, if you're interested, you'll often find car-rental offices or travel agencies at or near the terminal that are accustomed to renting cars for short time periods to cruisers. You can also look for deals online (on rental companies' websites or travel-booking sites) in advance.

At some ports (especially on Greek islands like Mykonos), it can be fun to rent an **ATV** (four-wheeled all-terrain vehicle) or a

"Cruise" in Six Languages

Need to find your way back to port? Ask a local or look for these words on signs.

Spanish	*crucero*	kruh-THEH-roh
French	*croisière*	kwah-shee-yay
Italian	*crociere*	kroh-chee-AY-reh
Croatian	*krstarenje*	kur-STAH-rehn-yeh
Greek	κρουαζιέρα	krow-SHEH-rah
Turkish	*seyir*	seh-YEER

scooter—much cheaper and easier, but potentially more dangerous than renting a car. For details, see page 983. In some places, renting a **bicycle** can be a good option (though the typically hilly terrain and potentially sweltering heat in Mediterranean port areas can make it tough). A bike enables you to get out into the countryside or to zip around a city at your own pace without relying on public transit. Along the French Riviera, various shops rent bikes with supplemental electric power to help you over the hills—a nice boost when you need it.

With Fellow Passengers

The upside of traveling with so many other people is that you have ample opportunities to make friends. On a ship with thousands of people, I guarantee you'll find someone who shares your style of travel. If you and your traveling companion hit it off with others, consider teaming up for your shore time. This "double-dating" can save both money (splitting the cost of an expensive taxi ride) and stress (working together to figure out the best way into town). But be sure you're all interested in the same things before you head ashore—you don't want to end up on the corner in front of the Colosseum, bickering about whether to go to the Forum or the Vatican.

In-Port Travel Skills

Whether you're taking an excursion or tackling a port on your own, this practical advice will come in handy. This section includes tips on useful services, avoiding theft, using money, sightseeing, shopping, eating, and in general, making the most of your time in port.

Travel Smart

Europe is like a complex play—easier to follow and really appreciate on a second viewing. While no one does the same trip twice to gain that advantage, reading about the places you'll visit before you reach each destination accomplishes much the same thing.

Though you're bound to your ship's schedule, note the best times to visit various sights, and try to hit them as best you can. Pay attention to holidays, festivals, and days when sights are closed. For example, many museums are closed on Mondays. Big sights and museums often stop admitting people 30-60 minutes before closing time.

Sundays have the same pros and cons as they do for travelers in the US (special events, limited hours, banks and many shops closed, limited public transportation, no rush hour). Saturdays are virtually weekdays with earlier closing times and no rush hour (though transportation connections can be less frequent than on weekdays).

When in port, visit the TI. Find a place to get online to research sights, make reservations (maybe book a guide or tour for your next destination), keep in touch with home, and so on. Then head for the sights you came so far to see.

Most important, connect with the culture. Set up your own quest to find the tastiest gelato in Italy or the best baklava in Greece. Slow down and be open to unexpected experiences. Enjoy the hospitality of the European people. Ask questions—most locals are eager to point you in their idea of the right direction. Wear your money belt, learn the currency, and figure out how to estimate prices in dollars. Those who expect to travel smart, do.

Services

Tourist Information: No matter how well I know a town, my first stop is always the TI. TIs are usually located on the main square, in the city hall, or at the train station (just look for signs). Many cruise ports also have a temporary TI desk, which hands out maps and answers questions for arriving cruisers. Their job is to make sure your few hours in town are enjoyable, so you'll come back on your own later. At TIs, you can get information on sights and public transit, and pick up a city map and a local entertainment guide. Ask if guided walks, self-guided walking-tour brochures, or audioguides are available. If you need a quick place to eat, ask the TI staff where they go for lunch.

Medical Help: If you get sick or injured while in port—assuming you're not in need of urgent care—do as the Europeans do and go to a pharmacist for advice. European pharmacists diagnose and prescribe remedies for most simple problems. They are usually friendly and speak English, and some medications that are only available by prescription in the US are available over the counter (surprisingly cheaply) in Europe. If necessary, the pharmacist will send you to a doctor or the health clinic. For most destinations, I've listed pharmacies close to the cruise port.

Theft or Loss: To replace a **passport,** you'll need to go in person to a US embassy or consulate (neither of which is usually located in a port town) during their business hours, which are generally limited and restricted to weekdays. This can take a day or two. If you lose your passport, contact the port agent or the ship's guest services desk immediately—and be aware that you may not be able to continue your cruise if a replacement passport is not available before the ship sails. Having a photocopy of your passport and a backup form of ID such as your driver's license, as well as an extra passport photo, can speed up getting a replacement.

If your **credit and debit cards** disappear, cancel and replace them (see "Damage Control for Lost or Stolen Cards" on page 132). File a police report on the spot for any loss (you'll need it to submit an insurance claim). For more info, see www.ricksteves.com/help.

Internet Cafés and Wi-Fi HotSpots: Finding an Internet café in Europe is a breeze. While these places don't always serve food or drinks—sometimes they're just big, functional, sweaty rooms filled with computers—they are an easy and affordable way to get online. It's even easier if you have a Wi-Fi-enabled smartphone, tablet, or laptop. There are hotspots at cafés and at other businesses. Sometimes Wi-Fi is free; other times you may have to pay by the minute or buy something in exchange for the network password.

Public Phones: Because calling from the ship or a mobile phone can be costly (see page 87), you may want to seek out a pay phone in port to make calls. Coin-op phones are rare in Europe, so you'll need to purchase one of two types of prepaid phone cards. An **insertable phone card,** which you physically slide into the telephone, can be used only at pay phones. It offers reasonable rates for domestic calls, and steeper but still acceptable rates for international calls (rarely exceeding $1/minute). You use an **international phone card** by dialing a toll-free number, then punching in a scratch-to-reveal PIN. Though designed for international calls, which can cost less than a nickel a minute, they also work for domestic calls. Both types of cards are sold in various denominations at tobacco shops, newsstands, and hole-in-the-wall long-distance shops. Generally these work best—and sometimes only—in the country where you buy them.

Outsmarting Thieves

In Europe, it's rare to encounter violent crime, but petty purse-snatching and pickpocketing are quite common. Thieves target

Americans, especially cruise passengers—not because the thieves are mean, but because they're smart. Loaded down with valuables in a strange new environment, we stick out like jeweled thumbs. But being savvy and knowing what to look out for can dramatically reduce your risk of being targeted.

Pickpockets are your primary concern. To avoid them, be aware of your surroundings, don't keep anything valuable in your pockets, and wear a money belt (explained on page 56). In your money belt, carry your passport, credit and debit cards, and large cash bills. Keep just a day's spending money in your pocket—if you lose that, it's no big deal.

Many cruise lines hand out cloth bags emblazoned with their logo. Carrying these around town is like an advertisement for pickpockets and con artists (not to mention aggressive salesmen). Save them for supermarket runs back home.

Thieves thrive on tourist-packed public-transportation routes—especially buses that cover major sights (such as Rome's notorious #64). When riding the subway or bus, be alert at stops, when thieves can dash on and off with your day bag. Criminals—often dressed as successful professionals or even as tourists—will often block a bus or subway entry, causing the person behind you to "bump" into you.

Be wary of any unusual contact or commotion in crowded public places (especially touristy spots). For example, while being

jostled at a crowded market, you might end up with ketchup or fake pigeon poop on your shirt. The perpetrator then offers profuse apologies while dabbing it up—and pawing your pockets. Treat any disturbance (a scuffle breaking out, a beggar in your face, someone falling down an escalator) as a smokescreen for theft—designed to distract unknowing victims.

Europe also has its share of scam artists, from scruffy babushkas offering you sprigs of rosemary (and expecting money in return) to con artists running street scams, such as the shell game, in which players pay to guess which of the moving shells hides the ball (don't try it—you'll lose every time). Or somebody sells you an item, and turns around to put it in a box while you're getting out your money. Later on the ship, when you open the box, you find only...rocks. Always look inside the box before walking away.

IN PORT

The most rampant scams are more subtle, such as being over-charged by a taxi driver (see the "Taxi Tips" sidebar, earlier). Another common scam is the "slow count": A cashier counts change back with odd pauses, in hopes the rushed tourist will gather up the money quickly without checking that it's all there. Waiters may pad the bill with mysterious charges—carefully scan the itemized bill and account for each item. If paying a small total with a large bill, clearly state the amount you're handing over, and be sure you get the correct change back. Don't be upset about these little scams—treat them as sport.

Nearly all crimes suffered by tourists are nonviolent and avoidable. Be aware of the pitfalls of traveling, but relax and have fun.

Money

Whenever you leave the ship, you must use local currency. Most destinations in this book (Spain, France, Italy, and Greece) use the euro; stock up on euros early in your trip, and use them throughout the region.

Some popular cruise-ship destinations, including Croatia and Turkey, as well as Israel and North African countries, don't officially use the euro. I've occasionally heard cruise-line employees tell their passengers, "We're only in the country for a day, and everyone takes euros, so you don't need to change money." That's true in many cases: Many merchants in non-euro countries do accept euros. But exchange rates are bad, and some vendors might flat-out refuse euros. Plus, euros often aren't accepted on public transportation or at major sights and museums. That's why it's better to get local cash, even if you're in town just for a few hours. In most port cities, ATMs are easy to find (I've listed the nearest locations for each destination). But in some of the more out-of-way ports, exchanging a small amount of money for local currency at the cruise ship's front desk can save you time looking for an ATM.

Cash

Cash is just as desirable in Europe as it is at home. Small businesses (restaurants, shops, etc.) may prefer that you pay with cash. Some vendors may charge you extra for using a credit card, and some won't take credit cards at all. Cash is the best—and sometimes only—way to pay for bus fare, taxis, and local guides.

Throughout Europe, cash machines (ATMs) are the standard way for travelers to get cash. But stay away from "independent" ATMs such as Travelex, Euronet, Cardpoint, and Cashzone, which charge huge commissions and have terrible exchange rates.

When using an ATM, try to withdraw large sums of money to reduce the number of per-transaction bank fees you'll pay. Although you can use a credit card for ATM transactions, it only makes sense in an emergency because it's considered a cash advance (with a high fee) rather than a withdrawal. To safeguard your cash, wear a money belt (described on page 56). Don't waste time in every port tracking down a cash machine—withdraw several days' worth of money, stuff it in your money belt, and see the sights!

Credit and Debit Cards

For purchases, Visa and MasterCard are more commonly accepted than American Express. Just like at home, credit or debit cards are generally accepted by larger restaurants and shops (smaller, family-run places usually require cash). Some vendors will charge you extra for using a credit card. I typically use my debit card to withdraw cash to pay for most purchases. I use my credit card only in a few specific situations: to book hotel reservations by phone (when staying in Europe before or after a cruise), to cover major purchases, and to pay for things near the end of my trip (to avoid another visit to the ATM).

While you can use either a credit or a debit card for most purchases, using a credit card offers a greater degree of fraud protection (since debit cards draw funds directly from your bank account).

Chip and PIN: Europeans are increasingly using chip-and-PIN cards, which are embedded with an electronic security chip (in addition to the magnetic stripe found on American-style cards). With this system, the purchaser punches in a PIN rather than signing a receipt. Your American-style card might not work at automated payment machines, such as those at train and subway stations, toll roads, parking garages, luggage lockers, and self-serve gas pumps.

If you have problems using your American card in a chip-and-PIN machine, here are some suggestions: For either a debit card or a credit card, try entering that card's PIN when prompted. (Note that your credit-card PIN may not be the same as your debit-card PIN; you'll need to ask your bank for your credit-card PIN.) If your cards still don't work, look for a machine that takes cash, seek out a clerk who might be able to process the transaction manually, or ask a local if you can pay them cash to run the transaction on their card.

And don't panic. Many travelers who use only magnetic-stripe cards never have a problem. Still, it pays to carry plenty of cash (you can always use an ATM to withdraw cash with your magnetic-stripe debit card).

If you're still concerned, you can apply for a chip card in the

Damage Control for Lost or Stolen Cards

If you lose your credit, debit, or ATM card, you can stop people from using your card by reporting the loss immediately to the respective global customer-assistance centers. Call these 24-hour US numbers collect: Visa (tel. 303/967-1096), Master-Card (tel. 636/722-7111), and American Express (tel. 336/393-1111). European toll-free numbers (listed by country) can be found at the websites for Visa and MasterCard.

At a minimum, you'll need to know the name of the financial institution that issued you the card, along with the type of card (classic, platinum, or whatever). Providing the following information will allow for a quicker cancellation of your missing card: full card number, whether you are the primary or secondary cardholder, the cardholder's name exactly as printed on the card, billing address, home phone number, circumstances of the loss or theft, and identification verification (your birth date, your mother's maiden name, or your Social Security number—memorize this, don't carry a copy). If you are the secondary cardholder, you'll also need to provide the primary cardholder's identification-verification details (see www.ricksteves.com/help for more).

If you report your loss within two days, you typically won't be responsible for any unauthorized transactions on your account, although many banks charge a liability fee of $50.

US (though I think that's overkill). One option is the no-fee Globe-Trek Visa, offered by Andrews Federal Credit Union in Maryland (open to all US residents; see www.andrewsfcu.org).

Dynamic Currency Conversion: If merchants offer to convert your purchase price into dollars (called dynamic currency conversion, or DCC), refuse this "service." You'll pay even more in fees for the expensive convenience of seeing your charge in dollars.

At Sights

Most cruise passengers are faced with far more to see and do than they have time for. That's why it's helpful to know what you can typically expect when visiting sights:

Perhaps the biggest challenge (and frustration) is **long lines.** At sights such as the Uffizi Gallery and Accademia in Florence, St. Peter's Basilica and the Colosseum in Rome, the Sagrada Família in Barcelona, and the Blue Mosque in Istanbul, lines can be a real frustration. Study up, plan ahead, and use the information in this book to minimize time spent in line. For details on making **reservations** or **buying advance tickets** at major sights, see page 50.

Some important sights have a **security check**, where you must open your bag or send it through a metal detector. Some sights require you to check daypacks and coats. (If you'd rather not check your daypack, try carrying it tucked under your arm like a purse as you enter.)

A modest **dress code** (no bare shoulders, shorts, or above-the-knee skirts) is enforced at some larger churches in Spain, France, and Italy (such as St. Mark's in Venice and St. Peter's in Rome),

but is often overlooked elsewhere. This applies to everyone, including kids. If you are caught by surprise, you can improvise, using maps to cover your shoulders and a jacket tied around your waist to hide your legs. (I wear a super-lightweight pair of long pants rather than shorts for my hot and muggy, big-city Italian sightseeing.)

If the museum's photo policy isn't clearly posted, ask a guard. Generally, **taking photos** without a flash or tripod is allowed. However, some sights ban photos altogether.

Museums may have **special exhibits** in addition to their permanent collection. Some exhibits are included in the entry price, while others come at an extra cost (which you may have to pay even if you don't want to see that exhibit).

Expect changes—artwork can be on tour, on loan, out sick, or shifted at the whim of the curator. To adapt, pick up a floor plan as you enter, and ask museum staff if you can't find a particular item.

Many sights rent **audioguides,** which generally offer excellent recorded descriptions in English. If you bring your own earbuds,

you can enjoy better sound and avoid holding the device to your ear. To save money, bring a Y-jack and share one audioguide with your travel partner. Increasingly, museums are offering apps (often free) that you can download to your mobile device. I've produced free downloadable **audio tours** of the major sights in Florence, Rome, Venice, Athens, and Ephesus; see page 50.

Important sights may have an **on-site café** or **cafeteria** (usually a handy place to rejuvenate during a long visit). The WCs at sights are free and generally clean.

Many places sell **postcards** that highlight their attractions. Before you leave a sight, scan the postcards and thumb through a guidebook to be sure you haven't overlooked something you'd like to see.

Be warned that you may not be allowed to enter if you arrive 30 to 60 minutes before **closing time**. And guards start ushering people out well before the actual closing time, so don't save the best for last.

Every sight or museum offers more than what's covered in this book. Use the information in this book as an introduction—not the final word.

Shopping

Shopping can be a fun part of any traveler's European trip. To have a good experience when you go ashore, be aware of the ins and outs

of shopping in port.

At every stop, your cruise line will give you an information sheet that highlights local shopping specialties and where to buy them. Remember that these shops commonly give kickbacks to cruise lines and guides. This doesn't mean that the shop (or what it sells) isn't good quality; it

just means you're probably paying top dollar.

Regardless of whether a store is working with the cruise line or not, many places jack up their rates when ships arrive, knowing they're about to get hit with a tidal wave of rushed and desperate shoppers. Remember: Europe's cruise season lasts approximately six months, and many people who live and work in that town must extract a year's worth of earnings from visitors during that period.

Finding Deals

So how can you avoid paying over-the-top, inflated prices for your treasured souvenirs? Go ahead and patronize the obvious tourist shops, but be sure to check out local shopping venues, too. Large department stores often have a souvenir section with standard knickknacks and postcards at prices way below those at cruise-recommended shops. These large stores generally work just like ours, and in big cities, most department-store staff are accustomed to wide-eyed foreign shoppers and can speak some English.

If you're adept at bargaining, head over to some of Europe's vibrant outdoor flea markets, where you can find local specialties and soft prices. In much of the Mediterranean world, haggling is the accepted (and expected) method of finding a compromise between the wishful thinking of both the merchant and the tourist.

Bargaining Tips: To be a successful haggler-shopper, first

Calculating Clothing Sizes

When shopping for clothing, use these US-to-European comparisons as general guidelines (but note that no conversion is perfect).

- **Women's dresses and blouses:** Add 30
  (US size 10 = European size 40)
- **Men's suits and jackets:** Add 10
  (US size 40 regular = European size 50)
- **Men's shirts:** Multiply by 2 and add about 8
  (US size 15 collar = European size 38)
- **Women's shoes:** Add about 30
  (US size 8 = European size 38-39)
- **Men's shoes:** Add 32-34
  (US size 9 = European size 41;
  US size 11 = European size 45)

---

determine the item's value to you. Many tourists think that if they can cut the price by 50 percent they are doing great. So merchants quadruple their prices and the tourist happily pays double the fair value. The best way to deal with crazy prices is to ignore them. Show some interest in an item but say, "It's just too much money." You've put the merchant in a position to make the first offer.

Many merchants will settle for a nickel profit rather than lose a sale entirely. Work the cost down to rock bottom. When it seems to have fallen to a record low, walk away. That last price hollered out as you turn the corner is often the best price you'll get. If the price is right, go back and buy. And don't forget that prices often drop at the end of the day, when flea-market merchants have to think about packing up. For more specifics on haggling in Turkey—where bargaining is practically obligatory in the tourist zones—see page 1182.

Getting a VAT Refund

Every year, tourists visiting Europe leave behind millions of dollars of refundable sales taxes. While for some, the headache of collecting the refund is not worth the few dollars at stake, if you do any serious shopping, it's hard cash—free and easy.

Wrapped into the purchase price of your souvenirs is a Value-Added Tax (VAT) of between 18 and 25 percent, depending on the country (for details, see www.ricksteves.com/vat). Almost all European countries require a minimum purchase for a refund, ranging from about $30 to several hundred dollars. If you spend that minimum at a store that participates in the VAT-refund scheme, you're entitled to get most of that tax back. Typically, you must ring up the minimum at a single retailer—you can't add up your purchases from various shops to reach the required amount.

Getting your refund is usually straightforward and, if you buy a substantial amount of souvenirs, well worth the hassle. If you're lucky, the merchant will subtract the tax when you make your purchase. (This is more likely to occur if the store ships the goods to your home.) Otherwise, you'll need to:

Get the paperwork. Have the merchant completely fill out the necessary refund document (either an official VAT customs form, or the shop or refund company's own version of it). You'll have to present your passport at the store. Get the paperwork done before you leave the store to ensure you'll have everything you need (including your original sales receipt).

Get your stamp at the border or airport. Process your VAT document at your last stop (for example, at the airport) with the customs agent who deals with VAT refunds. For purchases made in EU countries (such as Spain, France, Italy, Greece, and Croatia), process your document when you leave the EU. It doesn't have to be the country where you made your purchases as long as you're still in the EU; if your flight connects through London's Heathrow airport, you can do it there. For non-EU countries such as Turkey, process your VAT document at your last stop in that country. Arrive an additional hour early before you need to check in for your flight, to allow time to find the local customs office—and to stand in line. It's best to keep your purchases in your carry-on. If they're too large or dangerous to carry on (such as knives), pack them in your checked bags and alert the check-in agent. You'll be sent (with your tagged bag) to a customs desk outside security, where they'll examine your bag, stamp your paperwork, and put your bag on the belt. You're not supposed to use your purchased goods before you leave. If you show up at customs wearing your chic Greek shirt, officials might look the other way—or deny you a refund.

Collect your refund. You'll need to return your stamped document to the retailer or its representative. Many merchants work with a service, such as Global Blue or Premier Tax Free, that has offices at major airports, ports, or border crossings (either before or after security, probably strategically located near a duty-free shop). These services, which extract a 4 percent fee, can refund your money immediately in cash or credit your card (within two billing cycles). If the retailer handles VAT refunds directly, it's up to you to contact the merchant for your refund. You can mail the documents from home, or more quickly, from your point of departure (using an envelope you've prepared in advance or one that's been provided by the merchant). You'll then have to wait—it can take months.

Customs for American Shoppers

You are allowed to take home $800 worth of items per person duty-free, once every 30 days. You can also bring in duty-free a liter of alcohol. As for food, you can take home many processed and packaged foods: vacuum-packed cheeses, dried herbs, jams, baked goods, candy, chocolate, oil, vinegar, mustard, and honey. Fresh fruits and vegetables and most meats are not allowed. Any liquid-containing foods must be packed in checked luggage, a potential recipe for disaster. To check customs rules and duty rates, visit http://help.cbp.gov.

Eating in Port

Eating in Europe is sightseeing for your taste buds. The memories of good meals can satisfy you for years. Even though most of your meals will be on the ship, you can still experience Europe's amazing cuisine when you're in port. Your options range from grabbing a lunch on the run to lingering over a leisurely meal at a sit-down restaurant. When deciding where to eat, be aware that table service in Europe is slow—sometimes painfully so—by American standards. Don't expect to dine and dash, but you can try explaining to the waitstaff that you're in a hurry.

Lunch on the Go

You can eat quickly and still have a local experience. Every country has its own equivalent of the hot-dog stand, where you can grab

a filling bite on the go: French *crêperies*, Greek souvlaki stands, Italian *pizza rustica* take-out shops, and Turkish-style *döner kebab* and falafel kiosks. Or stop in a heavenly smelling bakery and buy a pastry or sandwich.

Ethnic eateries are usually cheap; eat in, or get your meal to go. Cafeterias, delis, and fast-food chains with salad bars are tourist-friendly and good for a quick meal.

Like businesspeople, cruise travelers have a lot on their daytime agendas and want to eat well but quickly. A good bet is to eat lunch at a place that caters to the local business clientele. You'll find many fine little restaurants advertising fast, two-course business lunches. These are inexpensive and served quickly. Each neighborhood is also likely to have a favorite deli/sandwich place where you'll see a thriving crowd of office workers spilling out onto the curb, eating fine, small meals or gourmet sandwiches—and often sipping a glass of top-end wine with their food.

Picnicking takes a little more time and planning but can be an even more exciting cultural experience: It's fun to dive into a marketplace and actually get a chance to do business there. Europe's colorful markets overflow with varied cheeses, meats, fresh fruits, vegetables, and still-warm-out-of-the-oven bread. Most markets are not self-service: You point to what you want and let the merchant weigh and bag it for you. The unit of measure throughout the Continent is a kilo, or 2.2 pounds. A kilo has 1,000 grams. One hundred grams is a common unit of sale for cheese or meat—and just the right amount to tuck into a chunk of French bread for a satisfying sandwich.

Sit-Down Restaurants

For some cruisers, it's unimaginable to waste valuable port time lingering at a sit-down restaurant when they could be cramming their day with sightseeing. For others, a good European restaurant experience beats a cathedral or a museum by a mile.

To find a good restaurant, head away from the tourist center and stroll around until you find a place with a happy crowd of locals. Look for menus handwritten in the native language (usually posted outside) and offering a small selection. This means they're cooking what was fresh in the market that morning for loyal return customers.

Restaurants in Europe usually do not serve meals throughout the day, so don't wait too long to find a place for lunch. Typically restaurants close from the late afternoon (about 14:00) until the dinner hour.

When entering a restaurant, feel free to seat yourself at any table that isn't marked "reserved." Catch a server's eye and signal to be sure it's OK to sit there. If the place is full, you're likely to simply be turned away: There's no "hostess" standing by to add your name to a carefully managed waiting list.

If no English **menu** is posted, ask to see one. What we call the menu in the US usually goes by some variation on the word "card" in Europe—for instance, *la carte* in French.

Be aware that the word "menu" can mean a fixed-price meal, particularly in France and Italy. Many small eateries offer an economical "*menu* of the day" (*menú del día* in Spain, *plat du jour* in France, and *menù del giorno* in Italy)—a daily special with a fixed price. The "tourist *menu*" (*menù turistico* in Italy, *menu touristique* in France, *menú de turista* in Spanish), popular in restaurants throughout Europe's tourist zones, offers confused visitors a no-stress, three-course meal for a painless price that usually includes service, bread, and a drink. You normally get a choice of several options for each course. Locals rarely order this, but if the options intrigue you, the tourist *menu* can be a convenient way to sample some regional flavors for a reasonable, predictable price.

In restaurants, Europeans generally drink bottled **water** (for taste, not health), served with or without carbonation. You can normally get free tap water, but you may need to be polite, patient, inventive, and know the correct phrase. There's nothing wrong with ordering tap water, and it is safe to drink in all the countries in this book, except for Turkey.

One of the biggest surprises for Americans at Europe's restaurants is the service, which can seem excruciatingly slow when you're eager to get out and sightsee (or in a hurry to get back to your cruise ship). Europeans will spend at least two hours enjoying a good meal, and fast service is considered rude service. If you need to eat and run, make it very clear when you order.

To get the **bill,** you'll have to ask for it. Don't wait until you are in a hurry to leave. Catch the waiter's eye and, with raised hands, scribble with an imaginary pencil on your palm. Before it comes, make a mental tally of roughly how much your meal should cost. If the total is a surprise, ask to have it itemized and explained.

Tipping: At European restaurants, a base gratuity is already included in your bill. Virtually anywhere in Europe, if you're pleased with the service, you can round up a euro or more. In most restaurants, 5 percent is adequate and 10 percent is considered a big tip. Please believe me—tipping 15-20 percent in Europe is unnecessary, if not culturally insensitive. Tip only at restaurants with waitstaff; skip the tip if you order food at a counter. Servers prefer to be tipped in cash even if you pay with your credit card; otherwise the tip may never reach them (specifics on tipping are also provided in each country's introduction chapter).

Cafés

Europeans are into café-sitting, coffee-sipping, and people-watching. If you simply want to slam down a cup of coffee, order and drink it at the bar. If you want to sit a while and check out the scene, grab a table with a view, and a waiter will take your order. This will cost you about double what it would at the bar (and sometimes an outdoor table is more expensive than an indoor one). If you're on a budget, always confirm the price for a sit-down drink. If you pay for a seat in a café with an expensive drink, that seat's yours for the entire afternoon if you like.

Returning to the Ship

When it's time to head back to your ship, remember that the posted departure time is a bit misleading: The all-aboard time (when you absolutely, positively must be on your ship) is usually a half-hour before departure. And the last shuttle bus or tender back to the ship might leave an hour before departure...trimming your port time even more. If you want to max out on time ashore, research alternative options—such as a taxi or a public bus—that get you back to the ship even closer to the all-aboard time (but, of course, be cautious not to cut it *too* close). Before leaving the ship, make sure you understand when you need to be back on board, and (if applicable) when the last shuttle bus or tender departs.

All of that said, feel free to take every minute of the time you've got. If the last tender leaves at 16:30, don't feel you need to get back to the dock at 16:00. I make it a point to be the last person back on the ship at every port...usually five minutes or so before all-aboard time. I sometimes get dirty looks from early birds who've been waiting for a few minutes on that last tender, but I didn't waste their time...they did.

What If I Miss My Boat?

You can't count on the ship to wait for you if you get back late. If you're cutting it close, call ahead to the port agent (the phone number is on your ship's port-of-call information sheet and/or daily program) and let them know you're coming. They will notify the ship's crew, so at least they know they didn't miscount the returning passengers. And there's a possibility (though a very slim one) that the ship could wait for you. But if it sets sail, and you're not on it, you're on your own to reach the next port. The cruise line will not cover any of your transportation or accommodations expenses, and you will not be reimbursed for any unused portion of your cruise.

You have approximately 24 hours to reach the ship before it departs from its next destination. Be clear on where the next stop is. If you're lucky, it's an easy two-hour train ride away, giving you bonus time in both destinations. If you're unlucky, it's a 20-hour overland odyssey or an expensive last-minute flight—or worse, the ship is spending the day at sea, meaning you'll miss out on two full cruising days.

First, ask the **port agent** for advice. The agent can typically give you a little help or at least point you in the right direction. Be aware that you'll be steered to the easiest, but not necessarily the most affordable, solution. For example, the agent might suggest hiring a private driver for hundreds of dollars, rather than taking a $50 bus ride. If your ship's policy is to hold passenger passports during the cruise, he'll have it waiting for you.

You can also ask for help from the **TI**, if it's still open. Local

travel agencies should know most or all of your connection options and can book tickets for you (they'll charge you a small commission). Or—to do it yourself—find an **Internet café** and get online to research your train, flight, and bus options. German Rail's handy, all-Europe train timetables are a good place to start: www. bahn.com. Check the website of the nearest airport; these usually show the schedule of upcoming flights in the next day or two. To compare inexpensive flights within Europe, try www.skyscanner. com.

Don't delay in making your plans. The sooner you begin investigating your options, the more choices you may have. If you realize you've missed your ship at 20:00, there may be an affordable night train to the next stop departing from the train station across town at 21:00...and if you're not on it, you could pay through the nose for a last-minute flight instead.

Remember, most ships never leave anyone behind over the course of the entire cruise. While the prospect of missing your ship is daunting, don't let it scare you into not enjoying your shore time. As long as you keep a close eye on the time and are conservative in estimating how long it'll take you to get back to the ship, it's easy to enjoy a very full day in port and be the last tired but happy tourist sauntering back onto the ship.

Overnighting in Port

At some major destinations (most often in Barcelona, Rome, Venice, and Istanbul), the cruise ship might spend two days and an overnight in port. This allows you to linger in the evening and really feel like you've been to a place—treating your cruise ship like a hotel.

With two-day port stops—or with two ports in a row that are close to each other (such as the French Riviera and Toulon, or Naples and Civitavecchia)—some adventurous travelers might opt to spend a night off the ship in order to get a break from the cruising lifestyle or overnight in a town away from the seafaring crowds. This is extra credit for very eager travelers—not recommended in most situations, but possible. If you do this, be sure to notify the officials aboard your ship that you won't be back that night. Any expenses you incur on land (hotels, train tickets, and so on) will be out of your own pocket, and you won't get any money back from the cruise line for days not spent on board.

PART III: MEDITERRANEAN CRUISE PORTS

MEDITERRANEAN CRUISE PORTS

The rest of this book focuses on specific cruise ports where you'll be spending your days. For each one, I've provided specific instructions for getting from the port into town, and included my suggested self-guided tours and walks for the best one-day plan in that town.

Rick Steves' Mediterranean Cruise Ports is a personal tour guide in your pocket, organized by destination. Each major destination is a mini-vacation on its own, filled with exciting sights, strollable neighborhoods, and memorable places to eat. You'll find the following sections in most of the destination chapters (although, because cruise port details can vary from place to place, not every destination will include all of these elements):

Planning Your Time suggests a schedule for how to best use your limited time in port. These plans are what I'd do with my time if I had only a few hours to spend in a particular destination, and assume that you're ambitious about spending the maximum amount of time in port sightseeing, rather than relaxing, shopping, or dining. For each option, I've suggested the minimum amount of time you can reasonably expect to spend to get a good look at the highlights. If you find that my plan packs too much in, or short-changes something you'd like to focus on, modify the plan by skipping one or two time-consuming options (read the descriptions in the chapters to decide which items interest you).

The **Excursions** sidebars help you make informed, strategic decisions about which cruise-line excursions to outlying destinations best match your interests.

Arrival at the Port sections provide detailed, step-by-step instructions for getting from your cruise ship to wherever you're going (whether it's to the city center, or, in some cases, to a nearby town). Each one begins with a brief "Arrival at a Glance" section that outlines your options. I've also tracked down helpful services (such as ATMs, Internet access, and pharmacies) at or near each port.

Orientation includes specifics on public transportation, helpful hints, local tour options, easy-to-read maps, and tourist information.

Self-guided **Walks** and **Tours** take you through interesting neighborhoods and world-class museums.

Sights describes the top attractions and includes their cost and hours. The "At a Glance" sections offer a brief overview of the sightseeing options in town.

Eating serves up a range of options, from inexpensive eateries to fancy restaurants.

Shopping offers advice on the most authentic local souvenirs and where to buy them.

The **What If I Miss My Boat?** sections give you a quick list of options for reaching your next port, in case you get stranded.

The **Starting or Ending Your Cruise** sections in the most common embarkation/disembarkation ports (Barcelona, Rome/Civitavecchia, Venice, Athens/Piraeus, and Istanbul) give advice about how to get from the airport to the cruise port, and list a few of my favorite hotels.

I've also included **Practicalities** sections for each of the six countries with ports in this book (Spain, France, Italy, Croatia, Greece, and Turkey), providing basic facts and figures, along with useful notes (such as the local currency, time zone, phone system, and tipping customs).

Key to This Book
Updates
This book is updated regularly, but things change. For the latest, visit www.ricksteves.com/update.

Abbreviations and Times
I use the following symbols and abbreviations in this book:
Sights are rated:

▲▲▲	Don't miss
▲▲	Try hard to see
▲	Worthwhile if you can make it
No rating	Worth knowing about

Tourist information offices are abbreviated as **TI,** and bathrooms are **WCs.**

Like Europe, this book uses the **24-hour clock** for schedules. It's the same through 12:00 noon, then keeps going: 13:00, 14:00, and so on. For anything over 12, subtract 12 and add p.m. (14:00 is 2:00 p.m.).

When giving **opening times,** I include both peak season and off-season hours if they differ. So, if a museum is listed as "May-Oct daily 9:00-16:00," it should be open from 9:00 a.m. until 4:00 p.m. from the first day of May until the last day of October (but expect exceptions).

If you see a ❂ symbol near a sight listing, it means that sight is described in far greater detail elsewhere—either with its own self-guided tour, or as part of a self-guided walk.

For **transit** or **tour departures,** I first list the frequency, then the duration. So, a train connection listed as "2/hour, 1.5 hours" departs twice each hour, and the journey lasts an hour and a half.

Sleep Code

In each of the cities where you're likely to begin or end your trip, I list a few of my favorite accommodations. To help you easily sort through these listings, I've divided the accommodations into three categories, based on the price for a double room with bath:

$$$	**Higher Priced**
$$	**Moderately Priced**
$	**Lower Priced**

To give maximum information in a minimum of space, I use the following code to describe accommodations. Prices in this book are listed per room, not per person.

S = Single room, or price for one person in a double.

D = Double or twin room.

T = Three-person room.

Q = Four-person room.

b = Private bathroom with toilet and shower or tub.

s = Private shower or tub only. (The toilet is down the hall.)

BARCELONA
Spain

Spain Practicalities

Spain (*España*) is in Europe, but not *of* Europe—it has a unique identity and history, thanks largely to the Pyrenees Mountains that physically isolate it from the rest of the Continent. Spain's seclusion contributed to the creation of distinctive customs (bullfights, flamenco dancing, and a national obsession with ham), and a diverse parade of rulers have shaped its history. Roman emperors, Muslim sultans, hardcore Christians, conquistadors, French dandies, and Fascist dictators have all left their mark on Spain's art, architecture, and customs. The country's special charm lies in its people (about 47 million, mostly Roman Catholic) and their unique lifestyle. From the stirring communal *sardana* dance in Barcelona to the sizzling rat-a-tat-tat of flamenco in Sevilla, this country creates its own beat amid the heat.

Money: Spain uses the euro currency: 1 euro (€) = about $1.30. An ATM is called a *cajero automático*. The VAT (value-added sales tax) rate is 21 percent; the minimum purchase eligible for a VAT refund is €90.15 (for details, see page 135).

Language: Most of Spain speaks Spanish, but Barcelona favors the regional Catalan language. For useful Spanish phrases, see page 239; for a few essential Catalan words, see page 172.

Emergencies: Dial 112 for police, medical, or other emergencies. In case of theft or loss, see page 128.

Time Zone: Spain is on Central European Time (the same as most of the Continent, and six/nine hours ahead of the East/West Coasts of the US).

Consular Services in Barcelona: The US consulate is at Passeig Reina Elisenda 23 (tel. 932-802-227, after-hours emergency tel. 915-872-200, http://barcelona.usconsulate.gov). The Canadian consulate is at Plaça de Catalunya 9 (tel. 932-703-614, www.spain.gc.ca). Call ahead for passport services.

Phoning: All phone numbers in Spain are nine digits (no area codes) that can be dialed direct throughout the country. To **call within Spain,** just dial the nine-digit number. To **call to Spain,** start with the international access code (00 if calling from Europe, or 011 from North America), then dial 34 (Spain's country code), then the phone number. To **call home from Spain,** dial 00, 1, then your area code and phone number. For more help, see page 1242.

Tipping: Most sit-down restaurants include a service charge in the bill (*servicio incluido*). If you like to tip for good service, round up to about 5 percent extra. If service is not included (*servicio no incluido*), tip up to 10 percent. Tip a taxi driver by rounding up the fare a bit (pay €5 on a €4.60 fare).

Tourist Information: www.spain.info

BARCELONA

Barcelona may be Spain's second city, but it's undoubtedly the first city of the proud and distinct region of Catalunya. Catalan flags wave side by side with the Spanish flag, and locals, while fluent in both languages, stubbornly insist on speaking Catalan first. This lively culture is on an unstoppable roll in Spain's most cosmopolitan and European corner.

Barcelona bubbles with life in its narrow Barri Gòtic alleys, along the pedestrian boulevard called the Ramblas, in the funky bohemian quarter of El Born, and throughout the chic, grid-planned new part of town called the Eixample. Its Old City is made for seeing on foot, full of winding lanes that emerge into secluded squares dotted with palm trees and ringed with cafés and boutiques. The waterfront bristles with life, overlooked by the park-like setting of Montjuïc. Everywhere you go, you'll find the city's architecture to be colorful, playful, and unique. Rows of symmetrical ironwork balconies are punctuated with fanciful details: bay windows, turrets, painted tiles, hanging lanterns, flower boxes, and carved reliefs.

Barcelona is full of history. You'll see Roman ruins, a medieval cathedral, twisty Gothic lanes, and traces of Columbus and the sea trade. As the Age of Exploration steered trade from the Mediterranean to the Atlantic, things got pretty quiet here (kept carefully under the thumb of Spanish rulers). But by the late 19th century, the city had boomed into an industrial powerhouse, and it was incubating a new artistic style—Modernism. Pablo Picasso lived in Barcelona as a teenager, right as he was on the verge of reinventing painting; his legacy is today's Picasso Museum. Catalan architects including Antoni Gaudí, Lluís Domènech i Montaner, and Josep Puig i Cadafalch forged the Modernista style and remade the city's

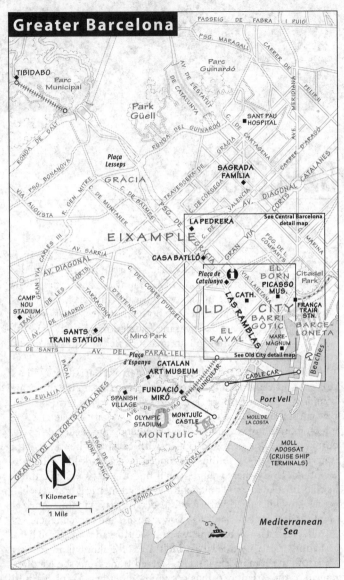

Greater Barcelona

PASSEIG DE FABRA I PUIG
PSG. MARAGALL
CARRER DE FELIP II
TIBIDABO
Parc Municipal
AV. DE L'ESTATUT
Parc Guinardó
Park Güell
RONDA DE DALT
RONDA DEL GUINARDÓ
C. DE CARTAGENA
SANT PAU HOSPITAL
AV. MERIDIANA
CARRER D'ARAGÓ
PSG. BONANOVA
VIA AUGUSTA
Plaça Lesseps
GRÀCIA
C. DE MUNTANER
R. GEN. MITRE
PSG. DE GRÀCIA
C. DE BALMES
TRAVESSERA DE GRÀCIA
C. DE CÓRSEGA
SAGRADA FAMÍLIA
VALÈNCIA
AV. DIAGONAL
GRAN VIA CARLES III
AV. SÀRRIA
AV. DIAGONAL
AV. DE LES CORTS
C. DE MADRID
C. DEL COMTE D'URGELL
C. D'ENTENÇA
GRAN VIA DE LES CORTS CATALANES
LA PEDRERA
See Central Barcelona detail map
EIXAMPLE
PSG. DE GRÀCIA
C. DE
GRAN VIA
PSG. DE L. COMPANYS
AV. MARINA
CASA BATLLÓ
Plaça de Catalunya
EL BORN
PICASSO MUS.
Citadel Park
CAMP NOU STADIUM
TARRAGONA
CATH.
VIA LAIETANA
OLD CITY
BARRI GÒTIC
FRANÇA TRAIN STN.
SANTS TRAIN STATION
Miró Park
LAS RAMBLAS
BARCE-LONETA
C. DE SANTS
AV. DEL PARAL·LEL
Plaça d'Espanya
EL RAVAL
MARE-MÀGNUM
Beaches
C. S. EULÀLIA
CATALAN ART MUSEUM
See Old City detail map
CABLE CAR
FUNICULAR
Port Vell
BADAL
SPANISH VILLAGE
FUNDACIÓ MIRÓ
AV.
MONTJUÏC CASTLE
MOLL DE LA COSTA
OLYMPIC STADIUM
MONTJUÏC
MOLL ADOSSAT (CRUISE SHIP TERMINALS)
GRAN VIA DE LES CORTS CATALANES
ZONA FRANCA
PSG. DE LA
RONDA DEL LITORAL
N
1 Kilometer
1 Mile
Mediterranean Sea

skyline with curvy fantasy buildings—culminating in Gaudí's over-the-top Sagrada Família, a church still under construction. Salvador Dalí and Joan Miró join the long list of world-changing 20th-century artists with ties to this city. Meanwhile, world's fairs in 1888 and 1929 helped spruce up the city, and in 1992, Barcelona hosted the Summer Olympics—an event that once again re-energized this dynamic city and left it with a wealth of attractive public areas and great sights.

Today's Barcelona is as vibrant as ever. Locals still join hands and dance the everyone's-welcome *sardana* in front of the cathedral every weekend. Neighborhood festivals jam the events calendar. The cafés are filled by day, and people crowd the streets at night, pausing to fortify themselves with a perfectly composed bite of seafood and a drink at a tapas bar. Every hidden back lane provides shelter for an array of inviting shops. If you're in the mood to surrender to a city's charms, let it be in Barcelona.

Many cruises start or end in Barcelona. If that's the case for you, check the end of this chapter for airport information and recommended hotels.

Planning Your Time

You have several good options:

• Follow my self-guided walk down **the Ramblas,** the city's colorful pedestrian drag. Allow one hour.

• Visit the **Sagrada Família** church-in-progress started by Modernista architect Antoni Gaudí (by far the single best Gaudí sight in town). Figure two hours.

• Tour the **Picasso Museum.** Allow 1.5 hours (but note that it's closed Mon).

• Take my self-guided walk of the **Barri Gòtic** (historical center), including the cathedral. Allow two hours total.

Crowd Warning: Expect lines at the Sagrada Família and Picasso Museum, particularly in the morning. Consider booking ahead.

Possible Itineraries

Gaudí Fans: Go to the Sagrada Família first (by Metro or taxi), then head to Plaça de Catalunya (by taxi or on foot), and take the self-guided walk down the Ramblas. (It's three miles from the Sagrada Família to the bottom of the Ramblas.) With any additional time, explore the Barri Gòtic. Allow at least five hours total.

If you want to see other Gaudí sights, start with the Sagrada Família, taxi to Passeig de Gràcia to see La Pedrera and Casa Batlló, then taxi or walk to Plaça de Catalunya and stroll down the Ramblas. Allow an additional hour to tour the interior of either La Pedrera (better choice) or Casa Batlló.

Picasso Fans: Go to the Picasso Museum (by foot or taxi), then walk through the Barri Gòtic to Plaça de Catalunya, and take the self-guided walk down the Ramblas. Figure on a minimum of five hours.

Combining Picasso and Gaudí: Walk (or taxi) to the Picasso

Museum, taxi to Sagrada Família, taxi to Plaça de Catalunya, and walk down the Ramblas. Allow six hours.

Arrival at the Port of Barcelona

Arrival at a Glance: Shuttle bus #T3 (also called Portbús) zips you right to the center of town, within walking distance (or an easy Metro ride) of most sights. Or pay €15 for a taxi downtown.

Port Overview

Cruise ships tie up about two miles southwest of the Old City, beneath the hill called Montjuïc. Nearly all of the big ships use the main Moll Adossat port ("Muelle Adosado" in Spanish). It's basically a very long dock with four modern, airport-like terminals (lettered A through D). Each terminal has basic amenities (café, shops, some Internet access), a shaded curb to await taxis, and a stop for the #T3 bus that shuttles travelers to and from the Columbus Monument at the base of the Ramblas. From the monument you can walk (or hop on the Metro) to wherever you like in Barcelona.

    Tourist Information: There's a TI kiosk in each terminal, as well as at the foot of the Columbus Monument (see page 162).

    Alternate Ports: While the vast majority of cruise ships arrive at the main port described above, some smaller ships arrive at the **World Trade Center,** with Terminals N (north) and S (south). These are within a 10-minute walk of the Columbus Monument. Yet another port, called **Moll de la Costa,** is farther out, but ships arriving here shuttle their passengers to the World Trade Center.

Getting into Town

Barcelona's main cruise port is relatively close to the top sights, but it's easy to hop the bus or take a taxi.

By Taxi

Taxis meet each arriving ship and are waiting as you exit any of the terminal buildings. The short trip into town (to the bottom of the Ramblas) runs about €15—a good deal if you split the fare with other travelers. During high season (May-Sept), when as many as six ships dock on the same day, there can be very long lines at the taxi stand—and because of traffic congestion, a ride into town can take twice as long and cost €10 more. Legal supplements are posted on the taxi window: €4.20 port fee and €1 per bag.

    For a one-way journey to other parts of town, expect to pay these fares:

Excursions from Barcelona

Barcelona can easily occupy a visitor for a full day (and beyond). But you may also see ads for excursions to the following out-of-town sights. While they may appeal to someone with a topical interest, for most visitors, they pale in comparison to the sights in Barcelona.

The town of **Figueres,** two hours north of Barcelona, is of sightseeing interest only for its Salvador Dalí Theater-Museum. But if you like Dalí, this is one of Europe's most enjoyable museums. Painted pink, studded with golden loaves of bread, and topped with monumental eggs and a geodesic dome, the building exudes Dalí's outrageous public persona. Because it's so far from town, it's worth considering only if you're a die-hard Dalí devotee.

The resort town of **Sitges,** 45 minutes south of Barcelona, has two attractions: Its tight-and-tiny Old Town, crammed with cafés and boutiques, and its nine long, luxurious beaches, extending about a mile south from town. If beach-resort ambience is more appealing to you than big-city sights, this is a good option.

The dramatic mountaintop **Montserrat** monastery, about 1.5 hours northwest of Barcelona, has been Catalunya's most important pilgrimage site for a thousand years. A scenic cable-car ride takes you to the monastery, nestled in the jagged peaks at 2,400 feet. In a quick day trip, you can tour the basilica and museum, view a statue of the Black Virgin, hike to a sacred cave, and listen to Gregorian chants by the world's oldest boys' choir. Interesting as this site is, its substantial distance from Barcelona makes it worth a pilgrimage only for the faithful.

- To the Picasso Museum or Plaça de Catalunya: €15
- To the Sagrada Família: €20
- To the airport: €35-40
- To Montserrat: €65

As always, it can cost more in busy times. The hourly touring rate is about €40. A round-trip to Montserrat (including waiting time at the site) costs about €150-160.

By Public Transportation

Getting to the sights requires two steps: First, you'll head to the Columbus Monument, in the middle of the roundabout at the bottom of the Ramblas (at the square called Plaça de Colón). Then you'll connect—by foot, Metro, or bus—to wherever you're going in town.

BARCELONA

Step 1: From Your Ship to the Columbus Monument

From the main cruise port, the walk into town is mostly through dreary docklands and is long, hot, and boring (figure about 20 minutes from Terminal A, and double that from Terminal D). Instead, take the **#T3 shuttle bus** (a.k.a. Portbús, departs from parking lot in front of each terminal—follow *Public Bus* signs, €2.50 one-way, €3.50 round-trip, buses leave every 20 minutes, timed to cruise ship arrival, tel. 932-986-000). The bus drops you right on the waterfront near the Columbus Monument. Pay attention to where you get off, as the return bus leaves roughly from the same spot but heading back toward the port (look for blue-and-white sign). Note: If your cruise arrives very early (before 8:30 or so), the shuttle bus may not be operating yet.

Step 2: From the Columbus Monument to Barcelona's Top Sights

From the waterfront and the Columbus Monument, you can already see (across the roundabout) one of Barcelona's main attractions: the delightful, tree-lined pedestrian drag, the Ramblas. In summer, a TI kiosk is just steps from where you get off the bus (look for the red booth with an "I" on top); there's also a TI in the base of the Columbus Monument (pick up a free town map and get your questions answered at either one). Hop-on, hop-off tour buses also stop here (a handy way to get a quick look at this sprawling city—see page 166).

For most destinations in town (including the Barri Gòtic, cathedral, and Picasso Museum), the best plan is to walk to the Ramblas, then walk or take the Metro from there. For the Sagrada Família church, you can either take the Metro or grab a taxi.

To the Ramblas and Points Beyond: The Ramblas is just beyond the Columbus Monument. From the shuttle-bus stop, stand with the sea to your back, cross over to the roundabout with the monument, and continue straight ahead. You'll end up right at the bottom of the tree-lined Ramblas.

A few steps up the Ramblas, you'll come to the red "M" sign marking the Drassanes **Metro** stop. This is on the handy L3 (green) line, with connections to Plaça de Catalunya (city center, ex-

Services near the Columbus Monument

The cruise terminals offer an impressive array of services. But if you can't find what you want there, head for the Columbus Monument, which is the entry point into the city for cruise passengers.

ATMs: You'll find plenty of ATMs at banks along the Ramblas.

Internet Access: Barcelona has free Wi-Fi hotspots throughout the city; you can connect, for example, in the lobby of the Maritime Museum, just near the Columbus Monument (look for blue diamond-shaped signs with a big "W"; www.bcn.cat/barcelonawifi). Navega Web, with computer terminals and Wi-Fi, is farther up the Ramblas (see page 163).

Pharmacy: From the Columbus Monument (with your back to the sea), cross to the foot of the Ramblas, then turn right down the street called Carrer de Josep Anselm Clavé (at the red corner house); a pharmacy is a block down on your right-hand side. There are more pharmacies up and down the Ramblas (see page 164).

plained below), Passeig de Gràcia (at the Block of Discord; also the transfer point for the L2 (purple) line to Sagrada Família), and more. For a list of stops on this line—and how to buy and use tickets for the Metro—see page 164.

Before hopping on the Metro, consider your options: Both of this chapter's self-guided walks—of the Ramblas itself, and of the Barri Gòtic neighborhood—begin at the square called **Plaça de Catalunya,** which is at the top of the Ramblas, straight ahead. You can walk, following my Ramblas tour in reverse, or zip to the square on the Metro (two stops, to Plaça de Catalunya). If you choose to walk, you'll find it's an easy, fascinating, 30-minute stroll. While the Ramblas can get crowded, it's typically not too congested in the morning (when most cruise ships arrive).

To the Sagrada Família Church: Your best public-transit option for reaching Gaudí's fanciful cathedral is to take the **Metro:** Ride the L3 (green) line from the Drassanes stop (described earlier), change to the L2 (purple) line at Passeig de Gràcia, then ride to the Sagrada Família stop.

By Tour

There's a convenient stop for the hop-on, hop-off **Tourist Bus** (Bus Turístic) red route near the #T3 shuttle bus stop at the Columbus Monument. This is an easy way to simply watch the city sights roll by for one reasonable price (and the option to hop off when you like and hop on any other bus rolling by; €26, buy ticket from kiosk or as you board, see page 166).

For information on local tour options in Barcelona—including local guides for hire, walking tours, and bus tours—see "Tours in Barcelona" on page 168.

Returning to Your Ship

You're a quick €15-20 cab ride back to your ship from just about anywhere in central Barcelona. If you're riding the #T3 shuttle bus back to the main cruise port, you'll catch it near the Columbus Monument (as you face the water, buses going to the right head toward the port; look for the blue-and-white sign). If you miss your boat, see the sidebar at the end of this chapter.

If you have some time to kill before heading back, linger along the Ramblas. Or dip into the Maritime Museum, which is a block from the Columbus Monument.

Orientation to Barcelona

Bustling Barcelona is geographically big and culturally complex. Plan your time carefully, carving up the metropolis into manageable sightseeing neighborhoods.

Barcelona: A Verbal Map

Like Los Angeles, Barcelona is a basically flat city that sprawls out under the sun between the sea and the mountains. It's huge (1.6 million people, with about 5 million people in greater Barcelona), but travelers need only focus on four areas: the Old City, the harbor/ Barceloneta, the Eixample, and Montjuïc.

A large square, **Plaça de Catalunya,** sits at the center of Barcelona, dividing the older and newer parts of town. Below Plaça de Catalunya is the Old City, with the boulevard called the Ramblas running down to the harbor. Above Plaça de Catalunya is the modern residential area called the Eixample. The Montjuïc hill overlooks the harbor. Outside the Old City, Barcelona's sights are widely scattered, but with a map and a willingness to figure out the sleek Metro system (or a few euros for taxis), all is manageable.

Here are more details per neighborhood:

Old City (Ciutat Vella): This is the compact core of Barcelona—ideal for strolling, shopping, and people-watching—it's where you'll probably spend most of your time. It's a labyrinth of narrow streets that once were confined by the medieval walls. The

Barcelona Experiences for Cruisers

Barcelona's top museums and churches are well worth seeing—but even if you're in port for only a short visit, you can go beyond predictable sightseeing and experience a very local slice of Catalan life. Here are some suggestions.

Have a tapas lunch. When Spaniards eat out, they usually don't go to a sit-down restaurant; instead, they assemble a mix-and-match meal at a tapas bar. For pointers, see the sidebar on page 230; for recommended tapas bars, see "Eating in Barcelona," later in this chapter.

Talk to a young person to learn a little Catalan. The local language of this region—which sounds like a cross between Spanish and French—was in danger of going extinct just a generation ago. But these days, many kids learn it as their first language, even before they learn Spanish. For a few phrases to get you started, see page 172.

Drink a *horchata* (a.k.a. *orxata*). Served at various bars (including Café Granja Viader—see page 223, and Casa Colomina—see page 232), this refreshing, milky drink is made from the *chufa* nut.

Join the *sardana* dance. This traditional and uniquely Catalan circle dance is an engaging way to feel momentarily like part of the community. Unfortunately, it happens only on Sundays at noon and most Saturdays at 18:00 (none in August)—but if you happen to be in town for one, it's worthwhile. For details, see page 192.

lively pedestrian drag called the **Ramblas**—one of Europe's most entertaining streets—runs through the heart of the Old City from Plaça de Catalunya down to the harbor. The Old City is divided into thirds by the Ramblas and another major thoroughfare, Via Laietana. Between the Ramblas and Via Laietana is the characteristic **Barri Gòtic** (BAH-ree GOH-teek, Gothic Quarter), with the cathedral as its navel. Locals call it simply "El Gòtic" for short. To the east of Via Laietana is the trendy **El Born** district (a.k.a. "La Ribera"), a shopping, dining, and nightlife mecca centered on the Picasso Museum and the Church of Santa Maria del Mar. To the west of the Ramblas is the **Raval** (rah-VAHL), enlivened by its university and modern-art museum. The Raval is of least interest to tourists (and, in fact, some parts of it are quite seedy and should be avoided).

Harborfront: The old harbor, **Port Vell,** gleams with landmark monuments and new developments. A pedestrian bridge links the Ramblas with the modern Maremagnum shopping/aquarium/entertainment complex. On the peninsula across the quaint sailboat harbor is **Barceloneta,** a traditional fishing neighborhood with gritty charm and some good seafood restaurants. Beyond

BARCELONA

Barcelona at a Glance

▲▲▲**Ramblas** Barcelona's colorful, gritty, tourist-filled pedestrian thoroughfare, with the thriving La Boqueria market. **Hours:** Always open (but market closed Sun). See page 169.

▲▲▲**Picasso Museum** Extensive collection offering insight into the brilliant Spanish artist's early years. **Hours:** Tue-Sun 9:00-19:00, Thu until 21:30, closed Mon. See page 194.

▲▲▲**Sagrada Família** Gaudí's remarkable, unfinished church—a masterpiece in progress. **Hours:** Daily April-Sept 9:00-20:00, Oct-March 9:00-18:00. See page 205.

▲▲**Barri Gòtic** City's Gothic Quarter, with the cathedral, remnants of Barcelona's Roman past, and Picasso's old haunt. **Hours:** Always open. See page 180.

▲▲**Palace of Catalan Music** Best Modernista interior in Barcelona. **Hours:** 50-minute English tours daily every hour 10:00-15:00, plus frequent concerts. See page 195.

▲▲**La Pedrera** Barcelona's quintessential Modernista building and Gaudí creation. **Hours:** Daily March-Oct 9:00-20:00, Nov-Feb 9:00-18:30. See page 203.

▲▲**Park Güell** Colorful Gaudí-designed park overlooking the city. **Hours:** Daily April-Oct 8:00-21:30, Nov-March 8:30-18:00. See page 205.

▲**Cathedral of Barcelona** Colossal Gothic cathedral ringed by distinctive chapels. **Hours:** Generally open to visitors Mon-Fri 8:00-19:30, Sat-Sun 8:00-20:00. See page 190.

▲*Sardana* Dances Patriotic dance in which proud Catalans join

Barceloneta, a gorgeous man-made **beach** several miles long leads east to the commercial and convention district called the **Fòrum.**

Eixample: North of the Old City, beyond the bustling hub of Plaça de Catalunya, is the elegant Eixample (eye-SHAM-plah) district, its grid plan softened by cut-off corners. Much of Barcelona's Modernista architecture is found here—especially along the swanky artery Passeig de Gràcia, an area called the **Quadrat d'Or** ("Golden Quarter"). To the north is the **Gràcia** district and beyond that, Antoni Gaudí's **Park Güell.**

Montjuïc: The large hill overlooking the city to the southwest is Montjuïc (mohn-jew-EEK), home to a variety of attractions, in-hands in a circle, often held outdoors. **Hours:** Every Sun at 12:00, usually also Sat at 18:00, no dances in Aug. See page 192.

▲**Barcelona History Museum** One-stop trip through town history, from Roman times to today. **Hours:** Tue-Sat 10:00-19:00, Sun 10:00-20:00, closed Mon. See page 193.

▲**Santa Caterina Market** Fine market hall built on the site of an old monastery and updated with a wavy Gaudí-inspired roof. **Hours:** Mon 7:30-14:00, Tue-Wed and Sat 7:30-15:30, Thu-Fri 7:30-20:30, closed Sun. See page 196.

▲**Church of Santa Maria del Mar** Catalan Gothic church in El Born, built by wealthy medieval shippers. **Hours:** Daily 8:00-13:30 & 17:00-19:30. See page 196.

▲**Maritime Museum** A sailor's delight, housed in an impressive medieval shipyard (but permanent collection likely closed until late 2014). **Hours:** Temporary exhibits daily 10:00-20:00. See page 198.

▲**Barcelona's Beach** Fun-filled, man-made stretch of sand reaching from the harbor to the Fòrum. **Hours:** Always open. See page 199.

▲**Palau Güell** Exquisitely curvy Gaudí interior and fantasy rooftop. **Hours:** April-Sept Tue-Sun 10:00-20:00, Oct-March Tue-Sun 10:00-17:30, closed Mon year-round. See page 199.

▲**Block of Discord** Noisy block of competing Modernista facades by Gaudí and his rivals. **Hours:** Always viewable. See page 202.

▲**Casa Batlló** Gaudí-designed home topped with fanciful dragon-inspired roof. **Hours:** Daily 9:00-20:00. See page 203.

cluding some excellent museums and the Olympic Stadium. On a short visit, most cruisers skip this area in favor of other sights in town.

Apart from your geographical orientation, you'll need to orient yourself linguistically to a language distinct from Spanish. Although Spanish ("Castilian"/*castellano*) is widely spoken, the native tongue in this region is Catalan—nearly as different from Spanish as Italian (see the sidebar on page 172).

Central Barcelona

AVINGUDA DIAGONAL

PALAU BARÓ DE QUADRAS

LA CONCEPCIÓ MARKET

C. DE D'ARAGÓ

PSG. DE SANT JOAN

Diagonal ⓜ

LA PEDRERA

CARRER MALLORCA

CHURCH OF THE HOLY CONCEPTION

C. DEL CONSELL DE CENT

Provença ⓡ

Diagonal (to Sagrada Familia) ⓜ

C. DE ROSSELLÓ

C. DE VALÈNCIA

C. DE GIRONA

Provença Train Station ⒷⓂ ❷

PASSEIG DE GRÀCIA

Passeig de Gràcia Train Station ⓡ

C. DE PAU CLARIS

C. DEL ROGER DE LLÚRIA

Girona ⓜ

QUADRAT D'OR

C. DE DIPUTACIÓ

EIX

RAMBLA

CATALANES

C. DEL BRUC

Water Tower Gardens

Provença ⓡ

CASA BATLLÓ

Passeig de Gràcia ⓡ

C. PROVENÇA

CASA AMATLLER ←

CARRER DE BALMES

BLOCK OF DISCORD

CASA LLEÓ MORERA

CASA AMATLLER ❶◆

GRÀCIA

C. D'ENRIC GRANADOS

CARRER D'ARIBAU

DE

CORTS

CARRER DE CASP C. DEL

Urquinaona ⓜ

Plaça del Doctor Letamendi

❸ Ⓜ

Passeig de Gràcia

EL CORTE INGLÉS DEP'T STORE

VIA LAIETANA

C. DE VALÈNCIA

C. DE CASANOVA

CATALUNYA

❹◆

Catalunya ⓜ

Bus to Airport (& Taxis) Ⓑ

LES

LES JONQUERES

C. DE MUNTANER

CARRER DEL CONSELLO DE CENT

CARRER DE LA DIPUTACIÓ

Plaça de Catalunya

PORTAL DE L'ÀNGEL

FONTANELLA

DE

R. DE LA UNIVERSITAT

S. ANNA

COMTAL

VIA

Universitat ⓜ

Bergara

SANTA ANNA

GRAN

C. DE PELAI

FNAC ⓡ

Catalunya ⓜ

LAS

PORTAFERRISSA

C. DELS TALLERS

SANTA ANNA

FOUNTAIN

CARRER DE

C. DE LA CANUDA

RAMBLAS

Plaça del Pi

200 Meters
200 Yards

MACBA CONTEMPORARY ART MUSEUM

C. D'ELISABETS

MONTALEGRE

ROMAN NECROPOLIS

PORTAFERRISSA

Urgell ⓜ

RONDA DE SANT ANTONI

JOAQUIM

NOTARIAT

ⓘ BETLEM CHURCH

C. DE COMTE D'URGELL

Plaça dels Àngels

C. D'ÀNGELS

Liceu ⓜ

C. DEL VILLARROEL

FERLANDINA

PEU DE LA CREU

C. DEL CARME

LA BOQUERIA MARKET

S. MARIA DEL PI

COSTA

C. DE SANT VICENÇ

OLD

MIRÓ MOSAIC

C. DE FLORIDABLANCA

RIERA ALTA

Plaça del Pedró

L'HOSPITAL

EL

Liceu ⓜ

C. DEL COMTE BORRELL

CENDRA

C. DE SANT PAU

C'N ROBADOR

LICEU OPERA HOUSE

C. DE VILADOMAT

TAMARIT

SANT ANTONI MARKET

SANT ANTONI ABAT

RAVAL

SANT RAFAEL

RAMBLA DEL RAVAL

PALAU GÜELL

To Plaça d'Espanya

Sant Antoni ⓜ

DE

AVINGUDA DE MISTRAL

CALABRIA

C. DE MANSO

PARLAMENT DE CATALUNYA

RONDA DE SANT PAU

C. DE LA REINA AMALIA

C. DE SANT PAU

C. MARQUÈS DE BARBERÀ

C. DE LES TÀPIES

C. NOU DE LA RAMBLA

AV. DE LES

C. DEL CID

To Plaça d'Espanya & Sants Station

C. DE FLORIDABLANCA

BORRELL

C. MARQUÈS DE CAMPO SAGRADO

Poble Sec ⓜ

Paral·lel ⓜ

S. MADRONA

BARCELONA

AVINGUDA DEL PARAL·LEL

Plaça d'El Molino

FUNICULAR

CABANES

DE LA RAMBLA

PICART

Plaça de Santa Madrona

C. DE MARGARIT

CONCORDIA

C. DELS MOLERS

BLAI

POETA CABANYES

C. DEL ROSER

C. NOU DE LA RAMBLA

To Montjuïc

CABANES

PALAUDARIES

PUIG XURIGUER

J. BONAPLATA

MARE DE DÉU DEL REMEI

CREU DELS MOLERS

Plaça del Sortidor

C. DE PIQUER

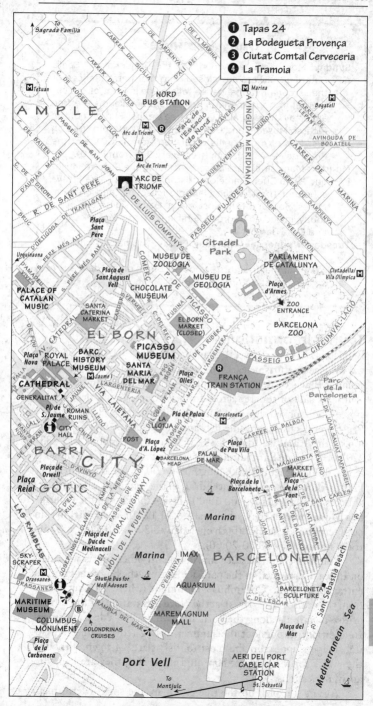

Daily Reminder

Sunday: Most sights are open, but the Boqueria and Santa Caterina markets are closed. Informal performances of the *sardana* national dance take place in front of the cathedral at noon (none in Aug). Some museums are free at certain times: Palau Güell (free on first Sun of month); Picasso Museum and Barcelona History Museum (free on first Sun of month plus other Sun from 15:00); and the Frederic Marès Museum (free every Sun from 15:00).

Monday: Many sights are closed, including the Picasso Museum, Palau Güell, Barcelona History Museum, *Santa Eulàlia* schooner (part of the Maritime Museum), and Frederic Marès Museum. But most major Gaudí sights are open today, including Sagrada Família, La Pedrera, Park Güell, and Casa Batlló.

Tuesday/Wednesday/Thursday/Friday: All major sights are open.

Saturday: All major sights are open. Barcelonans dance the *sardana* most Saturdays at 18:00.

Tourist Information

Barcelona's TI has several branches (central tel. 932-853-834, www.barcelonaturisme.cat). The primary one is beneath the main square, **Plaça de Catalunya** (daily 8:30-20:30, entrance along southeast side of square, across from El Corte Inglés department store—look for red sign and take stairs down, tel. 932-853-832).

Several other convenient branches include a kiosk near the top of the **Ramblas** (daily 8:30-20:30, at #115, mobile 618-783-479); on **Plaça de Sant Jaume,** just south of the cathedral (Mon-Fri 8:30-20:00, Sat 9:00-19:00, Sun 9:00-14:00, in the Barcelona City Hall at Ciutat 2); near the **cathedral,** in the Catalan College of Architects building (daily 9:00-19:00); inside the base of the **Columbus Monument** at the harbor (daily 8:30-19:30); at the **airport,** in both terminals 1 and 2B (both open daily 8:30-20:30); and at **Sants train station** (daily 8:00-20:00).

You'll also find smaller info kiosks in other touristy locales: on **Plaça d'Espanya,** in the park across from the **Sagrada Família** entrance, near the **Columbus Monument** (where the shuttle bus from the cruise port arrives), at the **Nord bus station,** at the various **cruise terminals** along the port, and two on **Plaça de Catalunya.** In addition, throughout the summer, young red-jacketed tourist-info helpers appear in the most touristy parts of town; although they work for the hop-on, hop-off Tourist Bus, they are happy to answer questions.

At any TI, pick up the free city map, the small Metro map,

the monthly *Barcelona Planning.com* guidebook (with basic tips on sightseeing, shopping, events, and restaurants), and the quarterly *See Barcelona* guide (with more in-depth practical information on museums and a neighborhood-by-neighborhood sightseeing rundown). The monthly *Time Out BCN Guide* offers a thorough but concise day-by-day list of events. And the monthly *Barcelona Metropolitan* magazine has timely and substantial coverage of local topics and events. All of these are free.

The TI is a handy place to buy tickets for the Tourist Bus (described later, under "Getting Around Barcelona") or for the TI-run walking tours (described later, under "Tours in Barcelona"). They also sell tickets to FC Barcelona soccer games.

Modernisme Route: Inside the Plaça de Catalunya TI is the privately run **Ruta del Modernisme** desk, which gives out a handy route map showing all 116 Modernista buildings and offers a sightseeing discount package (€12 for a great guidebook and 20-50-percent discounts to many Modernista sights—worthwhile if going beyond the biggies I cover in depth; for €18 you'll also get a guidebook to Modernista bars and restaurants; www.rutadelmodernisme.com).

Sightseeing Pass: The **Articket BCN** ticket covers admission to six art museums (including the Picasso Museum), letting you skip the ticket-buying lines (€30, sold at Plaça de Catalunya, Plaça de Sant Jaume, and Sants train station TIs and at participating museums; www.articketbcn.org).

Helpful Hints

Theft and Scam Alert: You're more likely to be pickpocketed here—especially on the Ramblas—than about anywhere else in Europe. Most crime is nonviolent, but muggings do occur. Leave valuables back on the ship and wear a money belt.

Street scams are easy to avoid if you recognize them. Most common is the too-friendly local who tries to engage you in conversation by asking for the time or whether you speak English. If a super-friendly man acts drunk and wants to dance because his soccer team just won, he's a pickpocket. Beware of thieves posing as lost tourists who ask for your help. Don't fall for any street-gambling shell games—you can be sure you'll lose if you play. Also beware of groups of women aggressively selling carnations, people offering to clean off a stain from your shirt, and people picking things up in front of you on escalators. If you stop for any commotion or show on the Ramblas, put your hands in your pockets before someone else does. Assume any scuffle is simply a distraction by a team of thieves. Don't be intimidated...just be smart.

Personal Safety: Some areas feel seedy and can be unsafe after dark; I'd avoid the southern part of the Barri Gòtic (basically the two or three blocks directly south and east of Plaça Reial), and I wouldn't venture too deep into the Raval (just west of the Ramblas). One block can separate a comfy tourist zone from the junkies and prostitutes.

Emergency Phone Numbers: General emergencies—112, police—092, ambulance—061 or 112.

Sight Reservations: To avoid standing in long lines, you can call or go online to book ahead for the Picasso Museum (see page 206), Sagrada Família (see page 211), Casa Batlló (see page 203), and La Pedrera (see page 203). An Articket BCN (described earlier) allows you to skip the lines at the Picasso Museum, but it doesn't cover any Gaudí sights. If you want to tour the Palace of Catalan Music, with its oh-wow Modernista interior, you'll need to reserve it in advance (see page 195). It's also smart to book ahead for Park Güell (see page 205).

Internet Access: The free city network, **Barcelona WiFi,** has hundreds of hotspots around town; just look for the blue diamond-shaped sign with a big "W" (for details, see www.bcn.cat/barcelonawifi). **Navega Web** has lots of computers and cheap Internet access (€2/hour); it's conveniently located across from La Boqueria market, downstairs in the bright Centre Comercial New Park (daily 10:00-24:00, Ramblas 88-94, tel. 933-179-193).

Pharmacy: A 24-hour pharmacy is across from La Boqueria market at #98 on the Ramblas. Another is on the corner of Passeig de Gràcia and Provença, just opposite the entrance to La Pedrera.

Updates to this Book: For any changes to this book's coverage since it was published, see www.ricksteves.com/update.

Getting Around Barcelona

Barcelona's Metro and bus system is run by **TMB**—Transports Metropolitans de Barcelona (tel. 902-075-027, www.tmb.cat). It's worth asking for TMB's excellent Metro/bus map at the TI (not always available).

By Metro

The city's Metro, among Europe's best, connects just about every place you'll visit. A single-ride ticket *(bitllet senzill)* costs €2. The T10 Card is a great deal—€9.80 gives you 10 rides (cutting the per-ride cost more than in half). The card is share-

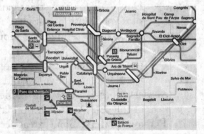

able, even by companions traveling with you (insert the card in the machine once for each passenger). The back of your T10 card will show how many trips were taken, with the time and date of each ride. One "ride" covers you for 1.25 hours of unlimited use on all Metro and local bus lines, as well as local rides on the RENFE and Rodalies de Catalunya train lines (including rides to the airport and train station) and the suburban FGC trains. Transfers made within your 1.25-hour limit are not counted as a new ride, but you still must revalidate your T10 Card whenever you transfer.

Multiday passes are also available (€13.40/2 days, €19.20/3 days, €24.40/4 days, €29/5 days). Machines at the Metro entrance have English instructions and sell all types of tickets (most machines accept credit/debit cards as well as cash).

Whatever type of ticket you use, keep it until you have exited the subway. You don't need the ticket to go through the exit, but inspectors occasionally ask riders to show it.

Barcelona has several color-coded lines, but most useful for tourists is the **L3 (green)** line. Handy city-center stops on this line include (in order):

Sants Estació—Main train station

Espanya—Plaça d'Espanya, with access to the lower part of Montjuïc and trains to Montserrat

Paral-lel—Funicular to the top of Montjuïc

Drassanes—Bottom of the Ramblas, near Maritime Museum and Maremagnum mall

Liceu—Middle of the Ramblas, near the heart of the Barri Gòtic and cathedral

Plaça de Catalunya—Top of the Ramblas and main square with TI, airport bus, and lots of transportation connections

Passeig de Gràcia—Classy Eixample street at the Block of Discord; also connection to L2 (purple) line to Sagrada Família and L4 (yellow) line

Diagonal—Gaudí's La Pedrera

The **L4 (yellow)** line, which crosses the L3 (green) line at Passeig de Gràcia, is also useful. Helpful stops include **Joanic** (bus #116 to Park Güell), **Jaume I** (between the Barri Gòtic/cathedral and El Born/Picasso Museum), and **Barceloneta** (at the south end of El Born, near the harbor action).

Before riding the Metro, study a map (available at TIs and posted at entrances) to get familiar with the system. Look for your line number and color, and find the end stop for your direction of travel. Enter the Metro by inserting your ticket into the turnstile (with the arrow pointing in), then reclaim it. Then, follow signs for your line and direction. On board, most trains have handy lighted displays that indicate upcoming destinations. Because the lines cross one another multiple times, there can be several ways to make

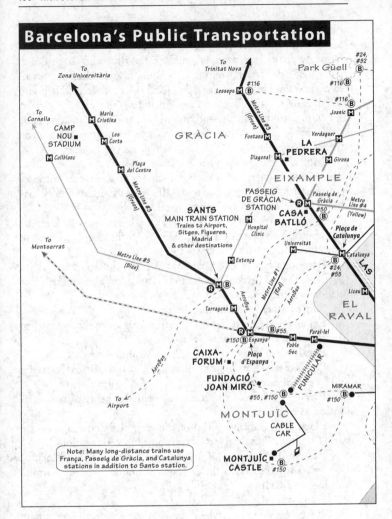

Barcelona's Public Transportation

any one journey. (It's a good idea to keep a general map with you—especially if you're transferring.)

Watch your valuables. If I were a pickpocket, I'd set up shop along the made-for-tourists L3 (green) line.

By Bus

Given the excellent Metro service, it's unlikely you'll take a **local bus** (also €2, covered by T10 Card, insert ticket in machine behind driver), although I've noted places where the bus makes sense.

The handy **hop-on, hop-off Tourist Bus** (Bus Turístic) offers three multistop circuits in colorful double-decker buses that go topless in sunny weather. The two-hour blue route covers north

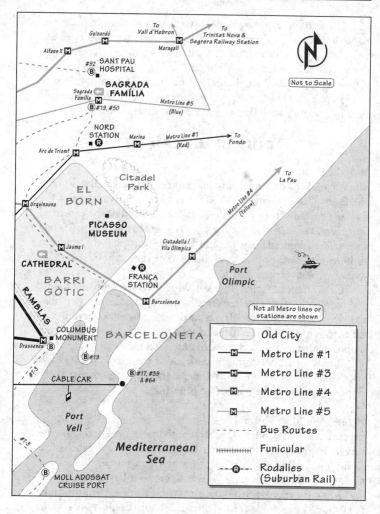

Barcelona (most Gaudí sights); the two-hour red route covers south Barcelona (Barri Gòtic, Montjuïc). All have headphone commentary (€26, daily 9:00-20:00 in summer, 9:00-19:00 in winter, buses run every 5-25 minutes, most frequent in summer, www.barcelonabusturistic.cat). Ask for a brochure (includes city map) at the TI or at a pick-up point. From Plaça de Catalunya, the blue route leaves from El Corte Inglés; the red route leaves from the west—Ramblas—side of the square.

By Taxi

Barcelona is one of Europe's best taxi towns. Taxis are plentiful (there are more than 11,000) and honest, whether they like it or not. The light on top shows which tariff they're charging; a green light on the roof indicates that a taxi is available. Cab rates are reasonable (€2.50 drop charge, €1/kilometer, these *"Tarif 2"* rates are in effect 8:00-20:00, pay higher *"Tarif 1"* rates off-hours, luggage-€1/piece, €2.10 surcharge to/from train station, €4.20 surcharge for airport or cruise port, other fees posted in window). Save time by hopping a cab (figure €10 from Ramblas to Sants Station).

Tours in Barcelona

Walking Tours

The TI at Plaça de Sant Jaume offers great guided walks through the **Barri Gòtic** in English. You'll learn the medieval story of the city as you walk from Plaça de Sant Jaume through the cathedral neighborhood (€15, daily at 9:30, 2 hours, groups limited to 35, buy your ticket 15 minutes early at the TI desk—not from the guide, in summer stop by the office a day ahead to reserve, tel. 932-853-832, www.barcelonaturisme.cat).

Other themed walks (**Picasso, Modernisme, gourmet foods,** and many others) depart from the TI at Plaça de Catalunya (check the website for departure days and times; smart to reserve in advance in summer). A **Maritime** tour that includes a boat trip on the harbor begins at the TI at the Columbus Monument.

The Ruta del Modernisme desk inside the Plaça de Catalunya TI also does tours of specific **Modernista buildings** that are otherwise not open to the public (see page 162).

"Free" Walking Tours

Several companies offer "free" walks that rely on—and expect—tips to stay in business. Though led by young people who've basically memorized a clever script (rather than trained historians), these walks can be a fun, casual way to get your bearings.

I like **Runner Bean Tours,** run by Gorka, Ann-Marie, and a handful of local guides. They offer 2.5-hour, English-only walks covering the Old City and Gaudí (both tours depart from Plaça Reial at 11:00 daily year-round, plus daily at 16:30 in April-Oct, www.runnerbeantours.com, mobile 636-108-776).

Discover Walks does similar tours, with three different two-hour itineraries: Gaudí (daily at 10:30, meet in front of Casa Batlló); Ramblas and Barri Gòtic (daily at 15:00, meet in front of Liceu Opera House on the Ramblas); and Picasso's Barcelona, covering the El Born neighborhood (daily at 17:00, meet at Plaça de l'Angel next to Jaume I Metro stop). This company distinguishes itself by using exclusively native-born guides—no expats (suggested tips: €5/person for a bad guide, €10 for a good one, €15 for a great one, www.discoverwalks.com, tel. 931-816-810).

Local Guides

The **Barcelona Guide Bureau** is a co-op with about 20 local guides who give personalized four-hour tours; **Joana Wilhelm** and **Carles Picazo** are excellent (€102/person for 2, €53/person for 4, per-person price continues to drop as group gets bigger, these prices include public-transportation costs, Via Laietana 54, tel. 932-682-422 or 933-107-778, www.bgb.es).

José Soler is a great and fun-to-be-with local guide who enjoys tailoring a walk through his hometown to your interests (€195/half-day per group, mobile 615-059-326, www.pepitotours.com, info@pepitotours.com). He can also take up to six people by car for a four-hour Barcelona Highlights tour (€395) and will meet you at the cruise port or airport.

Cristina Sanjuán of Live Barcelona is another good, professional guide who leads walking tours and can also arrange cruise excursions. It's best to reserve by email (€155/2 hours, €20/each additional hour; €195 extra for a car for up to 2 people, €220 extra for up to 6, can combine with airport transfer; tel. 936-327-259, mobile 609-205-844, www.livebarcelona.com, info@livebarcelona.com).

Guided Bus Tours

The **Barcelona Guide Bureau** offers several sightseeing tours leaving from Plaça de Catalunya. Tours are designed to end at a major sight in case you'd like to spend more time there. The Gaudí tour, for example, visits Casa Batlló and Sagrada Família, as well as the facade of La Pedrera (€62, includes Sagrada Família and Casa Batlló admission, daily at 9:00, 3.5 hours). You can get detailed information, confirm times, and book tickets at a TI, on their website (10 percent discount for 7-day advance purchase), or simply by showing up at their departure point on Plaça de Catalunya in front of the Deutsche Bank (next to the Hard Rock Café—look for the guides holding orange umbrellas; tel. 933-152-261, www.barcelonaguidebureau.com).

For information on **hop-on, hop-off bus tours,** see "Getting Around Barcelona," earlier.

The Ramblas Ramble

This self-guided walk begins at Barcelona's main square and leads you down the city's main drag: the Ramblas. Together with my second walk (see page 180), which guides you into the heart of the Barri Gòtic, you'll get a taste of the atmospheric Old City and an introduction to places you may want to explore further.

BARCELONA

Ramblas Ramble

EIXAMPLE

To Casa Batlló & La Pedrera

PASSEIG DE GRÀCIA

Urquinaona

M Urquinaona

GRAN VIA DE LES CORTS CATALANES

EL CORTE INGLÉS DEP'T STORE

VIA LAIETANA

DE LES JONQUERES

C. FONTANELLA

Catalunya M

Bus to Airport (& Taxis) B

C. DE DESTRUC

CARRER COMTAL

PORTAL DE L'ANGEL

ServiCaixa ATM

Plaça de Catalunya

WALK BEGINS

ELS 4 GATS

MONTSIÓ

DURANBAS

RONDA DE LA UNIVERSITAT

C. DE BERGARA

FNAC

R

S. ANNA

M Catalunya

C. DE SANTA ANNA

Universitat M

CARRER DE PELAI

C. DELS TALLERS

CARRER DE LA CANUDA

CARRER DE LA CANUDA

C. DEL DUC

FOUNTAIN

R. DE SANT ANTONI

C. DE VALLDONZELLA

C. MONTALEGRE

Plaça de la Vila de Madrid

BONSUCCÉS

CLOCK

ROMAN NECROPOLIS

C. DE LA PORTAFERRISSA

C. DE LA FORTALISSA

MACBA CONTEMPORARY ART MUSEUM

C. D'EN XUCLÀ

GROCERY

LAS RAMBLAS

CIGAR SHOP

C. PETRIXOL

Plaça del Pi

Plaça dels Àngels

C. D'ELISABETS

P. D'ELISA

C. NOTARIAT

DOCTOR DOU

DEL PINTOR FORTUNY

GRANJA CAFÉ VIADER

BETLEM CHURCH

C. DEL BOT

Plaça S. Josep Oriol

C. DEL CARME

CULTURAL INFO PALAU DE LA VIRREINA

Liceu M

C. D'EN ROCA

S. MARIA DEL PI

LA BOQUERIA MARKET

C. DE LA

OLD

C. DE JERUSALEM

MIRÓ MOSAIC

Liceu M

CAFÉ DE L'OPERA

Plaça S. Agustí

LICEU OPERA HOUSE

EL RAVAL

PALAU GÜELL

Legend

1 Plaça de Catalunya
2 Fountain of Canaletes
3 Rambla of the Little Birds
4 Betlem Church
5 Rambla of Flowers
6 La Boqueria
7 Heart of the Ramblas (Liceu)
8 Plaça Reial
9 Raval Neighborhood
10 Columbus Monument

To Plaça d'Espanya & Sants Station

Paral·lel M AVINGUDA DEL PARAL·LEL

Funicular To Montjuïc

C. D'ORTIGOSA TRAF.
C. DE SANT PERE MES ALT
Plaça Sant Pere
C. D. DEL PORTAL NOU
Citadel Park

D'AMADEU VIVES
CARRER DE SANT PERE MES BAIX
C. DEL COMERÇ
MUSEU DE ZOOLOGIA

PALACE OF CATALAN MUSIC
CARRER SANT PERE MES BAIX
C. DE FONOLLAR
C. L'ALLADA VERMELL
C. TANTARANTANA
MUSEU DE GEOLOGIA

DR. J. POU
SAGRIS.
AV. FRANCESC CAMBO
C. PELLISSER
C. CARDERS
C. ASSAONADORS
C. FUSINA
PASSEIG DE PICASSO

ARCH. COLL.
Plaça Maura
Santa CATERINA MARKET
C. MERCADERS
Plaça Santa Caterina
CARRER DE LA PRINCESA
C. FLASSADERS
EL BORN MARKET (CLOSED)

Plaça Nova
AV. CATEDRAL
C. COMTES
ROYAL PALACE
Plaça del Rei
EL BORN
TEXTILE MUSEUM
C. MONTCADA
PICASSO MUSEUM
C. DE LA RIBERA

SHOE MUSEUM
CLOISTER
CATHEDRAL
BARC. HISTORY MUSEUM
[M] Jaume I
C. BANYS VELLS
FASSEIG DEL BORN
C. A. SANT JOAN
C. DEL REC
FRANÇA TRAIN STATION
[R]

GENERALITAT
C. LLIBRETERIA
Pl. de l'Angel
L'ARGENTERIA
SANTA MARIA DEL MAR
Plaça Olles
AV. MARQUES DE L'ARGENTERA

C. S. SEVER
C. S. HONORAT
ROMAN RUINS
JAUME
VIA LAIETANA
C. DE LA NAU
Plaça S. Maria Anisadeta
LA LLOTJA
Pla de Palau
Barceloneta [M]

EL CALL
BANYS NOUS
Pl. de Sant Jaume
CITY HALL
C. DEL SOTS-TINENT NAVARRO
PASSEIG D'ISABEL II

BOQUERIA
FERRAN
C. CIUTAT
Plaça de Sant Miquel
C. DIATAUF
Plaça Traginers
POST
Plaça d'Antoni López
To Barceloneta
PALAU DE MAR

BARRI
CARRER
C. GEGANTS
C. FUSTERIA
BARCELONA HEAD

CITY
C. ESC. BLANCS
Plaça de George Orwell
D'AVINYO
C. MARQUET
C. PLATA

Plaça Reial
(8)
GOTIC
C. VIDRE
C. CARABASSA
C. SERRA
AMPLE
PASSEIG DE COLÓM
LOBSTER SCULPTURE
Marina

LAS RAMBLAS
C. ESCUDELLERS
C. NOU D'EN RULL
C. DELS CODOLS
C. DE LA MERCE

(9)
TEATRE
C. DE LA PAU
Plaça del Duc de Medinaceli
Marina
IMAX

Drassanes [M]
SKY-SCRAPER
WALK ENDS
SANTA EULÀLIA
AQUARIUM

DRASSANES
PORT AUTHORITY
MOLL. D'ESPANYA

MARITIME MUSEUM
(10)
GOLONDRINAS CRUISES
RAMBLA DEL MAR
MAREMAGNUM MALL

Plaça de la Carbonera
200 Meters
200 Yards
Port Vell

BARCELONA

"You're Not in Spain, You're in Catalunya!"

The region of Catalunya—with Barcelona as its capital—has its own language, history, and culture, and the people have a proud, independent spirit. Historically, Catalunya ("Cataluña" in Spanish, sometimes spelled "Catalonia" in English) has often been at odds with the central Spanish government in Madrid. The Catalan language and culture were discouraged or even outlawed at various times in history, as Catalunya often chose the wrong side in wars and rebellions against the kings in Madrid. In the Spanish Civil War (1936-1939), Catalunya was one of the last pockets of democratic resistance against the military coup of the fascist dictator Francisco Franco, who punished the region with four decades of repression.

After the end of the Franco era in the mid-1970s, the language made a huge comeback. Schools are now required by law to conduct all classes in Catalan; most school-age children learn Catalan first and Spanish second. While all Barcelonans still speak Spanish, nearly all understand Catalan, three-quarters speak Catalan, and half can write it.

Here are a few essential Catalan words:

English	Catalan	Pronounced
Hello	*Hola*	OH-lah
Please	*Si us plau*	see oos plow
Thank you	*Gracies*	GRAH-see-es
Goodbye	*Adéu*	ah-DAY-oo
exit	*sortida*	sor-TEE-dah
square	*Plaça*	PLAS-sah
street	*carrer*	kah-REHR
boulevard	*passeig*	PAH-sage
avenue	*avinguda*	ah-veen-GOO-dah

From Plaça de Catalunya to the Waterfront

For more than a century, the walk down Barcelona's main boulevard has drawn locals and visitors alike. While its former elegance has been tackified somewhat by tourist shops and fast-food joints, this still has the best people-watching in town.

The word "Ramblas" is plural; the street is actually a succession of five separately named segments. But street signs and addresses treat it as a single long street—"La Rambla," singular. On this pedestrian-only Champs-Elysées, you'll raft the river of Barcelonese life, passing a grand opera house, elegant cafés, flower stands, retread prostitutes, brazen pickpockets, power-dressing con men, artists, street mimes, an outdoor pet market, great shopping, and people looking to charge more for a shoeshine than what you paid for the shoes.

• *Start your ramble on Plaça de Catalunya, at the top of the Ramblas.*

❶ Plaça de Catalunya

Dotted with fountains, statues, and pigeons, and ringed by grand Art Deco buildings, this plaza is Barcelona's center. The square's stern, straight lines are a reaction to the curves of Modernisme

(which predominates in the Eixample district, just to the north). Plaça de Catalunya is the hub for the Metro, bus, airport shuttle, and Tourist Bus. It's where Barcelona congregates to watch soccer matches on the big screen, to demonstrate, to celebrate, and to enjoy outdoor concerts and festivals. It's the center of the world for 10 million Catalan people.

Geographically, the 12-acre square links old Barcelona (the narrow streets to the south) with the new (the broad boulevards to the north). Four great thoroughfares radiate from here. The Ramblas is the popular pedestrian promenade. Passeig de Gràcia has fashionable shops and cafés (and noisy traffic). Rambla de Catalunya is equally fashionable but cozier and more pedestrian-friendly. Avinguda Portal de l'Angel (shopper-friendly and traffic-free) leads to the Barri Gòtic (note that my self-guided "Barri Gòtic Walk" begins from right here).

Historically, Plaça de Catalunya links the modern city with its past. In the 1850s, when Barcelona tore down its medieval walls to expand the city, this square on the edge of the walls was one of the first places to be developed.

At the Ramblas end of the square, the odd, inverted-staircase **monument** represents the shape of Catalunya and honors one of its former presidents, Francesc Macià i Llussà, who declared independence for the breakaway region in 1931. (It didn't quite stick.) Sculptor Josep Maria Subirachs, whose work you'll see at the Sagrada Família (see page 214), designed it.

The venerable Café Zürich, just across the street from the monument, is a popular downtown rendezvous spot for locals. Homesick Americans might prefer the nearby Hard Rock Café.

• *Cross the street and start heading down the Ramblas. To get oriented, pause 20 yards down, at the ornate lamppost with a fountain as its base (on the right, near #129).*

❷ Fountain of Canaletes

The black-and-gold fountain has been a local favorite for more than a century. When Barcelona tore down its medieval wall and transformed the Ramblas from a drainage ditch into an elegant promenade, this fountain was one of its early attractions. Legend says that a drink from the fountain ensures that you'll come back to Barcelona one day. Watch the tourists—eager to guarantee a return trip—struggle with the awkwardly high water pressure. It's still a popular let's-meet-at-the-fountain rendezvous spot and a gathering place for celebrations and demonstrations. Fans of the Barcelona soccer team rally here before a big match—some touch their hand to their lips, then "kiss" the fountain with their hand for good luck. It's also a good spot to fill up your water bottle.

• Continue strolling.

All along the Ramblas are **newsstands** (open 24 hours). Among their souvenirs, you'll see soccer paraphernalia, especially the scar-

let-and-blue of FC Barcelona (known as "Barça"). The team is owned by its more than 170,000 "members"—fans who buy season tickets, which come with a share of ownership (the team's healthy payroll guarantees that they're always in contention). Their motto, "More than a club" *(Mes que un club)*, suggests that Barça represents not only athletic prowess but Catalan cultural identity. This comes to a head during a match nicknamed "El Clásico," in which they face their bitter rivals, Real Madrid (whom many Barça fans view as stand-ins for Castilian cultural chauvinism).

Walk 100 yards farther to #115 and the venerable **Royal Academy of Science and Arts building** (it's now home to a performing-arts theater). Look up: The clock high on the facade marks official Barcelona time—synchronize. No-

tice the **TI** kiosk right on the Ramblas—a handy stop for any questions. The **Carrefour** supermarket just behind it has cheap groceries (at #113, Mon-Sat 10:00-22:00, closed Sun).

• You're now standing at the...

❸ Rambla of the Little Birds

Traditionally, kids brought their parents here to buy pets, especially on Sundays. But animal-rights groups lobbied to cut back on the stalls be-

cause so many families were making impulse buys with no serious interest in taking care of these cute little critters—and many
ended up being flushed. Today, only a couple of traditional pet
stalls survive—and there's not a bird in sight. Now you'll find tourists oohing and aahing over little bunnies, hamsters, goldfish, and
turtles—easier for Barcelona's apartment-dwellers to care for than
dogs and cats.

• *At #122 (the big, modern Citadines Hotel on the left, just behind a pet
kiosk), take a 100-yard detour through a passageway marked* Passatge
de la Ramblas *to a recently discovered...*

Roman Necropolis: Look down and imagine a 2,000-year-
old tomb-lined road. In Roman cities, tombs (outside the walls)
typically lined the roads leading into town. Emperor Augustus
spent a lot of time in modern-day Spain conquering new land, so
the Romans were sure to incorporate Hispania into the empire's
infrastructure. This road, Via Augusta, led into the Roman port
of Barcino (today's highway to France still follows the route laid
out by this Roman thoroughfare). Looking down at these ruins,
you can see how Roman Barcino was about 10 feet lower than today's street level. For more on this city's Roman chapter, follow my
"Barri Gòtic Walk," later.

• *Return to the Ramblas and continue 100 yards or so to the next street,
Carrer de la Portaferrissa (across from the big church). Turn left a few
steps and look right to see the* **decorative tile** *over a fountain still in use
by locals. The scene shows the original city wall with the gate that once
stood here and the action on what is today's Ramblas. Now cross the
boulevard to the front of the big church.*

❹ Betlem Church

It's dedicated to Bethlehem,
and for centuries locals have
flocked here at Christmas-
time to see Nativity scenes.
The church is 17th-century
Baroque: Check out the sloping roofline, ball-topped pinnacles, corkscrew columns, and
scrolls above the entrance. The
Baroque and also Renaissance styles are relatively unusual in Bar-
celona because it missed out on several centuries of architectural
development. Barcelona enjoyed two heydays: during the medieval
period (before the Renaissance) and during the turn of the 20th
century (after Baroque). In between those periods, from about
1500 until 1850, the city's importance dropped—first, New World
discoveries shifted lucrative trade to ports on the Atlantic, and then
the Spanish crown kept unruly Catalunya on a short leash.

For a sweet treat, head around to the narrow lane on the far side of the church (running parallel to the Ramblas) to the recommended **Café Granja Viader,** which has specialized in baked and dairy delights since 1870. Step inside to see Viader family photos and early posters advertising Cacaolat—the local chocolate milk Barcelonans love. (For more sugary treats nearby, follow "A Short, Sweet Walk" on page 232.)

• *Continue down the boulevard, through the stretch called the...*

❺ Rambla of Flowers

This colorful block, lined with flower stands, is the Rambla of Flowers. Besides admiring the blossoms on display, gardeners will

covet the seeds sold here for varieties of radishes, greens, peppers, and beans seldom seen in the US—including the iconic green Padrón pepper of tapas fame (if you buy seeds, you're obligated to declare them at US customs when returning home). On the left, at #100, **Gimeno** sells cigars. Step inside and appreciate the dying art of cigar boxes. Go ahead, do something forbidden in America but perfectly legal here...buy a Cuban (little singles for €1). Tobacco shops sell stamps and phone cards, plus bongs and marijuana gear—the Spanish approach to pot is very casual. While people can't legally sell marijuana, they're allowed to grow it for personal use and consume it.

• *Continue to the Metro stop marked by the red M. At #91 (on the right) is the arcaded entrance to Barcelona's great covered market, La Boqueria. If this main entry is choked with visitors (as it often is), you can skirt around the sides by entering one block in either direction (look for the round arches that mark passages into the market colonnade).*

❻ La Boqueria

This lively market hall is an explosion of chicken legs, bags of live snails, stiff fish, delicious oranges, odd odors, and sleeping dogs.

The best day for a visit is Saturday, when the market is thriving. It's closed on Sundays, and locals avoid it on Mondays, when it's open but (they believe) vendors are selling items that aren't necessarily fresh—especially seafood, since fishermen stay home on Sundays.

Since as far back as 1200, Barcelonans have bought their animal parts here. The market was originally located by the walled city's entrance, as many medieval markets were (since it was more expensive to trade within the walls). It later expanded into the colonnaded courtyard of a now-gone monastery before being topped with a colorful arcade in 1850.

While tourists are drawn like moths to a flame to the area around the main entry (below the colorful stained-glass sign), locals know that the stalls up front pay the highest rent—and therefore have to inflate their prices and cater to out-of-towners. For example, the juices along the main drag just inside the entrance are tempting, but if you venture to the right a couple of alleys, the clientele gets more local and the prices drop dramatically.

Stop by the recommended **Pinotxo Bar**—it's just inside the market, under the sign—and snap a photo of Juan. Animated Juan and his family are always busy feeding shoppers. Getting Juan to crack a huge smile and a thumbs-up for your camera makes a great shot...and he loves it. The stools nearby are a fine perch for enjoying both your coffee and the people-watching.

The market and lanes nearby are busy with tempting little eateries (several are listed on page 224). Drop by a café for an *espresso con leche* or breakfast *tortilla española* (potato omelet). Once you get past the initial gauntlet, do some exploring. The small square on the north side of the market hosts a farmers market in the mornings. Wander around—as local architect Antoni Gaudí used to—and gain inspiration.

• *Head back out to the street and continue down the Ramblas.*

It's clear that, as you walk the Ramblas, you're skirting along the western boundary of the old Barri Gòtic neighborhood. As you walk, glance to the left through a modern archway for a glimpse of the medieval church tower of **Santa Maria del Pi,** a popular venue for guitar concerts (see "Nightlife in Barcelona" on page 221). This also marks Plaça del Pi and a great shopping street, Carrer Petritxol, which runs parallel to the Ramblas.

Now look across to the other side of the Ramblas. At the corner, find the highly regarded **Escribà** bakery, with its fine Modernista facade and interior (look for the *Antigua Casa Figueras* sign arching over the doorway). Notice the beautiful mosaics of twining plants, the stained-glass peacock displaying his tail feathers, and the undulating woodwork. In the sidewalk in front of the door, a plaque dates the building to 1902 (plaques like this identify historic shops all over town).

• *After another block, you reach the Liceu Metro station, marking the...*

❼ Heart of the Ramblas (Liceu)

At the Liceu Metro station's elevators, the Ramblas widens a bit into a small, lively square (Plaça de la Boqueria). Liceu marks the midpoint of the Ramblas, halfway between Plaça de Catalunya and the waterfront.

Underfoot in the center of the Ramblas, find the much-trod-upon red-white-yellow-and-blue **mosaic** by homegrown abstract artist Joan Miró. The mosaic's black arrow represents an anchor, a reminder of the city's attachment to the sea. Miró's simple, colorful designs are found all over the city, from murals to mobiles to the La Caixa bank logo. The best place in Barcelona to see his work is in the Fundació Joan Miró at Montjuïc.

The surrounding buildings have playful ornamentation typical of the city. The **Chinese dragon** holding a lantern (at #82) deco-rates a former umbrella shop (notice the fun umbrella mosaics high up). While the dragon may seem purely decorative, it's actually an important symbol of Catalan pride for its connection to the local patron saint, St. Jordi (George).

Hungry? Swing around the back of the umbrella shop to the recommended **Taverna Basca Irati** tapas bar (a block up Carrer del Cardenal Casanyes). This is one of many user-friendly, Basque-style tapas bars in town; instead of ordering, you can just grab or point to what looks good on the display platters, then pay per piece.

Back on the Ramblas, a few steps down (on the right) is the **Liceu Opera House** (Gran Teatre del Liceu), which hosts world-class opera, dance, and theater (box office around the right side, open Mon-Fri 13:30-20:00). Opposite the opera house is Café de l'Opera (#74), an elegant stop for an expensive beverage. This bus-tling café, with Modernista decor and a historic atmosphere, boasts that it's been open since 1929, even during the civil war.

• *We've seen the best stretch of the Ramblas; to cut this walk short, you could catch the Metro back to Plaça de Catalunya. Otherwise, let's con-tinue to the port. The wide, straight street that crosses the Ramblas in another 30 yards (Carrer de Ferran) leads left to Plaça de Sant Jaume, the government center.*

But we'll head down the Ramblas another 50 yards (to #46), and turn left down an arcaded lane (Correr de Colom) to the square called...

❽ Plaça Reial

Dotted with palm trees, surrounded by an arcade, and ringed by yellow buildings with white Neoclassical trim, this elegant square has a colonial ambience. It comes complete with old-fashioned taverns, modern bars with patio seating, and a Sunday coin-and-stamp mar-ket (10:00-14:00). Completing the picture are Gaudí's first public works (the two colorful hel-meted lampposts). While this used to be a seedy and dangerous part of town, recent gentrification efforts have given it new life, making it inviting and accessible. (The small streets stretching toward the water from the square remain a bit sketchier.) It's a lively hangout by day or by night. Big spaces like this (as well as the site of La Boqueria market) often originated as monasteries. When these were dissolved in the 19th century, their fine colonnaded squares were incorporated into what were considered generally more useful public spaces.

Head back out to the Ramblas. Across the boulevard, a half-block detour down Carrer Nou de la Rambla brings you to **Palau Güell,** designed by Antoni Gaudí (on the left, at #3-5). Even from the outside, you get a sense of this innovative apartment, the first of Gaudí's Modernista buildings. As this is early Gaudí (built 1886-1890), it's darker and more Neo-Gothic than his more famous later work. The two parabolic-arch doorways and elaborate wrought-iron work signal his emerging nonrectangular style. Recently renovated, Palau Güell offers an informative look at a Gaudí interior (see listing on page 199). Pablo Picasso had a studio at #10 (though there's nothing to see there today).

• *Proceed along the Ramblas.*

❾ Raval Neighborhood (Barri Xines)

The neighborhood on the right-hand side of this stretch of the Ramblas is El Raval. Its nickname was Barri Xines—the world's only Chinatown with nothing even remotely Chinese in or near it. Named for the prejudiced notion that Chinese immigrants went hand-in-hand with poverty, prostitution, and drug dealing, the neighborhood's actual inhabitants were poor Spanish, North African, and Roma (Gypsy) people. At night, the Barri Xines was frequented by prostitutes, many of them transvestites, who catered to sailors wandering up from the port. Today, it's becoming gentrified, but it's still a pretty rough neighborhood.

At about this part of the Ramblas, you may see the first of the drag's medley of surreal and goofy **human statues.** These performers—with creative and elaborate costumes—must audition and be registered by the city government; to avoid overcrowding, only 15 can work along the Ramblas at any one time. To enliven your Ramblas ramble, stroll with a pocket full of small change. As you wander along, drop coins into their cans (the money often kicks them into entertaining gear). Warning: Wherever people stop to gawk, pickpockets are at work.

You're also likely to see some good old-fashioned **shell games** in this part of town. Stand back and observe these nervous no-necks at work. They swish around their little boxes, making sure to show you the pea. Their shills play and win. Then, in hopes of making easy money, fools lose big time.

Near the bottom of the Ramblas, take note of the Drassanes Metro stop, which can take you back to Plaça de Catalunya when this walk is over. The skyscraper to the right of the Ramblas is the Edificio Colón. When it was built in 1970, the 28-story structure was Barcelona's first high-rise. Near the skyscraper is the Maritime Museum, housed in what were the city's giant medieval shipyards (see listing on page 198).

• *Up ahead is the...*

❿ Columbus Monument

The 200-foot column commemorates Christopher Columbus' stop in Barcelona after his first trip to America (see listing on page 198).

Continue ahead to the **waterfront.** Barcelona is one of Europe's top 10 ports, though this stretch of the harbor is a pleasant marina with sailboats.

The pedestrian bridge jutting into the harbor is a modern extension of the Ramblas called La Rambla del Mar ("Rambla of the Sea"). This popular wooden bridge—with waves like the sea—leads to Maremagnum, a shopping mall with a cinema, a huge aquarium, restaurants, and piles of people. Late at night, it's a rollicking youth hangout.

• *Your ramble is over. If you'd like to continue on to my self-guided walk of the Barri Gòtic (next), you'll need to retrace your steps back up the Ramblas to Plaça de Catalunya; to get there faster, take the Metro from the nearby Drassanes station, or ride bus #14 or #59 up the Ramblas. The Metro also takes you to other points in town, including some of the Modernista architecture sights in the Eixample.*

Barri Gòtic Walk

From Plaça de Catalunya to the Cathedral

Barcelona's Barri Gòtic, or Gothic Quarter, is a bustling world of shops, bars, and nightlife packed into narrow, winding lanes and undiscovered courtyards. This is Barcelona's birthplace—where the ancient Romans built a city, where medieval Christians built their cathedral, and where Barcelonans lived within a ring of protective walls until the 1850s, when the city expanded.

Today, this area—nicknamed simply "El Gòtic"—is Barcelona's most historic neighborhood. Concentrate on the area around the cathedral (since the section near the port is somewhat dull and seedy). The Barri Gòtic is a tangled-yet-inviting grab bag of grand squares, schoolyards, Art Nouveau storefronts, musty junk shops, classy antique shops (on Carrer de la Palla), street musicians strumming Catalan folk songs, and balconies with domestic jungles behind wrought-iron bars. Go on a cultural scavenger hunt. Write a poem. Take artsy pictures. This self-guided walk gives you a structure, covering the major sights and offering a historical overview before you get lost.

• *Start on Barcelona's grand, main square, Plaça de Catalunya (described on page 173). From the southeast corner (near El Corte Inglés), head down the broad pedestrian boulevard called...*

❶ Avinguda Portal de l'Angel

For much of Barcelona's history, this was one of the main boulevards leading into town. A medieval wall enclosed the city, and there was an entrance here—the "Gate of the Angel"—that gave the street its name. An angel statue atop the gate kept the city safe from plagues and bid voyagers safe journey as they left the security of the city. Imagine the fascinating scene here at the Gate of the Angel, where Barcelona stopped and the wilds began.

Today's street is pretty globalized and sanitized, full of international chain stores. Pause at Carrer de Santa Anna to admire the Art Nouveau awning at (another) El Corte Inglés store.

• *A half-block detour to the right on Carrer de Santa Anna (at #32) leads to a pleasant, flower-fragrant courtyard with the...*

❷ Church of Santa Anna

This 12th-century gem was an *extra muro* church (outside the Roman walls), with its marker cross still standing. As part of a convent, the church has a fine cloister, an arcaded walkway around a leafy courtyard (viewable through the gate to the left of the church). Climb the modern stairs for views of the bell tower.

If the church is open, you'll see a bare Romanesque interior and Greek-cross floor plan, topped with an octagonal wooden roof. The recumbent-knight tomb is of Miguel de Boera, renowned admiral of Charles V. The door at the far end of the nave leads to the cloister (€2 donation requested, church hours vary but usually daily 11:00-19:00).

• *Backtrack to Avinguda Portal de l'Angel. At Carrer de Montsió (on the left), side-trip half a block to...*

❸ Els Quatre Gats ("The Four Cats")

This restaurant (at #3) is a historic monument, tourist attraction, nightspot, and one of my recommended eateries. It's famous for being the circa-1900 bohemian-artist hangout where Picasso nursed drinks with friends and had his first one-man show (in 1900). The building itself, by prominent architect Josep Puig i

BARCELONA

Barri Gòtic Walk

EL CORTE INGLÉS
DEP'T STORE

B Bus to Airport
(& Taxis)

To Casa Batlló
& La Pedrera

WALK
BEGINS

N

100 Meters

100 Yards

CARRER DE LES MOLES

CARRER D'ESTRUC

C. FONTANELLA

CARRER COMTAL

AVINGUDA DEL PORTAL DE L'ANGEL

SANTA
ANNA

❶

❷

ELS
QUATRE
GATS

❸

CARRER DE MONTSIÓ

DURAN I BAS

BARRI

CARRER DE SANTA ANNA

CARRER DE LA CANUDA

❹

ATM

C. DELS

REIAL
CERCLE
ARTISTIC
MUSEUM

CARRER CUCURULLA

Plaça de la
Vila de Madrid

ROMAN
NECROPOLIS

CARRER DEL DUC

GÒTIC

CARRER D'EN BOT

LAS
RAMBLAS

BETLEM
CHURCH

CARRER DE LA PORTAFERRISSA

CARRER DEL PI

CARRER DE LA PALLA

CULTURAL INFO
PALAU DE LA VIRREINA

CARRER D'EN ROCA

CARRER
D'EN

PETRITXOL

Ⓜ Liceu

Plaça
del Pi

Plaça
S. Josep
Oriol

BARCELONA

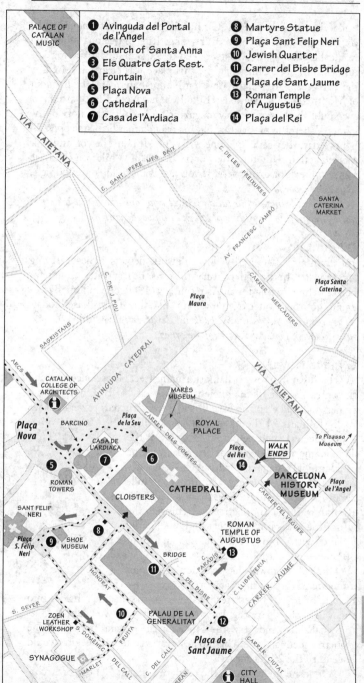

1 Avinguda del Portal de l'Àngel
2 Church of Santa Anna
3 Els Quatre Gats Rest.
4 Fountain
5 Plaça Nova
6 Cathedral
7 Casa de l'Ardiaca
8 Martyrs Statue
9 Plaça Sant Felip Neri
10 Jewish Quarter
11 Carrer del Bisbe Bridge
12 Plaça de Sant Jaume
13 Roman Temple of Augustus
14 Plaça del Rei

PALACE OF CATALAN MUSIC

VIA LAIETANA

C. SANT PERE MÉS BAIX

C. DE LES FREIXURES

SANTA CATERINA MARKET

AV. FRANCESC CAMBÓ

C. DE J. POU

Plaça Maura

CARRER MERCADERS

Plaça Santa Caterina

SAGRISTANS

AVINGUDA CATEDRAL

VIA LAIETANA

ARCS

CATALAN COLLEGE OF ARCHITECTS

MARÈS MUSEUM

Plaça Nova

BARCINO

Plaça de la Seu

CARRER DELS COMTES

ROYAL PALACE

Plaça del Rei

To Picasso Museum

CASA DE L'ARDIACA

5

7

6

14

WALK ENDS

BARCELONA HISTORY MUSEUM

Plaça de l'Àngel

ROMAN TOWERS

CLOISTERS

CATHEDRAL

CARRER DEL VEGUER

SANT FELIP NERI

8

SHOE MUSEUM

ROMAN TEMPLE OF AUGUSTUS

Plaça S. Felip Neri

9

HONORAT

11

BRIDGE

C. PARADIS

13

C. DEL BISBE

C. LLIBRETERIA

CARRER JAUME

S. SEVER

ZOEN LEATHER WORKSHOP

10

S. DOMÈNEC

PALAU DE LA GENERALITAT

12

CARRER CIUTAT

FRUITA

Plaça de Sant Jaume

SYNAGOGUE

MARLET

DEL CALL

C. DEL CALL

FERRAN

CITY HALL

BARCELONA

Cadafalch, represents Neo-Gothic Modernisme. Stepping inside, you feel the turn-of-the-century vibe. Rich Barcelona elites and would-be avant-garde artists looked to Paris, not Madrid, for cultural inspiration. Consequently, this place was clearly inspired by the Paris scene (especially Le Chat Noir cabaret/café, the hangout of Montmartre intellectuals). Like Le Chat Noir, Els Quatre Gats even published its own artsy magazine for a while. The story of the name? When the proprietor told his friends that he'd stay open 24 hours a day, they said, "No one will come. It'll just be you and four cats" (Catalan slang for "a few crazy people"). While you can have a snack, meal, or drink here, if you just want to look around, ask, "Solo mirar, por favor?"

• Return to Avinguda Portal de l'Angel and continue down the street until you run into a building at a fork in the road, with a...

❹ Fountain

The fountain's blue-and-yellow tilework depicts ladies carrying jugs of water. In the 17th century, this was the last watering stop for horses before leaving town. As recently as 1940, one in nine Barcelonans got their water from fountains like this. It's still used today.

• Take the left fork, passing by the Reial Cercle Artistic Museum (temporary exhibits). Enter the large square called...

❺ Plaça Nova

Two bold **Roman towers** flank the main street. These once guarded the entrance gate of the ancient Roman city of Barcino. The big stones that make up the base of the (reconstructed) towers are actually Roman. At the base, find the **modern bronze letters** spelling out "BARCINO." The city's name may have come from Barca, one of Hannibal's generals, who is said to have passed through during Hannibal's roundabout invasion of Italy. At Barcino's peak, the **Roman wall** (see the section stretching to the left of the towers) was 25 feet high and a mile around, with 74 towers. It enclosed an area of 30 acres—population 4,000.

One of the towers has a section of **Roman aqueduct** (a modern reconstruction). These bridges of stone carried fresh water from the distant hillsides into the walled city. Here the water supply split into two channels, one to feed Roman industry, the other for the general populace. The Roman aqueducts would be the best water system Barcelona would have until the 20th century.

Opposite the towers is the modern Catalan College of Architects building (TI inside) with a **frieze designed by Picasso** (1960).

In Picasso's distinctive, simplified style, it shows branch-waving kings and children celebrating a local festival. Picasso spent his formative years (1895-1904, age 14-23) in the Barri Gòtic. He had a studio a block east of here (where the big Caixa Catalunya building stands today). He drank with fellow bohemians at Els Quatre Gats (which we just passed) and frequented brothels a few blocks south of here on Carrer d'Avinyo ("Avignon"), which inspired his seminal Cubist painting *Les Demoiselles d'Avignon*. Picasso's Barri Gòtic was a hotbed of trend-setting art, propelling Picasso forward just before he moved to Paris and remade modern art.

• *Now head to the left and take in the mighty facade of the...*

❻ Cathedral of Barcelona (Catedral de Barcelona)

This location has been the center of Christian worship since the fourth century, and this particular building dates (mainly) from the 14th century. The facade is a virtual catalog of Gothic motifs: a pointed arch over the entrance, robed statues, tracery in windows, gargoyles, and bell towers with winged angels. The style is French Flamboyant (meaning "flame-like"), and the roofline sports the prickly spires meant to give the impression of a church flickering with spiritual fires. The facade is typically Gothic...but not medieval. It's a Neo-Gothic work from the 19th century. The area in front of the cathedral is where Barcelonans dance the *sardana* (see page 192). Standing in front of the Barcelona cathedral, if you look left, you can see the colorful swooping roof of the Santa Caterina Market (described on page 196).

The cathedral's interior—with its vast size, peaceful cloister, and many ornate chapels—is worth a visit. For specifics, see the listing on page 190.

• *The Frederic Marès Museum (see page 194 for details) is just to the left of the cathedral. But for now, return to the Roman towers. Pass between the towers up Carrer del Bisbe, and take an immediate left, up the ramp to the entrance of the...*

❼ Casa de l'Ardiaca (Archivo)

It's free to enter this mansion, which was once the archdeacon's house and today functions as the city archives. The elaborately carved doorway is Renaissance. To the right of the doorway is a carved mail slot by 19th-century Modernist architect Lluís Domènech i Montaner. Enter through a small courtyard with a fountain. Notice how the century-old palm tree seems to be held captive by urban man. Next, step inside the lobby of the city archives, where there are often free temporary exhibits. At the left end of the lobby, step through the archway and look down into the stairwell—this is the back side of the ancient Roman wall. Back in the courtyard, head up to the balcony for closer views of the cathedral steeple and gargoyles.

• *Return to Carrer del Bisbe and turn left. After a few steps you reach a small square with a bronze statue ensemble.*

❽ Martyrs Statue

Five Barcelona patriots calmly receive their last rites before being garroted (strangled) for resisting Napoleon's 1809 invasion of Spain. The plaque marking their mortal remains says these martyrs to independence gave their lives *"por Dios, por la Patria, y por el Rey"*—for God, country, and king.

The plaza offers interesting views of the cathedral's towers. The doorway here is the (not-always-open) "back door" entrance to the cathedral (at the cloister), letting you avoid the long lines at the cathedral's main entrance.

• *Exit the square down tiny Carrer de Montjuïc del Bisbe. This leads to the cute...*

❾ Plaça Sant Felip Neri

This shady square serves as the playground of an elementary school and is often bursting with youthful energy. The Church of Sant Felip Neri, which Gaudí attended, is still pocked with bomb damage from the Civil War. As a stronghold of democratic, anti-Franco forces, Barcelona saw a lot of fighting. The shrapnel that damaged this church was meant for the nearby Catalan government building (Palau de la Generalitat, which we'll see later on this walk).

The buildings here were paid for by the guilds that powered the local economy. On the corner where you entered the square is the former home of the shoemakers' guild; today it's the fun little **Shoe Museum** (€2.50, Tue-Sun 11:00-14:00, closed Mon).

• *Exit the square down Carrer de Sant Felip Neri. At the T-intersection, you have a choice:*

You can turn left, returning to the square with the Martyrs Statue, then turn right, walking along Carrer del Bisbe toward its little overpass bridge (described later).

Or if you're curious about the Jewish chapter of Barcelona's story, turn right at the T-intersection onto Carrer de Sant Sever, then immediately left on Carrer de Sant Domènec del Call (look for the blue El Call sign). You've entered the...

❿ Jewish Quarter (El Call)

In Catalan, a Jewish quarter goes by the name El Call—literally "narrow passage," for the tight lanes where medieval Jews were forced to live, under the watchful eye of the nearby cathedral. At its peak, some 4,000 Jews were crammed into just a few alleys.

Walk down Carrer de Sant Domènec del Call. You'll pass (on the right) the **Zoen leather workshop and showroom** (at #15), where everything is made on the spot, followed by a charming square. At the next lane (Carrer de Marlet), turn right. On the right-hand side is the low-profile entrance to what (most likely) was Barcelona's **main synagogue** during the Middle Ages (€2.50 requested donation). The structure dates from the third century, but it was destroyed during a brutal pogrom in 1391. The city's remaining Jews were expelled in 1492, and artifacts of their culture—including this synagogue—were forgotten for centuries. In the 1980s, a historian tracked down the synagogue using old tax-collector records. Another clue that this was the main synagogue: In accordance with Jewish traditions, it stubbornly faces east (toward Jerusalem), putting it at an angle that's at odds with surrounding structures. The sparse interior includes access to two small subterranean rooms with Roman walls topped by a medieval Catalan vault. Look through the glass floor to see dyeing vats used for a later shop on this site (run by former Jews who had forcibly been converted to Christianity).

• *From the synagogue, start back the way you came but continue straight ahead, onto Carrer de la Fruita. At the T-intersection, turn left, then right, to find your way back to the Martyrs Statue. From here, turn right down Carrer del Bisbe to the...*

⓫ Carrer del Bisbe Bridge

This Bridge-of-Sighs-like structure connects the Catalan government building on the right with the Catalan president's residence (ceremonial, not actual). Though the bridge looks medieval, it was constructed in the 1920s by Joan Rubió, who also did the carved ornamentation on the buildings.

It's a photographer's dream. Check out the jutting angels on the bridge, the basket-carrying maidens on the president's house, the gargoyle-like faces on the government building. Zoom in even closer. Find monsters, skulls, goddesses, old men with beards, climbing vines, and coats of arms—a Gothic museum in stone.

• *Continue along Carrer del Bisbe to...*

⓬ Plaça de Sant Jaume

Once the Roman forum, the stately Plaça de Sant Jaume (JOW-mah) has been the seat of city government for 2,000 years. Today the two top governmental buildings in Catalunya face each other.

For more than six centuries, **Palau de la Generalitat** has housed the autonomous government of Catalunya. It always flies the Catalan flag (red and yellow stripes) next to the obligatory Spanish one. Above the doorway is Catalunya's patron saint—St. Jordi (George), slaying the dragon. From these balconies, the nation's leaders (and soccer heroes) greet the people on momentous days. The square is often the site of demonstrations, from a single aggrieved citizen with a megaphone to thousands of riotous protesters.

The **Barcelona City Hall** (Casa de la Ciutat) sports a statue of the king "Jaume el Conqueridor"—not to be confused with Sant Jaume, the plaza's namesake (free, open Sun 10:00-13:30). King Jaume I (1208-1276, also called "the Just") is credited with freeing Barcelona from French control, granting self-government, and setting it on a course to become a major city. He was the driving force behind construction of the Royal Palace (which we'll see shortly).

Locals treasure the independence these two government buildings represent. In the 20th century, Barcelona opposed the dictator Francisco Franco (who ruled from 1939 to 1975), and Franco retaliated. He abolished the regional government and (effectively) outlawed the Catalan language and customs. Two years after Franco's death, joyous citizens packed this square to celebrate the return of self-rule.

Look left and right down the main streets branching off the square. Carrer de Ferran (which leads to the Ramblas) is classic Barcelona—lined with ironwork streetlamps and balconies draped with plants.

In ancient Roman days, Plaça de Sant Jaume was the town's forum, or central square, located at the intersection of the two main streets—the *decumanus* (Carrer del Bisbe) and the *cardus* (Carrer de la Llibreteria). The forum's biggest building was a massive temple of Augustus, which we'll see next.

• *Facing the Generalitat, exit the square to the right, heading uphill on tiny Carrer del Paradís. Follow this street as it turns right. When it swings left, pause at #10, the entrance to the...*

⑨ Roman Temple of Augustus (Temple Roma d'August)

You're standing at the summit of Mont Tàber. A plaque on the wall says it all: "Mont Tàber, 16.9 meters"—elevation 55 feet. The Barri Gòtic's highest spot is also marked with a millstone inlaid in the pavement at the doorstep of #10. It was here, atop this lofty summit, that the Romans founded the town of Barcino around 15 B.C. They built a *castrum* (fort) on the hilltop, protecting the harbor.

Step inside for a peek at the imposing

Roman temple. These four huge columns, from the late first century B.C., are as old as Barcelona itself. They were part of the ancient town's biggest structure, a temple dedicated to the Emperor Augustus, worshipped as a god. These Corinthian columns (with deep fluting and topped with leafy capitals) were the back corner of a 120-foot-long temple that extended from here to the Fòrum (free, good English info, Mon 10:00-14:00, Tue-Sat 10:00-19:00, Sun 10:00-20:00).

• *Continue down Carrer del Paridís one block. When you bump into the back end of the cathedral, take a right, and go downhill a block (down Baixada de Santa Clara) until you emerge into a square called...*

⓮ Plaça del Rei

The buildings that enclose this square once housed Spain's kings and queens. The central section (topped by a four-story addition) was the core of the Royal Palace. It has a vast hall on the ground floor that served as the throne room and reception room. From the 13th to the 15th century, the Royal Palace housed Catalunya's counts as well as resident Spanish kings. In 1493, a triumphant Christopher Columbus, accompanied by six New World natives (whom he called "Indians") and several pure-gold statues, entered the Royal Palace. King Ferdinand and Queen Isabel rose to welcome him home and honored him with the title "Admiral of the Oceans."

To the right is the palace's church, the Chapel of St. Agatha. It sits atop the foundations of the Roman wall.

To the left is the Viceroy's Palace (for the ruler's right-hand man), which also served as the archives of the Kingdom of Aragon. After Catalunya became part of Spain in the 15th century, the Royal Palace became a small regional residence, and the Viceroy's Palace became the headquarters of the local Inquisition. Today the Viceroy's Palace is once again home to the archives. Step inside to see an impressive Renaissance courtyard, a staircase with coffered wood ceilings, and a temporary exhibit space. Among the archive's treasures (though it's rarely on display) is the 1491 Santa Fe Capitulations, a contract between Columbus and the monarchs about his upcoming voyage.

Ironically, Columbus and the Kingdom of Aragon played a role in Barcelona's decline as an independent kingdom. When Ferdinand of Aragon married Isabel of Castile, Catalunya got swallowed up in greater Spain. Columbus' discovery of new trade routes made Barcelona's port less important, and soon the royals moved elsewhere.

The Barcelona History Museum's entrance is just around the corner from Plaça del Rei (see listing on page 193). It gives visitors the only peek they'll get of the palace interior (and there's disap-

BARCELONA

pointingly little to see), but more important, provides a fine way to retrace all the history we've seen on this walk—from modern to medieval to the Roman foundations of Barcino.

• Your walk is over. It's easy to get your bearings by backtracking to either Plaça de Sant Jaume or the cathedral. The Jaume I Metro stop is two blocks away (leave the square on Carrer del Veguer and turn left). Or simply wander and enjoy Barcelona at its Gothic best.

Sights in Barcelona

While Barcelona's attractions could easily fill a longer stopover, for a one-day cruiser visit, I've listed just the sights that are most important and centrally located. Within the Old City, choose from sights in these neighborhoods: the Barri Gòtic (Cathedral of Barcelona), El Born (Picasso Museum), and the harborfront (Maritime Museum). If you're interested in an overview of Barcelona's famous architecture, skip ahead to "Modernista Sights" (page 199).

In the Barri Gòtic

For an interesting route from Plaça de Catalunya to the cathedral neighborhood, see my self-guided walk of the Barri Gòtic (described earlier). And if you're in town on a weekend, don't miss the sardana dances (see sidebar).

▲Cathedral of Barcelona

Although Barcelona's most important church doesn't rank among Europe's finest cathedrals (frankly, it barely cracks the top 20), it's important, easy to visit, and—at certain times of the day—free.

Cost and Hours: Generally open to visitors Mon-Fri 8:00-19:30, Sat-Sun 8:00-20:00. Free to enter Mon-Sat before 12:45, Sun before 13:45, and daily after 17:15, but you must pay to enter the cathedral's three minor sights (museum-€2, terrace-€3, choir-€2.50). The church is officially "closed" for a few hours each afternoon (Mon-Sat 13:00-17:00, Sun 14:00-17:00), but you can still get in by paying for the interior sights. These sights have shorter hours than the church itself: museum daily 10:00-19:00; terrace Mon-Sat 9:00-18:00, closed Sun; choir Mon-Sat 9:00-19:00, closes in the afternoon on Sun. Tel. 933-151-554, www.catedralbcn.org.

Dress Code: The dress code is strictly enforced—no tank tops, shorts, or skirts above the knee.

Getting There: The huge, can't-miss-it cathedral is in the center of the Barri Gòtic, on Plaça de la Seu, Metro: Jaume I.

Getting In: The main, front door is open most of the time. While it can be crowded, the line generally moves fast. Sometimes you can also enter directly into the cloister around back (through door facing the Martyrs Statue on the small square along Carrer del Bisbe).

WCs: A tiny, semi-private WC is in the center of the cloister.

Visiting the Church: This has been Barcelona's holiest spot for 2,000 years. The Romans built their Temple of Jupiter here. In A.D. 343, the pagan temple was replaced with a Christian cathedral. That building was supplanted by a Romanesque-style church (11th century). The current Gothic structure was built in the 14th century (1298-1450), during the medieval glory days of the Catalan nation. The facade was humble, so in the 19th century the proud local bourgeoisie redid it in a more ornate, Neo-Gothic style. Construction was capped in 1913 with the central spire, 230 feet tall.

Inside, the nave is ringed with 28 **side chapels,** financed by local guilds eager to display their wealth—if not to ingratiate themselves to God. Besides being worship spaces, these serve as interior buttresses supporting the roof (which is why the exterior walls are smooth, without the normal Gothic buttresses outside). Barcelona—the city of 32 official public holidays—honors many of the homegrown saints found in these chapels.

In the middle of the nave, the 15th-century **choir** *(coro)* features ornately carved stalls. During the standing parts of the Mass, the chairs were folded up, but VIPs still had those little wooden ledges to lean on. Each was creatively carved and—since you couldn't sit on sacred things—the artists were free to enjoy some secular and naughty fun here.

Look behind the **high altar** (beneath the crucifix) to find the archbishop's chair, or cathedra. As a cathedral, this church is the archbishop's seat—hence its Catalan nickname of *La Seu.* To the left of the altar are the organ and the elevator up to the **terrace.**

The steps beneath the altar lead to the **crypt,** featuring the marble-and-alabaster sarcophagus (1327-1339) with the remains of St. Eulàlia. The cathedral is dedicated to this saint.

Exit out the right transept and into the circa-1450 **cloister**—the arcaded walkway surrounding a lush courtyard. Ahhhh. It's a tropical atmosphere of palm, orange, and magnolia trees; a fish pond; trickling fountains; and squawking geese. The nearby fountain has a tiny statue of St. Jordi slaying the dragon. During the Corpus Christi festival (June), kids come here to watch a hollow egg dance atop the fountain's spray. As you wander the cloister (clockwise), check out the coats of arms as well as the tombs in the pavement. These were rich merchants who paid good money to be buried as close to the altar as possible. Notice the symbols of their trades: scissors, shoes, bakers, and so on. The resident geese have

Circle Dances in Squares
and Castles in the Air

A memorable Barcelona experience is watching (or participating in) the patriotic *sardana* dances (worth ▲). For some it's a highly symbolic, politically charged action representing Catalan unity—but for most it's just a fun chance to kick up their heels. Participants gather in circles after putting their things in the center—symbolic of community and sharing (and the ever-present risk of theft). All are welcome, even tourists cursed with two left feet. The dances are held in the square in front of the cathedral every Sunday at 12:00 and usually also on Saturdays at 18:00 (none in Aug); the event lasts between one and two hours.

Holding hands, dancers raise their arms—slow-motion, *Zorba the Greek*–style—as they hop and sway gracefully to the music. The band *(cobla)* consists of a long flute, tenor and soprano oboes, strange-looking brass instruments, and a tiny bongo-like drum *(tambori)*. The rest of Spain mocks this lazy circle dance, but considering what it takes for a culture to survive within another culture's country, it is a stirring display of local pride and patriotism. During 36 years of Franco dictatorship, the *sardana* was forbidden.

Another Catalan tradition is the *castell*, a tower erected solely of people. *Castells* pop up on special occasions, such as the Festes de Gràcia in August and the Mercè festival in September. Towers can be up to 10 humans high. Imagine balancing 50 or 60 feet in the air, with nothing but a pile of flesh and bone between you and the ground. The base is formed by burly supports called *baixos*; above them are the *manilles* ("handles"), which help haul up the people to the top. The *castell* is capped with a human steeple—usually a child—who extends four fingers into the air, representing the four red stripes of the Catalan flag. A scrum of spotters (called *pinyas*) cluster around the base in case anyone falls. *Castelleres* are judged both on how quickly they erect their human towers and how fast they can take them down. You may also see people forming these towers in front of the cathedral on summer Saturdays around 19:00 (confirm locally before showing up).

One thing that these two traditions have in common is their communal nature. Perhaps it's no coincidence, as Catalunya is known for its community spirit, team building, and socialistic bent.

been here for at least 500 years. There are always 13, in memory of Eulàlia's 13 years and 13 torments.

The little **museum,** at the far end of the cloister, has the six-foot-tall 14th-century Great Monstrance, a ceremonial display case for the communion wafer that's paraded through the streets during the Corpus Christi festival. The next room, the Sala Capitular, has several altarpieces, including a *pietá* (a.k.a. *Desplà*) by Bartolomé Bermejo (1490).

▲Barcelona History Museum (Museu d'Història de Barcelona: Plaça del Rei)

At this main branch of the city history museum (MUHBA for short), you can walk through the history of Barcelona, with a focus on the city's Roman roots.

Cost and Hours: €7; ticket includes English audioguide and other MUHBA branches; free all day first Sun of month and other Sun from 15:00—but no audioguide during free times; open Tue-Sat 10:00-19:00, Sun 10:00-20:00, closed Mon; last entry 30 minutes before closing, Plaça del Rei, enter on Vageur street, Metro: Jaume I, tel. 932-562-122.

Visiting the Museum: Though the museum is housed in part of the former Royal Palace complex, you'll see only a bit of that grand space. Instead, the focus is on the exhibits in the cellar. While posted information is only in Catalan and Spanish, you'll find abundant English handouts, and the included English audioguide provides informative, if dry, descriptions of the exhibits.

Start by watching the nine-minute introductory video in the small theater (at the end of the first floor); it plays alternately in Catalan, Spanish, and English, but it's worth viewing in any language. Then take an elevator down 65 feet (and 2,000 years—see the date spin back while you descend) to stroll the streets of Roman Barcino—founded by Emperor Augustus around 10 B.C.

The history is so strong here, you can smell it. This was a working-class part of town. The archaeological route leads you through areas used for laundering clothes and dyeing garments, the remains of a factory that salted fish and produced garum (a fish-derived sauce used extensively in ancient Roman cooking), and winemaking facilities.

Next, you'll wander through bits of a seventh-century early Christian church and an exhibit in the 11th-century count's palace that shows you Barcelona through its glory days in the Middle Ages.

BARCELONA

Finally, head upstairs (or ride the elevator to floor 0) to see a model of the city from the early 16th century. From here, you can also enter **Tinell Hall** (part of the Royal Palace), with its long, graceful, rounded vaults. Nearby, step into the 14th-century **Chapel of St. Agatha,** if it's hosting a temporary exhibit.

Frederic Marès Museum (Museu Frederic Marès)

This museum, with the eclectic collection of local sculptor and packrat Frederic Marès (1893-1991), sprawls around a peaceful courtyard through several old Barri Gòtic buildings. The biggest part of the collection, on the ground and first floors, consists of sculpture—from ancient works to beautiful, evocative Gothic pieces to items from the early 20th century. Even more interesting is the extensive "Collector's Cabinet," consisting of items Marès found representative of everyday life in the 19th century. Lovingly displayed on the second and third floors, the collection contains rooms upon rooms of scissors, keys, irons, fans, nutcrackers, stamps, pipes, snuff boxes, opera glasses, pocket watches, bicycles, toy soldiers, dolls, and other bric-a-brac. And in Marès' study are several sculptures by the artist himself. The tranquil courtyard café offers a pleasant break, even when the museum is closed (café open in summer only, until 22:00).

Cost and Hours: €4.20, free Sun from 15:00, 1.5-hour audioguide-€1; open Tue-Sat 10:00-19:00, Sun 11:00-20:00, closed Mon; Plaça de Sant Iu 5-6, Metro: Jaume I, tel. 932-563-500, www.museumares.bcn.cat.

In El Born

The Old City's El Born neighborhood (also known as "La Ribera") is home to several great sights, including the Picasso Museum. But even without those, the neighborhood is a joy to explore. El Born's narrow lanes are crammed with artsy boutiques, inviting cafés and restaurants, funky one-off shops, rollicking nightlife, and a higher ratio of locals to tourists than in most other city-center zones.

▲▲▲Picasso Museum (Museu Picasso)

Pablo Picasso may have made his career in Paris, but the years he spent in Barcelona—from ages 14 through 23—were among the most formative of his life. It was here that young Pablo mastered the realistic painting style of his artistic forebears—and it was also here that he first felt the freedom that allowed him to leave that all behind and give in to his creative, experimental urges. When he left Barcelona, Picasso headed for Paris...and revolutionized art forever.

The pieces in this excellent museum capture that priceless moment just before this bold young thinker changed the world. While you won't find Picasso's famous, later Cubist works here, you will enjoy a representative sweep of his early years, from art-school prodigy to the gloomy hues of his Blue Period to the revitalized cheer of his Rose Period. You'll also see works from his twilight years, including dozens of wild improvisations inspired by Diego Velázquez's seminal *Las Meninas,* as well as a roomful of works that reflect the childlike exuberance of an old man playing like a young kid on the French Riviera. It's undoubtedly the top collection of Picassos here in his native country and the best anywhere of his early years.

Cost and Hours: €14, free all day first Sun of month and other Sun from 15:00; open Tue-Sun 9:00-19:00, Thu until 21:30, closed Mon, last entry 30 minutes before closing, Carrer de Montcada 15-23, ticket office at #21, Metro: Jaume I, tel. 932-563-000, www.museupicasso.bcn.cat. Buy a ticket online to skip the line at the admission desk or use an Articket BCN pass (see page 163).

 For a self-guided tour, see page 206.

▲▲Palace of Catalan Music (Palau de la Música Catalana)
This concert hall, built in just three years and finished in 1908, features an unexceptional exterior but boasts my favorite Modernista interior in town (by Lluís Domènech i Montaner). Its inviting arches lead you into the 2,138-seat hall (accessible only with a tour). A kaleidoscopic skylight features a choir singing around the sun, while playful carvings and mosaics celebrate music and Catalan culture. If you're interested in Modernisme, taking this tour (which starts with a relaxing 12-minute video) is one of the best experiences in town—and helps balance the hard-to-avoid overfocus on Gaudí as "Mr. Modernisme."

Cost and Hours: €17, 50-minute tours in English run daily every hour 10:00-15:00, tour times may change based on performance schedule, about 6 blocks northeast of cathedral, Carrer Palau de la Música 4-6, Metro: Urquinaona, tel. 902-442-882, www.palaumusica.cat.

Advance Tour Reservations Required: You must buy your ticket in advance to get a spot on an English guided tour (tickets available up to 4 months in advance—ideally buy yours at least 2 days before, though they're sometimes available the same day or day before—especially Oct-March). You can buy the ticket in person at the concert hall box office (less than a 10-minute walk from the cathedral or Picasso Museum, open daily 9:30-15:30); by phone with your credit card (no extra charge, tel. 902-475-485); or online at the concert hall website (€1 fee, www.palaumusica.cat).

Concerts: The other way to see the hall is by attending a concert (300 per year, €22-49 tickets, see website for details, box office tel. 902-442-882).

▲Santa Caterina Market

This eye-catching market hall was built on the ruins of an old monastery, then renovated in 2006 with a wildly colorful, swooping, Gaudí-inspired roof and shell built around its original white walls (a good exhibition at the far corner provides a view of the foundations and English explanations). The much-delayed construction took so long that locals began calling the site the "Hole of Shame." Come for the outlandish architecture, but stay for a chance to shop for a picnic without the tourist logjam of La Boqueria market on the Ramblas.

Cost and Hours: Free, Mon 7:30-14:00, Tue-Wed and Sat 7:30-15:30, Thu-Fri 7:30-20:30, closed Sun, Avinguda de Francesc Cambó 16, www.mercatsantacaterina.cat.

▲Church of Santa Maria del Mar

This so-called "Cathedral of the Sea" was built entirely with local funds and labor, in the heart of the wealthy merchant El Born quar-

ter. Proudly independent, the church features a purely Catalan Gothic interior that was forcibly uncluttered of its Baroque decor by civil war belligerents.

Cost and Hours: Free admission daily 9:00-13:30 & 16:30-20:00, also open 13:30-16:30 with €3 ticket; €5 guided rooftop tours in summer, English tours on the hour Mon-Fri 13:00-19:00, Sat-Sun at 11:00 and 12:00; Plaça Santa Maria, Metro: Jaume I, tel. 933-435-633, www.stamariadelmar.org.

Visiting the Church: Before entering, look at the figures on the front door. These represent the *bastaixos* who hauled the stone used to build the church all the way from Montjuïc quarries.

Step inside, to the largely unadorned Gothic space. It used to be more highly decorated with Baroque frills. But during the civil war (1936-1939), the Catholic Church sided with the conservative forces of Franco against the people. In retaliation, the working class took their anger out on this church, burning all of its wood furnishings and decor (carbon still blackens the ceiling).

Today the church remains stripped down—naked in all its Gothic glory. This is where shipwrights and merchants came to worship. The tree-like columns inspired Gaudí (their influence on the columns inside his Sagrada Família church is obvious). Sixteenth-century sailors left models of their ships at the foot of the altar for Mary's protection. Even today a classic old Catalan ship remains at Mary's feet. As within Barcelona's cathedral, here you can see the characteristic Catalan Gothic buttresses flying inward, defining the chapels that ring the nave. Brilliant stained glass—most notably the rose window over the main entry—flood the interior with soft light.

Nearby: Around the right side of the church is a poignant memorial to the "Catalan Alamo" of September 11, 1714, when the Spanish crown besieged and conquered Barcelona, slaughtering Catalan insurgents and kicking off more than two centuries of cultural suppression.

Passeig del Born

This long boulevard is the neighborhood center. Formerly a jousting square (as its Roman circus-esque shape indicates), it got its name, "El Born," from an old Catalan word for "tournament" (the name was eventually given to the entire neighborhood). These days, Passeig del Born is a popular springboard for exploring tapas bars, fun restaurants, and nightspots in the narrow streets all around. Wandering around here at night, you'll find piles of inviting and intriguing little restaurants (I've listed my favorites later, under "Eating in Barcelona"). At the far end of Passeig del Born is the vast-but-vacant, steel-frame, 19th-century El Born Market, which served as the city's main produce market hall until 1971, when it was relocated to the suburbs. Plans are under way to convert the market hall into a cultural center and museum.

You'll also find great shopping near this strip—be sure to venture up **Carrer dels Flassaders** (funky shops, to the left as you face the old market hall) and down **Carrer del Rec** (fashionable boutiques, to the right as you face the market). For more tips, see "Shopping in Barcelona," later.

Chocolate Museum (Museu de la Xocolata)

This museum, only a couple of blocks from the Picasso Museum, is fun for chocolate lovers. Operated by the local confectioners' guild, it tells the story of chocolate from Aztecs to Europeans via the port of Barcelona, where it was first unloaded and processed. But the history lesson is just an excuse to show off a series of remarkably ornate candy sculptures. These works of edible art—which change every year but often include such Spanish themes as Don Quixote or bullfighting—begin as store-window displays for Easter or Christmas. Once the holiday passes, the confectioners bring the sculptures here to be enjoyed.

Cost and Hours: €4.30, Mon-Sat 10:00-19:00 (until 20:00 mid-June-mid-Sept), Sun 10:00-15:00, Carrer del Comerç 36, Metro: Jaume I, tel. 932-687-878, www.museuxocolata.cat.

On the Harborfront
▲Maritime Museum
(Museu Marítim)

Barcelona's medieval shipyard, the best preserved in the entire Mediterranean, is home to an excellent museum at the bottom of the Ramblas. Its permanent collection is closed for renovation (until late 2014), but the museum is hosting a series of worthwhile temporary exhibits during the revamp.

The building's cavernous halls evoke the 14th-century days when Catalunya was a naval and shipbuilding power, cranking out 30 huge galleys each winter. As in the US today, military and commercial ventures mixed and mingled as Catalunya built its trading empire. When the permanent collection reopens, it'll cover the salty history of ships and navigation from the 13th to the 20th century. In the meantime, an impressively huge and richly decorated royal galley remains on display.

Cost and Hours: Museum price depends on exhibits but usually €5, daily 10:00-20:00, last entry 30 minutes before closing, nice café with seating inside or out on the museum courtyard (free to enter), Avinguda de la Drassanes, Metro: Drassanes, tel. 933-429-920, www.mmb.cat.

Nearby: Your ticket also includes entrance to the *Santa Eulàlia,* an early 20th-century schooner docked just a short walk from the Columbus Monument (€1 for entry without museum visit, April-Oct Tue-Fri and Sun 10:00-20:30, Sat 14:00-20:30, closes at 17:30 in Nov-March, closed Mon year-round). On Saturday mornings, the schooner sets sail around the harbor for three hours—reserve well in advance; spots book up weeks in advance (Sat 10:00-13:00, adult-€12, children 6-14-€6, family rates available, tel. 933-429-920, reserves.mmaritim@diba.cat).

Columbus Monument
(Monument a Colóm)

Located where the Ramblas hits the harbor, this 200-foot-tall monument was built for the 1888 world's fair and commemorates Columbus' visit to Barcelona following his first trip to America. A tight four-person elevator takes you to a glassed-in observation area at the top for congested but sweeping views—but the elevator is often closed; ask at any TI before making a special trip here to ride it. There is a small and usually uncrowded TI inside the base of the monument.

Cost and Hours: Monument—free and always open; elevator ride-€4, daily May-Oct 8:30-20:30, Nov-April 8:00-20:00.

▲Barcelona's Beach

Starting from the near-in Barceloneta neighborhood, Barcelona's beach extends for miles along the sea. The scene is a bit like a resort island—complete with lounge chairs, volleyball, showers, WCs, bike paths, Wi-Fi, and inviting beach bars called *chiringuitos*.

Getting There: The Barceloneta Metro stop will leave you blocks from the sand. To get to the nearest stretch of beach without a hike, take bus #59 from the bottom of the Ramblas (near the Columbus Monument).

Modernista Sights

For many visitors, Modernista architecture is Barcelona's main draw. And one name tops them all: Antoni Gaudí (1852-1926). Barcelona is an architectural scrapbook of Gaudí's galloping gables and organic curves. A devoted Catalan and Catholic, he immersed himself in each project, often living on-site. At various times, he called Park Güell, La Pedrera, and the Sagrada Família home. For more on Gaudí and some of his contemporaries, see the sidebar on page 201.

I've covered the main Gaudí attractions in the order you'd reach them from the harbor to the outskirts—starting along the Ramblas and in the Eixample before heading out to Sagrada Família and Park Güell (farther afield, but worth the trip).

Note that Lluís Domènech i Montaner's **Palace of Catalan Music** is described on page 195. For information on even more Modernista sights, you can visit the Plaça de Catalunya TI, where you'll find a special desk set aside just for Modernisme seekers (see page 162).

In the Old City, just off the Ramblas
▲Palau Güell

Just as the Picasso Museum reveals a young genius on the verge of a breakthrough, this early Gaudí building (completed in 1890) shows the architect taking his first tentative steps toward what would become his trademark curvy style. Dark and masculine, with its castle-like rooms, Palau Güell (Catalans pronounce it "gway") was custom-built to house the Güell clan and gives an insight into Gaudí's artistic genius. The included 24-stop audioguide provides all the details. Despite the eye-catching roof (visible from the street

BARCELONA

Modernista Sights

Guinardo Park

Park Güell
SIDE ENTRANCE
#24 & #92
(B)
GAUDÍ HOUSE MUSEUM
TERRACE ◆
MAIN ENTRANCE (B)
#116

AVE. DE L'ESTATUT DE CATALUNYA

HOSPITAL DE LA SANTA CREU I SANT PAU

Tourist Bus (B)

C. DE DALT

GUINARDÓ

TRAVESSERA

C. DEL TORRENT DE L'OLLA

C. DE L'ESCORIAL

DE L'OR

(B) #92

CARRER DE CARTAGENA

Plaça Lesseps
(B) M
#116   Lesseps

Joanic
M
#116

TRAVESSERA DE GRÀCIA

SAGRADA FAMÍLIA
◆ M Sagrada Família
(B)
#19, #50

CASA VICENS ◆
M
Fontana

GRÀCIA

HOTEL CASA FUSTER
◆

C. DE CÒRSEGA

CASA DE LES PUNXES
◆

AV. DIAGONAL

PALAU BARÓ DE QUADRAS
◆

C. DE VALÈNCIA

Diagonal ◆ **LA PEDRERA**
M

PSG. DE

COMPANYS

E I X A M P L E

CARRER DE MUNTANER

PSG. DE GRÀCIA

C. D'ARAGÓ

Passeig de Gràcia

CASA CALVET
◆

EL BORN

FUNDACIÓ TÀPIES
◆

Urquinaona
M

PALACE OF CATALAN MUSIC

CASA BATLLÓ & BLOCK OF DISCORD
◆

#24
(B)

VIA LAIETANA

CARRER

DEL

Catalunya M
Plaça de Catalunya
ℹ

PICASSO MUSEUM
■

BARRI GÒTIC
M Jaume I

GRAN VIA DE LES CORTS CATALANES

COMTE D'URGELL

OLD

M Liceu

LAS RAMBLAS

CITY

CARRER D'ENTENÇA

EL RAVAL

PALAU GÜELL
◆

Drassanes

Miró Park

M

COLUMBUS MONUMENT
■

Plaça d'Espanya
M Espanya

AV. DEL PARAL·LEL

FUNICULAR

CABLE CAR

MAGIC FOUNTAINS

CATALAN ART MUSEUM

FUNDACIÓ JOAN MIRÓ

Port Vell

MONTJUÏC

SPANISH VILLAGE

AV. DE L'ESTADI

OLYMPIC STADIUM

CABLE CAR

To Montjuïc Castle

To Moll Adossat (Cruise Ship Terminal)

Modernisme and Barcelona

Modernisme is Barcelona's unique contribution to the Europe-wide Art Nouveau movement. Meaning "a taste for what is modern"—things like streetcars, electric lights, and big-wheeled bicycles—this free-flowing organic style lasted from 1888 to 1906.

Antoni Gaudí (1852-1926), Barcelona's most famous Modernisme artist, was descended from four generations of metalworkers—a lineage of which he was quite proud. He in-

corporated ironwork into his architecture and came up with novel approaches to architectural structure and space. Gaudí's work strongly influenced his younger Catalan contemporary, Salvador Dalí. Notice the similarities: While Dalí was creating unlikely and shocking juxtapositions of photorealistic images, Gaudí did the same in architecture—using the spine of a reptile for a bannister or a turtle shell design on windows. Entire trips (and lives) are dedicated to seeing the works of Gaudí, but on a brief visit in Barcelona, the ones most worth considering are his great unfinished church, Sagrada Família; several mansions in the town center, including La Pedrera, Casa Batlló, and Palau Güell; and Park Güell, his ambitious and never-completed housing development (all described in this chapter).

While Gaudí gets 90 percent of the tourists' attention, two other great Modernista architects were just as important: Lluís Domènech i Montaner (1850-1923) and Josep Puig i Cadafalch (1867-1956). Gaudí was a remarkable innovator, but these two were perhaps more purely representative of the Modernista style. You'll see their work on the Block of Discord (see page 202).

if you crane your neck), I'd skip Palau Güell if you plan to see the more interesting La Pedrera (described later).

Cost and Hours: €12, includes audioguide, free first Sun of the month, open April-Sept Tue-Sun 10:00-20:00, Oct-March Tue-Sun 10:00-17:30, closed Mon year-round, last entry one hour before closing, a half-block off the Ramblas at Carrer Nou de la Rambla 3-5, Metro: Liceu or Drassanes, tel. 933-173-974, www.palauguell.cat.

Buying Tickets: As with any Gaudí sight, you may encounter lines. Since it's not possible to reserve tickets in advance, you'll have to buy them at the ticket window to the left of the entryway, then line up to the right. Each ticket has an entry time, so at busy times you may have to return later, even after buying your ticket.

In the Eixample

The Eixample ("Expansion") was built when a bulging Barcelona burst out of its medieval walls in the mid-19th century. With wide sidewalks, hardy shade trees, chic shops, and plenty of Art Nouveau fun, this carefully planned "new town," just north of the Old City, has a rigid grid plan cropped back at the corners to create space and lightness at each intersection. Conveniently, all of this new construction provided a generation of Modernista architects with a blank canvas for creating boldly experimental designs.

▲Block of Discord

Three colorful Modernista facades compete for your attention along a single block: Casa Lleó Morera, Casa Amatller, and Casa Batlló (the only one you can get inside). All were built by well-known architects at the end of the 19th century. Because the mansions look as though they are trying to outdo each other in creative twists, locals nicknamed the noisy block the "Block of Discord." You'll find the houses on Passeig de Gràcia (at the Metro stop of the same name), between Carrer del Consell de Cent and Carrer d'Aragó—three blocks above Plaça de Catalunya and four blocks below La Pedrera.

Casa Lleó Morera (#35): This paella-like mix of styles is the work of the architect Lluís Domènech i Montaner, who also designed the Palace of Catalan Music (you'll notice similarities). The lower floors have classical columns and a Greek-temple-like bay window. Farther up are Gothic balconies of rosettes and tracery, while the upper part has faux Moorish stucco work. The whole thing is ornamented with fantastic griffins, angels, and fish. Flanking the third-story windows are figures holding the exciting inventions of the day—the camera, lightbulb, and gramophone—designed to demonstrate just how modern the homeowners were in this age of Modern-isme. Unfortunately, the wonderful interior is closed to the public.

Casa Amatller (#41): Josep Puig i Cadafalch custom-designed this house for the Amatller family. The facade features a creative mix of three of Spain's historical traditions: Moorish-style pentagram-and-vine designs; Gothic-style tracery, gargoyles, and bay windows; and the step-gable roof from Spain's Habsburg connection to the Low Countries. Notice the many layers of the letter "A": The house itself (with its gable) forms an A, as does the decorative frieze over the bay window on the right side of the facade. Within that frieze, you'll see several more As sprouting from branches (*amatller* means "almond tree"). The reliefs above the smaller windows show off the hobbies of the Amatller clan: Find the cherubs holding the early box camera, the open book, and the amphora jug (which the family collected). Look through the second-floor bay window to see the corkscrew column. If you want, you can pop inside for a closer look at the elaborate entrance hall.

Casa Batlló (#43): The most famous facade on the block, rated ▲, is the green-blue, ceramic-speckled Casa Batlló, designed by

Antoni Gaudí, with an interior that's open to the public. It has tibia-like pillars and skull-like balconies, inspired by the time-tested natural forms that Gaudí knew made the best structural supports. The tiled roof has a soft-ice-cream-cone turret topped with a cross. The humpback roofline suggests a cresting dragon's back. It's thought that Gaudí based the work on the popular legend of St. Jordi (George) slaying the dragon. But some see instead a Mardi Gras theme, with mask-like balconies, a colorful confetti-like facade, and the ridge of a harlequin's hat up top. The inscrutable Gaudí preferred to leave his designs open to interpretation.

While the highlight is the roof, the interior of this Gaudí house is also interesting—and even more over-the-top than La Pedrera's (described next). Paid for with textile industry money, the house features a funky mushroom-shaped fireplace nook on the main floor, a blue-and-white-ceramic-slathered atrium, and an attic (with more parabolic arches). There's barely a straight line in the house. You can also get a close-up look at the dragon-inspired rooftop. Because preservation of the place is privately funded, the entrance fee is steep—but it includes a good (if long-winded) audioguide.

Cost and Hours: €20.35, daily 9:00-20:00, may close early for special events—closings posted in advance at entrance, tel. 932-160-306, www.casabatllo.cat. Purchase a ticket online to avoid lines—which are especially fierce in the morning. Your eticket isn't a timed reservation (it's good any time), but it will let you skip to the front of the queue.

▲▲La Pedrera (Casa Milà)

One of Gaudí's trademark works, this house—built between 1906 and 1912—is an icon of Modernisme. The wealthy industrialist Pere Milà i Camps commissioned it, and while some still call it "Casa

Milà," most take one look at its jagged, rocky facade and opt for the more colorful nickname, La Pedrera—"The Quarry." While it's fun to ogle from the outside, it's also worth going inside, as it features the city's purest Gaudí interior. And buying a ticket also gets you access to the delightful rooftop, with its forest of colorfully tiled chimneys (note that the roof may close when it rains).

Cost and Hours: €16.50, good audioguide-€4, daily March-Oct 9:00-20:00, Nov-Feb 9:00-18:30, last entry 30 minutes before closing, at the corner of Passeig de Gràcia and Provença (visitor entrance at Provença 261-265), Metro: Diagonal, info tel. 902-400-973, www.lapedrera.com.

Crowd-Beating Tips: As lines can be long (up to a 1.5-hour wait to get in), it's best to reserve ahead at www.lapedrera.com (tickets come with an assigned entry time and let you skip the line). If you come without a ticket, the best time to arrive is right when it opens.

Free Entrance to Atrium: For a peek at the interior without paying for a ticket, find the door directly on the corner, which leads to the main atrium. Upstairs on the first floor are temporary exhibits (generally free, open daily 10:00-20:00, may be closed between exhibitions).

Visiting the House: A visit to La Pedrera covers three sections: the apartment, the attic, and the rooftop. Enter and head upstairs to the apartment. If it's near closing time, continue up to see the attic and rooftop first to make sure you have enough time to enjoy Gaudí's works and the views.

The typical bourgeois **apartment** is decorated as it might have been when the building was first occupied by middle-class urbanites (a seven-minute video explains Barcelona society at the time). Notice Gaudí's clever use of the atrium to maximize daylight in all of the apartments.

The **attic** houses a sprawling multimedia exhibit tracing the history of the architect's career with models, photos, and videos of his work. It's all displayed under distinctive parabola-shaped arches. While evocative of Gaudí's style in themselves, the arches are formed this way partly to support the multilevel roof above. This area was also used for ventilation, helping to keep things cool in summer and warm in winter. Tenants had storage spaces and did their laundry up here.

From the attic, a stairway leads to the undulating, jaw-dropping **rooftop,** where 30 chimneys and ventilation towers play volleyball with the clouds.

Back at the **ground level** of La Pedrera, poke into the dreamily painted original entrance courtyard.

▲▲▲Sagrada Família (Holy Family Church)

Antoni Gaudí's grand masterpiece sits unfinished in a residential Eixample neighborhood 1.5 miles north of Plaça de Catalunya. An icon of the city, the Sagrada Família boasts bold, wildly creative, unmistakably organic architecture and decor inside and

out—from its melting-in-the-rain Glory Facade to its skull-like Passion Facade to its rainforest-like interior. Begun under Gaudí's careful watch in 1883, the project saw some setbacks in the mid-20th century, but lately the progress has been remarkable. The city has set a goal of finishing by 2026, the centennial of Gaudí's death. For now, visitors get a close-up view of the dramatic exterior flourishes, the chance to walk through the otherworldly interior, and access to a fine museum detailing the design and engineering behind this one-of-a-kind architectural marvel.

Cost and Hours: Church–€13.50, tower elevators–€4.50 each, €17 combo-ticket also includes Gaudí House Museum at Park Güell (see next listing), daily April-Sept 9:00-20:00, Oct-March 9:00-18:00, last entry 15 minutes before closing, Metro: Sagrada Família, exit toward Plaça de la Sagrada Família, tel. 932-073-031, www.sagradafamilia.cat.

✪ For a self-guided tour, see page 211.

Beyond the Eixample

▲▲Park Güell

Gaudí fans enjoy the artist's magic in this colorful park, located on the outskirts of town. While it takes a bit of effort to get here, Park Güell (Catalans pronounce it "gway") offers a unique look at Gaudí's style in a natural rather than urban context. Designed as an upscale housing development for early-20th-century urbanites, the park is home to some of Barcelona's most famous symbols, including a whimsical staircase guarded by a dragon and a wavy bench, covered with fragments of vivid tile, which encircles a

panoramic view terrace supported by a forest of columns. Much of the park is free, but the part visitors want to see, the Monumental

Zone—with all the iconic Gaudí features—has an entry fee and time-limited admission. Also in the park is the **Gaudí House Museum,** where Gaudí lived for a time. Although he did not design the house, you can see a few examples of his furniture here (the house is within the free portion of the park, but charges admission). Even without its Gaudí connection, Park Güell is simply a fine place to enjoy a break from a busy city, where green space is relatively rare.

Cost and Hours: Monumental Zone—€8 at the gate or €7 online, smart to reserve tickets in advance, daily April-Oct 8:00-21:30, Nov-March 8:30-18:00, www.parkguell.cat. Gaudí House Museum—€5.50, €17 combo-ticket also includes Sagrada Família, daily April-Sept 10:00-20:00, Oct-March 10:00-18:00, www.casamuseugaudi.org.

Getting There: To reach Park Güell—about 2.5 miles north of Plaça de Catalunya—it's easiest to take a **taxi** from downtown (around €12). Otherwise, the blue Tourist Bus stops about two blocks below the main entrance, and public **bus** #24 goes from Plaça de Catalunya to the park's side entrance. Or you can ride the Metro to Joanic, exit toward Carrer de l'Escorial, and find the bus stop in front of #20, where you can catch bus #116 to the park's main entrance.

Picasso Museum Tour

This is the best collection in the country of the work of Spaniard Pablo Picasso (1881-1973). And, since Picasso spent his formative years (from the ages of 14 to 23) in Barcelona, it's the best collection of his early works anywhere. The museum is sparse on later, better-known works from his time of international celebrity; visit this museum not to see famous canvases but to get an intimate portrait of the young man finding his way as an artist. By experiencing his youthful, realistic art, you can better understand his later, more challenging art and more fully appreciate his genius.

Orientation

Cost and Hours: €14, free all day first Sun of month and other Sun from 15:00; open Tue-Sun 9:00-19:00, Thu until 21:30, closed Mon, last entry 20 minutes before closing, Carrer de Montcada 15-23, ticket office at #21, Metro: Jaume I, tel. 932-563-000, www.museupicasso.bcn.cat.

Crowd-Beating Tips: There's almost always a line, sometimes with waits of more than an hour. The busiest times are mornings before 13:00, all day Tuesday, and during the free entry times on Sundays (see above). If you have an Articket BCN (see page 163), skip the line by going to the "Meeting Point" entrance (30 yards to the right of the main entrance). You can also skip the line by buying your ticket online at www.museupicasso.bcn.cat (no additional booking fee). Stuck in line without a ticket? Figure that about 25 people are admitted every 10 minutes.

Getting There: From the Jaume I Metro stop, it's a quick five-minute walk. Just head down Carrer de la Princesa (across the busy Via Laietana from the Barri Gòtic), turning right on Carrer de Montcada.

Audioguide: The 1.5-hour audioguide costs €3 and offers ample detail about the collection.

Services: The ground floor, which is free to enter, has a required bag check, as well as a handy array of other services (bookshop, WC, and cafeteria).

Cuisine Art: The museum itself has a good **café** (€8 sandwiches and salads). Outside the museum, right along Carrer de Montcada in either direction, are two great recommended tapas bars (both closed Mon): With your back to the museum, a few steps to the left is **El Xampanyet,** while to the right (across Carrer de la Princesa and up a block) is **Bar del Pla.**

The Tour Begins

The Picasso Museum's collection of paintings is presented more or less chronologically (though specific pieces may be out for restoration or on tour, and the rooms are sometimes rearranged). But with the help of thoughtful English descriptions for each stage (and guards who don't let you stray), it's easy to follow the evolution of Picasso's work. This tour is arranged by the stages of his life and art.

Boy Wonder

Pablo's earliest art is realistic and earnest. His work quickly advances from childish pencil drawings (such as *Hercules,* 1890), through a series of technically skilled art-school works (copies of plaster feet and arms), to oil paintings of impressive technique. Even at a young age, his **portraits** of grizzled peasants demonstrate surprising psychological insight. Because his dedicated father—himself a curator and artist—kept everything his son ever did, Picasso must have the best-documented youth of any great painter.

Developing Talent (Adolescence)

During a summer trip to Málaga, Picasso dabbles in a series of fresh, Impressionistic-style landscapes (relatively rare in Spain at the time). As a 15-year-old, Pablo dutifully enters art-school competitions. His first big work, *First Communion,* features a prescribed religious subject, but Picasso makes it an excuse to paint his family. His sister Lola is the model for the communicant, and the features of the man beside her belong to Picasso's father. Notice Lola's exquisitely painted veil. This piece was heavily influenced by the academic style of local painters.

Picasso's relatives star in a number of portraits from this time. If it's on view, find the **portrait of his mother** (this and other family portraits may be out on loan to the Picasso Museum in Málaga). The teenage Pablo is working on the fine details and gradients of white in her blouse and the expression in her cameo-like face. Notice the signature. Spaniards keep both parents' surnames, with the father's first, followed by the mother's: Pablo Ruiz Picasso.

Early Success

Science and Charity, which won second prize at a fine-arts exhibition, got Picasso the chance to study in Madrid. Now Picasso con-

veys real feeling. The doctor (modeled on Pablo's father) represents science. The nun represents charity and religion. From her hopeless face and lifeless hand, it seems that Picasso believes nothing will save this woman from death. Pablo painted a little perspective trick: Walk back and forth across the room to see the bed stretch and shrink. Three small studies for this painting (on the right) show how this was an exploratory work. The frontier: light.

Picasso travels to Madrid for further study. Stifled by the stuffy fine-arts school there, he hangs out instead in the Prado Museum and learns by copying the masters. (An example of his impressive mimicry is coming up in a later room.) Having absorbed the wisdom of the ages, in 1898 Pablo visits **Horta de San Juan**, a rural Catalan village, and finds his artistic independence. (See the small landscapes and scenes of village life he did there.) Poor and without a love in his life, he returns to Barcelona.

Barcelona Freedom (1900)

Art Nouveau is all the rage in Barcelona. Upsetting his dad, Pablo quits art school and falls in with the avant-garde crowd. These bohemians congregate daily at Els Quatre Gats ("The Four Cats," a popular restaurant to this day—see page 225). Picasso even created the **menu cover** for this favorite hangout (it's sometimes on view).

Further establishing his artistic freedom, he paints **portraits** of his new friends (including one of Jaume Sabartés, who later became his personal assistant and donated the works to establish this museum). Still a teenager, Pablo puts on his first one-man show at Els Quatre Gats in 1900.

Notice young Picasso's nearly perfect **copy** of a portrait of Philip IV by an earlier Spanish master, Diego Velázquez. Near the end of the museum, we'll see a much older Picasso—now confident in his boldly idiosyncratic style—riffing on another Velázquez painting.

Paris (1900-1901)

In 1900 Picasso makes his first trip to Paris, a city bursting with life, light, and love. Dropping the paternal surname Ruiz, Pablo establishes his commercial brand name: "Picasso." Here the explorer Picasso goes bohemian and befriends poets, prostitutes, and artists. He paints **cancan dancers** like Toulouse-Lautrec, **still lifes** like Paul Cézanne, brightly colored Fauvist works like Henri Matisse, and Impressionist **landscapes** like Claude Monet. In *The Wait (Margot)*, the subject—with her bold outline and strong gaze—pops out from the vivid, mosaic-like background.

Blue Period (1901-1904)

Picasso continues traveling to Paris. But the bleak weather, the suicide of his best friend, and his own poverty lead Picasso to abandon jewel-bright color for his Blue Period. He cranks out stacks of blue art just to stay housed and fed. With blue backgrounds (the coldest color) and depressing subjects, this period was revolutionary in art history. Now the artist is painting not what he sees, but what he feels. Look for the touching portrait of a mother and child, *Motherhood* (this very fragile pastel is only displayed intermittently), which captures the period well. Painting misfits and street people, Picasso, like Velázquez and Toulouse-Lautrec, sees "the beauty in ugliness."

Back home in Barcelona, Picasso paints his hometown at night from **rooftops.** The painting is still blue, but here we see proto-Cubism...five years before the first real Cubist painting.

Rose Period (1904-1907)

Picasso is finally lifted out of his funk after meeting a new lady, Fernande Olivier. He moves out of the blue and into the happier Rose Period. For a fine example, see the portrait of a woman wearing a classic Spanish mantilla *(Portrait of Bernadetta Bianco).* Its soft pink and reddish tones are the colors of flesh and sensuality.

Barcelona (1917)

Picasso spent six months back in Barcelona in 1917 (his girlfriend, a Russian dancer with the Ballets Russes, had a gig in town). The paintings from this time demonstrate the artist's irrepressible versatility: He's already developed Cubism (with his friend Georges Braque; more on this below), but he also continues to play with other styles. In *Woman with Mantilla*, we see a little Post-Impressionistic Pointillism in a portrait that is as elegant as a classical statue. Nearby, *Gored Horse* has all the anguish and power of his iconic *Guernica* (painted years later).

Pablo's role in the invention of the revolutionary Cubist style is well known—at least I hope so, since this museum has no true Cubist paintings. A Cubist work gives not only the basics of a subject—it shows every aspect of it simultaneously. The technique of "building" a subject with "cubes" of paint simmered in Picasso's artistic stew for years. In this museum, you'll see some so-called **Synthetic Cubist paintings**—a later variation that flattens the various angles, as opposed to the purer, original Analytical Cubist paintings, in which you can simultaneously see several 3-D facets of the subject.

Picasso and Velázquez (1957)

A series of Picasso's works relate to what many consider the greatest painting by anyone, ever: Diego Velázquez's *Las Meninas* (the original is displayed in Madrid's Prado Museum). Heralded as the first completely realistic painting, *Las Meninas* became an obsession for Picasso centuries later.

Picasso, who had great respect for Velázquez, painted more than **50 interpretations** of this piece. These two Spanish geniuses were artistic equals. Picasso seems to enjoy a relationship with Velázquez. Like artistic soul mates, they spar and tease. He deconstructs Velázquez and then injects light, color, and perspective to horse around with the earlier masterpiece. In the big black-and-white canvas, the king and queen (reflected in the mirror in the back of the room) are hardly seen, while the self-portrait of the painter towers above everyone. The two women of the court on the right look like they're in a tomb—but they're wearing party shoes. Browse the various studies, a playground of color and perspective. See the fun Picasso had playing paddleball with Velázquez's tour de force—filtering Velázquez's realism through the kaleidoscope of Cubism.

The French Riviera (Last Years)

The Spaniard spends the last 36 years of his life living simply in the south of France. Picasso said many times that "Paintings are like windows open to the world." We see his sunny Riviera world: With simple black outlines and Crayola colors, Picasso paints sun-splashed nature, peaceful doves, and the joys of the beach. He dabbles in the timeless art of ceramics, shaping bowls and vases into fun animals decorated with simple, playful designs. He's enjoying life with his second (and much younger) wife, Jacqueline Roque, whose portraits hang nearby.

Picasso died with brush in hand, still growing artistically. Sadly, since Picasso vowed never to set foot in a fascist, Franco-ruled Spain, the artist never returned to his homeland...and never saw this museum (his death came in 1973—two years before Franco's). However, to the end, Picasso continued exploring and loving life through his art.

Sagrada Família Tour

Architect Antoni Gaudí's most famous and awe-inspiring work is this unfinished, super-sized church. With its cake-in-the-rain facade and otherworldly spires, the church is not only an icon of Barcelona and its trademark Modernista style, but also a symbol of this period's greatest practitioner. As an architect, Gaudí's foundations were the classics, nature, and religion. The church represents all three.

Gaudí labored on the Sagrada Família for 43 years, from 1883 until his death in 1926. Nearly a century after his death, people continue to toil to bring Gaudí's designs to life. There's something powerful about a community of committed people with a vision, working on a church that won't be finished in their lifetime—as was standard in the Gothic age. The progress of this remarkable building is a testament to the generations of architects, sculptors, stonecutters, fund-raisers, and donors who've been caught up in the audacity of Gaudí's astonishing vision. After paying the steep admission price (becoming a partner in this building project), you will actually feel good. If there's any building on earth I'd like to see, it's the Sagrada Família...finished.

Orientation

Cost and Hours: Church-€13.50, tower elevators-€4.50 each, €17 combo-ticket also includes Gaudí House Museum at Park Güell (see page 205), daily April-Sept 9:00-20:00, Oct-March 9:00-18:00, last entry 15 minutes before closing, Metro: Sagrada Família, exit toward Plaça de la Sagrada Família, tel. 932-073-031, www.sagradafamilia.cat.

Getting There: The Sagrada Família Metro stop puts you right on the doorstep: Exit toward Plaça de la Sagrada Família. The ticket windows and entrance for individuals (not groups) are on the west side of the church (at the Passion Facade). Inviting parks flank the building, facing the two completed facades.

Crowd-Beating Tips: Though the ticket line can seem long (often curving around the block), it generally moves quickly; you can ask for an estimate from the guards at the front of the line. Still, waits can be up to 45 minutes at peak times (most crowded in the morning). To minimize your wait, arrive right at 9:00 (when it opens) or after 16:00. To skip the line, buy advance tickets, take a tour, or hire a private guide.

Advance Tickets: To avoid the ticket-buying line, you can reserve an entry time and buy tickets in advance. The best option is to book online at www.sagradafamilia.cat, which allows you to print tickets at home. With prepurchased tickets, head straight for the "online ticket office" window, to the right of the main ticket line, and show your ticket to the guard.

Tours: The 50-minute English tours (€4.50) run May-Oct daily at 11:00, 12:00, 13:00, and 15:00; Nov-April Mon-Fri at 11:00, 13:00, and 15:00, Sat-Sun at 11:00, 12:00, 13:00, and 15:00. Or rent the good 1.5-hour audioguide (€4.50). Good English information is posted throughout.

Tower Elevators: Two different elevators (€4.50 each, pay at main ticket office, each ticket comes with an entry time) take you partway up the towers for a great view of the city and a gargoyle's-eye perspective of the loopy church.

The easier option is the **Passion Facade elevator,** which takes you 215 feet up and down. If you want, you can climb higher, but expect the spiral stairs to be tight, hot, and congested.

The **Nativity Facade elevator** is more exciting and demanding. You'll get the opportunity to cross the dizzying bridge between the towers, but you'll need to take the stairs all the way down.

The Tour Begins

Start at the ticket entrance (at the Passion Facade) on the western side of the church. The view is best from the park across the street. Before heading to the ticket booth, take in the...

❶ Exterior

For over 130 years, Barcelona has labored to bring Antoni Gaudí's vision to reality. Local craftsmen often cap off their careers by spending a couple of years on this exciting construction site, while the present architect has been at it since 1985. Like Gothic churches of medieval times, the design has evolved over the decades. At heart, it's Gothic, a style much admired by Gaudí. He added his own Art Nouveau/Modernisme touches, guided by nature and engineering innovations. Today the site bristles with cranking cranes, rusty forests of rebar, and scaffolding. Sagrada Família offers a fun look at a living, growing, bigger-than-life building.

Stand and imagine how grand this church will be when completed. The four 330-foot spires topped with crosses are just a fraction of this mega-church. When finished, the church will have 18 spires. Four will stand at each of the three entrances. Rising above those will be four taller towers, dedicated to the four Evangelists. A tower dedicated to Mary will rise still higher—400 feet. And in the very center of the complex will stand the grand 560-foot Jesus tower, topped with a cross that will shine like a spiritual lighthouse, visible even from out at sea.

The Passion Facade that tourists enter today is only a side entrance to the church. The grand main entrance will be around to the right. That means that the nine-story apartment building will eventually have to be torn down to accommodate it. The three facades—Nativity, Passion, and Glory—will chronicle Christ's life from birth to death to resurrection. Inside and out, a goal of the church is to bring the lessons of the Bible to the world. Despite his boldly modern architectural vision, Gaudí was fundamentally traditional and deeply religious. He designed the Sagrada Família to be a bastion of solid Christian values in the midst of what was a humble workers' colony in a fast-changing city.

When Gaudí died, only one section (on the Nativity Facade) had been completed. The rest of the church has been inspired by Gaudí's long-range vision, but designed and executed by others. This artistic freedom was amplified in 1936, when civil war shelling burned many of Gaudí's blueprints. Supporters of the ongoing work insist that Gaudí, who enjoyed saying, "My client [God] is not in a hurry," knew he wouldn't live to complete the church and recognized that later architects and artists would rely on their own muses for inspiration. Detractors maintain that the church's design is a uniquely, intensely personal one and that it's folly (if not disrespectful) for anyone to try to guess what Gaudí would have intended. Studying the various plans and models in the museum below the church, it's clear that Gaudí's plan evolved dramatically the longer he worked. Is it appropriate to keep implementing a century-old vision that can no longer be modified by its creator? Discuss.

• *Pass through the ticket entrance into the complex, approaching closer to the...*

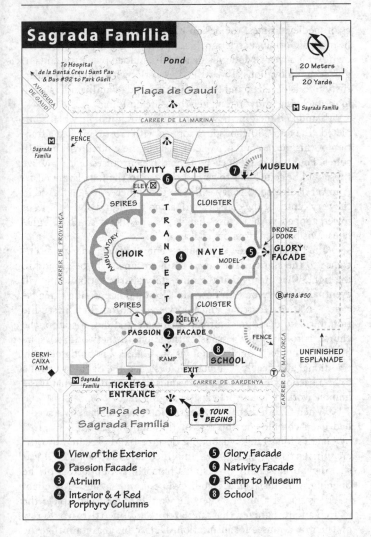

Sagrada Família

- Pond
- To Hospital de la Santa Creu i Sant Pau & Bus #92 to Park Güell
- AVINGUDA DE GAUDÍ
- Plaça de Gaudí
- Ⓜ Sagrada Família
- 20 Meters
- 20 Yards
- CARRER DE LA MARINA
- Ⓜ Sagrada Família
- FENCE
- NATIVITY FACADE
- ⑦ MUSEUM
- ELEV.⊠ ⑥
- SPIRES
- CLOISTER
- CARRER DE PROVENÇA
- AMBULATORY
- CHOIR
- T R A N S E P T
- ④
- NAVE
- MODEL
- ⑤ GLORY FACADE
- BRONZE DOOR
- Ⓑ #19 & #50
- SPIRES
- CLOISTER
- ③ ⊠ELEV.
- PASSION ② FACADE
- FENCE
- ⑧
- RAMP
- SCHOOL
- UNFINISHED ESPLANADE
- SERVI-CAIXA ATM
- EXIT
- CARRER DE SARDENYA
- Ⓣ
- CARRER DE MALLORCA
- Ⓜ Sagrada Família
- TICKETS & ENTRANCE
- Plaça de Sagrada Família
- ① TOUR BEGINS

① View of the Exterior
② Passion Facade
③ Atrium
④ Interior & 4 Red Porphyry Columns
⑤ Glory Facade
⑥ Nativity Facade
⑦ Ramp to Museum
⑧ School

❷ Passion Façade

Judge for yourself how well Gaudí's original vision has been carried out by later artists. The Passion Facade's four spires were designed by Gaudí and completed (quite faithfully) in 1976. But the lower part was only inspired by Gaudí's designs. The stark sculptures were interpreted freely (and controversially) by Josep Maria Subirachs (b. 1927), who completed the work in 2005.

Subirachs tells the story of Christ's torture and execution. The various scenes—Last Supper, betrayal, whipping, and so on—zigzag up from bottom to top, culminating in Christ's crucifixion over the doorway. The style is severe and unadorned, quite

different from Gaudí's signature playfulness. But the bone-like archways are closely based on Gaudí's original designs. And Gaudí had made it clear that this facade should be grim and terrifying.

The facade is full of symbolism. A stylized Alpha-and-Omega is over the door (which faces the setting sun). Jesus, hanging on the cross, has hair made of an open book, symbolizing the word of God. To the left of the door, there's a grid of numbers, always adding up to 33—Jesus' age at the time of his death. The distinct face of the man below and just left of Christ is a memorial to Gaudí. Now look high above: The two-ton figure suspended between the towers is the soul of Jesus, ascending to heaven.

• *Enter the church. As you pass through the* ❸ *Atrium, look down at the fine porphyry floor (with scenes of Jesus' entry into Jerusalem), and look right to see one of the* **elevators** *up to the towers. For now, continue into the...*

❹ Interior

Typical of even the most traditional Catalan and Spanish churches, the floor plan is in the shape of a Latin cross, 300 feet long and 200 feet wide. Ultimately, the church will encompass 48,000 square feet, accommodating 8,000 worshippers. The nave's roof is

150 feet high. The crisscross arches of the ceiling (the vaults) show off Gaudí's distinctive engineering. The church's roof and flooring were only completed in 2010—just in time for Pope Benedict XVI to arrive and consecrate the church.

Part of Gaudí's religious vision was a love for nature. He said, "Nothing is invented; it's written in nature." Like the trunks of trees, these **columns** (56 in all) blossom with life, complete with branches, leaves, and knot-like capitals. The columns are a variety of colors—brown clay, gray granite, dark-gray basalt. The taller columns are 72 feet tall; the shorter ones are exactly half that.

The angled columns form many **arches.** You'll see both parabolas (U-shaped) and hyperbolas (flatter, elliptical shapes). Gaudí's starting point was the Gothic pointed arch used in medieval churches. But he tweaked it after meticulous study of which arches are best at bearing weight.

Little **windows** let light filter in like the canopy of a rainforest, giving both privacy and an intimate connection with God. The clear glass is temporary and will gradually be replaced by stained glass. As more and more stained glass is installed, splashes of color will breathe even more life into this amazing space. Gaudí envisioned an awe-inspiring canopy with a symphony of colored light to encourage a contemplative mood.

High up at the back half of the church, the U-shaped **choir**—suspended above the nave—can seat 1,000. The singers will eventually be backed by four organs (there's one now).

Work your way up the grand nave, walking through this forest of massive columns. At the center of the church stand four **red porphyry columns,** each marked with an Evangelist's symbol and name in Catalan: angel (Mateu), lion (Marc), bull (Luc), and eagle (Joan). These columns support a ceiling vault that's 200 feet high—and eventually will also support the central steeple, the 560-foot Jesus tower with the shining cross. The steeple will be further supported by four underground pylons, each consisting of 8,000 tons of cement. It will be the tallest church steeple in the world, though still a few feet shorter than the city's highest point at the summit of Montjuïc hill, as Gaudí believed that a creation of man should not attempt to eclipse the creation of God.

Stroll behind the altar through the **ambulatory** to reach a small chapel set aside for prayer and meditation. Look through the windows down at the **crypt** (which holds the tomb of Gaudí). Peering down into that surprisingly traditional space, imagine how the church was started as a fairly conventional, 19th-century Neo-Gothic building until Gaudí was given the responsibility to finish it.

• *Head to the far end of the church, to what will eventually be the main entrance. Just inside the door, find the* **bronze model** *of the eventual floor plan of the completed church. Facing the doors, look high up to see Subirachs' statue of one of Barcelona's patron saints,* **Jordi**. *Go through the doors to imagine what will someday be the...*

❺ Glory Facade

As you exit, study the fine **bronze door,** emblazoned with the Lord's Prayer in Catalan, surrounded by "Give us this day our daily bread" in 50 languages. Once outside, you'll be face-to-face with... drab, doomed apartment blocks. In the 1950s, the mayor of Barcelona, figuring this day would never really come, sold the land destined for the church project. Now the city must buy back these buildings in order to complete Gaudí's vision: that of a grand esplanade leading to this main entry. Four towers will rise up. The facade's sculpture will represent how the soul passes through death, faces the Last Judgment, avoids the pitfalls of hell, and finds its way to eternal glory with God. Gaudí purposely left the facade's design open for later architects—stay tuned.

• *Re-enter the church, backtrack up the nave, and exit through the right transept. Once outside, back up as far as you can to take in the...*

❻ Nativity Facade

This is the only part of the church essentially finished in Gaudí's lifetime. The four spires decorated with his unmistakably non-linear sculpture mark this facade as part of his original design. Mixing Gothic-style symbolism, images from nature, and Modernista asymmetry, the Nativity Facade is the best example of Gaudí's original vision, and it established the template for future architects.

The theme of this facade, which faces the rising sun, is Christ's birth. A statue above the doorway shows Mary, Joseph, and Baby Jesus in the manger, while curious cows peek in. It's the Holy Family—or "Sagrada Família"—to whom this church is dedicated. Flanking the doorway are the three Magi and adoring shepherds. Other statues show Jesus as a young carpenter and angels playing musical instruments. Higher up on the facade, in the arched niche, Jesus crowns Mary triumphantly.

The facade is all about birth and new life, from the dove-covered Tree of Life on top to the turtles at the base of the columns flanking the entrance. At the bottom of the Tree of Life is a white pelican. Because it was believed that this noble bird would kill itself to feed its young, it was often used in the Middle Ages as a symbol for the self-sacrifice of Jesus. The chameleon gargoyles at the outer corners of the facade (just above door level) represent the change-ability of life. It's as playful as the Passion Facade is grim. Gaudí's plans were for this facade to be painted. Cleverly, this attractive facade was built and finished first to bring in financial support for the project.

The four **spires** are dedicated to Apostles, and they repeatedly bear the word "Sanctus," or holy. Their colorful ceramic caps symbolize the miters (formal hats) of bishops. The shorter spires (to the left) symbolize the Eucharist (communion), alternating between a chalice with grapes and a communion host with wheat.

To the left of the facade is one section of the **cloister.** Whereas most medieval churches have their cloisters attached to one side of the building, the Sagrada Família's cloister will wrap around the church, more than 400 yards long.

• *Notice the second **elevator** up to the towers. But for now, head down the ramp to the left of the facade, where you'll find WCs and the entrance to the...*

❼ Museum

Housed in what will someday be the church's crypt, the museum displays Gaudí's original **models and drawings,** and chronicles the progress of construction over the last 130 years. Wander among the plaster models used for the church's construction, including a model of the nave so big you walk beneath it. The models make clear the influence of nature. The columns seem light, with branches springing forth and capitals that look like palm trees. You'll notice that the models don't always match the finished product—these are ideas, not blueprints set in stone. The Passion Facade model (near the entrance) shows Gaudí's original vision, with which Subirachs tinkered very freely (see page 214).

Turn up the main hallway. On the left you can peek into a busy **workshop** still used for making the same kind of plaster models Gaudí used to envision the final product in 3-D. Farther along, a small hallway on the right leads to some original Gaudí architectural **sketches** in a dimly lit room and a worthwhile 20-minute **movie** (generally shown in English at :50 past each hour).

From the end of this hall, you have another opportunity to look down into the crypt and at **Gaudí's tomb.** Gaudí lived on the site for more than a decade and is buried in the Neo-Gothic 19th-century crypt. There's a move afoot to make Gaudí a saint. Perhaps someday his tomb will be a place of pilgrimage.

Back in the main hallway, on the right is the intriguing **"Hanging Model"** for Gaudí's unfinished Church of Colònia Güell (in a suburb of Barcelona), featuring a similar design to the Sagrada Família. The model illustrates how the architect used gravity to calculate the arches that support the church. Wires dangle like suspended chains, forming perfect hyperbolic arches. Attached to these are bags, representing the weight the arches must support. Flip these arches over, and they can bear the heavy weight of the roof. The mirror above the model shows how the right-side-up church is derived from this. Across the hall is a small exhibit commemorating **Pope Benedict XVI**'s 2010 consecration visit.

After passing some original sculptures from the Glory Facade (on the right) and continuing beneath a huge plaster model, turn right to find **three different visions** for this church. Notice how the arches evolved as Gaudí tinkered, from the original, pointy Neo-Gothic arches, to parabolic ones, to the hyperbolic ones he eventually settled on. Also in this hall are replicas of the **pulpit** and **confessional** that Gaudí, the micromanager, designed for his church. Before exiting at the far end of the hall, scan the photos (including one of the master himself) and timeline illustrating how construction work has progressed from Gaudí's day to now.

• *You'll exit near where you started, at the Passion Facade.*

❽ School

The small building outside the Passion Facade was a school Gaudí erected for the children of the workers building the church. Today it includes more exhibits about the design and engineering of the church, along with a classroom and a replica of Gaudí's desk as it was the day he died. Pause for a moment to pay homage to the man who made all this possible. Gaudí—a faithful Catholic whose medieval-style mysticism belied his Modernista architecture career—was certainly driven to greatness by his passion for God.

Shopping in Barcelona

Barcelona is a fantastic shopping destination, whether you prefer high-end fashion, department stores stocked with everyday European fashions, artisan shops with a centuries-long tradition, or funky little boutiques.

Most shops are open Monday through Friday from about 9:00 or 10:00 until lunchtime (around 13:00 or 14:00). After the siesta, they reopen in the late afternoon, around 16:30 or 17:00, and stay open until 20:00 or 21:00. Large stores and some smaller shops in touristy zones may remain open through the afternoon—but don't count on it. On Saturdays, many shops are open in the morning only. On Sundays, most shops are closed (though the Maremagnum complex on the harborfront is open).

For information on **VAT refunds** and **customs regulations,** see page 135.

Souvenir Ideas

In this very artistic city, consider picking up prints, books, posters, decorative items, or other keepsakes featuring works by your favorite **artist** (Picasso, Dalí, Miró, Gaudí, etc.). Gift shops at major museums can be entered gratis (such as the Picasso Museum and at Gaudí's La Pedrera) and are a bonanza for art and design lovers; model-ship builders will be fascinated by the offerings at the Maritime Museum shop.

Foodies might enjoy shopping for local **food items**—olive oil, wine, spices (such as saffron or sea salts), high-quality canned foods and preserves, dried beans, and so on. Remember, food items must be sealed to make it back through US customs. Cooks can look for Euro-style gadgets at **kitchen-supply** stores.

In this design-oriented city, **home decor** shops are abundant and fun to browse, offering a variety of Euro housewares unavailable back home. For something more classic, look for glassware or other items with a dash of Modernista style.

Fashionistas can shop for **espadrilles** (*espadenya* in Catalan). These soft-canvas, rope-soled shoes originated as humble Catalan peasant footwear but have become trendy as a lightweight summer shoe. A few shops in Barcelona, such as La Manual Alpargatera (in

BARCELONA

the Barri Gòtic at 7 Carrer d'Avinyó), still make these the traditional way.

Sports fans love jerseys, scarves, and other gear associated with the wildly popular **Barça** soccer team.

Shopping Neighborhoods and Streets

Barri Gòtic

Stay off of the wide, touristy Carrer de la Portaferrissa between the cathedral and the Ramblas unless you are looking for a mainstream shopping experience. For a far more colorful route that leads past many fun-to-browse shops, try this: Facing the Roman towers and big BARCINO letters (on Plaça Nova, near the cathedral), turn 90 degrees to the right and head up Carrer de la Palla (antiques, art galleries). At the fork, you can either detour left, down Carrer dels Banys Nous, or head right, continuing along Carrer de la Palla. That street pops you out into the delightful Plaça de Sant Josep Oriol, facing the Church of Santa Maria del Pi. Jog around the right side of the church, through the cute little Plaça del Pi (cutlery, menswear), and head up Carrer Petritxol (jewelry, shoes, kids' clothes). You'll wind up on Carrer de la Portaferrissa, one block from the Ramblas.

Other Barri Gòtic streets are loaded with fun shopping opportunities. On the other side of the Ramblas (two blocks below Plaça de Catalunya), stroll down skinny Carrer de Bonsuccés (it turns into Carrer d'Elisabets) and poke into the little boutiques along the way (such as the tiny, fashionable clothing store Passé Composé, at #12).

For department and chain stores, simply wander down **Avinguda Portal de l'Angel,** the street that connects Plaça de Catalunya with the cathedral, at the northern edge of the Barri Gòtic. In a few short blocks, you'll find the big El Corte Inglés department store, Zara (clothing), and a branch of practically every Spanish chain store.

El Born

For a slightly edgier and less touristy shopping experience, head to the El Born neighborhood. The main spines of El Born—Carrer de la Princesa, the perpendicular Carrer de Montcada, and the diagonal Carrer de l'Argenteria—are largely disappointing for shoppers. But if you lose yourself in the smaller back lanes between those arteries, you'll discover a world of artsy, funky little boutiques. Stroll along Carrer dels Flassaders (which runs behind the Picasso Museum), Carrer dels Banys Vells (between Montcada and l'Argenteria), and Carrer del Rec (just south of Passeig del Born)—and all of the little lanes crossing each of these streets.

Eixample

This ritzy area is home to many of the city's top-end shops. In general, you'll find a lot of big international names along Passeig de Gràcia, the main boulevard that runs north from Plaça de Catalunya to the Gaudí sights—an area fittingly called the Golden Quarter (Quadrat d'Or). Appropriately enough, the "upper end" of Passeig de Gràcia has the fancier shops—Gucci, Louis Vuitton, Escada, Chanel, and so on—while the southern part of the street is relatively "low-end" (Zara, Mango). One block to the west, Rambla de Catalunya holds more local (but still expensive) options for fashion, home decor, jewelry, perfume, and so on. The streets that connect Rambla de Catalunya to Passeig de Gràcia also have some fine shops.

This neighborhood is also home to some fun kitchen stores: Try Gadgets & Cuina (Carrer d'Aragó 249) or Cooking (Carrer de Provença 246).

Nightlife in Barcelona

Like all of Spain, Barcelona is extremely lively after hours. People head out for dinner at 22:00, then bar-hop or simply wander the streets until well after midnight (*matinada* is the Catalan word for "the wee hours" or "dawn").

If you want a more high-brow activity, consult the free *Time Out BCN Guide* (available at TI, in English). The TI's culture website (www.barcelonacultura.bcn.cat) is also helpful.

After-Hours Hangout Neighborhoods

El Born

Passeig del Born, a broad, park-like strip stretching from the Church of Santa Maria del Mar up to the old market hall, is lined with inviting bars and nightspots, as are the surrounding side streets. Right on Passeig del Born is **Miramelindo,** a local favorite—mellow yet convivial, with two floors of woody ambience and a minty aura from all those mojitos the bartenders are mashing up (Passeig del Born 15). **Palau Dalmases,** in the atmospheric courtyard of an old palace, slings cocktails when it's not hosting flamenco shows. **La Vinya del Senyor,** one of my recommended eateries, is a fine place for a good glass of wine out on the square in front of the Church of Santa Maria del Mar.

Plaça Reial (in the Barri Gòtic)

This charmingly trendy square is buried deep in the Barri Gòtic just off the Ramblas. Once seedy, it now bustles with popular bars and restaurants offering inflated prices at inviting outdoor tables. While not a great place to eat (the only one worth seriously considering for a meal is the recommended **Les Quinze Nits**), this is a great place to sip a before- or after-dinner drink. **Ocaña Bar,** at #13, has a dilapidated-mod interior, a see-through industrial kitchen, and rickety-chic secondhand tables out on the square (€4-9 tapas, reasonable drinks, open nightly). Or there's always the student option: Buy a cheap €1 beer from a convenience store (you'll find several just off the square, including a few along Carrer dels Escudellers, just south of Plaça Reial), then grab a free spot on the square.

The Beach at Barceloneta

A broad beach stretches for miles from the former fishermen's quarter at Barceloneta to the Fòrum. Every 100 yards or so is a *chiringuito*—a shack selling drinks and light snacks. It's a very fun, lively scene on a balmy summer evening. Barceloneta itself has a broad promenade facing the harbor, lined with interchangeable seafood restaurants. But the best beach experience is beyond the tip of Barceloneta. From here, a double-decker boardwalk runs the length of the beach, with a cool walkway up above and a series of fine seafood restaurants with romantic candlelit beachfront seating tucked down below.

Music

Serious Concerts

The **Palace of Catalan Music** (Palau de la Música Catalana), with one of the finest Modernista interiors in town (see listing on page 195), offers a full slate of performances, ranging from symphonic to Catalan folk songs to chamber music to flamenco (€22-49 tickets, box office open daily 9:30-21:00, Carrer Palau de la Música 4-6, Metro: Urquinaona, box office tel. 902-442-882, www.palaumusica.cat).

The **Liceu Opera House** (Gran Teatre del Liceu), right on the heart of the Ramblas, is a pre-Modernista, sumptuous venue for opera, dance, children's theater, and concerts (tickets from €12, La Rambla 51-59, box office just around the corner at Carrer Sant Pau 1, Metro: Liceu, box office tel. 934-859-913, www.liceubarcelona.cat).

Flamenco

For touristy but riveting performances of flamenco, check out **Tarantos,** on Plaça Reial in the heart of the Barri Gòtic (€8, nightly at 20:30, 21:30, and 22:30; Plaça Reial 17, tel. 933-191-789, www.masimas.com/en/tarantos); **Tablao Cordobés** on the Ramblas (€42 includes a drink, €77 includes mediocre buffet dinner and better seats, 2-3 performances/day, La Rambla 35, tel. 933-175-711, www.tablaocordobes.com); or **Palau Dalmases** in the heart of the El Born district (€20 includes a drink, daily at 19:30 and 21:30, in atmospheric old palace courtyard, Carrer de Montcada 20, tel. 933-100-673, www.palaudalmases.com).

Spanish Guitar

"Masters of Guitar" concerts are offered nearly nightly at 21:00 in the Barri Gòtic's Church of Santa Maria del Pi (€21 at the door, €3 less if you buy at least 3 hours ahead—look for ticket sellers in front of church and scattered around town, Plaça del Pi 7; sometimes in Sant Jaume Church instead, Carrer de Ferran 28; tel. 647-514-513, www.maestrosdelaguitarra.com).

Eating in Barcelona

Barcelona, the capital of Catalan cuisine—starring seafood—offers a tremendous variety of colorful eateries, ranging from basic and filling to chic and trendy. Most of my listings are lively spots with a busy tapas scene at the bar, along with restaurant tables for *raciones*. A regional specialty is *pa amb tomàquet* (pah ahm too-MAH-

kaht), toasted bread rubbed with a mix of crushed tomato and olive oil.

Along or near the Ramblas

Within a few steps of the Ramblas, you'll find handy lunch places and an inviting market hall. For locations, see the map on page 226.

Taverna Basca Irati serves 40 kinds of hot and cold Basque *pintxos* for €1.95 each. These are small open-faced sandwiches—like sushi on bread. Muscle in through the hungry local crowd, get an empty plate from the waiter, and then help yourself. Every few minutes, waiters circulate with platters of new, still-warm munchies. Grab one as they pass by...it's addictive (you'll be charged by the number of toothpicks left on your plate when you're done). Wash it down with €3-4 glasses of Rioja (full-bodied red wine), Txakolí (sprightly Basque white wine) or *sidra* (apple wine) poured from on high to add oxygen and bring out the flavor (daily 11:00-24:00, a block off the Ramblas, behind arcade at Carrer del Cardenal Casanyes 17, Metro: Liceu, tel. 933-023-084).

Restaurant Elisabets is a rough little neighborhood eatery packed with antique radios. It's popular with locals for its €12 "home-cooked" three-course lunch special; even cheaper *menú*

BARCELONA

rapid options are also available (13:00-16:00 only). Stop by for lunch, survey what those around you are enjoying, and order what looks best. Apparently, locals put up with the service for the tasty food (Mon-Sat 7:30-23:00, closed Sun and Aug, €3 tapas all day, 2 blocks west of Ramblas on far corner of Plaça del Bonsuccés at Carrer d'Elisabets 2, Metro: Catalunya, tel. 933-175-826, run by Pilar).

Biocenter, a Catalan soup-and-salad restaurant busy with local vegetarians, takes its cooking very seriously (€8-10 weekday lunch specials include soup or salad and plate of the day, €15 dinner specials, otherwise €7-9 salads and €11-13 main dishes, Mon-Sat 13:00-23:00, Sun 13:00-16:00, 2 blocks off the Ramblas at Carrer del Pintor Fortuny 25, Metro: Liceu, tel. 933-014-583).

Café Granja Viader is a quaint time capsule, family-run since 1870. They boast about being the first dairy business to bottle and distribute milk in Spain. This place—specializing in baked and dairy treats, toasted sandwiches, and light meals—is ideal for a traditional breakfast. Or indulge your sweet tooth: Try a glass of *orxata* (or *horchata*—*chufa*-nut milk, summer only), *llet mallorquina* (Majorca-style milk with cinnamon, lemon, and sugar), *crema catalana* (crème brûlée, their specialty), or *suis* ("Swiss"—hot chocolate with a snowcap of whipped cream). *Mel y mató* is fresh cheese with honey...very Catalan (Mon-Sat 9:00-13:15 & 17:00-21:15, closed Sun, a block off the Ramblas behind Betlem Church at Xuclà 4, Metro: Liceu, tel. 933-183-486).

Cafeteria: For a quick, affordable lunch with a view, the ninth-floor cafeteria at **El Corte Inglés** can't be beat (€10 salads and sandwiches, also café with €1.50 coffee and sit-down restaurant with €20 fixed-price meals, Mon-Sat 10:00-22:00, closed Sun, Plaça de Catalunya, Metro: Catalunya, tel. 933-063-800).

Picnics: Shoestring tourists buy groceries at **El Corte Inglés** (described above, supermarket in basement), **Carrefour Market** (Mon-Sat 10:00-22:00, closed Sun, Ramblas 113, Metro: Liceu), and **La Boqueria** market (closed Sun, described next).

In and near La Boqueria Market

Try eating at La Boqueria market at least once (#91 on the Ramblas). Like all farmers markets in Europe, this place is ringed by colorful, good-value eateries. Lots of stalls sell fun take-away food—especially fruit salads and fresh-squeezed juices—ideal for picnickers. There are several good bars around the market busy with shoppers munching at the counter (breakfast, tapas all day, coffee). The market, and most of the eateries listed here (unless noted), are open Monday through Saturday from 8:00 until 20:00 (though things get very quiet after about 16:00) and are closed on Sunday (nearest Metro: Liceu). For a more complete description of the market itself, see page 176 of my "Ramblas Ramble."

Pinotxo Bar is just to the right as you enter the market. It's a great spot for coffee, breakfast (spinach *tortillas,* or whatever's cooking with toast), or tapas. Fun-loving Juan and his family are La Boqueria fixtures. Grab a stool across the way to sip your drink with people-watching views. Be careful—this place can get expensive.

Kiosko Universal is popular for its great prices on wonderful fish dishes. As you enter the market from the Ramblas, it's all the way to the left. If you see people waiting, ask who's last in line *("¿El último?")*. You'll eat immersed in the spirit of the market (€7-14 dishes of the day with different fresh-fish options, €7 mixed veggies, €10 mushroom stir-fries, always packed but better before 12:30, tel. 933-178-286).

Restaurant la Gardunya, at the back of the market, offers tasty meat and seafood meals made with fresh ingredients bought directly from the market (€13.50 fixed-price lunch includes wine and bread, €16.50 three-course dinner specials include wine, €10-20 à la carte dishes, kitchen serves Mon-Sat 13:00-16:00 & 20:00-24:00 but open from 7:00, closed Sun, mod seating indoors or outside watching the market action, Carrer Jerusalem 18, tel. 933-024-323).

In the Barri Gòtic

These eateries populate Barcelona's atmospheric Gothic Quarter, near the cathedral. Choose between a sit-down meal at a restaurant or a string of tapas bars. For locations, see the map on page 226.

Café de l'Academia is a delightful place on a pretty square tucked away in the heart of the Barri Gòtic—but patronized mainly by the neighbors. They serve refined cuisine with Catalan roots using what's fresh from the market. The candlelit, air-conditioned interior is rustic yet elegant, with soft jazz, flowers, and modern art. And if you want to eat outdoors on a convivial, mellow square... this is the place. Reservations can be smart (€10-13 first courses, €12-16 second courses, fixed-price lunch for €10 at the bar or €14 at a table, Mon-Fri 13:30-16:00 & 20:30-23:30, closed Sat-Sun, near the City Hall square, off Carrer de Jaume I up Carrer de la Dagueria at Carrer dels Lledó 1, Metro: Jaume I, tel. 933-198-253).

Els Quatre Gats ("The Four Cats") was once the haunt of the Modernista greats—including a teenaged Picasso, who first publicly displayed his art here, and architect Josep Puig i Cadafalch, who designed the building. Inspired by Paris' famous Le Chat Noir

Barcelona's Old City Restaurants

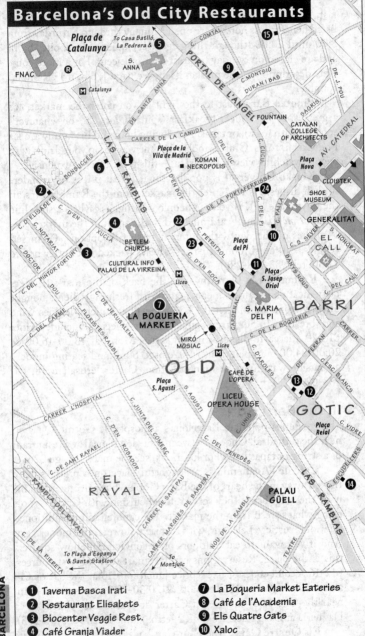

1 Taverna Basca Irati	**7** La Boqueria Market Eateries
2 Restaurant Elisabets	**8** Café de l'Academia
3 Biocenter Veggie Rest.	**9** Els Quatre Gats
4 Café Granja Viader	**10** Xaloc
5 To El Corte Inglés	**11** Bar del Pi
6 Carrefour Market	**12** Les Quinze Nits

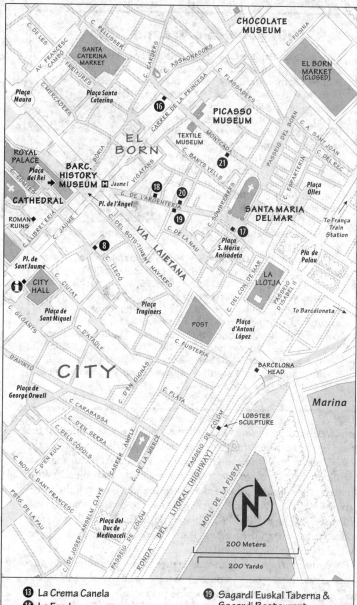

13 La Crema Canela

14 La Fonda

15 La Dolça Herminia

16 Bar del Pla

17 La Vinya del Senyor

18 El Senyor Parellada

19 Sagardi Euskal Taberna & Sagardi Restaurant

20 Taller de Tapas

21 El Xampanyet

22 Casa Colomina

23 Granja La Pallaresa

24 Fargas Chocolate Shop

Budget Meals Around Town

Sandwiches: Bright, clean, and inexpensive sandwich shops proudly hold the cultural line against the fast-food invasion that has hamburgerized the rest of Europe. Catalan sandwiches are made to order with crunchy French bread. Rather than butter, locals prefer *tomàquet* (a spread of crushed tomatoes). You'll see two big local chains (Bocatta and Pans & Company) everywhere, but these serve mass-produced McBaguettes ordered from a multilingual menu. I've had better luck with hole-in-the-wall sandwich shops—virtually as numerous as the chains—where you can see exactly what you're getting.

the best sandwiches in town

International Options: Try **Mucci's Pizza** for good, fresh €2 pizza slices and empanadas (two locations just off the Ramblas, at Bonsuccés 10 and Tallers 75, www.muccis.com). **Wok to Walk** makes tasty food on the run, serving up noodles and rice in takeaway containers with your choice of meat and/or veggies and finished with a savory sauce (€6-9, 3 locations—by the main door of the Boqueria Market, two steps from the Liceu Opera House, and near Plaça de Sant Jaume, www.woktowalk.com). **Kebab** places are another good, super-cheap standby; you'll see them all over town, offering a quick and tasty meal for about €3-4.

café/cabaret, Els Quatre Gats celebrated all that was modern at the turn of the 20th century (for more on the illustrious history of the place, see page 180 in the "Barri Gòtic Walk"). You can snack or drink at the bar, or go into the back for a sit-down meal. While touristy (less so later), the food and service are good, and the prices aren't as high as you might guess (€17 three-course lunch special Mon-Fri 13:00-16:00, €12-22 plates, daily 10:00-24:00, just steps off Avinguda Portal de l'Angel at Carrer de Montsió 3, Metro: Catalunya, tel. 933-024-140).

Xaloc is *the* place in the old center for nicely presented gourmet tapas. It's a classy, woody, modern dining room with a fun energy, good service, and reasonable prices. The walls are covered with *Ibérica* hamhocks and wine bottles. They focus on homestyle Catalan classics and serve only one quality of ham—and it's tops. A gazpacho, plank of ham, *pa amb tomàquet*, and nice glass of wine make a terrific light meal (€2-6 tapas, €5-12 main dishes, open daily 11:00-23:00, kitchen serves 13:00-17:00 & 19:00-23:00, a block toward the cathedral from Plaça de Sant Josep Oriol at Carrer de la Palla 13, Metro: Catalunya, tel. 933-011-990).

Bar del Pi is a simple, hardworking bar serving good salads, sandwiches, and tapas. It has just a handful of tables on the most inviting little square in the Barri Gòtic (Tue-Sun 9:00-23:00, closed Mon, on Plaça de Sant Josep Oriol 1, Metro: Liceu, tel. 933-022-123).

Andilana Restaurants: A local chain called Andilana (www.grupandilana.com) has several bright, modern eateries that are wildly popular for their artfully presented Spanish and Mediterranean cuisine, crisp ambience, and three-course €10 lunches and €16-21 dinners (both with wine). All are crowded with locals and in-the-know tourists—arrive 30 minutes before opening, or be prepared to wait. **Les Quinze Nits** has great seating right on atmospheric Plaça Reial (daily 12:30-23:30, at #6—you'll see the line, tel. 933-173-075, Metro: Liceu). Two others are within a block (also Metro: Liceu): **La Crema Canela,** a few steps above Plaça Reial, takes reservations (Mon-Thu 13:00-23:00, Fri-Sun until 23:30, Passatge de Madoz 6, tel. 933-182-744). **La Fonda** is a block below Plaça Reial (daily 13:00-23:30, Carrer dels Escudellers 10, tel. 933-017-515). Another location, **La Dolça Herminia,** is near the Palace of Catalan Music in El Born (daily 13:00-15:45 & 20:30-23:30, 2 blocks toward Ramblas from Palace of Catalan Music at Carrer de les Magdalenes 27, Metro: Jaume I, tel. 933-170-676).

In El Born, near the Picasso Museum

El Born (a.k.a. La Ribera), the hottest neighborhood in town, sparkles with eclectic and trendy as well as subdued and classy little restaurants hidden in the small lanes surrounding the Church of Santa Maria del Mar. Many restaurants and shops in this area are, like the Picasso Museum, closed on Mondays. For locations, see the map on page 227.

Bar del Pla is a local favorite—near the Picasso Museum but far enough away from the tourist crowds. This classic diner/bar, overlooking a tiny crossroads next to Barcelona's oldest church, serves traditional Catalan dishes, *raciones,* and tapas. Prices are the same at the bar or at a table, but eating at the bar puts you in the middle of a great scene (€4-11 tapas, Tue-Sun 12:00-24:00, closed Mon; with your back to the Picasso Museum, head right 2 blocks, past Carrer de la Princesa, to Carrer de Montcada 2; Metro: Jaume I, tel. 932-683-003).

La Vinya del Senyor is recommendable for its location—with wonderful tables on the square facing the Church of Santa Maria del Mar in the middle of a charming and lively pedestrian zone.

BARCELONA

Tips on Eating in Spain

By our standards, Spaniards eat late. Restaurants generally serve lunch from 13:00 to 16:00 and dinner from 20:00 or even later (Spaniards don't start dinner until about 22:00).

For a quick and inexpensive meal, stop at a bar any time of day. Besides *bocadillos* (sandwiches), bars often have slices of *tortilla española* (potato omelet) and fresh-squeezed orange juice. For a fun early dinner at a bar, build a light meal out of tapas—small appetizer-sized portions of seafood, salads, meat-filled pastries, deep-fried tasties, and so on. While the smaller "tapa" size is handiest for maximum tasting opportunities, many bars sell only larger sizes: the *ración* (full portion) and *media-ración* (half-portion).

Jamón, an air-dried ham similar to prosciutto, is a Spanish staple. Other key terms include *queso* (cheese), *tortilla* (omelet), *frito* (fried), *a la plancha* (grilled), and *surtido* (assortment).

Many bars have three price tiers. It's cheapest to eat or drink while standing at the bar *(barra)*, slightly more to sit at a table inside (*mesa* or *salón*), and most expensive to sit outside *(terraza)*. Wherever you are, be assertive or you'll never be served. Saying *"Por favor"* (please) grabs the attention of the server or bartender.

If you're having tapas, don't worry about paying as you go (the bartender keeps track). When you're ready to leave, ask for the bill: *"¿La cuenta?"*

For a budget meal in a restaurant, try a *plato combinado* (combination plate), which usually includes portions of one or two main dishes, a vegetable, and bread for a reasonable price. The *menú del día* (menu of the day, also known as *menú turístico*) is a substantial three- to four-course meal that usually comes with a carafe of house wine.

Their wine list is extensive—7 cl gives you a few sips, while 14 cl is a standard serving. They also have good cheeses, hams, and tapas (Tue-Sun 12:00-24:00, closed Mon, Plaça de Santa Maria 5, Metro: Jaume I or Barceloneta, tel. 933-103-379).

El Senyor Parellada, filling a former cloister, is an elegant restaurant with a smart, tourist-friendly waitstaff. It serves a fun menu of Mediterranean and Catalan cuisine with a modern twist, all in a classy chandeliers-and-white-tablecloths setting (€10-18 plates, open daily 13:00-15:45 & 20:30-23:30, Carrer de l'Argenteria 37, 100 yards from Metro: Jaume I, tel. 933-105-094).

Sagardi Euskal Taberna offers a wonderful array of Basque goodies—tempting *pintxos* and *montaditos* (miniature sandwiches) at €1.95 each—along its huge bar. Ask for a plate and graze (just take whatever looks good). You can sit on the square with your plunder for 20 percent extra. Wash it down with Txakolí, a Basque white wine poured from the spout of a huge wooden barrel into a glass as you watch. When you're done, they'll count your toothpicks to tally your bill. Hiding behind the thriving tapas bar is **Sagardi,** a mod, rustic, and minimalist woody restaurant committed to serving Basque T-bone steaks and grilled specialties with only the best ingredients. A big open kitchen with sizzling grills contributes to the ambience. Reservations are smart (€12-24 first courses, €20-28 second courses, plan on €50 for dinner; tapas daily 12:00-24:00, restaurant 13:00-16:00 & 20:00-24:00, Carrer de l'Argenteria 62, Metro: Jaume I, tel. 933-199-993, www.sagardi.com).

Taller de Tapas ("Tapas Workshop") is an upscale, trendier tapas bar and restaurant that dishes up well-presented, sophisticated morsels and light meals in a medieval-stone-yet-mod setting. Pay 15 percent more to sit on the square. Elegant, but a bit stuffy, it's favored by local office workers who aren't into the Old World Gothic stuff. Four plates will fill a hungry diner for about €20 (daily 8:30-24:00, Carrer de l'Argenteria 51, Metro: Jaume I, tel. 932-688-559, www.tallerdetapas.com).

El Xampanyet ("The Little Champagne Bar"), a colorful family-run bar with a fun-loving staff (Juan Carlos, his mom, and the man who may be his father), specializes in tapas and anchovies. Don't be put off by the seafood from a tin: Catalans like it this way. A *sortido* (assorted plate) of *carne* (meat) or *pescado* (fish) with *pa amb tomàquet* makes for a fun meal. It's filled with tourists during the sightseeing day, but this is a local favorite after dark. The scene is great but—especially during busy times—it's tough without Spanish skills. When I asked about the price, Juan Carlos said, "Who cares? The ATM is just across the street." Plan on spending €25 for a meal with wine (same price at bar or table, Tue-Sat 12:00-15:30 & 19:00-23:00, Sun 12:00-16:00 only, closed Mon, a half-block beyond the Picasso Museum at Carrer de Montcada 22, Metro: Jaume I, tel. 933-197-003).

Tapas Bars in the Eixample

Many trendy and touristic tapas bars in the Eixample offer a cheery welcome and slam out the appetizers. These four are particularly handy to Plaça de Catalunya and the Passeig de Gràcia artery (for easy access, the closest Metro stops are Catalunya, Provença, Diagonal, and Passeig de Gràcia).

Tapas 24 makes eating fun. This local favorite, with a few street tables, fills a spot a few steps below street level with happy energy, funky decor (white counters and mirrors), and absolutely excellent tapas. The menu has all the typical standbys and quirky inventions (such as the McFoie burger), plus daily specials. Service is friendly, and the owner, Carles Abellan, is one of Barcelona's hot chefs. This is a chance to eat his food at reasonable prices, which are the same whether you dine at the bar, a table, or outside. Figure about €45 for lunch for two with wine (€4-12 tapas, €12-15 plates, Mon-Sat 9:00-24:00, closed Sun, just off Passeig de Gràcia at Carrer de la Diputació 269, tel. 934-880-977).

La Bodegueta Provença is a lively tapas bar/café with a multigenerational clientele and a pleasant buzz. Sit at a stool at the marble counter or grab a table, indoors or out. If you and your partner are hungry, order the half-kilo grilled steak piled high with Padrón peppers—wow! (€5-8.50 tapas, Mon-Sat 7:00-24:00, Sun 13:00-24:00, Carrer de Provença 233, tel. 932-151-725).

Ciutat Comtal Cerveceria brags that it serves the best *montaditos* (€2-4 little open-faced sandwiches) and beers in Barcelona. It's an Eixample favorite, with an elegant bar and tables plus good seating out on the Rambla de Catalunya for all that people-watching action. It's packed 21:00-23:00, when you'll likely need to put your name on a list and wait. While it has no restaurant-type menu, the list of tapas and *montaditos* is easy, fun, and comes with a great variety (including daily specials). This place is a cut above your normal tapas bar, but with reasonable prices (most tapas around €4-10, daily 8:00-24:00, facing the intersection of Gran Via de les Corts Catalanes and Rambla de Catalunya at Rambla de Catalunya 18, tel. 933-181-997).

La Tramoia, at the opposite corner from Ciutat Comtal Cerveceria, serves piles of €1.75 *montaditos* and tapas at its ground-floor bar and at nice tables inside and out. If Ciutat Comtal Cerveceria is jammed, you're more likely to find a seat here. The brasserie-style restaurant upstairs bustles with happy local eaters enjoying grilled meats (€9-20 plates), but I'd stay downstairs for the €4-9 tapas (daily 12:00-24:00 for tapas, 13:00-16:00 & 17:30-24:00 for meals, also facing the intersection of Gran Via de les Corts Catalanes and Rambla de Catalunya at Rambla de Catalunya 15, tel. 934-123-634).

A Short, Sweet Walk

Let me propose this three-stop dessert (or, since these places close well before the traditional Barcelona dinnertime, a late-afternoon snack). Start with a chunk of *torr* or a glass of *orxata,* then munch some *churros con chocolate,* and end with a visit to a fine *xocolateria*—all within a three-minute walk of one another in the Barri Gòtic just off the Ramblas (Metro: Liceu). Start at the corner of Carrer de la Portaferrissa midway down the Ramblas. For the best atmosphere, begin your walk at about 18:00 (note that the last place is closed on Sun). For locations, see the map on page 226.

Torró **at Casa Colomina:** Walk down Carrer de la Portaferrissa to #8 (on the right). Casa Colomina, founded in 1908, specializes in homemade *torr* (or *turrn* in Spanish)—a variation of nougat made with almond, honey, and sugar, brought to Spain by the Moors 1,200 years ago. Three different kinds are sold in €8-12 slabs: *blando, duro,* and *yema*—soft, hard, and yolk (€2 prewrapped chunks on the counter). In the summer, the shop also sells ice cream and the refreshing *orxata* (or *horchata*, a drink made from *chufa* nuts—a.k.a. earth almonds or tiger nuts). Order a glass and ask to see and eat a *chufa* nut (Mon-Sat 10:00-20:30, Sun 12:30-20:30, tel. 933-122-511).

Churros con Chocolate **at Granja La Pallaresa:** Continue down Carrer de la Portaferrissa, taking a right at Carrer Petritxol to this fun-loving *xocolateria*. Elegant, older ladies gather here for the Spanish equivalent of tea time—dipping their greasy *churros* into pudding-thick cups of hot chocolate (€4.50 for five *churros con chocolate*). Or, for a more local treat, try an *ensamada* (a Mallorca-style croissant with powdered sugar) or the *crema catalana*, like a crème brûlée (Mon-Fri 9:00-13:00 & 16:00-21:00, Sat-Sun 9:00-13:00 & 17:00-21:00, Carrer Petritxol 11, tel. 933-022-036).

Homemade Chocolate at Fargas: For your last stop, head for the ornate Fargas chocolate shop. Continue down Carrer Petritxol to the square, hook left through the two-part square, and then left up Carrer del Pi to the corner of Carrer de la Portaferrissa. Since the 19th century, gentlemen with walking canes have dropped by here for their chocolate fix. Founded in 1827, this is one of the oldest and most traditional chocolate shops in Barcelona. If they're not too busy, ask to see the old chocolate mill *(Puedo ver el molino?)* to the right of the counter. (It's still used, but nowadays it's powered by a machine rather than a donkey in the basement.) They sell even tiny quantities (one little morsel) by the weight, so don't be shy. A delicious chunk of the crumbly semisweet house specialty costs €0.50 (glass bowl on the counter). The tempting bonbons in the window cost about €1-2 each (Mon-Sat 9:30-13:30 & 16:00-20:00, closed Sun).

Starting or Ending Your Cruise in Barcelona

If your cruise begins and/or ends in Barcelona, you'll want some extra time here; for most travelers, two days is a minimum to see the highlights of this grand, sprawling city. For a longer visit here, pick up my *Rick Steves' Barcelona* guidebook—or, if your trip extends to other points in the country, consider my *Rick Steves' Spain* guidebook.

Airport Connections

El Prat de Llobregat Airport

Barcelona's primary airport, El Prat de Llobregat (airport code: BCN), is eight miles southwest of town and has two large terminals linked by shuttle buses. Most major carriers use the newer Terminal 1. EasyJet and minor airlines use Terminal 2 (which is divided into sections A, B, and C). Terminal 1 and sections A and B of Terminal 2 each have a post office, pharmacy, left-luggage office, plenty of good cafeterias in the gate areas, and ATMs (use the bank-affiliated ATMs in the arrivals hall). Airport info: Tel. 913-211-000, www.aena.es.

Getting from Barcelona's Airport to Downtown

If you're spending the night in Barcelona before your cruise (see "Hotels in Barcelona," later), you can ride the **Aerobus** from the airport to downtown (#A1 and #A2, corresponding with Terminals 1 and 2, stops immediately outside the arrivals lobby of both terminals and in each section of Terminal 2). The bus takes about 30 minutes to go downtown, where it makes several stops, including Plaça d'Espanya and Plaça de Catalunya (departs every 5 minutes, from airport 6:00-1:00 in the morning, from downtown 5:30-24:15, €5.90 one-way, €10.30 round-trip, buy ticket from machine or from driver, tel. 934-100-104, www.aerobusbcn.com).

Alternatively, from Terminal 2, you could take the RENFE **train** (on the "R2 Sud" Rodalies line), which involves more walking (head down the long orange-roofed overpass between sections A and B to reach the station; 2/hour at about :08 and :38 past the hour, 20 minutes to Sants Station, 25 minutes to Passeig de Gràcia Station—near Plaça de Catalunya and some recommended hotels, 30 minutes to França Station; €3.80 or covered by T10 Card, which you can purchase at automated machines at the airport train station).

A **taxi** between the airport and downtown or the cruise port costs about €36 (about €30 on the meter plus a €4.20 airport supplement and fee of €1 per bag). For good service, add an additional 10 percent tip.

Getting from Downtown to the Cruise Port: If you spend the night in Barcelona before your cruise, in the morning you can ride the Metro to the Drassanes stop and catch the #T3 shuttle bus to your ship (for details, see next section).

Getting from Barcelona's Airport to the Cruise Port

There's no direct **public-transportation** connection between the airport and the cruise port, but the route can be done in three affordable (€11/person) but time-consuming steps. First, ride the

Aerobus (described earlier) to Plaça de Catalunya. Then, from Plaça de Catalunya, find the Metro station (look for red *M* sign), and ride the L3 (green) line two stops to Drassanes. Finally, from the bottom of the Ramblas, cross to the far side of the Columbus Monument roundabout, and catch the #T3 shuttle bus (a.k.a. Portbús) from the stop on the harborfront to Barcelona's main cruise port (Moll Adossat—Terminals A, B, C, or D; bus costs €2.50 one-way, €3.50 round-trip, runs every 20 minutes). If your boat is docked at one of the smaller ports at the World Trade Center, you can walk there from the Columbus Monument; here you'll also find a free shuttle bus to the more distant Moll de la Costa port.

For a more direct connection, take a **taxi** (about €36). Some cruise lines arrange **shuttle buses** between the airport and cruise port (for a fee).

Departing from Barcelona's Airport

If you're taking **public transportation** from your cruise terminal to the airport, simply reverse the directions given above: Take the #T3 shuttle bus to the Columbus Monument, cross over to the bottom of the Ramblas, walk or take the Metro up to Plaça de Catalunya, and catch the Aerobus to the airport.

There can be extremely long lines at the port for **taxis** to the airport. You may save time by riding the #T3 shuttle bus to the Columbus Monument and catching a taxi from there.

Alternate Airport

Some budget airlines, including Ryanair, use **Girona-Costa Brava Airport,** located 60 miles north of Barcelona near Girona (airport code: GRO, tel. 972-186-600, www.aena-aeropuertos.es). Ryanair runs a **bus,** operated by Sagalés, to the Barcelona Nord bus station (€16, departures timed to meet flights, 1.25 hours, tel. 902-361-550, www.sagales.com). You can also go from the airport to Girona on a Sagalés bus (hourly, 25 minutes, €3) or in a taxi (€25), then catch a train to Barcelona (at least hourly, 1.25 hours, €15-20). A taxi between the Girona airport and Barcelona costs at least €120.

Hotels in Barcelona

If you need a hotel in Barcelona before or after your cruise, here are a few to consider.

Business-Class Comfort near Plaça de Catalunya

$$$ Hotel Catalonia Plaça Catalunya has four stars, an elegant old entryway with a modern reception area, splashy public spaces, slick marble and hardwood floors, 140 comfortable but simple rooms, and a garden courtyard with a pool a world away from the big-city noise. It's a bit pricey for the quality of the rooms—you're paying for the posh lobby (Db-€200 but can swing much higher or lower with demand, extra bed-€38, breakfast-€19, air-con, elevator, guest computer, Wi-Fi, a half-block off Plaça de Catalunya at Carrer de Bergara 11, Metro: Catalunya, tel. 933-015-151, www. hoteles-catalonia.com, catalunya@hoteles-catalonia.es).

$$ Hotel Reding, on a quiet street a 10-minute walk west of the Ramblas and Plaça de Catalunya action, is a slick and sleek place renting 44 mod rooms at a reasonable price (Db-€125, breakfast-€14, prices go up during trade fairs, extra bed-€38, air-con, elevator, guest computer, Wi-Fi, Carrer de Gravina 5-7, Metro: Universitat, tel. 934-121-097, www.hotelreding.com, recepcion@hotelreding.com).

Affordable Hotels with "Personality" on or near the Ramblas

$$ Hotel Continental Barcelona, in a building overlooking the top of the Ramblas, offers classic, tiny view-balcony opportunities if you don't mind the noise. Its 39 comfortable but faded rooms come with clashing carpets and wallpaper, and perhaps one too many clever ideas. Choose between your own little Ramblas-view balcony (where you can eat your breakfast) or a quieter back room. J. M.'s (José María's) free breakfast and all-day snack-and-drink bar are a plus (Sb-€98, Db-€108, twin Db-€118, Db with Ramblas balcony-€128, extra bed-€40/adult or €20/child, includes breakfast, air-con, elevator, quiet terrace, guest computer, Wi-Fi, Ramblas 138, Metro: Catalunya, tel. 933-012-570, www.hotelcontinental.com, barcelona@hotelcontinental.com).

$ Hostal el Jardí offers 40 clean, remodeled rooms on a breezy square in the Barri Gòtic. Many of the tight, plain, comfy rooms come with petite balconies (for an extra charge) and enjoy an almost Parisian ambience. It's a good deal only if you value the quaint-square-with-Barri-Gòtic ambience—you're definitely paying for the location. Book well in advance, as this family-run place has an avid following (small basic interior Db-€75, nicer interior Db-€90, outer Db with balcony or twin with window-€95, large outer Db with balcony or square-view terrace-€110, no charge for extra bed, breakfast-€6, air-con, elevator, some stairs, Wi-Fi, halfway between Ramblas and cathedral at Plaça Sant Josep Oriol 1, Metro: Liceu, tel. 933-015-900, www.eljardi-barcelona.com, reservations@eljardi-barcelona.com).

Places in the Old City

$$$ Hotel Neri is posh, pretentious, and sophisticated, with 22 rooms spliced into the ancient stones of the Barri Gòtic, overlooking an overlooked square (Plaça Sant Felip Neri) a block from the cathedral. It has big flat-screen TVs, pricey modern art on the bedroom walls, dressed-up people in its gourmet restaurant, and stuffy service (Db-€260-300, suites-€320-400, generally cheaper on weekdays, breakfast-€22, air-con, elevator, Wi-Fi, rooftop tanning deck, Carrer de Sant Sever 5, Metro: Liceu or Jaume I, tel. 933-040-655, www.hotelneri.com, info@hotelneri.com).

$$$ Hotel Nouvel, in an elegant, Victorian-style building on a handy pedestrian street, is less business-oriented and offers more character than the others listed here. It boasts royal lounges and 78 comfy rooms (Sb-€132, Db-€205, online deals can be much much cheaper, extra bed-€35, includes breakfast, €20 deposit for TV remote, air-con, elevator, guest computer, pay Wi-Fi, Carrer de Santa Anna 20, Metro: Catalunya, tel. 933-018-274, www.hotelnouvel.com, info@hotelnouvel.com).

$$ Hotel Banys Orientals, a modern, boutique-type place, has a people-to-people ethic and refreshingly straight prices. Its 43 restful rooms are located in the El Born district on a pedestrianized street between the cathedral and Church of Santa Maria del Mar (Sb-€87, Db-€105, breakfast-€10, air-con, guest computer, Wi-Fi, Carrer de l'Argenteria 37, 50 yards from Metro: Jaume I, tel. 932-688-460, www.hotelbanysorientals.com, reservas@hotelbanysorientals.com). They also run the adjacent, recommended El Senyor Parellada restaurant.

In the Eixample

$$ Hotel Granvía, filling a palatial 1870s mansion, offers a large, peaceful sun patio and 58 spacious rooms (Sb-€75-185, Db-€90-150, superior Db-€105-225, family room-€120-245, mention Rick Steves to get best available rate, breakfast-€14, air-con, elevator, Wi-Fi, Gran Via de les Corts Catalanes 642, Metro: Passeig de Gràcia, tel. 933-181-900, www.hotelgranvia.com, hgranvia@nnhotels.com).

$$ Hotel Continental Palacete, with 19 small rooms, fills a 100-year-old chandeliered mansion. With flowery wallpaper and ornately gilded stucco, it's gaudy in the city of Gaudí, but it's also friendly, quiet, and well located. Guests have unlimited access to the outdoor terrace and the "cruise-inspired" fruit, veggie, and drink buffet (Sb-€108, Db-€145, €35-45 more for bigger and brighter view rooms, extra bed-€55/adult or €40/child, includes breakfast, air-con, guest computer, Wi-Fi, 2 blocks north of Plaça de Catalunya at corner of Rambla de Catalunya and Carrer de la Diputació, 30 Rambla de Catalunya, Metro: Passeig de Gràcia, tel. 934-457-657, www.hotelcontinental.com, palacete@hotelcontinental.com).

$ BCN Fashion House B&B is a meditative place with 10

What If I Miss My Boat?

Remember that you can get help from the cruise line's port agent (listed on the destination information sheet distributed on the ship) and the local TI (see page 162). If the port agent suggests a costly solution (such as a private car with a driver), you may want to consider public transit.

Frequent **trains** leave from Barcelona's Sants Station to points all over Spain and France, including **Valencia**, **Málaga**, **Nice**, **Marseille**, **Toulon**, and more. To look up specific connections, check www.renfe.com or www.bahn.com (Germany's excellent all-Europe website), or call Spain's train-info toll number (tel. 902-320-320). Note that some trains also stop at Barcelona stations closer to the downtown tourist zone: França, Passeig de Gràcia, or Plaça de Catalunya.

You can take a **ferry** to **Ibiza** or **Palma de Mallorca**. For more information, see www.directferries.es.

If you need to catch a **plane** to your next destination, see page 234 for information on Barcelona's airport.

For more advice on what to do if you miss the boat, see page 140.

rooms, a peaceful lounge, and a leafy backyard terrace on the first floor of a nondescript old building (S-€36-56, D-€56-83, bigger "veranda" D-€73-93, Db-€90-125, 2-night minimum stay, breakfast-€6, Wi-Fi, between Carrer d'Ausiàs Marc and Ronda de Sant Pere at Carrer del Bruc 13, just steps from Metro: Urquinaona, mobile 637-904-044, www.bcnfashionhouse.com, info@bcnfashionhouse.com).

Spanish Survival Phrases

Spanish has a guttural sound similar to the J in Baja California. In the phonetics, the symbol for this clearing-your-throat sound is the italicized *h*.

English	Spanish	Pronunciation
Good day.	*Buenos días.*	**bway**-nohs **dee**-ahs
Do you speak English?	*¿Habla Usted inglés?*	**ah**-blah oo-**stehd** een-**glays**
Yes. / No.	*Sí. / No.*	see / noh
I (don't) understand.	*(No) comprendo.*	(noh) kohm-**prehn**-doh
Please.	*Por favor.*	por fah-**bor**
Thank you.	*Gracias.*	**grah**-thee-ahs
I'm sorry.	*Lo siento.*	loh see-**ehn**-toh
Excuse me.	*Perdóneme.*	pehr-**doh**-nay-may
(No) problem.	*(No) problema.*	(noh) proh-**blay**-mah
Good.	*Bueno.*	**bway**-noh
Goodbye.	*Adiós.*	ah-dee-**ohs**
one / two	*uno / dos*	**oo**-noh / dohs
three / four	*tres / cuatro*	trays / **kwah**-troh
five / six	*cinco / seis*	**theen**-koh / says
seven / eight	*siete / ocho*	see-**eh**-tay / **oh**-choh
nine / ten	*nueve / diez*	**nway**-bay / dee-**ayth**
How much is it?	*¿Cuánto cuesta?*	**kwahn**-toh **kway**-stah
Write it?	*¿Me lo escribe?*	may loh ay-**skree**-bay
Is it free?	*¿Es gratis?*	ays **grah**-tees
Is it included?	*¿Está incluido?*	ay-**stah** een-kloo-**ee**-doh
Where can I buy / find...?	*¿Dónde puedo comprar / encontrar...?*	**dohn**-day **pway**-doh kohm-**prar** / ayn-kohn-**trar**
I'd like / We'd like...	*Quiero / Queremos...*	kee-**ehr**-oh / kehr-**ay**-mohs
...a room.	*...una habitación.*	**oo**-nah ah-bee-tah-thee-**ohn**
...a ticket to ___.	*...un billete para ___.*	oon bee-**yeh**-tay **pah**-rah ___
Is it possible?	*¿Es posible?*	ays poh-**see**-blay
Where is...?	*¿Dónde está...?*	**dohn**-day ay-**stah**
...the train station	*...la estación de trenes*	lah ay-stah-thee-**ohn** day **tray**-nays
...the bus station	*...la estación de autobuses*	lah ay-stah-thee-**ohn** day ow-toh-**boo**-says
...the tourist information office	*...la oficina de turismo*	lah oh-fee-**thee**-nah day too-**rees**-moh
Where are the toilets?	*¿Dónde están los servicios?*	**dohn**-day ay-**stahn** lohs sehr-**bee**-thee-ohs
men	*hombres, caballeros*	**ohm**-brays, kah-bah-**yay**-rohs
women	*mujeres, damas*	moo-**heh**-rays, **dah**-mahs
left / right	*izquierda / derecha*	eeth-kee-**ehr**-dah / day-**ray**-chah
straight	*derecho*	day-**ray**-choh
When do you open / close?	*¿A qué hora abren / cierran?*	ah kay **oh**-rah **ah**-brehn / thee-**ay**-rahn
At what time?	*¿A qué hora?*	ah kay **oh**-rah
Just a moment.	*Un momento.*	oon moh-**mehn**-toh
now / soon / later	*ahora / pronto / más tarde*	ah-**oh**-rah / **prohn**-toh / mahs **tar**-day
today / tomorrow	*hoy / mañana*	oy / mahn-**yah**-nah

In a Spanish Restaurant

English	Spanish	Pronunciation
I'd like / We'd like...	Quiero / Queremos...	kee-**ehr**-oh / kehr-**ay**-mohs
...to reserve...	...reservar...	ray-sehr-**bar**
...a table for one / two.	...una mesa para uno / dos.	**oo**-nah **may**-sah **pah**-rah **oo**-noh / dohs
Non-smoking.	No fumador.	noh foo-mah-**dohr**
Is this table free?	¿Está esta mesa libre?	ay-**stah** ay-stah **may**-sah **lee**-bray
The menu (in English), please.	La carta (en inglés), por favor.	lah **kar**-tah (ayn een-**glays**) por fah-**bor**
service (not) included	servicio (no) incluido	sehr-**bee**-thee-oh (noh) een-kloo-**ee**-doh
cover charge	precio de entrada	**pray**-thee-oh day ayn-**trah**-dah
to go	para llevar	**pah**-rah yay-**bar**
with / without	con / sin	kohn / seen
and / or	y / o	ee / oh
menu (of the day)	menú (del día)	may-**noo** (dayl **dee**-ah)
specialty of the house	especialidad de la casa	ay-spay-thee-ah-lee-**dahd** day lah **kah**-sah
tourist menu	menú turístico	meh-**noo** too-**ree**-stee-koh
combination plate	plato combinado	**plah**-toh kohm-bee-**nah**-doh
appetizers	tapas	**tah**-pahs
bread	pan	pahn
cheese	queso	**kay**-soh
sandwich	bocadillo	boh-kah-**dee**-yoh
soup	sopa	**soh**-pah
salad	ensalada	ayn-sah-**lah**-dah
meat	carne	**kar**-nay
poultry	aves	**ah**-bays
fish	pescado	pay-**skah**-doh
seafood	marisco	mah-**ree**-skoh
fruit	fruta	**froo**-tah
vegetables	verduras	behr-**doo**-rahs
dessert	postres	**poh**-strays
tap water	agua del grifo	**ah**-gwah dayl **gree**-foh
mineral water	agua mineral	**ah**-gwah mee-nay-**rahl**
milk	leche	**lay**-chay
(orange) juice	zumo (de naranja)	**thoo**-moh (day nah-**rahn**-hah)
coffee	café	kah-**feh**
tea	té	tay
wine	vino	**bee**-noh
red / white	tinto / blanco	**teen**-toh / **blahn**-koh
glass / bottle	vaso / botella	**bah**-soh / boh-**tay**-yah
beer	cerveza	thehr-**bay**-thah
Cheers!	¡Salud!	sah-**lood**
More. / Another.	Más. / Otro.	mahs / **oh**-troh
The same.	El mismo.	ehl **mees**-moh
The bill, please.	La cuenta, por favor.	lah **kwayn**-tah por fah-**bor**
tip	propina	proh-**pee**-nah
Delicious!	¡Delicioso!	day-lee-thee-**oh**-soh

For hundreds more pages of survival phrases for your trip to Spain, check out *Rick Steves' Spanish Phrase Book*.

PROVENCE
France

France Practicalities

France is a place of gentle beauty. At 215,000 square miles (roughly 20 percent smaller than Texas), it is Western Europe's largest nation, with luxuriant forests, forever coastlines, truly grand canyons, and Europe's highest mountain ranges. You'll also discover a dizzying array of artistic and architectural wonders—soaring cathedrals, chandeliered châteaux, and museums filled with the cultural icons of the Western world.

For the French, *l'art de vivre*—the art of living—is more than just a pleasing expression. Though they produce nearly a quarter of the world's wine, the French drink much of it themselves. Come here to experience subtle pleasures, including fine cuisine, velvety wines, and linger-long pastimes such as people-watching from sun-dappled cafés.

Money: France uses the euro currency: 1 euro (€) = about $1.30. An ATM is called a *distributeur*. The local VAT (value-added sales tax) rate is 20 percent; the minimum purchase eligible for a VAT refund is €175.01 (for details on refunds, see page 135).

Language: For useful French phrases, see page 293

Emergencies: Dial 17 for police or 112 for medical or other emergencies. In case of theft or loss, see page 128.

Time Zone: France is on Central European Time (the same as most of the Continent, and six/nine hours ahead of the East/West Coasts of the US).

Consular Services: The US consulate in Marseille is at Place Varian Fry (tel. 04 91 54 90 84, after-hours emergency tel. 01 43 12 22 22, http://marseille.usconsulate.gov); limited services are also available in Nice (tel. 04 93 88 89 55). The Canadian consulate in Nice is at 2 Place Franklin (tel. 04 93 92 93 22, www.france.gc.fr). Call ahead for passport services.

Phoning: France has a direct-dial 10-digit phone system (no area codes). To **call within France,** just dial the 10-digit number. To **call to France,** dial the international access code (00 if calling from Europe, or 011 from North America), then 33 (France's country code) then the phone number (but drop the initial zero). To **call home from France,** dial 00, 1, then your area code and phone number. For more help, see page 1242.

Tipping: At cafés and restaurants, a 12-15 percent service charge is typically included in the bill (*service compris*), and most French never tip. However, if you feel the service was exceptional, it's fine to tip up to 5 percent. To tip a cabbie, round up to about 10 percent of the metered fare (for a €13 fare, pay €14).

Tourist Information: www.us.rendezvousenfrance.com

PROVENCE

"*There are treasures to carry away in this land, which has not found a spokesman worthy of the riches it offers.*"
—Paul Cézanne

This magnificent region is shaped like a giant wedge of quiche. From its sunburned crust, fanning out along the Mediterranean coast from the Camargue to Marseille, it stretches north along the Rhône Valley to Orange. The Romans were here in force and left many ruins—some of the best anywhere. Seven popes, artists such as Vincent van Gogh and Paul Cézanne, and author Peter Mayle all enjoyed their years in Provence. This destination features a splendid recipe of arid climate, oceans of vineyards, dramatic scenery, lively cities, and adorable hill-capping villages.

On a cruise, you'll enter this region through one of two gloomy port cities that (let's be frank) are not representative of

the world-renowned romanticism of Provence: Marseille or Toulon. While some travelers enjoy exploring Marseille's swiftly rejuvenating cityscape, most prefer to get out of town—on the train, with a shore excursion, or with a rental car—to experience some of Provence's more famous stops. For a Provençal beach fix, find Cassis, between Marseille and Toulon. Stylish and self-confident Aix-en-Provence lies 45 minutes from the sea (an easy train ride from Marseille). Or delve deeper into the Proven-

Excursions from Marseille or Toulon

Fascinating and varied destinations abound in this region. The following are best done with an excursion or rental car:

Arles has an impressive Roman arena, an eclectic assortment of museums, and evocative Van Gogh sites.

Avignon, a fashionable walled city, is famous for its medieval bridge and Palace of the Popes.

Pont du Gard, a well-preserved ancient aqueduct, is one of the most remarkable surviving Roman ruins anywhere.

Les Baux is a medieval castle and hill town packed with boutiques and cafés.

The **Hill Towns of Provence** are villages that are pretty to look at and fun to explore, including Roussillon, Gordes, Lourmarin, and Isle-sur-la-Sorgue.

St-Tropez is a trendy seaside experience (see page 369 in the French Riviera chapter), but it's far from the Provençal ports, especially Marseille—Cassis is much closer. Resist your inclination to spend your day (and a very long bus ride) visiting this jet-set tourist trap.

çal interior on an excursion. Admire the skill of ball-tossing *boules* players in small squares in every Provençal village and city.

Planning Your Time

Provence's ports are Marseille and Toulon, about 40 miles apart. Marseille is within striking distance of several great destinations, but your choices from Toulon are more limited.

Docking at **Marseille,** you can stay put, or head to the train station and make a quick visit to Aix-en-Provence or Cassis.

Docking at **Toulon,** take the train either to Cassis or Marseille—or, for minimum effort, just hang out in Toulon. To go farther, it's best to take a cruise-line excursion or rent a car.

Here are descriptions, with time estimates, of three convenient destinations; you'll probably have to choose just one:

• **Cassis** is a seaside, Riviera-like resort town that's an easy 25-minute train ride from Marseille's station, or a 35-minute ride from Toulon's. It's pleasant to stroll, but with more time, hike or take a boat to the beaches tucked between the cliffs called *calanques* (access can be limited during busy times). Allow five hours for a quick visit from either port, and add up to two hours for the *calanques*.

• **Aix-en-Provence** is a manicured city just a 45-minute train ride away from Marseille's station. With no major sights, Aix is purely Provençal life on display. Follow my self-guided walk through town. Allow a total of six hours from Marseille's cruise

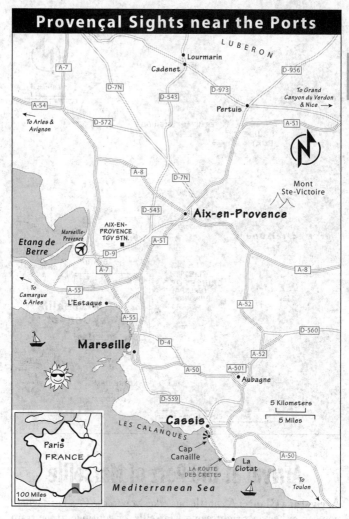

Provençal Sights near the Ports

port; make sure your train stops at Aix's Centre-Ville station. Because of the lengthy travel time, Aix isn't practical from Toulon.

• **Marseille,** a seedy port city with some interesting sights, can fill four hours: Explore the street called La Canebière, wander the Old Port, visit La Charité Museum (lunch café) and the cathedral, then head to Notre-Dame de la Garde. If coming from Toulon, skip Notre-Dame, and allow up to six hours, including transportation.

Greater Marseille

To Airport, Aix-en-Provence & Avignon

A-55

E-714

Bassin Mirabeau

TERMINAL BUILDINGS

CRUISE PORT 4

BREAKWATER

Bassin Nationale

D-4

Mediterranean Sea

ST-CHARLES TRAIN STATION

To Cassis, Toulon & Nice

LA JOLIETTE CRUISE PORT & TERMINAL BUILDING

Ⓜ Joliette

Ⓜ

Marseille Center

Ⓜ Old Port

See detail map

Les Iles

TOLL TUNNEL

A-50

To Toulon & Nice

NOTRE-DAME DE LA GARDE

1 Kilometer

1 Mile

Note: Not all Metro stations shown

To Cassis   D-559

Arrival at the Port of Marseille

Arrival at a Glance: A shuttle bus takes you to the Old Port, where you can either start sightseeing Marseille, or continue to the train station (a 20-minute walk or quick Métro ride). From the station, trains head for Cassis (25 minutes) and Aix-en-Provence (45 minutes). Taxis are available for outlying towns, but they're pricey.

Port Overview

Marseille's enormous port sprawls for miles beneath a bluff west of downtown. In this gritty industrial zone, most cruise ships tuck themselves in between cargo vessels at **Porte 4.** This cruise pier has several terminals (called *poste,* or "dock"): Poste 163, Poste 181, and Poste 186 feed into a new, modern terminal complex near the tip

┌───┐

Services near the Port of Marseille

The main terminal at Porte 4 has **Wi-Fi** and an **ATM** outside the front door. The smaller terminals have fewer services. Instead, head into town on the cruise line's shuttle bus, and find the nearest services from the Old Port (ask at the TI near the Old Port).

   Renting a car for the day can be an efficient use of your time in this region. There are car-rental offices at Marseille's train station, including Europcar (toll tel. 08 25 82 56 80), Avis (toll tel. 08 20 61 16 36), and Hertz (tel. 04 91 14 04 24).

└───┘

of the pier. A bit closer to the base of the pier, Poste 162 and Postes 2/3 each have their own, much smaller terminal buildings.

Tourist Information: There is no TI at the cruise port, but there is one near the shuttle drop-off at the Old Port (see page 257).

Alternative Port: On busy days, a few cruises may anchor offshore and tender passengers to a pier much closer to the town center (just below the cathedral), called **La Joliette.** Smaller ships may even dock here. La Joliette has two docks (Poste 94 and Poste 95). To reach the Old Port from here, walk 15 minutes (simply stroll with the port area on your right) or hop on bus #60.

Getting to the Sights

Choose between seeing Marseille or heading to a nearby town via train or bus. The best plan may be to begin the day out of town, then work your way back to Marseille and spend any remaining time sightseeing here before returning to your ship.

By Taxi

Taxis meet arriving ships and take passengers all over Marseille and Provence. Here are some average rates:

   • To the Old Port, train station, or Notre-Dame de la Garde church (20 minutes): €15-20
   • To Aix-en-Provence (45 minutes): €55
   • To Cassis (45 minutes): €63

If possible, agree on the above rates up front. If the cabbie uses the meter, make sure its set to the correct tariff: You'll most likely be charged "one-way" fares: tariff C on weekdays (Mon-Sat), or tariff D on Sundays, holidays, or at night. Round-trip fares are cheaper: tariff A on weekdays; tariff B on Sundays, holidays and at night. For any trip, you will pay about 20 percent more on Sundays and holidays. For rides in town, there's a legitimate €1.10 port supplement. The official hourly rate is €22.20.

PROVENCE

French Experiences for Cruisers

The South of France is famously touristy, but even those who have just a few hours in this region can find ways to meaningfully experience French culture. Here are some ideas that go beyond the predictable sightseeing rut.

Sip a *pastis* or a coffee at an outdoor café. The French are champions at relaxed yet refined people-watching from a scenic perch. Find a café with a view you like—on a shaded square or overlooking a sunny patch of beach—and invest a half-hour and a few euros in the delightfully French knack for good living. While a cup of coffee is an easy choice (for something resembling an American-style latte, order *café au lait*), you could really go local with a *pastis:* a sweet anise (licorice) liqueur that comes on the rocks with a glass of water (usually accompanied by black olives). Cut it with lots of water.

Assemble a picnic lunch at an outdoor market. French markets are a colorful potpourri of unique edibles. I've mentioned several markets in this book, but you can also ask around to find a *marché* (mar-shay) when you land; some run daily, while others are open only on certain days. Wander from stall to stall, filling your basket with anything that looks good. Then find a scenic bench for your feast. Remember to bring your Swiss Army knife ashore for opening wine bottles and slicing cheese and salami.

Swim (or at least wade) at an idyllic beach. The famed glittering beaches of the South of France are extremely inviting, and the French, along with tourists, love basking at the seafront. Consider bringing your swimsuit for your day in port to join in. While there are some public beaches (bring your own towel, or buy one as a souvenir), many French beaches have rentable chaise lounges, umbrellas, and towels—look for signs.

Watch the old guys play *boules* in a park. Also called *pétanque,* the game of *boules* is the horseshoes of the South of France, played in every city and village. Each player gets three heavy metal balls (*boules,* about the size of baseballs). They take turns trying to get their *boules* closest to the small wooden target ball (*le cochonnet*—"piglet," about the size of a table tennis ball). Watch a game and cheer—or groan—along with the other spectators. For extra credit, invite yourself into the mix to toss a few balls with local instruction.

By Public Transportation

First you'll go to the Old Port, and from there you'll either begin exploring town, or head to the train station to get to another Provençal destination.

Step 1: To Marseille's Old Port

The easiest solution by far is to take the cruise line's **shuttle bus** into downtown Marseille (around €7-14 round-trip, departs every 20 minutes, 15-20-minute trip). The bus deposits you at the Old Port in the heart of town, within walking distance of most of Marseille's sights, and a quick Métro ride from the train station (see "Step 2," next). The TI is just up the main street (La Canebière) on the left.

It's possible but obnoxiously time-consuming to get into town on your own (involving a 30-minute walk plus a bus-and-Métro ride). Doing it yourself could easily eat up an hour or more—spring for the shuttle bus instead.

Step 2: From the Old Port
to Marseille's Train Station

To reach the train station from the Old Port, **walk** straight uphill on the main drag (La Canebière), turn left up Boulevard Dugommier, and follow it to the station (it becomes Boulevard d'Athènes along the way). It's about a 20-minute walk.

To save time and sweat, zip to the station on the **Métro:** Find an entrance to the Vieux-Port Métro stop (there are several; a handy one is right on the Old Port). Go down into the Métro, buy a €1.50 ticket at the ticket machine, and board a train going toward La Rose. Ride it two stops, to the St. Charles stop, and escalate up into the train station.

Step 3: From Marseille's Train Station
to Provençal Sights

The main train station is called Marseille St. Charles. It has both ticket machines and staffed ticket windows; electronic boards show upcoming departures. Before taking off, be sure to plan your return journey. Frequent trains go to **Cassis** (20/day, 25 minutes) and **Aix-en-Provence Centre-Ville** station (2/hour, 45 minutes).

From the train station, you can also take a bus to **Aix-en-Provence** (at least 4/hour, 30-50 minutes).

By Tour

For information on hiring a local guide or joining a tour of the region, see the "Tours in..." section for each destination. Most guides and tour companies are based in Aix, Arles, or Avignon, but Mike Rijken's Wine Safari can pick you up in Marseille (see page 259).

Returning to Your Ship

If you stay in Marseille for the day, simply catch the cruise shuttle bus at the Old Port and ride it back to your terminal.

If you left Marseille and are returning by train, get off at Marseille's St. Charles Station and take the Métro back to the Old Port, where you can catch the shuttle bus: Buy a €1.50 ticket at the machine, descend the long escalator, and take the blue line 1 (direction: La Fourragère) two stops to Vieux-Port. Exiting the subway train, follow *Sortie la Canebière* signs to emerge near the TI and find your shuttle. (If you have time to spare, consider walking 20 minutes downhill from the train station instead of taking the Métro—see page 258.)

See page 290 for help if you miss your boat.

Arrival at the Port of Toulon

Arrival at a Glance: Ships dock either in Toulon itself (a 5-minute walk from the town center), or across the harbor in La Seyne-sur-Mer (take the cruise-line shuttle bus or a public ferry into Toulon). From Toulon's town center, you can walk (25-30 minutes) or ride a local bus to the train station for connections to Cassis (35 minutes) or Marseille (45-60 minutes).

Port Overview

The pleasant if unspectacular city of Toulon (pop. 170,000), situated between mountains and a large bay, is used by some cruise lines to access the sights of Provence. The Toulon cruise terminal is an air-conditioned little oasis with a WC and a parking lot for excursion buses.

Tourist Information: The TI desk in the terminal is open only when ships arrive. Toulon's city TI is a short walk from the port (see the "Services in Toulon" sidebar, later).

Alternative Port: Some ships dock across the water at **Le Seyne-sur-Mer** (which has no real terminal of its own).

Getting to the Sights

Considering the relative remoteness of Toulon, your best strategy is to take the train to Marseille or Cassis, or, if venturing farther afield, join a cruise-line excursion. If time is short, Toulon itself offers some sightseeing opportunities (see "Sights in Toulon," later).

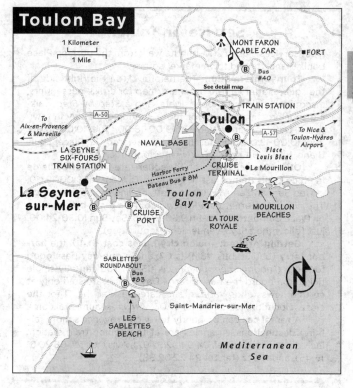

From Toulon's Cruise Terminal

The main part of Toulon's old town (and the TI) is just a 10-minute walk from the cruise terminal; to reach the train station, it's a 25-minute walk or a ride on a local bus. If there are no taxis waiting, you can call one at tel. 04 94 93 51 51; figure about €7-10 one-way to the train station.

Step 1: From the Cruise Terminal to the Old Town Market Square (Place Louis Blanc)

It's an easy walk from your cruise ship to the small, old town market square called Place Louis Blanc, where you'll find the TI, ATMs, a pharmacy, and the stop for buses headed to the train station. (If you get turned around, just look for signs to *Office du Tourisme*.) From the cruise terminal, walk toward the row of apartment blocks that line the top of the harbor. When you reach this embankment, swing left and walk alongside the apartments until you reach the big gap in the buildings. Hook right between the buildings; Place Louis Blanc is straight ahead, across the busy street. The TI is on the right side of the square, and other services are nearby. The mostly traffic-free old town sprawls beyond this square.

Services in Toulon

Most services cluster a 10-minute walk from the port, on Place Louis Blanc, the old town market square.

Tourist Information: The helpful TI, on the right side of the square, offers a free brochure/map for cruise passengers, discounted tickets to local sights, and a *Step by Step* walking tour brochure handy for those spending the day in town (April-Oct Mon and Wed-Sat 9:00-18:00, Tue 10:00-18:00, Sun 10:00-12:00; shorter hours Nov-March; 12 Place Louis Blanc, tel. 04 94 18 53 00, www.toulontourisme.com).

Other Services: Also on the square are the **Pharmacie de la Place Louis Blanc** (just beyond the TI, Mon-Sat 8:00-19:00, closed Sun) and an **ATM** (on the left, behind the flower stand). The nearest Internet café—**www@com**—is three blocks away on Place Gambetta (Mon-Fri 9:30-24:00, Sat-Sun 10:30-24:00, just follow the busy Avenue de la République).

Getting Around: Toulon **city buses** cost €1.40, the **harbor ferry** (bateau bus #8M) is €2, and a one-day pass good for both (*l'abonnement un jour*) is €3.90. You can buy single tickets on board the bus or ferry. Day passes are sold only at certain newsstands, *tabacs*, and cafés (ask at the TI for the closest location, tel. 04 94 03 87 03, www.reseaumistral.com).

A **rental car** can be handy to reach Provence's more far-flung destinations. Agencies are at the Toulon train station, including Europcar (tel. 04 94 92 52 92), Avis (toll tel. 08 20 61 16 45), and Hertz (tel. 04 94 22 02 88).

Step 2: From the Old Town Market Square (Place Louis Blanc) to Toulon's Train Station

From Place Louis Blanc, the walk to the train station takes about 25 minutes through not-very-interesting neighborhoods. Buses also run to the station from the square.

By Foot: With your back to Place Louis Blanc, turn right onto busy Avenue de la République and follow it a few blocks to a major intersection. At this point, swing right with the road up Rue Anatole France—passing the square called Place d'Armes on your left—and continue straight up to the big square called Place de la Liberté. Cross diagonally through this square, exiting at the top-right corner, on Rue Dumont d'Urville. You'll pop out on Boulevard de Tessé; the train station is just to your left.

By Bus: Buses #7 and #23 run frequently from Place Louis Blanc to the train station (€1.40, buy ticket from driver, 10-15-minute trip depending on traffic). You can catch either bus just a few steps off Place Louis Blanc (look for the bus stop signed *Louis Blanc* alongside the church, on Avenue de la République; #7 direction: Gare, #23 direction: Siblas). Take either bus to the Gare stop; #7 drops you two blocks below the train station—from there, walk up Avenue Vauban to the station; #23 stops at the station.

Step 3: From Toulon's Train Station to Marseille or Cassis

The only destinations close enough for an easy side-trip by train are **Marseille** (hourly, 45-60 minutes) and **Cassis** (about hourly, 35 minutes). While St-Tropez is sometimes offered as an excursion from Toulon, there's no convenient public-transportation connection.

From La Seyne-sur-Mer

If your ship docks at La Seyne-sur-Mer, it's easy to get across the harbor into Toulon proper. Cruise lines offer a **shuttle bus,** which takes you to the Toulon cruise terminal (from that point, follow the "From Toulon's Cruise Terminal" instructions earlier). There's also a **harbor ferry** (bateau bus #8M) that works like a city bus, shuttling passengers across the harbor from La Seyne to Toulon (€2, pay on boat, 2/hour, tel. 04 94 03 87 03, www.reseaumistral.com). This ferry starts in the center of La Seyne, but you can catch it at Espace Marine, a dock that's a 10-minute walk from your cruise ship (follow the waterfront to the right). The ferry cruises scenically across the harbor to Toulon's town center in 10 minutes, where you're dropped off at a pier near the TI. From the old town market square (Place Louis Blanc), follow the directions on the previous page to reach the train station.

By Tour

For information on hiring a local guide or joining a tour of the region, see the "Tours in..." sections for Marseille and Aix-en-Provence.

Sights in Toulon

If your time here is brief—and you don't have the energy to venture far—you could simply enjoy half a day in this easygoing, very French-feeling town, and then luxuriate back on the ship. Don't expect oodles of Old World charm; Toulon's port was devastated during World War II, and much of the city was rebuilt more modern than quaint. But if you simply walk across the busy waterfront street, you can be in the characteristic old quarter in minutes. Toulon feels like a mini-Marseille, with a strong North African flavor due to the many immigrant workers who call this part of France home.

For a short Toulon visit, I'd drop by the TI (pick up the *Step by Step* walking tour brochure), then get hands-on in the market (try olives or fruit). From the top of the market, loop through the town (circling generally counterclockwise), tour the National Naval

PROVENCE

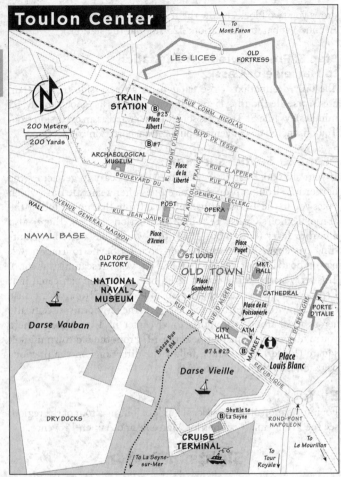

Toulon Center

To Mont Faron

LES LICES

OLD FORTRESS

TRAIN STATION

(B) #23

Place Albert I

(B) #7

RUE COMM. NICOLAS

BLVD. DE TESSE

ARCHAEOLOGICAL MUSEUM

R. DUMONT D'URVILLE

Place de la Liberté

RUE ANATOLE FRANCE

RUE CLAPPIER

RUE PICOT

BOULEVARD DU

GENERAL LECLERC

200 Meters
200 Yards

WALL

AVENUE GENERAL MAGNON

RUE JEAN JAURES

POST

OPERA

NAVAL BASE

Place d'Armes

ST. LOUIS

Place Puget

OLD ROPE FACTORY

OLD TOWN

MKT. HALL

NATIONAL NAVAL MUSEUM

Place Gambetta

CATHEDRAL

Darse Vauban

RUE DE LA

RUE D'ALGERS

Place de la Poissonerie

PORTE D'ITALIE

AVE DE BESAGNE

CITY HALL

ATM

Bateau Bus #8M

#7 & #23

MARKET

Place Louis Blanc

Darse Vieille

REPUBLIQUE

DRY DOCKS

Shuttle to La Seyne

ROND-PONT NAPOLEON

To Le Mourillon

CRUISE TERMINAL

To La Seyne-sur-Mer

To Tour Royale

Museum, and then nurse a drink or have lunch on the harborfront before returning to your ship.

▲▲The Market and Old Toulon

Toulon's colorful market fills a long square running inland from the center of the harbor (daily except Monday, until 13:00). Strolling here in the morning, you feel a part of a workaday town in southern France—with barely a hint of cruise culture. From the top of the market, you can wander the characteristic streets deeper into town. Bronze arrows in the cobbles direct you along the TI's walking tour.

▲▲National Naval Museum
(Musée National de la Marine)

This amazing little museum, housed in the 18th-century Royal Arsenal at the edge of a current naval base (a three-minute walk from the town center), tells the story of this important port. Toulon's harbor is considered one of the most beautiful and best-protected in the entire Mediterranean, which explains its impressive 600-year history as a leading French naval port.

Cost and Hours: €6, €4.50 for cruisers, includes audioguide; July-Aug daily 10:00-18:00; Sept-June Wed-Mon 10:00-18:00, closed Tue; Place Monsenergue, tel. 04 22 42 02 01, www.musee-marine.fr/toulon.html.

Visiting the Museum: With the help of the wonderful included audioguide, you'll learn of the 17th-century birth of the navy here under Louis XIII (who considered the Brittany port of Brest his defense to the west, and Toulon his defense to the east). Napoleon sailed from here to Egypt with 177 vessels in 1798. In 1900, this was Europe's leading military port, but it was devastated in World War II, when the French navy scuttled 77 ships in Toulon harbor to prevent them from falling into the hands of the Nazis. Today, 20,000 people still work here as part of the navy. You're likely to see France's only aircraft carrier, the nuclear-powered *Charles de Gaulle*, moored here. (There are navy harbor boat tours, but only in French.) Note the skinny, 400-yard-long building next door to the museum. It was a rope factory back when rope was a vital industry.

Tourist Train

The goofy little tourist train circles a district called Le Mourillon with a stop at a pleasant beach: Plage du Mourillon. You can catch it near the TI on the waterfront at square Germain Nouveau. While the tourist train gets cruisers to sand and surf, the only way to explore the old town is on foot.

Cost and Hours: €6; 3-6/day, more in summer, none Nov-March; 45 minutes, mobile 06 20 77 44 43, www.traintoulon.com.

Mont Faron Cable Car

By American or Swiss standards, this cable car (*téléphérique* in French) isn't much—but it's highly promoted in Toulon. Visitors ride to a 540-foot summit for commanding views of the bay and pleasant walks.

Cost and Hours: €7, special €6 *téléphérique* ticket includes transit day-pass—sold only at TI; daily 10:00-18:30, July-Aug until 19:45, May-June and Sept until 19:00, closed Mon off-season, closed Dec-mid-Feb and in high winds; tel. 04 94 92 68 25, www.telepherique-faron.com.

Getting There: Take bus #40 from Place Louis Blanc near the TI (direction: Mas du Faron, 20-minute bus ride to Téléphérique stop).

La Seyne-sur-Mer and Sablettes Beach

La Seyne-sur-Mer, once a mighty shipyard (established in 1711), was destroyed in World War II and rebuilt after the war. It closed for good in 1989. Today it's a modern and easygoing harbor town with a big park, relaxed marina, and fine waterfront promenade. From the La Seyne cruise port, it's a 20-minute walk to the town center—or you can walk 10 minutes to the Espace Marine dock and take the harbor ferry (bateau bus #8M). Nearby is Sablettes, with the best beach for cruise travelers based in La Seyne (take bus #83 from the main road next to the cruise ship dock, direction: Sablettes, 2/hour, 15 minutes, bus route ends at Sablettes roundabout, then follow Corniche Georges Pompidou to the south beach).

Returning to Your Ship

From Toulon's train station, it's a 30-minute downhill walk through town back to the cruise port, or you can catch bus #23 and take it to the Louis Blanc stop, near the TI and a 10-minute stroll from the port. If returning to La Seyne, your shuttle bus stop is at the Toulon cruise terminal, or you can ride the public ferry (bateau bus #8M) from the pier near the TI to the Espace Marine stop. See page 290 for help if you miss your boat.

Marseille

Those who think of Marseille as the "Naples of France"—a big, gritty, dangerous port—are missing the boat. Today's Marseille (mar-say), though hardly pristine, is closer to the "Barcelona of France." It's a big, gritty port, *sans* question, but it has a distinct culture, a proud spirit, and a populace determined to clean up its act. That's a tall order, but they're off to a fair start. Over the last few years, dozens of Marseille's historic buildings have been renovated and several new public buildings and exhibition spaces have been constructed (three of which are described in this chapter). The pedestrian zone around the Old Port was redesigned, and is now as wide as the Champs-Elysées. A new tramway system is up and running. This massive facelift was all in preparation for a year-long program as the European Capital of Culture in 2013, which attracted more than 10 million visitors to the city and cost roughly €3.5 billion. Marseille is on the move.

France's oldest (600 B.C.) and second-biggest city (and Europe's third-largest port) owns a history that goes back to ancient Greek times—and challenges you to find its charm. Marseille is a world apart from France's other leading cities, and has only one essential sight to visit—Notre-Dame de la Garde. Here the city is the museum, the streets are its paintings, and the happy-go-lucky residents provide its ambience.

The influence of immigrants matters in this city teeming with authentic ambience. More than 25 percent of the city's population came from countries in North Africa. You're likely to hear as much Arabic as French. These migrants have created residential ghettos where nary a word of French is uttered—infuriating anti-immigrant French people certain that this will be the destiny for the rest of "their" country.

Most tourists leave Marseille off their itinerary—it doesn't fit their idea of the French Riviera or of Provence (and they're right). But it would be a shame to come to the south of France and not experience the region's leading city and namesake of the French national anthem. This much-maligned city seems eager to put on a welcoming face.

Orientation to Marseille

Marseille is big, with 860,000 people, so keep it simple and focus on the area immediately around the Old Port (Vieux Port). A main boulevard (La Canebière) meets the colorful Old Port near a cluster of small (and skippable) museums and the TI. The Panier district is the old town, blanketing a hill that tumbles down to the port. Marseille's three new museums, anchored between the port and the cathedral, are impossible to miss. The harborside is a lively, broad promenade lined with inviting eateries, amusements, and a morning fish market. Everything described here is within a 30-minute walk of the Old Port.

Tourist Information

The main TI is two blocks up from the Old Port on La Canebière (Mon-Sat 9:00-19:00, Sun 10:00-17:00, 11 La Canebière, toll tel. 08 26 50 05 00, www.marseille-tourisme.com). In summer, two satellite offices are open: One's at the St. Charles train station (see next) and a kiosk is at the Old Port. Pick up the good city map, the flier with a self-guided walk through the old town, and information on museums and weekly walking tours.

Arrival in Marseille

By Train: If you're coming from Toulon, get off at St. Charles Station (Gare St. Charles). To reach the Old Port, you can walk, take the Métro, or catch a taxi.

On **foot** it's an exhilarating 15-minute downhill gauntlet along grimy streets. Leave the station through the exit at track A (past the big departure board), veer right, walk down the stairs, and go straight on Boulevard d'Athènes, which becomes Boulevard Dugommier. Turn right at McDonald's onto the grand boulevard, La Canebière, which leads directly to the main TI and the Old Port.

By **Métro** it's an easy subterranean trip from the train station to the Old Port: Go down the escalator opposite track E and then take a longer escalator to your left. Buy a ticket from a ticket machine (look for one that accepts coins—some take only credit cards) or the Accueil office (closed 12:40-13:40). Your €1.50 ticket is good for one hour of travel on Métro; buses and all-day passes cost €5 (www.rtm.fr). At the turnstile, touch your ticket to the yellow pads to get the green light, and walk through. Take blue line 1 (direction: La Fourragère) two stops to Vieux Port (Old Port). Following *Sortie* signs, then *la Canebière* exit signs, you'll pop out within sight of the TI (and not far from the smell of the fish market). To return to the station from here, take blue line 1 (direction: La Rose) two stops and get off at Gare St. Charles.

Taxis are out the front doors of the station, down the escalator opposite track E. Allow €15 to the port and €20 to Notre-Dame de la Garde—though train station cabbies may refuse these short trips if business is hopping (tel. 04 91 02 20 20). Taxis along the port will take you on shorter rides.

Helpful Hints

Pickpockets: As in any big city, thieves thrive in crowds and target tourists. Wear your money belt, and assume any commotion is a smokescreen for theft.

Car Rental: All the major companies are represented at St. Charles Station (see "Arrival in Marseille," earlier).

Bus #60 to the Basilica: This handy bus scoots you from the Old Port up to Notre-Dame de la Garde in 10 minutes (€1.50 ticket is good for one hour, pay driver, 3/hour). Ask the driver for the Notre-Dame de la Garde stop (where most are going). To return to the port, board the bus at this same stop. You can also catch this bus on the north side of the port, along the Quai du Port terminal (see "From the Old Port to the New Town" later).

Navigating French Food: For tips on eating in France, see the sidebar on page 276.

Bike Cabs: In summer, look for advertisement-slathered bicycle cabs that will zip you up and down the Old Port for free (tip optional).

Local Guide: **Pascale Benguigui** is a terrific guide for Marseille, Aix-en-Provence, St-Tropez, and anything in between (€156/half-day, €248/day, mobile 06 20 80 07 51, macpas@club-internet.fr).

Tours in Marseille

Ask at the TI about occasional **walking tours** conducted in English and French (usually Sat afternoons, about €7, covers the Panier district).

Le Petit Train's helpful little tourist trains with skimpy recorded information make two routes through town. Both leave at least hourly from the northeast corner of the Old Port. The more interesting Notre-Dame de la Garde route (#1) saves you the 30-minute climb to the basilica's fantastic view and runs along a nice section of Marseille's waterfront (€7; allow 80 minutes for round-trip, including 20-30 minutes to visit the church; runs daily, April-Nov usually every 20 minutes 10:00-12:20 & 13:40-18:20, less-frequent Dec-March; tel. 04 91 25 24 69, www.petit-train-marseille.com). I'd skip the Vieux Marseille route (#2), which toots you through the Panier district—better done on foot (€6, 65 minutes, includes one 30-minute stop, April-Oct only).

Two companies run pricey **big bus tours** that I don't recommend. **L'Open Tour**'s double-decker buses with open seating up top offer a 13-stop, hop-on, hop-off route that is very similar to Le Petit Train's routes. Buses depart from next to the Petit Train stop and run only every 45 minutes, leaving you too long at most stops, and there's a 1.5-hour gap in service at lunch (€18 for one-day pass, 70 minutes round-trip). **City Tour** red buses do a longer route, including La Canebière, in a two-hour round-trip (€18, departures at 10:30, 14:30, and 18:00 July-Sept, same stop locations at the Old Port).

Dutchman Mike Rijken's **Wine Safari** is a one-man show, taking travelers through the region he adopted more than 20 years ago. Mike came to France to train as a chef, later became a wine steward, and has now found his calling as a driver/guide. His English is fluent, and though his focus is on wine and wine villages, Mike knows the region thoroughly and is a good teacher of its history (€75/half-day, €130/day, priced per person, group size varies from 2 to 6; pickups possible in Marseille; tel. 04 90 35 59 21, mobile 06 19 29 50 81, www.winesafari.net, mikeswinesafari@orange.fr).

PROVENCE

Sights in Marseille

I've listed these sights starting at the Old Port, jogging up and back on La Canebière, and then wandering in the Panier district. I've also included some commentary to help you connect the dots (see the map on page 262).

• *Start where the cruise ship's shuttle bus (or the Métro from the train station) deposits you—in the heart of town, the...*

Old Port (Vieux Port)

Protected by two impressive fortresses at its mouth, Marseille's Vieux Port has long been the economic heart of town. These citadels were built in the 17th cen-
tury under Louis XIV, supposedly to protect the city. But locals figured the forts were actually designed to keep an eye on Marseille—a city that was essentially autonomous until 1660—and challenge Marseille to thoroughly incorporate into the growing kingdom of France.

Today, the serious shipping is away from the center, and the Old Port is the happy domain of pleasure craft. The fish market

along Quai des Belges (where you're standing) thrives each morning (unless the wind kept the boats home the day before). The stalls are gone by 13:00, but the smells linger. Looking out to sea from here, Le Panier (the old town) rises to your right. The harborfront below Le Panier was destroyed in 1943 by the Nazis, who didn't want a tangled refuge for resistance fighters so close to the harbor. It's now rebuilt with modern condos and trendy restaurants.

• *Walk uphill on the busy retail street called...*

La Canebière

The Boulevard La Canebière (pronounced "can o' bee-air") with its recent facelift—and classy tramway—is the celebrated main drag of Marseille. Strolling this stubby thoroughfare, you feel surrounded by a teeming, diverse city. Along this street, you'll find a

thriving international market scene, two museums, the TI, and a stylish shopping district.

• *For a taste of Africa, head five blocks up La Canebière and turn right at Rue Longue des Capucins. Walk down this street a few blocks to Rue d'Aubagne.*

Arab Markets

Marseille's huge Moroccan, Algerian, and Tunisian populations give the city a special spice. Strolling this area, you're immersed in an exotic and fragrant little medina filled with commotion—and no one's speaking French. Stop by **Soleil d'Egypte** and try a *bourek* wrap (potato and ground round) or, better, try the *pastilla* wrap (chicken, almonds, onions, and egg). You'll see them being made in the kitchen behind the counter. Double back to La Canebière on Rue d'Aubagne, stopping to pick up dessert (Tunisian pastries) at **La Carthage** bakery.

• *Return to La Canebière and walk back toward the Old Port. The grand triumphal arch you see far to the right down Cours Belsunce marks the historic gateway to the city of Aix-en-Provence. Two blocks before you hit the water, on the right side, you can't miss the spacious Office de Tourisme. After checking in at the TI, head next door to the tall, grandiose building.*

▲Chamber of Commerce Building (Le Palais de la Bourse) and Marine Museum

Step inside and take in the grand 1860s interior. A relief on the ceiling shows great moments in Marseille's history and a large court with a United Nations of plaques, reminding locals how their commerce comes from trade around the world.

The small ground-floor exhibit on the city's maritime history starts (to the right as you enter) with an impressive portrait of Emperor Napoleon III (who called for the building's construction) and his wife. Sketches show the pomp surrounding its grand opening. The next room traces the growth of the city through charts of its harbor, and the following rooms display models of big ships over the centuries.

Cost and Hours: Free entry to building, museum—€2, daily 10:00-18:00, tel. 04 91 39 33 33.

• *In La Centre Bourse, the modern shopping center behind the chamber of commerce, you'll find the...*

Marseille History Museum (Musée d'Histoire de Marseille)

This newly renovated museum—one of the largest history museums in France—provides a good introduction to Marseille's remarkable history, including the remains of an old Roman ship and bits of a Greek vessel—both found here.

Cost and Hours: €5, Tue-Sun 10:00-18:00, closed Mon, no English information, 2 Rue Henri-Barbusse, tel. 04 91 55 36 00, http://musee-histoire.marseille.fr.

PROVENCE

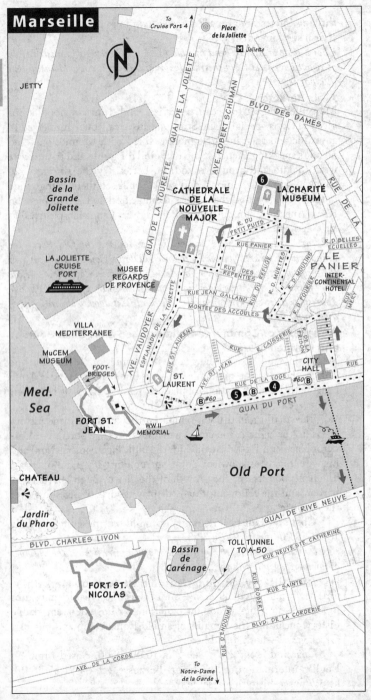

Marseille

To
Cruise Port 4

Place
de la Joliette

Ⓜ Joliette

JETTY

BLVD. DES DAMES

QUAI DE LA JOLIETTE

AVE. ROBERT SCHUMAN

RUE DE LA

Bassin
de la
Grande
Joliette

CATHEDRALE
DE LA
NOUVELLE
MAJOR

❻ LA CHARITÉ
MUSEUM

LA JOLIETTE
CRUISE PORT

R. DU
PETIT PUITS

R.D. BELLES
ECUELLES

RUE PANIER

LE
PANIER

MUSEE
REGARDS
DE PROVENCE

RUE
DES
REPENTIES

RUE DU REFUGE

R.D. MUETTES

R.D. MOULINS

INTER-
CONTINENTAL
HOTEL

QUAI DE LA TOURETTE

RUE JEAN GALLAND

R.D. POIRIER

RUE
MÉRY

MONTEE DES ACCOULES

VILLA
MEDITERRANEE

AVE. VAUDOYER

ESPLANADE DE LA TOURETTE

RUE ST. LAURENT

RUE

R. CAISSERIE

R. DE LA
PRISON

CITY
HALL

RUE

MuCEM
MUSEUM

FOOT-
BRIDGES

ST.
LAURENT

RUE ST. JEAN

RUE DE LA LOGE

Ⓑ #60

Med.
Sea

FORT ST.
JEAN

WW II
MEMORIAL

Ⓑ #60

❺ Ⓑ ❹

QUAI DU PORT

CHATEAU

Old Port

Jardin
du Pharo

QUAI DE RIVE NEUVE

BLVD. CHARLES LIVON

Bassin
de
Carénage

TOLL TUNNEL
TO A-50

RUE NEUVE STE. CATHERINE

RUE ROBERT

RUE SAINTE

FORT ST.
NICOLAS

RUE DENDOUME

BLVD. DE LA CORDERIE

AVE. DE LA CORSE

To
Notre-Dame
de la Garde

PROVENCE

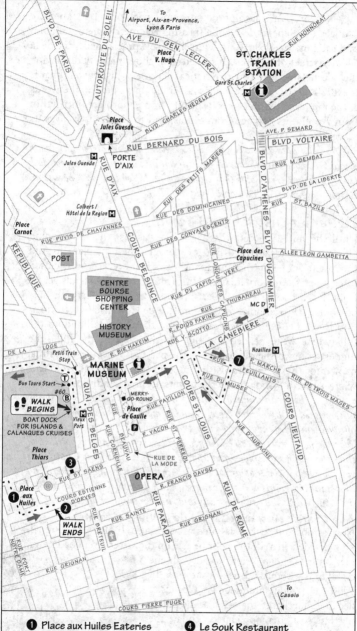

① Place aux Huiles Eateries
② Cours d'Estienne d'Orves Eateries
③ La Daurade & other Rue Saint-Saëns Eateries
④ Le Souk Restaurant
⑤ Les Galinettes Chez Madie Rest.
⑥ La Charité Museum Café
⑦ Arab Markets

Nearby: For a fashion detour, cross back over La Canebière to Place du Général de Gaulle (passing the merry-go-round), and find the tiny Rue de la Tour, Marseille's self-proclaimed "Rue de la Mode" (street of fashion). It's lined with shops proudly displaying the latest fashions, mostly from local designers. Just beyond that is the 1920s Art Deco facade of Marseille's opera house. The words at the top read: "Art receives its beauty from Aphrodite, its rhythm from Apollo, its balance from Pallas, and to Dionysus it owes its movement and life."

• *Now head back the way you came. When La Canebière ends, walk around the port with the water on your left and find the small ferry dock (La Ligne du Ferry Boat) that crosses the port. You'll be back here soon. But for now, turn around and find City Hall.*

Le Panier District (Old Town)

Until the mid-19th century, Marseille was just the hill-capping old town and its fortified port. Today, it's the best place to find the town's soul—but not at lunchtime, when everything is closed (except cafés). The ornate **City Hall** (Hôtel de Ville) stands across from the three-masted sailboat and the little shuttle ferry. Its bust of Louis XIV overlooks the harbor. Rue de la Mairie (which turns into Rue de la Guirlande) leads behind the City Hall and up the hill (where we're headed shortly). At the crest of the hill—the highest point in the old town—is the peaceful Place des Moulins, named for the 15 windmills that used to spin and grind from this windy summit. (Today, only the towers of three windmills remain.)

• *Walk up the broad stairway, passing City Hall. At the top is the shiny, just-restored 18th-century Hôtel Dieu (formerly a hospital), now an In-tercontinental Luxury Hotel with 194 rooms, most with view terraces over the port, starting at €320 per night. Turn left at the hotel, then track the brown signs up—and up some more—to la Vieille Charité. As you walk, read the thoughtful English-information plaques (posted on iron stands at points of historic interest) and listen for the sounds of local life being played out, on the streets and in the rooms just above.*

▲La Charité Museum (Centre de la Vieille Charité)

Now a museum, this was once a poorhouse. In 1674 the French king decided that all the poor people on the streets were bad news. He built a huge triple-arcaded home to take in a thousand needy subjects. In 1940 the famous architect Le Corbusier declared it a shame that such a fine building was so underappreciated. Today, the striking building—wonderfully renovated and beautiful in its arcaded simplicity—is used as a collection of art galleries surrounding a Pantheonesque church.

PROVENCE

You can stroll around the courtyard for free. (Good WCs are in the far-left corner.)

The pediment of the church features the figure of Charity taking care of orphans (as the state did with this building). She's flanked by pelicans (symbolic of charity, for the way they were said to pick flesh from their own bosom to feed their hungry chicks, according to medieval legend). The ground floor outside the church houses temporary exhibits. Upstairs you'll find rooms with interesting collections of Celtic (c. 300 B.C.), Greek, and Roman artifacts from this region. There's also a surprisingly good Egyptian collection, along with masks from Africa and the South Pacific.

Cost and Hours: €3-6 depending on exhibits, Tue-Sun June-Sept 11:00-18:00, Oct-May 10:00-17:00, closed Mon year-round, no English information, idyllic café/bar, tel. 04 91 14 58 80.

• *From La Charité, cross the small cobbled triangular square, turn right on Rue du Petit Puits, and walk all the way to the end, where you'll run into a charming square with Le Bar des 13 Coins (open daily, free Wi-Fi, tel. 04 91 91 56 49). Have a drink at this eclectic little bar—the inspiration for the main setting of France's most famous soap opera,* Plus Belle La Vie. *Take the stairs to Rue de l'Evêché, go left and walk downhill, then take your first right to find...*

Cathédrale de la Nouvelle Major

Bam. This huge, striped cathedral seems lost out here, away from the action and above the nondescript cruise-ship port. The cathedral was built in the late 1800s to replace the old cathedral that the city had outgrown. It's more impressive from the outside, but worth a quick peek inside for its floor and wall mosaics over the nave.

Cost and Hours: Free, Tue-Sun 10:00-19:00, closed Mon.

• *Return to the Old Port by walking up the tree-lined Esplanade de la Tourette. Marseille's sprawling modern port is behind you and becomes visible as you climb.*

The Great Maritime Port of Marseille (GPMM)

The economy of Marseille is driven by its modern commercial ports, which extend 30 miles west from here (a nearby canal links Marseille inland via the Rhône River, adding to the port's importance). Over 100 million tons of freight pass through this port each year (60 percent of which is petroleum), making this one of Europe's top three ports. Container traffic is significant but is hampered by crippling strikes for which the left-leaning city is famous. By contrast, cruise-ship tourism has taken off in a big way, bringing more than 550,000 passengers to Marseille each year.

• *From this street you can also see three of Marseille's newest sights, built for the European Culture Capital city program in 2013, but remaining as permanent additions to the city.*

Musée Regards de Provence

Next to the cathedral, this new museum has a colorful collection of art and media from the 18th to 21st centuries, devoted to life along the Mediterranean. Don't miss the rooftop restaurant with sensational views over the cathedral. The building housing the museum was formerly the sanitary building for immigration, where immigrants were inspected and their clothing was disinfected.

Cost and Hours: €3.50 for permanent collection, more for temporary exhibits, daily 10:00-18:00, tel. 04 96 17 40 40, www.museeregardsdeprovence.com.

Villa Méditerranée

This center hosts rotating exhibitions, lectures, films, and forums all focused on inspiring peace, brotherhood, and understanding between Mediterranean cultures. Its building, with a cantilevered top floor, was designed by Milanese architect Stefano Boeri. With the goal of "bringing a part of the Mediterranean sea into the building," the entire basement floor is below sea level.

Cost and Hours: €7, Tue-Thu 12:00-19:00, Fri 12:00-22:00, Sat-Sun 10:00-19:00, closed Mon, tel. 04 95 09 42 52, www.villa-mediterranee.org.

Museum of European and Mediterranean Civilizations

This national museum, in a lacework-covered building, houses art and artifacts from cultures surrounding the Mediterranean Sea. It's known as MuCEM to locals (Musée des Civilisations de l'Europe et de la Méditerranée). This "vertical casbah," as the architect calls it, is connected by a rooftop footbridge to the Fortress St. Jean, where the exhibition space continues.

Cost and Hours: €8, more for special events and performances, May-Oct Wed-Mon 11:00-19:00, Nov-April Wed-Mon 11:00-18:00, Fri until 22:00, closed Tue, tel. 04 84 35 14 00, www.mucem.org.

• *Keep walking uphill. A fabulous view awaits you at the bend.*

View Terrace

Voilà! This is one of the best views of Marseille, with Notre-Dame de la Garde presiding above, and twin forts below protecting the entrance to the Old Port. The ugly, boxy building marked "Memorial" at the base of the fort (below and to your right) is a memorial to those lost during the Nazi occupation of the city in World War II. The small church to your left is the Church of St. Laurent, which once served as a parish church for sailors and fishermen—notice the lighthouse-like tower.

• *After you've soaked it all in, continue down the steps back to the Old Port.*

From the Old Port to the New Town

From the bottom of the stairs, you have options. If you are pressed for time or want to save some steps, hop on bus #60 here (€1.50, direction: Nôtre-Dame de la Garde). In 20 minutes, you'll circle around the Old Port and head directly up to the basilica. Or you can walk 10 minutes, halfway along the promenade (Quai du Port) to the City Hall, where you'll see the fun little **ferry boat** that shuttles locals across the harbor to the new town (free, every 10 minutes 8:00-17:00, lunch break from about 12:30-13:15). Note the unusual two-way steering wheel as you sail. You'll dock in the new town—which, because of the 1943 bombings, is actually older than the "old" town along the harborfront.

Directly in front of the ferry landing across the port, you'll find popular bars and brasseries, good for a quick meal or memorable drink. Wander in along Place aux Huiles, make your way left, and find a smart pedestrian zone crammed with cafés and restaurants (see "Eating in Marseille," later).

• *Don't miss a trip up to Notre-Dame de la Garde, described next.*

Overlooking the Old Port

▲▲Notre-Dame de la Garde

Crowning Marseille's highest point, 500 feet above the harbor, is the city's landmark sight. This massive Neo-Romanesque-Byzantine basilica, built in the 1850s during the reign of Napoleon III, is a radiant collection of domes, gold, and mosaics. The monumental statue of Mary and the Baby Jesus towers above everything (Jesus' wrist alone is 42 inches around, and the statue weighs 9 tons). And though people come here mostly for the commanding city view, the interior will bowl you over. This hilltop has served as a lookout, as well as a place of worship, since ancient times. Climb to the highest

lookout for an orientation table and the best views. Those islands straight ahead are the Iles du Frioul, including the island of If—where the Count of Monte Cristo spent time.

Cost and Hours: Free, daily April-Sept 7:00-20:00, until 19:00 Oct-March, last entry 45 minutes before closing, cafeteria and WCs are just below the view terrace.

Getting There: To reach the church, you can hike 30 minutes straight up from the harbor. To save some sweat, catch a taxi (about €10), hop on bus #60, or ride the tourist train—all stop on the harborfront near the fish market (see map on page 262 and "Helpful Hints" on page 258).

Eating in Marseille

For general tips on eating in France, see page 276.

In the New Town: For the best combination of trendiness, variety, and a fun people scene, eat in the new town, on or near Quai de Rive-Neuve (on the left side of the Old Port as you look out to sea). Look for **Place aux Huiles, Cours d'Estienne d'Orves,** and **Rue Saint-Saëns** for a melting pot of international eateries ranging from giant salads and fresh seafood to crêpes, Vietnamese dishes, Belgian waffles, and Buffalo wings. Come here for ambience, not for top cuisine. **La Daurade** is worth considering, with fresh seafood at fair prices served in a classy setting (€18 *menus*, €30 bouillabaisse—requires two orders, closed Wed, 8 Rue Fortia, tel. 04 91 33 82 42).

Near the Old Port: For good views *en terrasse*, go to the quieter, other side of the port. Have a real Moroccan dinner at **Le Souk** (€18-20 couscous and *tajine* dishes, €29 three-course *menu*, vegetarian options, intimate and authentic interior, closed Mon, 100 Quai du Port, tel. 04 91 91 29 29, http://lesouk.idhii.net). If you want bouillabaisse, try **Les Galinettes Chez Madie** (€35/person for bouillabaisse, €25 *menu*, €17 lunch *menu*, closed Sun, 138 Quai du Port, tel. 04 91 90 40 87, http://chezmadie.idhii.net).

At La Charité Museum: The lovely, quiet courtyard has a kiosk-café with a few tables (lunch only).

Cassis

Hunkered below impossibly high cliffs, Cassis (kah-see) is an unpretentious port town that gives travelers a sunny time-out from their busy vacation. Two hours away from the fray of the Côte d'Azur, Cassis is a prettier, poor man's St-Tropez. Outdoor cafés line the small port on three

sides, where boaters clean their crafts as they chat up café clients. Cassis is popular with the French and close enough to Marseille to be busy on weekends and all summer. Come to Cassis to dine portside, swim in the glimmering-clear water, and explore its rocky *calanques* (inlets).

Orientation to Cassis

The Massif du Puget mountain hovers over little Cassis, with hills spilling down to the port. Cap Canaille cliff rises from the southeast, and the famous *calanques* inlets hide along the coast northwest of town. Hotels, restaurants, and boats line the attractive little port.

Tourist Information

The TI is in the modern building in the middle of the port among the boats. They have free Wi-Fi, good maps for sale, and the latest information on the conditions of the *calanques* (May-Sept Mon-Sat 9:00-18:30, until 19:00 July-Aug, Sun 9:30-12:30 & 15:00-18:00; Oct-April Mon-Sat 9:30-12:30 & 14:00-18:00, Sun 10:00-12:30, Quai des Moulins, toll tel. 08 92 39 01 03-€0.34/minute, www.ot-cassis.fr, info@ot-cassis.com).

Arrival in Cassis

By Train: Cassis' hills forced the train station to be built two miles away, and those last two miles can be a challenge. It's a small station with limited hours (no baggage storage, ticket windows open Mon-Fri 6:15-13:15 & 13:45-20:45, Sat-Sun 9:50-12:45 & 13:45-17:55). If you need to buy tickets when the station is closed, use the machines (coins only).

A **taxi** into town costs €12 and is well worth the expense unless a Marcouline bus is soon to arrive (see below). If there's no taxi waiting, call 04 42 01 78 96 (a pay phone is outside the train station). Otherwise, it's a 50-minute walk into town (turn left out of the station and follow signs).

Marcouline **buses** link the station with the town center, but service is spotty (€1, about hourly with longer intervals in the afternoon, schedule posted at all stops). Call the TI in advance to get the schedule (or check online at www.ot-cassis.com/fr/bus-intra-urbain-la-marcouline.html) and plan your arrival accordingly—but be ready to take a taxi. The bus drops you at the Casino stop in Cassis: From here, turn right on Rue de l'Arène and walk downhill five minutes to reach the port.

By Bus: Regional buses (including those from Marseille) run limited hours (check with the TI before taking one). The bus stop is a five-minute walk from the port on Avenue du 11 Novembre (stop is labeled Gendarmerie).

Helpful Hints

Market Days: The market hops on Wednesdays and Fridays until 12:30 (on the streets around the Hôtel de Ville).

PROVENCE

Cassis

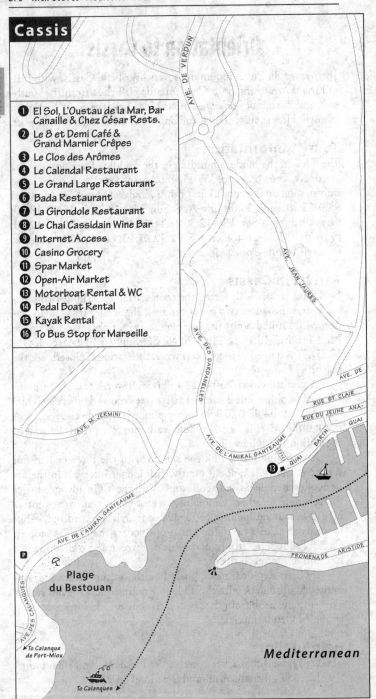

1 El Sol, L'Oustau de la Mar, Bar Canaille & Chez César Rests.

2 Le 8 et Demi Café & Grand Marnier Crêpes

3 Le Clos des Arômes

4 Le Calendal Restaurant

5 Le Grand Large Restaurant

6 Bada Restaurant

7 La Girondole Restaurant

8 Le Chai Cassidain Wine Bar

9 Internet Access

10 Casino Grocery

11 Spar Market

12 Open-Air Market

13 Motorboat Rental & WC

14 Pedal Boat Rental

15 Kayak Rental

16 To Bus Stop for Marseille

AVE. DE VERDUN

AVE. JEAN JAURES

AVE. DES DARDANELLES

AVE. M. JERMINI

AVE. DE L'AMIRAL GANTEAUME

RUE ST. CLAIR

RUE DU JEUNE ANA.

QUAI BARTH.

QUAI

AVE. DE

13

PROMENADE ARISTIDE

P

Plage du Bestouan

AVE. DES CALANQUES

To Calanque de Port-Miou

Mediterranean

To Calanques

PROVENCE

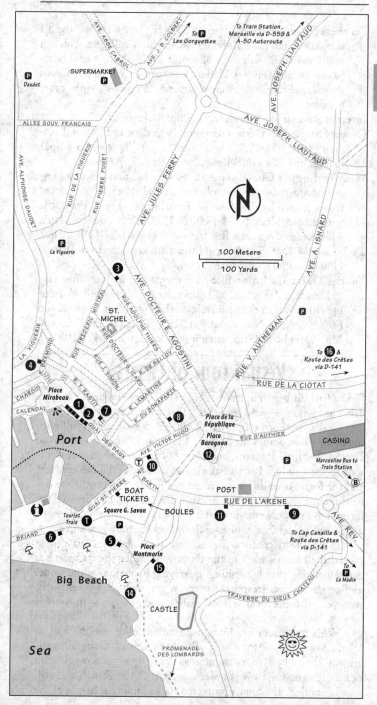

AVE. J. B. COLBERT

To P Les Gorguettes

To Train Station, Marseille via D-559 & A-50 Autoroute

AVE. ABBÉ CABROL

AVE. JOSEPH LIAUTAUD

P Daudet

SUPERMARKET P

ALLÉE SOUV. FRANÇAIS

AVE. JOSEPH LIAUTAUD

AVE. ALPHONSE DAUDET

RUE DE LA VIGUERIE

RUE PIERRE PUGET

AVE. JULES FERRY

N

100 Meters

100 Yards

AVE. A. ISNARD

LA VIGUERIE

P La Viguerie

3

ST. MICHEL

RUE FRÉDÉRIC MISTRAL

RUE ADOLPHE THIERS

AVE. DOCTEUR E. AGOSTINI

RUE DOCTEUR S. ICARD

R. K. DE BELLOY

RUE J. SIMON

R. T. RASTIT

R. LAMARTINE

R. DU BONAPARTE

RUE V. AUTHEMAN

To 16 & Route des Crêtes via D-141

P

RUE DE LA CIOTAT

CHARSIS

PUITS BRÉMOND

4

Place Mirabeau

CALENDAL

1 2 7

QUAI DES BAUX

8

Place de la République

RUE D'AUTHIER

Place Baragnon

12

CASINO

Port

AVE. VICTOR HUGO

T 10

R. BARTH

POST

Marcouline Bus to Train Station

B

P

BOAT TICKETS

RUE DE L'ARÈNE

QUAI ST. PIERRE

Square G. Savon

BOULES

11

9

AVE. REV.

i

Tourist Train T

P

BRIAND

6

5

Place Montmorin

15

To Cap Canaille & Route des Crêtes via D-141

To P La Madie

Big Beach

14

CASTLE

Sea

PROMENADE DES LOMBARDS

TRAVERSE DU VIEUX CHÂTEAU

Beaches: Cassis' beaches are pebbly. The big beach behind the TI is sandier than others, though water shoes still help. You can rent a mattress with a towel (about €17/day) and pedal boats (about €8/30 minutes). Underwater springs just off the Cassis shore make the water clean, clear, and a bit cooler than at other beaches.

Internet Access: The TI offers 30 minutes of free Wi-Fi.

Grocery Store: The **Casino** market is next door to Hôtel le Liautaud (daily 8:30-19:30, Sun until 19:00). There's also a **Spar** market just past Hôtel Laurence on Rue de l'Arène.

Wine Tasting: Le Chai Cassidain is a wine bar that welcomes visitors, with red-leather stools and a good selection of regional wines offered by the glass (€5, healthy pours) or by the bottle with nibbles (daily 10:00-13:00 & 15:00-22:00 and often later, 4 blocks from port at 6 Rue Séverin Icard, tel. 04 42 01 99 80).

Taxi: Call 04 42 01 78 96 or find the main taxi stand across from Hôtel Cassitel by the *boules* court.

Tourist Train: The little white *train touristique*, with commentary in French and English, will take you on a worthwhile 45-minute circuit out to the peninsula on the Port-Miou *calanque* and back (€7, April-Nov, usually at 11:15, 12:15, 14:15, 17:15 and May-Oct also at 18:15, catch it next to TI, tel. 04 42 01 09 98).

Visual Tour of Cassis

Find a friendly bench in front of Hôtel le Golfe—or, better, enjoy a drink at their café—and read this quick town intro.

Cassis was born more than 2,500 years ago (on the hill with the castle ruins, across the harbor). Ligurians, Phoenicians, maybe Greeks, certainly Romans, and plenty of barbarians all found this spot to their liking. Parts of the castle date from the 8th century, and the **fortress walls** were constructed in the 13th century to defend against seaborne barbarian raids. The Michelin family sold the fortress to investors who turned it into a luxury five-suite *chambres d'hôtes*, where celebrities often hole up looking for peace and quiet.

In the 18th century life became more secure, and people moved their homes back to the waterfront. Since then, Cassis has made its living through fishing, quarrying its famous white stone, and producing well-respected white wines—which, conveniently, pair well with the local seafood dishes, and *bien sûr*, with tourists like us.

With improvements in transportation following the end of World War II, tourism rose gradually in Cassis, though crowds are still sparse by Riviera standards. While foreigners overwhelm nearby resorts, Cassis is popular mostly with the French and still feels unspoiled. The town's protected status limits the height of the buildings along the waterfront. Cassis' port is home to some nice boats...but they're chump change compared to the glitzier harbors farther east.

The big cliff towering above the castle hill is **Cap Canaille.** Europe's highest maritime cliff, it was sculpted by receding glaciers (wrap your brain around that concept), and today drops 1,200 feet straight down. You can—and should—take a taxi along the top for staggering views.

If you can overcome your inertia, walk to your right, then veer left on top of the short wall in front of the public WCs. The rocky shore over your right shoulder looks cut away just for sunbathers. But Cassis was once an important **quarry,** and stones were sliced right out of this beach for easy transport to ships. The Statue of Liberty's base sits on this rock, and even today, Cassis stone remains highly valued throughout the world...but yesterday's quarrymen have been replaced by today's sunbathers.

Sights in Cassis

▲▲▲The *Calanques*

Until you see these exotic Mediterranean fjords—with their translucent blue water, tiny intimate beaches, and stark cliffs plunging into the sea or forming rocky promontories—it's hard to understand what all the excitement is about.

Calanques (kah-lahnk) are narrow, steep-sided valleys partially flooded by the sea, surrounded by rugged white cliffs usually made of limestone (quarries along the *calanques* have provided building stone for centuries). The word comes from the Corsican word *calanca,* meaning "inlet"—the island of Corsica also has *calanques.* These inlets began as underwater valleys carved by the seaward flow of water at river mouths, and were later gouged out deeper by glaciers. About 12,000 years ago, when the climate warmed and glaciers retreated at the end of the last Ice Age, the sea level rose partway up the steep rocky sides of the *calanques.* Today the cliffs harbor a unique habitat that includes rare plants and nesting sites for unusual raptors.

The most famous inlets are in the Massif des Calanques, which runs along a 13-mile stretch of the coast from Marseille to Cassis. This area and part of the surrounding region became a national park in 2012.

You can hike, or cruise by boat or kayak, to many *calanques.*

Bring plenty of water, sunscreen, and anything else you need for the day, as there's nary a baguette for sale. Don't dawdle—to limit crowds and because of fire hazards, the most popular *calanques* can be closed to visitors between 11:00 and 16:00 in high season (mid-June-mid-Sept) and on weekends. When they are "closed," the only way to see the *calanques* is by boat or kayak. The TI can give you plenty of advice.

Cruising the *Calanques*: Several boats offer trips of various lengths (three *calanques*-€15, 2/hour, 45 minutes; five *calanques*-€18, 3/day, 1 hour; 8-10 *calanques*-€25, 1-3/day, 1.5 hours, cash only; tel. 04 42 01 90 83, www.calanques-cassis.com). The three-*calanques* tour is the most popular. Tickets are sold (and boats depart) from a small booth on the port opposite the Hôtel Lieu-taud. *Prochain départ* means "next departure." Boats vary in size (some seat up to 100).

Hiking to the *Calanques*: Plan ahead. From June to September, many of the *calanques* are closed in certain weather conditions due to the high risk of brush fires. For information, check with the TI or call toll tel. 08 11 20 13 13; wait 30 seconds for English instructions. Conditions and closures are announced starting at 18:00 the day before.

The trail lacing together *calanques* Port-Miou, Port-Pin, and d'En-Vau will warm a hiker's heart. Views are glorious, and the trail is manageable if you have decent shoes (though shade is minimal).

For most, the best *calanque* by foot is **Calanque Port-Pin,** about an hour from Cassis (30 minutes after the linear, boat-lined Calanque Port-Miou, which also works as a destination if time is short). Calanque Port-Pin is intimate and well-forested, with a small beach.

The TI's map of Cassis gives a general idea of the *calanques* trail, though you don't really need a map. Start along the road behind Hôtel le Golfe and walk past Plage du Bestouan, then look for green hiker signs to *Calanque Miou* (pay attention to your route for an easier return). You'll climb up, then drop down through residential streets, eventually landing at the foot of Calanque de Port-Miou, where the dirt trail begins. Follow signs to *Calanques Port-Pin* and *d'En-Vau,* walking 500 yards along a wide trail and passing through an old quarry.

You're now on the *GR (Grande Randonnée)* trail, indicated by red, white, and green markers painted on rocks, trees, and other landmarks. Follow those markers as they lead uphill (great views at top), then connect to a rough stone trail leading down to Calanque Port-Pin (nice beach, good scampering). *Bonne route!*

Other Ways to Reach the *Calanques*: From about mid-April to mid-October, you can rent a **kayak** in Cassis—or in nearby Port-Miou, which is closer to the *calanques*. In Cassis, try Club

Sports Loisirs Nautiques on Place Montmorin, behind the merry-go-round (one-seater-€30/4 hours, two-seater-€45/4 hours, tel. 04 42 01 80 01). In Port-Miou, call mobile 06 75 70 00 73. The TI has brochures for more kayak companies. You can also take a **kayak tour** (€35/half-day, €55/day, depart from nearby town of La Ciotat, advance reservations smart, mobile 06 12 95 20 12, www.provencekayakmer.fr). If the hiking trails are closed, this is the only way you'll be able to get to those *calanques* beaches.

You can rent a small **motorboat** without a special boating license (€100/half-day, €140/day, €700 cash or credit-card imprint as deposit; at Loca'Bato office, a few steps away from Hôtel le Golfe; mobile 06 89 53 15 62 or 06 43 88 19 07). Another option is a **skippered boat rental** with JCF Boat Services (up to 8 people, about €350/half-day, €410/day, English-speaking captains, mobile 06 75 74 25 82 or 06 62 46 73 16, www.jcf-boat-services.com, contact@jcf-boat-services.com).

Eating in Cassis

Peruse the lineup of tempting restaurants along the port, window-shop the recommended places below, and then decide for yourself (all have good interior and exterior seating). You can have a ham-and-cheese crêpe or go all-out for bouillabaisse with the same great view. Picnickers can enjoy a beggars' banquet at the benches at Hôtel le Golfe or on the beach, or discover your own quiet places along the lanes away from the port (small grocery stores open until 19:30). Local wines are terrific: red from Bandol and whites/rosés from Cassis.

Dining Portside

The first four places are ideally situated side by side, allowing diners to comparison shop. I've enjoyed good meals at each of them.

El Sol is sharp and popular with discerning diners (*menus*-€21-30, closed Sun eve off-season, all day Mon year-round, and sometimes Tue for lunch, 20 Quai des Baux, tel. 04 42 01 76 10, www.restaurant-el-sol.fr).

L'Oustau de la Mar has a loyal following and fair prices (*menu*-€22, closed Mon eve and all day Tue, 20 Quai des Baux, tel. 04 42 01 78 22).

Bar Canaille specializes in fresh seafood platters, oysters, and other shellfish (open daily in summer, closed Wed off-season, 22 Quai des Baux, tel. 04 42 01 72 36).

Chez César was most popular with locals on my last visit, with good prices and selection (€26 *marmite de pêcheur*—a poor man's bouillabaisse, €12.50 *plats*, *menus* from €23, closed Sun-Mon, 21 Quai des Baux, tel. 04 42 01 75 47).

Tips on Eating in France

The French eat long and well—nowhere more so than in the south. Relaxed and tree-shaded lunches with a chilled rosé and endless afternoons at outdoor cafés are the norm.

But busy sightseers can easily get food on the go. You'll find bakeries and small stands selling baguette sandwiches, quiche, and pizza-like items for about €4. Sandwich varieties include *fromage* (cheese), *jambon beurre* (ham and butter), *jambon* or *poulet crudités* (ham or chicken with tomatoes, lettuce, cucumbers, and mayonnaise), *saucisson beurre* (sausage and butter), and *thon crudités* (tuna with tomatoes, lettuce, and mayonnaise). Typical quiches at shops and bakeries are *fromage, lorraine* (ham and cheese), *aux oignons* (onion), *aux poireaux* (leek), *aux champignons* (mushroom), *au saumon* (salmon), or *au thon* (tuna).

If you're planning to gather supplies for a picnic lunch, start early: Many small stores close at noon. Be daring. Try the smelly cheeses, ugly pâtés, and miniscule yogurts. Shopkeepers are accustomed to selling small quantities. Get a tasty salad to go, and ask for a plastic fork *(une fourchette en plastique)*. A small container is *une barquette*. A slice is *une tranche.*

Cafés and brasseries provide user-friendly meals. At either, feel free to order only a bowl of soup or a salad or *plat* (main

Le 8 et Demi serves crêpes, pizza, salads, and good Italian gelato on plastic tables with front-and-center portside views (closed Thu off-season, 8 Quai des Baux, tel. 04 42 01 94 63).

The **Grand Marnier crêpe stand** cooks delicious dessert crêpes to go for €3—the Grand Marnier crêpe rules. This is ideal for strollers (next to Le 8 et Demi, daily April-Sept 15:00-23:30).

Dining Away from the Port

Le Clos des Arômes is the place to come for a refined, candlelit dinner. Dine on a lovely enclosed terrace (€26 *menu*, closed all day Wed, closed Thu for lunch, near Parking la Viguerie at 10 Rue Abbé Paul Mouton, tel. 04 42 01 71 84, www.le-clos-des-aromes.com).

Le Calendal serves up *menus* that feature local dishes in a warm, charming, and cozy setting. Don't be surprised if the chef visits your table (indoor or terrace seating available). If you want bouillabaisse, you must order it a day ahead of time (€33 *menu*, closed Sun for lunch and all day Mon, 3 Rue Brémond, tel. 04 42 01 17 70).

course) at any time of day. The daily special—*plat du jour*—is a fast, hearty, and garnished hot plate for €10-15. Unlike restaurants, which open only for lunch and dinner and close in between,

some cafés and all brasseries serve food throughout the day, making them the best option if you want a late lunch or an early dinner. There are two sets of prices: You'll pay more for the same drink if you're seated at a table *(salle)* than if you're at the bar or counter *(comptoir)*.

Restaurants are generally more formal and pricier; you're expected to order more of a meal. If a restaurant serves lunch, it generally begins at 11:30 and goes until 14:00, with last orders taken about 13:30. Dinner service usually begins at 19:00.

To get a waiter's attention, say, *"s'il vous plaît."* A *menu* is a fixed-price meal that usually includes two or three courses; these are a good value, particularly at lunch (the same menu costs more at dinner). Ask for *la carte* if you'd rather see a menu and order à la carte.

Service seems slow to Americans, but the French consider it polite not to rush you. When you're ready for the bill, ask for it: *"L'addition, s'il vous plaît."*

Le Grand Large is indeed large and owns the scenic beachfront next to the TI. Come here for a quiet drink, or to dine seaside rather than portside (€32 *menu* with good choices, open daily, Plage de Cassis, tel. 04 42 01 81 00, www.cassis-grand-large.com).

Bada is a trendy beachfront place right behind the TI, serving breakfast with the sounds of crashing waves, and €14-17 salads at lunch (no dinner service). It's open only in good weather since it's not covered and the wind can be strong (Promenade Aristide Briand, tel. 04 42 83 70 09).

La Girondole is an easy place for families, with cheap pizza, pasta, and salads. It's a block off the port (open daily in summer, take-away also possible, closed Tue off-season, 1 Rue Thérèse Rastit, tel. 04 42 01 13 39).

PROVENCE

Aix-en-Provence

Aix-en-Provence is famous for its outdoor markets and handsome pedestrian lanes, as well as its cultivated residents and their ability to embrace the good life. Nowhere else in France is *l'art de vivre* (the art of living) so well on display. It was that way when the French king made the town his administrative capital of Provence, and it's that way today. For a tourist, Aix-en-Provence (the "Aix" is pronounced "X") is happily free of any obligatory turnstiles. And there's not a single ancient site to see. It's just a wealthy town filled with 140,000 people—most of whom, it seems, know how to live well and look good. Aix-en-Provence's 40,000 well-dressed students (many from other countries) give the city a year-round youthful energy, and its numerous squares, lined with cafés and fine shops, allow everyone a comfortable place to pose.

Orientation to Aix-en-Provence

With no "must-see" sights, Aix works well as a day trip, and is best on days when the most markets thrive (Tue, Thu, and Sat). The city can be seen in a 1.5-hour stroll from the TI or train station, though connoisseurs of southern French culture will want more time to savor this lovely place.

Cours Mirabeau (the grand central boulevard) divides the stately, quiet Mazarin Quarter from the lively old town (where all the action is). In the old half, picturesque squares are connected by fine pedestrian shopping lanes, many of which lead to the cathedral. Right-angle intersections are rare in the old half—expect to get turned around regularly.

Tourist Information

The TI, France's grandest, is located at La Rotonde traffic circle. Get the walking-tour brochure *In the Footsteps of Cézanne*, with the best city-center map and a good overview of excursions in the area. The TI has other maps that cover areas beyond old Aix (Mon-Sat 8:30-19:00, Sun 10:00-13:00 & 14:00-18:00, longer hours in the summer, shorter hours in the winter, 300 Avenue Giuseppe Verdi, tel. 04 42 16 11 61, www.aixenprovencetourism.com).

English-language **walking tours** (shown on monitors in the TI) of the old town are offered at 10:00 on Tuesdays; Cézanne walking tours leave at 10:00 on Thursdays and Saturdays (€8, two hours, depart from the TI).

Arrival in Aix-en-Provence

By Train: Aix-en-Provence has two train stations: Centre-Ville, near the city center, and the faraway TGV station, which cruisers should avoid. From the Centre-Ville Station, it's a breezy 10-minute stroll to the TI and pedestrian area. Cross the boulevard in front of the station and walk up Avenue Victor Hugo; turn left at the first intersection (you're still on Victor Hugo). At the large fountain (La Rotonde), turn left and go about a quarter of the way around the fountain to find the TI.

By Bus: Aix-en-Provence's bus station is located on Avenue de l'Europe near its intersection with Avenue des Belges (toll tel. 08 21 20 22 03). From the bus station, it's a 10-minute walk to the TI. Head slightly uphill to the flowery roundabout, turn left on Avenue des Belges, and walk to the splashing fountain (La Rotonde, the big traffic circle by the TI).

Helpful Hints

Markets: Aix-en-Provence bubbles over with photogenic open-air morning markets in several of its squares: **Richelme** (produce daily, my favorite), **Palace of Justice** (produce and flea market Tue, Thu, and Sat), **L'Hôtel de Ville** (flower market Tue, Thu, and Sat; book market first Sun of each month), and along **Cours Mirabeau** (textiles and crafts, Tue and Thu morning). Most pack up at 13:00, except the book market, which runs all day. Saturday market days are the biggest. It's well worth planning your visit for a market day, as these markets are the sightseeing highlights of the town. Jennifer Dugdale leads market tours (see "Tours in Aix-en-Provence," later).

Internet Access: There are many options; ask the TI for suggestions.

Services: Public WCs, as they're not stylish, are nonexistent in Aix. Take advantage of WCs in every restaurant, museum, or other stop you make.

English Bookstore: Located on the quiet side of Aix-en-Provence, the atmospheric **Book in Bar** has a great collection of adult and children's books, and a good selection of tourist guides (Cassis, Arles, Avignon, and so on). It's a good way to connect with the expat community; events such as author lectures and book-club meetings are held regularly. They also serve fine coffee and scones (Mon-Sat 9:00-19:00, closed Sun, 4 Rue Joseph Cabassol, where it crosses Rue Goyrand, tel. 04 42 26 60 07).

Supermarket: Monoprix, on Cours Mirabeau, two long blocks up from La Rotonde, has a grocery store in the basement (Mon-

PROVENCE

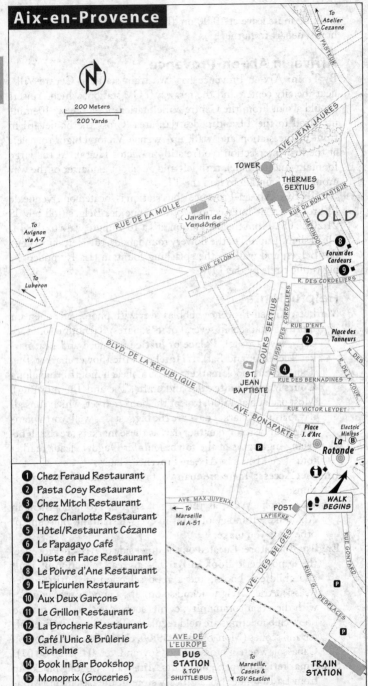

Aix-en-Provence

200 Meters
200 Yards

To Atelier Cézanne

AVE. PASTEUR

AVE. JEAN JAURES

TOWER

THERMES SEXTIUS

RUE DU BON PASTEUR

RUE DE LA MOLLE

Jardin de Vendôme

OLD

To Avignon via A-7

RUE MERINDOL

❽ Forum des Cardeurs

RUE CELONY

R. DES CORDELIERS

To Luberon

❾

RUE LISSE DES CORDELIERS

COURS SEXTIUS

RUE D'ENT.

Place des Tanneurs

❷

R. DES

BLVD. DE LA REPUBLIQUE

❹ RUE DES BERNADINES

ST. JEAN BAPTISTE

R. DE LA COUR

RUE VICTOR LEYDET

AVE. BONAPARTE

Place J. d'Arc

Electric Minibus

P

La Rotonde

ℬ

🛈

AVE. MAX JUVENAL

Place LAPIERRE

POST

WALK BEGINS

To Marseille via A-51

AVE. DES BELGES

RUE GONTARD

RUE G. DESPLACES

P

- ❶ Chez Feraud Restaurant
- ❷ Pasta Cosy Restaurant
- ❸ Chez Mitch Restaurant
- ❹ Chez Charlotte Restaurant
- ❺ Hôtel/Restaurant Cézanne
- ❻ Le Papagayo Café
- ❼ Juste en Face Restaurant
- ❽ Le Poivre d'Ane Restaurant
- ❾ L'Epicurien Restaurant
- ❿ Aux Deux Garçons
- ⓫ Le Grillon Restaurant
- ⓬ La Brocherie Restaurant
- ⓭ Café l'Unic & Brûlerie Richelme
- ⓮ Book In Bar Bookshop
- ⓯ Monoprix (Groceries)

P

AVE. DE L'EUROPE

BUS STATION
& TGV SHUTTLE BUS

To Marseille, Cassis & TGV Station

TRAIN STATION

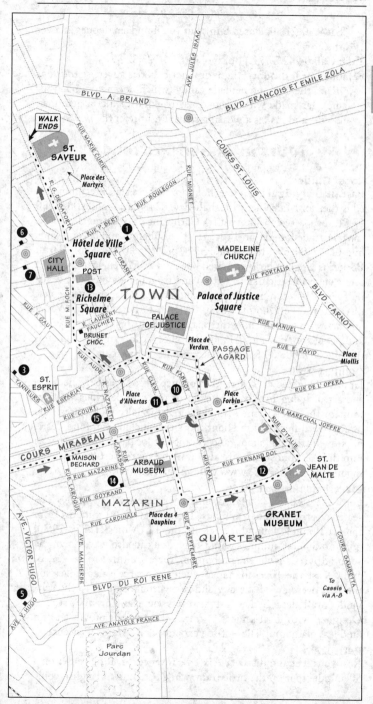

WALK
ENDS

ST.
SAVEUR

Place des
Martyrs

BLVD. A. BRIAND

AVE. JULES ISAAC

BLVD. FRANCOIS ET EMILE ZOLA

COURS ST. LOUIS

RUE MARIE CURIE

RUE BOULEGON

RUE MIGNET

R. G. DESAPORTA

RUE P. BERT

6

7

CITY HALL

POST

13
Richelme
Square

Hôtel de Ville
Square

1

R. CRANET

TOWN

MADELEINE
CHURCH

RUE PORTALIS

**Palace of Justice
Square**

BLVD. CARNOT

RUE M. FOCH

R. LAURENT
FAUCHIER

BRUNET
CHOC.

PALACE
OF JUSTICE

RUE MANUEL

RUE E. DAVID

Place
Miollis

3
ST.
ESPRIT

RUE TANNEURS

RUE ESPARIAT

R. NAZARETH

RUE AUDE

Place
d'Albertas

RUE CLEM.

RUE FABROT

Place de
Verdun

PASSAGE
AGARD

RUE DE L'OPERA

11

10

Place
Forbin

RUE MARECHAL JOFFRE

15

RUE COURT

COURS MIRABEAU

MAISON
BECHARD

RUE MAZARINE

RUE LAROQUE

RUE CABASSOL

ARBAUD
MUSEUM

14

RUE GOYRAND

MAZARIN

RUE CARDINALE

Place des 4
Dauphins

RUE F. MISTRAL

RUE D'ITALIE

RUE FERNAND DOL

12

ST.
JEAN DE
MALTE

QUARTER

RUE 4e SEPTEMBRE

**GRANET
MUSEUM**

COURS GAMBETTA

AVE. VICTOR HUGO

AVE. MALHERBE

5

AVE. Y. HUGO

BLVD. DU ROI RENE

AVE. ANATOLE FRANCE

Parc
Jourdan

To
Cassis
via A-8

Sat 8:30-21:30, closed Sun), but you'll find small ones all over the city.

Taxi: Call 04 42 27 71 11 or mobile 06 16 23 82 39.

Famous Local Product: Signs at fancy bakeries advertise *calissons d'Aix,* the city's homemade candy (which doesn't do much for me). It's made with almond paste—kind of like a marzipan cake—and makes a pleasing souvenir. I prefer the *macarons.*

Tours in Aix-en-Provence

Local Guides
Pascale Benguigui is a good choice for this area (also recommended earlier for Marseille; €156/half-day, €248/day, mobile 06 20 80 07 51, macpas@club-internet.fr). **Catherine d'Antuono** is a smart, capable guide for Aix-en-Provence, the Luberon, and beyond (mobile 06 17 94 69 61, tour.designer@provence-travel.com). **Sarah Pernet** is English born and bred but lives in Aix-en-Provence and offers enjoyable excursions within and from her adopted city (€80/half-day, €140/day, priced per person, www.discover-provence.net, discoverprovence@hotmail.com). Art historian **Daniela Wedel** and her team eagerly show their passion for the history, food, wine, and people of Avignon, Aix-en-Provence, Arles, and the Luberon (mobile 06 43 86 30 83, daniela@treasure-europe.com).

Culinary Tours
Jennifer Dugdale at **Tastes of Provence** introduces her clients to the art of living in Aix, with informative and delicious walking tours of the city's farmers' markets and specialty food stores. She offers two different three-hour tours that include top food destinations, intriguing shops, and tastings of local treats. Excursions into the Aix countryside are also available on request (€60/person, mobile 06 33 69 42 95, www.tastesofprovence.com).

Electric Minibus Joyride
For a mere €0.50, take an orientation ride on a *Diabline*—a six-seater electric-powered minibus. It leaves every 10 minutes from the La Rotonde fountain, opposite the TI (Mon-Sat 8:30-19:30, none on Sun, 40 minutes round-trip). You can also wave down the young drivers anywhere and hop on. There are three routes (A, B, and C); ask the driver for a map when you board. Line A gives you the best overview of the city and runs a route similar to the self-guided walk described next. It also gets you near Cézanne's studio. Designed with local seniors in mind, the minibus provides a fun (and less glamorous) slice-of-life experience in Aix-en-Provence.

Petit Train
Rest your feet and discover Aix-en-Provence's historic center on a 50-minute tour on the little train, while listening to English com-

mentary (€7, departs from La Rotonde fountain). Ask about the longer tours that cover Cézanne's steps.

Aix-en-Provence Town Walk

I've listed these streets, squares, and sights in the order of a handy, lazy orientation stroll. This self-guided walk is highlighted on the map on page 280.

• *Start on Cours Mirabeau at La Rotonde, near the statues on either side of the street, and face...*

La Rotonde: In the 1600s, the roads from Paris and Marseille met just outside the Aix-en-Provence town wall at a huge round-about called La Rotonde. From here locals enjoyed a sweeping view of open countryside before entering the town. As time passed, Aix-en-Provence needed space more than fortifications. The wall was destroyed and replaced by a grand boulevard (Cours Mirabeau). A modern grid-plan town, the Mazarin Quarter, arose across the boulevard from the medieval town (to the right as you look up Cours Mirabeau). In 1860, to give residents water and shade, the town graced La Rotonde with a fountain and a grand boulevard lined with trees. The three figures on top of the fountain represent Justice, Agriculture, and Fine Arts. *Voilà:* The modern core of Aix-en-Provence was created. The new Apple store facing La Rotonde is the latest feather in Aix's style cap, assuring locals that they are still among the chosen few.

• *Saunter slowly up the right side of Cours Mirabeau.*

Cours Mirabeau: This "Champs-Elysées of Provence" divides the higgledy-piggledy old town and the stately Mazarin Quarter.

Designed for the rich and famous to strut their fancy stuff, Cours Mirabeau survives much as it was: a single lane for traffic and an extravagant pedestrian promenade, shaded by plane trees and lined by 17th- and 18th-century mansions for the nobility. Rich folks lived on the right side (in the Mazarin Quarter); common folk lived on the left side (in the old town). Cross-streets were gated to keep everyone in their place.

The street follows a plan based on fours: 440 meters long, 44 meters wide, plane trees (originally elms) 4 meters apart, and decorated by 4 fountains. The "mossy fountains," covered by 200 years of neglect, trickle with water from the thermal spa that gave Aix its first name (in France, "Aix" refers to a city built over a hot spring).

Cours Mirabeau was designed for showing off. Today, it remains a place for *tendance* (trendiness)—or even *hyper-tendance*. Show your stuff and strut the broad sidewalk. As you stroll up the boulevard, stop in front of Aix's oldest and most venerated *patisserie*, **Maison Béchard** (on the right side at 12 Cours Mirabeau) and get a whiff coming from the vent under the entry.

• *Keep on strutting. From the mossy fountain at Rue du 4 Septembre, turn right onto Aix-en-Provence's quiet side, the pleasing little Place des Quatre Dauphins. This marks the center of the...*

Mazarin Quarter (Quartier Mazarin): Built in a grid plan during the reign of King Louis XIV, the Mazarin Quarter remains a peaceful, elegant residential neighborhood—although each of its mansions now houses several families rather than just one. Study the quarter's Baroque and Neoclassical architecture (from the 17th and 18th centuries). The square's Fountain of the Four Dolphins, inspired by Bernini's fountains in Rome, dates from an age when Italian culture set the Baroque standard across Europe. Appreciate how calm this half of the city feels.

Wander up Rue Cardinale to the vertical church, St. Jean-de-Malte, which faces a handsome square. The **Musée Granet** sits next door and features Aix's homegrown artists (including several "lesser" paintings by Cézanne—see sidebar). The museum is most popular for its selection of works from the Planque Collection, often including some by Picasso, Dufy, Monet, Van Gogh, and Braque. Check its website to see what works are on display and to learn about current exhibits, or ask at the TI (museum open June-Sept Tue-Sun 10:00-19:00, Oct-May Tue-Sun 12:00-18:00, closed Mon year-round, www.museegranet-aixenprovence.fr).

• *Turn left on Rue d'Italie behind the church and return to Cours Mirabeau. At the top of the boulevard, a statue celebrates the last count of Provence, under whose rule this region joined France. Stroll down the right side of the street to #53, and spot the venerable...*

Aux Deux Garçons: This café, once frequented by Paul Cézanne, is now popular with—and controlled by—the local mafia. Don't take photos here (and don't open a competing café—the mafia is a serious problem for many independent restaurateurs in Aix). Still, it's worth a peek for its beautiful circa-1790 interior and, for many, worth the higher (mafia-inflated) prices for the sidewalk setting. The Cézanne family hat shop was next door (#55). Cézanne's dad must have been some hatter. He parlayed that successful business into a bank, then into greater wealth, setting up his son to be free to enjoy his artistic pursuits.

• *From here we'll enter the lively Old Town, where pedestrian streets are filled with fine food stores and boutiques, and romantic street musi-*

cians. This is the place in Aix-en-Provence for shopping. Leave Cours Mirabeau at #55, through the tiny Passage Agard. It leads to the **Palace of Justice Square,** *which hosts a bustling flea market (Tue, Thu, and Sat mornings). If the market is on, dally awhile. Leave this square heading left along the first street you crossed as you came into the square. The street you're on, Rue Marius Reinaud, hosts the top designer shops in town. Pause several blocks down when you hear the gurgling of water at the peaceful courtyard square called...*

Place d'Albertas: This sweet little square was created by the guy who lived across the street. He hated the medieval mess of buildings facing his mansion, so he drew up a harmonious facade with a fountain, and hired an architect to build his ideal vision and mask the ugly neighborhood. The neighbors got a nice new facade, and the rich guy got the view of his dreams. The long-overdue restoration of this once run-down square is making a remarkable difference. But since only two-thirds of the property owners agreed to help fund the work, one-third remains undone.

With your back to the fountain, find the large wooden door on the building across the street. Take a look at the names on the door buzzers—the Albertas family still lives here. Behind this door is one of the most beautiful private courtyards in Aix.

• *From here turn right on Rue Aude, the main street of medieval Aix-en-Provence (which turns into Rue du Maréchal Foch). Notice the side streets, with their traffic-barrier stumps that lower during delivery hours. Turn right at Rue Laurent Fauchier, and detour down a few steps for a decadent* macaron *sensation at...*

Brunet Chocolatier and Macarons (closed Sun-Mon): Here you'll find *macarons,* those wonderful cookies made of cloud-like almond meringue sandwiched between luscious butter creams. They're the rage throughout France, no more than here in Aix. You'll find them in every color and flavor imaginable. Try the caramel with salted butter, pistachio, or black-currant violet. Though this confection's origins are vague (some claim they came from Italy in the 16th century), what matters is that they're delicious.

• *Try one or two, then continue on to...*

Richelme Square (Place Richelme): This wonderful square hosts a lively market, as it has since the 1300s (daily 8:00-13:00). It's the perfect Provençal scene—lovely buildings, plane trees, and farmers selling local produce. You'll also find two famous goat-cheese merchants. Bruno is a former marketing executive who purchased goats rather than a Ferrari during his midlife crisis. You can find his cheese (as well as pictures of his herd) on Tuesdays, Thursdays, and Saturdays on the Rue Maréchal Foch side of the market. The other famous goat-cheese stall is near the Bar de l'Horloge; the owner looks just like Paul Cézanne—or Jerry Garcia, if that's more your style. (He works Saturdays only and is fully aware of his

PROVENCE

Paul Cézanne in Aix-en-Provence

Post-Impressionist artist Paul Cézanne (1839-1906) loved Aix-en-Provence. He studied law at the university (opposite the cathedral), and produced most of his paintings in and around Aix-en-Provence—even though this conservative town didn't understand him or his art. Today the city fathers milk anything remotely related to his years here. But because the conservative curator of the town's leading art gallery, the Granet Museum, decreed "no Cézannes," you can see only some of Cézanne's lesser original paintings in Aix-en-Provence. Bad curator.

Instead, fans of the artist will want to pick up the *In the Footsteps of Cézanne* self-guided-tour flier at the TI, and follow the bronze pavement markers around town.

Atelier Cézanne, the artist's last studio, has been preserved as it was when he died and is open to the public. It's a 30-minute walk from the TI, or you can get there on electric minibus A (see "Tours in Aix-en-Provence," earlier). Although there is no art here, his tools and personal belongings make it almost interesting for enthusiasts—I'd skip it. If you must go, it's best (and essential in high season) to reserve a visit time in advance at the TI or at www.aixenprovencetourism.com.

Cost and Hours: €6, daily July-Aug 10:00-18:00, April-June and Sept 10:00-12:00 & 14:00-18:00, Oct-March until 17:00, English-language tours usually at 17:00, 2 miles from TI at 9 Avenue Cézanne, tel. 04 42 16 10 91, www.atelier-cezanne.com.

special good looks; drop by for a sample and a photo if you like.) The cafés at the end of the square are ideal for market observation. To savor the market scene, pause for a drink at Café l'Unic (also draws a lively and young pre-dinner crowd). To experience the best coffee and hot chocolate in Aix, grab an outdoor stool and go local at Brûlerie Richelme (Tue-Sat 8:30-19:00, closed Sun-Mon).

• *One block uphill is the stately...*

L'Hôtel de Ville Square (Place de l'Hôtel de Ville): This square, also known as Place de la Mairie, is anchored by a Roman column. Stand with your back to the column and face the Hôtel de Ville. The center niche of this 17th-century City Hall once featured a bust of Louis XIV. But since the Revolution, Marianne (the Lady of the Republic) has taken his place. As throughout Europe, the three flags represent the region (Provence), country (France), and the

European Union. Provence's flag carries the red and yellow of Catalunya (the region in Spain centered on Barcelona) because the counts of Provence originated there. Aix-en-Provence's coat of arms over the doorway combines the Catalan flag and the French fleur-de-lis.

The 18th-century building on your left was once the town's corn exchange (today it's a letter exchange). Its exuberant pediment features figures representing the two rivers of Provence: old man Rhône and madame Durance. While the Durance River floods frequently (here depicted overflowing its frame), it also brings fertility to the fields (hence the cornucopia).

Back toward Hôtel de Ville, the 16th-century bell tower was built in part with stones scavenged from ancient Roman buildings—notice the white stones at the tower's base. The niche above the arch once displayed the bust of the king. Since the Revolution, it has housed a funerary urn that symbolically honors all who gave their lives for French liberty. Walk under the arch to see a small plaque honoring the American 3rd Division that liberated the town in 1944 (with the participation of French troops; Aix-en-Provence got through World War II relatively unscathed).

History aside, the square is a delight for its vintage French storefronts and colorful morning markets: flowers (Tue, Thu, and Sat) and old books (first Sun of the month). On non-market days and each afternoon, café tables replace the market stalls.

• *Stroll under the bell tower and up Rue Gaston de Saporta to the...*

Cathedral of the Holy Savior (Saint-Sauveur): This church was built atop the Roman forum—likely on the site of a pagan temple. As the cathedral grew with the city, its interior became a parade of architectural styles. The many-faceted interior is at once confusing and fascinating, with three distinct sections: Standing at the entrance, you face the Romanesque section; to the left are the Gothic and then the Baroque sections. We'll visit each in turn (church open Mon-Sat 8:00-12:00 & 14:00-18:00, Sun 9:00-12:00 & 14:00-19:00).

In the **Romanesque section,** step down to the right to find the baptistery, with its early Christian (fourth-century) Roman font. It was located outside the church until the 14th century, when the church was expanded to house the baptistery. The font is big enough for immersion, which was the baptismal style in Roman times. Also notice that it's eight-sided, symbolizing eternity: one side more than the seven days it took God to create everything. The font is surrounded by ancient columns with original fourth-century capitals below a Renaissance cupola.

Farther down is the door to the 12th-century cloister (visits on the half-hour except 12:00-14:00). After passing a side chapel, find the closet-sized architectural footprint of the original Christian chapel from the Roman era several feet below floor level. Like the baptistery, this would have been outside the current church walls until the 14th century.

In the **Gothic section,** two organs flank the nave: One works, but the other is a prop, added for looks...an appropriately symmetrical Neoclassical touch, as was the style in the 18th century (notice the lack of depth in one of them). The precious door (facing the street from this section) is carved of chestnut with a Gothic top (showing sibyls, or ancient female prophets) and Renaissance lower half (depicting prophets). Because it faces the street, it's covered by a second, protective door (viewable on request).

In the **Baroque section,** don't miss the three-paneled altar painting of the burning bush (*Buisson Ardent,* 15th century, by Nicolas Froment). This finely detailed painting was rescued from a convent that was flattened during the French Revolution. The central panel shows the Virgin and Child on the burning bush as Moses looks on in amazement.

• *Your walk is over. Strolling back through town, drop by a designer bakery to try a* calisson, *Aix-en-Provence's local candy (see "Helpful Hints," earlier). Or, for fewer calories and just as much fun, marvel at a town filled with people who seem to be living life very, very well.*

Eating in Aix-en-Provence

In Aix-en-Provence, you can dine on bustling squares, along a grand boulevard, or in little restaurants on side streets (where you'll find the best values). Cours Mirabeau is good for desserts and drinks, as are many of the outdoor places lining leafy squares. Aix is filled with tempting but mediocre restaurants. To eat higher on the food chain, try one of the following places.

For general tips on eating in France, see page 276.

In the Old Town

Chez Feraud, in a lovely vine-covered building that requires some extra time to find, is a good choice for a traditional dinner of authentic Provençal dishes. While maybe past its prime, this Old World place features a mother-son team: Mama serves with formal grace while son handles the grill (€30 *menu,* 8 Rue du Puits Juif, tel. 04 42 63 07 27).

Pasta Cosy is unique, serving a Franco-Italian fusion of original dishes in a small, cozy setting (inside and out). It's also family-

and tourist-friendly, thanks to welcoming owner Fabien. He greets every client with the same enthusiasm—and with fluent English—and loves taking care of his guests. Split the antipasta-tapas appetizer (up to nine items), and be tempted by his rich Pastacosy dish (pasta cooked inside a wheel of parmesan cheese). Try the *fiocchetti* (pasta cooked with pears and gorgonzola) or the gourmet white truffle pasta. Desserts are homemade and delicious. The reasonably priced wine list features wines from Burgundy and Provence (closed Sun-Mon except open Mon in summer, across from Hôtel le Manoir at 5 Rue d'Entrecasteaux, tel. 04 42 38 02 28).

Chez Mitch is a fine choice for classic French cuisine with modern flair. Overlook the trendy decor, and savor the seasonal dishes, excellent wine list, and top-notch service that Mitch assures. Book ahead for weekends (€30-50 *menus*, closed Sun, vaulted dining room downstairs, 26 Rue des Tanneurs, tel. 04 42 26 63 08, www.mitchrestaurant.com).

Chez Charlotte is Aix's low-key, down-and-dirty diner, where old-school residents come for a good meal at a good price. A young couple, Laurent and Nathalie, are your hosts (he cooks, she makes pastry). The dining area is simple and convivial; come early to snag a cheery garden table (€19 three-course *menu* only, no à la carte, closed Sun-Mon, 32 Rue des Bernardines, tel. 04 42 26 77 56).

Hôtel Cézanne serves up a gourmet champagne brunch *à la française*. For €20 you can feast on a great selection of omelets (made with caramelized goat cheese or truffles) and sample real French toast (brunch served daily 7:00-12:00, 40 Avenue Victor Hugo, tel. 04 42 91 11 11, www.hotelaix.com).

On Forum des Cardeurs: Just off L'Hôtel de Ville Square, the Forum des Cardeurs is café-crammed. Browse the selection from top to bottom, then decide. At the top, **Le Papagayo** has a good selection of salads and a quiche of the day (big €14 salads, open daily for lunch and dinner, 22 Forum des Cardeurs, tel. 04 42 23 98 35). **Juste en Face,** facing Papagayo, features grilled meats (the duck and rabbit are tasty) and Mediterranean cuisine, specializing in North African *tajine*—a vegetable-based stew usually served with meat (€16-20 *plats*, open daily, 6 Rue Verrerie, tel. 04 42 96 47 70).

Discerning diners should try one of these two places that face each other at the lower end of the big square. These restaurants are the talk of the city, so book ahead on weekends:

Le Poivre d'Ane has a stylish interior and good terrace tables. *Le chef* describes his cuisine as inventive and audacious (€30 three-course *menu*, €45 five-course *menu*, 40 Forum des Cardeurs, tel. 04 42 21 32 66, www.restaurantlepoivredane.com).

L'Epicurien has just eight tables, allowing the chef to main-

What If I Miss My Boat?

Remember that you can get help from the cruise line's port agent (listed on the destination information sheet distributed on the ship) and the local TI (see page 257 for Marseille or page 252 for Toulon). If the port agent suggests a costly solution (such as a private car with a driver), you may want to consider public transit.

Frequent **trains** leave from Marseille's St. Charles Station to **Barcelona** (some direct, more with changes in Montpellier) and **Nice**. Toulon also has frequent, direct trains to **Nice**. Italian ports—such as **Livorno**, **Civitavecchia**, and **Naples**—are also reachable from Marseille and Toulon, but require multiple changes. To look up specific connections, use http://en.voyages-sncf.com/en (domestic journeys only) or www.bahn.com (Germany's excellent all-Europe schedule website).

For other ports (in Croatia, Greece, and Turkey), you'll probably need to catch a **plane**. Marseille's airport (Aéroport Marseille-Provence), about 16 miles north of the city center, is small and easy to navigate (airport code: MRS, tel. 04 42 14 14 14, www.marseille.aeroport.fr).

Local **travel agents** in Marseille and Toulon can also help you. For more advice on what to do if you miss the boat, see page 140.

tain his top-quality standards. The cuisine is elegant and creatively Provençal (*menus* from €33-46, open Wed-Sat for dinner and Mon-Sat for lunch, closed Sun, 13 Forum des Cardeurs, mobile 06 89 33 49 83).

Along Cours Mirabeau

If you're interested in a delicious view more than delicious food, eat with style on Cours Mirabeau.

Aux Deux Garçons has always been the place to see and be seen: a vintage brasserie with door-to-door waiters in aprons, a lovely interior, and well-positioned outdoor tables with properly placed silverware on white tablecloths. It's busy at lunch (€20-30 *plats*, three-course *menus* from €25, great steak *tartare*, open daily, 53 Cours Mirabeau, tel. 04 42 26 00 51, www.les2garcons.fr). Even if you're not eating here, pop in to see the decor.

Le Grillon is a younger, more boisterous choice for dining on Cours Mirabeau (white tablecloths, €20 *plats*, €15-30 *menu*). Its bar is a hit with locals for the prime seating: front and center on the boulevard's strolling fashion show (open daily for lunch and dinner, corner of Rue Clémenceau and Cours Mirabeau, tel. 04 42 27 58 81, http://cafelegrillon.free.fr).

In the Mazarin Quarter

La Brocherie dishes up French rather than Provençal cuisine. Its stone-rustic, indoors-only ambience is best for cooler days. This family-owned bistro—run by Messieurs Soudain and Tourville—is deep in the Mazarin Quarter and highlights food from the farm (it's about beef). Dig into the hearty self-service salad buffet (all you can eat, €12) and meats grilled over a wood fire (skip the fish options). The €20 *menu* includes the salad bar (closed Sat for lunch and Sun all day, indoor seating only, 5 Rue Fernand Dol, tel. 04 42 38 33 21).

PROVENCE

French Survival Phrases

When using the phonetics, try to nasalize the n sound.

English	French	Pronunciation
Good day.	*Bonjour.*	bohn-zhoor
Mrs. / Mr.	*Madame / Monsieur*	mah-dahm / muhs-yur
Do you speak English?	*Parlez-vous anglais?*	par-lay-voo ahn-glay
Yes. / No.	*Oui. / Non.*	wee / nohn
I understand.	*Je comprends.*	zhuh kohn-prahn
I don't understand.	*Je ne comprends pas.*	zhuh nuh kohn-prahn pah
Please.	*S'il vous plaît.*	see voo play
Thank you.	*Merci.*	mehr-see
I'm sorry.	*Désolé.*	day-zoh-lay
Excuse me.	*Pardon.*	par-dohn
(No) problem.	*(Pas de) problème.*	(pah duh) proh-blehm
It's good.	*C'est bon.*	say bohn
Goodbye.	*Au revoir.*	oh vwahr
one / two	*un / deux*	uhn / duh
three / four	*trois / quatre*	twah / kah-truh
five / six	*cinq / six*	sank / sees
seven / eight	*sept / huit*	seht / weet
nine / ten	*neuf / dix*	nuhf / dees
How much is it?	*Combien?*	kohn-bee-an
Write it?	*Ecrivez?*	ay-kree-vay
Is it free?	*C'est gratuit?*	say grah-twee
Included?	*Inclus?*	an-klew
Where can I buy / find...?	*Où puis-je acheter / trouver...?*	oo pwee-zhuh ah-shuh-tay / troo-vay
I'd like / We'd like...	*Je voudrais / Nous voudrions...*	zhuh voo-dray / noo voo-dree-ohn
...a room.	*...une chambre.*	ewn shahn-bruh
...a ticket to ___.	*...un billet pour ___.*	uhn bee-yay poor ___
Is it possible?	*C'est possible?*	say poh-see-bluh
Where is...?	*Où est...?*	oo ay
...the train station	*...la gare*	lah gar
...the bus station	*...la gare routière*	lah gar root-yehr
...tourist information	*...l'office du tourisme*	loh-fees dew too-reez-muh
Where are the toilets?	*Où sont les toilettes?*	oo sohn lay twah-leht
men	*hommes*	ohm
women	*dames*	dahm
left / right	*à gauche / à droite*	ah gohsh / ah dwaht
straight	*tout droit*	too dwah
When does this open / close?	*Ça ouvre / ferme à quelle heure?*	sah oo-vruh / fehrm ah kehl ur
At what time?	*À quelle heure?*	ah kehl ur
Just a moment.	*Un moment.*	uhn moh-mahn
now / soon / later	*maintenant / bientôt / plus tard*	man-tuh-nahn / bee-an-toh / plew tar
today / tomorrow	*aujourd'hui / demain*	oh-zhoor-dwee / duh-man

In a French Restaurant

English	French	Pronunciation
I'd like / We'd like...	Je voudrais / Nous voudrions...	zhuh voo-dray / noo voo-dree-ohn
...to reserve...	...réserver...	ray-zehr-vay
...a table for one / two.	...une table pour un / deux.	ewn tah-bluh poor uhn / duh
Is this seat free?	C'est libre?	say lee-bruh
The menu (in English), please.	La carte (en anglais), s'il vous plaît.	lah kart (ahn ahn-glay) see voo play
service (not) included	service (non) compris	sehr-vees (nohn) kohn-pree
to go	à emporter	ah ahn-por-tay
with / without	avec / sans	ah-vehk / sahn
and / or	et / ou	ay / oo
special of the day	plat du jour	plah dew zhoor
specialty of the house	spécialité de la maison	spay-see-ah-lee-tay duh lah may-zohn
appetizers	hors d'oeuvre	or duh-vruh
first course (soup, salad)	entrée	ahn-tray
main course (meat, fish)	plat principal	plah pran-see-pahl
bread	pain	pan
cheese	fromage	froh-mahzh
sandwich	sandwich	sahnd-weech
soup	soupe	soop
salad	salade	sah-lahd
meat	viande	vee-ahnd
chicken	poulet	poo-lay
fish	poisson	pwah-sohn
seafood	fruits de mer	frwee duh mehr
fruit	fruit	frwee
vegetables	légumes	lay-gewm
dessert	dessert	day-sehr
mineral water	eau minérale	oh mee-nay-rahl
tap water	l'eau du robinet	loh dew roh-bee-nay
milk	lait	lay
(orange) juice	jus (d'orange)	zhew (doh-rahnzh)
coffee / tea	café / thé	kah-fay / tay
wine	vin	van
red / white	rouge / blanc	roozh / blahn
glass / bottle	verre / bouteille	vehr / boo-tay
beer	bière	bee-ehr
Cheers!	Santé!	sahn-tay
More. / Another.	Plus. / Un autre.	plew / uhn oh-truh
The same.	La même chose.	lah mehm shohz
The bill, please.	L'addition, s'il vous plaît.	lah-dee-see-ohn see voo play
Do you accept credit cards?	Vous prenez les cartes?	voo pruh-nay lay kart
tip	pourboire	poor-bwahr
Delicious!	Délicieux!	day-lee-see-uh

For more user-friendly French phrases, check out *Rick Steves' French Phrase Book and Dictionary* or *Rick Steves' French, Italian & German Phrase Book.*

THE FRENCH RIVIERA

France

France Practicalities

France is a place of gentle beauty. At 215,000 square miles (roughly 20 percent smaller than Texas), it is Western Europe's largest nation, with luxuriant forests, forever coastlines, truly grand canyons, and Europe's highest mountain ranges. You'll also discover a dizzying array of artistic and architectural wonders—soaring cathedrals, chandeliered châteaux, and museums filled with the cultural icons of the Western world.

For the French, *l'art de vivre*—the art of living—is more than just a pleasing expression. Though they produce nearly a quarter of the world's wine, the French drink much of it themselves. Come here to experience subtle pleasures, including fine cuisine, velvety wines, and linger-long pastimes such as people-watching from sun-dappled cafés.

Money: France uses the euro currency: 1 euro (€) = about $1.30. An ATM is called a *distributeur*. The local VAT (value-added sales tax) rate is 20 percent; the minimum purchase eligible for a VAT refund is €175.01 (for details on refunds, see page 135).

Language: For useful French phrases, see page 371.

Emergencies: Dial 17 for police or 112 for medical or other emergencies. In case of theft or loss, see page 128.

Time Zone: France is on Central European Time (the same as most of the Continent, and six/nine hours ahead of the East/West Coasts of the US).

Consular Services: The US consulate in Marseille is at Place Varian Fry (tel. 04 91 54 90 84, after-hours emergency tel. 01 43 12 22 22, http://marseille.usconsulate.gov); limited services are also available in Nice (tel. 04 93 88 89 55). The Canadian consulate in Nice is at 2 Place Franklin (tel. 04 93 92 93 22, www.france.gc.fr). Call ahead for passport services.

Phoning: France has a direct-dial 10-digit phone system (no area codes). To **call within France,** just dial the 10-digit number. To **call to France,** dial the international access code (00 if calling from Europe, or 011 from North America), then 33 (France's country code, then the phone number (but drop the initial zero). To **call home from France,** dial 00, 1, then your area code and phone number. For more help, see page 1242.

Tipping: At cafés and restaurants, a 12-15 percent service charge is typically included in the bill *(service compris),* and most French never tip. However, if you feel the service was exceptional, it's fine to tip up to 5 percent. To tip a cabbie, round up to about 10 percent of the metered fare (for a €13 fare, pay €14).

Tourist Information: www.us.rendezvousenfrance.com

THE FRENCH RIVIERA

La Côte d'Azur

A hundred years ago, celebrities from London to Moscow flocked to the French Riviera to socialize, gamble, and escape the dreary weather at home. Today, cruise passengers, budget vacationers, and heat-seeking Europeans fill belle-époque resorts at France's most sought-after fun-in-the-sun destination.

The region got its nickname from turn-of-the-20th-century vacationing Brits, who simply extended the Italian Riviera west to France to include Nice. Today, the Riviera label stretches even farther westward, running (for our purposes) from the Italian border to St-Tropez. To the French, this summer fun zone is known as La Côte d'Azur.

Three main cruise ports line up along a 12-mile seafront stretch in this region: Nice, Villefranche-sur-Mer, and Monaco. Smaller ships dock at the pier in Nice; larger ships anchor in Villefranche-sur-Mer's harbor; and Monaco handles ships either at anchor or at its pier. A few cruises tender to Cannes.

Once ashore at any of these spots, the region's biggest draw is Nice—with world-class museums, a splendid beachfront promenade, a seductive old town, and all the headaches of a major city (traffic, crime, pollution, and so on). Monaco welcomes everyone and will happily take your cash. Between Nice and Monaco lies the Riviera's richest stretch of real estate, paved with famously scenic roads (called the Three Corniches) and peppered with cliff-hanging villages, million-dollar vistas, and sea-view walking trails connecting beach towns. Fifteen minutes from Nice (on the way to Monaco), little Villefranche-sur-Mer stares across the bay to woodsy and exclusive Cap Ferrat. The eagle's-nest Eze-le-Village surveys the same scene from high above. West of Nice (and practi-

Excursions from French Riviera Ports

The best destinations are all doable by public transportation. **Nice** is better than nice—it's tops. Other winners are peaceful **Villefranche-sur-Mer,** and glitzy **Monaco.** (All three are covered at greater length in this chapter.) Other excursions east of Nice include the elegant peninsula of **Cap Ferrat** and the hilltop town of **Eze-le-Village.**

Other than Antibes, the following destinations west of Nice are not as appealing. They're farther afield and more suited for excursions, but why bother when Nice is near?

Antibes is a ramparted medieval town of narrow streets and red-tiled roofs, with a big yacht harbor, sandy beaches, and the prized Picasso Museum. It's the best stop west of Nice.

Cannes is a wealthy seafront town, catering to the rich and famous, and made for window-shopping. Go here only if your ship docks here.

St-Tropez is a trendy, busy, traffic-free port town smothered with fashion boutiques, fancy restaurants, and luxury boats. Other seafront resorts are at least as good, and closer, to the main Riviera ports.

St-Paul-de-Vence is a cobblestoned hill town jammed with shops and waves of tourists, and near the Fondation Maeght's modern-art collection. Difficult to reach on your own, this worthwhile town is usually bundled into an excursion with other sights.

cal to visit only if your ship arrives in Nice) are more options: Antibes has a thriving port and silky sand beaches; image-conscious Cannes (also a port for some smaller cruise ships) is the Riviera's self-appointed queen, with an elegant veneer hiding...very little; and yacht-happy St-Tropez swims alone at the western fringe of the region.

Planning Your Time

If Arriving at Nice, Villefranche-sur-Mer, or Monaco: Conveniently, these three ports are easily connected to each other by frequent trains and buses—so your sightseeing options are effectively the same from any of them. It can be hard to choose among the many good destinations described in this chapter. If it's a toss-up, an easy plan is to visit **your port city plus Nice.** If your ship docks at Nice, you could consider a speedy side-trip to Monaco or Antibes; either is within 15-30 minutes one-way by train.

If Arriving at Cannes: Your best, nearest option is to visit Antibes (with its Picasso Museum), just 15 minutes away by train. Nice is about 40 minutes away. Or just enjoy relaxing in Cannes.

Your Top Options

Here are quick descriptions, with time estimates, of your choices:

• The big city of **Nice** has a beachfront promenade, an atmospheric old town (Vieux Nice), and two excellent art museums (Chagall and Matisse). With a day here, start with my two self-guided walks: "Welcome to the Riviera" and "Scratch-and-Sniff Walk Through Vieux Nice" (allow an hour each). Art lovers can spend an hour apiece in the Chagall and Matisse museums (plus 15-20 minutes each way by taxi or bus—but note that both museums are closed Tue), while others can just relax at the beach. Allow six to seven hours for everything. If you have a half-day, choose between the walks or the museums.

• **Villefranche-sur-Mer** is simply an easygoing harbor town of steep narrow streets on a lovely bay filled with sailing yachts. You can spend anywhere from a few minutes to a few hours here, enjoying the ambience or hitting the beach. It's just 10 minutes by train from Nice.

• The glamorous principality of **Monaco** has two main sightseeing zones: Monaco-Ville, a cliff-capping old town with great views (follow my self-guided walk and allow up to two hours), and the glitzy district of Monte Carlo, with little to see except its famous casino (which doesn't open until 14:00; allow one hour or less). All said, figure on a total of three hours in Monaco for a satisfying experience. It's 20 minutes from Nice by train.

• **Cap Ferrat**, a 30-minute bus ride from Nice (and next door to Villefranche), is an exclusive, beautiful peninsula where groomed trails pass by villas, beaches, and a village port.

• **Antibes**, with its Picasso Museum, is a fine side-trip, particularly if you're arriving in Nice or Cannes. Figure on four or five hours round-trip from either destination, including train time (15-30 minutes from Nice, 15 minutes from Cannes).

Tips: If your destination is accessible by either train or bus, it's substantially faster to take the train (although the bus from Nice to Villefranche can be more convenient and memorable). And no matter where you go, bring along a swimsuit if the weather's sunny—good beaches are plentiful.

Getting Around the Riviera

If taking the train or bus, have coins handy. Ticket machines don't take US credit cards or euro bills, smaller train stations may be unstaffed, and bus drivers can't make change for large bills.

By Public Transportation: Trains and buses do a good job of connecting places along the coast, with bonus views along many routes. Buses also provide reasonable service to some inland hill towns. Choose the bus for convenience and economy, or the pricier but faster train when you want to save time.

Buses are an amazing deal. The Côte d'Azur has a single regional transportation network—Lignes d'Azur (www.lignesdazur.com). Any one-way bus or tram ride costs €1.50 (€10 for 10 tickets) whether you're riding 20 minutes to Villefranche-sur-Mer, 45 minutes to Monaco, or an hour to Antibes. The €1.50 ticket is good for 74 minutes of travel in one direction anywhere within the bus system except for airport buses (and can't be used for a round-trip). Buy your bus ticket from the driver (be sure to carry small bills or coins) or from the machines at stops, and validate your ticket in the machine on board. You can even transfer between the buses of the Lignes d'Azur and the smaller TAM (Transports Alpes-Maritimes) system; if you board a TAM bus and need a transfer, ask for *un ticket correspondance*. A €6 all-day ticket is good on Nice's city buses, tramway, and airport express bus, plus selected buses serving nearby destinations (such as Villefranche and Eze-le-Village).

The **train** is more expensive, but there's no quicker way to move about the Riviera (http://en.voyages-sncf.com/en). Speedy trains link the Riviera's beachfront destinations—Cannes, Antibes, Nice, Villefranche-sur-Mer, Monaco, and Menton. If in Nice, Villefranche, or Monaco, you can assume trains marked for *Vintimille* or *Menton* are going east, and those marked for *Grasse, Cannes,* or *Nice* are going west. Never board a train without a ticket or valid pass—fare inspectors don't accept any excuses, and the minimum fine is €70.

For an overview of many Riviera train and bus connections, see the "Public Transportation in the French Riviera" chart on page 302.

By Boat: Trans Côte d'Azur offers boat service from Nice to Monaco or to St-Tropez from June into September (tel. 04 92 98 71 30, www.trans-cote-azur.com).

By Car: While public transportation is easy in this region, some cruisers enjoy renting a car to joyride between towns—especially along the three dramatically scenic roads, called the Corniches, that connect Nice and Monaco (for car-rental offices in Nice, see "Helpful Hints," page 312).

Tours of the French Riviera

To see several Riviera destinations efficiently in one short day, consider hiring a guide or joining a tour.

Local Guides: Agnès Dumartin, a top guide for the region, is a good teacher who understands Nice particularly well and loves all forms of art (€205/half-day, €295/day, mobile 06 81 82 17 67, agnes.dumartin@orange.fr). **Sylvie Di Cristo** offers terrific full-day tours throughout the French Riviera in a car or minivan. She adores educating people about this area's culture and history, and loves adapting her tour to your interests, from overlooked hill

Public Transportation in the French Riviera

Many key Riviera destinations are connected by bus or train service, and some are served by both. See the chart on the following pages for a summary of available services. While bus fare for any trip is only €1.50, the pricier train can be a better choice because it saves you time. The bus frequencies are for Monday-Saturday (Sun often has limited or no bus service)—confirm all connections and last train/bus times locally. I've listed some connections as "not recommended" due to the amount of time spent in transit; for example, while it is possible to connect Cannes and Monaco by train, at over two hours round-trip, you'd spend a good portion of your day on the train instead of enjoying the sights. Stick closer to your port.

THE FRENCH RIVIERA

Public Transportation in the French Riviera

From	To Cannes	To Antibes	
Cannes by Train	N/A	2/hr, 15 min	
Cannes by Bus	N/A	#200, 2-4/hr, 35 min	
Antibes by Train	2/hr, 15 min	N/A	
Antibes by Bus	#200, 2-4/hr, 35 min	N/A	
Nice by Train	2/hr, 30-40 min	2/hr, 15-30 min	
Nice by Bus	#200, 2-4/hr, 1.5-1.75 hrs	#200, 2-4/hr, 1-1.5 hrs	
Villefranche-sur-Mer by Train	2/hr, 50 min	2/hr, 40 min	
Villefranche-sur-Mer by Bus	Not recommended	Not recommended	
Monaco by Train	2/hr, 70 min	2/hr, 50 min	
Monaco by Bus	Not recommended	Not recommended	

towns to wine, cuisine, art, or perfume (€200-250/person for 2-3 people, €120-150/person for 4-6 people, €90-100/person for 7-8 people, 2-person minimum, mobile 06 09 88 83 83, www.frenchrivieraguides.net, dicristosylvie@gmail.com).

Sofia Villavicencio is a pleasant guide who makes the Riviera's art come alive (€145/half-day, €200/day, mobile 06 68 51 55 52, sofia.villavicencio@laposte.net). **Boba Vukadinovic** enjoys sharing her passion for her adoptive home. Her good tours of Nice and the Riviera are tailored to the sights and topics that appeal to you (€250/half-day, €350/day, mobile 06 27 45 68 39, www.yourguideboba.com, boba@yourguideboba.com).

Cooking Tour and Classes: Charming Canadian Francophile Rosa Jackson, a food journalist, Cordon Bleu-trained cook, and longtime resident of France, runs **Les Petits Farcis,** which offers three-hour "Taste of Nice" food tours for €90. She also teaches popular cooking classes in Vieux Nice, which include a morning trip to the open-air market on Cours Saleya to pick up ingredients, and an afternoon session spent creating an authentic Niçois meal from your purchases (€195/person, mobile 06 81 67 41 22, www.petitsfarcis.com).

Minivan Tours: The Nice TI has information on minivan excursions from Nice (roughly €50-70/half-day, €80-110/day). **Revelation Tours** takes pride in its guides (mobile 06 27 05 67 77, www.revelation-tours.com). **Med-Tour** is one of many (tel. 04 93 82 92 58, mobile 06 73 82 04 10, www.med-tour.com); **Tour Azur**

To Nice	To Villefranche-sur-Mer	To Monaco
2/hr, 30-40 min	2/hr, 50 min	2/hr, 70 min
#200, 2-4/hr, 1.5-1.75 hrs	Not recommended	Not recommended
2/hr, 15-30 min	2/hr, 40 min	2/hr, 50 min
#200, 2-4/hr, 1-1.5 hrs	Not recommended	Not recommended
N/A	2/hr, 10 min	2/hr, 20 min
N/A	#100, 3-5/hr, 20 min; also #81, 2-4/hr, 20 min	#100, 3-5/hr, 45 min
2/hr, 10 min	N/A	2/hr, 10 min
#100, 4-5/hr, 20 min; also #81, 2-4/hr, 20 min	N/A	#100, 4-5/hr, 25 min
2/hr, 20 min	2/hr, 10 min	N/A
#100, 3-5/hr, 45 min	#100, 3-5/hr, 25 min	N/A

THE FRENCH RIVIERA

is another (tel. 04 93 44 88 77, www.tourazur.com). All also offer private tours by the day or half-day (check with them for their outrageous prices, about €100/hour).

Helpful Hints

Medical Help: Riviera Medical Services has a list of English-speaking physicians all along the Riviera. They can help you make an appointment or call an ambulance (tel. 04 93 26 12 70, www.rivieramedical.com).

Closed Days: The following sights are closed on Mondays: the Modern and Contemporary Art Museum, Fine Arts Museum, Russian Cathedral, and Cours Saleya market in Nice, along with Antibes' Picasso Museum and Marché Provençal market (Sept-June). On Tuesdays these museums are closed: the Chagall, Matisse, and Archaeological museums in Nice.

Events: The Riviera is famous for staging major events. Unless you're actually taking part in the festivities, these occasions give you only room shortages and traffic jams. Here are the three biggies: **Nice Carnival** (late Feb-early March, www.nicecarnaval.com), Festival de Cannes, better known as the **Cannes Film Festival** (mid-May, www.festival-cannes.com), and the **Grand Prix of Monaco** (late May, www.grand-prix-monaco.com).

Navigating French Food: For tips on eating in France, see sidebar on page 276.

Experiences: For ideas on experiencing French culture, see the sidebar on page 248.

Updates to this Book: For news about changes to this book's coverage since it was published, see www.ricksteves.com/update.

Nice

Nice (sounds like "niece"), with its spectacular Alps-to-Mediterranean surroundings, is an enjoyable big-city highlight of the Riviera. Its traffic-free old city mixes Italian and French flavors to create a spicy Mediterranean dressing, while its big squares, broad seaside walkways, and long beaches invite lounging and people-watching. Nice may be nice, but it's hot and jammed in July and August. Everything you'll want to see in Nice is either within walking distance, or a short bus or tram ride away.

Travelers arriving in Nice by cruise ship should read the next section to get oriented. Side-trippers visiting from elsewhere in the Riviera can skip down to "Orientation to Nice" on page 310.

Arrival at the Port of Nice

Arrival at a Glance: You can easily walk or take public transit (bus or tram) to most sights in Nice. To reach nearby towns, the train is faster than the bus. Go to Nice's train station (walk 10 minutes, then take the tram; or pay €15-20 for a taxi), where you can catch a train to Villefranche-sur-Mer (10 minutes), Monaco (20 minutes), or Antibes (15-30 minutes). Or, at the top of the port, you can catch bus #100 to Villefranche-sur-Mer (15 minutes) or Monaco (45 minutes); additional regional buses depart near Place Masséna (a 20-25-minute walk away). Taxis are available for any of these (€35-40 one-way to Villefranche, €80-90 one-way to Monaco).

Port Overview

Nice's port is at the eastern edge of the town center, below the landmark Castle Hill. Cruise ships dock at either end of the mouth of this port: **Terminal 1** to the east (along the embankment called Quai du Commerce), or **Terminal 2** to the west (along Quai Infernet). From either terminal, it's a free shuttle bus ride or about a

Services at the Port of Nice

As the port is close to Nice's city center, you'll easily find ample ATMs, Internet cafés, and other services, either at or near the port. For some of the options in town, see "Helpful Hints" on page 312.

Internet Access: You may be able to pick up a free Wi-Fi signal at the port (though this is sporadic). Several places around the port have Internet terminals.

Pharmacy: There are several within a block or two of the port, including Pharmacie Port Lympia (a block from Terminal 2, at 50 Boulevard de Stalingrad); Pharmacie du Port (at the top-left corner of the port, on the street leading to Place Garibaldi at Rue Cassini 17); and Pharmacie du Mont Boron at 3 Boulevard Carnot (at the top-right corner of the port).

10-minute walk to the top of the port. The picturesque port is filled with yachts, sailboats, and fishing boats, and surrounded by seafood restaurants and brasseries. There's a tiny, rocky, partially nude beach at the mouth of the port, just beyond Terminal 1.

A free **shuttle bus** *(navette)* circles the port, connecting the two terminals and Place Ile de Beauté, the street that runs along the top of the port (where you'll find bus stops—including for Villefranche and Monaco—and easy access to Place Garibaldi, Nice's entry square). The shuttle bus can save you a few minutes' walk, but the port area is charming enough that walking is an enjoyable alternative.

Tourist Information: TI kiosks at both terminals are timed to be open when cruises arrive—just look for the TI attendants under the pointy white tents. For TIs in town, see page 311.

Getting into Town

The atmospheric streets of Vieux Nice (Old Nice)—and the beaches and grand promenade that stretch between the city and the sea—are just on the other side of Castle Hill from the port. The tram and all city and regional buses cost only €1.50 per trip, making this one of the cheapest and easiest cities in France to get around in. Note that the **Le Grand Tour Bus** hop-on, hop-off bus circuit, which conveniently connects many of Nice's major sights, has a stop at the top of the port (for details, see "Tours in Nice," later).

By Taxi

Taxis meet arriving cruise ships; if you can't find one, ask the TI at the terminal to call one for you. Rates can be slippery, but expect to pay about €25-30 to points within Nice (such as to the train sta-

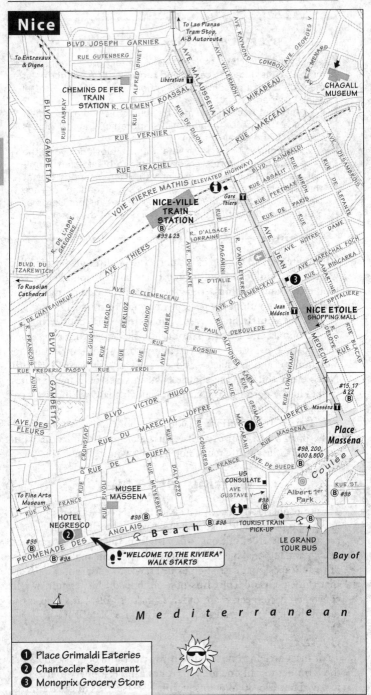

THE FRENCH RIVIERA

Nice

To Las Planas
Tram Stop,
A-8 Autoroute

To Entrevaux
& Digne

BLVD. JOSEPH GARNIER

RUE GUTENBERG

Libération T

CHEMINS DE FER
TRAIN
STATION

R. CLEMENT ROASSAL

RUE DE DIJON

CHAGALL
MUSEUM

AVE. MALAUSSENA

AVE. RAYMOND

AVE. VILLERMONT

AVE. MIRABEAU

AVE. KATYMOND

COMBOUL

AVE. GEORGES V

AVE. P. MENARD

RUE DABRAY

RUE VERNIER

RUE CLEMENT

RUE MARCEAU

AVE. DESAMBROIS

RUE TRACHEL

BLVD. RAIMBALDI

RUE ASSALIT

RUE MIRON

RUE DE LEPANTE

BLVD. GAMBETTA

VOIE PIERRE MATHIS (ELEVATED HIGHWAY)

i

NICE-VILLE
TRAIN STATION
B
#99 & 23

Gare
Thiers T

RUE PERTINAX

RUE DE PARIS

RUE NOTRE DAME

AVE. JEAN

AVE. MARECHAL FOCH

RUE PIBCARRA

R. DE L'ABBE
GREGOIRE

AVE. THIERS

R. D'ALSACE-
LORRAINE

R. PAGANINI

R. D'ANGLETERRE

AVE. DURANTE

R. D'ITALIE

AVE. G. CLEMENCEAU

3

LAMARTINE

SPITALIERE

BLVD. DU
TZAREWITCH

To Russian
Cathedral

R. DE CHATEAUNEUF

AVE. G. CLEMENCEAU

Jean
Médecin

NICE ETOILE
SHOPPING MALL

R. G. DELOYE

R. FRANÇOIS
AUNE

BLVD. GAMBETTA

RUE GIUGLIA

RUE HEROLD

RUE BERLIOZ

RUE GOUNOD

AVE. AUBER

R. PAUL DEROULEDE

RUE BLACAS

RUE FREDERIC PASSY

RUE VERDI

RUE ROSSINI

MEDECIN

AVE. DES
FLEURS

BLVD. VICTOR HUGO

RUE GRIMALDI

RUE KARL

LIBERTE

#15, 17
& 22
B

Masséna T

RUE DU MARECHAL JOFFRE

RUE MACCARANI

RUE MASSENA

Place
Masséna

RUE DE CRONSTADT

RUE DE LA BUFFA

RUE DALPOZZO

R. FRANCE

1

AVE. DE SUEDE

#98, 200,
400 & 500
B

Coulée

To Fine Arts
Museum

RUE DE
FRANCE

MUSEE
MASSENA

RUE RIVOLI

RUE MEYERBEER

#98 B

US
CONSULATE

AVE
GUSTAVE V

#98
B

i

Albert 1er
Park

RUE ST.

#98 B

HOTEL
NEGRESCO

2

PROMENADE DES

ANGLAIS

Beach

B #98

#98 B

TOURIST TRAIN
PICK-UP

LE GRAND
TOUR BUS

B

Bay of

#98 B

"WELCOME TO THE RIVIERA"
WALK STARTS

M e d i t e r r a n e a n

1 Place Grimaldi Eateries
2 Chantecler Restaurant
3 Monoprix Grocery Store

THE FRENCH RIVIERA

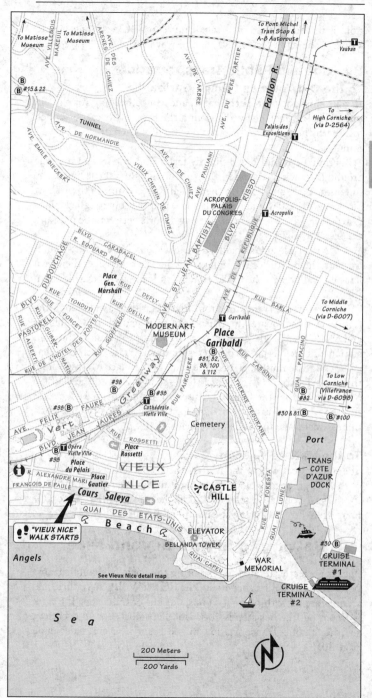

tion or to the Matisse or Chagall museums), €35-40 one-way to Villefranche-sur-Mer, or €80-90 one-way to Monaco.

By Foot and Public Transportation

To the Old Town and Place Garibaldi

If your ship docks at **Terminal 2,** and you're heading for the old town (Vieux Nice), just walk around the base of the castle-topped hill (with the sea on your left), and you'll be there in about 10-15 minutes.

From **Terminal 1,** it's slightly faster (but less scenic) to circle around the back of Castle Hill. Walk or ride the shuttle bus to the top of the port, and head up the angled Rue Cassini. In three short blocks and 15-20 minutes, you'll pop out at the square called **Place Garibaldi,** which serves as a gateway of sorts between the port and the rest of the city.

Once in Place Garibaldi, to reach **Vieux Nice,** walk straight through the middle of the square and out the other side, then turn left and walk down the broad Boulevard Jean Jaurès; the old town sprawls to your left.

To reach the **tram stop** from Place Garibaldi, walk along the right side of the square, then turn right on Avenue de la République and walk a half-block. From here, you can ride the tram to the train station and various points of interest in town. Or, to reach the Chagall or Matisse museums, take the tram to the Place Masséna stop, then transfer to bus #15 or #22 (bus #17 also goes to the Matisse Museum, but not the Chagall Museum); for details, see pages 328 (for the Matisse Museum) or 326 (for the Chagall Museum). For a more direct route to Matisse, see below.

To the Matisse Museum

The most direct way to the Matisse Museum is to walk to the top of the port, then go a block to the right to Boulevard de Stalingrad. From here, you can catch bus #20 to the Arènes-Matisse stop (3/hour Mon-Fri, 1-2/hour Sat-Sun, 30 minutes).

Getting to Sights Beyond Nice

Nice is perfectly situated for exploring the Riviera by public transport. Monaco, Villefranche-sur-Mer, Eze-le-Village, Antibes, and Cannes are all within about a one-hour bus or train ride. The train is faster, but the bus stop is closer to Nice's port. For an overview, see the "Public Transportation in the French Rivera" sidebar on page 301.

By Train

Trains go from Nice eastward to **Villefranche-sur-Mer** (2/hour, 10 minutes) and **Monaco** (2/hour, 20 minutes); and westward to **Antibes** (2/hour, 15-30 minutes) and **Cannes** (2/hour, 30-40 minutes).

From the cruise port, you can get to the train station by bus or by tram (the bus is closer but departs less frequently).

Bus #30 goes from the top of the port to the train station (2/hour, 15 minutes). If you arrive at Terminal 2, you'll catch the bus at the top-left corner of the port, along Place Ile de Beauté (the bus stop is to your left, with the port to your back). If you arrive at Terminal 1, you can catch bus #30 closer to the terminal: As you walk along the port, look for the steps on your right leading up to Boulevard de Stalingrad; once on that street, find the bus stop. From either stop, take bus #30 in the direction of Gare SNCF to the end of the line (Gare SNCF stop), right at the train station.

Rather than wait for the bus, it can be faster to walk three blocks from the top of the port to catch the more frequent **tram** on Place Garibaldi (see directions to Place Garibaldi, earlier): Hop on a tram marked *Las Planas* (going back the direction you just came from), and ride to the Gare Thiers stop. From that stop, cross the tracks and walk straight one long block on Avenue Thiers; you'll see the train station on the right.

By Bus

Exiting either terminal, walk up to the top of the port (Place Ile de Beauté). Near the right end of this strip (with your back to the port) is the stop for bus #100, which runs about every 15 minutes to **Villefranche-sur-Mer** (15 minutes), **Cap Ferrat** (20 minutes), or **Monaco** (45 minutes). Other buses departing at or near Place Ile de Beauté include bus #81 for Cap Ferrat (2-3/hour, 40 minutes, offers more stops on the Cap than bus #100) and bus #82 or #112 for **Eze-le-Village** (16/day, Mon-Sat, 8/day Sun, 40 minutes). For **Cannes** and other points west, take the tram to Place Masséna and then walk to the stop for bus #200 on Avenue de Verdun near Albert 1er Park (see the map on page 322). For more details on bus travel, consult with the TI at the port.

By Boat to Monaco

From June to mid-September, Trans Côte d'Azur offers scenic boat trips from Nice to Monaco (Tue, Thu, and Sat only, 45 minutes each way). The boat departs at 9:30; you can either come straight back (€29, arriving back in Nice at 11:00), or you can disembark in Monaco and return to Nice on an afternoon boat (€35, arriving at 18:00—do this only if your ship is departing late and you'll have plenty of time to absorb any potential delays). Reservations are required, so try to book a few days ahead (tel. 04 92 98 71 30 or 04 92 00 42 30, www.trans-cote-azur.com, croisieres@trans-cote-azur. com). The boat leaves from the port, near Terminal 2—look for the blue ticket booth (billeterie) on Quai de Lunel. The same company also runs one-hour round-trip cruises along the coast to Cap Ferrat (see "Tours in Nice," later), as well as boats to St-Tropez (but the return boat from St-Tropez likely won't get you back in time to catch your ship—I'd skip this option).

By Tour

For information on local tour options around the French Riviera, see page 300; for options within Nice—including bus tours, guided boat cruises, walking tours, and more—see "Tours in Nice" on page 314.

Returning to Your Ship

From Vieux Nice, walk around Castle Hill to find the port. If you're coming on bus #100 from Villefranche-sur-Mer or Monaco, get off at the "Le Port" stop, right at the top of the port. If arriving by train, take a taxi to the port, or ride the tramway to Place Garibaldi and walk 15-20 minutes from there (down Rue Cassini straight to the port).

Orientation to Nice

The main points of interest lie between the beach and the train tracks (about 15 blocks apart—see map on page 306). The city revolves around its grand Place Masséna, where pedestrian-friendly Avenue Jean Médecin meets Vieux (Old) Nice and the Albert 1er parkway (with quick access to the beaches). It's a 20-minute walk (or a €15 taxi ride) from the train station to the beach, and a 20-minute walk along the promenade from the fancy Hôtel Negresco to the heart of Vieux Nice.

A 10-minute ride on the smooth-as-silk tramway through the center of the city connects the train station, Place Masséna, Vieux Nice, and the port (from nearby Place Garibaldi). The tram and all city and regional buses cost only €1.50 per trip, making this one of the cheapest and easiest cities in France to get around in (see "Getting Around Nice," later). When you visit, work may be underway on a new tramway line along (or under) the Promenade des Anglais.

Tourist Information

Nice's helpful TIs share a phone number and website (tel. 08 92 70 74 07, www.nicetourisme.com). There are TI branches at the **airport** (desks in both terminals, typically quiet, daily 9:00-18:00, until 20:00 April-Sept); next to the **train station** (busy, summer Mon-Sat 8:00-20:00, Sun 9:00-19:00, rest of year Mon-Sat 9:00-19:00, Sun 10:00-17:00); facing the **beach** at 5 Promenade des Anglais (moderately busy, daily 9:00-18:00, until 20:00 July-Aug, closed Sun off-season); and in a kiosk at the south end of **Place Masséna** (less busy, mid-June-Sept, typically daily 10:00-19:00). Pick up the thorough *Practical Guide to Nice* and a free Nice map. You can also get day-trip information at any TI (including maps of Monaco or Antibes, details on boat excursions, and bus schedules to Eze-le-Village, La Turbie, Vence, and other destinations).

Arrival in Nice by Train or Bus

By Train: All trains stop at Nice's main station, Nice-Ville (baggage storage at the far right with your back to the tracks, lockers open daily 8:00-21:00). Don't get off at the suburban Nice Riquier station, which is one stop east of the main station. The station area is gritty and busy: Never leave your bags unattended and don't linger here longer than necessary. The area in front of the station was recently under construction, but should be looking sharp by the time you visit. Because of this work, bus and taxi stops may be different from what I've described here.

Turn left out of the station to find a **TI** next door. Continue a few more blocks down Avenue Jean Médecin for the Gare Thiers **tram stop** (this will take you to Place Masséna, the old city, and the port). Board the tram heading toward the right, direction: Pont Michel (see "Getting Around Nice," later).

To walk to the beach opposite Promenade des Anglais, cross Avenue Thiers in front of the station, go down the steps by Hôtel Interlaken, and continue walking down Avenue Durante which turns into Rue des Congrés. You'll soon reach the heart of Nice's beachfront promenade.

Taxis and **buses to the airport** (#23 and #99) wait in front of the train station. **Car rental** offices are to the right as you exit the station.

By Bus: Nice's bus station was demolished as part of a major project to expand the city's central parkway. Most stops for bus routes important to travelers (those serving Antibes, the airport, Vence, Villefranche-sur-Mer, Monaco, and St-Jean-Cap-Ferrat) have been moved to other locations (see map on page 322). As work continues along the parkway, bus stop locations are subject to change; confirm locally.

Helpful Hints

Theft Alert: Nice has its share of pickpockets. Thieves target fanny packs: Have nothing important on or around your waist, unless it's in a money belt tucked out of sight. Don't leave things unattended on the beach while swimming, and stick to main streets in Vieux Nice after dark.

Sightseeing Tips: The following sights are closed on Mondays: the Modern and Contemporary Art Museum, the Fine Arts Museum, the Russian Cathedral, and the Cours Saleya market. On Tuesdays the Chagall, Matisse, and Archaeological museums are closed. All of the sights in Nice—except the Chagall Museum—are free to enter, making rainy-day options a swinging deal here.

Internet Access: There's no shortage of places to get online; look for one of these establishments, all with free Wi-Fi: Quick Hamburger, Häagen Dazs, and McDonald's (multiple locations), or the Nice Etoile Shopping Center and Virgin Megastore (on Avenue Jean Médecin).

Grocery Store: The big **Monoprix** on Avenue Jean Médecin and Rue Biscarra has it all, including a deli counter, bakery, and cold drinks (Mon-Sat 8:30-21:00, closed Sun, see map on page 306).

Boutique Shopping: The chic streets where Rue Alphonse Karr meets Rue de la Liberté and then Rue de Paradis are known as the "Golden Square." If you need pricey stuff, shop here.

SNCF Boutique: There's a handy French rail ticket office a half-block west of Avenue Jean Médecin at 2 Rue de la Liberté (Mon-Fri 10:00-17:50, closed Sat-Sun).

Renting a Bike (and Other Wheels): Roller Station rents bikes (*vélos*, can be taken on trains, €5/hour, €10/half-day, €15/day), rollerblades, skateboards, and Razor-style scooters (*trotinettes*, €7/half-day, €9/day). You'll need to leave your ID as a deposit (daily March-May and Sept-Oct 10:00-19:00, June-Aug 10:00-20:30, Nov-Feb 10:00-18:00, next to yellow awnings of Pailin's Asian restaurant at 49 Quai des Etats-Unis—see map on page 322, tel. 04 93 62 99 05, owner Eric). If you need more power, the TI has a list of places renting electric scooters.

You'll notice blue bikes **(Vélos Bleu)** stationed at various points in the city. A thousand of these bikes, available for locals to use when running errands, rent cheaply for short-term use (first 30 minutes free, European-style chip-and-PIN credit card or American Express card required).

Car Rental: You'll find most companies represented at Nice's train station and near Albert 1er Park.

English Radio: Tune in to Riviera-Radio at FM 106.5.

Views: For panoramic views, climb Castle Hill (see page 320), or take a one-hour boat trip (described later, under "Tours in Nice").

Beach Gear: To make life tolerable on the rocks, swimmers should buy a pair of the cheap plastic beach shoes sold at many shops (flip-flops fall off in the water). **Go Sport** at #13 on Place Masséna sells beach shoes, flip-flops, and cheap sunglasses (Mon-Sat 9:30-19:30, Sun 10:30-19:00—see map on page 322).

Getting Around Nice

Although you can walk to most attractions in Nice, smart travelers make good use of the buses and tram. Both are covered by the same €1.50 single-ride ticket (€10 for 10 tickets that can be shared, good for 74 minutes in one direction, including transfers between bus and tram; can't be used for a round-trip or airport express bus). The **bus** is particularly handy for reaching the Chagall and Matisse museums and the Russian Cathedral. Pick up timetables at Nice's TIs (or view them online at www.lignesdazur.com) and buy tickets from the driver. Make sure to validate your ticket in the machine just behind the driver—watch locals do it and imitate.

The €5 all-day pass is valid on city buses and trams, as well as buses to some nearby destinations. The all-day ticket makes sense if you plan to take the bus to museums or use the tramway several times (you must validate your ticket on every trip). Express buses to and from the airport (#98 and #99) require the €6 Aéro ticket.

Nice's **tramway** makes an "*L*" along Avenue Jean Médecin and Boulevard Jean Jaurès, and connects the main train station (Gare

Thiers stop), Place Masséna (Masséna stop, near many regional bus stops and a few blocks' walk from the sea), Vieux Nice (Opéra-Vieille Ville, Cathédrale-Vieille Ville), and the Modern and Contemporary Art Museum and port (Place Garibaldi).

Boarding the tram in the direction of Pont Michel takes you from the train station toward the beach and Vieux Nice (direction: Las Planas goes the other way). Buy tickets at the machines on the platforms (coins only, no credit cards). Choose the English flag to change the display language, turn the round knob and push the green button to select your ticket, press it twice at the end to get your ticket, or press the red button to cancel. Once you're on the tram, validate your ticket by inserting it into the top of the white box, then reclaiming it (http://tramway.nice.fr).

Taxis are useful for getting to Nice's less-central sights, and worth it if you're nowhere near a bus or tram stop (figure €15 from Promenade des Anglais). Cabbies normally only pick up at taxi stands *(tête de station)*, or you can call 04 93 13 78 78.

The hokey **tourist train** gets you up Castle Hill (see "Tours in Nice," next).

Tours in Nice

Bus Tour

Le Grand Tour Bus provides an 11-stop, hop-on, hop-off service on an open-deck bus with headphone commentary (2/hour, 1.5-hour loop) that includes the Promenade des Anglais, the old port, Cap de Nice, and the Chagall and Matisse museums on Cimiez Hill (€21/1-day pass, €23/2-day pass, cheaper for seniors and students, €12 for last tour of the day at about 18:00, buy tickets on bus, main stop is near where Promenade des Anglais and Quai des Etats-Unis meet, across from the Plage Beau Rivage lounge, tel. 04 92 29 17 00, www.nicelegrandtour.com). This tour is a pricey way to get to the Chagall and Matisse museums, but it's an acceptable option if you also want a city overview. Check the schedule if you plan to use this bus to see the Russian Cathedral, as it may be faster to walk there.

Tourist Train

For €8 (€4 for children under age 9), you can spend 45 embarrassing minutes on the tourist train tooting along the promenade, through the old city, and up to Castle Hill. This is a sweat-free way to get to the top of the hill—but so is the elevator, which is free (train runs every 30 minutes, daily 10:00-18:00, June-Aug until 19:00, recorded English commentary, meet train near Le Grand Tour Bus stop on Quai des Etats-Unis, tel. 02 99 88 47 07, www.ttdf.com).

▲Boat Cruise

On this one-hour star-studded tour run by Trans Côte d'Azur, you'll cruise in a comfortable yacht-size vessel to Cap Ferrat and past Villefranche-sur-Mer, then return to Nice with a final lap along Promenade des Anglais. It's a scenic trip (the best views are from the seats on top), and worthwhile if you won't be hiking along the Cap Ferrat trails that provide similar views.

French (and sometimes English-speaking) guides play Robin Leach, pointing out mansions owned by some pretty famous people, including Elton John (just as you leave Nice, it's the soft-yellow square-shaped place right on the water), Sean Connery (on the hill above Elton, with rounded arches and tower), and Microsoft co-founder Paul Allen (in the saddle of Cap Ferrat hill—look above

Nice at a Glance

▲▲▲**Chagall Museum** The world's largest collection of Marc Chagall's work, popular even with people who don't like modern art. **Hours:** Wed-Mon 10:00-17:00, May-Oct until 18:00, closed Tue year-round. See page 326.

▲▲▲**Promenade des Anglais** Nice's four-mile sun-struck seafront promenade. **Hours:** Always open. See page 324.

▲▲**Vieux Nice** Charming old city offering enjoyable atmosphere and a look at Nice's French-Italian cultural blend. **Hours:** Always open. See page 320.

▲**Matisse Museum** Small but worthwhile collection of Henri Matisse's paintings, sketches, paper cutouts, and more. **Hours:** Wed-Mon 10:00-18:00, closed Tue. See page 328.

▲**Modern and Contemporary Art Museum** Ultramodern museum with enjoyable collection from the 1960s-1970s, including Warhol and Lichtenstein. **Hours:** Tue-Sun 10:00-18:00, closed Mon. See page 330.

▲**Russian Cathedral** Finest Orthodox church outside of Russia. **Hours:** Tue-Sat 9:00-12:00 & 14:00-19:00, Sun 9:00-12:00, closed Mon. See page 331.

▲**Castle Hill** Site of an ancient fort boasting great views—especially in early mornings and evenings. **Hours:** Park closes at 20:00 in summer, earlier off-season. Elevator runs daily 10:00-19:00, until 20:00 in summer. See page 320.

Fine Arts Museum Lush villa shows off impressive paintings by Monet, Sisley, Bonnard, and Raoul Dufy. **Hours:** Tue-Sun 10:00-18:00, closed Mon. See page 330.

Molinard Perfume Museum Two-room museum in a storefront boutique tracing the history of perfume. **Hours:** Daily April-Sept 10:00-19:00, Oct-March 10:00-13:00 & 14:00-18:00, sometimes closed Sun off-season. See page 330.

the umbrellas of Plage de Passable beach and find the house with a sloping red-tile roof). I wonder if this gang ever hangs out together. Guides also like to point out the mansion between Villefranche-sur-Mer and Cap Ferrat where the Rolling Stones recorded *Exile on Main Street* (€17; April-Oct Tue-Sun 2/day, usually at 11:00 and 15:00, no boats Mon or in off-season; call ahead to verify schedule, arrive 30 minutes early to get best seats, drinks and WCs available).

Walking Tours

The TI on Promenade des Anglais organizes weekly walking tours of Vieux Nice in French and English (€12, May-Oct only, usually Sat morning at 9:30, 2.5 hours, reservations necessary, depart from TI, tel. 08 92 70 74 07). They also have evening art walks on Fridays at 19:00.

Local Guides and Cooking Classes

See page 300 for a list of guides for Nice and other regional destinations, plus "Taste of Nice" food tours and Vieux Nice cooking classes.

Welcome to the Riviera Walk

This leisurely, level self-guided walk begins on the Promenade des Anglais (near the landmark Hôtel Negresco) and ends on Castle Hill above Vieux Nice. While the entire walk is enjoyable at any time, the first half makes a great pre- or post-dinner stroll. Timing your stroll to end up on Castle Hill (this walk's grand finale) at sunset is ideal. Allow one hour at a promenade pace to reach the elevator up to Castle Hill (which stops running at 20:00 in summer).
• *Begin at the walkway running along Nice's beach. This is the...*

Promenade des Anglais

Welcome to the Riviera. There's something for everyone along this four-mile-long seafront circus. Watch Europeans at play, admire the azure Mediterranean, anchor yourself on a blue seat, and prop your feet up on the made-to-order guardrail. Later in the day, come back to join the evening parade of tans along the promenade.

For now, stroll like the belle-époque English aristocrats for whom the promenade was paved (see map on page 306). The broad sidewalks of the Promenade des Anglais ("Walkway of the English") were financed by upper-crust English tourists who wanted a secure and comfortable place to stroll and admire the view. The

walk was done in marble in 1822 for aristocrats who didn't want to dirty their shoes or smell the fishy gravel. This grand promenade leads to the old city and Castle Hill.
• *Check out the pink-domed...*

Hôtel Negresco

Nice's finest hotel is also a historic monument, offering up the city's most expensive beds and a museum-like interior that, sadly, has been made off-limits to non-guests—at least in high season. But, it's worth a try to enter—dress well, appear confident, and march in. (Or, you can always get in by patronizing the hotel's Le Relais bar, which opens at 15:00.)

The exquisite **Salon Royal** lounge is an elegant place for a drink and frequently hosts modern art exhibits (opens at 11:00). The chandelier hanging from the Eiffel-built dome is made of 16,000 pieces of crystal. It was built in France for the Russian czar's Moscow palace...but thanks to the Bolshevik Revolution in 1917, he couldn't take delivery (portraits of Czar Alexander III and his wife, Maria Feodorovna—who returned to her native Denmark after the revolution—are to the right, under the dome). Saunter around the perimeter counterclockwise.

If the **Le Relais bar** door is open (after about 15:00), wander up the marble steps for a look. Farther along, nip into the toilets for either an early 20th-century powder room or a Battle of Waterloo experience. The chairs nearby were typical of the age (cones of silence for an afternoon nap sitting up).

The hotel's **Chantecler restaurant** is one of the Riviera's best (allow €100 per person before drinks; described on page 333). In France, big-time chefs are like famous athletes: People know about them and talk about who's hot and who's not. Cooking is serious business—about 10 years ago, a famous Burgundian chef lost a star and committed suicide. On your way out, pop into the **Salon Louis XIV** (right of entry lobby as you leave), where the embarrassingly short Sun King models his red platform boots (English descriptions explain the room).

Outside, walk away from the sea with the hotel to your left to find the hotel's original **entrance** on Rue Berretta (grander than today's)—in the 19th century, classy people stayed out of the sun, and any posh hotel that cared about its clientele would design its entry on the shady north side.

• *Cross the Promenade des Anglais, and—before you begin your seaside promenade—grab a blue seat and gaze out to the...*

Bay of Angels (Baie des Anges)

Face the water. The body of Nice's patron saint, Réparate, was supposedly escorted into this bay by angels in the fourth century. To your right is where you might have been escorted into France—Nice's airport, built on a massive landfill. On that tip of land way beyond the runway is Cap d'Antibes. Until 1860, Antibes and Nice were in different countries—Antibes was French, but Nice was a protectorate of the Italian kingdom of Savoy-Piedmont, a.k.a. the Kingdom of Sardinia. (During that period, the Var River—just west of Nice—was the geographic border between these two peoples.) In 1850 the people here spoke Italian and ate pasta. As Italy was uniting, the region was given a choice: Join the new country of Italy or join good old France (which was enjoying good times under the rule of Napoleon III). The vast majority voted in 1860 to go French...and voilà!

The lower green hill to your left (Castle Hill) marks the end of this walk. Farther left lies Villefranche-sur-Mer (marked by the tower at land's end, and home to lots of millionaires), then Monaco (which you can't see, with more millionaires), then Italy (with lots of, uh, Italians). Behind you are the foothills of the Alps (Alpes-Maritimes), which trap threatening clouds, ensuring that the Côte d'Azur enjoys sunshine more than 300 days each year. While half a million people live here, pollution is carefully treated—the water is routinely tested and very clean.

• *With the sea on your right, begin...*

Strolling the Promenade

The block next to Hôtel Negresco houses a lush park and the Masséna Museum of city history. Nearby sit two other belle-époque establishments: the West End and Westminster **hotels,** both boasting English names to help those original guests feel at home (the West End is now part of the Best Western group...to help American guests feel at home). These hotels symbolize Nice's arrival as a tourist mecca a century ago, when the combination of leisure time and a stable economy allowed visitors to find the sun even in winter. Hotel rooms back then were much larger than they are now—today, even the grandest hotels have sliced and diced floor plans to create more rooms.

As you walk, be careful to avoid the green bike lane. The promenade you're walking on was originally much narrower. It's been widened over the years to keep up with tourist demand, including increased bicycle use. You'll pass a number of separate **beaches**—some private, others public. In spite of the rocks, they're still a popular draw. You can go local and rent gear—about €15 for a *chaise longue* (long chair) and a *transat* (mattress), €5 for an umbrella, and €4 for a towel.  You'll also pass several beach restaurants (a highly recommended experience). Some of these eateries serve breakfast, all serve lunch, some do dinner, and a few have beachy bars...tailor-made for a break from this walk (the coolest lounge is Plage Beau Rivage, farther along on Quai des Etats-Unis). A few promote package deals, including a lounge chair, an umbrella, a locker, and a meal, all for about €28. Why all this gear rental? In Europe, most beach-going families take planes or trains, since parking and gas are *très* pricey, and traffic is ugly. So, unlike my family on a beach trip, they can't stuff chairs, coolers, and the like in the trunk of their car and park right near the beach.

Even a hundred years ago, there was sufficient tourism in Nice to justify building its first **casino** (a leisure activity imported from Venice). Part of an elegant casino, La Jetée Promenade stood on those white-covered pilings just offshore, until the Germans destroyed it during World War II. When La Jetée was thriving, it took gamblers two full days to get to the Riviera by train from Paris—so if you had a week off, four of those days were spent getting to and from this Promised Land.

Although La Jetée Promenade is gone, you can still see the striking 1927 Art Nouveau facade of the Palais de la Méditerranée, a grand casino, hotel, and theater. This intimidating edifice was built during the Great Depression by American financier Frank Jay Gould, who was looking for a better return on his investments when America's economy was tanking. It soon became the grandest casino in Europe, and today it is one of France's most exclusive hotels, though the casino feels cheap and cheesy.

The unappealing Casino Ruhl stands in the next block. Anyone can drop in for some one-armed-bandit fun, but to play the tables at night you'll need to dress better and bring your passport. **Albert 1er Park** is named for the Belgian king who enjoyed wintering here—these were his private gardens. While the English came first, the Belgians and Russians were also big fans of 19th-century Nice. That tall statue at the edge of the park commemorates the 100-year anniversary of Nice's union with France.

Continue along the promenade, past the park. You're now on **Quai des Etats-Unis** ("Quay of the United States"). This name was given as a tip-of-the-cap to the Americans for finally entering World War I in 1917. Check out the laid-back couches at the Plage Beau Rivage lounge, and look for sections of public beach with imported sand (and be amazed that most locals still prefer lying on the rocks—I don't get it). The tall rusted steel girders reaching for the sky (across the street, to the left) were designed to celebrate the 150th anniversary of Nice's union with France. The same artist created the Arc of the Riviera sculpture in the parkway near Place Masséna.

Five minutes past the Hôtel Suisse (brilliant views as you walk), there's a monumental **war memorial** sculpted from the rock in honor of the thousands of local boys who died serving their country in World Wars I and II.

• *Take the elevator next to the Hôtel Suisse up to Castle Hill (free, elevator runs daily 10:00-19:00, until 20:00 in summer).*

THE FRENCH RIVIERA

Castle Hill (Colline du Château)

This hill—in an otherwise flat city center—offers sensational views over Nice, the port (to the east), the foothills of the Alps, and the Mediterranean. The views are best early or at sunset, or whenever the weather's clear (park closes at 20:00 in summer, earlier off-season). Nice was founded on this hill. Its residents were crammed onto the hilltop until the 12th century, as it was too risky to live in the flatlands below. Today you'll find a waterfall, a playground, two cafés (with fair prices), and a cemetery—but no castle—on Castle Hill.

• *Your tour is finished. Enjoy the vistas. To walk down to Vieux Nice, follow signs from just below the upper café to Vieille Ville (not Le Port), turn right at the cemetery, and then look for the walkway down on your left. To make a beeline back to the port, wrap around the base of Castle Hill with the beach on your right.*

A Scratch-and-Sniff Walk Through Vieux Nice

This approximately hour-long self-guided walk leads you through the delights of Vieux (Old) Nice.

• *See the map on page 322, and start at Nice's main market square...*

Cours Saleya (koor sah-lay-yuh): Named for its broad exposure to the sun *(soleil)*, this commotion of color, sights, smells, and people has been Nice's main market square since the Middle Ages (produce market held Tue-Sun until 13:00—on Mon, an antiques market takes center stage). Amazingly, part of this square was a parking lot until 1980, when the mayor of Nice had an underground garage built.

The first section is devoted to the Riviera's largest flower market (all day Tue-Sun and in operation since the 19th century). Here you'll find plants and flowers that grow effortlessly and ubiquitously in this climate, including the local favorites: carnations, roses, and jasmine. Not long ago, this region supplied all of France with its flowers; today, many are imported from Africa (the glorious orchids are from Kenya). Still, fresh flowers are perhaps the best value in this city.

The boisterous produce section trumpets the season with mushrooms, strawberries, white asparagus, zucchini flowers, and more—whatever's fresh gets top billing. Find your way down the center and buy something healthy.

The market opens up at Place Pierre Gautier (also called Plassa dou Gouvernou—bilingual street signs include the old Niçois language, an Italian dialect). This is where farmers set up stalls to sell their produce and herbs directly.

Continue down the center of Cours Saleya, stopping when you see La Cambuse restaurant on your left. In front, hovering over the black-barrel fire with the paella-like pan on top, is the self-proclaimed **Queen of the Market,** Thérèse, cooking *socca*, Nice's chickpea crêpe specialty (until about 13:00). Spend €3 for a wad (careful—it's hot, but good). If Thérèse doesn't have a pan out, it's on its way (watch for the frequent scooter deliveries). Wait in line... or else it'll be all gone when you return.

• *Continue down Cours Saleya. The fine golden building that seals the end of the square is where Henri Matisse spent 17 years with a brilliant view onto Nice's world. The Café les Ponchettes is perfectly positioned for a people-watching break. Turn at the café onto...*

Rue de la Poissonnerie: Look up at the first floor of the first building on your right. **Adam and Eve** are squaring off, each holding a zucchini-like gourd. This scene (post-apple) represents the annual rapprochement in Nice to make up for the sins of a too-much-fun Carnival (Mardi Gras, the pre-Lenten festival). Residents of Nice have partied hard during Carnival for more than 700 years.

A few steps ahead, check out the small **Baroque church** (Notre-Dame-de-l'Annonciation) dedicated to Ste. Rita, the patron saint of desperate causes. She holds a special place in locals' hearts, making this the most popular church in Nice.

• *Turn right on the next street, where you'll pass Vieux Nice's most happening café/bar **(Distilleries Ideales)**, with a lively happy hour (18:00-21:00) and a Pirates of the Caribbean-style interior. Now turn left on "Right" Street (Rue Droite), and enter an area that feels like a Little Naples.*

Rue Droite: In the Middle Ages, this straight, skinny street provided the most direct route from wall to wall, or river to sea. Stop at **Espuno's bakery** (at Place du Jésus, closed Mon-Tue) and say *bonjour* to the friendly folks. Decades ago, this baker was voted the best in France—the trophies you see were earned for breadmaking, not bowling. His son now runs the place. Notice the firewood stacked behind the oven. Try the house specialty, *tourte aux blettes*—a Swiss chard tart. It's traditionally made with jam (a sweet, tasty breakfast treat), but there's also a savory version, stuffed with pine nuts, raisins, and white beets (my favorite for lunch).

Farther along, at #28, Thérèse (whom you met earlier) cooks her *socca* in the wood-fired oven before she carts it to her barrel on Cours Saleya. The balconies of the mansion in the next block mark the **Palais Lascaris** (c. 1647, gorgeous at night), a rare souvenir

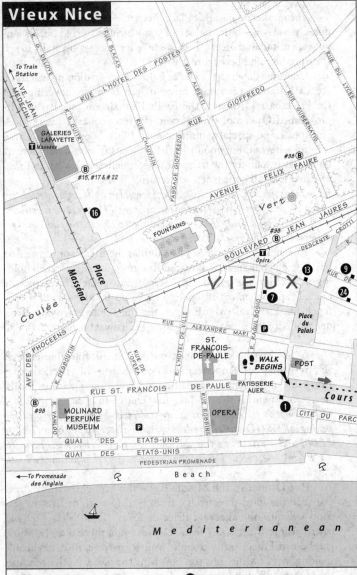

THE FRENCH RIVIERA

Vieux Nice

Legend:
1. La Voglia Restaurant
2. Le Safari Restaurant
3. Chez Palmyre Restaurant
4. Le Bistrot du Fromager
5. Oliviera Shop/Restaurant
6. Bistrot D'Antoine
7. La Merenda Restaurant
8. L'Acchiardo Restaurant
9. Ville de Siena Restaurant
10. Lou Pilha Leva Restaurant
11. Restaurant Castel
12. Fenocchio's Gelato (2)
13. Oui, Jelato
14. Distilleries Ideales
15. Bike Rental
16. Go Sport

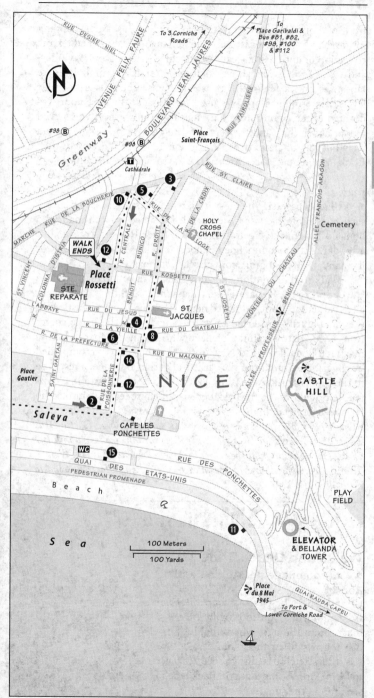

from one of Nice's most prestigious families. It's worth popping inside (handy WCs) for its Baroque Italian architecture and terrific collection of antique musical instruments—harps, guitars, violins, and violas (good English explanations). You'll also find elaborate tapestries and a few well-furnished rooms. The palace has four levels: The ground floor was used for storage, the first floor was devoted to reception rooms (and musical events), the owners lived a floor above that, and the servants lived at the top—with a good view but lots of stairs (free, Wed-Mon 10:00-18:00, closed Tue). Look up and make faces back at the guys under the balconies.

• *Turn left on the Rue de la Loge, then left again on Rue Centrale to reach...*

Place Rossetti: The most Italian of Nice's piazzas, Place Rossetti feels more like Rome than Nice. Named for the man who donated his land to create this square, Place Rossetti comes alive after dark. The recommended Fenocchio gelato shop is popular for its many flavors, ranging from classic to innovative.

Walk to the fountain and stare back at the church. This is the **Cathedral of St. Réparate**—an unassuming building for a major city's cathedral. It was relocated here in the 1500s, when Castle Hill was temporarily converted to military use only. The name comes from Nice's patron saint, a teenage virgin named Réparate whose martyred body floated to Nice in the fourth century accompanied by angels. The interior of the cathedral gushes Baroque, a response to the Protestant Reformation. With the Catholic Church's Counter-Reformation, the theatrical energy of churches was cranked up with re-energized, high-powered saints and eye-popping decor.

• *Our walk is over. If you're re-energized, take a walk up* **Castle Hill**. *To get there, cross Place Rossetti and follow the lane leading uphill (see Castle Hill description at the end of the "Welcome to the Riviera Walk"). To visit the Chagall or Matisse museums, return to Place Masséna to catch a bus there.*

Sights in Nice

Walks and Beach Time

▲▲▲Promenade des Anglais and Beach

Meandering along Nice's four-mile sea-front promenade on foot or by bike is a must. From the days when wealthy English tourists filled the grand seaside hotels, this stretch has always been *the* place to be in Nice. Europeans still flock here to seek fun in the sun.

For a self-guided walk of this strip, see the "Welcome to the Riviera Walk," earlier. To rev up the pace of your promenade saunter, rent a bike and glide along the coast in either or both directions (about 30 minutes each way; for rental info, see "Helpful Hints," earlier).

And of course, there's the **beach.** Settle in on the smooth rocks or find a section with imported sand, and consider your options: You can play beach vol-leyball, table tennis, or *boules;* rent paddleboats, personal wa-tercraft, or windsurfing equip-ment; explore ways to use your zoom lens for some revealing people-watching; or snooze on a comfy beach bed.

To rent a spot on the beach, compare rates, as prices vary—beaches on the east end of the bay are usually cheaper (chair and mattress—*chaise longue* and *transat*—about €15, umbrella-€5, towel-€4). Have lunch in your bathing suit (€12 salads and pizzas in bars and restaurants all along the beach). Or, for a peaceful café au lait on the Mediterranean, stop here first thing in the morning before the crowds hit. *Plage Publique* signs explain the 15 beach no-nos (translated into English).

▲▲Wandering Vieux Nice (Old Nice)
Offering an intriguing look at Nice's melding of French and Italian cultures, the old city is a fine place to linger. Enjoy its narrow lanes, bustling market squares, and colorful people.

For details on this neighborhood, see the "Scratch-and-Sniff Walk Through Vieux Nice," earlier.

Museums and Monuments
To bring culture to the masses, the city of Nice has nixed entry fees to all municipal museums—so it's free to enter all the following sights except the Chagall Museum and the Russian Cathedral. Cool.

The first two museums (Chagall and Matisse) are a long walk northeast of Nice's city center. Because they're in the same direction and served by the same bus line (buses #15 and #22 stop at both museums), it makes sense to visit them on the same trip. From Place Masséna, the Chagall Museum is a 10-minute bus ride or a 30-minute walk, and the Matisse Museum is a 20-minute bus ride or a one-hour walk.

▲▲▲Chagall Museum
(Musée National Marc Chagall)

Even if you're suspicious of modern art, this museum—with the world's largest collection of Marc Chagall's work in captivity—is

a delight. After World War II, Chagall returned from the United States to settle in Vence, not far from Nice. Between 1954 and 1967 he painted a cycle of 17 large murals designed for, and donated to, this museum. These paintings, inspired by the biblical books of Genesis, Exodus, and the Song of Songs, make up the "nave,"
or core, of what Chagall called the "House of Brotherhood."

Each painting is a lighter-than-air collage of images that draws from Chagall's Russian folk-village youth, his Jewish heritage, biblical themes, and his feeling that he existed somewhere between heaven and earth. He believed that the Bible was a synonym for nature, and that color and biblical themes were key for understanding God's love for his creation. Chagall's brilliant blues and reds celebrate nature, as do his spiritual and folk themes. Notice the focus on couples. To Chagall, humans loving each other mirrored God's love of creation.

Although Chagall would suggest that you explore his works without help, the free audioguide gives you detailed explanations of his works and covers temporary exhibits. The free *Plan du Musée* helps you locate the rooms, though you can do without, as the museum is pretty simple.

Cost and Hours: €7.50, €1-2 more with (frequent) special exhibits, free first Sun of the month (but crowded), open Wed-Mon 10:00-17:00, May-Oct until 18:00, closed Tue year-round, Avenue Docteur Ménard, tel. 04 93 53 87 20, www.musees-nationaux-alpesmaritimes.fr/chagall/.

Getting to the Chagall Museum: You can reach the museum, located on Avenue Docteur Ménard, by bus or on foot.

Buses #15 and #22 serve the Chagall Museum from the Masséna Guitry stop, near Place Masséna (5-7/hour Mon-Sat, 3/hour Sun, €1.50, immediately behind Galeries Lafayette department store—see map on page 306). The museum's bus stop (called Musée Chagall, shown on the bus shelter) is on Boulevard de Cimiez (walk uphill from the stop and cross the street to find the museum).

To **walk** from central Nice to the Chagall Museum (30 minutes), go to the train-station end of Avenue Jean Médecin and turn right onto Boulevard Raimbaldi. Walk four long blocks along the elevated road, then turn left onto Avenue Raymond Comboul, and follow *Musée Chagall* signs.

Chagall's Style

Chagall uses a deceptively simple, almost childlike style to paint a world that's hidden to the eye—the magical, mystical world below the surface. Here are some of the characteristics of his paintings:

- **Deep, radiant colors,** inspired by Expressionism and Fauvism (an art movement pioneered by Matisse and other French painters).
- **Personal imagery,** particularly from his childhood in Russia—smiling barnyard animals, fiddlers on the roof, flower bouquets, huts, and blissful sweethearts.
- **A Hasidic Jewish perspective,** the idea that God is everywhere, appearing in everyday things like nature, animals, and humdrum activities.
- **A fragmented Cubist style,** multifaceted and multidimensional, a perfect style to mirror the complexity of God's creation.
- **Overlapping images,** like double-exposure photography, with faint imagery that bleeds through, suggesting there's more to life under the surface.
- **Stained-glass-esque technique** of dark, deep, earthy, "potent" colors, and simplified, iconic, symbolic figures.
- **Gravity-defying compositions,** with lovers, animals, and angels twirling blissfully in midair.
- **Happy (not tragic) mood** depicting a world of personal joy, despite the violence and turmoil of world wars and revolution.
- **Childlike simplicity,** drawn with simple, heavy outlines, filled in with Crayola colors that often spill over the lines. Major characters in a scene are bigger than the lesser characters. The grinning barnyard animals, the bright colors, the magical events presented as literal truth...Was Chagall a lightweight? Or a lighter-than-air-weight?

Cuisine Art and Services: An idyllic café (€10 salads and *plats*) awaits in the corner of the garden. A spick-and-span WC is next to the ticket desk. Another WC is inside.

Leaving the Museum: To take **buses** #15 or #22 back to downtown Nice, turn right out of the museum, then make another right down Boulevard de Cimiez, and catch the bus heading downhill. To continue on to the Matisse Museum, catch buses #15 or

#22 using the uphill stop located across the street. **Taxis** usually wait in front of the museum. It's about €12 for a ride to the city center.

To **walk** to the train station area from the museum (20 minutes), turn left out of the museum grounds on Avenue Docteur Ménard, and follow the street to the left at the first intersection, continuing to hug the museum grounds. Where the street curves right (by #32), take the ramps and staircases down on your left, turn left at the bottom, cross under the freeway and the train tracks, then turn right on Boulevard Raimbaldi to reach the station.

▲Matisse Museum (Musée Matisse)

This small museum contains a sampling of works from the various periods of Henri Matisse's long artistic career. The museum offers a painless introduction to the artist's many styles and materials, both shaped by Mediterranean light and by fellow Côte d'Azur artists Pablo Picasso and Pierre-Auguste Renoir. The collection is scattered throughout several rooms with a few worthwhile works, though it lacks a certain *je ne sais quoi* when compared to the Chagall Museum.

Cost and Hours: Free, Wed-Mon 10:00-18:00, closed Tue, 164 Avenue des Arènes de Cimiez, tel. 04 93 81 08 08, www.musee-matisse-nice.org. The museum is housed in a beautiful Mediterranean mansion set in an olive grove amid the ruins of the ancient Roman city of Cemenelum.

Getting to the Matisse Museum: It's a long uphill walk from the city center. Take the bus (details follow) or a cab (€20 from Promenade des Anglais). Once here, walk into the park to find the pink villa. **Buses #15, #17,** and **#22** offer regular service to the Matisse Museum from just off Place Masséna on Rue Sacha Guitry (Masséna Guitry stop, at the east end of the Galeries Lafayette department store—see map on page 306, 20 minutes; note that bus #17 does not stop at the Chagall Museum). **Bus #20** connects the port to the museum. On any bus, get off at the Arènes-Matisse bus stop (look for the crumbling Roman wall).

Background: Henri Matisse (1869-1954), the master of leaving things out, could suggest a woman's body with a single curvy line—letting the viewer's mind fill in the rest. Ignoring traditional 3-D perspective, he expressed his passion for life through simplified but recognizable scenes in which dark outlines and saturated, bright blocks of color create an overall decorative pattern. You don't look "through" a Matisse canvas, like a window; you look "at" it, like wallpaper.

Matisse understood how colors and shapes affect us emotionally. He could create either shocking, clashing works (early Fauvism) or geometrical, balanced, harmonious ones (later cutouts). Whereas other modern artists reveled in purely abstract design,

Matisse (almost) always kept the subject matter at least vaguely recognizable. He used unreal colors and distorted lines not just to portray what an object looks like, but to express its inner nature (even inanimate objects). Meditating on his paintings helps you connect with life—or so Matisse hoped.

As you tour the museum, look for Matisse's favorite motifs—including fruit, flowers, wallpaper, and sunny rooms—often with a window opening onto a sunny landscape. Another favorite subject is the *odalisque* (harem concubine), usually shown sprawled in a seductive pose and with a simplified, masklike face. You'll also see a few souvenirs from his travels, which influenced much of his work.

Visiting the Museum: Enter the museum at park level from the door opposite the olive grove (not the basement entry). The museum features temporary exhibits about Matisse that change frequently.

Rooms on the entry level usually house paintings from Matisse's formative years as a student (1890s). Notice how quickly his work evolves: from dark still lifes *(nature mortes)*, to colorful Impressionist scenes, to more abstract pieces, all in a matter of a few years. A beige banner describes his "Découverte de la Lumière" (discovery of light), which the Riviera (and his various travels to sun-soaked places like Corsica, Collioure, and Tahiti) brought to his art. You may see photographs of his apartment on cours Saleya, which is described in my "Scratch-and-Sniff Walk Through Vieux Nice," earlier.

Other rooms on this floor highlight Matisse's fascination with dance and the female body (these subjects may be upstairs). You'll see pencil and charcoal drawings, and a handful of bronze busts; he was fascinated by sculpture. *The Acrobat*—painted only two years before Matisse's death—shows the artist at his minimalist best. A room devoted to two 25-foot-long watery cutouts for an uncompleted pool project *(La Piscine)* for the city of Nice shows his abiding love of deep blue.

The floor above features sketches and models of Matisse's famous Chapel of the Rosary, located in nearby Vence, and related religious works. On the same floor, you may find paper cutouts from his *Jazz* series, more bronze sculptures, various personal objects, and linen embroideries inspired by his travels to Polynesia.

The bookshop, WCs, and additional temporary exhibits are on the basement level. The fantastic wall-hanging near the bookshop—Matisse's colorful paper cutout *Flowers and Fruits*—shouts, "Riviera!"

Leaving the Museum: When leaving the museum, find the stop for buses #15 and #22 (frequent service to downtown, stops en route at the Chagall Museum): Turn left from the Matisse Museum into the park and keep straight on Allée Barney Wilen, exiting the park at the Archeological Museum, then turn right. Pass the bus stop across the street (#17 goes to the city center but not the Chagall Museum, and #20 goes to the port), and walk to the small roundabout. Cross the roundabout to find the shelter (facing downhill) for buses #15 and #22.

▲Modern and Contemporary Art Museum (Musée d'Art Moderne et d'Art Contemporain)

This ultramodern museum features an explosively colorful, far-out, yet manageable collection focused on American and European-American artists from the 1960s and 1970s (Pop Art and New Realism styles are highlighted). The exhibits cover three floors and include a few works by Andy Warhol, Roy Lichtenstein, and Jean Tinguely, and small models of Christo's famous wrappings. You'll find rooms dedicated to Robert Indiana, Yves Klein, and Niki de Saint Phalle (my favorite). The temporary exhibits can be as appealing to modern-art lovers as the permanent collection: Check the museum website for what's playing. Don't leave without exploring the rooftop terrace.

Cost and Hours: Free, Tue-Sun 10:00-18:00, closed Mon, about a 15-minute walk from Place Masséna, near Vieux Nice on Promenade des Arts, tel. 04 93 62 61 62, www.mamac-nice.org.

Fine Arts Museum (Musée des Beaux-Arts)

Housed in a sumptuous Riviera villa with lovely gardens, this museum holds 6,000 artworks from the 17th to 20th centuries. Start on the first floor and work your way up to experience an appealing array of paintings by Monet, Sisley, Bonnard, and Raoul Dufy, as well as a few sculptures by Rodin and Carpeaux.

Cost and Hours: Free, Tue-Sun 10:00-18:00, closed Mon; inconveniently located at the western end of Nice, take bus #12 or #23 from the train station to the Rosa Bonheur stop and walk to 3 Avenue des Baumettes; tel. 04 92 15 28 28, www.musee-beaux-arts-nice.org.

Molinard Perfume Museum

The Molinard family has been making perfume in Grasse (about an hour's drive from Nice) since 1849. Their Nice store has a small museum in the rear that illustrates the story of their industry. Back when people believed water spread the plague (Louis XIV supposedly bathed less than once a year), doctors advised people to rub fragrances into their skin and then powder their bodies. At that time, perfume was a necessity of everyday life. The museum's two rooms describe the distillation process and explain the important role of the "nose"—the perfume mastermind (most of whom are French).

Cost and Hours: Free, daily April-Sept 10:00-19:00, Oct-March 10:00-13:00 & 14:00-18:00, sometimes closed Sun off-season, just between beach and Place Masséna at 20 Rue St. François de Paule, see map on page 322, tel. 04 93 62 90 50, www.molinard.com.

▲Russian Cathedral (Cathédrale Russe)

Nice's Russian Orthodox church— claimed by some to be the finest outside Russia—is worth a visit. Five hundred rich Russian families wintered in Nice in the late 19th century, and they needed a worthy Orthodox house of worship. Czar Nicholas I's widow provided the land (which required tearing down her house), and Czar Nicholas II gave this church to the Russian community in  1912. (A few years later, Russian comrades who *didn't* winter on the Riviera assassinated him.) Here in the land of olives and anchovies, these proud onion domes seem odd. But, I imagine, so did those old Russians.

Cost and Hours: Free; Tue-Sat 9:00–12:00 & 14:00–19:00, Sun 9:00-12:00, closed Mon; chanted services Sat at 17:30 or 18:00, Sun at 10:00; no tourist visits during services, no shorts allowed, 17 Boulevard du Tzarewitch, tel. 04 93 96 88 02, www.acor-nice.com. The park around the church stays open at lunch and makes a fine setting for picnics.

Getting There: It's a 10-minute walk from the train station. Head west on Avenue Thiers, turn right on Avenue Gambetta, go under the freeway, and turn left following *Eglise Russe* signs. Or, from the station, take any bus heading west on Avenue Thiers and get off at Avenue Gambetta (then follow the previous directions).

Eating in Nice

For general tips on eating in France, see page 276.

In Vieux Nice

Nice's dinner scene converges on Cours Saleya (koor sah-lay-yuh), which is entertaining enough in itself to make the generally mediocre food a good deal. It's a fun, festive spot to compare tans and mussels. Even if you're eating elsewhere, wander through here in the evening. For locations, see the map on page 322.

La Voglia has figured out a winning formula: Good food + ample servings + fair prices = good business. Come here early for top-value Italian cuisine, or plan on waiting for a table. There's fun seating inside and out (€12-14 pizza and pasta, €15-25 *plats*, open daily, at the western edge of Cours Saleya at 2 Rue St. Francois de Paule, tel. 04 93 80 99 16).

Le Safari is a fair option for outdoor dining on Cours Saleya, with a few more locals than tourists. The cuisine is Niçois, and the service is professional (€18-30 *plats*, open daily, 1 Cours Saleya, tel. 04 93 80 18 44, www.restaurantsafari.fr).

Chez Palmyre is the place to eat on a budget in the old town. It's popular, so book this one ahead. The ambience is rustic but intimate, and the menu changes every two weeks. The three-course *menu* is only €15, and the food could not be more homemade (closed Sun, cash only, 5 Rue Droite, tel. 04 93 85 72 32).

Le Bistrot du Fromager's owner, Hugo, is crazy about cheese and wine. Come here to escape the heat and dine in cozy, cool, vaulted cellars surrounded by shelves of wine. All dishes use cheese as their base ingredient, although you'll also find pasta, ham, and salmon (with cheese, of course). This is a good choice for vegetarians (€10-14 starters, €15-21 *plats*, €6 desserts, closed Sun, just off Place du Jésus at 29 Rue Benoît Bunico, tel. 04 93 13 07 83).

Oliviera venerates the French olive. This shop/restaurant sells a variety of oils, offers free tastings, and serves a menu of dishes paired with specific oils (think of a wine pairing). Welcoming owner Nadim, who speaks excellent English, knows all his producers, and provides "Olive Oil 101" explanations with his tastings (best if you buy something afterward or have a meal). You'll learn how passionate he is about his products, and once you've had a taste, you'll want to stay and eat—so go early (or reserve ahead), as tables fill fast (allow €40 with wine, €16-24 main dishes, Tue-Sat 10:00-22:00, closed Sun-Mon, indoor seating only, 8 bis Rue du Collet, tel. 04 93 13 06 45).

Bistrot D'Antoine is a welcoming, vine-draped option whose delightful menu emphasizes Niçois cuisine and good grilled selections. The food is delicious and the prices are reasonable, so call ahead to reserve a table (€7-10 starters, €13-18 *plats*, €6 desserts, closed Sun-Mon, 27 Rue de la Préfecture, tel. 04 93 85 29 57).

La Merenda is a tiny place on the edge of the old town. Dine on simple, home-style dishes in a communal environment. The menu, presented tableside on a small blackboard, changes with the season. This place fills fast, so go early (opens at 19:00) or, since they don't have a phone, drop by to reserve (€10-12 starters, €12-20 *plats*, €6 desserts, closed Sat-Sun, cash only, 4 Rue Raoul Bosio, www.lamerenda.net).

L'Acchiardo, hidden away in the heart of Vieux Nice, is a homey eatery that does a good job mixing a loyal clientele with hungry tourists. Its simple, hearty Niçois cuisine is served at fair prices by gentle Monsieur Acchiardo. The small plaque under the menu outside says the restaurant has been run by father and son since 1927 (€8 starters, €15-20 *plats*, €7 desserts, cash only, closed Sat-Sun, indoor seating only, 38 Rue Droite, tel. 04 93 85 51 16).

Ville de Siena draws young travelers who dig this place for its big portions, open kitchen, and raucous atmosphere, with tables crammed outside on a narrow lane. The food is Italian and hearty (€12-17 *plats*, closed Sun, 10 Rue St. Vincent, tel. 04 93 80 12 45).

Lou Pilha Leva delivers fun and cheap lunch or dinner options with Niçois specialties and always busy outdoor-only picnic-table dining (daily, located where Rue de la Loge and Rue Centrale meet in Vieux Nice).

Restaurant Castel is a fine eat-on-the-beach option, thanks to its location at the very east end of Nice looking over the bay. Lose the city hustle and bustle by dropping down the steps below Castle Hill. The views are unforgettable even if the cuisine is not; you can even have lunch at your beach chair if you've rented one here (€15/half-day, €18/day). Dinner here is best: Arrive before sunset and find a waterfront table perfectly positioned to watch evening swimmers get in their last laps as the sky turns pink and city lights flicker on. Linger long enough to justify the few extra euros the place charges (€18 salads and pastas, €20-28 main courses, 8 Quai des Etats-Unis, tel. 04 93 85 22 66, www.castelplage.com).

And for Dessert...

Gelato lovers should save room for the tempting ice-cream stands in Vieux Nice. **Fenocchio** is the city's favorite, with mouthwatering displays of 86 flavors ranging from tomato to lavender to avocado—all of which are surprisingly good (daily March-Nov, until 24:00 in summer, two locations: 2 Place Rossetti and 6 Rue de la Poissonnerie). Gelato connoisseurs should head for **Oui, Jelato,** where the selection may be a fraction of Fenocchio's but the quality is superior (5 Rue de la Préfecture, on the Place du Palais).

Near Promenade des Anglais

Worthwhile restaurants are few and far between in this area. Either head for Vieux Nice or try one of these good places.

On Place Grimaldi: This square nurtures a lineup of appealing restaurants with good indoor and outdoor seating along a broad sidewalk under tall, leafy sycamore trees. **Crêperie Bretonne** is the only *crêperie* I list in Nice (€11 dinner crêpes, closed Sun, 3 Place Grimaldi, tel. 04 93 82 28 47). **Le Grimaldi** delivers basic café fare (€17 pasta, €15-25 *plats*, closed Sun, 1 Place Grimaldi, tel. 04 93 87 98 13).

Chantecler has Nice's most prestigious address—inside the Hôtel Negresco. This is everything a luxury restaurant should be: elegant, soft, and top quality (*menus* from €100, closed Mon-Tue, 37 Promenade des Anglais, tel. 04 93 16 64 00, www.hotel-negres-co-nice.com).

Villefranche-sur-Mer

In the glitzy world of the Riviera, Villefranche-sur-Mer offers travelers an easygoing slice of small-town Mediterranean life. From here, convenient day trips allow you to gamble in style in Monaco, saunter the Promenade des Anglais in Nice, or drink in immense views from Eze-le-Village. Villefranche-sur-Mer feels Italian, with soft-orange buildings; steep, narrow streets spilling into the sea; and pasta on most menus. Luxury sailing yachts glisten in the bay—an inspiration to those lazing along the harborfront to start saving when their trips are over. Sand-pebble beaches and a handful of interesting sights keep other visitors just busy enough.

Originally a Roman port, Villefranche-sur-Mer was overtaken

by fifth-century barbarians. Villagers fled into the hills, where they stayed and farmed their olives. In 1295 the Duke of Provence—like many in coastal Europe—was threatened by the Saracen Turks. He asked the hillside olive farmers to move down to the water and establish a front line against the invaders, thus denying the enemy a base from which to attack Nice. In return for tax-free status, they stopped farming, took up fishing, and established Ville- (town) franche (without taxes). Since there were many such towns, this one was specifically "Tax-free town on the sea" (sur Mer). In about 1560, the Duke of Savoy built an immense, sprawling citadel in the town (which you can still tour). And today, while the town has an international following (including Tina Turner), two-thirds of its 8,000 people call it their primary residence. That makes Villefranche-sur-Mer feel more like a real community than many neighboring Riviera towns.

Travelers arriving in Villefranche-sur-Mer by cruise ship should read the next section to get oriented. Side-trippers from elsewhere in the Riviera can skip down to "Orientation to Villefranche-sur-Mer" on page 340.

Arrival at the Port of Villefranche-sur-Mer

Arrival at a Glance: Villefranche's sights and beach are easily walkable from the cruise terminal. To reach other towns, you can walk 10 minutes to the train station for trains to Nice (10 minutes) or Monaco (10 minutes); or hike 10 minutes up to the main road to

Services at the Port of Villefranche-sur-Mer

You'll find several helpful services inside the terminal building, including a phone that lets you make a free call to local excursion companies to see if you can join a last-minute tour of the region. Right at the terminal building is a fun, characteristic little **"Exposition Marine,"** displaying old nautical paintings and model ships, with a very local-feeling, hole-in-the-wall bar in the back (free entry).

Wi-Fi and Internet: There's a tight little Internet shop in the terminal (popular with ship crew but also welcoming the public). Otherwise, two places with both Internet terminals and Wi-Fi sit side by side on Place du Marché: **Chez Net,** an "Australian International Sports Bar Internet Café," has American keyboards, whereas **L'Ex Café** has French keyboards (both are open daily).

ATM: An ATM is on Place Wilson, near the cruise terminal.

Pharmacy: The nearest pharmacy is on the main road up above, near the TI.

Bike Rental: If you want to go for a bike ride around the area (such as the nearby Cap Ferrat) but don't feel like pedaling too hard, consider renting an electric bike from Henri at Eco-Loc. The adventurous can also try this as an alternative to taking the bus to Cap Ferrat, Eze-le-Village, or even Nice (although the road to Nice is awfully busy). You get about 25 miles on a fully charged battery (less on hilly terrain—after that you're pedaling; €15/half-day, €20/day, early April-Sept daily 9:00-17:00, deposit and ID required, best to call for reservations 24 hours in advance; helmets, locks, baskets, and child seats available; find the small tent on the port next to Café Calypso, mobile 06 66 92 72 41, www.ecoloc06.fr).

Boat Rental: You can be your own skipper and rent a motor boat at Dark Pelican (€100/half-day, €160/day, deposit required, on the harbor at the Gare Maritime, tel. 04 93 01 76 54, www.darkpelican.com).

catch bus #100 to Nice (20 minutes) or Monaco (25 minutes). Cap Ferrat's lush hiking trails are a 50-minute walk or 15-minute bus ride away. Taxis go to Nice (€35-40), Monaco (€50-60), and Cap Ferrat (€20-25)—all one-way rates.

Port Overview

Tenders deposit passengers at a slick terminal building (Gare Maritime) at the Port de la Santé, right in front of Villefranche-sur-Mer's old town. The main road (with the main TI and bus stop) is a steep hike above.

Smaller and less famous than its neighbors Nice and Monaco,

Villefranche-sur-Mer hustles to impress its cruise passengers. On days when cruises are in town, local vendors set up kiosks to show off their wares on Place Amélie Pollonnais (just to the left as you exit the terminal). Because Villefranche is a small town, it's a low-impact, pleasant place to arrive. And, while it lacks flashy sights and big-name museums, Villefranche is simply a delightful place to kill time. Leave yourself some time at the end of the day to just hang out in Villefranche as you wait for that last tender.

Tourist Information: There's a TI inside the terminal building (opening timed to cruise-ship arrivals). Pick up the free town map that's tailor-made for arriving cruise passengers. The main TI is on the main road up above, near the bus stops (see page 340).

Getting into Town

Your tender leaves you in the heart of town—staring right at the main square. A pleasant maze of tight streets climbs the hill behind Hôtel Welcome. The walls of the imposing citadel squat boldly just down the coast (just walk with the water on your left), with the Port de la Darse beyond. For details on all of these sights, see "Sights in Villefranche-sur-Mer," later.

It's easy to **walk** to various points in town. Leaving the terminal, you'll see directional signs pointing left, to *Town center/bus* (a 10-minute, steeply uphill walk); and right, to *Gare SNCF/train station* (a 10-minute, mostly level stroll with some stairs up at the end).

Little **minibus #80,** which departs from in front of the cruise terminal, saves you the sweat of going from the harbor up the hill to the TI and main road—but it only runs once per hour (daily 7:00-19:00; €1.50 ticket also covers bus to Nice—but to go to Monaco, you'll need to buy a separate €1.50 ticket on that bus). The minibus travels from the port to the top of the hill, stopping near Hôtel la Fiancée du Pirate and the Col de Villefranche stop for buses #82 and #112 to Eze-le-Village.

It's possible to **taxi** to points in town (see "By Taxi," below), but it's overpriced and unnecessary, given the small size of the place.

Skip the useless white **Petit Train,** which goes nowhere interesting (€7, 20-minute ride).

Getting to Sights Beyond Villefranche-sur-Mer

To reach Nice, Monaco, and other Riviera sights, your options include taxi, train, and bus.

By Taxi

Taxis wait in the parking lot in front of the cruise terminal. Their exorbitant rates start with a minimum €10-20 charge for a ride to the train station (an easy 10-minute stroll along the beach), but many drivers will flat-out refuse such a short ride. For farther-flung trips, here are the likely one-way rates:

- To Nice: €35-40
- To Cap Ferrat: €20-25
- To Eze-le-Village: €35-40
- To Monaco: €50-60

Ask your driver to write down the price before you get in, and get a receipt when you pay. For an all-day trip, you can try negotiating a flat fee (e.g., €300 for a 4-hour tour). For a reliable taxi in Villefranche-sur-Mer, call or email **Didier** (mobile 06 15 15 39 15, taxididier.villefranchesurmer@orange.fr). Other numbers to try are mobile 06 09 33 36 12 or mobile 06 39 32 54 09.

By Public Transportation

Villefranche's train station and bus stop are both a short walk from the cruise terminal. There's some uphill climbing to either one; the bus stop is closer but steeper, while the train station has fewer stairs.

By Train

To reach the train station from the terminal, simply stroll with the water on your right for about 10 minutes along the sun-drenched promenade, then look for the stairs on your left leading steeply up to the station. From here, trains go west to **Nice** (2/hour, 10 minutes), **Antibes** (2/hour, 40 minutes), and **Cannes** (2/hour, 50 minutes); and east to **Monaco** (2/hour, 10 minutes).

By Bus

Villefranche's primary bus stop is uphill from the cruise terminal: Follow signs for *Octroi/centre-ville/TI* up the switchback path through the park, pass the soccer field and the TI, and find the Octroi bus stop (just above the TI). From here, buses go to **Monaco** (#100, 4-5/hour Mon-Sat, 3-4/hour Sun, 25 minutes) and Nice (#100, 4-5/hour Mon-Sat, 3-4/hour Sun, 20 minutes; or #81, 2-4/hour daily, 20 minutes).

To reach **Eze-le-Village,** you have two bus options, either of which requires a transfer. (For more on this cliff-capping village,

THE FRENCH RIVIERA

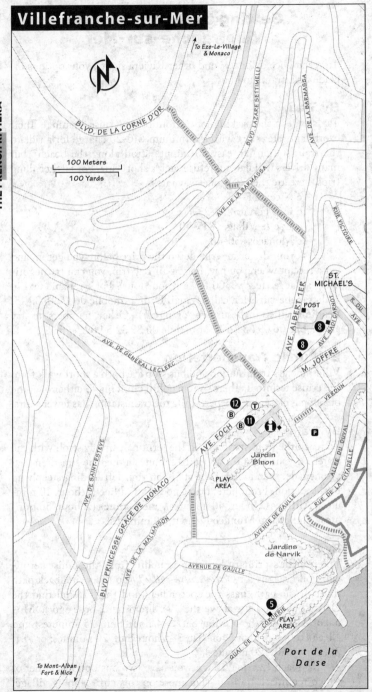

Villefranche-sur-Mer

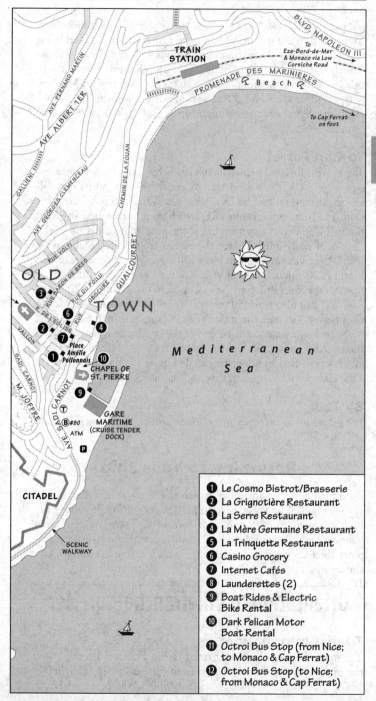

1 Le Cosmo Bistrot/Brasserie
2 La Grignotière Restaurant
3 La Serre Restaurant
4 La Mère Germaine Restaurant
5 La Trinquette Restaurant
6 Casino Grocery
7 Internet Cafés
8 Launderettes (2)
9 Boat Rides & Electric Bike Rental
10 Dark Pelican Motor Boat Rental
11 Octroi Bus Stop (from Nice; to Monaco & Cap Ferrat)
12 Octroi Bus Stop (to Nice; from Monaco & Cap Ferrat)

see page 368.) Take bus #80 from the center of Villefranche-sur-Mer uphill to the Col de Villefranche stop in front of Hôtel la Fiancée du Pirate, where you can catch bus #82 or #112 to Eze-le-Village (14/day Mon-Sat, 10/day Sun, 25 minutes). Alternatively, ride bus #100 or the train (both explained above) toward Monaco, but get off at the Gare d'Eze stop (in Eze-Bord-du-Mer). Then catch the #83 shuttle bus straight up to Eze-le-Village (8/day, 15 minutes).

To Cap Ferrat

The nearby, forested peninsula of Cap Ferrat is a magnet for hikers (see page 343). The easiest way to get there is by bus: First, follow the directions for "By Bus," above, to Villefranche's Octroi bus stop. The best option is **bus #81,** which goes to Beaulieu-sur-Mer, then all Cap Ferrat stops, ending at the port in St-Jean-Cap-Ferrat (2-3/hour daily until 20:15, 20 minutes from Villefranche to St. Jean). The twice-as-frequent **bus #100** leaves you at the edge of Cap Ferrat (a 20-minute walk to Villa Ephrussi de Rothschild).

A **taxi** from Villefranche to Cap Ferrat costs about €20-25.

You can also **walk** 50 minutes from Villefranche-sur-Mer to Cap Ferrat: Go past the train station along the small beach lane, then climb the steps at the far end of the beach and walk parallel to the tracks. Continue straight past the mansions (with ornate gates) and take the first right on Avenue de Grasseuil. You'll see signs to *Villa Ephrussi de Rothschild*, then to Cap Ferrat's port.

By Tour

For information on local tour options around the French Riviera, see page 300.

Returning to Your Ship

To return to Villefranche's port, see the "Arrival in Villefranche-sur-Mer by Bus or Train" section in the next section. If you're early back to town, consider yourself fortunate. There are few ports where it's more enjoyable to linger before catching your tender. Explore the back streets or sip a coffee until it's time to stroll back to the terminal.

Orientation to Villefranche-sur-Mer

Tourist Information

The main TI is in the park named Jardin François Binon, below the main bus stop, labeled *Octroi* (mid-June-mid-Sept daily 9:00-18:00; mid-Sept-mid-June Mon-Sat 9:00-12:00 & 14:00-17:00, closed Sun; 20-minute walk or €10 taxi ride from train station, tel. 04 93 01 73 68, www.villefranche-sur-mer.com). Pick up regional bus schedules here (buses #80, #81, #82, #83, #100, #112, and #114). Also ask for the brochure detailing a self-guided walking tour of Villefranche-sur-Mer and information on boat rides (usually mid-June-Sept). A smaller TI is on the port (mid-May-mid-Sept Mon-Fri 10:00-17:00, Sat-Sun 10:00-16:00, closed off-season).

Arrival in Villefranche-sur-Mer by Bus or Train

By Bus: Whether you've taken bus #100 or #81 from Nice, or bus #100 from Monaco, hop off at the Octroi stop, at the Jardin François Binon, just above the TI. To reach the old town, walk past the TI down Avenue Général de Gaulle, take the first stairway on the left, then make a right at the street's end.

By Train: Not all trains stop in Villefranche-sur-Mer (you may need to transfer to a local train in Nice or Monaco). Villefranche-sur-Mer's train station is a 15-minute walk along the water from the old town. Find your way down toward the water, and turn right to walk into town.

Helpful Hints

Market Day: A fun bric-a-brac market enlivens Villefranche-sur-Mer on Sundays (on Place Amélie Pollonnais by Hôtel Welcome, and in Jardin François Binon by the TI). On Saturday mornings, a small food market sets up near the TI (only in Jardin François Binon).

Last Call: If your ship is staying late in town, be aware that the last bus back from Nice or Monaco is at about 20:00. After that, take the train or a cab.

Villefranche Beach: For some beach time in Villefranche, find the town's decent, if humble, beach just below the train station (a 5-minute stroll from where your tender drops you).

Tender Congestion: To avoid delays getting off your ship, consider skipping breakfast on board and eating in Villefranche. There are several options on Place du Marché (the little square near Hôtel Welcome).

Laundry: The town has two launderettes, both owned by Laura and located just below the main road on Avenue Sadi Carnot. At the upper *pressing moderne,* Laura does your wash for you—for a price (Tue-Sat 9:00-12:30 & 15:00-19:00, closed Sun-Mon, next to Hôtel Riviera, tel. 04 93 01 73 71). The lower *laverie* is self-service only (daily 7:00-20:00, opposite 6 Avenue Sadi Carnot).

Sights in Villefranche-sur-Mer

Conveniently, most of Villefranche-sur-Mer's modest sights cluster near the cruise terminal.

The Harbor

Browse Villefranche-sur-Mer's minuscule harbor. Although the town was once an important fishing community, only a few families still fish here to make money. Find the footpath that leads beneath the citadel to the sea (by the port parking lot). Stop where the path hits the sea and marvel at the scene: a bay filled with beautiful sailing yachts. (You might see well-coiffed captains being ferried in by dutiful mates to pick up their statuesque call girls.) Local guides keep a list of the world's 100 biggest yachts and talk about some of them as if they're part of the neighborhood.

Looking far to the right, that last apartment building on the sea was the headquarters for the US Navy's Sixth Fleet following World War II, and remained so until 1966, when de Gaulle pulled France out of the military wing of NATO. (The Sixth Fleet has been based in Naples ever since.) A wall plaque at the bottom of Rue de l'Eglise commemorates the US Navy's presence in Villefranche-sur-Mer.

Citadel

The town's mammoth castle was built in the 1500s by the Duke of Savoy to defend against the French. When the region joined France in 1860, it became just a barracks. In the 20th century, the city had no military use for the space, and started using the citadel to house its police station, city hall, a summer outdoor theater, and two art galleries. There's still only one fortified entry to this huge complex.

Chapel of St. Pierre (Chapelle Cocteau)

This chapel, decorated by artist Jean Cocteau, is the town's cultural highlight. Cocteau was a Parisian transplant who adored little Villefranche-sur-Mer and whose career was distinguished by his work as an artist, poet, novelist, playwright, and filmmaker. Influenced by his pals Marcel Proust, André Gide, Edith Piaf, and Pablo Picasso, Cocteau was a leader among 20th-century avant-garde intellectuals. At the door, Marie-France—who is passionate about Cocteau's art—collects a €2.50 donation for a fishermen's charity. She then sets you free to enjoy the chapel's small but intriguing interior. She's happy to give some explanations if you ask.

In 1955 Jean Cocteau covered the barrel-vaulted chapel with

heavy black lines and pastels. Each of Cocteau's surrealist works—the Roma (Gypsies) of Stes-Maries-de-la-Mer who dance and sing to honor the Virgin, girls wearing traditional outfits, and three scenes from the life of St. Peter—is explained in English. Is that Villefranche-sur-Mer's citadel in the scene above the altar?

Cost and Hours: Wed-Mon 10:00-12:00 & 15:00-19:00, usually closed Tue (varies with cruise-ship traffic) and when Marie-France is tired, below Hôtel Welcome at 1 Quai de l'Amiral Courbet, tel. 04 93 76 90 70.

Nearby: A few blocks north along the harbor (past Hôtel Welcome), Rue de May leads to the mysterious **Rue Obscure**—a covered lane running 400 feet along the medieval rampart. This street served as an air-raid shelter during World War II. Much of the lane is closed indefinitely for repair.

St. Michael's Church

The town church, a few blocks up Rue de l'Eglise from the harbor, features an 18th-century organ and a fine statue of a recumbent Christ—carved, they say, from a fig tree by a galley slave in the 1600s.

Seafront Walks

A seaside walkway originally used by customs agents to patrol the harbor leads under the citadel and connects the old town with the workaday harbor (Port de la Darse). At the port you'll find a few cafés, France's Institute of Oceanography (an outpost for the University of Paris oceanographic studies), and an 18th-century dry dock. This scenic walk turns downright romantic after dark. You can also wander the other direction along Villefranche-sur-Mer's waterfront and continue beyond the train station for postcard-perfect views back to Villefranche-sur-Mer (ideal in the morning—go before breakfast). You can even extend your walk to Cap Ferrat (the wooded peninsula across the bay from Villefranche, described next).

Near Villefranche-sur-Mer: Cap Ferrat

An exclusive peninsula across the bay from Villefranche-sur-Mer, Cap Ferrat is a peaceful eddy off the busy Nice-Monaco highway. You could spend a leisurely day on this peninsula, wandering the sleepy port village of St-Jean-Cap-Ferrat (usually called "St. Jean"), touring the Villa Ephrussi de Rothschild mansion and gardens and the nearby Villa Kérylos, and walking on sections of the beautiful trails that follow the coast.

The Cap's **Villa Ephrussi de Rothschild** seems like the ultimate in Riviera extravagance—Venice, Versailles, and the Côte d'Azur come together in a pastel-pink 1905 mansion. While the interior is opulent, the gorgeous gardens are why most come here. Designed in the shape of a ship, there are seven lush sections re-created from locations all over the world. The sea views from here are jaw-dropping (open daily, www.villa-ephrussi.com).

The peaceful little beach called **Plage de Passable,** located below the Villa Ephrussi, comes with great views of Villefranche-sur-Mer and a rough, pebbly surface. Half is public (free, with shower), and the other half is run by a small restaurant (pay to rent a chair and locker). If ever you were to do the French Riviera rent-a-beach ritual, this would be the place.

It's a lovely 30-minute stroll, mostly downhill and east, from the Villa Ephrussi to the Villa Kérylos in Beaulieu-sur-Mer; or south, to the port of St. Jean-Cap-Ferrat.

Villa Kérylos was built in 1902 by an eccentric millionaire who modeled his new mansion after a Greek villa from the island of Delos from about 200 B.C. No expense was spared in re-creating this Greek fantasy, from the floor mosaics to Carrara marble columns to exquisite wood furnishings (open daily, good audioguide, www.villa-kerylos.com).

The quiet village port of **St-Jean-Cap-Ferrat** lies in Cap Ferrat's center, yet off most tourist itineraries. St. Jean houses yachts, boardwalks, views, and boutiques packaged in a "take your time, darling" atmosphere. A string of restaurants line the port, with just enough visitors to keep them in business.

Hiking is a popular pastime on the Cap. Popular routes include the 30-minute, level stroll between St. Jean and Beaulieu-sur-Mer; the 45-minute, sea-soaked, view-loaded Plage de la Paloma Loop Trail, just east of St. Jean's port; and the more challenging, two- to three-hour hike that circles the Cap from Plage de Passable to St. Jean. Ask local TIs for tips on each of these.

Eating in Villefranche-sur-Mer

For general tips on eating in France, see page 276.

Le Cosmo Bistrot/Brasserie takes center stage on Place Amélie Pollonnais with a great setting—a few tables have views to the harbor and to the Chapel of St. Pierre's facade (after some wine, the Cocteau art really pops). This tight but friendly place offers well-presented, tasty meals with good wines (I love their red Bandol). Ask for the daily suggestions and consider the €13 *omelette niçoise* (€16 fine salads  and pastas, €16-29 *plats*, daily, Place Amélie Pollonnais, tel. 04 93 01 84 05, www.restaurant-lecosmo.fr).

Disappear into Villefranche-sur-Mer's walking streets and find cute little **La Grignotière,** serving generous and delicious

€21 *plats*, and plenty of other options. Gregarious Michel speaks English fluently and runs the place with his sidekick Brigitte. The mixed seafood grill is a smart order, as are the spaghetti and *gambas* (shrimp), and Michel's personal-recipe bouillabaisse (€23). They also offer a hearty €33 *menu*, but good luck finding room for it. Dining is primarily inside, making this a good choice for cooler days (daily April-Oct, closed Wed Nov-April, 3 Rue du Poilu, tel. 04 93 76 79 83).

La Serre, nestled in the old town below St. Michael's Church, is a simple place with a hardworking owner. Sylvie serves well-priced dinners to a loyal local clientele, always with a smile. Choose from the many pizzas (all named after US states and €10 or less), salads, and meats; or try the good-value, €17 three-course *menu* (open daily, evenings only, cheap house wine, 16 Rue de May, tel. 04 93 76 79 91).

La Mère Germaine, right on the harbor, is the only place in town classy enough to lure a yachter ashore. It's dressy, with formal service and a price list to match. The name commemorates the current owner's grandmother, who fed hungry GIs during World War II. Try the bouillabaisse, served with panache (€79/person with 2-person minimum, €51 mini-version for one, €45 *menu*, open daily, reserve harborfront table, 9 Quai de l'Amiral Courbet, tel. 04 93 01 71 39, www.meregermaine.com).

La Trinquette is a relaxed, low-key place away from the fray on the "other port," next to the Hôtel de la Darse (a lovely 10-minute walk from the other recommended restaurants). The cuisine is good and weekends bring a cool live music scene (€11-20 *plats*, daily in summer, closed Wed off-season, 30 Avenue Général de Gaulle, tel. 04 93 16 92 48).

There's a handy **Casino supermarket/grocery store** a few blocks above Hôtel Welcome at 12 Rue du Poilu (Mon-Tue and Thu-Sat 7:30-12:30 & 15:30-19:00, Sun 7:30-12:30 only, closed Wed).

Monaco

Despite high prices, wall-to-wall daytime tourists, and a Disney-esque atmosphere, Monaco is a Riviera must. Monaco is on the go. Since 1929, cars have raced around the port and in front of the casino in one of the world's

THE FRENCH RIVIERA

most famous auto races, the Grand Prix de Monaco. The modern breakwater—constructed elsewhere and towed in by sea—enables big cruise ships to dock here. The district of Fontvieille, reclaimed from the sea, bristles with luxury high-rise condos. But don't look for anything too deep in this glittering tax haven. Two-thirds of its 30,000 residents live here because there's no income tax—leaving fewer than 10,000 true Monegasques.

This minuscule principality (0.75 square mile) borders only France and the Mediterranean. The country has always been tiny, but it used to be...less tiny. In an 1860 plebiscite, Monaco lost two-thirds of its territory when the region of Menton voted to join France. To compensate, France suggested that Monaco build a fancy casino and promised to connect it to the world with a road (the Low Corniche) and a train line. This started a high-class tourist boom that has yet to let up.

Although "independent," Monaco is run as a piece of France. A French civil servant appointed by the French president—with the blessing of Monaco's prince—serves as state minister and manages the place. Monaco's phone system, electricity, water, and so on, are all French.

The glamorous romance and marriage of the American actress Grace Kelly to Prince Rainier added to Monaco's fairy-tale mystique. Princess Grace (Prince Albert's mother) first came to Monaco to star in the 1955 Hitchcock movie *To Catch a Thief*, in which she was filmed racing along the Corniches. She married the prince in 1956 and adopted the country, but tragically, the much-loved princess died in 1982 after suffering a stroke while driving on one of those same scenic roads. She was just 52 years old.

The death of Prince Rainier in 2005 ended his 56-year career of enlightened rule. Today Monaco is ruled by Prince Rainier's unassuming son, Prince Albert Alexandre Louis Pierre, Marquis of Baux. Prince Albert had long been considered Europe's most eligible bachelor—until he finally married on July 2, 2011, at age 53. His bride, known as Princess Charlene, is a South African commoner twenty years his junior. Sadly for Monaco, this rare royal event was overshadowed by the London wedding of Prince William and Kate Middleton.

A graduate of Amherst College, Albert is a bobsled enthusiast who raced in several Olympics, and an avid environmentalist who seems determined to clean up Monaco's tarnished tax-haven, money-laundering image. (Monaco is infamously known as a "sunny place for shady people.") Monaco is big business, and Prince Albert is its CEO. Its famous casino contributes only 5 percent of the state's revenue, whereas its 43 banks—which offer an attractive way to hide your money—are hugely profitable. The prince also makes

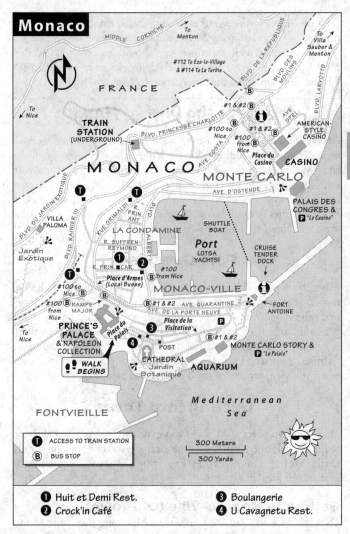

Monaco

To Menton

MIDDLE CORNICHE

BLVD. DE LA RÉPUBLIQUE

To Villa Sauber & Menton

BLVD. DES MOULINS

BLVD. LARVOTTO

#112 To Eze-le-Village & #114 To La Turbie

B

FRANCE

#1 & #2 **B**

To Nice

TRAIN STATION (UNDERGROUND)

BLVD. PRINCESSE CHARLOTTE

i #1 & #2 **B**

AVE. SPEL

AMERICAN-STYLE CASINO

M O N A C O

#100 to Nice **B**

AVE. COSTA

#100 from Nice **B**

Place du Casino

CASINO

MONTE CARLO

AVE. D'OSTENDE

T **T**

BLVD DU JARDIN EXOTIQUE

BLVD. RAINIER III

RUE GRIMALDI

R. PRIN. ANT.

BLVD. ALBERT

PALAIS DES CONGRÈS & **P** *"Le Casino"*

VILLA PALOMA

Jardin Exotique

LA CONDAMINE

R. SUFFREN-REYMOND

1

2

SHUTTLE BOAT

Port LOTSA YACHTS!

CRUISE TENDER DOCK

T

R. PRIN. CAR.

Place d'Armes (Local Buses)

B

#100 from Nice

MONACO-VILLE

#100 to Nice **B**

B

#100 from Nice

B RAMPE MAJOR

B

B #1 & #2 AVE. QUARANTINE

AVE. DE LA PORTE NEUVE

FORT ANTOINE

i

To Nice

PRINCE'S PALACE & NAPOLEON COLLECTION

Place du Palais

3 *Place de la Visitation*

P

B #1 & #2

4

WALK BEGINS

POST

CATHEDRAL

Jardin Botanique

MONTE CARLO STORY & **P** *"Le Palais"*

AQUARIUM

FONTVIEILLE

M e d i t e r r a n e a n   S e a

T ACCESS TO TRAIN STATION

B BUS STOP

300 Meters

300 Yards

1 Huit et Demi Rest.
2 Crock'in Café
3 Boulangerie
4 U Cavagnetu Rest.

money with a value-added tax (19.6 percent, the same as in France), plus real estate and corporate taxes.

Monaco is a special place: There are more people in Monaco's philharmonic orchestra (about 100) than in its army (about 80 guards). The princedom is well-guarded, with police and cameras on every corner. (They say you could win a million dollars at the casino and walk to the train station in the wee hours without a worry...and I believe it.) Stamps are so few that they increase in value almost as soon as they're printed. And collectors snapped up the rare Monaco versions of euro coins (with Prince Rainier's portrait) so quickly that many Monegasques have never even seen one.

Travelers arriving by cruise ship should read the next section on the port of Monaco. Those side-tripping from elsewhere in the Riviera can skip down to "Orientation to Monaco" on page 351.

Arrival at the Port of Monaco

Arrival at a Glance: It's a long walk or a short bus ride to most sights in town (including Monaco-Ville—the old town—and the ritzy Monte Carlo casino district). To reach other towns, you can walk 20 minutes to the train station for trains to Villefranche-sur-Mer (10 minutes) and Nice (20 minutes); or walk 10 minutes to Place d'Armes to catch bus #100 to Villefranche-sur-Mer (25 minutes) and Nice (45 minutes).

Port Overview

Monaco's big, modern cruise-ship terminal is just below the old town at the end of the yacht harbor—a pleasant harborside stroll from the modern town center. Your ship will either tie up at the pier or moor in the harbor and tender its passengers to the terminal.

Tourist Information: The seasonal TI right next to the cruise terminal is open on busy days May through September. If it's closed when you visit, try one of the TIs listed on page 352.

Getting into Town

There are two parts of Monaco you may want to visit: the cliff-top old town, **Monaco-Ville;** and the ritzy skyscraper zone of **Monte Carlo,** with its famous casino. Everything in town is accessible by foot and/or local bus.

Getting to Monaco-Ville (Old Town)

To reach Monaco-Ville, which towers high over the cruise terminal, you can either hike steeply and scenically up to the top of the hill, or walk 10 level minutes to meet a bus that will take you up top sweat-free.

By Foot: A series of sidewalks, stairs, escalators, and elevators links the terminal to the old town. The fastest, steepest ascent (with an elevator option partway) is near the tip of the Monaco-Ville peninsula, just above the harbor: From the terminal, head toward downtown, but keep an eye out on your left for the easy-to-miss steps at the corner of the port, set back right before the Yacht Club de Monaco. These stairs take you steeply up to the base of the hill. Turn left, then curl to the right around the bluff (with the water on

Services at the Port of Monaco

Taxis: To summon a taxi (assuming none are waiting at the terminal when you disembark), look for the gray taxi-call box. Press the button and wait for your cab to arrive.

Electric Car Rental: Golf-cart-like electric cars can be rented at the terminal (€25/hour, €50/half-day, credit card required for security deposit, 2-person capacity, about 25-mile-range per battery charge). These can be a fun way to tool around Monaco. Because they are electric, you can park for free in any car or scooter space.

your left), following signs for *Palais/Musées*. Eventually you'll reach a parking garage; you can either bypass the garage and keep hiking up through the manicured park, or enter the garage and ride up the elevator, then the escalator. Either way, you'll emerge near the venerable Cousteau Aquarium, close to the end of my self-guided walk. (It's a 5-minute walk through town to Palace Square, grand Monaco viewpoints, and the start of the walk; you can also catch the tourist train here—described on page 353.)

By Bus from Place d'Armes: To ride bus #1 or #2 up to Monaco-Ville, first walk to the bus stop near the market square called Place d'Armes: Head straight along the yacht harbor until you reach the busy Boulevard Albert 1er. Use the white overpass (with an elevator) to cross the street, then follow green *Gare S.N.C.F./Ferroviare* signs through a maze of skyscrapers, across the street, and up a charming lane lined with motorcycle shops. Continue straight into the peach-and-yellow building, and ride the free public elevator up to *Marché Place d'Armes* (level 0). As you exit the elevator into Place d'Armes, turn left and cross the street, then continue up to the second, uphill street (which leads up to the hilltop). Cross this second street and bear right to find the bus stop (see "Getting Around Monaco," later, for more on bus service). Note: Don't take bus #1 and #2 from the stop on the lower street—from here, the bus runs in the opposite direction and will just take you farther from the old town.

Getting to Monte Carlo

Monte Carlo (and its landmark casino) is basically across the harbor from the cruise ship terminal. While the casino doesn't open until 14:00, its architecture is easy to appreciate, and the genteel gardens that sprawl behind it are an elegant place to stroll. You can **walk** to the casino area in about 25 minutes—just go all the way around the harbor. To shave some time off the hike, ride the little "bateau-bus" **shuttle boat** that plies back and forth across the harbor from near the cruise terminal (to find it, walk toward town, then go right along the pier extending into the harbor). It drops you on the far side near a bus stop and below Monte Carlo (and the casino zone). The €2 boat ticket is good for 30 minutes and includes a transfer to the bus system (buy on board, €5/all-day pass, 3/hour); you can quickly "sail" round-trip on the shuttle—just to confuse the pilot—and still catch a city bus with your ticket.

To ride **bus** #1 or #2 to the upper part of Monte Carlo—with the TI, views down over the casino gardens, and handy bus stops (including the one for Eze-le-Village)—walk along the harbor toward town. When you reach Boulevard Albert 1er, look for the Princess Stéphanie stop for bus #1 and #2 at the top of the yacht harbor. In Monte Carlo, bus #1 stops at "Place du Casino" (near the lower end of the casino gardens), while bus #2 goes to the "Casino" stop (near the upper end of the gardens); both buses continue uphill to the "Casino Tourisme" stop, which is handier for the TI (and the bus stop for Eze-le-Village).

Getting to Sights Beyond Monaco

Monaco is connected to most nearby sights by both train and bus. Remember, the bus is more scenic, but the train is faster.

By Train

Monaco's long, mostly underground train station sits unobtrusively about a 20-minute walk from the harbor—but it's a pleasant stroll. First, follow the directions to Place d'Armes (given above, under "Getting to Monaco-Ville—By Bus from Place d'Armes"). Head up to the far end of Place d'Armes, cross the busy Rue Grimaldi, and continue on the narrow lane (Rue de la Turbie) angling up from the pharmacy at the corner. Go up the stairs (or ride the elevator) into the little plaza, where you'll see a small TI kiosk (open only in peak season). Turn left, walk up more stairs, and enter the train station (the big, pink building on your right; the easy-to-miss entrance is at the far end—look for *Accès Gare* signs). You'll go down a long marble hallway with moving walkways to the tracks, then hike to the right along the tracks to reach the ticket offices. From here, the train goes twice hourly to **Villefranche-sur-Mer** (10 minutes), then on to **Nice** (20 minutes). Any train labeled *Grasse* is heading west and will stop in Villefranche and Nice.

By Bus

The stop for bus #100—which conveniently connects Monaco along the Lower Corniche to most other sights in this chapter—is near Place d'Armes (follow the instructions to that square given earlier, under "Getting to Monaco-Ville—By Bus from Place d'Armes"). Once in Place d'Armes, head up to the far end of the square, along Rue Grimaldi. Across the roundabout on the left, on the right-hand side of the street, is the stop for bus #100 to Nice, Villefranche-sur-Mer, and Cap Ferrat; cross the street two times in either direction (circling halfway around the roundabout) to get there. While the stop may not be marked for bus #100, it's the right one. If you're concerned, verify with a local by asking, *"A Nice?"* From here, the bus runs every 15 minutes (less on Sun) to **Cap Ferrat** (20 minutes), **Villefranche-sur-Mer** (25 minutes), and **Nice** (45 minutes). A ticket for any ride costs €1.50.

If you're going first to the TI and Monte Carlo area, and want to catch bus #100 to Nice from there, you'll find a stop a few blocks above the casino on Avenue de la Costa (under the arcade to the left of Barclays Bank).

By Tour

For information on local tour options around the French Riviera, see page 300.

Returning to Your Ship

If you have some time to kill before "all aboard," notice that Monaco-Ville is directly above the cruise terminal. You could linger up there, then head toward the Cousteau Aquarium, ride down the escalator, then transfer to the elevator (inside the parking garage), and finally walk around the point to the stairs leading down to the terminal. To stick closer, you can luxuriate along the harbor in front of the Yacht Club.

Orientation to Monaco

The principality of Monaco has three distinct tourist areas: Monaco-Ville, Monte Carlo, and La Condamine. **Monaco-Ville** fills the rock high above everything else and is referred to by locals as Le Rocher ("The Rock"). This is the oldest section, home to the Prince's Palace and all the sights except the casino. **Monte Carlo** is the area around the casino. **La Condamine** is the port (which lies between Mo-

naco-Ville and Monte Carlo). From here it's a 25-minute walk up to the Prince's Palace or to the casino, or three minutes by local bus (see "Getting Around Monaco," later). A fourth, less-interesting area, **Fontvieille,** forms the west end of Monaco and was reclaimed from the sea by Prince Rainier in the 1970s.

The surgical-strike plan for most travelers is to start at Monaco-Ville (where you'll spend the most time), wander down along the port area, and finish by gambling away whatever you have left in Monte Carlo (the casino doesn't open until 14:00). You can walk the entire route in about 1.5 hours, or take three bus trips and do it in 15 minutes.

Tourist Information

The main TI is at the top of the park, above the casino (Mon-Sat 9:00-19:00, Sun 11:00-13:00, 2 Boulevard des Moulins, tel. 00-377/92 16 61 16 or 00-377/92 16 61 66, www.visitmonaco.com). Branch TIs may be open in the train station (Tue-Sat 9:00-17:00, until 18:00 in summer, closed Sun-Mon except July-Aug).

Arrival in Monaco by Bus or Train

By Bus from Nice and Villefranche-sur-Mer: Bus riders need to pay attention, since stops are not announced. Cap d'Ail is the town before Monaco, so be on the lookout after that (the last stop before Monaco is called Cimetière). You'll enter Monaco through the modern cityscape of high-rises of the Fontvieille district. When you see the rocky outcrop of old Monaco, be ready to get off.

There are three stops in Monaco. Listed in order from Nice, they are Place d'Armes (in front of a tunnel at the base of Monaco-Ville's rock), Stade Nautique (closest stop to Monaco-Ville on the port), and Office de Tourisme (near the casino and the TI on Avenue d'Ostende). The Place d'Armes stop is the best starting point, and is the only signed stop (otherwise, verify with locals that you're at the right stop). From the Place d'Armes stop, you can walk up to Monaco-Ville and the palace (10 minutes straight up), or catch a quick local bus (line #1 or #2—see "Getting Around Monaco," later). To reach the bus stop and steps up to Monaco-Ville, cross the street right in front of the tunnel and walk with the rock on your right for about 200 feet (good WCs at the local-bus stop). To begin at the Office de Tourisme stop, pass through the port, and get off the bus when you see the Häagen-Dazs, walk past it, and turn right.

For directions on returning to Nice by bus, see "Getting to Sights Beyond Monaco—By Bus," earlier.

By Train from Nice and Villefranche-sur-Mer: This looooong underground train station is in central Monaco, about a 15-minute walk to the casino or to the port, and about 25 minutes to the palace. The TI and ticket windows are up the escalator at the Italy end of the station. There are three exits from the train platform level (one at each end and one in the middle).

To reach Monaco-Ville and the palace from the station, take the platform-level exit at the Nice end of the tracks (signed *Sortie Fontvieille/Monaco Ville*), which leads through a long tunnel (TI annex at end); as you emerge from the tunnel, turn right, turn left at the end of the walkway, and cross the busy intersection. From here, it's a 15-minute hike up to the palace, or take the bus (#1 or #2).

To reach Monaco's port and the casino, take the mid-platform exit, closer to the Italy end of the tracks. Follow *Sortie la Condamine* signs down the steps and escalators, then follow *Accès Port* signs until you pop out at the port, where you'll see the stop for buses #1 and #2. It's a 25-minute walk from the port to the palace (to your right) or 20 minutes to the casino (up Avenue d'Ostende to your left), or a short trip via buses #1 or #2 to either.

If you plan to return to Nice by train after 20:30, when ticket windows close, buy your return tickets now or be sure to have about €4 in coins (the ticket machines only take coins).

Helpful Hints

Combo-Ticket: If you plan to see all three of Monaco's big sights (Prince's Palace, Napoleon Collection, and the Cousteau Aquarium), buy the €19 combo-ticket at the first sight you visit.

Telephone Tip: To call Monaco from France, dial 00, then 377 (Monaco's country code) and the eight-digit number. Within Monaco, simply dial the eight-digit number.

Pharmacy: You'll find one at the top-right corner of Place d'Armes, and another one just across the street.

Getting Around Monaco

By Local Bus: Buses #1 and #2 link all areas with fast and frequent service (single ticket-€2, 6 tickets-€10, day pass-€5, pay driver, slightly cheaper if bought from machine, 10/hour, fewer on Sun, buses run until 21:00, www.cam.mc). You can split a six-ride ticket with your travel partners (which is handy, since you're unlikely to take more than two or three rides in Monaco). Bus tickets are good for a free transfer if used within 30 minutes.

By Open Bus Tour: You could pay €18 for a hop-on, hop-off open-deck bus tour that makes 12 stops in Monaco, but I wouldn't. This tour doesn't go to the best view spot in the Jardin Exotique (described on page 356) and, besides, most of Monaco is walkable. If you want a scenic tour of the principality that includes its best views, pay €2 to take local bus #2, and stay on board for a full loop (or hop on and off as you please).

By Tourist Train: "Monaco Tour" tourist trains are an efficient way to enjoy a blitz tour of Monaco. They begin at the aquarium and pass by the port, casino, and palace (€8, 2/hour, 40 minutes, recorded English commentary).

By Taxi: If you've lost all track of time at the casino, you can call the 24-hour taxi service (tel. 08 20 20 98 98)...provided you still have enough money to pay for the cab fare.

By Electric Car: Tiny golf-cart-like electric cars can be rented just outside the cruise terminal (described earlier).

Monaco-Ville Walk

All of Monaco's sights (except the casino) are in Monaco-Ville, packed within a few cheerfully tidy blocks. This self-guided walk makes a tight little loop, starting from the palace square.

• *To get from anywhere in Monaco to the palace square (Monaco-Ville's sightseeing center, home of the palace and the Napoleon Collection), take bus #1 or #2 to the end of the line at Place de la Visitation. Turn right as you step off the bus and walk five minutes down Rue Emile de Loth. You'll pass the post office, a worthwhile stop for its collection of valuable Monegasque stamps.*

Palace Square (Place du Palais): This square is the best place to get oriented to Monaco. Facing the palace, go to the right and

look out over the city (er... principality). This rock gave birth to the little pastel Hong Kong look-alike in 1215, and it's managed to remain an independent country for most of its nearly 800 years. Looking beyond the glitzy port, notice the faded green roof above and to the right: It belongs to the casino that put Monaco on the map. The famous Grand Prix runs along the port, and then up the ramp to the casino. And Italy is so close, you can almost smell the pesto. Just beyond the casino is France again (which flanks Monaco on both sides)—you could walk one-way from France to France, passing through Monaco in about 60 minutes.

The odd statue of a woman with a fishing net is dedicated to **Prince Albert I's** glorious reign (1889-1922). Albert was a Renaissance man with varied skills and interests. He had a Jacques Cousteau-like fascination with the sea (and built Monaco's famous aquarium), and was a determined pacifist who made many attempts to dissuade Germany's Kaiser Wilhelm II from becoming involved in World War I. It was Albert I's dad, Charles III, who built the casino.

• *Now walk toward the palace and find the statue of the monk grasping a sword.*

Meet **François Grimaldi,** a renegade Italian dressed as a monk, who captured Monaco in 1297 and began the dynasty that still rules the principality. Prince Albert is his great-great-great... grandson, which gives Monaco's royal family the distinction of being the longest-lasting dynasty in Europe.

• *Make your way to the...*

Prince's Palace (Palais Princier): A medieval castle sat where Monaco's palace is today. Its strategic setting has had a lot to do with Monaco's ability to resist attackers. Today, Prince Albert and his bride live in the palace, while poor Princesses Stephanie and Caroline live down the street. The palace guards protect the prince 24/7 and still stage a **Changing of the Guard** ceremony with all the pageantry of an important nation (daily at 11:55, fun to watch but jam-packed). Audioguide tours take you through part of the prince's lavish palace in 30 minutes. The rooms are well-furnished and impressive, but interesting only if you haven't seen a château lately (€8 combo-ticket includes audioguide and Napoleon Collection, €19 combo-ticket also includes Cousteau Aquarium; hours vary but generally April-Oct daily 10:00-18:00, closed Nov-March, last entry 30 minutes before closing; tel. 00-377/93 25 18 31).

• *Next to the palace entry is the...*

Napoleon Collection: Napoleon occupied Monaco after the French Revolution. This is the prince's private collection of items Napoleon left behind: military medals, swords, guns, letters, and— best—his hat. I found this collection more interesting than the palace (€4 includes audioguide, €8 combo-ticket includes Prince's Palace, €19 combo-ticket also includes Cousteau Aquarium; same hours as palace).

• *With your back to the palace, leave the square through the arch to the right side of the square (under the most beautiful police station I've ever seen) and find the...*

Cathedral of Monaco (Cathédrale de Monaco): The somber but beautifully lit cathedral, rebuilt in 1878, shows that Monaco cared for more than just its new casino. It's where centuries of Grimaldis are buried, and where Princess Grace and Prince Rainier were married. Circle slowly behind the altar (counterclockwise). The second tomb is that of Albert I, who did much to put Monaco on the world stage. The second-to-last tomb—inscribed *"Gratia Patricia, MCMLXXXII"*—is where Princess Grace was buried in 1982. Prince Rainier's tomb lies next to Princess Grace's (daily 8:30-19:15).

• *As you leave the cathedral, find the 1956 wedding photo of Princess Grace and Prince Rainier (keep an eye out for other photos of the couple as you walk), then dip into the immaculately maintained Jardin Botanique, with more fine views. In the gardens, turn left. Eventually you'll find the...*

Cousteau Aquarium (Musée Océanographique): Prince Albert I built this impressive, cliff-hanging aquarium in 1910 as a monument to his enthusiasm for things from the sea. The aquarium, which Captain Jacques Cousteau directed for 32 years, has 2,000 different specimens, representing 250 species. The bottom floor features Mediterranean fish and colorful tropical species (all nicely described in English). My favorite is the zebra lionfish, though I'm keen on eels, too. Rotating exhibits occupy the entry floor. Upstairs, the fancy Albert I Hall houses a museum (included in entry fee, very little English information) and features ship models, whale skeletons, oceanographic instruments and tools, and scenes of Albert and his beachcombers hard at work. Find the display on Christopher Columbus with English explanations.

Don't miss the elevator to the rooftop terrace view, where you'll also find convenient WCs and a reasonable café (aquarium-€14, kids-€7, €19 combo-ticket includes Prince's Palace and Napoleon Collection; daily July-Aug 10:00-19:30, April-June and Sept 10:00-19:00, Oct-March 10:00-18:00; down the steps from Monaco-Ville bus stop, at the opposite end of Monaco-Ville from the palace; tel. 00-377/93 15 36 00, www.oceano.mc).

• *The red-brick steps, across from the aquarium and a bit to the right, lead up to stops for buses #1 and #2, both of which run to the port, the casino, and the train station. To walk back to the palace and through the old city, turn left at the top of the brick steps. For a brief movie break, as you leave the aquarium, take the escalator to the right and drop into the parking garage, then take the elevator down and find the...*

Monte Carlo Story: This informative 35-minute film gives an entertaining and informative account of Monaco's fairy-tale history, from fishing village to jet-set principality, and offers a comfortable, soft-chair break from all that walking. The last part of the film was added to the original version after the death of Prince Rainier, which is why your sound stops early (€8, headphone commentary in English; daily showings usually at 14:00, 15:00, 16:00, and 17:00; there may be a morning showing for groups that you can join—ask, tel. 00-377/93 25 32 33).

Sights in Monaco

Above Monaco-Ville

Jardin Exotique

This cliffside municipal garden, located above Monaco-Ville, has eye-popping views from France to Italy. It's a fascinating home to more than a thousand species of cacti (some giant) and other suc-

Le Grand Prix Automobile de Monaco

Each May, the Grand Prix de Monaco focuses the world's attention on this little country. The race started as an enthusiasts' car rally by the Automobile Club of Monaco (and is still run by the same group, more than 80 years later). The first race, held in 1929, was won by a Bugatti at a screaming average speed of...48 mph (today's cars double that speed). To this day, drivers consider this one of the most important races on their circuits.

By Grand Prix standards, it's an unusual course, running through the streets of this tiny principality, sardined between mountains and sea. The hilly landscape means that the streets are narrow, with tight curves, steep climbs, and extremely short straightaways. Each lap is about two miles, beginning and ending at the port. Cars climb along the sea from the port, pass in front of the casino, race through the commercial district, and do a few dandy turns back to the port. The race lasts 78 laps, and whoever is still rolling at the end wins (most don't finish).

The Formula 1 cars look like overgrown toys that kids might pedal up and down their neighborhood street (if you're here a week or so before the race, feel free to browse the parking structure below Monaco-Ville, where many race cars are kept). Time trials to establish pole position begin three days before the race, which is always on a Sunday in late May (for dates, see www.grand-prix-monaco.com). More than 150,000 people attend the gala event; like the nearby film festival in Cannes, it's an excuse for yacht parties, restaurant splurges, and four-digit bar tabs at luxury hotels.

culent plants, but probably worth the entry only for view-loving botanists (some posted English explanations provided). Your ticket includes entry to a skippable natural cave and an anthropological museum, as well as a not-to-be-missed view snack bar/café. Bus #2 runs here from any stop in Monaco, and makes a worthwhile mini tour of the country, even if you don't visit the gardens. You can get similar views over Monaco for free from behind the souvenir stand at the Jardin's bus stop; or, for even grander vistas, cross the street and hike toward La Turbie.

Cost and Hours: €7.20, €10 combo-ticket with New National Museum of Monaco, daily May-Sept 9:00-19:00, Oct-April 9:00-18:00 or until dusk, tel. 00-377/93 15 29 80, www.jardin-exotique. com.

New National Museum of Monaco (Nouveau Musée National de Monaco)

This two-branch museum, which opened in 2011, hosts a series of rotating exhibits that highlight Monaco's cultural heritage, from works by famous artists to exhibits on the development of Monaco to current challenges facing the principality. The collection is split between two historic villas (ticket includes entrance to both): Villa Paloma (next to the Jardin Exotique at 56 Boulevard du Jardin Exotique) and Villa Sauber (17 Avenue Princesse Grace), east of the casino. To reach Villa Paloma, take bus #2 from any stop in Monaco; for Villa Sauber, take bus #6 from Place du Casino.

Cost and Hours: €6, €10 combo-ticket with Jardin Exotique, free first Sun of the month, daily June-Sept 11:00-19:00, Oct-May 8:00-18:00, Villa Paloma tel. 00-377/98 98 48 60, Villa Sauber tel. 00-377/98 98 91 26, www.nmnm.mc.

In Monte Carlo

▲Casino

Monte Carlo, which means "Charles' Hill" in Spanish, is named for the prince who presided over Monaco's 19th-century makeover. Begin your visit opposite Europe's most famous casino, in the park above the pedestrian-unfriendly traffic circle. In the mid-1800s, olive groves stood here. Then, with the construction of the casino and spas, and easy road and train access, one of Europe's poorest countries was on the Grand Tour map—*the* place for the vacationing aristocracy to play. Today, Monaco has the world's highest per-capita income.

The casino is intended to make you feel comfortable while losing money. Charles Garnier designed the place (with an opera house inside) in 1878, in part to thank the prince for his financial

help in completing Paris' Opéra Garnier (which the architect also designed). The central doors provide access to slot machines, private gaming rooms, and the opera house. The private gaming rooms occupy the left wing of the building.

The scene, flooded with camera-toting tourists during the day, is great at night—and downright James Bond-like in the private rooms. This is your chance to rub elbows with some high rollers—provided you're 18 or older (bring your passport as proof).

If paying an entrance fee to lose money is not your idea of fun, you can access all games for free in the plebeian, American-style casino, adjacent to the old casino.

Cost and Hours: The casino opens daily at 9:30 and stays open until the wee hours (there is no official closing time), but gambling is not allowed until 14:00. The **first gaming rooms** (Salle Renaissance, Salon de l'Europe, and Salle des Amériques) are free to enter after 14:00, with European and English roulette, blackjack, craps, and slot machines. You can pay €10 to visit in the morning to gawk—but not gamble—in the same rooms (daily 9:00-12:30, no dress code). The more glamorous **private game rooms** (Salons Touzet, Salle Medecin, and Terrasse Salle Blanche) cost €10 to enter and have the same games as above, plus Trente et Quarante, Ultimate Texas Hold 'Em poker, and Punto Banco—a version of baccarat.

Information: Tel. 00-377/92 16 20 00, www.montecarlocasinos.com.

Dress Code: During gambling hours, men need to wear a jacket and slacks. Dress standards for women are more relaxed—only tennis shoes and beach attire are definite no-no's.

Take the Money and Run: The stop for buses returning to Nice and Villefranche-sur-Mer, and for local buses #1 and #2, is at the top of the park, above the casino on Avenue de la Costa (under the arcade to the left). To get back to the train station from the casino, take bus #1 or #2 from this stop, or walk about 15 minutes down Avenue d'Ostende (just outside the casino) toward the port, and follow signs to *Gare SNCF* (see map).

Eating in Monaco

For general tips on eating in France, see page 276.

Several cafés serve basic, inexpensive fare (day and night) on the port. I prefer the eateries that line the flowery and traffic-free Rue de la Princesse Caroline, which runs between Rue Grimaldi and the port. The best this street has to offer is **Huit et Demi**. It has a white-tablecloth-meets-director's-chair ambience, mostly outdoor tables, and cuisine worth returning for (€15 salads, €15 pizzas, €18-24 *plats*, closed Sat for lunch and all day Sun, 7 Rue de la Princesse Caroline, tel. 00-377/93 50 97 02). For a simple and cheap salad or sandwich, find the **Crock'in** café farther down at 2 Rue de la Princesse Caroline (closed Sat, tel. 00-377/93 15 02 78).

In Monaco-Ville, You'll find incredible *pan bagnat* (*salade niçoise* sandwich), quiche, and sandwiches at the yellow-bannered **Boulangerie,** a block off Place du Palais (open daily until 21:00, 8 Rue Basse). Try a *barbajuan* (a spring roll-size beignet with wheat, rice, and Parmesan), the *tourta de bléa* (pastry stuffed with pine nuts, raisins, and white beets), or the focaccia sandwich (salted bread with herbs, mozzarella, basil, and tomatoes, all drenched in olive oil). For dessert, order the *fougasse monégasque* (a soft-bread pastry topped with sliced almonds and anise candies).

The best-value restaurant in Monaco-Ville is **U Cavagnetu**—and it's no secret. You'll dine very cheaply on specialties from Monaco just a block from Albert's palace (€13-18 *plats*, €26 *menu*, daily, 14 Rue Comte Félix Gastaldi, tel. 00-377/97 98 20 40). Monaco-Ville has other pizzerias, *crêperies*, and sandwich stands, but the neighborhood is dead at night.

Cannes

Located to the west of Nice, Cannes (pronounced "can")—famous for its film festival—is the sister city of Beverly Hills. That says it all. When I asked at the TI for a list of museums and sights,

they just smiled. Cannes—with big, exclusive hotels lining mostly private stretches of perfect, sandy beach—is for strolling, shopping, dreaming of meeting a movie star, and lounging on the seafront. Cannes has little that's unique to offer the traveler...except a mostly off-limits film festival and quick access to two undeveloped islands. Money is what Cannes has always been about—wealthy people come here to make the scene, so there's always enough *scandale* to go around. The king of Saudi Arabia purchased a serious slice of waterfront just east of town and built his compound with no regard to local zoning regulations. Money talks on the Riviera...and always has.

Arrival at the Port of Cannes

Cruise ships tender passengers to the west side of Cannes' port. From here, it's an easy walk into town: Just head inland, with the port on your right-hand side. As you walk, you'll pass ticket windows selling seats for various offshore excursions, and across the port you'll see the Film Festival Hall. (The tender dock is near the end of my self-guided walk; you can either start the walk here and do it in reverse; or you can stroll about 10 minutes around the port to the walk's starting point—in the park just beyond the Film Festival Hall.)

Tourist Information: There's no TI at the port, but you will find TIs at the film festival office (see "Orientation to Cannes," later).

Getting into Town

It's about a 15-minute walk from the tender dock to the **train station:** Go up to the square at the top of the port. Walk to the far end of the square, and exit at its top-right corner, onto Rue Maréchal. Bear right up Rue Vénizélos, and you'll pop out at the train station. From here, trains run twice hourly to **Antibes** (15 minutes), **Nice** (30-40 minutes), **Villefranche-sur-Mer** (50 minutes), and points beyond.

Orientation to Cannes

It's a breeze to visit Cannes—you can buy an ice-cream cone at the train station and see everything before you've had your last lick.

Arrival in Cannes by Train or Bus: Trains pull into the centrally located station on Place de la Gare, and buses arrive right next door.

Tourist Information: Cannes' glamorously quiet TI is located in the Film Festival Hall at 1 Boulevard de la Croisette (daily July-Aug 9:00-20:00, Sept-June 10:00-19:00).

Cannes Walk

This self-guided walking tour will take you to Cannes' sights in a level, one-hour walk at a movie-star pace. Well-kept WCs are available in the lobbies of any large hotel you pass.

• *From the train station, cross the street and walk for five unimpressive minutes down Rue des Serbes to the beachfront. Cross the busy Boulevard de la Croisette and make your way past snack stands to the sea. Find the round lookout and get familiar with...*

The Lay of the Land: Cannes feels different from its neighbors to the east. You won't find the distinctive pastel oranges and pinks of Old Nice and Villefranche-sur-Mer. Cannes was never part of Italy—and through its architecture and cuisine, it shows.

Face the water. The land jutting into the sea on your left is actually two islands, St. Honorat and Ste. Marguerite. **St. Honorat** has been the property of monks for over 500 years; today its abbey, vineyards, trails, and gardens can be visited by peace-seeking travelers. **Ste. Marguerite,** which you also can visit, is famous for the stone prison that housed the 17th-century Man in the Iron Mask (whose true identity remains unknown).

Handy Cannes Phrases

Where is a movie star?	Où est une vedette?
I am a movie star.	Je suis une vedette.
I am rich and single.	Je suis riche et célibataire.
Are you rich and single?	Etes-vous riche et célibataire?
Are those real?	Ils sont des vrais?
How long is your yacht?	Quelle est la longeur de votre yacht?
How much did that cost?	Combien coûtait-il?
You can always dream...	On peut toujours rêver...

Now look to your right. Those striking mountains sweeping down to the sea are the Massif de l'Esterel. Their red-rock outcrops oversee spectacular car and train routes. Closer in, the hill with the medieval tower caps Cannes' old town (Le Suquet). This hilltop offers grand views and pretty lanes, but little else. Below the old town, the port welcomes yachts of all sizes...provided they're big.

Face inland. On the left, find the modern, cream-colored building that's home to the famous film festival (we'll visit there soon). Back the other way, gaze up the boulevard. That classy building with twin black-domed roofs is Hôtel Carlton, our eventual target and as far as we'll go together in that direction.

• *Continue with the sea on your right and stroll the...*

Promenade (La Croisette): You're walking along Boulevard de la Croisette—Cannes' famed two-mile-long promenade. First popular with kings who wintered here after Napoleon fell, the elite parade was later joined by British aristocracy. Today, Boulevard de la Croisette is fronted by some of the most expensive apartments and hotels in Europe. If it's lunchtime, you might try one of the beach cafés—Brad Pitt did. **Plage le**

Goéland's café has fair-enough prices and appealing decor (daily, closest private beach to the Film Festival Hall, tel. 04 93 38 22 05).

• *Stop when you get to...*

Hôtel Carlton: This is the most famous address on Boulevard de la Croisette (allow €1,300-6,000 per night). Face the beach. The iconic Cannes experience is to slip out of your luxury hotel (preferably this one), into a robe (ideally, monogrammed with your ini-

THE FRENCH RIVIERA

tials), and onto the beach—
or, better yet, onto the pier
(this avoids getting irritating
sand on your carefully oiled
skin). While you may not be
doing the "fancy hotel and
monogrammed robe" ritual
on this Cannes excursion,
you can—for about €25—
rent a chair and umbrella and

pretend you're tanning for a red-carpet premiere. Cannes does have
a few token public beaches, but most beaches are private and run by
hotels like the Carlton. You could save money by sunning among
the common folk, but the real Cannes way to flee the rabble and
paparazzi is to rent a spot on a private beach (best to reserve ahead
in July-Aug).

Cross over and wander into the hotel—you're welcome to
browse (except during the festival). Ask for a hotel brochure, verify
room rates, check for availability. Can all these people really afford
this? Imagine the scene here during the film festival (see anyone
famous?). A surprisingly affordable café (considering the cost of a
room) lies just beyond.

• *You can continue your stroll down La Croisette, but I'm doubling back
to the cream-colored building that is Cannes'...*

Film Festival Hall: Cannes' film festival (Festival de Cannes),
staged since 1946, completes the "Big Three" of Riviera events
(with Monaco's Grand Prix
and Nice's Carnival). The hall
where the festival takes place—
a busy-but-nondescript convention center that also hosts
the town TI—sits like a plump
movie star on the beach. You'll
recognize the formal grand
entryway—but the red carpet
won't be draped for your visit.

Find the famous (Hollywood-style) handprints in the sidewalk all
around. To get inside during the festival, you have to be a star (or
a photographer—some 3,000 paparazzi attend the gala event, and
most bring their own ladders to get above the crowds).

The festival originated in part as an anti-fascist response to
Mussolini's Venice Film Festival. Cannes' first festival was due to
open in 1939, on the very day Hitler invaded Poland. Thanks to
what followed (World War II), the opening was delayed until 1946
(in 2002 they screened the films that would have been shown in
1939). Cannes' film festival is also famous as the first festival to

give one vote per country on the jury (giving films from smaller countries a fighting chance).

Though off-limits to us, the festival is all that matters around here—and is worth a day trip to Cannes if you happen to be in the region when it's on. The town buzzes with mega-star energy, press passes, and revealing dresses. Locals claim that it's the world's third-biggest media event, after the Olympics and the World Cup (soccer). The festival prize is the Palme d'Or (like the Oscar for Best Picture). The French press can't cover the event enough, and the average Jean in France follows it as Joe would the World Series in the States.

• *Around the other side of the festival hall is the port (Gare Maritime).*

The Port and Old Town (Le Suquet): The big-boy yachts line up closest to the Film Festival Hall. After seeing this yacht frenzy, everything else looks like a dinghy. Boat service to St-Tropez and the nearby islands of St. Honorat and Ste. Marguerite depart from the far side of the port (at Quai Laubeuf; for boat info, see "Sights in Cannes," later).

Cannes' oldest neighborhood, Le Suquet, crowns the hill past the port. Locals refer to it as their Montmartre. It's artsy and charming, but it's a steep 15-minute walk above the port, with little of interest except the panoramic views from its ancient church, Notre-Dame-de-l'Espérance (Our Lady of Hope).

• *To find the views in Le Suquet, walk past the bus station at the northwest corner of the port and make your way up cobbled Rue Saint-Antoine (next to the Café St. Antoine). Turn left on Place du Suquet, and then follow signs to* Traverse de la Tour *for the final leg.*

Cue music. Roll end credits. Our film is over. For further exploration, look for Cannes' "underbelly" between Le Suquet and the train station—narrow lanes with inexpensive cafés and shops that regular folks can afford.

Sights in Cannes

Shopping

Cannes is made for window-shopping (the best streets are between the station and the waterfront). For the trendiest boutiques, stroll down handsome Rue d'Antibes (it parallels the sea about three blocks inland). Rue Meynadier anchors a pedestrian zone with more affordable shops closer to the port. To bring home a real surprise, consider cosmetic surgery. Cannes is well-known as *the* place on the Riviera to have your face (or other parts) realigned.

Excursions to St. Honorat and Ste. Marguerite Islands

Boats ferry tourists 15 minutes to these twin islands just off Cannes' shore (€13 round-trip, daily 9:00-18:00, 1-2/hour, www.trans-cote-azur.com, no ferry runs between the 2 islands). The islands

offer a refreshing change from the frenetic mainland, with almost no development, good swimming, and peaceful walking paths. On Ste. Marguerite you can visit the castle and cell where the mysterious Man in the Iron Mask was imprisoned (good little museum with decent English explanations featuring cargo from a sunken Roman vessel). On St. Honorat you can hike seafront trails and visit the abbey where monks still live and pray.

Excursions to St-Tropez

Trans Côte d'Azur runs boat excursions from Cannes to St-Tropez (€46 round-trip, 1.25 hours each way; July-Aug daily 1/day; June and Sept 1/day Tue, Thu, and Sat-Sun only; no service Oct-May; tel. 04 92 98 71 30, www.trans-cote-azur.com). This boat trip is popular—book a few days ahead from June to September.

Eating in Cannes

For a tasty, easy lunch in Cannes, consider **Fournil St. Nicholas.** You'll get mouthwatering quiche and sandwiches and exquisite salads at affordable prices (leaving the train station, turn right and walk a few blocks to 5 Rue Venizelos, tel. 04 93 38 81 12).

Antibes

Antibes has a down-to-earth, easygoing ambience that's rare in this area. Its old town is a maze of narrow streets and red-tile roofs rising above the blue Med, protected by twin medieval towers and wrapped in extensive ramparts. Visitors can browse Europe's biggest yacht harbor, snooze on a sandy beach, loiter through an enjoyable old town, and hike along a sea-swept trail. The town's cultural claim to fame, the Picasso Museum, shows off its great collection in a fine old building.

Antibes' old town lies between the port and Boulevard Albert 1er and Avenue Robert Soleau. Place Nationale is the old town's hub of activity. The restaurant-lined Rue Aubernon connects the port and the old town. Stroll along the sea between the old port and Place Albert 1er (where Boulevard Albert 1er meets the water). The best beaches lie just beyond Place Albert 1er, and the walk is beautiful. Good play areas for children are along this path and on Place des Martyrs de la Résistance.

Orientation to Antibes

Tourist Information

Antibes has two TIs: one in a kiosk across the street from the **train station** (May-Sept only, Mon-Sat 9:00-12:00 & 14:00-18:00, closed Sun), and the main TI on **Place Général de Gaulle** where the fountains squirt (July-Aug daily 9:00-19:00; Sept-June Mon-Fri 9:00-12:30 & 13:30-18:00, Sat 9:00-12:00 & 14:00-18:00, Sun 10:00-12:30 & 14:30-17:00; tel. 04 97 23 11 11, www.antibesjuan-lespins.com). At either TI, pick up the excellent city map and the self-guided walking tour of old Antibes. The Nice TI has Antibes maps and the Antibes TI has Nice maps—plan ahead.

Arrival in Antibes by Train and Bus

By Train: Bus #14 runs every 30 minutes from the train station (bus stop 50 yards to right as you exit station) to the *gare routière* (bus station; near the main TI and old town), and continues to the fine Plage de la Salis with quick access to the Phare de la Garoupe trail. **Taxis** are usually waiting in front of the train station.

To **walk** to the port, the old town, and the Picasso Museum (15-20 minutes), cross the street in front of the station, skirting left of Piranha's Café, and follow Avenue de la Libération downhill as it bends left. At the end of the street, head right along the port, and continue until you reach the end of the parking lots, then turn right into the old town.

By Bus: Buses from most destinations use the **bus station** at the edge of the old town on Place Guynemer, a block below the main TI on Place Général de Gaulle (info desk open Mon-Fri 7:30-19:00, Sat 8:30-12:00 & 14:30-17:30, closed Sun, www.envibus.fr).

Helpful Hints

Monday, Monday: Avoid Antibes on Mondays, when all sights are closed.

Internet Access: Centrally located **l'Outil du Web** is two blocks from the Place Général de Gaulle TI—walk toward the train station (Mon-Fri 9:30-18:30, closed Sat-Sun, 11 Avenue Robert Soleau, tel. 04 93 74 11 86).

English Bookstore: Heidi's English Bookshop has a welcoming vibe and a great selection of new and used books, with many guidebooks—including mine (Tue-Sat 9:00-19:00, Sun-Mon 11:00-18:00, 24 Rue Aubernon, tel. 04 93 34 74 11).

Grocery Stores: Picnickers will appreciate **L'Épicerie du Marché** on Cours Masséna, up the hill as you exit the Marché Provençal (daily until 23:00). **L'Épicerie de la Place** has a smaller selection (daily until 22:00 in summer, until 21:00 off-season, where Rue Sade meets Place Nationale). A large **Monoprix** is located next door to the TI on Place Général de Gaulle (Mon-Sat 8:30-20:30, Sun 9:00-12:30).

Taxi: For a taxi, call tel. 04 93 67 67 67.

Car Rental: The big-name agencies have offices in Antibes (all close Mon-Sat 12:00-14:00 and all day Sun). The most central are **Avis** (at the train station, tel. 04 93 34 65 15) and **Hertz** (across from the train station at 46 Avenue Robert Soleau, tel. 04 92 91 28 00). **Europcar** is about 1.5 miles northwest of town at 106 Route de Grasse (tel. 04 93 34 79 79).

Boat Rental: You can motor your own seven-person yacht thanks to **Antibes Bateaux Services** (€300/half-day, at the small fish market on the port, mobile 06 15 75 44 36, www.antibes-bateaux.com).

Getting Around Antibes

Though most sights and activities are walkable, buses are a great value in Antibes, allowing one hour of travel for €1 (one-way or round-trip, unlimited transfers, www.envibus.fr). **Bus #2** provides access to the best beaches and hikes. It runs from the bus station down Boulevard Albert 1er, with stops every few blocks (daily 7:00-19:00, every 40 minutes). **Bus #14** is also useful, linking the train station, bus station, old town, and Plage de la Salis.

A **tourist train** offers circuits around old Antibes, the port, and the ramparts (€8, departs from pedestrian-only Rue de la République, mobile 06 15 77 67 47).

Sights in Antibes

Antibes' port was enlarged in the 1970s to accommodate ever-expanding yacht dimensions. The work was financed by wealthy yacht owners (mostly Saudi Arabian) eager for a place to park their aircraft carriers. That old four-pointed structure crowning the opposite end of the port is **Fort Carré**, which protected Antibes from foreigners for more than 500 years. The pathetic remains of a once-hearty **fishing fleet** are moored in front of you. The Mediterranean is pretty much fished out. Most of the seafood you'll eat here comes from fish farms or the Atlantic.

Antibes' **old town** is the haunt of a large community of English, Irish, and Aussie boaters who help crew those giant yachts in Antibes' port. (That explains the Irish pubs and English bookstores.) Continue straight and uphill (halfway up on the right, you'll pass Rue Clemenceau, which leads to the heart of the old town), and you'll arrive at Antibes' **market hall**. This hall does double duty—market by day, restaurants by night (a fun place for dinner). Near the market is the pretty pastel **Church of the Immaculate Conception,** built on the site of a Greek temple (worth a peek inside). A church has stood on this site since the 12th century. This one served as the area's cathedral until the mid-1200s.

Looming above the church on prime real estate is the whitestone **Château Grimaldi.** This site has been home to the acropolis of the Greek city of Antipolis, a Roman fort, and a medieval bishop's palace (once connected to the cathedral below). Today this is where you'll find the compact three-floor **Picasso Museum,** which offers a manageable collection of Picasso's paintings, sketches, and ceramics. Picasso lived in this castle for four months in 1946, when he cranked out an amazing amount of art. He was elated by the end of World War II, and his works show a celebration of color and a rediscovery of light after France's long nightmare of war (€6; mid-June-mid-Sept Tue-Sun 10:00-18:00, July-Aug Wed and Fri until 20:00; mid-Sept-mid-June Tue-Sun 10:00-12:00 & 14:00-18:00, closed Mon year-round, last entry 30 minutes before closing, tel. 04 92 90 54 20, www.antibes-juanlespins.com).

The best **beaches** stretch between Antibes' port and Cap d'Antibes. The first you'll cross is Plage Publique (no rentals required). Next are the groomed Plage de la Salis and Plage du Ponteil (with mattress, umbrella, and towel rental). All are busy but manageable in summer and on weekends, with cheap snack stands and exceptional views of the old town. The closest beach to the old town is at the port (Plage de la Gravette), which seems calm in any season.

More Sights on the French Riviera

Eze-le-Village

Floating high above the sea, flowery and flawless Eze-le-Village (don't confuse it with the seafront town of Eze-Bord-de-Mer) is entirely consumed by tourism. This *village d'art et de gastronomie* (as it calls itself) nurtures perfume outlets, stylish boutiques, steep cobbled lanes, and magnificent views. Touristy as this place certainly Eze, its stony state of preservation and magnificent hilltop setting over the Mediterranean may lure you away from the beaches. Day-tripping by bus to Eze-le-Village from Nice, Monaco, or Villefranche-sur-Mer works well, provided you know the bus schedules (ask at TIs).

What If I Miss My Boat?

Remember that you can get help from the cruise line's port agent (listed on the destination information sheet distributed on the ship) and the local TI (see page 311 for Nice, page 340 for Villefranche-sur-Mer, page 361 for Cannes, or page 352 for Monaco). If the port agent suggests a costly solution (such as a private car with a driver), you may want to consider public transit.

Frequent **trains** connect **Nice, Villefranche-sur-Mer, Monaco,** and **Cannes.** The train is also a good option for **Marseille** and **Toulon.** Spanish and Italian ports—such as **Barcelona, Livorno, Civitavecchia,** and **Naples**—are also reachable, but require multiple changes.

To look up specific connections, use http://en.voyages-sncf.com/en (domestic journeys only) or www.bahn.com (Germany's excellent all-Europe schedule website). For other ports (in Croatia, Greece, and Turkey), you'll probably have to fly.

Nice's easy-to-navigate **airport** (Aéroport de Nice Côte d'Azur) is a 20- to 30-minute taxi or bus ride west of the city center (airport code: NCE, toll tel. 08 20 42 33 33, www.nice.aeroport.fr).

Any local **travel agent** also should be able to help. For more advice on what to do if you miss the boat, see page 140.

St-Tropez

St-Tropez is a busy, charming, and traffic-free port town smothered with fashion boutiques, elegant restaurants, and luxury boats. The village itself is the attraction, as the nearest big beach is miles away. Wander the harborfront, where fancy yachts moor stern-in, their carefully coiffed captains and first mates enjoying *pu-pus* for happy hour—they're seeing and being seen. Take time to stroll the back streets while nibbling a chocolate-and-Grand Marnier crêpe.

In St-Tropez, window-shopping, people-watching, tan maintenance, and savoring slow meals fill people's days, weeks, and, in some cases, lives. Here, one dresses up, sizes up one another's yachts, and trolls for a partner. While the only models you'll see are in the shop windows, Brigitte Bardot sometimes hangs out on a bench in front of the TI signing autographs.

St-Paul-de-Vence

The most famous of Riviera hill towns is also the most visited village in France. And it feels that way—like an overrun and over-restored artist-shopping-mall. Its attraction is understandable, as every cobble and flower seems *just-so*, and the setting is memorable.

The inviting, pricey, and far-out Fondation Maeght, a private museum, is situated a steep 20-minute walk or short taxi ride above St-Paul-de-Vence.

Fondation Maeght offers an excellent introduction to modern Mediterranean art by gathering many of the Riviera's most famous artists under one roof. The unusual museum building is purposefully low-profile, to let its world-class modern-art collection take center stage. Works by Fernand Léger, Joan Miró, Alexander Calder, Georges Braque, and Marc Chagall are thoughtfully arranged in well-lit rooms. The backyard of the museum has views, a Gaudí-esque sculpture labyrinth by Miró, and a courtyard filled with the wispy works of Alberto Giacometti.

French Survival Phrases

When using the phonetics, try to nasalize the n̲ sound.

English	French	Pronunciation
Good day.	Bonjour.	bohn̲-zhoor
Mrs. / Mr.	Madame / Monsieur	mah-dahm / muhs-yur
Do you speak English?	Parlez-vous anglais?	par-lay-voo ahn̲-glay
Yes. / No.	Oui. / Non.	wee / nohn̲
I understand.	Je comprends.	zhuh kohn̲-prahn̲
I don't understand.	Je ne comprends pas.	zhuh nuh kohn̲-prahn̲ pah
Please.	S'il vous plaît.	see voo play
Thank you.	Merci.	mehr-see
I'm sorry.	Désolé.	day-zoh-lay
Excuse me.	Pardon.	par-dohn̲
(No) problem.	(Pas de) problème.	(pah duh) proh-blehm
It's good.	C'est bon.	say bohn̲
Goodbye.	Au revoir.	oh vwahr
one / two	un / deux	uhn̲ / duh
three / four	trois / quatre	twah / kah-truh
five / six	cinq / six	sank / sees
seven / eight	sept / huit	seht / weet
nine / ten	neuf / dix	nuhf / dees
How much is it?	Combien?	kohn̲-bee-an̲
Write it?	Ecrivez?	ay-kree-vay
Is it free?	C'est gratuit?	say grah-twee
Included?	Inclus?	an̲-klew
Where can I buy / find...?	Où puis-je acheter / trouver...?	oo pwee-zhuh ah-shuh-tay / troo-vay
I'd like / We'd like...	Je voudrais / Nous voudrions...	zhuh voo-dray / noo voo-dree-ohn̲
...a room.	...une chambre.	ewn shahn̲-bruh
...a ticket to ___.	...un billet pour ___.	uhn̲ bee-yay poor ___
Is it possible?	C'est possible?	say poh-see-bluh
Where is...?	Où est...?	oo ay
...the train station	...la gare	lah gar
...the bus station	...la gare routière	lah gar root-yehr
...tourist information	...l'office du tourisme	loh-fees dew too-reez-muh
Where are the toilets?	Où sont les toilettes?	oo sohn̲ lay twah-leht
men	hommes	ohm
women	dames	dahm
left / right	à gauche / à droite	ah gohsh / ah dwaht
straight	tout droit	too dwah
When does this open / close?	Ça ouvre / ferme à quelle heure?	sah oo-vruh / fehrm ah kehl ur
At what time?	À quelle heure?	ah kehl ur
Just a moment.	Un moment.	uhn̲ moh-mahn̲
now / soon / later	maintenant / bientôt / plus tard	man̲-tuh-nahn̲ / bee-an̲-toh / plew tar
today / tomorrow	aujourd'hui / demain	oh-zhoor-dwee / duh-man̲

THE FRENCH RIVIERA

In a French Restaurant

English	French	Pronunciation
I'd like / We'd like...	Je voudrais / Nous voudrions...	zhuh voo-dray / noo voo-dree-oh<u>n</u>
...to reserve...	...réserver...	ray-zehr-vay
...a table for one / two.	...une table pour un / deux.	ewn tah-bluh poor uh<u>n</u> / duh
Is this seat free?	C'est libre?	say lee-bruh
The menu (in English), please.	La carte (en anglais), s'il vous plaît.	lah kart (ah<u>n</u> ah<u>n</u>-glay) see voo play
service (not) included	service (non) compris	sehr-vees (noh<u>n</u>) koh<u>n</u>-pree
to go	à emporter	ah ah<u>n</u>-por-tay
with / without	avec / sans	ah-vehk / sah<u>n</u>
and / or	et / ou	ay / oo
special of the day	plat du jour	plah dew zhoor
specialty of the house	spécialité de la maison	spay-see-ah-lee-tay duh lah may-zoh<u>n</u>
appetizers	hors d'oeuvre	or duh-vruh
first course (soup, salad)	entrée	ah<u>n</u>-tray
main course (meat, fish)	plat principal	plah pra<u>n</u>-see-pahl
bread	pain	pa<u>n</u>
cheese	fromage	froh-mahzh
sandwich	sandwich	sah<u>n</u>d-weech
soup	soupe	soop
salad	salade	sah-lahd
meat	viande	vee-ah<u>n</u>d
chicken	poulet	poo-lay
fish	poisson	pwah-soh<u>n</u>
seafood	fruits de mer	frwee duh mehr
fruit	fruit	frwee
vegetables	légumes	lay-gewm
dessert	dessert	day-sehr
mineral water	eau minérale	oh mee-nay-rahl
tap water	l'eau du robinet	loh dew roh-bee-nay
milk	lait	lay
(orange) juice	jus (d'orange)	zhew (doh-rah<u>n</u>zh)
coffee / tea	café / thé	kah-fay / tay
wine	vin	va<u>n</u>
red / white	rouge / blanc	roozh / blah<u>n</u>
glass / bottle	verre / bouteille	vehr / boo-tay
beer	bière	bee-ehr
Cheers!	Santé!	sah<u>n</u>-tay
More. / Another.	Plus. / Un autre.	plew / uh<u>n</u> oh-truh
The same.	La même chose.	lah mehm shohz
The bill, please.	L'addition, s'il vous plaît.	lah-dee-see-oh<u>n</u> see voo play
Do you accept credit cards?	Vous prenez les cartes?	voo pruh-nay lay kart
tip	pourboire	poor-bwahr
Delicious!	Délicieux!	day-lee-see-uh

For more user-friendly French phrases, check out *Rick Steves'
French Phrase Book and Dictionary* or *Rick Steves' French, Italian
& German Phrase Book*.

FLORENCE
Italy

Italy Practicalities

Stretching 850 miles long and 150 miles wide, art-drenched Italy is the cradle of European civilization. Visitors here come face to face with some of the world's most iconic images: Rome's ancient Colosseum, Pisa's medieval Leaning Tower, Venice's romantic canals.

Italy's 61 million inhabitants are more social and communal than most other Europeans. Because they're so outgoing and their language is so fun, Italians are a pleasure to communicate with. This boot-shaped country has all the elements that make travel to Europe forever fresh and rewarding: visible history, lively people, and fun by the minute.

Money: Italy uses the euro currency: 1 euro (€) = about $1.30. An ATM is called a *bancomat.* The local VAT (value-added sales tax) rate is 22 percent; the minimum purchase eligible for a VAT refund is €155 (for details on refunds, see page 135).

Language: For useful Italian phrases, see page 485.

Emergencies: Dial 113 for police or 118 for medical emergencies. In case of theft or loss, see page 128.

Time Zone: Italy is on Central European Time (the same as most of the Continent, and six/nine hours ahead of the East/West Coasts of the US).

Theft Alert: Assume that beggars are pickpockets and any scuffle is simply a distraction by a team of thieves. For more on outsmarting thieves, see page 128.

Consular Services: The US embassy in Rome is at Via Vittorio Veneto 121 (24-hour tel. 06-46741, http://italy.usembassy. gov); consular services are also available in Florence (tel. 055-266-951) and Naples (tel. 081-583-8111). The Canadian Embassy in Rome is at Via Zara 30 (tel. 06-854-441, www.italy. gc.ca). Call ahead for passport services.

Phoning: Italy has a direct-dial phone system (no area codes). To **call within Italy,** just dial the number (keep in mind that Italian phone numbers vary in length). To **call to Italy,** dial the international access code (00 if calling from Europe, or 011 from North America), then dial 39 (Italy's country code), then the phone number. To **call home from Italy,** dial 00, 1, then your area code and phone number. For more help, see page 1242.

Dress Code: Some major churches enforce a modest dress code (no bare shoulders or shorts).

Tipping: A service charge *(servicio)* of about 10 percent is usually built into your restaurant bill. If you are pleased with the service, you can add an extra euro or two for each person in your party. If service isn't included *(servizio non incluso)*, add a tip of about 10 percent. To tip a cabbie, round up your fare a bit (to pay a €4.50 fare, give €5).

Tourist Information: www.italia.it

FLORENCE, PISA, LUCCA
and the Port of Livorno

The port of Livorno gives cruisers access to Italy's justifiably famous region of Tuscany. While there are many Tuscan treats to consider, for most the top attraction is Florence.

Florence is Europe's cultural capital. As the home of the Renaissance and the birthplace of the modern world, Florence practiced the art of civilized living back when the rest of Europe was rural and crude. Democracy, science, and literature, as well as painting, sculpture, and architecture, were all championed by the proud and energetic Florentines of the 1400s.

Today, Florence is geographically small but culturally rich, with more artistic masterpieces per square mile than anyplace else.

In a single day, you could look Michelangelo's *David* in the eyes, fall under the seductive sway of Botticelli's *Birth of Venus,* and climb the modern world's first dome, which still dominates the skyline.

The port of Livorno is also within easy striking distance of two other great cities. Pisa's famous Field of Miracles (Leaning Tower, Duomo, and Baptistery) is touristy but worth a visit. Lucca, contained within its fine Renaissance wall, has a charm that causes many connoisseurs of Italy to claim it as a favorite stop.

And Livorno itself, while extensively bombed during World War II, has a charm of its own. If you've already seen both Florence and Pisa, and want to split your day between seeing the action on shore and relaxing on your cruise ship's pool deck, it's easy to spend a couple of hours enjoying Italy

Excursions from Livorno

The top choices, of course, are **Florence, Pisa,** and **Lucca.**

The following destinations are farther afield, with less-straightforward public-transportation connections—they're best done by shore excursion or with a hired driver.

Siena is a red-brick hilltop city known for its pageantry, Palio horse race, and a stunning traffic-free main square.

The Cinque Terre consists of five idyllic Riviera hamlets along a rugged coastline, connected by scenic hiking trails and dotted with beaches.

San Gimignano is a small, picturesque hill town, spiked with medieval towers and swarming with tourists.

Volterra, a more remote hill town, has wine bars, alabaster workshops, Etruscan sights, and few crowds.

in port. If you don't need famous sights, Livorno is as good as any other Italian city.

Planning Your Time

For most travelers, the best choice is to make a beeline to Florence. Another good option is going to Pisa and, if you're interested, the neighboring town of Lucca as well. Read the descriptions in this book to decide which destination(s) most appeals to you.

If you choose Florence, don't try to combine it with any other destination; it'll take you two hours just to get from the port of Livorno to Florence. You have three good options for getting into town: take the train; share a minibus taxi (arrange this at the dock); or take a cruise-line excursion (either fully guided or transportation-only—see page 108).

No matter where you go, if you're taking the train, keep in mind that it takes 30-45 minutes just to get from Livorno's cruise port to the train station across town. Also, be sure to plan your day conservatively, as trains can be delayed.

Florence

Florence's sights are concentrated in its compact core. The city's two top sights—the Accademia and Uffizi Gallery—are plagued with long ticket-buying lines; it's smart to book entry times in advance or get a Firenze Card (see page 396). If you don't reserve ahead and plan to wait in line, visit your preferred sight first, then see if you have time for the other. Note that both sights are closed on Monday.

Allow nine hours for visiting Florence, including transportation from your cruise ship and back. I'd suggest seeing the sights in this order, following my self-guided walk and tours:

Destinations Near Livorno

• Tour the Accademia, starring Michelangelo's *David*. Allow 30 minutes inside. Then head down Via Ricasoli to the Duomo (10-minute walk).

• Take my self-guided Florence Renaissance Walk, starting at the Duomo. If you're in a hurry, you can walk to the Uffizi Gallery in 10 minutes, but I'd allow up to two hours.

• Tour the Uffizi Gallery, famous for its Renaissance art. Allow up to two hours inside.

• Any additional time is well spent at Ponte Vecchio (shop-lined bridge over the Arno), the Bargello (sculpture museum near the Uffizi), or shopping at the San Lorenzo Market (a short walk north of the Duomo). If you're more interested in shopping than sightseeing, see page 449.

Pisa and Lucca

You can visit either or both towns easily from Livorno using public transportation. At a bare minimum, Pisa and Lucca each deserve at least a two-hour stop (plus transportation time from your ship).

For **Pisa,** allow a minimum of four hours, including transportation from your cruise ship and back. If you want to climb the Leaning Tower, add an hour—or potentially longer, if you didn't reserve ahead (see page 467).

Lucca alone deserves at least five hours (including transportation), which gives you enough time to stroll the town and rent a bike for a spin around the wall.

To do **both Pisa and Lucca,** allow yourself six hours mini-mum (including transportation), and skip climbing Pisa's Leaning Tower; you'll need more time to make it satisfying.

Below are details for each of these options.

FLORENCE

Italian Experiences for Cruisers

Beyond the "must-see" sights in Italy, there are also countless small ways to taste authentic Italian culture. Try these activities.

Sample some gelato. Gelato is a type of ice cream made with less fat and more sugar than typical American ice creams, and—thanks to inventive gelato makers—often more pungent flavors. For the top gelato parlors in Florence (which has, purists claim, the best gelato in Italy), see the sidebar on page 456.

Step inside a church to ogle some art. Italian churches have some astonishing masterpieces by some of the greatest names in art history. Even better, many can be viewed in situ—in the place for which the art was designed. I've described some of the most famous churches in this book, but even off-the-beaten-path churches can contain some remarkable artwork. Just remember that you'll likely need to cover your knees and shoulders when you enter a church.

Assemble a cheap lunch at a deli. Find a hole-in-the-wall shop with an enticing window display, and head inside to order 50 grams each of cheese and salami. Don't get just the basic kind—try something you've never had before.

Pisa Only

If you're going only to Pisa, you'll have time to see the city beyond its famous tower. After arriving at the train station, follow this plan:

• Take my self-guided walk (allow up to an hour) from the train station to the Field of Miracles to see the Leaning Tower. To get there quicker, take the city bus from the station (15 minutes).

• If you want to climb the Leaning Tower and don't have a reservation, go straight to the Tower's ticket office to snag an appointment—usually for a couple of hours later. Allow an hour to ascend the Tower.

• Visit the sights on the Field of Miracles—specifically the Baptistery (eerie acoustics) and Duomo (distinctive architecture). Allow one hour.

Lucca Only

Lucca is a pleasant town with a walkable wall. Note that many of the town's stores and museums are closed on Sundays and Mondays.

When in Lucca, consider the following:

• Walk part or all of the 2.5-mile wall that encircles the city. Or do it by rental bike.

• Stroll the town, dipping into a few churches or museums if you like.

Both Pisa and Lucca

It's logistically wise to begin in Lucca (the farthest point), then work your way back toward Livorno. Starting in Livorno, catch the train to the Pisa Centrale Station, where you'll change to the Lucca-bound train. After you visit Lucca, take the hourly, 30-minute, direct bus from Lucca's Piazzale Verdi to Pisa's Field of Miracles and Leaning Tower. When you're done, ride the city bus across town to the Pisa Centrale train station for the 20-minute ride back to Livorno's station (remember, it's another 30-45 minutes from Livorno's station back to your ship).

If you have your heart set on Pisa, but are only so-so on Lucca, head straight to Pisa, then decide if you have enough time to squeeze in a side-trip to Lucca—you'll be halfway there already.

Arrival at the Port of Livorno

FLORENCE

Arrival at a Glance: Ride the port shuttle bus (or walk) into Livorno's town center, Piazza del Municipio. From here, you can catch a local public bus to the train station (10 minutes). Inexpensive trains go to Florence (1.5 hours), Pisa (20 minutes), and Lucca (about 1 hour, change in Pisa). There's also a direct bus from downtown Livorno to Pisa (1 hour). Taxis cost €60 to Pisa, €80 to Lucca, and €200 to Florence (all one-way rates); sharing a minibus taxi with other cruisers can bring the round-trip cost to Florence down to about €50 per person.

Port Overview

The city of Livorno (sometimes called "Leghorn" in English), with 160,000 inhabitants, is located on Italy's west coast, about 60 miles

from Florence. If you're just looking for an accessible slice of Italy without the famous sights, Livorno can be a delight. Like many other Mediterranean seaside towns that function as cruise ports today, it was an important naval port in World War II—so it was thoroughly bombed. Though the town was later rebuilt with the help of the American army, Livorno's unkempt postwar architecture still suggests its rough past. While this Tuscan city does have an interesting history—particularly in the time of the Renaissance—it pales in comparison to the tidier and more compelling nearby destinations. More than one million cruise passengers pass through Livorno each year. Most of them are side-tripping into Florence, Pisa, and Lucca, but it's also possible to reach farther destinations, including Siena, Tuscan hill towns (such as San Gimignano and Volterra), and the Cinque Terre.

Livorno's port (at the western edge of town) is vast and sprawling, but most arriving cruise ships dock in one of two places: Molo 75, at the **Porto Mediceo**; or the adjacent **Molo Capitaneria.** At either pier, you'll find cruise-line excursion buses, a tiny TI desk, drivers hustling to fill their minibus taxis for trips into Florence, and a shuttle bus leaving every few minutes for Piazza del Municipio in the center of Livorno.

Tourist Information: While there is no formal TI at the port, small TI desks are often set up on the pier to help arriving cruisers. For details about Livorno's TI, see the "Services in Downtown Livorno" sidebar, later.

Getting into Florence, Pisa, and Lucca

If this is the one time in your life that you're this close to Michelangelo's *David* or Pisa's famous Leaning Tower, it's worth the effort to see them. Taxis to Florence, Pisa, and Lucca are very expensive (but become more affordable if you split the fare with other cruisers). Any budget-minded traveler with patience can use public transportation to go from Livorno to any of these places and back again before the ship departs.

By Taxi and Shared Minibus

Taxis wait at the dock to hustle up business as travelers disembark. While a private taxi is costly, enterprising drivers with eight-seat minibuses gather groups to split their €400 round-trip fee for Florence; €50 per person (as part of a group of eight) is a great deal. You'll be driven one hour into Florence, dropped off near the center for four or five hours of free time, and then taken back to the port. Some groups cram in a stop at Pisa on the way back, which (while rushing a tour of Florence) is doable. If you make friends on board, this is a smart option worth considering and talking up before you arrive in Livorno.

Here are some ballpark fares for a four-seat car:

- One-way to Pisa: €60
- Round-trip to Pisa: €120
- One-way to Lucca: €80
- One-way between Pisa and Lucca: €50
- Round-trip from Livorno to both Pisa and Lucca: €220
- One-way to Florence: €200
- Round-trip to Florence, including four hours of free time: €320
- Wait fee: €30/hour (if not included in flat fare)

In general, drivers at the port prefer to take passengers who will pay them for the whole day, so it can be difficult to get one to

Livorno

To More
Cruise
Docks

Bacino Firenze

Piazza del
Portuale

Bacino
Cappellini

VIA DELLA CINTA ESTERNA

Fosso Reale

QUARTIERE
DELLA
VENEZIA

FORTEZZA
NUOVA

Piazza
Garibaldi

To
Central
Train
Station

FORTEZZA
VECCHIA

Piazza della
Fort. Vecchia

CITY
HALL
🚻

VIA AVVALORATI

VIA D. POSTA

VIA D. GALERE

Piazza della
Repubblica

Piazza dei
Marmi

**Piazza del
Municipio**

①

Piazza
Unità d'Italia

**Piazza
Grande**

VIA GRANDE

Darsena
Vecchia

Piazza del
Pamiglione

VIA FIUME

① ATM

②

PHARMACY

VIA BUONTALENTI

COVERED
MARKET

MOLO
CAPITINERIA

Piazza
Micheli

VIA GRANDE

DUOMO

③

Piazza
Cavallotti

④

VIA DEL
CARDINALE

MOLO 75

Piazza
Arsenale

VIA S. FRANCESCO

V. TEMPIO

POST

PRODUCE
MARKET

**Porto
Mediceo**

VIA CRISPI

200 Meters

200 Yards

To Molo
Mediceo
Cruise Terminal

Darsena
Nuova

SCALI D'AZEGLIO

① Shuttle to/from Port   **③** Bus to Pisa
② Bus to Train Stn.   **④** Pizzeria da Gagari

FLORENCE

take you just one-way (especially the long haul into Florence); you might have better luck for shorter trips if you take the shuttle bus into downtown Livorno, and then catch a taxi there. Taxis both at the port and in the city offer the same rates. Clarify the fare beforehand, even though by law the driver must have the meter on (the quoted price will usually be less than the meter). The fare can vary, depending on the number of people and the season. Don't pay for a round-trip excursion until your cabbie has returned you to your ship...safe, sound, and on time.

By Excursion

Most cruise lines offer a "transportation-only" excursion from the ship to Florence. This includes a bus ride from the ship directly to a point in downtown Florence, free time to explore the city, then a bus ride back to your ship. This is extremely convenient, but relatively expensive (around $100-125—which is about €75-95). Sharing a minibus taxi (explained above) offers a similar transfer for a lower price. Alternatively, you can buy a similar excursion on your own at the shuttle-bus stop in downtown Livorno for much less. A "transportation-only" excursion from the cruise line is worth considering only if you appreciate the peace of mind of being guaranteed that you'll make it back to the ship on time. (While shared taxis or excursions available locally do this trip all the time and are smart about anticipating traffic patterns, they can't guarantee the ship will wait for you in case of unexpected delays.)

By Public Transportation

The basic plan is this: Ride the cruise line's shuttle bus from the port to downtown Livorno; catch a public bus to Livorno's train station; then take the train to wherever you're going. It's cheap and fun, but a bit time-consuming.

When planning your day, factor in the 30-45 minutes it takes each way to get from Livorno's dock to its train station, Livorno Centrale. It's about 15 minutes from the port to the town center on the shuttle bus, then another 15 minutes on bus #1 or #1R to the station (plus the time you'll spend transferring and waiting for buses).

Beware: Pickpockets plague downtown Livorno, especially around the bus stops. Wear your money belt and use caution.

Step 1: From the Ship to Downtown Livorno

From the port, you can either ride the cruise line's shuttle bus or walk to downtown.

Most cruise lines offer a **shuttle bus** to the center of Livorno, dropping you off at a big, canvas-covered bus stop near the TI on Piazza del Municipio (about €5-8 round-trip, 15 minutes). Particularly if your boat is docked at the far end of the port, this is a handy option. Stepping off the shuttle bus, you'll find plenty of transportation and tour deals being hawked by a gaggle of small-time guides and tour operators eager to win your business.

If the line for the shuttle bus is too long—or if you're in the mood for a stroll—you can **walk** from most areas of the port to downtown Livorno in about 10-20 minutes. From Molo 75/Porto Mediceo, walk around the little sailboat harbor, then bear right over the wide bridge and up Via Grande. From Molo Capitaneria, walk through the port area, cross the wide bridge, and continue straight up Via Grande. Via Grande—an elegant-feeling, arcaded street lined with local shops and fashion boutiques—takes you straight to Piazza Grande in the heart of town (where you can catch bus #1 or #1R to the train station).

Note: When there are multiple cruise ships in town, it can be hard to predict where your ship will dock. On very busy days, or if your ship is very large, you might put in at the cargo docks of Porto Industriale, much farther out from the two piers described earlier. If this is the case, the shuttle bus is your only option.

Step 2: From Downtown Livorno to the Train Station

Livorno's city center clusters around two squares, a quick two-

Services in Downtown Livorno

All cruise-line shuttle buses drop off at Piazza del Municipio in the center of Livorno. You'll find the following services either on this square or nearby. If you decide to linger in Livorno, see "Sights in Livorno," later.

Tourist Information: The TI is inside the covered pedestrian mall just off Piazza del Municipio, a few steps from the port shuttle-bus stop (daily May-Oct 8:00-19:00, Nov-April 8:00-17:30, tel. 0586-894-236, www.costadeglietruschi.it). The TI arranges local guides and hands out a free *Livorno* brochure with self-guided Livorno walks. They can also inform you about local tours, such as a boat trip around the canals of Livorno plus a visit to Pisa (€20).

ATMs: The handiest ATM is at UniCreditBanca, next to the port shuttle-bus stop on Via Cogorano (between Piazza Grande and Piazza del Municipio). You'll also find plenty of other ATMs around Livorno.

Pharmacy: The **Farmacia Internazionale** is on Via Grande, between the port area and downtown (Mon-Fri 8:30-13:00 & 15:00-19:30, Sat 8:30-12:30, closed Sun, one block before Piazza Grande, on the left with your back to the port, Via Grande 140, tel. 0586-890-346). Another pharmacy is on Via Cogorano between Piazza Grande and Piazza del Municipio (open 24 hours daily).

WCs: Public bathrooms are in the stark city hall, across the street from the TI on Piazza del Municipio.

block walk apart: **Piazza del Municipio** (public WCs, shuttle-bus stop) and **Piazza Grande** (stop for buses #1 and #1R to train station). The squares are connected by a long, covered pedestrian mall (with the helpful TI inside). For specifics on local services, see the sidebar.

Public **buses** #1 and #1R to the train station depart from the middle of Piazza Grande (in front of the cathedral). To reach Piazza Grande from the port shuttle-bus stop on Piazza del Municipio, turn right out of the bus and walk two short blocks on Via Cogorano to Piazza Grande, or simply stroll through the pedestrian mall (and visit the TI on the way). From here, the bus heads to Livorno Centrale Station, the end of the line (€1.20, €1.70 if bought from driver, 8/hour Mon-Sat, 4-6/hour Sun, 15 minutes). Before boarding, buy your bus ticket at a tobacco shop *(tabacchi)* or newsstand; at the same place, you can also buy regional train tickets to Pisa, Lucca, or Florence (buying a train ticket now could help save time and avoid lines later at the train station).

The 35-minute **walk** from Piazza Grande to the train station is long and boring; don't do it—the bus is simple.

Pisa Bus Alternative: If you want to go straight to Pisa, consider taking a bus. The Livorno TI arranges cheap and efficient shuttle buses for cruisers bound for the Leaning Tower. Cheaper still is the public bus labeled *PISA*, which connects downtown Livorno and Pisa (€2.75, departs hourly on the hour, fewer buses Sat-Sun, 1 hour, schedule posted at stop). In Livorno, you can catch the Pisa bus at the Largo Duomo stop behind the cathedral (from Piazza Grande, walk around the left side of the cathedral to find the stop by the CPT bus office). The bus drops you off about a block from Pisa's train station at Piazza Santo Antonio, across town from the Field of Miracles and Leaning Tower (see "Arrival in Pisa," page 461). Notice that the bus runs less frequently than the train, and weekend service is limited. It also takes more than twice as long as the train—but it saves you the trip from downtown Livorno to the train station.

Step 3: From Livorno Centrale Train Station to Florence, Pisa, and Lucca

From Livorno Centrale, trains zip to Florence, Pisa, Lucca, and other points in Italy. Check the *partenze* (departures) board for the next train to your destination. In Italian, Florence is "Firenze." If you're going to Pisa, note that it's usually listed as an intermediate station (for example, on the way to Firenze, Milano, or Torino) rather than the final destination. All Florence-bound trains stop in Pisa.

While the lines can be long at the ticket windows, the self-service machines are fast and generally less crowded. There are two types of machines: The green machines, marked *Biglietto Regionale Veloce*, sell tickets for regional trains (not the faster IC or ES trains to Pisa—explained next). The gray TrenItalia machines, marked *Biglietto Veloce*, sell all tickets. Both machines accept credit cards and cash. Before boarding the train, be sure to validate your ticket by sticking it in the *convalida* slot. Remember, you can also buy regional train tickets (along with your local bus ticket) at any tobacco shop or newsstand.

Most trains are regional and cheap, but a few Pisa-bound trains are high-speed InterCity (IC) or Eurostar (ES) trains; if you take these to Pisa—even if it's just to transfer to a Lucca- or Florence-bound train—you'll pay a premium (about €5 extra on IC, €6 extra on ES; these tickets not available from tobacco shops/ newsstands), and it will only save you a few minutes.

To Florence: Hourly, usually departs at :12 after the hour, arrives in Florence at :32 past the following hour—about 1.5 hours total, €9 on a regional train. (A few additional departures also run; try to avoid the pricier premium tickets, which require a connection at Pisa and don't save you any time.) For details on what to do when you get to Florence, see "Arrival in Florence," page 389.

To Pisa: 2-3/hour, 20 minutes, €2.50 on a regional train. Once in Pisa, turn to "Arrival in Pisa," page 461.

To Lucca: About hourly, 1 hour, transfer at Pisa Centrale, €5.10 on a regional train. See "Arrival in Lucca," page 476.

To Both Lucca and Pisa: If you want to visit Lucca and Pisa in one day, take the train to Lucca first. From there, a handy bus connects Lucca's Piazzale Giuseppe Verdi to Pisa's Field of Miracles (Mon-Sat hourly, fewer on Sun, 30 minutes, €3).

To Other Destinations: From Livorno Centrale station, you can ride to **Monterosso** on the **Cinque Terre** (nearly hourly, 1.5 hours, some direct, others transfer at La Spezia Centrale, €14) or **Siena** (hourly, 2-2.5 hours, transfer in Empoli)—though both of these are too far to be particularly convenient as a side-trip from Livorno.

By Tour

Karin Kibby, an Oregonian living in Livorno who leads Rick Steves tours, offers a morning "slice of Italian life" walk (including Livorno's fantastic food market) and day trips from the cruise port throughout Tuscany. She'll work with you to find the best solution for your budget and interests (2-10 people, mobile 333-108-6348, karinkintuscany@yahoo.it).

For information on local tours in Florence, see "Tours in Florence" on page 395. There are also tour options in Pisa (page 463) and Lucca (page 477).

Sights in Livorno

Like many European ports, Livorno was severely damaged during WWII bombings. Despite that, it still possesses an energy and charm that make it a delight to explore. If you find yourself with extra time to spend in Livorno itself, you have a few options.

The TI's *Livorno* brochure includes worthwhile **self-guided walks,** including one that ends at the waterfront a 15-minute walk from the cruise docks. You'll meander through the "Quartiere della Venezia," a historic district with canals (though that's about all it has in common with Venice). Starting at the TI, and ending at the harbor's fortress, the walk takes you by 18th-century palaces and churches, including buildings still displaying damage from World War II (allow 45 minutes).

A touristy **hop-on, hop-off** bus offers recorded tours in three languages, covering the city plus the nearby coastline (€12, runs April-Oct, www.city-sightseeing.it, details at TI).

Livorno's 19th-century **covered market hall** (*mercato coperto*) is Tuscany's largest (dead in the afternoon, closed Sun). This venerable market hall, which is surrounded by a colorful cluster of outdoor markets, is a 10-minute walk southeast of Piazza Grande. Other Livorno markets include produce on Piazza Cavallotti (Mon-Sat mornings, closed Sun) and home goods and clothes on Via Buontalenti (Mon-Sat all day, closed Sun).

The Giro in Battello **canal boat tour** makes a lazy circle, giving you a look at Livorno's old town from its canal system. You and 50 other tourists perch on hard wooden benches in a salty open boat while the live guide rattles off his or her spiel in three languages (€10, 50 minutes, departs daily at 10:00, 11:00, 12:00, and 15:30 from TI at shuttle-bus stop, tel. 348-738-2094).

The **Aquarium di Livorno** is a child-friendly option with a 1950s American-style diner nearby (€12, kids-€6, daily April-Sept 10:00-18:00, weekends only Oct-March, www.acquariodilivorno. it). From the port itself, the aquarium is a 20-minute walk: Head to the right, following Viale Italia along the coast. Along the way, you'll pass several beaches with facilities for sunbathing and swimming. Or you can take bus #1 from Piazza Grande (direction: Miramare).

Grab a taste of the local culinary specialty, *torta di ceci*—a savory chickpea-flour crêpe with oil and pepper. Get a piece "to go" at Pizzeria da Gagari (10-minute walk from Piazza Grande at Via del Cardinale 24, Mon-Sat 8:30-14:00 & 16:00-21:00, closed Sun). Seafood lovers will want to seek out *cacciucco*, a flavorful stew made from seasonal fish swimming in a zesty garlic tomato broth. A handy seafood place at the port itself is **Ristorante Aragosta** (€8 pastas, €11 *secondi*, Wed-Mon 12:00-15:00 & 19:00-23:00, closed Tue, Piazza Arsenale 6, tel. 0586-895-395).

Returning to Your Ship

Remember, trains can be delayed, and it's a several-step process to get back to your ship (train to Livorno train station, then bus to downtown Livorno, then shuttle bus or walk to the port). Schedule your day conservatively. If you wind up with extra time in Livorno, check out the options under "Sights in Livorno," earlier.

If returning by train from Florence, Pisa, or Lucca, get off at Livorno Centrale and head straight out the front door to the awaiting bus #1 or #1R, which brings you back to Piazza Grande (buy ticket on board, last bus leaves station at 20:45). From Piazza Grande, walk straight up Via Grande to the port (generally 10-20 minutes, depending on where your ship is docked), or walk two short blocks (down Via Cogorano or through the pedestrian mall) to Piazza del Municipio to catch the shuttle bus back to your ship. If you're tight on time, you can grab a taxi outside the station.

See page 483 for help if you miss your boat.

Florence

Florence, the home of the Renaissance and birthplace of our modern world, has the best Renaissance art in Europe. In a single day, you could look Michelangelo's *David* in the eyes, fall under the seductive sway of Botticelli's *Birth of Venus,* and climb the modern world's first dome, which still dominates the skyline.

Get your bearings with a Renaissance walk. Florentine art goes beyond paintings and statues—enjoy the food, fashion, and street markets. You can lick Italy's best gelato while enjoying some of Europe's best people-watching.

Orientation to Florence

The best of Florence (*Firenze* in Italian) lies on the north bank of the Arno River. The main historical sights cluster around the red-brick dome of the cathedral (Duomo). Everything is within a 20-minute walk of the train station, cathedral, or Ponte Vecchio (Old Bridge). The less famous but more characteristic Oltrarno area (south bank) is just over the bridge.

Though small, Florence is intense. Prepare for scorching summer heat, slick pickpockets, few WCs, steep prices, and long lines. Easy tourist money has corrupted some locals, making them greedy and dishonest (check your bill carefully). Visitors to Florence will enjoy the city's newfound passion for traffic-free zones. Once brutal for pedestrians, the city is now a delight on foot.

Tourist Information

Florence has two separate TI organizations, which are equally helpful.

One TI has two different branches, both with a focus on the city. The main branch is across the square from the **train station** and very crowded (Mon-Sat 8:30-19:00, Sun 8:30-14:00; with

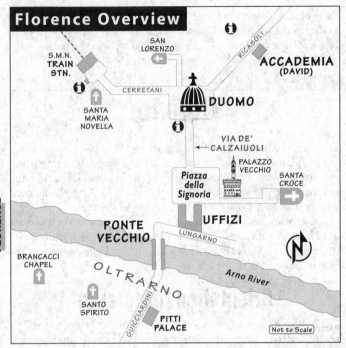

Florence Overview

S.M.N. TRAIN STN.

SAN LORENZO

RICASOLI

ACCADEMIA (DAVID)

CERRETANI

SANTA MARIA NOVELLA

DUOMO

VIA DE' CALZAIUOLI

PALAZZO VECCHIO

SANTA CROCE

Piazza della Signoria

PONTE VECCHIO

UFFIZI

LUNGARNO

BRANCACCI CHAPEL

OLTRARNO

Arno River

N

SANTO SPIRITO

GUICCIARDINI

PITTI PALACE

Not to Scale

FLORENCE

your back to tracks, exit the station—it's 100 yards away, across the square in wall near corner of church at Piazza Stazione 4; if you see a "tourist information" desk inside the train station, it's a hotel-booking service in disguise; tel. 055-212-245, www.firenze-turismo.it). The smaller branch is very centrally located at **Piazza del Duomo,** at the west corner of Via Calzaiuoli (it's inside the Bigallo Museum/Loggia; Mon-Sat 9:00-19:00, Sun 9:00-14:00, tel. 055-288-496).

The other TI organization covers both the city and the greater province of Florence. Its main branch is a couple of blocks **north of the Duomo** and is often less crowded than the others (Mon-Sat 8:30-18:30, closed Sun, just past Medici-Riccardi Palace at Via Cavour 1 red, tel. 055-290-832, international bookstore across street); a second branch is at the **airport** (daily 8:30-20:30).

At any TI, pick up the city map, the transit map (which has bus routes of interest to tourists on the back), a current museum-hours listing (very important; you can also download this list at www.firenzeturismo.it), and your choice of other brochures.

The TIs across from the train station and on Via Cavour sell the **Firenze Card,** an expensive but handy sightseeing pass that allows you to skip the lines at top museums (see page 396).

Arrival in Florence

Florence's main train station (called Firenze S.M.N. to distinguish it from Florence's two smaller stations) is on the western edge of the historic center, an easy 15-minute walk to the Duomo.

With your back to the tracks, get oriented. Look left to see the green cross of a 24-hour pharmacy *(farmacia)* and a small food court. Directly ahead—outside the station—is a TI, located straight across the square, 100 yards away. To the right (also outside the station) is the handy Margherita/Conad supermarket, for sandwiches and salads to go.

To get into town, exit the station to the left. There you'll find taxis (€8 to the Duomo) and city buses (buy tickets at the small ATAF ticket office outside). To walk into town, exit the station to the left and find the escalators down to the underground mall called Galleria S.M. Novella. Pass through the mall toward the Church of Santa Maria Novella. Watch for pickpockets. When you emerge from the tunnel, head east down Via dei Panzani, which leads directly to the Duomo.

Helpful Hints

Theft Alert: Florence has particularly hardworking thief gangs who hang out where you do: near the train station, the station's underpass (especially where the tunnel surfaces), and at major sights. American tourists—especially older ones—are considered easy targets. Some thieves even dress like tourists to fool you. Be on guard at two squares frequented by drug pushers (Santa Maria Novella and Santo Spirito).

Medical Help: There's no shortage of English-speaking medical help in Florence. To reach a doctor who speaks English, call **Medical Service Firenze** at 055-475-411; the phone is answered 24/7. Rates are reasonable. For a doctor to come to you within an hour of your call, you'd pay €100-200 (higher rates apply on Sun, holidays, or for late visits). You pay only €50 if you go to the clinic when the doctor's in (Mon-Fri 11:00-12:00, 13:00-15:00 & 17:00-18:00, Sat 11:00-12:00 & 13:00-15:00, closed Sun, no appointment necessary, Via Roma 4, between the Duomo and Piazza della Repubblica).

Dr. Stephen Kerr is an English doctor specializing in helping sick tourists (drop-in clinic open Mon-Fri 15:00-17:00, other times by appointment, €50/visit, Piazza Mercato Nuovo 1, between Piazza della Repubblica and Ponte Vecchio, tel. 055-288-055, mobile 335-836-1682, www.dr-kerr.com). The TI has a list of other English-speaking doctors.

There are 24-hour **pharmacies** at the train station and on Borgo San Lorenzo (near the Baptistery).

Visiting Churches: Some churches operate like museums, charg-

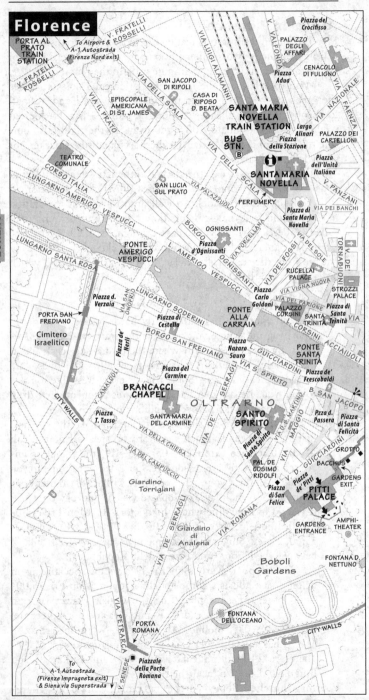

Florence

FLORENCE

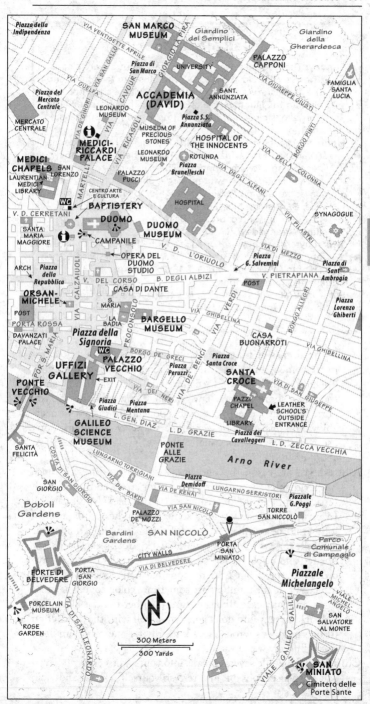

FLORENCE

Daily Reminder

Sunday: The Duomo's dome and Mercato Centrale are closed. These sights close early: Duomo Museum (at 13:45) and the Baptistery's interior (at 14:00). Many churches—including the Duomo—are open only in the afternoon. The Bargello is closed on the first, third, and fifth Sundays of the month.

Monday: The biggies are closed, including the Accademia (David) and the Uffizi Gallery. The Bargello closes on the second and fourth Mondays. The San Lorenzo Market is closed Mondays in winter. Target these sights on Mondays: the Duomo and its dome, Duomo Museum, Campanile, Baptistery, Mercato Nuovo, Mercato Centrale, Palazzo Vecchio, and churches. Or take a walking tour.

Tuesday/Wednesday: All sights are open.

Thursday: All sights are open, though the following close early: the Palazzo Vecchio (14:00) and off-season, the Duomo (16:00 May and Oct, 16:30 Nov-April).

Friday: All sights are open.

Saturday: All sights are open, but the Duomo's dome closes earlier than usual, at 17:40.

ing an admission fee to see their art treasures. Modest dress for men, women, and even children is required in some churches (including the Duomo). I recommend no bare shoulders, short shorts, or short skirts at any church. Many churches let you borrow or buy a cheap, disposable poncho for instant respectability. Be respectful of worshippers and the paintings; don't use a flash. Churches usually close from 12:00 or 12:30 to 15:00 or 16:00.

Addresses: For reasons beyond human understanding, Florence has a ridiculously confusing system for street addresses, with separate numbering for businesses (red) and residences (black). In print, this designation is sometimes indicated by a letter following the number: "r" = red, for *rosso*; no indication or "n" = black, for *nero*. While usually black, B&Bs can be either. The red and black numbers each appear in roughly consecutive order on streets but bear no apparent connection with each other. While the numbers are sometimes color-coded on street signs, in many cases they appear in neither red nor black, but in blue! I'm lazy and don't concern myself with the distinction (if one number's wrong, I look nearby for the other) and can easily find my way around.

Chill Out: Schedule several breaks into your sightseeing when you can sit, pause, cool off, and refresh yourself with a sandwich, gelato, or coffee. Carry a water bottle to refill at Florence's twist-the-handle public fountains (near the Duomo dome entrance, around the corner from the "Piglet" at the Mercato Nuovo, or in front of the Pitti Palace). Try the *fontanello* (dispenser of free cold water, *frizzante* or *naturale*) on Piazza della Signoria, behind the statue of Neptune (on the left side of the Palazzo Vecchio).

Internet Access: Bustling, tourist-filled Florence has many small Internet cafés. **VIP Internet** has cheap rates, numerous terminals, and long hours (€1.50/hour, daily 9:00-24:00, Via Faenza 49 red, tel. 055-264-5552). An increasing number of cafés and restaurants offer Wi-Fi. If you have a smartphone with an Italian mobile number, you can access free Wi-Fi for two hours a day at various hotspots around town, including most major squares and along the river (the TI can give you a list of hotspots and instructions).

Bookstores: For a good selection of brand-name guidebooks (including mine), try one of these shops. The first two are locally owned and carry only English books. **Paperback Exchange** has the widest selection and also deals in used books (Mon-Fri 9:00-19:30, Sat 10:30-19:30, closed Sun, just south of the Duomo on Via delle Oche 4 red, tel. 055-293-460). **B & M Books & Fine Art** is a bit smaller but also has a great Italian interest section (Tue-Sat 11:00-19:00, closed Sun-Mon, near Ponte alla Carraia at Borgo Ognissanti 4 red, tel. 055-294-575). The local branch of **Feltrinelli International** has a relatively small English section (Mon-Sat 9:00-19:30, closed Sun, a few blocks north of the Duomo, across the street from TI and Medici-Riccardi Palace at Via Cavour 12 red, tel. 055-219-524).

WCs: Public restrooms are scarce. Use them when you can, in any café or museum you patronize. A convenient pay WC (€1) is located near the Duomo, at the Baptistery ticket office.

Updates to this Book: For updates to this book, check www.ricksteves.com/update.

Getting Around Florence

I organize my sightseeing geographically and do it all on foot. I think of Florence as a Renaissance treadmill—it requires a lot of walking. You likely won't need public transit. But just in case...

Buses: A single ticket is €1.20 and good for 90 minutes. A 24-hour pass is €5, and Firenze Card holders ride free. Buy tickets at tobacco shops *(tabacchi),* newsstands, the ATAF bus office just east of the train station, or on board for a bit more (€2, exact change). Validate your ticket in the machine on board. Most buses leave

Florence at a Glance

▲▲▲**Accademia** Michelangelo's *David* and powerful (unfinished) *Prisoners*. Reserve ahead or get a Firenze Card. **Hours:** Tue-Sun 8:15-18:50, closed Mon. See page 415.

▲▲▲**Duomo Museum** Underrated cathedral museum with sculptures (under renovation until fall of 2015). **Hours:** Mon-Sat 9:00-19:30, Sun 9:00-13:45. See page 418.

▲▲▲**Bargello** Underappreciated sculpture museum (Michelangelo, Donatello, Medici treasures). **Hours:** Tue-Sat 8:15-13:50, until 16:50 during special exhibits (typically April-Oct); also open first, third, and fifth Mon and second and fourth Sun of each month. See page 418.

▲▲▲**Uffizi Gallery** Greatest collection of Italian paintings anywhere. Reserve well in advance or get a Firenze Card. **Hours:** Tue-Sun 8:15-18:35, closed Mon. See page 420.

▲▲**Duomo** Gothic cathedral with colorful facade and the first dome built since ancient Roman times. **Hours:** Mon-Fri 10:00-17:00, Thu until 16:00 May and Oct, until 16:30 Nov-April; Sat 10:00-16:45, Sun 13:30-16:45. See page 417.

▲▲**Palazzo Vecchio** Fortified palace, once the home of the Medici family, wallpapered with history. **Hours:** Fri-Wed 9:00-19:00, until 24:00 April-Sept, Thu 9:00-14:00 year-round. See page 420.

▲**Climbing the Duomo's Dome** Grand view into the cathedral, close-up of dome architecture, and, after 463 steps, a glorious city vista. **Hours:** Mon-Fri 8:30-19:00, Sat 8:30-17:40, closed Sun. See page 417.

▲**Campanile** Bell tower with views similar to Duomo's, 50 fewer steps, and shorter lines. **Hours:** Daily 8:30-19:30. See page 417.

▲**Baptistery** Bronze doors fit to be the gates of paradise. **Hours:** Doors always viewable; interior open Mon-Sat 11:15-19:00 except first Sat of each month 8:30-14:00, Sun 8:30-14:00. See page 417.

▲**Ponte Vecchio** Famous bridge lined with gold and silver shops. **Hours:** Bridge always open (shops closed at night). See page 421.

from two major hubs: the train station or Piazza San Marco (near the Accademia). For bus information, get a transit map at the TI, call 800-424-500, or check www.ataf.net.

I find these to be most helpful bus lines:

#C2 twists through the congested old center from the train station to the Santa Croce neighborhood. Just €1.20 gets you a 90-minute joyride.

#C1 stops near the Palazzo Vecchio and Piazza Santa Croce, then heads north to Piazza Libertà.

#D goes from the train station to Ponte Vecchio, then cruises through Oltrarno as far east as Ponte San Niccolò.

#12 and **#13** go from the train station to the Pitti Palace, Piazzale Michelangelo, and Santa Croce.

Taxi: The minimum cost is €5 (€6 after 22:00 and on Sun). Taxi fares and supplements are clearly explained on signs in each taxi—rides in the center of town should be charged as tariff #1. A typical taxi ride from the train station to the Duomo costs about €8; from Ponte Vecchio to Piazzale Michelangelo costs about €10. It can be hard to hail a cab on the street. To call one (€2 extra), dial 055-4390 or 055-4242.

Tours in Florence

To sightsee on your own, download my series of free audio tours that illuminate some of Florence's top sights and neighborhoods: my Renaissance Walk, the Accademia, and the Uffizi Gallery (see sidebar on page 50 for details).

For insight with a personal touch, consider the tour companies and individual Florentine guides listed here. Hardworking and creative, they offer a worthwhile array of organized sightseeing activities. Study their websites for details. If you're taking a city tour, remember that individuals save money with a scheduled public tour (such as those offered daily by Florencetown or ArtViva). If you're traveling as a family or small group, however, you're likely to save money by booking a private guide (since rates are hourly for any size of group).

Walking (and Biking) Tours
ArtViva Walking Tours
This company offers up to 12 tours per day year-round, featuring downtown Florence and museum highlights. Their guides are native English speakers. Museum tours include the Uffizi Gallery (€49, includes admission, 2 hours) and the Accademia ("Original *David*" tour, €36, includes admission, 1 hour). They also lead biking and hiking tours (office open Mon-Sat 8:00-18:00, Sun 8:30-13:30

Avoiding Lines at Major Sights in Florence

Florence offers several options to help you bypass the lengthy ticket-buying lines that can plague its most popular sights in peak season. You can spend less time in line and more time seeing the sights if you make use of Florence's official sightseeing pass (the Firenze Card) or make advance reservations.

Firenze Card

The Firenze Card (€72) is pricey but convenient. This three-day sightseeing pass gives you admission to many of Florence's sights, including the Uffizi Gallery and Accademia. Just as important, it lets you skip the ticket-buying lines without making reservations. Even if you're in town for only a few hours on a cruise (in which case, this pass almost certainly won't save you money), skipping the lines without having to make a reservation may be worth the high price tag. (But if you only want to see the Uffizi and Accademia, you'll save by making individual reservations instead; described below.)

With the card, you simply go to the entrance at a covered sight (if there's a "with reservations" door, use it), show the card, and they let you in (though there still may be delays at popular sights with bottleneck entryways or capacity limits). At some sights, you must first present your card at the ticket booth or information desk to get a physical ticket before proceeding to the entrance. For a complete list of included sights, see www.firenzecard.it.

Many outlets around town sell the card, including the TIs at the train station and at Via Cavour 1 red (a couple of blocks north of the Duomo) and at some sights: the Uffizi Gallery's door #2 (enter to the left of the ticket-buying line), back entrance of Santa Maria Novella (near the train station), Bargello, and Palazzo Vecchio. Lines are shortest at the Via Cavour TI and the Church of Santa Maria Novella (around back at Piazza della Stazione 4); if you're doing the Uffizi first, door #2 is relatively quick. You can also pay for the card online (www.firenzecard.it), obtain a voucher, and pick up the card at any of the above locations.

Accademia and Uffizi Reservations

If you don't get a Firenze Card, it's smart to make reservations at the often-crowded Accademia and Uffizi Gallery—particularly because your time in town will be very limited, and you'll be competing for space with everyone else on your cruise ship. Reserve as soon as you know when you'll be in town. You can generally get an entry time for the Accademia a few days before your visit, but reserve for the Uffizi well in advance. To avoid being rushed, I'd choose a time at least three hours after your scheduled arrival time in Livorno (giving you ample time for the train connection into town, plus getting to the sights themselves).

There are several ways to make a reservation:

• **By Phone:** For either sight, reserve by phone before you leave the States (from the US, dial 011-39-055-294-883, or within Italy call 055-294-883; €4/ticket reservation fee; booking office open Mon-Fri 8:30-18:30, Sat 8:30-12:30, closed Sun). The reservation line is often busy. Be persistent. When you get through, an English-speaking operator walks you through the process—a few minutes later you say *grazie*, having secured an entry time and a confirmation number. You'll present your confirmation number at the museum and pay cash for your ticket. Note that you pay nothing up front when you phone.

• **Online:** Using a credit card, you can reserve your Accademia or Uffizi visit online via the city's official site (€4/ticket reservation fee, www.firenzemusei.it). To start, click on the gray "B-ticket" strip, and make sure you "Add" your ticket to the cart before you "Buy" it. You'll receive an immediate confirmation email, which is followed within three days by a voucher. Bring your voucher to the ticket desk to swap for an actual ticket.

Pricey middleman sites—such as www.uffizi.com and www.tickitaly.com—are reliable and more user-friendly than the official site, but their booking fees run about €10 per ticket. (Tip: When ordering from these broker sites, don't confuse Florence's Accademia with Venice's gallery of the same name.)

• **Private Tour:** Take a tour that includes your museum admission. For example, ArtViva Walking Tours offers tours of the Uffizi and Accademia (see listing on page 395).

• **Last-Minute Strategies:** If you arrive without a reservation, call the reservation number (see "By Phone" above); or head to a booking window, either at Orsanmichele Church (€4 reservation fee, daily 10:00-17:00, along Via de' Calzaiuoli—see location on map on page 402) or at the My Accademia Libreria bookstore across from the Accademia's exit (€4 reservation fee, Tue-Sun 8:15-17:30, closed Mon, Via Ricasoli 105 red—see map on page 424). It's also possible to go to the Uffizi's official ticket office (use door #2 and skirt to the left of the long ticket-buying line), ask if they have any short-notice reservations available, and pay cash (€4 fee, Tue-Sun 8:15-18:35).

May-Oct only, near Piazza della Repubblica at Via de' Sassetti 1, second floor, above Odeon Cinema, tel. 055-264-5033 during day or mobile 329-613-2730 from 18:00-20:00, www.artviva.com).

Florencetown Tours on Foot or by Bike

This well-organized company runs a variety of English-language tours. The boss, Luca Perfetto, offers student rates (10 percent discount) to anyone with this book, with an additional 10 percent off for second tours (if booking on their website, enter the code "RICKSTEVES2014" when prompted). Their "I Bike Florence" tour gives you 2.5 hours on a vintage one-speed bike following a fast-talking guide on a blitz of the town's top sights (€25, daily at 10:00 and 15:00, helmets optional, 15 stops on both sides of the river; in bad weather, the bike tours go as a walking tour). Their office is two blocks from the Palazzo Vecchio at Via de Lamberti 1 (find steps off Via de' Calzaiuoli on the river side of Orsanmichele Church); they also have a "Tourist Point" kiosk on Piazza della Repubblica, under the arches at the corner with Via Pellicceria (tel. 055-012-3994, www.florencetown.com).

Walks Inside Florence

Three art historians—Paola Barubiani and her partners Emma Molignoni and Marzia Valbonesi—provide quality guiding. Their company offers a daily 2.5-hour introductory tour (€50/person, 6 people maximum; outside except for a visit to see *David*, Accademia entry fee not included) and three-hour private tours (€180, €60/hour for more time, price is for groups of up to 4 people). They also offer an artisans-and-shopping tour, a guided evening walk, cooking classes with a market visit, private cruise excursions from the port of Livorno, and more—see their website for details (ask about Rick Steves rate for any tour, Paola's mobile 335-526-6496, www.walksinsideflorence.com, paola@walksinsideflorence.it).

Florentia

Top-notch private walking tours—geared for thoughtful, well-heeled travelers with longer-than-average attention spans—are led by Florentine scholars. The tours range from introductory city walks and museum visits to in-depth thematic walks, such as the Oltrarno neighborhood, Jewish Florence, and family-oriented tours (tours start at €250, includes personal assistance by email as you plan your trip, reserve in advance, www.florentia.org, info@florentia.org).

Context Florence

This scholarly group of graduate students and professors leads "walking seminars," such as a 3.5-hour study of Michelangelo's work and influence (€80/person, plus museum admission) and a two-hour evening orientation stroll (€65/person). I enjoyed the fascinating three-hour fresco workshop (€75/person plus materials, you take home a fresco you make yourself). See their website for other innovative offerings: Medici walk, lecture series, food walks, kids' tours, and other programs throughout Europe (tel. 06-9672-7371, US tel. 800-691-6036, www.contexttravel.com, info@contexttravel.com).

Local Guides for Private Tours

Alessandra Marchetti, a Florentine who has lived in the US, gives private walking tours of Florence and driving tours of Tuscany (€60-75/hour, mobile 347-386-9839, aleoberm@tin.it).

Paola Migliorini and her partners offer museum tours, city walking tours, private cooking classes, wine tours, and Tuscan excursions by van—you can tailor tours as you like (€60/hour without car, €70/hour in an 8-seat van, tel. 055-472-448, mobile 347-657-2611, www.florencetour.com, info@florencetour.com); they also do private tours from the cruise-ship port of Livorno.

Also consider Livorno-based **Karin Kibby** (see page 385).

Hop-on, Hop-off Bus Tours

Around town, you'll see big double-decker sightseeing buses double-parking near major sights. Tourists on the top deck can listen to brief recorded descriptions of the sights, snap photos, and enjoy a drive-by look at major landmarks (€20/1 calendar day, €25/48 hours, pay as you board, www.firenze.city-sightseeing.it). As the name implies, you can hop off when you want and catch the next bus (usually every 30 minutes, less frequently off-season). But since the most important sights are buried in the old center where big buses can't go, Florence doesn't really lend itself to this kind of tour bus. Look at the route map before committing.

Florence Renaissance Walk

Florence is a walker's paradise—and it's even better now that traffic has been banned from the area near the Duomo. To begin discovering this wonderful city, take this self-guided two-hour stroll through the heart of Florence.

From the Duomo to the Arno River

After centuries of labor, Florence gave birth to the Renaissance. We'll start with the soaring church dome that stands as the proud symbol of the Renaissance spirit. Just opposite, you'll find the Baptistery doors that opened the Renaissance. Finally, we'll reach Florence's political center, dotted with monuments of that proud

FLORENCE

time. As great and rich as this city is, it's easily covered on foot. This walk through the top sights is less than a mile long, running from the Duomo to the Arno River.

Orientation

Duomo (Cathedral): Free; Mon-Fri 10:00-17:00, Thu until 16:00 May and Oct, until 16:30 Nov-April; Sat 10:00-16:45, Sun 13:30-16:45. A modest dress code is enforced.

Climbing the Dome: €10 ticket covers all Duomo sights, also covered by Firenze Card, Mon-Fri 8:30-19:00, Sat 8:30-17:40, closed Sun, last entry 40 minutes before closing, 463 steps.

Campanile (Giotto's Tower): €10 ticket covers all Duomo sights, also covered by Firenze Card, daily 8:30-19:30, last entry 40 minutes before closing, 414 steps.

Baptistery: €10 ticket covers all Duomo sights, also covered by Firenze Card (get free paper ticket from ticket office), interior open Mon-Sat 11:15-19:00 except first Sat of month 8:30-14:00, Sun 8:30-14:00, last entry 30 minutes before closing. The facsimiles of the famous *Gates of Paradise* bronze doors on the exterior are always viewable (and free to see; the original panels are in the Duomo Museum).

Orsanmichele Church: Free, daily 10:00-17:00 (except closed Mon in Aug), free upstairs museum open only Mon 10:00-17:00. The niche sculptures are always viewable from the outside. At the door facing Via de' Calzaiuoli is a ticket box office, where you can check if there are any available tickets for the Uffizi or Accademia.

Palazzo Vecchio: Courtyard—free, museum—€6.50, covered by Firenze Card, Fri-Wed 9:00-19:00, until 24:00 April-Sept, Thu 9:00-14:00 year-round, ticket office closes one hour earlier.

Information: There's a TI right on Piazza del Duomo (just south of Baptistery, at the corner of Via de' Calzaiuoli), and another one on Via Cavour 1, a couple of blocks north of the Duomo (immediately beyond the Medici-Riccardi Palace). At either TI, ask for an updated list of museum hours.

Audio Tour: You can download this walk as a free Rick Steves audio tour (see page 50).

Services: Many cafés along the walk have WCs, and public pay toilets (€1) are at the Baptistery ticket office. You can refill your water bottle at public twist-the-handle fountains at the Duomo (left side, by the dome entrance), the Palazzo Vecchio (behind the Neptune fountain), and on Ponte Vecchio.

Photography: In churches and other sights along this walk, photos without a flash are generally OK.

Eating: You'll find plenty of cafés, self-service cafeterias, bars, and gelato shops along the route. Several of my recommended eateries are also along this walk, including Self-Service Ristorante Leonardo (near the Duomo) and the popular L'Antico Trippaio tripe-selling sandwich cart (also has non-tripe fare, a block east of Orsanmichele on Via Dante Alighieri; other cheap options are nearby); for details, see page 451.

Starring: Brunelleschi's dome, Ghiberti's doors, the Medici palaces, and the city of Florence—old and new.

The Walk Begins

The Duomo, the cathedral with the distinctive red dome, is the center of Florence and the orientation point for this walk. If you ever get lost, home's the dome. We'll start here, see several sights in the area, and then stroll down the city's pedestrian-only main street to the Palazzo Vecchio and the Arno River. Consider prefacing this walk with a visit to the ultimate Renaissance Man: Michelangelo's *David* (❂ see the "Accademia Gallery Tour" on page 421).

• *Stand in front of the Duomo as you get your historical bearings.*

The Florentine Renaissance

In the 13th and 14th centuries, Florence was a powerful center of banking, trading, and textile manufacturing. The resulting wealth fertilized the cultural soil. Then came the Black Death in 1348. Nearly half the population died, but the infrastructure remained strong, and the city rebuilt better than ever. Led by Florence's chief family—the art-crazy Medici—and propelled by the naturally aggressive and creative spirit of the Florentines, it's no wonder that the long-awaited Renaissance finally took root here.

The Renaissance—the "rebirth" of Greek and Roman culture that swept across Europe—started around 1400 and lasted about 150 years. In politics, the Renaissance meant democracy; in science, a renewed interest in exploring nature. The general mood was optimistic and "humanistic," with a confidence in the power of the individual.

In medieval times, poverty and ignorance had made life "nasty, brutish, and short" (for lack of a better cliché). The church was the people's opiate, and their lives were only a

FLORENCE

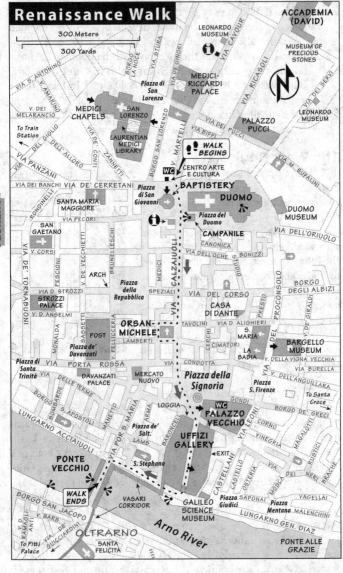

Renaissance Walk

300 Meters
300 Yards

ACCADEMIA
(DAVID)

LEONARDO
MUSEUM

MUSEUM OF
PRECIOUS
STONES

MEDICI-
RICCARDI
PALACE

Piazza di
San
Lorenzo

PALAZZO
PUCCI

LEONARDO
MUSEUM

MEDICI
CHAPELS

SAN
LORENZO

LAURENTIAN
MEDICI
LIBRARY

WALK
BEGINS

WC CENTRO ARTE
E CULTURA

SANTA MARIA
MAGGIORE

Piazza di
San Giovanni

BAPTISTERY

DUOMO

DUOMO
MUSEUM

SAN
GAETANO

Piazza del
Duomo

CAMPANILE

CANONICA

STROZZI
PALACE

ARCH

Piazza
della
Repubblica

VIA DELL'OCHE BONIZZI

VIA DEL CORSO

CASA
DI DANTE

ORSAN-
MICHELE

S.
MARIA
LA
BADIA

BARGELLO
MUSEUM

POST

Piazza de'
Davanzati

MERCATO
NUOVO

Piazza della
Signoria

Piazza di
Santa
Trinità

DAVANZATI
PALACE

Piazza
S. Firenze

To Santa
Croce

LOGGIA

WC

PALAZZO
VECCHIO

Piazza de'
Salt.

UFFIZI
GALLERY

PONTE
VECCHIO

WALK
ENDS

S. Stephano

EXIT

VASARI
CORRIDOR

GALILEO
SCIENCE
MUSEUM

Piazza
Giudici

Piazza
Mentana

OLTRARNO

SANTA
FELICITA

Arno River

To Pitti
Palace

PONTE ALLE
GRAZIE

preparation for a happier time in heaven after leaving this miserable vale of tears.

Medieval art was the church's servant. The noblest art form was architecture—churches themselves—and other arts were considered most worthwhile if they embellished the house of God. Painting and sculpture were narrative and symbolic, designed to tell Bible stories to the devout and illiterate masses.

As prosperity rose in Florence, so did people's confidence in life and themselves. Middle-class craftsmen, merchants, and bankers felt they could control their own destinies, rather than be at the whim of nature. They found much in common with the ancient Greeks and Romans, who valued logic and reason above superstition and blind faith.

Renaissance art was a return to the realism and balance of Greek and Roman sculpture and architecture. Domes and round arches replaced Gothic spires and pointed arches. In painting and sculpture, Renaissance artists strove for realism. Merging art and science, they used mathematics, the laws of perspective, and direct observation of nature to paint the world on a flat surface.

This was not an anti-Christian movement, though it was a logical and scientific age. Artists saw themselves as an extension of God's creative powers. At times, the church even supported the Renaissance and commissioned many of its greatest works—for instance, Raphael frescoed images of Plato and Aristotle on the walls of the Vatican. But for the first time in Europe since Roman times, there were rich laymen who wanted art simply for art's sake.

After 1,000 years of waiting, the smoldering fires of Europe's classical heritage burst into flames in Florence.

• *The dome of the Duomo is best viewed just to the right of the facade, from the corner of the pedestrian-only Via de' Calzaiuoli.*

The Duomo and Its Dome

The dome of Florence's cathedral—visible from all over the city—inspired Florentines to do great things. (Most recently, it inspired

the city to make the area around the cathedral delightfully traffic-free.) The big church itself (called the Duomo) is Gothic, built in the Middle Ages by architects who left it unfinished.

Think of the confidence of the age: The Duomo was built with a big hole in its roof, just waiting for a grand dome to cover it—but the technology needed to create such a dome had yet to be invented. *No problema.* The Florentines knew that someone would soon be able to handle the challenge. In the 1400s, the architect Filippo Brunelleschi was called on to finish the job. Brunelleschi capped the church Roman-style—with a tall, self-supporting dome as grand as the ancient Pantheon's (which he had studied).

He used a dome within a dome. First, he built the grand white skeletal ribs, which you can see, then filled them in with interlocking bricks in a herringbone pattern. The dome grew upward like

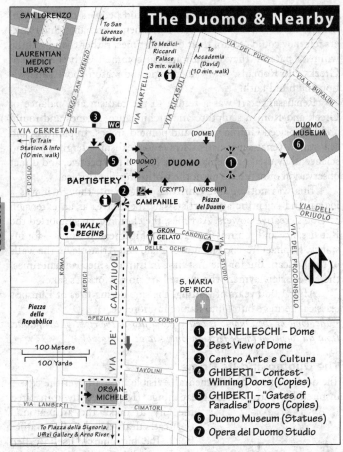

The Duomo & Nearby

① BRUNELLESCHI – Dome
② Best View of Dome
③ Centro Arte e Cultura
④ GHIBERTI – Contest-Winning Doors (Copies)
⑤ GHIBERTI – "Gates of Paradise" Doors (Copies)
⑥ Duomo Museum (Statues)
⑦ Opera del Duomo Studio

an igloo, supporting itself as it proceeded from the base. When the ribs reached the top, Brunelleschi arched them in and fixed them in place with the cupola at the top. His dome, built in only 14 years, was the largest since Rome's Pantheon.

Brunelleschi's dome was the wonder of the age, the model for many domes to follow, from St. Peter's to the US Capitol. People gave it the ultimate compliment, saying, "Not even the ancients could have done it." Michelangelo, setting out to construct the dome of St. Peter's, drew inspiration from the dome of Florence. He said, "I'll make its sister...bigger, but not more beautiful."

The church's facade looks old, but is actually Neo-Gothic—only from 1870. The facade was rushed to completion (about 600 years after the building began) to celebrate Italian unity, here in the city that for a few years served as the young country's capital. Its "retro" look captures the feel of the original medieval facade,

with green, white, and pink marble sheets that cover the brick construction; Gothic (pointed) arches; and three horizontal stories decorated with mosaics and statues. Still, the facade is generally ridiculed. (While one of this book's authors thinks it's the most beautiful church facade this side of heaven, the other one naively agrees with those who call it "the cathedral in pajamas.")

The interior feels bare after being cleaned out during the Neoclassical age and by the terrible flood of 1966 (free entry, but not worth a long wait). To climb the dome, enter from outside the church on the north side (see page 417).

FLORENCE

Campanile (Giotto's Tower)

The bell tower (to the right of the cathedral's front) offers an easier, less crowded, and faster climb than the Duomo's dome, though the unobstructed views from the Duomo are better. Giotto, like any good pre-Renaissance genius, wore several artistic hats. Not only is he considered the father of modern painting, he's also the one who designed this 270-foot-tall bell tower for the Duomo two centuries before the age of Michelangelo. In his day, Giotto was called the ugliest man to ever walk the streets of Florence, but he designed for the city what many in our day call the most beautiful bell tower in all of Europe.

The bell tower served as a sculpture gallery for Renaissance artists—notice Donatello's four prophets on the side that faces the piazza (west). These are copies—the originals are at the wonderful **Duomo Museum,** just behind the church (see the Duomo Museum listing on page 418). In the museum, you'll also get a close-up look at Brunelleschi's wooden model of his dome, Ghiberti's doors (described next), and a late *Pietà* by Michelangelo. A couple of blocks south of the Duomo, at the Opera del Duomo Studio, workers sculpt and restore statues for the cathedral (Via dello Studio 23a—see location on map on the previous page; you can peek through the doorway).

• *The Baptistery is the small octagonal building in front of the church. First, view the doors from the outside. Then, if you decide to go inside, buy your ticket across the square and enter through the north door.*

Ghiberti's Bronze Doors

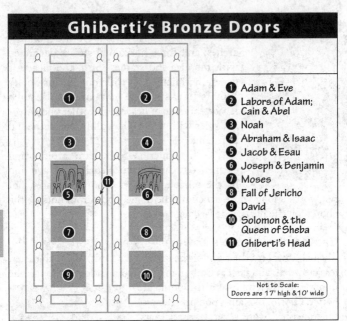

1 Adam & Eve
2 Labors of Adam; Cain & Abel
3 Noah
4 Abraham & Isaac
5 Jacob & Esau
6 Joseph & Benjamin
7 Moses
8 Fall of Jericho
9 David
10 Solomon & the Queen of Sheba
11 Ghiberti's Head

Not to Scale:
Doors are 17' high & 10' wide

FLORENCE

Baptistery and Ghiberti's Bronze Doors

Florence's Baptistery is dear to the soul of the city. In medieval and Renaissance times, the locals—eager to link themselves to the classical past—believed (wrongly) that this was a Roman building. It is, however, Florence's oldest building (11th century). Most festivals and parades either started or ended here.

Doors: The Baptistery's bronze doors bring us out of the Middle Ages and into the Renaissance. Some say the Renaissance

began precisely in the year 1401, when Florence staged a competition to find the best artist to create the Baptistery's **north doors** (the door panels are being restored and may not be visible when you visit). Florence had strong civic spirit, with different guilds (powerful trade associations) and merchant groups embellishing their city with superb art. All the greats entered the contest, but 25-year-old Lorenzo Ghiberti won easily, beating out heavyweights such as Brunelleschi (who, having lost the Baptistery gig, was free to go to Rome, study the Pantheon, and later design the Duomo's dome). The original entries of Brunelleschi and Ghiberti are in the Bargello, where you can judge them for yourself.

Later, in 1425, Ghiberti was given another commission, for the **east doors**. This time there was literally no contest. The bronze panels of these doors (the ones with the crowd of tourists looking on) added a whole new dimension to art—depth. Michelangelo said these doors were fit to be the "Gates of Paradise." (These panels are copies; the originals are in the nearby Duomo Museum.) Here we see how the Renaissance masters merged art and science. Realism was in, and Renaissance artists used math, illusion, and dissection to create it.

In the Jacob and Esau panel (just above eye level on the left), receding arches, floor tiles, and banisters create a background for

a realistic scene. The figures in the foreground stand and move like real people, telling the Bible story with human details. Amazingly, this spacious, 3-D scene is made from bronze only a few inches deep.

Ghiberti spent 27 years (1425-1452) working on these panels. That's him in the center of the door frame, atop the second row of panels—the head on the left with the shiny male-pattern baldness.

Interior: You'll see a fine example of pre-Renaissance mosaic art (1200s-1300s) in the Byzantine style. Workers from St. Mark's in Venice came here to make the remarkable ceiling mosaics (of Venetian glass) in the late 1200s.

The Last Judgment on the ceiling gives us a glimpse of the medieval worldview. Life was a preparation for the afterlife, when you would be judged and saved, or judged and damned—with no in-between. Christ, peaceful and reassuring, blessed those at his right hand with heaven (thumbs up) and sent those on his left to hell (the ultimate thumbs-down), to be tortured by demons and gnashed between the teeth of monsters. This hellish scene looks like something right out of the *Inferno* by Dante, who was dipped into the baptismal waters right here.

The rest of the ceiling mosaics tell the history of the world, from Adam and Eve (over the north/entrance doors, top row) to Noah and the Flood (over south doors, top row), to the life of Christ (second row) to the beheading of John the Baptist (bottom row), all bathed in the golden glow of pre-Renaissance heaven.

• *From the Duomo, head south, entering the pedestrian-only street that runs from here toward the Arno River.*

Via de' Calzaiuoli

The pedestrian-only Via de' Calzaiuoli (kahlts-ay-WOH-lee) is lined with high-fashion shops, as Florence is a trendsetting city in trendsetting Italy. This street has always been the main axis of the city, and it was part of the ancient Roman grid plan that became Florence. In medieval times, this street connected the religious center (where we are now) with the political center (where we're heading), a five-minute walk away. In the 20th century, this historic core was a noisy snarl of car traffic. But traffic jams have been replaced by potted plants, and now this is a pleasant place to stroll, people-watch, window-shop, lick the drips on your gelato cone, and wonder why American cities can't become more pedestrian-friendly.

And speaking of gelato...the recommended **Grom,** which keeps its *gelati* in covered metal bins, the old-fashioned way, is just a half-block detour away (daily 10:30-24:00, take your first left, to Via delle Oche 24 red). Or you could drop by any of the several nearby gelato shops. *Perché no?* (Why not?)

Continue down Via de' Calzaiuoli. Two blocks down from the Baptistery, look right on Via degli Speziali to see a triumphal arch that marks **Piazza della Repubblica.** The arch celebrates the unification of Italy in 1870 and stands as a reminder that, in ancient Roman times, this piazza was the city center. For more on this square, see page 419.

• *A block farther, at the intersection with Via Orsanmichele, is the...*

Orsanmichele Church

The Orsanmichele Church provides an interesting look at Florence's medieval roots. It's a combo church/granary. Originally, this was an open loggia (covered porch) with a huge grain warehouse upstairs. The arches of the loggia were artfully filled in (14th century), and the building gained a new purpose—as a church. This was prime real estate on what had become the main drag between the church and palace.

The niches in the walls stood empty for decades before sponsors filled them in with statues. That role fell to the rising middle class of merchants and their guilds.

Florence in 1400 was a republic, a government working for the interests not of a king, but of these guilds (much as modern America caters to corporate interests). Over time, various guilds commissioned statues as PR gestures, hiring the finest artists of the generation. As a result, the statues that ring the church (generally copies of originals stored safely in nearby museums) function as a textbook of the evolution of Florentine art.

In earlier Gothic times, statues were set deep into church niches, simply embellishing the house of God. Here at the Orsan-

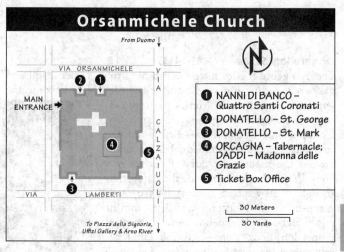

Orsanmichele Church

From Duomo

VIA ORSANMICHELE

MAIN ENTRANCE

V I A   C A L Z A I U O L I

VIA LAMBERTI

To Piazza della Signoria,
Uffizi Gallery & Arno River

❶ NANNI DI BANCO –
Quattro Santi Coronati

❷ DONATELLO – St. George

❸ DONATELLO – St. Mark

❹ ORCAGNA – Tabernacle;
DADDI – Madonna delle
Grazie

❺ Ticket Box Office

30 Meters

30 Yards

FLORENCE

michele Church, we see statues—as restless as man on the verge of the Renaissance—stepping out from the protection of the Church.
• *Head up Via Orsanmichele and circle the church exterior counterclockwise, looking out for these statues. Be careful not to stand right in the middle of the road—or at least keep an eye out for minibuses and horses.*

Nanni di Banco's *Quattro Santi Coronati* (c. 1415-1417)

These four early Christians were sculptors martyred by the Roman emperor Diocletian because they refused to sculpt pagan gods. They seem to be contemplating the consequences of the fatal decision they're about to make. Beneath some of the niches, you'll find the symbol of the guilds that paid for the art. Art historians differ here. Some think the work was commissioned by the carpenters' and masons' guild. Others contend it was by the guys who did discount circumcisions.

Donatello's *St. George* (c. 1417)

George is alert, perched on the edge of his niche, scanning the horizon for dragons and announcing the new age with its new outlook. His knitted brow shows there's a drama unfolding. Sure, he's anxious, but he's also self-assured. Comparing this Renaissance-style *St. George* to *Quattro Santi Coronati,* you can psychoanalyze the heady changes underway. This is humanism. This *St. George* is a copy of the c. 1417 original (now in the Bargello).

• *Continue around the corner of the church (bypassing the entrance for now), all the way to the opposite side.*

Donatello's *St. Mark* (1411-1413)

The evangelist cradles his gospel in his strong, veined hand and gazes out, resting his weight on the right leg while bending the left. Though subtle, St. Mark's twisting *contrapposto* pose was the first seen since antiquity. Commissioned by the linen-sellers' guild, the statue has elaborately detailed robes that drape around the natural contours of his weighty body. When the guild first saw the statue, they thought the oversized head and torso made it top-heavy. Only after it was lifted into its raised niche did Donatello's cleverly designed proportions look right—and the guild accepted it. Eighty years after young Donatello carved this statue, a teenage Michelangelo Buonarroti stood here and marveled at it.

• *Backtrack to the entrance and go inside.*

Orsanmichele Interior

Here's a chance to step into Florence, circa 1350. The church has a double nave because it was adapted from a granary. Look for the pillars (on the left) with rectangular holes in them about three feet off the ground. These were once used as chutes for delivering grain from the storage rooms upstairs. Look up to see the rings hanging from the ceiling, likely used to make pulleys for lifting grain, and the iron bars spanning the vaults for support.

The fine **tabernacle** is by Andrea Orcagna. Notice how it was designed exactly for this space: Like the biggest Christmas tree possible, it's capped by an angel whose head touches the ceiling. Take in the Gothic tabernacle's medieval elegance.

Upstairs is a free museum (open only Mon 10:00-17:00) displaying most of the originals of the statues you just saw outside. Each one is identified by the subject, year, and sculptor, representing virtually every big name in pre-Michelangelo Florentine sculpture: Donatello, Ghiberti, Brunelleschi, Giambologna, and more.

• *The Bargello, with Florence's best collection of sculpture, is a few blocks east, down Via dei Tavolini (see page 418). But let's continue down the mall 50 more yards, to the huge and historic square...*

Piazza della Signoria

The main civic center of Florence is dominated by the Palazzo Vecchio, the Uffizi Gallery, and the marble greatness of old Florence littering the cobbles. Piazza della Signoria still vibrates with the

Palazzo Vecchio & Nearby

1. Chart of Roman City Plan
2. MICHELANGELO – David (Copy)
3. GIAMBOLOGNA – The Rape of the Sabine Women; CELLINI – Perseus; other statues
4. AMMANATI – Neptune Fountain
5. Savonarola Plaque
6. Courtyard Statues
7. View of Ponte Vecchio
8. Bust of Cellini

FLORENCE

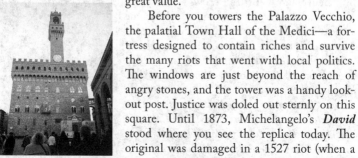

echoes of the city's past—executions, riots, and great celebrations. There's even Roman history: Look for the **chart** showing the ancient city (on a waist-high, freestanding display to your right as you enter the square). Today, it's a tourist's world with pigeons, postcards, horse buggies, and tired hubbies. If it would make your weary companion happy, stop in at the expensive **Rivoire** café to enjoy its fine desserts, pudding-thick hot chocolate, and the best view seats in town. It's expensive—but if you linger, it can be a great value.

Before you towers the Palazzo Vecchio, the palatial Town Hall of the Medici—a fortress designed to contain riches and survive the many riots that went with local politics. The windows are just beyond the reach of angry stones, and the tower was a handy lookout post. Justice was doled out sternly on this square. Until 1873, Michelangelo's *David* stood where you see the replica today. The original was damaged in a 1527 riot (when a bench thrown from a palace window knocked its left arm off), but it remained here for several centuries, vulnerable to erosion and pollution, before being moved indoors for protection.

Step past the replica *David* through the front door into the **Palazzo Vecchio**'s courtyard (free). This palace was Florence's symbol of civic power. You're surrounded by art for art's sake—a cherub frivolously marks the courtyard's center, and ornate stuccoes and frescoes decorate the walls and columns. Such luxury represented a big change 500 years ago. (For more on touring the *palazzo*, see page 420.)

• *Back outside, check out the statue-filled...*

Loggia dei Lanzi (a.k.a. Loggia della Signoria)

The loggia, once a forum for public debate, was perfect for a city that prided itself on its democratic traditions. But later, when the Medici figured that good art was more desirable than free speech, it was turned into an outdoor sculpture gallery. Notice the squirming Florentine themes—conquest, domination, rape, and decapitation. The statues lining the back are Roman originals brought back to Florence by a Medici when he moved home after living in

Rome. Two statues in the front deserve a closer look.

The Rape of the Sabine Women, with its pulse-quickening rhythm of muscles, is from the restless Mannerist period, which followed the stately and confident Renaissance (c. 1583). The sculptor, Giambologna, proved his mastery of the medium by sculpting three entangled bodies from one piece of marble. The composition is best viewed from below and in front. The relief panel below shows a wider view of the terrible scene. Note what looks like an IV tube on the arm of the horrified husband. It's an electrified wire that effectively keeps the pigeons away.

Benvenuto **Cellini's** *Perseus* (1545-1553), the loggia's most noteworthy piece, shows the Greek hero who decapitated the snake-headed Medusa. They say Medusa was so ugly she turned humans who looked at her to stone—though one of this book's authors thinks she's kinda cute.

• *Cross the square to the big fountain of Neptune by Bartolomeo Ammanati that Florentines (including Michelangelo) consider a huge waste of marble—though one of this book's authors...*

The guy on the horse, to the left, is Cosimo I, one of the post–Renaissance Medici. Find the round bronze plaque on the ground 10 steps in front of the fountain.

Savonarola Plaque

The Medici family was briefly thrown from power by an austere monk named Savonarola, who made Florence a constitutional republic. He organized huge rallies lit by roaring bonfires here on the square where he preached. While children sang hymns, the devout brought their rich "vanities" (such as paintings, musical instruments, and playing cards) and threw them into the flames.

But not everyone wanted a return to the medieval past. Encouraged by the pope, the Florentines fought back and arrested Savonarola. For two days, they tortured him, trying unsuccessfully to persuade him to see their side of things. Finally, on the very spot where Savonarola's followers had built bonfires of vanities, the monk was burned. The bronze plaque, engraved in Italian *("Qui dove...")*, reads, "Here, Girolamo Savonarola and his Dominican brothers were hanged and burned" in the year "MCCCCXCVIII" (1498).

• *Stay cool, we have 200 yards to go. Follow the gaze of the fake David into the courtyard of the two-tone horseshoe-shaped building.*

Uffizi Courtyard

The top floor of this building, known as the *uffizi* (offices) during Medici days, is filled with the greatest collection of Florentine painting anywhere. It's one of Europe's top four or five art galleries (✪ see the "Uffizi Gallery Tour" on page 427).

The Uffizi courtyard, filled with merchants and hustling young artists, is watched over by 19th-century statues of the great figures of the Renaissance. Tourists zero in on the visual accomplishments of the era—not realizing that it was many-faceted. Let's pay tribute to the nonvisual Renaissance as well, as we wander through Florence's Renaissance Hall of Fame.

LORENZO IL MAGNIFICO

• *Stroll down the left side of the courtyard from the Palazzo Vecchio to the river, noticing the following greats.*

1. Lorenzo de' Medici (the Magnificent) was a great art patron and cunning power broker. Excelling in everything except modesty, he set the tone for the Renaissance. His statue is tucked under the arcade, by a Uffizi doorway.

2. Giotto, holding the plan to the city's bell tower (which is named for him) was the great pre-Renaissance artist whose paintings foretold the future of Italian art.

3. Donatello, the sculptor who served as a role model for Michelangelo, holds a hammer and chisel.

4. Alberti wrote a famous book, *On Painting*, which taught early Renaissance artists the mathematics of perspective.

5. Leonardo da Vinci was a scientist, sculptor, musician, engineer...and not a bad painter either.

6. Michelangelo ponders the universe and/or stifles a belch.

7. Dante, with the laurel-leaf crown and lyre of a poet, says, "I am the father of the Italian language." He was the first Italian to write a popular work *(The Divine Comedy)* in the Florentine dialect, which soon became "Italian" throughout the country (until Dante, Latin had been the language of literature).

8. The poet **Petrarch** wears laurel leaves from Greece, a robe from Rome, and a belt from Wal-Mart.

9. Boccaccio wrote *The Decameron,* stories told to pass the time during the 1348 Black Death.

10. The devious-looking **Machiavelli** is hatching a plot—his book *The Prince* taught that the end justifies the means, paving the way for the slick-and-cunning "Machiavellian" politics of today.

11. Vespucci (in the corner) was an explorer who gave his first name, Amerigo, to a fledgling New World.

12. Galileo (in the other corner) holds the humble telescope he used to spot the moons of Jupiter.

• *Pause at the Arno River, overlooking Ponte Vecchio.*

Ponte Vecchio

Before you is Ponte Vecchio (Old Bridge). A bridge has spanned this narrowest part of the Arno since Roman times. While Rome
"fell," Florence never really did, remaining a bustling trade center along the river. To get into the exclusive little park below (on the north bank), you'll need to join the Florence rowing club.

• *Finish your walk by hiking to the center of the bridge.*

A fine bust of the great goldsmith Cellini graces the central point of the bridge. This statue is a reminder that, in the 1500s, the Medici booted out the bridge's butchers and tanners and installed the gold- and silversmiths who still tempt visitors to this day. This is a very romantic spot late at night (when lovers gather, and a top-notch street musician performs).

Look up to notice the protected and elevated passageway that led the Medici from the Palazzo Vecchio through the Uffizi, across Ponte Vecchio, and up to the immense Pitti Palace, four blocks beyond the bridge. During World War II, the Nazi occupiers were ordered to blow up Ponte Vecchio. An art-loving German consul intervened and saved the bridge. The buildings at either end were destroyed, leaving the bridge impassable but intact. *Grazie.*

• *From here, explore some of Florence's main sights, described next.*

Sights in Florence

While Florence has a wealth of interesting museums well worth knowing about on a longer visit, for a one-day cruiser visit, I've listed just the main sights within walking distance of each other in the center. Don't let the length of my descriptions determine your sightseeing priorities. In this section, Florence's most important sights may have the shortest listings. Sights marked with a ✪ in the listings below are covered in much more detail either in the self-guided walk (earlier) or in one of the self-guided tours (later). If your time is limited, remember that you can beat the crowds at two of Florence's top sights (the Uffizi Gallery and the Accademia) either by buying a Firenze Card or by making a reservation (both explained in the sidebar on page 396).

North of the Duomo

▲▲▲Accademia (Galleria dell'Accademia)

This museum houses Michelangelo's *David*, the consummate Renaissance statue of the buff, biblical shepherd boy ready to take on the giant. Nearby are some of the master's other works, including his powerful (unfinished) *Prisoners*, *St. Matthew*, and a *Pietà* (possibly by one of his disciples).

Cost and Hours: €6.50, €11 with mandatory special exhibits, additional €4 for recommended reservation, covered by Firenze Card; Tue-Sun 8:15-18:50, closed Mon, last entry 30 minutes before closing; audioguide-€6, Rick Steves audio tour available—see page 50, Via Ricasoli 60, reservation tel. 055-294-883, www.polo-museale.firenze.it. To avoid long lines in peak season, get the Firenze Card or make reservations (see sidebar).

✪ For a self-guided tour, see page 421.

▲San Lorenzo Market

Florence's vast open-air market sprawls around the Piazza del Mercato Centrale. Most of the leather stalls are run by Iranians selling South American leather that was tailored in Italy. Prices are soft (daily 9:00-19:00, closed Mon in winter, between the Duomo and train station).

▲Mercato Centrale (Central Market)

Florence's giant iron-and-glass-covered central market, a wonderland of picturesque produce, is fun to explore. While the San Lorenzo Market—with its garment stalls in the piazza just outside—feels like a step up from a haphazard flea market, the Mercato Centrale retains a Florentine elegance. Wander around. You'll see parts of the cow you'd never dream of eating (no, that's not a turkey neck), enjoy generous free samples, watch pasta being made, and have your pick of plenty of fun eateries sloshing out cheap and tasty pasta to locals (Mon-Fri 7:00-14:00, Sat 7:00-17:00, closed Sun). For eating ideas in and around the market, see "Eating in Florence," later.

Duomo and Nearby

The following Duomo-related sights are all covered by a single €10 combo-ticket. This ticket admits you to the Baptistery, dome, Campanile, Duomo Museum, and church crypt (the Duomo itself is free). Tickets are sold online (www.operaduomo.firenze.it) and at the cathedral (inside), Campanile, Duomo Museum (rarely crowded), and the Centro Arte e Cultura (a few steps north of the Baptistery at Piazza di San Giovanni 7).

The Firenze Card (see page 396) also covers all of these sights (except the uninteresting crypt).

❂ For more details on the exterior features of these sights, see the "Florence Renaissance Walk" on page 399.

▲▲Duomo (Cattedrale di Santa Maria del Fiore)

Florence's Gothic cathedral has the third-longest nave in Christendom. The church's noisy neo-Gothic facade from the 1870s is covered with pink, green, and white Tuscan marble. In the interior, you'll see a huge *Last Judgment* by Giorgio Vasari and Federico Zuccari (inside the dome). Much of the church's great art is stored behind the church in the Duomo Museum (which is partially closed for renovation until 2015).

The cathedral's claim to artistic fame is Brunelleschi's magnificent **dome**. While the dome is impressive from down below, you can also climb up inside it (see next listing).

Massive crowds line up to see the huge church's **interior**. Although it's a major sight (and free), it's not worth a long wait.

Cost and Hours: Cathedral interior—free; Mon-Fri 10:00-17:00, Thu until 16:00 May and Oct, until 16:30 Nov-April; Sat 10:00-16:45, Sun 13:30-16:45, audioguide—€5, free English tours offered but fill up fast, modest dress code enforced, tel. 055-230-2885, www.operaduomo.firenze.it.

▲Climbing the Duomo's Dome

For a grand view into the cathedral from the base of the dome, a peek at some of the tools used in the dome's construction, a chance to see Brunelleschi's "dome-within-a-dome" construction, a glorious Florence view from the top, and the equivalent of 463 plunges on a Renaissance StairMaster, climb the dome.

Cost and Hours: €10 ticket covers all Duomo sights, covered by Firenze Card, Mon-Fri 8:30-19:00, Sat 8:30-17:40, closed Sun, last entry 40 minutes before closing, arrive by 8:30 or drop by very late for the fewest crowds, enter from outside church on north side, tel. 055-230-2885.

▲Campanile (Giotto's Tower)

The 270-foot bell tower has 50-some fewer steps than the Duomo's dome (but that's still 414 steps—no elevator); offers a faster, relatively less-crowded climb; and has a view of that magnificent dome to boot. On the way up, there are several intermediate levels where you can catch your breath and enjoy ever-higher views. The stairs narrow as you go up, creating a mosh-pit bottleneck near the very top—but the views are worth the hassle. While the various viewpoints are enclosed by cage-like bars, the gaps are big enough to let you snap great photos.

Cost and Hours: €10 ticket covers all Duomo sights, covered by Firenze Card, daily 8:30-19:30, last entry 40 minutes before closing.

▲Baptistery

Michelangelo said the bronze doors of this octagonal building were fit to be the gates of paradise. Check out the gleaming copies of Lorenzo Ghiberti's bronze doors facing the Duomo (the original panels are in the Duomo Museum). Making a breakthrough in perspective, Ghiberti used mathematical laws to create the illusion of receding distance on a basically flat surface. Inside, sit and savor the medieval mosaic ceiling, where it's always Judgment Day and Jesus is giving the ultimate thumbs-up and thumbs-down.

Cost and Hours: €10 ticket covers all Duomo sights, covered by Firenze Card (get free paper ticket from ticket office), interior open Mon-Sat 11:15-19:00 except first Sat of month 8:30-14:00, Sun 8:30-14:00, last entry 30 minutes before closing, audioguide-€2, photos allowed inside, tel. 055-230-2885. The (facsimile) bronze doors are on the exterior, so they are always "open" and viewable.

▲▲▲Duomo Museum (Museo dell'Opera del Duomo)

The underrated cathedral museum, behind the church, is great if you like sculpture. The building will be undergoing extensive upgrades, so what's on display may change. The museum is home to many of the original creations that defined the 1400s (the Quattrocento) in Florence, when the city blossomed and classical arts were reborn. On the ground floor, look for a late Michelangelo *Pietà*, which was intended as his sculptural epitaph, and statues from the original Baptistery facade. The museum also features Ghiberti's original bronze "Gates of Paradise" panels (the ones on the Baptistery's doors today are replicas). The original sculptured masterpieces that decorated the exterior of the Duomo and the Campanile are now restored and displayed safely indoors at the Duomo Museum (copies are installed on the cathedral and bell tower). Upstairs, you'll find Brunelleschi's models for

his dome, as well as Donatello's anorexic *Mary Magdalene* and his playful choir loft. Though overlooked by most visitors to Florence, this museum is a delight.

Cost and Hours: €10 ticket covers all Duomo sights, covered by Firenze Card, Mon-Sat 9:00-19:30, Sun 9:00-13:45, last entry 45 minutes before closing, one of the few museums in Florence always open on Mon, audioguide-€5, guided tours-€3 summer only (schedule varies, stop by or call to ask), Via del Proconsolo 9, tel. 055-282-226 or 055-230-7885, www.operaduomo.firenze.it.

Between the Duomo and Piazza della Signoria

▲▲▲Bargello (Museo Nazionale del Bargello)

This underappreciated sculpture museum is in a former police station-turned-prison that looks like a mini-Palazzo Vecchio. The Renaissance began with sculpture—the great Florentine painters were "sculptors with brushes." You can see the birth of this revolution of 3-D in the Bargello (bar-JEL-oh), which boasts the best collection of Florentine sculpture. It's a small, uncrowded museum and a pleasant break from the intensity of the rest of Florence.

The Bargello has Donatello's very influential, painfully beautiful *David* (the first male nude to be sculpted in a thousand years), works by Michelangelo, and rooms of Medici treasures. Moody Donatello, who embraced realism with his lifelike statues, set the personal and artistic style for many Renaissance artists to follow. The best pieces are in the ground-floor room at the foot of the outdoor staircase (with fine works by Michelangelo, Cellini, and Giambologna) and in the "Donatello room" directly above (with plenty by Donatello, including two different *David*s, plus Ghiberti and Brunelleschi's revolutionary dueling door panels and yet another *David* by Verrocchio).

Cost and Hours: €4, €7 with mandatory exhibits, covered by Firenze Card, Tue-Sat 8:15-13:50, until 16:50 during special exhibits (generally April-Oct); also open first, third, and fifth Mon and the second and fourth Sun of each month; last entry 30 minutes before closing, reservations possible but unnecessary, audioguide-€6 (€10/2 people), photos in courtyard only, Via del Proconsolo 4, reservation tel. 055-238-8606, www.polomuseale.firenze.it.

▲Mercato Nuovo (a.k.a. the Straw Market)

This market loggia is how Orsanmichele looked before it became a church. Originally a silk and straw market, Mercato Nuovo still functions as a rustic yet touristy market (at the intersection of Via Calimala and Via Porta Rossa). Prices are soft, but the San Lorenzo Market (listed earlier) is much better for haggling. Notice the circled X in the center, marking the spot where people hit after being hoisted up to the top and dropped as punishment for bankruptcy. You'll also find *Il Porcellino* (a statue of a wild boar nicknamed "The Piglet"), which people rub and give coins to ensure their return to Florence. This new copy, while only a few years old, already has a polished snout. At the back corner, a wagon sells tripe (cow innards) sandwiches—a local favorite (daily 9:00-20:00).

▲Piazza della Repubblica and Nearby

This large square sits on the site of the original Roman Forum. Florence was a riverside garrison town set below the older town

of Fiesole—essentially a rectangular fort with the square marking the intersection of the two main roads (Via Corso and Via Roma). The square's lone column—nicknamed the "belly button of Florence"—once marked the intersection (the Roman streets were about nine feet below the present street level). Above ground, all that survives of Roman Florence is this column and the city's street plan. But beneath the stones lie the remains of the ancient city. Look at

FLORENCE

any map of Florence today, and you'll see the ghost of Rome in its streets: a grid-plan city center surrounded by what was the Roman wall. The Braille model of the city (in front of the Paszkowski café) makes the design clear.

Venerable cafés and stores line the square. During the 19th century, intellectuals met in cafés here. Gilli, on the northeast corner, is a favorite for its grand atmosphere and tasty sweets (cheap if you stand at the bar, expensive to sit down) while the recommended Paszkowski has good lunch options (see page 458). The department store La Rinascente, facing Piazza della Repubblica, is one of the city's mainstays (WC on fourth floor, continue up the stairs from there to the bar with a rooftop terrace for great Duomo and city views).

On and near Piazza della Signoria

✪ For more information on Florence's main civic square, Piazza della Signoria, see my "Florence Renaissance Walk" on page 399.

▲▲▲Uffizi Gallery

This greatest collection of Italian paintings anywhere features works by Giotto, Leonardo, Raphael, Caravaggio, Titian, and Michelangelo, and a roomful of Botticellis, including the *Birth of Venus*. Northern Renaissance masters (Dürer, Rembrandt, and Rubens) are also well represented.

Cost and Hours: €6.50, €11 with mandatory special exhibits, extra €4 for recommended reservation, cash required to pick up tickets reserved by phone, covered by Firenze Card, Tue-Sun 8:15-18:35, closed Mon, last entry 30 minutes before closing, audioguide-€6, free Rick Steves audio tour available—see page 50, museum info tel. 055-238-8651, reservation tel. 055-294-883, www.uffizi.firenze.it. To avoid the long ticket lines, get a Firenze Card or make reservations (see page 396).

✪ For a self-guided tour, see page 427.

▲▲Palazzo Vecchio

This castle-like fortress with the 300-foot spire dominates Florence's main square. In Renaissance times, it was the Town Hall, where citizens pioneered the once-radical notion of self-rule. Its official name—the Palazzo della Signoria—refers to the elected members of the city council. In 1540, the tyrant Cosimo I de' Medici made the building his personal palace, redecorating the interior in lavish style. Today the building functions once again as the Town Hall.

Entry to the ground-floor courtyard is free, so even if you don't go upstairs to the museum, you can step inside and feel the essence of the Medici. Paying customers can see Cosimo's (fairly) lavish royal apartments, decorated with (fairly) top-notch paintings and statues by Michelangelo and Donatello. The highlight is the Grand Hall (Salone dei Cinquecento), a 13,000-square-foot hall lined with huge frescoes and interesting statues.

Cost and Hours: Courtyard—free to enter, museum—€6.50, tower climb-€6.50 (418 steps), museum plus tower-€10, museum and tower covered by Firenze Card (first pick up ticket at ground-floor information desk before entering museum); Fri-Wed 9:00-19:00, until 24:00 April-Sept, Thu 9:00-14:00 year-round; tower keeps similar but shorter hours, ticket office closes one hour earlier, videoguide-€5, English tours available, Piazza della Signoria, tel. 055-276-8224, www.museicivicifiorentini.it.

▲Ponte Vecchio

Florence's most famous bridge has long been lined with shops. Originally these were butcher shops that used the river as a handy disposal system. Then, when the powerful and princely Medici built the Vasari Corridor over the bridge, the stinky meat market was replaced by the more elegant gold and silver shops that remain there to this day. A statue of Benvenuto Cellini, the master goldsmith of the Renaissance, stands in the center, ignored by the flood of tacky tourism. This is a very romantic spot late at night (when lovers gather, and a top-notch street musician performs).

FLORENCE

Accademia Gallery Tour: Michelangelo's *David*

One of Europe's great thrills is seeing Michelangelo's *David* in the flesh at the Accademia Gallery. Seventeen feet high, gleaming white, and exalted by a halo-like dome over his head, *David* rarely disappoints, even for those with high expectations. And the Accademia doesn't stop there. With a handful of other Michelangelo statues and a few other interesting sights, it makes for an uplifting visit that isn't overwhelming. *David* is a must-see on any visit to Florence, so plan for it.

Orientation

Cost: €6.50, temporary exhibits raise price to €11, additional €4 fee for recommended reservation; covered by Firenze Card.

Hours: Tue-Sun 8:15-18:50, closed Mon, last entry 30 minutes before closing.

Avoiding Lines: In peak season (April-Oct), it's smart to buy a Firenze Card or reserve ahead (see page 396 for info on both options, as well as some last-minute alternatives). Those with reservations or the Firenze Card line up at the entrance labeled *With Reservations*. In peak season, the museum is most crowded on Sun, Tue, and between about 11:00 and 13:00.

Getting There: It's at Via Ricasoli 60, a 15-minute walk from the train station or a 10-minute walk northeast of the Duomo. Taxis are reasonable.

Information: Exhibits are explained in English, and a small bookstore sells guidebooks near the ticket booths at the entrance. Another bookstore (inside and near the exit) and several shops outside sell postcards, books, and posters. Reservation tel. 055-294-883, www.polomuseale.firenze.it.

Audioguide: A €6 audioguide (€10/2 people) is available in the ticket lobby. You can also download a free Rick Steves audio tour (see page 50).

Length of This Tour: While *David* and the *Prisoners* can be seen in 30 minutes, allow an hour if you wish to linger and explore other parts of the museum.

Services: The museum has no bag-check service, and large backpacks are not allowed. WCs are downstairs near the entrance/exit.

Photography: Photos and videos are prohibited.

Cuisine Art: Gelateria Carabè, popular for its sumptuous *granite* (fresh-fruit Italian ices) is a block toward the Duomo, at Via Ricasoli 60 red. Picnickers can stock up at Il Centro Supermercati, a half-block north (open daily, also has curbside sandwich bar, Via Ricasoli 109). At Piazza San Marco, you can get pizza by the slice from Pugi (#10) and refill your water bottle (in the traffic circle park).

Starring: Michelangelo's *David* and *Prisoners*.

The Tour Begins

• *From the entrance lobby, show your ticket, turn left, and look right down the long hall with* David *at the far end, under a halo-like dome. Yes, you're really here. With* David *presiding at the "altar," the* Prisoners *lining the "nave," and hordes of "pilgrims" crowding in to look, you've arrived at Florence's "cathedral of humanism."*

    Start with the ultimate...

David (1501-1504)

When you look into the eyes of Michelangelo's *David*, you're looking into the eyes of Renaissance Man. This 17-foot-tall symbol of divine victory over evil represents a new century and a whole new Renaissance outlook. This is the age of Columbus and classicism, Galileo and Gutenberg, Luther and Leonardo—of Florence and the Renaissance.

In 1501, Michelangelo Buonarroti, a 26-year-old Florentine, was commissioned to carve a large-scale work for the Duomo. He was given a block of marble that other sculptors had rejected as too tall, shallow, and flawed to be of any value. But Michelangelo picked up his hammer and chisel, knocked a knot off what became *David*'s heart, and started to work.

The figure comes from a Bible story. The Israelites, God's chosen people, are surrounded by barbarian warriors led by a brutish giant named Goliath. The giant challenges the Israelites to send out someone to fight him. Everyone is afraid except for one young shepherd boy—David. Armed only with a sling, which he's thrown over his shoulder, David gathers five smooth stones from the stream and faces Goliath.

The statue captures David as he's sizing up his enemy. He stands relaxed but alert, leaning on one leg in a classical pose known as *contrapposto*. In his powerful right hand, he fondles the handle of the sling, ready to fling a stone at the giant. His gaze is steady—searching with intense concentration, but also with extreme confidence. Michelangelo has caught the precise moment when David is saying to himself, "I can take this guy."

Note that while the label on *David* indicates that he's already slain the giant, the current director of the Accademia believes, as I do, that Michelangelo has portrayed David facing the giant. Unlike most depictions of David after the kill, this sculpture does not show the giant's severed head. There's also a question of exactly how David's sling would work. Is he holding the stone in his right or left hand? Does the right hand hold the sling's pouch or the retention handle of a sling? Scholars debate Sling Theory endlessly.

David is a symbol of Renaissance optimism. He's no brute. He's a civilized, thinking individual who can grapple with and overcome problems. He needs no armor, only his God-given body and wits. Look at his right hand, with the raised veins and strong, relaxed fingers—

FLORENCE

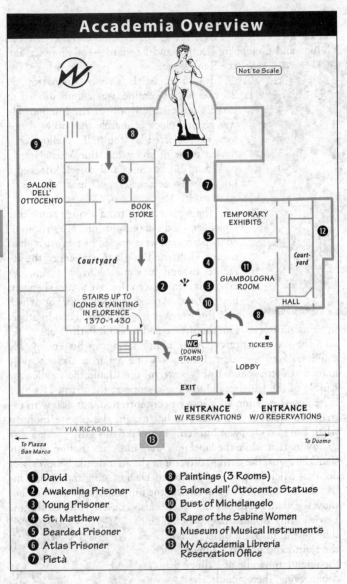

Accademia Overview

Not to Scale

SALONE DELL' OTTOCENTO

BOOK STORE

Courtyard

STAIRS UP TO ICONS & PAINTING IN FLORENCE 1370-1430

TEMPORARY EXHIBITS

GIAMBOLOGNA ROOM

Court-yard

HALL

WC (DOWN STAIRS)

TICKETS

LOBBY

EXIT

ENTRANCE W/ RESERVATIONS

ENTRANCE W/O RESERVATIONS

VIA RICASOLI

← To Piazza San Marco

To Duomo →

1 David
2 Awakening Prisoner
3 Young Prisoner
4 St. Matthew
5 Bearded Prisoner
6 Atlas Prisoner
7 Pietà

8 Paintings (3 Rooms)
9 Salone dell' Ottocento Statues
10 Bust of Michelangelo
11 Rape of the Sabine Women
12 Museum of Musical Instruments
13 My Accademia Libreria Reservation Office

many complained that it was too big and overdeveloped. But this is the hand of a man with the strength of God. No mere boy could slay the giant. But David, powered by God, could...and did.

Originally, the statue was commissioned to stand along the southern roofline of the Duomo. But during the three years it took to sculpt, they decided instead to place it guarding the entrance of Town Hall—the Palazzo Vecchio. (If the relationship between

David's head and body seems a bit out of proportion, it's because Michelangelo designed it to be seen "correctly" from far below the rooftop of the church.)

The colossus was placed standing up in a cart and dragged across rollers from Michelangelo's workshop (behind the Duomo) to the Palazzo Vecchio, where it replaced a work by Donatello. There *David* stood—naked and outdoors—for 350 years. In the right light, you can see signs of weathering on his shoulders. Also, note the crack in *David*'s left arm where it was broken off during a 1527 riot near the Palazzo Vecchio. In 1873, to conserve the masterpiece, the statue was finally replaced with a copy (see photo on bottom of page 423) and moved here. The real *David* now stands under a wonderful Renaissance-style dome designed just for him.

Circle *David* and view him from various angles. From the front, he's confident, but a little less so when you gaze directly into his eyes. Around back, see his sling strap, buns of steel, and Renaissance mullet. Up close, you can see the blue-veined Carrara marble and a few cracks and stains. From the sides, Michelangelo's challenge becomes clear: to sculpt a figure from a block of marble other sculptors said was too tall and narrow to accommodate a human figure.

Renaissance Florentines could identify with *David*. Like him, they considered themselves God-blessed underdogs fighting their city-state rivals. In a deeper sense, they were civilized Renaissance people slaying the ugly giant of medieval superstition, pessimism, and oppression.

• *Hang around a while. Eavesdrop on tour guides. The Plexiglas shields at the base of the statue went up after an attack by a frustrated artist, who smashed the statue's feet in 1991.*

Lining the hall leading up to David are other statues by Michelangelo—his Prisoners, St. Matthew, and Pietà. Start with the Awakening Prisoner, the statue at the end of the nave (farthest from David). He's on your left as you face David.

The Prisoners (*Prigioni*, c. 1516-1534)

These unfinished figures seem to be fighting to free themselves from the stone. Michelangelo believed the sculptor was a tool of God, not creating but simply revealing the powerful and beautiful figures that God had encased in the marble. Michelangelo's job was to chip away the excess, to reveal. He needed to be in tune with God's will, and whenever the spirit came upon him, Michelangelo worked in a frenzy, without sleep, often for days on end.

FLORENCE

The *Prisoners* give us a glimpse of this fitful process, showing the restless energy of someone possessed, struggling against the rock that binds him. Michelangelo himself fought to create the image he saw in his mind's eye. You can still see the grooves from the chisel, and you can picture Michelangelo hacking away in a cloud of dust. Unlike most sculptors, who built a model and then marked up their block of marble to know where to chip, Michelangelo always worked freehand, starting from the front and working back. These figures emerge from the stone (as his colleague Vasari put it) "as though surfacing from a pool of water."

The so-called *Awakening Prisoner* (the names are given by scholars, not Michelangelo) seems to be stretching after a long nap, still tangled in the "bedsheets" of uncarved rock. He's more block than statue.

On the right, the *Young Prisoner* is more finished. He buries his face in his forearm, while his other arm is chained behind him.

The *Prisoners* were designed for the never-completed tomb of Pope Julius II (who also commissioned the Sistine Chapel ceiling). Michelangelo may have abandoned them simply because the project itself petered out, or he may have deliberately left them unfinished. Having perhaps satisfied himself that he'd accomplished what he set out to do, and seeing no point in polishing them into their shiny, finished state, he went on to a new project.

Walking up the nave toward *David,* you'll pass by Michelangelo's *St. Matthew* (1503), on the right. Though not one of the *Prisoners* series, he is also unfinished, perfectly illustrating Vasari's "surfacing" description.

The next statue (also on the right), the *Bearded Prisoner,* is the most finished of the four, with all four limbs, a bushy face, and even a hint of daylight between his arm and body.

Across the nave on the left, the *Atlas Prisoner* carries the unfinished marble on his stooped shoulders, his head still encased in the block.

As you study the *Prisoners,* notice Michelangelo's love and understanding of the human body. His greatest days were spent sketching the muscular, tanned, and sweating bodies of the workers in the Carrara marble quarries. The prisoners' heads and faces are the least-developed part—they "speak" with their poses. Comparing the restless, claustrophobic *Prisoners* with the serene and confident *David* gives an idea of the sheer emotional range in Michelangelo's work.

Pietà

In the unfinished *Pietà* (the threesome closest to *David*), the figures struggle to hold up the sagging body of Christ. Michelangelo (or, more likely, one of his followers) emphasizes the heaviness of

Jesus' dead body, driving home the point that this divine being suffered a very human death. Christ's massive arm is almost the size of his bent and broken legs. By stretching his body—if he stood up, he'd be more than seven feet tall—the weight is exaggerated.

• *Michelangelo's statues are far and away the highlight of the Accademia; if your time is short, you can end your tour now and move on to the next item on your sightseeing list. From here, it's a 10-minute walk to the Duomo—the starting point of my "Florence Renaissance Walk" (see page 399).*

If you have a bit of time to spare, you could take a quick look around...

The Rest of the Museum

Here are a few highlights: a **bust of Michelangelo** at age 89 by his friend and colleague Daniele da Volterra (at the far end of the hall from *David*); in the Salone dell'Ottocento, **plaster statues and busts** that were the "final exams" of the Academy art students; in the Giambologna Room, a full-size plaster model of *Rape of the Sabines* (1582; this guided Giambologna's assistants in completing the marble version in the loggia next to the Palazzo Vecchio), plus minor paintings by Botticelli, Filippino Lippi, Domenico Ghirlandaio, Fra Bartolomeo, and Benozzo Gozzoli; the **Museum of Musical Instruments,** with late-Renaissance cellos, dulcimers, violins, woodwinds, and harpsichords; and, upstairs, a collection of **Florentine Paintings** from just before the Renaissance bloomed (1370-1430).

Uffizi Gallery Tour

In the Renaissance, Florentine artists rediscovered the beauty of the natural world. Medieval art had been symbolic, telling Bible stories. Realism didn't matter. But Renaissance people saw the beauty of God in nature and the human body. They used math and science to capture the natural world on canvas as realistically as possible.

The Uffizi Gallery (oo-FEED-zee) has the greatest overall collection anywhere of Italian painting. We'll trace the rise of realism and savor the optimistic spirit that marked the Renaissance.

FLORENCE

Orientation

Cost: €6.50, €11 with mandatory special exhibits, additional €4 fee for recommended reservation (if you've reserved tickets by phone, bring cash to pick them up), covered by Firenze Card.

Hours: Tue-Sun 8:15-18:35, closed Mon, last entry 30 minutes before closing.

Renovation: The Uffizi is undergoing a massive, years-long renovation that may affect your visit. Some of the items described in this tour may be displayed in different rooms, on loan to other museums, or out for restoration—pick up a floor plan as you enter, and if you need help finding a particular piece of art, ask the guards in each room.

Avoiding Lines: To skip the notoriously long ticket-buying lines, either get a Firenze Card or reserve ahead (for details on both, see page 396). During summer and on weekends, the Uffizi can be booked up a month or more in advance. If you don't have a reservation or a Firenze Card in peak season (April-Oct), the wait can be hours; the busiest days are Tuesday, Saturday, and Sunday.

Getting There: It's on the Arno River between the Palazzo Vecchio and Ponte Vecchio, a 15-minute walk from the train station.

Getting In: There are several entrances (see map on next page). Which one you use depends on whether you have a Firenze Card, a reservation, or neither.

Firenze Card holders enter at door #1 (labeled *Reservation Entrance*), close to the Palazzo Vecchio. Read the signs carefully, as there are two lines at this entrance; get in the line for individuals, not groups.

People **buying a ticket on the spot** line up with everyone else at door #2. (The wait can be hours long.)

To **buy a Firenze Card,** or to see if there are any same-day reservations available (€4 extra, but could save you time in the ticket line), enter door #2 to the left of the ticket-buying line (marked *Booking Service and Today*).

If you've **already made a reservation** and need to pick up your ticket, go to door #3 (labeled *Reservation Ticket Office*, across the courtyard from doors #1 and #2). Tickets are available for pick-up 10 minutes before your appointed time. If you booked online and have already prepaid, you'll just exchange your voucher for a ticket. If you booked by phone, give them your confirmation number and pay for the ticket (cash only). Once you have your ticket, walk briskly past the 200-yard-

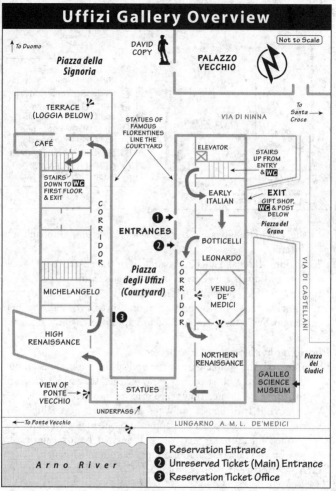

Uffizi Gallery Overview

To Duomo ↑

Piazza della Signoria

DAVID COPY

PALAZZO VECCHIO

Not to Scale

TERRACE (LOGGIA BELOW)

STATUES OF FAMOUS FLORENTINES LINE THE COURTYARD

VIA DI NINNA

To Santa Croce →

CAFÉ

ELEVATOR

STAIRS UP FROM ENTRY & WC

STAIRS DOWN TO WC FIRST FLOOR & EXIT

EARLY ITALIAN

EXIT
GIFT SHOP, WC & POST BELOW

Piazza del Grana

CORRIDOR

❶ → ❷ → ENTRANCES

BOTTICELLI

LEONARDO

Piazza degli Uffizi (Courtyard)

CORRIDOR

MICHELANGELO

VENUS DE' MEDICI

VIA DI CASTELLANI

❸ HIGH RENAISSANCE

NORTHERN RENAISSANCE

Piazza dei Giudici

VIEW OF PONTE VECCHIO →

STATUES

GALILEO SCIENCE MUSEUM

UNDERPASS ↗

← To Ponte Vecchio

LUNGARNO A. M. L. DE'MEDICI

Arno River

FLORENCE

❶ Reservation Entrance
❷ Unreserved Ticket (Main) Entrance
❸ Reservation Ticket Office

long ticket-buying line—pondering the IQ of this gang—to door #1. Show your ticket and walk in.

Information: English information is posted in many rooms. You can buy Uffizi guidebooks (a nice souvenir) at the ground-floor bookstore (€10 small book, €16 bigger version). Museum info tel. 055-238-8651, reservation tel. 055-294-883, www.uffizi.firenze.it.

Audioguides: A 1.5-hour audioguide costs €6 (€10/2 people; must leave ID). You can also download a free Rick Steves audio tour (see page 50).

Length of This Tour: Allow two hours. With less time, see the Florentine Renaissance rooms (Botticelli and Leonardo) and

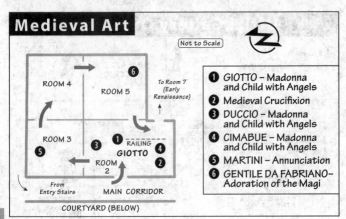

Medieval Art

Not to Scale

ROOM 4

ROOM 5

To Room 7
(Early
Renaissance)

ROOM 3

ROOM 2

RAILING
GIOTTO

From
Entry Stairs

MAIN CORRIDOR

COURTYARD (BELOW)

1. **GIOTTO** – Madonna and Child with Angels
2. **Medieval Crucifixion**
3. **DUCCIO** – Madonna and Child with Angels
4. **CIMABUE** – Madonna and Child with Angels
5. **MARTINI** – Annunciation
6. **GENTILE DA FABRIANO** – Adoration of the Magi

FLORENCE

the High Renaissance section (Michelangelo, Raphael, and Titian).

Cloakroom: Baggage check is available in the entrance lobby. No bottled liquids are allowed inside the museum.

Services: A WC, post office, and book/gift shop are in the entrance/exit hall on the ground floor. Once in the gallery, there are no WCs until the end of our tour, downstairs from the café.

Photography: No photos are allowed.

Cuisine Art: The simple café at the end of the gallery has an outdoor terrace with stunning views of the Palazzo Vecchio and the Duomo's dome. They serve pricey sandwiches, salads, desserts, and fruit cups. You'll pay more to sit at a table or on the view terrace, but a €5 cappuccino outside, with that view, is one of Europe's great treats. Plenty of handy eateries are nearby and described later, under "Eating in Florence."

Starring: Botticelli, Venus, Raphael, Giotto, Titian, Leonardo, and Michelangelo.

The Tour Begins

• *Walk up the four long flights of the monumental staircase to the top floor (those with limited mobility can take the elevator). Your brain should be fully aerated from the hike up. Past the ticket taker, look out the window.*

The Uffizi is U-shaped, running around the courtyard. This left wing contains Florentine paintings from medieval to Renaissance times. The right wing (which you can see across the courtyard) has art from the Roman and Venetian High Renaissance, works from the Baroque period that followed, and a café terrace facing the Duomo. A short hallway with sculpture connects the two wings. We'll concentrate on the Uffizi's forte, the Florentine section, then get a taste of the art it inspired.

• *Head up the long hallway, enter the first door on the left, and face Giotto's giant* Madonna and Child *(straight ahead).*

Medieval—When Art Was as Flat as the World (1200-1400)

Giotto (c. 1266-1337)—*Madonna and Child with Angels (Madonna col Bambino in Trone e Angeli)*

Mary and Baby Jesus sit on a throne in a golden never-never land symbolizing heaven. It's as if medieval Christians couldn't imagine holy people inhabiting our dreary material world. It took Renaissance painters to bring Mary down to earth and give her human realism. For the Florentines, "realism" meant "three-dimensional." In this room, pre-Renaissance paintings show the slow process of learning to paint a 3-D world on a 2-D surface.

Before concentrating on the Giotto, look at some others in the room. The **crucifixion** (on your right as you face the Giotto; may be in restoration) was medieval 3-D: paint a crude two-dimensional work, then physically tilt the head forward. Nice try.

The three similar-looking Madonna-and-Bambinos in this room—all painted within a few decades of each other in about the year 1300—show baby steps in the march to realism. **Duccio**'s piece (on the left as you face Giotto) is the most medieval and two-dimensional. There's no background. The angels are just stacked one on top of the other, floating in the golden atmosphere. Mary's throne is crudely drawn—the left side is at a three-quarter angle while the right is practically straight on. Mary herself is a wispy cardboard-cutout figure seemingly floating just above the throne.

On the opposite wall, the work of **Cimabue**—mixing the iconic Byzantine style with budding Italian realism—is an improvement. The large throne creates an illusion of depth. Mary's foot actually sticks out over the lip of the throne. Still, the angels are stacked totem-pole-style, serving as heavenly bookends.

FLORENCE

Giotto (JOT-oh) employs realism to make his theological points. He creates a space and fills it. Like a set designer, he builds a three-dimensional "stage"—the canopied throne—then peoples it with real beings. The throne has angels in front, prophets behind, and a canopy over the top, clearly defining its three dimensions. The steps up to the throne lead from our space to Mary's, making the scene an extension of our world. But the real triumph here is Mary herself—big and monumental, like a Roman statue. Beneath her robe, she has a real live body, with knees and breasts that stick out at us. This three-dimensionality

was revolutionary in its day, a taste of the Renaissance a century before it began.

Giotto was one of the first "famous" artists. In the Middle Ages, artists were mostly unglamorous craftsmen, like carpenters or cable-TV repairmen. They cranked out generic art and could have signed their work with a bar code. But Giotto was recognized as a genius, a unique individual. He died in a plague that devastated Florence. If there had been no plague, would the Renaissance have started 100 years earlier?

• *Enter Room 3, to the left of Giotto.*

Simone Martini (c. 1284-1344)—*Annunciation (Annunciazione con i Santi Ansano e Massima)*

Simone Martini boils things down to the basic figures needed to get the message across: (1) The angel appears to sternly tell (2) Mary

that she'll be the mother of Jesus. In the center is (3) a vase of lilies, a symbol of purity. Above is (4) the Holy Spirit as a dove about to descend on her. If the symbols aren't enough to get the message across, Simone Martini has spelled it right out for us in Latin: *"Ave Gratia Plena..."* or, "Hail, favored one, the Lord is with you." Mary doesn't exactly look pleased as punch.

This is not a three-dimensional work. The point was not to re-create reality but to teach religion, especially to the illiterate masses. This isn't a beautiful Mary or even a real Mary. She's a generic woman without distinctive features. We know she's pure—

not from her face, but only because of the halo and symbolic flowers. Before the Renaissance, artists didn't care about the beauty of individual people.

Simone Martini's *Annunciation* has medieval features you'll see in many of the paintings in the next few rooms: (1) religious subject, (2) gold background, (3) two-dimensionality, and (4) meticulous detail.

• *Pass through Room 4, full of golden altarpieces, stopping at the far end of Room 5.*

Gentile da Fabriano (c. 1370-1427)—*Adoration of the Magi (Adorazione dei Magi)*

Look at the incredible detail of the Three Kings' costumes, the fine horses, and the cow in the cave. The canvas is filled from top

to bottom with realistic details—but it's far from realistic. While the Magi worship Jesus in the foreground, their return trip home dangles over their heads in the "background."

This is a textbook example of the International Gothic style popular with Europe's aristocrats in the early 1400s: well-dressed, elegant people in a colorful, design-oriented setting. The religious subject is just an excuse to paint secular luxuries such as jewelry and clothes made of silk brocade. And the scene's background and foreground are compressed together to create an overall design that's pleasing to the eye.

Such exquisite detail work raises the question: Was Renaissance three-dimensionality truly an improvement over Gothic, or simply a different style?

• *Exit to your right and hang a U-turn left into Room 7.*

Early Renaissance (mid-1400s)

Paolo Uccello (1397-1475)—*The Battle of San Romano (La Battaglia di San Romano)*

(Consider yourself lucky if this painting, long under restoration, has returned for your visit.) In the 1400s, painters worked out the problems of painting realistically, using mathematics to create the illusion of three-dimensionality. This colorful battle scene is not so much a piece of art as an exercise in perspective. Paolo Uccello (oo-CHEL-loh) has challenged himself with every possible problem.

The broken lances at left set up a 3-D "grid" in which to place this crowded scene. The fallen horses and soldiers are experiments

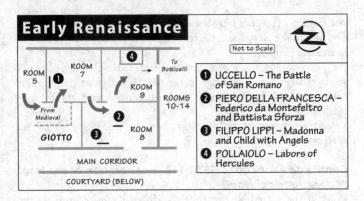

FLORENCE

in "foreshortening"—diminishing the things that are farther away from us (which appear smaller) to create the illusion of distance. Some of the figures are definitely A-plus material, like the fallen gray horse in the center and the white horse at the far right walking away. But some are more like B-minus work—the kicking red horse's legs look like ham hocks at this angle, and the fallen soldier at the far right would be child-size if he stood up.

And then there's the D-minus "Are you on drugs?" work. The converging hedges in the background create a nice illusion of a distant hillside maybe 250 feet away. So what are those soldiers the size of the foreground figures doing there? And jumping the hedge, is that rabbit 40 feet tall?

Paolo Uccello almost literally went crazy trying to master the three dimensions (thank God he was born before Einstein discovered one more). Uccello got so wrapped up in it he kind of lost... perspective.

• *Enter Room 8. In the center of the room stands a double portrait.*

Piero della Francesca (c. 1412-1492)—*Federico da Montefeltro and Battista Sforza (Federico da Montefeltro e Battista Sforza)*

In medieval times, only saints and angels were worthy of being painted. In the humanistic Renaissance, however, even nonreligious folk like this husband and wife had their features preserved for posterity. Usually the man would have appeared on the left, with his wife at the right. But Federico's right side was definitely not his best—he lost his right eye and part of his nose in a tournament. Renaissance artists discovered the beauty in ordinary people and painted them, literally, warts and all.

Fra Filippo Lippi (1406-1469)—*Madonna and Child with Angels (Madonna col Bambino e Angeli)*

Compare this Mary with the generic female in Simone Martini's *Annunciation*. We don't need the wispy halo over her head to tell

us she's holy—she radiates sweetness and light from her divine face. Heavenly beauty is expressed by a physically beautiful woman.

Fra (Brother) Lippi, an orphan raised as a monk, lived a less-than-monkish life. He lived with a nun who bore him two children. He spent his entire life searching for the perfect Virgin. Through his studio passed Florence's prettiest girls, many of whom decorate the walls here in this room.

Lippi painted idealized beauty, but his models were real flesh-and-blood human beings. You could look through all the thousands of paintings from the Middle Ages and not find anything so human as the mischievous face of one of Lippi's little angel boys.

• *Enter Room 9, with two small works by Pollaiolo in the glass case between the windows.*

Antonio del Pollaiolo (c. 1431-1498)—*Labors of Hercules (Fatiche di Ercole)*

Hercules gets a workout in two small panels showing the human form at odd angles. The poses are the wildest imaginable, to show how each muscle twists and tightens. While Uccello worked on perspective, Pollaiolo studied anatomy. In medieval times, dissection of corpses was a sin and a crime (the two were the same then).

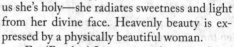

Dissecting was a desecration of the human body, the temple of God. But Pollaiolo was willing to sell his soul to the devil for artistic knowledge. He dissected.

There's something funny about this room that I can't put my finger on...I've got it—no Madonnas. Not one. (No, that's not a Madonna; she's a Virtue.)

We've seen how Early Renaissance artists worked to conquer reality. Now let's see the fruits of their work, the flowering of Florence's Renaissance.

• *Enter the large Botticelli room and take a seat.*

The Renaissance Blossoms (1450-1500)

Florence in 1450 was in a Firenz-y of activity. There was a can-do spirit of optimism in the air, led by prosperous merchants and bankers and a strong middle class. The government was reasonably democratic, and Florentines saw themselves as citizens of a strong republic—like ancient Rome. Their civic pride showed in the public monuments and artworks they built. Man was leaving the protection of the church to stand on his own two feet.

Lorenzo de' Medici, head of the powerful Medici family, epitomized this new humanistic spirit. Strong, decisive, handsome, poetic, athletic, sensitive, charismatic, intelligent, brave, clean, and reverent, Lorenzo was a true Renaissance man, deserving of the nickname he went by—the Magnificent. He gathered Florence's best and brightest around him for evening wine and discussions of great ideas. One of this circle was the painter Botticelli (bot-i-CHEL-ee).

Sandro Botticelli (1445-1510)—*Allegory of Spring* (*Primavera*)

It's springtime in a citrus grove. The winds of spring blow in (Mr. Blue, at right), causing the woman on the right to sprout flowers from her lips as she morphs into Flora, or Spring—who walks by, spreading flowers from her dress. At the left are Mercury and the Three Graces, dancing a delicate maypole dance. The Graces may be symbolic of the three forms of love—love of beauty, love of people, and sexual love, suggested by the raised intertwined fingers. (They forgot love of peanut butter on toast.) In the center stands Venus, the Greek goddess of love. Above her flies a blindfolded Cupid, happily shooting his arrows of love without worrying about whom they'll hit.

Here is the Renaissance in its first bloom, its "springtime" of

The Renaissance Blossoms

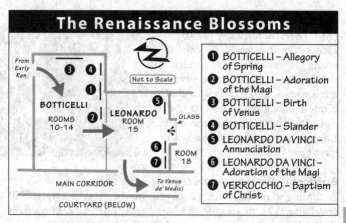

From Early Ren.

BOTTICELLI
ROOMS 10-14

LEONARDO
ROOM 15

GLASS

Not to Scale

ROOM 18

MAIN CORRIDOR

To Venus de' Medici

COURTYARD (BELOW)

❶ BOTTICELLI – Allegory of Spring
❷ BOTTICELLI – Adoration of the Magi
❸ BOTTICELLI – Birth of Venus
❹ BOTTICELLI – Slander
❺ LEONARDO DA VINCI – Annunciation
❻ LEONARDO DA VINCI – Adoration of the Magi
❼ VERROCCHIO – Baptism of Christ

innocence. Madonna is out, Venus is in. Adam and Eve hiding their nakedness are out, glorious flesh is in. This is a return to the pre-Christian pagan world of classical Greece, where things of the flesh are not sinful. But this is certainly no orgy—just fresh-faced innocence and playfulness.

Botticelli emphasizes pristine beauty over gritty realism. The lines of the bodies, especially of the Graces in their see-through nighties, have pleasing, S-like curves. The faces are idealized but have real human features. There's a look of thoughtfulness and even melancholy in the faces—as though everyone knows that the innocence of spring will not last forever.

• *Look at the next painting to the right.*

Botticelli—*Adoration of the Magi (Adorazione dei Magi)*

Here's the rat pack of confident young Florentines who reveled in the optimistic pagan spirit—even in a religious scene. Botticelli included himself among the adorers, at the far right, looking vain in the yellow robe. Lorenzo is the Magnificent-looking guy at the far left.

Botticelli—*Birth of Venus (Nascita di Venere)*

According to myth, Venus was born from the foam of a wave. Still only half awake, this fragile, newborn beauty floats ashore on a clam shell, blown by the winds, where her maid waits to dress her. The pose is the same S-curve of classical statues (as we'll soon see). Botticelli's pastel colors make the world itself seem fresh and newly born.

This is the purest expression of Renaissance beauty. Venus' naked body is not sensual, but innocent. Botticelli thought that physical beauty was a way of appreciating God. Remember Michelangelo's poem: Souls will never ascend to heaven "...unless the sight of Beauty lifts them there."

Botticelli finds God in the details—Venus' windblown hair, her translucent skin, the maid's braided hair, the slight ripple of the wind god's abs, and the flowers tumbling in the slowest of slow motions, suspended like musical notes, caught at the peak of their brief life.

Mr. and Mrs. Wind intertwine—notice her hands clasped around his body. Their hair, wings, and robes mingle like the wind. But what happened to those splayed toes?

• *"Venus on the Half-Shell" (as many tourists call this) is one of the masterpieces of Western art. Take some time with it. Then find the small canvas on the wall to the right, near the* Allegory of Spring.

Botticelli—*Slander (La Calunnia)*

The spring of Florence's Renaissance had to end. Lorenzo died young. The economy faltered. Into town rode the monk Savonarola, preaching medieval hellfire and damnation for those who embraced the "pagan" Renaissance spirit. "Down, down with all gold and decoration," he roared. "Down where the body is food for the worms." He presided over huge bonfires, where the people threw in their fine clothes, jewelry, pagan books...and paintings.

Slander spells the end of the Florentine Renaissance. The architectural setting is classic Brunelleschi, but look what's taking place beneath those stately arches. These aren't proud Renaissance men and women but a ragtag, medieval-looking bunch, a Court of Thieves in an abandoned hall of justice. The accusations fly, and everyone is condemned. The naked man pleads for mercy, but the hooded black figure, a symbol of his execution, turns away. The figure of Truth (naked Truth)—straight out of *The Birth of Venus*—looks up to heaven as if to ask, "What has happened to us?" The classical statues in their niches look on in disbelief.

Botticelli listened to Savonarola. He burned some of his own paintings and changed his tune. The last works of his life were darker, more somber, and pessimistic about humanity.

The 19th-century German poet Heinrich Heine said, "When they start by burning books, they'll end by burning people." After four short years of power, Savonarola was burned in 1498 on his own bonfire in Piazza della Signoria, but by then the city was in shambles. The first flowering of the Renaissance was over.

• *Enter the next room.*

Leonardo da Vinci (1452-1519)—*Annunciation (Annunciazione)*

A scientist, architect, engineer, musician, and painter, Leonardo was a true Renaissance Man. He worked at his own pace rather than to please an employer, so he often left works unfinished. The two paintings in this room aren't his best, but even a lesser Leonardo is enough to put a museum on the map, and they're definitely worth a look.

In the *Annunciation*, the angle Gabriel has walked up to Mary, and now kneels on one knee like an ambassador, saluting her. See how relaxed his other hand is, draped over his knee. Mary, who's been reading, looks up with a gesture of surprise and curiosity.

Leonardo constructs a beautifully landscaped "stage" and puts his characters in it. Look at the bricks on the right wall. If you extended lines from them, the lines would all converge at the center of the painting, the distant blue mountain. Same with the edge of the sarcophagus and the railing. This subtle touch creates a subconscious feeling of balance, order, and spaciousness in the viewer.

Think back to Simone Martini's *Annunciation* to realize how much more natural, relaxed, and realistic Leonardo's version is. He's taken a miraculous event—an angel appearing out of the blue—and presented it in a very human way.

Leonardo da Vinci—*Adoration of the Magi* (*Adorazione dei Magi*)

(This piece may be under restoration during your visit.) Leonardo's human insight is even more apparent here, in this unfinished work.

The poor kings are amazed at the Christ child—even afraid of him. They scurry around like chimps around a fire. This work is as agitated as the *Annunciation* is calm, giving us an idea of Leonardo's range. Leonardo was pioneering a new era of painting, showing not just outer features but the inner personality.

The next painting to the right, **Baptism of Christ**, is by Andrea del Verrocchio, Leonardo's teacher. Leonardo painted the angel on the far left when he was only a teenager. Legend has it that when Verrocchio saw that some kid had painted an angel better than he ever would...he hung up his brush for good.

Florence saw the first blossoming of the Renaissance. But when the cultural climate turned chilly, artists flew south to warmer climes. The Renaissance shifted to Rome.

• *Exit into the main hallway. Breathe. Sit. Admire the ceiling. Look out the window. See you in five.*

Back already? Now continue down the hallway. On your left is a

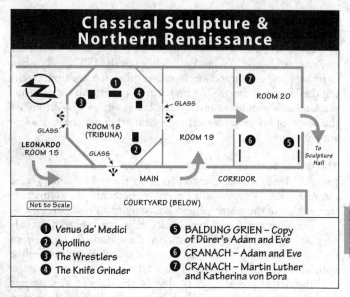

Classical Sculpture & Northern Renaissance

ROOM 18 (TRIBUNA)

ROOM 19

ROOM 20

LEONARDO ROOM 15

GLASS

GLASS

GLASS

MAIN   CORRIDOR

To Sculpture Hall

Not to Scale   COURTYARD (BELOW)

❶ Venus de' Medici
❷ Apollino
❸ The Wrestlers
❹ The Knife Grinder

❺ BALDUNG GRIEN – Copy of Dürer's Adam and Eve
❻ CRANACH – Adam and Eve
❼ CRANACH – Martin Luther and Katherina von Bora

FLORENCE

doorway to the recently renovated Tribuna (a.k.a. Room 18). Gazing inside, you'll see the famous Venus de' Medici statue.

Classical Sculpture

If the Renaissance was the foundation of the modern world, the foundation of the Renaissance was classical sculpture. Sculptors, painters, and poets alike turned for inspiration to these ancient Greek and Roman works as the epitome of balance, 3-D perspective, human anatomy, and beauty.

Venus de' Medici (Venere dei Medici)

Is this pose familiar? Botticelli's *Birth of Venus* has the same position of the arms, the same S-curved body, and the same lifting of the right leg. A copy of this statue stood in Lorenzo the Magnificent's garden, where Botticelli used to hang out. This one is a Roman copy of the lost original by the great Greek sculptor Praxiteles. Balanced, harmonious, and serene, the statue embodies the attributes of Greece's "Golden Age," when balance was admired in every aspect of life.

Perhaps more than any other work of art, this statue has been the epitome of both ideal beauty and sexuality. In the 18th and 19th centuries, sex was "dirty," so the sex drive of cultured aristocrats was channeled into a love of pure beauty. Wealthy sons and daughters of Europe's aristocrats made the pilgrimage to the

Uffizi to complete their classical education...where they swooned in ecstasy before the cold beauty of this goddess of love.

Louis XIV had a bronze copy made. Napoleon stole her away to Paris for himself. And in Philadelphia in the 1800s, a copy had to be kept under lock and key to prevent the innocent from catching the Venere-al disease. At first, it may be difficult for us to appreciate such passionate love of art, but if any generation knows the power of sex to sell something—be it art or underarm deodorant—it's ours.

The Other Statues

Venus de' Medici's male counterpart is on the right, facing Venus. *Apollino* (a.k.a. "Venus with a Penis") is another Greco-Roman interpretation of the master of smooth, cool lines: Praxiteles.

The other works are later Greek (Hellenistic), when quiet balance was replaced by violent motion and emotion. *The Wrestlers,* to the left of Venus, is a study in anatomy and twisted limbs—like Pollaiolo's paintings a thousand years later.

The drama of *The Knife Grinder* to the right of Venus stems from the off-stage action—he's sharpening the knife to flay a man alive.

This fine room was a showroom, or a "cabinet of wonders," back when this building still functioned as the Medici offices. Filled with family portraits, it's a holistic statement that symbolically links the Medici family with the four basic elements: air (weathervane in the lantern), water (inlaid mother of pearl in the dome), fire (red wall), and earth (inlaid stone floor).

• *Enter the next room past the Tribuna, then turn right into Room 20.*

Northern Renaissance

Baldung Grien (c. 1484-1545)—Copy of Dürer's
Adam and Eve

The warm spirit of the Renaissance blew north into Germany. Albrecht Dürer (1471-1528), the famous German painter and engraver, traveled to Venice, where he fell in love with all things Italian. Returning home, he painted the First Couple in the Italian style—full-bodied, muscular (check out Adam's abs and Eve's knees), "carved" with strong shading, fresh-faced, and innocent in their earthly Paradise.

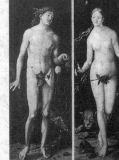

This copy of Dürer's original (it's in the Prado) by Hans Baldung Grien was a training exercise. Like many of Europe's artists—including Michelangelo and Raphael—Baldung Grien learned technique by studying Dürer's meticulous engravings, spread by the newly invented printing press.

Lucas Cranach (1472-1553)—*Adam and Eve*

Eve sashays forward, with heavy-lidded eyes, to offer the forbidden fruit. Adam stretches to display himself and his foliage to Eve.

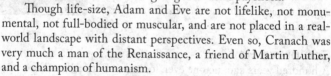

The two panels are linked by smoldering eye contact, as Man and Woman awaken to their own nakedness. The Garden of Eden is about to be rocked by new ideas that are both liberating and troubling.

Though the German Lucas Cranach occasionally dabbled in the "Italian style," he chose to portray his Adam and Eve in the now-retro look of International Gothic.

They are slimmer than Dürer's, as well as smoother, more S-shaped, elegant, graceful, shapely, and erotic, with the dainty pinkies of the refined aristocrats who were signing Cranach's paycheck.

Though life-size, Adam and Eve are not lifelike, not monumental, not full-bodied or muscular, and are not placed in a real-world landscape with distant perspectives. Even so, Cranach was very much a man of the Renaissance, a friend of Martin Luther, and a champion of humanism.

• *Find a small, two-panel portrait featuring Martin Luther with his wife (or possibly a panel featuring Luther's colleague, Melanchthon; the museum rotates these two).*

Cranach—*Martin Luther*

Martin Luther—German monk, fiery orator, and religious whistle-blower—sparked a century of European wars by speaking out against the Catholic Church.

Luther (1483-1546) lived a turbulent life. In early adulthood, the newly ordained priest suffered a severe personal crisis of faith, before finally emerging "born again." In 1517, he openly protested against Church corruption and was excommunicated. Defying both the pope and the emperor, he lived on the run as an outlaw, watching as his ideas sparked peasant riots. He still found time to translate the New Testament from Latin to modern German, write hymns such as "A Mighty Fortress," and spar with the humanist Erasmus and fellow-Reformer Zwingli.

In Cranach's portrait, Martin Luther (at age 46) is easing out of the fast lane. Recently married to an ex-nun, he has traded his monk's habit for street clothes, bought a house, had several kids... and has clearly been enjoying his wife's home cooking and home-brewed beer.

Cranach—*Katherina von Bora*

When "Katie" (well, Käthe) decided to leave her convent, the famous Martin Luther agreed to help find her a husband. She rejected his nominees, saying she'd marry no one...except Luther himself. In 1525, the 42-year-old ex-priest married the 26-year-old ex-nun "to please my father and annoy the pope." Martin turned his checkbook over to "my lord Katie," who also ran the family farm, raised their 6 children and 11 adopted orphans, and hosted Martin's circle of friends (including Cranach) at loud, chatty dinner parties.

• *Pass through the next couple of rooms, exiting to a great view of the Arno and Ponte Vecchio. Stroll through the...*

Sculpture Hall

A hundred years ago, no one even looked at Botticelli—they came to the Uffizi to see the sculpture collection. And today, these 2,000-year-old Roman copies of 2,500-year-old Greek originals are hardly noticed...but they should be. Only a few are displayed here now.

The most impressive is the male nude, *Doriforo* ("spear carrier"), a Roman copy of the Greek original by Polykleitos.

The purple statue in the center of the hall—headless and limbless—is a **female wolf** (*lupa,* c. A.D. 120) done in porphyry stone. This was the animal that raised Rome's legendary founders and became the city's symbol. Renaissance Florentines marveled at the ancient Romans' ability to create such lifelike, three-dimensional works. They learned to reproduce them in stone...and then learned to paint them on a two-dimensional surface.

• *Gaze out the windows from the hall for a...*

View of the Arno

Enjoy Florence's best view of the Arno and Ponte Vecchio. You can also see the red-tiled roof of the Vasari Corridor, the "secret" passage connecting the Palazzo Vecchio, Uffizi, Ponte Vecchio, and Pitti Palace on the other side of the river—a half-mile in all. This was a private walkway, wallpapered in great art, for the Medici family's commute from home to work.

As you appreciate the view (best at sunset), remember that it's this sort of pleasure that Renaissance painters wanted you to get from their paintings. For them, a canvas was a window you looked through to see the wide world. Their paintings re-create natural perspective: Distant objects (such as bridges) are smaller, dimmer, and higher up the "canvas," while closer objects are bigger, clearer, and lower.

We're headed down the home stretch now. If your little U-feetsies are killing you, and it feels like torture, remind yourself that it's a pleasant torture and smile...like the statue next to you.

• *In the far hallway, turn left into the first room (#25) to find the works by Titian and Parmigianino.*

High Renaissance (1500-1550)

Titian (Tiziano Vecellio, c. 1490-1576)—*Venus of Urbino (Venere di Urbino)*

Compare this *Venus* with Botticelli's newly hatched *Venus,* and you get a good idea of the difference between the Florentine and Vene-

tian Renaissance. Botticelli's was pure, innocent, and otherworldly. Titian's should have a staple in her belly button. This isn't a Venus, it's a centerfold—with no purpose but to please the eye and other organs. While Botticelli's allegorical *Venus* is a message, this is a massage. The bed is used.

Titian and his fellow Vene-
tians took the pagan spirit pioneered in Florence and carried it to its logical hedonistic conclusion. Using bright, rich colors, they captured the luxurious life of happy-go-lucky Venice.

While other artists may have balanced their compositions with a figure on the left and one on the right, Titian balances his painting in a different way—with color. The canvas is split down the middle by the curtain. The left half is dark, the right half lighter. The two halves are connected by a diagonal slash of luminous gold—the nude woman. The girl in the background is trying to find her some clothes.

By the way, visitors from centuries past also panted in front of this Venus. The Romantic poet Byron called it *"the* Venus." With her sensual skin, hey-sailor look, and suggestively placed hand, she must have left them blithering idiots.

• *Find a n-n-n-nearby painting...*

FLORENCE

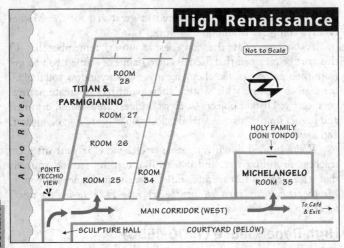

High Renaissance

Not to Scale

Arno River

ROOM 28

TITIAN & PARMIGIANINO

ROOM 27

ROOM 26

HOLY FAMILY (DONI TONDO)

PONTE VECCHIO VIEW

ROOM 25   ROOM 34

MICHELANGELO ROOM 35

MAIN CORRIDOR (WEST)

To Café & Exit

SCULPTURE HALL   COURTYARD (BELOW)

Parmigianino (1503-1540)—*Madonna with the Long Neck (Madonna della Collo Lungo)*

Once Renaissance artists had mastered reality, where could they go from here?

Mannerists such as Parmigianino tried, by going beyond realism, exaggerating it for effect. Using brighter colors and twisting poses, they created scenes more elegant and more exciting than real life.

By stretching the neck of his Madonna, Parmigianino (like the cheese) gives her an unnatural, swanlike beauty. She has the same pose and position of hands as Botticelli's *Venus* and the *Venus de' Medici*. Her body forms an arcing S-curve—down her neck as far as her elbow, then back the other way along Jesus' body to her knee, then down to her foot. Baby Jesus seems to be blissfully gliding down this slippery slide of sheer beauty.

• *Return to the hallway and continue down a few steps to Room 35, the Michelangelo Room.*

Michelangelo Buonarroti (1475-1564)—*Holy Family (Sacra Famiglia)*, a.k.a. *Doni Tondo*

This is the only completed easel painting by the greatest sculptor in history. Florentine painters were sculptors with brushes; this shows it. Instead of a painting, it's more like three clusters of statues with some clothes painted on.

The main subject is the holy family—Mary, Joseph, and Baby

Jesus—and in the background are two groups of nudes looking like classical statues. The background represents the old pagan world, while Jesus in the foreground is the new age of Christianity. The figure of young John the Baptist at right is the link between the two.

This is a "peasant" Mary, with a plain face and sunburned arms. Michelangelo shows her from a very unflattering angle—we're looking up her nostrils. But Michelangelo himself was an ugly man, and he was among the first artists to recognize the beauty in everyday people.

Michelangelo was a Florentine—in fact, he was like an adopted son of the Medici, who recognized his talent—but much of his

greatest work was done in Rome as part of the pope's face-lift of the city. We can see here some of the techniques he used on the Sistine Chapel ceiling that revolutionized painting—monumental figures; dramatic angles (looking up Mary's nose); accentuated, rippling muscles; and bright, clashing colors (all the more apparent since both this work and the Sistine Chapel ceiling have recently been cleaned). These elements added a dramatic tension that was lacking in the graceful work of Leonardo and Botticelli.

Michelangelo painted this for his friend Agnolo Doni for 70 ducats. (Michelangelo designed, but didn't carve, the elaborate frame.) When the painting was delivered, Doni tried to talk Michelangelo down to 40. Proud Michelangelo took the painting away and would not sell it until the man finally agreed to pay double...140 ducats.

In the Uffizi, we've seen many images of female beauty: from ancient goddesses to medieval Madonnas and wicked Eves, from Botticelli's pristine nymphs to Titian's sensuous centerfold, from Parmigianino's cheesy slippery-slide to Michelangelo's peasant Mary. Their physical beauty expresses different aspects of the human spirit.

• *Consider your essential Uffizi tour over. But on your way to the exit, you'll pass by much more art, including one high-power stop—Raphael.*

> *But first, continue down the hallway to the café. Here you can enjoy a truly aesthetic experience...*

Little Capuchin Monk (Cappuccino)

This drinkable art form, born in Italy, is now enjoyed all over the world. It's called the "Little Capuchin Monk" because the coffee's

frothy light- and dark-brown foam looks like the two-toned cowls of the Capuchin order. Sip it on the terrace in the shadow of the towering Palazzo Vecchio, and be glad we live in an age where you don't need to be a Medici to enjoy all this fine art. *Salute.*

*• When you're ready to move on, go down the staircase near the café, to the first floor. Like it or not, you'll be walking through a dozen or more rooms and a lot more art as you make your way to the exit (uscita)—including the **Foreign Painters Section** (with a couple of Rembrandt self-portraits in Room 49) and, in Room 66...*

Raphael (Raffaello Sanzio, 1483-1520)—*Madonna of the Goldfinch (La Madonna del Cardellino)*

Raphael brings Mary and bambino down from heaven and into the real world of trees, water, and sky. He gives Baby Jesus (right) and John the Baptist a realistic, human playfulness. It's a tender scene painted with warm colors and a hazy background that matches the golden skin of the children.

Raphael perfected his craft in Florence, following the graceful style of Leonardo. In typical Leonardo fashion, this group of Mary, John the Baptist, and Jesus is arranged in the shape of a pyramid, with Mary's head at the peak.

The two halves of the painting balance perfectly. Draw a line down the middle, through Mary's nose and down through her knee. John the Baptist on the left is balanced by Jesus on the right. Even the trees in the background balance each other, left and right. These things aren't immediately noticeable, but they help create the subconscious feelings of balance and order that reinforce the atmosphere of maternal security in this domestic scene—pure Renaissance.

Raphael—Leo X and Cardinals (*Ritratta del Papa Leone X con i Cardinali*)

Raphael was called to Rome at the same time as Michelangelo, working next door in the Vatican apartments while Michelangelo painted the Sistine Chapel ceiling. Raphael peeked in from time to time, learning from Michelangelo's monumental, dramatic figures, and his later work is grittier and more realistic than the idealized, graceful, and "Leonardoesque" Madonna.

Pope Leo X is big, like a Michelangelo statue. And Raphael captures some of the seamier side of Vatican life in the cardinals' eyes—shrewd, suspicious, and somewhat cynical. With Raphael, the photographic realism pursued by painters since Giotto was finally achieved.

The Florentine Renaissance ended in 1520 with the death of Raphael. Raphael (you may see his **self-portrait** in the room) is considered both the culmination and conclusion of the Renaissance. The realism, balance, and humanism we associate with the Renaissance are all found in Raphael's work. He combined the grace of Leonardo with the power of Michelangelo. With his death, the High Renaissance ended as well.

• *Continue on through a dozen more rooms to the exit. Before leaving, check out the nearby **Caravaggio Rooms** (81-82), which include the shocking ultra-realism of Caravaggio's Sacrifice of Isaac.*

> *When you're ready to leave, the exit takes you back down to the WCs/bookstore/post office, and the way out to the street. When you re-enter the real world, you may see it with new eyes.*

Shopping in Florence

Florence is a great shopping town—known for its sense of style since the Medici days. Many people spend entire days shopping.

Smaller stores are generally open 9:00-13:00 and 15:30-19:30, usually closed on Sunday, often closed on Monday, and sometimes closed for a couple of weeks around August 15. Many stores have promotional stalls in the market squares.

For shopping ideas, ads, and a list of markets, see *The Florentine* newspaper or *Florence Concierge Information* magazine (free from TI and many hotels). For a list of bookstores, see page 393. For information on VAT refunds and customs regulations, see page 135.

Where to Shop

Markets

Busy street scenes and markets abound. Prices are soft in the markets—go ahead and bargain. Perhaps the biggest market is the one that fills the Piazza del Mercato Centrale (see page 415), with countless stalls selling lower-end leather, clothing, T-shirts, handbags, and souvenirs (daily 9:00-19:00, closed Mon in winter, between the Duomo and train station). Beware of fake "genuine" leather (good quality shouldn't smell like "leather") and "Venetian" glass. The neighboring Mercato Centrale (Central Market) is a giant covered food market (see "Edible Goodies," later).

Other popular shopping centers include the following: the Santa Croce area, known for leather (check out the leather school actually inside Santa Croce Church); Ponte Vecchio's gold and silver shops; and the old, covered Mercato Nuovo (three blocks north of Ponte Vecchio, described on page 419).

Wander the city's "Left Bank," the Oltrarno, for antiques and artisan shops (on Via Toscanella and neighboring streets, south of the river).

A **flea market** litters Piazza dei Ciompi with antiques and odds and ends daily; it gets really big on the last Sunday of each month (9:00-19:30, north of Piazza Santa Croce).

Boutiques and High Fashion

The entire area between the river and the cathedral is busy with inviting boutiques that show off ritzy Italian fashions. The street Via de' Tornabuoni is best for boutique browsing.

The main **Ferragamo** store fills a classy 800-year-old building with a fine selection of shoes and bags (daily 10:00-19:30, Via de' Tornabuoni 2). They have an interesting, four-room **shoe museum** (€5, daily 10:00-18:00, near the Santa Trinità bridge at Piazza Santa Trinità 5, tel. 055-356-2846).

The **Gucci Museum,** right on Piazza della Signoria, stylishly tells the story of the famous designer, showcasing everything from clothing and bags to a limited-edition Cadillac (visible without going in). With a swanky café and contemporary art exhibits, it's the better choice for fashionistas with time for only one of these museums (€6, daily 10:00-20:00, tel. 055-7592-3302).

For more boutiques, meander the following streets: Via della Vigna Nuova (runs west from Via de' Tornabuoni), Via del Parione, and Via Strozzi (runs east from Via de' Tornabuoni to Piazza della Repubblica).

Department Stores

Typical chain department stores are **Coin,** the Italian equivalent of Macy's (Mon-Sat 10:00-19:30, Sun 10:30-19:30, on Via de' Calzaiuoli, near Orsanmichele Church); the similar, upscale **La Rinascente** (Mon-Sat 9:00-22:00, Sun 10:00-21:00, on Piazza della Repubblica); and **Oviesse,** a discount clothing chain, the local

JCPenney (Mon-Sat 9:00-19:30, Sun 10:00-19:30, near train station at intersection of Via Panzani and Via del Giglio).

What to Buy

Souvenir Ideas

Shoppers in Florence can easily buy art reproductions (posters, calendars, books, prints, and so on—a breeze to find in and near the Uffizi and Accademia museums). With its history as a literary center, Florence offers traditional marbled stationery and leather-bound journals (try the Il Papiro chain stores), plus reproductions of old documents, maps, and manuscripts. Find silk ties, scarves, and Tuscan ceramics at the San Lorenzo street market, where haggling is expected. Goofy knickknacks featuring Renaissance masterpieces are fun gifts: Botticelli mouse pads, Raphael lipstick-holders, and plaster *David*s. For soaps, skin creams, herbal remedies, and perfumes, sniff out the antique and palatial perfumery, **Farmacia di Santa Maria Novella** (Via della Scala 16).

Edible Goodies

The **Mercato Centrale** is a prime spot for stocking up on culinary souvenirs (Mon-Fri 7:00-14:00, Sat 7:00-17:00, closed Sun, a block north of the Church of San Lorenzo). Classic purchases include olive oil and balsamic vinegar, unusually shaped and colored pasta, dried porcini mushrooms, spices, and jars of pestos and sauces (such as pesto *genovese* or *tartufo*—truffle).

While many bring home a special bottle of Chianti Classico or Brunello di Montalcino, I take home only the names of my favorite wines—and buy them later at my hometown wine shop. Remember that all liquids—wine, olive oil, or otherwise—need to be placed in checked luggage. Also, your cruise ship may require you to hand over any alcohol for them to hold until you disembark.

Eating in Florence

Remember, restaurants like to serve what's fresh. If you're into flavor, go for the seasonal best bets—featured in the *piatti del giorno* ("specials of the day") section on menus. For dessert, it's gelato (see sidebar later in this section).

To save money and time for sights, keep lunches fast and simple, eating in one of the countless pizzerias and self-service cafeterias. Picnicking is easy—there's no shortage of corner *supermercatos,* or you can picnic your way through the Mercato Centrale.

FLORENCE

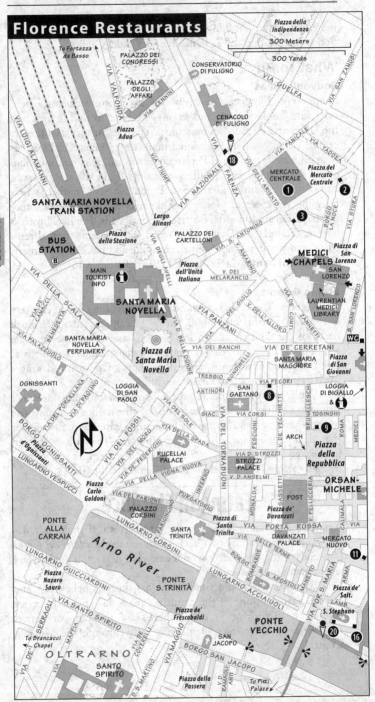

Florence Restaurants

Piazza della Indipendenza

300 Meters

300 Yards

To Fortezza da Basso

PALAZZO DEI CONGRESSI

CONSERVATORIO DI FULIGNO

VIA GUELFA

VIA VALFONDA

PALAZZO DEGLI AFFARI

VIA S. ZANOBI

VIA LUIGI ALAMANNI

VIA CENNINI

CENACOLO DI FULIGNO

VIA TADDEA

Piazza Adua

VIA PANICALE

VIA FIUME

VIA NAZIONALE

VIA DELL'ARIENTO

VIA FAENZA

18

MERCATO CENTRALE 1

Piazza del Mercato Centrale

2

BORGO LA NOCE

VIA STURA

SANTA MARIA NOVELLA TRAIN STATION

Largo Alinari

3

VIA S. ANTONINO

VIA DEGLI AVELLI

PALAZZO DEI CARTELLONI

VIA S. ANTONINO

Piazza di San Lorenzo

MEDICI CHAPELS

SAN LORENZO

BUS STATION B

Piazza della Stazione

VIA PANZANI

Piazza dell'Unità Italiana

V. DEI MELARANCIO

VIA DEL GIGLIO

V. DEL CONTI

VIA DE' ZANNETTI

B. SAN LORENZO

LAURENTIAN MEDICI LIBRARY

VIA DELLA SCALA

VIA DE' CARACCI

MAIN TOURIST INFO

SANTA MARIA NOVELLA

VIA DELL'ALLORO

WC

VIA DE' BENEDETTA

SANTA MARIA NOVELLA PERFUMERY

Piazza di Santa Maria Novella

VIA D. BELLE DONNE

VIA DEI BANCHI

VIA DE' CERRETANI

SANTA MARIA MAGGIORE

Piazza di San Giovanni

VIA PALAZZUOLO

OGNISSANTI

VIA DEL PORCELLANA

VIA DI PAOLINO

LOGGIA DI SAN PAOLO

TREBBIO

ANTINORI

RONDINELLI

VIA PECORI

SAN GAETANO 8

VIA DE' VECCHIETTI

BRUNELLESCHI

LOGGIA DI BIGALLO & i

TOSINGHI

BORGO OGNISSANTI

Piazza d'Ognissanti

VIA DEL SOLE

VIA DELLA SPADA

GIAC.

VIA CORSI

VIA PESCIONI

ARCH

9

ROMA

MEDICI

LUNGARNO VESPUCCI

N

VIA DEL MORO

VIA DE' FEDERIGHI

VIA DELLA VIGNA NUOVA

RUCELLAI PALACE

VIA DELLE BELLE DONNE

VIA D. STROZZI

STROZZI PALACE

V. D. ANSELMI

Piazza della Repubblica

ORSAN-MICHELE

CALIMALA

VIA

Piazza Carlo Goldoni

VIA DEL PARIONE

PALAZZO CORSINI

PURGATORIO

INFERNO

FARGINONGO

MONALDA

SASSETTI

V. PELLICCERIA

POST

Piazza de' Davanzati

DAVANZATI PALACE

MERCATO NUOVO

11

LUNGARNO CORSINI

SANTA TRINITA

Piazza di Santa Trinita

VIA PORTA ROSSA

VIA DELLE TERME

Arno River

Piazza Nazaro Sauro

PONTE ALLA CARRAIA

PONTE S. TRINITA

BORGO S.S. APOSTOLI

LUNGARNO ACCIAIUOLI

MANETTO

BORGO

BOMBARDE

VIA POR S. MARIA

Piazza de' Salt.

S. Stephano

ARMA

LAMB

Piazza Guicciardini

VIA SANTO SPIRITO

VIA MAGGIO

Piazza de' Frescobaldi

PONTE VECCHIO

20

16

To Brancacci Chapel

SERRAGLI

VIA MAFFIA

S. S. MARTINO

VIA D. COVERELLI

VIA DEI CAVELLI

SAN JACOPO

BORGO SAN JACOPO

V. D. RAMAGLIANTI

OLTRARNO

SANTO SPIRITO

Piazza della Passera

To Pitti Palace

FLORENCE

Gelateria

1. Mercato Centrale & Nerbone in the Market
2. Trattoria Mario's
3. Casa del Vino
4. Pugi Pizza
5. Pasticceria Robiglio
6. La Mescita Fiaschetteria
7. Il Centro Supermercati
8. Self-Service Rist. Leonardo
9. Paszkowski Café
10. Turkuaz Döner Kebab
11. Rivoire Café
12. Cantinetta dei Verrazzano & Perchè No! Gelateria
13. Osteria Vini e Vecchi Sapori
14. I Fratellini
15. L'Antico Trippaio, Pizzeria Totò & Supermarket
16. 'Ino Wine Bar
17. Gelateria Carabè
18. Il Triangolo della Bermuda
19. Gelateria Grom
20. Gelateria Carrozze
21. Vivoli's Gelateria
22. Gelateria de' Neri

In and near the Mercato Centrale

Mercato Centrale (Central Market) is great for an ad-lib lunch. It offers colorful piles of picnic produce, people-watching, and rustic sandwiches (Mon-Sat 7:00-14:00, Sat in winter until 17:00, closed Sun, a block north of San Lorenzo Church). The thriving eateries within the market (such as Nerbone, described next) serve some of the cheapest hot meals in town. The fancy deli, Perini, is famous for its quality (pricey) products and enticing display. Buy a picnic of fresh mozzarella cheese, olives, fruit, and crunchy bread to munch on the steps of the nearby Church of San Lorenzo, overlooking the bustling street market.

Nerbone in the Market is a venerable café and the best place for a sit-down meal within the Mercato Centrale. Join the shoppers and workers who crowd up to the bar to grab their €4-7 plates, and then find a stool at the cramped shared tables nearby. Of the several cheap market diners, this feels the most authentic. As intestines are close to Florentines' hearts, it's a good place to try tripe. For the less adventurous, *porchetta* (roast pork with herbs) and *bollito* (stewed beef with broth) are tasty alternatives (lunch menu served Mon-Sat 12:00-14:00, sandwiches available from 8:00 until the bread runs out, closed Sun, cash only, inside Mercato Centrale on the side closest to the Church of San Lorenzo, mobile 339-648-0251).

Trattoria Mario's has been serving hearty lunches to market-goers since 1953 (Fabio and Romeo are the latest generation). Their simple formula: no-frills, bustling service, old-fashioned good value, and shared tables. It's *cucina casalinga*—home cooking *con brio*. This place is high-energy and jam-packed. Their best dishes often sell out first, so go early. If there's a line, put your name on the list (€5-6 pastas, €8 *secondi*, cash only, Mon-Sat 12:00-15:30, closed Sun and Aug, no reservations, Via Rosina 2, tel. 055-218-550).

Casa del Vino, Florence's oldest operating wine shop, offers glasses of wine from among 25 open bottles (see the list tacked to the bar). Owner Gianni, whose family has owned the Casa for more than 70 years, is a class act. Gianni's *carta dei panini* lists delightful €3.50 sandwiches and €1 crostini; the *I Nostri Panini* (classic sandwiches) richly reward adventurous eaters. During busy times, it's a mob scene. You'll eat standing outside alongside workers on a quick lunch break (Mon-Fri 9:30-20:00 year-round, Sat 9:30-17:00 Sept-June only, closed Sun year-round and Sat in summer, Via dell'Ariento 16 red, tel. 055-215-609).

Budget Lunch Places Surrounding the Accademia

For pizza by the slice, try **Pugi,** at Piazza San Marco 9B.

Pasticceria Robiglio, a smart little café, opens up its stately dining area and sets out a few tables on the sidewalk for lunch. They

Tips on Eating in Italy

Italians eat lunch from about 12:00 to 14:00. They eat dinner a bit later than we do; better restaurants start serving around 19:00.

For a quick bite any time of day, stop by an Italian "bar." These aren't taverns, but small cafés selling sandwiches, cof-

fee, and other drinks. At bars, it's cheaper to eat and drink while standing at the counter (*banco*) rather than sitting at a table (*tavolo*) or outside (*terrazza*). This tiered pricing system is clearly posted on the wall. Sometimes you'll pay for your meal at a cash register, then take the receipt to another counter to claim your drink. Watch the locals and imitate.

Take-away food from pizza shops and delis (such as a *rosticcería* or *tavola calda*) makes an easy picnic. You can stop by a gelato shop for dessert. An *enoteca* is a wine bar with snacks and light meals.

If you have time to dine, look for a *ristorante*, *trattoria*, or *osteria*. A full meal consists of an appetizer (antipasto), a first course (*primo piatto*, pasta or soup), and a second course (*secondo piatto*, meat and fish dishes). Steak and seafood are sometimes sold by weight, priced by the kilogram (just over 2 pounds) or *etto* (100 grams, or nearly a quarter-pound); the let-ters "s.q." mean according

to quantity. Make sure you're really clear on the price before ordering. Vegetables (*verdure*) may come with the *secondo* or cost extra, as a side dish (*contorno*). The euros can add up in a hurry, but you don't have to order each course. A good rule of thumb is for each person to order any two courses. For example, a couple can order and share one *antipasto*, one *primo*, one *secondo*, and one dessert; or two *antipasti* and two *primi*; or whatever combination appeals.

For an unexciting but hearty meal, look for a *menù turistico* (or *menù del giorno*), a three- or four-course, fixed-price deal.

When you want the bill, ask for "*il conto.*"

Gelato

Italy's best ice cream is in Florence. But beware of scams at touristy joints on busy streets that turn a simple request for a cone into a €10 "tourist special" rip-off. To avoid this, survey the size options and specify what you want—for example, *un cono da tre euro* (a €3 cone).

All of these places, which are a cut above, are open daily for long hours.

Near the Accademia: A Sicilian choice on a tourist thoroughfare, **Gelateria Carabè** is particularly famous for its luscious granite—Italian ices made with fresh fruit. A *cremolata* is a *granita* with a dollop of gelato—a delicious combination (from the Accademia, it's a block toward the Duomo at Via Ricasoli 60 red).

Near the Mercato Centrale: **Il Triangolo della Bermuda** is a hit both for its fresh ingredients and for the big-hearted energy of its owner, Vetulio (Via Nazionale 61 red, where it crosses Via Faenza, tel. 055-287-490).

Near the Duomo: Grom uses organic ingredients and seasonal fresh fruit, along with biodegradable spoons and tubs. This

have a small menu of daily pasta and *secondi* specials, and seem determined to do things like they did in the elegant, pre-tourism days (generous €9-10 plates, a great €8 *niçoise*-like "fantasy salad," pretty pastries, smiling service, daily 12:00-15:00, longer hours as a café, a block toward the Duomo off Piazza S.S. Annunziata at Via dei Servi 112 red, tel. 055-212-784). Before you leave, be tempted by their pastries—famous among Florentines.

La Mescita Fiaschetteria is a characteristic hole-in-the-wall just around the corner from *David*—but a world away from all the tourism. It's where locals and students enjoy daily pasta specials and hearty sandwiches with good €1.50 house wine. You can trust Mirco and Alessio (as far as you can throw them—check your bill)—just point to what looks good (such as their €5-6 pasta plate or €6-8 *secondi*), and you'll soon be eating well and inexpensively. The place can either be mobbed by students or in a peaceful time warp, depending on when you stop by (Mon-Sat 10:45-16:00, closed Sun, Via degli Alfani 70 red, mobile 347-795-1604 or 338-992-2640).

Picnic on the Ultimate Renaissance Square: **Il Centro Supermercati,** a handy supermarket a half-block north of the Accademia, has a curbside sandwich bar (Panineria) with an easy

clever Italy-wide chain markets its traditional approach, although purists grumble that a chain *gelateria* can't possibly compare with a local one-off. Still, it's good and has maintained a high quality—likely because the menu follows what's in season, changing every month (Via delle Oche 24 red).

Near Orsanmichele Church: **Perchè No!** is located just off the busy main pedestrian drag, Via de' Calzaiuoli, and serves a wide array of flavors (Via dei Tavolini 19).

Near Ponte Vecchio: **Gelateria Carrozze** is a longtime favorite (on riverfront 30 yards from Ponte Vecchio toward the Uffizi at Piazza del Pesce 3).

Near the Church of Santa Croce: The venerable favorite, **Vivoli's** still has great gelato—but it's more expensive, and stingy in its servings. Before ordering, try a free sample of their rice flavor—*riso* (closed Mon, Aug, and Jan; opposite the Church of Santa Croce, go down Via Torta a block and turn right on Via Stinche). Florentines flock to **Gelateria de' Neri** (Via dei Neri 22 red; if not there, it might have moved slightly east—ask a local).

Across the River: If you want an excuse to check out the little village-like neighborhood across the river from Santa Croce (or are walking to Piazzale Michelangelo), enjoy a gelato at the tiny **Il Gelato di Filo** (named for Filippo and Lorenzo) at Via San Miniato 5 red, a few steps toward the river from Porta San Miniato. Gelato chef Edmir is proud of his fruity sorbet as well.

FLORENCE

English menu that includes salads to go (Mon-Sat 9:00-19:30, Sun 10:00-19:00, Sat-Mon closed 15:00-16:30, sandwich bar may close earlier, Via Ricasoli 109). With your picnic in hand, hike around the block and join the bums on Piazza S.S. Annunziata, the first Renaissance square in Florence (don't confuse this with the less-interesting Piazza San Marco, closer to the supermarket). There's a fountain for washing fruit on the square. Grab a stony seat anywhere you like, and savor one of my favorite cheap Florence eating experiences. Or, drop by any of the places listed earlier for an easy lunch to go.

Fast and Cheap near the Duomo

Self-Service Ristorante Leonardo is an inexpensive, air-conditioned, quick, and handy cafeteria. Eating here, you'll get the sense that they're passionate about the quality of their food. Stefano and Luciano (like Pavarotti) run the place with enthusiasm and put out free pitchers of tap water. It's just a block from the Duomo, southwest of the Baptistery (€5 *primi*, €6 main courses, lots of veggies, Sun-Fri 11:45-14:45 & 18:45-21:45, closed Sat, upstairs at Via Pecori 11, tel. 055-284-446).

Paszkowski, a grand café on Piazza della Repubblica, serves up inexpensive, quick lunches. At the display case, order a salad or €7 plate of pasta or cooked veggies (or half and half), pay the cashier, and find a seat upstairs. Better yet, eat at one of the tables on the square. Note that table service prices are much more expensive (daily 7:00-24:00, lunch served 12:00-15:00, closed Mon off-season, Piazza della Repubblica 35 red—northwest corner, tel. 055-210-236).

Döner Kebab: A good place to try this cheap Middle Eastern specialty is **Turkuaz**, a couple of blocks northeast of the Duomo (Via dei Servi 65).

Near Piazza della Signoria

Piazza della Signoria, the scenic square facing Palazzo Vecchio, is ringed by beautifully situated yet touristy eateries serving overpriced, bad-value, and probably microwaved food. If you're determined to eat on the square, have pizza at Ristorante il Cavallino or bar food from the Irish pub next door. Piazza della Signoria's saving grace is **Rivoire** café, famous for its fancy desserts and thick hot chocolate. While obscenely expensive, it has the best view tables on the square. Stand at the bar with the locals and pay way less (Tue-Sun 7:30-24:00, closed Mon, tel. 055-214-412).

Here are some more-affordable options nearby:

Cantinetta dei Verrazzano, a long-established bakery/café/wine bar, serves delightful sandwich plates in an old-time setting. Their *selezione Verrazzano* is a fine plate of four little crostini (like mini-bruschetta) proudly featuring different breads, cheeses, and meats from the Chianti region (€7.50). The *tagliere di focacce,* a sampler plate of mini-focaccia sandwiches, is also fun (€16 for big plate for two). Add a €5 glass of Chianti to either of these dishes to make a fine, light meal. Office workers pop in for a quick lunch, and it's traditional to share tables. Be warned: Prices can add up here in a hurry (Mon-Sat 8:00-21:00, Sun 10:00-16:30, no reservations taken, just off Via de' Calzaiuoli, across from Orsanmichele Church at Via dei Tavolini 18, tel. 055-268-590). They also have benches and tiny tables for eating at take-out prices. Simply step to the back and point to a hot *focacce* sandwich (€3), order a drink at the bar, and take away your food or sit with Florentines and watch the action while you munch.

Osteria Vini e Vecchi Sapori, half a block north of the Palazzo Vecchio, is a colorful eatery serving Tuscan food with a fun, accessible menu of delicious €8-10 pastas and €9-15 *secondi* (Mon-Sat 12:00-14:30 & 19:00-22:30, closed Sun, reserve for dinner; facing the bronze equestrian statue in Piazza della Signoria, go behind its tail into the corner and to your left; Via dei Magazzini 3 red, tel. 055-293-045, run by Mario while wife Rosanna cooks and son Thomas serves).

I Fratellini is a hole-in-the-wall where the "little brothers" have served peasants 29 different kinds of sandwiches and cheap glasses of Chianti wine (see list on wall) since 1875. Join the local crowd to order, then sit on a nearby curb to eat, placing your glass on the wall rack before you leave (€2.50-3 sandwiches, daily 9:00-19:30 or until the bread runs out, closed Sun in winter, 20 yards in front of Orsanmichele Church on Via dei Cimatori, tel. 055-239-6096). Be adventurous with the menu (easy-order by number). Consider *finocchiona e caprino* (#15, a Tuscan salami and soft goat cheese), *lardo di Colonnata* (#22, cured lard aged in Carrara marble), and *cinghiale* (#19, spicy wild boar salami) sandwiches. Order the most expensive wine they're selling by the glass (Brunello for €5; bottles are labeled).

Cheap Takeout on Via Dante Alighieri: Three handy places line up on this street, just a couple of blocks from the Duomo. **L'Antico Trippaio,** a tripe stand, is a fixture in the town center. Cheap and authentic as can be, this is where locals come daily for €4-7 sandwiches *(panino),* featuring specialties like *trippa alla fiorentina* (tripe), *lampredotto* (cow's stomach), and a list of more appetizing options. Lisa and Maurizio offer a free plastic glass of rotgut Chianti with each sandwich for travelers with this book (daily 9:00-21:00, on Via Dante Alighieri, mobile 339-742-5692). If tripe isn't your cup of offal, **Pizzeria Totò,** just next to the tripe stand, has good €2.50-3 slices (daily 10:30-23:00, Via Dante Alighieri 28 red, tel. 055-290-406). And a few steps in the opposite direction is a **Metà supermarket,** with cheap drinks and snacks and a fine *antipasti* case inside (daily 8:30-21:30, Sun from 9:00, Via Dante Alighieri 20-24). If you pick up lunch at any of these, the best people-watching place to enjoy your sandwich is three blocks away, on Piazza della Signoria.

Wine Bar near Ponte Vecchio: 'Ino is a mod little shop filled with gifty edibles. Alessandro and his staff serve sandwiches and wine—you'll get your €5-8 sandwich on a napkin with an included glass of their wine of the day as you perch on a tiny stool. They can also make a fine €12 *piatto misto* of cheeses and meats with bread (daily 11:30-16:30, immediately behind Uffizi Gallery on Ponte Vecchio side, between the olive tree and the river, Via dei Georgofili 7 red, tel. 055-219-208).

Pisa

In A.D. 1200, Pisa's power peaked. For nearly three centuries (1000-1300), Pisa rivaled Venice and Genoa as a sea-trading power, exchanging European goods for luxury items in Muslim lands. As a port near the mouth of the Arno River (six miles from the coast), the city enjoyed easy access to the Mediterranean, plus the protection of sitting a bit upstream. The Romans had made it a naval base, and by medieval times the city was a major player.

Pisa's 150-foot galleys cruised the Mediterranean, gaining control of the sea, establishing outposts on the islands of Corsica, Sardinia, and Sicily, and trading with other Europeans, Muslims, and Byzantine Christians as far south as North Africa and as far east as Syria. European Crusaders hired Pisan boats to carry them and their supplies as they headed off to conquer the Muslim-held Holy Land. The Pisan "Republic" prided itself on its independence from both popes and emperors. The city used its sea-trading wealth to build the grand monuments of the Field of Miracles, including the now-famous Leaning Tower. But the Pisan fleet was routed in battle by Genoa (1284, at Meloria, off Livorno), and their overseas outposts were taken away. Then the port silted up, and Pisa was left high and dry, with only its Field of Miracles and its university keeping it on the map.

Pisa's three important sights—the Duomo, Baptistery, and the Tower—float regally on the best lawn in Italy. The style throughout is Pisa's very own "Pisan Romanesque." Even as the church was being built, Piazza del Duomo was nicknamed the "Campo dei Miracoli," or Field of Miracles, for the grandness of the undertaking.

The Tower recently underwent a decade of restoration and topple-prevention. To ascend, you have to get your ticket and book a time at least a couple of hours in advance (for details, see page 467).

Orientation to Pisa

The city of Pisa is framed on the north by the Field of Miracles (Leaning Tower) and on the south by the Pisa Centrale train station. The Arno River flows east to west, bisecting the city. Walking from Pisa Centrale directly to the Tower takes about 30 minutes (but allow up to an hour if you take my self-guided walk). The two main streets for tourists  and shoppers are Via Santa Maria (running south from the Tower) and Corso Italia/Borgo Stretto (running north from the station).

Tourist Information

The TI is about 200 yards from Pisa Centrale train station—exit and walk straight up the left side of the street to the big, circular Piazza Vittorio Emanuele II. The TI is on the left at #14 (daily April-Oct 9:00-18:00, Nov-March 9:00-17:00, tel. 050-42291, www.pisaunicaterra.it). There's also a TI at the airport, in the arrivals hall (daily April-Oct 9:00-23:00, Nov-March 9:00-20:00, tel. 050-502-518).

Arrival in Pisa
By Train

Most trains (and visitors) arrive at Pisa Centrale Station, about a mile south of the Tower and Field of Miracles. A few trains, particularly those from Lucca, also stop at the smaller Pisa San Rossore Station, which is just four blocks from the Tower (not all trains stop here, but if yours does, hop off).

Pisa Centrale Station: To get to the Field of Miracles, you can **walk** (get free map from TI, 30 minutes direct, one hour if you follow my self-guided walk), take a **taxi** (€7-10, tel. 050-541-600, taxi stand at station), or go by **bus.** At all bus stops in Pisa, be cautious of pickpockets, who take advantage of crowds to operate.

Bus **LAM Rossa** (4-6/hour, runs until 20:30, 15 minutes) stops across the street from the train station, in front of the NH Cavalieri Hotel. Buy a €1.10 bus ticket from the tobacco/magazine kiosk in the train station's main hall or at any tobacco shop (€1.50 if you buy it on board, smart to have exact change, good for 70 minutes, round-trip permitted). Before getting on the bus, confirm that it is indeed going to "Campo dei Miracoli" (ask driver, a local, or TI) or risk taking a long tour of Pisa's suburbs. The correct buses let you off at Piazza Manin, in front of the gate to the Field of Miracles; drivers make sure tourists don't miss the stop.

To return to the train station from the Tower, catch bus LAM Rossa in front of the BNL bank, across the street from where you got off (again, confirm the destination—"Stazione Centrale," staht-see-OH-nay chen-TRAH-lay). You'll also find a taxi stand 30 yards from the Tower (at Bar Duomo).

Pisa San Rossore Station: It's just a four-block walk to the Field of Miracles. Take the underground walkway to Piazza Fancelli, and turn left onto Via Andrea Pisano. Continue for about 150 yards, and you'll see the Tower ahead of you, a few minutes away.

By Bus

From Livorno: Buses from Livorno (see "Pisa Bus Alternative" on page 383) leave you at Gate 2 at the bus station, which is two blocks in front of the train station. Exit the bus station straight ahead and bear left around the building to reach the circular Piazza Vittorio

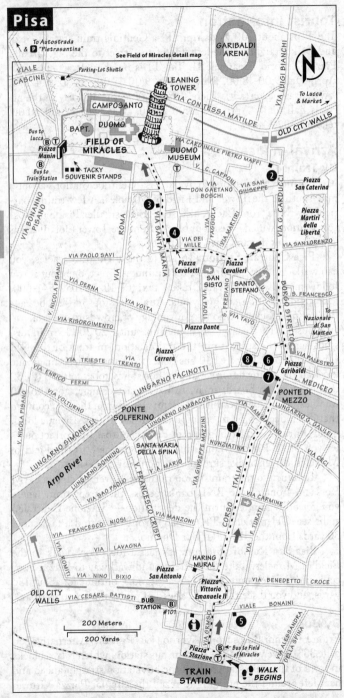

Pisa

To Autostrada & P "Pietrasantina"

See Field of Miracles detail map

GARIBALDI ARENA

To Lucca & Market

VIALE CASCINE

Parking-Lot Shuttle

LEANING TOWER

VIA CONTESSA MATILDE

CAMPOSANTO

DUOMO

OLD CITY WALLS

Bus to Lucca

B T

Piazza Manin

FIELD OF MIRACLES

BAPT.

B

Bus to Train Station

TACKY SOUVENIR STANDS

VIA CARDINALE PIETRO MAFFI

DUOMO MUSEUM

T

VIA C. CAPPONI

VIA SAN GIUSEPPE

VIA DON GAETANO BOSCHI

Piazza San Caterina

VIA G. CARDUCCI

VIA SAN GIUSEPPE

Piazza Martiri della Libertà

VIA SAN LORENZO

VIA BONANNO PISANO

ROMA

VIA SANTA MARIA

VIA FAGGIOLA

VIA MARTIRI

VIA DEI MILLE

Piazza Cavalotti

Piazza Cavalieri

SAN SISTO

SANTO STEFANO

U. DINI

BORGO STRETTO

S. FRANCESCO

VIA PAOLO SAVI

VIA NICOLA PISANO

VIA DERNA

VIA

S. FREDIANO

To Nazionale di San Matteo

V. NICOLA PISANO

VIA RISORGIMENTO

VIA VOLTA

VIA PAOLI

VIA TAVO

Piazza Dante

VIA PALESTRO

VIA TRIESTE

VIA TRENTO

Piazza Carrara

Piazza Garibaldi

VIA ENRICO FERMI

LUNGARNO PACINOTTI

L. MEDICEO

VIA VOLTURNO

PONTE DI MEZZO

V. NICOLA PISANO

LUNGARNO SIMONELLI

PONTE SOLFERINO

LUNGARNO GAMBACORTI

LUNGARNO G. GALILEI

VIA SAN MARTINO

VIA CECI

Arno River

LUNGARNO SONNINO

SANTA MARIA DELLA SPINA

V. A. MARIO

V. FRANCESCO CRISPI

VIA GIUSEPPE MAZZINI

NUNZIATINA

CORSO ITALIA

VIA CARMINE

LUNGARNO PACINOTTI

VIA SAO PAOLO

VIA FRANCESCO NIOSI

VIA MANZONI

VIA F. TURATI

VIA LAVAGNA

HARING MURAL

VIA ROMITI

VIA NINO BIXIO

Piazza San Antonio

Piazza Vittorio Emanuele II

VIA BENEDETTO CROCE

OLD CITY WALLS

VIA CESARE BATTISTI

BUS STATION #101

B

VIALE BONAINI

VIA ALESSANDRA DELLA SPINA

VIA GRIMSI

200 Meters

200 Yards

i

Piazza d. Stazione

B Bus to Field of Miracles

T

TRAIN STATION

WALK BEGINS

FLORENCE

Pisa Key

① Ristorante Bagus
② Pizzeria al Bagno di Nerone
③ Paninoteca il Canguro
④ Panetteria Antiche Tradizioni

⑤ La Lupa Ghiotta Tavola Calda
⑥ Via delle Colonne Produce Market & Restaurants
⑦ La Bottega del Gelato
⑧ Caffè dell'Ussero

Emanuele II. The TI and train station are to your right, and the Field of Miracles is a 25-minute walk to your left (see "Piazza Vittorio Emanuele II" in my self-guided walk, later).

From Lucca: Direct buses from Lucca's Piazzale Giuseppe Verdi drop you near the Leaning Tower outside the walls behind the Baptistery at the Field of Miracles (Mon-Sat hourly, fewer on Sun, 30 minutes, buy €3 ticket on bus); the stop is called Via Bonanno (see map on page 469).

Helpful Hints

Markets: An open-air **produce market** attracts picnickers to Piazza della Vettovaglie, one block north of the Arno River near Ponte di Mezzo, and nearby Piazza Sant'Uomobuono (Mon-Sat 7:00-18:00, main section closes at 13:00, closed Sun). A **street market**—with more practical goods than food—bustles on Wednesday and Saturday mornings between Via del Brennero and Via Paparrelli (8:00-13:00, just outside of wall, about 6 blocks east of the Tower).

Local Guide: Dottore Vincenzo Riolo is a great guide for Pisa and the surrounding area (€130/3 hours, mobile 338-211-2939, www.pisatour.it, info@pisatour.it).

Tours: The TI coordinates with local guides to offer walking tours most days. The theme and schedule change every day; check with the TI for the latest information. Ask about touring the old city walls; if open, a walk up top offers great views.

Welcome to Pisa Walk

From Pisa Centrale Train Station to the Tower

This leisurely one-hour self-guided walk from the station to the Tower is a great way to get acquainted with the more subtle virtues of this Renaissance city. Because the hordes who descend daily on the Tower rarely bother with the rest of the town, you'll find most of Pisa to be delightfully untouristy—a student-filled, classy, Old World town with an Arno-scape much like its upstream rival, Florence. Pisa is pretty small, with just 100,000 people. But its 45,000 students keep it lively.

FLORENCE

The Walk Begins

• *From Pisa Centrale train station, walk north up Viale Antonio Gramsci to the circular square called...*

Piazza Vittorio Emanuele II

The Allies considered Pisa to be strategically important in World War II, and both the train station and its main bridge were target-ed for bombing. Forty percent of this district was destroyed. The piazza has been recently rebuilt, and now this generous public space with grass and benches is actually a lid for an under-ground parking lot. The TI is on this piazza, in the arcade. The entire wall of a building just to the left of the pi-azza, by the Credito Artigiano bank, was painted by American artist Keith

Haring in 1989 to create *Tuttomondo (Whole Wide World)*. Haring (who died of AIDS in 1990) brought New York City graffiti into the mainstream. This painting is a celebration of diversity, chaos, and the liveliness of our world, vibrating with energy.

• *Walk up Corso Italia to the river.*

Corso Italia

Cutting through the center of town, this is Pisa's main drag. As you leave Piazza Vittorio Emanuele II, look to the right to see the circa-1960 wall map of Pisa with a steam train (on the wall of the bar on the corner). You'll also see plenty of youthful fashions, as kids are out making the scene here. Be on guard for pickpockets—too young to arrest, they can only be kicked out of town. Pushed out of their former happy hunting grounds, the Field of Miracles, they now work the crowds here, often dressed as tourists.

• *Follow the pedestrianized Corso Italia straight north to the Arno River and Ponte di Mezzo. Stop in the center of the bridge.*

Ponte di Mezzo

This modern bridge, constructed on the same site where the Ro-mans built one, marks the center of Pisa. In the Middle Ages, this bridge (like Florence's Ponte Vecchio) was lined with shops. It's been destroyed several times by floods and in 1943 by British and American bombers. Enjoy the view from the center of the bridge of the elegant mansions that line the riverbank, recalling Pisa's days of trading glory—the cityscape feels a bit like Venice's Grand Canal. Pisa sits on shifting delta sand, making construction tricky. The entire town leans. With innovative arches above ground and below,

architects didn't stop the leaning—but they have made buildings that wobble without being threatened.
• *Cross the bridge to...*

Piazza Garibaldi

This square is named for the charismatic leader of the Risorgimento, the unification movement that led to Italian independence in 1870. Knowing Pisa was strongly nationalist, Garibaldi came here when wounded to be nursed back to health; many Pisans died in the national struggle. **La Bottega del Gelato,** Pisa's favorite gelato place, is on Piazza Garibaldi (daily 11:00-24:00). You can side-trip about 100 yards downstream to **Caffè dell'Ussero** (famous for its fine 14th-century red terra-cotta original facade, at #28, Sun-Fri 7:00-21:00, closed Sat) and browse its time-warp interior, lined with portraits and documents from the struggle for Italian independence.
• *Continue north up the elegantly arcaded...*

Borgo Stretto

Welcome to Pisa's main shopping street. On the right, the Church of St. Michael, with its fine Pisan Romanesque facade, still sports some 16th-century graffiti. I'll bet you can see some modern graffiti across the street. Students have been pushing their causes here—or simply defacing things—for five centuries.

From here, look farther up the street and notice how it undulates like a flowing river. In the sixth century B.C., Pisa was born when two parallel rivers were connected by canals. This street echoes the flow of one of those canals. An 11th-century landslide rerouted the second river, destroying ancient Pisa, and the entire city had to regenerate.
• *After a few steps, detour left onto Via delle Colonne, and walk one block down to...*

Piazza delle Vettovaglie

Pisa's historic market square, Piazza delle Vettovaglie, is lively day and night. Its Renaissance loggia has hosted the fish and vegetable market for generations. The stalls are set up in this piazza during the morning (Mon-Sat 7:00-13:00, closed Sun) and stay open later in the neighboring piazza to the west (Piazza Sant'Uomobuono, Mon-Sat 7:00-18:00, closed Sun). You could cobble together a picnic from the sandwich shops and fruit-and-veggie stalls ringing these squares.
• *Continue north on Borgo Stretto another 100 yards, passing an ugly bomb site on the right, with its horrible 1960s reconstruction. Take the second left on nondescript Via Ulisse Dini (it's not obvious—turn left*

immediately at the arcade's end, just before the pharmacy). This leads to Pisa's historic core, Piazza dei Cavalieri.

Piazza dei Cavalieri

With its old clock and colorfully decorated palace, this piazza was once the seat of the independent Republic of Pisa's government. In around 1500, Florence conquered Pisa and made this square the training place for the knights of its navy. The statue of Cosimo I de' Medici shows the Florentine who ruled Pisa in the 16th century. With a foot on a dolphin, he reminded all who passed that the Florentine navy controlled the sea—at least a little of it. The frescoes on the exterior of the square's buildings, though damaged by salty sea air and years of neglect, reflect Pisa's fading glory under the Medici.

With Napoleon, this complex of grand buildings became part of the University of Pisa. The university is one of Europe's oldest, with roots in a law school that dates back as far as the 11th century. In the mid-16th century, the city was a hotbed of controversy, as spacey professors like Galileo Galilei studied the solar system—with results that challenged the church's powerful doctrine. More recently, the blind tenor Andrea Bocelli attended law school in Pisa before embarking on his well-known musical career.

From here, take Via Corsica (to the left of the clock). The humble **Church of San Sisto,** ahead on the left (side entrance on Via Corsica), is worth a quick look. With simple bricks, assorted reused columns, heavy walls, and few windows, this was the typical Romanesque style that predated the more lavish Pisan Romanesque style of the Field of Miracles structures.

• *Follow Via Corsica as it turns into Via dei Mille, then turn right on Via Santa Maria, which leads north (and grab a quick bite at the recommended **Panetteria Antiche Tradizioni**). You'll pass through increasingly touristy claptrap, directly to the Field of Miracles and the Tower.*

Sights in Pisa

▲▲▲Leaning Tower

A 15-foot lean from the vertical makes the Tower one of Europe's most recognizable images. You can see it for free; it's always viewable, or you can pay to climb its roughly 280 stairs to the seventh-floor viewing platform (one story below the top).

Cost and Hours: Free to look, €18 to go inside and climb to the seventh-floor viewing platform, one level below the top—the belfry is not currently accessible (see age restrictions in "Reservations to Climb the Tower," next), always viewable from the outside; open to climb daily April-Sept 8:00-20:00 (until 22:00 mid-June-Aug), Oct 9:00-19:00, Nov-Feb 10:00-17:00, March 9:00-18:00, ticket office opens 30 minutes early, last entry 30 minutes before closing. For details on how to get to the Tower from the train station, see page 461.

Reservations to Climb the Tower: Entry to the tower is by a timed ticket good for a 30-minute visit. Every 20 minutes, 45 people can clamber up the tilting steps (about 280 total—while belfry is closed). Children under age eight are not allowed to go up. Children ages 8-12 must be accompanied by—and hold hands at all times with—an adult. Teenagers (up to and including 18-year-olds) must also be accompanied by an adult.

Reserve your timed entry in person at either ticket office (see below), or choose your entry time and buy your ticket online at www.opapisa.it.

Online bookings are accepted no earlier than 20 days and no later than 12 days in advance. You must pick up your ticket(s) at least 30 minutes before your entry time. Show up 10 minutes before your appointment at the meeting point outside the ticket office.

To reserve in person, go to the **ticket office,** behind the Tower on the left (in the yellow building), or to the Museum of the Sinopias ticket office, hidden behind the souvenir stalls. In summer, for same-day entry, you'll likely need to wait a couple of hours before going up (see the rest of the monuments and grab lunch while waiting). The wait is usually much shorter at the beginning or end of the day.

At the Tower: In 2013, the room at the bottom of the tower, known as the *Sala del Pesce* for the Christian fish symbol on the

FLORENCE

Field of Miracles Tickets

Pisa has a combo-ticket scheme designed to get you into its neglected secondary sights: the Baptistery, Camposanto Cemetery, Duomo Museum, and Museum of the Sinopias (fresco pattern museum). For €5, you get your choice of one of these sights; for two of these sights, the cost is €7; and for the works, you'll pay €9 (credit cards accepted except AmEx). No matter which ticket you get, you have to pay an additional €18 if you want

to climb the Tower. Entry into the Duomo is free, but you'll need a free voucher or you can show your combo-ticket.

You can get the Duomo voucher (good for up to two people) and any of these tickets from either ticket office on the Field of Miracles: One is behind the Leaning Tower and the other is at the Museum of the Sinopias (near Baptistery, almost suffocated by souvenir stands). Both ticket offices have big, yellow, triangle-shaped signs. You can buy tickets in advance online at www.opapisa.it (no sooner than 20 days but at least 12 days ahead of your visit; the free voucher for the Duomo is not available online).

wall, was opened to visitors after a long period of restoration. Here, guides offer a short explanation of the Tower's construction and history before you wind your way up the outside along a spiraling ramp, climbing 280 or so stairs. For your 30-minute time slot, figure about a 5-minute presentation by the guide, 10 minutes to climb, and 10 to descend. This leaves about 5 minutes for vertigo on the seventh-floor viewing platform. (The belfry at the top of the tower is currently not accessible.) Even though this is technically a "guided" visit, the "guide" is a museum guard who makes sure you don't stay past your scheduled time.

Baggage Check: You can't take any bags up the Tower, but day-bag-size lockers are available at the ticket office—show your Tower ticket to check your bag. You may check your bag 10 minutes before your reservation time and must pick it up immediately after your Tower visit.

Caution: The railings are skinny, the steps are slanted, and rain makes the marble slippery. Anyone with balance issues of any sort should think twice before ascending.

◐ Self-Guided Tour: Rising up alongside the cathedral, the Tower is nearly 200 feet tall and 55 feet wide, weighing 14,000 tons

Pisa's Field of Miracles

To Autostrada
& **P** "Pietrasantina"

VIALE CASCINE

VIA CONTESSA MATILDE

100 Meters
100 Yards

Largo Griffi

PARKING-LOT SHUTTLE

Jewish Cemetery

VIA CARLO CAMMEO

VIA NICOLINI

CAMPOSANTO CEMETERY **WC** ❷ ❶

OLD CITY WALLS

❹ B

BAPTISTERY

PORTA S. MARIA

Piazza Manin

❸ B T

DUOMO

Grassy Lawn

Piazza del Duomo

❶

LEANING TOWER

VIA C. P. MAFFI

DUOMO MUSEUM

T BAR DUOMO

Piazza Archivescovado

TACKY SOUVENIR STANDS

MUSEUM OF THE SINOPIAS

VIA ROMA

VIA BONANNO PISANO

VIA SANTA MARIA

VIA TASSI

To rest of town & train station

❶ Ticket Offices (2) ❸ Bus to Train Station
❷ Baggage Check ❹ Bus to Lucca

FLORENCE

and currently leaning at a five-degree angle (15 feet off the vertical axis). It started to lean almost immediately after construction began. Count the eight stories—a simple base, six stories of columns (forming arcades), and a belfry on top. The inner structural core is a hollow cylinder built of limestone bricks, faced with white marble barged here from San Giuliano, northeast of the city. The thin columns of the open-air arcades make the heavy Tower seem light and graceful.

The Tower was built over two centuries by at least three different architects. You can see how each successive architect tried to correct the leaning problem—once halfway up (after the fourth story), once at the belfry on the top.

The first stones were laid in 1173, probably under the direction of the architect Bonanno Pisano (who also designed the Duomo's bronze back door). Five years later, just as the base and the first arcade were finished, someone said, "Is it just me, or does that look crooked?" The heavy Tower—resting on a very shallow 13-foot foundation—was obviously sinking on the south side into the marshy, multilayered, unstable soil. (Actually, all the Campo's buildings tilt somewhat.) The builders carried on anyway, until they'd finished four stories (the base, plus three arcade floors). Then, construction suddenly halted—no one knows why—and for a century the Tower sat half-finished and visibly leaning.

Around 1272, the next architect continued, trying to correct the problem by angling the next three stories backward, in the opposite direction of the lean. The project then again sat mysteriously idle for nearly another century. Finally, Tommaso Pisano put the belfry on the top (c. 1350-1372), also kinking it backward.

After the Tower's completion, several attempts were made to stop its slow-motion fall. The architect/artist/writer Giorgio Vasari reinforced the base (1550), and it actually worked. But in 1838, well-intentioned engineers pumped out groundwater, destabilizing the Tower and causing it to increase its lean at a rate of a millimeter per year.

It got so bad that in 1990 the Tower was closed for repairs, and $30 million was spent trying to stabilize it. Engineers dried the soil with steam pipes, anchored the Tower to the ground with steel cables, and buried 600 tons of lead on the north side as a counterweight (not visible)—all with little success. The breakthrough came when they drilled 15-foot-long holes in the ground on the north side and sucked out 60 tons of soil, allowing the Tower to sink on the north side and straighten out its lean by about six inches.

In addition to gravity, erosion threatens the Tower. Since its construction, 135 of the Tower's 180 marble columns have had to be replaced. Stone decay, deposits of lime and calcium phosphate, accumulations of dirt and moss, cracking from the stress of the lean—all of these are factors in its decline.

Thanks to the Tower's lean, there are special trouble spots. The lower south side (which is protected from cleansing rain and wind) is a magnet for dirty airborne particles, while the stone on the upper areas has more decay (from eroding rain and wind).

The Tower, now stabilized, has been cleaned as well. Cracks were filled, and accumulations of dirt removed with carefully formulated atomized water sprays and poultices of various solvents.

All the work to shore up, straighten, and clean the Tower has probably turned the clock back a few centuries. In fact, art historians figure it leans today as much as it did when Galileo reputedly conducted his gravity experiments here some 400 years ago.

▲▲Duomo (Cathedral)

The huge Pisan Romanesque cathedral, with its carved pulpit by Giovanni Pisano, is artistically more important than its more famous bell tower.

Cost and Hours: Free; you can enter using any of the combo-tickets (see sidebar on page 468) or pick up a free voucher

(valid for up to two people) at one of the ticket offices nearby; daily April-Sept 10:00-20:00, Oct 10:00-19:00, Nov-Feb 10:00-13:00 & 14:00-17:00, March 10:00-18:00, last entry 30 minutes before closing.

Information: Shorts are OK as long as they're not too short, and shoulders should be covered (although it's not really enforced). Big backpacks are not allowed, nor is storage provided. If you have a day bag, carry it. Don't let the sparkle of the new coin-operated "phone guides" tempt you. These €2 machines still use narration from a bygone era.

❷ Self-Guided Tour: Begun in 1063, the Duomo is the centerpiece of the Field of Miracles' complex of religious buildings. Start by admiring its facade.

Exterior: The architect Buschetto created the Pisan Romanesque style that set the tone for the Baptistery and Tower. Five decades later (1118), the architect Rainaldo added the impressive main-entrance facade (which also leans out about a foot).

The **bronze back doors** (Porta San Ranieri, at the Tower end) were designed by Bonanno Pisano (c. 1186). The doors have 24 different panels that show Christ's story using the same simple, skinny figures found in Byzantine icons. (The doors are actually copies; the originals are housed—but not always on display—in the Duomo Museum.) Cast using the lost-wax technique, these doors were an inspiration for Lorenzo Ghiberti's bronze doors in Florence.

Nave: Inside, the 320-foot nave was the longest in Christendom when it was built. The striped marble and arches-on-columns give it an exotic, almost mosque-like feel. Dim light filters in from the small upper windows of the galleries, where the women worshipped.

At the center of the gilded coffered ceiling is the shield of Florence's Medici family. This powerful merchant and banking family took over Pisa after its glory days.

In the apse (behind the altar) is a **mosaic** (c. 1300, partly done by the great artist Cimabue) showing Christ as the Ruler of All (Pantocrator), between Mary and St. John the Evangelist. The Pantocrator image of Christ is standard fare among Eastern

Orthodox Christians—that is, the "Byzantine" people who were Pisa's partners in trade.

Giovanni's Pulpit: The 15-foot-tall, octagonal pulpit is by Giovanni Pisano (c. 1250-1319), who left no stone uncarved in his

pursuit of beauty. Four hundred intricately sculpted figures smother the pulpit, blurring the architectural outlines. In addition, the relief panels are actually curved, making it look less like an octagon than a circle. The creamy-white Carrara marble has the look and feel of carved French ivories, which the Pisanos loved. At the base, lions roar and crouch over their prey, symbolizing how Christ (the lion) triumphs over Satan (the horse, as in the Four Horsemen of the Apocalypse). Four of the pulpit's support "columns" are statues. The central "column" features three graceful ladies representing Faith, Hope, and Charity, the three pillars of Christianity. Around the top of the pulpit, Christ's life unfolds in a series of panels saturated with carvings.

Galileo's Lamp: The bronze incense burner that hangs from the ceiling of the north transept (to the left of the altar) is a replica of the one that supposedly caught teenage Galileo's attention when a gust of wind set the lamp swinging. He timed the swings and realized that the burner swung back and forth in the same amount of time regardless of how wide the arc. (This pendulum motion was a constant that allowed Galileo to measure our ever-changing universe.)

St. Ranieri's Body: In a glass-lined casket on the altar, Pisa's patron saint lies mummified, encased in silver at his head and feet, with his hair shirt covering his body. The silver, mask-like face dates from 2000 and is as realistic as possible—derived from an FBI-style computer scan of Ranieri's skull. The son of a rich sea-trader, Ranieri (1117-1161) was a hard-partying, touring musician who one night was inspired to set fire to his musical instrument, open his arms to the heavens (à la Jimi Hendrix), and return to his father's shipping business, where he amassed a fortune. He later gave away his money, joined a monastery, and delivered spirited sermons from the Duomo pulpit.

Tomb of Holy Roman Emperor Henry VII: Pause at the tomb of this German king (c. 1275-1313), who invaded Italy and was welcomed by the Pisans as a leader of unity and peace. Unfortunately, Henry took ill and died young, leaving Ghibelline Pisa at the mercy of its Guelph rivals, such as rising Florence. Pisa never recovered.

▲▲▲Field of Miracles (Campo dei Miracoli)

Scattered across a golf-course-green lawn are five grand buildings: the cathedral (or Duomo), its bell tower (the Leaning Tower), the Baptistery, the hospital (today's Museum of the Sinopias), and the Camposanto Cemetery. The buildings are constructed from similar materials—bright white marble—and have comparable decoration.

Each has a simple ground floor and rows of delicate columns and arches that form open-air arcades, giving the Campo a pleasant visual unity.

The style is called Pisan Romanesque. Unlike traditional Romanesque, with its heavy fortress-like feel—thick walls, barrel arches, few windows—Pisan Romanesque is light and elegant. At ground level, most of the structures have simple half-columns and arches. On the upper levels, you'll see a little of everything—tight rows of thin columns; pointed Gothic gables and prickly spires; Byzantine mosaics and horseshoe arches; and geometric designs (such as diamonds) and striped, colored marbles inspired by mosques in Muslim lands.

Architecturally, the Campo is unique and exotic. Theologically, the Campo's buildings mark the main events of every Pisan's life: christened in the Baptistery, married in the Duomo, honored in ceremonies at the Tower, healed in the hospital, and buried in the Camposanto Cemetery.

Lining this field of artistic pearls is a gauntlet of Europe's tackiest souvenir stands, as well as dozens of amateur mimes "propping up" the Leaning Tower while tourists take photos. Although the smooth green carpet looks like the ideal picnic spot, lounging on this lawn can result in a €25 fine.

Secondary Sights on the Field of Miracles

The next four sights—the Baptistery, Camposanto Cemetery, Museum of the Sinopias, and Duomo Museum—share the same pricing and schedule.

Cost and Hours: €9 combo-ticket includes all the sights, plus the Duomo (credit cards accepted; see sidebar on page 468 for run-down on various combo-tickets). Open daily April-Sept 8:00-20:00, Oct 9:00-19:00, Nov-Feb 10:00-17:00, March 9:00-18:00, last entry 30 minutes before closing.

Getting There: The Baptistery is located in front of the Duomo's facade. The Camposanto Cemetery is behind the church on the north side of the Field of Miracles. The Museum of the Sinopias is hidden behind souvenir stands, across the street from the

FLORENCE

Baptistery entrance. The Duomo Museum is housed behind the Tower.

▲Baptistery

The round Baptistery is the biggest in Italy. It's interesting for its superb acoustics and fine Pisano pulpit. The building is 180 feet tall—John the Baptist is almost eye-to-eye with the tourists looking out from the nearly 200-foot-tall Leaning Tower. Inside, it's simple, spacious, and baptized with light. Tall arches encircle just a few pieces of religious furniture. In the center sits the beautiful, marble **octagonal font** (1246). A statue of the first Baptist, John the Baptist, stretches out his hand and says, "Welcome to my Baptistery." The **pulpit** by Nicola Pisano, Giovanni's father, is arguably the world's first Renaissance sculpture. The freestanding sculpture has classical columns, realistic people and animals, and 3-D effects in the carved panels. The relief panels, with scenes from the life of Christ, are more readable than the Duomo pulpit. Read left to right, starting from the back: Nativity, Adoration of the Magi, Presentation in the Temple, Crucifixion, Last Judgment. The **acoustics** are impressive. Make a sound in here and it echoes for a good 10 seconds. A priest standing at the baptismal font (or a security guard today) can sing three tones within the 10 seconds—"Ave Maria"—and make a chord, singing haunting harmonies with himself.

Camposanto Cemetery

This site has been a cemetery since at least the 12th century. The building's cloistered open-air courtyard, lined with traces of fresco on the bare-brick walls, is surrounded by an arcade with intricately carved tracery in the arches and dozens of ancient Roman sarcophagi. The courtyard's grass grows on special dirt (said to turn a body into bones in a single day), shipped here by returning Crusaders from Jerusalem's Mount Calvary, where Christ was crucified. The 1,000-square-foot fresco, *The Triumph of Death* (c. 1340), captures late-medieval Europe's concern with death—predating but still accurately depicting Pisa's mood in reaction to the bubonic plague (1348), which killed one in three Pisans. Grim stuff, but appropriate for the Camposanto's permanent residents.

Museum of the Sinopias (Museo delle Sinopie)

Housed in a 13th-century hospital, this museum features the preparatory sketches (sinopias) for the Camposanto's WWII-damaged frescoes (including *The Triumph of Death*, described earlier). Sinopias are sketches made in red paint directly on the wall, designed to guide the making of the final colored fresco. The master always did the sinopia himself; if he liked the results, his assistants made a "cartoon" by tracing the sinopia onto large sheets of paper *(cartone)*. Then the sinopia was plastered over, and the assistants redrew the outlines, using the cartoon as a guide. While the plaster was still wet, the master and his team quickly filled in the color and details, producing the final frescoes (now on display at the Camposanto).

Duomo Museum (Museo dell'Opera del Duomo)

This museum behind the Leaning Tower is big on Pisan art, displaying treasures of the cathedral, paintings, silverware, and sculptures (from the 12th to 14th centuries, particularly by the Pisano dynasty), as well as ancient Egyptian, Etruscan, and Roman artifacts. It houses many of the original statues and much of the artwork that once adorned the Campo's buildings (where copies stand today), notably the statues by Nicola and Giovanni Pisano. You can stand face-to-face with the Pisanos' very human busts, which once ringed the outside of the Baptistery. The museum's grassy interior courtyard has a two-story, tourist-free view of the Tower, Duomo, and Baptistery.

Eating in Pisa

For general tips on eating in Italy, see page 455.

At **Ristorante Bagus,** the specialties are an extra-rare burger made with the famous Chianina beef and trendy twists on typical Tuscan fare (€30 fixed-price meal, Mon-Fri 12:30-14:30 & 19:30-23:00, Sat 19:30-23:00 only, closed Sun; heading south on Corso Italia, turn right on Via Nunziata and take your first right after Piazza Griletti to Piazza dei Facchini 13; tel. 050-26196).

Pizzeria al Bagno di Nerone is a local favorite and particularly popular with students. Belly up to the bar and grab a slice to go, or sit in their small dining room for a whole pie. Try the *cecina,* a crêpe-like garbanzo-bean cake (Wed-Mon 12:00-14:30 & 18:00-22:30, closed Tue, a 5-minute walk from the Tower at Largo Carlo Fedeli 26, tel. 050-551-085).

At **Paninoteca il Canguro,** Fabio makes warm, hearty sandwiches to order. Check the chalkboard for seasonal specials, such as *porchetta* (daily 9:00-24:00, may be closed Sun in winter, Via Santa Maria 151, tel. 050-561-942).

Panetteria Antiche Tradizioni—not to be confused with another *panetteria* across the street—is a sandwich/bread shop with complete fixings for a picnic. Build your own sandwich with homemade bread or focaccia, then choose fruit from the counter, fresh pastries from the window, and cold drinks or wine to round out your meal (daily 8:00-20:00, Via Santa Maria 66, mobile 327-570-5210).

Drop by cheery **La Lupa Ghiotta Tavola Calda** for a cheap, fast, and tasty meal a few steps from Pisa Centrale train station. It's got everything you'd want from a *ristorante* at half the price and with faster service (build your own salad—five ingredients for €4.50; Mon-Sat 12:15-15:00 & 19:15-23:30, closed Sun, Viale F. Bonaini 113, tel. 050-21018).

FLORENCE

The street that houses the daily market, **Via delle Colonne** (a block north of the Arno, west of Borgo Stretto), has a few atmospheric, mid-priced restaurants and several fun, greasy take-out options.

Lucca

Surrounded by well-preserved ramparts, layered with history, alternately quaint and urbane, Lucca charms its visitors. The city is a paradox. Though it hasn't been involved in a war since 1430, it is Italy's most impressive fortress city, encircled by a perfectly intact wall. Most cities tear down their wall to make way for modern traffic, but Lucca's effectively keeps out both traffic and, it seems, the stress of the modern world. Locals are very protective of their wall, which they enjoy like a community roof garden. Romanesque churches seem to be around every corner, as do fun-loving and shady piazzas filled with soccer-playing children.

Orientation to Lucca

Tourist Information: The main TI is on Piazzale Giuseppe Verdi (daily April-Oct 9:00-19:00, Nov-March 9:00-17:00, futuristic WC-€0.60, tel. 0583-583-150, www. luccaitinera.it). It also has Internet access, baggage storage, bike rentals, and guided city walks (see "Tours in Lucca," later).

Arrival in Lucca: To reach the city center from the train station, walk toward the walls and head left, to the entry at Porta San Pietro. Taxis are sparse, but try calling 025-353 (ignore any recorded message—just wait for a live operator); a ride from the station to Piazza dell'Anfiteatro costs about €10.

Connecting Lucca and Pisa: Direct buses from Lucca's Piazzale Giuseppe Verdi drop you right at the Leaning Tower, making Pisa an easy connection (Mon-Sat hourly, fewer on Sun, 30 minutes, also stops at Pisa's airport, €3).

Helpful Hints

Combo-Tickets: A €7 combo-ticket includes visits to the Ilaria del Carretto tomb in San Martino Cathedral (€3), Cathedral Museum (€4), and San Giovanni Church (€4). A €6 combo-ticket combines the Guinigi Tower (€4) and the Clock Tower (€4).

Shops and Museums Alert: Shops close most of Sunday and Monday mornings. Many museums are closed on Monday as well.

Markets: Lucca's atmospheric markets are worth visiting. Every third weekend of the month (whenever the third Sun falls), one of the largest **antique markets** in Italy sprawls in the blocks between Piazza Antelminelli and Piazza San Giovanni (8:00-19:00). The last weekend of the month, local artisans sell **arts and crafts** around town, mainly near the cathedral (also 8:00-19:00). At the **general market,** held Wednesdays and Saturdays, you'll find produce and household goods (8:30-13:00, from Porta Elisa to Porta San Jacopo on Via dei Bacchettoni).

Bike Rental: A one-hour rental (ID required) gives you time for two leisurely loops around the ramparts. Several places with identical prices cluster around Piazza Santa Maria (€3/hour, €15/day, tandem bikes available, helmets available on request, daily about 9:00-19:00 or sunset). Try these easygoing shops: **Antonio Poli** (Piazza Santa Maria 42, tel. 0583-493-787, enthusiastic Cristiana) and, right next to it, **Cicli Bizzarri** (Piazza Santa Maria 32, tel. 0583-496-682, Australian Dely). At the west end of town, the **TI** on Piazzale Giuseppe Verdi rents bikes (€3/hour). At the south end, at Porta San Pietro, you'll find **Chrono** (same rates and hours as the competition, Corso Garibaldi 93, tel. 0583-490-591, www.chronobikes.com) and **Tourist Center Lucca** (near the train station).

Guided Tours: The TI offers two-hour **city walks** with a local guide, departing from the office on Piazzale Giuseppe Verdi (€10, daily at 14:00, tel. 0583-583-150). Otherwise, local guide **Gabriele Calabrese** knows and shares his hometown well (€120/3 hours, by foot or bike, mobile 347-788-0667, www.turislucca.com, turislucca@turislucca.com).

Sights in Lucca

▲▲Bike the Ramparts

Lucca's most remarkable feature, its Renaissance wall, is also its most enjoyable attraction—especially when circled on a rental bike. Stretching for 2.5 miles, this is an ideal place to come for an overview of the city by foot or bike.

Lucca has had a protective wall for 2,000 years. You can read three walls into today's map: the first rectangular Roman wall, the later medieval wall (nearly the size of today's), and the 16th-century Renaissance wall that still survives.

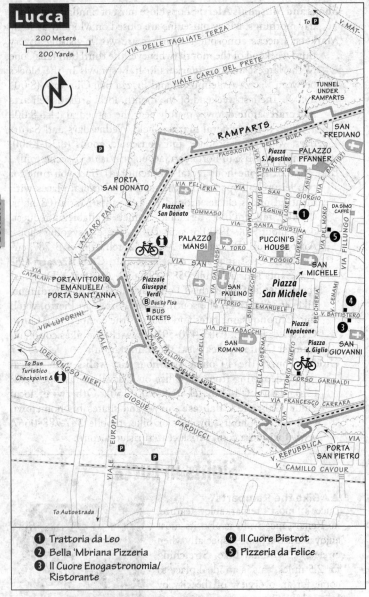

Lucca

200 Meters
200 Yards

To P

V. MAT-

VIA DELLE TAGLIATE TERZA

VIALE CARLO DEL PRETE

TUNNEL UNDER RAMPARTS

RAMPARTS

SAN FREDIANO

PASSAGGIATA DELLE MURA

Piazza S. Agostino

PALAZZO PFANNER

PANIFICIO

VIA DELLE STUFE

VIA SAN GIORGIO

VIA DEGLI ASILI

VIA C. BATTISTI

PORTA SAN DONATO

VIA PELLERIA

VIA LORETO

TEGNINI

DA SIMO CAFFÈ

Piazzale San Donato

TOMMASO

VIA COLOMBAIA

SANTA GIUSTINA

VIA DEL MORO

VIA FILLUNGO

1

PUCCINI'S HOUSE

5

PALAZZO MANSI

V. TORO

VIA SAN

VIA GALLI/ASSI

PAOLINO

VIA POGGIO

CALDERIA

SAN MICHELE

PORTA VITTORIO EMANUELE/ PORTA SANT'ANNA

V. LAZZARO PAPI

VIA CATALANI

Piazzale Giuseppe Verdi

B Bus to Pisa

BUS TICKETS

SAN PAULINO

VIA BURLAMACCHI

Piazza San Michele

BECCHERIA

V. CENAMI

4

V. BATTISTERO

3

VIA VITTORIO EMANUELE II

Piazza Napoleone

VIA LUPORINI

VIALE

VIA DEL FALLONE

PASSAGGIATA DELLE MURA

VIA DEI TABACCHI

CITTADELLA

SAN ROMANO

VIA DELLA CASERMA

Piazza d. Giglio

SAN GIOVANNI

To Bus Turistico Checkpoint &

V. IDELFONGSO NIERI

VIA VITTORIO VENETO

CORSO GARIBALDI

GIOSUE

CARDUCCI

VIA FRANCESCO CARRARA

VIALE EUROPA

P

P

V. REPUBBLICA

VIA

PORTA SAN PIETRO

V. CAMILLO CAVOUR

To Autostrada

1 Trattoria da Leo
2 Bella 'Mbriana Pizzeria
3 Il Cuore Enogastronomia/ Ristorante
4 Il Cuore Bistrot
5 Pizzeria da Felice

FLORENCE

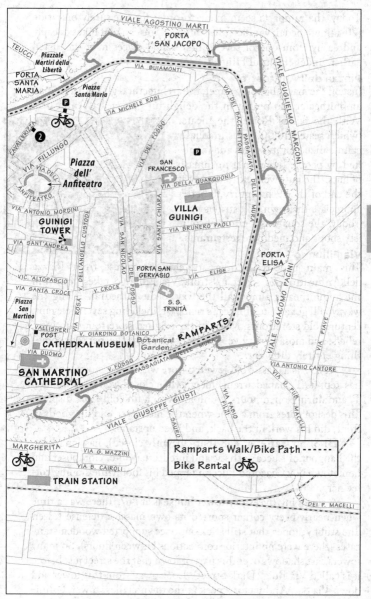

VIALE AGOSTINO MARTI

PORTA
SAN JACOPO

TEUCCI

*Piazzale
Martiri della
Libertà*

PORTA
SANTA
MARIA

VIA BUIAMONTI

*Piazza
Santa Maria*

VIA MICHELE ROSI

VIALE GUGLIELMO MARCONI

VIA DEL BACCHETTONI

PASSAGGIATA DELLE MURA

CAVALLERIZZA

VIA FILLUNGO

2

*Piazza
dell'
Anfiteatro*

VIA DELL' ANFITEATRO

VIA DEL FOSSO

SAN
FRANCESCO

VIA DELLA QUARQUONIA

**VILLA
GUINIGI**

VIA ANTONIO MORDINI

**GUINIGI
TOWER**

VIA SANT'ANDREA

VIA SAN NICOLAO

V. DELL'ANGELO CUSTODE

VIA SANTA CHIARA

VIA DEL FOSSO

VIA BRUNERO PAOLI

VIC. ALTOPASCIO

VIA SANTA CROCE

V. ROSA

V. CROCE

PORTA SAN
GERVASIO

VIA ELISE

PORTA
ELISA

VIA GIACOMO PACINI

*Piazza
San
Martino*

VALLISNERI

POST

V. GIARDINO BOTANICO

S. S.
TRINITÀ

VIA PIAVE

CATHEDRAL MUSEUM

*Botanical
Garden*

RAMPARTS

VIA DUOMO

**SAN MARTINO
CATHEDRAL**

V. FOSSO

PASSAGGIATA DELLE MURA

VIA ANTONIO CANTORE

VIA D. PUB MACELLI

VIALE GIUSEPPE GIUSTI

V. SAURO

VIA FABIO FILZI

MARGHERITA

VIA G. MAZZINI

VIA B. CAIROLI

Ramparts Walk/Bike Path ------
Bike Rental

TRAIN STATION

VIA DEI P. MACELLI

FLORENCE

Today, the ramparts seem made-to-order for a leisurely bike ride (20-minute pedal, wonderfully smooth). You can rent bikes cheaply and easily from one of several bike-rental places in town (listed earlier, under "Helpful Hints").

Piazza dell'Anfiteatro

Just off the main shopping street, the architectural ghost of a Roman amphitheater can be felt in the delightful Piazza dell'Anfiteatro.

With the fall of Rome, the theater (which seated 10,000) was gradually cannibalized for its stones and inhabited by people living in a mishmash of huts. The huts were cleared away at the end of the 19th century to better appreciate the town's illustrious past. Today, the square is a circle of touristy shops and mediocre restaurants.

Via Fillungo

This main pedestrian drag stretches southwest from Piazza dell'Anfiteatro. *The* street to stroll, Via Fillungo takes you from the amphitheater almost all the way to the cathedral. Along the way, you'll get a taste of Lucca's rich past, including several elegant, century-old storefronts. Many of the original storefront paintings, reliefs, and mosaics survive—even if today's shopkeeper sells something entirely different.

At #97 is a classic old **jewelry store** with a rare storefront that has kept its T-shaped arrangement (when closed, you see a wooden T, and during open hours it unfolds with a fine old-time display). This design dates from a time when the merchant sold his goods in front, did his work in the back, and lived upstairs.

Di Simo Caffè, at #58 (but currently closed), has long been the hangout of Lucca's artistic and intellectual elite. Composer and hometown boy Giacomo Puccini tapped his foot while sipping coffee here.

A surviving five-story **tower house** is at #67. There was a time when nearly every corner sported its own massive defense tower. The stubby stones that still stick out once supported wooden staircases (there were no interior connections between floors). So many towers cast shadows over this part of town that the street just before it is called Via Buia (Dark Street). Look away from this tower and down Via San Andrea for a peek at the town's tallest tower, Guinigi, in the distance—with its characteristic oak trees sprouting from the top.

At #45 and #43, you'll see two more good examples of tower houses. Across the street, the **Clock Tower** (Torre delle Ore) has a hand-wound Swiss clock that has clanged four times an hour since 1754 (€4 to climb up and see the mechanism flip into action on the

quarter-hour—if it's actually working, daily April-Oct 9:30-18:30, Nov-March 9:30-17:30, last entry 20 minutes before closing, corner of Via Fillungo and Via del'Arancio).

The intersection of Via Fillungo and Via Roma/Via Santa Croce marks the center of town (where the two original Roman roads crossed). As you go right down Via Roma, you'll pass the fine Edison Bookstore on your left before reaching Piazza San Michele.

Piazza San Michele

This square has been the center of town since Roman times, when it was the forum. It's dominated by the Church of San Michele. Towering above the church's fancy Pisan Romanesque facade, the archangel Michael stands ready to flap his wings—which he was known to do on special occasions.

▲San Martino Cathedral

This cathedral, begun in the 11th century, is an entertaining mix of architectural and artistic styles. It's also home to the exquisite 15th-century tomb of Ilaria del Carretto, who married into the wealthy Guinigi family.

Cost and Hours: Cathedral—free, Ilaria tomb—€3, €7 combo-ticket includes Cathedral Museum and San Giovanni Church; Mon-Fri 9:30-17:45, Sat 9:30-18:45, Sun 11:00-17:00; Piazza San Martino.

Cathedral Museum (Museo della Cattedrale)

This beautifully presented museum houses original paintings, sculptures, and vestments from the cathedral and other Lucca churches. The exhibits in this museum have very brief descriptions and are meaningful only with the slow-talking €1 audioguide—if you're not in the mood to listen, skip the place altogether.

Cost and Hours: €4, €7 combo-ticket includes Ilaria tomb and San Giovanni Church; April-Oct daily 10:00-18:00; Nov-March Mon-Fri 10:00-14:00, Sat-Sun 10:00-17:00; to the left of the cathedral as you're facing it, Piazza Antelminelli, tel. 0583-490-530, www.museocattedralelucca.it.

San Giovanni Church

This first cathedral of Lucca is interesting only for its archaeological finds. The entire floor of the 12th-century church has been excavated in recent decades, revealing layers of Roman houses, ancient hot tubs that date back to the time of Christ, early churches, and theological graffiti. Sporadic English translations help you understand what you're looking at. As you climb under the church's present-day floor and wander the lanes of Roman Lucca, remember that the entire city sits on similar ruins. If it's open, climb the *campanile* (bell tower) of the church for a panoramic view of the city.

Cost and Hours: €4, €7 combo-ticket includes Ilaria tomb and Cathedral Museum, audioguide-€1; mid-March-Oct daily 10:00-18:00; Nov-mid-March Sat-Sun 10:00-17:00, closed Mon-Fri; kitty-corner from cathedral at Piazza San Giovanni.

Church of San Frediano

This impressive church was built in 1112 by the pope to counter Lucca's bishop and his spiffy cathedral. Lucca was the first Mediterranean stop on the pilgrim route from northern Europe, and the pope wanted to remind pilgrims that the action, the glory, and the papacy awaited them in Rome. Therefore, he had the church made "Roman-esque." The pure marble facade frames an early Christian Roman-style mosaic of Christ with his 12 apostles. Step inside and you're struck by the sight of 40 powerful (if recycled) ancient Roman columns. The message: Lucca may be impressive, but the finale of your pilgrimage—in Rome—is worth the hike.

Cost and Hours: Free, Mon-Sat 8:30-12:00 & 15:00-17:30, Sun 9:00-11:30 & 15:00-17:30, Piazza San Frediano, tel. 0583-493-627.

Eating in Lucca

For general tips on eating in Italy, see page 455.

Trattoria da Leo packs in chatty locals for typical, cheap home-cooking in a hash-slingin' Mel's-diner atmosphere. This place is a high-energy winner...you know it's going to be good as soon as you step in. Arrive early or reserve in advance (€6 pastas, €10 *secondi*, daily 12:00-14:30, Mon-Sat also 19:30-22:30, cash only, leave Piazza San Salvatore on Via Asili and take the first left to Via Tegrimi 1, tel. 0583-492-236).

Bella 'Mbriana Pizzeria focuses on doing one thing very well: turning out piping-hot, wood-fired pizzas to happy locals in a welcoming wood-paneled dining room. Order and pay at the counter, take a number, and they'll call you when your pizza's ready. Consider take-out to munch on the nearby walls (Wed-Mon 12:30-14:30 & 18:30-23:00, closed Tue, to the right as you face the Church of San Frediano, Via della Cavallerizza 29, tel. 0583-495-565).

Il Cuore Enogastronomia/Ristorante includes a delicatessen and restaurant. For a fancy picnic, drop in the deli for ready-to-eat lasagna, saucy meatballs, grilled and roasted vegetables, vegetable soufflés, Tuscan bean soup, fruit salads, and more, sold by weight

---

What If I Miss My Boat?

Remember that you can get help from the cruise line's port agent (listed on the destination information sheet distributed on the ship) and local TIs (for Florence, see page 388; for Pisa, see page 461; for Lucca, see page 476). If the port agent suggests a costly solution (such as a private car with a driver), you may want to consider public transit.

Florence is Tuscany's transportation hub, with fine train, bus, and plane connections to virtually anywhere in Italy. The city has several train stations, a bus station (next to the main train station), and Amerigo Vespucci Airport. Pisa is on a main train line and has a major airport (Galileo Galilei Airport); Lucca is on a minor train line. It's easy to reach Florence by train from Pisa or from Lucca.

Frequent trains leave from Florence's Santa Maria Novella Station (the same one with train connections to Livorno) to **Venice, Civitavecchia** (transfer in Rome), **Naples,** and **Sorrento** (transfer to Circumvesuviana commuter train in Naples). The French ports—including **Nice** and **Marseille**—are also reachable by rail, but require multiple changes. To look up specific connections, use www.trenitalia.it (domestic journeys only) or www.bahn.com (Germany's excellent all-Europe schedule website). For other ports (in Spain, Croatia, Greece, and Turkey), you'll probably have to fly.

FLORENCE

---

and dished up in disposable trays to go. Ask them to heat your order *(riscaldare),* then picnic on nearby Piazza Napoleone. For curious traveling foodies on a budget who want to eat right there, they can assemble a €10 "degustation plate"—just point to what you want from among the array of tasty treats under the glass (Tue-Sun 9:30-19:30, closed Mon, Via del Battistero 2, tel. 0583-493-196, Cristina).

Il Cuore Bistrot, located across the way, is a trendy find for wine-tasting or a meal on a piazza. Try the €8 *aperitivo* (available 18:00-20:00), which includes a glass of wine and a plate of cheese, *salumi,* and snacks, or feast on fresh pastas and other high-quality dishes from their lunch and dinner menus (Wed-Sun 12:00-22:00 with limited menu 15:00-19:30, Tue 12:00-15:00, closed Mon, Via del Battistero, tel. 0583-493-196).

Pizzeria da Felice is a little mom-and-pop hole-in-the-wall serving *cecina* (garbanzo-bean crêpes) and slices of freshly baked pizza to throngs of snackers. Grab an *etto* of *cecina* and a short glass of wine for €2.50 (Mon-Sat 10:00-20:30, closed Sun and 3 weeks in Aug, Via Buia 12, tel. 0583-494-986).

Italian Survival Phrases

English	Italian	Pronunciation
Good day.	*Buon giorno.*	bwohn **jor**-noh
Do you speak English?	*Parla inglese?*	**par**-lah een-**gleh**-zay
Yes. / No.	*Sì. / No.*	see / noh
I (don't) understand.	*(Non) capisco.*	(nohn) kah-**pees**-koh
Please.	*Per favore.*	pehr fah-**voh**-ray
Thank you.	*Grazie.*	**graht**-see-ay
You're welcome.	*Prego.*	**preh**-go
I'm sorry.	*Mi dispiace.*	mee dee-spee-**ah**-chay
Excuse me.	*Mi scusi.*	mee **skoo**-zee
(No) problem.	*(Non) c'è un roblema.*	(nohn) cheh oon proh-**bleh**-mah
Good.	*Va bene.*	vah **beh**-nay
Goodbye.	*Arrivederci.*	ah-ree-veh-**dehr**-chee
one / two	*uno / due*	**oo**-noh / **doo**-ay
three / four	*tre / quattro*	tray / **kwah**-troh
five / six	*cinque / sei*	**cheeng**-kway / **seh**-ee
seven / eight	*sette / otto*	**seh**-tay / **oh**-toh
nine / ten	*nove / dieci*	**noh**-vay / dee-**ay**-chee
How much is it?	*Quanto costa?*	**kwahn**-toh **koh**-stah
Write it?	*Me lo scrive?*	may loh **skree**-vay
Is it free?	*È gratis?*	eh **grah**-tees
Is it included?	*È incluso?*	eh een-**kloo**-zoh
Where can I buy / find...?	*Dove posso comprare / trovare...?*	**doh**-vay poh-soh kohm-**prah**-ray / troh-**vah**-ray
I'd like / We'd like...	*Vorrei / Vorremmo...*	voh-**reh**-ee / voh-**reh**-moh
...a room.	*...una camera.*	**oo**-nah **kah**-meh-rah
...a ticket to ____.	*...un biglietto per ____.*	oon beel-**yeh**-toh pehr ____
Is it possible?	*È possibile?*	eh poh-**see**-bee-lay
Where is...?	*Dov'è...?*	doh-**veh**
...the train station	*...la stazione*	lah staht-see-**oh**-nay
...the bus station	*...la stazione degli autobus*	lah staht-see-**oh**-nay **dehl**-yee ow-toh-boos
...tourist information	*...informazioni per turisti*	een-for-maht-see-**oh**-nee pehr too-**ree**-stee
...the toilet	*...la toilette*	lah twah-**leh**-tay
men	*uomini / signori*	**woh**-mee-nee / seen-**yoh**-ree
women	*donne / signore*	**doh**-nay / seen-**yoh**-ray
left / right	*sinistra / destra*	see-**nee**-strah / **deh**-strah
straight	*sempre dritto*	**sehm**-pray **dree**-toh
What time does this open / close?	*A che ora apre / chiude?*	ah kay **oh**-rah ah-**pray** / kee-**oo**-day
At what time?	*A che ora?*	ah kay **oh**-rah
Just a moment.	*Un momento.*	oon moh-**mehn**-toh
now / soon / later	*adesso / presto / più tardi*	ah-**deh**-soh / **preh**-stoh / pew **tar**-dee
today / tomorrow	*oggi / domani*	**oh**-jee / doh-**mah**-nee

In an Italian Restaurant

English	Italian	Pronunciation
I'd like...	Vorrei...	voh-**reh**-ee
We'd like...	Vorremmo...	vor-**reh**-moh
...to reserve...	...prenotare...	preh-noh-**tah**-ray
...a table for one / two.	...un tavolo per uno / due.	oon **tah**-voh-loh pehr **oo**-noh / **doo**-ay
Is this seat free?	È libero questo posto?	eh **lee**-beh-roh **kweh**-stoh **poh**-stoh
The menu (in English), please.	Il menù (in inglese), per favore.	eel meh-**noo** (een een-**gleh**-zay) pehr fah-**voh**-ray
service (not) included	servizio (non) incluso	sehr-**veet**-see-oh (nohn) een-**kloo**-zoh
cover charge	pane e coperto	**pah**-nay ay koh-**pehr**-toh
to go	da portar via	dah **por**-tar **vee**-ah
with / without	con / senza	kohn / **sehnt**-sah
and / or	e / o	ay / oh
menu (of the day)	menù (del giorno)	meh-**noo** (dehl **jor**-noh)
specialty of the house	specialità della casa	speh-chah-lee-**tah deh**-lah **kah**-zah
first course (pasta, soup)	primo piatto	**pree**-moh pee-**ah**-toh
main course (meat, fish)	secondo piatto	seh-**kohn**-doh pee-**ah**-toh
side dishes	contorni	kohn-**tor**-nee
bread	pane	**pah**-nay
cheese	formaggio	for-**mah**-joh
sandwich	panino	pah-**nee**-noh
soup	zuppa	**tsoo**-pah
salad	insalata	een-sah-**lah**-tah
meat	carne	**kar**-nay
chicken	pollo	**poh**-loh
fish	pesce	**peh**-shay
seafood	frutti di mare	**froo**-tee dee **mah**-ray
fruit / vegetables	frutta / legumi	**froo**-tah / lay-**goo**-mee
dessert	dolce	**dohl**-chay
tap water	acqua del rubinetto	**ah**-kwah dehl roo-bee-**neh**-toh
mineral water	acqua minerale	**ah**-kwah mee-neh-**rah**-lay
milk	latte	**lah**-tay
(orange) juice	succo (d'arancia)	**soo**-koh (dah-**rahn**-chah)
coffee / tea	caffè / tè	kah-**feh** / teh
wine	vino	**vee**-noh
red / white	rosso / bianco	**roh**-soh / bee-**ahn**-koh
glass / bottle	bicchiere / bottiglia	bee-kee-**eh**-ray / boh-**teel**-yah
beer	birra	**bee**-rah
Cheers!	Cin cin!	cheen cheen
More. / Another.	Di più. / Un altro.	dee pew / oon **ahl**-troh
The same.	Lo stesso.	loh **steh**-soh
The bill, please.	Il conto, per favore.	eel **kohn**-toh pehr fah-**voh**-ray
Do you accept credit cards?	Accettate carte di credito?	ah-cheh-**tah**-tay **kar**-tay dee **kreh**-dee-toh
tip	mancia	**mahn**-chah
Delicious!	Delizioso!	day-leet-see-**oh**-zoh

For more user-friendly Italian phrases, check out *Rick Steves' Italian Phrase Book & Dictionary* or *Rick Steves' French, Italian, and German Phrase Book*.

ROME
Italy

Italy Practicalities

Stretching 850 miles long and 150 miles wide, art-drenched Italy is the cradle of European civilization. Visitors here come face to face with some of the world's most iconic images: Rome's ancient Colosseum, Pisa's medieval Leaning Tower, Venice's romantic canals.

Italy's 61 million inhabitants are more social and communal than most other Europeans. Because they're so outgoing and their language is so fun, Italians are a pleasure to communicate with. This boot-shaped country has all the elements that make travel to Europe forever fresh and rewarding: visible history, lively people, and fun by the minute.

Money: Italy uses the euro currency: 1 euro (€) = about $1.30. An ATM is called a *bancomat*. The local VAT (value-added sales tax) rate is 22 percent; the minimum purchase eligible for a VAT refund is €155 (for details on refunds, see page 136).

Language: For useful Italian phrases, see page 611.

Emergencies: Dial 113 for police or 118 for medical emergencies. In case of theft or loss, see page 504.

Time Zone: Italy is on Central European Time (the same as most of the Continent, and six/nine hours ahead of the East/West Coasts of the US).

Theft Alert: Assume that beggars are pickpockets and any scuffle is simply a distraction by a team of thieves. For more on outsmarting thieves in Rome, see page 503; for general tips, see page 128.

Consular Services: The US embassy in Rome is at Via Vittorio Veneto 121 (24-hour tel. 06-46741, http://italy.usembassy.gov); consular services are also available in Florence (tel. 055-266-951) and Naples (tel. 081-583-8111). The Canadian Embassy in Rome is at Via Zara 30 (tel. 06-854-441, www.italy.gc.ca). Call ahead for passport services.

Phoning: Italy has a direct-dial phone system (no area codes). To **call within Italy,** just dial the number (keep in mind that Italian phone numbers vary in length). To **call to Italy,** dial the international access code (00 if calling from Europe, or 011 from North America), then dial 39 (Italy's country code), then the phone number. To **call home from Italy,** dial 00, 1, then your area code and phone number. For more help, see page 1242.

Dress Code: Some major churches enforce a modest dress code (no bare shoulders or shorts).

Tipping: A service charge *(servicio)* of about 10 percent is usually built into your restaurant bill. If you are pleased with the service, you can add an extra euro or two for each person in your party. If service isn't included *(servizio non incluso),* add a tip of about 10 percent. To tip a cabbie, round up your fare a bit (to pay a €4.50 fare, give €5).

Tourist Information: www.italia.it

ROME
and the Port of Civitavecchia

Rome is magnificent and brutal at the same time. It's a showcase of Western civilization, with astonishingly ancient sights and a modern vibrancy. But if you're careless, you'll be run down or pickpocketed. And with the wrong attitude, you'll be frustrated by the kind of chaos that only an Italian can understand. On my last visit, a cabbie struggling with the traffic said, *"Roma chaos."* I responded, *"Bella chaos."* He agreed.

While Paris is an urban garden, Rome is a magnificent tangled forest. If you pace yourself; if you're well-organized for sightseeing; and if you protect yourself and your valuables with extra caution and discretion, you'll love it. (And Rome is much easier to live with if you can avoid the midsummer heat.)

For me, Rome is in a three-way tie with Paris and London as Europe's greatest city. Two thousand years ago, the word "Rome" meant civilization itself. Everything was either civilized (part of the Roman Empire, Latin- or Greek-speaking) or barbarian. Today, Rome is Italy's political capital, the capital of Catholicism, and the center of the ancient world, littered with evocative remains. As you peel through its fascinating and jumbled layers, you'll find Rome's buildings, cats, laundry, traffic, and 3.4 million people endlessly entertaining. And then, of course, there are its stupendous sights.

Visit St. Peter's, the greatest church on earth, and scale Michelangelo's 448-foot-tall dome, the world's tallest. Learn something about eternity by touring the huge Vatican Museum. You'll find the story of creation—bright as the day it was painted—in the restored Sistine Chapel. Do the "Caesar Shuffle" through ancient

Excursions from Civitavecchia

The top options are **Rome, Rome,** and **Rome.** You could easily fill a week without ever leaving the city limits.

Other typical excursions offered by cruise lines include the following:

The excavated ancient city **Ostia Antica** (one hour south of Civitavecchia) was a working port town, and its ruins show a more complete and grittier view of Roman life than wealthier Pompeii (near Naples). Wandering around today, you'll see ruins of warehouses, apartments, shopping arcades, and baths that once served 60,000 inhabitants.

The Etruscan necropolis of **Tarquinia,** about a half-hour north of Civitavecchia, contains 6,000 graves cut in the rock; the earliest date from the seventh century B.C. (that's pre-"ancient Rome"). Aristocratic tombs contain large-scale wall paintings rich in details. Excavated treasures are displayed in the Tarquinian National Museum.

Lake Bracciano, an hour's ride east of Civitavecchia, is part of the Parco Bracciano Nature Reserve. As pretty as it is, it's hard to imagine missing Rome for this excursion.

The grand, classic hill town of **Orvieto** (1.75 hours north of Civitavecchia), perched high above a vineyard-filled valley, is famous for its white wine, colorful ceramics, and resplendent Gothic cathedral. Take this side-trip only if you'd rather see a charming hill town than the enormous city of Rome.

ROME

Rome's Forum and Colosseum, or enjoy a walk from Campo de' Fiori to the Spanish Steps.

Many cruises start or end in Rome. If yours does, check the end of this chapter for airport information and recommended hotels.

Planning Your Time

Rome is wonderful, but it's huge and exhausting. With just a few hours, you'll have to be very selective—getting just a first nibble of this grand city. You'll also want to plan ahead, as several major sights have notoriously long lines: St. Peter's Basilica, the Vatican Museum, and the Colosseum (and often the Forum as well). In this chapter, I've explained how best to get around the long waits; read these tips well before you arrive. Don't just show up at Rome's top sights—do what you can to avoid wasting precious time in line.

Keep in mind that it takes approximately 1.5 hours each way to get between your ship and downtown Rome—so you'll need to mentally subtract at least 3 hours from the time you have in port.

Even if all you have left is a few hours, they'll be full and memorable. For a brief first-time visit to Rome, I'd recommend

Civitavecchia

To Tarquinia
VIA SANGALLO
VIA XX SETTEMBRE

100 Meters
100 Yards

BOATS TO
SARDINIA
& CORSICA

Piazzetta
S. Maria

Piazza V.
Emanuele

Piazza
Regina
Magherita

MKT.

Piazza del
Conservatoria

CENTOCELLE

CORSO

CRUISE
TERMINAL

PORT
GATE

Largo
Plebiscito

FORTE
MICHELANGELO

B
5

3
B
i

Piazza
d. Troi

Piazza
Fratti

V. IOFI

DIRECT ROUTE
TO/FROM
TRAIN STATION

SHUTTLE
BUS

4
Piazza degli
Eventi

P

ATM

2

V. BRUNO

VIALE

P

1
VIA DELLA
REPUBBLICA

TRAIN
STATION

P

PEDESTRIAN
PROMENADE

GARIBALDI

VIA

VITTORIA

B
To
Rome

Mediterranean   Sea

VIA DUCA D'AOSTA

1 Hotel de La Ville
2 Hotel Mediterraneo
3 Cruises Services Center
(Internet Access, Etc.)

4 Mr. G Cafè (Wi-Fi)
5 Casa del Gelato (Wi-Fi)

ROME

two main sightseeing plans, each taking several hours. For a short stop, you'll need to choose between the two. I've also included a third option, a mile-long "Heart of Rome Walk," which could be the focus of your visit, or could be added to the end of one of the other plans. If shopping is your main interest, see page 590.

• **Ancient Roman Sites** (in this order): Colosseum, Forum, and Pantheon. Allow three hours. (If you have extra time, it's easy to add on much of the "Heart of Rome Walk.")

• **Vatican City:** St. Peter's Basilica and the Vatican Museum (with the Sistine Chapel). Tour the Vatican Museum first; ideally, reserve your tickets online before your trip (see page 577). Allow four hours, and up to five hours if you haven't reserved ahead for the Vatican Museum and have to wait in line.

• **Heart of Rome:** Take my self-guided walk from Campo de' Fiori to the Spanish Steps, exploring the characteristic squares, Pantheon, and Trevi Fountain en route. Allow two hours or more, especially if you tour the Pantheon.

If you're up for a **semi-insane, do-it-all plan,** try this: Take the train from Civitavecchia to Roma Ostiense, ride the Metro two stops to Colosseo, then walk past the Colosseum, through the Forum (entry fee required), across Capitol Hill, and through the bustling, magical heart of the city to the Pantheon. Then taxi to

Vatican City to see St. Peter's Basilica (no time for the Vatican Museum), before walking to the San Pietro train station to return to Civitavecchia. If you do this, plan on a very busy day, with lots of walking—and little to no time to actually enjoy any of the sights (at best, you could attempt quick visits inside the Pantheon and St. Peter's). If you have one day in your life to spend in Rome, this will at least give you a fleeting taste of its many splendors.

Arrival at the Port of Civitavecchia

Arrival at a Glance: Ride a shuttle bus from your ship to the port entrance, then walk 10 minutes to the train station and catch a train into Rome (40-80 minutes, depending on type of train and destination in Rome). A taxi straight into Rome (which takes 1.5 hours and costs around €110-150) is a bad value compared to the handy, cheap, and direct train.

Port Overview

Cruise ships dock at Civitavecchia (chee-vee-tah-VEH-kyah), a small, manageable port city about 45 miles northwest of Rome.

Civitavecchia is historic: With foundations dating back to Etruscan times, this "Ancient Town" (as its name means) was built up by Emperor Trajan, then favored by the popes with "free port" status. By the 20th century, it had become Rome's main port before being leveled by Allied bombs in World

War II, and later rebuilt. Today, this town of 50,000 has little for visitors to see. Virtually every cruise passenger disembarking at Civitavecchia is headed for Rome.

Civitavecchia's large port area stretches west from its main crossroads, a square called Largo Plebiscito. Several cruise terminals line up along a long pier. The stout 16th-century Michelangelo Fortress (Forte Michelangelo) stands where the port area meets the town, next to the port gate. Tourist services cluster just outside the port gate, on Largo Plebiscito; others line the main road (Viale Garibaldi) between the gate and the train station (a 10-minute walk away).

Tourist Information: A small Civitavecchia **TI** is just beyond the shuttle bus stop. It's a green octagonal kiosk outside the port gate across from McDonald's (daily 9:00-13:00, opens earlier on days with early cruise arrivals, tel. 0766-679-619).

Immediately outside the port gate, the **Cruises Services Cen-**

Services in Civitavecchia

Here are the nearest services to the port, though if you can wait, Rome has everything you need (see "Helpful Hints" on page 502).

ATM: There are ATMs at **Intesa San Paolo** (behind the TI) and **Banca delle Marche,** between the port gate and the train station on Viale Garibaldi.

Internet Access: As you exit the port gate, the first shop on your right, **Cruises Services Center**, has Internet terminals (€3/hour), cheap telephone cards and calling cabins, and other basic services. Two nearby places offer free Wi-Fi with a purchase: **Mr. G Cafè** (near Cruises Services Center) and **Casa del Gelato** (across the small square). You'll also find Wi-Fi at many other restaurants and cafés around town.

Pharmacy: A pharmacy is behind McDonald's and the National Archaeological Museum (Largo Cavour 4).

Baggage Storage: If Civitavecchia is your first or last stop, and you need a place to store bags, you can stow them at the Cruises Services Center (€5/day per bag).

ter has a privately owned info desk with a very helpful, efficient staff that gives good advice for anyone heading into Rome (daily 9:00-19:00). They also offer Internet access and baggage storage, and sell regional train tickets (including the good-value BIRG ticket) for the same price as the station. Check the train schedule, decide which train to catch, and buy your ticket here.

Consider picking up a copy of the *Target Civitavecchia* magazine at the TI or the Cruises Service Center, in case you have time to kill in town when you return in the afternoon (when the TI will be closed).

Getting into Rome

Road traffic between Civitavecchia and Rome is terrible, making the train faster and much more economical than a taxi. After disembarking from your ship, you'll have to make your way to the port gate. From here, you have several options.

Getting from Your Ship to the Port Gate: It's a long walk or quick shuttle-bus ride to the port gate. Ships provide this free shuttle service to the gate (they run each way every 15 minutes or so, with the ship's name in the front window). You'll leave the port through a single small gate in the port fence; shuttle buses back to the ship line up right by this gate. Stepping through the gate, past the people hustling taxi services and rides to the airport, you meet the actual town. On your immediate right is the very helpful Cruises Services Center (described earlier). The TI is ahead, just across the street.

By Taxi

I'd avoid taxis here. But if you want to take one, you'll find them waiting at the port gate, attempting to extort €15 for the very short ride to the train station (at least triple the fair metered rate), or significantly more for the ride into Rome (figure about 1.5 hours each way, depending on traffic; the going rate should be €110-150 one-way, or €300-400 for an all-day Rome city tour, but many cabbies inflate their prices dramatically). Taxis generally meet arriving ships, or you can call 076-626-121. Beware of unlicensed taxis offering a huge price break; local police sometimes follow these "gypsy" cabs and impose hefty fines on both the driver and the passengers.

By Train

It's really quite simple: From the port gate, walk about 10 minutes to Civitavecchia's train station; ride the train into Rome; then connect by taxi or public transportation to what you'd like to see in Rome. Your main decision is about how to structure your time in Rome, which will determine the train station where you'll disembark. For a preview before your trip, you can check out the Rome Walks website (www.romewalks.com), which has a useful step-by-step video on this approach.

Step 1: Walk from the Port Gate to the Train Station

From the shuttle-bus stop, **walk** through the security checkpoint at the port gate to Largo Plebiscito, Civitavecchia's hub of activity. From here, it's about a 10-minute walk to the train station: Exit the port gate straight ahead, passing a row of hole-in-the-wall shops and businesses catering to cruise passengers, and continue straight along the broad sidewalk next to the main road, Viale Garibaldi (with the sea on your right). After about three blocks, at Hotel de La Ville, bear left and uphill through a long parking lot to the pale-orange train station (marked *Civitavecchia*—see photo). If you get turned around, look for signs to *Stazione FF. SS.*

Local **buses** #B, #C, and #D go from just above the port gate on Largo Plebiscito (Viale Garibaldi stop) one stop to the train station (Stazione FF. SS. stop; 3-4/hour, 5 minutes, €1, buy ticket at tobacco shop before you board). The bus only saves you a few minutes of walking; unless it happens to be departing just as you arrive, you'll likely spend more time waiting for the next bus than you would simply walking to the station. Take the bus only if you're carrying heavy bags or have limited mobility.

Step 2: Take the Train from Civitavecchia to Rome

Inside the **Civitavecchia train station,** you'll find the Food Village café and cafeteria, a tobacco shop, and a newsstand, but no lockers or baggage storage (the nearest baggage storage is at the port gate—described earlier). *Partenze* screens show upcoming departures. The columns show each train's destination *(destinazione)*; category *(cat)*; time of departure *(ore)*; delay, if any *(rit)*; and which track the train leaves from *(bin)*. Frequent trains (2-3/hour) connect Civitavecchia with several stations in Rome.

Just outside the station, the **Agenzie 365** travel agency sells transportation tickets of all types (including the BIRG ticket, described later). It also often has Vatican and Colosseum "skip the line" tickets available. You'll pay a premium (€27.50 for the Vatican, €25 for the Colosseum), but if you haven't made reservations in advance, it's worth considering if you'd rather not risk having to stand in line (daily 8:00-14:00, tel. 0766-220-239).

Choosing Between Rome's Stations: Depending on your sightseeing plans, you'll likely be best off heading either to **Ostiense Station** (with a handy Metro station, just two stops from the Colosseum) or **San Pietro Station** (a short walk from Vatican City). **Roma Termini,** the city's biggest station, serves as the main hub for the city's transit (including shuttle trains to the airport)—but overshoots the key city-center sights a bit.

Choosing Between Trains: Regional trains (marked *REG*) head into Rome roughly twice an hour, stopping at San Pietro and Ostiense stations on their way to Termini (40-55 minutes to San Pietro, 55-70 minutes to Ostiense, 65-80 minutes to Termini). The **Intercity train** (marked *IC*) is somewhat faster (40-50 minutes to Ostiense, 50-60 minutes to Termini), but doesn't stop at San Pietro Station, and isn't covered by the good-value BIRG ticket (described next). When there are enough ships in port to justify it, there's also a special **"Vatican train non-stop" express to San Pietro Station**, offering one daily round-trip designed for cruise travelers (times in 2013: departs Civitavecchia 9:30, arrives San Pietro 10:13; return trip: departs San Pietro 16:40, arrives Civitavecchia 17:20). While a bit more expensive (€10 one-way, €16 round-trip, not covered by the BIRG ticket), the ride is comfortable, air-conditioned, and limited to cruise passengers only (so it's not crowded, as regular trains often are), and it can save you up to 20 minutes each way. Since this train is operated by the cruise lines, ships know to wait for you if it's delayed.

Choosing Between Ticket Options: If you're taking a regional

ROME

train, save money by getting the wonderful BIRG ticket: a €12 day pass covering second-class, round-trip train travel between Civitavecchia and Rome as well as unlimited travel on Rome's buses, Metro, and trams—a great convenience (not valid on fast Intercity trains or the express train to San Pietro Station). Otherwise, expect to pay about €5 each way for regional trains or €10 on the Intercity.

Buying Tickets: Buy your BIRG ticket from the ticket desk at the Cruises Services Center (as you exit the port gate) or at the train station (available at the ticket counter but not at machines; also available at the Agenzie 365 travel agency, newsstand, and Food Village café); be sure to write your name on the back of your BIRG ticket.

If you're not getting a BIRG ticket, you can avoid the long ticket-window lines by using the station's **self-service machines.** Look for those labeled *Biglietto Veloce/Fast Ticket,* which are easy to use and sell tickets for all types of trains (except the special express train to San Pietro); on these machines, when prompted, select "base" fare. (Machines labeled *Biglietti Self-Service/Rete Regionale* have instructions only in Italian, accept only cash, and sell tickets only for regional trains.) Train tickets (including BIRG) must be validated in the green or yellow box before getting on the train. For the express to San Pietro Station, buy your ticket from a ticket window or on the train (same price).

Platforms: Be sure you're waiting at the correct platform (clearly indicated on the schedule). The Civitavecchia train station has five main platforms (*binario,* or *bin;* numbered 1 through 5), connected by an underground tunnel. There are also two "short" *(tronco)* platforms, 1T and 2T, at the far-right end of the station as you face the tracks; these are *not* the same as tracks 1 and 2.

Step 3: From Rome's Train Stations to the Sights

Once you arrive in Rome, your plan depends on which station you ride to: Ostiense (easy Metro connection to the Colosseum), San Pietro (best if you plan to start at the Vatican), or Termini (Rome's main station—huge, bustling and relatively overwhelming).

From Ostiense Station to the Colosseum

This practical little commuter hub connects the train system with Rome's subway system, serving also as the Piramide Metro stop. For anyone coming from the cruise port, this is the fastest connection to the Colosseum. Simply leave the train at Roma Ostiense, follow signs to the Metro (look for the red *M*), and ride two stops (direction: Rebibbia or Conca d'Oro/Jonio) to Colosseo. Assuming you purchased the BIRG ticket in Civitavecchia, you're already covered for the Metro ride. Just insert it into the front of the turnstile—magnetic strip side up, arrow first—retrieve it from the top, and you're on your way. Stepping out of the Metro at Colosseo, you come face-to-face with the most impressive sight of ancient Rome and are nicely positioned to walk from here through the Forum, over Capitol Hill, and on to the Pantheon.

Note that at Ostiense, a branch of the gourmet supermarket **Eataly** is adjacent to track 15a. Over three floors, you'll find every edible Italian goodie imaginable and a number of different food stations where you can eat in or take away (daily 10:00-24:00).

Near Ostiense Station: Just outside Ostiense Station, you can see the Pyramid of Gaius Cestius, built in about 15 B.C. by a rich Roman magistrate who wanted a stylish tomb (the occupation of Egypt had sparked ancient Romans' interest in all things Egyptian). It later was incorporated into Rome's mighty Aurelian Wall, which once encircled the city. Begun in the third century, the wall was 12 miles long and averaged about 26 feet high, with 14 main gates and 380 72-foot-tall towers. Across the street is the castle-esque Porta San Paulo, a key city gate in the Aurelian Wall, as it served Via Ostiense, the road to Rome's seaport.

From San Pietro Station to Vatican City

This small station has basic services (ticket window, ticket machines, WC, and café).

On Foot: From the station, **St. Peter's Basilica** is about a 10-minute walk. With your back to the station, head out and to the right for 50 yards to the first corner, then turn left and follow Via della Stazione San Pietro toward the huge dome towering in the distance. After a long block, follow the right side of the street (now Via Alcide de Gasperi) as it curves around to the right toward Via delle Fornaci, which leads directly to the vast, oval St. Peter's Square.

If you're going directly to the **Vatican Museum,** on the far side of Vatican City from here, it's smart to take a taxi to avoid the 30-minute walk from the station (taxi stand to the right as you exit the station). If you do decide to hoof it, follow the directions above, then cross St. Peter's Square and pass through the colonnades at the far side of the square. Go through the arches of the brick wall and continue straight ahead, following the wall north another 10-15 minutes along Via di Porta Angelica until it turns left at Viale Vaticano, where you'll find the main museum entrance.

By Bus: Bus #64 goes from San Pietro Station to the Caval-leggeri stop near St. Peter's Square, and then winds through the heart of the city, stopping at Largo Argentina (for the Pantheon), Piazza Venezia (for the Roman Forum and Colosseum), and on to

ROME

Termini train station. If you've already validated your BIRG ticket, you can just hop on (no need to validate again).

Returning to the Station: To walk from St. Peter's Square back to San Pietro Station, leave the square, keeping the church to your right, and follow yellow signs for *Stazione S. Pietro.*

From Termini Station to Various Points in Rome

Termini, Rome's main train station, is a buffet of tourist services; however, it's undergoing renovation, so some services might have moved by the time you arrive. On a short visit, it's too huge to be handy—try to avoid it by using one of the smaller stations described earlier.

If you do land at Termini, don't panic. While information desks are jammed with travelers, the staff at red info kiosks at the head of the tracks can answer your simple questions. Along track 24, about 100 yards down, you'll find the **TI** (daily 8:00-19:30) and **car rental** desks. A snack bar and good self-service **cafeteria,** Ciao, is near the head of track 24, upstairs (daily 11:00-22:30). Near track 1, you'll find a **pharmacy** (daily 7:30-22:00); along the same track is an often cramped **waiting room** and **Despar Express,** selling groceries and toiletries (daily 7:00-21:30). The handy **Conad,** selling everything from groceries to electronics, is just downstairs (daily 6:00-24:00; closest to track 1). Pricey **WCs** (€1) are also downstairs, just below the main exits on the north or south side.

Elsewhere in the station are **ATMs,** late-hours banks, and 24-hour thievery. In the station's main entrance lobby, **Borri Books** sells books in English, including popular fiction, Italian history and culture, and kids' books, plus maps upstairs (daily 7:00-23:00). The station has some sleazy sharks with official-looking business cards; avoid anybody selling anything unless they're in a legitimate shop at the station.

Termini is a local transportation hub, ideal for using Rome's excellent public transit network—which includes the Metro (subway), buses, and trams—to reach whatever you'd like to see in Rome. For all the details on this system and its tickets, see page 505. The Metro and bus areas are a work in progress and change frequently—look for signs directing you to the nearest Metro platform or bus stop.

Metro lines (A and B) intersect downstairs at Termini Metro station. If you're heading for the Colosseum and ancient sites, ride line B (direction: Laurentina) two stops to Colosseo. For the Vatican, ride line A (direction: Battisini) six stops to Ottaviano (still a 10-minute walk from the Vatican)—or take a bus, described next.

Buses (including Rome's hop-on, hop-off bus tours—see page 512) leave across the square directly in front of the main station hall. To reach the Pantheon or the Vatican, hop on bus #64 or #40 (requires an additional 10- to 15-minute walk to the Vatican Museum, or a 5-minute walk to the Pantheon).

Consider hiring a **taxi** to save time getting around Rome. Taxis queue in front and outside both the north and south side exits; if there's a long taxi line in front, try a side exit instead. Avoid con men hawking "express taxi" services in unmarked cars (only use cars marked with the word *taxi* and a phone number). For details on taking taxis in Rome, see page 494.

By Tour or Private Driver

A small company called **Can't Be Missed** offers Rome tours from the port (€62 plus €21.50 for Vatican Museum admission, 10 percent discount when you book using promo code "RICKSTEVES" and then show this book, includes BIRG ticket to cover all public transit, small groups, mobile 329-129-8182, www.cantbemissedtours.com, info@cantbemissedtours.com). On these tours you'll see the Colosseum from the outside unless you spring for the optional 30-minute unguided visit (€13.50). Your guide first meets you at the Civitavecchia train station (in time to catch the 8:41 train), then, once in town, leads you on a walk through Rome's ancient city center, passing the area's major sights. After a lunch break, you'll tour the Vatican Museum, including the Sistine Chapel (tickets are pre-reserved, so no waiting), and then visit St. Peter's Basilica before being put on a train back to the port (arriving by 17:15). This is a good deal considering you're sharing the services of a good, hardworking local guide.

Miles & Miles Private Tours also offers tours from the port to Rome by private car or van; see "Car and Minibus Tours" on page 514.

If you want to pay a premium for door-to-door service, recommended driver Ezio of **Autoservizi Monti Concezio** takes cruise travelers to Rome in a private car (€130/2 people, €20 for each additional person) and offers full-day tours of the city (€380/2 people, €30 for each additional person; see "Car and Minibus Tours" on page 514).

For information on other tour options in Rome—including local guides for hire, walking tours, and hop-on, hop-off bus tours—see "Tours in Rome" on page 510.

Sights in Civitavecchia

There are a few ways you can enjoyably kill any remaining time in Civitavecchia before catching the shuttle bus back to your ship. For a **stroll** through town, walk from the port gate directly inland through Largo Plebiscito and up Corso Centocelle (the TI's *Tar-*

ROME

get Civitavecchia magazine has more info on the town). For some **beach** time, handy little Pirgo Beach is directly in front of the train station.

Civitavecchia's humble three-floor **National Archaeological Museum**, just a block in front of the port gate, focuses on its ancient past, with a small exhibit described in English (free, Tue-Sun until 19:30, closed Mon, air-con, just beyond the McDonald's, across the street from Casa del Gelato).

Returning to Your Ship

Depending upon where you are at the end of your Roman holiday, you may find it easier to catch your Civitavecchia train from **Ostiense Station** (two Metro stops from the Colosseum) or **San Pietro Station** (a 10-minute walk from St. Peter's Square; Civitavecchia trains leave from track 5, generally around the top and bottom of the hour). Both stations are easily reached by taxi. Remember, with a BIRG ticket, you can simply hop on any train bound for Civitavecchia. If you're returning from **Termini Station,** note that trains to Civitavecchia generally leave from tracks 27-30, a 10- to 15-minute walk from the main station entrance...seriously. Allow plenty of time to make this hike.

Once back at Civitavecchia's train station, exit to the right and head straight back down to the port. After going through the gate, look for the free shuttle bus—before boarding, check to make sure it's the right one (marked with the name of your cruise ship on the front window).

Note: Not all taxis have permission to enter the port area (they can only go as far as the port gate). If you're taking a taxi *to* the port, ensure that they have authorization to the pier *(molo)* to bring you all the way to your ship; otherwise, you'll have to ride the shuttle bus.

See page 610 for help if you miss your boat.

Orientation to Rome

Sprawling Rome actually feels manageable once you get to know it. The old core, with most of the tourist sights, sits in a diamond formed by Termini train station (in the east), the Vatican (west), Villa Borghese Gardens (north), and the Colosseum (south). The Tiber River runs through the diamond from north to south. In the center of the diamond sits Piazza Venezia, a busy square and traffic hub. It takes about an hour to walk from Termini Station to the Vatican.

Rome: A Verbal Map

Think of Rome as a series of neighborhoods, huddling around major landmarks.

Ancient Rome: In ancient times, this was home for the grandest buildings of a city of a million people. Today, the best of the classical sights stand in a line from the Colosseum to the Forum to the Pantheon.

Pantheon Neighborhood: The Pantheon anchors the neighborhood I like to call the heart of Rome. It stretches eastward from the Tiber River through Campo de' Fiori and Piazza Navona, past the Pantheon to the Trevi Fountain.

Vatican City: Located west of the Tiber, it's a compact world of its own, with two great, huge sights: St. Peter's Basilica and the Vatican Museum.

North Rome: With the Spanish Steps, Villa Borghese Gardens, and trendy shopping streets (Via Veneto and the "shopping triangle"—the area between the Spanish Steps, Piazza Venezia, and Piazza del Popolo), this is a more modern, classy area.

East Rome: This includes the area around Termini Station, with its many public-transportation connections. Nearby is the neighborhood I call "Pilgrim's Rome," with several prominent churches dotting the area south of the station.

South Rome: South of Vatican City is Trastevere, the colorful, wrong-side-of-the-river neighborhood that provides a look at village Rome. It's the city at its crustiest—and perhaps most "Roman." Across the Tiber River, directly south of the city center, are the gritty/colorful Testaccio neighborhood, the 1930s suburb of E.U.R., and the Appian Way, home of the catacombs.

Tourist Information

Rome has two TI offices and several TI kiosks. The TI offices are at the airport (Terminal 3, daily 8:00-19:30) and Termini train station (daily 8:00-19:30, 100 yards down track 24, look for signs). Little kiosks (generally open daily 9:30-19:00) are near the Forum (on Piazza del Tempio della Pace), on Via Nazionale (at Palazzo delle Esposizioni), near Castel Sant'Angelo (at Piazza Pia), near Piazza Navona (at Piazza delle Cinque Lune), and near the Trevi Fountain (at Via del Corso and Via Minghetti). The TI's website is www.turismoroma.it.

At any TI, ask for a city map and a listing of sights and hours (in the free *Evento* booklet with English-language pages listing the month's cultural events—also includes a bus map; if they're out, ask for last month's issue as much of the info is still valid). The best map I found is published by Rough Guide (€9 in bookstores).

Rome's single best source of up-to-date tourist information is

Rome's Neighborhoods

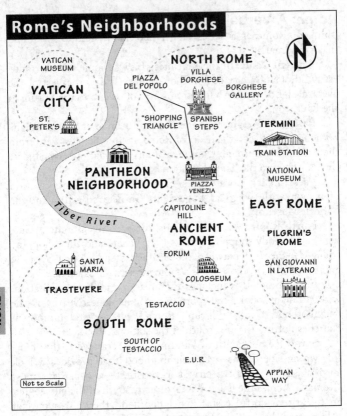

VATICAN MUSEUM

NORTH ROME

VILLA BORGHESE

PIAZZA DEL POPOLO

BORGHESE GALLERY

VATICAN CITY

ST. PETER'S

"SHOPPING TRIANGLE"

SPANISH STEPS

TERMINI

TRAIN STATION

NATIONAL MUSEUM

PANTHEON NEIGHBORHOOD

PIAZZA VENEZIA

Tiber River

CAPITOLINE HILL

ANCIENT ROME

FORUM

COLOSSEUM

EAST ROME

PILGRIM'S ROME

SAN GIOVANNI IN LATERANO

SANTA MARIA

TRASTEVERE

TESTACCIO

SOUTH ROME

SOUTH OF TESTACCIO

E.U.R.

APPIAN WAY

Not to Scale

ROME

its **call center,** with English-speakers on staff. Dial 06-0608 (answered daily 9:00-21:00, press 2 for English, www.060608.it).

Several English-oriented **websites** provide insight into events and daily life in the city: www.inromenow.com (light tourist info on lots of topics) and www.wantedinrome.com (events).

Helpful Hints

Sightseeing Tips: If you're in Rome on a Sunday, note that the Vatican Museum is closed (except for last Sun of the month, when it's free and even more crowded), and the Porta Portese flea market hops in the morning. On Mondays, the Capitoline Museums are closed. On Wednesdays, St. Peter's Basilica may be closed in the morning for a papal audience.

Bookstores: The following stores sell travel guidebooks, including mine (all open daily except Anglo American and Open Door closed Sun). The first two are chains, while the others have a more personal touch. **Borri Books** is at Termini Station, and **Feltrinelli** has two branches (at Largo Argentina 11, with a limited English section, and the larger Feltrinelli International, just off Piazza della Repubblica at Via Vittorio Emanuele Orlando 78-81, tel. 06-487-0171). **Anglo American Bookshop** has great art and history sections (closed all day Sun and Mon morning, a few blocks south of Spanish Steps at Via della Vite 102, tel. 06-679-5222). **Libreria Fanucci** has a small selection, but is centrally located (a block toward the Pantheon from Piazza Navona at Piazza Madama 8, tel. 06-686-1141). In Trastevere, Irishman Dermot at the **Almost Corner Bookshop** stocks an Italian-interest section (Via del Moro 45, tel. 06-583-6942), and the **Open Door Bookshop** carries the only used books in English in town (closed Sun, Via della Lungaretta 23, tel. 06-589-6478).

Laundry: The **Ondablu** chain usually comes with Internet access (€2/hour); one of their more central locations is near Termini Station (about €8 to wash and dry a 15-pound load, usually open daily 8:00-22:00, Via Principe Amedeo 70b, tel. 06-474-4647).

Travel Agencies: You can get train tickets and railpass-related reservations and supplements at travel agencies (at little or no additional cost), avoiding a trip to a train station.

Theft Alert: While violent crime is rare in the city center, petty theft is rampant. With sweet-talking con artists meeting you at the station, well-dressed pickpockets on buses, and thieving gangs of children at the ancient sites, Rome is a gauntlet of rip-offs. Although it's not as bad as it was a few years ago, and pickpockets don't want to hurt you—they usually just want your money—green or sloppy tourists will be scammed. Thieves strike when you're distracted. Don't trust kind strangers. Keep nothing important in your pockets.

Be most on guard while boarding and leaving buses and subways. Thieves crowd the door, then stop and turn while others crowd and push from behind. You'll find less crowding and commotion—and less risk—waiting for the end cars of a subway rather than the middle cars. The sneakiest thieves pretend to be well-dressed businessmen (generally with something in their hands), or tourists wearing fanny packs and toting cameras and even Rick Steves guidebooks.

If you know what to look out for, fast-fingered moms with babies and gangs of children picking the pockets and handbags of naive tourists are not a threat, but an interesting, albeit sad, spectacle. Pickpockets troll through the tourist crowds around the Colosseum, Forum, Vatican, and train and Metro stations. Watch them target tourists who are overloaded with bags or distracted with a video camera. The kids look like beggars and hold up newspapers or cardboard signs to confuse their victims. They scram like stray cats if you're on to them.

Scams abound: Always be clear about what paper money you're giving someone, demand clear and itemized bills, and count your change. Don't give your wallet to self-proclaimed "police" who stop you on the street, warn you about counterfeit (or drug) money, and ask to see your cash. If a bank machine eats your ATM card, see if there's a thin plastic insert with a tongue hanging out that thieves use to extract it.

Reporting Losses: To report lost or stolen items, file a police report (at Termini Station, with *polizia* at track 11 or with Carabinieri at track 20; offices are also at Piazza Venezia). You'll need the report to file an insurance claim for lost gear, and it can help with replacing your passport—first file the police report, then call your embassy to make an appointment (see page 488). For information on how to report lost or stolen credit cards, see page 132.

Pedestrian Safety: Your main safety concern in Rome is crossing streets safely. Use extreme caution. Scooters don't need to stop at red lights, and even cars exercise what drivers call the "logical option" of not stopping if they see no oncoming traffic. Each year, as noisy gasoline-powered scooters are replaced by electric ones, the streets get quieter (hooray) but more dangerous for pedestrians. Follow locals like a shadow when you cross a street (or spend a good part of your visit stranded on curbs). When you do cross alone, don't be a deer in the headlights. Find a gap in the traffic and walk with confidence while making eye contact with approaching drivers—they won't hit you if they can tell where you intend to go.

Staying/Getting Healthy: In the heat of summer, take frequent rest breaks. I drink lots of cold, refreshing water from Rome's many drinking fountains (the Forum has three).

Pharmacies: There's a pharmacy (marked by a green cross) in every neighborhood. Pharmacies stay open late in Termini Station (daily 7:30-22:00) and at Piazza dei Cinquecento 51 (Mon-Fri 7:00-23:30, Sat-Sun 8:00-23:00, next to Termini Station on the corner of Via Cavour, tel. 06-488-0019). There's also a 24-hour pharmacy several blocks down from Piazza della Repubblica at Via Nazionale 228 (tel. 06-488-4437).

Updates to This Book: For updates to this book, check www.ricksteves.com/update.

Getting Around Rome

Sightsee on foot, by city bus, by Metro, or by taxi. I've grouped your sightseeing into walkable neighborhoods. Make it a point to visit sights in a logical order. Needless backtracking wastes precious time.

The public transportation system, which is cheap and efficient, consists primarily of buses, a few trams, and the two underground subway (Metro) lines. Consider it part of your Roman experience.

The walking-tour company, Rome Walks, has produced an orientation video to Rome's transportation system; find it on YouTube by searching for "Understanding Rome's Public Transport."

For information, visit www.atac.roma.it, which has a useful route planner in English, or call 06-57003. If you have a smartphone and an international data plan, consider downloading the free Roma Bus app by Movenda, which also has a route planner and real-time updates on the bus schedule. The ATAC mobile website has similar info (www.muovi.roma.it).

Buying Tickets

All public transportation uses the same ticket. It costs €1.50 and is valid for one Metro ride—including transfers underground—plus unlimited city buses and trams during a 100-minute period. A one-day pass for buses and the Metro is €6 (good until midnight). Remember, if you bought a €12 BIRG ticket to cover your regional train ride from Civitavecchia, it's good for your Metro and bus travel in Rome.

You can purchase transit tickets and passes at some newsstands, tobacco shops (*tabacchi*, marked by a black-and-white *T* sign), and major Metro stations and bus stops, but not on board. It's smart to stock up on tickets so you don't have to run around searching for an open tobacco shop when you spot your bus approaching. Metro stations rarely have human ticket-sellers, and the machines are unreliable (it helps to insert your smallest coin first).

Validate your ticket by sticking it in the Metro turnstile (magnetic-strip-side up, arrow-side first) or in the machine when you board the bus (magnetic-strip-side down, arrow-side first)—watch others and imitate. It'll return your ticket with your expiration time printed. To get through a Metro turnstile with a transit pass, use it just like a ticket; on buses and trams, however, you need to validate your pass only if that's your first time using it.

By Metro

The Roman subway system (Metropolitana, or "Metro") is simple, with two clean, cheap, fast lines—A and B—that intersect at Termini Station. The Metro runs from 5:30 to 23:30 (Fri-Sat until

ROME

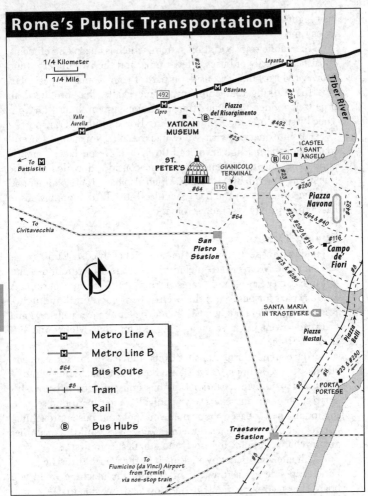

Rome's Public Transportation

1/4 Kilometer
1/4 Mile

Lepanto M

#23

Ottaviano M   #280

492 M
Cipro

Valle
Aurelia M

Piazza
del Risorgimento   B   #492

VATICAN
MUSEUM   #23

← To M
Battistini

Tiber River

CASTEL
SANT'
ANGELO

B 40

ST.
PETER'S   GIANICOLO
TERMINAL   #25   #280

#64   116   #8

Piazza
Navona   #492

← To
Civitavecchia

#64   #23 & #40
#280 & #116

#116

Campo
de'
Fiori   #8

San
Pietro
Station   #23 & #280

SANTA MARIA
IN TRASTEVERE

Piazza
Mastai

Piazza
Belli

#8   #23 & #280

PORTA
PORTESE

Legend:

- —M— Metro Line A
- ···M··· Metro Line B
- ‑‑ #64 ‑‑ Bus Route
- ├─ #8 ─┤ Tram
- ······ Rail
- Ⓑ Bus Hubs

Trastevere
Station

To
Fiumicino (da Vinci) Airport
from Termini
via non-stop train

1:30 in the morning). Remember, the subway's first and last compartments are generally the least crowded, and the least likely to harbor pickpockets.

You'll notice lots of big holes in the city while a new line is being built to run across town, including the historic heart. It will likely not be completed until 2020.

While much of Rome is not served by its skimpy subway, the following stops are helpful:

Termini (intersection of lines A and B): Termini Station, shuttle train to airport

Repubblica (line A): Baths of Diocletian and Via Nazionale

Barberini (line A): Trevi Fountain and Villa Borghese

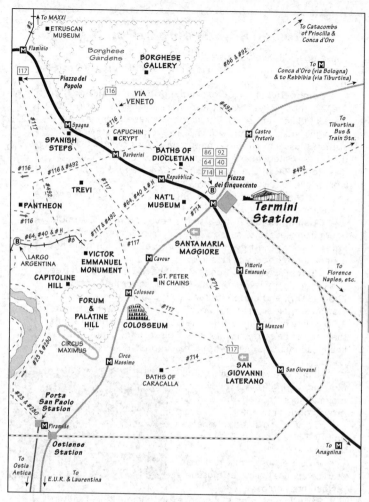

Spagna (line A): Spanish Steps and classy shopping area

Flaminio (line A): Piazza del Popolo

Ottaviano (line A): St. Peter's Basilica and Vatican Museum

Tiburtina (line B): Tiburtina train and bus station

Colosseo (line B): Colosseum, Roman Forum, bike rental

Piramide (line B): Ostiense Station with trains to Civita-vecchia

By Bus

The Metro is handy, but it won't get you everywhere—take the bus (or tram). Bus routes are clearly listed at the stops. TIs usually don't have bus maps, but with some knowledge of major stops, you won't

ROME

Tips on Sightseeing in Rome

These tips will help you use your time and money efficiently, making the Eternal City seem less eternal and more entertaining.

Combo-Ticket for Colosseum, Forum, and Palatine Hill: A €12 combo-ticket covers these three adjacent sights (no individual tickets are sold). The combo-ticket allows one entry per sight and is valid for two days. To avoid ticket-buying lines at the Colosseum and Forum, purchase your combo-ticket at the lesser-visited Palatine Hill or in advance online.

Roma Pass: The Roma Pass (€34, valid 3 days) isn't worthwhile for a short, one-day visit to Rome.

Vatican Museum: To avoid long lines at this sight, reserve in advance online (see page 577).

Opening Hours: Rome's sights have notoriously variable hours from season to season. Get a current listing of opening times—ask for the free booklet *Evento* at a TI. On holidays, expect shorter hours or closures.

Churches: Many churches, which have divine art and free entry, open early (around 7:00-7:30), close for lunch (roughly 12:00-15:00), and close late (about 19:00). Kamikaze tourists maximize their sightseeing hours by visiting churches before 9:00 or late in the day; during the siesta, they see major sights that stay open all day (St. Peter's, Colosseum, Forum, Capitoline Museums, and Pantheon). Dress modestly for church visits.

Picnic Discreetly: Public drinking and eating is not allowed at major sights, though the ban has proven difficult to enforce. To avoid the risk of being fined, choose an empty piazza for your picnic, or keep a low profile.

WCs: Because public restrooms are scarce, use toilets at museums, restaurants, and bars.

Experiences: For ideas on experiencing Italian culture beyond the sights, see the sidebar on page 378.

necessarily need one (though if you do want a route map, find one printed inside the *Evento* magazine—free at TIs and hotels—or buy it from tobacco shops).

Buses—especially the touristy #40 and #64—are havens for thieves and pickpockets. Assume any commotion is a thief-created distraction. If one bus is packed, there's likely a second one on its tail with far fewer crowds and thieves.

The tram lines are of limited use for most tourists, but a few lines can save some walking. For all intents and purposes, they function identically to buses. Once you know the bus/tram system, you'll find it's easier than searching for a cab.

Tickets have a barcode and must be stamped on the bus in the yellow box with the digital readout (be sure to retrieve your ticket). Validate your ticket as you board (magnetic-strip-side down, arrow-side first), otherwise you're cheating. While relatively safe, riding without a stamped ticket on the bus is stressful. Inspectors fine even innocent-looking tourists €50. There's no need to validate a transit pass on the bus, unless your pass is new and hasn't yet been stamped elsewhere in the transit system. Bus etiquette (not always followed) is to board at the front or rear doors and exit at the middle.

Regular bus lines start running at about 5:30, and during the day they run every 5-10 minutes. After 23:30, and sometimes earlier (such as on Sundays), buses are less frequent but still dependable.

These are the major bus routes:

Bus #64: This bus cuts across the city, linking Termini Station with the Vatican, stopping at Piazza della Repubblica (sights), Via Nazionale, Piazza Venezia (near Forum), Largo Argentina (near Pantheon and Campo de' Fiori), St. Peter's Basilica (get off just past the tunnel), and San Pietro Station. Ride it for a city overview and to watch pickpockets in action. The #64 can get horribly crowded.

Bus #40: This express bus, which mostly follows the #64 route (but ends near the Castel Sant'Angelo on the Vatican side of the river), is especially helpful—fewer stops and crowds.

***Elettrico* Minibuses:** Two cute *elettrico* minibuses that wind through the narrow streets of old and interesting neighborhoods are great for transport or simple joyriding. *Elettrico* **#116** runs through the medieval core of Rome: Ponte Vittorio Emanuele II (near Castel Sant'Angelo) to Campo de' Fiori, Pantheon, Piazza Barberini, and the southern edge of the scenic Villa Borghese Gardens. *Elettrico* **#117** connects San Giovanni in Laterano, Colosseo, Via dei Serpenti, Trevi Fountain, Piazza di Spagna, and Piazza del Popolo—and vice versa.

By Taxi

I use taxis in Rome more often than in other cities. They're reasonable and useful for efficient sightseeing in this big, hot metropolis. Taxis start at €3, then charge about €1.50 per kilometer (surcharges: €1.50 on Sun, €3.50 for nighttime hours of 22:00-7:00, one regular suitcase or bag rides free, tip by rounding up to the nearest euro). Sample fares: Termini area to Vatican-€11; Termini area to Colosseum-€7; (or look up your route at www.worldtaximeter.com). Three or four companions with more money than time should taxi almost everywhere.

It's tough to wave down a taxi in Rome. Find the nearest taxi stand by asking a passerby or a clerk in a shop, *"Dov'è una fermata dei taxi?"* (doh-VEH OO-nah fehr-MAH-tah DEH-ee TAHK-see). Some taxi stands are listed on my maps. To call a cab on your own, dial 06-3570, 06-4994, or 06-6645. It's routine for Romans to ask the waiter in a restaurant to call a taxi when they ask for the bill. The waiter will tell you how many minutes you have to enjoy your coffee.

Beware of corrupt taxis. First, make sure the meter *(tassametro)* is turned on. If it isn't, get out and hail another cab. Check that the meter is reset to the basic drop charge (should be around €3, or around €5 if you or your restaurant phoned for the taxi). Many meters show both the fare and the time elapsed during the ride, and some tourists—mistaking the time for the fare—end up paying more than the fair meter rate. Keep an eye on the fare on the meter as you near your destination; some cabbies turn the meter off instantly when they stop and tell you a higher price.

When you arrive at the train station, beware of hustlers conning naive visitors into unmarked, rip-off "express taxis." Only use official taxis, with a *taxi* sign and phone number marked on the door. By law, they must display a multilingual official price chart; point to the chart and ask the cabbie to explain it if the fare doesn't seem right. A common cabbie scam is to take your €20 note, drop it, and pick up a €5 note (similar color), claiming that's what you gave him. To avoid this scam, pay in small bills; if you only have a large bill, show it to the cabbie as you state its face value.

If you encounter any problems with a taxi, making a show of writing down the taxi number (to file a complaint) can motivate a driver to quickly settle the matter.

Tours in Rome

On Foot

Finding the best guided tours in Rome is challenging. Local guides are good but pricey. Tour companies are cheaper, but quality and organization are unreliable. To sightsee on your own, download my series of **free audio tours** that illuminate some of Rome's top sights and neighborhoods (see sidebar on page 50 for details).

If you do hire a private Italian guide, consider organizing a group of four to six people to split the cost (around €180 for a three-hour tour); this ends up costing about the same per person as going on a scheduled tour from one of the walking-tour companies listed below (about €25, generally expat guides).

Local Guides

I've worked with each of these licensed independent local guides. They're worth every euro. They speak excellent English and enjoy tailoring tours to your interests. Their prices (roughly €55-60/hour) flex with the day, season, and demand. Arrange your date and price by email.

Francesca Caruso loves to teach and share her appreciation of her city, and has contributed generously to this chapter (www. francescacaruso.com, francescainroma@gmail.com). Popular with my readers, Francesca understandably books up quickly; if she's busy, she'll recommend one of her colleagues. **Carla Zaia** is an engaging expert on all things Roman (carlaromeguide@gmail.com). **Cristina Giannicchi** has an archaeology background (mobile 338-111-4573, www.crisromanguide.com, crisgiannicchi@gmail. com). **Sara Magister,** a Roman with doctorates in art history and archaeology, leads tours throughout the city (a.magister@iol.it). **Giovanna Terzulli** is a personable, knowledgeable art historian (gioterzulli@gmail.com). **Alessandra Mazzoccoli** is experienced, easygoing, and good with all ages (alemazzoccoli@gmail.com). Italian-American **Sean Finelli,** known as "The Roman Guy," offers several walking tours and a trip-planning service (www.theromanguy.com).

Walking-Tour Companies

Rome has many highly competitive tour companies, each offering a series of themed walks through various slices of Rome. Three-hour guided walks generally cost €25-30 per person. Guides are usually native English speakers, often American expats. Tours are limited to small groups, geared to American tourists, and given in English only. I've listed some here, but without a lot of details on their offerings. Before your trip, spend some time on these companies' websites to get to know your options, as each company has a particular teaching and guiding personality. Some are highbrow, and others are less scholarly. It's sometimes required, and always smart, to book a spot in advance (easy online). I must add that we get a lot of negative feedback on some tour companies. Readers report that advertising can be misleading, and scheduling mishaps are common. Make sure you know what you are booking and when.

Context Rome's walking tours are more intellectual than most, designed for travelers with longer-than-average attention spans. They are more expensive than others and are led by "docents" rather than guides (tel. 06-9672-7371, US tel. 800-691-6036, www.contextrome.com). **Enjoy Rome** offers a number of different walks and a website filled with helpful information (Via Marghera 8a, tel. 06-445-1843, www.enjoyrome.com, info@enjoyrome.com). **Rome Walks** has put together several particularly

Rome at a Glance

▲▲▲**Colosseum** Huge stadium where gladiators fought. **Hours:** Daily 8:30 until one hour before sunset: April-Aug until 19:15, Sept until 19:00, Oct until 18:30, off-season closes as early as 16:30. See page 522.

▲▲▲**Roman Forum** Ancient Rome's main square, with ruins and grand arches. **Hours:** Same hours as Colosseum. See page 523.

▲▲▲**Pantheon** The defining domed temple. **Hours:** Mon-Sat 8:30-19:30, Sun 9:00-18:00, holidays 9:00-13:00, closed for Mass Sat at 17:00 and Sun at 10:30. See page 534.

▲▲▲**St. Peter's Basilica** Most impressive church on earth, with Michelangelo's *Pietà* and dome. **Hours:** Church—daily April-Sept 7:00-19:00, Oct-March 7:00-18:00, often closed Wed mornings; dome—daily April-Sept 8:00-18:00, Oct-March 8:00-16:45. See page 536.

▲▲▲**Vatican Museum** Four miles of the finest art of Western civilization, culminating in Michelangelo's glorious Sistine Chapel. **Hours:** Mon-Sat 9:00-18:00. Closed on religious holidays and Sun, except last Sun of the month (open 9:00-14:00). May be open some Fri nights by online reservation only. Hours are subject to change. See page 537.

ROME

creative itineraries (mobile 347-795-5175, www.romewalks.com, info@romewalks.com, Annie). **Europe Odyssey,** formerly named Roman Odyssey, gives readers of this book a 10 percent discount on their walks (tel. 06-580-9902, mobile 328-912-3720, www.europeodyssey.com, Rahul). **Through Eternity** offers travelers with this book a 10 percent discount on most tours and a 20 percent discount on its Underground Rome; book through their website and enter the promotional code "RICKSTEVES" for the best discount (tel. 06-700-9336, mobile 347-336-5298, www.througheternity.com, office@througheternity.com, Rob). **Walks of Italy** has fun guides who lead a variety of good walks for groups of no more than 12 people at a time (10 percent discount for readers of this book, enter the code "10ricksteves" if booking online, US tel. 202/684-6916, Italian mobile 334-974-4274, tel. 06-9558-3331, www.walksofitaly.com, Jason Spiehler).

On Wheels

Hop-on, Hop-off Bus Tours

Several different agencies, including the ATAC public bus company, run hop-on, hop-off tours around Rome. These tours are

▲▲▲**Capitoline Museums** Ancient statues, mosaics, and expansive view of Forum. **Hours:** Tue-Sun 9:00-20:00, closed Mon. See page 530.

▲▲**Palatine Hill** Ruins of emperors' palaces, Circus Maximus view, and museum. **Hours:** Same hours as Colosseum. See page 526.

▲**Arch of Constantine** Honors the emperor who legalized Christianity. **Hours:** Always viewable. See page 523.

▲**Piazza del Campidoglio** Square atop Capitoline Hill, designed by Michelangelo, with a museum, grand stairway, and Forum overlooks. **Hours:** Always open. See page 528.

▲**Victor Emmanuel Monument** Gigantic edifice celebrating Italian unity, with Rome from the Sky elevator ride up to 360-degree city view. **Hours:** Monument open daily 9:30-18:30; elevator open Mon-Thu 9:30-18:30, Fri-Sun 9:30-19:30. See page 532.

▲**Trevi Fountain** Baroque hot spot into which tourists throw coins to ensure a return trip to Rome. **Hours:** Always flowing. See page 536.

ROME

constantly evolving and offer varying combinations of sights. You can grab one (and pay as you board) at any stop; Termini Station and Piazza Venezia are handy hubs. Although the city is perfectly walkable and traffic jams can make the bus dreadfully slow, these open-top bus tours remain popular.

The **110open Bus** seems to be the best. Operated by the ATAC city-bus lines, it offers an orientation tour on big red double-decker buses with an open-air upper deck. In less than two hours, you'll have 80 sights pointed out to you, with a next-to-worthless recorded narration. While you can hop on and off, the service can be erratic (mobbed midday, not ideal in bad weather), and it can be very slow in heavy traffic. It's best to think of this as a 90-minute quickie orientation with scant information and lots of images. Stops include the Colosseum, Circus Maximus, Bocca della Verità (the Mouth of Truth from *Roman Holiday* fame), Piazza Venezia, St. Peter's Square, Via del Tritone (Trevi Fountain), and Piazza Barberini. The 110open Bus departs roughly every 20 minutes (less frequent off-season). You can catch it at any stop, including Termini Station. Buy the ticket as you board (runs daily April-Oct 8:30-20:30, Nov-March 8:30-19:00, single tour-€12, 1-day ticket-€15, 48-hour ticket-€20, family tickets available, kids 9 and under ride free, tel. 800-281-281, www.trambusopen.com).

Archeobus is an open-top bus, also operated by ATAC, that runs twice hourly from Termini Station out to the Appian Way (with stops at the Colosseum, Baths of Caracalla, San Callisto, San Sebastiano, and the Tomb of Cecilia Metella). This is a handy way to see the sights down this ancient Roman road, but it can be frustrating for various reasons—sparse narration, sporadic service, and not ideal for hopping on and off (single tour-€10, 48-hour ticket-€12, €25 combo-ticket with 110open Bus valid 72 hours, deals for families and children, 1.5-hour loop, daily April-mid-Oct 9:00-16:30, bus runs Fri-Sun only mid-Oct-March, from Termini Station and Piazza Venezia, tel. 800-281-281, www.trambusopen. com). A similar bus laces together all the Christian sights.

Car and Minibus Tours

Autoservizi Monti Concezio, run by gentle, capable, and English-speaking Ezio, offers private cars or minibuses with driver/guides (car-€40/hour, minibus-€45/hour, 3-hour minimum for city sightseeing, long rides outside Rome are more expensive, mobile 335-636-5907 or 349-674-5643, www.tourservicemonti.it, info@tourservicemonti.it).

Miles & Miles Private Tours, a family-run company, offers a number of tours (all explained on their website) in Mercedes vans and cars, all with good English-speaking driver/guides (€60/hour for up to 8 people, 5-hour minimum, mention Rick Steves when booking direct then show the book on the day of service to get a discount, mobile 331-466-4900, www.milesandmiles.net, info@milesandmiles.net, Francesco answers the mobile phone, while Kimberly—an American—runs the office). They can also provide unguided long-distance transportation; if traveling with a small group or a family from Rome to Florence, the Amalfi Coast, or elsewhere, consider paying extra to turn the trip into a memorable day tour with door-to-door service.

Heart of Rome Walk

From Campo de' Fiori to the Spanish Steps

Rome's most colorful neighborhood features narrow lanes, intimate piazzas, fanciful fountains, and some of Europe's best people-watching. During the day, this self-guided walk shows off the colorful Campo de' Fiori market and trendy fashion boutiques as it meanders past major monuments such as the Pantheon and the Spanish Steps.

But, when the sun sets, unexpected magic happens. A stroll in the cool of the evening brings out all the romance of the Eternal City. Sit so close to a bubbling fountain that traffic noise evaporates. Jostle with kids to see the gelato flavors. Watch lovers straddling more than the bench. Jaywalk past *polizia* in flak-proof vests. And marvel at the ramshackle elegance that softens this brutal city for those who were born here and can't imagine living anywhere else. These are the flavors of Rome, best tasted after dark.

Orientation

Pantheon: Free, open Mon-Sat 8:30-19:30, Sun 9:00-18:00, holidays 9:00-13:00, closed for Mass Sat at 17:00 and Sun at 10:30.

Getting There: The walk begins at Campo de' Fiori, a few blocks east of Largo Argentina, a major transportation hub. Buses #40, #64, and #492 stop at both Largo Argentina and along Corso Vittorio Emanuele II, a long block north of Campo de' Fiori. A taxi from Termini Station costs about €8.

Length of This Walk: Allow anywhere from one to three hours for this mile-long walk, depending on whether you linger (yes, do) and tour the Pantheon (another good idea).

Other Options: This walk is equally pleasant in reverse order. You could ride the Metro to the Spanish Steps and finish at Campo de' Fiori, near many recommended restaurants.

The Walk Begins

• *Start this walk at Campo de' Fiori, my favorite outdoor dining room (especially after dark—see "Eating in Rome," page 594).*

Campo de' Fiori

One of Rome's most colorful spots, this bohemian piazza hosts a fruit and vegetable **market** in the morning, cafés in the evening,

and pub-crawlers at night. In ancient times, the "Field of Flowers" was an open meadow. Later, Christian pilgrims passed through on their way to the Vatican, and a thriving market developed.

Lording over the center of the square is a statue of **Giordano Bruno,** an intellectual heretic who was burned on this spot in 1600. The pedestal shows scenes from Bruno's trial and execution, and reads, "And the flames rose up." When this statue honoring a heretic was erected in 1889, the Vatican protested, but they were overruled by angry Campo locals. The neighborhood is still known for its free spirit and anti-authoritarian demonstrations.

Campo de' Fiori is the product of centuries of unplanned

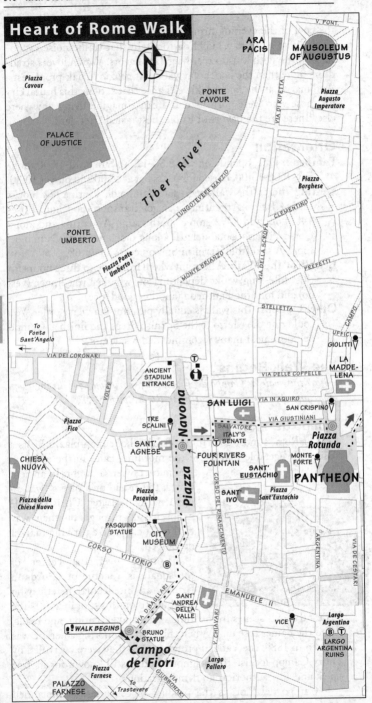

Heart of Rome Walk

ROME

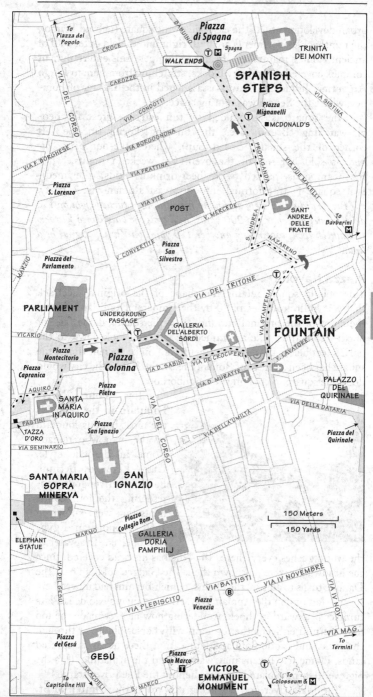

To Piazza del Popolo

Piazza di Spagna

TRINITÀ DEI MONTI

CROCE

VIA DEL CORSO

BABUINO

Spagna

WALK ENDS

SPANISH STEPS

CAROZZE

VIA SISTINA

VIA CONDOTTI

Piazza Mignanelli

MCDONALD'S

VIA BORGOGNONA

PROPAGANDA

VIA DUE MACELLI

VIA F. BORGHESE

VIA FRATTINA

Piazza S. LORENZO

VIA VITE

POST

V. MERCEDE

S. ANDREA

SANT' ANDREA DELLE FRATTE

To Barberini M

MARZIO

V. CONVERTITE

Piazza San Silvestro

NAZARENO

Piazza del Parlamento

PARLIAMENT

UNDERGROUND PASSAGE

GALLERIA DEL'ALBERTO SORDI

VIA DEL TRITONE

VIA STAMPERIA

TREVI FOUNTAIN

VICARIO

Piazza Montecitorio

Piazza Colonna

VIA D. SABINI

VIA DE CROCIFER.

V. LAVATORE

ROME

Piazza Capranica

AQUIRO

Piazza Pietra

VIA D. MURATTE

PALAZZO DEL QUIRINALE

PASTINI

SANTA MARIA IN AQUIRO

VIA DELLA DATARIA

TAZZA D'ORO

Piazza San Ignazio

VIA DELL'UMILTÀ

Piazza del Quirinale

VIA SEMINARIO

SANTA MARIA SOPRA MINERVA

SAN IGNAZIO

VIA DEL CORSO

ELEPHANT STATUE

MARMO

Piazza Collegio Rom.

GALLERIA DORIA PAMPHILJ

150 Meters

150 Yards

VIA DEL GESÙ

VIA BATTISTI

VIA IV NOVEMBRE

VIA IV NOV.

VIA PLEBISCITO

Piazza Venezia

VIA MAG.

To Termini

Piazza del Gesù

GESÙ

Piazza San Marco

ARACOELI

S. MARCO

To Capitoline Hill

VICTOR EMMANUEL MONUMENT

To Colosseum & M

urban development. At the east end of the square (behind Bruno), the ramshackle apartments are built right into the old outer wall of ancient Rome's mammoth Theater of Pompey. This entertainment complex covered several city blocks, stretching from here to Largo Argentina. Julius Caesar was assassinated in the Theater of Pompey, where the Senate was renting space.

The square is surrounded by fun eateries, great for people-watching. Bruno faces the bustling **Forno** (in the left corner of the square, closed Sun), where take-out *pizza bianco* is sold hot out of the oven. On weekend nights, when the Campo is packed with beer-drinking kids, the medieval square is transformed into one vast Roman street party. • *If Bruno did a hop, step, and jump forward, then turned right on Via dei Baullari and marched 200 yards, he'd cross the busy Corso Vittorio Emanuele; then, continuing another 150 yards on Via Cuccagna, he'd find...*

Piazza Navona

This oblong square retains the shape of the original racetrack that was built around A.D. 80 by the Emperor Domitian. (To see the ruins of the original entrance, exit the square at the far—or north—end, then take an immediate left, and look down to the left 25 feet below the current street level.) Since ancient times, the square has been a center of Roman life. In the 1800s, the city would flood the square to cool off the neighborhood.

The **Four Rivers Fountain** in the center is the most famous fountain by the man who remade Rome in Baroque style, Gian Lorenzo Bernini. Four burly river gods (representing the four continents that were known in 1650) support an Egyptian obelisk. The water of the world gushes everywhere. The Nile has his head covered, since the headwaters were unknown then. The Ganges holds an oar. The Danube turns to admire the obelisk, which Bernini had moved here from a stadium on the Appian Way. And Uruguay's Río de la Plata tumbles backward in shock, wondering how he ever made the top four. Bernini enlivens the fountain with horses plunging through the rocks and exotic flora and fauna from these newly discovered lands. Homesick Texans may want to find the armadillo. (It's the big, weird, armor-plated creature behind the Plata river statue.)

The Plata river god is gazing upward at the **Church of St.**

Agnes, worked on by Bernini's former student-turned-rival, Francesco Borromini. Borromini's concave facade helps reveal the dome and epitomizes the curved symmetry of Baroque. Tour guides say that Bernini designed his river god to look horrified at Borromini's work. Or maybe he's shielding his eyes from St. Agnes' nakedness, as she was stripped before being martyred. But either explanation is unlikely, since the fountain was completed two years before Borromini even started work on the church.

Piazza Navona is Rome's most interesting night scene, with street music, artists, fire-eaters, local Casanovas, ice cream, and outdoor cafés that are worthy of a splurge if you've got time to sit and enjoy Italy's human river.

• *Leave Piazza Navona directly across from Tre Scalini (famous for its rich chocolate ice cream), and go east down Corsia Agonale, past rose peddlers and palm readers. Jog left around the guarded building (the Palazzo Madama, where Italy's senate meets), and follow the brown sign to the Pantheon, which is straight down Via del Salvatore.*

The Pantheon

Sit for a while under the portico of the Pantheon (romantically floodlit and moonlit at night). The 40-foot, single-piece granite

columns of the Pantheon's entrance show the scale the ancient Romans built on. The columns support a triangular Greek-style roof with an inscription that says "M. Agrippa" built it. In fact, it was built *(fecit)* by Emperor Hadrian (A.D. 120), who gave credit to the builder of an earlier structure. This impressive entranceway gives no clue that the greatest wonder of the building is inside—a domed room that inspired later domes, including Michelangelo's St. Peter's and Brunelleschi's Duomo (in Florence).

If it's open, pop into the Pantheon for a look around (described on page 534). If you have extra time, consider detouring to several interesting churches near the Pantheon (listed on page 535).

• *With your back to the Pantheon, veer to the right, uphill toward the yellow sign that reads* Casa del Caffè *at the Tazza d'Oro coffee shop on Via Orfani.*

From the Pantheon to the Trevi Fountain

Tazza d'Oro Casa del Caffè, one of Rome's top coffee shops, dates back to the days when this area was licensed to roast coffee beans. Locals come here for a shot of espresso or, when it's hot, a refreshing *granita di caffè con panna* (coffee slush with cream).

• *Continue up Via Orfani to...*

Piazza Capranica is home to the big, plain Florentine Renaissance-style Palazzo Capranica (directly opposite as you enter the square). Big shots, like the Capranica family, built towers on their palaces—not for any military use, but just to show off.

• *Leave the piazza to the right of the palace, heading down Via in Aquiro.*

The street Via in Aquiro leads to a sixth-century B.C. **Egyptian obelisk** taken as a trophy by Augustus after his victory in Egypt over Mark Antony and Cleopatra. The obelisk was set up as a sundial. Follow the zodiac markings to the well-guarded front door. This is Italy's **parliament building,** where the lower house meets; you may see politicians, political demonstrations, and TV cameras.

• *To your right is Piazza Colonna, where we're heading next—unless you like gelato...*

A one-block detour to the left (past Albergo Nazionale) brings you to Rome's most famous *gelateria.* **Giolitti's** is cheap for takeout or elegant and splurge-worthy for a sit among classy locals (open daily until past midnight, Via Uffici del Vicario 40); get your gelato in a cone *(cono)* or cup *(coppetta).*

Piazza Colonna features a huge second-century column. Its reliefs depict the victories of Emperor Marcus Aurelius over the barbarians. When Marcus died in A.D. 180, the barbarians began to get the upper hand, beginning Rome's long three-century fall. The big, important-looking palace houses the headquarters for the prime minister's cabinet.

Noisy **Via del Corso** is Rome's main north-south boulevard. It's named for the Berber horse races—without riders—that took place here during Carnevale. This wild tradition continued until the late 1800s, when a series of fatal accidents (including, reportedly, one in front of Queen Margherita) led to its cancellation. Historically the street was filled with meat shops. When it became one of Rome's first gas-lit streets in 1854, these butcher shops were banned and replaced by classier boutiques, jewelers, and antique dealers. Nowadays the northern part of Via del Corso is closed to traffic, and for a few hours every evening it becomes a wonderful parade of Romans out for a stroll.

• *Cross Via del Corso to enter a big palatial building with columns, which houses the Galleria Alberto Sordi shopping mall (with convenient WCs). Inside, take the fork to the right and exit at the back. (If you're here after 22:00, when the mall is closed, circle around the right side of the Galleria on Via dei Sabini.) Once out the back, head up Via de Crociferi, to the roar of the water, lights, and people at the...*

Trevi Fountain

The Trevi Fountain shows how Rome took full advantage of the abundance of water brought into the city by its great aqueducts.

 This watery Baroque avalanche by Nicola Salvi was completed in 1762. Salvi used the palace behind the fountain as a theatrical backdrop for the figure of "Ocean," who represents water in every form. The statue surfs through his wet kingdom—with water gushing from 24 spouts and tumbling over 30 different kinds of plants—while Triton blows his conch shell.

The magic of the square is enhanced by the fact that no streets directly approach it. You can hear the excitement as you draw near, and then—*bam!*—you're there. The scene is always lively, with lucky Romeos clutching dates while unlucky ones clutch beers. Romantics toss a coin over their shoulder, thinking it will give them a wish and assure their return to Rome. That may sound silly, but every year I go through this tourist ritual...and it actually seems to work.

Take some time to people-watch (whisper a few breathy *bellos* or *bellas*) before leaving. There's a peaceful zone at water level on the far right.

• *From the Trevi Fountain, we're 10 minutes from our next stop, the Spanish Steps. Just use a map to get there, or follow these directions: Facing the Trevi Fountain, go forward, walking along the right side of the fountain on Via della Stamperia. Cross busy Via del Tritone. Continue 100 yards and veer right at Via Sant'Andrea delle Fratte, a street that changes its name to Via Propaganda before ending at the...*

Spanish Steps

Piazza di Spagna, with the very popular Spanish Steps, is named for the Spanish Embassy to the Vatican, which has been here for 300 years. It's been the hangout of many Romantics over the years (Keats, Wagner, Openshaw, Goethe, and others). In the 1700s, British aristocrats on the "Grand Tour" of Europe came here to ponder Rome's decay. The British poet John Keats pondered his mortality, then died of tuberculosis at age 25 in the pink building on the right side of the steps. Fellow Romantic Lord Byron lived across the square at #66.

The **Sinking Boat Fountain** at the foot of the steps, built by Bernini or his father, Pietro, is powered by an aqueduct. Actually, all of Rome's fountains are aqueduct-powered; their spurts are determined by the water pressure provided by the various aqueducts. This one, for instance, is much weaker than Trevi's gush.

ROME

The piazza is a thriving scene at night. Window-shop along Via Condotti, which stretches away from the steps. This is where Gucci and other big names cater to the trendsetting jet set. It's clear that the main sight around here is not the famous steps, but the people who sit on them.

• *Our walk is finished. If you'd like to reach the top of the steps sweat-free, take the free elevator just outside the Spagna Metro stop (to the left, as you face the steps; elevator closes at 21:00). A free WC is underground in the piazza near the Metro entrance, by the middle palm tree (10:00–19:30). The nearby McDonald's (as you face the Spanish Steps, go right one block) is big and lavish, with a salad bar and WC. When you're ready to leave, you can zip home on the Metro (usually open until 23:30, Fri–Sat until 1:30 in the morning), or grab a taxi at either the north or south side of the piazza.*

Sights in Rome

I've clustered Rome's sights into walkable neighborhoods, some quite close together (see "Rome's Neighborhoods" map on page 502). Save transit time by grouping your sightseeing according to location. For example, the Colosseum and the Forum are a few minutes' walk from Capitoline Hill; a 15-minute walk beyond that is the Pantheon.

While Rome has other sights worth knowing about on a longer visit, for a one-day cruiser visit, I've listed just the main sights within the city center.

Don't let the length of my descriptions determine your sightseeing priorities. In this section, Rome's most important sights have the shortest listings and are marked with a ✪. These sights are covered in much more detail either in my "Heart of Rome Walk" or in a self-guided tour.

Ancient Rome

The core of ancient Rome, where the grandest monuments were built, is between the Colosseum and Capitoline Hill. Among the ancient forums, a few modern sights have popped up.

The Colosseum and Nearby
▲▲▲Colosseum (Colosseo)

This 2,000-year-old building is the classic example of Roman engineering. Used as a venue for entertaining the masses, this colossal, functional stadium is one of Europe's most recognizable landmarks.

Cost and Hours: €12 combo-ticket includes Roman Forum and Palatine Hill (see page 508), open daily 8:30 until one hour before sunset—for specifics, see "Hours" on page 537, last entry one hour before closing, Metro: Colosseo, tel. 06-3996-7700, www.archeoroma.beniculturali.it/en.

✪ For a self-guided tour, see page 537.

▲Arch of Constantine

If you are a Christian, were raised a Christian, or simply belong to a so-called "Christian nation," ponder this arch. It marks one  of the great turning points in history: the military coup that made Christianity mainstream. In A.D. 312, Emperor Constantine defeated his rival Maxentius in the crucial Battle of the Milvian Bridge. The night before, he had seen a vision of a cross in the sky. Constantine—whose mother and sister had already become Christians—became sole emperor and legalized Christianity. With this one battle, a once-obscure Jewish sect with a handful of followers became the state religion of the entire Western world. In A.D. 300, you could be killed for being a Christian; a century later, you could be killed for not being one. Church enrollment boomed.

The restored arch is like an ancient museum. It's decorated entirely with recycled carvings originally made for other buildings. By covering it with exquisite carvings of high Roman art—works that glorified previous emperors—Constantine put himself in their league. Hadrian is featured in the round reliefs, with Marcus Aurelius in the square reliefs higher up. The big statues on top are of Trajan and Augustus. Originally, Augustus drove a chariot similar to the one topping the modern Victor Emmanuel II Monument. Fourth-century Rome may have been in decline, but Constantine clung to its glorious past.

The Roman Forum and Nearby

▲▲▲Roman Forum (Foro Romano)

This is ancient Rome's birthplace and civic center, and the common ground between Rome's famous seven hills. As just about anything important that happened in ancient Rome happened here, it's arguably the most important piece of real estate in Western civilization.  While only a few fragments of that glorious past remain, history seekers find plenty to ignite their imaginations amid the half-broken columns and arches.

Cost and Hours: €12 combo-ticket includes Colosseum and Palatine Hill (see page 508), open daily 8:30 until one hour before—for spe-

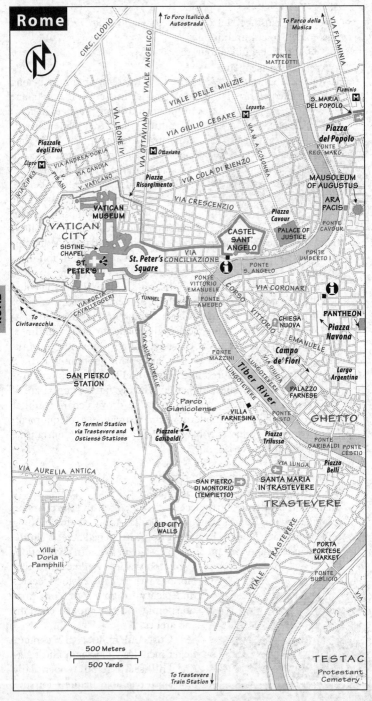

Rome

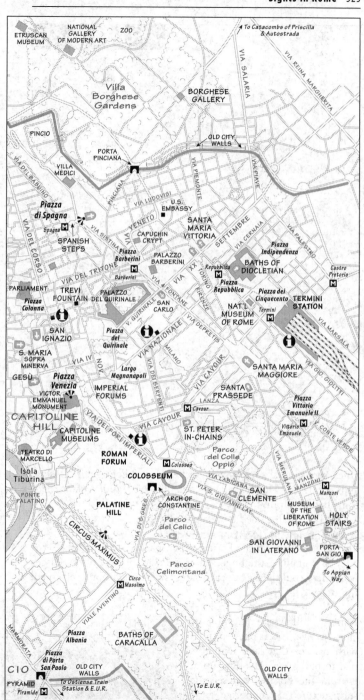

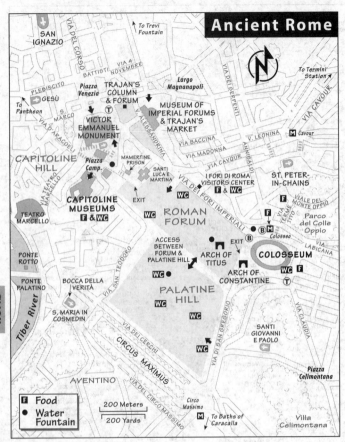

Ancient Rome

SAN IGNAZIO

To Trevi Fountain

VIA DEL CORSO

BATTISTI

VIA 4 NOVEMBRE

VIA DEI SERPENTI

To Termini Station

VIA CAVOUR

PLEBISCITO

Piazza Venezia

TRAJAN'S COLUMN & FORUM

Largo Magnanapoli

To Pantheon

GESÙ

S. MARCO

VICTOR EMMANUEL MONUMENT

VIA D'ARACOELI

T

VIA ALESSANDRINA

MUSEUM OF IMPERIAL FORUMS & TRAJAN'S MARKET

VIA BACCINA

VIA MADONNA

LEONINA

M Cavour

VIA CAVOUR

ANNIBALDI

CAPITOLINE HILL

Piazza Camp.

MAMERTINE PRISON

SANTI LUCA E MARTINA

I FORI DI ROMA VISITORS CENTER
F & WC

ST. PETER-IN-CHAINS

F

VIALE DEL MONTE OPPIO

VIA TEATRO MARCELLO

CAPITOLINE MUSEUMS
F & WC

EXIT

WC

ROMAN FORUM

WC

VIA DEI FORI IMPERIALI

F

VIA TERME TITO

Parco del Colle Oppio

TEATRO MARCELLO

B M Colosseo

VIA LABICANA

PONTE ROTTO

ACCESS BETWEEN FORUM & PALATINE HILL

EXIT

ARCH OF TITUS

COLOSSEUM

WC F

PONTE PALATINO

BOCCA DELLA VERITÀ

VIA SAN TEODORO

WC

ARCH OF CONSTANTINE

T

S. MARIA IN COSMEDIN

PALATINE HILL

WC

VIA DI SAN GREGORIO

VIA CLAUDIA

Tiber River

VIA DEL CERCHI

WC

SANTI GIOVANNI E PAOLO

CIRCUS MAXIMUS

WC

Piazza Celimontana

AVENTINO

VIA DEL CIRCO MASSIMO

Circo Massimo

M To Baths of Caracalla

Villa Celimontana

F Food
● Water Fountain

200 Meters
200 Yards

ROME

cifics, see "Hours" on page 548, last entry one hour before closing, audioguide—€5, Metro: Colosseo, tel. 06-3996-7700, www.archeo-roma.beniculturali.it/en.

🟢 For a self-guided tour, see page 548.

▲▲Palatine Hill (Monte Palatino)

The hill overlooking the Forum is jam-packed with history—"the huts of Romulus," the huge Imperial Palace, a view of the Circus Maximus—but there's only the barest skeleton of rubble left to tell the story.

We get our word "palace" from this hill, where the emperors chose to live. It was once so filled with palaces that later emperors had to build out. (Looking up at it from the Forum, you see the substructure that supported these

long-gone palaces.) The Palatine museum contains statues and frescoes that help you imagine the luxury of the imperial Palatine. From the pleasant garden, you'll get an overview of the Forum. On the far side, look down into an emperor's private stadium and then beyond at the grassy Circus Maximus, once a chariot course. Imagine the cheers, jeers, and furious betting.

While many tourists consider Palatine Hill just extra credit after the Forum, it offers an insight into the greatness of Rome that's well worth the effort. (And, if you're visiting the Colosseum or Forum, you've got a ticket whether you like it or not.)

Cost and Hours: €12 combo-ticket includes Roman Forum and Colosseum—see page 508, open same hours as Forum and Colosseum, audioguide-€5, guided tours may be available—ask, Metro: Colosseo, tel. 06-3996-7700, www.archeoroma.benicul-turali.it/en.

Getting In: The main entrance is on Via di San Gregorio (facing the Forum with the Colosseum at your back, it's down the street to your left). You can also enter Palatine from within the Roman Forum—just climb the hill from the Arch of Titus.

Services: WCs are at the ticket office when you enter, up the hill near the stadium, at the museum in the center of the site, and hiding among the orange trees in the Farnese Gardens.

Bocca della Verità

The legendary "Mouth of Truth" at the Church of Santa Maria in Cosmedin draws a playful crowd. Stick your hand in the mouth of the gaping stone face in the porch wall. As the legend goes (and was popularized by the 1953 film *Roman Holiday*, starring Gregory Peck and Audrey Hepburn), if you're a liar, your hand will be gobbled up. The mouth is only accessible when the church gate is open, but it's always (partially) visible through the gate, even when closed. If the church itself is open, step inside to see one of the few unaltered medieval church interiors in Rome. Notice the mismatched ancient columns and beautiful cosmatesque floor—a centuries-old example of recycling.

Cost and Hours: €0.50 suggested donation, daily 9:30-17:50, closes earlier off-season, Piazza Bocca della Verità, near the north end of Circus Maximus, tel. 06-678-7759.

Imperial Forums

As Rome grew from a village to an empire, it outgrew the Roman Forum. Several energetic emperors built their own forums—which stood in a line from the Colosseum to Trajan's Column—complete with temples, shopping malls, government buildings, statues, monuments, and piazzas. While the Roman Forum (which gets all the touristic focus) was built with no grand plan over 1,200 years, these new imperial forums were distinct modules, with a cohesive plan stamped with the emperor's unique personality. Julius Caesar built the first one (46 B.C.), and over the next 150 years, it was added onto by Augustus (2 B.C.), Vespasian (A.D. 75), Nerva (A.D. 97), and Trajan (A.D. 112). What you see today are mostly the remains of Trajan's great building campaign.

The ruins are always visible and free to look at from viewpoints at Piazza Venezia, along Via dei Fori Imperiali, and at Via IV Novembre. Trajan's Forum, with its impressive column and market, is the main sight to see. To view other (heavily ruined) forums, stroll down Via dei Fori Imperiali. Visiting here is especially nice, because the once-busy street is now closed to private car traffic. If you want a close-up look at some excavated statues and more information about the forums, you can pay admission to the Museum of the Imperial Forums (closed Mon). If not paying to go in, the best original ancient street is perfectly viewable from Via IV Novembre.

Capitoline Hill

Of Rome's famous seven hills, this is the smallest, tallest, and most famous—home of the ancient Temple of Jupiter and the center of city government for 2,500 years.

There are several ways to get to the top of Capitoline Hill. If you're coming from the north (from Piazza Venezia), take Michelangelo's impressive stairway to the right of the big, white Victor Emmanuel Monument. Coming from the southeast (the Forum), take the steep staircase near the Arch of Septimius Severus. From near Trajan's Forum along Via dei Fori Imperiali, take the winding road. All three converge at the top, in the square called Campidoglio (kahm-pee-DOHL-yoh).

▲Piazza del Campidoglio

This square atop the hill, once the religious and political center of ancient Rome, is still the home of the city's government. In the 1530s, the pope called on Michelangelo to re-establish this square as a grand center. Michelangelo placed the ancient equestrian statue of Marcus Aurelius as its focal point. Effective. (The original statue is now in the adjacent museum.) The twin buildings on either side are the Capitoline Museums. Behind the replica of the statue is the mayoral palace (Palazzo Senatorio).

Michelangelo intended that people approach the square from his grand stairway off Piazza Venezia. From the top of the stairway, you see the new Renaissance face of Rome, with its back to the Forum. Michelangelo gave the buildings the "giant order"—huge pilasters make the existing two-story buildings feel one-storied and more harmonious with the new square. Notice how the statues atop these buildings welcome you and then draw you in.

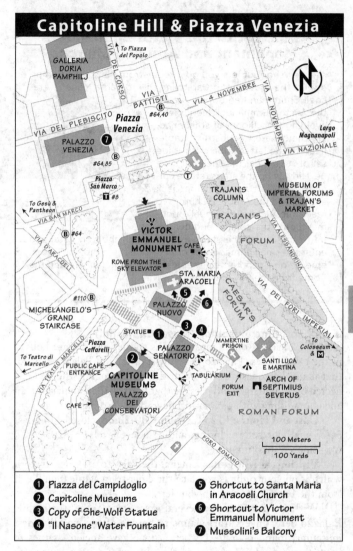

Capitoline Hill & Piazza Venezia

GALLERIA DORIA PAMPHILJ

To Piazza del Popolo

VIA DEL CORSO

VIA BATTISTI

#64,40

VIA 4 NOVEMBRE

VIA 4 NOVEMBRE

VIA DEL PLEBISCITO

Piazza Venezia

Largo Magnanapoli

VIA NAZIONALE

PALAZZO VENEZIA ⓻

#64,85

Piazza San Marco Ⓣ #8

TRAJAN'S COLUMN

MUSEUM OF IMPERIAL FORUMS & TRAJAN'S MARKET

To Gesù & Pantheon

VIA SAN MARCO

TRAJAN'S FORUM

Ⓑ #64

VIA D'ARACOELI

VICTOR EMMANUEL MONUMENT

CAFÉ

VIA ALESSANDRINA

ROME FROM THE SKY ELEVATOR

STA. MARIA ARACOELI

CAESAR'S FORUM

VIA DEI FORI IMPERIALI

#110 Ⓑ

MICHELANGELO'S GRAND STAIRCASE

Ⓢ

PALAZZO NUOVO

Ⓖ

STATUE ■ ❶

❸ ❹

Piazza Caffarelli

To Teatro di Marcello

VIA TEATRO MARCELLO

PUBLIC CAFÉ ENTRANCE

❷

PALAZZO SENATORIO

MAMERTINE PRISON

SANTI LUCA E MARTINA

To Colosseum & Ⓜ

CAPITOLINE MUSEUMS

PALAZZO DEI CONSERVATORI

TABULARIUM

FORUM EXIT

ARCH OF SEPTIMIUS SEVERUS

CAFÉ →

ROMAN FORUM

FORO ROMANO

100 Meters
100 Yards

❶ Piazza del Campidoglio
❷ Capitoline Museums
❸ Copy of She-Wolf Statue
❹ "Il Nasone" Water Fountain
❺ Shortcut to Santa Maria in Aracoeli Church
❻ Shortcut to Victor Emmanuel Monument
❼ Mussolini's Balcony

ROME

The terraces just downhill (past either side of the mayor's palace) offer grand views of the Forum. To the left of the mayor's palace is a copy of the famous she-wolf statue on a column. Farther down is *il nasone* ("the big nose"), a refreshing water fountain (see photo). Block the spout with your fingers, and water spurts up for drinking. Romans joke that a cheap Roman boy takes his date out for a drink at *il nasone*. Near the she-wolf statue is the staircase leading to a shortcut to the Victor Emmanuel Monument (see sidebar).

Shortcut to the Victor Emmanuel Monument and Aracoeli Church

A clever shortcut lets you go directly from Piazza del Campidoglio, the square atop Capitoline Hill, to Santa Maria in Aracoeli Church and an upper level of the Victor Emmanuel Monument, avoiding long flights of stairs. Facing the square's equestrian statue, head to the left, climbing the wide set of stairs near the she-wolf statue. Midway up the stairs (at the column), turn left to reach the back entrance to the Aracoeli Church. To reach the Victor Emmanuel Monument, pass the column and contin-  ue to the top of the steps, pass through the iron gate, and enter the small unmarked door at #13 on the right. You'll soon emerge on a café terrace that leads to the monument and the Rome from the Sky elevator.

ROME

▲▲▲Capitoline Museums (Musei Capitolini)

Some of ancient Rome's most famous statues and art are housed in the two palaces (Palazzo dei Conservatori and Palazzo Nuovo) that flank the equestrian statue in the Campidoglio. They're connected by an underground passage that leads to the Tabularium, an ancient building with panoramic views of the Roman Forum.

Cost and Hours: €12, Tue-Sun 9:00-20:00, closed Mon, last entry one hour before closing, audioguide-€5, tel. 06-8205-9127, www.museicapitolini.org.

Visiting the Museums: Enter at the Palazzo dei Conservatori, which is on your right as you face the equestrian statue (you'll exit from the Palazzo Nuovo, on your left).

With lavish rooms and several great statues, the worthwhile **Palazzo dei Conservatori** claims to be one of the world's oldest museums, founded in 1471 when a pope gave ancient statues to the citizens of Rome. Many of the museum's statues have gone on to become instantly recognizable cultural icons, including the 13th-century *Capitoline She-Wolf* (the little statues of Romulus and Remus were added in the Renaissance). Don't miss the *Boy Extracting a Thorn* and the enchanting *Commodus as Hercules*. Behind Commodus is a statue of his dad, Marcus Aurelius, on a horse. The greatest surviving equestrian statue of antiquity, this was the original centerpiece of the square (where a copy stands today). Christians in the Dark Ages thought that the statue's hand was raised in blessing, which probably led to their misidentifying him as Constantine, the first Christian emperor. While most pagan statues were destroyed by Christians, "Constantine" was spared.

The museum's second-floor café, **Caffè Capitolino,** has a splendid patio offering city views. It's lovely at sunset (public entrance for non-museum-goers off Piazza Caffarelli and through door #4).

The **Tabularium,** built in the first century B.C., once held the archives of ancient Rome. (The word Tabularium comes from "tablet," on which Romans wrote their laws.) You won't see any tablets, but you will see a stunning head-on view of the Forum from the windows. The **Palazzo Nuovo** houses mostly portrait busts of forgotten emperors. But it also has two must-see statues: the *Dying Gaul* and the *Capitoline Venus* (both on the first floor up).

Santa Maria in Aracoeli Church

The church atop Capitoline Hill is old and dear to the hearts of Romans. It stands on the site where Emperor Augustus (supposedly) had a premonition of the coming of Mary and Christ standing on an "altar in the sky" *(ara coeli)*. The church is Rome in a nutshell, where you can time-travel across 2,000 years by standing in one spot.

Cost and Hours: Free, daily April-Oct 9:00-12:30 & 15:00-18:30, Nov-March 9:00-12:30 & 14:30-17:30, tel. 06-6976-3839.

Piazza Venezia

This vast square, dominated by the big, white Victor Emmanuel Monument, is a major transportation hub and the focal point of modern Rome.

With your back to the monument (you'll get the best views from the terrace by the guards and eternal flame), look down Via del Corso, the city's axis, surrounded by Rome's classiest shopping district. In the 1930s, Benito Mussolini whipped up Italy's nationalistic fervor from a balcony above the square (it's the less-grand balcony on the left). Fascist masses filled the square screaming, "Four more years!"—or something like that. Mussolini created the boulevard Via dei Fori Imperiali (to your right, capped by Trajan's Column) to open up views of the Colosseum in the distance. Mussolini lied to his people, mixing fear and patriotism to push his country to the right and embroil the Italians in expensive and regrettable wars. In 1945, they shot Mussolini and hung him from a meat hook in Milan.

With your back still to the monument, circle around the left side. At the back end of the monument, look down into the ditch on your left to see the ruins of an ancient apartment building from the first century A.D.; part of it was transformed into a tiny church (faded frescoes and bell tower). Rome was built in layers—almost everywhere you go, there's an earlier version beneath your feet. (The hop-on, hop-off 110open Bus stops just downhill from here.)

Continuing on, you reach two staircases leading up Capitoline Hill. One is Michelangelo's grand staircase up to the Campidoglio. The steeper of the two leads to Santa Maria in Aracoeli, a good example of the earliest style of Christian church (described earlier). The contrast between this climb-on-your-knees ramp to God's house and Michelangelo's elegant stairs illustrates the changes Renaissance humanism brought civilization.

From the bottom of Michelangelo's stairs, look right several blocks down the street to see a condominium actually built upon the surviving ancient pillars and arches of Teatro di Marcello.

▲Victor Emmanuel Monument

This oversize monument to Italy's first king, built to celebrate the 50th anniversary of the birth of his kingdom in 1861, was part of Italy's push to overcome the new country's strong regionalism and create a national identity.

The scale of the monument is over-the-top: 200 feet high, 500 feet wide. The 43-foot-long statue of the king on the horse is one of the biggest equestrian statues in the world. The king's moustache forms an arc five feet long, and a person could sit within the horse's hoof. At the base of this statue, Italy's Tomb of the Unknown Soldier (flanked by Italian flags and armed guards) is watched over by the goddess Roma (with the gold mosaic background).

With its gleaming white sheen (from a recent scrubbing) and enormous scale, the monument provides a vivid sense of what Ancient Rome looked like at its peak—imagine the Forum filled with shiny, grandiose buildings like this one.

Cost and Hours: Monument—Free, daily 9:30-18:30, a few WCs scattered throughout, tel. 06-679-3598. Elevator—€7, Mon-Thu 9:30-18:30, Fri-Sun 9:30-19:30, ticket office closes 45 minutes earlier, WC at entrance, tel. 06-6920-2049; follow *ascensori panoramici* signs inside the Victor Emmanuel Monument or take the shortcut from Capitoline Hill (no elevator access from street level).

Visiting the Monument: To see the "Vittoriano" (as locals call it), simply climb the front stairs, or go inside from one of several entrances: midway up the monument through doorways flanking the central statue, on either side at street level, and at the base of the colonnade (two-thirds of the way up, near the shortcut from Capitoline Hill). The little-visited **Museum of the Risorgimento** fills several floors with displays (free, well-described in English) on the movement and war that led to the final unification of Italy in 1870. A section on the lower east side hosts temporary exhibits of minor works by major artists (free to enter museum, exhibits around €10, tel. 06-322-5380, www.comunicareorganizzando.it). A café is at the base of the top colonnade, on the monument's east side.

You can climb the stairs to the midway point for a decent view, keep climbing to the base of the colonnade for a better view, or, for the best view, ride the **Rome from the Sky** (Roma dal Cielo) elevator, which zips you from the top of the stair climb (at the back of the monument) to the rooftop for the grandest, 360-degree view of the center of Rome—even better than from the top of St. Peter's dome. Helpful panoramic diagrams describe the skyline, with powerful binoculars available for zooming in on particular sights. It's best in late afternoon, when it's beginning to cool off and Rome glows.

Pantheon Neighborhood

Besides being home to ancient sights and historic churches, this neighborhood gives Rome its urban-village feel. Wander narrow streets, sample the many shops and eateries, and gather with the locals in squares marked by bubbling fountains. Exploring is especially good in the evening, when the restaurants bustle and streets are jammed with foot traffic. For a self-guided walk of this neighborhood, from Campo de' Fiori to the Trevi Fountain (and ending at the Spanish Steps), see my "Heart of Rome Walk" on page 514.

Getting There: The Pantheon neighborhood is a 15-minute walk from Capitoline Hill. Taxis and buses stop at a chaotic square called Largo Argentina, a few blocks south of the Pantheon—from here you can walk north on either Via dei Cestari or Via di Torre Argentina to the Pantheon. Buses #40 and #64 carry tourists and pickpockets frequently between the Termini train station and Vatican City (#492 serves the same areas via a different route). Bus #87 connects to the Colosseum. The *elettrico* minibus #116 runs between Campo de' Fiori and Piazza Barberini via the Pantheon.

Pantheon Neighborhood

(Map labels:) PONTE UMBERTO, Piazza Ponte Umberto I, BRIANZO, VIA D. ORSO, VIA D. SCROFA, To Piazza del Popolo, To Spanish Steps, V. S. AND., To M Barberini, ANCIENT STADIUM ENTRANCE, CORONARI, PARLIAMENT, UFF. VICARIO, VIA DEL TRITONE, VIA TRITONE, TREVI FOUNTAIN, Piazza Montecitorio, Piazza Colonna, SABINA, VIA D. COPPELLE, AQUIRO, Piazza di Pietra, CORSO, MURATTE, SAN LUIGI, TRE SCALINI GELATERIA, Piazza Navona, SALV., GIUST., Piazza Rotunda, PASTINI, Piazza San Ignazio, SEMINARIO, SAN IGNAZIO, S. EUST., PANTHEON, FOUR RIVERS FOUNTAIN, SANT' AGNESE, S. IVO, Piazza S. Eust., ELEPHANT OBELISK, SANTA MARIA SOPRA MINERVA, Piazza Collegio Rom., Piazza Pasquino, CITY MUSEUM, CORSO, VITTORIO, ARGENTINA, CESTARI, GALLERIA DORIA PAMPHILJ, Campo de' Fiori, EMANUELE II, Largo Argentina, VIA PLEBISCITO, Piazza Venezia, Piazza Farnese, CHIAVARI, V. M. D. FARINA, LARGO ARGENTINA RUINS, GESÙ, VIA DI SAN MARCO, To Colosseum & M, PALAZZO FARNESE, VIA GIUBBONARI, VIA D. B. OSCURE, ARACOELI, VICTOR EMMANUEL MONUMENT, 200 Meters, 200 Yards, SPECCHI, VIA ARENULA, VIA DEL PORTICO D'OTTAVIA, CAPITOLINE HILL, Piazza Campidoglio

▲▲▲Pantheon

For the greatest look at the splendor of Rome, antiquity's best-preserved interior is a must. Built two millennia ago, this domed building served as the model for many others.

Because the Pantheon became a church dedicated to the martyrs just after the fall of Rome, the barbarians left it alone, and the locals didn't use it as a quarry. The portico is called "Rome's umbrella"—a fun local gathering in a rainstorm. Walk past its one-piece granite columns (biggest in Italy, shipped from Egypt) and through the original bronze doors. Sit inside under the glorious skylight and enjoy classical architecture at its best.

Cost and Hours: Free, Mon-Sat 8:30-19:30, Sun 9:00-18:00, holidays 9:00-13:00, closed for Mass Sat at 17:00 and Sun at 10:30, audioguide-€5, tel. 06-6830-0230. You can download a free Rick Steves audio tour of the Pantheon to your mobile device; see page 50.

When to Go: Visit before 9:00, and you'll have it all to yourself. Don't go midday, when the Pantheon is packed.

Visiting the Pantheon: The Pantheon was a Roman temple

dedicated to all *(pan)* of the gods *(theos)*, a one-stop-shopping temple where you could worship any of the gods whose statues decorated the niches. The original temple was built in 27 B.C. by Augustus' son-in-law, Marcus Agrippa (as the Latin inscription above the columns proclaims). The structure we see today dates from around A.D. 120, built by Emperor Hadrian. The 40-foot-high columns were taken from an Egyptian temple.

Step inside. The awe-inspiring **dome** is mathematically perfect: 142 feet tall and 142 feet wide. It rests atop a circular base; imagine a basketball set inside a wastebasket so that it just touches bottom. The dome is constructed from concrete, a Roman invention. The base is 23 feet thick and made from heavy travertine concrete, while the top is five feet thick and made from light volcanic pumice. The square indentations (or coffers) reduce the weight of the dome without compromising strength. At the top, the oculus, or eye-in-the-sky, is the building's only light source and is almost 30 feet across. The Pantheon also contains the world's greatest Roman column—the pillar of light from the oculus. This dome is perhaps the most influential in art history. It inspired Brunelleschi's Florence cathedral dome, Michelangelo's dome of St. Peter's, and even the capitol dome of Washington, D.C.

The marble **floor**—with its design of alternating circles and squares—is largely original. It has holes in it and slants toward the edges to let the rainwater drain.

Early in the Middle Ages, the Pantheon became a Christian church (from "all the gods" to "all the martyrs"), which means it's been in continual use for nearly 1,900 years. To the right of the altar is the **tomb** of Italy's first modern king, Victor Emmanuel II ("Padre della Patria," father of the fatherland), and to the left is Umberto I (son of the father). Also to the left of the altar, the artist Raphael lies buried, in a lighted glass niche.

When you leave, notice that the building is sunken below current street level, showing how the rest of the city has risen on 20 centuries of rubble.

▲▲Churches near the Pantheon

The **Church of San Luigi dei Francesi** has a magnificent chapel painted by Caravaggio (free, daily 10:00-12:30 & 15:00-19:00 except closed Thu afternoon, between the Pantheon and the north end of Piazza Navona). The only Gothic church in Rome is the **Church of Santa Maria sopra Minerva,** with a little-known Michelangelo statue, *Christ Bearing the Cross*, on a little square behind Pantheon, to the east). The **Church of San Ignazio,** several blocks east of the Pantheon, is a riot of Baroque illusions with a false dome (free, Mon-Sat 7:30-19:00, Sun 9:00-19:00). A few blocks away, across Corso Vittorio Emanuele, is the rich and Baroque **Gesù**

Church, headquarters of the Jesuits in Rome (free, daily 7:00-12:30 & 16:00-19:45, interesting daily service at 17:30).

▲Trevi Fountain

The bubbly Baroque fountain, worth ▲▲ by night, is a minor sight to art scholars...but a major nighttime gathering spot for teens on the make and tourists tossing coins. Those coins are collected daily to feed Rome's poor.

✪ For more information, see page 521 in the "Heart of Rome Walk."

Vatican City

Vatican City, the world's smallest country, contains St. Peter's Basilica (with Michelangelo's exquisite *Pietà*) and the Vatican Mu-

seum (with Michelangelo's Sistine Chapel). A helpful **TI** is just to the left of St. Peter's Basilica as you're facing it (Mon-Sat 8:30-18:15, closed Sun, tel. 06-6988-1662, Vatican switchboard tel. 06-6982, www.vatican. va). The entrances to St. Peter's and to the Vatican Museum are a 15-minute walk apart (follow the outside of the Vatican wall, which links the two sights). The nearest Metro stop—Ottaviano—still involves a 10-minute walk to either sight.

Modest dress is required of men, women, and children throughout Vatican City, even outdoors. Otherwise, the Swiss Guard can turn you away. Cover your shoulders; bring a light jacket or cover-up if you're wearing a tank top. Wear long pants instead of shorts. Skirts or dresses should extend below your knee.

▲▲▲St. Peter's Basilica (Basilica San Pietro)

There is no doubt: This is the richest and grandest church on earth. To call it vast is like calling Einstein smart.

Cost: Free entry to basilica and crypt. Dome climb–€5 if you take the stairs all the way up, or €7 to ride an elevator partway (to the roof), then climb to the top of the dome (for details, see "Dome Climb," page 560). Treasury Museum–€7 (cash only).

Hours: Church—daily April-Sept 7:00-19:00, Oct-March 7:00-18:00, closed Wed mornings during papal audiences; dome *(cupola)*—daily April-Sept 8:00-18:00, Oct-March 8:00-16:45 (last entry 30 minutes before closing); treasury museum—daily April-

Sept 9:00-18:15, Oct-March 9:00-17:15; crypt *(grotte)*—daily April-Sept 7:00-18:00, Oct-March 7:00-17:00.

✪ For a self-guided tour, see page 559.

▲▲▲Vatican Museum (Musei Vaticani)

The four miles of displays in this immense museum—from ancient statues to Christian frescoes to modern paintings—culminate in the Raphael Rooms and Michelangelo's glorious Sistine Chapel.

Cost and Hours: €16, €4 online reservation fee, Mon-Sat 9:00-18:00, last entry at 16:00 (though the official closing time is 18:00, the staff starts ushering you out at 17:30), closed on religious holidays and Sun except last Sun of the month (when it's free, more crowded, and open 9:00-14:00, last entry at 12:30); open Fri nights May-July and Sept-Oct 19:00-23:00 (last entry at 21:30) by online reservation only. Hours are subject to constant change and frequent holidays; check http://mv.vatican.va for current times.

✪ For a self-guided tour, see page 576.

Colosseum Tour

Rome has many layers—modern, Baroque, Renaissance, Christian. But let's face it: "Rome" is Caesars, gladiators, chariots, centurions, *"Et tu, Brute,"* trumpet fanfares, and thumbs-up or thumbs-down. This self-guided tour covers the downtown core of ancient Rome, the Colosseum.

Orientation

Cost: €12 combo-ticket covers both the Colosseum and the Roman Forum/Palatine Hill. The combo-ticket is valid for two consecutive days, but once your ticket is scanned for either the Colosseum or the Forum/Palatine Hill (grouped as one sight for the purposes of the ticket), you can't re-enter that sight (even the next day).

Hours: The Colosseum, Roman Forum, and Palatine Hill are all open daily 8:30 until one hour before sunset: April-Aug until 19:15, Sept until 19:00, Oct until 18:30, Nov-mid-Feb until 16:30, mid-Feb-mid-March until 17:00, mid-March-late March until 17:30; last entry one hour before closing.

Restoration: The arena is being cleaned from top to bottom, given permanent lighting, and outfitted with new shops and services. Long-range plans include building a free-standing ticket booth/visitors center outside the Colosseum. These ongoing renovations, scheduled to last several years, may affect your visit.

Avoiding Lines: Crowds tend to be thinner (and lines shorter) in the afternoon (especially after 15:00 in summer); this is also true at the Forum.

You can save lots of time by buying your combo-ticket in advance, booking a guided tour, or renting an audioguide or videoguide. Here are the options:

1. Buy your combo-ticket at the less-crowded Palatine Hill entrance, 150 yards away on Via di San Gregorio (facing the Forum, with Colosseum at your back, go left down the street). Avoid buying your ticket at the Forum, which also tends to have lines.

2. Buy a combo-ticket online at www.coopculture.it (€2 booking fee, not changeable). The "free tickets" you'll see listed are valid only for EU citizens with ID.

3. Pay to join an official guided tour, or rent an audioguide or videoguide (see "Tours," next page). This lets you march right up to the Colosseum's guided visits *(Visite Guidate)* desk, thus bypassing the ticket lines. Even if you don't use the device or accompany the guided tour, the extra cost might be worth it just to skip the ticket line.

4. Hire a private walking-tour guide. Guides of varying quality linger outside the Colosseum, offering tours that allow you to skip the line. Be aware that these private guides may try to mislead you into thinking the Colosseum lines are longer than they really are. For more on this option, see "Tours" on the next page.

Warning: Beware of the **greedy gladiators.** For a fee, the incredibly crude, modern-day gladiators snuff out their cigarettes and pose for photos. They're officially banned from panhandling in this area, but you may still see them, hoping to intimidate easy-to-swindle tourists into paying too much money for a photo op. (If you go for it, €4-5 for one photo usually keeps them appeased.) Also, look out for **pickpockets** and con artists in this prime tourist spot.

Getting There: The Colosseo Metro stop on line B is just across the street from the monument.

Getting In: If you need to buy a ticket or sign up for a guided tour, follow the signs for the appropriate line. With a combo-ticket in hand, look for signs for *ticket holders*, allowing you to bypass the long lines.

Information: Tel. 06-3996-7700, www.archeoroma.beniculturali. it/en.

Tours: A dry but fact-filled **audioguide** is available just past the turnstiles (€5.50/2 hours). A handheld **videoguide** senses where you are in the site and plays related video clips (€6).

Official **guided tours** in English depart nearly hourly between 10:00 and 17:00, and last 45-60 minutes (€5 plus Colosseum ticket, purchase inside the Colosseum near the ticket booth marked *Visite Guidate;* if you're lost, ask a guard to direct you to the desk).

A 1.5-hour **"Colosseum, Underground and Third Ring" tour** takes you through restricted areas, including the top floor and underground passageways, which are off-limits to regular Colosseum visitors. While interesting, this tour certainly isn't essential to appreciating the Colosseum. Although it's possible to sign up for the tour at the Colosseum's guided tours window, it's strongly advised you reserve at least a day in advance, either by phone or online. The tour is operated by CoopCulture, a private company (€8 plus Colosseum ticket, www.coopculture.it). Call 06-3996-7700 during business hours: Mon-Fri 9:00-18:00, Sat 9:00-14:00 (closed Sun, no same-day reservations). After dialing, wait for English instructions on how to reach a live operator, then reserve a time and pre-pay with a credit card. Without a reservation, you can try to join the next available tour (may be in Italian): Once you have your Colosseum entrance ticket and are at the turnstiles, look for the tour meeting point just past the ticket desk; pay the guide directly.

Private guides stand outside the Colosseum looking for business (€25-30/2-hour tour of the Colosseum, Forum, and Palatine Hill). If booking a private guide, make sure that your tour will start right away and that the ticket you receive covers all three sights: the Colosseum, Forum, and Palatine Hill.

You can also download this tour as a free Rick Steves **audio tour** (see page 50).

Length of This Tour: Allow an hour. If you're short on time, you can basically see the entire interior with a single glance. It's not necessary to go upstairs or circle the place.

Services: There's a WC (often crowded) inside the Colosseum. For more tips on where to eat, drink, and find a WC in the area, see the sidebar on page 544.

ROME

The Tour Begins

Exterior

• *View the Colosseum from the Forum fence, across the street from the Colosseo Metro station.*

Built when the Roman Empire was at its peak in A.D. 80, the Colosseum represents Rome at its grandest. The Flavian Amphitheater (the Colosseum's real name) was an arena for gladiator contests and public spectacles. When killing became a spectator sport, the Romans wanted to share the fun with as many people as possible, so they stuck two semicircular theaters together to create a freestanding amphitheater. The outside (where slender cypress trees stand today) was decorated with a 100-foot-tall bronze statue of Nero that gleamed in the sunlight. In a later age, the colossal structure was nicknamed a "coloss-eum," the wonder of its age. Towering 150 feet high, it could accommodate 50,000 roaring fans (100,000 thumbs).

The Romans pioneered the use of concrete and the rounded arch, which enabled them to build on this tremendous scale. The exterior is a skeleton of 3.5 million cubic feet of travertine stone. (Each of the pillars flanking the ground-level arches weighs five tons.) It took 200 ox-drawn wagons shuttling back and forth every day for four years just to bring the stone here from Tivoli. They stacked stone blocks (without mortar) into the shape of an arch, supported temporarily by wooden scaffolding. Finally, they wedged a keystone into the top of the arch—it not only kept the arch from falling, it could bear even more weight above. Iron pegs held the larger stones together; notice the small holes—the result of medieval peg poachers—that pockmark the sides.

The exterior says a lot about the Romans. They were great engineers, not artists, and the building is more functional than beautiful. (If ancient Romans visited the US today as tourists, they might send home postcards of our greatest works of "art"—freeways.) While the essential structure of the Colosseum is Roman, the four-story facade is decorated with mostly Greek columns—Doric-like Tuscan columns on the ground level, Ionic on the second story, Corinthian on the next level, and at the top, half-columns with a mix of all three. Originally, copies of Greek statues stood in the arches of the middle two stories, giving a veneer of sophistication to this arena of death.

Only a third of the original Colosseum remains. Earthquakes destroyed some of it, but most was carted off as easy pre-cut stones for other buildings during the Middle Ages and Renaissance.

• *To enter, line up in the correct queue: the one for ticket buyers or the one for those who already have a ticket (plus people looking to take a guided tour or rent an audio or videoguide). The third line is for groups. Once*

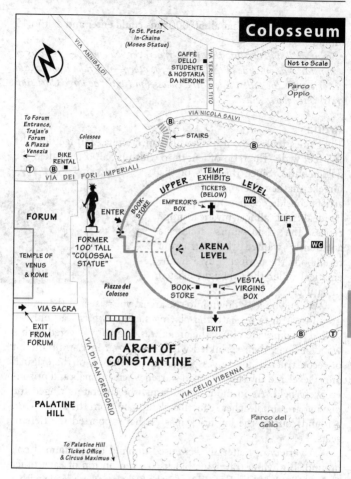

*past the turnstiles, there may be signs directing you on a specific visitors'
route. Follow the flow of traffic, making your way into the arena.*

Interior

Entrances and Exits

As you walk through passageways and up staircases, admire the
ergonomics. Fans could pour in through ground-floor entrances;
there were 76 numbered ones in addition to the emperor's private
entrance on the north side. Your ticket (likely a piece of pottery)
was marked with your entrance, section, row, and seat number.
You'd pass by concession stands selling fast food and souvenirs,
such as wine glasses with the names of famous gladiators. A hallway leading to the seats was called a *vomitorium*. At exit time, the
Colosseum would "vomit" out its contents, giving us the English

word. It's estimated that all 50,000 fans could enter and exit in 15 minutes.

• *Soon you'll spill out into the arena. Wherever you end up—upstairs or downstairs, at one side of the arena or the other—just take it all in and get oriented. The tallest side of the Colosseum (with the large Christian cross) is the north side.*

Arena

The games took place in this oval-shaped arena, 280 feet long by 165 feet wide. The ratio of length to width is 5:3, often called the golden ratio. Since the days of the Greek mathematician Pythagoras, artists considered that proportion to be ideal, with almost mystical properties. The Colosseum's architects apparently wanted their structure to embody the perfect 5-by-3 mathematical order they thought existed in nature.

When you look down into the arena, you're seeing the underground passages beneath the playing surface (which can only be visited on a private tour). The arena was originally covered with a wooden floor, then sprinkled with sand (*arena* in Latin). The bit of reconstructed floor gives you an accurate sense of the original arena level and the subterranean warren where animals and prisoners were held. As in modern stadiums, the spectators ringed the playing area in bleacher seats that slanted up from the arena floor. Around you are the big brick masses that supported the tiers of seats.

A variety of materials were used to build the stadium. Look around. Big white travertine blocks stacked on top of each other formed the skeleton. The pillars for the bleachers were made with a shell of brick, filled in with concrete. Originally the bare brick was covered with marble columns or ornamental facing, so the interior was a brilliant white (they used white plaster for the upper-floor cheap seats).

The Colosseum's seating was strictly segregated. At ringside, the emperor, senators, Vestal Virgins, and VIPs occupied marble

seats with their names carved on them (a few marble seats have been restored, at the east end). The next level upheld those of noble birth. The level tourists now occupy was for ordinary free Roman citizens, called plebeians. Up at the very top (a hundred yards from the action), there were once wooden bleachers for the poorest people—foreigners, slaves, and women. While no seats survive and you're likely viewing the arena from what was a passageway that ran under the seats, you can imagine the scene.

The top story of the Colosseum is mostly ruined—only the north side still retains its high wall. This was not part of the origi-

nal three-story structure, but was added around A.D. 230 after a fire necessitated repairs. Picture the awning that could be stretched across the top of the stadium by armies of sailors. Strung along horizontal beams that pointed inward to the center, the awning only

covered about a third of the arena—so those at the top always enjoyed shade, while many nobles down below roasted in the sun.

Looking into the complex web of passageways beneath the arena, you can imagine how busy the backstage action was. Gladiators strolled down the central passageway, from their warm-up yard on the east end to the arena entrance on the west. Some workers tended wild animals. Others prepared stage sets of trees or fake buildings, allowing the arena to be quickly transformed from an African jungle to a Greek temple. Props and sets were hauled up to arena level on 80 different elevator shafts via a system of ropes and pulleys. (You might be able to make out some small rectangular shafts, especially near the center of the arena.) That means there were 80 different spots from which animals, warriors, and stage sets could pop up and magically appear.

The games began with a few warm-up acts—dogs bloodying themselves attacking porcupines, female gladiators fighting each other, or a one-legged man battling a dwarf. Then came the main event—the gladiators.

"Hail, Caesar! *(Ave, Cesare!)* We who are about to die salute you!" The gladiators would enter the arena from the west end, parade around to the sound of trumpets, acknowledge the Vestal Virgins (on the south side), then stop at the emperor's box (supposedly marked today by the cross that stands at the "50-yard line" on the north side—although no one knows for sure where it was). They would then raise their weapons, shout, and salute—and begin fighting. The fights pitted men against men, men against beasts, and beasts against beasts. Picture 50,000 screaming people around

Modern Amenities in the Ancient World

The area around the Colosseum, Forum, and Palatine Hill is rich in history, but pretty barren when it comes to food, shelter, and WCs. Here are a few options:

The Colosseum has a crowded **WC** inside. A nice, big WC is behind (east of) the structure (facing ticket entrance, go clockwise; WC is under stairway). If you can wait, the best WCs in the area are at Palatine Hill—at the Via di San Gregorio entrance, outside the stadium, in the museum, and in the Farnese Gardens. The Forum has WCs at the main entrance, near the Arch of Titus (in the "Soprintendenza" office), and in the middle of the Forum (near #8 on the map on page 551).

Because the area's **eating** options are limited, consider assembling a small picnic. The Colosseo Metro stop has forgettable €5 hot sandwiches. Snack stands on street corners sell overpriced drinks, sandwiches, fruit, and candy. If you prefer to dine in, you'll find a few restaurants behind the Colosseum (with expansive views of the structure), several recommended places within a few blocks (no views but a better value—see page 601), and a cluster of places near the Forum's main entrance (where Via Cavour spills into Via dei Fori Imperiali).

To refill your **water** bottle, stop at one of the water fountains in the area. You'll find them along a few city streets, as well as inside the Forum and Palatine Hill.

A nice oasis is the free visitors center, **I Fori di Roma,** located near the Forum entrance. It's across Via dei Fori Imperiali and a bit east, toward the Colosseum. It has a small café, a WC, and a few exhibits.

If your sightseeing takes you as far as **Capitoline Hill,** you'll find services at the Capitoline Museums, including a nice view café (see page 530).

Several **public buses** (#85, #87, etc.) traverse Via dei Fori Imperiali between the Colosseum and Piazza Venezia, making it easy to hop on for a stop or two. If you need a **taxi,** use the stand near the southeast corner of the Colosseum. The taxi drivers parked near the Colosseo Metro stop (on Via dei Fori Imperiali) have a reputation for being sharks.

you (did gladiators get stage fright?), and imagine that they want to see you die.

Some gladiators wielded swords, protected only with a shield and a heavy helmet. Others represented fighting fishermen, with a net to snare opponents and a trident to spear them. The gladiators were usually slaves, criminals, or poor people who got their chance for freedom, wealth, and fame in the ring. They learned to fight in

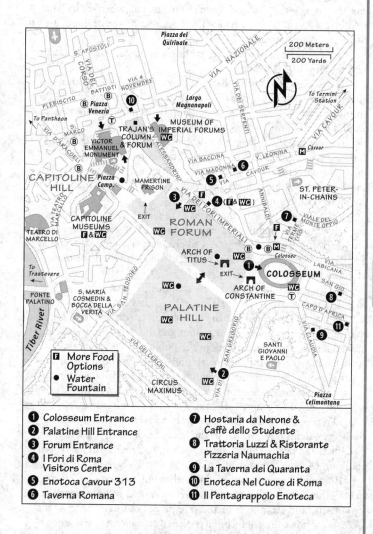

200 Meters
200 Yards

1 Colosseum Entrance
2 Palatine Hill Entrance
3 Forum Entrance
4 I Fori di Roma Visitors Center
5 Enotoca Cavour 313
6 Taverna Romana
7 Hostaria da Nerone & Caffè dello Studente
8 Trattoria Luzzi & Ristorante Pizzeria Naumachia
9 La Taverna dei Quaranta
10 Enoteca Nel Cuore di Roma
11 Il Pentagrappolo Enoteca

F More Food Options
• Water Fountain

ROME

training schools, then battled their way up the ranks. The best were rewarded like our modern sports stars, with fan clubs, great wealth, and, yes, product endorsements.

The animals came from all over the world: lions, tigers, and bears (oh my!), crocodiles, elephants, and hippos (not to mention exotic human "animals" from the "barbarian" lands). They were kept in cages beneath the arena floor, then lifted up in the elevators.

Released at floor level, animals would pop out from behind blinds into the arena—the gladiator didn't know where, when, or by what he'd be attacked. Many a hapless warrior met his death here, and never even knew what hit him. (This sometimes brought howls of laughter from the hardened fans in the cheap upper seats, who had a better view of the action.)

Nets ringed the arena to protect the crowd. The stadium was inaugurated with a 100-day festival in which 2,000 men and 9,000 animals were killed. Colosseum employees squirted perfumes around the stadium to mask the stench of blood.

If a gladiator fell helpless to the ground, his opponent would approach the emperor's box and ask: Should he live or die? Sometimes the emperor left the decision to the crowd, who would judge based on how valiantly the man had fought. They would make their decision: thumbs-up or thumbs-down.

Consider the value of these games in placating and controlling the huge Roman populace. Imagine never having seen an actual lion, and suddenly one jumps out to chase a prisoner in the arena. Seeing the king of beasts slain by a gladiator reminded the masses of man's triumph over nature.

In an age without a hint of a newsreel, it was hard for local Romans to visualize and appreciate the faraway conquests their empire was so dedicated to. The Colosseum spectacles were a way to bring home the environments, animals, and people of these conquered lands, parade them before the public, and make them real. And having the thumbs-up or thumbs-down authority over another person's life gave the spectators a real sense of power. Imagine the psychological boost the otherwise downtrodden masses felt when the emperor granted them this thrilling decision.

Did they throw Christians to the lions as in the movies? Christians were definitely thrown to the lions, made to fight gladiators, crucified, and burned alive...but probably not here in this particular stadium. Maybe, but probably not.

Rome was a nation of warriors that built an empire by conquest. The battles fought against Germans and other barbarians, Egyptians, and strange animals were played out daily here in the Colosseum for the benefit of city-slicker bureaucrats, who got vicarious thrills by watching brutes battle to the death. The contests were always free, sponsored by the government to bribe the people's favor or to keep Rome's growing masses of unemployed rabble off the streets.

• *With these scenes in mind, wander around, then check out the upper level. There are stairs on both the east and west sides, as well as an elevator at the east end (only accessible to those who really need it). The upper deck offers more colossal views of the arena, plus a bookstore and temporary exhibits.*

The Colosseum's Legacy

With the coming of Christianity to Rome, the Colosseum and its deadly games slowly became politically incorrect. However, some gladiator contests continued here sporadically until they were completely banned in A.D. 435. Animal hunts continued a few decades longer. As the Roman Empire dwindled and the infrastructure crumbled, the stadium itself was neglected. Finally, around A.D. 523—after nearly 500 years of games—the last animal was killed, and the Colosseum shut its doors.

For the next thousand years, the structure was inhabited by various squatters. It was used for makeshift apartments or shops, as a church, a cemetery, and as a refuge during invasions and riots. Over time, the Colosseum was eroded by wind, rain, and the strain of gravity. Earthquakes weakened it, and a powerful quake in 1349 toppled the south side.

More than anything, the Colosseum was dismantled by the Roman citizens themselves, who carted off pre-cut stones to be reused for palaces and churches, including St. Peter's. The marble facing was pulverized into mortar, and 300 tons of iron brackets were pried out and melted down, resulting in the pockmarking you see today.

After centuries of neglect, a series of 16th-century popes took pity on the pagan structure. In memory of the Christians who may (or may not) have been martyred here, they shored up the south and west sides with bricks and placed the big cross on the north side of the arena.

Today, the Colosseum links Rome's glorious past with its vital present. Major political demonstrations begin or end here, providing protesters with an iconic backdrop for the TV cameras. On Good Friday, the pope comes here to lead pilgrims as they follow the Stations of the Cross.

The legend goes that as long as the Colosseum shall stand, the city of Rome shall also stand. For nearly 2,000 years, the Colosseum has been the enduring symbol of Rome, the Eternal City.

• *The Roman Forum is 100 yards to the right of the arch. You can enter it through the Forum entrance on Via dei Fori Imperiali or from the Palatine Hill entrance along Via di San Gregorio—see the map on page 545. (Note that what looks like an entrance gate up Via Sacra is currently exit-only.)*

ROME

Roman Forum Tour

The Forum was the political, religious, and commercial center of the city. Rome's most important temples and halls of justice were here. This was the place for religious processions, political demonstrations, elections, important speeches, and parades by conquering generals. As Rome's empire expanded, these few acres of land became the center of the civilized world.

Orientation

Cost: €12 combo-ticket covers both the Roman Forum/Palatine Hill (grouped as one sight for the purposes of the ticket) and the Colosseum.

Hours: The Roman Forum, Palatine Hill, and Colosseum are all open daily 8:30 until one hour before sunset: April-Aug until 19:15, Sept until 19:00, Oct until 18:30, Nov-mid-Feb until 16:30, mid-Feb-mid-March until 17:00, mid-March-late March until 17:30; last entry one hour before closing.

Avoiding Lines: See tips on page 538.

Getting There: The closest Metro stop is Colosseo. The Forum has two entrances. The main entrance is on Via dei Fori Imperiali ("Road of the Imperial Forums"). From the Colosseo Metro stop, walk away from the Colosseum on Via dei Fori Imperiali to find the low-profile Forum ticket office (look closely), located where Via Cavour spills into Via dei Fori Imperiali. Buses #53, #85, #87, and #175 stop along Via dei Fori Imperiali near the entrance, the Colosseum, and Piazza Venezia.

While the Forum has four exits, there are only two ways in. The second entrance—which may be more convenient if you're coming from the Colosseum—is at the Palatine Hill ticket office on Via di San Gregorio. After buying your ticket, take the path to the right (not up the hill), which leads to the Forum at the Arch of Titus.

Information: A free visitors center (called I Fori di Roma), located across Via dei Fori Imperiali from the Forum's main entrance, has a TI, bookshop, small café, WCs, and a film (daily 9:30-18:30). A bookstore is at the Forum entrance. Vendors outside sell *Rome: Past and Present* books with plastic overlays that restore the ruins (includes DVD; smaller book marked €15, prices soft, so offer €10). Info office tel. 06-3996-7700, http://archeoroma.beniculturali.it/en.

Tours: An unexciting yet informative **audioguide** helps decipher the rubble (€5/2 hours, €7 version includes Palatine Hill and lasts 3 hours, must leave ID), but you'll have to return it to one of the Forum entrances instead of being able to exit directly to Capitoline Hill or the Colosseum. Official **guided tours** in English might be available (inquire at ticket office). You can download this tour as a free Rick Steves **audio tour** (see page 50).

Length of This Tour: Allow 1.5 hours. If you have less time, end the tour at the Arch of Septimius Severus. Don't miss the Basilica of Constantine hiding behind the trees.

Services: WCs are at the main entrance, near the Arch of Titus (in the "Soprintendenza" office), and in the middle of the Forum, near #8 on the map.

Plan Ahead: The ancient paving at the Forum is uneven; wear sturdy shoes. I carry a water bottle and refill it at the Forum's public drinking fountains.

Improvise: Because of ongoing restoration, paths through the Forum are often rerouted. Use this walk as a starting point, but be prepared for a few detours and backtracking.

The Tour Begins

• *Start at the Arch of Titus (Arco di Tito). It's the white triumphal arch that rises above the rubble on the east end of the Forum (closest to the Colosseum). Stand at the viewpoint alongside the arch and gaze over the valley known as the Forum.*

As you begin this Forum tour, here's a hint for seeing things with "period eyes." We imagine the structures in ancient Rome as mostly white, but ornate buildings and monuments like the Arch of Titus were originally more colorful. Through the ages, builders scavenged stone from the Forum, and the finest stone—the colored marble— was cannibalized first. If any was left, it was generally the  white stone. Statues that filled the niches were vividly painted, but the organic paint rotted away as statues lay buried for centuries. Lettering was inset bronze and eyes were inset ivory. Even seemingly intact structures, like the Arch of Titus, have been reassembled. Notice the columns are half smooth and half fluted. The fluted halves are original; the smooth parts are reconstructions— intentionally not trying to fake the original.

❶ Arch of Titus (Arco di Tito)

The Arch of Titus commemorated the Roman victory over the province of Judaea (Israel) in A.D. 70. The Romans had a reputa-

tion as benevolent conquerors who tolerated
the local customs and rulers. All they required
was allegiance to the empire, shown by worshipping the emperor as a god. No problem
for most conquered people, who already had
half a dozen gods on their prayer lists anyway.
But Israelites believed in only one god, and
it wasn't the emperor. Israel revolted. After a
short but bitter war, the Romans defeated the
rebels, took Jerusalem, destroyed their tem-

ple (leaving only the foundation wall—today's revered "Wailing
Wall"), and brought home 50,000 Jewish slaves...who were forced
to build this arch (and the Colosseum).

• *Walk down Via Sacra into the Forum. Imagine Roman sandals on
these original basalt stones—the oldest street you'll ever walk. After
about 50 yards, turn right and follow a path uphill to the three huge
arches of the...*

❷ Basilica of Constantine (Basilica Maxentius)

Yes, these are big arches. But they represent only one-third of the
original Basilica of Constantine, a mammoth hall of justice. The
arches were matched by a similar set along the Via Sacra side (only
a few squat brick piers remain). Between them ran the central hall,
which was spanned by a roof 130 feet high—about 55 feet higher
than the side arches you see. (The stub of brick you see sticking up
began an arch that once spanned the central hall.) The hall itself
was as long as a football field, lavishly furnished with colorful inlaid marble, a gilded bronze ceiling, and statues, and filled with
strolling Romans. At the far (west) end was an enormous marble
statue of Emperor Constantine on a throne. (Pieces of this statue,
including a hand the size of a man, are on display in Rome's Capitoline Museums.)

The basilica was begun by the Emperor Maxentius, but after
he was trounced in battle, the victor Constantine completed the

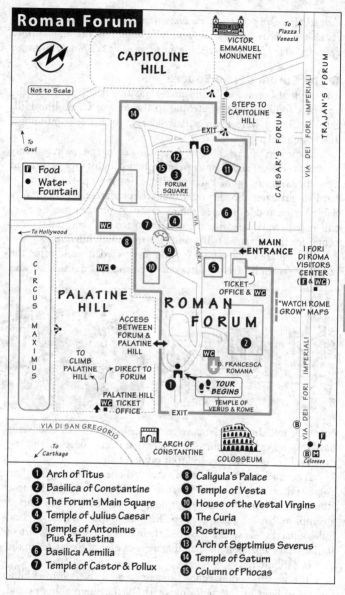

Roman Forum

Not to Scale

CAPITOLINE HILL

VICTOR EMMANUEL MONUMENT

To Piazza Venezia

STEPS TO CAPITOLINE HILL

EXIT

To Gaul

F Food
● Water Fountain

TRAJAN'S FORUM

VIA DEI FORI IMPERIALI

CAESAR'S FORUM

⑭

⑬
⑫
⑮ ③
FORUM SQUARE
⑪

⑥

To Hollywood

WC
⑦ ④
⑧
⑨

VIA SACRA

MAIN ENTRANCE

I FORI DI ROMA VISITORS CENTER (**F** & **WC**)

WC ●
⑩
⑤

TICKET OFFICE & **WC**

"WATCH ROME GROW" MAPS

CIRCUS MAXIMUS

PALATINE HILL

ROMAN FORUM

②

ROME

ACCESS BETWEEN FORUM & PALATINE HILL

TO CLIMB PALATINE HILL

DIRECT TO FORUM

WC
S. FRANCESCA ROMANA

PALATINE HILL TICKET OFFICE
WC

①
TOUR BEGINS

TEMPLE OF VENUS & ROME

VIA DEI FORI IMPERIALI

EXIT

VIA DI SAN GREGORIO

To Carthage

ARCH OF CONSTANTINE

COLOSSEUM

Ⓑ

F

Ⓑ Ⓜ
Colosseo

① Arch of Titus
② Basilica of Constantine
③ The Forum's Main Square
④ Temple of Julius Caesar
⑤ Temple of Antoninus Pius & Faustina
⑥ Basilica Aemilia
⑦ Temple of Castor & Pollux
⑧ Caligula's Palace
⑨ Temple of Vesta
⑩ House of the Vestal Virgins
⑪ The Curia
⑫ Rostrum
⑬ Arch of Septimius Severus
⑭ Temple of Saturn
⑮ Column of Phocas

massive building. No doubt about it, the Romans built monuments on a more epic scale than any previous Europeans, wowing their "barbarian" neighbors.

• Now stroll deeper into the Forum, downhill along Via Sacra, through the trees. Many of the large basalt stones under your feet were walked on by Caesar Augustus 2,000 years ago. Pass by the only original bronze *door still swinging on its ancient hinges (the green door at the Tempio di Romolo, on the right—if it happens to be open, peek in), and continue between ruined buildings until Via Sacra opens up to a flat, grassy area.*

❸ The Forum's Main Square

The original Forum, or main square, was this flat patch about the size of a football field, stretching to the foot of Capitoline Hill. Surrounding it were temples, law courts, government buildings, and triumphal arches.

Rome was born right here. According to legend, twin brothers Romulus (Rome) and Remus were orphaned in infancy and raised by a she-wolf on top of Palatine Hill. Growing up, they found it hard to get dates. So they and their cohorts attacked the nearby Sabine tribe and kidnapped their women. After they made peace, this marshy valley became the meeting place and then the trading center for the scattered tribes on the surrounding hillsides.

The square was the busiest and most crowded—and often the seediest—section of town. Besides the senators, politicians, and

currency exchangers, there were even sleazier types—souvenir hawkers, pickpockets, fortune-tellers, gamblers, slave marketers, drunks, hookers, lawyers, and tour guides.

Ancient Rome's population exceeded one million, more than any city until London and Paris in the 19th century. All those Roman masses lived in tiny apartments as we would live in tents at a campsite, basically just to sleep. The public space—their Forum, today's piazza—is where they did their living. To this day, urban Italians have a passion for spending a major part of their time in the streets and squares.

The Forum is now rubble, but imagine it in its prime: blindingly brilliant marble buildings with 40-foot-high columns and shining metal roofs; rows of statues painted in realistic colors; processional chariots rattling down Via Sacra. Mentally replace tourists in T-shirts with tribunes in togas. Imagine the buildings towering and the people buzzing around you while an orator gives a rabble-rousing speech from the Rostrum. If things still look like

ROME

just a pile of rocks, at least tell yourself, "But Julius Caesar once leaned against these rocks."

• *At the near (east) end of the main square (the Colosseum is to the east) are the foundations of a temple now capped with a peaked wood-and-metal roof.*

❹ Temple of Julius Caesar (Tempio del Divo Giulio, or Ara di Cesare)

On March 15, in 44 B.C., Julius Caesar was stabbed 23 times by political conspirators. After his assassination, Caesar's body was cre-

mated on this spot (under the metal roof). Afterward, this temple was built to honor him. Peek behind the wall into the small apse area, where a mound of dirt usually has fresh flowers—given to remember the man who, more than any other, personified the greatness of Rome.

Caesar (100-44 B.C.) changed Rome—and the Forum—dramatically. He cleared out many of the wooden market stalls and began to ring the square with even grander buildings. Caesar's house was located behind the temple, near that clump of trees. He walked right by here on the day he was assassinated ("Beware the Ides of March!" warned a street-corner Etruscan preacher).

Though he was popular with the masses, not everyone liked Caesar's urban design or his politics. When he assumed dictatorial powers, he was ambushed and stabbed to death by a conspiracy of senators, including his adopted son, Brutus *("Et tu, Brute?")*.

The funeral was held here, facing the main square. The citizens gathered, and speeches were made. Mark Antony stood up to say (in Shakespeare's words), "Friends, Romans, countrymen, lend me your ears. I come to bury Caesar, not to praise him." When Caesar's body was burned, his adoring fans threw anything at hand on the fire, requiring the fire department to come put it out. Later, Emperor Augustus dedicated this temple in his name, making Caesar the first Roman to become a god.

• *Behind and to the left of the Temple of Julius Caesar are 10 tall columns. These belong to the...*

❺ Temple of Antoninus Pius and Faustina

The Senate built this temple to honor Emperor Antoninus Pius (A.D. 138-161) and his deified wife, Faustina. The 50-foot-tall Corinthian (leafy) columns must have been awe-inspiring to out-of-towners who grew up in thatched huts. Although the temple has been inhabited by a church, you can still see the basic layout—a

ROME

staircase led to a shaded porch (the columns), which admitted you to the main building (now a church), where the statue of the god sat. Originally, these columns supported a triangular pediment decorated with sculptures.

Picture these columns, with gilded capitals, supporting brightly painted statues in the pediment, and the whole building capped with a gleaming bronze roof. The stately gray rubble of today's Forum is a faded black-and-white photograph of a 3-D Technicolor era.

The building is a microcosm of many changes that occurred after Rome fell. In medieval times, the temple was pillaged. Note the diagonal cuts high on the marble columns—a failed attempt by scavengers to cut through the pillars to pull them down for their precious stone. (They used vinegar and rope to cut the marble... but because vinegar also eats through rope, they abandoned the attempt.) In 1550, a church was housed inside the ancient temple. The green door shows the street level at the time of Michelangelo. The long staircase was underground until excavated in the 1800s.

• *Next, explore the ruins of the Basilica Aemilia. You can view it from a ramp next to the Temple of Antoninus Pius and Faustina, or find the entrance near the Curia.*

❻ Basilica Aemilia

A basilica was a covered public forum, often serving as a Roman hall of justice. In a society that was just as legal-minded as America

is today, you needed a lot of lawyers—and a big place to put them. Citizens came here to work out matters such as inheritances and building permits, or to sue somebody.

Notice the layout. It was a long, rectangular building. The stubby columns all in a row form one long, central hall flanked by two side aisles.

Medieval Christians required a larger meeting hall for their worship services than Roman temples provided, so they used the spacious Roman basilica as the model for their churches. Cathedrals from France to Spain to England, from Romanesque to Gothic to Renaissance, all have the same basic floor plan as a Roman basilica.

• *Return again to the Temple of Julius Caesar. To the right of the temple are the three tall columns of the...*

❼ Temple of Castor and Pollux

These three columns—all that remain of a once-prestigious temple—have become the most photographed sight in the Forum. The temple was one of the city's oldest, built in the fifth century B.C. It commemorated the Roman victory over the Tarquin, the notorious Etruscan king who oppressed them. As a symbol of Rome's self-governing Republic, the temple was often used as a meeting place of senators, and its front steps served as a podium for free speech. The three columns are Corinthian style, featuring leafy capitals and fluting. They date from a later incarnation of the temple (first century).

• *Beyond the three columns is Palatine Hill—the corner of which may have been...*

❽ Caligula's Palace (Palace of Tiberius)

Emperor Caligula (ruled A.D. 37-41) had a huge palace on Palatine Hill overlooking the Forum. It actually sprawled down the hill into

the Forum (some supporting arches remain in the hillside).

Caligula was not a nice person. He tortured enemies, stole senators' wives, and parked his chariot in handicap spaces. But Rome's luxury-loving emperors only added to the glory of the Forum, with each one trying to make his mark on history.

• *To the left of the Temple of Castor and Pollux, find the remains of a small white circular temple.*

❾ Temple of Vesta

This is perhaps Rome's most sacred spot. Rome considered itself one big family, and this temple represented a circular hut, like the kind that Rome's first families lived in. Inside, a fire burned, just as in a Roman home. And back in the days before lighters and butane, you never wanted your fire to go out. As long as the sacred flame burned, Rome would stand. The flame was tended by priestesses known as Vestal Virgins.

• *Around the back of the Temple of Vesta, you'll find two rectangular brick pools. These stood in the courtyard of the...*

ROME

⑩ House of the Vestal Virgins

The Vestal Virgins lived in a two-story building surrounding a long central courtyard with two pools at one end. Rows of statues depicting leading Vestal Virgins flanked the courtyard. This place was the model—both architecturally and sexually—for medieval convents and monasteries.

Chosen from noble families before they reached the age of 10, the six Vestal Virgins served a 30-year term. Honored and revered

by the Romans, the Vestals even had their own box opposite the emperor in the Colosseum. The statues that line the courtyard honor dutiful Vestals. As the name implies, a Vestal took a vow of chastity. If she served her term faithfully—abstaining for 30 years—she was given a huge dowry and allowed to marry. But if they found any Virgin who wasn't, she was strapped to a funeral car, paraded through the streets of the Forum, taken to a crypt, given a loaf of bread and a lamp...and buried alive. Many women suffered the latter fate.

• *Return to the Temple of Julius Caesar and head to the Forum's west end (opposite the Colosseum). As you pass alongside the big open space of the Forum's main square, consider how the piazza is still a standard part of any Italian town. It has reflected and accommodated the gregarious and outgoing nature of the Italian people since Roman times.*

Stop at the big, well-preserved brick building (on right) with the triangular roof—the Curia. (Ongoing archaeological work may restrict access to the Curia, as well as the Arch of Septimius Severus—described later—and the exit to Capitoline Hill.)

⑪ The Curia (Senate House)

The Curia was the most important political building in the Forum. While the present building dates from A.D. 283, this was the site of Rome's official center of government since the birth of the republic. Three hundred senators, elected by the citizens of Rome, met here to debate and

create the laws of the land. Their wooden seats once circled the building in three tiers; the Senate president's podium sat at the far end. The marble floor is from ancient times. Listen to the echoes in this vast room—the acoustics are great.

Rome prided itself on being a republic. Early in the city's history, its people threw out the king and established rule by elected representatives. Each Roman citizen was free to speak his mind and have a say in public policy. Even when emperors became the supreme authority, the Senate was a power to be reckoned with. The Curia building is well-preserved, having been used as a church since early Christian times. In the 1930s, it was restored and opened to the public as a historic site. (Note: Although Julius Caesar was assassinated in "the Senate," it wasn't here—the Senate was temporarily meeting across town.)

A statue and two reliefs inside the Curia help build our mental image of the Forum. The statue, made of porphyry marble in about A.D. 100 (with its head, arms, and feet now missing), was a tribute to an emperor, probably Hadrian or Trajan. The two relief panels may have decorated the Rostrum. Those on the left show people (with big stone tablets) standing in line to burn their debt records following a government amnesty. The other shows the distribution of grain (Rome's welfare system), some buildings in the background, and the latest fashion in togas.

• *Go back down the Senate steps and find the 10-foot-high wall just to the left of the big arch, marked...*

⓮ Rostrum

Nowhere was Roman freedom more apparent than at this "Speaker's Corner." The Rostrum was a raised platform, 10 feet high and 80 feet long, decorated with statues, columns, and the prows of ships.

On a stage like this, Rome's orators, great and small, tried to draw a crowd and sway public opinion. Mark Antony rose to offer Caesar the laurel-leaf crown of kingship, which Caesar publicly (and hypocritically) refused while privately becoming a dictator. Men such as Cicero railed against the corruption and decadence that came with the city's newfound wealth. In later years, daring citizens even spoke out against the emperors, reminding them that Rome was once free. Picture the backdrop these speakers would have had—a mountain of marble buildings piling up on Capitoline Hill.

In front of the Rostrum are trees bearing fruits that were sacred to the ancient Romans: olives (provided food, light, and preservatives), figs (tasty), and wine grapes (made a popular export product).

• *The big arch to the right of the Rostrum is the...*

ROME

⑬ Arch of Septimius Severus

In imperial times, the Rostrum's voices of democracy would have been dwarfed by images of the empire, such as the huge six-story-high Arch of Septimius Severus (A.D.

203). The reliefs commemorate the African-born emperor's battles in Mesopotamia. Near ground level, see soldiers marching captured barbarians back to Rome for the victory parade. Despite Severus' efficient rule, Rome's empire was crumbling under the weight of its own corruption, disease, decaying infrastructure, and the constant attacks by foreign "barbarians."

• *Pass underneath the Arch of Septimius Severus and turn left. If the path is blocked, backtrack toward the Temple of Julius Caesar and around the square. On the slope of Capitoline Hill are the eight remaining columns of the...*

⑭ Temple of Saturn

These columns framed the entrance to the Forum's oldest temple (497 B.C.). Inside was a humble, very old wooden statue of the god Saturn. But the statue's pedestal held the gold bars, coins, and jewels of Rome's state treasury, the booty collected by conquering generals.

• *Standing here, at one of the Forum's first buildings, look east at the lone, tall...*

⑮ Column of Phocas

This is the Forum's last monument (A.D. 608), a gift from the powerful Byzantine Empire to a fallen empire—Rome. Given to com-

memorate the pagan Pantheon's becoming a Christian church, it's like a symbolic last nail in ancient Rome's coffin. After Rome's 1,000-year reign, the city was looted by Vandals, the population of a million-plus shrank to about 10,000, and the once-grand city center—the Forum—was abandoned, slowly covered up by centuries of silt and dirt. In the 1700s, an English historian named Edward Gibbon overlooked this spot from Capitoline Hill. Hearing Christian monks singing at these pagan ruins, he looked out at the few columns poking up

from the ground, pondered the decline and fall of the Roman Empire, and thought, "Hmm, that's a catchy title..."

• *From here, you have several options:*

1. Exiting past the Arch of Titus lands you at the Colosseum (page 522).

2. Exiting past the Arch of Septimius Severus leads you to the stairs up to Capitoline Hill (page 528).

3. The Forum's main entrance spills you back out onto Via dei Fori Imperiali; from there you can head to Trajan's Column, Trajan's Market, and Museum of the Imperial Forums (page 527).

4. From the Arch of Titus, you can climb Palatine Hill to the top (page 526).

St. Peter's Basilica Tour

St. Peter's Basilica (Basilica San Pietro) is the greatest church in Christendom. It represents the power and splendor of Rome's 2,000-year domination of the Western world. Built on the memory and grave of the first pope, St. Peter, this is where the grandeur of ancient Rome became the grandeur of Christianity.

Orientation

Cost: Free entry to basilica and crypt. Dome climb-€5 if you take the stairs all the way up, or €7 to ride an elevator partway (to the roof), then climb to the top of the dome (for details, see "Dome Climb," later). Treasury Museum-€7 (cash only).

Hours: The **church** is open daily April-Sept 7:00-19:00, Oct-March 7:00-18:00. It closes on Wednesday mornings during papal audiences.

The **dome** *(cupola)* is open to climbers daily April-Sept 8:00-18:00, Oct-March 8:00-16:45 (last entry 30 minutes before closing).

The **Treasury Museum** is open daily April-Sept 9:00-18:15, Oct-March 9:00-17:15.

The **crypt** *(grotte)* is open daily April-Sept 7:00-18:00, Oct-March 7:00-17:00.

When to Go: The best time to visit the church is early or late—but unfortunately, your cruise schedule is unlikely to have you here at those times. If you do have the flexibility to be here later in the day, aim for about 17:00—when the church is fairly empty, sunbeams can work their magic, and the late-afternoon Mass fills the place with spiritual music.

Avoiding Lines: The security-checkpoint lines can get quite long and there's no sure-fire way to avoid them. Note that the checkpoint can switch locations; it's typically on the north side of the square, but can be closer to the church or tucked under the south colonnade.

Occasionally, St. Peter's is accessible directly from the Sistine Chapel inside the Vatican Museum—a great time-saving trick, but unfortunately not a reliable one (for details, see page 579).

Dress Code: No shorts, above-the-knee skirts, or bare shoulders (this applies to men, women, and children). Attendants strictly enforce this dress code, even in hot weather. Carry a cover-up, if necessary.

Getting There: If you're taking a regional train from Civitavecchia, it's easiest to get off at San Pietro Station (see page 497). Coming from Termini or elsewhere in town, take the Metro to Ottaviano, then walk 10 minutes south on Via Ottaviano. The #40 express bus drops off at Piazza Pio, next to Castel Sant'Angelo—a 10-minute walk from St. Peter's. The more crowded bus #64 is convenient for pickpockets and stops just outside St. Peter's Square to the south (get off the bus after it crosses the Tiber, at the first stop past the tunnel; backtrack toward the tunnel and turn left when you see the rows of columns). Bus #492 heads through the center of town, stopping at Largo Argentina, and gets you near Piazza Risorgimento (get off when you see the Vatican walls). A taxi from Termini train station to St. Peter's costs about €11.

Information: The TI on the left (south) side of the square is excellent (Mon-Sat 8:30-18:15, closed Sun, free Vatican and church map). Tel. 06-6988-1662, www.saintpetersbasilica.org (this unofficial site provides a detailed map and latest opening hours and Mass times; the official site isn't any more reliable, and is far less user-friendly).

Church Services: Mass is performed daily, generally in Italian and in just a small area of the vast church: usually either in the south (left) transept, the Blessed Sacrament Chapel (on right side of nave), or the apse (where the 17:00 service is held Mon-Sat). Sunday morning Mass tends to take place at the main altar. Typical schedule: Mon-Sat at 8:30, 9:00, 10:00, 11:00, 12:00, and 17:00 (in Latin, in the apse); and on Sun and holidays at 9:00, 10:30 (in Latin), 11:30, 12:15, 13:00, 16:00, and 17:45.

Tours: The Vatican TI conducts free 1.5-hour **tours of St. Peter's** (depart from TI Mon-Fri at 14:15, plus Tue and Thu at 9:45, confirm schedule at TI, tel. 06-6988-1662). **Audioguides** can be rented near the checkroom (€5 plus ID, for church only, daily 9:00-17:00). Or you can download this tour as a free Rick Steves **audio tour** (see page 50).

Dome Climb: You can take the elevator or stairs to the roof (231

Vatican City

This tiny independent country of little more than 100 acres, contained entirely within Rome, has its own postal system, armed guards, helipad, mini-train station, and radio station (KPOP). It also has two huge sights: St. Peter's Basilica (with Michelangelo's *Pietà*) and the Vatican Museum (with the Sistine Chapel). Politically powerful, the Vatican is the religious capital of 1.2 billion Roman Catholics. If you're not a Catholic, become one for your visit.

The pope is both the religious and secular leader of Vatican City. For centuries, locals referred to him as "King Pope." Italy and the Vatican didn't always have good relations. In fact, after unification (in 1870), when Rome's modern grid plan was built around the miniscule Vatican, it seemed as if the new buildings were designed to be just high enough so no one could see the dome of St. Peter's from street level. Modern Italy was created in 1870, but the Holy See didn't recognize it as a country until 1929, when the pope and Mussolini signed the Lateran Pact, giving sovereignty and a few nearby churches to the Vatican.

Like every European country, Vatican City has its own versions of the euro coin (with a portrait of Pope Francis I and, before him, of Benedict XVI). You're unlikely to find one in your pocket, though, as they're snatched up by collectors before falling into circulation.

Post Offices: The Vatican postal service is famous for its stamps, which you can get from offices on St. Peter's Square (next to TI or between the columns just before the security checkpoint) or in the Vatican Museum (Mon-Sat 8:30-18:30, closed Sun). Vatican stamps are good throughout Rome, but to use the Vatican's mail service, you need to mail your cards from the Vatican itself; write your postcards ahead of time. (Note that the Vatican won't mail cards with Italian stamps.)

ROME

steps), then climb another 323 steps to the top of the dome. The entry to the elevator is just outside the basilica, on the north side of St. Peter's (near the secret exit from the Sistine Chapel). Look for signs to the *cupola*. Note that the dome-climb exit may not be located near the entrance—if you're not climbing the dome with your travel partner, ask about the current exit spot before you split up. For more on the dome, see page 576.

Length of This Tour: Allow one hour, plus another hour if you climb the dome (or a half-hour to the roof). If you have less time, skip the crypt and the dome climb, but at least stroll the nave, glance up at the dome and down at the marker of St. Peter's tomb. Don't miss the *Pietà*.

Baggage Check: The free bag check (mandatory for bags larger

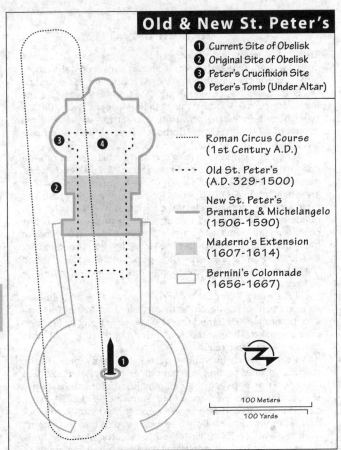

Old & New St. Peter's

1. Current Site of Obelisk
2. Original Site of Obelisk
3. Peter's Crucifixion Site
4. Peter's Tomb (Under Altar)

.... Roman Circus Course
(1st Century A.D.)

- - - - Old St. Peter's
(A.D. 329-1500)

New St. Peter's
Bramante & Michelangelo
(1506-1590)

Maderno's Extension
(1607-1614)

Bernini's Colonnade
(1656-1667)

100 Meters

100 Yards

ROME

than a purse or daypack) is outside the basilica (to the right as you face the entrance) just inside the security checkpoint.

Services: WCs are to the right and left on St. Peter's Square (just outside the security checkpoint and exit), near baggage storage down the steps on the right side of the entrance, and on the roof. **Drinking fountains** are at the obelisk and near WCs. **Post offices** are next to the TI and just outside the security checkpoint (you can buy stamps and postcards and drop them into a postbox).

Starring: Michelangelo, Bernini, St. Peter, a heavenly host...and, occasionally, the pope.

Background

Nearly 2,000 years ago, St. Peter's oval-shaped "square" was the site of Nero's Circus—a huge, cigar-shaped Roman chariot racecourse.

The Romans had no marching bands, so for halftime entertainment they killed Christians. This persecuted minority was forced to fight wild animals and gladiators, or they were simply crucified. Some were tarred up, tied to posts, and burned—human torches to light up the evening races.

One of those killed here, in about A.D. 65, was Peter, Jesus' right-hand man, who had come to Rome to spread the message of

love. At his own request, Peter was crucified upside down, because he felt unworthy to die as his master had. His remains were buried in a cemetery located where the main altar in St. Peter's is today. For 250 years, these relics were quietly and secretly revered.

Peter had been recognized as the first "pope," or bishop of Rome, from whom all later popes claimed their authority as head of the Church. When Christianity was finally legalized in 313, the Christian Emperor Constantine built a church on the site of Peter's martyrdom. "Old St. Peter's" lasted 1,200 years (A.D. 329-1500).

ROME

By the time of the Renaissance, Old St. Peter's was falling apart and was considered unfit to be the center of the Western Church. The new, larger church we see today was begun in 1506 by the architect Bramante. He was succeeded by Michelangelo and a number of other architects, each with his own designs. Later, Carlo Maderno took Michelangelo's Greek cross-shaped church and lengthened it, adding a long nave. As the construction proceeded, the new church rose around the old one (see diagram on

preceding page). The project was finally finished 120 years later, and Old St. Peter's was dismantled and carried out of the new church.

Michelangelo designed the magnificent dome. Unfortunately, although it soars above St. Peter's, it's barely visible from the center of the square because of Maderno's extended nave. To see the entire dome, you'll need to step outside the open end of the square, where in the 1930s Benito Mussolini opened up the broad boulevard, finally letting people

see the dome that had been hidden for centuries by the facade. Though I don't make a habit of thanking fascist dictators, in this case I'll make an exception: *"Grazie, Benito."*

The Tour Begins

• Ideally, you should head out to the obelisk at the center of the square and read this. But let me guess—it's 95 degrees outside, right? OK, find a shady spot under one of these stone sequoias. If the pigeons have left a clean spot, sit on it.

St. Peter's Square

St. Peter's Square, with its ring of columns, symbolizes the arms of the church welcoming everyone—believers and non-believers—with its motherly embrace. It was designed a century after Michelangelo by the Baroque architect Gian Lorenzo Bernini, who did much of the work that we'll see inside. Numbers first: 284 columns, 56 feet high, in stern Doric style. Topping them are Bernini's 140 favorite saints, each 10 feet tall. The "square" itself is actually elliptical, 660 by 500 feet (roughly the same dimensions as the Colosseum). Though large, it's designed like a saucer, a little higher around the edges, so that even when full of crowds (as it often is), it allows those on the periphery to see above the throngs.

The **obelisk** in the center is 90 feet of solid granite weighing more than 300 tons. It once stood about 100 yards from its current location, in the center of the circus course (to the left of where St. Peter's is today). Think for a second about how much history this monument has seen. Originally erected in Egypt more than 2,000 years ago, it witnessed the fall of the pharaohs to the Greeks and then to the Romans. Then the Emperor Caligula moved it to imperial Rome, where it stood impassively watching the slaughter of Christians at the racecourse and the torture of Protestants by the Inquisition (in the yellow-and-rust building just outside the square, to the left of the church). Today, it watches over the church, a reminder that each civilization builds on the previous ones. The puny cross on top reminds us that Christian culture has cast but a thin veneer over our pagan origins.

• Now venture out across the burning desert to the obelisk, which provides a narrow sliver of shade.

As you face the church, the gray building to the right at two o'clock, rising up behind Bernini's colonnade, is, at least officially, the **pope's abode.** The last window on the right

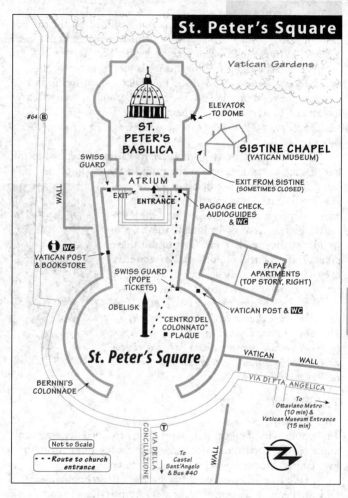

St. Peter's Square

Vatican Gardens

#64 (B)

ST. PETER'S BASILICA

ELEVATOR TO DOME

SISTINE CHAPEL
(VATICAN MUSEUM)

SWISS GUARD

ATRIUM

EXIT FROM SISTINE
(SOMETIMES CLOSED)

EXIT ENTRANCE

WALL

BAGGAGE CHECK,
AUDIOGUIDES
& WC

VATICAN POST
& BOOKSTORE

SWISS GUARD
(POPE TICKETS)

PAPAL APARTMENTS
(TOP STORY, RIGHT)

OBELISK

VATICAN POST & WC

"CENTRO DEL
COLONNATO"
PLAQUE

St. Peter's Square

VATICAN WALL

VIA DI PTA. ANGELICA

BERNINI'S COLONNADE

To
Ottaviano Metro
(10 min) &
Vatican Museum Entrance
(15 min)

Not to Scale

- - - Route to church
entrance

VIA DELLA CONCILIAZIONE

To
Castel
Sant'Angelo
& Bus #40

ROME

of the top floor is the papal bedroom; to the left of that window is the study window, where popes have often appeared to greet the masses. Pope Francis, however, seems to prefer a more modest residence that houses other cardinals, and has so far expressed no interest in moving into these grand apartments (upon first seeing them, he exclaimed, "You could fit 300 people in here!").

On more formal occasions (which you may have seen on TV), the pope appears from the church itself, on the small balcony above the central door.

The Sistine Chapel is just to the right of the facade—the small gray-brown building with the triangular roof, topped by an antenna. The tiny chimney—the pimple along the roofline midway up the left side—is where the famous smoke signals announce the election of each new pope (an extension is added on for the occasion). If the smoke is black, a two-thirds majority hasn't been reached. White smoke means a new pope has been selected.

Walk to the right, five pavement plaques from the obelisk, to one marked *Centro del Colonnato*. From here, all of Bernini's columns on the right side line up. The curved Baroque square still pays its respects to Renaissance mathematical symmetry.

• *Climb the gradually sloping pavement past crowd barriers and the security checkpoint.*

On the square are two entrances to Vatican City: one to the left of the facade, and one to the right in the crook of Bernini's "arm" (the same entrance that hands out pope-viewing tickets). Guarding this small but powerful country's border crossing are the mercenary guards from Switzerland. You have to wonder if they really know how to use those pikes. Their colorful uniforms are said to have been designed by Michelangelo, though he was not known for his sense of humor.

• *Continue up, passing the huge statues of St. Paul (with his two-edged sword) and St. Peter (with his bushy hair and keys). Along the way, you'll pass by the dress-code enforcers and a gaggle of ticked-off tourists in shorts. Enter the atrium (entrance hall) of the church.*

The Basilica
The Atrium

The atrium is itself bigger than most churches. The huge white columns on the portico date from the first church (fourth century). Five famous bronze doors lead into the church.

Made from the melted-down bronze of the original door of Old St. Peter's, the central door was the first Renaissance work in Rome (c. 1450). It's only opened on special occasions. The panels (from the top down) feature Jesus and Mary, Paul and Peter, and (at the bottom) how each was martyred: Paul decapitated, Peter crucified upside down.

The far-right entrance is the **Holy Door,** opened only during Holy Years. On Christmas Eve every 25 years, the pope knocks three times with a silver hammer and the door opens, welcoming pilgrims to pass through. After Pope John Paul II opened the door on Christmas Eve, 1999, he bricked it up again with a ceremonial

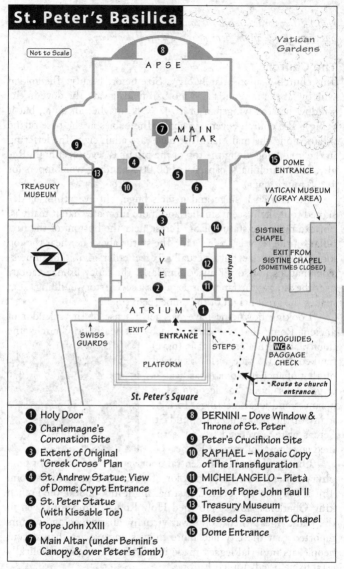

St. Peter's Basilica

Not to Scale

VATICAN GARDENS

APSE

❽

❾

❼ MAIN ALTAR

❹

❺

❻

⓭

⓾

TREASURY MUSEUM

❸ NAVE

❷

⓮

⓬

⓫

⓯ DOME ENTRANCE

VATICAN MUSEUM (GRAY AREA)

SISTINE CHAPEL

EXIT FROM SISTINE CHAPEL (SOMETIMES CLOSED)

Courtyard

ATRIUM ❶

SWISS GUARDS

EXIT **ENTRANCE** STEPS

PLATFORM

AUDIOGUIDES, **WC** & BAGGAGE CHECK

St. Peter's Square

- - - Route to church entrance

ROME

❶ Holy Door

❷ Charlemagne's Coronation Site

❸ Extent of Original "Greek Cross" Plan

❹ St. Andrew Statue; View of Dome; Crypt Entrance

❺ St. Peter Statue (with Kissable Toe)

❻ Pope John XXIII

❼ Main Altar (under Bernini's Canopy & over Peter's Tomb)

❽ BERNINI – Dove Window & Throne of St. Peter

❾ Peter's Crucifixion Site

⓾ RAPHAEL – Mosaic Copy of The Transfiguration

⓫ MICHELANGELO – Pietà

⓬ Tomb of Pope John Paul II

⓭ Treasury Museum

⓮ Blessed Sacrament Chapel

⓯ Dome Entrance

trowel a year later to wait another 24 years. (A plaque above the door fudges a bit for effect: It says that Pope "IOANNES PAULUS II" opened the door in the year "MM"—2000—and closed it in "MMI.") On the door itself, note the crucified Jesus and his shiny knees, polished by pious pilgrims who touch them for a blessing.

• *Now for one of Europe's great "wow" experiences. Enter the church. Gape for a while. But don't gape at Michelangelo's famous* Pietà *(on the*

*right). I'll cover it later in the tour. I'll wait for you at the round maroon
pavement stone on the floor near the central doorway.*

The Church

This church is appropriately huge. Size before beauty: The golden
window at the far end is two football fields away. The dove in the
window has the wingspan of a 747 (OK, maybe not quite, but it
is big). The church covers six acres. The babies at the base of the
pillars along the main hall (the nave) are adult-size. The lettering
in the gold band along the top of the pillars is seven feet high. Really. The church has a capacity of 60,000 standing worshippers (or
1,200 tour groups).

The church is huge and it feels huge, but everything is designed to make it seem smaller and more intimate than it really is.
For example, the statue of St. Teresa near the bottom of the first
pillar on the right is 15 feet tall. The statue above her near the top
looks the same size, but is actually six feet taller, giving the impression that it's not so far away. Similarly, the fancy bronze canopy
over the altar at the far end is as tall as a seven-story building. That
makes the great height of the dome seem smaller.

Looking down the nave, we get a sense of the splendor of
ancient Rome that was carried on by the Catholic Church. The

floor plan, with a central aisle (nave)
flanked by two side aisles, is based
on that of ancient Roman basilicas—
large halls built to accommodate
business and legal meetings. In fact,
many of the stones used to build St.
Peter's were scavenged from the ruined law courts of ancient Rome.

On the floor near the central doorway is a round slab of **porphyry stone** in the maroon color of ancient Roman officialdom.
This is the spot where, on Christmas night in A.D. 800, the French
king Charlemagne was crowned Holy Roman Emperor. Even in
the Dark Ages, when Rome was virtually abandoned and visitors
reported that the city had more thieves and wolves than decent
people, its imperial legacy made it a fitting place to symbolically
establish a briefly united Europe.

St. Peter's was very expensive to build and decorate. The popes
financed it by selling "indulgences," allowing the rich to buy forgiveness for their sins from the Church. This kind of corruption
inspired an obscure German monk named Martin Luther to rebel
and start the Protestant Reformation.

The ornate, Baroque-style interior decoration—a riot of marble, gold, stucco, mosaics, columns of stone, and pillars of light—
was part of the Church's "Counter" Reformation. Baroque art and

architecture served as cheery propaganda, impressing followers with the authority of the Church and giving them a glimpse of the heaven that awaited the faithful.

• *Now, walk straight up the center of the nave toward the altar.*

"Michelangelo's Church"—The Greek Cross

The plaques on the floor show where other, smaller churches of the world would end if they were placed inside St. Peter's: St. Paul's Cathedral in London (Londinense), Florence's Duomo, and so on.

You'll also walk over circular golden grates. Stop at the second one (at the third pillar from the entrance). Look back at the entrance and realize that if Michelangelo had had his way, this whole long section of the church wouldn't exist. The nave was extended after his death.

Michelangelo was 71 years old when the pope persuaded him to take over the church project and cap it with a dome. He agreed,

intending to put the dome over Donato Bramante's original "Greek Cross" floor plan, with four equal arms. In optimistic Renaissance times, this symmetrical arrangement symbolized perfection—the orderliness of the created world and the goodness of man (who was created in God's image). But Michelangelo was a Renaissance Man in Counter-Reformation times. The Church, struggling against Protestants and its own corruption, opted for a plan designed to impress the world with its grandeur—the Latin cross of the Crucifixion, with its nave extended to accommodate the grand

religious spectacles of the Baroque period.

• *Continue toward the altar, entering "Michelangelo's church." Park yourself in front of the statue of St. Andrew to the left of the altar, the guy holding an X-shaped cross. Like Andrew, gaze up into the dome, and also like him, gasp. (Never stifle a gasp.)*

Note: *The entrance to the crypt is usually down the stairs beside the statue of St. Andrew. Save the crypt for later, though, as it exits outside the basilica (see the end of this tour for more details).*

The Dome

The dome soars higher than a football field on end, 448 feet from the floor of the cathedral to the top of the lantern. It glows with light from its windows, the blue and gold mosaics creating a cool, solemn atmosphere. In this majestic vision

of heaven (not painted by Michelangelo), we see (above the windows) Jesus, Mary, and a ring of saints, rings of more angels above them, and, way up in the ozone, God the Father (a blur of blue and red, unless you have binoculars).

When Michelangelo died (1564), he'd completed only the drum of the dome—the circular base up as far as the windows—but the next architects were guided by his designs.

Listen to the hum of visitors echoing through St. Peter's and reflect on our place in the cosmos: half animal, half angel, stretched between heaven and earth, born to live only a short while, a bubble of foam on a great cresting wave of humanity.

• *But I digress.*

Peter's Remains

The base of the dome is ringed with a gold banner telling us in massive blue letters why this church is so important. According to Catholics, Peter was selected by Jesus to head the church. The banner in Latin quotes from the Bible where Jesus says to him, "You are Peter *(Tu es Petrus)* and upon this rock I will build my church, and to you I will give the keys of the kingdom of heaven" (Matthew 16:18). (Every quote from Jesus to Peter found in the Bible is written out in seven-foot-tall letters that continue around the entire church.)

Peter was the first bishop of Rome. His prestige and that of the city itself made this bishopric more illustrious than all others, and Peter's authority has supposedly passed in an unbroken chain to each succeeding bishop of Rome—that is, the 250-odd popes that followed.

Under the dome, under the bronze canopy, under the altar, some 23 feet under the marble floor, rest the bones of St. Peter, the "rock" upon which this particular church was built. You can't see the tomb, but go to the railing and look down into the small, lighted niche below the altar with a box containing bishops' shawls—a symbol of how Peter's authority spread to the other churches. Peter's tomb (not visible) is just below this box.

Are they really the bones of Jesus' apostle? According to a papal pronouncement: definitely maybe. The traditional site of his tomb was sealed when Old St. Peter's was built on it in A.D. 326, and it remained sealed until 1940, when it was opened for archaeological study. Bones were found, dated from the first century, of a robust man who died in old age. His body was wrapped in expensive cloth. A third-century tag artist had graffitied a wall near the tomb with "Peter is here," indicating that early visitors thought this was Peter's tomb. Does that mean it's really Peter? Who am I to disagree with the pope? Definitely maybe.

If you line up the cross on the altar with the dove in the window, you'll notice that the niche below the cross is just off-center compared with the rest of the church. Why? Because Michelangelo built the church around the traditional location of the tomb, not the actual location—about two feet away—discovered by modern archaeology.

Back in the nave sits a bronze **statue of Peter** under a canopy. This is one of a handful of pieces of art that were in the earlier church. In one hand he holds the keys, the symbol of the authority given him by Christ, while with the other hand he blesses us. He's wearing the toga of a Roman senator. It may be that the original statue was of a senator and that the bushy head and keys were added later to make it Peter. His big right toe has been worn smooth by the lips of pilgrims and foot-fetishists. Stand in line and kiss it, or, to avoid foot-and-mouth disease, touch your hand to your lips, then rub the toe. This is simply an act of reverence with no legend attached, though you can make one up if you like.

• *Circle to the right around the statue of Peter to find another stop that's popular among pilgrims: the lighted glass niche with the red-robed body of...*

ROME

Pope John XXIII

Pope John XXIII, whose papacy lasted from 1958 to 1963, is nicknamed "the good pope." He is best known for initiating the landmark Vatican II Council (1962-1965) that instituted major reforms, bringing the Church into the modern age. The Council allowed Mass to be conducted in the vernacular rather than in Latin. Lay people were invited to participate more in services, Church leadership underwent some healthy self-criticism, and a spirit of ecumenism flourished. Pope John was a populist, referring to people as "brothers and sisters"...a phrase popular today among popes. In 2000, during the beatification process (a stop on the way to sainthood), Church authorities checked his body, and it was surprisingly fresh. So they moved it upstairs, put it behind glass, and now old Catholics who remember him fondly enjoy another stop on their St. Peter's visit.

We'll visit the tomb of another beloved pope—John Paul II—near the end of this tour.

The Main Altar

The main altar beneath the dome and canopy (the white marble slab with cross and candlesticks) is used only when the pope himself says Mass. He sometimes conducts the Sunday morning service when he's in town.

The tiny altar would be lost in this enormous church if it weren't for Gian Lorenzo Bernini's seven-story bronze canopy (God's "four-poster bed"), which "extends" the altar upward and reduces the perceived distance between floor and ceiling. The corkscrew columns echo the marble ones that surrounded the altar/tomb in Old St. Peter's. Some of the bronze used here was taken and melted down from the ancient Pantheon. On the marble base of the columns are three bees on a shield, the symbol of the Barberini family, who commissioned the work and ordered the raid on the Pantheon. As the saying went, "What the barbarians didn't do, the Barberini did."

Starting from the column to the left of the altar, walk clockwise around the canopy. Notice the female faces on the marble bases, about eye level above the bees. Someone in the Barberini family was pregnant during the making of the canopy, so Bernini put the various stages of childbirth on the bases. Continue clockwise to the last base to see how it came out.

Bernini (1598-1680), the Michelangelo of the Baroque era, is the man most responsible for the interior decoration of the church. The altar area was his masterpiece, a "theater" for holy spectacles. Bernini did: 1) the bronze canopy; 2) the dove window in the apse, surrounded by bronze work and statues; 3) the massive statue of lance-bearing St. Longinus ("The hills are alive..."), which became the model for the other three statues in the niches around the main altar; 4) much of the marble floor decoration; and 5) the balconies above the four statues, incorporating some of the actual corkscrew columns from Old St. Peter's, said to have been looted by the Romans from the Temple of Herod (called "Solomon's Temple") in Jerusalem. Bernini, the father of Baroque, gave an impressive unity to an amazing variety of pillars, windows, statues, chapels, and aisles.

• *Approach the apse, the front area with the golden dove window.*

The Apse

Bernini's **dove window** shines above the smaller front altar used for everyday services. The Holy Spirit, in the form of a six-foot-high dove, pours sunlight onto the faithful through the alabaster windows, turning into artificial rays of gold and reflecting off swirling gold clouds, angels, and winged babies. During a service, real sunlight passes through real clouds of incense, mingling with Bernini's sculpture. This is the epitome of Baroque—an ornate, mixed-media work designed to overwhelm the viewer.

Beneath the dove is the centerpiece of this structure, the so-called Throne of St. Peter, an oak chair built in medieval times for a king. Subsequently, it was encrusted with tradition and encased in bronze by Bernini as a symbol of papal authority. Statues of four early Church Fathers support the chair, a symbol of how bishops should support the pope in troubled times—times like the Counter-Reformation.

Remember that St. Peter's is a church, not a museum. In the apse, Mass is said daily for pilgrims, tourists, and Roman citizens alike (for Mass times, see "Church Services" on page 560). Wooden confessional booths are available in the north transept (to the right of the main altar) for Catholics to tell their sins to a listening ear and receive forgiveness and peace of mind (daily, usually mornings and late afternoons—see website). The faithful renew their faith, and the faithless gain inspiration. Look at the light streaming through the windows, turn and gaze up into the dome, and quietly contemplate your deity (or lack thereof).

• *To the left of the main altar is the south transept. It may be roped off for worship, but anyone can step past the guard if you're there "for prayer." At the far end, left side, find the dark "painting" of St. Peter crucified upside down.*

ROME

South Transept—Peter's Crucifixion Site

This marks the exact spot (according to tradition) where Peter was killed 1,900 years ago. Peter had come to the world's greatest city to preach Jesus' message of love to the pagan, often hostile, Romans. During the reign of Emperor Nero, he was arrested and brought to Nero's Circus so all of Rome could witness his execution. When the authorities told Peter he was to be crucified just like his Lord, Peter said essentially, "I'm not worthy" and insisted they nail him on the cross upside down.

The Romans were actually quite tolerant of other religions, but they required their conquered peoples to worship the Roman emperor as a god. For most religions, this was no problem, but monotheistic Christians refused to worship the emperor even when they were burned alive, crucified, or thrown to the lions. Their bravery, optimism in suffering, and message of love struck a chord among slaves and members of the lower classes. The religion started by a poor carpenter grew, despite occasional pogroms (persecution of minorities) by fanatical emperors. In three short centuries, Christianity went from a small Jewish sect in Jerusalem to the official religion of the world's greatest empire.

This and all the other "paintings" in the church are actually mosaic copies made from thousands of colored chips the size of your little fingernail. Smoke and humidity would damage real paintings. Around the corner on the right (heading back toward the central nave), pause at the copy of Raphael's huge "painting" (mosaic) of *The Transfiguration*, especially if you won't be seeing the original in the Vatican Museum.

• *Back near the entrance of the church, in the far corner, behind bulletproof glass, is the sculpture everyone has come to see, the...*

Pietà

Michelangelo was 24 years old when he completed this *pietà* (peeay-TAH) of Mary with the body of Christ taken from the cross. It was Michelangelo's first major commission (by the French ambassador to the Vatican), done for Holy Year 1500.

Pietà means "pity." Michelangelo, with his total mastery of the real world, captures the sadness of the moment. Mary cradles her crucified son in her lap. Christ's lifeless right arm drooping down lets us know how heavy this corpse is. His smooth skin is accented by the rough folds of Mary's robe. Mary tilts her head down, looking at her dead son with sad tenderness. Her left hand turns upward, asking, "How could they do this to you?"

Michelangelo didn't think of sculpting as creating a figure, but as simply freeing the God-made figure from the prison of marble around it. He'd attack a project like this with an inspired passion, chipping away to find what God had placed inside.

The bunched-up shoulder and rigor-mortis legs show that Michelangelo learned well from his studies of cadavers. But realistic as this work is, its true power lies in the subtle "unreal" features. Life-size Christ looks childlike compared with larger-than-life Mary. Unnoticed at first, this accentuates the subconscious impression of Mary enfolding Jesus in her maternal love. Mary—the mother of a 33-year-old man—looks like a teenager, emphasizing how Mary was the eternally youthful "handmaiden" of the Lord, always serving him, even at this moment of supreme sacrifice. She accepts God's will, even if it means giving up her son.

The statue is a solid pyramid of maternal tenderness. Yet within this, Christ's body tilts diagonally down to the right and Mary's hem flows with it. Subconsciously, we feel the weight of this dead God sliding from her lap to the ground.

At 11:30 on May 23, 1972, a madman with a hammer entered St. Peter's and began hacking away at the *Pietà*. The damage was repaired, but that's why there's now a shield of bulletproof glass in front of the sculpture.

This is Michelangelo's only signed work. The story goes that he overheard some pilgrims praising his finished *Pietà*, but attributing it to a second-rate sculptor from a lesser city. He was so enraged that he grabbed his chisel and chipped "Michelangelo Buonarroti of Florence did this" in the ribbon running down Mary's chest.

On your right (covered in gray concrete with a gold cross) is the inside of the Holy Door. It won't be opened until Christmas Eve, 2024, the dawn of the next Jubilee Year. If there's a prayer inside you, ask that St. Peter's will no longer need security checks or bulletproof glass when this door is next opened.

• *In the chapel to the left is the...*

Tomb of Pope John Paul II

Originally located in the crypt beneath the church, the tomb of John Paul II was moved to the Chapel of San Sebastian in 2011, after he was beatified by Pope Benedict XVI. Beatification, a step on the road to sainthood, meant that John Paul was considered "blessed" *(beatus)* and had miracles attributed to him. In 2013, the Vatican announced that John Paul would be elevated to the next level—sainthood.

John Paul II (1920-2005) was one of the most beloved popes of recent times. During his papacy (1978-2005), he was the highly visible face of the Catholic Church as it labored to stay relevant in an increasingly secular world. The first non-Italian pope in four centuries, he traveled widely. He was the first pope to visit a mosque and a synagogue. He oversaw the fall of communism in his native Poland. He survived an assassination attempt, and

he publicly endured his slow decline from Parkinson's disease with great stoicism.

When John Paul II died in 2005, hundreds of thousands lined up outside the church, waiting up to 24 hours to pay their respects. At his funeral in St. Peter's Square, the crowd began chanting *"Santo subito, santo subito!"* insisting he be made a saint *(santo)* right now *(subito)*. By Vatican standards, the honorific process is moving at light speed.

The tomb has no monument—just a simple stone slab with the inscription *Beatus Ioannes Paulus PP. II (1920-2005)*. John Paul II lies beneath a painting of the steadfast St. Sebastian—the martyr who calmly suffered the slings and arrows of outrageous Romans. Sebastian was John Paul's favorite saint. There's also a plaque in the floor on the opposite side of the church honoring the man. Of 250-plus popes, two have been given the title "Great." That elite group may soon grow by 50 percent, as there's talk of calling him "John Paul the Great."

Up to the Dome (Cupola)

A good way to finish a visit to St. Peter's is to go up to the dome

for the best view of Rome anywhere. The entrance to the dome is along the right side of the church, but the line begins to form out front, at the church's right door (as you face the church).

There are two levels: the rooftop of the church and the very top of the dome. Climb (for €5) or take an elevator (€7) to the first level, on the church roof just above the facade. From the roof, you have a commanding view of St. Peter's Square, the statues on the colonnade, Rome across the Tiber in front of you, and the dome itself—almost terrifying in its nearness—looming behind you. (This view from the roof may only be accessible after you've descended from the dome—the route changes.)

From here, you can also go inside to the gallery ringing the interior of the dome, where you can look down inside the church. Notice the dusty top of Bernini's seven-story-tall canopy far below. Study the mosaics up close—and those huge letters! It's worth the elevator ride for this view alone.

From this level, if you're energetic, continue all the way up to the top of the dome. The staircase actually winds between the outer shell and the inner one. It's a sweaty, crowded, claustrophobic 15-minute, 323-step climb, but worth it. The view from the summit is great, the fresh air even better. Admire the arms of Bernini's colonnade encircling St. Peter's Square. Find the big, white Victor Emmanuel Monument, with the two statues on top; and the Pantheon, with its large, light, shallow dome. The large rectangular building to the

left of the obelisk is the Vatican Museum, stuffed with art. Survey the Vatican grounds, with its mini-train system and lush gardens. Look down into the square at the tiny pilgrims buzzing like electrons around the nucleus of Catholicism.

Vatican Museum Tour

The four miles of displays in the Vatican Museum (Musei Vaticani)—from ancient statues to Christian frescoes to modern paintings—culminate in the Raphael Rooms and Michelangelo's glorious Sistine Chapel. This is one of Europe's top three or four houses of art. It can be exhausting, so plan your visit carefully, focusing on a few themes. Allow two hours for a quick visit, three or four hours for enough time to enjoy it.

Orientation

Cost: €16, €4 online reservation fee, free on the last Sun of each month (when it's very crowded).

Hours: Mon-Sat 9:00-18:00, last entry at 16:00 (though the official closing time is 18:00, the staff starts ushering you out at 17:30). Closed Sun, except last Sun of the month, when it's open 9:00-14:00, last entry at 12:30. May be open Fri nights May-July and Sept-Oct 19:00-23:00 (last entry at 21:30) by online reservation only—check the website; note that during evening visits, parts of the museum—including the Pinacoteca—are often closed.

Individual rooms may close at odd hours, especially in the afternoon. The rooms described here are usually open.

Reservations: Bypass the long ticket lines by reserving an entry time online at http://mv.vatican.va. It costs €20 (€16 ticket plus €4 booking fee, pay with credit card). It's easy. You choose your day and time, they email you a confirmation immediately, and you print out the voucher. At the Vatican Museum, bypass the ticket-buying line and queue up at the "Entrance with Reservations" line (to the right). Show your voucher to the guard and go in. Once inside the museum, present your voucher (and ID) at a ticket window *(cassa)*, either in the lobby or upstairs, and they'll issue your ticket.

When to Go: The museum is generally hot and crowded, with shoulder-to-shoulder sightseeing through much of it. There can be waits of up to two hours to buy tickets (figure about a 10-minute wait for every 100 yards in line). The best (or least-worst) time to visit is a weekday late-afternoon. The worst days are Saturdays, the last Sunday of the month (when it's free), Mondays, rainy days, and any day before or after a holiday closure. Mornings are most crowded.

More Line-Beating Tips: If you've booked a **guided tour** (see next page), you can show the guard your voucher and go right in.

You can often buy **same-day, skip-the-line tickets** (for the same €20 online price) through the TI in St. Peter's Square (to the left, as you face the basilica). Also, the "Roma Cristiana" tour company sells same-day tickets from their kiosk at St. Peter's Square (for a pricey €26.50, entrances almost hourly, tel. 06-6980-6380, www.operaromanapellegrinaggi.org). If their kiosk is closed, try the nearby storefront labeled *Opera Romana Pellegrini,* just in front of the square, which also sometimes sells these tickets.

If you don't have a reservation, **try arriving after 14:00,** when crowds subside somewhat. Another good time is during the papal audience, on Wednesday at 10:30, when many tourists are at St. Peter's.

Make sure you get in the right line. Generally, individuals without tickets line up against the Vatican City wall (to the left of the entrance as you face it), and reservation holders (both individuals and groups) enter on the right.

Dress Code: Modest dress is required (no shorts, above-knee skirts, or bare shoulders). This dress code is strictly enforced here, at St. Peter's Basilica, and throughout Vatican City.

Getting There: If you're taking a regional train from Civitavecchia, get off at San Pietro Station (see page 497). If you're coming from Termini or elsewhere in town, you can catch the Metro to the Ottaviano stop, a 10-minute walk from the entrance. Bus #492 heads from the city center past Piazza Risorgimento and the Vatican walls, and stops on Via Leone IV, just downhill from the entrance. Bus #64 stops on the other side of St. Peter's Square, a 15- to 20-minute walk (facing the church from the obelisk, take a right through the colonnade and follow the Vatican Wall). Taxis are reasonable (hop in and say, "moo-ZAY-ee vah-tee-KAH-nee").

Information: At http://mv.vatican.va, you can reserve an entry time, sign up for a tour, get general info, and see which days the museum is closed. You can virtually tour the Sistine Chapel ceiling at www.vatican.va (click on "Basilicas and Papal Chapels"). Tel. 06-6988-3860 or 06-6988-1662.

As you enter the main lobby of the museum, an info desk is to your left, and TV screens list which rooms are open or closed. Bookstores are scattered throughout the museum, and many exhibits have English explanations.

Tours: A €7 **audioguide** is available at the top of the spiral ramp/escalator (ID required). If you rent an audioguide, you lose the option of taking the shortcut from the Sistine Chapel to St. Peter's (described later, under "Museum Strategies"), since audioguides must be returned to the museum entrance/exit.

You can download the Sistine Chapel portion of this tour as a free Rick Steves **audio tour** (see page 50).

The Vatican offers **English tours** that are easy to book online (€32, includes admission, http://mv.vatican.va). As with individual ticket reservations, present your confirmation voucher to a guard to the right of the entrance; then, once inside, go to the Guided Tours desk (in the lobby, up a few stairs).

For a list of **private tour** companies and guides, see page 510.

Length of This Tour: Until you expire, the museum closes, or 2.5 hours, whichever comes first. If you're short on time, see the octagonal courtyard *(Laocoön)*, then follow the crowd flow directly to the Sistine Chapel, sightseeing along the way; skip the Etruscan Wing and the Pinacoteca. From the Sistine Chapel, head straight to St. Peter's via the shortcut, if open (see "Museum Strategies," below).

Security and Baggage Check: To enter the museum, you pass through a metal detector (no pocket knives allowed). The baggage check (to the right after security) takes only bigger bags, not day bags.

Services: The post office, with stamps that make collectors drool, is upstairs. WCs are mainly at the entrance/exit, plus a few scattered within the collection.

Museum Strategies: The museum has two exits, and you'll want to decide which you'll take before you enter. The **main exit** is right near the entrance. Use this one if you want to rent an audioguide (which you must return at the entrance).

The other exit is a handy (but sometimes closed) **shortcut** that leads from the Sistine Chapel directly to St. Peter's Basilica (spilling out alongside the church; see map on next page). This route saves you a 30-minute walk (15 minutes back to the Vatican Museum entry/exit, then 15 minutes to St. Peter's) and lets you avoid the often-long security line at the basilica's main entrance. If you take this route, you'll have to forgo an audioguide and skip the Pinacoteca (or tour it earlier). Officially, this exit is for Vatican guides and their groups only. However, it's often open to anyone (depending on how crowded the chapel is and how the guards feel). It's worth a shot (try blending in with a group that's leaving), but be prepared for the possibility that you won't get through.

Photography: No photos allowed in the Sistine Chapel, but photos without flash are permitted elsewhere.

Cuisine Art: A self-service cafeteria is inside, near the Pinacoteca. Smaller cafés are in the outdoor Cortile della Pigna and near the Sistine Chapel.

Starring: World history, a pope's palace, Michelangelo, Raphael, the Greek masters, and their Roman copyists.

The Tour Begins

Start, as civilization did, in **Egypt and Mesopotamia.** Decorating the museum's courtyard are some of the best **Greek and Roman statues** in captivity, including the *Laocoön* group (first century B.C., Hellenistic) and the *Apollo Belvedere* (a second-century Roman copy of a Greek original).

The centerpiece of the next hall is the *Belvedere Torso* (just a 2,000-year-old torso, but one that had a great impact on the art of Michelangelo). Finishing off the classical statuary are two fine fourth-century porphyry sarcophagi. These royal purple tombs were made (though not used) for the Roman Emperor Constantine's mother and daughter. They were Christians—and therefore outlaws—until Constantine made Christianity legal in A.D. 312, and they became saints. Both sarcophagi were quarried and worked in Egypt. The technique for working this extremely hard stone (a special tempering of metal was required) was lost after this, and porphyry marble was not chiseled again until Renaissance times in Florence.

After long halls of tapestries, old maps, broken penises, and fig leaves, you'll come to what most people are looking for: the Raphael Rooms and Michelangelo's Sistine Chapel.

Raphael Rooms

The highlight of these rooms, frescoed by Raphael and his assistants, is the restored *School of Athens*. It is remarkable for its blatant pre-Christian classical orientation, especially since it originally wallpapered the apartments of Pope Julius II. Raphael honors the great pre-Christian thinkers—Aristotle, Plato, and company—who are portrayed as the leading artists of Raphael's day. There's Leonardo da Vinci, whom Raphael worshipped, in the role of Plato. Michelangelo broods in the foreground, added later. When Raphael snuck a peek at the Sistine Chapel, he decided that his arch-competitor was so good that he had to put their personal differences aside and include him in this tribute to the artists of his generation. Today's St. Peter's was under construction as Raphael was working. In the *School of Athens*, he gives us a sneak preview of the unfinished church.

• Next stop: the Sistine Chapel, just a five-minute walk away. Exit the final Raphael Room through a passageway, bear right, and go down the stairs. At the foot of the stairs you'll find several quiet rooms with benches. Have a seat and read ahead before entering the hectic Sistine Chapel.

The Sistine Chapel

The Sistine Chapel contains Michelangelo's ceiling and his huge *Last Judgment*. The Sistine is the personal chapel of the pope and the place where new popes are elected. (The small, old-fashioned stove that burns pope-vote ballots—which sends out puffs of telltale smoke—is placed near today's shortcut exit.)

When Pope Julius II asked Michelangelo to take on this important project, he said, "No, grazie." Michelangelo insisted he was a sculptor, not a painter. The Sistine ceiling was a vast undertaking, and he didn't want to do a half-vast job. But the pope pleaded, bribed, and threatened until

Vatican Museum Overview

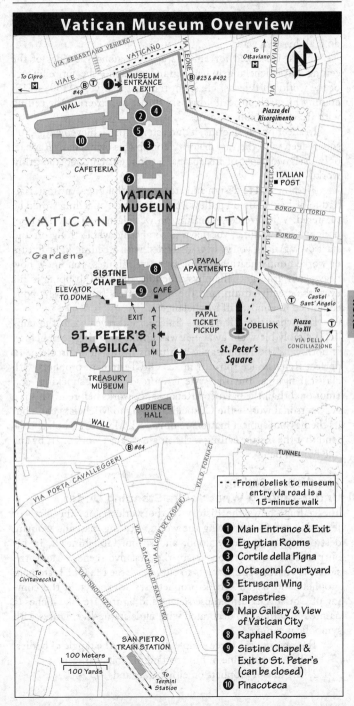

- - - From obelisk to museum entry via road is a 15-minute walk

❶ Main Entrance & Exit
❷ Egyptian Rooms
❸ Cortile della Pigna
❹ Octagonal Courtyard
❺ Etruscan Wing
❻ Tapestries
❼ Map Gallery & View of Vatican City
❽ Raphael Rooms
❾ Sistine Chapel & Exit to St. Peter's (can be closed)
❿ Pinacoteca

ROME

Michelangelo finally consented, on the condition that he be able to do it all his own way.

Julius had asked for only 12 apostles along the sides of the ceiling, but Michelangelo had a grander vision—the entire history of the world until Jesus. He spent the next four years (1508-1512) craning his neck on scaffolding six stories up, covering the ceiling with frescoes of biblical scenes.

In sheer physical terms, it's an astonishing achievement: 5,900 square feet, with the vast majority done by his own hand. (Raphael only designed most of his rooms, letting assistants do the grunt work.)

First, he had to design and erect the scaffolding. Any materials had to be hauled up on pulleys. Then, a section of ceiling would be plastered. With fresco—painting on wet plaster—if you don't get it right the first time, you have to scrape the whole thing off and start over. And if you've ever struggled with a ceiling light fixture or worked underneath a car for even five minutes, you know how heavy your arms get. The physical effort, the paint dripping in his eyes, the creative drain, and the mental stress from a pushy pope combined to almost kill Michelangelo.

But when the ceiling was finished and revealed to the public, it simply blew 'em away—it was unlike anything seen before. It both caps the Renaissance and turns it in a new direction. In perfect Renaissance spirit, it mixes Old Testament prophets with classical figures. But the style is more dramatic, shocking, and emotional than the balanced Renaissance works before it. This is a very personal work—the Gospel according to Michelangelo—but its themes and subject matter are universal. Many art scholars contend that the Sistine ceiling is the single greatest work of art by any one human being.

The Sistine Ceiling: Understanding What You're Standing Under

The ceiling shows the history of the world before the birth of Jesus. We see God creating the world, creating man and woman, destroying the earth by flood, and so on. God himself, in his purple robe, actually appears in the first five scenes. Along the sides (where the ceiling starts to curve), we see the Old Testament prophets and pagan Greek prophetesses who foretold the coming of Christ. Dividing these scenes and figures are fake niches (a painted 3-D illusion) decorated with nude statue-like figures with symbolic meaning.

The key is to see three simple divisions in the tangle of bodies:
1. The central spine of nine rectangular biblical scenes;
2. The line of prophets on either side; and

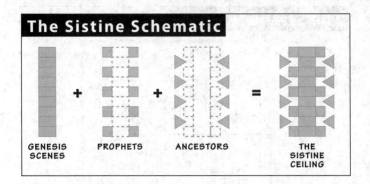

The Sistine Schematic

GENESIS SCENES + PROPHETS + ANCESTORS = THE SISTINE CEILING

3. The triangles between the prophets showing the ancestors of Christ.

• *Ready? Within the chapel, grab a seat along the side (when there's room—people come and go). Face the altar with the big* Last Judgment *on the wall (more on that later). Now look up to the ceiling and find the central panel of...*

The Creation of Adam

God and man take center stage in this Renaissance version of creation. Adam, newly formed in the image of God, lounges dreamily in perfect naked innocence. God, with his entourage, swoops in with a swirl of activity (which—with a little imagination—looks like a cross-section of a human brain...quite a strong humanist statement). Their reaching hands are the center of this work. Adam's is limp and passive; God's is strong and forceful, his finger twitching upward with energy. Here is the very moment of creation, as God passes the spark of life to man, the crowning work of his creation.

This is the spirit of the Renaissance. God is not a terrifying giant reaching down to puny and helpless man from way on high. Here they are on an equal plane, divided only by the diagonal bit of sky. God's billowing robe and the patch of green upon which Adam is lying balance each other. They are like two pieces of a jigsaw puzzle, or two long-separated continents, or like the yin and yang symbols finally coming together—uniting, complementing each other, creating wholeness. God and man work together in the divine process of creation.

• *This celebration of man permeates the ceiling. Notice the Adonises-come-to-life on the pedestals that divide the central panels. And then came woman.*

The Garden of Eden

In one panel, we see two scenes from the Garden of Eden: *Temptation* and *Expulsion*. On the left is the leafy garden of paradise where Adam and Eve lie around blissfully. But the devil comes along—a

ROME

The Sistine Ceiling

WALL

DAVID & GOLIATH

ZACHA-RIAH

JUDITH & HOLOFERNES

JOEL

DRUNKENNESS OF NOAH

DELPHICA

ZORO-BABEL

THE FLOOD

JOSIAH

ERYTH-RAEA

SACRIFICE OF NOAH

ISAIAH

OZIAS

TEMPTATION AND EXPULSION

EZEKIAS

EZEKIEL

CREATION OF EVE

CUMAEA

ROBOAM

CREATION OF ADAM

ASA

PERSICA

SEPARATION OF LAND FROM WATER

DANIEL

SALMON

CREATION OF SUN, MOON & PLANETS

JESSE

See photo on facing page

JEREMIAH

SEPARATION OF LIGHT FROM DARKNESS

LIBICA

W A L L

W A L L

DEATH OF HAMAN

JONAH

BRAZEN SERPENT

ROME

LAST JUDGMENT WALL

ENTRY DOOR →
FROM RAPHAEL ROOMS &
MODERN RELIGIOUS ART...

☆ TO USE THIS DIAGRAM:
FACE THE LAST JUDGMENT &
HOLD THE BOOK UP TO THE CEILING.

serpent with a woman's torso—and winds around the forbidden Tree of Knowledge. The temptation to gain new knowledge is too great for these Renaissance people. They eat the forbidden fruit.

At right, a sword-wielding angel drives them from Paradise into the barren plains. They're grieving, but they're far from helpless. Adam's body is thick and sturdy, and we know they'll survive in the cruel world. Adam firmly gestures to the angel, like he's saying, "All right, already! We're going!"

The Nine Scenes from Genesis

Take some time with these central scenes to understand the story that the ceiling tells. They run in sequence, starting at the front:

1. God, in purple, divides the light from darkness.
2. God creates the sun (burning orange) and the moon (pale white, to the right). Oops, I guess there's another moon.
3. God bursts toward us to separate the land and water.
4. God creates Adam.
5. God creates Eve, who dives into existence out of Adam's side.
6. Adam and Eve are tempted, then expelled, from the Garden of Eden.
7. Noah kills a ram and stokes the altar fires to make a sacrifice to God.
8. The great flood, sent by God, destroys the wicked, who desperately head for higher ground. In the distance, the Ark carries Noah's family to safety.
9. Noah's sons see their drunken father. (Perhaps Michelangelo chose to end his work with this scene as a reminder that even the best of men are fallible.)

Prophets

You'll notice that the figures at the far end of the chapel are a bit smaller than those over *The Last Judgment*.

Michelangelo started at the far end, with the Noah scenes. By 1510, he'd finished the first half of the ceiling. When they took the scaffolding down and could finally see what he'd been working on for two years, everyone was awestruck—except Michelangelo. As powerful as his figures are, from the floor they didn't look dramatic enough for Michelangelo. For the other half, he pulled out all the stops.

Compare the Noah scenes (far end), with their many small figures, to the huge images of God at the other end. Similarly,

Isaiah (near the lattice screen, marked "Esaias") is stately and balanced, while Jeremiah ("Hieremias," in the corner by *The Last Judgment*) is a dark, brooding figure. This prophet who witnessed the destruction of Israel slumps his chin in his hand and ponders the fate of his people.

The Last Judgment

When Michelangelo returned to paint the altar wall 23 years later (1535), the mood of Europe—and of the artist—was completely different. The Protestant Reformation had forced the Catholic Church to clamp down on free thought, and religious wars raged. Rome had recently been pillaged by roving bands of mercenaries. The Renaissance spirit of optimism was fading. Michelangelo himself had begun to question the innate goodness of mankind.

It's Judgment Day, and Christ—the powerful figure in the center, raising his arm to spank the wicked—has come to find out

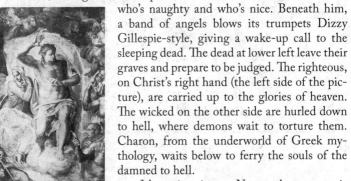

who's naughty and who's nice. Beneath him, a band of angels blows its trumpets Dizzy Gillespie-style, giving a wake-up call to the sleeping dead. The dead at lower left leave their graves and prepare to be judged. The righteous, on Christ's right hand (the left side of the picture), are carried up to the glories of heaven. The wicked on the other side are hurled down to hell, where demons wait to torture them. Charon, from the underworld of Greek mythology, waits below to ferry the souls of the damned to hell.

It's a grim picture. No one, but no one, is smiling. Even many of the righteous being resurrected (lower left) are either skeletons or cadavers with ghastly skin. The angels have to play tug-of-war with subterranean monsters to drag them from their graves.

Over in hell, the wicked are tortured by gleeful demons. One of the damned (to the right of the trumpeting angels) has an utterly lost expression, as if saying, "Why did I cheat on my wife?!" Two demons grab him around the ankles to pull him down to the bowels of hell, condemned to an eternity of constipation.

But it's the terrifying figure of Christ that dominates this scene. He raises his arm to smite the wicked, sending a ripple of fear through everyone. Even the saints around him—even Mary beneath his arm (whose interceding days are clearly over)—shrink back in terror from this uncharacteristic outburst from loving Jesus. His expression is completely closed, and he turns his head, refusing to even listen to the whining alibis of the damned.

When *The Last Judgment* was unveiled to the public in 1541, it

The Last Judgment

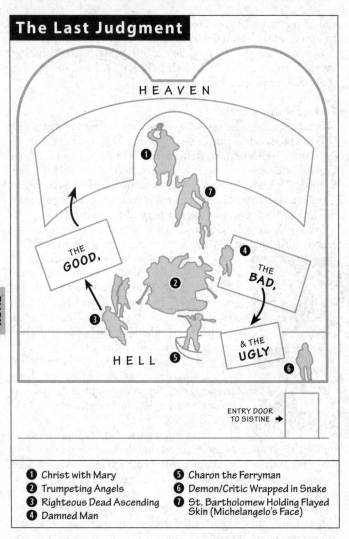

HEAVEN

THE GOOD,

THE BAD,

& THE UGLY

HELL

ENTRY DOOR
TO SISTINE →

① Christ with Mary
② Trumpeting Angels
③ Righteous Dead Ascending
④ Damned Man
⑤ Charon the Ferryman
⑥ Demon/Critic Wrapped in Snake
⑦ St. Bartholomew Holding Flayed Skin (Michelangelo's Face)

ROME

caused a sensation. The pope is said to have dropped to his knees and cried, "Lord, charge me not with my sins when thou shalt come on the Day of Judgment."

And it changed the course of art. The complex composition, with more than 300 figures swirling around the figure of Christ, went far beyond traditional Renaissance balance. The twisted figures shown from every imaginable angle challenged other painters to try and top this master of 3-D illusion. And the sheer terror and drama of the scene was a striking contrast to the placid optimism of, say, Raphael's *School of Athens*. Michelangelo had Baroque-en all the rules of the Renaissance, signaling a new era of art.

With the Renaissance fading, the fleshy figures in *The Last Judgment* aroused murmurs of discontent from Church authorities. Michelangelo rebelled by painting his chief critic into the scene—in hell. He's the jackassed demon in the bottom-right corner, wrapped in a snake. Look at how Michelangelo covered his privates. Sweet revenge.

The Last Judgment marks the end of Renaissance optimism epitomized in *The Creation of Adam,* with its innocence and exaltation of man.

Michelangelo himself must have wondered how he would be judged—had he used his God-given talents wisely? Look at St. Bartholomew, the bald, bearded guy at Christ's left foot (our right). In the flayed skin he's holding is a barely recognizable face—the twisted self-portrait of a self-questioning Michelangelo.

• *There are two exits from the Sistine Chapel.*

1. To return to the main entrance/ exit, leave the Sistine through the side door next to the screen. You'll soon find yourself facing the **Long March back to the museum's entrance** *(about 15 minutes away) and the Pinacoteca (the Vatican's small but fine collection of paintings, with Raphael's* Transfiguration, *Leonardo's unfinished St. Jerome, and Caravaggio's* Deposition*). Along this corridor (located one floor below the long corridor that you walked to get here), you'll see some of the wealth amassed by the popes, mostly gifts from royalty. Find your hometown on the 1529 map of the world—look in the land labeled "Terra Incognita." The elaborately decorated library that branches off to the right contains rare manuscripts. The corridor eventually spills back outside.*

2. To take the **shortcut directly to St. Peter's Basilica** *(see "Museum Strategies," page 579), you'll exit at the far-right corner of the Sistine Chapel (with your back to the altar). This route saves you a 30-minute walk and the wait in the St. Peter's security line, but you can't get back to the main entrance/exit or the Pinacoteca. Though this corner door is likely labeled "Exit for private tour groups only," you can probably just slide through with the crowds (or protest that your group has left you behind). If this exit is closed (which can happen without notice), hang out in the Sistine Chapel for a few more minutes—it'll likely reopen shortly.*

ROME

Shopping in Rome

Traditionally, shops are open from 9:00 to 13:00 and from 15:30 or 16:30 to 19:00 or 19:30. They're often closed on Sundays, summer Saturday afternoons, and winter Monday mornings. But in the city center, you'll find that many are now staying open through lunch (generally 10:00-19:00).

For information on VAT refunds and customs regulations, see page 135.

Where to Shop

Department Stores

To conveniently peruse clothes, bags, shoes, and perfume at several major Italian chain stores, wander the shopping complex under Termini train station (most stores open daily 8:00-22:00).

Large department stores offer relatively painless one-stop shopping. A good upscale department store is **La Rinascente** (like Nordstrom or Macy's). Its main branch is on Piazza Fiume, and a smaller store is on Via del Corso in the **Galleria Alberto Sordi,** an elegant 19th-century "mall" (across from Piazza Colonna). **UPIM** is a popular mid-range department store (many branches, including inside Termini train station, Via Nazionale 111, Piazza Santa Maria Maggiore, and Via del Tritone 172). **Oviesse,** a cheap clothing outlet, is near the Vatican Museum (on the corner of Via Candia and Via Mocenigo, Metro: Cipro).

Affordable Shopping

An affordable shopping area is all along **Via del Corso,** with prices increasing as you head toward Piazza di Spagna. **Via Nazionale** also features a range of reasonably priced shops, especially for clothes and shoes. Near the bottom of Via Nazionale, **Via Boschetto** and **Via dei Serpenti** are more unique, with a mix of clothing shops and designer bric-a-brac. The back lanes of **Trastevere** have a similar feel. **Via Cola di Rienzo**, near the Vatican, is good for mid-range clothes. Cheapskates scrounge through the junky but dirt-cheap shops in the gritty area around **Piazza Vittorio.**

Boutique Shopping

For top fashion, stroll the streets around the Spanish Steps, including **Via Condotti, Via Borgognona** (for the big-name shops), and **Via del Babuino** (more big names and a few galleries). For antiques and vintage items, wander **Via dei Coronari** (between Piazza Navona and the bend in the river), **Via Giulia** (between Campo de' Fiori and the river), **Via dei Banchi Vecchi** (parallel to Via Giulia), and the classier **Via Margutta**, with art galleries too (hidden parallel to Via del Babuino and running from the Spanish Steps to Piazza del Popolo). For funkier, unique finds, try **Via Giubbonari**—it's packed with artsy little boutiques—and other streets near Campo de' Fiori.

Flea Markets

For antiques and fleas, the granddaddy of markets is the **Porta Portese** *mercato delle pulci* (flea market). This Sunday-morning market

is long and spindly, running between the actual Porta Portese (a gate in the old town wall) and the Trastevere train station. While the shopping gets old (and the vendor food will make you sick), the people-watching is endlessly entertaining (6:30-13:00 Sun only, on Via Portuense and Via Ippolito Nievo; to get to the market, catch bus #75 from Termini train station or tram #8 from Piazza Venezia, get off the bus or tram on Viale di Trastevere, and walk toward the river—and the noise).

At the **Via Sannio** market, you'll find new and used clothing and leather goods, some handicrafts, and random items that were probably stolen. You won't find antiques (Mon-Sat 9:00-13:30, closed Sun, behind Coin department store, just outside the walls of San Giovanni in Laterano, Metro: San Giovanni).

Open-Air Produce Markets

Rome's outdoor markets provide a fun and colorful dimension of the city that even the most avid museumgoer should not miss. Wander through the easygoing neighborhood produce markets that clog certain streets and squares every morning (7:00-13:30) except Sunday. Consider the huge **Mercato Trionfale** (three blocks north of Vatican Museum at Via Andrea Doria). Another great food market is the **Mercato Esquilino** (Via Turati near Piazza Vittorio). Smaller but equally charming slices of everyday Roman life are at markets on these streets and squares: **Piazza delle Coppelle** (near the Pantheon), **Via Balbo** (near Termini train station), and **Via della Pace** (near Piazza Navona). The covered **Mercato di Testaccio** sells produce and housewares and is a hit with photographers and people-watchers (Metro: Piramide). And **Campo de' Fiori,** despite having become quite touristy, is still a fun scene.

ROME

Nightlife in Rome

Many cruises begin or end at Rome's port of Civitavecchia. If you are staying in Rome, try to experience it after dark. Romans get dressed up and eat out in casual surroundings for their evening entertainment. For most visitors, the best after-dark activity is simply to grab a gelato and stroll the medieval lanes that connect the romantic, floodlit squares and fountains. Head for Piazza Navona, the Pantheon, Campo de' Fiori, Trevi Fountain, the Spanish Steps, Via del Corso, Trastevere (around the Santa Maria in Trastevere Church), or Monte Testaccio.

Performances

Get a copy of the entertainment guide *Evento* (free at TIs and many hotels). Look at the current listings of concerts, operas, dance, and films. Posters around town also advertise upcoming events. For the most up-to-date events calendar, check these English-language websites: www.inromenow.com, www.wantedinrome.com, and www.rome.angloinfo.com.

Music

Music lovers will seek out the mega-music complex of the Rome **Auditorium** (Auditorium Parco della Musica), designed by contemporary architect Renzo Piano (€20-60 tickets, check availability in advance—concerts often sell out, Viale Pietro de Coubertin 30, take Metro to Flaminio and then catch tram #2 to Apollodoro, from there it's a 5-minute walk east, just beyond the elevated road, tram/metro runs until 23:30, box office tel. 06-8024-1281, www.auditorium.com). Nicknamed the Park of Music, it's a place where many Romans go just for the scene—music store, restaurants, cafés, and fresh modern architecture with three state-of-the-art auditoriums (known as "the beetles" for their appearance). If you want to see today's Rome enjoying today's culture, an evening here is the best you'll do.

Classical Music and Opera

The **Teatro dell'Opera** has an active schedule of opera and classical concerts. In the summer, the productions move to the Baths of Caracalla, where ancient ruins make an evocative backdrop. You'll see locals in all their finery, so pull your fanciest outfit from your backpack (near Via Nazionale at Via Firenze 72, tel. 06-4816-0255, www.operaroma.it).

Musical events at the Episcopal **Church of St. Paul's Within the Walls** range from orchestral concerts (usually Tue and Fri) to full operatic performances, which are usually on Saturdays (€20-30, performances at 20:30, tickets usually available on day of show, arrive 30-45 minutes early for a good seat, lasts 1.5-2.5 hours, corner of Via Nazionale at Via Napoli 58, near Termini train station, tel. 06-482-6296, www.musicaemusicasrl.com). On Sunday evenings at 18:30, the church occasionally hosts hour-long candlelit *Luminaria* concerts (€10-20, buy tickets at the church on Sunday, www.stpaulsrome.it).

Jazz

Rome has a relatively small but vibrant jazz scene. **Alexanderplatz** is the venerable club in town, with performances most evenings (Sun-Thu concerts at 21:45, Fri-Sat at 22:30, closed in summer, Via Ostia 9, Ottaviano Metro stop, tel. 06-3972-1867 or 06-3974-2171, www.alexanderplatz.it).

Il Pentagrappolo is an intimate *enoteca,* serving light meals (proudly, no pasta) to go with their selection of quality wines, many organic. Thursday through Saturday, they host live music (often jazz) starting around 22:00 (open Tue-Sun 18:00-24:00, closed Mon, music Sept-June, best to reserve on weekends, three blocks east of the Colosseum at Via Celimontana 21, www.ilpentagrappolo.com, tel. 06-709-6301, Simone).

Nightclubs and Bars

An interesting place for club-hopping is **Monte Testaccio.** After 21:00, ride the Metro to the Piramide stop and follow the noise. Monte Testaccio, once an ancient trash heap, is now a small hill whose cool caves house funky restaurants and trendy clubs. (It stands amid a pretty rough neighborhood, though.)

Evening Sightseeing

Some **museums** have later opening hours (especially on Sat in summer), offering a good chance to see art in a cooler, less-crowded environment. See the "Rome at a Glance" sidebar on page 512, and ask the TI if any museums are currently open late.

The **Scuderie del Quirinale** stays open late when it's hosting major art exhibitions (€12, Sun-Thu 10:00-20:00, Fri-Sat 10:00-20:30, last entry one hour before closing, Via XXIV Maggio 16, tel. 06-696-271, www.scuderiequirinale.it). The same goes for the nearby **Palazzo delle Esposizioni** (€12, Tue-Thu and Sun 10:00-20:00, Fri-Sat 10:00-20:30, closed Mon, last entry one hour before closing, Via Nazionale 194, tel. 06-399-6750, www.palazzoesposizioni.it). A €20 combo-ticket (good for three days) gets you into both sites.

ROME

Eating in Rome

For general tips on eating in Italy, see page 455.

In the Pantheon Neighborhood

For the restaurants in this central area, I've listed them based on which landmark they're closest to: Campo de' Fiori, Piazza Navona, or the Pantheon itself.

On and near Campo de' Fiori

By day, Campo de' Fiori hosts one of the few markets in downtown Rome, selling fruit and veggies (and an increasing number of tourist knickknacks; Mon-Sat closes around 13:30, closed Sun). Combined with a sandwich and sweet from the Forno (bakery) in the west corner of the square (behind the fountain), you can assemble a nice picnic.

By night, while it is touristy, Campo de' Fiori offers a sublimely romantic setting. And, since it's so close to the heart of the Roman people, it remains popular with locals, even though its restaurants offer greater atmosphere than food value. The square is lined with popular and interesting bars, pizzerias, and small restaurants—all great for people-watching over a glass of wine. Later at night it's taken over by a younger clubbing crowd.

Ristorante ar Galletto is nearby, on the more elegant and peaceful Piazza Farnese. Angelo entertains an upscale Roman clientele and has magical outdoor seating. Regrettably, service can be brusque, you need to double-check the bill, and single diners aren't treated very well. Still, if you're in no hurry and ready to savor my favorite al fresco setting in Rome (while humoring the waiters), this can be a good bet (€10-12 pastas, €16-22 *secondi*, daily 12:15-15:00 & 19:30-23:00, reservations smart for outdoor seating, Piazza Farnese 104, tel. 06-686-1714, www.ristoranteargallettoroma.com).

Vineria Salumeria Roscioli is an elegant *enoteca* that's a hit with local foodies, so reservations are a must. While it's just a salami toss away from touristy Campo de' Fiori, you'll dine with classy locals, and feel like you're sitting in a romantic (and expensive) deli after hours. They have a good selection of fine cheeses, meats, local dishes, and top-end wines by the glass (€15-25 plates, Mon-Sat 12:30-16:00 & 19:00-24:00, closed Sun, 3 blocks east of Campo de' Fiori at Via dei Giubbonari 21, tel. 06-687-5287, www.salumeriaroscioli.com). Their nearby **Forno Roscioli** is a favorite for a quick slice of pizza or pastry to go (Mon-Sat 6:00-20:00, closed Sun, Via dei Chiavari 34, tel. 06-686-4045).

Trattoria der Pallaro, an eccentric and well-worn eatery that has no menu, has a slogan: "Here, you'll eat what we want to feed you." Paola Fazi—with a towel wrapped around her head turban-style—and her gang dish up a five-course meal of homey Roman food. You have three menu choices: €25 for the works; €20 for appetizers, *secondi*, and dessert; or €15 for appetizers and pasta. Any option is filling, includes wine and coffee, and is capped with a thimble of mandarin juice. While the service can be odd and the food is rustic, the experience is fun (daily 12:00-16:00 & 19:00-24:00, reserve if dining after 20:00, cash only, indoor/outdoor seating on quiet square, a block south of Corso Vittorio Emanuele, down Largo del Chiavari to Largo del Pallaro 15, tel. 06-6880-1488).

Filetti di Baccalà is a cheap and basic Roman classic, where nostalgic regulars cram into wooden tables and savor their old-school favorites—fried cod finger-food fillets (€5 each) and raw, slightly bitter *puntarelle* greens (slathered with anchovy sauce, available in spring and winter). Study what others are eating, and order from your grease-stained server by pointing at what you want. Sit in the fluorescently lit interior or try to grab a seat out on the little square, a quiet haven a block east of Campo de' Fiori (Mon-Sat 17:30-23:00, closed Sun, cash only, Largo dei Librari 88, tel. 06-686-4018). If you're not into greasy spoons, avoid this place.

Pizzeria da Baffetto 2 makes pizza Roman-style: thin crust, crispy, and wood-fired. Eat in the cramped informal interior, or outside on the busy square (€7-10 pizzas, daily 18:30-24:00, Sat-Sun also open for lunch 12:30-15:30, a block north of Campo de' Fiori at Piazza del Teatro di Pompeo 18, tel. 06-6821-0807).

Open Baladin is a modern pub featuring a few dozen Italian craft beers on tap and menu of burgers, salads, and freshly cooked potato chips. As this is a relatively new concept in Italy, prices are somewhat high—and the food can be hit or miss—but it's a nice break if you're parched and ready for pub grub (€9-15 plates, daily 12:00-24:00, Via degli Specchi 5, tel. 06-683-8989, www.open-baladinroma.it).

Near Piazza Navona

Piazza Navona is the quintessential setting for dining on a Roman square. Whether you eat here or not, you'll want to stroll the piazza before or after your evening meal. This is where many people fall in love with Rome. The tangled streets just to the west are lined with popular eateries of many stripes.

Ciccia Bomba is a simple, traditional trattoria where Gianpaolo, Gianluca, and their crew serve up tasty homemade pasta, wood-fired pizza, and other Roman specialties (consider their daily-special sheet)—all at a good price. While downstairs you can sit at a table on ancient pavement next to your own column,

ROME

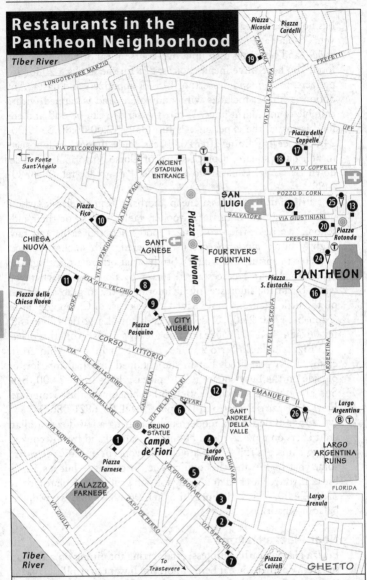

Restaurants in the Pantheon Neighborhood

1. Ristorante ar Galletto
2. Vineria Salumeria Roscioli
3. Forno Roscioli
4. Trattoria der Pallaro
5. Filetti di Baccalà
6. Pizzeria da Baffetto 2
7. Open Baladin Pub
8. Ciccia Bomba
9. Cul de Sac & L'Insalata Ricca
10. Rist. Pizzeria "da Francesco"
11. Pizzeria da Baffetto
12. L'Insalata Ricca
13. Ristorante da Fortunato
14. Enoteca Corsi

ROME

15 Trattoria dal Cavalier Gino
16 Miscellanea
17 Osteria da Mario
18 Taverna le Coppelle
19 Ristorante la Campana
20 Antica Salumeria
21 Super Mkt. Carrefour Express

22 Supermercato Despar
24 Gelateria Giolitti
24 Crèmeria Monteforte
25 Gelateria San Crispino
26 Gelateria Vice

I like the ambience on the main level. Reserve at least a week in advance for their 45-minute pizza-making "lesson" that costs €25 (€8 pastas, €10-16 *secondi*, Thu-Tue 12:30-15:00 & 19:00-24:00, closed Wed, Via del Governo Vecchio 76, a block west of Piazza Navona, just north from Piazza Pasquino, tel. 06-6880-2108).

Cul de Sac, a corridor-wide trattoria lined with wine bottles, is packed with an enthusiastic crowd enjoying a wide-ranging menu, from pasta to homemade pâté. They have fun tasting-plates of *salumi* and cheese, more than a thousand different wines, and fine outdoor seating. It's small, and they don't take reservations—come early to avoid a wait (€7-15 plates, daily 12:00-24:00, a block off Piazza Navona on Piazza Pasquino, tel. 06-6880-1094).

Ristorante Pizzeria "da Francesco," bustling and authentic, has a 50-year-old tradition, a hardworking young waitstaff, great indoor seating, and classic outdoor seating on a cluttered little square that makes you want to break out a sketchpad. Their blackboard explains the daily specials (€9 pizzas and pastas, €15-20 *secondi*, daily 12:00-15:30 & 19:00-24:00, 3 blocks west of Piazza Navona at Piazza del Fico 29, tel. 06-686-4009).

Pizzeria da Baffetto, buried deep in the old quarter behind Piazza Navona, is a Roman favorite, offering tasty pizza and surly service. Its tables are tightly arranged amid the mishmash of photos and sketches littering the walls. The pizza-assembly kitchen keeps things energetic, and the pizza oven keeps the main room warm (you can opt for a table on the cobbled street). Come early or late, or be prepared to wait (€7 pizzas, daily from 18:30, cash only; order "P," "M," or "D"—small, medium, or large; west of Piazza Navona on the corner of Via Sora at Via del Governo Vecchio 114, tel. 06-686-1617).

L'Insalata Ricca is a popular local chain that specializes in healthy, filling €8 salads and less-healthy pastas and main courses (daily March-Oct 12:00-24:00, closes between lunch and dinner in off-season). They have a handy branch on Piazza Pasquino (next to the recommended Cul de Sac, tel. 06-6830-7881) and a more spacious and enjoyable location a few blocks away, on a bigger square next to busy Corso Vittorio Emanuele (near Campo de' Fiori at Largo dei Chiavari 85, tel. 06-6880-3656).

Close to the Pantheon

Eating on the square facing the Pantheon is a temptation, and I'd consider it just to relax and enjoy the Roman scene. But if you walk a block or two away, you'll get less view and better value. Here are some suggestions.

Ristorante da Fortunato is an Italian classic, with fresh flowers on the tables and white-coated, black-tie career waiters politely serving good meat and fish to politicians, foreign dignitaries, and tourists with good taste. Don't leave without perusing the photos of their famous visitors—everyone from former Iraqi Foreign Minister Tariq Aziz to Bill Clinton seems to have eaten here. All are pictured with the boss, Fortunato, who, since 1975, has been a master of simple edible elegance. (His son Jason is now on the team.) The outdoor seating is fine for watching the river of Roman street life flow by, but the real atmosphere is inside. For a dressy night out, this is a reliable and surprisingly reasonable choice—but be sure to reserve ahead (plan to spend €45 per person, daily 12:30-15:30 & 19:30-23:30, a block in front of the Pantheon at Via del Pantheon 55, tel. 06-679-2788, www.ristorantefortunato.it).

Enoteca Corsi is a wine shop that grew into a thriving lunch-only restaurant. The Paiella family serves straightforward, traditional cuisine to an appreciative crowd of office workers. Check the board for daily specials (gnocchi on Thursday, fish on Friday, and so on). Friendly Giuliana, Claudia, Sara, and Manuela welcome eaters to step into their wine shop and pick out a bottle. For the cheap take-away price, plus €4-8 (depending on the wine), they'll uncork it at your table. With €9 pastas, €13 main dishes, and fine wine at a third of the price you'd pay in normal restaurants, this can be a good value. And guests with this book finish their meal with a free glass of homemade *limoncello* (Mon-Sat 12:00-15:30, closed Sun, no reservations possible, a block toward the Pantheon from the Gesù Church at Via del Gesù 87, tel. 06-679-0821).

Trattoria dal Cavalier Gino, tucked away on a tiny street behind the Parliament, has been a favorite since 1963. Photos on the wall recall the days when it was the haunt of big-time politicians. Grandpa Gino shuffles around grating the parmesan cheese while his English-speaking children Carla and Fabrizio serve up traditional Roman favorites and make sure things run smoothly. Reserve ahead, even for lunch, as you'll be packed in with savvy locals (€8 pastas, €11 *secondi,* cash only, Mon-Sat 13:00-14:45 & 20:00-22:30, closed Sun, behind Piazza del Parlamento and just off Via di Campo Marzio at Vicolo Rosini 4, tel. 06-687-3434).

Miscellanea is run by much-loved Mikki, who's on a mission to keep foreign students well-fed. Welcoming travelers as well as locals, he offers hearty €4 sandwiches and a long list of €7 salads, along with pasta and other staples. This is a great value for a cheap and hearty dinner featuring typical rustic Roman cuisine. Mikki (and his son Romeo) often tosses in a fun little extra, including—if you have this book on the table—a free glass of Mikki's "sexy wine" (from *fragoline*—strawberry-flavored grapes). While basic, it's convenient (€7 pastas, €10 *secondi,* daily 11:00-24:00, indoor/outdoor seating, facing the rear of the Pantheon at Via della Palombella 34, tel. 06-6813-5318).

Osteria da Mario, a homey little mom-and-pop joint with a no-stress menu, serves traditional favorites in a fun dining room or on tables spilling out onto a picturesque old Roman square (€9 pastas, €12-15 *secondi*, Mon-Sat 12:30-15:30 & 19:00-23:00, closed Sun; from the Pantheon walk 2 blocks up Via del Pantheon, go left on Via delle Coppelle, and take first right to Piazza delle Coppelle 51; tel. 06-6880-6349, Marco).

Taverna le Coppelle is simple, basic, family-friendly, and inexpensive—especially for pizza—with a checkered-tablecloth ambience (€9 pizzas, daily 12:30-15:00 & 19:30-23:30, Via delle Coppelle 39, tel. 06-6880-6557, Alfonso).

Ristorante la Campana is a plain and honest little place—an authentic slice of Rome with a local following and no pretense. It serves classic dishes and daily specials, plus it has a good self-service *antipasti* buffet (€10 pastas, €15 *secondi*, Tue-Sun 12:30-15:00 & 19:30-23:00, closed Mon, inside seating only, reserve for dinner, just off Via della Scrofa and Piazza Nicosia at Vicolo della Campana 18, tel. 06-687-5273, www.ristorantelacampana.com).

Picnicking Close to the Pantheon

It's fun to munch a picnic with a view of the Pantheon. (Remember to be discreet.) Here are some options.

Antica Salumeria is an old-time *alimentari* (grocery store) on the Pantheon square. While they hustle most tourists into premade €5 sandwiches, you can make your own picnic. Find your way to the back to buy artichokes, mixed olives, bread, cheese, and meat (daily 8:00-21:00, mobile 334-340-9014).

Supermarkets near the Pantheon: Food is relatively cheap at Italian supermarkets. **Super Market Carrefour Express** is a convenient place for groceries a block from the Gesù Church (Mon-Sat 8:00-20:30, Sun 9:00-19:30, 50 yards off Via del Plebiscito at Via del Gesù 59). Another place, **Supermercato Despar,** is half a block from the Pantheon toward Piazza Navona (daily 8:30-22:00, Via Giustiniani 18).

Gelato Close to the Pantheon

Several fine *gelaterie* are within a five-minute walk of the Pantheon.

Giolitti is Rome's most famous and venerable ice-cream joint (although few would say it has the best gelato). Take-away prices are reasonable, and it has elegant Old World seating (daily 7:00-24:00, just off Piazza Colonna and Piazza Monte Citorio at Via Uffici del Vicario 40, tel. 06-699-1243).

Crèmeria Monteforte is known for its traditional gelato and super-creamy sorbets *(cremolati)*. The fruit flavors are especially refreshing—think gourmet slushies (Tue-Sun 10:00-24:00, off-season closes earlier, closed Mon and Dec-Jan, faces the west side of the Pantheon at Via della Rotonda 22, tel. 06-686-7720).

Gelateria San Crispino serves small portions of particularly tasty gourmet gelato. Because of their commitment to natural ingredients, the colors are muted; gelato purists consider bright colors a sign of unnatural chemicals used to attract children (daily 12:00-24:00, a block in front of the Pantheon on Piazza della Maddalena, tel. 06-6889-1310).

Gelateria Vice is a relative newcomer but might be the best of all. Using top-quality ingredients in innovative ways, the flavors change with the seasons (daily 11:00-24:00, around the northwest corner of Largo Argentina at Corso Vittorio Emanuele II 96, tel. 06-8117-3023).

Near the Colosseum and Forum

Within a block of the Colosseum and Forum, you'll find convenient eateries catering to weary sightseers, offering neither memorable food nor good value. To get your money's worth, stick with one of these good choices or head farther away. The characteristic Monti neighborhood, with a number of casual options, is several blocks north of the Forum (head up Via Cavour and then left on Via dei Serpenti; the action centers on Piazza della Madonna dei Monti and unfolds along Via dei Serpenti, Via del Boschetto, and Via Leonina/Urbana). For a map of the area, see page 545.

Enoteca Cavour 313 is a wine bar with a mission: to offer good wine and food with an old-fashioned commitment to value and friendly service. Its slightly unconventional menu, ranging from couscous and salads to high-quality *affettati* (cold cuts) and cheese, makes a nice alternative to the usual pasta/pizza choices. With a mellow ambience under lofts of wine bottles, it's a favorite at any time but especially for a convenient lunch (€7-14 basic plates, daily 12:30-14:45 & 19:00-24:00, 100 yards off Via dei Fori Imperiali at Via Cavour 313, tel. 06-678-5496, Angelo, Massimo, and Pulika).

Taverna Romana, run by the same folks as Cavour 313, is small and simple, serving traditional classics made with quality ingredients. Reserve for the earliest seating or join the locals and add your name to the waitlist for the later seating (€8 pastas, €12 *secondi*, Mon-Sat 12:30-14:45 & 19:00-23:00, closed Sun, cash only, Via Madonna dei Monti 79, tel. 06-474-5325).

Hostaria da Nerone is a traditional place serving hearty classics, including tasty homemade pasta dishes. Their *antipasti* plate— with a variety of veggies, fish, and meat—is a good value for a quick lunch. While the *antipasti* menu indicates specifics, you can have a plate of whatever's out—just direct the waiter to assemble the €10 *antipasti* plate of your lunchtime dreams (€11 pastas, €13-15 *secondi*, Mon-Sat 12:00-15:00 & 19:00-23:00, closed Sun, indoor/outdoor seating, Via delle Terme di Tito 96, tel. 06-481-7952, Teo and Eugenio).

Caffè dello Studente, next door to Hostaria da Nerone, is popular with engineering students attending the nearby University of Rome. The owners—Pina, Mauro, their perky daughter Simona, and their son-in-law Emiliano (the last two speak English)—give my readers a friendly welcome. They serve average, microwaved *bar gastronomia* fare—toasted sandwiches, salads, and mixed bruschetta. If it's not busy, show this book when you order at the bar and sit at a table without paying extra (Mon-Sat 7:30-21:00, April-Oct Sun 9:00-20:00, Nov-March closed Sun, Via delle Terme di Tito, tel. 06-488-3240).

Trattoria Luzzi is a well-worn, no-frills eatery serving simple food in a high-energy environment (as they've done since 1945). With good prices, big portions, and proximity to the Colosseum, it draws a crowd—reserve or expect a short wait at lunch and after 19:30 (€5-7 pastas, €7 pizzas, €7-12 *secondi*, Thu-Tue 12:00-24:00, closed Wed, Via San Giovanni in Laterano 88, tel. 06-709-6332). If Luzzi is jam-packed, as it often is, **Ristorante Pizzeria Naumachia** (next door at Via Celimontana 7, tel. 06-700-2764) is a bit more upscale and serves good quality pizza and pastas at good prices.

La Taverna dei Quaranta, a casual neighborhood favorite, has a humble, red-checkered tablecloth ambience. In the evening, they fire up the wood oven for pizza, to go along with a basic menu of Roman classics and seasonal specialties. As the place caters mostly to locals, service can be a bit slow and straightforward—but it's a good bet in this touristy area (€8 pastas, €8-13 *secondi*, daily 12:00-15:30 & 19:00-23:30, Via Claudia 24, tel. 06-700-0550).

Enoteca Nel Cuore di Roma sits overlooking Trajan's Column. It's a modern little place with a cool, peaceful, and well-lit dining room and a few outside tables. It celebrates Roman cuisine with fresh local produce and daily €13 specials including wine (daily 11:00-23:30, Foro Traiano 82, tel. 06-6994-0273).

Near Vatican City

As in the Colosseum area, eateries near the Vatican cater to exhausted tourists. Avoid the restaurant-pushers handing out fliers: They're usually hawking places with bad food and expensive menu tricks. Instead, tide yourself over with a slice of pizza or at any of these eateries and save your splurges for elsewhere.

Handy Lunch Places near Piazza Risorgimento

These are a stone's throw from the Vatican wall, located halfway between St. Peter's Basilica and the Vatican Museum. They're all fast and cheap, with a good *gelateria* next door.

Hostaria dei Bastioni, run by Antonio while Emilio cooks, has noisy street-side seating and a quiet interior (€8 pastas, €8-12

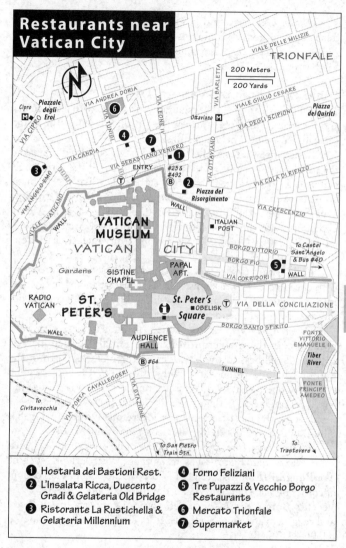

Restaurants near Vatican City

TRIONFALE

200 Meters

200 Yards

Cipro Piazzale degli Eroi

VIALE PELLE MILIZIE

VIA BARLETTA

VIALE GIULIO CESARE

VIA ANDREA DORIA

VIA LEONE IV

Ottaviano M

VIA DEGLI SCIPIONI

Piazza dei Quiriti

VIA CIPRO

VIA TUNISI

VIA OTTAVIANO

VIA CANDIA

VIA SEBASTIANO VENIERO

ENTRY

#23 & #492

VIA COLA DI RIENZO

VIA ANGELO EMO

VIA CRESCENZIO

Piazza del Risorgimento

WALL

ITALIAN POST

VATICAN MUSEUM

VATICAN   CITY

VIALE VATICANO

BORGO VITTORIO

BORGO PIO

To Castel Sant'Angelo & Bus #40

WALL

Gardens

SISTINE CHAPEL

PAPAL APT.

VIA CORRIDORI

RADIO VATICAN

ST. PETER'S

OBELISK

St. Peter's Square

VIA DELLA CONCILIAZIONE

WALL

BORGO SANTO SPIRITO

AUDIENCE HALL

#64

TUNNEL

PONTE VITTORIO EMANUELE II

Tiber River

VIA PORTA CAVALLEGGERI

VIA STAZIONE

PONTE PRINCIPE AMEDEO

To Civitavecchia

To San Pietro Train Stn.

To Trastevere

ROME

❶ Hostaria dei Bastioni Rest.

❷ L'Insalata Ricca, Duecento Gradi & Gelateria Old Bridge

❸ Ristorante La Rustichella & Gelateria Millennium

❹ Forno Feliziani

❺ Tre Pupazzi & Vecchio Borgo Restaurants

❻ Mercato Trionfale

❼ Supermarket

secondi, Mon-Sat 12:00-15:30 & 18:30-23:00, closed Sun, at corner of Vatican wall at Via Leone IV 29, tel. 06-3972-3034).

L'Insalata Ricca is another branch of the popular chain that serves hearty salads and pastas (daily April-Oct 12:30-23:30, closes between lunch and dinner in off-season, across from Vatican walls at Piazza Risorgimento 5, tel. 06-3973-0387).

Duecento Gradi is a good bet for fresh and creative €5 sandwiches. Munch your lunch on a stool or take it away (daily 11:00-24:00, Piazza Risorgimento 3, tel. 06-3975-4239).

Gelato: **Gelateria Old Bridge** scoops up hearty portions of fresh gelato for tourists and nuns alike—join the line (daily 10:00-23:00, just off Piazza Risorgimento across from Vatican walls at Via Bastioni 3).

Other Options in the Vatican Area

The first three listings—the restaurant, the streets with pizza shops, and the covered market—are near the Vatican Museum. The Borgo Pio eateries are near St. Peter's Basilica.

Ristorante La Rustichella serves tasty wood-fired pizza and the usual pasta in addition to their *antipasti* buffet (€8 for a single plate) in a no-frills, neighborhood setting. Do like the Romans do—take a moderate amount of *antipasti* and make one trip only (Tue-Sun 12:30-15:00 & 19:00-24:00, closed Mon, near Metro: Cipro, opposite church at end of Via Candia, Via Angelo Emo 1, tel. 06-3972-0649). Consider the fun and fruity **Gelateria Millennium** next door.

Viale Giulio Cesare and *Via Candia:* These streets are lined with cheap *pizza rustica* shops, self-serve places, and basic eateries. **Forno Feliziani** (Via Candia 61, tel. 06-3973-7362) is a good bet for pizza by the slice and simple cafeteria-style dishes.

Covered Market: As you collect picnic supplies, turn your nose loose in the wonderful **Mercato Trionfale** covered market. It's one of the best in the city, located three blocks north of the Vatican Museum (Mon-Sat roughly 7:00-14:00, Tue and Fri some stalls stay open until 19:00, closed Sun, corner of Via Tunisi and Via Andrea Doria). If the market is closed, try several nearby supermarkets; the most convenient is **Carrefour Express** (Mon-Sat 8:00-20:00, Sun 9:00-20:00, Via Sebastiano Veniero 16).

Along Borgo Pio: The pedestrians-only Borgo Pio—a block from Piazza San Pietro—has restaurants worth a look, such as **Tre Pupazzi** (Mon-Sat 12:00-15:00 & 19:00-23:00, closed Sun, at corner of Via Tre Pupazzi and Borgo Pio, tel. 06-686-8371). At **Vecchio Borgo,** across the street, you can get pasta, pizza slices, and veggies to go (Mon-Sat 9:00-21:00, closed Sun, Borgo Pio 27a, tel. 06-8117-3585).

Starting or Ending Your Cruise in Rome

If your cruise begins or ends in Rome, you'll want some extra time here; for most travelers, two days is a minimum to see the highlights of the Eternal City. If you're planning a longer visit, pick up my *Rick Steves' Rome* guidebook—or, if your trip extends beyond Rome, consider my *Rick Steves' Italy* guidebook.

Airport Connections

You'll need to take two trains to link Civitavecchia and Fiumicino Airport: one between the airport and Rome's Termini Station, and another between Termini and Civitavecchia. Rome's two airports—**Fiumicino** (a.k.a. Leonardo da Vinci, airport code: FCO) and the small **Ciampino** (airport code: CIA)—share the same website (www.adr.it).

Fiumicino Airport

Rome's primary airport has a TI (in Terminal 3, daily 8:00-19:30), ATMs, banks, luggage storage, shops, and bars. The Rome Walks website (www.romewalks.com) has a useful video on options for getting into the city from the airport. Allow lots of time going in either direction; there's a fair amount of transportation involved (e.g., getting to Termini, the ride to the airport, the walk from the airport train station to check-in, etc.). Flying to the US involves an extra level of security—plan on getting to the airport even earlier than normal (I like to arrive 2.5 hours ahead of my flight).

Getting from Fiumicino Airport to Downtown

The slick, direct **Leonardo Express train** connects the airport and Rome's central Termini train station in 30 minutes for €14. Trains run twice hourly in both directions from roughly 6:00 to 23:00. It leaves the airport at :08 and :38 past each hour, arriving at Termini train station about a half-hour later. From the airport's arrival gate, follow signs to the train car icon or *Stazione/Railway Station*. Buy your ticket from a machine, the Biglietteria office, or a newsstand at the platform, then validate it in a green or yellow machine near the track. Make sure the train you board is going to the central "Roma Termini" station, not "Roma Orte" or others. Once at Termini Station, you can continue by taxi, bus, or Metro to your accommodations, or by train to Civitavecchia (see below).

A Rome city **taxi** between the airport and central Rome should cost €48 (for four people and their normal-size bags). Cabbies not based in Rome can charge €70. Look for a Rome city cab, with the words *"Roma Capitale"* and an "SPQR" shield on the door. By law, they can charge only €48 for the ride (still, be sure to establish the price before you get in). If you're staying the night in Rome, check with your hotel about an airport **shuttle van.**

Getting from Fiumicino Airport (or Downtown) to Civitavecchia

There is no direct **public-transportation** connection to Civitavecchia; you'll have to transfer at Rome's Termini train station. First, take the Leonardo Express train from the airport to Termini

Station. From Termini, you'll ride another train to Civitavecchia (€5-15, 2-3/hour, 40-80 minutes). Be warned that Civitavecchia trains generally leave from tracks 27-30, a long 10- to 15-minute walk from the station entrance. There are moving walkways underground, but it's often easier to walk along track 24. If you're catching the Civitavecchia-bound train at Termini Station, you'll likely be approached on the platform by bogus "porters" who offer to help you get your bags into the train and find your seat, then demand an exorbitant tip. These are not railway employees; there are no official porters. Don't use them unless you really need to; then, if you do, tip them only what you think is fair (and always keep a close eye on your belongings).

Once in Civitavecchia, you can walk 10 minutes to the port entrance, following the directions under "Returning to Your Ship," on page 500. Go through the port gate and find the cruise line's shuttle-bus stop across the street from the big fortress. Wait for a bus marked with your cruise ship's name.

Shuttle van services run between the port and Rome's airport, such as **Rome Airport Shuttle** (€90/1-2 people, €15 each additional person up to 8, share with others and save, much more for pickup between 21:00 and 7:00, tel. 06-4201-4507 or 06-4201-3469, www.airportshuttle.it). A **taxi** costs about €120 one-way between Civitavecchia and Fiumicino Airport.

Departing from Fiumicino Airport

If your cruise ends in Civitavecchia, follow the directions on page 492 to reach the Civitavecchia train station, and ride the train to Rome's Termini train station. Once at Termini, the Leonardo Express train to the airport departs at about :22 and :52 past the hour, usually from track 24. Check the departure boards for "Fiumicino Aeroporto"—the local name for the airport—and confirm with an official or a local on the platform that the train is indeed going to the airport (€14, buy ticket from any tobacco shop or newsstand in the station, or at the self-service machines, Termini-Fiumicino trains run 5:52-22:52). Read your ticket: If it requires validation, stamp it in the green or yellow machines near the platform before boarding. From the train station at the airport, you can access most of the terminals. American airlines flying direct to the US depart from Terminal 5, which is a separate building not connected to the rest of the terminals. If you arrive by train, catch the T5 shuttle bus *(navetta)* on the sidewalk in front of Terminal 3—it's too far to walk with luggage.

Alternate Airport (Ciampino)

Rome's smaller airport (tel. 06-6595-9515) handles charter flights and some budget airlines (including all Ryanair flights). The Terravision Express Shuttle connects Ciampino and Termini train station (€6 one-way, €8 round-trip, about 2/hour, 45 minutes, Termini to Ciampino pickup on Via Marsala outside the station next to the Terracafé, tel. 06-9761-0632, www.terravision.eu). The SIT Bus Shuttle also connects Termini to Ciampino (€6 one-way, €8 round-trip, about 2/hour, 45 minutes, pickup on Via Marsala just outside the train exit closest to track 1, tel. 06-592-3507, www.sitbusshuttle.com). A taxi should cost €30 to downtown (within the old city walls). Once at Termini, follow the instructions under "Getting from Fiumicino Airport (or Downtown) to Civitavecchia," earlier.

Hotels in Rome

If you need a hotel in Rome for before or after your cruise, here are a few suggestions.

Getting to Civitavecchia: For those overnighting in Rome, many of my recommended hotels are near the Termini train station—to meet your cruise, just follow the directions "Getting from the Airport (or Downtown) to Civitavecchia," earlier. However, if you're staying near Vatican City, you catch a Civitavecchia-bound train from the San Pietro Station; if you're staying near the Colosseum, ride the Metro two stops to Piramide, which is next to the Ostiense Station, where you also can catch a train to Civitavecchia. For details on these stations, and ticket options between Rome and Civitavecchia, see page 495.

Near Termini Train Station

While not as atmospheric as other areas of Rome, the hotels near Termini train station are less expensive, and public-transportation options link these places easily with the entire city. The city's two Metro lines intersect at the station, and most buses leave from here. Piazza Venezia is a 20-minute walk down Via Nazionale.

$$$ Hotel Modigliani, a delightful 23-room place, is energetically run in a clean, bright, minimalist yet in-love-with-life style that its artist namesake would appreciate. It has a vast and plush lounge, a garden, and a newsletter introducing you to each of the staff (Db-€202, check website for deals and ask about Rick Steves discount when you book direct, air-con, elevator, Wi-Fi; northwest of Via Firenze—from Tritone Fountain on Piazza Barberini, go 2 blocks up Via della Purificazione to #42; tel. 06-4281-5226, www.hotelmodigliani.com, info@hotelmodigliani.com, Giulia and Marco).

$$ Hotel Oceania is a peaceful slice of air-conditioned heaven. This 24-room manor house-type hotel is spacious and quiet, with tastefully decorated rooms. Stefano runs a fine staff, serves wonderful coffee, provides lots of thoughtful extra touches, and works hard to maintain a caring family atmosphere (Sb-€135, Db-€168, Tb-€198, Qb-€220, 5 percent discount if you pay cash, deep discounts summer and winter, family suite, elevator, guest computer, Wi-Fi, videos in the TV lounge, Via Firenze 38, third floor, tel. 06-482-4696, www.hoteloceania.it, info@hoteloceania.it; Anna and Radu round out the staff).

$$ Hotel Aberdeen, which perfectly combines quality and friendliness, is warmly run by Annamaria, with support from sister Laura and cousin Cinzia, and staff members Mariano and Costel. The 37 comfy, modern rooms are a fine value (Sb-€102, Db-€170, Tb-€180, Qb-€200, for these rates—or better—book direct via email or use the "Rick Steves reader reservations" link on their website, air-con, guest computer, Wi-Fi, Via Firenze 48, tel. 06-482-3920, www.hotelaberdeen.it, info@hotelaberdeen.it).

$$ Hotel Opera Roma, with contemporary furnishings and marble accents, boasts 15 spacious, modern, and thoughtfully appointed rooms. It's quiet and just a stone's throw from the Opera House (Db-€150, Tb-€165, for these rates book direct and mention Rick Steves, 5 percent discount if you pay cash, air-con, elevator, guest computer, Wi-Fi, Via Firenze 11, tel. 06-487-1787, www.hoteloperaroma.com, info@hoteloperaroma.com, Rezza, Litu, and Federica).

$ Hotel Nardizzi Americana, with a small rooftop terrace and 40 standard rooms spread throughout the building, is another decent value (Sb-€95, Db-€125, Tb-€155, Qb-€175; to get the best rates, check their "Rick Steves readers reservations" link along with the rest of their website; additional 10 percent off any price if you pay cash, air-con, elevator, guest computer, Wi-Fi, Via Firenze 38, reception on fourth floor, tel. 06-488-0035, www.hotelnardizzi.it, info@hotelnardizzi.it; friendly Stefano, Fabrizio, Mario, and Giancarlo).

$ Hotel Montreal is a basic three-star place with 27 small rooms on a big street a block southeast of Santa Maria Maggiore (Sb-€90, Db-€110, Tb-€135, email direct and ask for a Rick Steves discount, air-con, elevator, guest computer, Wi-Fi, small garden terrace, good security, Via Carlo Alberto 4, 1 block from Metro: Vittorio Emanuele, 3 blocks from Termini train station, tel. 06-445-7797, www.hotelmontrealroma.it, info@hotelmontrealroma.it, Pasquale).

$ The Beehive gives vagabonds—old and young—a cheap, clean, and comfy home in Rome, thoughtfully and creatively run by Steve and Linda, a friendly American couple, and their hard-working staff. They offer six great-value artsy-mod double rooms (D-€80, T-€105) and an eight-bed dorm (€30 bunks). Their nearby annex, **The Sweets,** has similar style and several rooms with private baths (Sb-€60, Db-€100, air-con-€10, breakfast extra, guest computer, Wi-Fi, private garden terrace, 2 blocks from Termini train station at Via Marghera 8, tel. 06-4470-4553, www.the-bee-hive.com, info@the-beehive.com). They're also a good resource for apartments across the city (www.cross-pollinate.com).

Elsewhere in Rome

Near the Colosseum: **$$$ Hotel Lancelot** is a comfortable yet elegant refuge—a 60-room hotel with the ambience of a B&B. It's quiet and safe, with a shady courtyard, restaurant, bar, and tiny communal sixth-floor terrace. It's well-run by Faris and Lubna Khan, who serve a good €25 dinner—a chance to connect with your hotel neighbors and the friendly staff. No wonder it's popular with returning guests (Sb-€128, Db-€196, Tb-€226, Qb-€266, €20 extra for sixth-floor terrace room with a Colosseum view, ask about discount if you book direct and mention Rick Steves, air-con, elevator, wheelchair-accessible, free Wi-Fi, parking-€10/day, 10-minute walk behind Colosseum near San Clemente Church at Via Capo d'Africa 47, tel. 06-7045-0615, www.lancelothotel.com, info@lancelothotel.com). Faris and Lubna speak the Queen's English.

Near the Pantheon: **$$$ Albergo Santa Chiara,** in the old center, is big, solid, and hotelesque. Flavia, Silvio, and their fine staff offer marbled elegance (but basic furniture) and all the hotel services. Its ample public lounges are dressy and professional, and its 99 rooms are quiet and spacious (Sb-€138, Db-€215, Tb-€260, check website for discounts, book online direct and request special Rick Steves rates, elevator, air-con, free Wi-Fi, behind Pantheon at Via di Santa Chiara 21, tel. 06-687-2979, www.albergosanta-chiara.com, info@albergosantachiara.com).

Near Vatican City: **$$ Hotel Alimandi Tunisi** is a good value, run by other members of the friendly and entrepreneurial Alimandi family—Paolo, Luigi, Marta, and Barbara. They have 27 modest but comfortable rooms and vast public spaces, including a piano lounge, pool table, and rooftop terrace where the grand buffet breakfast is served (Sb-€90, Db-€175, 5 percent discount if you pay cash, elevator, air-con, guest computer, Wi-Fi, down the stairs directly in front of Vatican Museum, Via Tunisi 8, Metro: Ottaviano, tel. 06-3972-3941, www.alimandi.com, alimandi@tin.it).

In Civitavecchia

With the glories of one of Europe's best after-dark cities just a short train-ride away (and the ease of getting from Rome to its port), I'd never sleep in ho-hum Civitavecchia. But if you must, two decent hotels are midway between the train station and the cruise port, just a five-minute walk from each and overlooking the gritty har-

ROME

What If I Miss My Boat?

Remember that you can get help from the cruise line's port agent (listed on the destination information sheet distributed on the ship) and the local TI (see page 501). If the port agent suggests a costly solution (such as a private car with a driver), you may want to consider public transit.

Frequent **trains** leave from Rome's very central Termini Station (the same one with train connections to Civitavecchia) to points all over Italy and beyond: to **Venice, Livorno, Naples, Sorrento** (transfer in Naples to Circumvesuviana train), **Nice,** and more. A few trains depart from Rome's Tiburtina Station, four Metro stops from Termini. To look up specific connections, use www.trenitalia.com (domestic journeys only) or www.bahn.com (Germany's excellent all-Europe schedule website). For other ports (in France, Spain, Croatia, Greece, and Turkey), you'll probably have to fly.

If you need to catch a **plane** to your next destination, see "Airport Connections" for information on Rome's two airports.

For help booking travel to your next port, look for a travel agency in Rome; if you're in Civitavecchia, try the Cruises Services Center or Agenzie 365 (see page 495). For more advice on what to do if you miss the boat, see page 140.

bor (both hotels have air-con, elevators, and Wi-Fi). **Hotel de La Ville** rents 40 four-star rooms in a classy 19th-century building (Db-€150, Viale della Repubblica 4, tel. 0766-580-507, www.roseshotels.it). Its simpler and cheaper three-star sister, **Hotel Mediterraneo,** is next door (50 rooms, Db-€120, Viale Garibaldi 38, tel. 076-623-156, www.roseshotels.it).

Italian Survival Phrases

English	Italian	Pronunciation
Good day.	*Buon giorno.*	bwohn **jor**-noh
Do you speak English?	*Parla inglese?*	**par**-lah een-**gleh**-zay
Yes. / No.	*Sì. / No.*	see / noh
I (don't) understand.	*(Non) capisco.*	(nohn) kah-**pees**-koh
Please.	*Per favore.*	pehr fah-**voh**-ray
Thank you.	*Grazie.*	**graht**-see-ay
You're welcome.	*Prego.*	**preh**-go
I'm sorry.	*Mi dispiace.*	mee dee-spee-**ah**-chay
Excuse me.	*Mi scusi.*	mee **skoo**-zee
(No) problem.	*(Non) c'è un roblema.*	(nohn) cheh oon proh-**bleh**-mah
Good.	*Va bene.*	vah **beh**-nay
Goodbye.	*Arrivederci.*	ah-ree-veh-**dehr**-chee
one / two	*uno / due*	**oo**-noh / **doo**-ay
three / four	*tre / quattro*	tray / **kwah**-troh
five / six	*cinque / sei*	**cheeng**-kway / **seh**-ee
seven / eight	*sette / otto*	**seh**-tay / **oh**-toh
nine / ten	*nove / dieci*	**noh**-vay / dee-**ay**-chee
How much is it?	*Quanto costa?*	**kwahn**-toh **koh**-stah
Write it?	*Me lo scrive?*	may loh **skree**-vay
Is it free?	*È gratis?*	eh **grah**-tees
Is it included?	*È incluso?*	eh een-**kloo**-zoh
Where can I buy / find...?	*Dove posso comprare / trovare...?*	**doh**-vay **poh**-soh kohm-**prah**-ray / troh-**vah**-ray
I'd like / We'd like...	*Vorrei / Vorremmo...*	voh-**reh**-ee / voh-**reh**-moh
...a room.	*...una camera.*	**oo**-nah **kah**-meh-rah
...a ticket to ____.	*...un biglietto per ____.*	oon beel-**yeh**-toh pehr ____
Is it possible?	*È possibile?*	eh poh-**see**-bee-lay
Where is...?	*Dov'è...?*	doh-**veh**
...the train station	*...la stazione*	lah staht-see-**oh**-nay
...the bus station	*...la stazione degli autobus*	lah staht-see-**oh**-nay **dehl**-yee ow-toh-boos
...tourist information	*...informazioni per turisti*	een-for-maht-see-**oh**-nee pehr too-**ree**-stee
...the toilet	*...la toilette*	lah twah-**leh**-tay
men	*uomini / signori*	**woh**-mee-nee / seen-**yoh**-ree
women	*donne / signore*	**doh**-nay / seen-**yoh**-ray
left / right	*sinistra / destra*	see-**nee**-strah / **deh**-strah
straight	*sempre dritto*	**sehm**-pray **dree**-toh
What time does this open / close?	*A che ora apre / chiude?*	ah kay **oh**-rah ah-**pray** / kee-**oo**-day
At what time?	*A che ora?*	ah kay **oh**-rah
Just a moment.	*Un momento.*	oon moh-**mehn**-toh
now / soon / later	*adesso / presto / più tardi*	ah-**deh**-soh / **preh**-stoh / pew **tar**-dee
today / tomorrow	*oggi / domani*	**oh**-jee / doh-**mah**-nee

In an Italian Restaurant

English	Italian	Pronunciation
I'd like...	Vorrei...	voh-**reh**-ee
We'd like...	Vorremmo...	vor-**reh**-moh
...to reserve...	...prenotare...	preh-noh-**tah**-ray
...a table for one / two.	...un tavolo per uno / due.	oon **tah**-voh-loh pehr **oo**-noh / **doo**-ay
Is this seat free?	È libero questo posto?	eh **lee**-beh-roh **kweh**-stoh **poh**-stoh
The menu (in English), please.	Il menù (in inglese), per favore.	eel meh-**noo** (een een-**gleh**-zay) pehr fah-**voh**-ray
service (not) included	servizio (non) incluso	sehr-**veet**-see-oh (nohn) een-**kloo**-zoh
cover charge	pane e coperto	**pah**-nay ay koh-**pehr**-toh
to go	da portar via	dah **por**-tar **vee**-ah
with / without	con / senza	kohn / **sehnt**-sah
and / or	e / o	ay / oh
menu (of the day)	menù (del giorno)	meh-**noo** (dehl **jor**-noh)
specialty of the house	specialità della casa	speh-chah-lee-**tah** **deh**-lah **kah**-zah
first course (pasta, soup)	primo piatto	**pree**-moh pee-**ah**-toh
main course (meat, fish)	secondo piatto	seh-**kohn**-doh pee-**ah**-toh
side dishes	contorni	kohn-**tor**-nee
bread	pane	**pah**-nay
cheese	formaggio	for-**mah**-joh
sandwich	panino	pah-**nee**-noh
soup	zuppa	**tsoo**-pah
salad	insalata	een-sah-**lah**-tah
meat	carne	**kar**-nay
chicken	pollo	**poh**-loh
fish	pesce	**peh**-shay
seafood	frutti di mare	**froo**-tee dee **mah**-ray
fruit / vegetables	frutta / legumi	**froo**-tah / lay-**goo**-mee
dessert	dolce	**dohl**-chay
tap water	acqua del rubinetto	**ah**-kwah dehl roo-bee-**neh**-toh
mineral water	acqua minerale	**ah**-kwah mee-neh-**rah**-lay
milk	latte	**lah**-tay
(orange) juice	succo (d'arancia)	**soo**-koh (dah-**rahn**-chah)
coffee / tea	caffè / tè	kah-**feh** / teh
wine	vino	**vee**-noh
red / white	rosso / bianco	**roh**-soh / bee-**ahn**-koh
glass / bottle	bicchiere / bottiglia	bee-kee-**eh**-ray / boh-**teel**-yah
beer	birra	**bee**-rah
Cheers!	Cin cin!	cheen cheen
More. / Another.	Di più. / Un altro.	dee pew / oon **ahl**-troh
The same.	Lo stesso.	loh **steh**-soh
The bill, please.	Il conto, per favore.	eel **kohn**-toh pehr fah-**voh**-ray
Do you accept credit cards?	Accettate carte di credito?	ah-cheh-**tah**-tay **kar**-tay dee **kreh**-dee-toh
tip	mancia	**mahn**-chah
Delicious!	Delizioso!	day-leet-see-**oh**-zoh

For more user-friendly Italian phrases, check out *Rick Steves' Italian Phrase Book & Dictionary* or *Rick Steves' French, Italian, and German Phrase Book*.

ROME

NAPLES
Italy

Italy Practicalities

Stretching 850 miles long and 150 miles wide, art-drenched Italy is the cradle of European civilization. Visitors here come face to face with some of the world's most iconic images: Rome's ancient Colosseum, Pisa's medieval Leaning Tower, Venice's romantic canals.

Italy's 61 million inhabitants are more social and communal than most other Europeans. Because they're so outgoing and their language is so fun, Italians are a pleasure to communicate with. This boot-shaped country has all the elements that make travel to Europe forever fresh and rewarding: visible history, lively people, and fun by the minute.

Money: Italy uses the euro currency: 1 euro (€) = about $1.30. An ATM is called a *bancomat*. The local VAT (value-added sales tax) rate is 22 percent; the minimum purchase eligible for a VAT refund is €155 (for details on refunds, see page 135).

Language: For useful Italian phrases, see page 701.

Emergencies: Dial 113 for police or 118 for medical emergencies. In case of theft or loss, see page 128.

Time Zone: Italy is on Central European Time (the same as most of the Continent, and six/nine hours ahead of the East/West Coasts of the US).

Theft Alert: Assume that beggars are pickpockets and any scuffle is simply a distraction by a team of thieves. For more on outsmarting thieves, see page 128.

Consular Services: The US embassy in Rome is at Via Vittorio Veneto 121 (24-hour tel. 06-46741, http://italy.usembassy.gov); consular services are also available in Florence (tel. 055-266-951) and Naples (tel. 081-583-8111). The Canadian Embassy in Rome is at Via Zara 30 (tel. 06-854-441, www.italy.gc.ca). Call ahead for passport services.

Phoning: Italy has a direct-dial phone system (no area codes). To **call within Italy,** just dial the number (keep in mind that Italian phone numbers vary in length). To **call to Italy,** dial the international access code (00 if calling from Europe, or 011 from North America), then dial 39 (Italy's country code), then the phone number. To **call home from Italy,** dial 00, 1, then your area code and phone number. For more help, see page 1242.

Dress Code: Some major churches enforce a modest dress code (no bare shoulders or shorts).

Tipping: A service charge (*servicio*) of about 10 percent is usually built into your restaurant bill. If you are pleased with the service, you can add an extra euro or two for each person in your party. If service isn't included (*servizio non incluso*), add a tip of about 10 percent. To tip a cabbie, round up your fare a bit (to pay a €4.50 fare, give €5).

Tourist Information: www.italia.it

NAPLES,
Sorrento, and Capri

Naples is southern Italy's leading city, offering a fascinating, gritty mix of museums, churches, and lively street scenes. Just beyond Naples you'll find the impressive ruins of Pompeii and Herculaneum...and see the brooding volcano that did them both in, Mount Vesuvius. Farther away are the resort town of Sorrento, the holiday isle of Capri, and the scenic Amalfi Coast—each of these is, up to a point, reachable from Naples on a day in port.

These destinations are well-connected by Circumvesuviana train, taxi, or boat. Long-distance buses are possible but less reliable if you're on a tight cruising timetable. If time permits, consider taking a boat—it's faster, cooler, and more scenic, and you'll enjoy coastline views you won't get from land.

Planning Your Time
Ships call at either Naples or Sorrento. While you have essentially the same options from either port, some destinations are easier to reach from one than from the other.

If you dock at **Naples,** an easy choice is to spend your day in the city, visiting the Archaeological Museum and following my self-guided walk through the downtown. The ruins at Pompeii and Herculaneum are each a short train ride away. Or you can take a boat across the bay to the island of Capri. Sorrento and the Amalfi Coast are farther away, and harder to squeeze into a single day.

From **Sorrento,** you're a short boat ride away from the island of Capri, and a train ride from Pompeii and Herculaneum. You're also near the dramatic Amalfi Coast (easiest with a hired driver or cruise-line excursion).

Excursions from Naples or Sorrento

In this region, the best excursions are those to **Naples,** the ancient Roman archaeological sites of **Pompeii** or the smaller **Herculaneum,** the romantic island of **Capri,** or the dramatic and staggeringly vertical **Amalfi Coast.** The following two options—a bit farther afield—round out the possibilities.

To escape the heat and the crowds, visit the desolate, lunar-like 4,000-foot-high **Vesuvius** (an hour southeast of Naples), mainland Europe's only active volcano (it last erupted in 1944). A steep 30-minute climb takes you from the parking lot to the often cold and windy top for a sweeping view of the Bay of Naples. Walk the entire crater lip for the most interesting views; the far end overlooks Pompeii.

Paestum (2 hours southeast of Naples) has one of the best collections of Greek temples anywhere, and its archaeological museum offers the rare opportunity to see beautifully crafted artifacts—dating from prehistoric to Greek to Roman times—at the site where they were discovered.

Note that some cruise lines advertise a stop in **"Capri,"** but actually dock across the bay, in Naples.

Your Top Options

Here are quick descriptions, with time estimates, of your top choices:

• **Naples** has two major experiences: first, its excellent Archaeological Museum, with Pompeii's best art (worth two hours, museum closed on Tue); and second, my self-guided walk through Naples' vibrant streets, from the museum to Piazza del Plebiscito, near the port (Parts 1 and 2; allow 1 hour), and with extra time, on to the train station (Part 3; allow 2 more hours, with stops in churches). If arriving in Naples, you can reach these sights in a matter of minutes by public transportation or taxi. From Sorrento, add 70 minutes each way by train or 35 minutes by express boat (the boat runs only every 2 hours).

• Allow up to five hours to tour **Pompeii**'s ruins (2-3 hours at the site, plus the train from either Naples or Sorrento—the site is roughly between these two ports).

• Fans of Roman antiquity can spend a marvelous day combining **Pompeii** and **Naples' Archaeological Museum** (allow up to 9 hours total, including the Circumvesuviana train between them; if coming from Sorrento, add about 30 minutes to reach Pompeii, then 70 minutes by train or 35 minutes by infrequent express boat from Naples back to Sorrento).

• If time is tight, **Herculaneum**—which is like a small Pompeii—takes only an hour to tour (allow a total of 3 hours from Naples or 3.5 hours from Sorrento).

• The resort town of **Sorrento** is pleasant, but has little actual sightseeing (my self-guided walk takes about an hour). If you're docking in Naples, it's not worth coming to Sorrento just to see the town (about 2 hours round-trip by boat or 2.5 hours round-trip by train). If your ship docks in Sorrento, and you want to visit Pompeii and Naples' Archaeological Museum by Circumvesuviana train, allow up to 9 hours.

• The island of **Capri** will fill an entire day. Be careful to factor in transportation time for the boat trip from either Sorrento (about 20-25 minutes) or Naples (about 50 minutes); only a few cruises tender passengers directly to Capri. If you want to see Capri's Blue Grotto, check that the tide isn't too high or the water too rough—ask at the TI in Naples or Sorrento before you go.

• The scenic **Amalfi Coast** takes a full day to see. From Sorrento, it's most easily done with a hired driver. From Naples, it's best to hire one of the taxis waiting eagerly at the terminal (with reasonable and fixed rates for the trip) or join a shore excursion.

Naples

Neapolis ("new city") was a thriving Greek commercial center 2,500 years ago. Today it's Italy's third-largest city, with more than

one million people. Walking through its colorful Old Town is one of my favorite sightseeing experiences anywhere in Italy.

The pulse of Italy throbs in Naples (*Napoli* in Italian). Like Cairo or Mumbai, it's appalling and captivating at the same time, the closest thing to "reality travel" that you'll find in Western Europe. But this tangled mess still somehow manages to breathe, laugh, and sing—with a captivating Italian accent.

In Naples, like almost no other port, the ship docks in the center of town. You are literally a five-minute walk from the terminal into the intensity of this wild and exciting Italian city.

Arrival at the Port of Naples

Arrival at a Glance: If you want to see Naples, take a taxi, bus (or, if it's running, the subway) to the Archaeological Museum, which is also the start of my self-guided walk. For other sights in the region, take a taxi or tram to the train station, then take the Circum-vesuviana commuter train to Herculaneum (20 minutes), Pompeii (40 minutes) or Sorrento (70 minutes). You can also take a boat to Capri (50 minutes) or Sorrento (35 minutes; boats depart from near the cruise terminal). A round-trip taxi to Pompeii (including waiting time) costs €90; one-way to Sorrento costs €100.

Port Overview

Naples' cruise terminal (Stazione Marittima) is conveniently located at the southeast edge of downtown Naples, immediately below

the Castel Nuovo and near the grand square called Piazza del Plebiscito. The terminal complex is a stern, blocky, fascist-style bunker with two separate buildings connected by a second-story concourse that forms a covered, garage-like area containing some helpful services.

Walking straight out from the cruise terminal, you're facing the old center of Naples. A busy street runs along the waterfront in front of the terminal area (called Via Ammiraglio Ferdinando Acton to the left and Via Cristoforo Colombo to the right). To the left is the Molo Beverello dock, with boats to Sorrento and Capri. To the right is the stop for tram #1 to Centrale Station as well as Porta Nolana Station (Circumvesuviana terminus). The square straight ahead (across the road) is called Piazza Municipio, and off it to the right is the stop for bus #R4 to Naples' world-class Archaeological Museum. All of these options are explained in detail later.

Tourist Information: The cruise terminal is well set up for independent travelers. As you exit the terminal complex, you'll pass through a little checkpoint (marked *Molo Angioino*) that has a small TI with maps and helpful, knowledgeable attendants who can get you oriented and answer questions. There are other TIs elsewhere in Naples (see page 623), but they're no better than this one.

Getting to the Sights

Whether you're staying in Naples or heading to nearby sights, you can either pay for a taxi or use public transport.

By Taxi

As you leave the cruise terminal, you'll find a taxi stand ahead and to the left. Taxis offer various sightseeing tours at fixed, govern-

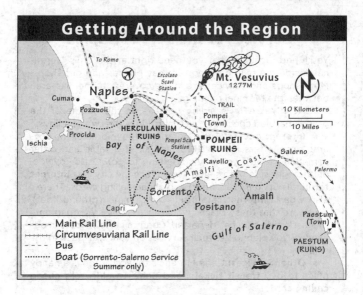

Getting Around the Region

To Rome

Naples

Cumae

Pozzuoli

Ercolano
Scavi
Station

Mt. Vesuvius
1277M

TRAIL

10 Kilometers

10 Miles

Pompei
(Town)

HERCULANEUM
RUINS

Ischia

Procida

Bay of Naples

Pompei Scavi
Station

POMPEII
RUINS

Salerno

To
Palermo

Ravello

Amalfi Coast

Sorrento

Capri

Positano

Amalfi

Paestum
(Town)

Gulf of Salerno

PAESTUM
(RUINS)

- - - - - Main Rail Line
+++++ Circumvesuviana Rail Line
- - - Bus
.... Boat (Sorrento-Salerno Service
          Summer only)

ment-set prices, which can be split by up to four passengers. These taxis are super-competitive and, especially when shared with other travelers, can be very economical. Here are the standard rates to points both in Naples and throughout the region:

- To the Archaeological Museum or the train station: €12-15
- Two-hour tour around Naples: €70
- Round-trip to Pompeii including a two-hour wait: €90
- Round-trip to Herculaneum including a two-hour wait: €70
- Round-trip to Pompeii and Herculaneum including waiting time: €130
- One-way to Sorrento: €100

Agree on a set price *(tariffa predeterminata)* without the meter. Pay only when you're back safely and happily at the port. You'll be charged a legitimate supplement on Sundays and holidays.

You can also arrange to join a tour or hire a driver before you arrive in Naples; for details, see "By Tour," later.

By Public Transportation

If you'll be taking a public bus, tram, or subway in Naples, get your **tickets** at the tobacco shop inside the terminal complex, within the Caffè Moreno in the covered area between the two buildings. Local transit tickets cost €1.30 apiece; day passes cost €3.70. Validate the ticket in the yellow box as you board. For now, only trams and buses serve the port, but when the new Metro station under Piazza Municipio opens (possibly in 2015), you'll be able to jump on the Metro from here as well.

However, if you'd like to stretch your legs, you can **walk—**

Services at the Port of Naples

You'll find most of what you need right at the cruise terminal. Inside the twin buildings are pay phones and gift shops. More shops and services are in the covered, tunnel-like area between the terminal buildings.

ATM: An ATM is hiding upstairs, in the middle of the grand, marbled check-in area that bridges the two buildings.

Internet Access: Caffè Moreno, in the middle of the covered area, offers free **Wi-Fi** if you sit at a table and order something (not if you buy something to go). Caffè Tovaldo, on the right side of this area as you face the city, has **Internet terminals** upstairs (€3/hour) and cheap calling cards. There's also a basic **Internet café** inside the terminal (ground floor). Be aware that these places won't necessarily stay open until the last cruise ship has departed: Confirm closing hours in advance if you plan to use their services on your way back to the ship.

Other Services: Caffè Moreno's tobacco shop is a handy place to buy **transit tickets,** and Caffè Tovaldo sells **cheap calling cards.**

both the Archaeological Museum and the train station are about 45 gently uphill minutes away (in different directions).

To Sights in Naples

The **Archaeological Museum** stands at the top of town. Head here either to tour its impressive collection or to begin my self-guided walk downhill through old Naples. You can get to the museum by taxi, bus, or Metro.

To reach the stop for bus #R4 (and, en route, check on the progress of the new Municipio Metro stop), walk straight out of the cruise terminal and to the busy road. Bear right to the traffic-light crosswalk and cross this road to Piazza Municipio. If the new Metro station is open, hop on line 1 and ride it three stops to Museo. If the Metro isn't open, continue straight up Piazza Municipio for three short blocks to the busy street called Via Agostino Depretis. Cross this street, then turn right and walk along it about a half-block to the Depretis stop (in front of a single palm tree) for bus #R4 (departs every 10-15 minutes). Ride this bus six stops to Piazza Museo.

Another way to reach the museum is to walk all the way up to the top of Piazza Municipio, then another five minutes along Via San Giacomo to reach Via Toledo, Naples' shopping boulevard. There you'll see the Toledo Metro station a block away (look for the red *M* signs). Board the Metro and take it two stops to Museo (you may have to switch trains at the intermediate Dante stop).

From the museum, you can take my self-guided walk through Naples. If you only do Parts 1 and 2 of the walk, you'll end up near Piazza del Plebiscito, an easy 10-minute walk from the cruise terminal. Part 3 immerses you even more deeply (and enjoyably) in the quirky urban world of Naples, taking you across town and ending near Centrale Station. From Piazza Garibaldi (the giant square in front of the train station), you can catch tram #1 back to the port.

If you're more interested in the city of Naples than in the Archaeological Museum, you can join my self-guided walk partway through, at **Piazza del Plebiscito**, a 10-minute walk from the port: After crossing the busy street in front of the port, head up the ramp just to the right of the castle. At the top, angle left, past Teatro di San Carlo, to Piazza del Plebiscito.

To Herculaneum, Pompeii, or Sorrento by Circumvesuviana Train

Trains to Herculaneum, Pompeii, and Sorrento run on the Circumvesuviana line, which terminates in Naples at the Porta Nolana Station. (Trains to other points in Italy—such as Rome—leave from Centrale Station, very close by.) Be warned that the Circumvesuviana is popular among thieves—keep a close eye on your belongings. Circumvesuviana tickets are sold at newsstands (including in the cruise terminal) and at the station itself.

To reach the Circumvesuviana train from the cruise terminal, you can either take a taxi (€12-15) or ride tram #1 (€1.30, 6/hour; it leaves from a platform in the middle of the big road just to the right as you walk toward the city from the terminal). Take the tram a couple of stops to the Circumvesuviana terminus (at Porta Nolana Station). Look for trains marked *Sorrento* (the end point), which depart twice hourly. These take you to **Herculaneum/Ercolano Scavi** (about 20 minutes, €2.20 one-way), **Pompeii** (about 40 minutes, €2.90 one-way), and **Sorrento,** the end of the line (70 minutes, €4.20 one-way). Not every train goes as far as Sorrento; check the schedule and confirm with a local before boarding. Express trains marked *DD* (6/day) get you to Sorrento 15 minutes faster (and also stop at Herculaneum and Pompeii).

If you're going to the ancient site of Pompeii, be sure to use the Circumvesuviana train's Pompei Scavi stop. Don't use national train connections from Centrale Station to the modern-day city of Pompei (which might seem convenient, but is far from the ruins).

Catching the Circumvesuviana from Centrale Station: If you miss the Circumvesuviana terminus, you can also catch the Circumvesuviana from within Centrale Station on Piazza Garibaldi. Go into the station and follow the signs to *Circumvesuviana* (across from track 13, downstairs and down the corridor to the

NAPLES

left), where you'll find the ticket office and info booth. The train platforms are downstairs.

To Capri or Sorrento by Boat

Naples is well-connected by boat to Capri (1-2/hour, 50 minutes, €19-21) and Sorrento (6 hydrofoils/day, more in summer, leaves roughly every 2 hours starting at 9:00, 35 minutes, €12-13). While there are several competing companies, all boats are essentially the same speed and price. Taking the hydrofoil between Naples and Sorrento is faster—and safer from pickpockets—than the Circum-vesuviana train, though it doesn't run as frequently.

Conveniently, Naples' local boat dock (called Molo Beverello) is almost right next to the cruise terminal: As you exit the cruise terminal, bear left, following the well-marked crosswalks to *Molo Beverello*. Pass the row of cafés to reach the blue-and-white Molo Beverello building. The big info screen between the ticket building and the cafés (close to the water) shows the next six boat departures. Because the competing company sales windows show nothing but their own departures, this screen is a handy summary of what's leaving and when. There's a low-key info point (offering the best unbiased info on departures) and a left-luggage desk on the water side of the ticket building (at the far end).

Before taking the boat anywhere, first be absolutely certain that you can make it back to your cruise ship with plenty of time to spare. Ask and double-check with the ticket sellers. Buy a ticket for whichever boat is leaving soonest to your destination, and also buy your return ticket, reserving a seat in advance if possible. If crowds are expected on the return boat, arrive at the dock early. The last boat usually leaves before 19:00, and trips are cancelled in bad weather.

By Tour

Consider the **Can't Be Missed** tour company, which gives you a quick look at Naples, Sorrento, and Pompeii with a small group and local guide for €65 (meet at 8:30 in front of port, bus leaves at 9:00, returns at 17:00, Pompeii ticket extra, mobile 329-129-8182, www.cantbemissedtours.com).

For private car service, try **SeeAmalfiCoast,** which specializes in cruise-ship excursions from Naples to the Amalfi Coast (tel. 081-622-517, www.seeamalficoast.com). You can also try one of the drivers specializing in the Amalfi Coast (listed on page 668).

For information on hiring a **local guide** in Naples, see page 626; for Pompeii, see page 652.

Returning to Your Ship

If you end up on Naples' **Piazza del Plebiscito,** you're about a 10-minute walk from your ship: Simply go to the bottom corner of the palace, walk down the stairs to the embankment, then head straight to the cruise terminal—you can see your ship from here.

If you end my self-guided walk near **Piazza Garibaldi** (near Centrale Station), just hop on tram #1 back to Stazione Marittima.

If you're returning to Naples on the **Circumvesuviana,** stay on until the last stop and head out the front door to the street called Corso Garibaldi. Take a taxi, or hop on any tram heading to the left and ride it to Stazione Marittima. (If the new Municipio Metro station is up and running, another option is to hop off the Circumvesuviana one stop earlier, at Garibaldi, and take Metro line 1 from the Garibaldi stop to the Municipio stop, a few minutes' walk above the port. However, unless you're sure the Municipio Metro stop is open, the first option is better.)

If you're returning by **boat,** it's very easy: You'll dock in the shadow of your towering cruise ship.

For information on what to do if you've missed your boat, see the sidebar on page 699.

Orientation to Naples

Naples is set deep inside the large and curving Bay of Naples, with Mount Vesuvius looming just five miles away. Although Naples is a sprawling city, its fairly compact core contains the most interesting sights. The tourist's Naples is a triangle, with its points at the Centrale train station in the east, the Archaeological Museum to the west, and Piazza del Plebiscito (with the Royal Palace) and the port to the south. Steep hills rise above this historic core, including San Martino, capped with a mighty fortress.

Tourist Information

Take full advantage of the small tourist info desk as you exit the cruise port. Otherwise, there's a TI in Naples' Centrale train station (daily 9:00-19:00, near track 23, operated by a private agency, tel. 081-268-779).

Arrival in Naples
By Boat
If you're arriving by cruise ship or by boat from Sorrento or Capri, see "Arrival at the Port of Naples," earlier.

By Circumvesuviana Train
If your cruise ship docks in Sorrento, and you're taking the Cir-

cumvesuviana train to Naples, you can ride it all the way to the Circumvesuviana terminus at Napoli Porta Nolana (the last stop, which faces the thriving Porta Nolana market and is close to the old town action).

Or, if you're going directly to the Archaeological Museum and the start of my self-guided walk, get off one stop earlier, at the Garibaldi commuter rail station on the lower level of the Centrale Station complex. To take a **taxi** from here to the museum, ride the escalator up into Centrale Station, where you'll find a TI (near track 23) and an ATM (at Banco di Napoli near track 24). Taxis wait outside; figure on €12 for a ride to the museum (insist on the meter—*tassametro*).

To take the **subway** to the museum, follow *Metropolitana* signs to the Metro, located downstairs at the Garibaldi subway station (across from track 13). You can use your Circumvesuviana train ticket to cover all public transit within three hours of validation (no need to validate again). Ask which track—*"Quale binario?"* (KWAH-lay bee-NAH-ree-oh)—to Piazza Cavour (direction: Pozzuoli, usually track 4). Validate your ticket in one of the small yellow boxes near the escalator going down to the tracks. Hop on any train that comes through (confirm by its sign or with a local that it's going to the museum), and ride the subway one stop to Cavour. As you leave the Metro, exit and hike five minutes uphill through the park along the busy street. Look for a grand old red building up a flight of stairs at the top of the block.

To return by Metro to Centrale Station, make sure to catch your train in the Cavour subway station, rather than at the connected Museo stop (which is on a different line).

Helpful Hints

Theft Alert: Err on the side of caution. Don't venture into neighborhoods that make you uncomfortable. Walk with confidence, as if you know where you're going and what you're doing. Assume able-bodied beggars are thieves.

Stick to busy streets and beware of gangs of hoodlums. A third of the city is unemployed, and past local governments have set an example that the Mafia would be proud of. Assume con artists are more clever than you. Any jostle or commotion is probably a thief-team smokescreen. To keep bags safe, it's probably best to leave them at the left-luggage office in Centrale Station.

Always walk on the sidewalk (even if the locals don't) and carry your bag on the side away from the street—thieves on scooters have been known to snatch bags as they swoop by. The less you have dangling from you (including cameras and necklaces), the better.

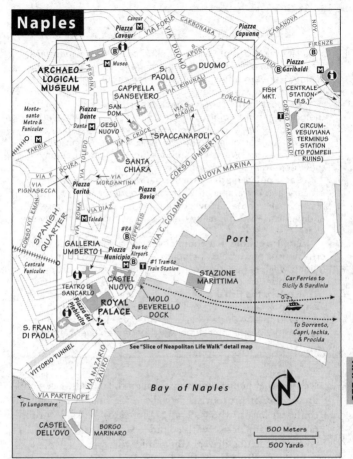

Naples

Piazza Cavour
Piazza Capuana
VIA FORIA
CARBONARA
CASANOVA
NOV.
Cavour
FIRENZE
Piazza Garibaldi
VIA DUOMO
ARCHAEO-LOGICAL MUSEUM
Museo
S. PAOLO
DUOMO
S. APOST.
VIA TRIBUNALI
POERIO
CENTRALE STATION (F.S.)
CAPPELLA SANSEVERO
SAN DOM.
VIA S. BIAGIO
FORCELLA
FISH MKT.
CIRCUM-VESUVIANA TERMINUS STATION (TO POMPEII RUINS)
Monte-santo Metro & Funicular
Piazza Dante
Dante
GESÙ NUOVO
"SPACCANAPOLI"
VIA P. CROCE
CORSO GARIBALDI
TAKSIA
VIA P. SCURA
VIA TOLEDO
SANTA CHIARA
VIA MORGANTINA
Piazza Bovio
CORSO UMBERTO I
NUOVA MARINA
VIA P. SCURA
Piazza Carità
SPANISH QUARTER
CORSO VITEMAN
VIA PIGNASECCA
VIA ROMA
VIA DIAZ
Toledo
#R4
VIA DEPRETIS
VIA C. COLOMBO
Port
Centrale Funicular
GALLERIA UMBERTO I
Piazza Municipio
Bus to Airport
#1 Tram to Train Station
STAZIONE MARITTIMA
Car Ferries to Sicily & Sardinia
TEATRO DI SANCARLO
CASTEL NUOVO
Piazza del Plebiscito
ROYAL PALACE
MOLO BEVERELLO DOCK
S. FRAN. DI PAOLA
VITTORIO TUNNEL
VIA NAZARIO SAURO
See "Slice of Neapolitan Life Walk" detail map
To Sorrento, Capri, Ischia, & Procida
VIA PARTENOPE
To Lungomare
Bay of Naples
N
CASTEL DELL'OVO
BORGO MARINARO
500 Meters
500 Yards

NAPLES

Perhaps your biggest risk of theft is while catching or riding the Circumvesuviana commuter train. It's prime hunting ground for thieves. While I ride the Circumvesuviana comfortably and safely, each year I hear of many travelers who get ripped off on this ride. You won't be mugged—but you may be conned or pickpocketed. For maximum safety and peace of mind, sit in the front car, where the driver will double as your protector, and avoid riding after dark.

Con artists may say you need to "transfer" by taxi to catch the Circumvesuviana; you don't. Wear your money belt, hang on to your bag, and don't display any valuables.

Traffic Safety: In Naples, red lights are discretionary, and pedestrians need to be wary, particularly of motor scooters. Even on "pedestrian" streets, stay alert to avoid being sideswiped by

Naples Experiences for Cruisers

While it boasts one of Europe's best archaeological museums, Naples is one place that's about experiences more than sight-seeing. Here are a few suggestions for a "cultural scavenger hunt" of untouristy Naples, doable even with just a day in port.

Get lost in the tangled back lanes. Naples has some of the grittiest, most colorful street life this side of the developing world. Go for a stroll through a workaday neighborhood, noticing the balconies lining the walls of the urban canyon high above you. Wave at someone up high on a balcony; if they seem friendly, strike up a conversation.

Seek out a made-to-order sandwich. Step into a tiny grocery and communicate with the proprietor that you want him to make you a sandwich with his favorite meat, cheese, and garnish. Pay for it all by the weight...without getting over-charged.

Light a candle in a church. Naples has particularly powerful houses of worship (including some described on my self-guided walk, page 628). Visit one of these—or just drop into any neighborhood church—and light a candle.

Explore the fish market. If you're here in the morning and want a look at colorful, workaday Naples, stroll through the lively (and smelly) Porta Nolana fish market. Listen to the droning sales pitches of the fishmongers, perfected over centuries.

NAPLES

scooters that nudge their way through the crowds. Keep children close. Smart tourists jaywalk in the shadow of bold and confident locals, who generally ignore crosswalks. Wait for a break in traffic, cross with confidence, and make eye contact with approaching drivers. The traffic will stop.

Local Guides: Pina Esposito knows her ancient archaeology and art and does fine private walking and driving tours of Naples and the region (Pompeii, Capri, etc.), including Naples' Archaeological Museum (€60/hour, 2-hour minimum, 10 percent off with this book, lower rates for full-day tours, mobile 366-622-8217, giuseppina.esposito20@istruzione.it). The team at **Mondo Tours** also offers private tours of the museum (€120/2 hours), city (€240/4 hours), and region, along with special group tours for my readers—see page 628 (tel. 081-751-3290, www.mondoguide.it, info@mondoguide.it).

Supermarket: Superò is a block off Piazza Dante (Mon-Sat 8:30-20:30, Sun 8:30-14:00, Via San Domenico Soriano 20e).

Laundry: Laundry DIY, between Piazza Dante and the Archaeological Museum, will—despite their name—do your laundry for you (€8/load, Mon-Fri 8:00-19:30, Sat 8:00-13:15, closed Sun, Via Vincenzo Bellini 50, mobile 339-318-0876).

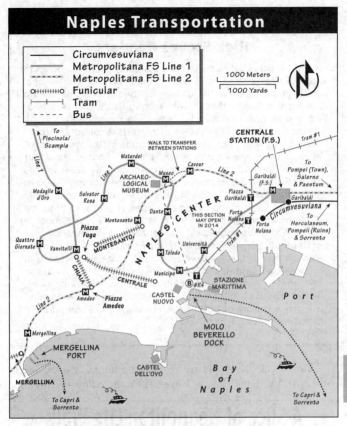

Naples Transportation

——— Circumvesuviana
——— Metropolitana FS Line 1
- - - - Metropolitana FS Line 2
o⊦⊦⊦⊦⊦⊦o Funicular
⊢⊢⊢⊢⊢ Tram
- - - - - Bus

1000 Meters
1000 Yards

Getting Around Naples

Naples' subway, the Metropolitana, has three main lines.

Line 2 runs from Centrale Station (catch it downstairs at the Garibaldi stop) through the center of town (direction: Pozzuoli), stopping at Piazza Cavour (a five-minute walk from the Archaeological Museum) and Montesanto (top of Spanish Quarter and Spaccanapoli street). Line 1 is being extended, adding new stations that may be open when you visit. From the Museo stop (Archaeological Museum), line 1 heads to Dante (at Piazza Dante, between the museum and Spaccanapoli), Toledo (south end of Via Toledo, near Piazza del Plebiscito), Municipio (possibly opening in 2015; at Piazza Municipio, just above the cruise terminal), Università (the university), Duomo (likely to open in 2016; near the cathedral and the end of my self-guided walk), and Garibaldi (on Piazza Garibaldi, in front of Centrale Station). Line 6 is not yet complete; it will begin at Municipio and head west—unlikely to be of much use to tourists.

Mondo Tours Offers Shared Tours for Rick Steves Readers

Mondo Tours, a big Naples-based company, offers co-op tours for Rick Steves readers. These include a private, professional guide at a fraction of the usual cost (because you're sharing the expense with other travelers using this book). A schedule of offerings is on their website, www.mondoguide.it (look for the Rick Steves tab). Pre-registration is required, and tours depart only if at least eight people sign up (16-person maximum). Call or email a day or two ahead to confirm your tour will run, then pay cash to the guide (tel. 081-751-3290, mobile 340-460-5254, info@mondoguide.it). Note that you'll have to make your own way to the starting point for each tour. Tours run April-October and include **Pompeii** (€12, doesn't include €11 Pompeii entry, likely Mon-Fri at 10:00, 1.5 hours, meet in Pompeii at Ristorante Suisse on Piazza Esedra), a walking tour of **Naples** (€20; likely Mon, Wed, and Fri at 15:00; 3 hours, meet at the steps of the Archaeological Museum—not included in the walk), a **Pompeii and Naples** combo (€30; Mon, Wed, and Fri); and an **Amalfi Coast minibus tour** from Sorrento (€45, likely Mon-Fri at 9:00, 9 hours, meet in Sorrento overlooking the gorge in front of Hotel Antiche Mura at Via Fuorimura 7, a block inland from Piazza Tasso).

Tickets cost €1.30 and are good for 1.5 hours. All-day tickets cost €3.70. Validate tickets as you enter (in the yellow machines).

A Slice of Neapolitan Life Walk

Naples, a living medieval city, is its own best sight. Couples artfully make love on Vespas surrounded by more fights and smiles per cobblestone than anywhere else in Italy. Rather than seeing Naples as a list of sights, start by visiting its one great museum—the Archaeological Museum (see my self-guided tour on page 639)—and then capture the essence of Naples by taking this walk through the core of the city.

From the Archaeological Museum to Centrale Station

This self-guided walk takes you from the Archaeological Museum through the heart of town to near the port (Part 1 and Part 2), then across town to Centrale Station (Part 3). Allow at least three hours, plus time for pizza and sightseeing stops. If you're in a rush, do just Part 1 and Part 2, ending close to the port. Should you become overwhelmed or lost, step into a store and ask for directions. For example, "Where is the Centrale Station?" in Italian is

"A Slice of Neapolitan Life" Walk

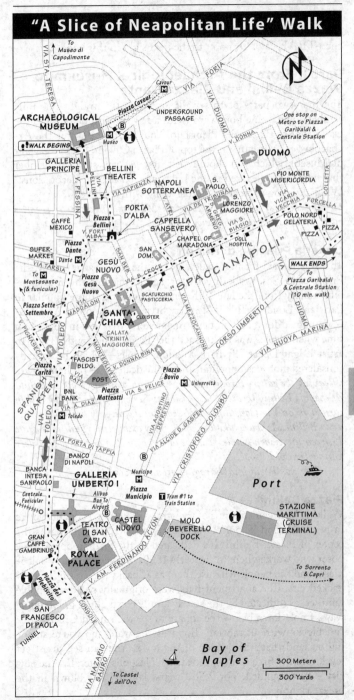

To Museo di Capodimonte

To Sta. Teresa

VIA FORIA

Cavour

Piazza Cavour

VIA DUOMO

UNDERGROUND PASSAGE

V. DONNA

One stop on Metro to Piazza Garibaldi & Centrale Station

ARCHAEOLOGICAL MUSEUM

Museo

WALK BEGINS

DUOMO

GALLERIA PRINCIPE

BELLINI THEATER

NAPOLI SOTTERRANEA

S. PAOLO

PIO MONTE MISERICORDIA

VIA SAPIENZA

VIA DEI TRIBUNALI

S. LORENZO MAGGIORE

VICARIA VECCHIA

FORCELLA

COLLETTA

CAFFÈ MEXICO

PORTA D'ALBA

Piazza Bellini

CAPPELLA SANSEVERO

VIA S. BIAGIO

DOLL HOSPITAL

POLO NORD GELATERIA

PIZZA

PIZZA

SUPER-MARKET

Piazza Dante

Dante

SAN DOM.

CHAPEL OF MARADONA

"SPACCANAPOLI"

WALK ENDS

To Piazza Garibaldi & Centrale Station (10 min. walk)

GESÙ NUOVO

Piazza Gesù Nuovo

VIA B. CROCE

To Montesanto (& funicular)

VIA TARSIA

SCATURCHIO PASTICCERIA

VIA MEZZOCANNONE

CORSO UMBERTO I

VIA NUOVA MARINA

Piazza Sette Settembre

SANTA CHIARA

CLOISTER

CALATA TRINITÀ MAGGIORE

VIA TOLEDO

FASCIST BLDG.

V. DONNALBINA

Piazza Bovio

Università

Piazza Carità

POST

Piazza Matteotti

VIA S. FELICE

BNL BANK

VIA A. DIAZ

SPANISH QUARTER

VIA AGOSTINO DEPRETIS

VIA ALCIDE D. GASPERI

VIA CRISTOFORO COLOMBO

Toledo

VIA PORTA DI TAPPIA

BANCO DI NAPOLI

Municipio

B

Port

BANCA INTESA SANPAOLO

Centrale Funicular

GALLERIA UMBERTO I

Alibus Bus To Airport

Piazza Municipio

Tram #1 to Train Station

STAZIONE MARITTIMA (CRUISE TERMINAL)

GRAN CAFFÈ GAMBRINUS

TEATRO DI SAN CARLO

CASTEL NUOVO

MOLO BEVERELLO DOCK

ROYAL PALACE

V. AM. FERDINANDO ACTON

To Sorrento & Capri

Piazza del Plebiscito

SAN FRANCESCO DI PAOLA

CONSOLE

TUNNEL

VIA NAZARIO SAURO

Bay of Naples

To Castel dell'Ovo

300 Meters

300 Yards

NAPLES

"Dov'è la Stazione Centrale?" (DOH-vay lah staht-zee-OH-nay chen-TRAH-lay). Or point to the next sight in this book.

Part 1: From the Archaeological Museum to Piazza Bellini and Piazza Dante

The first two parts of this walk are a mostly straight one-mile ramble down a fine boulevard (with a few colorful detours) to the waterfront at Piazza del Plebiscito. Your starting point is the Archaeological Museum (at the top of Piazza Cavour, Metro: Cavour or Museo), which you should visit first. As you stroll, remember that here in Naples, red traffic lights are considered "decorations." When crossing a street, try to tag along with a native.

• *From the door of the Archaeological Museum, cross the street, veer right, and pass through the fancy mall.*

Galleria Principe di Napoli

This was named for first male child of the royal Savoy family, the Prince of Naples. Walk directly through it, enjoying this fine shopping gallery from the late 19th century, similar to those popular in Paris and London. This is "Liberty Style," a variation of Art Nouveau (named for a British department store) that was in vogue at a time when Naples was nicknamed the "Paris of the South." Parisian artist Edgar Degas left Paris to adopt Naples—which he actually considered more cosmopolitan and sophisticated—as his hometown.

• *Leaving the gallery through the opposite end, walk one block downhill. At the fine Bellini Theater (in the Liberty Style), jog left one block, then turn right on Via Constantinopoli, continuing directly downhill to Piazza Bellini. As you walk, look up to enjoy architecture built in the late 19th century, when Naples was the last stop on Romantic Age travelers' Grand Tour of Europe.*

Soon you'll run into the ragtag urban park called...

Piazza Bellini

Walking between columns of two grand churches, suddenly you're in neighborhood Napoli. A statue of Vincenzo Bellini marks the center of Piazza Bellini. It's dedicated to the Sicilian opera composer who worked here in the early 1800s. Survey the many balconies—and the people who use them as a "backyard" in this densely packed city. The apartment flats were originally palaces of noble families, as indicated by the stately family crests above grand doorways. Look down below the square to see the ruined Greek walls: tuff blocks without mortar. This was the wall, and you're standing on land that was outside of the town. You can see the street level from the fifth century B.C., when Neapolis—literally "the new city"—was founded. For 2,500 years, laundry has blown in the breeze right here.

• *Walk 30 yards downhill. Stop at the horseshoe-shaped Port'Alba gate (on the right). Spin slowly 360 degrees and take in the scene. The proud tile across the street shows Piazza Bellini circa 1890. Learn to ignore graffiti (as the locals do). Pass through the gate, and stroll past the book stalls down Via Port'Alba to the next big square...*

Piazza Dante

This square is marked by a statue of Dante, the medieval poet. Fittingly, half the square is devoted to bookstores. Old Dante looks out over an urban area that was once grand, then chaotic, and is now slowly becoming grand again.

While this square feels perfectly Italian to me, for many Neapolitans it represents the repression of the central Italian state. When Napoleon was defeated, Naples briefly became its own independent kingdom. But within a few decades of Italian unification in 1861, Naples went from being a thriving cultural and political capital to a provincial town, its money used to help establish the industrial strength of the north, its dialect considered backward, and its bureaucrats transferred to Rome.

Originally, a statue of a Spanish Bourbon king stood in the square. (The grand red-and-gray building is typical of Bourbon structures from that period.) But with the unification of Italy, the king, symbolic of Naples' colonial subjugation, was replaced by Dante, the father of the unified Italian language—a strong symbol of nationalism (and yet another form of subjugation).

The Neapolitan people are survivors. A long history of corrupt and greedy colonial overlords (German, Norman, French, Austrian, and Spanish) has taught Neapolitans to deal creatively with authority. Many credit this aspect of Naples' past for the strength of organized crime here.

Across the street, **Caffè Mexico** (at #86) is an institution known for its espresso, which is served already sweetened—ask for *senza zucchero* if you don't want sugar (pay first, then take receipt to the counter and hand it over). Most Italians agree that Neapolitan coffee is the best anywhere.

• *Walk downhill on...*

Via Toledo

The long, straight street heading downhill from Piazza Dante is Naples' principal shopping drag. It originated as a military road built under Spanish rule (hence the name) in the 16th century. Via Toledo skirted the old town wall to connect the Spanish military headquarters (now the museum where you started this walk) with the Royal Palace (down by the bay, where you're heading). As you stroll, peek into lovely atriums, an ancient urban design feature providing a break from the big street.

NAPLES

After a couple of hundred yards, you'll reach **Piazza Sette Settembre.** In 1860, from the white marble balcony of the Neoclassical building overlooking the square, the famous revolutionary Giuseppe Garibaldi declared Italy united and Victor Emmanuel II its first king. Only in 1870, a decade later, was the dream of Italian unity fully realized when Rome fell to unification forces.

• *Continue straight on Via Toledo. About three blocks below Piazza Dante and a block past Piazza Sette Settembre, you'll come to Via Maddaloni, which marks the start of the long, straight, narrow street nicknamed...*

Spaccanapoli

Before crossing the street—whose name translates as "split Naples"—look left (toward the train station). Then look right (to see San Martino hill rising steeply above the center). Since ancient times, this thin street has bisected the city. It changes names several times: Via Maddaloni (as it's called here), Via B. Croce, Via S. Biagio dei Librai, and Via Vicaria Vecchia.

Part 2: Monumental Naples (Via Toledo, the Spanish Quarter, and Piazza del Plebiscito)

• *We'll detour off of Via Toledo for just a couple of blocks (rejoining it later). At the Spaccanapoli intersection, go right (toward the church facade on the hill, up Via Pasquale Scura). After about 100 yards, you hit a busy intersection. Stop. You're on one of Naples' most colorful open-air market streets...*

Via Pignasecca Market

Snoop around from here if you are so inclined. Then, turn left down Via Pignasecca and stroll this colorful strip. You'll pass meat and fish stalls, produce stands, street-food vendors, and much more. This is a taste of Naples' famous Spanish Quarter, which we'll experience more of later in this walk.

• *Via Pignasecca meets back up with Via Toledo at the square called...*

Piazza Carità

This square, built for an official visit by Hitler to Mussolini in 1938, is full of stern, straight, obedient lines. The big building belonged to an insurance company. (For the best fascist architecture in town, take a slight detour from here: With your back to Via Toledo, leave Piazza Carità downhill on the right-hand corner and walk a block to the Poste e Telegrafi building. There you'll see several government buildings with stirring reliefs singing the praises of lobotomized workers and a totalitarian society.)

In Naples—long a poor and rough city—rather than being heroic, people learn from the cradle the art of survival. The modern memorial statue in the center of the square celebrates Salvo d'Acquisto, a rare hometown hero. In 1943, he was executed after falsely confessing to sabotage...in order to save 22 fellow Italian soldiers from a Nazi revenge massacre.

• *From Piazza Carità, continue south down Via Toledo for a few blocks, looking to your left for more...*

Fascist Architecture (Banks)

You can't miss the two big, blocky bank buildings. First comes the chalky-white BNL Bank. A bit farther down, past the Metro, imagine trying to rob the even more imposing Banco di Napoli (Via Toledo 178). Step across the street and check out its architecture: typical fascist arches and reliefs, built to celebrate the bank's 400th anniversary (est. 1539—how old is *your* bank?).

The street here was pedestrianized after the Toledo Metro stop opened in 2012. Now, the street is even more popular for strolling, property values have risen, and international brands such as H&M and the Disney Store have moved in.

• *On the next block (at #184) is the...*

Banca Intesa Sanpaolo

This fills an older palace—take a free peek at the opulent atrium. In the entry hall, you can buy a ticket for the **Galleria d'Italia Palazzo Zevallos Stigliano,** a small collection located in the upper two floors. The gallery's only piece worth seeing—on the second floor—is a great late Caravaggio painting. *The Martyrdom of Saint Ursula* shows a terrible scene: His marriage proposal rejected, the king of the Huns shoots an arrow into Ursula's chest. Blood spurts, Ursula is stunned but accepts her destiny sweetly, and Caravaggio himself—far right, his last self-portrait—screams to symbolize the rejection of evil. The rest of the second floor holds opulent chandeliered apartments, a few Neapolitan landscapes, and little else. The first floor has temporary exhibits (€4, Tue-Sun 10:00-18:00, closed Mon; entry includes 40-minute audioguide, a look at old Naples paintings, and a fine WC; Via Toledo 185, tel. 800-454-229, www.palazzozevallos.com).

• *Feeling bold? From here, you could side-trip uphill a couple of blocks into the...*

Spanish Quarter

This is a classic world of *basso* (low) living. The streets—which were laid out in the 16th century for the Spanish military bar-racks outside the city walls—are unbelievably narrow (and cool in summer), and the buildings rise five stories high. In such tight quarters, life—flirting, fighting, playing, and loving—happens in the road. This is *the* cliché of life in Naples, as shown in so many movies. The Spanish Quarter is Naples at its most characteristic.

The shopkeepers are friendly, and the mopeds are bold (watch out). Concerned locals will tug on their lower eyelids, warning you to be wary. Hungry? Pop into a grocery shop and ask the clerk to make you his best prosciutto-and-mozzarella sandwich (the price should be about €4).

• *Return to Via Toledo and work your way down. Across the street is the impressive Galleria Umberto I—but don't go in now, as you'll see it in a minute from the other side.*

For now, just keep heading down the main drag and through the smaller Piazza Trieste e Trento to the immense...

NAPLES

Piazza del Plebiscito

This square celebrates the 1861 vote (*plebiscito*, plebiscite) where Naples chose to join Italy. Dominating the top of the square is the **Church of San Francesco di Paola,** with its Pantheon-inspired dome and broad, arcing colonnades. If it's open, step inside to ogle the vast interior—a Neoclassical recreation of one of ancient Rome's finest buildings (free, daily 8:30-12:00 & 16:00-19:00).

• *Opposite is the...*

Royal Palace (Palazzo Reale)

Having housed Spanish, French, and even Italian royalty, this building displays statues of all those who stayed here. Look for eight kings in the niches, each from a different dynasty (left to right): Norman, German, French, Spanish, Spanish, Spanish, French (Napoleon's brother-in-law), and, finally, Italian—Victor Emmanuel II, King of Savoy. The statues were done at the request of V. E. II's son, so his dad is the most dashing of the group. While you could consider touring the interior, it's relatively unimpressive (described under "Sights in Naples," later).

• *Continue 50 yards past the Royal Palace (toward the trees) to enjoy a...*

Fine Harbor View

While boats busily serve Capri and Sorrento, Mount Vesuvius smolders ominously in the distance. (Hey, look—there's your cruise ship in the foreground!) Look back to see the vast "Bourbon red" palace—its color inspired by Pompeii. The hilltop above Piazza del Plebiscito is San Martino, home to a Carthusian monastery-turned-museum and the Castle of St. Elmo. This street continues to Naples' romantic harborfront—the fishermen's quarter (Borgo Marinaro)—a fortified island connected to the mainland by a stout causeway, with its fanciful, ancient Castel dell'Ovo (Egg Castle) and trendy harborside restaurants. Farther along the harborfront stretches the Lungomare promenade and Santa Lucia district.

• *Head back through the piazza and pop into...*

Gran Caffè Gambrinus

This coffee house, facing the piazza, takes you back to the elegance of 1860. It's a classic place to sample a unique Neapolitan treat called *sfogliatella* (crispy scallop shell-shaped pastry filled with sweet ricotta cheese). Or you might prefer the mushroom-shaped, rum-soaked bread-like cakes called *babà*, which come in a huge variety. Stand at the bar *(banco)*, pay double to sit *(tavola)*, or just wander around as you imagine the café buzzing with the ritzy in-tellectuals, journalists, and artsy bohemian types who munched on *babà* here during Naples' 19th-century heyday (daily 7:00-24:00, Piazza del Plebiscito 1, tel. 081-417-582).

• *A block away, tucked behind the palace, you can peek inside the Neo-classical...*

Teatro di San Carlo

Built in 1737, 41 years before Milan's La Scala, this is Europe's old-est opera house and Italy's second-most-respected (after La Scala). The theater burned down in 1816, and was rebuilt within the year. Guided 35-minute visits in English basically just show you the fine auditorium with its 184 boxes—each with a big mirror to reflect the candlelight (€6; tours Mon-Sat at 10:30, 11:30, 12:30, 14:30, 15:30, and 16:30; Sun at 10:30, 11:30, and 12:30; tel. 081-797-468, www.teatrosancarlo.it).

Beyond Teatro di San Carlo and the Royal Palace is the huge, harborfront **Castel Nuovo,** which houses government bureaucrats and the **Civic Museum.** It feels like a mostly empty shell, with a couple of dusty halls of Neapolitan art, but the views over the bay from the upper terraces are impressive (€5, Mon-Sat 9:00-19:00, closed Sun, tel. 081-795-7722, www.comune.napoli.it).

Cross the street from Teatro di San Carlo and go through the tall yellow arch into the Victorian iron and glass of the 100-year-old

NAPLES

shopping mall, **Galleria Umberto I.**
It was built in 1892 to reinvigorate
the district after a devastating chol-
era epidemic occurred here. Gawk
up, then walk left to bring you back
out on Via Toledo.

• *For Part 3 of this walk, double back up
Via Toledo to Piazza Carità, veering
right (just above the first big fascist-style
building we saw earlier) on Via Morgantini through Piazza Monteoliveto. Cross the busy street, then angle up Calata Trinità Maggiore to
the fancy column at the top of the hill. (To avoid the backtracking and
uphill walk, catch a €10 taxi to the Church of Gesù Nuovo—JAY-zoo
noo-OH-voh.)*

Part 3: Spaccanapoli Back to the Station

You're back at the straight-as-a-Greek-arrow Spaccanapoli, formerly the main thoroughfare of the Greek city of Neapolis.
• *Stop at...*

Piazza Gesù Nuovo

This square is marked by a towering 18th-century Baroque monument to the Counter-Reformation. Although the Jesuit order was
powerful in Naples because of its Spanish heritage, locals never
attacked Protestants here with the full fury of the Spanish Inquisition.

   If you'd like, you can visit two bulky old churches, starting
with the dark, fortress-like, 17th-century **Church of Gesù Nuovo,**
followed by the simpler **Church of Santa Chiara** (in the courtyard
across the street). Both are described in more detail later, under
"Sights in Naples."

• *After touring the churches, continue along the main drag. Since this is a
university district, you'll see lots of students and bookstores. This neighborhood is also famously superstitious. Look for incense-burning women
with carts full of good-luck charms for sale.*

   *Farther down Spaccanapoli—passing Palazzo Venezia, the em-
bassy of Venice to Naples when both were independent powers—you'll
see the next square...*

Piazza San Domenico Maggiore

This square is marked by an ornate 17th-century monument built
to thank God for ending the plague. From this square, detour left
along the right side of the castle-like church, then follow yellow
signs, taking the first right and walking one block to the remarkable **Cappella Sansevero.** This Baroque chapel is well worth visiting (described later, under "Sights in Naples").

• *After touring the chapel, return to Via B. Croce (a.k.a. Spaccanapoli), turn left, and continue your cultural scavenger hunt. At the intersection of Via Nilo, find the...*

Statue of the Nile (on the left)

A reminder of the multiethnic make-up of Greek Neapolis, this statue is in what was the Egyptian quarter. Locals like to call this statue *The Body of Naples,* with the overflowing cornucopia symbolizing the abundance of their fine city. (I once asked a Neapolitan man to describe the local women, who are famous for their beauty, in one word. He replied simply, "Abundant.") This intersection is considered the center of old Naples.

• *Directly opposite the statue, between the two doors of Bar Nilo, is the...*

"Chapel of Maradona"

The small "chapel" on the wall is dedicated to Diego Maradona, a soccer star who played for Naples in the 1980s. Locals consider soccer almost a religion, and this guy was practically a deity. You can even see a "hair of Diego" and a teardrop from the city when he went to another team for more money. Unfortunately, his reputation has since been sullied by problems he's had with organized crime, drugs, and police. Perhaps inspired by Maradona's example, the coffee bar has posted a quadrilingual sign (though strangely, not in English) threatening that those who take a picture without buying a cup of coffee may find their camera damaged...*Capisce*? (Note that this "chapel" is removable—if it's raining or they're just feeling grumpy, it may be gone.)

• *As you continue, you'll begin to see shops selling...*

Presepi (Nativity Scenes)

Just as many Americans keep an eye out year-round for Christmas-tree ornaments, Italians regularly add pieces to the family *presepe,* the centerpiece of their holiday decorations. Stop after a few blocks at the tiny square, where Via San Gregorio Armeno leads left into a colorful district with the highest concentration of shops selling fantastic *presepi* and their tiny components, including figurines caricaturing local politicians and celebrities.

• *Back on Spaccanapoli, as Via B. Croce becomes Via S. Biagio dei Librai, notice the...*

Gold and Silver Shops

Some say stolen jewelry ends up here, is melted down immediately, and gets resold in some other form as soon as it cools. At #95, find the Compro Oro ("I Buy Gold") shop. This is one of many pawn shops that have appeared recently, in concert with Italy's economic tough times. At #81, the Ospedale delle Bambole (Doll Hospital)

NAPLES

heals dolls that have been loved to pieces, and also sells restored classics.

• *Cross busy Via Duomo. If you have time and aren't already churched out, consider detouring five minutes north (left) up Via Duomo to visit Naples'* **Duomo**; *just around the corner is the* **Pio Monte della Misericordia Church**, *with a fine Caravaggio painting (both described later, under "Sights in Naples"). Afterwards, continue straight along Via Vicaria Vecchia. As you stroll, ponder Naples' vibrant...*

Street Life, Past and Present

Here along Via Vicaria Vecchia, the street and side-street scenes intensify. The area is said to be a center of the Camorra (organized crime), but as a tourist, you won't notice. Paint a picture with these thoughts: Naples has the most intact street plan of any ancient Greek or Roman city. Imagine this city during those times (and retain these images as you visit Pompeii), with streetside shop fronts that close up after dark, and private homes on upper floors. What you see today is just one more page in a 2,000-year-old story of a city: all kinds of meetings, beatings, and cheatings; kisses, near misses, and little-boy pisses.

You name it, it occurs right on the streets today, as it has since ancient times. People ooze from crusty corners. Black-and-white death announcements add to the clutter on the walls. Widows sell cigarettes from buckets. For a peek behind the scenes in the shade of wet laundry, venture down a few side streets. Buy two carrots as a gift for the woman on the fifth floor if she'll lower her bucket to pick them up. A few blocks on, at the tiny fenced-in triangle of greenery, hang out for a few minutes to just observe the crazy motorbike action and teen scene.

• *From here, veer right onto Via Forcella (which leads to the busy boulevard that leads to Centrale Station). A block down, a tiny, fenced-in traffic island protects a chunk of the ancient Greek wall of Neapolis. Turn right here on Via Pietro Colletta, walk 40 yards, and step into the North Pole, at the...*

Polo Nord Gelateria

The oldest *gelateria* in Naples has had four generations of family working here since 1931. Before you order, sample a few flavors, including their *bacio* or "kiss" flavor (chocolate and hazelnut)—all are made fresh daily. Low-sugar and soy ice creams are also available (Via Pietro Colletta 41). Via Pietro Colletta leads past two of

Napoli's most competitive **pizzerias** (see "Eating in Naples," later) to Corso Umberto I.

• *Turn left on the grand boulevard-like Corso Umberto I. From here to Centrale Station, it's at least a 10-minute walk (if you're tired, hop on a bus; they all go to the station). To finish the walk, continue on Corso Umberto I—past a gauntlet of purse/CD/sunglasses salesmen and shady characters hawking stolen mobile phones—to the vast, ugly Piazza Garibaldi. You made it.*

To reach the cruise port, you can catch tram #1 from this end of Piazza Garibaldi; or, if you're taking the train back to Sorrento, you can hike to the far end of the giant square to Centrale Station, then head downstairs to the Circumvesuviana train.

Sights in Naples

▲▲▲Archaeological Museum (Museo Archeologico)

This museum offers the best possible peek at the art and decorations of Pompeii and Herculaneum, the two ancient burgs that were buried in ash by the eruption of Mount Vesuvius in A.D. 79. When Pompeii was excavated in the late 1700s, Naples' Bourbon king bellowed, "Bring me the best of what you find!" The finest art and artifacts ended up here, and today, the ancient sites themselves are impressive but barren.

Cost and Hours: €8, sometimes more for temporary exhibits, cash only, Wed-Mon 9:00-19:30, closed Tue, last entry 30 minutes before closing. Early and temporary closures are noted on a board near the ticket office.

Getting There: For directions on how to get here from the cruise port, see page 620; from the Circumvesuviana station, see page 621.

Information: The shop sells a worthwhile *National Archaeological Museum of Naples* guidebook for €12. Tel. 081-442-2149.

Tours: My self-guided tour covers all the basics. For more detail, the decent **audioguide** costs €5 (at ticket desk). If you want a **guided tour**, book Pina Esposito (see "Helpful Hints," earlier).

Baggage Check: Bag check is obligatory and free.

Photography: Photos are allowed without a flash.

Eating: The museum has no café, but vending machines sell drinks and snacks at reasonable prices. There are several good places to grab a meal within a few blocks; see page 650.

❍ Self-Guided Tour: Entering the museum, stand at the base of the grand staircase and get oriented. To your right, on the ground floor, are the larger-than-life statues of the Farnese Collection, starring the *Toro Farnese* and the *Farnese Hercules*. Up the stairs on the mezzanine level (turn left at the lion) are mosaics and frescoes from Pompeii, including the *Battle of Alexander* and the Secret Room of erotic art. On the top floor are more frescoes, a scale model of Pompeii, and bronze statues from Herculaneum. WCs are behind the staircase.

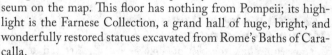

• *From the base of the grand staircase, turn right through the door marked* Collezione Farnese *and head to the far end—walking through a rich collection of idealistic and realistic ancient portrait busts—to reach the farthest room (Sala XIII).*

Ground Floor—The Farnese Collection: The museum's ground floor alone has enough Greek and Roman art to put any museum on the map. This floor has nothing from Pompeii; its highlight is the Farnese Collection, a grand hall of huge, bright, and wonderfully restored statues excavated from Rome's Baths of Caracalla.

Peruse the larger-than-life statues filling the hall. They were dug up in the 1540s at the behest of Alessandro Farnese (by then Pope Paul III) while he was building the family palace on the Campo dei Fiori in Rome. His main purpose in excavating the baths was to scavenge quality building stone. The sculptures were a nice extra and helped the palace come in under budget on decorations. In the 1700s, the collection ended up in the hands of Charles, the Bourbon king of Naples (whose mother was a Farnese). His son, the next king, had it brought to Naples.

• *Quick—look down to the left end of the hall. There's a woman being tied to a snorting bull.*

The tangled *Toro Farnese* tells a thrilling Greek myth. At 13 feet, it's the tallest ancient marble group ever found, and the largest

intact statue from antiquity. A third-century A.D. copy of a lost bronze Hellenistic original, it was carved out of one piece of marble. Michelangelo and others "restored" it at the pope's request—meaning that they integrated surviving bits into a new work. Panels on the wall show which pieces were actually carved by Michelangelo (in blue on the chart): the head of the woman in back, the torso of the aunt under the bull, and the dog. (Imagine how the statue would stand out if it was thoughtfully lit and not surrounded by white walls.)

Here's the tragic story behind the statue: Once upon an ancient Greek time, King Lycus was bewitched by Dirce. He abandoned his pregnant wife, Antiope (standing regally in the background). The single mom gave birth to twin boys (shown here). When they grew up, they killed their deadbeat dad and tied Dirce to the horns of a bull to be bashed against a mountain. Captured in marble, the action is thrilling: cape flailing, dog snarling, hooves in the air. You can almost hear the bull snorting. And in the back, Antiope oversees this harsh ancient justice with satisfaction.

At the opposite end of the hall stands the *Farnese Hercules.* The great Greek hero is exhausted. He leans wearily on his

club (draped with his lion skin) and bows his head. He's just finished the daunting Eleventh Labor, having traveled the world, fought men and gods, freed Prometheus from his rock, and carried Atlas' weight of the world on his shoulders. Now he's returned with the prize: the golden apples of the gods, which he cups behind his back. But, after all that, he's just been told he has to return the apples and do one final labor: descend into Hell itself. Oh, man.

• *Backtrack to the main entry hall, then head up to the mezzanine level (turning left at the lion).*

Mezzanine—Pompeiian Mosaics and the Secret Room: Most of these mosaics—of animals, musicians, and geometric designs—were taken from Pompeii's House of the Faun (see page 661). Walk into the third room and look for the 20-inch-high statue in a free-standing glass case: the house's delightful centerpiece, the *Dancing Faun.* This rare surviving Greek bronze statue (from the fourth century B.C.) is surrounded by some of the best mosaics of that age.

A museum highlight, just beyond the statue, is the grand *Battle of Alexander,* a second-century B.C. copy of the original Greek

fresco, done a century earlier. It decorated a floor in the House of the Faun and was found intact; the damage you see occurred as this treasure was moved from Pompeii to the king's collection here. Alexander (left side of the scene, with curly hair and sideburns) is about to defeat the Persians under Darius (central figure, in chariot with turban and beard). This pivotal victory allowed Alexander to quickly overrun much of Asia (331 B.C.). Alexander is the only one without a helmet...a confident master of the battlefield while

everyone else is fighting for their lives, eyes bulging with fear. Notice how the horses, already in retreat, add to the scene's propaganda value. Notice also the shading and perspective, which Renaissance artists would later work so hard to accomplish. (A modern reproduction of the mosaic is now back in Pompeii, at the House of the Faun.)

Further on, the **Secret Room (Gabinetto Segreto)** contains a sizable assortment of erotic frescoes, well-hung pottery, and perky statues that once decorated bedrooms, meeting rooms, brothels, and even shops at Pompeii and Herculaneum. These bawdy statues and frescoes—many of them once displayed in Pompeii's grandest houses—were entertainment for guests. (By the time they made it to this museum, in 1819, the frescoes could be viewed only with permission from the king—see the letters in the glass case just outside the door.) The Roman nobles commissioned the wildest scenes imaginable. Think of them as ancient dirty jokes.

• *So, now that your travel buddy is finally showing a little interest in art...finish up your visit by climbing the stairs to the top floor.*

Top Floor—Frescoes, Statues, Artifacts, and a Model of Pompeii: At the top of the stairs, go through the center door to enter a grand, empty hall. This was the **great hall** of the university (17th and 18th centuries) until the building became the royal museum in 1777. Walk to the center. The sundial (from 1791) still works. Look up to the far-right corner of the hall and find the tiny pinhole. At noon (13:00 in summer), a ray of sun enters the hall and strikes the sundial, showing the time of the year...if you know your zodiac.

To your left, you'll see a door marked *affreschi*. This leads to eight rooms showing off the museum's impressive and well-described collection of (non-erotic) **frescoes** taken from the walls of Pompeii villas. Pompeiians loved to decorate their homes with scenes from mythology (Hercules' labors, Venus and Mars in love), landscapes, everyday market scenes, and faux architecture.

Continue around this wing counterclockwise (with the courtyard on your left) through rooms of artifacts found at Pompeii. At the far end is a scale model of Pompeii as excavated in 1879 *(plastic di Pompeii)*. Another model (on the wall) shows the site in 2004, after more excavations.

• *Eventually you'll end up back in the great hall.*

Step out to the top landing of the staircase you climbed earlier.

Turn left and go down, then up, 16 steps and into the wing labeled *La Villa dei Papiri*. This exhibition shows off artifacts (particularly bronze statues) from the Herculaneum holiday home of Julius Caesar's father-in-law. In the second room (numbered CXVI), look into the lifelike blue eyes of the intense *Corridore* (athletes), bent on

doing their best. The *Five Dancers*, with their inlaid-ivory eyes and graceful poses, decorated a portico. The next room (CXVII) has more fine works: *Resting Hermes* (with his tired little heel wings) is taking a break. Nearby, the *Drunken Faun* (singing and snapping his fingers to the beat, a wineskin at his side) is clearly living for today—true to the *carpe diem* preaching of the Epicurean philosophy. Caesar's father-in-law was a fan of Epicurean philosophy, and his library—containing 2,000 papyrus scrolls—supported his outlook. Back by the entrance, check out the plans of the villa, and in the side room, see how the half-burned scrolls were unrolled and (with luck) read after excavation in the 1750s.

• *Return to the ground floor. The exit hall (right) leads around the museum courtyard and to the gift shop.*

Doriforo: For extra credit on your way out, find *Doriforo*. He was last spotted on the right as you walk down the exit hall. (If

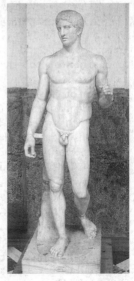

he's been moved, ask a guard, *"Dov'è il Doriforo?"*) This seven-foot-tall "spear-carrier" (the literal translation of *doriforo*) just stands there, as if holding a spear. What's the big deal about this statue, which looks like so many others? It's a marble replica made by the Romans of one of the most-copied statues of antiquity, a fifth-century B.C. bronze Greek original by Polyclitus. This copy once stood in a Pompeii gym, where it inspired ancient athletes by showing the ideal proportions of Greek beauty. So full of motion, and so realistic in its *contrapposto* pose (weight on one foot), the *Doriforo* would later inspire Donatello and Michelangelo, helping to trigger the Renaissance. And so the glories of ancient Pompeii, once buried and forgotten, live on today.

Churches on or near Spaccanapoli

These churches are linked—in this order—on "Part 3" of my self-guided walk, earlier.

▲Church of Gesù Nuovo

This church's unique pyramid-grill facade survives from a fortified 15th-century noble palace. Step inside for a brilliant Neapolitan Baroque interior. The second chapel on the right features a much-adored **statue of St. Giuseppe Moscati** (1880-1927), a Christian doctor famous for helping the poor. In 1987, Moscati became the first modern doctor to be canonized. Sit and watch a steady stream of Neapolitans taking turns to kiss and touch the altar, then hold the good doctor's highly polished hand.

Continue on to the third chapel and enter the **Sale Moscati.** Look high on the walls of this long room to see hundreds of "Ex Votos"—tiny red-and-silver plaques of thanksgiving for prayers answered with the help of St. Moscati (each has a symbol of the ailment cured). Naples' practice of using Ex Votos, while incorporated into its Catholic rituals, goes back to its pagan Greek roots. Rooms from Moscati's nearby apartment are on display, and a glass case shows possessions and photos of the great doctor. As you leave the Sale Moscati, notice the big bomb casing that hangs in the left corner. It fell through the church's dome in 1943, but caused almost no damage...yet another miracle.

Cost and Hours: Free, daily 7:00-13:00 & 16:00-19:30, Piazza del Gesù Nuovo, www.gesunuovo.it.

Church of Santa Chiara

Dating from the 14th century, this church is from a period of French royal rule under the Angevin dynasty. Consider the stark contrast between this church (Gothic) and the Gesù Nuovo (Baroque), across the street. Inside, notice the huge inlaid-marble Angevin coat of arms on the floor. The faded Trinity on the back wall (on the right as you face the door), shows a dove representing the Holy Spirit between the heads of God the Father and Christ (c. 1414). This is an example of the fine frescoes that once covered the walls. Most were stuccoed over during Baroque times or destroyed in 1943 by Allied bombs. The altar is adorned with four finely carved Gothic tombs of Angevin kings. A chapel stacked with Bourbon royalty is just to the right.

Cost and Hours: Free, daily 7:00-13:00 & 16:30-20:00, Piazza del Gesù Nuovo. Its tranquil cloistered courtyard, around back, is not worth its €6 entry fee.

▲▲Cappella Sansevero

This small chapel is a Baroque explosion mourning the body of Christ, who lies on a soft pillow under an incredibly realistic veil. It's also the personal chapel of Raimondo de Sangro, an eccentric Freemason, containing his tomb and the tombs of his family.

Like other 18th-century Enlightenment figures, Raimondo was a wealthy man of letters, scientist and inventor, and patron of the arts—and he was also a grand master of the Freemasons of the Kingdom of Naples. His chapel—filled with Freemason symbolism—is a complex ensemble, with statues representing virtues such as self-control, religious zeal, and the Freemason philosophy of freedom through enlightenment. Though it's a pricey private enterprise, the chapel is worth a visit.

Cost and Hours: €7, buy tickets at office at the corner, Mon and Wed-Sat 10:00-18:00, Sun 10:00-13:30, closed Tue, last entry 20 minutes before closing, no photos, Via de Sanctis 19, tel. 081-551-8470, www.museosansevero.it. Good English explanations are posted throughout; when you buy your ticket, pick up the free floor plan, which identifies each of the statues lining the nave.

▲Duomo

Naples' historic cathedral, built by imported French Anjou kings in the 14th century, boasts a breathtaking Neo-Gothic facade. Step into the vast interior to see the mix of styles along the side chapels—from pointy Gothic arches to rounded Renaissance ones to gilded Baroque decor.

Cost and Hours: Free, daily 8:30-13:30 & 14:30-20:00, Via Duomo.

Visiting the Church: Explore the two largest side-chapels—each practically a church in its own right. On the left, the Chapel of St. Restituta stands on the site of the original, early-Christian church that predated the cathedral (at the far end, you can pay €1.50 to see its sixth-century baptismal font under mosaics and go downstairs to see its even earlier foundations; chapel open Mon-Sat 8:30-12:30 & 16:30-18:30, Sun 8:30-13:00). On the right is the Chapel of San Gennaro—dedicated to the beloved patron saint of Naples—decorated with silver busts of centuries of bishops, and seven paintings done on bronze.

Back out in the main nave, the altar at the front is ringed by carved wooden seats, filled three times a year by clergy to witness the Miracle of the Blood. Thousands of Neapolitans cram into this church for a peek at two tiny vials with the dried blood of St. Gennaro. As the clergy roots—or even jeers—for the miracle to occur, the blood temporarily liquefies. Neapolitans take this ritual with deadly seriousness, and believe that if the blood remains solid, it's terrible luck for the city. Sure enough, on the rare occasion that the miracle fails, locals can point to a terrible event soon after—such as an earthquake or an eruption of Mount Vesuvius.

The stairs beneath the altar take you to a crypt with the relics of St. Gennaro and (across the room) a statue of the bishop who rescued the relics from a rival town and returned them to Naples.

Pio Monte della Misericordia

Art lovers come to this small church (near the Duomo, and run by a charitable foundation) to appreciate one of the best works by Caravaggio, *The Seven Works of Mercy*, which hangs over the main altar. In one crowded canvas, the great early-Baroque artist illustrates seven virtues: burying the dead (the man carrying a corpse by the ankles), visiting the imprisoned, feeding the hungry (Pero breastfeeding her starving father—a scene from a famous Roman story), sheltering the homeless (a pilgrim on the Camino de Santiago, with his floppy hat, negotiates with an innkeeper), caring for the sick, clothing the naked (St. Martin offers part of his cloak to the injured man in the foreground), and giving drink to the thirsty (Samson chugs from a jawbone in the background)—all of them set in a dark Neapolitan alley, and watched over by Mary, Jesus, and a pair of angels. Caravaggio painted this work in Naples in 1607, while in exile from Rome, where he had been sentenced to death for killing a man in a duel. Your ticket also lets you in to the foundation's pleasant upper-floor museum, with some minor Neapolitan paintings.

Cost and Hours: €6, includes audioguide, Thu-Tue 9:00-14:30, closed Wed, Via dei Tribunali 253, tel. 081-446-944, www.piomontedellamisericordia.it.

In the City Center

Royal Palace (Palazzo Reale)

Facing Piazza del Plebiscito, this huge, lavish palace welcomes the public. The palace's grand Neoclassical staircase leads up to a floor with 30 plush rooms. You'll follow a one-way route (with some English descriptions) featuring the palace theater, paintings by "the Caravaggio Imitators," Neapolitan tapestries, fine inlaid-stone tabletops, chandeliers, gilded woodwork, and more. The rooms do feel quite grand, but lack the personality and sense of importance of Europe's better palaces. Don't miss the huge, tapestry-laden Hercules Hall. On the way out, stop into the chapel, with a fantastic nativity scene—a commotion of 18th-century ceramic figurines.

Cost and Hours: €4, includes painfully dry audioguide, Thu-Tue 9:00-20:00, closed Wed, last entry one hour before closing, tel. 848-800-288.

Porta Nolana Open-Air Fish Market

Naples' fish market squirts and stinks as it has for centuries under the Porta Nolana (gate in the city wall), immediately in front of the Napoli Porta Nolana Circumvesuviana Station and four long blocks from Centrale

Station. Of the town's many boisterous outdoor markets, this will net you the most photos and memories. From Piazza Nolana, wander under the medieval gate and take your first left down Vico Sopramuro, enjoying this wild and entirely edible cultural scavenger hunt (Tue-Sun 8:00-14:00, closed Mon).

Two other markets with more clothing and fewer fish are at Piazza Capuana (several blocks northwest of Centrale Station and tumbling down Via Sant'Antonio Abate, Mon-Sat 8:00-18:00, Sun 9:00-13:00) and a similar cobbled shopping zone along Via Pignasecca (just off Via Toledo, west of Piazza Carità).

Eating in Naples

For general tips on eating in Italy, see page 455.

Cheap and Famous Pizza

Naples is the birthplace of pizza. Its pizzerias bake just the right combination of fresh dough, mozzarella, and tomatoes in traditional wood-burning ovens. An average one-person pie costs €4-6; most places offer both take-out and eat-in.

Near the Station

These two pizzerias—the most famous—are both a few long blocks from the train station, and at the end of my "Slice of Neapolitan Life" self-guided walk.

Antica Pizzeria da Michele is for pizza purists. Filled with locals (and tourists), it serves just two varieties: *margherita* (tomato sauce and mozzarella) and *marinara* (tomato sauce, oregano, and garlic, no cheese). Come early to sit and watch the pizza artists in action. A pizza with beer costs €6-7. As this place is often jammed with a long line, arrive early or late to get a seat. If there's a mob, head inside to get a number. If it's just too crowded to wait, the less-exceptional Pizzeria Trianon (described next) generally has room (Mon-Sat 10:30-24:00, closed Sun; look for the vertical red *Antica Pizzeria* sign at the intersection of Via Pietro Colletta and Via Cesare Sersale at #1; tel. 081-553-9204).

Pizzeria Trianon, across the street and left a few doors, has been da Michele's archrival since 1923. It offers more choices, slightly higher prices (€5-7), air-conditioning, and a cozier atmosphere. For less chaos, head upstairs. While waiting for your meal, you can survey the transformation of a humble wad of dough into a smoldering bubbly feast in their entryway pizza kitchen (daily 11:00-15:30 & 19:00-23:00, Via Pietro Colletta 42, tel. 081-553-9426, Giuseppe).

NAPLES

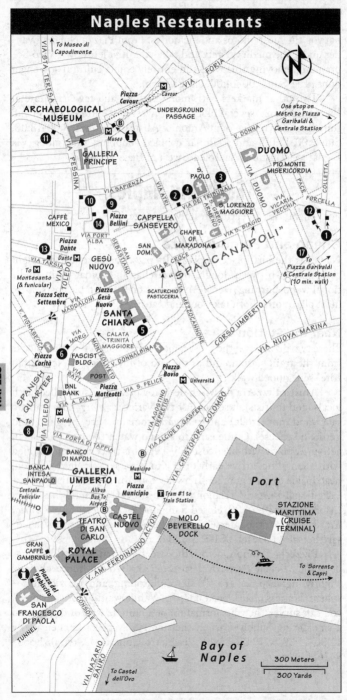

Naples Restaurants

NAPLES

Naples Restaurants Key

❶ Antica Pizzeria da Michele
  & Pizzeria Trianon
❷ Gino Sorbillo Pizzeria
❸ Pizzeria di Matteo
❹ Pizzeria I Decumani &
  Trattoria Campagnola
❺ Ecomesarà
❻ Osteria il Garum
❼ Valù

❽ To Trattoria da Nennella
❾ La Stanza del Gusto
❿ Caffetteria Angela
⓫ Salumeria Pasquale Carrino
⓬ Polo Nord Gelateria
⓭ Supermarket
⓮ Laundry

On Via dei Tribunali

This street, which runs a couple of blocks north of Spaccanapoli, is home to several pizzerias that are more convenient to sightseeing. Three in particular are on all the "best pizza in Naples" lists...as you'll learn the hard way if you show up at peak mealtimes, when huge mobs crowd outside the front door waiting for a table. **Gino Sorbillo** is a local favorite (closed Sun, Via dei Tribunali 32—don't confuse this with his relatives' similarly named places on the same street, tel. 081-446-643). At **Pizzeria di Matteo,** people waiting out front snack on €0.50 croquettes *(crocché),* sold at the little window (closed Sun, Via dei Tribunali 94, tel. 081-455-262). **Pizzeria I Decumani** has a bit nicer seating and is open seven days a week (facing Piazza San Gaetano at Via dei Tribunali 58, tel. 081-557-1309).

Restaurants

If you want a full meal rather than a pizza, consider these options, which I've organized by neighborhood.

Near Spaccanapoli and Via Toledo

Ecomesarà serves up Neapolitan and *meridionale* (southern Italian) dishes in a modern setting just below the Santa Chiara cloister, a long block south of Spaccanapoli. The atmosphere is mellow, modern, and international. Cristiano and his staff are happy to explain the menu, which refreshingly dispenses with the traditional Italian *primi/secondi* distinction. Cristiano—who abides by the Slow Food ethic—explains that separate *contorni* (vegetable sides) aren't necessary because *all* of their dishes have vegetables (€9-16 main courses, Tue-Sun 13:00-15:00 & 19:30-23:00, closed Mon, Via Santa Chiara 49, tel. 081-1925-9353).

Trattoria Campagnola is a classic family place with a daily home-cooking-style chalkboard menu on the back wall, mama busy cooking in the back, and wine on tap. Here you can venture away from pastas, be experimental with a series of local dishes, and not go wrong (€7 main courses, Wed-Mon 12:00-16:00 & 19:00-

NAPLES

23:00, closed Tue, between the famous pizzerias at Via Tribunali 47, tel. 081-459-034 but no reservations).

Osteria il Garum is great if you'd like to eat on a classic Neapolitan square. It's named for the ancient fish sauce that was widely used in Roman cooking. These days, mild-mannered Luigi and his staff inject their pricey local cuisine with centuries of tradition, served in a cozy split-level cellar or outside on a covered terrace facing a neighborhood church. It's just between Via Toledo and Spaccanapoli, a short walk from the Church of Gesù Nuovo (€9-13 pastas, €14-17 *secondi,* daily 12:00-15:30 & 19:00-23:30, Piazza Monteoliveto 2A, tel. 081-542-3228).

Valù, with a modern red-and-black color scheme and a wine-bar vibe, sits sane and romantic in the colorful and rowdy Spanish Quarter just a block off Via Toledo. This *risotteria* specializes in risotto (which is not a local dish), serving 20 different variations. Choose between the interior or a few outdoor tables along a tight alley (€10-12 risottos, €8-16 meat dishes, Mon-Sat 12:30-15:00 & 19:00-24:00, closed Sun, Vico Lungo del Gelso 80, up alley directly opposite Banco di Napoli entrance, tel. 081-038-1139).

Trattoria da Nennella is fun-loving chaos, with red-shirted waiters barking orders, a small festival anytime someone puts a tip in the bucket, and the fruit course served in plastic bidets. There's one price—€12 per person—and you choose three courses plus a fruit. House wine is served in tiny plastic cups, the crowd is ready for fun, and the food's good. It's buried in the Spanish Quarter. You can sit indoors, or on a cobbled terrace under a trellis (closed Sun, leave Via Toledo a block down from the BNL bank and walk up Vico Teatro Nuovo three blocks to the corner of Vico Lungo Teatro Nuovo, Vico Lungo Teatro Nuovo 103, tel. 081-414-338 but no reservations).

Near the Archaeological Museum

La Stanza del Gusto, two blocks downhill from the museum, tackles food creatively and injects crusty Naples with a little modern color and irreverence. The downstairs is casual, trendy, and playful, while the upstairs is more refined yet still polka-dotted (€5-8 *panini,* €10-15 *secondi*; fixed-price meals: €35 five-course vegetarian, €65 seven-course meat; Tue-Sat 12:00-15:30 & 19:30-23:30, closed Sun-Mon, Via Santa Maria di Constantinopoli 100, tel. 081-401-578).

Caffetteria Angela is a fun little eating complex: coffee bar; *tavola calda* with hot ready-to-eat dishes (€3-4); and a tiny meat, cheese, and bread shop with all you need for a cheap meal to go. It offers honest pricing and simple, peaceful, air-conditioned indoor seating (no cover, open Mon-Sat 7:00-21:00, Sun 9:00-14:00, 3 blocks below museum at Via Conte di Ruvo 21, between Via Pessina and Via Bellini, tel. 081-549-9660).

Salumeria Pasquale Carrino is a tiny *salumi* shop with an exuberant owner—the fun-loving and flamboyant Pasquale—who turns sandwich-making into a show (€3-7 sandwiches good for two people, Mon-Sat 8:00-15:00 & 17:00-20:00, closed Sun, 100 yards from museum—walk to the northwest corner of the building and cross two crosswalks to Via Salvator Rosa 10, tel. 081-564-0889).

Pompeii

Stopped in their tracks by the eruption of Mount Vesuvius in A.D. 79, Pompeii and Herculaneum offer the best look anywhere at what life in Rome must have been like around 2,000 years ago. Of the two sites, Pompeii is grander, while Herculaneum is smaller and more intimate; both are easily reached from Naples on the Circumvesuviana commuter train

(for details, see page 621). Vesuvius, smoldering ominously, rises up on the horizon. It last erupted in 1944, and is still an active volcano.

A once-thriving commercial port of 20,000, Pompeii (worth ▲▲▲) grew from Greek and Etruscan roots to become an important Roman city. Then, on August 24, A.D. 79, everything changed. Vesuvius erupted and began to bury the city under 30 feet of hot volcanic ash. For the archaeologists who excavated it centuries later, this was a shake-and-bake windfall, teaching them volumes about daily Roman life. Pompeii was accidentally rediscovered in 1599; excavations began in 1748.

Pompeii is a surprisingly big and impressive site, but its best art is in Naples' Archaeological Museum. If you want to deepen your understanding of Pompeii, try to visit the museum in Naples as well.

Orientation

Cost: €11, cash only; €20 combo-ticket includes Pompeii and three lesser sites (valid 3 consecutive days).

Hours: Daily April-Oct 8:30-19:30, Nov-March 8:30-17:00 (last entry 1.5 hours before closing).

Crowd-Beating Tips: On busy days, there can be a line of up to 30 minutes to buy a ticket. If you anticipate lines, buy your ticket at the "info point" kiosk at the train station (same price as at the site, credit cards accepted).

Getting There: Pompeii is roughly midway between Naples and Sorrento on the Circumvesuviana train line (2/hour, €2.90 and 40 minutes from Naples, one-way). Get off at the Pompei Scavi-Villa dei Misteri stop; from Naples, it's the stop after Torre Annunziata. The DD express trains (6/day) bypass several stations but do stop at Pompei Scavi, shaving 10 minutes off the trip from Naples. From the Pompei Scavi train station, it's just a two-minute walk to the Porta Marina entrance: Turn right and walk down the road about a block to the entrance (on your left).

Pompei vs. Pompei Scavi: Pompei is the name of a separate train station on the national rail network that's a long, dull walk from the ruins. Make sure you're taking the Circumvesuviana commuter train to Pompei Scavi (*scavi* means "excavations").

Information: The "info point" kiosk at the station is a private agency selling tours (not a real TI; see "Tours," below), but they can provide some information and also sell tickets for the site.

Be sure to pick up the free, helpful map at the entrance (ask for it when you buy your ticket, or check at the info window to the left of the WCs—the maps aren't available within the walls of Pompeii). Tel. 081-857-5347, www.pompeiisites.org.

The bookshop sells the small Pompeii and Herculaneum *Past and Present* book. Its plastic overlays allow you to re-create the ruins (€12; if you buy from a street vendor, pay no more than that).

Tours: My **self-guided tour** covers the basics and provides a good framework for exploring the site on your own, and is also available as a free Rick Steves **audio tour** (see page 50).

Guided tours leave every hour from the "info point" kiosk near the train station (€12). You can also sign up in advance for a group tour of Pompeii offered to Rick Steves readers through Naples-based Mondo Tours (€12, doesn't include entry fee, April-Oct Mon-Fri at 10:00, meet at Ristorante Suisse, on Piazza Esedra, down the hill from the Porta Marina entrance—see page 628).

Private guides (around €110/2 hours) of varying quality—there really is no guarantee of what you're getting—cluster near the ticket booth and may try to herd you into a group with other travelers, which makes the price more reasonable. For a private two-hour tour, consider **Gaetano Manfredi,** who is pricey but brings energy and theatricality to his tours (€120/up to 4 people, book in advance by email, www. pompeiitourguide.com, gaetanoguide@hotmail.it). **Antonio Somma** specializes in Pompeii (from €120, price varies with season and size of group, book in advance, evening tel. 081-850-1992, daytime mobile 393-406-3824 or 339-891-9489, www.pompeitour.com, info@pompeitour.com). Antonio can organize transport for visitors who want to fill up the rest of the day with a trip to the Amalfi Coast. The Naples-based guides recommended on page 626 can also guide you at Pompeii. Parents, note that the ancient brothel and its sexually explicit frescoes are included on tours; let your guide know if you'd rather skip that stop.

Audioguides are available from a kiosk near the ticket booth at the Porta Marina entrance (€6.50, €10/2 people, ID required), but they offer basically the same info as your free booklet.

Length of This Tour: Allow two hours, or three if you visit the theater and amphitheater. With less time, focus on the Forum, Baths of the Forum, House of the Faun, and brothel.

Services: There's a WC at the train station. The site has two WCs—one near the entrance and another in the cafeteria.

Eating: The Ciao cafeteria within the site serves good sandwiches, pizza, and pasta at a reasonable price. A few mediocre restaurants cluster between the entrance and the train station. Your cheapest bet may be to bring your own food for a discreet picnic.

Starring: Roofless (collapsed) but otherwise intact Roman buildings, plaster casts of hapless victims, a few erotic frescoes, and the dawning realization that these ancient people were not that different from us.

Background

Pompeii, founded in 600 B.C., eventually became a booming Roman trading city. Not rich, not poor, it was middle class—a perfect example of typical Roman life. Most streets would have been lined with stalls and jammed with customers from sunup to sundown. Chariots vied with shoppers for street space. Two thousand

years ago, Rome controlled the entire Mediterranean—making it a kind of free-trade zone—and Pompeii was a central and bustling port.

There were no posh neighborhoods in Pompeii. Rich and poor mixed it up as elegant houses existed side by side with simple homes. While nearby Herculaneum would

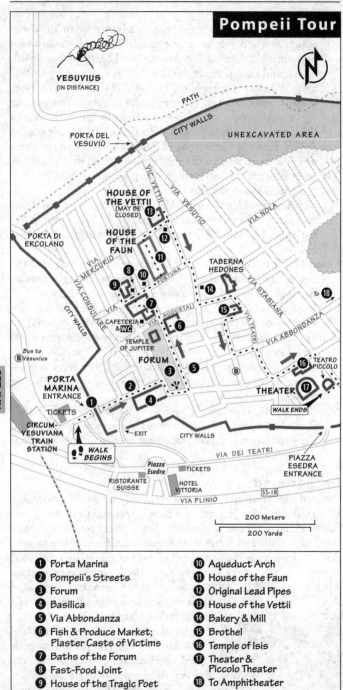

Pompeii Tour

VESUVIUS (IN DISTANCE)

PATH

CITY WALLS

PORTA DEL VESUVIO

UNEXCAVATED AREA

VIC. VETTII

VIA VESUVIO

VIA NOLA

HOUSE OF THE VETTII (MAY BE CLOSED) 13

PORTA DI ERCOLANO

HOUSE OF THE FAUN 12

VIA MERCURIO

11

VIA STABIANA

VIA FORTUNA

TABERNA HEDONES

To 18

8

10

9

14

VIA CONSOLARE

CITY WALLS

VIA 7

VIA AUGUSTALI

15

VIA TEATRI

VIA ABBONDANZA

CAFETERIA & WC

6

TEMPLE OF JUPITER

5

Bus to B Vesuvius

FORUM

3

B

16

TEATRO PICCOLO

PORTA MARINA ENTRANCE 1

2

4

THEATER 17

TICKETS

WALK ENDS

CIRCUM-VESUVIANA TRAIN STATION

WALK BEGINS

EXIT

CITY WALLS

VIA DEI TEATRI

PIAZZA ESEDRA ENTRANCE

Piazza Esedra

TICKETS

RISTORANTE SUISSE

HOTEL VITTORIA

SS-18

VIA PLINIO

200 Meters

200 Yards

NAPLES

① Porta Marina
② Pompeii's Streets
③ Forum
④ Basilica
⑤ Via Abbondanza
⑥ Fish & Produce Market; Plaster Casts of Victims
⑦ Baths of the Forum
⑧ Fast-Food Joint
⑨ House of the Tragic Poet

⑩ Aqueduct Arch
⑪ House of the Faun
⑫ Original Lead Pipes
⑬ House of the Vettii
⑭ Bakery & Mill
⑮ Brothel
⑯ Temple of Isis
⑰ Theater & Piccolo Theater
⑱ To Amphitheater

have been a classier place to live (traffic-free streets, fancier houses, far better drainage), Pompeii was the place for action and shopping. It served an estimated 20,000 residents with more than 40 bakeries, 30 brothels, and 130 bars, restaurants, and hotels. With most of its buildings covered by brilliant white ground-marble stucco, Pompeii in A.D. 79 was an impressive town.

The Tour Begins
• *Just past the ticket-taker, start your approach up to the...*

❶ Porta Marina
The city of Pompeii was born on the hill ahead of you. This was the original town gate. Before Vesuvius blew and filled in the harbor, the sea came nearly to here. Notice the two openings in the gate (ahead, up the ramp). Both were left open by day to admit major traffic. At

night, the larger one was closed for better security.
• *Pass through the Porta Marina and continue up to the top of the street, pausing at the three large stepping-stones in the middle.*

❷ Pompeii's Streets
Every day, Pompeiians flooded the streets with gushing water to clean them. These stepping-stones let pedestrians cross without

getting their sandals wet. Chariots traveling in either direction could straddle the stones (all had standard-size axles). A single stepping-stone in a road means it was a one-way street, a pair indicates an ordinary two-way, and three (like this) signifies a major

thoroughfare. The basalt stones are the original Roman pavement. The sidewalks (elevated to hide the plumbing) were paved with bits of broken pots (an ancient form of recycling) and studded with reflective bits of white marble. These "cats' eyes" helped people get around after dark, either by moonlight or with the help of lamps.
• *Continue straight ahead, don your mental toga, and enter the city as the Romans once did. The road opens up into the spacious main square: the Forum. Stand at the near end of this rectangular space and look toward Mount Vesuvius.*

❸ The Forum (Foro)

Pompeii's commercial, religious, and political center stands at the intersection of the city's two main streets. While it's the most ru-

ined part of Pompeii, it's grand nonetheless. Picture the piazza surrounded by two-story buildings on all sides. The pedestals that line the square once held statues (now safely displayed in the museum in Naples). In its heyday, Pompeii's citizens gathered here in the main square to shop, talk politics, and socialize. Business took place in the important buildings that lined the piazza.

The Forum was dominated by the **Temple of Jupiter,** at the far end (marked by a half-dozen ruined columns atop a stair-step base). Jupiter was the supreme god of the Roman pantheon—you might be able to make out his little white marble head at the center-rear of the temple.

At the near end of the Forum (behind where you're standing) is the **curia,** or city hall. Like many Roman buildings, it was built with brick and mortar, then covered with marble walls and floors. To your left (as you face Vesuvius and the Temple of Jupiter) is the **basilica,** or courthouse.

Since Pompeii was a pretty typical Roman town, it has the same layout and components that you'll find in any Roman city— main square, curia, basilica, temples, axis of roads, and so on. All power converged at the Forum: religious (the temple), political (the curia), judicial (the basilica), and commercial (this piazza was the main marketplace). Even the power of the people was expressed here, since this where they gathered to vote. Imagine the hubbub of this town square in its heyday.

Look beyond the Temple of Jupiter. Five miles to the north looms the ominous backstory to this site: **Mount Vesuvius.** Mentally draw a triangle up from the two remaining peaks to reconstruct the mountain before the eruption. When it blew, Pompeiians had no idea that they were living under a volcano, since Vesuvius hadn't erupted for 1,200 years. Imagine the wonder—then the horror—as a column of pulverized rock roared upward, and then ash began to fall. The weight of the ash and small rocks collapsed Pompeii's roofs later that day, crushing people who had taken refuge inside buildings instead of fleeing the city.

• *As you face Vesuvius, the basilica is to your left, lined with stumps of columns. Step inside and see the layout.*

❹ Basilica

Pompeii's basilica was a first-century palace of justice. This ancient law court has the same floor plan later adopted by many Christian churches (which are also called basilicas). The big central hall (or nave) is flanked by rows of columns marking off narrower side aisles. Along the side walls are traces of the original marble.

The columns—now stumps all about the same height—were not ruined by the volcano. Rather, they were left unfinished when Vesuvius blew. Pompeii had been devastated by an earthquake in A.D. 62, and was just in the process of rebuilding the basilica when Vesuvius erupted 17 years later. The half-built columns show off the technology of the day. Uniform bricks were stacked around a cylindrical core. Once finished, they would have been coated with marble

dust stucco to simulate marble columns—an economical construction method found throughout Pompeii (and the Roman Empire).

Besides the earthquake and the eruption, Pompeii's buildings have suffered other ravages over the years, including Spanish plunderers (c. 1800), 19th-century souvenir hunters, WWII bombs, wild vegetation, another earthquake in 1980, and modern neglect. The fact that the entire city was covered by the eruption of A.D. 79 actually helped preserve it, saving it from the sixth-century barbarians who plundered many other towns into oblivion.

• *Exit the basilica and cross the short side of the square, where the city's main street hits the Forum.*

❺ Via Abbondanza

Glance down Via Abbondanza, Pompeii's main street. Lined with shops, bars, and restaurants, it was a lively, pedestrian-only zone. The three "beaver-teeth" stones are traffic barriers that kept chariots out. On the corner (just to the left), take a close look at the dark travertine column standing next to the white one. Notice that the marble drums of the white column are not chiseled entirely round—another construction project left unfinished when Vesuvius erupted.

• *Head toward Vesuvius, walking along the right side of the Forum. Immediately to the right of the Temple of Jupiter (just before the four round arches), a door leads into the market hall, where you'll find two glass cases.*

➏ Fish and Produce Market—Plaster Casts of Victims

As the frescoes on the wall (just inside on the left) indicate, this is where Pompeiians came to buy their food—fish, bread, chickens, and so on. These fine examples of Roman art—with their glimpses of everyday life and their mastery of depth and illusion—would not be matched until the Renaissance, a thousand years after the fall of Rome.

The glass cases hold casts of Pompeiians, eerily captured in their last moments. They were quickly suffocated by a superheated avalanche of gas and ash, and their bodies were encased in volcanic debris. While excavating, modern archaeologists detected hollow spaces underfoot, created when the victims' bodies decomposed. By gently filling the holes with plaster, the archaeologists were able to create molds of the Pompeiians who were caught in the disaster.

• *Continue on, leaving the Forum through an arch behind the Temple of Jupiter. Here you'll find a pedestrian-only road sign (ahead on the right corner, above the* REG VII INS IV *sign) and more "beaver-teeth" traffic blocks. The modern cafeteria is the only eatery inside the archaeological site (with a coffee bar and WC upstairs). Twenty yards past the cafeteria, on the left-hand side at #24, is the entrance to the...*

➐ Baths of the Forum (Terme del Foro)

Pompeii had six public baths, each with a men's and a women's section. You're in the men's zone. The leafy courtyard at the entrance was the gymnasium. After working out, clients could relax with a hot bath *(caldarium),* warm bath *(tepidarium),* or cold plunge *(frigidarium).*

The first big, plain room you enter served as the **dressing room.** Holes on the walls were for pegs to hang clothing. High up, the window (with a faded Neptune underneath) was originally covered with a less-translucent Roman glass. Walk over the non-slip mosaics into the next room.

The ***tepidarium*** is ringed by mini-statues or *telamones* (male caryatids, figures used as supporting pillars), which divided the lockers. Clients would undress and warm up here, perhaps stretching out on one of the bronze benches near the bronze heater for a massage. Look at the ceiling—half crushed by the eruption and half intact, with its fine blue-and-white stucco work.

Next, admire the engineering in the steam-bath room, or ***caldarium.*** The double floor was heated from below—so nice with bare feet (look into the grate to see the brick support towers). The

The Eruption of Vesuvius

At about 1:00 in the afternoon on August 24, A.D. 79, Mount Vesuvius erupted, sending a mushroom cloud of ash, dust, and rocks 12 miles into the air. It spewed for 18 hours straight, as winds blew the cloud southward. The white-gray ash settled like a heavy snow on Pompeii, its weight eventually collapsing roofs and floors, but leaving the walls intact. While most of Pompeii's 20,000 residents fled that day, about two thousand stayed behind.

Although the city of Herculaneum was closer to the volcano—about four miles away—at first it largely escaped the rain of ash, due to the direction of the wind. However, 12 hours after Vesuvius awoke, the type of eruption suddenly changed. The mountain let loose a superheated avalanche of ash, pumice, and gas. This red-hot "pyroclastic flow" sped down the side of the mountain at nearly 100 miles per hour, engulfing Herculaneum and cooking its residents alive. Several more flows over the next few hours further entombed Herculaneum, burying it in nearly 60 feet of hot material that later cooled into rock, freezing the city in time. Then around 7:30 in the morning, another pyroclastic flow headed south and struck Pompeii, dealing a fatal blow to those who'd remained behind.

NAPLES

double walls with brown terra-cotta tiles held the heat. Romans soaked in the big tub, which was filled with hot water. Opposite the big tub is a fountain, which spouted water onto the hot floor, creating steam. The lettering on the fountain reminded those enjoying the room which two politicians paid for it...and how much it cost them (5,250 *sestertii*). To keep condensation from dripping annoyingly from the ceiling, fluting (ribbing) was added to carry water down the walls.

• *Today's visitors exit the baths through the original entry. If you're a bit hungry, immediately across the street is an ancient...*

❽ Fast-Food Joint

After a bath, it was only natural to want a little snack. So, just across the street is a fast-food joint, marked by a series of rectangular marble counters. Most ancient

Romans didn't cook for themselves in their tiny apartments, so to-go places like this were commonplace. The holes in the counters held the pots for food. Each container was like a thermos, with a wooden lid to keep the soup hot, the wine cool, and so on. Notice the groove in the front doorstep and the holes out on the curb. The holes likely accommodated cords for stretching awnings over the sidewalk to shield the clientele from the hot sun, while the grooves were for the shop's folding accordion doors. Look at the wheel grooves in the pavement, worn down through centuries of use. Nearby are more stepping-stones for pedestrians to cross the flooded streets.

• *Just a few steps uphill from the fast-food joint, at #5 (with a locked gate), is the...*

❾ House of the Tragic Poet (Casa del Poeta Tragico)

This house is typical Roman style. The entry is flanked by two family-owned shops (each with a track for a collapsing accordion door). The home is like a train running straight away from the street: atrium (with skylight and pool to catch the rain), den (where deals were made by the shopkeeper), and garden (with rooms facing it and a shrine to remember both the gods and family ancestors). In the entryway is the famous "Beware of Dog" *(Cave Canem)* mosaic.

Today's visitors enter the home by the back door (circle around to the left). On your way there, look for the modern exposed pipe on the left side of the lane; this is the same as ones used in the ancient plumbing system, hidden beneath the raised sidewalk. Inside the house, the grooves on the marble well-head in the entry hall (possibly closed) were formed by generations of inhabitants dragging the bucket up by rope. The richly frescoed dining room is off the garden. Diners lounged on their couches (the Roman custom) and enjoyed frescoes with fake "windows," giving the illusion of a bigger and airier room. Next to the dining room is a humble BBQ-style kitchen with a little closet for the toilet (the kitchen and bathroom shared the same plumbing).

• *Return to the fast-food place and continue about 10 yards downhill to the big intersection. From the center of the intersection, look left to see a giant arch, framing a nice view of Mount Vesuvius.*

❿ Aqueduct Arch—Running Water

Water was critical for this city of 20,000 people, and this arch was part of Pompeii's water-delivery system. A 100-mile-long aqueduct carried fresh water down from the hillsides to a big reservoir perched at the highest point of the city wall. Since overall water pressure was disappointing, Pompeiians built arches like the brick one you see here (originally covered in marble) with hidden water tanks at the top. Located just below the altitude of the main tank, these smaller tanks were filled by gravity, and provided each neighborhood with reliable pressure.

• *If you're thirsty, fill your water bottle from the modern fountain. Then continue straight downhill one block (50 yards) to #2 on the left.*

⓫ House of the Faun (Casa del Fauno)

Stand across the street and marvel at the grand entry with *"HAVE"* (hail to you) as a welcome mat. Go in. Notice the two shrines above the entryway—one dedicated to the gods, the other to this wealthy family's ancestors.

You are standing in Pompeii's largest home, where you're greeted by the delightful small bronze statue of the *Dancing Faun*, famed for its realistic movement and fine proportion. (The original, described on page 641, is in Naples' Archaeological Museum.) With 40 rooms and 27,000 square feet, the House of the Faun covers an entire city block. The next floor mosaic, with an intricate diamond-like design, decorates the homeowner's office. Beyond that is the famous floor mosaic of the *Battle of Alexander.* (The original is also at the museum in Naples.) In 333 B.C., Alexander the Great beat Darius and the Persians. Romans had great respect for Alexander, the first great emperor before Rome's. While most of Pompeii's nouveau riche had notoriously bad taste and stuffed their palaces with over-the-top, mismatched decor, this guy had class. Both the faun (an ancient copy of a famous Greek statue) and the Alexander mosaic show an appreciation for history.

The house's back courtyard leads to the exit in the far-right corner. It's lined with pillars rebuilt after the A.D. 62 earthquake. Take a close look at the brick, mortar, and fake marble stucco veneer.

• *Sneak out of the House of the Faun through its back door and turn right. (If this exit is closed, return to the entrance and make a U-turn left, around to the back of the house.) Thirty yards down, along the right-hand side of the street are metal cages protecting...*

⓬ Original Lead Pipes

These 2,000-year-old pipes (made of lead imported from Britannia) were part of the city's elaborate water system. From the aqueduct-fed water tank at the high end of town, three independent pipe systems supplied water to the city: one for baths, one for private homes, and one for public water fountains. If there was a water shortage, democratic priorities prevailed: First the baths were cut off, then the private homes. The last water supply to go was the public fountains, where all citizens could get drinking and cooking water.

• *If the street's not closed off, take your first left (on Vicolo dei Vettii), walk about 20 yards, and find the entrance (on the left) to the next stop. (If the street is closed, turn right down the street marked REG VI INS XIV and skip down to the next set of directions.)*

⓭ House of the Vettii (Casa dei Vettii)

Pompeii's best-preserved home has been completely blocked off for years; unfortunately it's unlikely to reopen in time for your

visit. The House of the Vettii was the bachelor pad of two wealthy merchant brothers. If you can see the entryway, you may spot the huge erection. This is not pornography. There's a meaning here: The penis and the sack of money balance each other on the goldsmith scale above a fine bowl of fruit. Translation: Only with a balance of fertility and money can you have abundance.

If it's open, step into the atrium with its ceiling open to the sky to collect light and rainwater. The pool, while decorative, was a functional water-supply tank. It's flanked by large money boxes anchored to the floor. The brothers were certainly successful merchants, and possibly moneylenders, too.

Exit on the right, passing the tight servant quarters, and go into the kitchen, with its bronze cooking pots (and an exposed lead pipe on the back wall). The passage dead-ends in the little Venus Room, which features erotic frescoes behind glass.

Return to the atrium and pass into the big colonnaded garden. It was replanted according to the plan indicated by the traces of roots that were excavated from the volcanic ash. Richly frescoed entertainment rooms ring this courtyard. Circle counterclockwise. The dining room is finely decorated in black and "Pompeiian red" (from iron rust). Study the detail. Notice the lead humidity seal between the wall and the floor, designed to keep the moisture-sensitive frescoes dry. (Had Leonardo da Vinci taken this clever step, his *Last Supper* in Milan might be in better shape today.) Continuing around, you'll see more of the square white stones inlaid in the floor. Imagine them reflecting like cats' eyes as the brothers and their friends wandered around by oil lamp late at night. Frescoes in the Yellow Room (near the exit) show off the ancient mastery of perspective, which would not be matched elsewhere in Europe for nearly 1,500 years.

• *Facing the entrance to the House of the Vettii, turn left and walk downhill one long block (along Vicolo dei Vettii) to a T-intersection (Via della Fortuna), marked by a stone fountain with a bull's head for a spout. Intersections like this were busy*

neighborhood centers, where the rent was highest and people gathered. With the fountain at your back, turn left, then immediately right, walking along a gently curving road (Vicolo Storto). On the left side of the street, at #22, find four big stone cylinders.

⑭ Bakery and Mill (Forno e Mulini)

The brick oven looks like a modern-day pizza oven. The stubby stone towers are flour grinders. Grain was poured into the top, and

donkeys or slaves pushed wooden bars that turned the stones. The powdered grain dropped out of the bottom as flour—flavored with tiny bits of rock. Each neighborhood had a bakery like this.

Continue to the next intersection (Via degli Augustali, where there's another fast-food joint, at #32) and turn left. As you walk, look at the destructive power of all the vines, and notice how deeply the chariot grooves have worn into the pavement. Deep grooves could break wagon wheels. The suddenly ungroovy stretch indicates that this road was in the process of being repaved when the eruption shut everything down.

• *Head about 50 yards down this (obviously one-way) street to #44 (on the left). Here you'll find the Taberna Hedones (with a small atrium, den, and garden). This bar still has its original floor and, deeper in, the mosaic arch of a grotto fountain. Just past the tavern, turn right and walk downhill to #18, on the right.*

Possible detour: If the road past the tavern is blocked off, here's another way to reach the next stop: First, backtrack to the Forum—go back the way you came, turn left at the bull's-head fountain, then turn left again at the aqueduct arch. Back in the Forum, head down to the far end and turn left onto the main street, Via dell'Abbondanza (which we looked down earlier—remember the beaver teeth?). Follow this, turning left up the second street (after the fountain, marked REG VII INS I, *with a small* Vicolo del Lupanare *sign). This leads to the entrance of the...*

⑮ Brothel (Lupanare)

You'll find the biggest crowds in Pompeii at a place that was likely popular 2,000 ago, too—the brothel. Prostitutes were nicknamed *lupe* (she-wolves), alluding to the call they made when trying to attract business. The brothel was a simple place, with beds and pillows made of stone. The ancient graffiti includes tallies and exotic names of the women, indicating the prostitutes came from all corners of the Mediterranean (it also served as feedback from satisfied customers). The faded frescoes above the cells may have

NAPLES

been a kind of menu for services offered. Note the idealized women (white, which was considered beautiful; one wears an early bra) and the rougher men (dark, considered horny). The bed legs came with little disk-like barriers to keep critters from crawling up.

• *Leaving the brothel, go right, then take the first left, and continue going downhill two blocks to the intersection with Pompeii's main drag, Via dell'Abbondanza. The Forum—and exit—are to the right, for those who may wish to opt out from here.*

The huge amphitheater—which is certainly skippable—is 10 minutes to your left. But for now, go left for 60 yards, then turn right just beyond the fountain, and walk down Via dei Teatri. Turn left before the columns, and head downhill another 60 yards to #28, which marks the...

⓰ Temple of Isis

This Egyptian temple served Pompeii's Egyptian community. The little white stucco shrine with the modern plastic roof housed holy water from the Nile. Isis, from Egyptian myth, was one of many foreign gods adopted by the eclectic Romans. Pompeii must have had a synagogue, too, but it has yet to be excavated.

• *Exit the temple where you entered, and go right. At the next intersection, turn right again, and head downhill to the adjacent theaters. Your goal is the large theater down the corridor at #20, but if it's closed, look at the smaller but similar theater (Teatro Piccolo) just beyond at #19.*

⓱ Theater

Originally a Greek theater (Greeks built theirs with the help of a hillside), this was the birthplace of the Greek port here in 470 B.C.

During Roman times, the theater sat 5,000 people in three sets of seats, all with different prices: the five marble terraces up close (filled with romantic wooden seats for two), the main section, and the cheap nosebleed section (surviving only on the high end, near the trees). The square stones above the cheap seats once supported a canvas rooftop. Take note of the high-profile boxes, flanking the stage, for guests of honor. From this perch, you can see the gladiator barracks—the colonnaded courtyard beyond the theater. They lived in tiny rooms, trained in the courtyard, and fought in the nearby amphitheater.

• *You've seen Pompeii's highlights. When you're ready to leave, backtrack to the main road and turn left, going uphill to the Forum, where you'll find the main entrance/exit.*

However, there's much more to see—three-quarters of Pompeii's 164 acres have been excavated, but this tour has covered only a third

*of the site. After the theater—if you still have energy to see more—go
back to the main road, and take a right toward the eastern part of the
site, where the crowds thin out. Go straight for about 10 minutes, likely
jogging right after a bit (just follow the posted maps). You'll wind up
passing through a pretty, forested area. At the far end is the...*

⑱ Amphitheater

If you can, climb to the upper level of the amphitheater (though
the stairs are often blocked). With Vesuvius looming in the background, mentally replace the tourists below with gladiators and
wild animals locked in combat. Walk
along the top of the amphitheater and
look down into the grassy rectangular
area surrounded by columns. This is the
Palaestra, an area once used for athletic
training. (If you can't get to the top of the
amphitheater, you can see the Palaestra
from outside—in fact, you can't miss it,
as it's right next door.) Facing the other
way, look for the bell tower that tops the
roofline of the modern city of Pompei,
where locals go about their daily lives in
the shadow of the volcano, just as their
ancestors did 2,000 years ago.

• *If it's too crowded to bear hiking back along uneven lanes to the entrance, you can slip out the site's "back door," which is next to the amphitheater. Exiting, turn right and follow the site's wall all the way back to
the entrance.*

Herculaneum

Smaller, less crowded, and not as ruined as its famous big sister,
Herculaneum (worth ▲▲; Ercolano in Italian) offers a closer, more
intimate peek into ancient Roman life but lacks the grandeur of
Pompeii (there's barely a colonnade).

Orientation

Cost and Hours: €11, daily April-Oct
8:30-19:30, Nov-March 8:30-17:00,
ticket office closes 1.5 hours earlier.

Getting There: Ercolano Scavi, the
nearest train station to Herculaneum, is about 20 minutes from
Naples and 50 minutes from Sor-

rento on the same Circumvesuviana train that goes to Pompeii (for details on the Circumvesuviana, see page 621. Leave the station and turn right, then left down the main drag; go eight blocks straight downhill to the end of the road, where you'll see the entrance to the ruins marked by a grand arch. (Skip the Museo MAV.)

Information: Pick up a free, detailed map and excellent booklet at the info desk next to the ticket window. The booklet gives you a quick explanation of each building, keyed to the same numbers as the audioguides. There's a bookstore inside the site, next to the audioguide stand. Tel. 081-777-7008, www.pompeiisites.org.

Audioguide: The informative and interesting audioguide sheds light on the ruins and life in Herculaneum in the first century A.D. (€6.50, €10/2 people, ID required, cheaper version available for kids ages 4-10, pick up 100 yards after the ticket turnstiles, uses same numbers as info booklet).

Services: There's a free WC in the ticket office building. The site doesn't have a café of its own, but there are several eateries on the way from the train station.

Visiting the Site

Caked and baked by the same A.D. 79 eruption that pummeled Pompeii, Herculaneum is a small community of intact buildings, surrounded on all sides by the modern town. Herculaneum got slammed about 12 hours after the eruption started by a superheated avalanche of ash and hot gases. The city was eventually buried under nearly 60 feet of boiling mud, which hardened into tuff, perfectly preserving the city until excavations began in 1748.

Highlights of the excavation site include the **Seat of the Augustali** (Sede degli Augustali, #24), which was a forum for freed slaves climbing their way up the ladder of Roman society, and the *thermopolium* (#22)—the Roman equivalent to a fast-food joint, with giant jars for wine, oil, and snacks. The **Bottega ad Cucumas** wine shop (#19) still has charred remains of beams, and its drink list remains frescoed on the outside wall. **The House of Neptune and Amphitrite** (Casa di Nettuno e Anfitrite, #29) has colorful mosaics and an intact "frame" made of shells.

Don't miss the **sports complex** *(palestra, #12)* and the **House of the Deer** (Casa dei Cervi, #8), with its colorfully frescoed walls. Ancient Herculaneum, like all Roman cities of that age, was filled with color, rather than the stark white we often imagine (even the statues were painted).

The **baths** (Terme Suburbane, #3, sometimes closed) illustrate the city's devastation. Back outside, make your way down the steps to the sunken area just below. As you descend, you're walking across what was formerly Herculaneum's **beach.** During excavations in 1981, hundreds of skeletons were discovered here, between the wall of volcanic stone behind you and the city in front of you. Some of Herculaneum's 4,000 citizens tried to escape by sea, but were overtaken by the pyroclastic flows.

Thankfully, your escape is easier. Either follow the sounds of the water and continue through the tunnel; or, more scenically, backtrack and exit the same way you entered.

Sorrento

Arriving in serene Sorrento—a welcoming mid-sized city with plenty of services but little bustle—presents the cruise traveler with an embarrassment of riches. While worth a stroll itself, the city is a jumping-off-place for several exciting destinations. The jet-setting island of Capri is just a short cruise from Sorrento, offering more charm and fun (outside of the crowded months of July and Aug) than its glitzy reputation would suggest. North of Sorrento, and easily accessible on the Circumvesuviana train line, are the ancient sites of Pompeii and Herculaneum, and big-city Naples with its impressive Archaeological Museum. To the east of Sorrento is the stunning Amalfi Coast, which you can tour with a hired driver or by public bus.

See "Your Top Options" on page 616 for approximate times to allow per destination.

Arrival at the Port of Sorrento

Arrival at a Glance: You can explore the town of Sorrento itself; walk or take a bus to the train station to ride the Circumvesuviana to Pompeii (30 minutes), Herculaneum (50 minutes), or Naples (70 minutes); or catch a boat to Capri (20-25 minutes) or Naples (35 minutes). A taxi or hired driver brings the glorious Amalfi Coast within reach.

Port Overview

Cruise ships tender passengers to Sorrento's main harbor, called Marina Piccola. From the boat dock, Sorrento's town center (the main square, Piazza Tasso) and its train station are both steeply uphill. For a description of the town and the services it offers, see page 670.

NAPLES

Getting to the Sights

By Taxi or Hired Car

Taxi: Taxis are expensive—charging at least €15 for the short ride from the port to the train station. Take the bus instead (see "By Public Transportation," later). But because of heavy traffic and the complex one-way road system, you can likely walk faster than you can ride in this city. If you do use a taxi, even if you agree to a set price, be sure it has a meter (all official taxis have one).

For a longer trip, especially to the Amalfi Coast, taxis are a good idea. Expect to pay €80 for up to four people in a car (or €90 for up to six in a minibus) for a one-way trip from Sorrento to Positano. While taxis must use a meter within a city, a fixed rate is OK otherwise. Negotiate—ask about a reduced rate for a round-trip.

Hired Car: If you'd like not just a taxi driver but someone happy to share their knowledge of the area, hire a driver for the day. This splurge is a particularly enticing option on the Amalfi Coast, given the tight turns, impossible parking, congested buses, and potential fun. (It makes much less sense to pay a premium for a driver to take you to Pompeii, Herculaneum, or Naples, as those places are conveniently served by the Circumvesuviana train, and only licensed guides, not drivers, are authorized to take you into the site at Pompeii.) These are worth reserving in advance:

The **Monetti** family does Amalfi Coast excursions, including pickup from cruise ports, for roughly €280 for eight hours (and as far as Paestum for €400 for 10 hours). These prices are for up to three people—they can take up to eight (at a higher price) in their air-conditioned Mercedes van. To get their best prices, mention this book. Payment is by cash only (Raffaele Monetti's mobile 335-602-9158 or 338-946-2860; "office" run by Raffaele's English-speaking wife, Susanna; fax 081-807-4531, www.monettitaxi17.it, monettitaxi17@libero.it).

Francesco del Pizzo is another smooth and honest driver. A classy young man who speaks English well, Francesco enjoys explaining things as he drives (9 hours in a car with up to 4 passengers, €280; up to 8 passengers in a minibus, €320; mobile 333-238-4144, francescodelpizzo@yahoo.it).

Umberto and Giovanni Benvenuto offer transport, narrated tours, and shore excursions throughout the Amalfi Coast, as well as to Rome, Naples, Pompeii, and more. They are based in Praiano (near Positano). While as friendly as the Monettis, they're more upmarket and formal, with steeper rates explained on their website (tel. 081-007-2114, mobile 346-684-0226, US tel. 310-424-5640, www.benvenutolimos.com, info@benvenutolimos.com).

Anthony Buonocore is based in Amalfi, but does excursions and transfers anywhere in the region in his air-conditioned eight-person Mercedes van (rates vary depending on trip, tel. 349-441-0336, www.amalfitransfer.com, buonocoreanthony@yahoo.it).

Sorrento Silver Star, with professional drivers and comfortable Mercedes cars and vans, offers custom trips throughout the area at prices between the Monettis' and Benvenutos' (tel. 081-877-1224, mobile 339-388-8143, www.sorrentosilverstar.com, luisa@sorrentosilverstar.com, Luisa).

By Public Transportation

From Sorrento's harbor, you can head up into the town center; catch a train to nearby destinations; or ride a boat to the isle of Capri or the city of Naples (for information on arrival at those destinations, see page 618 for Naples or page 685 for Capri).

To Sorrento's Town Center

To get from the harbor to Piazza Tasso, the easiest way is to follow the *Lift* signs a couple of hundred yards to the elevator. Pay €1 to ride it up to Villa Comunale city park. Exit through the park gate and bear left; Piazza Tasso is about four blocks away. Or, you can hike uphill along the road for 15 minutes. Other options are the red-and-white city bus #B or #C (buy €1 tickets at the tobacco shop, 3/hour), or the small, blue private bus (€1, buy ticket from driver, 4/hour). The train station is a five-minute walk from Piazza Tasso (head down Corso Italia).

To Pompeii, Herculaneum, or Naples by Circumvesuviana Train

The Circumvesuviana commuter train (explained on page 621) runs about every 30 minutes between Naples and Sorrento (less frequently on holidays, www.vesuviana.it). From Sorrento, it's about 30 minutes to Pompeii, 50 minutes to Herculaneum (€2.20 one-way for either trip), and 70 minutes to Naples (€4.20 one-way). The schedule is printed in the free *Surrentum* magazine (available at TI). Readers report a big problem with theft on this train, though the risk seems to be largely limited to travel in suburban Naples; going between Sorrento and Pompeii or Herculaneum is generally safer.

To Capri or Naples by Boat

In considering your options, note that the number of boats that run per day varies according to the season. The frequency indicated here is for roughly mid-May through mid-October, with a few more boats per day in summer and less off-season. The Caremar line, a subsidized state-run ferry company, takes cars, offers fewer departures, and is just a bit slower—but cheaper—than the other boat. All of the boats take several hundred people each—and frequently fill up.

From Sorrento to Capri: Boats run at least hourly. Your options include a fast **ferry** (*traghetto* or *nave veloce*, 4/day, 25 minutes, €15, run by Caremar, tel. 081-807-3077, www.caremar.it) or a faster but pricier **hydrofoil** (*aliscafi*, up to 20/day, 20 minutes, €17-18, run by Gescab, tel. 081-807-1812, www.gescab.it). To avoid the crowds on Capri, it's best to buy your ticket at 8:00 and take the 8:25 hydrofoil (try to depart by 9:30 at the very latest)—if your cruise arrives early enough. These early boats can be jammed, but it's worth it once you reach the island.

From Sorrento to Naples: 6/day, departs roughly every 2 hours, 35 minutes, €12-13; for more info, see page 617.

To Positano and the Amalfi Coast

Given your time constraints, I'd recommend seeing the Amalfi Coast by shore excursion or by taxi or hired driver (see page 668). Buses and boats can get overcrowded, forcing people to wait for the next departure and making these options risky.

Returning to Sorrento

If returning by train, simply walk or ride a bus back down to the port (see "Arrival in Sorrento," later).

NAPLES

Orientation to Sorrento

Wedged on a ledge under the mountains and over the Mediterranean, spritzed by lemon and olive groves, Sorrento is an attractive resort of 20,000 residents and, in summer, just as many tourists. As 90 percent of the town's economy is tourism, everyone seems to speak fluent English and work for the Chamber of Commerce. This gateway to the Amalfi Coast has an unspoiled old quarter, a lively main shopping street, and a spectacular cliffside setting.

Downtown Sorrento is long and narrow. Piazza Tasso marks the town's center. The main drag, Corso Italia, runs parallel to the sea, passing 50 yards below the train station, through Piazza Tasso, and then out toward the cape, where the road's name becomes Via Capo. Nearly everything mentioned here (except Meta beach) is within a 10-minute walk of the station. The town is perched on a cliff; the best real beaches are a couple of miles away.

Sorrento has two different port areas: The Marina Piccola, below Piazza Tasso, is the functional harbor with boats to Naples and Capri, as well as cruise-ship tenders. The Marina Grande, below the other end of downtown, is like a little fishing village, with recommended restaurants and more charm.

Tourist Information

The helpful TI (labeled *Soggiorno e Turismo*)—located inside the Foreigners' Club—hands out the free monthly *Surrentum* maga-zine, with a great city map and schedules of boats, buses, concerts, and festivals (Mon-Fri 8:30-19:00, Sat-Sun 9:00-13:00 except closed Sun Oct-May; Via Luigi de Maio 35, tel. 081-807-4033, www.sorrentotourism.com; Nino, Fabiola, and Peppe).

To get from Piazza Tasso to the TI, turn right at the end of the square, and go down Via Luigi de Maio through Piazza Sant'Antonino, bearing right downhill about 30 yards to the For-eigners' Club mansion at #35.

If you just need quick advice, the fake tourist office—located in a green caboose just outside the train station—can be of help. While they're a private business with hopes that you'll purchase one of their overpriced excursions, they're willing to give basic in-formation on directions, buses, and ferries.

Arrival in Sorrento

By Boat: Passenger boats from Naples or Capri dock at Sorrento's little harbor, Marina Piccola—which is also where cruise ships ten-der passengers. For details on arriving here, see page 667.

By Train: If you're arriving on the Circumvesuviana from Na-ples or Pompeii, you're a five-minute walk from the main square, Pi-azza Tasso: Exit the station straight ahead, then turn left on Corso Italia. From Piazza Tasso, you can walk a few minutes to the TI (see "Tourist Information," earlier, for directions), take my self-guided walk, or, if you're taking a boat to Capri or Naples, you can head for the harbor, Marina Piccola. To reach the harbor **on foot,** head down the stairs near the statue's left side (about 10 minutes). Or you can catch red-and-white city **bus** #B or #C (€1, buy ticket at tobacco shop near the dock, 3/hour) or the small, blue private bus (€1, buy ticket from driver, 4/hour). Boat tickets are sold only at the port.

Helpful Hints

Bookstore: Libreria Tasso has a decent selection of books in Eng-lish, including this one (June-Sept daily 10:00-22:00; Oct-May Mon-Sat 9:45-13:00 & 16:00-20:30, Sun 11:00-13:00 &

17:00-20:00; Via San Cesareo 96, one block north of cathedral, near Sorrento Men's Club; tel. 081-807-1639).

Laundry: Sorrento has two handy self-service launderettes (both charge about €8/load wash and dry, includes soap). One launderette is just down the alley next to Corso Italia 30 (daily May-Sept 7:00-24:00, Oct-April 8:00-23:00, Vico I Fuoro 3, mobile 338-506-0942). The other is near the station, at the corner of Corso Italia and Via degli Aranci (daily 7:00-22:00).

Guided Tours of Pompeii, Naples, and the Amalfi Coast: Naples-based **Mondo Tours** offers affordable tours of these destinations, including a nine-hour Amalfi Coast drive that starts from Sorrento. You'll sign up in advance and team up with fellow Rick Steves readers to split the cost (making it €45/person). For details, see page 628.

Local Guides: Giovanna Donadio is a good tour guide for Sorrento, Amalfi, and Capri (€100/half-day, €160/day, same price for any size group, mobile 338-466-0114, giovanna_dona@hotmail.com). **Giovanni Visetti** is a nature lover, mapmaker, and orienteer who organizes hikes and has a fine website describing local trails (mobile 339-694-2911, www.giovis.com, giovis@giovis.com).

Getting Around Sorrento

By Bus: City buses (either orange or red-and-white) all stop near the main square, Piazza Tasso. Bus #A runs east to Meta beach; buses #B and #C go to the port (Marina Piccola); and bus #D heads to the fishing village (Marina Grande). Buses #A and #D stop at the beginning of Corso Italia (west side of Piazza Tasso for Via Capo or Marina Grande, east side for Meta); #B and #C stop at the corner of Piazza Sant'Antonino, just down the hill toward the water. The trip between Piazza Tasso and Marina Piccola costs just €1 (see "Arrival in Sorrento," earlier); for other trips, tickets cost €2.50 and are good for 45 minutes (purchase at tobacco shops and newsstands). Stamp your ticket upon entering the bus. One-day passes (€7.60) are valid on buses along the entire Amalfi Coast.

By Rental Wheels: Many places rent motor scooters for about €35 per day, including two locations near the train station: **Europcar** (Mon-Sat 9:00-13:00 & 16:00-19:30, Sun by request 10:00-13:00, Corso Italia 210p, tel. 081-878-1386, www.sorrento.it) and **Penisola Rent,** a half-block away (Mon-Sat 9:00-13:00 & 16:00-20:30, Sun 9:00-13:00, located in Hotel Nice, Corso Italia 259, tel. 081-877-4664, www.penisolarent.com). Don't rent a car in summer unless you enjoy traffic jams.

By Taxi: See page 668.

Welcome to Sorrento Walk

From Piazza Tasso to Marina Grande

Get to know Sorrento with this lazy self-guided town stroll that ends down by the waterside at the small-boat harbor, Marina Grande.

• *Begin on the main square. Stand under the flags with your back to the sea, and face...*

Piazza Tasso

As in any southern Italian town, this "piazza" is Sorrento's living room. It may be noisy and congested, but locals want to be where the action is...and be part of the scene. The most expensive apartments and top cafés are on or near this square. City buses stop at or close to the square on their way to Marina Piccola and Via Capo. The train station is a five-minute walk to the left. A statue of St. Anthony, patron of Sorrento, faces north as if greeting those coming from Naples (he's often equipped with an armload of fresh lemons and oranges).

This square spans a gorge that divides downtown Sorrento. The newer section (to your left) was farm country just two centuries ago. The older part is to your right, with an ancient Greek gridded street plan (like much of southern Italy, Sorrento was Greek-speaking for centuries before it was Romanized). If you walk a block inland, go right up to the green railing, and look down, you'll see steps that were carved in the fifth century B.C. The combination of the gorge and the seaside cliffs made Sorrento easy to defend. A small section of wall (which you can find near Hotel Mignon) closed the landward gap in the city's defenses.

Sorrento's name may come from the Greek word for "siren," the legendary half-bird, half-woman who sang an intoxicating lullaby. According to Homer, the sirens lived on an island near here. No one had ever sailed by the sirens without succumbing to their incredible musical charms...and to death. But Homer's hero Ulysses was determined to hear the song. He put wax in his oarsmen's ears and had himself lashed to the mast of his ship. Oh, it was nice. The sirens, thinking they had lost their powers, threw themselves into the sea, and the place became safe to inhabit. Ulysses' odyssey was all about the westward expansion of Greek culture, and to the ancient Greeks, places like Sorrento were the wild, wild west.

• *With your back still to the sea, head to the far-right corner of the square, behind the statue of Torquato Tasso, the square's namesake. (A Sorrento native, he was a lively Renaissance poet—but today he seems only to wonder which restaurant to choose for dinner.) Peek into the big court-*

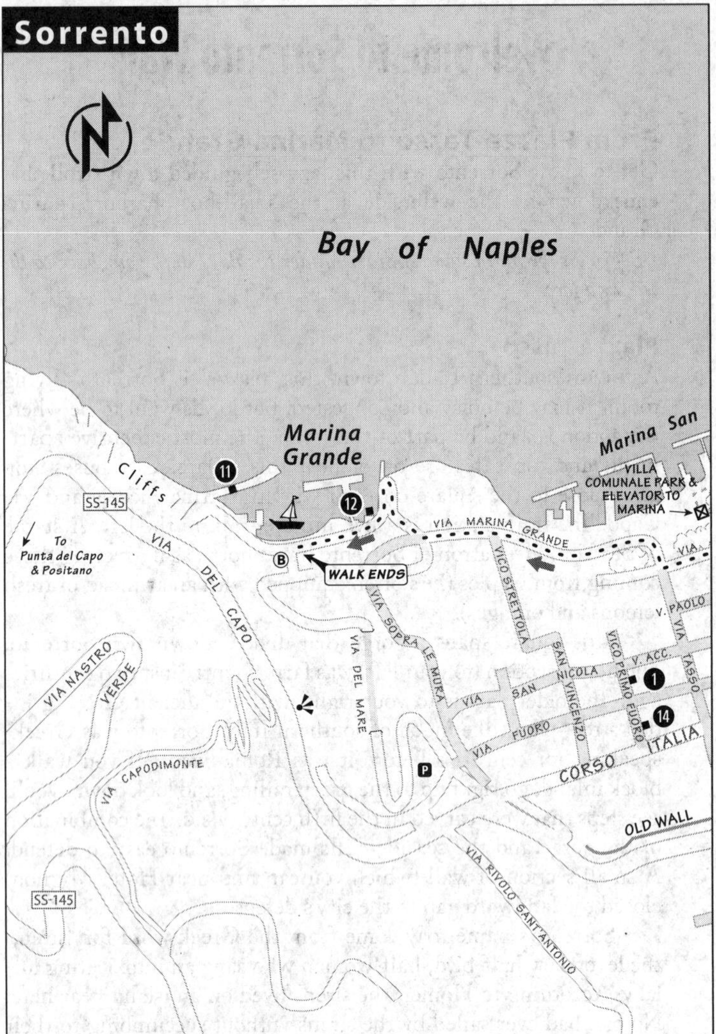

Sorrento

Bay of Naples

Marina Grande

Marina San

Cliffs

SS-145

To Punta del Capo & Positano

VIA DEL CAPO

VIA MARINA GRANDE

VILLA COMUNALE PARK & ELEVATOR TO MARINA

VICO STRETTOLA

V. PAOLO

VIA NASTRO VERDE

VIA CAPODIMONTE

VIA SOPRA LE MURA

VIA DEL MARE

WALK ENDS

VIA SAN

SAN NICOLA

VICO PRIMO FUORO

V. ACC.

CORSO ITALIA

VIA FUORO

SAN VINCENZO

OLD WALL

SS-145

VIA RIVOLO SANT'ANTONIO

To Positano

1 Inn Bufalito

2 Camera & Cucina Ristorante

3 Chantecler's Trattoria & Meating

4 Rist. Pizzeria da Gigino

5 Foreigners' Club Rest.

6 Pizzeria da Franco

7 Kebab Joint

8 Decò Supermarket

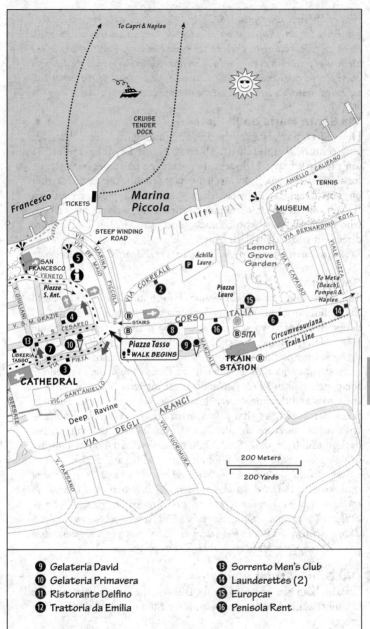

To Capri & Naples

CRUISE
TENDER
DOCK

*Marina
Piccola*

Francesco

TICKETS

STEEP WINDING
ROAD

VIA DE MAIO

VIA DI MARINA PICCOLA

Cliffs

VIA ANIELLO CALIFANO • TENNIS

MUSEUM

VIA BERNARDINO ROTA

VIA B CAPASSO

VIALE NIZZA

SAN
FRANCESCO
VENETO

Piazza
S. Ant.

V GIULIANI

V.S M GRAZIE

VIA S. CESAREO

LIBRERIA
TASSO

VIA PIETA

V SERSALE

CATHEDRAL

VIC. SANT'ANIELLO

Deep Ravine

VIA DEGLI ARANCI

VIA FUOROMURA

V PACANO

VIA CORREALE

Achille
Lauro

P

*Piazza
Lauro*

Lemon
Grove
Garden

To Meta
(Beach),
Pompeii &
Naples

CORSO   ITALIA

STAIRS

B

B

Piazza Tasso
WALK BEGINS

MARZIALE

Circumvesuviana
Train Line

B SITA

**TRAIN
STATION** B

200 Meters

200 Yards

9 Gelateria David
10 Gelateria Primavera
11 Ristorante Delfino
12 Trattoria da Emilia

13 Sorrento Men's Club
14 Launderettes (2)
15 Europcar
16 Penisola Rent

yard of Palazzo Correale (#18, behind the statue in the right corner) to get a feel for an 18th-century aristocratic palace's courtyard, its walls lined with characteristic tiles. In the same building, you'll see one of the zillions of fun, touristy shops in Sorrento that sells regional goodies and offers free biscuits and tastes of liqueurs. As you're leaving the courtyard, on your immediate left you'll see the narrow...

Via Santa Maria della Pietà

Here, just a few yards off the noisy main drag, is a street that goes back centuries before Christ. About 100 yards down the lane, at #24 (on the left), find a 13th-century palace (no balconies back then... for security reasons), now an elementary school. A few steps farther on, you'll see a tiny shrine across the street. Typical of southern Italy, it's where the faithful pray to their saint, who contacts Mary, who contacts Jesus, who contacts God. This shrine is a bit more direct—it starts right with Mary.

• *Continue down the lane, which ends at the delightful...*

Cathedral

This is the seat of the local bishop. Pop in for a cool stroll around the ambulatory, checking out the impressive *intarsio* (inlaid-wood) doors. There are two sets of doors—the main entry and the side entry, facing the big street. They're inlaid on both sides and show many scenes of the town and its industry. The doors facing the main street include an old town map. These were made to celebrate the pope's visit in 1992. Also notice the intricate inlaid Stations of the Cross and the fine *presepe* (manger scene) in the back. This one takes Bethlehem on that first Christmas and sets it in Naples— with pasta, mozzarella, salami, and even Mount Vesuvius in the background (free, daily 8:00-12:30 & 16:30-20:30, no visits during Mass daily at 8:30 and 18:00, plus Sun at 11:00 and 12:15).

• *Backtrack 10 yards down Via Santa Maria della Pietà, turn left, and cross busy Corso Italia. In the summer, this stretch of road is closed to traffic each evening, when it hosts the best of the* passeggiata. *Look back at the bell tower, with the scavenged ancient Roman columns at its base. Then go straight on Via P. Reginaldo Giuliani (pausing to see who's died lately on the poster board on your right) and follow the...*

Old Greek Street Plan

Locals claim the ancient Greeks laid out the streets east-west for the most sunlight and north-south for the prevailing and cooling breeze.

• *One block ahead on your right, the 14th-century loggia is home to the...*

Sorrento Men's Club

Once the meeting place of the town's nobles, this club has been a

retreat for retired working-class men for generations. Strictly no women—and no phones.

Italian men venerate their mothers. (Italians joke that Jesus must have been a southern Italian because his mother believed her son was God, he believed his mom was a virgin, and he lived at home with her until he was 30.) But Italian men have also built into their culture ways to be on their own. Here, men play cards and gossip under a historic emblem of the city and a finely frescoed 16th-century dome, with its marvelous 3-D scenes.

• *Turn right for a better view of the Men's Club and a historical marker describing the building. Then continue along...*

Via San Cesareo

This touristy pedestrian-only shopping street leads back to Piazza Tasso. It's lined with competitive little shops where you can peruse (and sample) lemon products. Notice the huge ancient doorways with their tiny doors—to let the right people in, carefully, during a more dangerous age.

• *After a block, take a left onto Via degli Archi, go under the arch, and then hang a right (under another arch) to the square with the...*

Statue of St. Anthony (Antonino)

Sorrento's town saint humbly looms among the palms, facing the basilica where the reliquary containing a few of his bones lies (free, downstairs in the crypt beneath the altar, surrounded by lots of votives).

• *Exit the square at the bottom-left (following the* lift to the port *signs; don't go down the street with the line of trees and the* porto *signs). After a block or so, on the right you'll see the trees in front of the Imperial Hotel Tramontano, and to their right a path leading to a...*

Cliffside Square

This fine public square, the Villa Comunale, overlooks the harbor. Belly up to the banister to enjoy the view of Marina Piccola and the Bay of Naples. From here, steps zigzag down to the harbor, where lounge chairs, filled by vacationers working on tans, line the sundecks (there's also a €1 elevator to the harbor). The Franciscan church fronting this square faces a fine modern statue of Francis across the street. Next to the church is a dreamy little cloister. Pop inside to see Sicilian Gothic—a 13th-century mix of Norman, Gothic, and Arabic styles, all around the old pepper tree. This is an understandably popular spot for weddings and concerts.

• *From here, you can quit the walk and stay in the town center, or continue another few minutes downhill to the waterfront at Marina Grande. To do that, return to the road and keep going downhill. At the next square (Piazza della Vittoria), which offers another grand view, cut over to the road closest to the water. After winding downhill for a few minutes, it turns into a wide stairway, and just before reaching the waterfront, you pass under an...*

Ancient Greek Gate

This gate marks the boundary between Sorrento and Marina Grande, technically a separate town with its own proud residents—it's said that even their cats look different. Because Marina Grande dwellers lived outside the wall and were more susceptible to rape, pillage, and plunder, Sorrentines believe that they come from Saracen (Turkish pirate) stock. Sorrentines still scare their children by saying, "Behave—or the Turks will take you away."

• *Now go all the way down the steps into Marina Grande, Sorrento's "big" small-boat harbor. (Confusingly, Capri also has a harbor called Marina Grande.)*

Marina Grande

Until recently, this little community was famously traditional, with its economy based on its fishing fleet. Locals recall when women wore black when a relative died (1 year for an uncle, aunt, or sibling; 2-3 years for a husband or parent). Men got off easy, just wearing a black memorial button.

There are two recommended restaurants on the harbor. **Trattoria da Emilia** has an old newspaper clipping, tacked near the door, about Sophia Loren filming here. On the far side of the harbor, **Ristorante Delfino** boasts a sundeck for a lazy drink before or after lunch.

• *From here, buses return to the center at Piazza Tasso every hour (€2.50, buy ticket at tobacco shop). Or you can walk back up.*

Sights in Sorrento

▲▲Strolling

Take time to explore the surprisingly pleasant old city between Corso Italia and the sea. Views from Villa Comunale, the public park next to Imperial Hotel Tramontano, are worth the detour.

Lemon Products Galore

Via San Cesareo is lined with hard-working rival shops selling a mind-boggling array of lemon prod-

Lemons

Around here, *limoni* are ubiquitous: screaming yellow painted on ceramics, dainty bottles of *limoncello,* and lemons the size of softballs at the fruit stand.

The Amalfi Coast and Sorrento area produces several different kinds of lemons. The gigantic, bumpy "lemons" are actually citrons, called *cedri,* and are

more for show—they're pulpier than they are juicy, and make a good marmalade. The juicy *sfusato sorrentino,* grown only in Sorrento, is shaped like an American football, while the *sfusato amalfitano,* with knobby points on both ends, is less juicy but equally aromatic. These two kinds of luscious lemons are used in sweets such as *granita* (shaved ice doused in lemonade), *limoncello* (a candy-like liqueur with a big kick, called *limoncino* on the Cinque Terre), *delizia* (a dome of fluffy cake filled and slathered with a thick whipped lemon cream), *spremuta di limone* (fresh-squeezed lemon juice), and, of course, gelato or *sorbetto alla limone.*

ucts and offering samples of lots of sour goodies. Poke around for a pungent experience.

▲Lemon Grove Garden (Giardini di Cataldo)

This small park consists of an inviting organic lemon and orange grove lined with shady, welcoming paths. The owners of the grove are seasoned green thumbs, having worked the orchard through many generations. You'll see that they've even grafted orange-tree branches onto a lemon tree so that both fruits now grow on the same tree. The garden is dotted with benches, tables, and an inviting little tasting (and buying) stand. You'll get a chance to sniff and taste the varieties of lemons, and enjoy free samples of chilled *limoncello* along with various other homemade liqueurs made from basil, mandarins, or fennel.

Cost and Hours: Enthusiastically free, daily April-Sept 9:30-sunset, Oct-March 10:00-sunset, closed in rainy weather, tel. 081-807-4040, www.igiardinidicataldo.it. Enter the garden either on Corso Italia (100 yards north of the train station—where painted tiles show lemon fantasies), or at the intersection of Via Capasso and Via Rota (next to the Hotel La Meridiana Sorrento). The main shop selling their organic homemade products, tasty gelato, and lemonade is across from the Corso Italia entrance at #267.

▲Swimming near Sorrento

If you require immediate tanning, you can rent a chair on a pier by the port. There are no great beaches in Sorrento—the gravelly, jam-packed private beaches of **Marina Piccola** are more for partying than pampering, and there's just a tiny spot for public use. The elevator in Villa Comunale city park (next to the Church of San Francesco) gets you down for €1. At **Marina Grande,** Restaurant Delfino has a pier lined with lounge chairs for sunbathing (free for those with this book who buy lunch there).

There's a classic, sandy Italian beach two miles away at **Meta,** but it's generally overrun by teenagers from Naples. While the Meta Circumvesuviana stop is a very long walk from the beach (or a €25 cab ride), the red-and-white bus #A goes directly from Piazza Tasso to the Meta beach (last stop, schedule posted for hourly returns). At Meta, you'll find pizzerias, snack bars, and a little free section of beach, but the place is mostly dominated by several sprawling private-beach complexes—if you go, pay for a spot in one of these. Lido Metamare seems best (open May-Sept, €2.50 entry; lockable changing cabins, lounge chairs, and more available for an extra fee; tel. 081-532-2505). It's a very Italian scene—locals complain that it's "too local" (i.e., inundated with Naples' riff-raff)—with light lunches, a playground, a manicured beach, loud pop music...and no international tourists.

Tarzan might take Jane to the wild and stony beach at **Punta del Capo,** a 15-minute bus ride from Piazza Tasso (the same bus #A explained above, but in the opposite direction from Meta; 2/hour, get off at stop in front of the American Bar, then walk 10 minutes past ruined Roman Villa di Pollio).

Scuba Diving

To escape the shops, dive deep into the Mediterranean. PADI-certified Futuro Mare offers a one-hour boat ride out to the protected marine zone that lies between Sorrento and Capri, where you can try the beginners' dive (€90, includes instruction and complete supervision, April-Oct usually daily at 9:30). The boat also takes experienced certified divers (1 dive-€65, 2 dives-€95, April-Oct daily at 9:30 and 14:00). The whole experience takes about three hours. Prices include all equipment, transportation, and the dive itself, which lasts about 40 minutes for both novices and experts (call a day or two in advance to reserve, tel. 349-653-6323, www. sorrentodiving.it, info@futuromare.it).

Boat Rental

You can rent motor boats big enough for four people (€150/day, plus gas—figure about €30 for a trip to Capri, more with a skipper; with your back to the ferry-ticket offices, it's to the left around the corner at Via Marina Piccola 43; tel. 081-807-2283, www.nauticasicsic. com).

Eating in Sorrento

For general tips on eating in Italy, see page 455.

Mid-Priced Restaurants Downtown

Inn Bufalito specializes in *mozzarella di bufala*, of course, but also features all things buffalo—steak, sausage, salami, carpaccio, buffalo-meat pasta sauce, and several different types of buffalo milk cheese. They serve more standard Italian food, too, but the buffalo theme is the reason to come. The smartly designed space has a modern, borderline-trendy, casual atmosphere and a fun indoor-outdoor vibe (€6-9 salads, €8-10 pastas, €9-14 *secondi*, no cover, don't miss the seasonal specialties on the blackboard, daily 12:00-24:00, closed Oct-April, Vico I Fuoro 21, tel. 081-365-6975).

Camera & Cucina is less traditional and more expensive, with mod atmosphere, a fine garden, and a creative menu that caters to trendy young locals (€9-13 pastas, €15-18 *secondi*, May-Nov daily 18:00-late, Dec-April open Fri-Sat only, reservations smart, Via Correale 19, 4-minute walk from Piazza Tasso, tel. 081-877-3686).

Chantecler's Trattoria, a hole-in-the-wall, family-run place on the narrow lane that leads to the cathedral, is particularly great for meat and vegetarian fare. They offer a €9 meal deal at lunch: your choice of one *primo* and one *secondo* (prices slightly higher at dinner—€7 pastas, €10 *secondi*, no cover charge, good vegetarian dishes, take out or eat in, Tue-Sun 12:00-15:00 & 19:00-24:00, closed Mon, Via Santa Maria della Pietà 38, tel. 081-807-5868, Luigi and family).

Ristorante Pizzeria da Gigino, lively and congested with a sprawling interior and tables spilling into the street, makes huge, tasty Neapolitan-style pizzas in their wood-burning oven (€8-10 pizzas and pastas, €8-13 *secondi*, no cover charge, daily 12:00-24:00, closed Jan-Feb; just off Piazza Sant'Antonino—take first road to the left of Sant'Antonino as you face him, pass under the archway, and take the first left to Via degli Archi 15; tel. 081-878-1927, Antonino).

Meating, as its name implies, focuses on top-quality meats, from homemade sausages to giant steaks on a wood-fired grill. You'll find no seafood or pasta here, but there are a variety of vegetable dishes and delicious local cheeses, along with a reasonably priced selection of wines (€10-18 steaks, daily 18:00-24:00, Via Santa Maria della Pietà 20, tel. 081-878-2891).

With a Sea View: The **Foreigners' Club Restaurant** has some of the best sea views in town (with a sprawling terrace under breezy palms), live music nightly at 20:00 (May-mid-Oct), and passable meals. It's a good spot for dessert or an after-dinner *limoncello* (€9-

14 pastas and pizzas, €12-23 *secondi*, daily, bar opens at 9:30, meals served 11:00-23:00, Via Luigi de Maio 35, tel. 081-877-3263). If you'd enjoy eating along the water (rather than just with a water view), see "Harborside in Marina Grande," later.

Cheap Eats Downtown

Pizza: **Pizzeria da Franco** seems to be Sorrento's favorite place for basic, casual pizza in a fun, untouristy atmosphere. There's nothing fancy about this place—just locals on benches eating hot sandwiches and great pizzas served on waxed paper in a square tin. It's packed to the rafters with a youthful crowd that doesn't mind the plastic cups (€6-8 pizzas and calzones, €5-7 salads, takeout possible, daily 8:00-2:00 in the morning, just across from Lemon Grove Garden on busy Corso Italia at #265, tel. 081-877-2066).

Kebabs: **Kebab Joint**, a little hole-in-the-wall, has a passionate following among eaters who appreciate Andrea's fresh bread, homemade sauces, and ethic of buying meat fresh each day (and closing when the supply is gone). This is your best non-Italian €5 meal in town. Choose beef or chicken—locals don't go for pork—and garnish as you like with fries and/or salad (nightly from 17:00, before the cathedral off Via Santa Maria della Pietà, at Vico il Traversa Pietà 23, tel. 081-807-4595).

Picnics: Get groceries at the **Decò supermarket** (Mon-Sat 8:30-20:30, Sun 9:30-13:00 & 16:30-20:00, Corso Italia 223).

Gelato: Near the train station, **Gelateria David** has many repeat customers (so many flavors, so little time). In 1957, Augusto Davide opened a *gelateria* in Sorrento, and his grandson, Mario, proudly carries on the tradition today (the gelato is still made on-site). Before choosing, sample *Profumi di Sorrento* (an explosive sorbet of mixed fruits), "Sorrento moon" (white almond with lemon zest), and lemon crème. They also serve sandwiches at fair prices (€2 cones, daily 9:00-24:00, shorter hours in spring and fall, closed Dec-Feb, a block below the train station at Via Marziale 19, tel. 081-807-3649). Don't mistake this place for the similarly named Gelateria Davide, in the town center—owned by a distant relative, but not as good.

At **Gelateria Primavera,** another local favorite, Antonio and Alberta whip up 70 exotic flavors—and still have time to make pastries for the pope (and everybody else—check out the photos). Try the *noci* (pronounced NO-chee) *di Sorrento*, made from local walnuts (€2.50 cones, daily 9:00-24:00, just west of Piazza Tasso at Corso Italia 142, tel. 081-807-3252).

Harborside in Marina Grande

For a meal *con vista*, head down to either of these restaurants by Sorrento's small-boat harbor, Marina Grande. To get to Marina

Grande, follow the directions from the cliffside square on the "Welcome to Sorrento" walk (described earlier). For a less scenic route, walk down Via del Mare, past the Ulisse Deluxe Hostel, to the harbor. Either way, it's about a 15-minute stroll from downtown. You can also take bus #D from Piazza Tasso (€2.50).

Ristorante Delfino serves fish in big portions to hungry locals in a quiet and bright, Seattle-style pier restaurant. The cooking, service, and setting are all top-notch. The restaurant is lovingly run by Luisa, her brothers Andrea and Roberto, and her husband Antonio. Show this book for a free glass of *limoncello* to cap the meal. If you're here for lunch, take advantage of the sundeck—show this book to get an hour of relaxation and digestion on the lounge chairs (€11-16 pastas, €17-30 *secondi*, daily 11:30-15:30 & 18:30-23:00, closed Nov-March; at Marina Grande, facing the water, go all the way to the left and follow signs; tel. 081-878-2038).

Trattoria da Emilia, at the opposite end of the tranquil Marina Grande waterfront, is considerably more rustic, less expensive, and good for straightforward, typical Sorrentine home-cooking, including fresh fish, lots of fried seafood, and *gnocchi di mamma*—potato dumplings with meat sauce, basil, and mozzarella (€7-12 pastas, €11-15 *secondi*, daily 12:15-15:00 & 19:00-22:30, Sept-Oct closed Tue, closed Nov-Feb, no reservations taken, indoor and outdoor seating, tel. 081-807-2720).

NAPLES

Capri

Capri was made famous as the vacation hideaway of Roman emperors Augustus and Tiberius. In the 19th century, it was the haunt of Romantic Age aristocrats on their Grand Tour of Europe. Later it was briefly a refuge for Europe's artsy gay community: Oscar Wilde, D. H. Lawrence, and company hung out here back when being gay could land you in jail...or worse. And these days, the island is a world-class tourist trap, packed with gawky, nametag-wearing visitors searching for the rich and famous, and finding only their prices.

The "Island of Dreams" is a zoo in July and August—overrun with tacky, low-grade group tourism at its worst. At other times of year, while still crowded, it can provide a relaxing and scenic break from the cultural gauntlet of Italy.

Planning Your Time
From Sorrento or Naples, you can reach Capri by ferry or hydrofoil; unfortunately, unless your cruise arrives very early, you'll be making this trip along with every other tourist in town. Do your best to

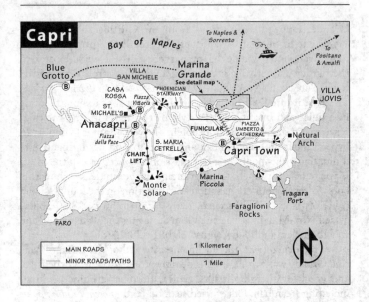

stay ahead of the crowds: Take the soonest, fastest boat possible on arrival. It's wise to get a round-trip boat ticket with a specific return (improving your odds of getting a spot on a boat when they're most crowded); you can use the ticket to return earlier if you like. Once on Capri, go directly to the Blue Grotto, then catch a bus from the grotto to Anacapri and ride the chairlift to Monte Solaro. From the summit, return by chairlift (or hike down). Stroll out from the base of the chairlift to Villa San Michele for the view, then catch a bus to Capri town for the rest of your stay.

At the end of the day, ride the funicular down to Marina Grande (kill time lazing on the free beach or wandering the yacht harbor) to catch the boat back to Sorrento or Naples. Be 20 minutes early for the boat, or you can be bumped. Confirm the schedule carefully—last boats usually leave between 18:30 and 19:30 (check the automated boat-departure board at the port, which notes exact dock locations for each departure—facing the taxis, the board is just around the corner from the TI).

Orientation to Capri

First thing—pronounce it right: Italians say KAH-pree, not kah-PREE like the song or the pants. The island is small—just four miles by two miles—and is separated from the Sorrentine Peninsula by a narrow strait. Home to 13,000 people, there are only two towns to speak of: Capri and Anacapri. The island also has some scant Roman ruins and a few interesting churches and villas. But its chief attraction is its famous Blue Grotto, and its best activity is the chairlift from Anacapri up the island's Monte Solaro.

Tourist Information

Capri's efficient English-speaking tourist information office has branches in Marina Grande, Capri town, and Anacapri. Their well-organized  website has schedules and practical information in English (www.capritourism.com).

The **Marina Grande TI** is by the Motoscafisti Capri tour boat dock (May-Sept Mon-Sat 9:30-13:30 & 15:30-18:45, Sun 9:00-15:00; Oct-April generally daily 9:00-15:00; pick up free map—or the better €1 map if you'll be venturing to the outskirts of Capri town or Anacapri, tel. 081-837-0634).

The **Capri town TI** fills a closet under the bell tower on Piazza Umberto and is less crowded than its sister at the port (Mon-Sat 9:30-13:30 & 15:30-18:45, Sun 9:00-15:00, shorter hours off-season, WC and baggage storage downstairs behind TI, tel. 081-837-0686).

The tiny **Anacapri TI** is at Via Orlandi 59 (Mon-Sat 9:00-15:00, closed Sun, may be closed Nov-Easter, tel. 081-837-1524).

Arrival in Capri

Approaching Capri: Get oriented on the boat before you dock, as you near the harbor with the island spread out before you. The port is a small community of its own, called **Marina Grande,** connected by a funicular and buses to the rest of the island. **Capri town** fills the ridge high above the harbor. The ruins of Emperor Tiberius' palace, **Villa Jovis,** cap the peak on the left. To the right, the dramatic *"Mamma mia!"* road arcs around the highest mountain on the island **(Monte Solaro),** leading up to **Anacapri** (the island's second town, just out of sight). Notice the old zigzag steps below that road. Until 1874, this was the only connection between Capri and Anacapri. (Though it's quite old, it's nowhere near as old as its nickname, "The Phoenician Stairway," implies.) The white house on the ridge above the zigzags is **Villa San Michele** (where you can go later for a grand view of boats like the one you're on now).

Arrival at Marina Grande: Upon arrival, get your bearings. Find the base of the **funicular railway** (signed *funicolare*) that runs up to Capri town, and stand facing it, with your back to the water.

To your right is a stand of ticket windows with counters for **funicular and bus tickets** (you can't buy tickets at the funicular itself) and for return **boat tickets** to Naples and Sorrento. Just beyond these is the **stop for buses** to the rest of the island. Across

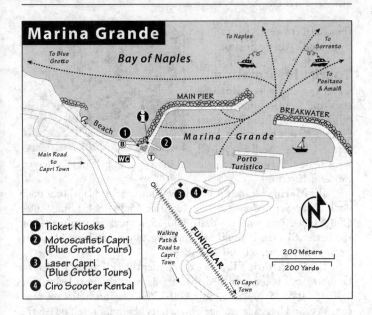

Marina Grande

Bay of Naples

To Naples
To Sorrento
To Positano & Amalfi
To Blue Grotto

MAIN PIER

BREAKWATER

Beach

Marina Grande

Porto Turistico

Main Road to Capri Town →

WC

1 Ticket Kiosks
2 Motoscafisti Capri (Blue Grotto Tours)
3 Laser Capri (Blue Grotto Tours)
4 Ciro Scooter Rental

Walking Path & Road to Capri Town

FUNICULAR

To Capri Town

200 Meters
200 Yards

the street is a **public WC** (€0.50), and a little farther on is Marina Grande's pebbly public beach.

Two competing companies offer **boat trips** around the island and to the Blue Grotto: Laser Capri and Motoscafisti Capri. You'll see Motoscafisti Capri's dock and ticket shed near the ticket windows; Laser Capri's office is halfway down the waterfront to the left at Via Cristoforo Colombo 69. Both offer similar services (see "Getting Around Capri," later).

The **TI** is near the ticket kiosks, right by the Motoscafisti Capri dock (for TI details, see "Tourist Information," earlier).

From the port, you can take a boat to the Blue Grotto (my recommended plan) or around the island, the funicular to Capri town, or a bus to various destinations on Capri. If you have energy to burn, you can follow the steep paved footpath that connects the port area with Capri town. It starts a block inland from the ferry dock (follow the signs to *Capri centro*; allow 30 minutes).

Helpful Hints

Cheap Tricks: A cheap day trip to Capri is tough. Hydrofoils from Sorrento or Naples cost €17-21 each way, and Blue Grotto tickets (plus boat transportation) come to €26—that's €60-68 per person. Using the bus to the Blue Grotto saves about €6 (see "Blue Grotto," later). After the boats stop running, anyone willing to swim the few yards in from the little dock can see the Blue Grotto for free (albeit illegally).

Best Real Hike: Serious hikers love the peaceful and scenic three-hour Fortress Hike, which takes you entirely away from the tourists. You'll walk under ruined forts along the rugged coast, from the Blue Grotto to the *faro* (lighthouse). From there, you can take a bus back to Anacapri (3/hour). The TI has a fine map/brochure.

Free Beach: Marina Grande has a free pebbly beach. You can get a shower at the bar for €1.

Local Guides: Anna Bilardi Leva lives on Capri and is licensed to guide both on the island, and elsewhere around Naples (€130/half-day, €200/day, mobile 339-712-7416, www.capritourinformation.com, annaleva@hotmail.it). **Giovanna Donadio** is a good tour guide for Sorrento, Amalfi, and Capri (€100/half-day, €160/day, same price for any size group, mobile 338-466-0114, giovanna_dona@hotmail.com). Naples-based **Pina Esposito** also does tours of the entire region (see listing on page 626).

Getting Around Capri

By Bus and Funicular: Tickets for the island's buses and funicular cost €1.80 per ride or €8.60 for an all-day pass (includes deposit—turn it in at the end of the day to get €1 back). Single-ride tickets are available at newsstands, tobacco shops, official ticket offices, or from the driver. All-day passes and funicular tickets are usually sold only at official ticket offices. The all-day pass pays for itself if you take at least five rides on the buses and funicular (possible if you go by bus to the Blue Grotto and spend some time in both towns).

Schedules are clearly posted at all bus stations. Buses from the port to Capri town, and from Capri town to Anacapri, are frequent (4/hour, 10 minutes). The direct bus between the port to Anacapri runs less often (every 30-40 minutes, 25 minutes). From Anacapri, branch bus lines run to the parking lot above the Blue Grotto and to the Faro lighthouse. Buses are teeny (because of the island's narrow roads) and often packed. At most stops, you'll see ranks for passengers to line up in. Drivers can push a button to change the bus's display to *completo* (full), in which case you just have to wait for the next one.

By Taxi: Taxis have fixed rates (Marina Grande to Capri town-€15; Marina Grande to Anacapri-€20 for 3 people, €2/additional person). You can hire a taxi for about €70 per hour—negotiate.

By Scooter: If you are experienced at riding a scooter, this is the perfect way to have the run of the island. (For novice riders, Capri's steep and narrow roads aren't a good place to start.) **Ciro** proudly rents bright-yellow scooters with 50cc engines—strong enough to haul couples. Rental includes a map and instructions with parking tips and other helpful information (€15/hour, €55/

NAPLES

day, ask about €5 discount with this book for 2 hours or more; includes helmet, gas, and insurance; daily April-Oct 9:30-19:00, may open in good weather off-season, look for the Ferrari logo at Via Don Giobbe Ruocco 55, Marina Grande, tel. 081-837-8018, mobile 338-360-6918, www.capriscooter.com).

Boat Trips Around the Island: Both **Laser Capri** and **Motoscafisti Capri** run quick one-hour trips that circle the island, passing stunning cliffs, caves, and views that most miss when they go only to the Blue Grotto (€16-17; see contact details under "Blue Grotto," later). With both companies, you can combine the boat trip with a visit to the Blue Grotto at no extra charge (figure another hour). As the trip just to the grotto already costs €13.50, the island circle is well worth the extra €3 if you have an hour to spare (boats leave daily from 9:00 until 13:00 or possibly later—whenever Blue Grotto rowboats stop running).

Sights in Capri

Capri Town

This is a cute but extremely clogged and touristy shopping town. It's worth a brief visit, including to the Giardini Augusto, before moving on to more interesting parts of the island.

The funicular drops you just around the corner from Piazza Umberto, the town's main square. With your back to the funicular, the bus stop is 50 yards straight ahead down Via Roma. You'll find the **TI** under the bell tower on Piazza Umberto (for TI details, see "Tourist Information," earlier). The footpath to the port starts just behind the TI (follow signs to *Il Porto*, 15-minute walk).

Capri town's multi-domed Baroque **cathedral,** which faces the square, is worth a quick look. (Its multicolored marble floor at the altar was scavenged from the Emperor Tiberius's villa in the 19th century.)

To the left of City Hall (Municipio, lowest corner), a lane leads into the medieval part of town, which has plenty of eateries and is the starting point for the walk to Villa Jovis.

The lane to the left of the cathedral (past Bar Tiberio, under the wide arch) is a fashionable shopping strip that's justifiably been dubbed "Rodeo Drive" by residents. Walk a few minutes down Rodeo Drive (past Gelateria Buonocore at #35, with its tempting fresh waffle cones) to Quisisana Hotel, the island's top old-time hotel. From there, head left for fancy shops and villas, and right for gardens and views. Downhill and to the right, a five-minute walk leads to a lovely public garden, Giardini Augusto, with superb views of the back side of the island (€1, April-Oct daily 9:00-19:30, May and early Nov daily 9:00-17:30, mid-Nov-March shorter hours and free admission, no picnicking).

Villa Jovis and the Emperor's Capri

Even before becoming emperor, Augustus loved Capri so much that he traded the family-owned Isle of Ischia to the (then-independent) Neapolitans in exchange for making Capri his personal property. Emperor Tiberius spent a decade here, A.D. 26-37. (Some figure he did so in order to escape being assassinated in Rome.)

Emperor Tiberius' ruined villa, Villa Jovis, is a scenic 45-minute hike from Capri town. You won't find any statues or mosaics here—just an evocative, ruined complex of terraces fitting a rocky perch over a sheer drop to the sea...and a lovely view. You can make out a large water reservoir for baths, the foundations of servants' quarters, and Tiberius' private apartments (fragments of marble flooring still survive). The ruined lighthouse dates from the Middle Ages.

Cost and Hours: €2, nearly daily 11:00-15:00, closed Tue from 1st to 15th of each month and closed Sun from the 16th to the end of each month, tel. 081-837-4549.

▲▲Blue Grotto

Three thousand tourists a day spend a couple of hours visiting Capri's Blue Grotto (Grotta Azzurra). I did—early (when the light is best), without the frustration of crowds, and with choppy waves nearly making entrance impossible...and it was great.

The actual cave experience isn't much: a five-minute dinghy ride through a three-foot-high entry hole to reach a 60-yard-long cave, where the sun reflects brilliantly blue

on its limestone bottom. But the experience—getting there, getting in, and getting back—is a scenic hoot. You get a fast ride on a 30-foot boat partway around the gorgeous island; along the way you see bird life and dramatic limestone cliffs with scant narration. You'll understand why Roman emperors appreciated the invulnerability of the island—it's surrounded by cliffs, with only one good access point, and therefore easy to defend.

Just outside the grotto, your boat idles as you pile into eight-foot dinghies that hold up to four passengers each. Next, you'll be taken to a floating ticket counter and asked to pass the €12.50 grotto entry fee over the side. From there, your ruffian rower will elbow his way to the tiny hole, then pull fast and hard on the cable at the low point of the swells to squeeze you into the grotto (keep your head down and hands in the boat). Then your man rows you around, spouting off a few descriptive lines and singing "O Sole Mio." Depending upon the strength of the sunshine that day, the blue light inside can be brilliant.

The grotto was actually an ancient Roman *nymphaeum*—a retreat for romantic hanky-panky. Many believe that, in its day, a tunnel led here directly from the palace, and that the grotto experience was enlivened by statues of Poseidon and company, placed half-underwater as if emerging from the sea. It was ancient Romans who smoothed out the entry hole that's still used to this day.

Sometimes, your boatman will try to extort an extra tip out of you before taking you back outside to your big boat (€1 is enough, but you don't need to pay a penny...you've already paid plenty). If you don't want to return by boat, ask your boatman to let you off at the little dock, where stairs lead up to a café and the Blue Grotto bus stop.

Cost: The €12.50 entry fee (separate from the €13.50 ride from Marina Grande) includes €8.50 for the rowboat service plus €4 to cover the admission to the grotto itself. Though signs forbid it, some people dive in for free from the little dock next to the grotto entrance after the boats stop running—a magical experience and a favorite among locals.

Timing: When the waves or high tide make entering dangerous, the boats don't go in—the grotto can close without notice, sending tourists (flush with anticipation) home without a chance to squeeze through the little hole. (If this happens to you, consider the one-hour boat ride around the island offered by both companies.)

If you're coming from Capri's port (Marina Grande), allow 1-3 hours for the entire visit, depending on the chaos at the caves. Going with the first trip will get you there at the same time as the boatmen in their dinghies—who hitch a ride behind your boat—resulting in less chaos and a shorter wait at the entry point.

Getting There: You can either take the boat directly from Marina Grande, as most people do, or save money by taking the bus via Anacapri.

By Boat from Marina Grande: Two companies make the boat trip from different parts of Marina Grande—Laser Capri and Motoscafisti Capri (€13.50 round-trip with either company, no discount for one-way; Motoscafista Capri—tel. 081-837-7714, www.motoscafisticapri.com; Laser Capri—tel. 081-837-5208, www.lasercapri.com). The first boats depart Marina Grande at 9:00, and they continue at least until 13:00—or often later, depending on when the rowboats stop running (likely 17:00 in summer, but earlier off-season).

By Bus via Anacapri: If you're on a budget, you can take the bus from Anacapri to the grotto (rather than a boat from Marina Grande). You'll save about €6 (assuming you take the direct Marina Grande-Anacapri bus and then change to the Anacapri-Blue Grotto bus), lose time, and see a beautiful, calmer side of the island.

Anacapri-Blue Grotto buses (roughly 3/hour, Nov-March 1-2/hour, 10 minutes) depart only from the Anacapri bus station at Piazza della Pace (not from the bus stop at Piazza Vittoria 200 yards away, which is more popular with tourists). If you're coming from Marina Grande or Capri town and want to transfer to the Blue Grotto buses, don't get off when the driver announces "Anacapri." Instead, ride one more stop to Piazza della Pace. If in doubt, ask the driver or a local.

Getting Back from the Blue Grotto: You can either take the boat back, or ask your boatman to drop you off on the small dock next to the grotto entrance, from where you climb up the stairs to the stop for the bus to Anacapri (if you came by boat, you'll still have to pay the full €13.50 round-trip boat fare).

Anacapri

Capri's second town has two or three hours' worth of interesting sights. Though higher up on the island ("ana" means "upper" in Greek), there are no sea views at street level in the town center.

When visiting Anacapri by bus, note that there are two stops: the bus stop by the cemetery (called Piazza della Pace—pronounced "PAH-chay"—though locals may call it by its former name, Piazza del Cimitero), and the more central Piazza Vittoria stop, 200 yards away, by the base of the chairlift to Monte Solaro. It doesn't matter which stop you get off at. But when leaving Anacapri for Capri town or Marina Grande, buses can be packed. Your best chance of getting a seat is to catch the bus from Piazza della Pace, one stop before where most people get on (stand at the street corner under the concrete awning).

Regardless of where you get off, make your way to Via Orlandi, Anacapri's pedestrianized main street. From Piazza della Pace, reach it via the crosswalk and then the small lane called Via Filietto; from Piazza Vittoria, head to the right of the statue of "Anacapri." Anacapri's tiny **TI** is at Via Orlandi 59 (Mon-Sat 9:00-15:00, closed Sun, may be closed Nov-Easter, tel. 081-837-1524).

To see the town, walk on this street for 10 minutes or so. Signs suggest a quick circuit that links the Casa Rossa, St. Michael's Church, and peaceful side streets. You'll also find a number of shops and eateries, including a couple of good choices for quick, inexpensive pizza, panini, and other goodies: **Sciué Sciué** (same price for informal seating or take-away, no cover charge, daily April-Oct, closed Nov-March, near the TI at #73, tel. 081-837-2068) and **Pizza e Pasta** (take-away only, daily March-Nov, closed Dec-Feb, just before the church at #157, tel. 328-623-8460).

▲Villa San Michele

This is the 19th-century mansion of Axel Munthe, Capri's grand personality, an idealistic Swedish doctor who lived here until 1943 and whose services to the Swedish royal family brought him into contact with high society. At the very least, walk the path from Piazza Victoria past the villa to a superb, free viewpoint over Capri town and Marina Grande. Paying to enter the villa lets you see a few rooms with a well-done but ho-hum exhibit on Munthe, plus a delightful and extensive garden with a chapel, Olivetum (a tiny museum of native birds and bugs), and a view that's slightly better than the free one outside. A café (also with a view) serves €6 sandwiches. Walking to the villa from Piazza Victoria, you pass the deluxe Capri Palace Hotel—venture in if you can get past the treacherously eye-catching swimming pool windows.

Cost and Hours: €7, May-Sept daily 9:00-18:00, closes earlier Oct-April, last entry 20 minutes before closing, tel. 081-837-1401, www.villasanmichele.eu.

Casa Rossa (Red House)

This "Pompeiian-red," eccentric home, a hodgepodge of architectural styles, is the former residence of John Clay MacKowen, a Louisiana doctor and ex-Confederate officer who moved to Capri in the 1870s and married a local girl. (MacKowen and Axel Munthe loathed each other, and even tried to challenge each other to a duel.) Its small collection of 19th-century paintings of scenes from around the island recalls a time before mass tourism. Don't miss the second floor, with its four ancient, sea-worn statues, which were recovered from the depths of the Blue Grotto in the 1960s and '70s.

Cost and Hours: €3; free with ticket stub from Blue Grotto, Villa San Michele, or Monte Solaro chairlift; June-Sept Tue-Sun 10:00-13:30 & 17:30-20:00, closed Mon; April-May Tue-Sun 10:00-17:00, closed Mon; Oct Tue-Sun 10:00-16:00, closed Mon; closed Nov-March, Via Orlandi 78, tel. 081-838-2193.

▲Church of San Michele

This Baroque church in the village center has a remarkable majolica floor showing paradise on earth in a classic 18th-century Neapolitan style. The entire floor is ornately tiled, featuring an angel (with flaming sword) driving Adam and Eve from paradise. The devil is wrapped around the trunk of a beautiful tree. The animals—happily ignoring this momentous event—all have human expressions.

For the best view, climb the spiral stairs from the postcard desk. Services are only held during the first two weeks of Advent, when the church is closed to visitors.

Cost and Hours: €2, daily April-Oct 9:00-19:00, Nov and mid-Dec-March 10:00-14:00, closed late Nov-mid Dec, in town center just off Via Orlandi—look for signs for *San Michele*, tel. 081-837-2396, www.chiesa-san-michele.com.

Faro

The lighthouse has a private beach, pool, small restaurants, and a few fishermen. Reach it by bus from Anacapri (3/hour, departs from Piazza della Pace stop).

▲▲Chairlift up to Monte Solaro

From Anacapri, ride the chairlift *(seggiovia)* to the 1,900-foot summit of Monte Solaro for a commanding view of the Bay of Naples.

Work on your tan as you float over hazelnut, walnut, chestnut, apricot, peach, kiwi, and fig trees, past a montage of tourists. Prospective smoochers should know that the lift seats are all single. As you ascend, consider how Capri's real estate has been priced out of the locals' reach. The ride takes 13 minutes each way, and you'll want at least 30 minutes on top, where there are picnic benches and a cafe with WCs.

Cost and Hours: €7.50 one-way, €10 round-trip, daily June-Oct 9:30-17:00, last run down at 17:30, closes earlier Nov-May, confirm schedule with TI, departs from top of the steps in Piazza Vittoria—the first Anacapri bus stop, tel. 081-837-1428, www.seggioviamontesolaro.it.

At the Summit: You'll enjoy the best panorama possible: lush cliffs busy with seagulls enjoying the ideal nesting spot. Find the Faraglioni Rocks—with tour boats squeezing through every few minutes—which are an icon of the island. The pink building nearest the rocks was an American R&R base during World War II. Eisenhower and Churchill met here. On the peak closest to Cape Sorrento, you can see the distant ruins of the Emperor Tiberius' palace, Villa Jovis. Pipes from the Sorrento Peninsula bring water to Capri (demand for fresh water here long ago exceeded the supply provided by the island's three natural springs). The Galli Islands mark the Amalfi Coast in the distance. Cross the bar terrace for views of Mount Vesuvius and Naples.

Hiking Down: A highlight for hardy walkers (with strong knees and good shoes) is the 40-minute downhill hike from the top of Monte Solaro, through lush vegetation and ever-changing views, past the 14th-century Chapel of Santa Maria Cetrella (at the trail's only intersection, it's a 10-minute detour to the right), and back into Anacapri. The trail starts downstairs, past the WCs (last chance). Down two more flights of stairs, look for the sign to *Anacapri e Cetrella*—you're on your way. While the trail is well-established, you'll encounter plenty of uneven steps, loose rocks, and few signs.

Amalfi Coast

With its stunning scenery, hill- and harbor-hugging towns, and historic ruins, Amalfi is Italy's coast with the most. The trip from Sorrento to Salerno along the breathtaking Amalfi Coast is one of the world's great scenic drives. It will leave your mouth open and your camera's memory card full. You'll gain respect for the 19th-century Italian engineers who built the roads—and even more respect for anyone who drives it today. Cantilevered garages, hotels, and villas cling to the vertical terrain, and beautiful sandy coves tease from far below and out of reach. As you hyperventilate, notice how the Mediterranean, a sheer 500-foot drop below, really twinkles. All this beautiful scenery apparently inspires local Romeos and Juliets, with the latex evidence of late-night romantic encounters littering the roadside turnouts. Over the centuries, the spectacular scenery and climate have been a siren call for the rich and famous, luring Roman emperor Tiberius, Richard Wagner, Sophia Loren, Gore Vidal, and others to the Amalfi Coast's special brand of *la dolce vita*.

Getting to the Amalfi Coast

Amalfi Coast towns are pretty, but they're generally touristy, congested, overpriced, and a long hike above tiny, pebbly beaches. Most beaches here are private, and access is expensive. The real thrill here is the scenic Amalfi drive.

Don't Get Stranded: When deciding how best to see the coast, consider foremost your time restrictions, and the fact that the coastal road is often clogged with gawking drivers, especially in July and August. Taking a **shore excursion** operated by your cruise ship is your safest option, as your ship will wait if you're caught in

Getting Around the Amalfi Coast

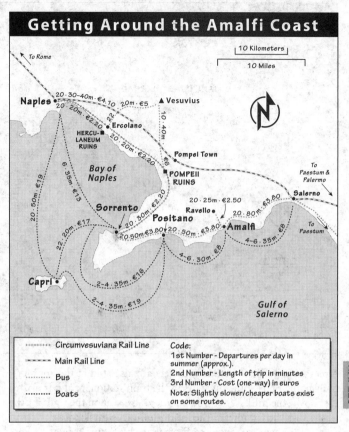

10 Kilometers

10 Miles

To Rome

Naples · 20 · 30-40m · €4.10 · 20m · €5 · ▲ **Vesuvius**

20 · 20m · €2.20

HERCU-LANEUM RUINS · **Ercolano**

10 · 40m

20 · 20m · €2.20 · **Pompei Town**

6 · 35m · €13

Bay of Naples · **POMPEII RUINS**

20 · 50m · €19

20 · 20m · €17

22 · 20m · €2.20

20 · 30m · €2.20 · **Sorrento**

Positano · 20 · 50m · €3.80

20.50m·€3.80 · 20 · 50m · €3.80 · **Amalfi**

20 · 25m · €2.50 · **Ravello** · 20 · 80m · €3.80 · **Salerno**

To Paestum & Palermo

To Paestum

4-6 · 35m · €8

4-6 · 30m · €8

2-4 · 35m · €16 · **Capri**

2-4 · 35m · €19

Gulf of Salerno

┄┄ Circumvesuviana Rail Line	**Code:**
╌╌╌ Main Rail Line	1st Number - Departures per day in summer (approx.).
⋯⋯ Bus	2nd Number - Length of trip in minutes
⋯⋯ Boats	3rd Number - Cost (one-way) in euros
	Note: Slightly slower/cheaper boats exist on some routes.

traffic. Your next best option is either taking a **taxi** or **hiring a driver,** which gives you the most flexibility (see page 668 for recommended services).

The **bus** is by far the cheapest option, and worth considering if you have at least eight hours for the coast. The bus runs fairly frequently from Sorrento (about hourly, daily 6:30-22:00 in summer, shorter hours off-season; 50 minutes to Positano; ticket prices vary with trip length: 1.5-hour ride, good for one-way ride to Positano, €3.80). It's probably best to go only as far as Positano. Buses carry a risk: Not only can they get stuck in traffic, but they can fill up in the afternoon. If your return bus is full, don't wait for the next one: Call a taxi (about €80-100 from Positano to Sorrento). Even better, don't cut it close; return earlier than you need to.

In Sorrento, look for the *Bus Stop SITA* sign across from the train station (10 steps down) and line up for the bus marked *Amalfi via Positano* (buy tickets at the info booth across from the bus stop at the Sorrento train station or at the tobacco shop/newsstand at

street level inside the station; tickets are also sold at the appropriately named Snack Bar, upstairs in the train station, or at Bar Frisby, just down the hill). When you board, grab a seat on the right for the best views; sitting toward the front minimizes carsickness.

While you can avoid traffic hassles by taking a **boat** to Positano, their infrequency makes them even less appealing for the cruise traveler (pick up schedule at TI, generally mid-April–mid-Oct only).

The Coastal Drive: Sorrento to Positano

The trip from Sorrento along the Amalfi Coast is one of the all-time great white-knuckle rides. Sit on the right side as you go out

and on the left as you return to Sorrento. (Those on the wrong side really miss out.) Traffic is so heavy that private tour buses are only allowed to go in one direction (southbound from Sorrento)—summer traffic is infuriating. Fluorescent-vested

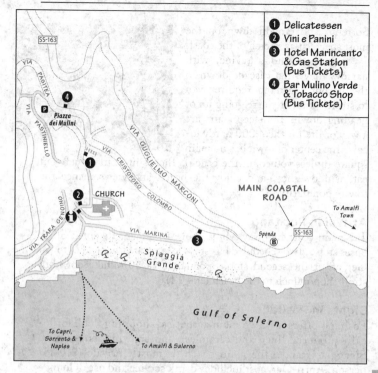

1 Delicatessen
2 Vini e Panini
3 Hotel Marincanto & Gas Station (Bus Tickets)
4 Bar Mulino Verde & Tobacco Shop (Bus Tickets)

SS-163

VIA PASITEA

VIA PASITELLO

Piazza dei Mulini

VIA CRISTOFORO COLOMBO

VIA GUGLIELMO MARCONI

MAIN COASTAL ROAD

To Amalfi Town

VIA TRARA GENOINO

CHURCH

VIA MARINA

Sponda SS-163

Spiaggia Grande

Gulf of Salerno

To Capri, Sorrento & Naples

To Amalfi & Salerno

NAPLES

policemen are posted at tough bends during peak hours to help fold in side-view mirrors and keep things moving.

Leaving Sorrento, the road winds up into the hills past lemon groves and hidden houses. Traveling the coast, you'll see several watchtowers placed within sight of each other, so that a relay of rooftop bonfires could spread word of a Saracen (Turkish pirate) attack. The gray-green trees are olives. Dark, green-leafed trees planted in dense groves are the source of the region's lemons—many destined to become *limoncello* liqueur. The black nets over the orange and lemon groves create a greenhouse effect, trapping warmth and humidity for maximum tastiness, while offering protection from extreme weather (preserving the peels used for *limoncello*).

As you approach the exotic-looking town of **Positano,** you know you've reached the scenic heart of the Amalfi Coast.

Positano

According to legend, the Greek god Poseidon created Positano for Pasitea, a nymph he lusted after. History says the town was founded when ancient Greeks at Paestum, nearby, decided to move out of the swamp (to escape the malaria carried by its mosquitoes). Specializing in scenery and sand, Positano hangs halfway between

Sorrento and Amalfi town on the most spectacular stretch of the coast.

Squished into a ravine, with narrow alleys that cascade down to the harbor, Positano requires you to stroll, whether you're going up or heading down. The steep stairs are a way of life for the 4,000 hardy locals. The center of town has no main square (unless you count the beach). There's little to do here but eat, window-shop, and enjoy the beach and views...hence the town's popularity.

Arrival in Positano

The main coast highway winds above the town. Regional SITA buses stop at two scheduled bus stops located at either end of town: Get off at the second stop, Sponda. It's a 20-minute downhill stroll/shop/munch to the beach (and TI).

Sights in Positano

Positano offers just two main activities: **shopping** (look for locally produced linen and ceramics), and enjoying its **beaches.** Spiaggia Grande, the main beach, is mostly private (€10-15/person, April-Oct, cost includes drink service and use of lounge chair and umbrella, free section near the middle—close to where the boats take off, nearest WC beneath the steps to the right as you face the water). Fornillo Beach, just around the bend (to the west), is less crowded, offers more affordable chair-and-umbrella rentals, and is lined by humble snack bars and lunch eateries.

Eating in Positano

Positano is an expensive place to dine. At the waterfront, several interchangeable restaurants with view terraces leave people fat and happy, albeit with skinnier wallets (figure €15-20 pastas and *secondi*, plus pricey drinks and sides, and a cover charge). Little distinguishes one place from the next; all are pleasant, convenient, and overpriced.

Sunny Emilia at the **Delicatessen** grocery store can supply picnic ingredients (*antipasto misto* to go at €1.40/100 grams, pasta for €1/100 grams, sandwiches made and sold by weight—about €3.50-4.50, she microwaves food and includes all the picnic ware, come early for best selection; daily March-Oct 7:00-22:00, Nov-Feb 8:00-20:00, just below car park at Via del Mulini 5, tel. 089-875-489).

What If I Miss My Boat?

Remember that you can get help from the cruise line's port agent (listed on the destination information sheet distributed on the ship) and local TIs (see pages 623, 671, and 685). If the port agent suggests a costly solution (such as a private car with a driver), you may want to consider public transit.

Naples is the region's transportation hub. If you miss your boat in Sorrento, your best bet is to head to Naples via the Circumvesuviana commuter train. Frequent **trains** leave from Naples' Centrale Station to points all over Italy, including **Civitavecchia** (most change in Rome), **Venice** (changes in Bologna or Rome, overnight options), and **Livorno** (most change in Rome or Florence). The French ports of **Nice** and **Marseille/Toulon** are reachable via overnight trains. To look up specific connections, use www.trenitalia.it (domestic journeys only), ask at the train station, or check www.bahn.com (Germany's excellent all-Europe website). Any travel agent can help you.

For more advice on what to do if you miss the boat, see page 140.

Vini e Panini, another small grocery, is a block from the beach a few steps above the TI. Daniela, the fifth-generation owner, speaks English and happily makes sandwiches to order. They also have a nice selection of well-priced regional wines (daily 8:00-20:00, until 22:00 in summer, closed mid-Nov-mid-March, just off church steps, tel. 089-875-175).

Getting Back to Sorrento by Bus

If you're catching the SITA bus back to Sorrento, be aware that it may leave from the Sponda stop up to five minutes before the printed departure. There's simply no room for the bus to wait, so in case the driver is early, you should be, too (€3.80, departures about hourly, daily 7:00-22:00, until 20:00 off-season). Buy tickets from the tobacco shop next to Bar Mulino Verde in the town center, or just below the Sponda bus stop at the Li Galli Bar or Total gas station (across from Hotel Marincanto).

If the walk up to the stop is too tough, take the dizzy little local red-and-white shuttle bus (marked *Interno Positano*), which constantly loops through Positano, connecting the lower town with the highway's two bus stops (2/hour, €1.20 at tobacco shop or €1.50 on board, catch it at convenient stop at the corner of Via Colombo and Via dei Mulini, heads up to Sponda). Bar Mulino Verde, located off Piazza dei Mulini (as close as cars, taxis, and the shuttle bus can get to the beach), is just across from the shuttle bus stop, with a fine, breezy terrace you can enjoy if you're waiting.

NAPLES

Italian Survival Phrases

English	Italian	Pronunciation
Good day.	Buon giorno.	bwohn **jor**-noh
Do you speak English?	Parla inglese?	**par**-lah een-**gleh**-zay
Yes. / No.	Sì. / No.	see / noh
I (don't) understand.	(Non) capisco.	(nohn) kah-**pees**-koh
Please.	Per favore.	pehr fah-**voh**-ray
Thank you.	Grazie.	**graht**-see-ay
You're welcome.	Prego.	**preh**-go
I'm sorry.	Mi dispiace.	mee dee-spee-**ah**-chay
Excuse me.	Mi scusi.	mee **skoo**-zee
(No) problem.	(Non) c'è un problema.	(nohn) cheh oon proh-**bleh**-mah
Good.	Va bene.	vah **beh**-nay
Goodbye.	Arrivederci.	ah-ree-veh-**dehr**-chee
one / two	uno / due	**oo**-noh / **doo**-ay
three / four	tre / quattro	tray / **kwah**-troh
five / six	cinque / sei	**cheeng**-kway / **seh**-ee
seven / eight	sette / otto	**seh**-tay / **oh**-toh
nine / ten	nove / dieci	**noh**-vay / dee-**ay**-chee
How much is it?	Quanto costa?	**kwahn**-toh **koh**-stah
Write it?	Me lo scrive?	may loh **skree**-vay
Is it free?	È gratis?	eh **grah**-tees
Is it included?	È incluso?	eh een-**kloo**-zoh
Where can I buy / find...?	Dove posso comprare / trovare...?	**doh**-vay **poh**-soh kohm-**prah**-ray / troh-**vah**-ray
I'd like / We'd like...	Vorrei / Vorremmo...	voh-**reh**-ee / voh-**reh**-moh
...a room.	...una camera.	**oo**-nah **kah**-meh-rah
...a ticket to ____.	...un biglietto per ____.	oon beel-**yeh**-toh pehr ____
Is it possible?	È possibile?	eh poh-**see**-bee-lay
Where is...?	Dov'è...?	doh-**veh**
...the train station	...la stazione	lah staht-see-**oh**-nay
...the bus station	...la stazione degli autobus	lah staht-see-**oh**-nay **dehl**-yee ow-toh-boos
...tourist information	...informazioni per turisti	een-for-maht-see-**oh**-nee pehr too-**ree**-stee
...the toilet	...la toilette	lah twah-**leh**-tay
men	uomini / signori	**woh**-mee-nee / seen-**yoh**-ree
women	donne / signore	**doh**-nay / seen-**yoh**-ray
left / right	sinistra / destra	see-**nee**-strah / **deh**-strah
straight	sempre dritto	**sehm**-pray **dree**-toh
What time does this open / close?	A che ora apre / chiude?	ah kay **oh**-rah **ah**-pray / kee-**oo**-day
At what time?	A che ora?	ah kay **oh**-rah
Just a moment.	Un momento.	oon moh-**mehn**-toh
now / soon / later	adesso / presto / più tardi	ah-**deh**-soh / **preh**-stoh / pew **tar**-dee
today / tomorrow	oggi / domani	**oh**-jee / doh-**mah**-nee

NAPLES

In an Italian Restaurant

English	Italian	Pronunciation
I'd like...	Vorrei...	voh-**reh**-ee
We'd like...	Vorremmo...	vor-**reh**-moh
...to reserve...	...prenotare...	preh-noh-**tah**-ray
...a table for one / two.	...un tavolo per uno / due.	oon **tah**-voh-loh pehr **oo**-noh / **doo**-ay
Is this seat free?	È libero questo posto?	eh **lee**-beh-roh **kweh**-stoh **poh**-stoh
The menu (in English), please.	Il menù (in inglese), per favore.	eel meh-**noo** (een een-**gleh**-zay) pehr fah-**voh**-ray
service (not) included	servizio (non) incluso	sehr-**veet**-see-oh (nohn) een-**kloo**-zoh
cover charge	pane e coperto	**pah**-nay ay koh-**pehr**-toh
to go	da portar via	dah **por**-tar **vee**-ah
with / without	con / senza	kohn / **sehnt**-sah
and / or	e / o	ay / oh
menu (of the day)	menù (del giorno)	meh-**noo** (dehl **jor**-noh)
specialty of the house	specialità della casa	speh-chah-lee-**tah** deh-lah **kah**-zah
first course (pasta, soup)	primo piatto	**pree**-moh pee-**ah**-toh
main course (meat, fish)	secondo piatto	seh-**kohn**-doh pee-**ah**-toh
side dishes	contorni	kohn-**tor**-nee
bread	pane	**pah**-nay
cheese	formaggio	for-**mah**-joh
sandwich	panino	pah-**nee**-noh
soup	zuppa	**tsoo**-pah
salad	insalata	een-sah-**lah**-tah
meat	carne	**kar**-nay
chicken	pollo	**poh**-loh
fish	pesce	**peh**-shay
seafood	frutti di mare	**froo**-tee dee **mah**-ray
fruit / vegetables	frutta / legumi	**froo**-tah / lay-**goo**-mee
dessert	dolce	**dohl**-chay
tap water	acqua del rubinetto	**ah**-kwah dehl roo-bee-**neh**-toh
mineral water	acqua minerale	**ah**-kwah mee-neh-**rah**-lay
milk	latte	**lah**-tay
(orange) juice	succo (d'arancia)	**soo**-koh (dah-**rahn**-chah)
coffee / tea	caffè / tè	kah-**feh** / teh
wine	vino	**vee**-noh
red / white	rosso / bianco	**roh**-soh / bee-**ahn**-koh
glass / bottle	bicchiere / bottiglia	bee-kee-**eh**-ray / boh-**teel**-yah
beer	birra	**bee**-rah
Cheers!	Cin cin!	cheen cheen
More. / Another.	Di più. / Un altro.	dee pew / oon **ahl**-troh
The same.	Lo stesso.	loh **steh**-soh
The bill, please.	Il conto, per favore.	eel **kohn**-toh pehr fah-**voh**-ray
Do you accept credit cards?	Accettate carte di credito?	ah-cheh-**tah**-tay **kar**-tay dee **kreh**-dee-toh
tip	mancia	**mahn**-chah
Delicious!	Delizioso!	day-leet-see-**oh**-zoh

For more user-friendly Italian phrases, check out *Rick Steves' Italian Phrase Book & Dictionary* or *Rick Steves' French, Italian, and German Phrase Book*.

VENICE
ITALY

Italy Practicalities

Stretching 850 miles long and 150 miles wide, art-drenched Italy is the cradle of European civilization. Visitors here come face to face with some of the world's most iconic images: Rome's ancient Colosseum, Pisa's medieval Leaning Tower, Venice's romantic canals.

Italy's 61 million inhabitants are more social and communal than most other Europeans. Because they're so outgoing and their language is so fun, Italians are a pleasure to communicate with. This boot-shaped country has all the elements that make travel to Europe forever fresh and rewarding: visible history, lively people, and fun by the minute.

Money: Italy uses the euro currency: 1 euro (€) = about $1.30. An ATM is called a *bancomat*. The local VAT (value-added sales tax) rate is 22 percent; the minimum purchase eligible for a VAT refund is €155 (for details on refunds, see page 135).

Language: For useful Italian phrases, see page 799.

Emergencies: Dial 113 for police or 118 for medical emergencies. In case of theft or loss, see page 714.

Time Zone: Italy is on Central European Time (the same as most of the Continent, and six/nine hours ahead of the East/West Coasts of the US).

Theft Alert: Assume that beggars are pickpockets and any scuffle is simply a distraction by a team of thieves. For more on outsmarting thieves, see page 128.

Consular Services: The US embassy in Rome is at Via Vittorio Veneto 121 (24-hour tel. 06-46741, http://italy.usembassy.gov); consular services are also available in Florence (tel. 055-266-951) and Naples (tel. 081-583-8111). The Canadian Embassy in Rome is at Via Zara 30 (tel. 06-854-441, www.italy.gc.ca). Call ahead for passport services.

Phoning: Italy has a direct-dial phone system (no area codes). To **call within Italy,** just dial the number (keep in mind that Italian phone numbers vary in length). To **call to Italy,** dial the international access code (00 if calling from Europe, or 011 from North America), then dial 39 (Italy's country code), then the phone number. To **call home from Italy,** dial 00, 1, then your area code and phone number. For more help, see page 1242.

Dress Code: Some major churches enforce a modest dress code (no bare shoulders or shorts).

Tipping: A service charge (*servicio*) of about 10 percent is usually built into your restaurant bill. If you are pleased with the service, you can add an extra euro or two for each person in your party. If service isn't included (*servizio non incluso*), add a tip of about 10 percent. To tip a cabbie, round up your fare a bit (to pay a €4.50 fare, give €5).

Tourist Information: www.italia.it

VENICE

Soak all day in this puddle of elegant decay. Venice (*Venezia* in Italian) is Europe's best-preserved big city. This car-free urban wonderland of a hundred islands—laced together by 400 bridges and 2,000 alleys—survives on the artificial respirator of tourism.

Born in a lagoon 1,500 years ago as a refuge from barbarians, Venice is overloaded with tourists and is slowly sinking (unrelated facts). In the Middle Ages, the Venetians became Europe's clever middlemen for East-West trade and created a great trading empire. By smuggling in the bones of St. Mark (San Marco) in A.D. 828, Venice gained religious importance as well. With the discovery of America and new trading routes to the Orient, Venetian power ebbed. But as Venice fell, her appetite for decadence grew. Through the 17th and 18th centuries, Venice partied on the wealth accumulated through earlier centuries as a trading power.

Today, Venice is home to 58,000 people in its old city, down from about twice that number just three decades ago. While there are about 270,000 in greater Venice (counting the mainland, not counting tourists), the old town has a small-town feel. Locals seem to know everyone. To see small-town Venice away from the touristic flak, escape the Rialto-San Marco tourist zone and savor the town without the hordes of vacationers day-tripping in from cruise ships and nearby beach resorts. A 10-minute walk from the madness puts you in an idyllic Venice that few tourists see.

Some cruises start or end in Venice. If yours does, see the end of the chapter for airport information and some recommended hotels.

Venice Overview

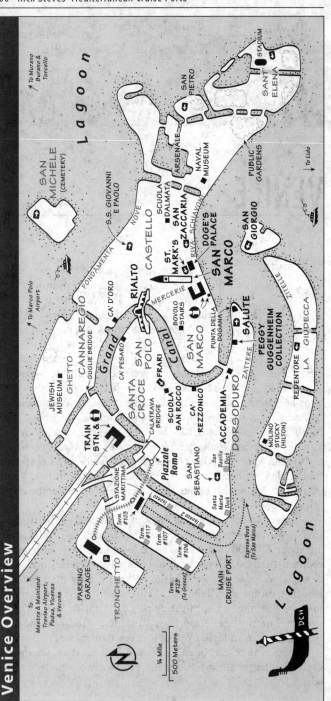

Excursions from Venice

Excursion offerings might appeal to cruisers with special interests, but their attractions can't touch the jewel-like confection that is **Venice.**

North of Venice are the islands of **Murano** (40 minutes by boat) and **Burano** (an additional 30 minutes from Murano). Visit the first for its world-class glass artisans and factories, and the second for its fine lace and picturesque pastel houses. Some travelers (especially those who have already spent time in Venice proper) enjoy these islands as a small-town alternative to Venice. As these towns are most famous for their respective products, expect any excursions here to be heavily focused on selling you glass and lace.

Padua is for art lovers; this elegantly arcaded university town (about an hour southwest of Venice) is home to the celebrated Scrovegni Chapel frescoes by the early Renaissance master Giotto.

Serious history buffs might choose to see the impressive Roman ruins in **Verona** (about two hours west of Venice), which is also the pick for star-crossed lovers retracing Romeo and Juliet's steps.

Planning Your Time

Venice is made to order for a wonderful day. I'd suggest tackling the city in this order:

• From the cruise port, head for Piazzale Roma, hop on a vaporetto, and take my self-guided **"Grand Canal Cruise,"** ending at St. Mark's Square. Allow an hour (15 minutes to Piazzale Roma, 45 minutes on the vaporetto).

• Take my self-guided walk through **St. Mark's Square** (allow 30 minutes) and self-guided tour of **St. Mark's Basilica** (1 hour).

• With more time, you could visit the **Doge's Palace** (on St. Mark's Square); take a 15-minute walk from St. Mark's Square to the **Rialto Bridge** and its open-air produce market; ride a gondola; or visit the **Accademia** art gallery. If you visit the Accademia, see it on your way in: Take the "Grand Canal Cruise," get off at the Accademia stop, tour the museum, then continue on the vaporetto to St. Mark's Square (or go by foot—it's a 15-minute walk). If you'd rather shop than sightsee, see page 775.

Allow at least an hour to get back to port. You can catch an express boat from St. Mark's Square directly back to the cruise port, or you can ride a vaporetto from St. Mark's Square or the Rialto to Piazzale Roma, then take the monorail to the port. It's also fun to walk back from St. Mark's Square—give yourself an hour, though allowing more time makes it more relaxing.

Arrival at the Port of Venice

Arrival at a Glance: Hop aboard an express boat to St. Mark's Square (30 minutes); or walk to the People Mover monorail and take it to the Grand Canal (10-15 minutes total), where you can ride a slow, scenic vaporetto to St. Mark's—following my self-guided "Grand Canal Cruise" (45 minutes). If all of these options are jammed up (as can happen when multiple cruise ships arrive), you can walk to the Grand Canal in about 15 minutes, or all the way to St. Mark's Square in about an hour. Water taxis downtown are expensive (likely around €70-80).

Port Overview

Most cruise ships dock at Venice's Stazione Marittima (also called Terminal Crociere, Venezia Terminal Passeggeri, or VTP), which is at the west end of town, roughly between the Tronchetto parking garage and Santa Lucia train station. The terminal forms the "fish's mouth" of Venice. The cruise port consists of one long, wide, rectangular pier, and a narrower, adjacent pier; together these form a harbor. There are several terminal buildings: #117 (along the north side of the main pier), #107 and #108 (along the south/harbor side of the main pier), #103 (at the top of the harbor), and Isonzo 1 and Isonzo 2 (along the narrower pier, used mostly by the MSC cruise line).

While everything is easily walkable from terminals #103, #107, and #108, the Isonzo terminals are much farther out; a free **shuttle bus** *(bus navetta del porto)* loops passengers between the terminals and a stop just below the People Mover tracks.

Wherever you arrive, the best strategy is to make your way to terminal #103 (the long, low-slung, modern, red building with the tall gray tower in the middle) at the top of the harbor. The waterfront strip in front of this terminal includes the dock for both *vaporetti* and taxi boats; the People Mover is a five-minute walk beyond this building.

Alternate Port: A few smaller cruise ships tie up at the **Santa Marta** and **San Basilio** docks, which sit side by side along the Giudecca Canal just southeast of the main port. From the nearby San Basilio stop, you can catch vaporetto #2, which does an express loop in both directions, linking the Giudecca Canal and the Grand Canal (including stops at Piazzale Roma, Rialto, and St. Mark's Square). The Port of Venice website has a map of the different docks (www.port.venice.it/en/terminals.html).

New Cruise Ship Restrictions: Citing environmental concerns and the risk of a catastrophic accident, the Italian government has begun limiting cruise ship traffic in the Venice lagoon. This means fewer large cruise vessels will be sailing close to Venice's shores. A ban on the very largest ships may take effect in November 2014. Regardless of the new rules, most cruise ships permitted to enter Venice's lagoon will continue to dock at the main cruise terminal for the foreseeable future.

Tourist Information: The local port authority sometimes operates small TI kiosks in the terminals; these dispense free maps of the city. For information on TIs in Venice itself, see page 713.

Getting Into Town

From Venice's main cruise port, public transportation is convenient and affordable, and there's little reason to pay for a water taxi. However, this is an extremely popular cruise port, and transportation can be uncomfortably crowded; decide in advance how you want to get into town (i.e., boat or People Mover), then disembark quickly and make a beeline for that option—hopefully before a line forms.

By Taxi

You can hire a **water taxi** to points in central Venice, but it's very expensive (figure around €70-80 minimum for up to six people to anywhere in Venice; book at the kiosks in front of terminal #103 at the top of the harbor). **Land taxis** wait in front of the cruise terminals, but because virtually nothing of interest in Venice is accessible by car, it's unlikely you'll need them (unless you're going to Marco Polo Airport—about €40).

By Public Transportation

Choose whether you want to go directly to St. Mark's Square (by express boat along the Giudecca Canal, around the bottom of Venice); or take the slower, more scenic approach via the more famous Grand Canal.

Directly to St. Mark's Square
(via the Giudecca Canal)

The handy Alilaguna express boat (blue line) conveniently connects the cruise port to St. Mark's Square (San Marco-Giardinetti dock) in just 30 minutes (€8 one-way, €15 round-trip, €3/big bag, 2/hour in each direction, www.alilaguna.it). This boat leaves from the small dock at the top of the harbor, in front of terminal building #103; before boarding, buy your ticket at the kiosk. While there's a small round-trip discount, I'd buy a one-way ticket in order to leave my options open for returning to the cruise port. Because this

---

Services at the Port of Venice

You'll find everything you need in downtown Venice. Here's a rundown on what you'll encounter at the port.

ATMs: These are inside the terminal buildings. A handy one is in a freestanding kiosk at the left end of terminal #103.

Internet Access: You'll find Wi-Fi in at least some of the terminal buildings (most likely in #103); ask for the password, or look to see if it's posted somewhere in the terminal.

Pharmacy: The nearest pharmacy is a five-minute walk from Piazzale Roma. With your back to the People Mover, walk straight ahead through the bus parking lot, and proceed through the little park. Cross two bridges, and you'll see a pharmacy on your right, facing a canal. Another option is across the Grand Canal, past the train station, on the main drag (Rio Terà Lista di Spagna).

---

service is understandably popular, the boats can fill up. If there's already a long line, consider one of the options described next.

To St. Mark's Square via the Grand Canal

First, make your way to Piazzale Roma—the bus station/parking lot on the Grand Canal—by shuttle bus, monorail, or on foot; from there, you can ride a vaporetto (water bus) to St. Mark's Square.

Step 1—From the Cruise Port to Piazzale Roma: Some cruise lines offer a free **shuttle bus** from near terminal building #103 to Piazzale Roma.

If there's no shuttle, you can take the **People Mover** monorail, which connects the cruise port to the rest of Venice. To reach it, head away from the water, and look for its white, elevated tracks and station (just beyond terminal building #103). From the harbor, it's about a five-minute, somewhat circuitous walk, following signs out of the port gate. From this stop (called Stazione Marittima), the monorail goes every few minutes (direction: Piazzale Roma, €1, buy ticket at machine as you enter the terminal, 3-minute ride). You'll exit into a busy bus parking lot. Turn left and head for the Grand Canal, where you'll find a vaporetto stop.

The People Mover can be crowded when several cruises arrive; if the line seems too long and you're feeling energetic, take a drab, urban 15-minute **walk** to Piazzale Roma: Continue straight past the People Mover station through the big parking lot, and walk up the red-brick traffic bridge (with a sidewalk for pedestrians). When you reach the busy road at the gas station, turn right and follow the road straight to Piazzale Roma, then continue straight ahead to the vaporetto stop.

Step 2—From Piazzale Roma via the Grand Canal to St.

Mark's Square: Walk to Piazzale Roma's waterfront and look for the vaporetto stop. Buy a vaporetto ticket (€7 one-way) and hop on the boat: Slower boat #1 takes about 45 minutes to St. Mark's, while express boat #2 skips several stops and gets there in 25 minutes. My self-guided "Grand Canal Cruise" is more enjoyable on #1, but workable on #2 if you're in a hurry. You'll hop off at the San Marco stop, right in the heart of historic Venice.

Alternate Plan—Walk to St. Mark's Square: If the *vaporetti* are too crowded and you'd like to stretch your legs and get a glimpse of untouristy Venice, consider walking from Piazzale Roma to St. Mark's along the city's back streets (1.5 miles, allow about 45 minutes, follow signs for *San Marco*). Note: It can be even more enjoyable to walk back to the ship at the end of the day.

By Tour

For information on local tour options in Venice—including walking tours and local guides for hire—see "Tours in Venice" on page 726.

Returning to Your Ship

Because every cruise passenger in town will be trying to get back to the port at the same time as you, your return options can be crowded. Plan ahead, keep an eye on lines at the boat docks, and be sure to leave yourself plenty of time. See page 797 for help if you miss your boat.

By Express Boat: The fastest way back to the cruise port is on the Alilaguna express boat (blue line, catch it at the San Marco dock: From St. Mark's, head for the waterfront, turn right, and walk into the small park; the boat zips straight to the cruise port in 30 minutes; for specifics, see "Directly to St. Mark's Square," earlier).

By Vaporetto: You can catch a vaporetto to Piazzale Roma (from which it's just a quick People Mover monorail ride to the port). From the San Zaccaria dock, *vaporetti* #4.2 and #5.2 both go to Piazzale Roma in about 20 minutes; vaporetto #2 will get you there in 40 minutes. From any vaporetto dock along the Grand Canal, you can take vaporetto #1 (slower) or vaporetto #2 (fewer stops, so faster) to Piazzale Roma. Once you make it to Piazzale Roma, just hop on the People Mover—look for the entrance along the right side of the square, near the top, between the parking garages.

If your ship is at the Santa Maria or San Basilio dock, take vaporetto #2, which stops at San Basilio.

On Foot: One of my favorite activities in Venice is walking through the back streets all the way to Piazzale Roma (from there, you can hop on the People Mover back to the port). Allow yourself about an hour for the whole trip (ideally more for lingering or getting lost). Refer constantly to a map to stay on track, and keep following signs for *Piazzale Roma*—or, if you don't see any, watch for *Ferrovia* (the train station, across the Grand Canal from Piazzale Roma).

By Water Taxi: In an emergency, you can pay a water taxi to zip you back to the cruise port—but it's expensive (€70-80 or more).

Orientation to Venice

The island city of Venice is shaped like a fish. Its major thoroughfares are canals. The Grand Canal winds through the middle of the fish, starting at the mouth where all the people and food enter, passing under the Rialto Bridge, and ending at St. Mark's Square (Piazza San Marco). Park your 21st-century perspective at the mouth and let Venice swallow you whole.

Venice is a car-less kaleidoscope of people, bridges, and odorless canals. It's made up of more than a hundred small islands—but for simplicity, I refer to the whole shebang as "the island."

Venice: A Verbal Map

There are six districts (*sestieri,* shown on map on page 706): **San Marco** (from St. Mark's Square to the Accademia Bridge), **Castello** (the area east of St. Mark's Square), **Dorsoduro** (the "belly" of the fish, on the far side the Accademia Bridge), **Cannaregio** (between the train station and the Rialto Bridge), **San Polo** (west of the Rialto Bridge), and **Santa Croce** (the "eye" of the fish, across the canal from the train station).

The easiest way to navigate is by landmarks. Many street corners have a sign pointing you to *(per)* the nearest major landmark, such as San Marco, Accademia, Rialto, and Ferrovia (train station). Obedient visitors stick to the main thoroughfares as directed by these signs...and miss the charm of back-street Venice.

Beyond the city's core lie several other islands, including San Giorgio (with great views of Venice), Giudecca (more views), San Michele (old cemetery), Murano (famous for glass), Burano (lacemaking), Torcello (old church), and the skinny Lido (with Venice's beach).

Tourist Information

With this book, a city map, and the events schedule on the TI's website, there's little need to make an in-person visit to a TI in Venice. That's fortunate, because the city's TIs can be crowded and don't have many free printed materials to hand out. If you need to check or confirm something, try phoning the TI at 041-529-8711 or visit www.turismovenezia.it (click on "Venezia," then the English icon). This website can be more helpful than the actual TI office.

If you must visit a TI, you'll find two convenient branches near **St. Mark's Square** (one in the far-left corner with your back to the basilica, the other next to the Giardinetti Reali park near the San Marco vaporetto stop; both of these are open daily 9:00-19:00). There's also a TI desk at the **airport** (daily 9:00-20:00).

At the **train station,** you'll find TI staffers in a big, white kiosk out front near the vaporetto #2 stop most of the year (from Carnevale—falling sometime in Feb—through Oct daily 9:00-14:30, closed off-season; as this kiosk is shared with the private Alilaguna boat company, be sure to seek out a TI representative). The TI inside the station is open on summer afternoons (daily 13:00-19:00) and all day long in winter (daily 9:00-19:00; likely near track 1, though this may change with station renovation).

Maps: Of all places, you need a good map in Venice. Hotels give away freebies (no better than the small color one at the front of this book). The TI sells a decent €2.50 map and miniguide—but you can find a wider range at bookshops, newsstands, and postcard stands. The cheap maps are pretty bad, but if you spend €5, you'll get a map that shows you everything. Investing in a good map can be the best €5 you'll spend in Venice. Map lovers should look for the book *Calli, Campielli e Canali*, sold at bookstores for €22.50, with 1:2,000 maps of the whole city.

Also consider a mapping **app** for your smartphone, which uses GPS to pinpoint your location—extremely useful if you get lost in twisty back streets. To avoid data-roaming charges, look for an offline map that can be downloaded in its entirety before your trip. **City Maps 2Go** has a huge number of searchable offline maps, including a fairly good Venice version ($2 pays for any/all of their maps).

Helpful History Timelines: For historical orientation, local guide Michael Broderick (listed later, under "Tours in Venice") has produced three poster-size timelines that cleverly map the city's history and art (sold at local bookstores; see www.venicescapes.org).

Daily Reminder

Sunday: While anyone is welcome to worship, most churches are closed to sightseers on Sunday morning. They re-open in the afternoon: St. Mark's Basilica (14:00-17:00, until 16:00 Nov-March), Frari Church (13:00-18:00), and the Church of San Zaccaria (16:00-18:00). The Church of San Polo is closed all day, and the Rialto open-air market consists mainly of souvenir stalls (fish and produce sections closed). It's a bad day for a pub crawl, as most pubs are closed.

Monday: All sights are open except the Rialto fish market, Lace Museum (on the island of Burano), and Torcello Museum (on the island of Torcello). The Accademia and Ca' d'Oro close at 14:00.

Tuesday: All sights are open except the Peggy Guggenheim Collection.

Wednesday/Thursday/Friday/Saturday: All sights are open.

Notes: The Accademia is open earlier (daily at 8:15) and closes later (19:15 Tue-Sun) than most sights in Venice. Some sights close earlier off-season (such as the Correr Museum, Campanile bell tower, St. Mark's Basilica, and the Church of San Giorgio Maggiore). Modest dress is recommended at churches and required at St. Mark's Basilica—no bare shoulders, shorts, or short skirts.

Crowd Control: The city is inundated with cruise-ship passengers and tours from mainland hotels daily from 10:00 to about 17:00. While major sights are busiest in the late morning, it's a delightful time to explore the back lanes. The sights that have crowd problems get even more packed when it rains.

    To avoid the worst of the crowds at **St. Mark's Basilica,** go early or late.

    At the **Doge's Palace,** purchase your ticket at the never-crowded Correr Museum across St. Mark's Square. You can also visit later in the day.

    For the **Campanile,** ascend first thing in the morning or go late (it's open until 21:00 July-Sept), or skip it entirely if you're going to the similar San Giorgio Maggiore bell tower.

    For the **Accademia,** you'll enjoy fewer crowds by going early or late.

Helpful Hints

Theft Alert: Pickpockets (often elegantly dressed) work the crowded main streets, docks, and *vaporetti*. Your biggest risk of pickpockets is inside St. Mark's Basilica, near the Accademia or Rialto bridges (especially if you're preoccupied with snapping photos), or on a tightly packed vaporetto.

A handy *polizia* station is on the right side of St. Mark's Square as you face the basilica (at #63, near Caffè Florian). To call the police, dial 113. The Venice TI handles complaints—which must be submitted in writing—about local crooks, including gondoliers, restaurants, and hotel rip-offs (fax 041-523-0399, complaint.apt@turismovenezia.it).

It's illegal for street vendors to sell knockoff handbags, and it's also illegal for you to buy them; both you and the vendor can get big fines.

Be Prepared to Splurge: Venice is expensive for residents as well as tourists, as everything must be shipped in and hand-trucked to its destination. But it's a unique place that's worth paying a premium to fully experience. I find that the best way to enjoy Venice is just to succumb to its charms and blow through a little money.

Take Breaks: Venice's endless pavement, crowds, and tight spaces are hard on tourists, especially in hot weather. Schedule breaks in your sightseeing. Grab a cool place to sit down, relax, and recoup—meditate on a pew in an uncrowded church, or stop in a café.

Etiquette: As ever-growing waves of tourists wash over Venice every year, its residents are struggling to ward off the trash (and trashiness) left in their wake. Picnicking is illegal anywhere on St. Mark's Square, and offenders can be fined. (The only place nearby for a legal picnic is in Giardinetti Reali, the small park along the waterfront west of the Piazzetta near St. Mark's Square. Elsewhere in Venice, picnicking is no problem.) On St. Mark's Square, police admonish snackers and sunbathers. You may see friendly guidelines posted around town discouraging litter, pigeon-feeding, and beachwear (or rather, "encouraging" good behavior, as city officials are hoping that sweet talk will prove more effective than admonishment has).

Dress Modestly: When visiting St. Mark's Basilica or other major churches, men, women, and even children must cover their shoulders and knees (or risk being turned away). Remove hats when entering a church.

Public Toilets: Handy public WCs (€1.50) are near major landmarks, including: St. Mark's Square (behind the Correr Museum and at the waterfront park, Giardinetti Reali), Rialto, and the Accademia Bridge. Use free toilets whenever you can—any museum you're visiting, or any café you're eating in. You could also get a drink at a bar (cheaper) and use their WC for free.

Best Views: A slow vaporetto ride down the Grand Canal on a sunny day—or a misty early morning—is a shutterbug's delight (try to sit in the front seats, available on some older boats; for narration, see my self-guided "Grand Canal Cruise," later). On St. Mark's Square, enjoy views from the soaring Campanile or the balcony of St. Mark's Basilica (both require admission). The Rialto and Accademia bridges provide free, expansive views of the Grand Canal, along with a cooling breeze. Or get off the main island for a view of the Venetian skyline: Ascend San Giorgio Maggiore's bell tower, or venture to Giudecca Island to visit the swanky bar of the Molino Stucky Hilton Hotel (free shuttle boat leaves from near the San Zaccaria-M.V.E. vaporetto dock).

Pigeon Poop: If your head is bombed by a pigeon, resist the initial response to wipe it off immediately—it'll just smear into your hair. Wait until it dries, and it should flake off cleanly. But if the poop splatters on your clothes, wipe it off immediately to avoid a stain.

Water: I carry a water bottle to refill at public fountains. Venetians pride themselves on having pure, safe, and tasty tap water piped in from the foothills of the Alps. You can actually see the mountains from Venice's bell towers on crisp, clear winter days.

Services

Internet Access: Almost all hotels have Wi-Fi, many have a computer that guests can use, and most provide these services for free. Otherwise, handy if pricey little Internet places are scattered around town (usually on back streets, marked with an @ sign, and charging €5/hour).

Post Office: Use post offices only as a last resort, as simple transactions can take 45 minutes if you get in the wrong line. You can buy stamps from tobacco shops and mail postcards at any of the red postboxes in town. The main post office is just north of the Rialto Bridge—on the San Marco side, near the Teatro Malibran on Calle de le Acque (Mon-Fri 8:30-19:10, Sat 8:30-12:30, closed Sun, Castello 5016). You'll find branch offices with shorter hours (generally mornings only) around town, including a handy one right behind St. Mark's Square (near the TI).

Bookstores: In keeping with its literary heritage, Venice has classy and inviting bookstores. To locate these three bookstores, see map on page 774. The small **Libreria Studium,** a block behind St. Mark's Basilica, has a carefully chosen selection of new English books, including my guidebooks (Mon-Sat 9:00-19:30, Sun 9:30-13:30 & 14:00-18:00, on Calle de la Canonica at #337, tel. 041-522-2382). Used-bookstore lovers shouldn't miss the funky **Acqua Alta** ("high water") bookstore, whose

Sightseeing Passes for Venice

Venice offers a dizzying array of combo-tickets and sightseeing passes. Determine roughly what you plan to see, do the math, and pick the pass that suits your plans. For most people, the best choice is the Museum Pass, which covers entry into the Doge's Palace, Correr Museum, and more. Note that some major sights are not covered on any pass, including the Accademia, Peggy Guggenheim Collection, Scuola San Rocco, and Campanile, along with the three sights within St. Mark's Basilica that charge admission.

The following passes (except for the combo-ticket) are sold at the TI, and most are available at participating sights.

Combo-Ticket: A €16 combo-ticket covers the Doge's Palace and the Correr Museum; to bypass the long line at the Doge's Palace, buy your combo-ticket at the never-crowded Correr Museum. The two sights are also covered by the Museum Pass and Venice Card.

Museum Pass: Busy sightseers may prefer this more expensive pass, which covers these museums: the Doge's Palace, Correr Museum, Ca' Rezzonico (Museum of 18th-Century Venice), Palazzo Mocenigo Costume Museum, Casa Goldoni (home of the Italian playwright), Ca' Pesaro (modern art), Museum of Natural History in the Santa Croce district, the Glass Museum on the island of Murano, and the Lace Museum on the island of Burano. At €24, this pass is the best value if you plan to see the Doge's Palace/Correr Museum and even just one of the other covered museums. (Families get a price break on multiple passes—ask.) You can buy it at any of the participating museums.

Venice Card: This pass combines the 11 city-run museums and 16 churches (including the Frari Church), plus a few minor discounts, for €40. A cheaper variation, the Venice Card San Marco, is more selective: It covers the Correr Museum, Doge's Palace, and your choice of any three churches for €25. But it's hard to make either of these passes pay off.

Transportation Passes: Venice sells transit-only passes that cover *vaporetti* and mainland buses. For a rundown on these, see "Getting Around Venice" on page 718.

quirky owner Luigi has prepared for the next flood by displaying his wares in a selection of vessels, including bathtubs and a gondola. Look for the "book stairs" in his back garden (daily 9:00-21:00, large and classically disorganized selection includes prints of Venice, just beyond Campo Santa Maria Formosa on Calle Lunga Santa Maria Formosa at #5176, tel. 041-296-0841). For a solid selection of used books in English, visit **Marco Polo,** on Calle del Teatro o de l'Opera, close to the St. Mark's side of the Rialto Bridge, just past the Coin department store and behind the church (Mon-Sat 9:30-13:00 & 15:30-19:30, closed Sun, Cannaregio 5886a, tel. 041-522-6343).

Travel Agencies: If you need to get train tickets, make seat reservations, or arrange a *cuccetta* (koo-CHET-tah—a berth on a night train), save a time-consuming trip to Venice's crowded train station by using a downtown travel agency. Most trains between Venice, Florence, and Rome require reservations, even for railpass holders. A travel agency can also give advice on cheap flights (book at least a week in advance for the best fares). Both of the following agencies charge a €4 per-ticket fee.

Along the embankment near St. Mark's Square (facing the San Zaccaria vaporetto stop), look for **Oltrex Change and Travel** (daily 9:00-13:00 & 14:00-18:00, closed Sun Nov-April; on Riva degli Schiavoni, one bridge past the Bridge of Sighs at San Marco 5097b; tel. 041-524-2828, Luca and Beatrice). Near Rialto, try **Kele & Teo Travel** (Mon-Fri 9:00-18:00, Sat 9:00-12:00, closed Sun; leaving the Rialto Bridge heading for St. Mark's, it's half a block away, tucked down a side street on the right; tel. 041-520-8722).

Getting Around Venice
On Foot
The city's "streets" are narrow pedestrian walkways connecting its docks, squares, bridges, and courtyards. To navigate, look for yellow signs on street corners pointing you to *(per)* the nearest major landmark. The first landmarks you'll get to know are San Marco (St. Mark's Square), Rialto (the bridge), Accademia (another bridge), Ferrovia (the train station), and Piazzale Roma (the bus station). Determine whether your destination is in the direction of a major signposted landmark, then follow the signs through the maze.

Dare to turn off the posted routes and make your own discoveries. While 80 percent of Venice is, in fact, not touristy, 80 percent of the tourists never notice. Escape the crowds and explore on foot. Walk and walk to the far reaches of the town. Don't worry about getting lost—in fact, get as lost as possible. Keep reminding yourself, "I'm on an island, and I can't get off." When it comes time to find your way, just follow the arrows on building corners or simply ask a local, *"Dov'è San Marco?"* ("Where is St. Mark's?") People in the tourist business (that's most Venetians) speak some English. If they don't, listen politely, watch where their hands point, say *"Grazie,"* and head off in that direction. If you're lost, refer to your map, or pop into a hotel and ask for their business card—it probably comes with a map and a prominent "You are here."

Every building in Venice has a house number. The numbers relate to the district (each with about 6,000 address numbers), not the street. Therefore, if you need to find a specific address, it helps to know its district, street, house number, and nearby landmarks.

Some helpful street terminology: *Campo* means square, a *campiello* is a small square, *calle* (pronounced "KAH-lay" with an "L" sound) means street, and a *ponte* is a bridge. A *fondamenta* is the embankment along a canal or the lagoon. A *rio* is a small canal, while a *rio terà* is a street that was once a canal and has been filled in (and a *piscina* is a filled-in former pond). A *sotoportego* is a covered passageway. *Salizzada* means "laid with cobblestones" (indicating it's among the first Venetian streets ever paved). Don't get hung up on the exact spelling of street and square names, which may sometimes appear in the Venetian dialect and other times in standard Italian.

By Vaporetto

Venice's public transit system, run by a company called ACTV, is a fleet of motorized bus-boats called *vaporetti*. They work like city

buses except that they never get a flat, the stops are docks, and if you get off between stops, you might drown.

For most travelers, only two vaporetto lines matter: line #1 and line #2. These lines leave every 10 minutes or so and go up and down the Grand Canal, between the "mouth" of the fish at one end and St. Mark's Square at the other. Line #1 is the slow boat, taking 45 minutes and making every stop along the way. Line #2 is the fast boat that zips down the

Grand Canal in 25 minutes, stopping only at Tronchetto (parking lot), Piazzale Roma (bus station), Ferrovia (train station), Rialto Bridge, San Tomà (Frari Church), San Samuele (opposite Ca' Rezzonico—an easy *traghetto* ride across), Accademia Bridge, and San Marco (west end of St. Mark's Square, end of the line).

Catching a vaporetto is very much like catching a city bus. You can buy either single-ride tickets (valid for 1 hour) or passes (valid for a variety of durations, from 12 hours to 7 days) from any ticket window or HelloVenezia office. HelloVenezia, run by ACTV, is a string of shops selling tickets and passes at the same prices as ticket windows (www.hellovenezia.com).

Before you board, validate your ticket by holding it up to the small white machine on the dock until you hear a pinging sound. The machine readout shows how long your ticket is valid—and inspectors do come by now and then to check tickets. If you board without a ticket (because ticket windows may be closed at odd

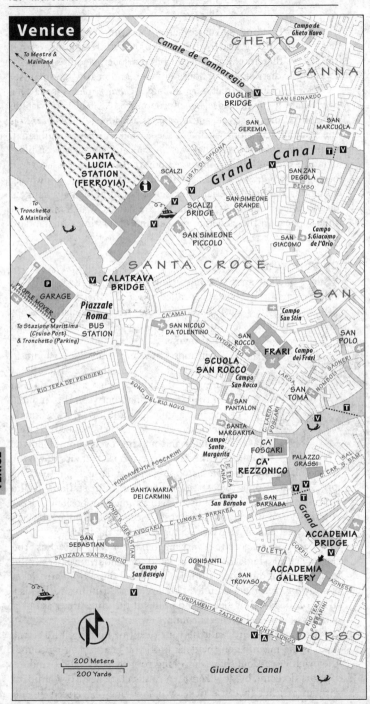

Venice

VENICE

GHETTO

Campo de
Gheto Novo

CANNA

Canale de Cannaregio

To Mestre &
Mainland

GUGLIE
BRIDGE V

SAN LEONARDO

SAN
MARCUOLA

SAN
GEREMIA

SANTA
LUCIA
STATION
(FERROVIA)

SCALZI

Grand Canal

T V

SAN ZAN
DEGOLA

BEMBO

To
Tronchetto
& Mainland

V

SCALZI
BRIDGE

SAN SIMEONE
GRANDE

Campo
S.Giacomo
de l'Orio

SAN SIMEONE
PICCOLO

SAN
GIACOMO

SANTA CROCE

SAN

PEOPLE MOVER

P
GARAGE

V CALATRAVA
BRIDGE

Piazzale
Roma
BUS
STATION

CA'AMAI

SAN NICOLO
DA TOLENTINO

Campo
San Stin

SAN
POLO

To Stazione Marittima
(Cruise Port)
& Tronchetto (Parking)

SAN
ROCCO

FRARI Campo
dei Frari

SCUOLA
SAN ROCCO

Campo
San Rocco

SAN
TOMA

T

RIO TERA DEI PENSIERI

FOND. DEL RIO NOVO

SAN
PANTALON

V

SANTA
MARGARITA

CA'
FOSCARI

PALAZZO
GRASSI

Campo
Santa
Margarita

CA'
REZZONICO

PONDAMENTA FOSCARINI

SANTA MARIA
DEI CARMINI

Campo
San Barnaba

SAN
BARNABA

V V
T

Grand

SAN
SEBASTIAN

OGNISSANTI

TOLETTA

ACCADEMIA
BRIDGE

SALIZADA SAN BASEGIO

Campo
San Basegio

SAN
TROVASO

V

ACCADEMIA
GALLERY

V

FONDAMENTA ZATTERE AL PONTE LONGO

V A

DORSO

N

V

200 Meters
200 Yards

Giudecca Canal

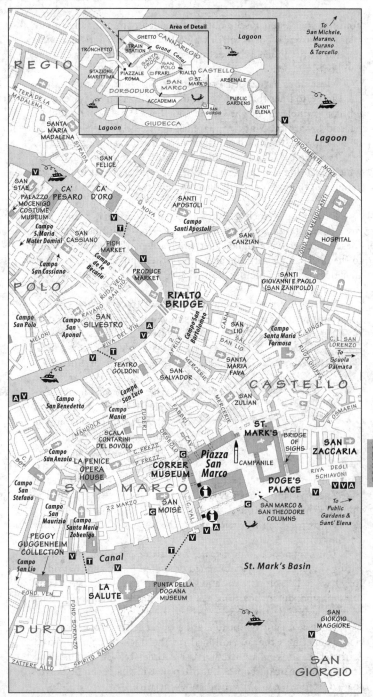

hours or small stops), seek out the conductor immediately to buy a single ticket on board (or risk a €50 fine). If you purchase a vaporetto pass, you need to touch the pass to the machine each time you board the boat.

Most stops have at least two docks. Signs on each dock show the vaporetto lines that stop there and the direction they are headed. For example, along the Grand Canal, a #1 or #2 boat might be headed toward St. Mark's Square (signposted *Lido* or *San Marco*), or back toward the mainland (signposted *Ferrovia, Piazzale Roma*, or *Tronchetto*). Helpful electronic boards at most stops display which boats are coming next, and when. Make a point to take advantage of these. Most boats also have electronic boards displaying this information.

Large stops—such as San Marco, San Zaccaria, Rialto, Ferrovia (train station), and Piazzale Roma—have multiple docks. At these, each berth is assigned a letter (clearly marked above the door to the dock, along with the numbers of the vaporetto lines that use that dock). Electronic boards will direct you to the letter of the dock you want.

Sorting out the different directions of travel can be confusing. Some boats have circular routes traveling in one direction only

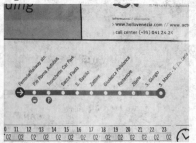

(true for lines #5.1 and #5.2, plus the non-Murano sections of lines #4.1 and #4.2). Be careful of the otherwise-handy express line #2, which runs in both directions and is almost, but not quite, a full loop. The #2 boat leaving from the San Marco stop goes in one direction (up the Grand Canal), while from the San Zaccaria stop—just a five-minute walk away—it goes in the opposite direction (around the tail of the "fish"). Make sure you use the correct stop to avoid taking the long way around to your destination.

You may notice some *vaporetti* sporting a *corsa bis* sign, indicating that it's running a shortened or altered route, and that riders may have to hop off partway and wait for the next boat. If you see a *corsa bis* sign, before boarding ask the conductor whether it's going to your desired destination.

To clear up any confusion, ask a ticket seller or conductor for help (sometimes they're stationed on the dock to help confused tourists), or look at a current ACTV timetable (in English and Italian, free at ticket booths but often unavailable—can be downloaded from the ACTV website, www.actv.it).

Tickets and Passes

Individual Vaporetto Tickets: A single ticket costs €7. Tickets are good for one hour in one direction; you can hop on and off at stops and change boats during that time. Tickets are electronic and refillable—don't toss your ticket after the first use. You can put more money on it at the automated kiosks and avoid waiting in line at the ticket window. The fare is reduced to €4 for a few one-stop runs *(corsa semplice)* that are hard to do by foot, including the route from San Marco to La Salute, from Fondamente Nove to Murano-Colonna, and from San Zaccaria to San Giorgio Maggiore.

Vaporetto Passes: You can buy a pass for unlimited use of *vaporetti:* €18/12 hours, €20/24 hours, €25/36 hours, €30/48 hours. All passes must be validated each time you board by touching it to the small white machine on the dock. Because single tickets cost a hefty €7 a pop, these passes can pay for themselves in a hurry. Think through your Venice itinerary before you step up to the ticket booth to pay for your first vaporetto trip. The 48-hour pass pays for itself with five rides. Keep in mind that smaller and/or outlying stops, such as Sant'Elena and Biennale, are unstaffed—another good reason to buy a pass. It's fun to be able to hop on and off spontaneously, and avoid long ticket lines. On the other hand, many tourists just walk and rarely use a boat.

Passes are also valid on ACTV's mainland buses, including bus #5 to the airport (but not the airport buses run by ATVO, a separate company).

More Vaporetto Tips

For fun, follow my self-guided "Grand Canal Cruise" (see page 727). But be warned: Grand Canal *vaporetti* in particular can be absolutely jam-packed, especially during the tourist rush hour (during mornings heading in from Piazzale Roma, and in evenings heading out to Piazzale Roma). Riding at night, with nearly empty boats and chandelier-lit palace interiors viewable from the Grand Canal, is an entirely different experience.

By *Traghetto*

Only four bridges cross the Grand Canal, but *traghetti* (shuttle gondolas) ferry locals and in-the-know tourists across the Grand Canal at seven handy locations (marked on the color map of Venice at the front of this book). Just step in, hand the gondolier €2, and enjoy the ride—standing or sitting. Note that some *traghetti* are seasonal, some stop running as early

VENICE

Handy *Vaporetti* from San Zaccaria, near St. Mark's Square

Several *vaporetti* leave from the San Zaccaria docks, located 150 yards east of St. Mark's Square. There are four separate San Zaccaria docks spaced about 70 yards apart, with a total of six different berths, lettered A to F: Danieli (E and F), Jolanda (C and D), M.V.E. (B), and Pietà (A). While this may sound confusing, in practice it's simple: Check the big electronic board (next to the Jolanda C/D dock), which indicates the departure time, line number, destination, and berth letter of upcoming *vaporetti*. Once you've figured out which boat you want, go to that letter berth and hop on. They're all within about a five-minute stroll of each other.

- **Line #1** goes up the Grand Canal, making all the stops, including San Marco, Rialto, Ferrovia (train station), and Piazzale Roma (but it does not go as far as Tronchetto). In the other direction, it goes from San Zaccaria to Arsenale and Giardini before ending on the Lido.
- **Line #2** zips over to San Giorgio Maggiore, the island church across from St. Mark's Square (5 minutes, €4 ride). From there, it continues on to stops on the island of Giudecca, the parking lot at Tronchetto, and then down the Grand Canal. Note: You cannot ride the #2 up the Grand Canal (for example, to Rialto or the train station) directly from this stop—you'll need to walk five minutes along the waterfront, past St. Mark's Square, to the San Marco-Giardinetti dock and hop the #2 from there.
- **Line #4.1** goes to San Michele and Murano in 45 minutes.
- **Line #7** is the summertime express boat to Murano (25 minutes).
- The **Molino Stucky shuttle boat** takes even non-guests to the Hilton Hotel, with its popular view bar (free, 20-minute ride, leaves at 0:20 past the hour from near the San Zaccaria-M.V.E. dock).

as 12:30, and all stop by 18:00. *Traghetti* are not covered by any transit pass.

By Water Taxi

Venetian taxis, like speedboat limos, hang out at busy points along the Grand Canal. Prices are regulated and listed on the TI's website: €15 for pickup, then €2 per minute; €5 per person for more than four passengers; and €10 between 22:00 and 6:00. Extra bags cost €3 apiece. (For information on taking the water taxi to/from the airport, see page 792.) Despite regulation, prices can be soft; negotiate and settle on the price or rate before stepping in. For travelers with lots of luggage or small groups who can split the cost,

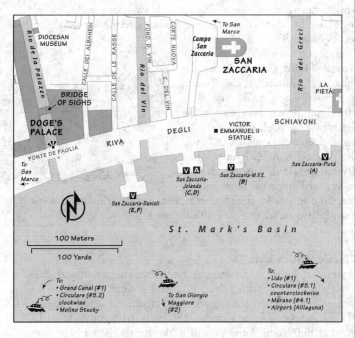

- **Lines #5.1** and **#5.2** are the *circulare* (cheer-koo-LAH-ray), making a loop around the perimeter of the island, with a stop at the Lido—perfect if you just like riding boats. Line #5.1 goes counterclockwise, and #5.2 goes clockwise.
- The **Alilaguna** shuttle to and from the airport stops here as well.

VENICE

taxi boat rides can be a worthwhile and time-saving convenience—and skipping across the lagoon in a classic wooden motorboat is a cool indulgence. For a little more than €100 an hour, you can have a private, unguided taxi-boat tour. You may find more competitive rates if you prebook through the Consorzio Motoscafi water taxi association (tel. 041-522-2303, www.motoscafivenezia.it)

By Gondola

If you're interested in hiring a gondolier for your own private cruise, see page 756.

Tours in Venice

Avventure Bellissime Venice Tours

This company offers several English-only two-hour walks, including a basic St. Mark's Square introduction called the "Original Venice Walking Tour" (€22, includes church entry, most days at 11:00, Sun at 14:00; 45 minutes on the square, 15 minutes in the church, one hour along back streets), a 70-minute private boat tour of the Grand Canal (€43, daily at 16:30, eight people maximum), a "Hidden Venice" tour (€22, in summer 3/week at 11:30, less off-season), and excursions on the mainland (10  percent discount for Rick Steves readers, see descriptions at www. tours-italy.com, tel. 041-970-499, info@tours-italy.com, Monica or Jonathan).

Classic Venice Bars Tour

If you're in Venice in the evening, consider taking a tour with debonair guide Alessandro Schezzini, a connoisseur of Venetian *bacari*—classic old bars serving wine and traditional *cicchetti* snacks. He organizes two-hour Venetian pub tours (€30, any night on request at 18:00, depart from top of Rialto Bridge, better to book by email—alessandro@schezzini.it—than by phone, mobile 335-530-9024, www.schezzini.it). Alessandro's tours include sampling *cicchetti* with wines at three different *bacari*. (If you think of this tour as a light dinner with a local friend, it's a particularly good value.)

Artviva Tours

This company offers a comprehensive program of tours, including Venice in a day, five themed tours (Grand Canal, Venice Walk, Doge's Palace, Gondola Tour, Food and Wine Tour with a sommelier), and a "Learn to Be a Gondolier" tour (for details, see www. italy.artviva.com).

Venicescapes

Michael Broderick's private theme tours of Venice are intellectually demanding and beyond the attention span of most mortal tourists. But travelers with a keen interest and a desire to learn find him passionate and engaging. Your time with Michael is like a rolling, graduate-level lecture (see his website for various 4-6-hour itineraries, 2 people-$250-290 or the euro equivalent, $60/person after that, admissions and transport not included, book in advance, tel. 041-850-5742, mobile 349-479-7406, www.venicescapes.org, info@venicescapes.org).

Local Guides

Plenty of licensed, trained guides are available. If you organize a small group to split the cost (figure on €70/hour with a 2-hour minimum), the fee becomes more reasonable. The following guides work with individuals, families, and small groups:

Walks Inside Venice is a dynamic duo of women—and their tour-guide colleagues—enthusiastic about teaching (€225/3 hours per group of up to 6 with this book, 3-hour minimum; Roberta: mobile 347-253-0560; Sara: mobile 335-522-9714; www.walksinsidevenice.com, info@walksinsidevenice.com). Roberta has been a big help in the making of this book. They also do side-trips to outlying destinations, and offer regularly scheduled small-group, English-only walking tours (€62.50, departs Mon-Sat at 14:30, 2.5 hours).

Alessandro Schezzini, mentioned earlier for his Classic Venice Bars Tour, isn't a licensed guide, so he can't take you into sights. But his relaxed, 1.5-hour back-streets tour gets you beyond the clichés and into off-beat Venice (€15/person, departs daily at 16:30, mobile 335-530-9024, www.schezzini.it, alessandro@schezzini.it). He also does lagoon tours in the morning.

Another good option is **Venice with a Guide,** a co-op of 10 good guides (www.venicewithaguide.com), including **Corine Govi** (mobile 347-966-8346, corine_g@libero.it) and **Elisabetta Morelli** (€70/hour, 2-hour minimum, tel. 041-526-7816, mobile 328-753-5220, bettamorelli@inwind.it).

Grand Canal Cruise

VENICE

From Piazzale Roma (or Ferrovia) to St. Mark's Square

Take a joyride and introduce yourself to Venice by boat. Cruise the Grand Canal all the way to the San Zaccaria stop (near St. Mark's Square), starting at the bus station, Piazzale Roma (or at the train station, Ferrovia, if you're not coming from the cruise port). If it's your first trip down the Grand Canal, you might want to stow this book and just take it all in—Venice is a barrage on the senses that hardly needs narration. But these notes give the cruise a little meaning and help orient you to this great city.

You can cruise the Grand Canal to St. Mark's Square, and launch straight into the self-guided walk of St. Mark's Square (see page 740). You could then top it off with my self-guided tour of St. Mark's Basilica (see page 759).

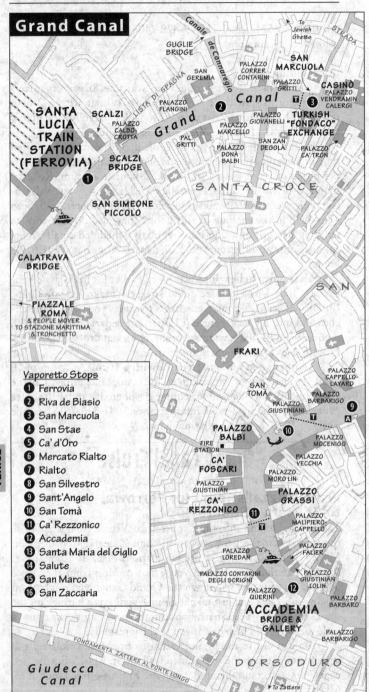

Grand Canal

VENICE

Canale de Cannaregio

To Jewish Ghetto

STRADA

GUGLIE BRIDGE

SAN GEREMIA

PALAZZO CORRER CONTARINI

SAN MARCUOLA

PALAZZO GRITTI

CASINÒ

PALAZZO VENDRAMIN CALERGI

Canal

PALAZZO FLANGINI

Grand

PALAZZO GIOVANELLI

TURKISH "FONDACO" EXCHANGE

SANTA LUCIA TRAIN STATION (FERROVIA)

SCALZI

PALAZZO CALBO-CROTTA

PAL. GRITTI

PALAZZO MARCELLO

SAN ZAN DEGOLÀ

PALAZZO CA'TRON

SCALZI BRIDGE

PALAZZO DONÀ BALBI

SANTA CROCE

SAN

SAN SIMEONE PICCOLO

CALATRAVA BRIDGE

PIAZZALE ROMA
& PEOPLE MOVER TO STAZIONE MARITTIMA & TRONCHETTO

FRARI

PALAZZO CAPPELLO-LAYARD

SAN TOMÀ

PALAZZO BARBARIGO

PALAZZO GIUSTINIANI

Vaporetto Stops

1. Ferrovia
2. Riva de Biasio
3. San Marcuola
4. San Stae
5. Ca' d'Oro
6. Mercato Rialto
7. Rialto
8. San Silvestro
9. Sant'Angelo
10. San Tomà
11. Ca' Rezzonico
12. Accademia
13. Santa Maria del Giglio
14. Salute
15. San Marco
16. San Zaccaria

PALAZZO BALBI

FIRE STATION

CA' FOSCARI

PALAZZO GIUSTINIAN

CA' REZZONICO

PALAZZO MOCENIGO

PALAZZO VECCHIA

PALAZZO MORO LIN

PALAZZO GRASSI

PALAZZO MALIPIERO-CAPPELLO

PALAZZO LOREDAN

PALAZZO FALIER

PALAZZO CONTARINI DEGLI SCRIGNI

PALAZZO QUERINI

PALAZZO GIUSTINIAN LOLIN

PALAZZO BARBARO

ACCADEMIA BRIDGE & GALLERY

PALAZZO BARBARIGO

FONDAMENTA ZATTERE AL PONTE LONGO

Giudecca Canal

DORSODURO

To Zattere

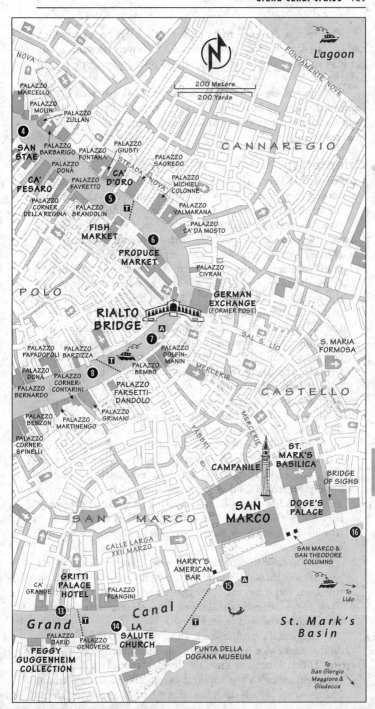

Lagoon

FONDAMENTE NOVE

N

200 Meters
200 Yards

NOVA

PALAZZO
MARCELLO

PALAZZO
MOLIN

PALAZZO
ZULLAN

CANNAREGIO

4

SAN
STAE

PALAZZO
BARBARIGO

PALAZZO
FONTANA

PALAZZO
GIUSTI

PALAZZO
SAGREDO

CA'
PESARO

PALAZZO
DONÀ

PALAZZO
FAVRETTO

CA'
D'ORO

STRADA NOVA

PALAZZO
MICHIEL
COLONNE

5

PALAZZO
CORNER
DELLA REGINA

PALAZZO
BRANDOLIN

PALAZZO
VALMARANA

FISH
MARKET

T

6

PALAZZO
CA' DA MOSTO

POLO

PRODUCE
MARKET

PALAZZO
CIVRAN

GERMAN
EXCHANGE
(FORMER POST)

RIALTO
BRIDGE

7

A

SAL S. LIO

S. MARIA
FORMOSA

PALAZZO
PAPADOPOLI

PALAZZO
BARZIZZA

T

PALAZZO
DOLFIN-
MANIN

PALAZZO
BEMBO

MERCERIE

PALAZZO
DONÀ

8

PALAZZO
CORNER-
CONTARINI

PALAZZO
FARSETTI-
DANDOLO

CASTELLO

PALAZZO
BERNARDO

PALAZZO
BENZON

PALAZZO
MARTINENGO

PALAZZO
GRIMANI

FABBRI

PALAZZO
CORNER-
SPINELLI

MERCERIE

ST.
MARK'S
BASILICA

CAMPANILE

BRIDGE
OF SIGHS

SAN
MARCO

DOGE'S
PALACE

SAN   MARCO

16

CALLE LARGA
XXII MARZO

SAN MARCO &
SAN THEODORE
COLUMNS

HARRY'S
AMERICAN
BAR

A

To
Lido

CA'
GRANDE

GRITTI
PALACE
HOTEL

PALAZZO
FLANGINI

15

St. Mark's
Basin

Grand

13

T

PALAZZO
DARIO

PALAZZO
GENOVESE

14

Canal

T

LA
SALUTE
CHURCH

PUNTA DELLA
DOGANA MUSEUM

To
San Giorgio
Maggiore &
Giudecca

PEGGY
GUGGENHEIM
COLLECTION

VENICE

This tour is designed to be done on the slow boat #1 (which takes about 45 minutes). The express boat #2 travels the same route, but it skips many stops and takes only 25 minutes, making it hard to sightsee.

To help you enjoy the visual parade of canal wonders, I've organized this tour by boat stop. I'll point out both what you can see from the current stop, and what to look forward to as you cruise to the next stop.

Orientation

Length of This Tour: Allow 45 minutes (25 minutes for an express version on vaporetto #2). With limited time, take the 25-minute express vaporetto #2. Or only do half the trip—choose either Ferrovia-to-Rialto or Rialto-to-San Marco.

Cost: €7 for a one-hour vaporetto ticket, or covered by a pass—best choice if you want to hop on and off (see page 723).

When to Go: Boats run every 10 minutes or so. If possible, ride late in the day to enjoy the best light and the fewest crowds. Avoid the morning rush hour (8:00-10:00), when local workers and tourists commute into town (from Ferrovia to San Marco—in the same direction as this tour). In the evening, the crowds head the opposite way, and boats to San Marco are less crowded. Sunset bathes the buildings in gold (particularly on the left side, which is the San Marco side). After dark, chandeliers light up building interiors.

Seating Strategies: As the *vaporetti* can be jammed, strategize about where to sit—then, when the boat pulls up, make a bee-line for your preference. Some *vaporetti* have seats in the bow (in front of the captain's bridge), which is the perfect vantage point for spotting sights left, right, and forward. However, many boats lack these seats, so you have to settle for another option: Sit inside (and view the passing sights through windows); stand in the open middle deck (you can try to move back and forth—almost impossible if the boat is crowded); or sit outside in the back (where you'll miss the wonderful forward views).

If you have to commit to one side, consider this: The left side has a slight edge in terms of seeing the sights described on this tour, and it has the best light late in the day. You're more likely to find an empty seat if you catch the vaporetto at Piazzale Roma—the stop *before* Ferrovia.

Because it's hard to see it all in one go, you may want to do this tour twice (perhaps once in either direction).

Getting There: From the Piazzale Roma monorail station, cross the parking lot to the vaporetto stop. Check the electronic boards to see which dock the next #1 or #2 is leaving from, hop on board, and start reading the tour when your vaporetto reaches Ferrovia.

Stops to Consider: You can break up the tour by hopping on and off at various sights described in greater depth elsewhere in this chapter (but remember, a single-fare vaporetto ticket is good for just one hour; passes let you hop on and off all day).

These are all worth considering as hop-off spots: San Marcuola (Jewish Ghetto), Mercato Rialto (fish market and famous bridge), Ca' Rezzonico (Museum of 18th-Century Venice), Accademia (art museum and the nearby Peggy Guggenheim Collection), and Salute (huge and interesting church and nearby Punta della Dogana contemporary art museum).

Information: Some city maps (on sale at postcard racks) have a handy Grand Canal map on the back.

Audio Tour: You can download this cruise as a free Rick Steves audio tour (see page 50).

Starring: Palaces, markets, boats, bridges—Venice.

The Cruise Begins

While you wait for your boat, here's some background on Venice's "Main Street."

At more than two miles long, nearly 150 feet wide, and nearly 15 feet deep, it's the city's largest canal, lined with its most impressive palaces. It's the remnant of a river that once spilled from the mainland into the Adriatic. The sediment it carried formed barrier islands that cut Venice off from the sea, forming a lagoon.

Venice was built on the marshy islands of the former delta, sitting on wood pilings driven nearly 15 feet into the clay (alder was the preferred wood). About 25 miles of canals drain the city, dumping like streams into the Grand Canal. Technically, Venice has only three canals: Grand, Giudecca, and Cannaregio. The 45 small waterways that dump into the Grand Canal are referred to as rivers (e.g., Rio Novo).

Venice is a city of palaces, dating from the days when the city was the world's richest. The most lavish palaces formed a grand architectural cancan along the Grand Canal. Once frescoed in reds and blues, with black-and-white borders and gold-leaf trim, they made Venice a city of dazzling color. This cruise is the only way to truly appreciate the palaces, approaching them at water level, where their main entrances were located. Today, strict laws prohibit any changes in these buildings, so while landowners gnash their teeth, we can enjoy Europe's best-preserved medieval city—

VENICE

slowly rotting. Many of the grand buildings are now vacant. Others harbor chandeliered elegance above mossy, empty (often flooded) ground floors.

❶ Ferrovia

The **Santa Lucia train station,** one of the few modern buildings in town, was built in 1954. It's been the gateway into Venice since

1860, when the first station was built. "F.S." stands for "Ferrovie dello Stato," the Italian state railway system.

More than 20,000 people a day commute in from the mainland, making this the busiest part of Venice during rush hour. The **Calatrava Bridge,** spanning the Grand Canal between the train station and Piazzale Roma upstream, was built in 2008 to alleviate some of the congestion and make the commute easier.

Opposite the train station, atop the green dome of **San Simeon Piccolo** church, St. Simeon waves *ciao* to whoever enters or leaves the "old" city. The pink church with the white Carrara-marble facade, just beyond the train station, is the **Church of the Scalzi** (Church of the Barefoot, named after the shoeless Carmelite monks), where the last doge (Venetian ruler) rests. It looks relatively new because it was partially rebuilt after being bombed in 1915 by Austrians aiming (poorly) at the train station.

❷ Riva de Biasio

Venice's main thoroughfare is busy with all kinds of **boats:** taxis, police boats, garbage boats, ambulances, construction cranes, and even brown-and-white UPS boats. Somehow they all manage to share the canal in relative peace.

About 25 yards past the Riva de Biasio stop, look left down the broad **Cannaregio Canal** to see what was the **Jewish Ghetto**. The twin, pale-pink, six-story "skyscrapers"—the tallest buildings you'll see at this end of the canal—are reminders of how densely populated the world's original ghetto was. Set aside as the local Jewish quarter in 1516, this area became extremely crowded. This urban island developed into one of the most closely knit business and cultural quarters of all the Jewish communities in Italy, and gave us our word "ghetto" (from *geto*, the copper foundry located here).

❸ San Marcuola

At this stop, facing a tiny square just ahead, stands the unfinished Church of San Marcuola, one of only five churches fronting the

Grand Canal. Centuries ago, this canal was a commercial drag of expensive real estate in high demand by wealthy merchants. About 20 yards ahead on the right (across the Grand Canal) stands the stately gray **Turkish "Fondaco" Exchange,** one of the oldest houses in Venice. Its horseshoe

arches and roofline of triangles and dingleballs are reminders of its Byzantine heritage. Turkish traders in turbans docked here, unloaded their goods into the warehouse on the bottom story, then went upstairs for a home-style meal and a place to sleep. Venice in the 1500s was very cosmopolitan, welcoming every religion and ethnicity, so long as they carried cash. (Today the building contains the city's Museum of Natural History—and Venice's only dinosaur skeleton.)

Just 100 yards ahead on the left, Venice's **Casinò** is housed in the palace where German composer Richard *(The Ring)* Wagner died in 1883. See his distinct, strong-jawed profile in the white plaque on the brick wall. In the 1700s, Venice was Europe's Vegas, with casinos and prostitutes everywhere. *Casinòs* ("little houses" in Venetian dialect) have long provided Italians with a handy escape from daily life. Today they're run by the state to keep Mafia influence at bay. Notice the fancy front porch, rolling out the red carpet for high rollers arriving by taxi or hotel boat.

❹ San Stae

The San Stae Church sports a delightful Baroque facade. Opposite the San Stae stop is a little canal opening—on the second building

to the right of that opening, look for the peeling plaster that once made up **frescoes** (you can barely distinguish the scant remains of little angels on the lower floors). Imagine the facades of the Grand Canal at their finest. Most of them would have been covered in frescoes by the best artists of the day. As colorful as the city is today, it's still only a faded, sepia-toned remnant of a long-gone era, a time of lavishly decorated, brilliantly colored palaces.

Just ahead, jutting out a bit on the right, is the ornate white facade of **Ca' Pesaro** (which houses the International Gallery of Modern Art). *"Ca'"* is short for *casa* (house). Because only the house of the doge (Venetian ruler) could be called a palace *(palazzo)*, all other Venetian palaces are technically "*Ca'*."

In this city of masks, notice how the rich marble facades along the Grand Canal mask what are generally just simple, no-nonsense brick buildings. Most merchants enjoyed showing off. However, being smart businessmen, they only decorated the side of the buildings that would be seen and appreciated. But look back as you pass Ca' Pesaro. It's the only building you'll see with a fine side facade. Ahead, on the left, with its glorious triple-decker medieval arcade (just before the next stop) is Ca' d'Oro.

❺ Ca' d'Oro

The lacy **Ca' d'Oro** (House of Gold) is the best example of Venetian Gothic architecture on the canal. Its three stories offer dif-

ferent variations on balcony design, topped with a spiny white roofline. Venetian Gothic mixes traditional Gothic (pointed arches and round medallions stamped with a four-leaf clover) with Byzantine styles (tall, narrow arches atop thin columns), filled in with Islamic frills. Like all the palaces, this was originally painted and gilded to make it even more glorious than it is now. Today the Ca' d'Oro is an art gallery.

Look at the Venetian chorus line of palaces in front of the boat. On the right is the arcade of the covered **fish market,** with the open-air **produce market** just beyond. It bustles in the morning but is quiet the rest of the day. This is a great scene to wander through—even though European Union hygiene standards have made it cleaner but less colorful than it once was.

Find the *traghetto* gondola ferrying shoppers—standing like Washington crossing the Delaware—back and forth. There are seven *traghetto* crossings along the Grand Canal, each one marked by a classy low-key green-and-black sign. Driving a *traghetto* isn't these gondoliers' normal day jobs. As a public service, all gondoliers are obliged to row the *traghetto* a few days a month. Make a point to use them. At €2 a ride, *traghetti* offer the cheapest gondola ride in Venice (but at this price, don't expect them to sing to you).

❻ Mercato Rialto

This stop was opened in 2007 to serve the busy market (boats only stop here between 8:00 and 20:00). The long and officious-looking building at this stop is the Venice courthouse. Straight ahead in the distance, rising above the huge post office, is the tip of the Campanile (bell tower), crowned by its golden angel at St. Mark's Square, where this tour will end. The **German Exchange** (100 yards directly ahead, on left side) was the trading center for German metal merchants in the early 1500s (once a post office, it will soon be a shopping center).

You'll cruise by some trendy and beautifully situated wine bars on the right, but look ahead as you round the corner and see the impressive Rialto Bridge come into view.

A major landmark of Venice, the **Rialto Bridge** is lined with shops and tourists. Constructed in 1588, it's the third bridge built on this spot. Until the 1850s, this was the only bridge crossing the Grand Canal. With a span of 160 feet and foundations stretching 650 feet on either side, the Rialto was an impressive engineering feat in its day. Earlier Rialto Bridges could open to let big ships in, but not this one. When this new bridge was completed, much of the Grand Canal was closed to shipping and became a canal of palaces.

When gondoliers pass under the fat arch of the Rialto Bridge, they take full advantage of its acoustics: *"Volare, oh, oh..."*

❼ Rialto

Rialto, a separate town in the early days of Venice, has always been the commercial district, while San Marco was the religious and governmental center. Today, a winding street called the Mercerie connects the two, providing travelers with human traffic jams and a mesmerizing gauntlet of shopping temptations. This is the only stretch of the historic Grand Canal with landings upon which you can walk. They unloaded the city's basic necessities here: oil, wine, charcoal, iron. Today, the quay is lined with tourist-trap restaurants.

Venice's sleek, black, graceful **gondolas** are a symbol of the city (for more on gondolas, see page 756). With about 500 gondoliers joyriding amid the churning *vaporetti*, there's a lot of congestion on the Grand Canal. Pay attention—this is where most of the gondola and vaporetto accidents take place. While the Rialto is the highlight of many gondola rides, gondoliers understandably prefer the quieter small canals. Watch your vaporetto driver curse the better-paid gondoliers.

Ahead 100 yards on the left, two gray-colored **palaces** stand side by side (the City Hall and the mayor's office). Their horseshoe-shaped, arched windows are similar and their stories are the same height, lining up to create the effect of one long balcony.

❽ San Silvestro

We now enter a long stretch of important **merchants' palaces,** each with proud and different facades. Because ships couldn't navigate

beyond the Rialto Bridge, the biggest palaces—with the major shipping needs—line this last stretch of the navigable Grand Canal.

Palaces like these were multi-functional: ground floor for the ware-house, offices and showrooms up-stairs, and the living quarters above the offices on the "noble floors" (with big windows designed to allow in maximum light). Servants lived and

worked on the top floors (with the smallest windows). For fire-safety reasons, the kitchens were also located on the top floors. Peek into the noble floors to catch a glimpse of their still-glorious chandeliers of Murano glass.

❾ Sant'Angelo

Notice how many buildings have a foundation of waterproof white stone *(pietra d'Istria)* upon which the bricks sit high and dry. Many

canal-level floors are abandoned as the rising water level takes its toll. The **posts**—historically painted gaily with the equivalent of family coats of arms—don't rot underwater. But the wood at the waterline, where it's ex-posed to oxygen, does. On the small-est canals, little blue gondola signs indicate that these docks are for gon-dolas only (no taxis or motor boats).

❿ San Tomà

Fifty yards ahead, on the right side (with twin obelisks on the rooftop) stands **Palazzo Balbi,** the palace of an early-17th-century captain general of the sea. These Venetian equivalents of five-star admirals were honored with twin obelisks decorating their pal-aces. This palace, like so many in the city, flies three flags: Italy (green-white-red), the European Union (blue with ring of stars), and Venice (a lion on a field of red and gold). Today it houses the administrative headquarters of the regional government.

Just past the admiral's palace, look immediately to the right, down a side canal. On the right side of that canal, before the bridge, see the traffic light and the **fire station** (the 1930s Mussolini-era building with four arches hiding fireboats parked and ready to go).

The impressive **Ca' Foscari,** with a classic Venetian facade (on the corner, across from the fire station), dominates the bend in the canal. This is the main building of the University of Venice, which has about 25,000 students. Notice the elegant lamp on the corner—needed in the old days to light this intersection.

The grand, heavy, white **Ca' Rezzonico,** just before the stop of the same name, houses the Museum of 18th-Century Venice. Across the canal is the cleaner and leaner **Palazzo Grassi,** the last major palace built on the canal, erected in the late 1700s. It was purchased by a French tycoon and now displays part of Punta della Dogana's contemporary art collection.

⓫ Ca' Rezzonico

Up ahead, the Accademia Bridge leads over the Grand Canal to the **Accademia Gallery** (right side), filled with the best Venetian paintings (described on page 752). The bridge was put up in 1934 as a temporary structure. Locals liked it, so it stayed. It was rebuilt in 1984 in the original style.

VENICE

⓬ Accademia

From here, look through the graceful bridge and way ahead to enjoy a classic view of **La Salute Church,** topped by a crown-shaped dome supported by scrolls. This Church of St. Mary of Good Health was built to thank God for delivering Venetians from the devastating plague of 1630 (which had killed about a third of the city's population).

The low, white building among greenery (100 yards ahead, on the right, between the Accademia Bridge and the church) is the **Peggy Guggenheim Collection.** The American heiress "retired" here, sprucing up a palace that had been abandoned in mid-construction. Peggy willed the city her fine collection of modern art (described on page 754).

As you approach the next stop, notice on the right how the fine line of higgledy-piggledy palaces evokes old-time Venice. Two doors past the Guggenheim, Palazzo Dario has a great set of characteristic **funnel-shaped chimneys.** These forced embers through a loop-the-loop channel until they were dead—required in the days when stone palaces were surrounded by humble, wooden buildings, and a live spark could make a merchant's workforce homeless. Notice this early Renaissance building's flat-feeling facade with "pasted-on" Renaissance motifs. Three doors later is the **Salviati building,** which once served as a glassworks. Its fine mosaic, done by Art Nouveau in the early 20th century, features Venice as a queen being appreciated by the big shots of society.

⓫ Santa Maria del Giglio

Back on the left stands the fancy Gritti Palace hotel. Hemingway and Woody Allen both stayed here (but not together).

Take a deep whiff of Venice. What's all this nonsense about stinky canals? All I smell is my shirt. By the way, how's your captain? Smooth dockings? To get to know him, stand up in the bow and block his view.

⓮ Salute

The huge La Salute Church towers overhead as if squirted from a can of Catholic Reddi-wip. Like Venice itself, the church rests upon pilings. To build the foundation for the city, more than a million trees were piled together, reaching beneath the mud to the solid clay. Much of the surrounding countryside was deforested by Venice. Trees were imported and consumed locally—to fuel the furnaces of Venice's booming glass industry, to build Europe's big-

gest merchant marine, to form light and flexible beams for nearly all of the buildings in town, and to prop up this city in the mud.

As the Grand Canal opens up into the lagoon, the last building on the right with the golden ball is the 17th-century **Customs House,** which now houses the Punta della Dogana contemporary art museum. Its two bronze Atlases hold a statue of Fortune riding the ball. Arriving ships stopped here to pay their tolls.

⓯ San Marco

Up ahead on the left, the green pointed tip of the Campanile marks **St. Mark's Square,** the political and religious center of Venice...

and the final destination of this tour. You could get off at the San Marco stop and go straight to St. Mark's Square. But I'm staying on the boat for one more stop, just past St. Mark's Square (it's a quick walk back).

Survey the lagoon. Opposite St. Mark's Square, across the water, the ghostly white church with the pointy bell tower is **San Giorgio Maggiore,** with great views of Venice (described on page 752). Next to it is the residential island of Giudecca, stretching from close to San Giorgio Maggiore past the Venice youth hostel (with a nice view, directly across) to the Hilton Hotel (good nighttime view, far right end of island).

Still on board? If you are, as we leave the San Marco stop, prepare for a drive-by view of St. Mark's Square. First comes the bold white facade of the old mint (marked by a tiny cupola, where Venice's golden ducat, the "dollar" of the Venetian Republic, was made) and the library facade. Then come the twin columns topped by St. Theodore and St. Mark, who've welcomed visitors since the 15th century. Between the columns, catch a glimpse of two giant figures atop the **Clock Tower**—they've been whacking their clappers every hour since 1499. The domes of **St. Mark's Basilica** are soon eclipsed by the lacy facade of the **Doge's Palace.** Next you'll see the **Bridge of Sighs** (leading from the palace to the prison—check out the maximum security bars), many gondolas with their green breakwater buoys, and then the grand harborside promenade—the **Riva.**

Follow the Riva with your eye, past elegant hotels to the green area in the distance. This is the largest of Venice's few **parks,** which hosts the annual art exhibition and festival called the Biennale. Much farther in the distance is the **Lido,** the island with Venice's beach. Its sand and casinos are tempting, but its car traffic disrupts the medieval charm of Venice.

⓰ San Zaccaria

OK, you're at your last stop. Quick—muscle your way off this boat! (If you don't, you'll eventually end up at the Lido.)

VENICE

Venice at a Glance

▲▲▲**St. Mark's Square** Venice's grand main square. **Hours:** Always open. See page 749.

▲▲▲**St. Mark's Basilica** Cathedral with mosaics, saint's bones, treasury, museum, and viewpoint of square. **Hours:** Mon-Sat 9:45-17:00, Sun 14:00-17:00 (until 16:00 Nov-March). See page 749.

▲▲▲**Doge's Palace** Art-splashed palace of former rulers, with prison accessible through Bridge of Sighs. **Hours:** Daily April-Oct 8:30-18:30, Nov-March 8:00-17:30. See page 750.

▲▲▲**Rialto Bridge** Distinctive bridge spanning the Grand Canal, with a market nearby. **Hours:** Bridge—always open; market—souvenir stalls open daily, produce market closed Sun, fish market closed Sun-Mon. See page 756.

▲▲**Correr Museum** Venetian history and art. **Hours:** Daily April-Oct 10:00-19:00, Nov-March 10:00-17:00. See page 751.

▲▲**Accademia** Venice's top art museum. **Hours:** Mon 8:15-14:00, Tue-Sun 8:15-19:15. See page 752.

▲▲**Peggy Guggenheim Collection** Popular display of 20th-century art. **Hours:** Wed-Mon 10:00-18:00, closed Tue. See page 754.

▲▲**Frari Church** Franciscan church featuring Renaissance masters. **Hours:** Mon-Sat 9:00-18:00, Sun 13:00-18:00. See page 756.

▲**Campanile** Dramatic bell tower on St. Mark's Square with elevator to the top. **Hours:** Daily Easter-June and Oct 9:00-19:00, July-Sept 9:00-21:00; Nov-Easter 9:30-16:45. See page 747.

VENICE

At San Zaccaria, you're right in the thick of the action. A number of other *vaporetti* depart from here (see page 724). Otherwise, it's a short walk back along the Riva to St. Mark's Square. Ahoy!

St. Mark's Square Walk

Venice was once Europe's richest city, and Piazza San Marco was its center. As middleman in the trade between Asia and Europe, wealthy Venice profited from both sides. In 1450, Venice had 180,000 citizens (far more than London) and a gross "national" product that exceeded that of entire countries.

The rich Venetians taught the rest of Europe about the good

▲**Bridge of Sighs** Famous enclosed bridge, part of Doge's Palace, near St. Mark's Square. **Hours:** Always viewable. See page 749.

Church of San Zaccaria Final resting place of St. Zechariah, plus a Bellini altarpiece and an eerie crypt. **Hours:** Mon-Sat 10:00-12:00 & 16:00-18:00, Sun 16:00-18:00.

Nearby Islands
▲**San Giorgio Maggiore** Island facing St. Mark's Square, featuring church with Palladio architecture, Tintoretto paintings, and fine views back on Venice. **Hours:** April-Oct Mon-Sat 9:00-19:00, Sun 9:00-11:00 & 12:00-19:00; Nov-March daily 9:00-17:30. See page 752.

San Michele Cemetery island on the lagoon. **Hours:** Daily April-Sept 7:30-18:00, Oct-March 7:30-16:30.

▲**Murano** Island famous for glass factories and glassmaking museum. **Hours:** Glass Museum open daily April-Oct 10:00-18:00, Nov-March 10:00-17:00 (may be under renovation when you visit).

▲▲**Burano** Sleepy island known for lacemaking and a lace museum. **Hours:** Lace Museum open April-Oct Tue-Sun 10:00-18:00, Nov-March Tue-Sun 10:00-17:00, closed Mon year-round.

▲**Torcello** Near-deserted island with old church, bell tower, and museum. **Hours:** Church open daily March-Oct 10:30-18:00, Nov-Feb 10:00-17:00, museum closed Mon.

VENICE

life—silks, spices, and jewels from the East, crafts from northern Europe, good food and wine, fine architecture, music, theater, and laughter. Venice was a vibrant city full of painted palaces, glittering canals, and impressed visitors. Five centuries after its power began to decline, Venice still has all of these, with the added charm of romantic decay. In this tour, we'll spend half an hour in the heart of this Old World superpower.

Orientation

Getting There: Signs all over town point to *San Marco*—meaning both the square and the basilica—located where the Grand Canal spills out into the lagoon. The Alilaguna express boat (blue line) from the cruise port zips you right here. Vaporetto stops: San Marco or San Zaccaria.

Campanile: If you ascend the bell tower, it'll cost you €8 (daily Easter-June and Oct 9:00-19:00, July-Sept 9:00-21:00; Nov-Easter 9:30-16:45).

Information: There are two TIs near St. Mark's Square. One is in the southwest corner of the square; the other is along the waterfront at the San Marco-Vallaresso vaporetto dock.

Audio Tour: You can download this chapter as a free Rick Steves audio tour (see page 50).

Services: Handy public WCs (€1.50) are behind the Correr Museum and also at the waterfront park, Giardinetti Reali (near the TI and San Marco-Vallaresso vaporetto dock).

Eating: Cafés with live music provide an engaging soundtrack for St. Mark's Square. The Correr Museum (at the end of the square opposite the basilica) has a quiet upstairs coffee shop overlooking the crowded square. For a list of restaurants in the area, see page 787.

Necessary Eyesores: Expect scaffolding and advertising billboards to cover parts of the square and its monuments when you visit.

Cardinal Points: The square is aligned (roughly) east-west. So, facing the basilica, north is to your left.

Starring: Byzantine domes, Gothic arches, Renaissance arches... and the wonderful, musical space they enclose.

The Walk Begins

• *For an overview of this grand square and the buildings that surround it, view it from the west end of the square (away from St. Mark's Basilica).*

The Piazza

St. Mark's Basilica dominates the square with its Eastern-style onion domes and glowing mosaics. Mark Twain said it looked like

"a vast warty bug taking a meditative walk." (I say it looks like tiara-wearing ladybugs copulating.) To the right of the basilica is its 325-foot-tall Campanile. Behind the Campanile, you can catch a glimpse of the pale-pink Doge's Palace.

VENICE

Lining the square are the former government offices *(procuratie)* that managed the treasury of St. Mark's, back when the church and state were one, and administered the Venetian empire's vast network of trading outposts, which stretched all the way to Turkey.

The square is big, but it feels intimate with its cafés and dueling orchestras. (The setting is spectacular, but the cafés are pricey—figure €6 for a basic cup of coffee, plus €6 extra per person cover charge if the musicians are playing.) By day, it's great for people-watching and pigeon-chasing. By night, under lantern light, it transports you to another century, complete with its own romantic soundtrack. The piazza draws Indians in saris, English nobles in blue blazers, and Nebraskans in shorts. Napoleon called the piazza "the most beautiful drawing room in Europe." Napoleon himself added to the intimacy by building the final wing, opposite the basilica, that encloses the square.

The arcade ringing the square, formerly lined with dozens of fine cafés, still provides an elegant promenade—complete with drapery that is dropped when necessary to provide relief from the sun.

Imagine this square full of water, with gondolas floating where people now sip cappuccinos. That happens every so often at very high tides *(acqua alta)*, a reminder that Venice and the sea are intertwined. (Now that one is sinking and the other is rising, they are more intertwined than ever.)

Venice became Europe's richest city from its trade with northern Europeans, Ottoman Muslims, and Byzantine Christians. Here in St. Mark's Square, the exact center of this East-West axis, we see both the luxury and the mix of Eastern and Western influences.

Watch out for pigeon speckle. The pigeons are not indigenous to Venice (they were imported by the Habsburgs) nor loved by residents. In fact, Venetians love seagulls because they eat pigeons. In 2008, Venice outlawed the feeding of pigeons. But tourists—eager for a pigeon-clad photo op—haven't gotten that message, so at least some pigeons persist.

• *Now approach the basilica. If it's hot and you're tired, grab a shady spot at the foot of the Campanile.*

St. Mark's Basilica

The facade is a wild mix of East and West, with round, Roman-style arches over the doorways, golden Byzantine mosaics, a roofline ringed with pointed Gothic pinnacles, and Muslim-shaped onion domes (wood, covered with lead)

VENICE

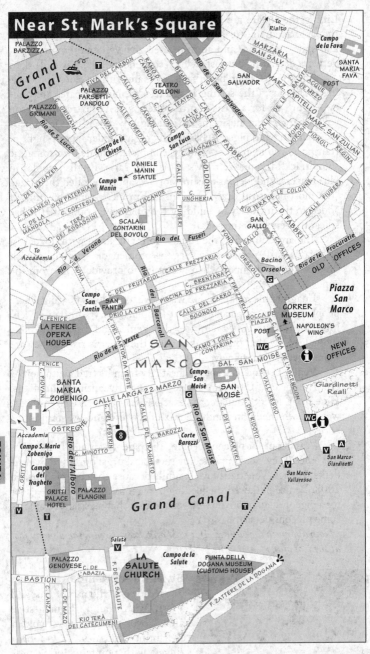

Near St. Mark's Square

VENICE

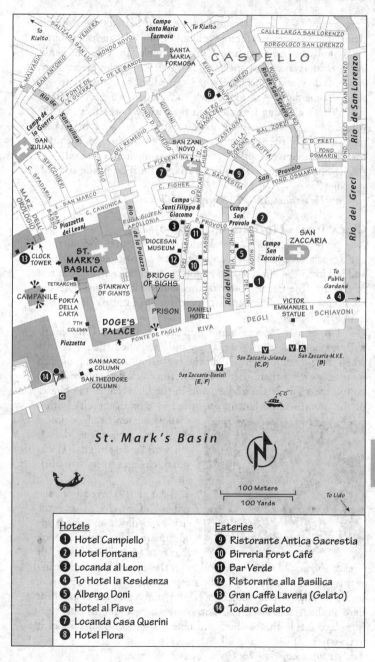

St. Mark's Basin

100 Meters
100 Yards

To Lido

To Rialto

VENICE

Hotels
1 Hotel Campiello
2 Hotel Fontana
3 Locanda al Leon
4 To Hotel la Residenza
5 Albergo Doni
6 Hotel al Piave
7 Locanda Casa Querini
8 Hotel Flora

Eateries
9 Ristorante Antica Sacrestia
10 Birreria Forst Café
11 Bar Verde
12 Ristorante alla Basilica
13 Gran Caffè Lavena (Gelato)
14 Todaro Gelato

on the roof. The brick-structure building is blanketed in marble that came from everywhere—columns from Alexandria, capitals from Sicily, and carvings from Constantinople. The columns flanking the doorways show the facade's variety—purple, green, gray, white, yellow, some speckled, some striped horizontally, some vertically, some fluted—all topped with a variety of different capitals.

What's amazing isn't so much the variety as the fact that the whole thing comes together in a bizarre sort of harmony. St. Mark's remains simply the most interesting church in Europe, a church that (to paraphrase Goethe) "can only be compared with itself."

✪ For a self-guided tour of St. Mark's Basilica, inside and out, see page 759.

• *Facing the basilica, turn 90 degrees to the left to see the...*

Clock Tower (Torre dell'Orologio)

Any proper Renaissance city wanted to have a fine, formal entry and a clock tower. In Venice's case, its entry was visible from the sea and led from the big religious and governmental center to the rest of the city. The Clock Tower retains some of its original blue and gold pigments, a reminder that, in centuries past, this city glowed with bright color.

Two bronze "Moors" stand atop the Clock Tower (built originally to be Caucasian giants, they only switched their ethnicity when their metal darkened over the centuries). At the top of each hour they swing their giant clappers. The clock dial shows the 24 hours, the signs of the zodiac, and in the blue center, the phases of the moon—important information, as a maritime city with a

shallow lagoon needs to know the tides. Above the dial is the world's first digital clock, which changes every five minutes.

An alert winged lion, the symbol of St. Mark and the city, looks down on the crowded square. He opens a book that reads *"Pax Tibi Marce,"* or "Peace to you, Mark." As legend goes, these were the comforting words that an angel spoke to the stressed evangelist, assuring him he would find serenity during a stormy night that the saint spent here on the island. Eventually, St. Mark's body found its final resting place inside the basilica, and now his winged-lion symbol is everywhere. (Find four in 20 seconds. Go.)

• *Across the square from the Clock Tower is the gigantic...*

VENICE

Campanile

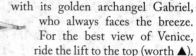

The original Campanile (cam-pah-NEE-lay, bell tower) was an observation tower and a marvel of medieval and Renaissance architecture until 1902, when it toppled into the center of the piazza. It had groaned ominously the night before, sending people scurrying from the cafés. The next morning...crash! The golden angel on top landed right at the basilica's front door, standing up.

The Campanile was rebuilt 10 years later complete with its golden archangel Gabriel, who always faces the breeze. For the best view of Venice, ride the lift to the top (worth ▲).

It's crowded at peak times, but well worth it.

Because St. Mark's Square is the first place in town to start flooding, there are tide gauges at the outside base of the Campanile (near the exit, facing St. Mark's Square) that show the current sea level *(livello marea)*.

• *The small square between the basilica and the water is the...*

Piazzetta

This "Little Square" is framed by the Doge's Palace on the left, the library on the right, and the waterfront of the lagoon. In former days, the Piazzetta was closed to the public for a few hours a day so that government officials and bigwigs could gather in the sun to strike shady deals.

The pale-pink **Doge's Palace** is the epitome of the style known as Venetian Gothic. Columns support traditional, pointed Gothic arches, but with a Venetian flair—they're curved to a point, ornamented with a trefoil (three-leaf clover), and topped with a round medallion of a quatrefoil (four-leaf clover). The pattern is found on buildings all over Venice and on the formerly Venetian-controlled Croatian coast, but nowhere else in the world (except Las Vegas).

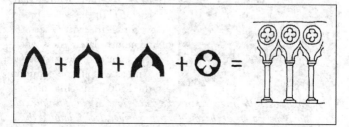

VENICE

The two large 12th-century **columns** near the water were looted from Constantinople. Mark's winged lion sits on top of one. The lion's body (nearly 15 feet long) predates the wings and is more than 2,000 years old. The other column holds St. Theodore (battling a crocodile), the former patron saint who was replaced by Mark. I guess stabbing crocs in the back isn't classy enough for an upwardly mobile world power. Criminals were executed by being hung from these columns in the hopes that the public could learn its lessons vicariously.

Venice was the "Bride of the Sea" because she depended on sea trading for her livelihood. This "marriage" was celebrated annually by the people on Ascension Day. The doge, in full regalia, boarded a ritual boat (his Air Force One equivalent) here at the edge of the Piazzetta and sailed out into the lagoon. There a vow was made, and he dropped a jeweled ring into the water to seal the marriage.

In the distance, on an island across the lagoon, is one of the grandest views in the city, of the **Church of San Giorgio Maggiore**. With its four tall columns as the entryway, the church, designed by the late-Renaissance architect Andrea Palladio, influenced the appearance of future government and bank buildings around the world.

Where the basilica meets the Doge's Palace is the traditional entrance to the palace, decorated with four small Roman statues—the **Tetrarchs**. No one knows for sure who they are, but I like the legend that says they're the scared leaders of a divided Rome during its fall, holding their swords and each other as all hell breaks loose around them.

About two-thirds of the way down the Doge's Palace, look for a **column** that's slightly shorter and fatter than the rest (it's the seventh from the water). Its carved capital tells a story of love, romance, and tragedy: 1) In the first scene (the carving facing the Piazzetta), a woman on a

balcony is wooed by her lover, who says, "Babe, I want *you!*" 2) She responds, "Why, little ol' *me?*" 3) They get married. 4) Kiss. 5) Hit the sack—pretty racy for 14th-century art. 6) Nine months later, guess what? 7) The baby takes its first steps. 8) And as was all too common in the 1300s...the child dies.

• *Continue down the Piazzetta to the waterfront. Turn left and walk (east) along the water. At the top of the first bridge, look inland at the...*

Bridge of Sighs

In the Doge's Palace (on your left), the government doled out justice. On your right are the prisons. (Don't let the palatial facade fool you—see the bars on the windows?) Prisoners sentenced in the palace crossed to the prisons by way of the covered bridge in front of you. This was called the Prisons' Bridge until the Romantic poet Lord Byron renamed it in the 19th century. From this bridge, the convicted got their final view of sunny, joyous Venice before entering the black and dank prisons. According to the Romantic legend, they sighed.

Venice has been a major tourist center for four centuries. Anyone who's ever come here has stood on this very spot, looking at the Bridge of Sighs. Lean on the railing leaned on by everyone from Casanova to Byron to Hemingway.

Sights in Venice

While Venice has many sights worth knowing about on a longer visit, for a one-day cruiser visit, I've listed just the top sights.

San Marco District

For information on the combo-ticket that covers most of the sights on the square, see page 717.

▲▲▲St. Mark's Square (Piazza San Marco)

This grand square is surrounded by splashy, historic buildings and sights: St. Mark's Basilica, the Doge's Palace, the Campanile bell tower, and the Correr Museum. The square is filled with music, lovers, pigeons, and tourists by day, and is your private rendezvous with the Venetian past late at night, when Europe's most magnificent dance floor is *the* romantic place to be.

✪ For a self-guided walk around this grand square—including the Campanile (bell tower) and the nearby Bridge of Sighs—see page 740.

▲▲▲St. Mark's Basilica (Basilica di San Marco)

Built in the 11th century to replace an earlier church, this basilica's distinctly Eastern-style architecture underlines Venice's connection with Byzantium (which protected it from the ambition of Charlemagne and

VENICE

his Holy Roman Empire). It's decorated with booty from returning sea captains—a kind of architectural Venetian trophy chest. The interior glows mysteriously with gold mosaics and colored marble. Since about A.D. 830, the saint's bones have been housed on this site.

Cost and Hours: Basilica entry is free, three interior sights charge admission, open Mon-Sat 9:45-17:00, Sun 14:00-17:00 (Sun until 16:00 Nov-March), interior brilliantly lit daily 11:30-12:30, St. Mark's Square, vaporetto: San Marco or San Zaccaria. No photos are allowed inside. Tel. 041-270-8311, www.basilicasanmarco.it. The dress code is strictly enforced for everyone (no bare shoulders or bare knees). Lines can be long, and bag check is mandatory, free, and can save you time in line; no photos are allowed inside.

> ✪ For a self-guided tour, see page 759.

▲▲▲Doge's Palace (Palazzo Ducale)

The seat of the Venetian government and home of its ruling duke, or doge, this was the most powerful half-acre in Europe for 400 years. The Doge's Palace was built to show off the power and wealth of

the Republic. The doge lived with his family on the first floor up, near the halls of power. From his once-lavish (now sparse) quarters, you'll follow the one-way tour through the public rooms of the top floor, finishing with the Bridge of Sighs and the prison. The place is wallpapered with masterpieces by Veronese and Tintoretto.

Don't worry too much about the great art. Enjoy the building.

Cost and Hours: €16 combo-ticket includes Correr Museum, also covered by Museum Pass—see page 717, daily April-Oct 8:30-18:30, Nov-March 8:00-17:30, last entry one hour before closing, café, no photos inside, next to St. Mark's Basilica, just off St. Mark's Square, vaporetto stops: San Marco or San Zaccaria, tel. 041-271-5911, http://palazzoducale.visitmuve.it.

Avoiding Lines: If the line is long at the Doge's Palace, buy your combo-ticket at the Correr Museum across the square; then you can go straight to the Doge's Palace turnstile, skirting along to the right of the long ticket-buying line and entering at the "prepaid tickets" entrance. It's also possible to buy your ticket online—at least 48 hours in advance—on the museum website (€0.50 fee).

Tours: The **audioguide** tour is dry but informative (€5, 1.5 hours, need ID or credit card for deposit). For a 1.25-hour live guided tour, consider the Secret Itineraries Tour, which takes you into palace rooms otherwise not open to the public (€20, includes Doge's Palace admission but not Correr Museum admission; €14 with combo-ticket; three English-language tours each morning). Though the tour skips the palace's main hall, you're welcome to visit the hall afterward on your own. Reserve ahead for this tour in peak season—it can fill up as much as a month in advance. Book online (http://palazzoducale.visitmuve.it, €0.50 fee), or reserve by phone (tel. 848-082-000, from the US dial 011-39-041-4273-0892), or you can try just showing up at the info desk.

Visiting the Doge's Palace: You'll see the restored facades from the **courtyard.** Notice a grand staircase (with nearly naked Moses and Paul Newman at the top). Even the most powerful visitors climbed this to meet the doge. This was the beginning of an architectural power trip.

In the **Senate Hall,** the 120 senators met, debated, and passed laws. Tintoretto's large *Triumph of Venice* on the ceiling (central painting, best viewed from the top) shows the city in all its glory. Lady Venice is up in heaven with the Greek gods, while barbaric lesser nations swirl up to give her gifts and tribute.

The **Armory**—a dazzling display originally assembled to intimidate potential adversaries—shows remnants of the military might that the empire employed to keep the East-West trade lines open (and the local economy booming).

The giant **Hall of the Grand Council** (175 feet by 80 feet, capacity 2,600) is where the entire nobility met to elect the senate and doge. It took a room this size to contain the grandeur of the Most Serene Republic. Ringing the top of the room are portraits of the first 76 doges (in chronological order). The one at the far end that's blacked out (in the left corner) is the notorious Doge Marin Falier, who opposed the will of the Grand Council in 1355. He was tried for treason, beheaded, and airbrushed from history.

On the wall over the doge's throne is Tintoretto's monsterpiece, *Paradise,* the largest oil painting in the world. Christ and Mary are surrounded by a heavenly host of 500 saints. The painting leaves you feeling that you get to heaven not by being a good Christian, but by being a good Venetian.

Cross the covered **Bridge of Sighs** over the canal to the **prisons.** Circle the cells. Notice the carvings made by prisoners—from olden days up until 1930—on some of the stone windowsills of the cells, especially in the far corner of the building.

Cross back over the Bridge of Sighs, pausing to look through the marble-trellised windows at all of the tourists.

▲▲Correr Museum (Museo Correr)

This uncrowded museum gives you a good, easy-to-manage overview of Venetian history and art. The doge memorabilia, armor, banners, statues (by Canova), and paintings (by the Bellini family and others) re-create the festive days of the Venetian Republic. And it's all accompanied—throughout the museum—by English descriptions and breathtaking views of St. Mark's Square. But the Correr Museum has one more thing to offer, and that's a quiet refuge—a place to rise above St. Mark's Square when the piazza is too hot, too rainy, or too overrun with tourists.

Cost and Hours: €16 combo-ticket also includes the Doge's Palace and the two lesser museums inside the Correr (National Archaeological Museum and the Monumental Rooms of the Marciana National Library); daily April-Oct 10:00-19:00, Nov-March 10:00-17:00, last entry one hour before closing; bag check free and mandatory for bags bigger than a large purse, no photos, elegant café, enter at far end of square directly opposite basilica, tel. 041-240-5211, http://correr.visitmuve.it.

Avoid long lines at the crowded Doge's Palace by buying your combo-ticket at the Correr Museum.

Across the Lagoon from St. Mark's Square
▲San Giorgio Maggiore
This is the dreamy church-topped island you can see from the waterfront by St. Mark's Square. The striking church, designed by Palladio, features art by Tintoretto, a bell tower, and good views of Venice.

Cost and Hours: Free entry to church; April-Oct Mon-Sat 9:00-19:00, Sun 9:00-11:00 & 12:00-19:00; Nov-March daily 9:00-17:30. The bell tower costs €6 and is accessible by elevator (runs until 30 minutes before the church closes).

Getting There: To reach the island from St. Mark's Square, take the five-minute ride on vaporetto #2 (€4, 6/hour, ticket valid for one hour; leaves from San Zaccaria stop—check the reader board to see which dock/berth it leaves from, direction: Tronchetto).

Dorsoduro District
▲▲Accademia (Galleria dell'Accademia)
Venice's top art museum, packed with highlights of the Venetian Renaissance, features paintings by the Bellini family, Titian, Tintoretto, Veronese, Tiepolo, Giorgione, Canaletto, and Testosterone. It's just over the wooden Accademia Bridge from the San Marco action.

Cost and Hours: €9, dull audioguide-€6, Mon 8:15-14:00, Tue-Sun 8:15-19:15, last entry 45 minutes before closing, no photos allowed. At Accademia Bridge, vaporetto: Accademia, tel. 041-522-2247, www.gallerieaccademia.org.

Avoiding Lines: Just 360 people are allowed into the gallery at one time, so you may have to wait. It's most crowded on Monday mornings and whenever it rains; it's least crowded Tue-Sun mornings (before about 10:00) and late afternoons (after about 17:00). While it's possible to book tickets in advance (€1.50/ticket surcharge; either book online at www.gallerieaccademia.org or call 041-520-0345), it's generally not necessary if you avoid the busiest times.

Renovation: This museum seems to be in a constant state of disarray. A major expansion and renovation has been dragging on for years. Paintings come and go, but the museum always contains sumptuous art—the best in Venice. If you can't find one of the items noted below, check in Room 23 at the end, where they tend to shuffle pieces that have been displaced by the renovation.

Visiting the Accademia: The Accademia is the greatest museum anywhere for Venetian Renaissance art and a good overview of painters whose works you'll see all over town. Venetian art is underrated and, I think, misunderstood. It's nowhere near as famous today as the work of the florescent Florentines, but—with historical slices of Venice, ravishing nudes, and very human Madonnas—it's livelier, more colorful, and simply more fun. The Venetian love of luxury shines through in this collection, which starts in the Middle Ages and runs to the 1700s. Look for grand canvases of colorful, spacious settings, peopled with happy locals in extravagant clothes having a great time.

Medieval highlights include elaborate altarpieces and golden-haloed Madonnas, all painted at a time when realism, depth of field, and emotion were considered beside the point. Medieval Venetians, with their close ties to the East, borrowed techniques such as gold-leafing, frontal poses, and "iconic" faces from the religious icons of Byzantium (modern-day Istanbul).

Among early masterpieces of the Renaissance are Mantegna's studly *St. George* and Giorgione's mysterious *Tempest*. As the Renaissance reaches its heights, so do the paintings, such as Titian's magnificent *Presentation of the Virgin*. It's a religious scene, yes, but it's really just an excuse to display secular splendor (Titian was the most famous painter of his day—perhaps even more famous than Michelangelo). Veronese's sumptuous *Feast in the House of Levi* also has an ostensibly religious theme (in the middle, find Jesus eating his final meal)—but it's outdone by the luxury and optimism of Renaissance Venice. Life was a good thing and beauty was to be enjoyed. (Veronese was hauled before the Inquisition for painting such a bawdy Last Supper...so he fine-tuned the title). End your tour with Guardi's and Canaletto's painted "postcards" of the city—landscapes for visitors who lost their hearts to the romance of Venice.

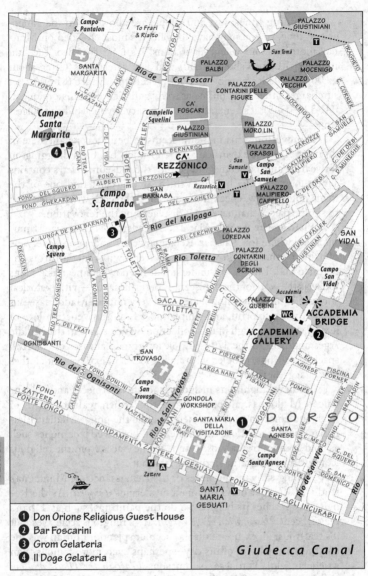

1 Don Orione Religious Guest House
2 Bar Foscarini
3 Grom Gelateria
4 Il Doge Gelateria

▲▲Peggy Guggenheim Collection

The popular museum of far-out art, housed in the American heiress' former retirement palazzo, offers one of Europe's best reviews of the art of the first half of the 20th century. Stroll through styles represented by artists whom Peggy knew personally—Cubism (Picasso, Braque), Surrealism (Dalí, Ernst), Futurism (Boccioni),

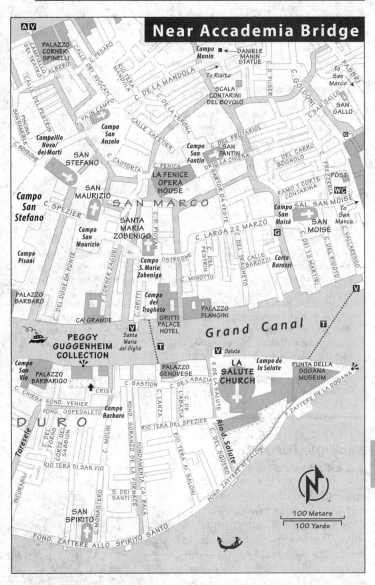

American Abstract Expressionism (Pollock), and a sprinkling of Klee, Calder, and Chagall.

Cost and Hours: €14, usually includes temporary exhibits, audioguide-€7, Wed-Mon 10:00-18:00, closed Tue, pricey café, 5-minute walk from the Accademia Bridge, vaporetto: Accademia or Salute, tel. 041-240-5411, www.guggenheim-venice.it.

Gondola Rides

Riding a gondola is simple, expensive, and one of the great experiences in Europe. Gondoliers hanging out all over town are eager to have you hop in for a ride. While this is a rip-off for some, it's a traditional must for romantics.

The price for a gondola starts at €80 for a 40-minute ride during the day. You can divide the cost—and the romance—among up to six people per boat, but only two get the love seat. Prices jump about 30 percent after 19:00—when it's most romantic and relaxing. Adding a singer and an accordionist will cost an additional €120. If you value budget over romance, you can save money by recruiting fellow travelers to split a gondola. Prices are standard and listed on the gondoliers' association website (go to www.gondolavenezia.it, click on "Using the Gondola," and look under *"charterage"*).

Dozens of gondola stations (*servizio gondole*) are set up along canals all over town. Because your gondolier might offer narration or conversation during your ride, talk with several and choose one you like. You're welcome to review the map and discuss the route. Doing so is also a good way to see if you enjoy the gondolier's personality and language skills. Establish the price, route, and duration of the trip before boarding, enjoy your ride, and pay only when you're finished. While prices are pretty firm, you might find them softer during the day. Most gondoliers honor the official prices, but a few might try to scam you out of some extra euros, particularly by insisting on a tip. (While not required or even expected, if your gondolier does the full 40 minutes and entertains you en route, a 5-10 percent tip is appreciated; if he's

San Polo District

▲▲▲Rialto Bridge

One of the world's most famous bridges, this distinctive and dramatic stone structure crosses the Grand Canal with a single confident span. The arcades along the top of the bridge help reinforce the structure...and offer some enjoyable shopping diversions, as does the **market**

surrounding the bridge (produce market closed Sun, fish market closed Sun-Mon).

▲▲Frari Church (Basilica di Santa Maria Gloriosa dei Frari)

My favorite art experience in Venice is seeing art in the setting for which it was designed—as it is at the Frari Church. The Franciscan "Church of the Brothers" and the art that decorates it are warmed

surly or rushes through the trip, skip it.)

If you've hired musicians and want to hear a Venetian song *(un canto Veneziano)*, try requesting *"Venezia La Luna e Tu."* Ask-

ing to hear *"O Sole Mio"* (which comes from Naples) is like asking a lounge singer in Cleveland to sing "The Eyes of Texas."

If you're in town at night, glide through Venice with your head on someone's shoulder. Follow the moon as it sails past otherwise unseen buildings. Silhouettes gaze down from bridges while window glitter spills onto the black water. You're anonymous in the city of masks, as the rhythmic thrust of your striped-shirted gondolier turns old crows into songbirds. This is extremely relaxing (and, I think, worth the extra cost to experience at night). Suggestion: Put the camera down and make a point for you and your partner to enjoy a threesome with Venice. Warning: Women, beware...while gondoliers can be extremely charming, local women say that anyone who falls for one of these Venetian Romeos "has slices of ham over her eyes."

For cheap gondola thrills during the day, stick to the €2 one-minute ferry ride on a Grand Canal *traghetto*. At night, *vaporetti* are nearly empty, and it's a great time to cruise the Grand Canal on the slow boat #1. Or hang out on a bridge along the gondola route and wave at romantics.

by the spirit of St. Francis. It features the work of three great Renaissance masters: Donatello, Giovanni Bellini, and Titian—each showing worshippers the glory of God in human terms.

Cost and Hours: €3, Mon-Sat 9:00-18:00, Sun 13:00-18:00, last entry 30 minutes before closing, modest dress recommended, no photos, on Campo dei Frari, near San Tomà vaporetto and *traghetto* stops, tel. 041-272-8618, www. basilicadeifrari.it.

Audio Tours: You can rent an audioguide for €2, or you can download a free Rick Steves audio tour of the Frari (see page 50).

Concerts: The church occasionally hosts evening concerts and small theatrical performances (usually around €15, buy tickets at church, for details see the church's website, above).

Visiting the Frari Church: In Do-

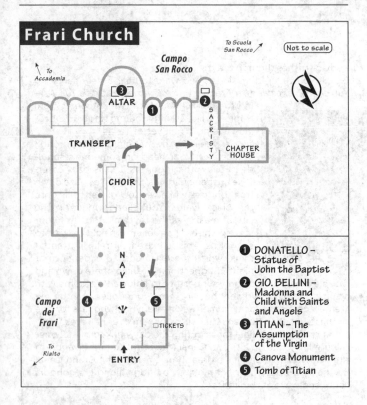

Frari Church

To Scuola San Rocco

(Not to scale)

Campo San Rocco

To Accademia

❸ ALTAR

❶

❷ SACRISTY

TRANSEPT

CHAPTER HOUSE

CHOIR

N A V E

Campo dei Frari

❹

❺

To Rialto

□TICKETS

ENTRY

❶ DONATELLO – Statue of John the Baptist
❷ GIO. BELLINI – Madonna and Child with Saints and Angels
❸ TITIAN – The Assumption of the Virgin
❹ Canova Monument
❺ Tomb of Titian

VENICE

natello's wood statue of **St. John the Baptist** (just to the right of the high altar), the prophet of the desert—dressed in animal skins and nearly starving from his diet of bugs 'n' honey—announces the coming of the Messiah. Donatello was a Florentine working at the dawn of the Renaissance.

Bellini's *Madonna and Child with Saints and Angels* painting (in the sacristy farther to the right) came later, done by a Venetian in a more Venetian style—soft focus without Donatello's harsh realism. While Renaissance humanism demanded Madonnas and saints that were accessible and human, Bellini places them in a physical setting so beautiful that it creates its own mood of serene holiness. The genius of Bellini, perhaps the greatest Venetian painter, is obvious in the pristine clarity, rich colors (notice Mary's clothing), believable depth, and reassuring calm of this three-paneled altarpiece.

Finally, glowing red and gold like a stained-glass window over the high altar, **Titian's *Assumption of the Virgin*** sets the tone of exuberant beauty found in the otherwise sparse church. Titian the Venetian—a student of Bellini—painted steadily for 60 years... you'll see a lot of his art. As stunned apostles look up past the swirl of arms and legs, the complex composition of this painting draws you right to the radiant face of the once-dying, now-triumphant Mary as she joins God in heaven.

Feel comfortable to discreetly freeload off passing tours. For many, these three pieces of art make a visit to the Accademia Gallery unnecessary (or they may whet your appetite for more). Before leaving, flanking the nave just inside the main entrance, check out the Neoclassical pyramid-shaped Canova monument and (opposite that) the grandiose tomb of Titian. Compare the carved marble *Assumption* behind Titian's tombstone portrait with the painted original above the high altar.

St. Mark's Basilica Tour

Among Europe's churches, St. Mark's is peerless. From the outside, it's a riot of domes, columns, and statues, completely unlike the towering Gothic churches of northern Europe or the heavy Baroque of much of the rest of Italy. Inside is a decor of mosaics, colored marbles, and oriental treasures that's rarely seen elsewhere. The Christian symbolism is unfamiliar to Western eyes, done in the style of Byzantine icons and even Islamic designs. Older than most of Europe's churches, it feels like a remnant of a lost world.

This is your best chance in Italy (outside of Ravenna) to glimpse a forgotten and somewhat mysterious part of the human story—Byzantium.

Orientation

Cost: Entering the church is free. Three separate, optional sights inside require paid admission: the Treasury (€3, includes audioguide), Golden Altarpiece (€2), and San Marco Museum—the sight most worth its entry fee (€5, enter museum up stairs from atrium either before or after you tour the church).

Hours: The church and its museums are open Mon-Sat 9:45-17:00, Sun 14:00-17:00 (Sun until 16:00 Nov-March). The interior is brilliantly lit daily from 11:30 to 12:30; although this also coincides with an especially busy time, the additional lighting brings the otherwise dim gold-leaf domes and mosaics to glowing life—it may be worth the extra crowds.

Lines: There's almost always a long line to get into St. Mark's; try going early or late. (It's very smart to check your day bag at the nearby church, which allows you to skip to the front of the line—see "Bag Check," later.) If you wind up in a long line, don't fret; it gives you time to enjoy one of Europe's finest squares as you read ahead in this tour—and besides, the line moves pretty fast. Once inside, it can be packed, and you just have to shuffle through on a one-way system (another good reason to read this tour before you enter).

Dress Code: Modest dress (no bare knees or bare shoulders) is strictly enforced, even for kids. Shorts are OK if they cover the knees.

Theft Alert: St. Mark's Basilica is the most dangerous place in Venice for pickpocketing—inside, it's always a crowded jostle.

Getting There: Signs throughout Venice point to *San Marco*, meaning both the square and the church (vaporetto: San Marco or San Zaccaria).

Information: Guidebooks are sold at the bookstand in the basilica's atrium. Tel. 041-270-8311, www.basilicasanmarco.it.

Tours: Free, hour-long English **tours** (heavy on the mosaics' religious symbolism) are offered many days at 11:00 (meet in atrium, schedule varies, see schedule board just inside entrance). You can download this tour as a free Rick Steves **audio tour** (see page 50).

Length of This Tour: Allow one hour. If you have less time, forgo one (or all) of the basilica's three museums. The most skippable is the Golden Altarpiece (elaborate gold altarpiece near Mark's burial place), followed by the Treasury (fascinating but obscure old objects).

Bag Check (and Skipping the Line): Small purses and shoulder-slung bags are allowed inside, but larger bags and backpacks are not. Check them for free for up to one hour at the nearby church called Ateneo San Basso, 30 yards to the left of the basilica, down narrow Calle San Basso (daily 9:30-17:00). Note that you can't check small bags that would be allowed inside.

Those with a bag to check actually get to skip the line, as do their companions (up to three or so). Leave your bag at Ateneo San Basso and pick up your claim tag. Take your tag to the basilica's tourist entrance. Keep to the left of the railing where the line forms and show your tag to the gatekeeper. He'll let you in, ahead of the line. After touring the church, come back and pick up your bag.

Services: A free WC is inside the San Marco Museum.

Photography: Although officially forbidden inside the church, it is allowed on the balcony of the San Marco Museum, which has great views overlooking the square.

Eating: No food is allowed inside the church. For suggestions nearby, see page 787.

Starring: St. Mark, Byzantium, mosaics, and ancient bronze horses.

The Tour Begins

• *Start outside in the square, far enough back to take in the whole facade. Then zero in on the details.*

St. Mark's Basilica

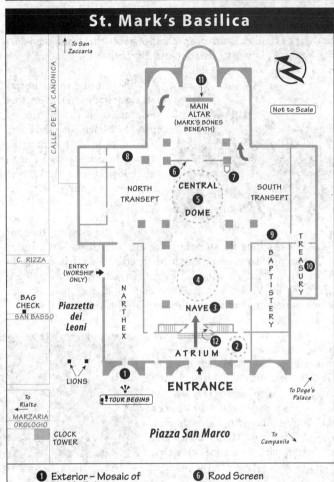

To San Zaccaria

CALLE DE LA CANONICA

Not to Scale

MAIN ALTAR (MARK'S BONES BENEATH) ⑪

⑧ NICOPEIA ICON

⑥ ⑦

NORTH TRANSEPT

CENTRAL DOME ⑤

SOUTH TRANSEPT

⑨

C. RIZZA

ENTRY (WORSHIP ONLY) ➤

N A R T H E X

NAVE ③

④

B A P T I S T E R Y

T R E A S U R Y ⑩

BAG CHECK
SAN BASSO

Piazzetta dei Leoni

⑫

②

A T R I U M

LIONS

①

ENTRANCE

To Doge's Palace

To Rialto

MARZARIA OROLOGIO

⑤ TOUR BEGINS

CLOCK TOWER

Piazza San Marco

To Campanile

VENICE

① Exterior – Mosaic of Mark's Relics
② Atrium – Mosaic of Noah's Ark & the Great Flood
③ Nave – Mosaics & Greek-Cross Floor Plan
④ Pentecost Mosaic
⑤ Central Dome – Ascension Mosaic

⑥ Rood Screen
⑦ Doge's Pulpit
⑧ Nicopeia Icon
⑨ Discovery of Mark Mosaic
⑩ Treasury
⑪ Golden Altarpiece
⑫ Stairs up to Loggia: San Marco Museum & Bronze Horses

❶ Exterior—Mosaic of Mark's Relics

St. Mark's Basilica is a treasure chest of booty that was looted during Venice's glory days. That's most appropriate for a church built on the stolen bones of a saint.

The **mosaic over the far left door** shows the theft that put Venice on the pilgrimage map. Two men (in the center, with crooked staffs) enter the church bearing a coffin with the body of St. Mark, who looks pretty grumpy from the long voyage.

St. Mark was the author of one of the Gospels, the four Bible books telling the story of Jesus' life (Matthew, Mark, Luke, and John). Seven centuries after his death, his holy body was in Muslim-occupied Alexandria, Egypt. In A.D. 828, two visiting merchants of Venice "rescued" the body from the "infidels," hid it in a pork barrel (which was unclean to Muslims), and spirited it away to Venice.

The merchants presented the body—not to a pope or bishop—but to the doge (with white ermine collar, on the right) and his wife, the dogaressa (with entourage, on the left), giving instant status to Venice's budding secular state. They built a church here over Mark's bones and made him the patron saint of the city. You'll see his symbol, the winged lion, all over Venice.

The original church burned down in A.D. 976. Today's structure was begun in 1063. The mosaic, from 1260, shows that the church hasn't changed much since then—you can see the onion domes and famous bronze horses on the balcony.

The St. Mark's you see today, mostly from the 11th century, was modeled after a great fourth-century church in Constantinople (Istanbul), the Church of the Holy Apostles (now long gone). Venice needed roots. By building a retro church, the city could imply that it had been around for longer than it actually had been. (Throughout European history, upstarts loved to fake deep roots this way. Germany embraced mystic, medieval lore as it emerged as a modern nation in the 19th century, England cooked up the King Arthur legend, and so on.)

In subsequent centuries, the church was encrusted with materials looted from buildings throughout the Venetian empire (see sidebar on page 768). Their prize booty was the four bronze horses that adorn the balcony, stolen from Constantinople during the Fourth Crusade (these are copies, as the originals are housed inside the church museum); the atrium you're about to enter was added on to the church as their pedestal. Later, it was decorated with a mish-mash of plundered columns. The architectural style of St. Mark's has been called "Early Ransack."

• *Enter the atrium (entrance hall) of the basilica, through a sixth-century, bronze-paneled Byzantine door—which likely once swung in Constantinople's Hagia Sophia church. Immediately after being admitted by the dress-code guard, look up and to the right into an archway decorated with fine mosaics.*

❷ Atrium—Mosaic of Noah's Ark and the Great Flood

St. Mark's famous mosaics, with their picture symbols, were easily understood in medieval times, even by illiterate masses. Today's literate masses have trouble reading them, so let's practice on these, some of the oldest (13th century), finest, and most accessible mosaics in the church.

In the scene to the right of the entry door, Noah and sons are sawing logs to build a boat. Venetians—who were great ship builders—related to the story of Noah and the Ark. At its peak, Venice's Arsenale warship-building plant employed several thousand.

Below that are three scenes of Noah putting all species of animals into the Ark, two by two. (Who's at the head of the line?

Lions.) Across the arch, the Flood hits in full force, drowning the wicked. Noah sends out a dove twice to see whether there's any dry land where he can dock. He finds it, leaves the Ark with a gorgeous rainbow overhead, and offers a sacrifice of thanks to God. Easy, huh?

Venture past Noah under the Creation Dome (if it's not blocked off), which tells the entire story of Genesis, including Adam and Eve and the original sin. In a scene-by-scene narration, we see Adam lonely in the garden, the creation of Eve, the happy couple in Eden, and then trouble: from apple to fig leaf to banishment.

• *Now that our medieval literacy rate has risen, rejoin the slow flow*

VENICE

of people. Notice the entrance to the San Marco Museum (Loggia dei Cavalli). You could follow the rest of this tour in a number of ways: For example, you can visit the San Marco Museum now or save it until after you've toured the main part of the church. Survey the lay of the (holy) land and consider the flow of the masses.

Assuming you're following the tour as written, climb seven steps, pass through the doorway, and enter the nave. Loiter somewhere just inside the door (crowd permitting) and let your eyes adjust.

❸ The Nave—Mosaics and Greek-Cross Floor Plan

The initial effect is dark and unimpressive (unless they've got the floodlights on). But as your pupils slowly unclench, notice that the  entire upper part is decorated in mosaic—nearly 5,000 square yards (imagine paving a football field with contact lenses). These golden mosaics are in the Byzantine style, though many were designed by artists from the Italian Renaissance and later. The often-overlooked lower walls are covered with green-, yellow-, purple-, and rose-colored marble slabs, cut to expose the grain, and laid out in geometric patterns. Even the floor is mosaic, with mostly geometrical designs. It rolls like the sea. Venice is sinking and shifting, creating these cresting waves of stone.

The church is laid out with four equal arms, topped with domes, radiating out from the center to form a Greek cross (+). Those familiar with Eastern Orthodox churches will find familiar elements in St. Mark's: a central floor plan, domes, mosaics, and iconic images of Mary and Christ as Pantocrator—ruler of all things. As your eyes adjust, the mosaics start to give off a "mystical, golden luminosity," the atmosphere of the Byzantine heaven. The air itself seems almost visible, like a cloud of incense. It's a subtle effect, one that grows on you as the filtered light changes. There are more beautiful, bigger, more overwhelming, and even holier churches, but none is as stately.

• *Find the chandelier near the entrance doorway (in the shape of a Greek cross cathedral space station), and run your eyes up the support chain to the dome above.*

❹ Pentecost Mosaic

In a golden heaven, the dove of the Holy Spirit shoots out a pinwheel of spiritual lasers, igniting tongues of fire on the heads of the 12 apostles below, giving them the ability to speak other lan-

guages without a Rick Steves phrase book. You'd think they'd be amazed, but their expressions are as solemn as...icons. One of the oldest mosaics in the church (c. 1125), it has distinct "Byzantine" features: a gold background and apostles with halos, solemn faces, almond eyes, delicate blessing hands, and rumpled robes, all facing forward.

This is art from a society still touchy about the Bible's commandment against making "graven images" of holy things. Byzantium had recently emerged from two centuries of Iconoclasm, in which statues and paintings were broken and burned as sinful "false gods." The Byzantine style emphasizes otherworldliness rather than literal human detail.

• *Shuffle along with the crowds up to the central dome.*

❺ Central Dome—Ascension Mosaic

Gape upward to the very heart of the church. Christ—having lived his miraculous life and having been crucified for man's sins—ascends into the starry sky on a rainbow. He raises his right hand and blesses the universe. This isn't the dead, crucified, mortal Jesus featured in most churches, but a powerful, resurrected God, the ruler of all.

Christ's blessing radiates, rippling down to the ring of white-robed apostles below. They stand amid the trees of the Mount of Olives, waving good-bye as Christ ascends. Mary is with them, wearing blue with golden Greek crosses on each shoulder and looking ready to play patty-cake. From these saints, goodness descends, creating the Virtues that ring the base of the dome between the windows. In Byzantine churches, the window-lit dome represented heaven, while the dark church below represented earth—a microcosm of the hierarchical universe.

Beneath the dome at the four corners, the four Gospel writers ("Matev," "Marc," "Luca," and "Ioh") thoughtfully scribble down the heavenly events. This wisdom flows down like water from the symbolic Four Rivers below them, spreading through the church's four equal arms (the "four corners" of the world), and baptizing the congregation with God's love. The church building is a series of perfect circles within perfect squares—the cosmic order—with Christ in the center solemnly blessing us. God's in his heaven, saints are on earth, and all's right with the world.

Under the Ascension Dome—The Church as Theater

Look around at the church's furniture and imagine a service here.

VENICE

The ❻ **rood screen,** topped with 14 saints, separates the congregation from the high altar, heightening the "mystery" of the Mass. The ❼ **pulpit on the right** was reserved for the doge, who led prayers and made important announcements.

The Venetian church service is a theatrical multimedia spectacle, combining words (prayers, biblical passages, Latin and Greek phrases), music (chants, a choir, organ, horns, strings), images (mosaics telling Bible stories), costumes and props (priests' robes, golden reliquaries, candles, incense), set design (the mosaics, rood screen, Golden Altarpiece), and even stage direction (processionals through the crowd, priests' motions, standing, sitting, kneeling, crossing yourself). The symmetrical church is itself part of the set design. The Greek-cross floor plan symbolizes perfection, rather than the more common Latin cross of the crucifixion (emphasizing man's sinfulness). Coincidentally or not, the first modern opera—also a multimedia theatrical experience—was written by St. Mark's *maestro di cappella,* Claudio Monteverdi (1567-1643).

North Transept

In the north transept (the arm of the church to the left of the altar), today's Venetians pray to a painted wooden icon of Mary and baby Jesus known as ❽ **Nicopeia,** or "Our Lady of Victory" (on the east wall of the north transept, it's a small painting crusted over with a big stone canopy). In its day, this was the ultimate trophy—the actual icon used to protect the Byzantine army in war, looted by the Crusaders. Supposedly painted by the evangelist Luke, it was once enameled with bright paint and precious stones, and Mary was adorned with a crown and necklace of gold and jewels (now on display in the Treasury). Now the protector of Venetians, this Madonna has helped the city persevere through plagues, wars, and crucial soccer games.

• *In the south transept (to the right of main altar), find the dim mosaic high up on the wall above the entrance to the treasury.*

❾ Discovery of Mark Mosaic

This mosaic isn't a biblical scene; it depicts the miraculous event that capped the construction of the present church.

It's 1094, the church is nearly complete (see the domes shown in cutaway fashion), and they're all set to re-inter Mark's bones under the new altar. There's just one problem: During the decades of construction, they forgot where they'd stored his body!

VENICE

So (in the left half of the mosaic), all of Venice gathers inside the church to bow down and pray for help finding the bones. The doge (from the Latin *dux,* meaning leader) leads them. Soon after (the right  half), the patriarch (far right) is inspired to look inside a hollow column where he finds the relics. Everyone turns and applauds, including the womenfolk (left side of scene), who stream in from the upper-floor galleries. The relics were soon placed under the altar in a ceremony that inaugurated the current structure.

The door under the rose window, with the green curtain, leads directly from the Doge's Palace. On important occasions, the doge entered the church through here, ascended the steps of his pulpit, and addressed the people.

St. Mark's Three Museums

Inside the church are three sights, each requiring a separate admission. These provide an easy way to experience the richness of Byzantium. The San Marco Museum also gives you access to great views over the inside of the church, as well as to St. Mark's Square outside.

⑩ Treasury (Tesoro)

• *The two-room Treasury is in the south transept. The admission fee includes an audioguide.*

If you're not into metalworking or religious objects, you may find the Treasury's cramped collection somewhat underwhelming, but the objects become more interesting when you consider their illustrious past. These rooms hold an amazing collection of precious items, most of them stolen from Constantinople: Byzantine chalices, silver reliquaries, monstrous monstrances (for displaying the Communion wafer), and icons done in gold, silver, enamels, gems, and semiprecious stones. These pieces, highlighting finely worked and translucent material, are the ones that show up in art textbooks as the finest surviving Byzantine treasures (assuaging any Venetian guilt). As Venice thought of itself as the granddaughter of Rome and the daughter of Byzantium, Venetians consider these treasures not stolen, but inherited—rock crystal, jasper, alabaster, and marble that was rightfully theirs. Less sophisticated thieves would have smelted these pieces, but the Venetians safely stored them here for posterity.

Some of the items represent the fruits of labor by different civilizations over a thousand-year period. For example, an ancient

Byzantium, the Fourth Crusade, and Venice

The Byzantine Empire was the eastern half of the ancient Roman Empire that *didn't* "fall" in A.D. 476. It remained Christian, Greek-speaking, and enlightened for another thousand years.

In A.D. 330, Constantine, the first Christian emperor, moved the Roman Empire's capital to the newly expanded city of Byzantium, which he humbly renamed Constantinople. With him went Rome's best and brightest. When the city of Rome decayed and fell, plunging Western Europe into its "Dark Ages," Constantinople lived on as the greatest city in Europe.

Venice had strong ties with Byzantium from its earliest days. In the sixth century, Byzantine Emperor Justinian invaded northern Italy, briefly reuniting East and West, and making Ravenna his regional capital. In 800, Venetians asked the emperor in Constantinople to protect them from Charlemagne's marauding Franks.

Soon Venetian merchants were granted trading rights to Byzantine ports in the Adriatic and eastern Mediterranean. They traded raw materials from Western Europe for luxury goods from the East. By the 10th century, about 10,000 Venetian merchants lived and worked in Constantinople. Meanwhile, relations between Byzantine Christians and Roman Catholics were souring across Europe over religious grounds—and because Constantinople's local merchants felt crowded out by the powerful Venetians, the corporate titans of the day. In 1171, the Byzantine emperor expelled Venetian merchants from the city; after a decade of conflict, the entire Roman Catholic population—about 60,000 people—was either slaughtered or expelled from Constantinople.

Powerful, rich Venice wasn't about to stand for it—the Venetians had virtually no economy without trade. Two decades later, they saw their chance: The pope was organizing a Crusade to "save" the Holy Land from Muslim influence. Venice offered her ships to transport more than 30,000 Crusaders. They set out bound for Jerusalem...but the ships, led by the Venetian doge, diverted to Constantinople. The Crusaders sacked the Byzantine capital and occupied it from 1204 to 1261, turning the city into a

rock-crystal chalice made by the Romans might have been decorated centuries later with Byzantine enamels and then finished still later with gold filigree by Venetian goldsmiths. This is marvelous handiwork, but all the more marvelous for having been done when Western Europe was still mired in mud.

In the **relics/sanctuary room,** the glass case over the glowing alabaster altar contains elaborate gold-and-glass reliquaries holding

quarry—one wide open for plunder. During that period, any ship traveling from Constantinople to Venice was required to bring with it a souvenir for the Venetian Republic. Eventually the riches of Constantinople ended up in Venice—much of it here, in St. Mark's Basilica.

You can still see much of what the Venetians carried home: the bronze horses, bronze doors of Hagia Sophia, Golden Altarpiece enamels, the Treasury's treasures, the Nicopeia icon, and much of the marble that now covers the (brick) church. A good portion of the artistic riches adorning the church and filling its treasury was 700 years old when it arrived here...800 years ago.

The Venetians were clearly thieves, albeit thieves with good taste. While you could say the treasures belong in Turkey today, a good Venetian would argue that had they not "rescued" it, much of it (especially anything made from precious metal) never would have survived the centuries.

After the Fourth Crusade, Venice rose while the Byzantine Empire faded. Then both civilizations nose-dived when Constantinople finally fell to the Ottomans in 1453, severely damaging Venice's trading empire and ending Byzantium entirely. Constantinople, however, soon began to thrive again—once a bustling Christian city of a thousand churches, it flourished again as the newly Islamic city of Istanbul.

relics of Jesus' Passion—his torture and execution. The reliquary showing Christ being whipped (from 1125) holds a stone from the column he was tied to. You may scoff, but of Europe's many "Pieces of the True Cross" and "Crown of Thorns" relics, these have at least some claim of authenticity. Legend has it that Christ's possessions were gathered up in the fourth century by Constantine's mother and taken to Constantinople. During the Crusade heist of 1204,

Venetians brought them here. They've been paraded through the city every Good Friday for 800 years.

Back by the room's entrance is a glass reliquary with the bones of Doge Orseolo (r. 976-978), who built the church that preceded the current structure. Another contains the bones of St. George, legendary dragon slayer.

⓫ Golden Altarpiece (Pala d'Oro)

• *The Golden Altarpiece is located behind the main altar. Join the line to pay, and then go through the turnstile.*

Under the green marble canopy, supported by four intricately carved alabaster columns, sits the **high altar**. Inside the altar

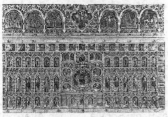

is an urn (not visible) with the mortal remains of Mark, the Gospel writer. (Look through the grate of the altar to read *Corpus Divi Marci Evangelistae,* or "Body of the Evangelist Mark.") He rests in peace, as an angel had promised him. Shh.

The **Golden Altarpiece** itself is a stunning golden wall made of 250 blue-backed enamels with religious scenes, all set in a gold frame and studded with 15 hefty rubies, 300 emeralds, 1,500 pearls, and assorted sapphires, amethysts, and topaz. The Byzantine-made enamels were part of the Venetians' plunder of 1204, subsequently pieced together by Byzantine craftsmen specifically for St. Mark's high altar. It's a bit much to take in all at once, but get up close and find several details you might recognize: Jesus as Ruler of the Cosmos sits on a golden throne; Old Testament prophets show off the books of the Bible they've written; Mark's story ends (in the bottom right panel) with the two Venetian merchants returning by ship, carrying his coffin here to be laid to rest.

Byzantium excelled in the art of *cloisonné* enameling. This kind of craftsmanship—and the social infrastructure that could afford it—made Byzantium seem like an enchanted world during Europe's dim Middle Ages.

⓬ San Marco Museum (Museo di San Marco)—Mosaics, Bronze Horses, View of the Piazza, and More

• *The staircase up to the museum is in the atrium near the main entrance. The sign says* Loggia dei Cavalli, Museo. *Ascend the steps, buy your ticket, and enter.*

In the first room, you'll see several models of the church at various stages of its history. Notice how the original domes, once squat, were made taller in the 13th century, leaving today's church with a dome-within-a-dome structure. Notice also the historic drawings here.

Next are the museum's three highlights: view of the interior (right), view of the square (out the door to the left), and bronze horses (directly ahead). Belly up to the stone balustrade (on the right) to survey the interior.

View of Church Interior

Scan the church, with its thousands of square meters of mosaics, then take a closer look at the Pentecost Mosaic (first dome above you, described on page 764). The unique design at the very top signifies the Trinity: throne (God), Gospels (Christ), and dove (Holy Spirit). The couples below the ring of apostles are the people of the world (I can find Judaea, Cappadocia, and Asia), who, despite their different languages, still understood the Spirit's message.

Appreciate the patterns of the mosaic floor—one of the finest in Italy—that covers the floor like a Persian carpet.

• *From here, the museum loops you along the left gallery to the far (altar) end of the church, then back to the bronze horses. Along the way, you'll see fragments of the mosaics that once hung in the church (many are accompanied by small photos that show where the fragment used to fit into a larger scene).*

Continuing on, down a set of stairs, you'll see other artwork and catch glimpses of the interior of the church from the north transept. Here you get a close-up view of the Tree of Jesse mosaic, showing Jesus' distant ancestor at the root and his mom at the top. This mosaic is from 1540, during the High Renaissance—it's much more modern than those decorating the domes, which date mostly from the 1200s. Continue on to the Sala dei Banchetti (WCs near the room's entrance).

Sala dei Banchetti

This large, ornate room—once the doge's banquet hall—is filled with religious objects, tapestries, and carpets that once adorned the church, Burano-made lace vestments, illuminated music manuscripts from the 16th century, a doge's throne, and much more. In the center of the hall stands the most prestigious artwork here, the *Pala Feriale*, by Paolo Veneziano (1345). The top row shows seven saints (including crucified Christ); below are seven episodes in Mark's life.

• *Now double back toward the museum entrance, through displays of stone fragments from the church, finally arriving at...*

The Bronze Horses (La Quadriga)

Stepping lively in pairs and with smiles on their faces, they exude energy and exuberance. Art historians don't know how old they are—they could be from ancient Greece (fourth century B.C.)

or from ancient Rome, during its Fall (fourth century A.D.). Professor Carbon Fourteen says they're from around 175 B.C. Originally, the horses pulled a chariot driven by an emperor, *Ben-Hur* style. Originally gilded, these bronze statues still have some streaks of gold. Long gone are the ruby pupils that gave the horses the original case of "red eye."

Megalomaniacs through the ages have coveted these horses not only for their artistic value, but because they symbolize Apollo, the Greco-Roman god of the sun...and of secular power. Legend says they were made in the time of Alexander the Great, then taken by Nero to Rome. Constantine took them to his new capital in Constantinople to adorn the chariot racecourse. The Venetians then stole them from their fellow Christians when they sacked the city in 1204 and brought them here to St. Mark's in 1255. The doge spoke to his people while standing between the horses when they graced the balcony atop the church's facade (where the copies—which you'll see next—stand today).

What goes around comes around, and Napoleon came around and took the horses when he conquered Venice in 1797. They stood atop a triumphal arch in Paris until Napoleon's empire was "blown-aparte" and they were returned to their "rightful" home. Their expressive faces seem to say, "Oh boy, Wilbur, have we done some travelin'."

The horses were again removed from their spot when they were attacked by their most dangerous enemy yet—modern man. The threat of oxidation from pollution sent them galloping for cover inside the church in 1975.

• *The visit ends outside on the balcony overlooking St. Mark's Square.*

The Loggia and View of St. Mark's Square

You'll be drawn repeatedly to the viewpoint of the square, but remember to look at the facade to see how cleverly all the looted architectural elements blend together. Ramble among the statues of wa-

ter-bearing slaves that serve as drain spouts. The horses are modern copies (note the 1978 date on the hoof of the horse to the right).

Be a doge, and stand between the bronze horses overlooking St. Mark's Square. Under the gilded lion of St. Mark, in front of the four great Evangelists (who once stood atop the columns), and flanked—like Apollo—by the four glorious horses, he inspired the Venetians in the square below to great things.

Admire the mesmerizing, commanding view of the center of this city, which so long ago was Europe's only superpower, and today is just a small town with a big history—one that's filled with tourists.

Shopping in Venice

In many areas, Venice feels like one big open-air shopping mall. Trinket stands tuck themselves between internationally famous designer and hole-in-the-wall artisan shops. While there are plenty of temptations, remember: Anything not made locally is brought in by boat—and therefore generally more expensive than elsewhere in Italy. And, given Venice's tourist cachet, even items made here are priced at a premium. The shops near St. Mark's Square charge the most.

In touristy areas, shops are typically open from 9:00 to 19:30 (sometimes with a break from about 13:00 until 15:00 or 16:00), and more stores are open on Sunday here than in the rest of the country. If you're buying a substantial amount from nearly any shop, bargain—it's accepted and almost expected. Offer less and offer to pay cash; merchants are very conscious of the bite taken by credit-card companies.

For shop locations, see the map on page 774. For information on VAT refunds and customs regulations, see page 135.

Where to Shop

San Marco

The San Marco area—between the back of St. Mark's Square and the Grand Canal—has Venice's highest concentration of shops. The streets closest to St. Mark's Square, and those between St. Mark's and the Rialto Bridge, are also the highest-trafficked, the highest-rent, and the highest-priced. This is where you'll see all of the big international names; it seems you can't be a fashion-world staple until you have a branch in San Marco.

Between St. Mark's Square and Rialto: This predictable Venetian shopping stretch starts on St. Mark's, where you can walk the entire colonnaded square past pricey jewelry, glass, lace, and clothing stores. **Galleria San Marco** (described later, under "Venetian Glass"), right on the square, sells glass items and does glassblowing demonstrations, while **Il Merletto**, just north of the square, has lace goods. **Daniela Ghezzo,** a few blocks northwest of the square, sells handmade shoes (tucked in an adorably cluttered hole-in-the-wall on Calle dei Fuseri, San Marco 4365, www.danielaghezzo.it).

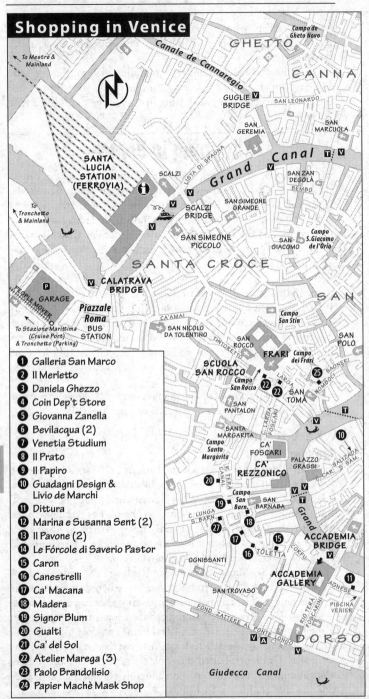

Shopping in Venice

1. Galleria San Marco
2. Il Merletto
3. Daniela Ghezzo
4. Coin Dep't Store
5. Giovanna Zanella
6. Bevilacqua (2)
7. Venetia Studium
8. Il Prato
9. Il Papiro
10. Guadagni Design & Livio de Marchi
11. Dittura
12. Marina e Susanna Sent (2)
13. Il Pavone (2)
14. Le Fórcole di Saverio Pastor
15. Caron
16. Canestrelli
17. Ca' Macana
18. Madera
19. Signor Blum
20. Gualti
21. Ca' del Sol
22. Atelier Marega (3)
23. Paolo Brandolisio
24. Papier Machè Mask Shop

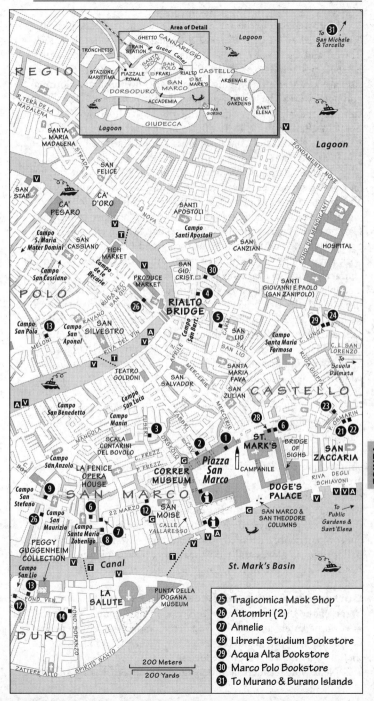

25 Tragicomica Mask Shop
26 Attombri (2)
27 Annelie
28 Libreria Studium Bookstore
29 Acqua Alta Bookstore
30 Marco Polo Bookstore
31 To Murano & Burano Islands

VENICE

The Mercerie is the main street between St. Mark's Square (also labeled as "Marzarie"; leave the square from under the Clock Tower) and the Rialto, noted for its fancy windows and designer labels. You'll wind up at Rialto Bridge, where the streets on either side are a cancan of shopping temptations. For ordinary clothing and housewares, the best all-purpose department store is the **Coin** store on the St. Mark's Square side of the Rialto Bridge (Mon-Sat 9:30-19:30, Sun 11:00-19:30; from the bridge, head north). For handmade shoes, check out **Giovanna Zanella,** just east of the Rialto (Castello 5641, www.giovannazanella.it).

West of St. Mark's Square: A half-block detour out the far end of the square leads to several high-fashion shops along Calle Vallaresso (southwest of St. Mark's, away from Rialto). For a somewhat lower-roller ambience, the streets and bridges connecting Campo Santa Maria Zobenigo, Campo San Maurizio, and Campo San Stefano (basically parallel to the Grand Canal) are scattered with a few shops that, while not quite "untouristy," are a bit more characteristic and affordable. Interesting places along here include a couple of textile shops: **Bevilacqua** (at San Marco 2520 and behind St. Mark's Basilica at San Marco 337b) and **Venetia Studium** (at San Marco 2445). For fine stationery, check out **Il Prato,** which specializes in vividly bound books, trays, and glass (near Campo Santa Maria Zobenigo, on Calle de le Ostreghe, San Marco 2456, www.ilpratovenezia.com), and **Il Papiro** (near Campo San Maurizio, on Calle del Piovan, San Marco 2764, www.ilpapirofirenze.it).

A bit farther west, you'll find a fascinating smattering of mostly cutting-edge art boutiques, in the zone north and west of Campo San Stefano, toward the Grand Canal. From that square, head west on Calle Botteghe, which becomes Crosera before it runs into the skinny square called Salizada San Samuele. Fronting this square are a half-dozen low-profile art galleries worth a browse. Halfway down the square, **Guadagni Design** sells sleek and unique housewares (at #3336, www.guadagnidesign.it). At the bottom, peek into the shop of **Livio de Marchi,** who specializes in outlandish and/or remarkably detailed wood-carvings—from handbags and ballet shoes to gloves and teddy bears to a bizarre phallus-medusa head (at #3157a, www.liviodemarchi.com).

Dorsoduro, Across the Accademia Bridge

Some of the best shopping in Venice is in Dorsoduro. While the area immediately around the Accademia and Peggy Guggenheim Collection is crowded and can feel tacky, within a few blocks things mellow out and feel a bit more local.

Near the Accademia and Guggenheim: For a strip of very

touristy (yet still worthwhile) shops—mostly selling glass and/or jewelry with an artistic bent—browse the busy streets connecting those two museums (Calle Nova Sant'Agnese, Piscina del Forner, and Fondamenta Venier). Interesting shops along here are the **Dittura** slipper shop (at Dorsoduro 871), the **Marina e Susanna Sent** jewelry gallery (described later), and the **Il Pavone** paper shop (at Dorsoduro 721 and at San Polo 1478, near the Rialto Bridge).

Nearby, one canal east of the Guggenheim Collection, detour south along Fondamenta Soranzo to reach **Le Fórcole di Saverio Pastor**, the workshop of a local craftsman who carves the uniquely curvy Venetian oarlocks called *fórcole*. You can watch Saverio work, and you can buy a scale model (closed Sun and usually Sat, Fondamenta Soranzo de la Fornace, Dorsoduro 341, www.forcole.com).

Near Campo San Barnaba: The area around Campo San Barnaba, about a 10-minute walk northwest of the Accademia, is a great place to window-shop, as it strikes the right balance between tourist-friendly and local. Crossing the canal west of the Accademia, angle up the street called La Toletta, passing several interesting shops: **Caron** handmade glass jewelry (open daily, at #1195); **Canestrelli,** where soft-spoken Stefano Coluccio makes unique convex mirrors in circular frames, like the ones in old paintings (at #1173, www.venicemirrors.com); and **Ca' Macana,** a mask shop that proudly designed masks for Stanley Kubrick's *Eyes Wide Shut* (they also offer mask-painting classes—arrange in advance; open daily, at #3172, www.camacana.com). The street leads straight to the delightful Campo San Barnaba.

Right on the square are two of my favorite shops. Next to Grom *gelateria* is **Madera,** a wonderful boutique that collects beautiful and practical items from around the world, with an emphasis on high-quality materials and smart design. It injects a bit of slick modernity to ye olde Venice (closed Sun, right on Campo San Barnaba at #2762, www.maderavenezia.it). To see more, check out their bigger showroom, just a few short blocks down Calle Lunga San Barnaba. At the bottom corner of the square, overlooking the canal, is **Signor Blum,** which makes and sells delightfully colorful wood-carved letters, symbols, mobiles, and scenes of Venice—fun for kids and grown-ups (open daily, at #2840, www.signorblum.com).

From here, consider crossing the bridge and continuing up Rio Terà Canal one block to the vast and lively Campo Santa Margarita. Along the way you'll pass **Gualti** boutique on the left (at #3111), worth a peek for its cutting-edge-contemporary accessories and shoes. After shopping 'til you drop, reward yourself with a gelato from **Il Doge,** located on the square (described on page 790). Popular souvenirs and gifts include Murano glass, Burano lace (fun lace umbrellas for little girls), Carnevale masks (fine shops and artisans all over town), art reproductions (posters, postcards, and books), prints of Venetian scenes, traditional stationery (pens and marbled paper products of all kinds), calendars with Venetian scenes (and sexy gondoliers), silk ties, scarves, and plenty of goofy knickknacks (Titian mouse pads, gondolier T-shirts, and little plastic gondola condom holders). But beyond the typical souvenirs, Venice has a wealth of unique and locally made items, such as artisan jewelry, handcrafted fabrics, and made-to-order shoes. Note that many shops selling artisan goods can be quite expensive. But they are still atmospheric, engaging places to window-shop and daydream.

Venetian Glass

Popular Venetian glass is available in many forms: vases, tea sets, decanters, glasses, jewelry, lamps, mod sculptures (such as solid-

glass aquariums), and on and on. Shops will ship it home for you, but you're likely to pay as much or more for the shipping as you are for the item(s), and you may have to pay duty on larger purchases. Make sure the shop insures their merchandise *(assicurazione)*, or you're out of luck if it breaks. If your item arrives broken and it has been insured, take a photo of the pieces, send it to the shop, and they'll replace it for free.

Some visitors feel that because they're in Venice, they ought to grab the opportunity to buy glass. Remember that you can buy fine glass back home, too (Venice stopped forbidding its glassblowers from leaving the republic a few centuries ago)—and under less time pressure.

Also be aware that much of the cheap glass you'll see in Venice is imported (a sore point for local vendors dealing in the more expensive, authentic stuff). Venetian glass producers, up in arms about the influx of Chinese glass, claim that a big percentage of the glass tourists buy is actually not Venetian. Genuine Venetian glass comes with the Murano seal.

If you'd like to watch a quick glassblowing demonstration, try **Galleria San Marco,** a tour-group staple on St. Mark's Square at #139, which offers great demos every few minutes. They let individual travelers flashing this book sneak in with tour groups to see the show (and sales pitch). If you buy anything, show this book and they'll take 20 percent off the listed price. The gallery faces the square behind the orchestra nearest to the church; come to the

Mask Making

In the 1700s, when Venice was Europe's party town, masks were popular—sometimes even mandatory—to preserve the  anonymity of visiting nobles doing things forbidden back home. At Carnevale (the weeks-long Mardi Gras leading up to Lent), everyone wore masks. The most popular were based on characters from the low-brow comedic theater called commedia dell'arte. We all know Harlequin (simple, Lone Ranger-type masks), but there were also long-nosed masks for the hypocritical plague doctor, pretty Columbina masks, and so on.

Masks are made with the simple technique of papier-mâché. You make a mold of clay, smear it with Vaseline (to make it easy to remove the finished mask), then create the mask by draping layers of paper and glue atop the clay mold.

You'll see mask shops all over town. Just behind St. Mark's Square, on a quiet canal just inland from the Church of San Zaccaria (on Fondamenta de l'Osmarin), is a corner with two fascinating mask and costume shops: **Ca' del Sol** at #4964 (two showrooms connected by a little bridge) and **Atelier Marega** at #4968 (two other locations near the Frari Church on Campo San Rocco at #3046 and around the corner on Calle Larga at #2940b). After you cross the bridge to the second Ca' del Sol shop, head to the next door farther on to the wood-carving shop of **Paolo Brandolisio.**

Just a bit north, a block off Campo Santa Maria Formosa (next to Acqua Alta bookstore—see map on page 774), is the **Papier Machè Mask Shop,** where Stefano Gottardo proudly sells only masks made in his store. The masks are both traditional and modern, and you're welcome to watch the artisans at work (daily 9:00-19:30, at the end of Calle Lunga Santa Maria Formosa, Castello 5174b, tel. 041-522-9995).

Out near the Frari Church, the **Tragicomica Mask Shop** is highly respected and likely to have artisans at work; the workshop is open to customers who've bought a mask (daily 10:00-19:00, 200 yards past Church of San Polo on Calle dei Nomboli at #2800, tel. 041-721-102). Another option is **Ca' Macana,** near Campo San Barnaba (for details, see "Dorsoduro, Across the Accademia Bridge," earlier).

door at #139, go through the shop, and climb the stairs (daily 9:00-18:00, tel. 041-271-8671, info@galleriasanmarco.it, manager Marino Busetto).

If you're serious about glass, visit the island of **Murano,** its glass museum, and many shops (see details in "Venice at a Glance" sidebar, page 740). You'll find greater variety on Murano, but prices are usually the same as in Venice.

Jewelry

Jewelers abound in Venice. Not surprisingly, glass jewelry and beadwork are particularly popular—you'll see references to *perle de Venezia* or *perle veneziane*, colorfully speckled glass beads. In addition to buying premade pieces, at many shops you can select the beads you like to create your own masterpiece. As with other glass, you can assume that cheap beads are imported, not local.

Because jewelry is such a subjective taste, I recommend that you browse around to find the styles and prices that suit you. But if you need help, here are some places to start: Several jewelers can be found under the arcades (behind the chintzy souvenir stands) on the west (market) side of the Rialto Bridge, including **Attombri,** selling pieces with a classic, filigree-plus-beads look (Sotoportego dei Orafi, San Polo 74; another location in San Marco on Campo San Maurizio, San Marco 2668a; www.attombri.com). **Marina e Susanna Sent** sells contemporary designs in two upscale-feeling showrooms (near St. Mark's next to Campo San Moisè at San Marco 2090, and near the Accademia on Campo San Vio at Dorsoduro 669, www.marinaesusannasent.com).

Lace

Lace, made from cotton or silk thread, is another Venetian specialty. Prior to the Industrial Revolution, the city was a major trading point for luxury fabrics like lace, silk, and satin. Venice was a European fashion hot spot, and Venetian Burano lace adorned the clothing of royalty. Venice is particularly known for "needle lace," with intricate flowers, leaves, and curling stems, which was used for cuffs, gowns, and frilly collars.

In recent decades the lace industry has been on life support as cheap imitations flood the market. But lately Venetians are attempting to revive the art. Today, popular lace goods include tablecloths, doilies, clothing, and even lace pictures suitable for framing.

But buyer beware. Note that much of the lace sold in Venice (and on the island of Burano) is cheap, machine-made, and imported—so stick to reputable shops to ensure that you are buying an authentic product.

The **Il Merletto** shop just off the northwest corner of St. Mark's Square is the most convenient. **Annelie,** in the Dorso-

Beware of Cheap Knockoff Bags

Along Venice's many shopping streets, you'll notice fly-by-night street vendors selling knockoffs of famous designer handbags (Louis Vuitton, Gucci, etc.). These vendors are willing to bargain. Beware: If you're caught purchasing fakes, you could get hit with a fine. Legitimate manufacturers are raising a stink about these street merchants, and the government is trying to rid the city of them. Caught up in a city-wide game of cat and mouse (with the police playing the role of cat), the vendors spend as much time lurking in alleys waiting for the coast to clear as they do selling. Authorities, frustrated in their attempts to actually arrest the merchants, have made it illegal to buy counterfeit items. Their hope: The threat of a huge fine will scare potential customers away—so unlicensed merchants will be driven out of business and off the streets.

duro district, is another well-respected shop (on Calle Lunga San Barnaba, Dorsoduro 2748). Lace lovers will find the journey out to Burano worthwhile. Here you'll find many shops (such as **Merletti d'arte dalla Lidia**) and the **Lace Museum** (see details in "Venice at a Glance" sidebar, page 740).

Nightlife in Venice

VENICE

Some cruises spend an overnight in Venice; many others begin or end here. If your schedule allows, try to experience Venice after dark. Gondolas cost more, but are worth the extra expense (see page 756).

Venice has a busy schedule of events, church concerts, festivals, and entertainment. Check at the TI or the TI's website (www.turismovenezia.it) for listings. The free monthly *Un Ospite di Venezia* lists all the latest happenings in English (free at fancy hotels, or check www.unospitedivenezia.it).

Performances

Baroque Concerts

Venice is a city of the powdered-wig Baroque era. For about €25, you can take your pick of traditional Vivaldi concerts in churches throughout town. Homegrown Vivaldi is as ubiquitous here as Strauss is in Vienna and Mozart is in Salzburg. In fact, you'll find frilly young Vivaldis hawking concert tickets on many corners. Most shows start at 20:30 and generally last 1.5 hours. You'll see posters in hotels all over town (hotels sell tickets at face-value). Tickets for Baroque concerts in Venice can usually be bought the same day as the concert, so don't bother with websites that sell tickets with a surcharge. The general rule of thumb: Musicians in wigs and tights offer better spectacle; musicians in black-and-white suits are better performers.

The **Interpreti Veneziani orchestra**, considered the best group in town, generally performs 1.5-hour concerts nightly at 21:00 inside the sumptuous San Vidal Church (€26, church ticket booth open daily 9:30-21:00, north end of Accademia Bridge, tel. 041-277-0561, www.interpretiveneziani.com).

Other Performances

Venice's most famous theaters are **La Fenice** (grand old opera house, box office tel. 041-2424), **Teatro Goldoni** (mostly Italian live theater), and **Teatro della Fondamenta Nuove** (theater, music, and dance).

Musica a Palazzo is a unique evening of opera at a Venetian palace on the Grand Canal. You'll spend about 45 delightful minutes in each of three sumptuous rooms (about 2.25 hours total) as eight musicians (generally four instruments and four singers) perform. They generally present three different operas on successive nights—enthusiasts can experience more than one. With these kinds of surroundings, under Tiepolo frescoes, you'll be glad you dressed up. As there are only 70 seats, you must book by phone or online in advance (€60, nightly at 20:30, Palazzo Barbarigo Minotto, Fondamenta Duodo o Barbarigo, vaporetto: Santa Maria del Giglio, San Marco 2504, mobile 340-971-7272, www.musicapalazzo.com).

St. Mark's Square

For tourists, St. Mark's Square is the highlight, with lantern light and live music echoing from the cafés. Just being here after dark is a thrill, as **dueling café orchestras** entertain. Every night, enthusiastic musicians play the same songs, creating the same irresistible magic. Hang out for free behind the tables (allowing you to move easily on to the next orchestra when the musicians take a break), or spring for a seat and enjoy a fun and gorgeously set concert. If you sit a while, it can be €12-22 well spent (for a drink and the cover charge for music). Dancing on the square is free—and encouraged.

Several venerable cafés and bars on the square serve expensive drinks outside but cheap drinks inside at the bar. The scene in a bar like **Gran Caffè Lavena** (in spite of its politically incorrect chandelier) can be great. The touristy **Bar Americano** is lively until late (under the Clock Tower). You'll hear people talking about the famous **Harry's American Bar,** which sells overpriced food and American cocktails to dressy tourists near the San Marco-Vallaresso vaporetto stop. But it's a rip-off...and the last place Hemingway would drink today. It's far cheaper to get a drink at any of the bars just off St. Mark's Square; you can get a bottle of beer or even prosecco-to-go in a plastic cup.

Wherever you end up, streetlamp halos, live music, floodlit history, and a ceiling of stars make St. Mark's magic at midnight. You're not a tourist, you're a living part of a soft Venetian night...an alley cat with money. In the misty light, the moon has a golden hue. Shine with the old lanterns on the gondola piers, where the sloppy lagoon splashes at the Doge's Palace...reminiscing.

Eating in Venice

While touristy restaurants are the scourge of Venice, the following places are popular with actual Venetians and respect the tourists who happen in. First trick: Walk away from triple-language menus. Second trick: For freshness, eat fish. Most seafood dishes are the catch-of-the-day. (But remember that seafood can be sold by weight—per 100 grams or *etto*—rather than a set price.) And, if you're staying in town, the third trick is: Eat later. A place may feel really touristy at 19:00, but if you come back at 21:00, it can be filled with locals. Tourists eat barbarically early, which is fine with the restaurants because they fill tables that would otherwise be used only once in an evening.

For general tips on eating in Italy, see page 455.

Near the Rialto Bridge
For locations, see the map on page 785.

East of the Rialto Bridge
Rosticceria San Bartolomeo is a cheap—if confusing—self-service diner. This throwback budget eatery has a surly staff: Don't take it personally. Notice that the different counters serve up different types of food—pastas, *secondi*, fried goodies, and so on. You can get it to go, grab one of the few tiny tables, or munch at the bar—but I'd skip their upper-floor restaurant option (€7-8 pastas, great fried *mozzarella al prosciutto* for €1.60, fruit salad, €2 glasses of wine, prices listed on wall behind counter, no cover and no service charge, daily 9:00-21:30, San Marco 5424, tel. 041-522-3569). To find it, imagine the statue on Campo San Bartolomeo walking backward 20 yards, turning left, and going under a passageway—now, follow him.

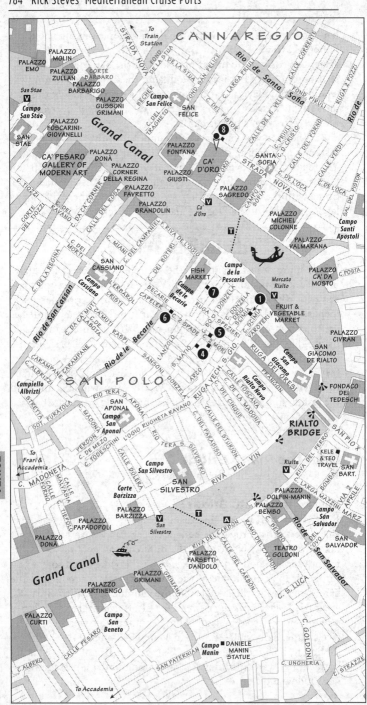

VENICE

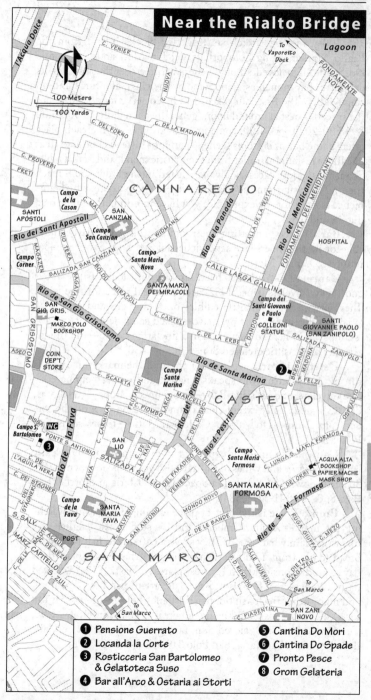

Near the Rialto Bridge

Lagoon

100 Meters
100 Yards

CANNAREGIO

CASTELLO

SAN MARCO

① Pensione Guerrato
② Locanda la Corte
③ Rosticceria San Bartolomeo
   & Gelatoteca Suso
④ Bar all'Arco & Ostaria ai Storti

⑤ Cantina Do Mori
⑥ Cantina Do Spade
⑦ Pronto Pesce
⑧ Grom Gelateria

VENICE

West of the Rialto Bridge

The 100-yard-long stretch starting two blocks inland from the Rialto Market (along Sotoportego dei Do Mori and Calle de le Do Spade) is beloved among Venetian *cicchetti* enthusiasts for its delightful bar munchies, good wine by the glass, and fun stand-up conviviality. The first four places I've listed serve food all day, but the spread is best at around noon (generally open daily 12:00-15:00 & 18:00-20:00 or 21:00; some are closed Sun). While each place offers a fine bar-and-stools scene, you might instead choose to treat one like a restaurant, order from their rustic menu, and grab a table. Scout these four places in advance (listed in the order you'll reach them, if coming from the Rialto Bridge) to help decide which ambience is right for the experience you have in mind. Then pick one, dig in, and drink up.

Bar all'Arco, a bustling one-room joint, is particularly enjoyable for its tiny open-face sandwiches (closed Sun, San Polo 436; Francisco, Anne, Matteo).

Cantina Do Mori has been famous with locals (since 1462) and savvy travelers (since 1982) as a convivial place for fine wine. They serve a forest of little edibles on toothpicks and *francobolli* (a spicy selection of 20 tiny, mayo-soaked sandwiches nicknamed "stamps"). Go here to be abused in a fine atmosphere—the frowns are part of the shtick (closed Sun, San Polo 430).

Osteria ai Storti, with a cool photo of the market in 1909, is run by Alessandro, who speaks English and enjoys helping educate travelers, and his sister Baby—pronounced "Bobby" (€8 pastas, €12-13 *secondi,* daily except closed Sun off-season, around the corner from Cantina Do Mori on Calle San Matio—follow signs, San Polo 819).

Cantina Do Spade is expertly run by Francesco, who clearly lists the *cicchetti* and wines of the day (also good for sit-down meals, 30 yards down Calle de le Do Spade from Osteria ai Storti at San Polo 860, tel. 041-521-0583).

Pronto Pesce is the perfect place to sample fish while watching the market action. Umberto and his staff speak English and like to explain what's good. They serve a €10 mixed fish plate with bread (daily from 13:00 until it's sold out) that locals plan their day around. Consider their "express plates" of pasta (€12-15, served daily 12:45-14:15), fish risotto specials, artful fish hors d'oeuvres, and many other fresh fish tidbits. This fancy hole-in-the-wall is fun for a quick bite—eat standing up or take it to go (Mon 11:30-15:00, Tue-Sat 10:00-15:00, closed Sun, facing the fish market on Calle de le Becarie o Panataria, San Polo 319, tel. 041-822-0298).

Near St. Mark's Square

While my first listing is a serious restaurant, the other places listed here are cheap-and-cheery options convenient to your sightseeing. For locations, see the map on page 744.

Ristorante Antica Sacrestia is a classic restaurant where the owner, Pino, takes a hands-on approach to greeting guests. His staff serve creative €33-50 fixed-price meals and a humdrum €20 *menù del giorno*. (Be warned: These meals seem designed to overwhelm you with too much food. You will not leave hungry.) You can also order à la carte; try the delightful €21 antipasto spread, which looks like a lagoon aquarium spread out on a plate. The entrance courtyard is a great place to sip a drink if you have to wait for a table. While the food isn't high cuisine, the service is animated and the experience is memorable. My readers are welcome to a free *sgroppino* (lemon vodka after-dinner drink) upon request (€13-18 pastas and pizzas, €20-30 *secondi*, Tue-Sun 11:30-15:00 & 18:00-23:00, closed Mon, behind San Zaninovo/Giovanni Novo Church on Calle Corona at Castello 4463, tel. 041-523-0749).

"Sandwich Row": On Calle de le Rasse, just steps away from the tourist intensity at St. Mark's Square, is a handy strip I call "Sandwich Row." Lined with sandwich bars, it's the closest place to St. Mark's to get a decent sandwich at an affordable price with a place to sit down (most places open daily 7:00-24:00, €1 extra to sit; from the Bridge of Sighs, head down the Riva and take the second lane on the left). I particularly like **Birreria Forst,** a pleasantly unpretentious café that serves a selection of meaty €3 sandwiches with tasty sauce on wheat bread, or made-to-order sandwiches for €4 (daily 9:30-22:00, air-con, rustic wood tables, Castello 4540, tel. 041-523-0557), and **Bar Verde,** a more modern sandwich bar with fun people-watching views from its corner tables (big €4-5 sandwiches, splittable €9 salads, fresh pastries, at the end of Calle de le Rasse at #4526, facing Campo Santi Filippo e Giacomo).

Ristorante alla Basilica, just one street behind St. Mark's Basilica, is a church-run, indoor, institutional-feeling place that serves a solid €14 fixed-price lunch (including water). It's not self-serve—you'll be seated and can choose a pasta, a *secondi,* and a vegetable side dish off the menu (Tue-Sun 11:45-15:00, closed Mon, air-con, Calle dei Albanesi 4255, tel. 041-522-0524).

Picnicking: Though you can't picnic on St. Mark's Square, you can legally take your snacks to the nearby Giardinetti Reali, the small park along the waterfront west of the Piazzetta.

In Dorsoduro, near the Accademia Bridge

Bar Foscarini, next to the Accademia Bridge and Galleria, offers decent €8-15 pizzas and €8-10 *panini* in a memorable Grand Canal-view setting. The food is decent but forgettable, and pricey

VENICE

The Stand-Up Progressive
Venetian Pub-Crawl Dinner

If you're in town at dinnertime, try my favorite Venetian dinner ritual. It's a pub crawl *(giro d'ombra)*—a tradition unique to Venice, where no cars means easy crawling. (*Giro* means stroll, and *ombra*—slang for a glass of wine—means shade, from the old days when a portable wine bar scooted with the shadow of the Campanile bell tower across St. Mark's Square.)

Venice's residential back streets hide plenty of characteristic bars *(bacari)* with countless trays of interesting toothpick munchies *(cicchetti)* and blackboards listing the wines that are uncorked and served by the glass. This is a great way to mingle and have fun with the Venetians. Bars don't stay open very late, and the *cic-*

chetti selection is best early, so start your evening by 18:00. Most bars are closed on Sunday. For a stress-free pub crawl, consider taking a tour with the charming Alessandro Schezzini (see page 726).

Cicchetti bars have a social stand-up zone and a cozy gaggle of tables where you can generally sit down with your *cicchetti* or order from a simple menu. In some of the more popular places, the crowds happily spill out into the street. Food generally costs the same price whether you stand or sit.

I've listed plenty of pubs in walking order for a quick or extended crawl. If you've crawled enough, most of these bars make

drinks pad your tab, but you're paying a premium for this premium location. On each visit to Venice, I grab a pizza lunch here while I ponder the Grand Canal bustle. They also serve a €10 breakfast (Wed-Mon 7:00-22:30, until 21:00 Nov-April, closed Tue year-round, on Rio Terà A. Foscarini at #878c—see map on page 755, tel. 041-522-7281, Paolo).

Cheap Meals

The keys to eating affordably in Venice are pizza, *döner kebabs*, bars/cafés, self-service cafeterias, and picnics. Sandwiches (*panini, piadini,* and *tramezzini*) are sold fast and cheap at bars everywhere and can stave off midmorning hunger. There's a great "sandwich row" of cheap cafés near St. Mark's Square (described earlier). For speed, value, and ambience, you can get a filling plate of typically Venetian appetizers at nearly any bar. I like small, fun, stand-up mini-meals at *cicchetti* **bars** best (see sidebar above).

Picnics: The **fruit and vegetable market** that sprawls for a few blocks just past the Rialto Bridge is a fun place to assemble a picnic

a fine one-stop, sit-down dinner.

While you can order a plate, Venetians prefer going one-by-one...sipping their wine and trying this...then give me one of those...and so on. Try deep-fried mozzarella cheese, gorgonzola, calamari, artichoke hearts, and anything ugly on a toothpick. *Crostini* (small toasted bread with a topping) are popular, as are marinated seafood, olives, and prosciutto with melon. Meat and fish (*pesce;* PESH-ay) munchies can be expensive; veggies *(verdure)* are cheap, at about €3 for a meal-sized plate. In many places, there's a set price per food item (e.g., €1.50). To get a plate of assorted appetizers for €8 (or more, depending on how hungry you are), ask for *"Un piatto classico di cicchetti misti da €8"* (oon pee-AH-toh KLAH-see-koh dee cheh-KET-tee MEE-stee dah OH-toh ay-OO-roh). Bread sticks *(grissini)* are free for the asking.

Bar-hopping Venetians enjoy an *aperitivo,* a before-dinner drink. Boldly order a Bellini, a *spritz con Aperol,* or a prosecco, and draw approving looks from the natives.

Drink the house wines. A small glass of house red or white wine *(ombra rosso* or *ombra bianco)* or a small beer *(birrino)* costs about €1. The house keg wine is cheap—€1 per glass, about €4 per liter. *Vin bon,* Venetian for fine wine, may run you from €2 to €6 per little glass. There are usually several fine wines uncorked and available by the glass. A good last drink is *fragolino,* the local sweet wine—*bianco* or *rosso.* It often comes with a little cookie *(biscotti)* for dipping.

(best Mon-Sat 8:00-13:00, liveliest in the morning, closed Sun). The adjacent **fish market** is wonderfully slimy (closed Sun-Mon). Side lanes in this area are speckled with fine little hole-in-the-wall munchie bars, bakeries, and cheese shops. Again, you're legally forbidden from picnicking anywhere on or near St. Mark's Square except for Giardinetti Reali, the waterfront park near the San Marco vaporetto docks.

Gelato

You'll find good *gelaterie* in every Venetian neighborhood, offering one-scoop cones for about €1.50. Look for the words *artigianale* or *produzione propria,* which indicates that a shop makes its own gelato. All of these are open long hours daily.

The popular, inventive, upscale **Grom** ice-cream chain has three branches in Venice: on Campo San Barnaba at #2761 (beyond the Accademia Bridge); on the Strada Nova at #3844, not far from the Rialto; and on Campo dei Frari at #3006, facing the Frari Church (all open long hours daily). A competing gourmet gelato shop, **Gelatoteca Suso,** serves up delectable flavors such as fig and nut (next to recommended Rosticceria San Bartolomeo on Calle de la Bissa, San Marco 5453). **Il Doge,** on the big and bustling Campo Santa Margarita, has a wide range of homemade flavors, as well as Sicilian-style *granita* (slushy ice flavored with fresh fruit; Dorsoduro 3058a, tel. 041-523-4607).

On St. Mark's Square, two venerable cafés have *gelato* counters: **Gran Caffè Lavena** (April-Oct daily until 24:00, no gelato Nov-March, at #134) and **Todaro** (on the corner of the Piazzetta at #5, near the water and just under the column topped by St. Theodore slaying a crocodile).

Starting or Ending Your Cruise in Venice

If your cruise begins and/or ends in Venice, you'll want some extra time here; for most travelers, two days is a minimum to see the highlights of this grand city. For a longer visit here, pick up my *Rick Steves' Venice* guidebook—or, if your trip extends to other points in the country, consider my *Rick Steves' Italy* guidebook.

Airport Connections

Marco Polo Airport

Venice's small, modern airport is on the mainland shore of the lagoon, six miles north of the city (airport code: VCE). There's one sleek terminal, with a TI (daily 9:00-20:00), car-rental agencies, ATMs, a bank, and a few shops and eateries. For flight information, call 041-260-9260, visit www.veniceairport.com, or ask your hotel.

Getting from Marco Polo Airport to Downtown

You have four options for getting between the airport and downtown Venice: two by sea (slow Alilaguna boats and speedy water taxis) and two by land (cheap ACTV/ATVO shuttle buses and pricier taxis or private minivans).

Both Alilaguna boats and water taxis leave from the airport's boat dock, an eight-minute walk from the terminal. Exit the arrivals hall and turn left, following signs along a paved, level, covered sidewalk (easy for wheeled bags).

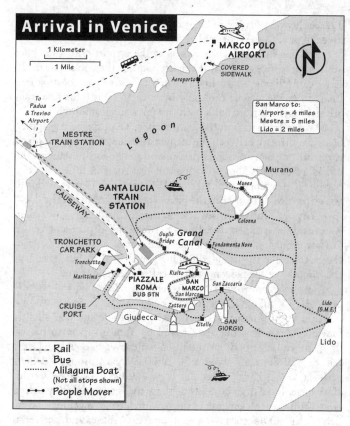

Arrival in Venice

1 Kilometer

1 Mile

MARCO POLO AIRPORT

COVERED SIDEWALK

Aeroporto

To Padua & Treviso Airport

San Marco to:
Airport = 4 miles
Mestre = 5 miles
Lido = 2 miles

L a g o o n

MESTRE TRAIN STATION

Murano

Museo

SANTA LUCIA TRAIN STATION

Colonna

CAUSEWAY

Fondamenta Nove

TRONCHETTO CAR PARK

Guglie Bridge

Grand Canal

Tronchetto

Rialto

Marittima

PIAZZALE ROMA BUS STN

SAN MARCO
San Marco

San Zaccaria

CRUISE PORT

Zattere

Lido (S.M.E.)

Giudecca

Zitelle

SAN GIORGIO

Lido

····· Rail
---- Bus
········· Alilaguna Boat (Not all stops shown)
•—• People Mover

Alilaguna Airport Boats (slowest trip, medium cost): These boats make the scenic (if slooooow) journey across the lagoon, each shuttling passengers between the airport and a number of different stops on the island of Venice (€15, €27 round-trip, €1 surcharge if bought on boat, roughly 2/hour, 1-1.5-hour trip depending on destination). Alilaguna boats are not part of the ACTV vaporetto system, so they aren't covered by city transit passes. But they do use the same docks and ticket windows as the regular *vaporetti*.

There are two Alilaguna lines—blue and orange—which take about the same amount of time to reach St. Mark's Square. From the airport, the blue line *(linea blu)* heads first to Fondamente Nove (on the "back" of Venice's fish, 40 minutes), then loops around the "tail" of the fish to San Zaccaria and San Marco (about 1.5 hours) before continuing on to Zattere and the cruise terminal (almost 2 hours). The orange line *(linea arancio)* runs down the Grand Canal, reaching Guglie (handy for Cannaregio hotels, 45 minutes), Rialto (1 hour), and San Marco (1.25 hours). For a full schedule, visit the

TI, see the website (www.alilaguna.it), call 041-240-1701, ask your hotelier, or scan the schedules posted at the docks.

You can buy Alilaguna tickets at the airport's TI, the ticket desk in the terminal, and at the ticket booth at the dock. Any ticket seller can tell you which line to catch to get to your destination. Boats from the airport run roughly twice an hour (blue line from 6:10, orange line from 8:00, both run until about midnight).

Water Taxis (fastest trip, most expensive): Luxury taxi speedboats zip directly between the airport and downtown, getting you to within steps of your final destination in about 30 minutes. The official price is €115 for up to four people; add €10 for every extra person (10-passenger limit). From the airport, arrange your ride at the water-taxi desk or with the boat captains lounging at the dock.

Airport Shuttle Buses (faster than Alilaguna, slower than water taxi, least expensive): Buses between the airport and Venice are fast, frequent, and cheap. They take you across the bridge from the mainland to the island, dropping you at Venice's bus station, at the "mouth" of the fish on a square called Piazzale Roma.

Two bus companies run between Piazzale Roma and the airport: ACTV and ATVO. ATVO buses take 20 minutes and go nonstop. ACTV buses make a few stops en route and take slightly longer (30 minutes) but are covered by Venice vaporetto passes. They are equally good; just jump on whichever one's leaving next (either bus: €6, runs about 5:00-24:00, 2/hour, drops to 1/hour early and late, check schedules at www.atvo.it or www.actv.it). Both buses leave from just outside the arrivals terminal. Buy tickets from the TI, the ticket desk in the terminal, ticket machines, or the driver. ATVO tickets are not valid on ACTV buses and vice versa. Double-check the destination; you want Piazzale Roma. If taking ACTV, you want bus #5.

The bus leaves you at Piazzale Roma. From here, *vaporetti* cruise down the Grand Canal—convenient for hotels near the Rialto Bridge and St. Mark's Square. When you arrive at Piazzale Roma, you'll find the vaporetto dock by walking to the six-story white building, then taking a right. Piazzale Roma is also the terminus of the People Mover monorail that zips you to the cruise port (€1, one stop to Stazione Marittima).

Land Taxi or Private Minivan (medium speed, medium cost): It takes about 20 minutes to drive from the airport to Piazzale Roma. A land taxi can get you from the airport to Piazzale Roma for about €40. Treviso Car Service offers a private minivan service between the airport and Piazzale Roma or the cruise port (minivan-€55, seats up to 8; car-€50, seats up to 3; mobile 348-900-0700 or 333-411-2840, www.tourleadervenice.com, info@tourleadervenice.com).

Getting from Downtown to the Cruise Port: If you're heading to the port from **St. Mark's Square,** you can ride the Alilaguna express boat. From elsewhere in Venice, it might be easier to take a vaporetto to Piazzale Roma and take the People Mover from there. (For details on either option, see "Returning to Your Ship" on page 711).

If arriving from other points in Italy at **Venezia Santa Lucia train station** and going directly to the port, exit the station, turn right, follow the Grand Canal to the modern Calatrava Bridge, cross it, walk through Piazzale Roma (big bus parking lot) to the People Mover station at the far-right corner, then ride the People Mover monorail one stop to Stazione Marittima (buy €1 People Mover ticket as you enter).

Getting from Marco Polo Airport to the Cruise Port

To get from the airport directly to your cruise ship, you can take a land taxi straight to the port (about €40). The cheaper option is to take an airport shuttle bus to Piazzale Roma (explained earlier), walk through its big bus parking lot to the People Mover station at the far-right corner, then take the People Mover monorail from there (buy €1 People Mover ticket as you enter, take it one stop to Stazione Marittima).

Checking in for Your Cruise at the Port

Once at the port, you'll need to drop off your bags at the baggage collection area. Follow signs for your cruise line, and ask representatives where you can drop bags (many of them use a huge but easy-to-miss white tented area set back from the piers, between buildings #107/#108 and #117). Once you've deposited your bags, you can head to your terminal building to check in. If your cruise starts in Venice, you may need to check in at the main terminal even if your ship docks outside the main port.

Departing from Marco Polo Airport

If flying out of Venice, allow yourself plenty of time to get to the airport. Water transport is slow. Plan to arrive at the airport at least two hours before your flight, and remember that getting there can easily take another two hours. Consider alternatives ahead of time, especially if you're planning to take one of the Alilaguna boats (which are small and can fill up).

The affordable public-transportation connection first involves making your way to the square called Piazzale Roma, which is a quick ride on the People Mover monorail from the cruise port (see "To St. Mark's Square via the Grand Canal" on page 710), and easy to reach on a Grand Canal vaporetto from other points in Venice.

VENICE

From Piazzale Roma, you can ride one of two different **airport shuttle buses** (€6, 20-30 minutes, operated by ACTV or ATVO). At Piazzale Roma, buy your ticket from the ACTV windows or ATVO office before heading out to the platforms. The newsstand in the center of the lot also sells tickets. ACTV buses leave from platform A1; ATVO buses leave from platforms near the center of the lot and are well-signed. For more details, see "Getting from Marco Polo Airport to Downtown," earlier.

You can also ride the slow **Alilaguna airport boat** from various stops in Venice (see "Getting from Marco Polo Airport to Downtown," earlier). If staying overnight, ask your hotelier which dock and which line is best. Blue line boats start leaving Venice as early as 3:40 in the morning for passengers with early flights. Scope out the dock and buy your ticket in advance to avoid last-minute stress.

A **land taxi** costs about €40 for the 30-minute ride to the airport (taxis wait in front of the cruise terminal). A pricey **taxi speedboat** can whisk you from the cruise port to the airport in about 30 minutes, but you'll pay a premium (€115 for up to four people, €10 extra per additional passenger). You can hire one at the kiosks in front of terminal #103 at the top of the harbor, or you can book directly with the Consorzio Motoscafi water taxi association (tel. 041-522-2303, www.motoscafivenezia.it).

Alternate Airport (Treviso)

Several budget airlines, such as Ryanair, Wizz Air, and Germanwings, use Treviso Airport, 12 miles northwest of Venice (airport code: TSF, tel. 042-231-5111, www.trevisoairport.it). The fastest option into Venice (Tronchetto parking lot) is on the **Barzi express bus,** which does the trip in just 40 minutes (€7, buy tickets on board, 1-2/hour, www.barziservice.com). From Tronchetto, hop on the People Mover monorail to Piazzale Roma for €1. **ATVO buses** are a bit more frequent and drop you right at Piazzale Roma (saving you the People Mover ride), but take nearly twice as long because they make more stops (€7, about 2/hour, 1.25 hours, www.atvo.it; buy tickets at the ATVO desk in the airport and stamp them on the bus). **Treviso Car Service** offers minivan service to Piazzale Roma (minivan-€75, seats up to 8; car-€65, seats up to 3; for contact info, see listing on page 792).

Hotels in Venice

If you need a hotel in Venice before or after your cruise, here are a few to consider.

Near St. Mark's Square

To locate all of these San Marco-area hotels, see the map on page 744.

East of St. Mark's Square

$$$ Hotel Campiello, lacy and bright, was once part of a 19th-century convent. Ideally located 50 yards off the waterfront, on a tiny square, its 16 rooms offer a tranquil, friendly refuge for travelers who appreciate comfort and professional service (Sb-€130, Db-€180, bigger "superior" rooms €20-30 more, 10 percent discount with this book if you reserve direct and pay cash on arrival, air-con, elevator, free Wi-Fi; from the San Zaccaria vaporetto stop, take Calle del Vin, between pink Hotel Danieli and Hotel Savoia e Jolanda, to Castello #4647; tel. 041-520-5764, www.hcampiello.it, campiello@hcampiello.it; family-run for four generations, currently by Thomas, Monica, Nicoletta, and Marco). They also rent three modern family apartments, under rustic timbers just steps away (up to €380/night).

$$$ Hotel Fontana, two bridges behind St. Mark's Square, is a pleasant family-run place with 15 sparse but classic-feeling rooms overlooking a lively square (Sb-€120, Db-€180, family rooms, 10 percent cash discount, quieter rooms on garden side, 2 rooms have terraces for €20 extra, air-con, elevator, free Wi-Fi in common areas, on Campo San Provolo at Castello 4701, tel. 041-522-0579, www.hotelfontana.it, info@hotelfontana.it, cousins Diego and Gabriele).

$$$ Hotel la Residenza is a grand old palace facing a peaceful square. It has 16 small rooms on three levels (with no elevator) and a huge, luxurious lounge that comes with a piano and a stingy breakfast. This is a good value for romantics—you'll feel like you're in the Doge's Palace after hours (Sb-€105, Db-€205, view Db-€215, air-con, free Wi-Fi, on Campo Bandiera e Moro at Castello 3608, tel. 041-528-5315, www.venicelaresidenza.com, info@venicelaresidenza.com, Giovanni).

$$ Locanda al Leon, which feels a little like a medieval tower house, is conscientiously run and rents 13 reasonably priced rooms just off Campo Santi Filippo e Giacomo (Db-€160, Db with square view-€180, Tb-€200, Qb-€240, these prices with cash and this book, air-con, free Wi-Fi, 2 apartments with kitchens, Campo Santi Filippo e Giacomo, Castello 4270, tel. 041-277-0393, www.hotelalleon.com, leon@hotelalleon.com, Giuliano and Marcella).

Their down-the-street annex, **B&B Marcella,** has three newer, classy, and spacious rooms for the same rates (check in at main hotel).

$ Albergo Doni, situated along a quiet canal, is dark and quiet. This time-warp—with 13 well-worn, once-classy rooms up a creaky stairway—is run by friendly Tessa and her brother, an Italian stallion named Nikos (S-€70, D-€105, Db-€130, T-€135, Tb-€170, ask about Rick Steves discount, ceiling fans, three Db rooms have air-con, free Wi-Fi in common areas, 3 nice overflow apartments are same price but no breakfast, on Fondamenta del Vin at Castello 4656, tel. 041-522-4267, www.albergodoni.it, albergodoni@hotmail.it).

North of St. Mark's Square

$$ Hotel al Piave, with 28 fine, air-conditioned rooms above a bright and classy lobby, is fresh, modern, and comfortable. You'll enjoy the neighborhood and always get a cheery welcome (Db-€155, larger "superior" Db-€200, Tb-€200, Qb-€260; family suites-€280 for 4, €300 for 5, or €310 for 6; €10 Rick Steves discount when you book direct and pay in cash, free Wi-Fi, on Ruga Giuffa at Castello 4838/40, tel. 041-528-5174, www.hotelalpiave. com, info@hotelalpiave.com, Mirella, Paolo, Ilaria, and Federico speak English).

$$ Locanda Casa Querini rents six bright, high-ceilinged rooms on a quiet square tucked away behind St. Mark's. You can enjoy your breakfast or a sunny picnic/happy hour sitting at their tables right on the sleepy little square (Db-€155, Tb-€180, one cheaper small double, ask about Rick Steves discount, air-con, free Wi-Fi, halfway between San Zaccaria vaporetto stop and Campo Santa Maria Formosa at Castello 4388 on Campo San Zaninovo/ Giovanni Novo, tel. 041-241-1294, www.locandaquerini.com, info@locandaquerini.com; Silvia, Patrizia, and Caterina).

West of St. Mark's Square

$$$ Hotel Flora sits buried in a sea of fancy designer boutiques and elegant hotels almost on the Grand Canal. It's formal, with uniformed staff and grand public spaces, yet the 40 rooms have a homey warmth and the garden oasis is a sanctuary for foot-weary guests (generally Db-€260, check website for special discounts or email Sr. Romanelli for 10 percent Rick Steves discount off standard prices, air-con, elevator, free Wi-Fi, fitness room, family apartment, on Calle Bergamaschi at San Marco 2283a, tel. 041-520-5844, www.hotelflora.it, info@hotelflora.it).

Near the Rialto Bridge

For locations, see the map on page 785.

VENICE

What If I Miss My Boat?

Remember that you can get help from the cruise line's port agent (listed on the destination information sheet distributed on the ship) and the local TI (see page 713). If the port agent suggests a costly solution (such as a private car with a driver), you may want to consider public transit instead.

Venice has train and plane connections to virtually anywhere in Italy. The city has a train station and two airports—Marco Polo and the small Treviso.

Frequent **trains** leave from Venice's **Santa Lucia train station** (on the Grand Canal) to points all over Italy and beyond: to **Florence** (often crowded so make reservations), **Rome** (overnight possible), **Naples** (with changes in Rome). To **Split** or **Dubrovnik,** overland connections are long (partly by night train to Split, much longer by train and bus to Dubrovnik); driving all the way is much shorter (consider hiring a driver), or look into flights.

For other connections, ask at the train station or check www.bahn.com (Germany's excellent all-Europe website).

For recommended local **travel agents,** see page 718. For more advice on what to do if you miss the boat, see page 140.

$$ Pensione Guerrato, above the colorful Rialto produce market and just two minutes from the Rialto Bridge, is run by friendly, creative, and hardworking Roberto and Piero. Their 800-year-old building—with 24 spacious, charming rooms—is simple, airy, and wonderfully characteristic (D-€95, Db-€135, Tb-€155, Qb-€175, Quint/b-€185, these prices with this book and cash, check website for special discounts, Rick Steves readers can ask for €5/night discount below online specials, air-con, free Wi-Fi in lobby, on Calle drio la Scimia at San Polo 240a, tel. 041-528-5927, www.pensioneguerrato.it, info@pensioneguerrato.it, Monica and Rosanna). My tour groups book this place for 60 nights each year. Sorry. The Guerrato also rents family apartments in the old center (great for groups of 4-8) for around €60 per person.

$$ Locanda la Corte is perfumed with elegance without being snooty. Its 17 attractive, high-ceilinged, wood-beamed rooms—Venetian-style, done in earthy pastels—circle a small, quiet courtyard (standard Db-€150, deluxe Db-€170, ask about Rick Steves discount, suites and family rooms available, air-con, free Wi-Fi, on Calle Bressana at Castello 6317, tel. 041-241-1300, www.locandalacorte.it, info@locandalacorte.it, Marco and Tommy the cat).

Near the Accademia Bridge

$$ Don Orione Religious Guest House is a big cultural center dedicated to the work of a local man who became a saint in modern times. With 80 rooms filling an old monastery, it feels cookie-cutter institutional (like a modern retreat center), but is also classy, clean, peaceful, and strictly run. It's beautifully located, comfortable, and a good value supporting a fine cause: Profits go to mission work in the developing world (Sb-€96, Db-€160, Tb-€207, Qb-€248, groups welcome, air-con, elevator, free Wi-Fi, on Rio Terà A. Foscarini, Dorsoduro 909a—for location see map on page 755, tel. 041-522-4077, www.donorione-venezia.it, info@donorione-venezia.it). From the Zattere vaporetto stop, turn right, then turn left. It's just after the church at #909a.

Italian Survival Phrases

English	Italian	Pronunciation
Good day.	*Buon giorno.*	bwohn **jor**-noh
Do you speak English?	*Parla inglese?*	**par**-lah een-**gleh**-zay
Yes. / No.	*Sì. / No.*	see / noh
I (don't) understand.	*(Non) capisco.*	(nohn) kah-**pees**-koh
Please.	*Per favore.*	pehr fah-**voh**-ray
Thank you.	*Grazie.*	**graht**-see-ay
You're welcome.	*Prego.*	**preh**-go
I'm sorry.	*Mi dispiace.*	mee dee-spee-**ah**-chay
Excuse me.	*Mi scusi.*	mee **skoo**-zee
(No) problem.	*(Non) c'è un roblema.*	(nohn) cheh oon proh-**bleh**-mah
Good.	*Va bene.*	vah **beh**-nay
Goodbye.	*Arrivederci.*	ah-ree-veh-**dehr**-chee
one / two	*uno / due*	**oo**-noh / **doo**-ay
three / four	*tre / quattro*	tray / **kwah**-troh
five / six	*cinque / sei*	**cheeng**-kway / **seh**-ee
seven / eight	*sette / otto*	**seh**-tay / **oh**-toh
nine / ten	*nove / dieci*	**noh**-vay / dee-**ay**-chee
How much is it?	*Quanto costa?*	**kwahn**-toh **koh**-stah
Write it?	*Me lo scrive?*	may loh **skree**-vay
Is it free?	*È gratis?*	eh **grah**-tees
Is it included?	*È incluso?*	eh een-**kloo**-zoh
Where can I buy / find...?	*Dove posso comprare / trovare...?*	**doh**-vay **poh**-soh kohm-**prah**-ray / troh-**vah**-ray
I'd like / We'd like...	*Vorrei / Vorremmo...*	voh-**reh**-ee / voh-**reh**-moh
...a room.	*...una camera.*	**oo**-nah **kah**-meh-rah
...a ticket to ____.	*...un biglietto per ____.*	oon beel-**yeh**-toh pehr ____
Is it possible?	*È possibile?*	eh poh-**see**-bee-lay
Where is...?	*Dov'è...?*	doh-**veh**
...the train station	*...la stazione*	lah staht-see-**oh**-nay
...the bus station	*...la stazione degli autobus*	lah staht-see-**oh**-nay **dehl**-yee ow-toh-boos
...tourist information	*...informazioni per turisti*	een-for-maht-see-**oh**-nee pehr too-**ree**-stee
...the toilet	*...la toilette*	lah twah-**leh**-tay
men	*uomini / signori*	**woh**-mee-nee / seen-**yoh**-ree
women	*donne / signore*	**doh**-nay / seen-**yoh**-ray
left / right	*sinistra / destra*	see-**nee**-strah / **deh**-strah
straight	*sempre dritto*	**sehm**-pray **dree**-toh
What time does this open / close?	*A che ora apre / chiude?*	ah kay oh-rah ah-**pray** / kee-**oo**-day
At what time?	*A che ora?*	ah kay **oh**-rah
Just a moment.	*Un momento.*	oon moh-**mehn**-toh
now / soon / later	*adesso / presto / più tardi*	ah-**deh**-soh / **preh**-stoh / pew **tar**-dee
today / tomorrow	*oggi / domani*	**oh**-jee / doh-**mah**-nee

VENICE

In an Italian Restaurant

English	Italian	Pronunciation
I'd like...	Vorrei...	voh-**reh**-ee
We'd like...	Vorremmo...	vor-**reh**-moh
...to reserve...	...prenotare...	preh-noh-**tah**-ray
...a table for one / two.	...un tavolo per uno / due.	oon **tah**-voh-loh pehr **oo**-noh / **doo**-ay
Is this seat free?	È libero questo posto?	eh **lee**-beh-roh **kweh**-stoh **poh**-stoh
The menu (in English), please.	Il menù (in inglese), per favore.	eel meh-**noo** (een een-**gleh**-zay) pehr fah-**voh**-ray
service (not) included	servizio (non) incluso	sehr-**veet**-see-oh (nohn) een-**kloo**-zoh
cover charge	pane e coperto	**pah**-nay ay koh-**pehr**-toh
to go	da portar via	dah **por**-tar **vee**-ah
with / without	con / senza	kohn / **sehnt**-sah
and / or	e / o	ay / oh
menu (of the day)	menù (del giorno)	meh-**noo** (dehl **jor**-noh)
specialty of the house	specialità della casa	speh-chah-lee-**tah deh**-lah **kah**-zah
first course (pasta, soup)	primo piatto	**pree**-moh pee-**ah**-toh
main course (meat, fish)	secondo piatto	seh-**kohn**-doh pee-**ah**-toh
side dishes	contorni	kohn-**tor**-nee
bread	pane	**pah**-nay
cheese	formaggio	for-**mah**-joh
sandwich	panino	pah-**nee**-noh
soup	zuppa	**tsoo**-pah
salad	insalata	een-sah-**lah**-tah
meat	carne	**kar**-nay
chicken	pollo	**poh**-loh
fish	pesce	**peh**-shay
seafood	frutti di mare	**froo**-tee dee **mah**-ray
fruit / vegetables	frutta / legumi	**froo**-tah / lay-**goo**-mee
dessert	dolce	**dohl**-chay
tap water	acqua del rubinetto	**ah**-kwah dehl roo-bee-**neh**-toh
mineral water	acqua minerale	**ah**-kwah mee-neh-**rah**-lay
milk	latte	**lah**-tay
(orange) juice	succo (d'arancia)	**soo**-koh (dah-**rahn**-chah)
coffee / tea	caffè / tè	kah-**feh** / teh
wine	vino	**vee**-noh
red / white	rosso / bianco	**roh**-soh / bee-**ahn**-koh
glass / bottle	bicchiere / bottiglia	bee-kee-**eh**-ray / boh-**teel**-yah
beer	birra	**bee**-rah
Cheers!	Cin cin!	cheen cheen
More. / Another.	Di più. / Un altro.	dee pew / oon **ahl**-troh
The same.	Lo stesso.	loh **steh**-soh
The bill, please.	Il conto, per favore.	eel **kohn**-toh pehr fah-**voh**-ray
Do you accept credit cards?	Accettate carte di credito?	ah-cheh-**tah**-tay **kar**-tay dee **kreh**-dee-toh
tip	mancia	**mahn**-chah
Delicious!	Delizioso!	day-leet-see-oh-zoh

For more user-friendly Italian phrases, check out *Rick Steves' Italian Phrase Book & Dictionary* or *Rick Steves' French, Italian, and German Phrase Book*.

SPLIT
Croatia

Croatia Practicalities

Unfamiliar as it might seem, Croatia (*Hrvatska*) has some of Europe's most spectacular natural wonders—many of them still off the beaten path. With thousands of miles of seafront and more than a thousand islands, Croatia's coastline is Eastern Europe's Riviera. Aside from its fun-in-the-sun status, Croatia is also historic. From ruined Roman arenas and Byzantine mosaics to Venetian bell towers, Habsburg villas, and even communist concrete, past rulers have left their mark on this country of 4.5 million (90 percent ethnic Croat—Catholic—and 4.5 percent Serb—Orthodox). A trip to Croatia offers thoughtful travelers the opportunity to understand this country's complicated role in Europe's most violent war in generations. But most visitors will focus on Croatia's beautiful nature: mountains, sun, sand, and sea.

Money: Croatia uses its traditional currency, the kuna: 1 kuna (kn, or HRK) = about 20 cents. One kuna is broken down into 100 lipa. Many Croatian businesses refuse to accept euros or dollars, so it's worth getting a few kunas for your time in port. An ATM is called a *bankomat*. The local VAT (value-added sales tax) rate is 25 percent; the minimum purchase eligible for a VAT refund is 740 kn (for details on refunds, see page 135).

Language: For useful Croatian phrases, see page 833.

Emergencies: Dial 92 for police; dial 112 for medical or other emergencies.

Time Zone: Croatia is on Central European Time (the same as most of the Continent, and six/nine hours ahead of the East/West Coasts of the US).

Consular Services in Zagreb: The US Embassy is at Ulica Thomasa Jeffersona 2 (tel. 01/661-2200, after-hours tel. 01/661-2400, http://zagreb.usembassy.gov). The Canadian Embassy is at Prilaz Đure Deželića 4 (tel. 01/488-1200, www.croatia.gc.ca). Call ahead for passport services.

Phoning: Croatia's phone system uses area codes. If you're dialing within an area code, use just the local number; for long-distance calls, dial the area code (which starts with 0), then the local number. To **call to Croatia,** dial the international access code (00 if calling from Europe, 011 from North America), then 385 (Croatia's country code), the area code (without the initial 0), and the local number. To **call home from Croatia,** dial 00, 1, then your area code and phone number. For more help, see page 1242.

Tipping: At a restaurant with table service, round up the bill 5-10 percent after a good meal. At some tourist restaurants, a 10-15 percent service charge may be added to your bill, in which case an additional tip is not necessary.

Tourist Information: http://us.croatia.hr.

SPLIT

Dubrovnik is the darling of the Dalmatian Coast, but Split (pronounced as it's spelled) is Croatia's "second city" (after Zagreb), bustling with 178,000 people. If you've been hopping along the coast, landing in urban Split feels like a return to civilization. While most Dalmatian coastal towns seem made for tourists, Split is real and vibrant—a shipbuilding city with ugly sprawl surrounding an atmospheric Old Town, which teems with Croatians living life to the fullest.

Though today's Split throbs to a modern, youthful beat, its history goes way back—all the way to the Roman Empire. Along with all the trappings of a modern city, Split has some of the best Roman ruins this side of Italy. In the fourth century A.D., the Roman Emperor Diocletian (245-313) wanted to retire in his native Dalmatia, so he built a huge palace here. Eventually, the palace was abandoned. Then locals, fleeing seventh-century Slavic invaders, moved in and made themselves at home, and a medieval town sprouted from the rubble of the old palace. In the 15th century, the Venetians took over the Dalmatian Coast. They developed and fortified Split, slathering the city with a new layer of Gothic-Renaissance architecture.

But even as Split grew, the nucleus remained the ruins of Diocletian's Palace. To this day, 2,000 people live or work inside the former palace walls. A maze of narrow alleys is home to fashionable boutiques and galleries, wonderfully atmospheric cafés, and Roman artifacts around every corner.

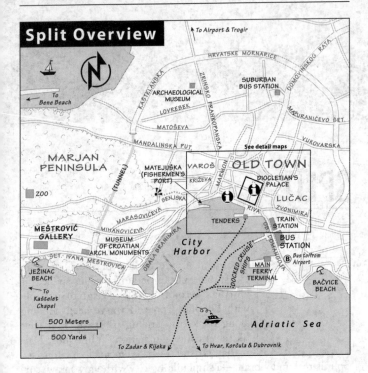

Split Overview

To Airport & Trogir

HRVATSKE MORNARICE

DOMOVINSKOG RATA

To Bene Beach

SUBURBAN
BUS STATION

ARCHAEOLOGICAL
MUSEUM
LOVREBEK

MAŽURANIĆEVO ŠET.

MATOŠEVA

VUKOVARSKA

MANDALINSKA PUT

See detail maps

MARJAN
PENINSULA

MATEJUŠKA
(FISHERMEN'S
PORT)

VAROŠ   OLD TOWN

DIOCLETIAN'S
PALACE

ZOO

KRIŽEVA

LUČAC

ZVONIMIRA

SENJSKA

RIVA

TRAIN
STATION

MARASOVIĆEVA

MEŠTROVIĆ
GALLERY

MIHANOVIĆEVA

TENDERS

BUS
STATION

MUSEUM
OF CROATIAN
ARCH. MONUMENTS

City
Harbor

B   Bus to/from
Airport

ŠET. IVANA MEŠTROVIĆA

MAIN
FERRY
TERMINAL

JEŽINAC
BEACH

BAČVICE
BEACH

To
Kaštelet
Chapel

500 Meters

500 Yards

Adriatic Sea

To Zadar & Rijeka

To Hvar, Korčula & Dubrovnik

Planning Your Time

Compact Split is made to order for a quick visit on a cruise. Here are the top activities, which I'd do in this order:

• **Tour Diocletian's Palace** in the Old Town; allow 1-1.5 hours. It's a short walk from the cruise terminal and tender dock. Stroll the remains of the palace, either using my self-guided walk or joining a walking tour (see page 810).

• Take a **coffee or ice-cream break** along the Riva promenade, or **lunch** in or near the Old Town.

• Browse the **shops** in the Old Town, or visit a couple of Split's **museums** (most can be seen in 30-60 minutes). The **Meštrović Gallery** is tops (allow 1 hour to tour the collection), but it's a 25-minute walk or short bus or taxi ride from the Old Town—leave yourself plenty of time to get back to your ship.

Arrival at the Port of Split

From a cruiser's perspective, Split is one of the easiest cities to arrive in. Cruise ships either dock or tender here; in either case, cruise passengers arrive in downtown Split, just a short walk from the main sights. From any entry point, you can see the church tower

Excursions from Split

Split itself offers enough diversions to fill an entire day, all within easy walking distance of the ship. But Split is also a place where cruise lines seem to cobble together excursions based on what's convenient to bus passengers, rather than on what's really worth seeing.

Of the many options near Split, the small town of **Trogir** is the most appealing (about a 30-minute ride by bus). Trogir is a tiny, medieval-architecture-packed town surrounded by water. Its proximity to Split makes it appealing to yachters; the proud masts of tall ships line the harbor three deep. Although Trogir is nothing to jump ship for, it's an easy day trip for those looking to get away from urban Split.

The Roman ruins at **Solin** (a.k.a. Ancient Salona), located on the outskirts of Split, pale in comparison to ancient ruins elsewhere—including those in the city center of Split. Unless you've never met a Roman ruin you didn't like, I'd skip Solin.

More nature-oriented options are farther afield: the gorgeous waterfalls at **Krka National Park,** where hikers can actually swim in a large natural pool at the base of thundering cascades (1.5 hours northwest of Split); the **Cetina River,** popular for canoe and white-water rafting trips (about 45 minutes southeast of Split); and the rustic island of **Brač,** with its famous sandy beaches (30-minute boat ride south from Split).

And finally, some cruise lines also offer side-trips to nearby towns and cities, including the resort town of **Omiš,** where the Cetina River empties into the Adriatic (about 30 minutes southeast of Split); and the city of **Šibenik,** with its impressive Cathedral of St. James (about 1.25 hours northwest of Split)... though, again, where Dalmatian cities are concerned, both of these decidedly play second fiddle to Split.

Bottom line: Unless you have a special interest in the above sights, save yourself some money and simply enjoy the urban charms, ancient wonders, and artistic gems of Split.

and waterfront promenade marking the Old Town: Just walk in that direction, and you're there.

Docking in Split: Cruise ships that dock in Split do so along a busy and very practical strip of land called Obala Kneza Domagoja, on the east side of the City Harbor. Also along here are docks for various passenger boats and car ferries to destinations throughout Croatia and Italy, the main bus station, the train station, and a wide range of services: travel agencies, ATMs, a post office, Internet cafés, shops, and cafés (see "Helpful Hints," later). On arrival, just walk around the harbor toward the big bell tower (about a 10-minute walk): Exit the ship, turn left onto the main embankment, and walk (with the harbor on your left) straight into town.

Tendering in Split: Tenders arrive at the Obala Lazareta embankment, right in front of the Old Town—just a three-minute walk from Diocletian's Palace.

Missing the Boat: For information on what to do if you miss your boat at the end of your visit, see the sidebar near the end of this chapter.

Orientation to Split

Split sprawls, but almost everything of interest to travelers is around the City Harbor (Gradska Luka). At the top of this harbor is the Old Town (Stari Grad). Between the Old Town and the sea is the Riva, a waterfront pedestrian promenade lined with cafés and shaded by palm trees.

Split's domino-shaped Old Town is made up of two square sections. The east half was once Diocletian's Palace, and the west half is the medieval town that sprang up next door. The shell of Diocletian's ruined palace provides a checkerboard street plan, with a gate at each end. But the streets built since are anything but straight, making the Old Town a delightfully convoluted maze (double-decker in some places). At the center of the former palace is a square called the Peristyle (Peristil), where you'll find the TI, cathedral, and the highest concentration of Roman ruins.

Tourist Information

Split has two TI locations: One is in the little chapel on the square called the Peristyle, in the very center of Diocletian's Palace, and the other is on the Riva at #9, facing the harbor (same hours for both: May-Sept Mon-Sat 8:00-21:00, Sun 8:00-13:00—longer if there's a cruise ship in town; April and Oct Mon-Sat 8:00-20:00, Sun 8:00-13:00; Nov-March Mon-Fri 9:00-16:00, Sat 9:00-13:00, closed Sun; Peristyle tel. 021/345-606, Riva tel. 021/360-066, www.visitsplit.com). The TIs hand out a stack of free info: a good town map, the *Discover Split* newspaper (with an even more detailed map), *Split in Your Pocket* mini-guidebooks and maps, and piles of brochures.

Helpful Hints

Festivals: For one week in late August, Split celebrates Diocletian Days, when 50 actors from Rome walk the streets in ancient garb. A boat brings "Diocletian" to the Riva, people wearing

Split Essentials

English	Croatian	Pronounced
Old Town	*Stari Grad*	STAH-ree grahd
City Harbor	*Gradska Luka*	GRAHD-skah LOO-kah
Harborfront promenade	*Riva*	REE-vah
Peristyle (old Roman square)	*Peristil*	PEH-ree-steel
Soccer team	*Hajduk*	HIGH-dook
Local sculptor	*Ivan Meštrović*	EE-vahn MESH-troh-veech
Adriatic Sea	*Jadran*	YAH-drahn

togas attend dinner in the palace cellars, and the Diocletian Games are staged along the Riva.

Internet Access: Internet cafés are plentiful in the Old Town; look for signs, especially around the Peristyle, or try **Modrulj Launderette** (described below). Closer to the stations and ferry terminal, **Backpacker C@fé** has Internet access, coffee and drinks with outdoor seating, luggage storage, and used paperbacks for sale (30 kn/hour, Wi-Fi-15 kn/hour, daily July-Aug 6:30-21:00, shoulder season 7:00-20:30, shorter hours off-season, near the beginning of Obala Kneza Domagoja, tel. 021/338-548). For locations, see map on page 808.

Post Office: A modern little post office is next to the bus station. They sell empty boxes, so this is a good opportunity to mail home any dead weight you've accumulated (Mon-Fri 7:00-20:00, Sat 7:00-13:00, closed Sun, on Obala Kneza Domagoja).

Laundry: Modrulj Launderette, a rare self-service launderette, is conveniently located in the Varoš neighborhood at the west end of the Old Town, near several recommended restaurants—handy if multitasking is your style (self-service-50 kn/load, full-service-75 kn/load, air-con, Internet access, left-luggage service; April-Oct daily 8:00-20:00; Nov-March Mon-Sat 9:00-17:00, closed Sun; Šperun 1—see map on page 808, tel. 021/315-888).

Bike Rental: Several places around town rent bikes; one central location is **Travel49** (60 kn/4 hours, 100 kn/day, Dioklecijan-

SPLIT

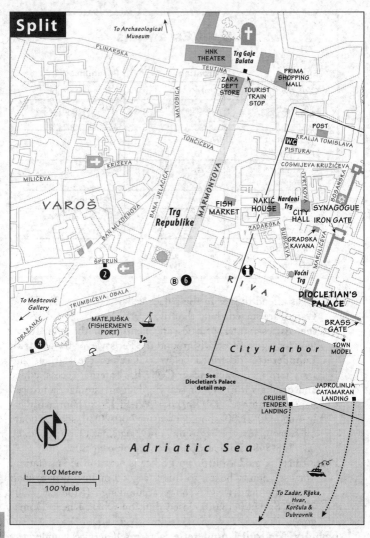

SPLIT

ova 5, mobile 098-858-141). They also plan to offer three-hour bike tours for "one penny" (but you pay for the bike rental, and the guide expects a tip). Another option is Baracuda (listed next). One good—if strenuous—option is a loop around the nearby Marjan peninsula, with a stop at a beach.

Boat Rental: As the transportation hub of the Dalmatian Coast, Split is a handy place to rent your own boat. **Baracuda,** which faces the Matejuška fishermen's port, rents a wide range of boats (one day costs €160-1,600, depending on the boat; you

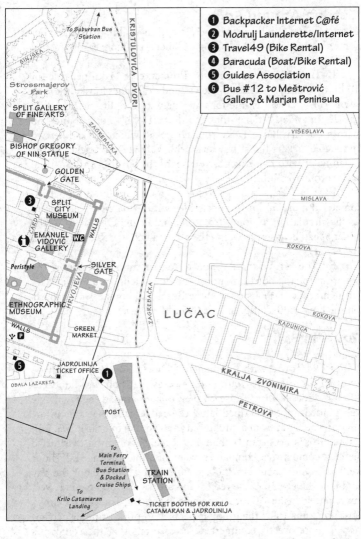

1. Backpacker Internet C@fé
2. Modrulj Launderette/Internet
3. Travel49 (Bike Rental)
4. Baracuda (Boat/Bike Rental)
5. Guides Association
6. Bus #12 to Meštrović Gallery & Marjan Peninsula

KRISTULOVIĆA DVORI

To Suburban Bus Station

SINJSKA

Strossmajerov Park

SPLIT GALLERY OF FINE ARTS

ZAGREBAČKA

VIŠESLAVA

BISHOP GREGORY OF NIN STATUE

GOLDEN GATE

MISLAVA

3 SPLIT CITY MUSEUM

CARDO

EMANUEL VIDOVIĆ GALLERY WC

1

Peristyle

WALLS

ROKOVA

SILVER GATE

HRVOJEVA

ETHNOGRAPHIC MUSEUM

LUČAC

ROKOVA

ZAGREBAČKA

RADUNICA

WALLS

GREEN MARKET

P

5

JADROLINIJA TICKET OFFICE

KRALJA ZVONIMIRA

OBALA LAZARETA

1

PETROVA

POST

To Main Ferry Terminal, Bus Station & Docked Cruise Ships

TRAIN STATION

To Krilo Catamaran Landing

TICKET BOOTHS FOR *KRILO* CATAMARAN & JADROLINIJA

SPLIT

can pay €80 extra to hire a skipper). They also offer transfers to the islands (e.g., €370 to Hvar, €710 to Korčula), scuba diving (€50/1.5 hours for beginners, €95/5 hours for licensed divers), fishing trips (€100/person for 1-2 people, €65/person for 3 or more, about 5 hours), and bike rental (20 kn/hour, 60 kn/4 hours; daily 8:00-20:00, closed Sun in winter, Trumbićeva Obala 13, tel. 021/362-462, mobile 091-566-5741, www.baracuda.hr, baracuda@st.t-com.hr).

Getting Around Split

Most of what you'll want to see is within walking distance, but some sights (such as the Meštrović Gallery) are more easily reached by bus or taxi.

By Bus: Local buses, run by Promet, cost 11 kn per ride (or 10 kn if you buy a ticket at a newsstand or Promet kiosk, ask for a *putna karta;* zone I is fine for any ride within Split, but you need the 21-kn zone IV ticket for the ride to Trogir). For a round-trip within the city, buy a 17-kn transfer ticket, which works like two individual tickets (must buy at kiosk). Validate your ticket in the machine or with the driver as you board the bus. Bus information: www.promet-split.hr.

By Taxi: Taxis start at 20 kn, then cost around 8 kn per kilometer. Figure 50 kn for most rides within the city—but due to traffic circulation, if going from one end of the Old Town to the other, it can be faster to walk. To call for a taxi, try Radio Taxi (tel. 021/1777).

By Tourist Train: An hourly tourist train leaves from the square at the top of Marmontova and does a loop around the Marjan peninsula, with a stop at Bene Beach (20 kn one-way, departs on the hour 9:00-20:00, mobile 095-530-6962).

Tours in Split

Walking Tours

Split's Old Town, with fragments of Diocletian's Palace, is made to order for a walking tour, and it seems that Split has hundreds of tour guides leading cruise-ship excursions around the town. My self-guided walk (described later) covers basically the same information you'll get from a guide. But if you'd like to hear it live, join a tour. This is a constantly changing scene, but on my last visit, two fiercely competitive companies were offering dueling 1.25-hour walks, leaving about every 60 to 90 minutes throughout the day and into the evening. The red **Sirena tours** cost 100 kn and have a more purely historical focus; the blue **"Walking Tour for a Penny"** cost one kuna (plus the guide expects a 30-50-kn tip per person) and is more overtly commercial, cross-promoting the company's other offerings. I'd pay a bit extra for a more serious operation, but you can chat with the umbrella-toting touts to find out what your options are. Yet another choice: The local **guides association** offers tours three times daily in summer (100 kn, May-Sept Mon-Sat at 10:00, 11:30, and 13:00); while these guides are usually more polished and professional, the starting point—at their office on the Riva (see map on page 808)—is a little less convenient.

Local Guides

You can hire an insider to show you around. **Maja Benzon** is a smart and savvy local guide; she leads good walking tours through the Old Town (500 kn/up to 2 hours, 600 kn/3 hours, mobile 098-852-869, maja.benzon@gmail.com). You can also hire a guide through the **guide association,** which has an office on the Riva (525 kn/1.5-2 hours; May-Sept Mon-Fri 8:30-17:30, Sat 9:00-15:00, closed Sun; off-season generally open weekday mornings only; Obala Lazareta 3, tel. 021/360-058 or 021/346-267, mobile 098-361-936, www.guides.hr, info@guides.hr).

Diocletian's Palace Walk

Split's top activity is visiting the remains of Roman Emperor Diocletian's enormous retirement palace, sitting on the harbor in the heart of the city. This monstrous complex, known as the Dioklecijanova Palača, was two impressive structures in one: luxurious villa and fortified Roman town.

My self-guided walk takes you through Diocletian's back door; down into the labyrinth of cellars that supported the palace; up to the Peristyle (the center of the palace); into Diocletian's mausoleum—now the town's cathedral, with a crypt, treasury/museum, and climbable tower; over to Jupiter's Temple (later converted into a baptistery); down the main artery of the palace; and finally to what was once the palace's front entrance. The ruins themselves are now integrated with the city's street plan, so exploring them is free—except for the cellars and the cathedral sights/temple, which you'll pay to enter. In peak season, the cellars are open late (on most days until 20:00 or 21:00), and the cathedral sights generally close at 19:00. If visiting off-season, do this walk as early as possible, because the cathedral sights close at noon. For exact hours, see the individual sight listings.

Fragments of the palace are poorly marked, and there are no good guidebooks or audioguides for understanding the remains. For most visitors, this walk provides enough details; for more in-depth information, you could join a walking tour or hire a guide (see "Tours in Split," earlier).

Background

Diocletian grew up just inland from Split, in the town of Salona (Solin in Croatian), which was then the capital of the Roman province of Dalmatia. He worked his way up the Roman hierarchy and ruled as emperor for the unusually long tenure of 20 years (A.D. 284-305). Despite all of his achievements, Diocletian is best remembered for two ques-

DIOCLETIANVS

SPLIT

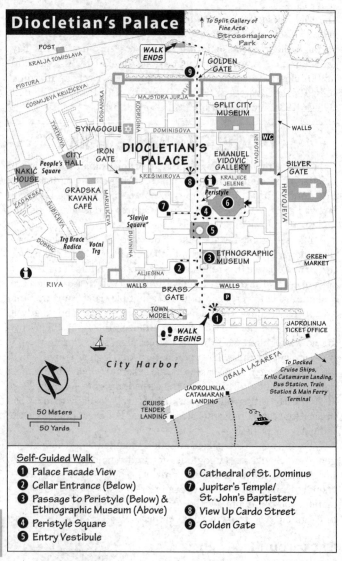

Diocletian's Palace

Self-Guided Walk

1. Palace Facade View
2. Cellar Entrance (Below)
3. Passage to Peristyle (Below) & Ethnographic Museum (Above)
4. Peristyle Square
5. Entry Vestibule
6. Cathedral of St. Dominus
7. Jupiter's Temple/ St. John's Baptistery
8. View Up Cardo Street
9. Golden Gate

tionable legacies: dividing the huge empire among four emperors (which helped administer it more efficiently, but began a splintering effect that arguably led to the empire's decline); and torturing and executing Christians, including thousands right here on the Dalmatian Coast. Soon after the end of Diocletian's reign, his successor, Constantine, not only legalized Christianity, but made it the official religion of the empire—effectively making Diocletian's purges some of the last in Roman history.

As Diocletian grew older, he decided to return to his home-land for retirement. Since he was in poor health, the medicinal sulfur spring here was another plus. His massive palace took only 11 years to build—and this fast pace required a big push (more than 2,000 slaves died during construction). Huge sections of his palace still exist, modified by medieval and modern developers alike.

• *Start in front of the palace, at the east end of the Riva. To get a sense of the original palace, check out the big illustration posted across from the palace entry. Across the street at the end of the Riva, notice the big car-size model of today's Old Town, which is helpful for orientation. (Both the sign and the model are usually crowded with tour groups.) Now study the...*

Palace Facade

The "front" of today's Split—facing the harbor—was actually the back door of Diocletian's Palace. There was no embankment in front of the palace back then, so the water came right up to this door—sort of an emergency exit by boat. Looking out to the water, appreciate the palace's strategic location: It's easy to fortify, and to spot enemies approaching either by land or by sea.

Visually trace the outline of the gigantic palace, which was more than 600 feet long on each side. On the corner to the right stands a big, rectangular guard tower (one of the original 16). To the left, the tower is gone and the corner is harder to pick out (look for the beginning of the newer-looking buildings). Mentally erase the ramshackle two-story buildings added 200 years ago, which obscure the grandeur of the palace wall.

Halfway up the facade, notice the row of 42 arched window frames (mostly filled in today). Diocletian and his family lived in the seaside half of the palace. Imagine him strolling back and forth along this fine arcade, enjoying the views of his Adriatic homeland. The inland, non-view half of the palace was home to 700 servants, bodyguards, and soldiers.

• *Go through the door in the middle of the palace (known as the "Brass Gate," located under* The Substructure of Diocletian's Palace *banner). Just inside the door and to the left is the entrance to...*

Diocletian's Cellars (Podromi)

Since the palace was constructed on land that sloped down to the sea, these chambers were built to level out a foundation for the massive structure above (like a modern "daylight basement"). These cellars were filled with water from three different sources: a fresh-water spring, a sulfur spring, and the sea. Later, medieval residents used them as a dump. Rediscovered only in the last century, the cellars enabled archaeologists to derive the floor plan of some of the palace's long-gone upper sections. These underground chambers now house art exhibits and a little strip of souvenir stands. One particularly well-preserved stretch can be toured, offering the best look in town at Roman engineering.

Cost and Hours: 40 kn, some posters inside explain the site; June-Sept daily 9:00-21:00; April-May and Oct Mon-Sat 9:00-20:00, Sun 9:00-18:00 except in April, when it closes Sun at 14:00; Nov-March Mon-Sat 9:00-18:00, Sun 9:00-14:00.

Visiting the Cellars: Use the free map you get at the entry to navigate this labyrinthine complex of cellars. First visit the **western cellars** (to the left as you enter). Near the ticket-seller, notice the big **topographical map** of the Split area, clearly showing the city's easily defensible location—with a natural harbor sheltered by tall mountains. You'll see the former Roman city of Salona, Diocletian's birthplace, just inland.

This network of cellars is quite a maze, so follow these instructions carefully: Head into the main part of the cellars by going through the door on the right, just past the ticket-seller. This takes you into the complex's vast, vaulted **main hall**—the biggest space in the cellars, with stout pillars to support everything upstairs. When those first villagers took refuge in the abandoned palace from the rampaging Slavs in 641, the elite lived upstairs, grabbing what was once the emperor's wing. They carved the rough holes you see in the ceiling to dump their garbage and sewage. Over the generations, the basement (where you're standing) filled up with layers of pungent waste that solidified, ultimately becoming a precious bonanza for 19th- and 20th-century archaeologists. Today this hall is used for everything from flower and book shows to fashion catwalks. (And, in 2013, it was used to film scenes for HBO's *Game of Thrones*.)

Exit the main hall through either of the doors on the left, cross through the narrow corridor, and enter the long room. Look just overhead—the holes you see once held beams to support floorboards, making this a two-story cellar. Face the giant replica of a golden Diocletian coin at the far end, and turn left, then immediately right into a small circular room, which has a headless, pawless black granite sphinx—one of 13 that Diocletian brought home from Egypt (only four survive, including a mostly intact one we'll see soon on the Peristyle). Look up to admire the circular brickwork. Then continue straight into another small room, which adjoins one that displays a stone olive-oil press.

Backtrack through the round room and into a room that displays two petrified beams, like the ones that once filled the double-decker holes we saw earlier. At the far (right) end of this room is an unexcavated wing—a compost pile of ancient lifestyles, awaiting the tiny shovels and toothbrushes of future archaeologists.

Facing the mound of ancient garbage, turn left into another round room, featuring a bust of Diocletian (or is it Sean Connery?). From here, turn left and go through another room (passing WCs on the right) to return to the long room you were in earlier, then turn right and exit out the bottom of this hall. On your right, look for original Roman sewer pipes—square outside and round inside—designed to fit into each other to create long pipes.

From here, head back out to the exit. If you'd like to see more cellars—mostly with their ceilings missing, so they're open to the air—cross over into the **eastern cellars** (same ticket). This section is less interesting than the western part, but worth a quick visit.

• *When you're finished, head back to the main gallery. Ignore the tacky made-in-Malaysia trinket shops as you head down the passage and up the chunky stairs into the...*

Peristyle (Peristil)

This square was the centerpiece of Diocletian's Palace. As you walk up the stairs, the entry vestibule into the residence is above your

head, Diocletian's mausoleum (today's Cathedral of St. Dominus) is to your right, and the street to Jupiter's Temple (supported by wooden beams) is on your left. The TI is in the small chapel, at the end of the square on the right. Straight ahead, beyond the TI/chapel, is the narrow street that leads to the palace's former main entrance, the Golden Gate.

Go to the middle of the square and take it all in. The red granite pillars—which you'll see all over Diocletian's Palace—are from Egypt, where Diocletian spent many of his pre-retirement years. Imagine the pillars defining fine arcades—now obscured by medieval houses. The black sphinx is the only one of Diocletian's collection of 13 that's still (mostly) intact.

"Roman soldiers" pose for tips (daily 9:00-17:00), and every day at noon in summer (mid-June-mid-Sept), an actor playing Diocletian appears at the top of the stairs to address the crowd in Latin.

Without realizing it, you're standing in the middle of one of Split's most inviting bars, Luxor. The red cushions on the steps ringing the square belong to the bar; if you want to sit on one, you have to buy a drink (especially worthwhile in the evening, when the Peristyle is less crowded and there's often live music).

• *Climb the stairs (above where you came in) into the domed, open-ceilinged...*

Entry Vestibule

Impressed? That's the idea. This was the grand entry to Diocletian's living quarters, meant to wow visitors. Emperors were believed

to be gods. Diocletian called himself "Jovius"—the son of Jupiter, the most powerful of all gods. Four times a year (at the changing of the seasons), Diocletian would stand here and overlook the Peristyle. His subjects would lie on the ground in worship, praising his name and kissing his scarlet robe. Notice the four big niches at floor level, which once held statues of the four tetrarchs who ruled the unwieldy empire after Diocletian retired. The empty hole in the ceiling was once capped by a dome (long since collapsed), and the ceiling itself was covered with frescoes and mosaics.

In this grand space, you'll likely run into an all-male band of *klapa* singers, performing traditional a cappella harmonies. Just stand and enjoy a few glorious tunes—you'll rarely find a better group or acoustics. A 100-kn *klapa* CD is the perfect souvenir.

Wander out back to the harborside through medieval buildings (some with seventh-century foundations), which evoke the way local villagers came in and took over the once-spacious and elegant palace. Back in this area, you'll find the beautifully restored home of the **Ethnographic Museum** (described later, under "Sights in Split").

• *Now go back into the Peristyle and turn right, climbing the steps to the...*

Cathedral of St. Dominus (Katedrala Sv. Duje)

The original octagonal structure was Diocletian's elaborate mausoleum, built in the fourth century. But after the fall of Rome, it was converted into the town's cathedral. Construction of the bell tower began in the 13th century and took 300 years to complete. Before you go inside, notice the sarcophagi ringing the cathedral. In the late Middle Ages, this was prime post-mortem real estate, since being buried closer to a cathedral improved your chances of getting to heaven.

Cost and Hours: Several sights associated with the cathedral require tickets: the cathedral interior, the unimpressive treasury/museum, the crypt, the tower climb, and—a block away—Jupiter's Temple (described later). While ticketing options always seem in flux, you'll likely have an option to pay 25 kn for the cathedral, crypt, and baptistery (the three most worthwhile parts); a 45-kn ticket adds the skippable treasury/museum and steep-but-scenic bell tower. (You can also pay 15 kn just for the tower climb—buy ticket at tower door.) All of the sights are open similar hours, but the cathedral can close unexpectedly for services. In general, hours are summer Mon-Sat 8:00-19:00, Sun 12:30-18:30, cathedral often closed Sat afternoons for weddings; winter daily 7:00-12:00, maybe later on request; Kraj Sv. Duje 5, tel. 021/345-602.

Visiting the Cathedral: To get inside in peak season (April-Oct), you must loop around the outside of the cathedral. Facing the main door at the bottom of the stairs, circle around the right side—passing the crypt (included in the cathedral ticket and described later)—to find the door in the building behind. Buy your ticket here and climb up the stairs. (In winter, you can usually enter the cathedral through the main door.) Once inside, the first flight of stairs leads to the cathedral interior (described below), but if you bought the 45-kn ticket and want to see the **treasury/museum** first, head up one more flight. The single-room museum contains dusty display cases of vestments, giant psalter books, icon-like paintings, reliquaries, chalices, monstrances, and other church art, with very sparse English descriptions. After visiting, head back down to the cathedral.

Step into the church **interior.** You'll enter into the apse; head around the side of the altar to reach the main (though still tiny) part of the church. This is the oldest—and likely smallest—building used as a cathedral anywhere in Christendom. Imagine the place in pre-Christian times, with Diocletian's tomb in the center. The only surviving pieces of decor from those days are the granite columns and the relief circling the base of the dome (about 50 feet up)—a ring of carvings heralding the greatness of the emperor. The

small red-marble pillars around the top of the pulpit (near the main door) were scavenged from Diocletian's sarcophagus. These pillars are all that remain of Diocletian's remains.

Diocletian brutally persecuted his Christian subjects. Just before he moved to the Dalmatian

SPLIT

Coast, he had Bishop Dominus of Salona killed, along with several thousand Christians. When Diocletian died, there were riots of happiness. In the seventh century, his mausoleum became a cathedral dedicated to the martyred bishop. The apse (behind the altar) was added in the ninth century. The sarcophagus of St. Dominus (to the right of the altar, with early-Christian carvings) was once the cathedral's high altar. To the left of today's main altar is the impressively detailed, Renaissance-era altar of St. Anastasius, who is lying on a millstone that is tied to his neck. On Diocletian's orders, this Christian martyr was drowned in A.D. 302. To the left of St. Anastasius' altar is the "new" altar of St. Dominus; his relics lie in the 18th-century Baroque silver reliquary, above a stone relief showing him about to be beheaded. Posthumous poetic justice: Now Christian saints are entombed in Diocletian's mausoleum... and Diocletian is nowhere to be found. As you exit through the 13th-century main doors, notice the 14 panels on each of the two wings—showing 28 scenes from the life of Christ.

Exiting the church, you'll see the entrance to the **bell tower** on your right. Climbing the 183 steep steps to the top of the 200-foot-tall bell tower rewards you with sweeping views of Split, but it's not for claustrophobes or those scared of heights.

To visit the **crypt** *(kripta)*, also included with your ticket, exit the main door of the cathedral, go down the stairs, and loop left to find its low-profile entrance. This musty, domed cellar (with eerie acoustics) was originally used to level the foundation of Diocletian's mausoleum. Later, Christians turned it into another chapel, dedicated to the Italian Saint Lucia, who was martyred by Diocletian. (The legend you'll likely hear about Diocletian torturing and murdering Christians in this very crypt, which began about the same time this became a church, is probably false.) Lucia stands above a small altar where the faithful have left scraps of paper scrawled with their prayers and their thanks. Ponder the contrast of this dark and gloomy space with Santa Lucia, whose name means "light." Notice the freshwater well in the middle of the room. Because this water was believed to have healing properties, the faithful would wash their eyes with it (particularly appropriate, since Santa Lucia is also the patron saint of eyesight).

• *Return to the middle of the Peristyle square. Remember that Diocletian believed himself to be Jovius (Jupiter, Jr.). As worshippers exited the mausoleum of Jovius, they would look straight ahead to the temple of Jupiter. (Back then, there were none of these medieval buildings cluttering up the view.) Make your way through the narrow alley (directly across from the cathedral entry), past another headless, pawless sphinx, to explore the small...*

Jupiter's Temple/St. John's Baptistery

About the time the mausoleum became a cathedral, this temple was converted into a baptistery (same ticket and hours as cathe-

dral; off-season, if it's locked, go ask the person at the cathedral to let you in). Inside, the big 12th-century baptismal font—large enough to immerse someone (as was the tradition in those days)—is decorated with the intricate, traditional woven-rope *pleter* design. Observant travelers will see examples of this motif all over the country. On the font, notice the engraving: a bishop (on the left) and the king on his throne (on the right).

At their feet (literally under the feet of the bishop) is a submissive commoner—neatly summing up the social structure of the Middle Ages. Standing above the font is a statue of St. John the Baptist counting to four, done by the great Croatian sculptor Ivan Meštrović (see page 824). The half-barrel vaulted ceiling, completed later, is considered the best-preserved of its kind anywhere. Every face and each patterned box is different.

• *Back at the Peristyle, stand in front of the little chapel with your back to the square. The small street just beyond the chapel (going left to right) connects the east and west gates. If you've had enough Roman history, head right (east) to go through the Silver Gate and find Split's busy, open-air Green Market. Or, head to the left (west), which takes you to the Iron Gate and People's Square (see "Sights in Split," later) and, beyond that, the fresh-and-smelly fish market. But if you want to see one last bit of Roman history, continue straight ahead up the...*

Cardo

A traditional Roman street plan has two roads: Cardo (the north-south axis) and Decumanus (the east-west axis). Split's Cardo street was the most important in Diocletian's Palace, connecting the main entry with the heart of the complex. As you walk, you'll pass several noteworthy sights: in the first building on the right, a bank with modern computer gear all around its exposed Roman ruins (look through window); at the first gate on the left, the courtyard of a Venetian merchant's palace (a reminder that Split was dominated by Venice from the 15th century on); farther along on the right, an alley to the **City Museum** (with a modest but interesting exhibit on local history); and, beyond that on the right, **Nadalina,** an artisan chocolatier selling mostly dark chocolate creations with some innovative Dalmatian flavors—such as dried fig and prosecco

(32 kn/100 grams, chocolate bars, Mon-Fri 8:30-20:30, Sat 9:00-14:00, closed Sun, mobile 091-210-8889).

At the end of the street, just before the Golden Gate, detour a few steps to the left along covered **Majstora Jurja** street—lined with some of the most appealing outdoor cafés in town, lively both day and night (described later, under "Nightlife in Split"). Near the start of this street, just after its initial jog, stairs climb to the miniscule **St. Martin's Chapel,** burrowed into the city wall. Dating from the fifth century, this is one of the earliest Christian chapels anywhere. St. Martin is the patron saint of soldiers, and the chapel was built for the troops who guarded this gate (free, sporadic hours—just climb the stairs to see if it's open).

• *Backtrack to the main drag and go inside the huge...*

Golden Gate (Zlatna Vrata)

This great gate was the main entry of Diocletian's Palace. Its name wasn't literal—rather, the "gold" suggests the importance of this gateway to Salona, the Roman provincial capital at the time. Standing inside the gate itself, you can appreciate the double-door design that kept the palace safe. Also notice how this ancient building is now being used in very different ways from its original purpose. Above, on the outer wall, you can see the bricked-in windows that contain part of a Dominican convent. At the top of the inner wall is somebody's garden terrace.

Go outside the gate and look back at the recently restored fortification—with all its structural elements gleaming. This mostly  uncluttered facade gives you the best opportunity in town to visualize how the palace looked before so many other buildings were grafted on. Straight ahead as you exit this gate is Salona (Solin), which was a major city of 60,000 (and Diocletian's hometown) before there was a Split. The big statue by Ivan Meštrović is **Bishop Gregory of Nin,** a 10th-century Croatian priest who tried to convince the Vatican to allow sermons during Mass to be said in Croatian, rather than Latin. People rub his toe for good luck (though only nonmaterial wishes are given serious consideration).

• *Our walk is finished. Now enjoy the rest of Split.*

Sights in Split

Inviting Public Spaces in or near the Old Town

My self-guided walk through Diocletian's Palace (described earlier) takes you through the main artery of town, but just a few steps away are some delightful squares and other public zones that are worth exploring.

▲▲▲The Riva

The official name for this seaside pedestrian drag is the "Croatian National Revival Embankment" (Obala Hrvatskog Narodnog

Preporoda), but locals just call it "Riva" (Italian for "harbor"). This is the town's promenade, an integral part of Mediterranean culture. After dinner, Split residents collect their families and friends for a stroll on the Riva. It offers some of the best people-watching in Croatia; make it a point to be here for an hour or two after dinner. The stinky smell that sometimes accompanies the stroll (especially at the west end) isn't from a sewer. It's sulfur—a reminder that the town's medicinal sulfur spas have attracted people here since the days of Diocletian.

The Riva is a broad, sleek, carefully landscaped people zone. A clean, synchronized line of modern white lampposts and sun screens sashays down the promenade. Some think that the starkly modern strip is at odds with the rest of the higgledy-piggledy Old Town, while others see this as simply the early-21st century's contribution to the architectural hodgepodge that is Split.

At the west end of the Riva, the people-parade of Croatian culture turns right and heads away from the water, up **Marmontova.** Although it lacks the seafront cachet, this drag is equally enjoyable and feels more local. As you walk up Marmontova, on the left is the plain-Jane outer facade of the arcade that defines Trg Republike, a grand and genteel Napoleonic-era square. Duck through the passage across from the fish market to bask in its "poor man's St. Mark's Square" ambience, and maybe to linger over a drink at the recommended Bajamonti café. A bit farther up Marmontova, on the right, look for the whimsical fountain nicknamed "The Teacup," with a hand squirting water across the sidewalk into a funnel. At the top of Marmontova are some department stores,

SPLIT

a lively café square, and the Croatian National Theater (Hrvatsko Narodno Kazalište, HNK).

▲People's Square (Narodni Trg)

Locals call this lively square at the center of the Old Town *Pjaca*, pronounced the same as the Italian *piazza* (PYAH-tsah). Stand in the center and enjoy the bustle. Look around for a quick lesson in

Dalmatian history. When Diocletian lived in his palace, a Roman village popped up here, just outside the wall. Face the former wall of Diocletian's Palace (behind and to the right of the 24-hour clock tower). This was the western entrance, or so-called "Iron Gate." By the 14th century, a medieval town had developed, making this the main square of Split.

On the wall just to the right of the lane leading to the Peristyle, look for the life-size relief of **St. Anthony.** Notice the creepy "mini-me" clutching the saint's left leg—depicting the sculptor's donor, who didn't want his gift to be forgotten. Above this strange statue, notice the smaller, faded relief of a man and a woman arguing.

Turn around and face the square. On your left is the city's grand old café, **Gradska Kavana,** which has been the Old Town's venerable meeting point for generations. Today it's both a café and a restaurant with disappointing food but the best outdoor ambience in town.

Across the square, the white building jutting into the square was once the **City Hall,** and now houses temporary exhibitions. The loggia is all that remains of the original Gothic building.

At the far end of the square is the out-of-place **Nakić House,** built in the early 20th-century Viennese Secession style—a reminder that Dalmatia was part of the Habsburg Empire, and ruled by Vienna, from Napoleon's downfall through World War I.

The lane on the right side of the Nakić House leads to Split's **fish market** (Ribarnica), where you can see piles of the still-wriggling catch of the day. No flies? It's thanks to the sulfur spring in the nearby spa building (with the gray statues, on the corner). Just beyond the fish market is the pedestrian boulevard, Marmontova (described earlier).

Radić Brothers Square (Trg Braće Radića)

This little piazza is just off the Riva between the two halves of the Old Town. Overhead is a **Venetian citadel.** After Split became part of the Venetian Republic, there was a serious danger of attack by the Ottomans, so octagonal towers like this were built all along the coast. But this imposing tower had a second purpose: to encourage citizens of Split to forget about any plans of rebellion. At its base is an inviting juice bar, invoking the more popular nickname of the square—Voćni Trg ("Fruit Square"), for the produce that was once sold here.

In the middle of the square is a studious sculpture by Ivan Meštrović of the 16th-century poet **Marko Marulić,** who is considered the father of the Croatian language. Marulić was the first to write literature in the Croatian vernacular, which before then had generally been considered a backward peasants' tongue.

On the downhill (harbor) side of the square is **Croata,** a necktie boutique that loves to explain how Croatian soldiers who fought with the French in the Thirty Years' War (1618-1648) had a distinctive way of tying their scarves. The French found it stylish, adopted it, and called it *à la Croate*—or eventually, *cravate*—thus creating the modern necktie that many people wear to work every day throughout the world. Croata's selection includes ties with traditional Croatian motifs, such as the checkerboard pattern from the flag or writing in the ninth-century Glagolitic alphabet. Though pricey, these ties make nice souvenirs. Basic ties run about 500 kn, while handmade ones with 24-carat gold accents can run 2,800-3,800 kn. The shop also sells women's scarves (Mon-Fri 8:00-20:00, Sat 8:00-13:00, closed Sun, Mihovilova Širina 7, tel. 021/346-336). Croata has a bigger, second location on the Peristyle.

Green Market

This lively open-air market bustles at the east end of Diocletian's Palace. Residents shop for produce and clothes here, and there are plenty of tourist souvenirs as well. Browse the wide selection of T-shirts, and ignore the sleazy black-market tobacco salesmen who mutter at you: *"Cigaretta?"*

Matejuška Fishermen's Port

While Split's harborfront Riva is where the beautiful people stroll, the city's fishermen roots still thrive just to the west. The neigh-

borhood called Matejuška—at the little harbor where the Varoš district hits the water (a five-minute walk beyond the end of the Riva, with the water on your left)—has long been Split's working fishermen's harbor. While the area has received a facelift to match the one along the Riva, it still retains its striped-collar character. The enclosed harbor area is filled with working fishing boats and colorful dinghies that bob in unison. Along the breakwater, notice the new fishermen's lockers,

Ivan Meštrović
(1883-1962)

Ivan Meštrović (EE-vahn MESH-troh-veech), who achieved international fame for his talents as a sculptor, was Croatia's answer to Rodin. You'll see Meštrović's works every-where, in the streets, squares, and museums of Croatia.

Meštrović came from humble begin-nings. He grew up in a family of poor, nomad-ic farm workers just inland from Split. At an early age, his drawings and wooden carvings showed promise, and a rich family took him in and made sure he was properly trained. He eventually went off to school in Vienna, where he fell in with the Secession movement and found fame and fortune. He lived in Prague, Paris, and Switzerland, fully engaged in the flourishing European artistic culture at the turn of the 20th century (he counted Rodin among his friends). After World War I, Meštrović moved back to Croatia and established an atelier, or workshop, in Zagreb.

Later in life—like Diocletian before him—Meštrović returned to Split and built a huge seaside mansion (today's Meštrović Gallery). The years between the World Wars were Meštrović's happiest and most productive. It was during this time that he sculpted his most internationally famous works, a pair of giant Native American warriors on horseback in Chicago's Grant Park. But when World War II broke out, Meštrović—an outspoken supporter of the ideals of a united Yugoslavia—was briefly imprisoned by the anti-Yugoslav Ustaše (Croatia's Nazi puppet government). After his release, Meštrović fled to Italy, then to the US, where he lectured at prominent universities such as Notre Dame and Syracuse. (President Eisenhower literally handed Meštrović his new US passport in 1954.) After the war, the Yugoslav dictator Tito invited Meštrović to return, but the very religious artist refused to cooperate with an atheist regime. (Meštrović was friends with the Archbishop Alojzije Stepinac, who was imprisoned by Tito.) Meštrović died in South Bend, Indiana.

Viewing Meštrović's works, his abundant talent is evident.

where people who earn their living from the Adriatic still keep their supplies. You'll see the most fisherman action here in the mornings.

The far side of the breakwater—all glitzy white marble—is another world, with a pebbly beach, attractive plaza, and some of the best views looking back on the Riva. After its recent renovation, this jetty has become a popular open-air, after-hours hangout for young people. Like Split itself, these two worlds—the grizzled

He worked in wood, plaster, marble, and bronze, and dabbled in painting. Meštrović's figures typically have long, angular fingers, arms, and legs. Whether whimsical or emotional, Meštrović's expressive, elongated faces—often with prominent noses—powerfully connect with the viewer.

Here are a few themes you'll see recurring in Meštrović's works as you tour his museum:

Religion: Meštrović was a devout Catholic.

Dalmatian traditions: Meštrović felt a poignant nostalgia for the simple lifestyles and customs of his home region of Drniš, and he used his art to elevate them to be on par with religious and mythological themes. This is most evident in the angular scarves many of his female subjects wear around their heads.

Yugoslav symbolism: Meštrović was a strong supporter of the first (pre-WWII) incarnation of Yugoslavia. He created sculptures not only in Croatia, but throughout Yugoslavia, many of them honoring heroes of Yugoslav tradition.

Secession: Living and studying in Vienna in the early 20th century, Meštrović was exposed to the slinky cultural milieu of the likes of Gustav Klimt.

Struggling men, serene women: While Meštrović frequently sculpted both male and female nudes, they often carry starkly different tones: Meštrović's ripped men tend to be toiling against an insurmountable challenge; his smooth and supple women are celebrating life, often through the medium of music (dancing, singing, playing musical instruments, and so on).

Tumult: Meštrović's life coincided with a time of great turmoil in Europe. He lived through World War I, the creation of the first Yugoslavia, World War II, the postwar/communist Yugoslavia, and the dawn of the Atomic Age in the United States. This early 20th-century angst—particularly surrounding his arrest and exile during World War II—comes through in his work.

Meštrović's works can be found throughout Split, Croatia, and the former Yugoslavia. In Split, in addition to the Meštrović Gallery and Kaštelet Chapel, you'll find his statues of Marko Marulić (see page 823), Gregory of Nin (page 820), and John the Baptist (page 819).

SPLIT

fishermen mending their nets, and the teenagers laughing and flirting—coexist more smoothly than anyone might have guessed.

Beyond Matejuška, the harborfront embankment (which runs toward the Marjan peninsula) has also been rejuvenated and is now spiffed up with cafés facing moored sailboats, creating a relaxing, scenic, largely tourist-free zone.

Marjan Peninsula

This huge, hilly, and relatively undeveloped spit of parkland—improbably located right next to Split's Old Town—feels like a chunk of Dalmatian island wilderness, a stone's throw from the big city. With out-of-the-way beaches and miles of hiking trails, the Marjan (MAR-yahn) Peninsula is where residents go to relax; most people here seem to have their favorite hidden paths and beach coves, so ask around for tips.

Beaches

Since it's more of a big city than a resort, Split's beaches aren't as scenic (and the water not as clear) as in many other Adriatic towns. But if you want to do some sunbathing and take a dip, you do have several options. The beach that's most popular—and crowded—is the family-friendly **Bačvice,** in a shallow, pebbly cove just a short walk east of the main ferry terminal. You'll find less crowded beaches just to the east of Bačvice. Each cove has its own little swimming zone; the fourth cove over, called **Trstenik,** is perhaps the most inviting, with rental chairs in front of a big hotel.

Or head in the other direction to Marjan, the peninsular city park (described earlier), which is ringed with several sunbathing beaches. Along the southern edge of Marjan, just below the Meštrović Gallery, is a rocky but more local-feeling and less crowded beach called **Ježinac** (Croatian for "sea urchin"...be sure to wear water shoes). **Bene Beach** is along the northern edge of Marjan—so it offers more shade. You can get to Bene Beach by bus #12 (the same one that goes to the Meštrović Gallery), tourist train (described earlier, under "Getting Around Split"), bike, or foot (about a 45-minute walk from the Old Town).

Ivan Meštrović Sights, West of the Old Town

The excellent Meštrović Gallery and nearby Kaštelet Chapel are just outside the Old Town. Both sights are covered by the same ticket and have the same hours.

Cost and Hours: 30 kn, covers both the gallery and the chapel; May-Sept Tue-Sun 9:00-19:00; Oct-April Tue-Sat 9:00-16:00, Sun 10:00-15:00; closed Mon year-round; gallery tel. 021/340-800, chapel tel. 021/358-185, www.mdc.hr/mestrovic.

Getting There: Both sights are located along Šetalište Ivana Meštrovića. You can take **bus** #12 from the little cul-de-sac at the west end of the Riva (departs hourly, likely at :50 past the hour—but check the schedule; get off at the stop in front of the gallery, just after your bus passes a museum prominently marked *Muzej Hrvatskih Arheoloških Spomenika*). You can also **walk** (about 30 minutes): Follow the harbor west of town toward the big marina, swing right with the road, and follow the park until you see the gallery on your right (at #46). A **taxi** from the west end of the Old

Town to the gallery costs about 50 kn (much more from the east end of the Old Town).

The chapel is a short walk past the gallery down Šetalište Ivana Meštrovića. To reach the chapel from the gallery, head down the stairs to the road, cross the street, turn right, and walk about five minutes. You'll see the low-profile entrance to the chapel on the left, through a doorway marked *39,* in an olive grove.

Cuisine Art: Café Galerija is just above the ticket office.

▲▲Meštrović Gallery (Galerija Meštrović)

Split's best art museum is dedicated to the sculptor Ivan Meštrović, the most important of all Croatian artists. Many of Meštrović's

finest works are housed in this palace, designed by the sculptor himself to serve as his residence, studio, and exhibition space. If you have time, it's worth the trek. Each work is labeled, but there's very little description otherwise (and the 80-kn guidebook is overkill for most visitors). Before you begin, read the sidebar (see page 824) for background on Meštrović's life; while the collection is presented thematically rather than chronologically, knowing the artist's journey helps to make sense of what you'll see.

▲▲Kaštelet Chapel

If you enjoy the gallery, don't miss the nearby Kaštelet Chapel ("Chapel of the Holy Cross"). Meštrović bought this 16th-century

fortified palace to display his 28 wood reliefs of Jesus' life. You can see how Meštrović's style changed over time, as he carved these over a nearly 30-year span, completing the last 12 when he was in the US. (However, note that he didn't carve the reliefs in chronological order; the ticket office sells a booklet identifying the topic and year for each one.) While the earlier pieces are well-composed and powerful, the later ones seem more hastily done, as Meštrović rushed to complete his opus. Work clockwise around the room, tracing the life of Christ. Notice that some of the Passion scenes are out of order (a side-effect of Meštrović's nonlinear schedule). The beautiful *pietà* back near the entrance still shows some of the original surface of the wood, demonstrating the skill required to create depth and emotion in just a few inches of medium. Dominating the chapel is an extremely powerful wooden crucifix, with Christ's arms, legs, fingers, and toes bent at unnatural angles—a typically expressionistic flair Meštrović used to exaggerate suffering.

Eating in Split

In and near the Old Town

Trattoria Bajamont, not to be confused with Bajamonti (listed below), is buried on a narrow lane deep in the Old Town. They offer unpretentious, affordable Dalmatian home cooking with an emphasis on fish. The handwritten menu informs you of the day's options—all fresh from the market. In this tight, casual, and cozy eatery, the busy kitchen and seven tables are all crammed into a single room (with more tables on the alley outside). Because the place can be crowded, you may have to share your table—and be prepared for the service to be chaotic and a bit quirky (90-120-kn pastas, 90-150-kn fish dishes, cash only, daily 8:00-24:00—but closed Sun outside peak season, Bajamontijeva 3, tel. 021/355-356).

Apetit serves up traditional Dalmatian cuisine in an appealingly modern, second-floor dining room. As there's no outdoor seating, this is a good bad-weather option (60-85-kn pastas, 60-125-kn main courses; 90-kn daily special includes soup, salad, and main dish; lots of groups, daily 10:00-24:00, Šubićeva 5, tel. 021/332-549).

Bajamonti sits regally at the top of Split's beautiful, arcaded square, Trg Republike, just off the west end of the Riva. This place brings a certain grand-café elegance to Split's otherwise rustic-*konoba*-heavy dining scene. The interior is classy, with checkerboard-tiled, split-level elegance, but the best seating is on the grand square out front, facing the sea. The food is pricey, with an emphasis on fish (90-120-kn pastas, 120-170-kn main courses, 75-95-kn lunches, daily 7:30-24:00, Trg Republike 1, tel. 021/341-033).

Uje Oilbar is the flagship restaurant of Croatia's popular chain of upscale olive-oil boutiques. Tucked away in a hidden corner of the Old Town, it serves simple plates and boards of Dalmatian *pršut* (prosciutto), cheeses, olives, and, of course, olive oils—50 different types. The menu is short, and it feels more like a big snack than a hearty meal; to assemble a filling meal, you'll run up quite a bill. But the rustic-mod interior, pleasant (if cramped) outdoor seating, and refreshingly good-quality local flavors can make a light meal here worthwhile (35-65-kn olive-oil tastings, 70-100-kn small plates and taster boards, daily 12:00-24:00, Dominisova 3, mobile 095-200-8008).

Maslina ("Olive"), an unpretentious family-run spot filled with locals, hides behind a shopping mall on the busy Marmontova pedestrian street. They serve a wide range of 45-70-kn pizzas and

Tips on Eating in Croatia

Croatia offers good food for reasonable prices. Choosing between strudel and baklava on the same menu, you're constantly reminded that this is a land where East meets West.

If you're in the mood for a picnic meal, look for bakeries selling *burek* (savory phyllo dough filled with meat, cheese, spinach, or apples), baklava (phyllo dough layered with honey and nuts), and other goodies, or try a shop advertising "pizza cut" (pizza by the slice to go). Many grocery stores sell premade sandwiches.

Cheap pizza or pasta joints are on every corner, offering an easy, quick, and inexpensive way to fill the tank. A Dalmatian specialty is *pašticada*—braised beef in a slightly sweet wine-and-herb sauce. Balkan-style grilled meats are also popular: You'll most often see *čevapčići,* minced meat formed into a sausage shape, and *ražnjići,* steak on a skewer. A nice veggie complement is *đuveđ,* a spicy mix of stewed vegetables, flavored with tomatoes and peppers. The perfect condiment for grilled meats is *ajvar,* made from red bell pepper and eggplant—like ketchup with a kick.

At fish restaurants, seafood is often priced by weight—either by kilogram (just over two pounds) or by hectogram (about 3.5 ounces). A one-kilogram portion feeds two hungry people or three light eaters.

When restaurant-hunting, venturing even a block or two off the main drag leads to local, higher-quality food for less than half the price of the tourist-oriented places. Only a rude waiter will rush you. Good service is relaxed (slow to an American).

pastas, plus 70-120-kn meat and fish dishes (Tue-Sat 11:00-24:00, Sun-Mon 12:00-24:00, Teutina 1A, tel. 021/314-988, Pezo family). It's virtually impossible to find on your own, so follow these directions carefully: Approaching the top of Marmontova from the harbor, look for the low-profile archway on the left beyond the café tables (just before the big Zara store). Walk along the skinny path between the building and the old wall to reach the restaurant.

Pizzerias: **Ristorante Pizzeria Galija,** at the west end of the Old Town, has a boisterous local following and good wood-fired

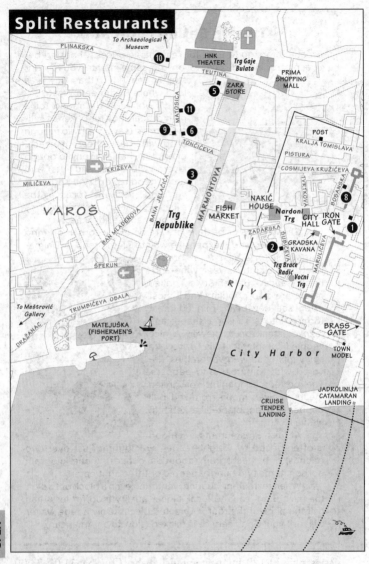

Split Restaurants

To Archaeological Museum

PLINARSKA

HNK THEATER

Trg Gaje Bulata

TEUTINA

PRIMA SHOPPING MALL

ZARA STORE

MATOŠICA

TONČIĆEVA

POST

KRALJA TOMISLAVA

PISTURA

COSMIJEVA   KRUŽIĆEVA

TKETKOVA

BOSANSKA

KRIŽEVA

BANA JELAČIĆA

MARMONTOVA

NAKIĆ HOUSE

MARULIĆEVA

IRON GATE

MILIČEVA

VAROŠ

FISH MARKET

Trg Republike

Nardoni Trg

CITY HALL

ZADARSKA

SUBIĆEVA

GRADSKA KAVANA

BAN MLADENOVA

ŠPERUN

Trg Braće Radić

Voćni Trg

DRAŽANAC

TRUMBIĆEVA OBALA

To Meštrović Gallery

MATEJUŠKA (FISHERMEN'S PORT)

R I V A

BRASS GATE

TOWN MODEL

City Harbor

CRUISE TENDER LANDING

JADROLINIJA CATAMARAN LANDING

pizza, pasta, and salads. They have a cozy interior and a terrace (40-75 kn, Mon-Sat 9:00-24:00, Sun 12:00-24:00, air-con, just a block off of Marmontova at Tončićeva 12, tel. 021/347-932; the recommended Hajduk ice-cream shop is nearby). **Zlatna Vrata** ("Golden Gate"), right in the Old Town, offers wood-fired pizzas and pasta dishes. The food and interior are nothing special, but there's wonderful outdoor seating in a tingle-worthy Gothic courtyard with pointy arches and lots of pillars. They plan to start serving a more

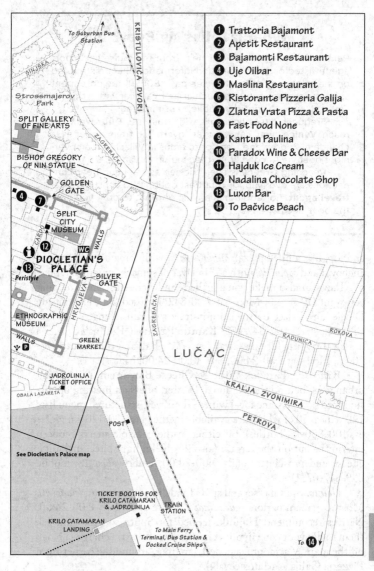

1 Trattoria Bajamont
2 Apetit Restaurant
3 Bajamonti Restaurant
4 Uje Oilbar
5 Maslina Restaurant
6 Ristorante Pizzeria Galija
7 Zlatna Vrata Pizza & Pasta
8 Fast Food None
9 Kantun Paulina
10 Paradox Wine & Cheese Bar
11 Hajduk Ice Cream
12 Nadalina Chocolate Shop
13 Luxor Bar
14 To Bačvice Beach

SPLIT

extensive and expensive menu in the near future, so prices may increase (50-75 kn, Mon-Sat 7:00-24:00, closed Sun, just inside the Golden Gate and—as you face outside—up the skinny alley to the left, on Majstora Jurja, tel. 021/345-015).

Take-Away: **Fast Food None** ("Grandma's") is a stand-up or take-away pizza joint handy for a quick bite in the Old Town. In addition to pizzas and bruschettas with various toppings, they serve up a pair of traditional pizza-like specialties (with crust on bottom

What If I Miss My Boat?

Remember that you can get help from the cruise line's port agent (listed on the destination information sheet distributed on the ship) and the local TI (see page 806). If the port agent suggests a costly solution (such as a private car with a driver), you may want to consider public transit instead.

Frequent buses link Split with train-less **Dubrovnik.** To reach **Venice,** you can take an overnight train (requires a change in Zagreb and transfer to a bus in Villach), or an overnight boat via Ancona, Italy, then a train to Venice.

Reaching **Greece** is even trickier, as train and boat connections are overly long. Your best option is to consult a local **travel agent.** For additional advice on what to do if you miss the boat, see page 140.

and top, like a filled pizza): *viška pogača,* with tomatoes, onion, and anchovy; and *soparnik,* with a thin layer of spinach, onion, and olive oil. They can also make you a grilled sandwich—just point to what you want (10-30 kn, Mon-Sat 7:00-23:00, closed Sun, just outside Diocletian's Palace on the skinny street that runs along the wall at Bosanska 4, tel. 021/347-252). **Kantun Paulina** ("Paulina's Corner") is a local favorite for take-away *ćevapčići*—Balkan grilled meats (17-20 kn, Mon-Sat 8:30-24:00, Sun 10:00-24:00, Matošića 1).

Wine Bar: **Paradox Wine & Cheese Bar,** in an unassuming urban zone behind the National Theater, offers an inviting opportunity to sample some local wines. Their well-structured menu lists 120 wines, 50 of which are available by the glass (20-120-kn glasses, 100-800-kn bottles). Sit either in the cozy old-meets-modern interior or out on the terrace (also 25-40-kn light bites, including cheese and prosciutto, daily 9:00-24:00, Dubrovačka 18, mobile 099-817-0711).

Gelato: Split has several spots for delicious ice cream *(sladoled).* Most ice-cream parlors *(kuća sladoleda)* are open daily 8:00-24:00. Natives recommend **Hajduk,** named for Split's soccer team; ask them to dip your cone in milk chocolate for no extra charge (a block off the main Marmontova pedestrian drag, around the corner from Pizzeria Galija at Matošićeva 4).

SPLIT

Croatian Survival Phrases

In the phonetics, ī sounds like the long *i* in "light," and bolded
syllables are stressed.

English	Croatian	Pronunciation
Hello. (formal)	Dobar dan.	**doh**-bahr dahn
Hi. / Bye. (informal)	Bok.	bohk
Do you speak English?	Govorite li engleski?	**goh**-voh-ree-teh lee **ehn**-glehs-kee
Yes. / No.	Da. / Ne.	dah / neh
I (don't) understand.	(Ne) razumijem.	(neh) rah-**zoo**-mee-yehm
Please. / You're welcome.	Molim.	**moh**-leem
Thank you (very much).	Hvala (ljepa).	**hvah**-lah (**lyeh**-pah)
Excuse me. / I'm sorry.	Oprostite.	oh-**proh**-stee-teh
problem	problem	proh-**blehm**
No problem.	Nema problema.	**neh**-mah proh-**bleh**-mah
Good.	Dobro.	**doh**-broh
Goodbye.	Do viđenja.	doh veed-**jay**-neeah
one / two	jedan / dva	**yeh**-dahn / dvah
three / four	tri / četiri	tree / **cheh**-teh-ree
five / six	pet / šest	peht / shehst
seven / eight	sedam / osam	**seh**-dahm / **oh**-sahm
nine / ten	devet / deset	**deh**-veht / **deh**-seht
hundred / thousand	sto / tisuća	stoh / **tee**-soo-chah
How much?	Koliko?	**koh**-lee-koh
local currency	kuna	**koo**-nah
Write it?	Napišite?	nah-**peesh**-ee-teh
Is it free?	Da li je besplatno?	dah lee yeh **beh**-splaht-noh
Is it included?	Da li je uključeno?	dah lee yeh **ook**-lyoo-cheh-noh
Where can I find / buy...?	Gdje mogu pronaći / kupiti...?	guh-**dyeh** moh-goo proh-nah-chee / **koo**-pee-tee
I'd like / We'd like...	Želio bih / Željeli bismo...	**zheh**-lee-oh beeh / **zheh**-lyeh-lee **bees**-moh
...a room.	...sobu.	**soh**-boo
...a ticket to ___.	...kartu do ___.	**kar**-too doh ___
Is it possible?	Da li je moguće?	dah lee yeh **moh**-goo-cheh
Where is...?	Gdje je...?	guh-**dyeh** yeh
...the train station	...kolodvor	**koh**-loh-dvor
...the bus station	...autobusni kolodvor	**ow**-toh-boos-nee **koh**-loh-dvor
...the tourist information office	...turističko informativni centar	**too**-ree-steech-koh **een**-for-mah-teev-nee **tsehn**-tahr
...the toilet	...vece (WC)	**veht**-seh
men	muški	**moosh**-kee
women	ženski	**zhehn**-skee
left / right	lijevo / desno	**lee**-yeh-voh / **dehs**-noh
straight	ravno	**rahv**-noh
At what time...	U koliko sati...	oo **koh**-lee-koh **sah**-tee
...does this open / close?	...otvara / zatvara?	**oht**-vah-rah / **zaht**-vah-rah
(Just) a moment.	(Samo) trenutak.	(**sah**-moh) treh-**noo**-tahk
now / soon / later	sada / uskoro / kasnije	**sah**-dah / **oos**-koh-roh / **kahs**-nee-yeh
today / tomorrow	danas / sutra	**dah**-nahs / **soo**-trah

In a Croatian Restaurant

English	Croatian	Pronunciation
I'd like to reserve...	Rezervirao bih...	reh-zehr-**veer**-ow beeh
We'd like to reserve...	Rezervirali bismo...	reh-zehr-**vee**-rah-lee **bees**-moh
...a table for one / two.	...stol za jednog / dva.	stohl zah **yehd**-nog / dvah
Non-smoking.	Za nepušače.	zah **neh**-poo-shah-cheh
Is this table free?	Da li je ovaj stol slobodan?	dah lee yeh **oh**-vī stohl **sloh**-boh-dahn
Can I help you?	Izvolite?	**eez**-voh-lee-teh
The menu (in English), please.	Jelovnik (na engleskom), molim.	yeh-**lohv**-neek (nah **ehn**-glehs-kohm) **moh**-leem
service (not) included	posluga (nije) uključena	**poh**-sloo-gah (**nee**-yeh) **ook**-lyoo-cheh-nah
cover charge	couvert	**koo**-vehr
"to go"	za ponjeti	zah **pohn**-yeh-tee
with / without	sa / bez	sah / behz
and / or	i / ili	ee / **ee**-lee
fixed-price meal (of the day)	(dnevni) meni	(duh-**nehv**-nee) **meh**-nee
specialty of the house	specijalitet kuće	speht-see-yah-**lee**-teht **koo**-cheh
half portion	pola porcije	**poh**-lah **port**-see-yeh
daily special	jelo dana	**yeh**-loh **dah**-nah
fixed-price meal for tourists	turistički meni	**too**-ree-steech-kee **meh**-nee
appetizers	predjela	**prehd**-yeh-lah
bread	kruh	krooh
cheese	sir	seer
sandwich	sendvič	**send**-veech
soup	juha	**yoo**-hah
salad	salata	sah-**lah**-tah
meat	meso	**may**-soh
poultry	perad	**peh**-rahd
fish	riba	**ree**-bah
seafood	morska hrana	**mohr**-skah **hrah**-nah
fruit	voće	**voh**-cheh
vegetables	povrće	**poh**-vur-cheh
dessert	desert	deh-**sayrt**
(tap) water	voda (od slavine)	**voh**-dah (ohd **slah**-vee-neh)
mineral water	mineralna voda	**mee**-neh-rahl-nah **voh**-dah
milk	mlijeko	mlee-**yeh**-koh
(orange) juice	sok (od naranče)	sohk (ohd **nah**-rahn-cheh)
coffee	kava	**kah**-vah
tea	čaj	chī
wine	vino	**vee**-noh
red / white	crno / bijelo	**tsehr**-noh / bee-**yeh**-loh
sweet / dry / semi-dry	slatko / suho / polusuho	**slaht**-koh / **soo**-hoh / **poh**-loo-soo-hoh
glass / bottle	čaša / boca	**chah**-shah / **boht**-sah
beer	pivo	**pee**-voh
Cheers!	Živjeli!	**zhee**-vyeh-lee
More. / Another.	Još. / Još jedno.	yohsh / yohsh **yehd**-noh
The same.	Isto.	**ees**-toh
Bill, please.	Račun, molim.	**rah**-choon **moh**-leem
tip	napojnica	**nah**-poy-neet-sah
Delicious!	Izvrsno!	**eez**-vur-snoh

SPLIT

DUBROVNIK
Croatia

Croatia Practicalities

Unfamiliar as it might seem, Croatia (*Hrvatska*) has some of Europe's most spectacular natural wonders—many of them still off the beaten path. With thousands of miles of seafront and more than a thousand islands, Croatia's coastline is Eastern Europe's Riviera. Aside from its fun-in-the-sun status, Croatia is also historic. From ruined Roman arenas and Byzantine mosaics to Venetian bell towers, Habsburg villas, and even communist concrete, past rulers have left their mark on this country of 4.5 million (90 percent ethnic Croat—Catholic—and 4.5 percent Serb—Orthodox). A trip to Croatia offers thoughtful travelers the opportunity to understand its complicated role in Europe's most violent war in generations. But most visitors will focus on Croatia's beautiful nature: mountains, sun, sand, and sea.

Money: Croatia uses its traditional currency, the kuna: 1 kuna (kn, or HRK) = about 20 cents. One kuna is broken down into 100 lipa. Many Croatian businesses refuse to accept euros or dollars, so it's worth getting a few kunas for your time in port. An ATM is called a *bankomat*. The local VAT (value-added sales tax) rate is 25 percent; the minimum purchase eligible for a VAT refund is 740 kn (for details on refunds, see page 135).

Language: For useful Croatian phrases, see page 881.

Emergencies: Dial 92 for police; dial 112 for medical or other emergencies.

Time Zone: Croatia is on Central European Time (the same as most of the Continent, and six/nine hours ahead of the East/West Coasts of the US).

Consular Services in Zagreb: The US Embassy is at Ulica Thomasa Jeffersona 2 (tel. 01/661-2200, after-hours tel. 01/661-2400, http://zagreb.usembassy.gov). The Canadian Embassy is at Prilaz Đure Deželića 4 (tel. 01/488-1200, www.croatia.gc.ca). Call ahead for passport services.

Phoning: Croatia's phone system uses area codes. If you're dialing within an area code, use just the local number; for long-distance calls, dial the area code (which starts with 0), then the local number. To **call to Croatia,** dial the international access code (00 if calling from Europe, 011 from North America), then 385 (Croatia's country code), the area code (without the initial 0), and the local number. To **call home from Croatia,** dial 00, 1, then your area code and phone number. For more help, see page 1242.

Tipping: At a restaurant with table service, round up the bill 5-10 percent after a good meal. At some tourist restaurants, a 10-15 percent service charge may be added to your bill, in which case an additional tip is not necessary.

Tourist Information: http://us.croatia.hr

DUBROVNIK

Dubrovnik is a living fairy tale that shouldn't be missed. It feels like a small town today, but 500 years ago, Dubrovnik was a major maritime power, with the third-biggest navy in the Mediterranean. Still jutting confidently into the sea and ringed by thick medieval walls, Dubrovnik deserves its nickname: the Pearl of the Adriatic. Within the ramparts, the traffic-free Old Town is a fun jumble of quiet, cobbled back lanes; low-impact museums; narrow, steep alleys; and kid-friendly squares. After all these centuries, the buildings still hint at old-time wealth, and the central promenade (Stradun) remains the place to see and be seen. If I had to pick just one place to visit in Croatia, this would be it.

The city's charm is the sleepy result of its no-nonsense past. Busy merchants, the salt trade, and shipbuilding made Dubrovnik rich. But the city's most valued commodity was always its freedom—even today, you'll see the proud motto *Libertas* displayed all over town.

Dubrovnik flourished in the 15th and 16th centuries, but an earthquake (and ensuing fire) destroyed nearly everything in 1667. Most of today's buildings in the Old Town are post-quake Baroque, although a few palaces, monasteries, and convents displaying a rich Gothic-Renaissance mix survive from Dubrovnik's earlier Golden Age. Dubrovnik remained a big tourist draw through the Tito years, bringing in much-needed hard currency from Western visitors. Consequently, the city never acquired the hard socialist patina of other Yugoslav cities (such as the nearby Montenegrin capital Podgorica, then known as "Titograd").

As Croatia violently separated from Yugoslavia in 1991, Dubrovnik became the only coastal city to be pulled into the fighting

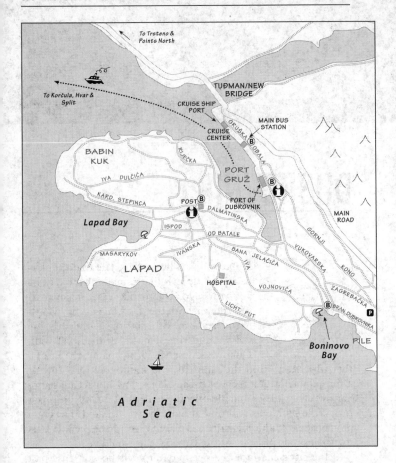

(see "The Siege of Dubrovnik" sidebar on page 856). Imagine having your youthful memories of good times spent romping in the surrounding hills replaced by visions of tanks and warships shelling your hometown. The city was devastated, but Dubrovnik has been repaired with amazing speed. The only physical reminders of the war are lots of new, bright-orange roof tiles. Locals, relieved the fighting is over but forever hardened, are often willing to talk openly about the experience with visitors—offering a rare opportunity to grasp the harsh realities of war from an eyewitness perspective.

Though the war killed tourism in the 1990s, today the crowds are most decidedly back—even exceeding prewar levels. In fact, Dubrovnik's biggest downside is the overwhelming midday crush of multinational tourists who converge on the Old Town when their cruise ships dock. These days the city's economy is based almost entirely on tourism, and most locals have moved to the sub-

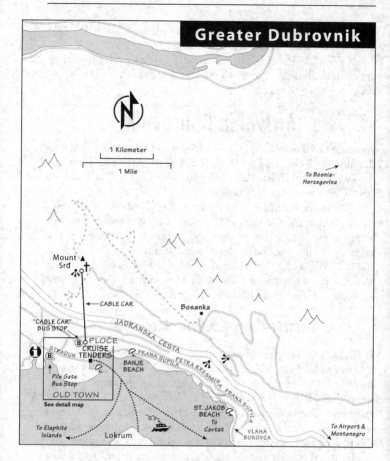

Greater Dubrovnik

1 Kilometer

1 Mile

To Bosnia-
Herzegovina

Mount
Srđ

CABLE CAR

Bosanka

JADRANSKA CESTA

"CABLE CAR"
BUS STOP

PLOČE
CRUISE
TENDERS

FRANA SUPILA

PETRA KREŠIMIRA

STRADUN

BANJE
BEACH

FRANA SUPILA

Pile Gate
Bus Stop

OLD TOWN
See detail map

ST. JAKOB
BEACH
To
Cavtat

To Elaphite
Islands

Lokrum

VLAHA
BUKOVCA

To Airport &
Montenegro

urbs so they can rent their Old Town apartments to travelers. All of this can make the Old Town feel, at times, like a very pretty but soulless theme park. But, like Venice, Dubrovnik rewards those who get off the beaten path.

Planning Your Time

You have four good choices, which I'd suggest doing in this order:

• Walk around the **city walls** (allow about 1.5 hours). Upon arrival, make a beeline to the walls before the crowds hit and it gets too hot. If there's already a long line, save the walls for later in the day, when the crowds subside (though afternoons can still be scorching).

• Follow my "Strolling the Stradun" **self-guided walk** through the heart of town (allow about an hour). Dip into any **museums or churches** that appeal to you.

DUBROVNIK

• Ride up the cable car to **Mount Srđ,** high above the Old Town (allow about 1.5 hours total round-trip).

• With any additional time, consider swimming or sunbathing at one of the **beaches** near the Old Town, or take a dip right below the city walls (see page 873).

Arrival in Dubrovnik

Arrival at a Glance: Cruise ships arriving in Dubrovnik either tender directly to the Old Port (right in the heart of the Old Town), or dock at Port Gruž (about two miles northwest of the Old Town—a 10- to 15-minute bus or taxi ride).

Currency Reminder: Remember that Croatia officially uses its own currency, the kuna ($1 = about 5 kunas, abbreviated *kn*). While some Croatian merchants and sights also accept euros, the majority do not—including local buses and major sights, such as the City Walls and the cable car to Mount Srđ. Even if you're in town for just a few hours, visit an ATM (which are abundant) and get some kunas to avoid hassles when it comes time to pay.

Tendering to the Old Port

It couldn't be simpler: Tenders deposit cruise passengers at Dubrovnik's Old Port, which forms the "mouth" of the city's stoutly walled Old Town. Just walk straight ahead up the small pier and through the hole in the wall, then bear left, and you'll find yourself right on Dubrovnik's main drag, the Stradun. Because the tenders put you right in the heart of town, this is a place where tendering might actually be better than docking—provided that you get your tender ticket as early as possible, and make it off the boat on one of the first tenders.

Docking at Port Gruž

Port Gruž is a long harbor that sits on the other side of a ridge from the Old Town. Cruise ships dock along a long, continuous embankment. Depending on where along this strip your ship docks, you'll exit through one of two terminal buildings—either at the Passenger Terminal building a bit closer to town, or at a smaller Cruise Center a bit farther out (these are about a 10-minute walk apart). Also along this harborfront are the docks for various passenger boats and car ferries to other points in Croatia, as well as the long-distance bus station *(autobusni kolodvor).* Several helpful services cluster near the Port Authority building (marked *Luka Dubrovnik*), which is at the south end of the harborfront strip—about a 5- to 15-minute walk from your ship (depending on where you

Services at (and near) Port Gruž

Most of these services are inside or next to the Port Authority building, at the south end of the harborfront embankment (about a 10-minute walk from your cruise ship). In addition to the services listed below, this area has a Konzum grocery store, travel agencies, car-rental offices, and a ticket office for the main Croatian ferry line, Jadrolinija. But if you can wait to get to the Old Town, you'll find all the services you need there.

ATMs: A cash machine is in front of the Jadrolinija office. (You'll need the local currency, kunas, if you want to take the public bus into town.)

Internet Access: You can get online inside the Port Authority building. For alternatives in the Old Town, see "Helpful Hints" on page 844.

Pharmacy: Ljekarna Gruž is across the street from the Port Authority, next to the steeple of the Dominican Monastery of the Holy Cross.

dock; walk along the main portside road, Gruška obala, with the water on your right).

Note: In the coming years, Dubrovnik plans to move its cruise arrivals area out to the far end of Port Gruž, around the corner and below the modern Tuđman Bridge. When this happens, public buses and taxis will continue to connect the new arrivals area with the Old Town.

Tourist Information: A TI is across the street from the Jadrolinija ferry dock (daily June-Sept 8:00-21:00, May and Oct 8:00-20:00, shorter hours Nov-April, Gruška obala, tel. 020/417-983). In town, there's a TI near the Pile Gate (see page 843).

Getting into Town

Your goal is to get from the cruise terminal to the Pile Gate (pronounced PEE-leh), which marks the western end of the Old Town (and is the starting point for my self-guided walk).

By Taxi

Taxis wait at the cruise terminal, charging about 60-80 kn for the ride to the Pile Gate. You'll pay about 220 kn to the airport or Cavtat, and a one-hour "panorama" tour to some gorgeous Old Town viewpoints costs around 350 kn. To hire a driver for a full day of sightseeing in the area, consider the options listed on page 848.

By Public Transportation

On the road in front of each cruise terminal, you'll find a city bus

Excursions from Dubrovnik

Croatia's finest town, **Dubrovnik** will easily keep you busy for however much time you have in port. While cruise lines sometimes push excursions to nearby towns and villages, none of them comes close to matching the epic history, engaging sights, and fun-loving ambience of Dubrovnik itself.

Most cruise-line excursions hype a "Croatian village experience" where they shuttle passengers to a "rustic" (but made-for-tour-groups) restaurant in Dubrovnik's hinterland, most often in the **Konavle Valley** (about a half-hour drive south of the city). While these excursions can offer a glimpse into traditional Croatian lifestyles, most of the clichés you'll see here are kept on life-support for cruise-line tour groups.

Another typical offering is **Cavtat,** a bayfront resort town about a half-hour's drive or 45-minute boat ride south of Dubrovnik's Old Town. Cavtat's main appeal is the opportunity to see fine works by a pair of talented local artists (Ivan Meštrović and Vlaho Bukovac), but on a short visit, Dubrovnik is more satisfying.

A few more interesting sights line up on the road north of Dubrovnik: Plant-lovers enjoy the surprisingly engaging **Trsteno Arboretum,** punctuated by a classical-style fountain and aqueduct (30 minutes north of Dubrovnik). A small town with giant fortifications, **Ston** offers the opportunity to scramble up its extensive walls (1 hour north of Dubrovnik). And just beyond Ston, the **Pelješac Peninsula** produces some of Croatia's best-regarded wines, with vineyards that offer tastings. While this area could fill an enjoyable day, again, Dubrovnik is far superior to any of the alternatives.

stop, where you can hop on a bus (#1, #1a, #1b, or #1c) to the Pile stop (12 kn if you buy ticket beforehand at a kiosk—ask for *autobusna karta,* ow-toh-BOOS-nah KAR-tah; or 15 kn if you buy one from the bus driver; only Croatian kunas are accepted—no euros or credit cards). Get out at Pile, at the end of the line (and at the start of my self-guided walk). For more details about Dubrovnik's public buses, see page 845.

Tour Options in Dubrovnik

For information on walking tours and local guides for hire, see "Tours in Dubrovnik" on page 847. Dubrovnik can also be a good place to hire a local driver to visit the surrounding area; I've listed some favorites on page 848.

Returning to Your Ship

If returning to Port Gruž, head back via the transportation hub just outside the Old Town's Pile Gate. Here you can hire a taxi to take you back to your ship, or you can ride bus #1, #1a, #1b, or #1c (the bus departs just across the little square from where it arrives; this stop is both the beginning and end of the line). If you miss the ship, see the sidebar at the end of this chapter.

Orientation to Dubrovnik

Nearly all of the sights worth seeing are in Dubrovnik's traffic-free, walled **Old Town** (Stari Grad) peninsula. The main pedestrian promenade through the middle of town is called the **Stradun;** from this artery, the Old Town climbs steeply uphill in both directions to the walls. The Old Town connects to the mainland through three gates: the **Pile Gate,** to the west; the **Ploče Gate,** to the east; and the smaller **Buža Gate,** at the top of the stepped lane called Boškovićeva. The **Old Port** (Gradska Luka), with cruise-ship tenders as well as leisure boats to nearby destinations, is at the east end of town. While greater Dubrovnik has about 50,000 people, the Old Town is home to just a few thousand in the winter—and even fewer in summer, when many residents move out to rent their apartments to tourists.

The **Pile** (PEE-leh) neighborhood, a pincushion of tourist services, is just outside the western end of the Old Town (through the Pile Gate). In front of the gate, you'll find the main TI, ATMs, a post office, taxis, buses (fanning out to all the outlying neighborhoods), a bus ticket kiosk, a cheap Konzum grocery store, and a DM pharmacy. This is also the starting point for my "Strolling the Stradun" self-guided walk.

A mile or two away from the Old Town are beaches peppered with expensive resort hotels. The closest area is **Boninovo Bay** (a 20-minute walk or 5-minute bus trip from the Old Town), but most cluster on the lush **Lapad Peninsula** to the west (a 15-minute bus trip from the Old Town). Across the bay from the Lapad Peninsula is **Port Gruž,** with the main bus station, ferry terminal, and cruise-ship port.

Tourist Information

Dubrovnik's main TI is just outside the Old Town's **Pile Gate,** at the far end of the big terrace with the modern video-screens sculpture (June-Sept daily 8:00-21:00; May and Oct daily 8:00-20:00; Nov-April Mon-Sat 8:00-19:00, Sun 9:00-15:00; Brsalje 5, tel. 020/312-011, www.tzdubrovnik.hr). There are also locations at **Port Gruž,** across the street from the Jadrolinija ferry dock (same

Dubrovnik Essentials

English	Croatian	Pronounced
Old Town	Stari Grad	STAH-ree grahd
Old Port	Stara Luka	STAH-rah LOO-kah
Pile Gate	Gradska Vrata Pile	GRAHD-skah VRAH-tah PEE-leh
Ploče Gate	Gradska Vrata Ploče	GRAHD-skah VRAH-tah PLOH-cheh
Main Promenade	Stradun	STRAH-doon
Adriatic Sea	Jadran	YAH-drahn

hours except closes earlier in Nov-April, Gruška obala, tel. 020/417-983); in the **Lapad** resort area, at the head of the main drag (June-Sept daily 8:00-20:00; May and Oct Mon-Fri 8:00-20:00, Sat-Sun 9:00-12:00 & 17:00-20:00; April Mon-Sat 9:00-12:00 & 17:00-20:00, closed Sun; closed Nov-March; Šetalište Kralja Zvonimira 7, tel. 020/437-460); on two of the Elaphite Islands, **Lopud** (Obala Iva Kuljevana 12, tel. 020/759-086) and **Šipan** (Luka b.b., tel. 020/758-084); and at the arrivals area of the **airport.**

All the TIs are government-run and legally can't sell you anything except a Dubrovnik Card (150 kn/24 hours, unlikely to pay for itself unless you're a very busy sightseer)—but they can answer questions and give you a copy of the free town map and two similar information booklets: the annual *Dubrovnik Riviera Info* and the monthly *The Best in Dubrovnik* (with a current schedule of events and performances); both contain helpful maps, bus and ferry schedules, museum hours, specifics on side-trip destinations, and more.

Helpful Hints

Crowd-Beating Tips: Dubrovnik has been discovered—especially by cruise ships (nearly 800 of which visit each year, bringing a total of around 900,000 passengers—in 2013, one September day brought 16,000 passengers on six ships). Cruise-ship crowds descend on the Old Town roughly between 8:30 and 14:00 (the streets are most crowded 9:00-13:00). If at all possible, try to avoid the big sights—especially walking around the wall—during these peak times, and hit the beach or take a siesta midday, when the town is hottest and most crowded.

Wine Shop: For the best wine-tasting selection in a cool bar atmosphere, don't miss **D'Vino Wine Bar** (described on page 879).

If you want to shop rather than taste, **Vinoteka Miličić** offers a nice variety of local wines; wry Dolores can explain your options, though she does tend to push Miličić wines (daily June-Aug 9:00-23:00, April-May and Sept-Oct 9:00-20:00, Nov-March 9:00-16:00, near the Pile end of the Stradun, tel. 020/321-777).

Internet Access: Several cafés and bars around town provide Wi-Fi for customers. In the Old Town, the modern **Buzz Bar** has free Wi-Fi and loaner laptops with the purchase of a drink (daily 9:00-24:00, Prijeko 21, tel. 020/321-025).

English Bookstore: The **Algoritam** shop, right on the Stradun, has a wide variety of guidebooks, nonfiction books about Croatia and the former Yugoslavia, novels, and magazines—all in English (July-Aug Mon-Sat 9:00-23:00, Sun 10:00-13:00 & 18:00-22:00; June and Sept Mon-Sat 9:00-21:00, Sun 10:00-14:00; shorter hours off-season; Placa 8, tel. 020/322-044).

Travel Agency: You'll see travel agencies all over town. At any of them, you can buy seats on an excursion, rent a car, or book a room. The most established company is **Atlas,** just off the Stradun in the Old Town (Mon-Fri 9:00-21:00, Sat-Sun 10:00-13:00 & 16:00-20:00, Boškovićeva 5, tel. 020/442-574, www.atlas-croatia.com).

Best Views: Walking the **City Walls** late in the day, when the city is bathed in rich light, is a treat. The cable car up to **Mount Srđ** provides bird's-eye panoramas over the entire region, from the highest vantage point without wings. The **Fort of St. Lawrence,** perched above the Pile neighborhood cove, has great views over the Old Town. The **panoramic cruises** that loop around the City Walls are another fine choice. A stroll up the road east of the city walls offers nice views back on the Old Town (best light early in the day). Better yet, if you have a car, head south of the city in the morning for gorgeously lit Old Town views over your right shoulder; various turn-offs along this road are ideal photo stops. The best one, known locally simply as **"panorama point,"** is where the road leading up and out of Dubrovnik meets the main road that passes above the town (look for the pull-out on the right, usually crowded with tour buses).

Updates to This Book: Check www.ricksteves.com/update for any significant changes that have occurred since this book was published.

Getting Around Dubrovnik

If you're tendering to the Old Town, everything is easily walkable. But those coming into town from Port Gruž will want to get com-

Dubrovnik at a Glance

▲▲▲**Stradun Stroll** Charming walk through Dubrovnik's vibrant Old Town, ideal for coffee, ice cream, and people-watching. **Hours:** Always open. See page 849.

▲▲▲**City Walls** Scenic mile-long walk along top of 15th-century fortifications encircling the city. **Hours:** July-Aug daily 8:00-19:30, progressively shorter hours off-season until 10:00-15:00 in mid-Nov-mid-March. See page 858.

▲▲▲**Mount Srđ** Napoleonic fortress above Dubrovnik with spectacular views and a modest museum on the recent war. **Hours:** Mountaintop—always open; cable car—daily June-Aug 9:00-24:00, Sept 9:00-22:00, April-May and Oct 9:00-20:00, Feb-March and Nov 9:00-17:00, Dec-Jan 9:00-16:00; museum—same hours as cable car. See page 870.

▲**Franciscan Monastery Museum** Tranquil cloister, medieval pharmacy-turned-museum, and a century-old pharmacy still serving residents today. **Hours:** Daily April-Oct 9:00-18:00, Nov-March 9:00-17:00. See page 864.

▲**Rector's Palace** Sparse antiques collection in the former home of rectors who ruled Dubrovnik in the Middle Ages. **Hours:** Daily May-Oct 9:00-18:00, Nov-April 9:00-16:00. See page 865.

▲**Cathedral** Eighteenth-century Roman Baroque cathedral and treasury filled with unusual relics, such as a swatch of Jesus' swaddling clothes. **Hours:** Church—daily 8:00-18:00, treasury—generally open same hours as church, both have shorter hours off-season. See page 866.

fortable using the buses. Once you understand the system, commuting to the Old Town is a breeze.

By Bus: Libertas runs Dubrovnik's public buses. Tickets, which are good for an hour, are cheaper if you buy them in advance from a newsstand (12 kn, ask for *autobusna karta*, ow-toh-BOOS-nah KAR-tah) than if you buy them from the bus driver (15 kn). A 24-hour ticket costs 35 kn (only sold at special bus-ticket kiosks, such as the one near the Pile Gate bus stop).

When you enter the bus, validate your ticket in the machine next to the driver (insert it with the orange arrow facing out and pointing down). Because most tourists can't figure out how to validate their tickets, it can take a long time to load the bus (which means drivers are understandably grumpy, and locals aren't shy about cutting in line).

▲**Dominican Monastery Museum** Another relaxing cloister with precious paintings, altarpieces, and manuscripts. **Hours:** Daily April-Oct 9:00-18:00, Nov-March 9:00-17:00. See page 866.

▲**Synagogue Museum** Europe's second-oldest synagogue and Croatia's only Jewish museum, with 13th-century Torahs and Holocaust-era artifacts. **Hours:** May-mid-Nov daily 10:00-20:00; mid-Nov-April Mon-Fri 10:00-13:00, closed Sat-Sun. See page 868.

▲**War Photo Limited** Thought-provoking photographic look at contemporary warfare. **Hours:** June-Sept daily 10:00-22:00; May and Oct Tue-Sun 10:00-16:00, closed Mon; closed Nov-April. See page 869.

▲**Serbian Orthodox Church and Icon Museum** Active church serving Dubrovnik's Serbian Orthodox community and museum with traditional religious icons. **Hours:** Church—daily May-Sept 8:00-14:00 & 16:00-21:00 or 22:00, until 19:00 in shoulder season, until 17:00 in winter; museum—May-Oct Mon-Sat 9:00-13:00, closed Sun; Nov-April Mon-Fri 9:00-13:00, closed Sat-Sun. See page 869.

▲**Rupe Granary and Ethnographic Museum** Good folk museum with tools, jewelry, clothing, and painted eggs above immense underground grain stores. **Hours:** Wed-Mon 9:00-18:00, until 14:00 off-season, closed Tue year-round. See page 870.

All buses stop near the Old Town, just in front of the Pile Gate (buy tickets at the newsstand). From here, they fan out to just about anywhere you'd want to go (including the cruise port). You'll find bus schedules and a map in the TI booklet (for more information, visit www.libertasdubrovnik.hr).

By Taxi: Taxis start at 25 kn, then charge 8 kn per kilometer. The handiest taxi stand for the Old Town is just outside the Pile Gate. The biggest operation is Radio Taxi (tel. 0800-0970).

Tours in Dubrovnik

Walking Tours

Two companies—**Dubrovnik Walking Tours** (www.dubrovnik-walking-tours.com) and **Dubrovnik Walks** (www.dubrovnikwalks.com)—offer similar one-hour walking tours of the Old Town daily

DUBROVNIK

at 10:00 and usually also at 13:00 and 18:00 or 18:30 (90 kn). I'd skip these tours—they're pricey and brief, touching lightly on the same information explained in this chapter. However, both companies also offer themed tours, typically covering wartime Dubrovnik and the historic Jewish quarter, which may be worthwhile. Pick up their fliers locally or check online for details.

Local Guides

For an in-depth look at the city, consider hiring your own local guide. **Roberto de Lorenzo** and his mother **Marija Tiberi** are both warm people enthusiastic about telling evocative stories from medieval Dubrovnik, including some off-the-beaten-path stops tailored to your interests (500 kn/2 hours, mobile 091-541-6637, bobdel70@yahoo.com); ask about guided transfers to Bosnia-Herzegovina or Split. **Štefica Curić Lenert** is a sharp professional guide who offers a great by-the-book tour and an insider's look at the city (550 kn/1.5 hours, other tour options explained on her website, reserve at least one day ahead, mobile 091-345-0133, www.dubrovnikprivateguide.com, stefe@ubrovnikprivateguide.com). If these guides are busy, they can refer you to another good guide for a similar price.

Hire Your Own Driver

I enjoy renting my own car to see the sights around Dubrovnik. But if you're more comfortable having someone else do the driving, hire a driver. While the drivers listed here are not licensed tour guides, they speak great English and offer commentary as you roll, and can help you craft a good day-long itinerary to Mostar, Montenegro, or anywhere else near Dubrovnik (typically departing around 8:00 and returning in the early evening).

Friendly **Pepo Klaić,** a veteran of the recent war, is enjoyable to get to know and has a knack for making the experience both informative and meaningful (€250/day, €125 for half-day trip to nearer destinations, airport transfer for about €30—cheaper than a taxi, these prices for up to four people—more expensive for bigger group, mobile 098-427-301, www.dubrovnikshoretrip.com, pepoklaic@yahoo.com). **Petar Vlašić** does similar tours for similar prices, and specializes in wine tours to the Pelješac Peninsula, with stops at various wineries along the way (€30 airport transfers, €190-200 for 2-person trip to Pelješac wineries, these prices for 1-3 people—more for larger groups, mobile 091-580-8721, www.dubrovnikrivieratours.com, info@dubrovnikrivieratours.com). **Pero Carević** also drives travelers on excursions (similar prices, mobile 098-765-634, villa.ragusa@du.t-com.hr).

Strolling the Stradun

Running through the heart of Dubrovnik's Old Town is the 300-yard-long Stradun promenade—packed with people and lined with sights.

This self-guided walk offers an ideal introduction to Dubrovnik's charms. It takes about a half-hour, not counting sightseeing stops.

• *Begin at the busy square in front of the west entrance to the Old Town, the Pile (PEE-leh) Gate.*

Pile Neighborhood

This bustling area is the nerve center of Dubrovnik's tourist industry—it's where the real world meets the fantasy of Dubrovnik (for  details on services offered here, see "Orientation to Dubrovnik," earlier). Behind the modern, mirrors-and-LED-screens monument (which honors the "Dubrovnik Defenders" who protected the city during the 1991-1992 siege) is a leafy café terrace. Wander over to the edge of the terrace and take in the imposing walls of the Pearl of the Adriatic. The huge, fortified peninsula just outside the city walls is the **Fort of St. Lawrence** (Tvrđava Lovrijenac), Dubrovnik's oldest fortress. Imagine how this fort and the stout walls worked together to fortify the little harbor—and the gate just behind you. You can climb this fortress for great views over the Old Town (30 kn, or covered by same ticket as City Walls on the same day).

• *Cross over the moat (now a shady park) to the round entrance tower in the City Walls. This is the...*

Pile Gate (Gradska Vrata Pile)

Just before you enter the gate, notice the image above the entrance of **St. Blaise** (Sveti Vlaho in Croatian) cradling Dubrovnik in his arm. You'll see a lot more of Blaise, the protector of Dubrovnik, during your time here—he is to Dubrovnik what the winged lion of St. Mark is to Venice.

Inside the first part of the gate, dead ahead you'll see another image of Blaise. Down the ramp to your left, look for the white **map** (next to the tourist map) that shows where each bomb

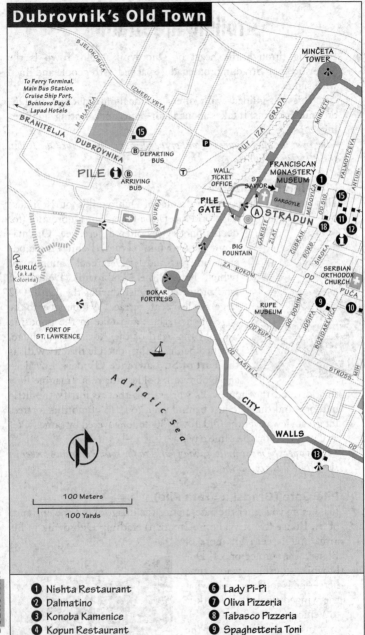

Dubrovnik's Old Town

1. Nishta Restaurant
2. Dalmatino
3. Konoba Kamenice
4. Kopun Restaurant
5. Azur Restaurant
6. Lady Pi-Pi
7. Oliva Pizzeria
8. Tabasco Pizzeria
9. Spaghetteria Toni
10. Taj Mahal Restaurant

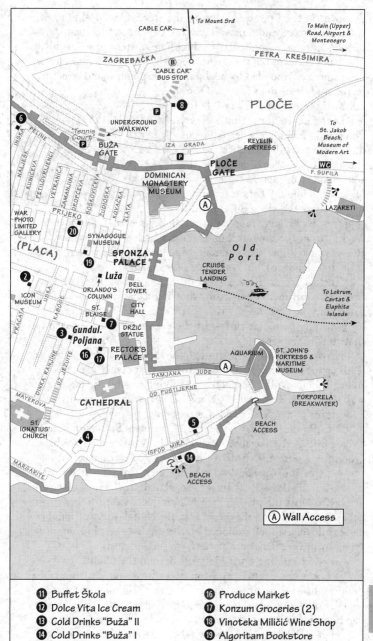

- ⑪ Buffet Škola
- ⑫ Dolce Vita Ice Cream
- ⑬ Cold Drinks "Buža" II
- ⑭ Cold Drinks "Buža" I
- ⑮ D'Vino Wine Bar
- ⑯ Produce Market
- ⑰ Konzum Groceries (2)
- ⑱ Vinoteka Miličić Wine Shop
- ⑲ Algoritam Bookstore
- ⑳ Atlas Travel Agency

DUBROVNIK

dropped on the Old Town during the siege. Once inside town, you'll see virtually no signs of the war—demonstrating the townspeople's impressive resilience in rebuilding so well and so quickly.

Passing the rest of the way through the gate, you'll find a lively little square surrounded by landmarks. The giant, round structure in the middle of the square is **Ono-frio's Big Fountain** (Velika Onofri-jea Fontana). In the Middle Ages, Dubrovnik had a complicated aqueduct system that brought water from the mountains seven miles away. The water ended up here, at the town's biggest fountain, before continuing through the city. This plentiful

supply of water, large reserves of salt (a key source of Dubrovnik's wealth, from the town of Ston), and a massive granary (now the Rupe Granary and Ethnographic Museum, described later) made little, independent Dubrovnik very siege-resistant.

Tucked across the square from the church is the **Visia Du-brovnik Multimedia Museum,** showing a badly produced 3-D film about the city's history that isn't worth your 35 minutes or 75 kn (schedule posted at entry). In the evening, the theater shows first-run 3-D movies.

To the left as you come through the Pile Gate, a steep stairway leads up to the imposing **Minčeta Tower.** It's possible to enter here to begin Dubrovnik's best activity, walking around the top of the wall (described later, under "Sights in Dubrovnik")—but this walk ends near a better, less crowded entry point.

Next to the stairway is the small **Church of St. Savior** (Crkva Svetog Spasa). Appreciative locals built this votive church to thank God after Dubrovnik made it through a 1520 earthquake. When the massive 1667 quake destroyed the city, this church was one of the only buildings left intact—its Renaissance interior stands at odds against the predominantly Baroque styles in other town churches. And during the recent war, the church survived another close call when a shell exploded on the ground right in front of it (you can still see faint pockmarks from the shrapnel).

The big building on the left just beyond the small Church of St. Savior is the **Franciscan Monastery Museum.** This tourable building has a delightful cloister and one of Europe's oldest continually operating pharmacies (described later; enter through the gap between the small church and the door of the big church).

Historically, the monastery's **Franciscan Church** was the house of worship for Dubrovnik's poor people, while the Dominican Church (down at the far end of the Stradun, where our walk ends) was for the wealthy. Services were staggered by 15 minutes to allow servants to drop off their masters there, then rush up the Stradun for their own service here. If you peek inside the church, you'll find a Baroque interior—typical of virtually all of the town's churches, which were rebuilt after the 1667 quake.

Looking up, notice the **bell tower** of the Franciscan Church—with its rounded top—which is integrated into the structure of the building. If your travels have taken you beyond Dubrovnik, you'll notice the difference from other Croatian towns, where church steeples follow Venetian convention: Set apart from the church, and with a pointy top. This is just the first of many contrasts we'll see between Dubrovnik and Venice—two powerful maritime republics who were rivals for control of the Adriatic.

Notice the stubby little, shin-high, mustachioed **gargoyle** embedded in the wall, just left of the Franciscan Church's door. You may see a commotion of tourists trying to balance on the small, slippery surface of the gargoyle's head. Tour guides enjoy spinning a variety of tall tales about this creature—if you can balance on one leg for three seconds, your fondest wish comes true—but these are a recent innovation. This legend began in the 1960s, when local teens tried to convince female tourists that balancing on the gargoyle and removing their blouse would grant them three wishes. (Why didn't I think of that in high school?) As for the gargoyle itself, it's simply a drain for rainwater. Why is it down here instead of up on the roofline? Perhaps simply to avoid deluging people who are on their way to church.

• *When you're finished taking in the sights on this square, continue along...*

The Stradun

Dubrovnik's main promenade—officially called the Placa, but better known as the Stradun—is alive with locals and tourists alike.

This is the heartbeat of the city: an Old World shopping mall by day and sprawling cocktail party after dark, when everybody seems to be doing the traditional evening stroll—flirting, ice-cream-licking, flaunting, and gawking. A coffee and some of Europe's best people-watching in a prime Stradun café is one of travel's great $4 bargains.

When Dubrovnik was just getting its start in the seventh century, this street was a canal. Romans fleeing from the invading Slavs lived on the island of Ragusa (on your right), and the Slavs settled on the shore. In the 11th century, the canal separating Ragusa from the mainland was filled in, the towns merged, and

DUBROVNIK

a unique Slavic-Roman culture and language blossomed. While originally much more higgledy-piggledy, this street was rebuilt in the current, more straightforward style after the 1667 earthquake. The ensuing fire raged for three weeks and consumed much of the city.

The distinctively shaped doors—with shop windows built right in, to provide maximum view of goods, but minimum access—indicate that this was the terrain of the merchants...and it still is.

The austerity of Dubrovnik's main drag disappoints some visitors. Rather than lavish funds on ostentatious palaces, as in Venice, Dubrovnik seems eager to downplay its wealth. For much of its history, Dubrovnik paid a hefty tribute to the sultan of the Ottoman Empire to maintain its independent status. Flaunting wealth would have raised Ottoman eyebrows...and, likely, Ottoman taxes. Unlike its rival Venice, which then as now is desperate to impress, Dubrovnik embodies a restraint that reflects the tumultuous time and place in which it thrived. Venice was surrounded by Italians, Austrians, Germans—some allies, some rivals, but all Christian. Dubrovnik sat five miles from the frontier of the Ottoman Empire; leaving the city felt like leaving the known world and the safety of what we'd today call "Western Civilization." Dubrovnik was, culturally and spiritually, an island of European Christianity surrounded on all sides by something so very different.

Today, you probably feel surrounded on all sides by hordes of international tourists. Things are worst on days when several cruise ships drop anchor—and when excursions into town feel more like incursions. But try some attitude adjustment: For much of its history, the maritime republic of Dubrovnik has been a crossroads of merchants, sailors, and other travelers from around the world. While today they may be following their tour guides' numbered paddles rather than trading exotic spices, the legions of visitors are still part of the city's tapestry of history.

If you're here in the summer (June-Sept), you'll periodically hear the rat-a-tat-tat of a drum echoing through the streets from the Stradun. This means it's time to head for this main drag to get a glimpse of the colorfully costumed **"town guards"** parading through (and the cavalcade of tourists running alongside them, trying to snap a clear picture). You may also see some of these characters standing guard outside the town gates. It's all part of the local tourist board's efforts to make their town even more atmospheric.

• *Branching off from this promenade are several museums and other attractions. At the end of the Stradun is a passageway leading to the Ploče Gate. Just before this passage is the lively Luža Square. Its centerpiece is the 20-foot-tall...*

Orlando's Column (Orlandov Stup)

Columns like this were typical of towns in northern Germany. Dubrovnik erected the column in 1417, soon after it had shifted allegiances from the oppressive Venetians to the Hungarians. By putting a northern European symbol in the middle of its most prominent square, Dubrovnik decisively distanced itself from Venice. Whenever a decision was made by the Republic, the town crier came to Orlando's Column and announced the news. The step he stood on indicated the importance of his message—the higher up, the more important the news. It was also used as the pillory, where people were publicly punished. The thin line on the top step in front of Orlando is exactly as long as the statue's forearm. This mark was Dubrovnik's standard measurement—not for a foot, but for an "elbow."

• *Now stand in front of Orlando's Column and orient yourself with a...*

Luža Square Spin-Tour

Orlando is looking toward the **Sponza Palace** (Sponza-Povijesni Arhiv). This building, from 1522, is the finest surviving example of

Dubrovnik's Golden Age in the 15th and 16th centuries. It's a combination of Renaissance (ground-floor arches) and Venetian Gothic (upstairs windows). Houses up and down the main promenade used to look like this, but after the 1667 earthquake and fire, they were replaced with boring uniformity. This used to be the customs office *(dogana)*, but now it's an exhaustive archive of the city's history, with temporary art exhibits and a war memorial. The poignant **Memorial Room of Dubrovnik Defenders** (inside and on the left) has photos of dozens of people from Dubrovnik who were killed fighting Yugoslav forces in 1991. A TV screen and images near the ceiling show the devastation of the city. Though the English descriptions are pointedly—if unavoidably—slanted to the Croat perspective, it's compelling to look in the eyes of the brave young men who didn't start this war...but were willing to finish it (free, long hours daily in peak season, shorter hours off-season). Beyond the memorial room, the impressive **courtyard,** which generally displays temporary exhibits, is worth a peek (25 kn, generally free after-hours).

To the right of Sponza Palace is the town's **Bell Tower** (Gradski Zvonik). The original dated from 1444, but it was rebuilt when it started to lean in the 1920s. The big clock may be an octopus, but only one of its hands tells time. Below that, the golden circle shows the phase of the moon. At the bottom, the old-fashioned digital readout tells the hour (in Roman numerals) and the minutes

DUBROVNIK

The Siege of Dubrovnik

In June 1991, Croatia declared independence from Yugoslavia. Within weeks, the nations were at war. Though warfare raged in the Croatian interior, nobody expected that the bloodshed would reach Dubrovnik.

As refugees from Vukovar (in northeastern Croatia) arrived in Dubrovnik that fall, telling horrific stories of the warfare there, local residents began fearing the worst. Warplanes from the Serb-dominated Yugoslav People's Army buzzed threateningly low over the town, as if to signal an impending attack.

Then, at 6:00 in the morning on October 1, 1991, Dubrovnik residents awoke to explosions on nearby hillsides. The first attacks were focused on Mount Srđ, high above the Old Town. First the giant cross was destroyed, then a communications tower (both have been rebuilt and are visible today). This first wave of attacks cleared the way for Yugoslav land troops—mostly Serbs and Montenegrins—who surrounded the city. The ragtag, newly formed Croatian army quickly dug in at the old Napoleonic-era fortress at the top of Mount Srđ, where just 25 or 30 soldiers fended off a Yugoslav takeover of this highly strategic position.

At first, shelling targeted military positions on the outskirts of town. But soon, Yugoslav forces began bombing residential neighborhoods, then the Pearl of the Adriatic itself: Dubrovnik's Old Town. Defenseless townspeople took shelter in their cellars, and sometimes even huddled together in the city wall's 15th-cen-

---

(in five-minute increments). At the top of each hour (and again three minutes later), the time is clanged out on the bell up top by two bronze bell-ringers, Maro and Baro. (If this all seems like a copy of the very similar clock on St. Mark's Square in Venice, locals are quick to point out that this clock predates that one by several decades.) The clock still has to be wound every two days. Notice the little window between the moon phase and the "digital" readout: The clock-winder opens this window to get some light. The Krasovac family was in charge of winding the clock for generations (1877-2005). During the 1991-1992 siege, their house was destroyed—with the winding keys inside. For days, the clock bell didn't run. But then, miraculously, the keys were discovered lying in the street. The excited Dubrovnik citizens came together in this square and cheered as the clock was wound and the bell chimed, signaling to the soldiers surrounding the city that they hadn't won yet.

To the right of the Bell Tower, you'll see the entrance to the Sloboda movie theater (the rainy-day location for cultural events in the summer), and next to that, **Onofrio's Little Fountain** (Mala Onofrijea Fontana), the little brother of the one at the other end of

tury forts. It was the first time in Dubrovnik's long history that the walls were actually used to defend against an attack.

Dubrovnik resisted the siege better than anyone expected. The Yugoslav forces were hoping that residents would flee the town, but the people of Dubrovnik stayed. Though severely outgunned and outnumbered, Dubrovnik's defenders managed to hold the fort atop Mount Srđ, while Yugoslav forces controlled the nearby mountaintops. All supplies had to be carried up to the fort by foot or by donkey. Dubrovnik wasn't prepared for war, so its citizens had to improvise their defense. Many brave young locals lost their lives when they slung old hunting rifles over their shoulders and, under cover of darkness, climbed the hills above Dubrovnik to meet Yugoslav soldiers face-to-face.

After eight months of bombing, Dubrovnik was liberated by the Croatian army, which attacked Yugoslav positions from the north. By the end of the siege, 100 civilians were dead, as well as more than 200 Dubrovnik citizens who lost their lives actively fighting for their hometown (much revered today as "Dubrovnik Defenders"); in the greater Dubrovnik area, 420 "Defenders" were killed, and another 900 wounded. More than two-thirds of Dubrovnik's buildings had been damaged, and more than 30,000 people had to flee their homes—but the failed siege was finally over.

the Stradun. The big building beyond the fountain is the **City Hall** (Vijećnica)—the only 19th-century building inside the Old Town. The terrace at the near end of City Hall is occupied by the **Gradska Kavana,** or "Town Café." This hangout—historically Dubrovnik's favorite spot for gossiping and people-watching—has pricey drinks and seating all the way through the wall to the Old Port. Just down the street from the Town Café is the Rector's Palace, and then the cathedral (for more on each, see "Sights in Dubrovnik").

Behind Orlando is **St. Blaise's Church** (Crkva Sv. Vlaha), dedicated to the patron saint of Dubrovnik. You'll see statues and paintings of St. Blaise all over

town, always holding a model of the city in his left hand. According to legend, a millennium ago St. Blaise came to a local priest in a dream and warned him that the up-and-coming Venetians would soon attack the city. The priest alerted the authorities, who prepared for war. Of course, the prediction came true. St. Blaise has been a Dubrovnik symbol—and locals have resented Venice—ever since.

The church, like most churches in this city, was built following the 1667 earthquake and fire. And, while we've heard plenty on this walk about Dubrovnik's rivalry with Venice, there's no denying that the Venetians were some of Europe's top cultural trendsetters at that time. So Dubrovnik invited a Venetian architect to design the church dedicated to their favorite saint. That's why St. Blaise's looks like it would be right at home reflected in a Venetian canal...right down to its bulbous dome, which seems transplanted here from the top of St. Mark's.

• *Our walk is finished. From here, you've got plenty of sightseeing options (all described next, under "Sights in Dubrovnik"). As you face the Bell Tower, you can go up the street to the right to reach the Rector's Palace and cathedral; you can walk straight ahead through the gate to reach the Old Port; or you can head through the gate and jog left to find the Dominican Monastery Museum. Even more sights—including an old synagogue, an Orthodox church, a modern exhibit of war photography, and the medieval granary—are in the steep streets between the Stradun and the walls.*

Sights in Dubrovnik

▲▲▲City Walls (Gradske Zidine)

Dubrovnik's single best attraction is strolling the scenic mile-and-a-quarter around the city walls. As you meander along this lofty perch—with a sea of orange roofs on one side, and the actual sea on the other—you'll get your bearings, peek down into secluded gardens, and snap pictures like mad of the ever-changing views. Bring your map, which you can use to pick out landmarks and get the lay of the land.

Cost: 100 kn to enter walls, also includes the Fort of St. Lawrence outside the Pile Gate (kunas or credit cards only—no euros).

Hours: July-Aug daily 8:00-19:30, progressively shorter hours off-season until mid-Nov-mid-March 10:00-15:00. Since the hours change with the season, confirm them by checking signs posted at the entrance (essential if you want to time your wall walk to avoid the worst crowds—explained below). The posted closing time indicates when the walls shut down, *not* the last entry—ascend well before this time if you want to make it all the way around. (If you want to linger, begin at least an hour ahead; if you're speedy, you can ascend 30

DUBROVNIK

minutes before closing time.) Attendants begin circling the walls at the posted closing time to lock the gates. There's talk of someday illuminating the walls at night, in which case the hours would be extended until after dark.

Entrances and Strategies: There are three entry points for the wall (see map on page 850), and wall-walkers are required to proceed counterclockwise. The best plan is to begin at the far side of the Old Town, using the entrance **near the Ploče Gate** and Dominican Monastery. This entrance is the least crowded, and you'll tackle the steepest part (and enjoy the best views) first, as you climb up to the landward side of the wall with magnificent views across the entire Old Town and the Adriatic. If you're wiped out, overheated, or fed up with crowds after that, you can bail out halfway (at the Pile Gate), having seen the best—or you can continue around the seaward side. The other two entrances are **just inside the Pile Gate** (by far the most crowded; for this location only, you must buy your tickets at the desk across the square; if you begin here, you'll reach the Minčeta Tower—with the steepest ascent and best views—last) and **near St. John's Fort** overlooking the Old Port (next to the Maritime Museum).

Crowd Control: Because this is Dubrovnik's top attraction, it's extremely crowded. Your best strategy is to avoid the walls during the times when the cruise ships are in town. If you arrive in the morning, try to get started as early as possible—be the first off your ship and make a beeline here. The walls are the most crowded from about 9:00 until 11:00. If it's already too crowded when you first arrive, consider waiting a few hours. There's generally an afternoon lull in the crowds (13:00-14:00)—but that's also the hottest time to be atop the walls. Crowds pick up again in the late afternoon (around 17:00), peaking about an hour before closing time (18:30 in high season).

Tips: Speed demons with no cameras can walk the walls in about an hour; strollers and shutterbugs should plan on longer. Because your ticket is electronically scanned as you enter, you can't leave and re-enter the wall later; you have to do it all in one go. If you have a Dubrovnik Card—even a multiple-day one—you can only use it to ascend the walls once.

Warning: The walls can get deliriously hot—all that white stone and seawater reflect blazing sunshine something fierce, and there's virtually no shade. It's essential to bring sunscreen, a hat, and water. Pace yourself: There are several steep stretches, and you'll be climbing up and down the whole way around. A few scant shops and cafés along the top of the wall (mostly on the sea side) sell water and other drinks, but it's safest to bring what you'll need with you. If you have trouble with the heat, save the walls for a cloudy day. In that hazy light, the red roof tiles seem more vivid, since they're not washed out by glaring sunshine.

Audioguide: You can rent an audioguide, separate from the admission fee, for a dryly narrated circular tour of the walls (look for vendors near the Pile Gate entrance—not available at other entrances). But I'd rather just enjoy the views and lazily pick out the landmarks with my map.

Background: There have been walls here almost as long as there's been a Dubrovnik. As with virtually all fortifications on the Croatian Coast, these walls were beefed up in the 15th century, when the Ottoman navy became a threat. Around the perimeter are several substantial forts, with walls rounded so that cannonballs would glance off harmlessly. These stout forts intimidated would-be invaders during the Republic of Dubrovnik's Golden Age, and protected residents during the 1991-1992 siege.

❍ Self-Guided Tour: It's possible to just wander the walls and snap photos like crazy as you go. And trying to hew too closely to guided commentary kind of misses the point of being high above the Dubrovnik rooftops. But this brief tour will help give you bearings to what you're seeing as you read Dubrovnik's unique and illustrious history into its street plan.

Part 1—Ploče Gate to Pile Gate: Begin by ascending near the **Ploče Gate** (go through the gate under the Bell Tower, walk along the stoutly walled passageway between the port and the Dominican Monastery, and look for the wall entrance on your right). Buy your ticket, head up, turn left, and start walking counterclockwise. Climbing stairs, you'll walk with Mount Srd and the cable car on your right. After passing the Dominican Monastery's fine courtyard on the left, you're walking above what was the poorest part of medieval Dubrovnik, the domain of the craftsmen—with narrow, stepped lanes that had shops on the ground floor and humble dwellings up above. Standing above the Buža Gate (one of just three places where people can enter and exit the walled Old Town), you have a great view down narrow Boškovićeva street, with its many little stone tabs sticking out next to windows. (These were used to hang banners during the city's Golden Age.)

As you walk, keep an eye on the different-colored **rooftops** for an illustration of the damage Dubrovnik sustained during the 1991-1992 siege. It's easy to see that nearly two-thirds of Dubrovnik's roofs were replaced after the bombings (notice the new, bright-orange tiles—and how some buildings salvaged the old tiles, but have 20th-century ones under-

DUBROVNIK

neath). The pristine-seeming Old Town was rebuilt using exactly the same materials and methods with which it was originally constructed.

The path you're on alternates between straight stretches and stairs; as you walk you're rewarded with higher and higher views.

Nearing the summit, you pass a juice bar (you can use the WCs if you buy a drink). At the very top, you enjoy the best possible view of the Old Town—you can see the rooftops, churches, and the sea. For an even better view, if you have the energy, huff up the steep stairs to the (empty) **Minčeta Tower.** From either viewpoint, observe the valley-like shape of Dubrovnik. It's easy to imagine how it began as two towns—one where you are now, and the other on the hilly island with the church spires across the way—originally separated by a seawater canal. Notice the relatively regular, grid-like pattern of houses on this side, but the more higgledy-piggledy arrangement on the far side (a visual clue that the far side is older).

The sports court at your feet is a reminder that Dubrovnik is a living city—though it's not as vibrant as it once was. While officially 2,000 people live within these walls, most locals estimate the real number at about half that; the rest rent out their homes to tourists. And with good reason: Imagine the challenges that come with living in such a steep medieval townscape well into the 21st century.

Delivery trucks rumble up and down the Stradun early each morning, and you'll see hardworking young men delivering goods on hand carts throughout the day. Looking up at the fortress atop Mount Srđ—seemingly custom-made for keeping an eye on a large swathe of coastline—the strategic position of Dubrovnik is clear. Independent Dubrovnik was not just this walled city, but an entire region.

Now continue downhill (you've earned it), noticing views on your right of the bustling Pile Gate area and the Fort of St. Lawrence (we'll reach better views of both of these soon). As the wall walk levels off, you'll pass an exit (on the left); if you're bushed and ready to head back to town, you can bail out here—but be aware that once you leave, you can't re-enter on the same ticket. Better yet, carry on straight for part 2.

Part 2—Pile Gate to Old Port: Pause to enjoy the full fron-

tal view of the **Stradun,** barreling right at you.
In the Middle Ages, lining this drag were the
merchants, and before that, this was a canal. At
your feet is Onfrio's Big Fountain, which supplied water to a thirsty town. From here, you
can see a wide range of church steeples representing the cosmopolitan makeup of a thriving
medieval trade town (from left to right): Dominican, Franciscan (near you), the town Bell
Tower, St. Blaise's (the round dome—hard to
see from here), Serbian Orthodox (twin domed
steeples), Cathedral, and (high on the hill)
Jesuit St. Ignatius. Sit and watch the river of

humanity, flowing constantly up and down one of Europe's finest
main streets. Now do a 180 for a good view of the Pile Gate chaos,
with a steady stream of buses lumbering up and down the hill, teth-
ering the Old Town to Port Gruž and the Lapad resort zone.

Carry on through the guard tower and along the wall, climbing uphill again. Looking to the wall ahead of you, notice that—
after we passed along a straighter, lower stretch—this wall is scampering up a mighty foundation of solid rock. We've left the canal
that once separated the two parts of Dubrovnik, and now we're
ascending what used to be a separate, very steep, rocky island.

On the right, across the little cove, is the **Fort of St. Lawrence,**
which worked in concert with these stout walls to make Dubrovnik
virtually impenetrable. (That fort is also climbable, and covered by
the same ticket as the walls.) Climbing higher and looking to your
left, into town, you'll see that this area is still damaged—not from
the 1991-1992 siege, but from the 1667 earthquake. Notice that,
unlike the extremely dense construction on the poorer far side of
town, this area has more breathing space and larger gardens. Originally this was also densely populated, but after the quake, rather
than rebuild, the wealthy folks who lived here decided to turn some
former homes into green space. Grates cover the openings to old
wells and grain stores that once supplied homes here—essential for
surviving a siege.

As the walkway sum-
mits and levels out, you
pass a drink stand. Farther
along, at the picturesque
little turret, is an artsy
souvenir boutique. You'll
stroll past local residents'
backyards, peering into
their inviting gardens
and checking the status

of their drying laundry. Looking down to your right (outside the wall), you'll begin to see tables and umbrellas clinging to the rocks at the base of the wall. This is the recommended Cold Drinks "Buža" II, the best spot in town for a scenic drink. (You can't enter from atop the wall—you'll have to wait until later.) On the horizon is the isle of Lokrum and—often—cruise ships at anchor, sending their passengers to and fro on tenders. After passing Buža, look down on the left to see the neighborhood kids' makeshift soccer pitch, wedged between the walls, and a little chapel—the best they can do in this vertical town. Soon you'll see the "other" Buža (technically Buža I) ahead; just above it, notice the little statue of St. Blaise, Dubrovnik's patron, enjoy some shade under the turret.

Rounding the bend, look left to see the facade of the Jesuit St. Ignatius Church. Notice that the homes in this area are much larger. These are aristocratic palaces—VIPs wanted to live as close as possible to the Cathedral and Rector's Palace, which are just below—and this also happens to be the oldest part of town, where "Ragusa" was born on a steep offshore island.

Continue around the wall, passing two more snack bars (the second with pay WCs) and more quake-ruined houses. Eventually you'll pop out at a high plateau, where *The City Walls—Continuation* signs lead down to the next part. From here, if you're bushed, you can bail out for the exit. (In the little plant-filled square at the bottom of these stairs is a sweet cat hospice, with a donation box for feeding some homeless feline residents.) But the final stretch of our wall walk is shorter than the other two, and mostly level.

Part 3—Old Port to Ploče Gate: Continuing along the wall, you'll pass near the entrance to the skippable Maritime Museum, then walk along the top of the wall overlooking the Old Port. Imagine how this heavily fortified little harbor (facing away from Dubrovnik's historic foes, the Venetians) was busy with trade in the Middle Ages. Today it's still the economic lifeline for town— watch the steady stream of cruise-ship tenders injecting dose after dose of tourist cash into town. As you curl around the far side of the port, you'll see the outdoor tables of 360°, a cocktail bar/restaurant catering to high-rolling yachters. While it looks appealing, it's a very exclusive place that frowns on would-be visitors who dress like normal people. Gussied-up jet-set diners enjoy coming here for good but extremely expensive designer fare. (One local told me, "The food is great—just eat a hamburger before you go.")

Just past 360°, you come to the stairs leading back down to where you started this wall walk. Nice work. Now head on down and reward yourself with an ice-cream cone...and some shade.

The "Other" Wall Climb: Your ticket for the City Walls also includes the Fort of St. Lawrence just outside the Old Town (valid same day only; fort described on page 849). If you've already bought a 30-kn ticket there, show it when buying your main wall ticket and you'll pay only the difference.

Near the Pile Gate

This museum is just inside the Pile Gate.

▲Franciscan Monastery Museum
(Franjevački Samostan-Muzej)

In the Middle Ages, Dubrovnik's monasteries flourished. And, as a part of their charity work, the monks at this monastery took on the responsibility of serving as pharmacists for the community. Visiting here today, you'll stroll through a delightful cloister and walk through a one-room museum in the old pharmacy.

Cost and Hours: 30 kn, daily April-Oct 9:00-18:00, Nov-March 9:00-17:00, Placa 2, tel. 020/321-410.

Visiting the Museum: Enter through the gap between the small church and the big monastery. Just inside the door (before the ticket-seller), a century-old **pharmacy** still serves residents. Notice the antique jars, advertisements (including one of the first known Aspirin ads), and other vintage pharmacist gear. By keeping this pharmacy open, the monastery maintains one of the world's oldest continually operating pharmacies.

Explore the peaceful, sun-dappled **cloister.** Examine the capitals at the tops of the 60 Romanesque-Gothic double pillars. Each one is different. Notice that some parts of the portals inside the courtyard are made with a lighter-colored stone—these had to be repaired after being hit during the 1991-1992 siege. The damaged 19th-century frescoes along the tops of the walls depict the life of St. Francis, who supposedly visited Dubrovnik in the early 13th  century. If you look closely, in a few panels you may see two layers of (different) scenes; beneath the 19th-century frescoes, restorers have found even more precious fragments of some early 18th-century paintings; where possible, these are also being resurrected.

In the far corner stands the monastery's original medieval **pharmacy.** The Franciscans opened this pharmacy in 1317, and it's been in continual operation ever since. On display are jars, pots, and other medieval pharmacists' tools. Notice the row of old pharmacists' books from the 16th, 17th, and 18th centuries—expertise imported from as far away as Venice, Frankfurt, Amsterdam, and Bologna. The sick would come to get their medicine at the little window (on the left side), which limited contact with the pharmacist and reduced the risk of passing on disease. On the right side, look for the glass case marked *venena*—where poisons were locked away and carefully doled out, with a record of who had what (if only modern gun dealers were so cautiously regulated).

Around the room, you'll also find some relics, old manuscripts, and a detailed painting of early 17th-century Dubrovnik. In the painting, notice that at the top of Mount Srđ—the highly strategic locale where Napoleon built a fortress that was key during the 1991 siege (see page 856)—is a chapel. Though Dubrovnik was always heavily fortified, they avoided putting a fortress on the mountaintop—fearing it might seem overly provocative to the Ottoman Empire that surrounded them, and upon whose favor they depended for their autonomy.

Leaving the museum room, turn right and walk to the end of this corridor. While you're walking upon tombs, look up to see one with privileged position, affixed high on the wall. The **Gučetić-Gozze** family donated vast sums to help rebuilt the monastery after the devastating 1667 earthquake. As thanks, the Franciscans helped them get just that much closer to God when they passed on, offering them this final resting place that was elevated...in every sense.

Near Luža Square

These sights are at the far end of the Stradun (nearest the Old Port). As you stand on Luža Square facing the Bell Tower, the Rector's Palace and cathedral are up the wide street called Pred Dvorom to the right, and the Dominican Monastery Museum is through the gate by the Bell Tower and to the left.

▲Rector's Palace (Knežev Dvor)

In the Middle Ages, the Republic of Dubrovnik was ruled by a rector (similar to a Venetian doge), who was elected by the nobility.

To prevent any one person from becoming too powerful, the rector's term was limited to one month. Most rectors were in their 50s—near the end of the average life span and when they were less likely to shake things up. During his term, a rector lived upstairs in this palace. Because it's been plundered twice (most recently by Napoleon's forces, who stole all the furniture), this empty-feeling museum isn't as interesting as most other European palaces. What little you'll see

was donated by local aristocrats to flesh out the pathetically empty complex. The palace collection, which requires a ticket and has good English explanations, is skippable, but it does offer a glimpse of Dubrovnik in its glory days. Even if you pass on the interior, the palace's exterior and courtyard are viewable at no charge.

Cost and Hours: 70 kn, ticket also includes Rupe Granary and Ethnographic Museum, daily May-Oct 9:00-18:00, Nov-April 9:00-16:00, some posted English information, 7-kn English booklet is helpful, Pred Dvorom 3, tel. 020/322-096.

Nearby: Just to the left as you face the entrance of the Rector's Palace, notice the statue of Dubrovnik poet **Marin Držić** (1508-1567). This beloved bard's most famous work concerns "Uncle Maro," an aristocrat who's as stingy as he is wealthy. His son cleans out his savings account and goes on a bender in Rome...until his father gets wind of it and comes calling. The shiny lap and bright nose of this statue, erected in 2008, might lead you to believe it's good luck to rub his schnozz—and, sure enough, you'll see a steady stream of tourists doing just that. But the truth is that when the statue went up, local kids were drawn to his prominent proboscis, and couldn't resist climbing up on his lap and grabbing it. Tourists saw the shine and assumed they were supposed to do it, too. A legend was born.

▲Cathedral (Katedrala)

Dubrovnik's original 12th-century cathedral was funded largely by the English King Richard the Lionheart. On his way back from the Third Crusade, Richard was shipwrecked nearby. He promised God that if he survived, he'd build a church on the spot where he landed—which happened to be on Lokrum Island, just offshore. At Dubrovnik's request, Richard agreed to build his token of thanks inside the city instead. It was the finest Romanesque church on the Adriatic...before it was destroyed by the 1667 earthquake. This version is 18th-century Roman Baroque. You can enter the building for free to see the interior, but you'll have to pay to peek into the small treasury, densely packed with silver, gold, and relics.

Cost and Hours: Church—free, open daily 8:00 until Mass begins at 18:00; treasury—15 kn, generally open same hours as church; both have shorter hours off-season.

▲Dominican Monastery Museum (Dominikanski Samostan-Muzej)

You'll find many of Dubrovnik's art treasures—paintings, altarpieces, and manuscripts—gathered around the peaceful Dominican Monastery cloister inside the Ploče Gate. As you climb the stairs up to the monastery, notice that the spindles supporting the railing are solid up until about two feet above the ground. This was to provide a modicum of modesty to ladies on their way to

church—and to prevent creeps down below from looking up their skirts.

Cost and Hours: 30 kn, art buffs enjoy the 50-kn English book, daily April-Oct 9:00-18:00, Nov-March 9:00-17:00.

Visiting the Museum: Turn left from the entry and work your way clockwise around the cloister. The room in the far corner contains paintings from the **"Dubrovnik School,"** the Republic's circa-1500 answer to the art boom in Florence and Venice. Though the 1667 earthquake destroyed most of these paintings, about a dozen survive, and five of those are in this room. Don't miss the triptych by Nikola Božidarović with St. Blaise holding a detailed model of 16th-century Dubrovnik (left panel)—the most famous depiction of Dubrovnik's favorite saint. You'll also see reliquaries shaped like the hands and feet that they hold.

Continuing around the courtyard, duck into the next room. Here you'll see a painting by **Titian** depicting St. Blaise, Mary Magdalene, and the donor who financed this work.

At the next corner of the courtyard is the entrance to the striking **church** at the heart of this still-active monastery. Step inside. The interior is decorated with modern stained glass, a fine 13th-century stone pulpit that survived the earthquake (reminding visitors of the intellectual approach to scripture that characterized the Dominicans), and a precious 14th-century Paolo Veneziano crucifix hanging above the high altar. Behind the altar, find the Vukovar Cross, embedded with panels painted by different artists from the Croatian school of Naïve Art—offering an enticing taste of this unique and fascinating style. Perhaps the finest piece of art in the church is the *Miracle of St. Dominic,* showing the founder of the order bringing a child back to life (over the altar to the right, as you enter). It was painted in the Realist style (late 19th century) by Vlaho Bukovac.

The Old Port (Stara Luka)

The picturesque Old Port, carefully nestled behind St. John's Fort, faces away from what was Dubrovnik's biggest threat, the Venetians. At the port, you can haggle with captains selling excursions to nearby towns and islands and watch cruise-ship passengers coming and going on their tenders. The long seaside building across the bay on the left is the Lazareti, once the me-

dieval quarantine house. In those days, all visitors were locked in here for 40 days before entering town. (Today it hosts folk-dancing shows—described later, under "Entertainment in Dubrovnik.") A bench-lined harborside walk leads around the fort to a breakwater, providing a peaceful perch. From the breakwater, rocky beaches curl around the outside of the wall.

Excursions

Various excursion boats depart from the Old Port. The basic option is a 50-minute **"panorama cruise"** out into the water and back again, most popular at sunset (75 kn, departures every hour; look for the old-fashioned 1878 cargo boat called *St. Ivan*, which offers a 20 percent discount to Rick Steves readers). Other popular trips are to **Lokrum Island,** just offshore, which offers the chance to hike through forests and swim at one of many rocky beaches (60 kn round-trip, 2/hour, 15-minute crossing, runs April-Oct 9:00-18:00, mid-June-Aug until 20:00, none Nov-March); and to the archipelago called the **Elaphite Islands,** with visits to three different islands (but most Elaphite trips are too long to work for cruise passengers).

Between the Stradun and the Mainland

These two museums are a few steps off the main promenade toward the mainland.

▲Synagogue Museum (Sinagoga-Muzej)

When the Jews were forced out of Spain in 1492, a steady stream of them passed through here en route to today's Turkey. Finding Dubrovnik to be a flourishing and relatively tolerant city, many stayed. Žudioska ulica ("Jewish Street"), just inside the Ploče Gate, became the ghetto in 1546. It was walled at one end and had a gate (which would be locked at night) at the other end. Today, the same street is home to the second-oldest continuously functioning synagogue in Europe (after Prague's), which contains Croatia's only Jewish museum. The top floor houses the synagogue itself. Notice the lattice windows that separated the women from the men (in accordance with Orthodox Jewish tradition). Below that, a small museum with good English descriptions gives meaning to the various Torahs (including a 14th-century one from Spain) and other items—such as the written orders *(naredba)* from Nazi-era Yugoslavia, stating that Jews were to identify their shops as Jewish-owned and wear armbands. (The Ustaše—the Nazi puppet government in Croatia—interned and executed not only Jews and Roma/Gypsies, but also Serbs and other people they considered undesirable.) Of Croatia's 24,000 Jews, only 4,000 survived the Holocaust. Today Croatia has about 2,000 Jews, including a dozen Jewish families who call Dubrovnik home.

Cost and Hours: 25 kn, 10-kn English booklet; May-mid-

Nov daily 10:00-20:00; mid-Nov-April Mon-Fri 10:00-13:00, closed Sat-Sun; Žudioska ulica 5, tel. 020/321-204.

▲War Photo Limited

If the tragic story of wartime Dubrovnik has you in a pensive mood, drop by this gallery with images of warfare from around the world. The brainchild of Kiwi-turned-Croatian photojournalist Wade Goddard, this thought-provoking museum attempts to show the ugly reality of war through raw, often disturbing photographs taken in the field. You'll find well-displayed exhibits on two floors; a small permanent exhibit (on the top floor) captures the wars in the former Yugoslavia through photography and video footage. Each summer, the gallery also houses various temporary exhibits. Note that the focus is not solely on Dubrovnik, but on war anywhere and everywhere.

Cost and Hours: 40 kn; June-Sept daily 10:00-22:00; May and Oct Tue-Sun 10:00-16:00, closed Mon; closed Nov-April; Antuninska 6, tel. 020/322-166, www.warphotoltd.com.

Between the Stradun and the Sea

▲Serbian Orthodox Church and Icon Museum
(Srpska Pravoslavna Crkva i Muzej Ikona)

Round out your look at Dubrovnik's major faiths (Catholic, Jewish, and Orthodox) with a visit to this house of worship—one of the most convenient places in Croatia to learn about Orthodox Christianity. People from the former Yugoslavia who follow the Orthodox faith are, by definition, ethnic Serbs. With all the hard feelings about the recent war, this church serves as an important reminder that all Serbs aren't bloodthirsty killers.

Dubrovnik never had a very large Serb population (an Orthodox church wasn't even allowed inside the City Walls until the mid-19th century). During the recent war, most Serbs fled, created new lives for themselves elsewhere, and saw little reason to return. But some old-timers remain, and Dubrovnik's dwindling, aging Orthodox population is still served by this **church.** The candles stuck in the sand (to prevent fire outbreaks) represent prayers: The ones at knee level are for the deceased, while the ones higher up are for the living. The gentleman selling candles encourages you to buy and light one, regardless of your faith, so long as you do so with the proper intentions and reverence.

A few doors down, you'll find the **Icon Museum.** This small collection features 78 different icons (stylized paintings of saints, generally on a golden background—a common feature of Orthodox churches) from the 15th through the 19th centuries, all identified in English. In the library—crammed with old shelves holding some 12,000 books—look for the astonishingly detailed calendar, with portraits of hundreds of saints. The gallery on the ground floor, run by Michael, sells original icons and reproductions (open longer hours than museum).

Cost and Hours: Church—free but donations accepted, good 20-kn English book explains church and museum; daily May-Sept 8:00-14:00 & 16:00-21:00 or 22:00, until 19:00 in shoulder season, until 17:00 in winter; short services daily at 8:30 and 19:00, longer liturgy Sun 10:00-11:00; museum—10 kn; May-Oct Mon-Sat 9:00-13:00 or possibly later, closed Sun; Nov-April Mon-Fri 9:00-13:00, closed Sat-Sun, Od Puča 8, tel. 020/323-283.

▲Rupe Granary and Ethnographic Museum (Etnografski Muzej Rupe)

This huge, 16th-century building was Dubrovnik's biggest granary, and today houses the best folk museum I've seen in Croatia. *Rupe* means "holes"—and it's worth the price of entry just to peer down into these 15 cavernous underground grain stores, designed to maintain the perfect temperature to preserve the seeds (63 degrees Fahrenheit). When the grain had to be dried, it was moved upstairs—where today you'll find a surprisingly well-presented Ethnographic Museum, with tools, jewelry, clothing, instruments, painted eggs, and other folk artifacts from Dubrovnik's colorful history. Borrow the free English information guide at the entry. The museum hides several blocks uphill from the main promenade, toward the sea (climb up Široka—the widest side street from the Stradun—which becomes Od Domina on the way to the museum).

Cost and Hours: Covered by 70-kn combo-ticket with Rector's Palace, Wed-Mon 9:00-18:00—or until 14:00 off-season, closed Tue year-round, od Rupa 3, tel. 020/323-013.

Above Dubrovnik

▲▲▲Mount Srđ

After adding Dubrovnik to his holdings, Napoleon built a fortress atop the hill behind the Old Town to keep an eye on his new subjects (in 1810). During the city's 20th-century tourism heyday, a cable car was built to effortlessly whisk visitors to the top so they could enjoy the fine views from the fortress and the giant cross nearby. Then, when war broke out in the 1990s, Mount Srđ (pronounced like "surge") be-

came a crucial link in the defense of Dubrovnik—the only high land that locals were able to hold. The fortress was shelled and damaged, and the cross and cable car were destroyed. Minefields and unexploded ordnance left the hilltop a dangerous no-man's land. But more recently, the mountain's fortunes have reversed. The landmines have been removed, and in 2010, the cable car was rebuilt to once again connect Dubrovnik's Old Town to its mountaintop. Visitors head to the top both for the spectacular sweeping views and to ponder the exhibits in a ragtag museum about the war.

Warning: While this area has officially been cleared of landmines, nervous locals remind visitors that this was once a war zone. Be sure to stay on clearly defined paths and roads.

Getting There: The **cable car** is easily the best option for reaching the summit of Mount Srđ (94 kn round-trip, 50 kn one-way, kunas or credit cards only—no euros; at least 2/hour—generally departing at :00 and :30 past each hour, more frequent with demand, 3-minute ride; daily from 9:00, June-Aug until 24:00, Sept until 22:00, April-May and Oct until 20:00, Feb-March and Nov until 17:00, Dec-Jan until 16:00; doesn't run in Bora wind or heavy rain, last ascent 30 minutes before closing, tel. 020/325-393, www.dubrovnikcablecar.com). The lower station is just above the Buža Gate at the top of the Old Town (from the main drag, huff all the way to the top of Boškovićeva, exit through gate, and climb uphill one block, then look right). You may see travel agencies selling tickets elsewhere in town, but there's no advantage to buying them anywhere but here. The line you may see at the cable-car station is not to buy tickets, but to actually ride up. For tips on avoiding a long wait, see below.

If you have a **car,** you can drive up. From the high road above the Old Town, watch for the turnoff to *Bosanka*, which leads you to that village, then up to the fortress and cross—follow signs for *Srđ* (it's twisty but not far—figure a 20-minute drive from the Old Town area). If you're coming south from the Old Town, once you reach the main road above, you'll have to turn left and backtrack a bit to reach the Bosanka turnoff. For **hikers,** a switchback trail (used to supply the fortress during the siege) connects the Old Town to the mountaintop—but it's very steep and provides minimal shade. (If you're in great shape and it's not too hot, you could ride the cable car up, then hike down.)

Crowd-Beating Tips: The cable car has a limited capacity, and lines can get long when several cruise ships are in town. It tends to be most crowded in the morning, shortly after the cruises arrive (peaking around 11:00). If you come during this peak time, you may have to wait your turn while watching several cable cars fill and ascend. But as the day goes on, the lines tend to get shorter.

DUBROVNIK

I'd aim to visit later in the day—particularly if you can do it at sunset.

Mountaintop: From the top cable-car station, head up the stairs to the panoramic terrace. The bird's-eye **view** is truly spectacular, looking straight down to the street plan of Dubrovnik's Old Town. From this lofty perch, you can see north to the Dalmatian islands (the Elaphite archipelago, Mljet, Korčula, and be-

yond); south to Montenegro; and east into Bosnia-Herzegovina. Gazing upon those looming mountains that define the border with Bosnia-Herzegovina—which, centuries ago, was also the frontier of the huge and powerful Ottoman Empire—you can appreciate how impressive it was that stubborn little Dubrovnik managed to remain independent for so much of its history.

The **cross** was always an important symbol in this very Catholic town. After it was destroyed, a temporary wooden one was

erected to encourage the townspeople who were waiting out the siege below. During a visit in 2003, Pope John Paul II blessed the rubble from the old cross; those fragments are now being used in the foundations of the city's newest churches. Nearby stands a huge red, white, and blue flagpole—the colors of the Croatian flag.

To reach the museum in the old fortress, walk behind the cable-car station along the rocky red soil.

Fort and Museum: The Napoleonic-era Fort Imperial (Trđava Imperijal) houses the **Dubrovnik During the Homeland War (1991-1995) Museum** (30 kn, various books for sale, same hours as cable car). As you enter, temporary exhibits are on the right, and the permanent exhibit is to the left. Photos, documents, and artifacts tell the story (with English descriptions) of the overarching war with Yugoslavia and how the people defended this fortress. The descriptions are too dense and tactical for casual visitors, but you'll see lots of photos and some actual items used in the fighting: primitive, rusty rifles (some dating from World War II) that the Croatians used for their improvised defense, and piles of spent mortar shells and other projectiles that Yugoslav forces hurled at the fortress and the city. Look for the wire-guided Russian rockets. After being launched at their target, the rockets would burrow into a wall, waiting to be detonated once their operators saw the opportunity for maximum destruction. The tattered Croatian flag seems soaked in local patriotism. A video screen shows breathless international news reports from the front line during the bombing. You'll also learn how a squadron of armed supply ships became besieged Dubrovnik's only tether to the outside world.

While the devastation of Dubrovnik was disturbing, this museum could do a far better job of fostering at least an illusion of impartiality. Instead, descriptions rant one-sidedly against "Serbian and Montenegrin aggression" and the "Serbian imperialist war," and the exhibits self-righteously depict Croats exclusively as victims (which was essentially true here in Dubrovnik, but ignores Croat atrocities elsewhere). All of this serves only to trivialize and distract from the human tragedy of this war.

After seeing the exhibit, climb up a few flights of stairs to the **rooftop** for the view. The giant communications tower overhead flew the Croatian flag during the war, to inspire the besieged residents below. You might see some charred trees around here—these were claimed not by the war, but more recently, by forest fires. (Fear of landmines and other explosives prevented locals from fighting the wildfires as aggressively as they might otherwise, making these fires more dangerous than ever.)

Eating: Boasting undoubtedly the best view in Dubrovnik, **Restaurant/Snack Bar Panorama** has reasonable prices and drop-dead, astonishing views over the rooftops of the Old Town and to the most beautiful parts of three different countries. While there's glassed-in seating inside, in good weather I'd exit the building to find the outdoor terrace—the Old Town floats just under your nose (25-35-kn drinks, 55-75-kn cocktails, 80-90-kn pastas, 100-160-kn main dishes, open same hours as cable car).

Activities in Dubrovnik

Swimming and Sunbathing

If the weather's good and you've had enough of museums, spend a sunny afternoon at the beach. There are no sandy beaches on the mainland near Dubrovnik, but there are lots of suitable pebbly options, plus several concrete perches.

The easiest and most atmospheric place to take a dip is right off the **Old Town**. From the Old Port and its breakwater, uneven steps clinging to the outside of the wall lead to a series of great sunbathing and swimming coves (and

DUBROVNIK

even a showerhead sticking out of the City Walls). Another delightful rocky beach hangs onto the outside of the Old Town's wall (at the bar called Cold Drinks "Buža" I; for more on this bar, and how to find it, see page 878).

A more convenient public beach is **Banje,** just outside the Ploče Gate, east of Old Town. While this is dominated by the EastWest nightclub, by day it's a public beach with an inviting swath of sand/pebbles, ideal for sunbathing and wading with a spectacular backdrop of Dubrovnik's Old Town. To reach the beach, leave the Old Town through the Ploče Gate, walk about five minutes gradually uphill on the main road, then watch for the two staircases marked *EastWest* and climb down. (While the stairs nearer the Old Town pass through the EastWest café/bar, it is public access.) The café/bar itself is slick and swanky (in keeping with its nightclub's exclusive vibe), serving pricey food and drink. You can also rent a very expensive sun bed (100-200 kn, depending on level of luxury), but it's much more affordable to bring your own towel and find a comfy patch of sand. Pay showers are nearby.

My favorite hidden beach—**St. Jakob**—takes a lot longer to reach, but if you're up for the hike, it's worth it to escape the crowds.

Figure about a 25-minute walk (each way) from the Old Town. Go through the Ploče Gate at the east end of the Old Town, and walk along the street called Frana Supila as it climbs uphill above the waterfront. At Hotel Argentina, take the right (downhill) fork and keep going on Vlaha Bukovca. Eventually you'll reach the small church of St. Jakob. You'll see the beach—in a cozy protected cove—far below. Curl around behind the church and keep an eye out for stairs going down on the right. Unfortunately, these stairs are effectively unmarked, so it might take some trial and error to find the right ones. (If you reach the rusted-white gateway of the old communist-era open-air theater, you've gone too far.) Hike down the very steep stairs to the gentle cove, which has rentable chairs and a small restaurant for drinks (and a WC). Enjoy the pebbly beach and faraway views of Dubrovnik's Old Town.

Locals prefer to swim on **Lokrum Island,** because there are (relatively) fewer tourists there. While there are no sandy or even pebbly beaches, there are several rocky ones, with ladders to lower yourself gingerly into the water. As the rocks here can be particularly jagged, you'll want to wear good water shoes, and beware of uneven footing (both underwater, and on your way to the ladders). For details on taking a boat to Lokrum, see page 868.

Sea Kayaking

Paddling a sleek kayak around the outside of Dubrovnik's imposing walls is a memorable experience. Several outfits in town offer half-day tours (most options 250-350 kn); popular itineraries include loops along the city walls, to secluded beaches, and around Lokrum Island; many include a break for snorkeling, and some are timed to catch the sunset while bobbing just offshore from the city walls. As this scene is continually evolving, look for fliers locally.

Shopping in Dubrovnik

Most souvenirs sold in Dubrovnik—from lavender sachets to plaster models of the Old Town—are pretty tacky. Whatever you buy,

prices are much higher along the Stradun than on the side streets.

A classy alternative to the knickknacks is a type of local jewelry called *Konavoske puce* ("Konavle buttons"). Sold as earrings, pendants, and rings, these distinctive and fashionable filigree-style pieces consist of a sphere with several small posts. Though they're sold around town, it's least expensive to buy them on Od Puča street, which runs parallel to the Stradun two blocks toward the sea (near the Serbian Orthodox Church). The high concentration of jewelers along this lane keeps prices reasonable. You'll find the "buttons" in various sizes, in both silver (affordable) and gold (pricey).

You'll also see lots of jewelry made from red coral, which can only be legally gathered in small amounts from two small islands in northern Dalmatia. If you see a particularly large chunk of coral, it's likely imported. To know what you're getting, shop at an actual jeweler instead of a souvenir shop.

Gift-Shop Chains: Several pleasant gift shops in Dubrovnik (with additional branches throughout Dalmatia) hawk fun, if sometimes made-in-China, items. Look for these chains, which are a bit classier than the many no-name shops around town: **Aqua** sells pleasant nautical-themed gifts, blue-and-white-striped sailor shirts, and other gear. **Bonbonnière Kraš** is Croatia's leading chocolatier, selling a wide array of tasty candies. **Uje** has artisan olive oils and other boutiquey edibles.

Eating in Dubrovnik

Dubrovnik disappoints diners with high prices, surly service, and mediocre quality. With the constant influx of deep-pocketed tour-

ists corrupting greedy res-taurateurs, places here tend to go downhill faster than a game of marbles on the *Titanic*. Promising new res-taurants open all the time, but most quickly fade, and what's great one year can be miserable the next. There-

fore, lower your expectations, take my suggestions with a grain of salt, and ask around locally for what's good this month. In general, seafood restaurants are good only at seafood; if you want pasta, go to a pasta place.

For restaurant locations, see map on pages 850-851.

Eateries in the Old Town

Nishta ("Nothing"), featuring a short menu of delicious vegetarian fusion cuisine with Asian flair, offers a welcome change of pace from the Dalmatian seafood-pasta-pizza rut. Busy Swiss owner/chef Gildas cooks, while his wife Ruža and their staff cheerfully serve a steady stream of return diners. This tiny place—which has been a reliable and affordable crowd-pleaser for years—has just a few cramped indoor and outdoor tables. Even if you're not a veg-etarian, it's worth a visit; reserve the day ahead in peak season (35-45-kn starters, 65-85-kn main courses, Mon-Sat 11:30-22:00, closed Sun and Jan-Feb, on the restaurant-clogged Prijeko street—near the Pile Gate end of the street, tel. 020/322-088).

Dalmatino offers some of the best traditional Dalmatian cooking in the city, combined with a few modern twists. This is quality food and attentive service at prices that won't blow your budget. South African-Croatian owner Robert prides himself on cooking each dish to order; while this may take a few minutes lon-ger, you can taste the results. While there are only a few outdoor tables tucked along the alley, there's a spacious, classy-but-not-stuffy dining room (50-160-kn pastas, 80-160-kn main dishes, daily 11:00-23:00, Miha Pracata 6, tel. 020/323-070, http://dal-matino-dubrovnik.com). Don't confuse Dalmatino's tables with its neighbors'.

On the Market Square: The square called Gundulićeva polja-na, tucked two short blocks from the Stradun, is filled with outdoor tables. **Konoba Kamenice**, a no-frills fish restaurant, is a local institution offering inexpensive, fresh, and good meals on a charming market square, as central as can be in the Old Town. On the limited menu, the seafood dishes are excellent (try their octopus salad, even if you don't think you like octopus), while the few non-seafood dishes are uninspired. Some of the waitstaff are notorious for their playfully brusque service, but loyal patrons happily put up with it. Arrive early, or you'll have to wait (45-75-kn main courses, daily 8:00-23:00, until 22:00 off-season, Gundulićeva poljana 8, tel. 020/323-682).

Kopun, with picturesque seating on the big square in front of the Jesuit St. Ignatius Church, serves up regional specialties not only from Dubrovnik, but from elsewhere in Croatia—all well-explained in the menu. Several dishes make use of the restaurant's namesake, *kopun*—a rooster that's castrated young and plumps up. While a bit pricey and new to the scene, this place is off to a promising start (60-130-kn pastas and starters, 80-160-kn main courses, daily 11:00-23:00, Poljana Ruđera Boškovića 7, tel. 020/323-969, www.restaurantkopun.com).

Azur, tucked high inside the City Walls (near the two Buža cocktail bars), offers relief to travelers needing a break from the typical Croatian menu. The sort-of-Asian-fusion menu might not fly in big cosmopolitan cities, but here on the Croatian coast, appreciative international diners cling to it like a sesame-oil life preserver (45-75-kn starters and snacks, 90-150-kn main dishes, daily 11:00-24:00, Pobijana 10, tel. 020/324-806).

Lady Pi-Pi, named for a comical, anatomically correct, and slightly off-putting statue out front, sits high above town just inside the wall. The food, prepared on an open grill, is just an excuse to sit out on their vine-covered terrace, with several tables overlooking the rooftops of Dubrovnik. Come early or be prepared to line up (70-75-kn pastas, 65-150-kn main dishes, daily May-Sept 9:00-24:00, closed Oct-April and in bad weather, Peline b.b., tel. 020/321-288).

Pizza: Dubrovnik seems to have a pizzeria on every corner. Little separates the various options—just look for a menu and outdoor seating option that appeals to you. **Oliva Pizzeria,** just behind St. Blaise's Church, puts out consistently good food (40-70-kn pizzas, Lučarica 5, daily 10:00-24:00, tel. 020/324-594; don't mistake this for their sister restaurant next door, Oliva Gourmet, with a pricier non-pizza menu). Around the side is a handy take-out window for a bite on the go. Close to the Old Town, but just far away to be frequented mostly by locals, **Tabasco Pizzeria** is tucked at the corner of the parking lot beneath the cable-car station. Unpretentious and affordable, this is the place to come if the pizza is more important than the setting—though the outdoor terrace does have views of the City Walls...over a sea of parked cars (40-50-kn pizzas, 70-85-kn "jumbo" pizzas, daily 9:00-23:00, Hvarska 48A, tel. 020/429-595).

Pasta: **Spaghetteria Toni** is popular with natives and tourists. While nothing fancy, it offers good pastas at reasonable prices. Choose between the cozy 10-table interior or the long alley filled with outdoor tables (50-95-kn pastas, 55-70-kn salads, daily in summer 11:00-23:00, closed Sun in winter, closed Jan, Nikole Božidarevića 14, tel. 020/323-134).

Bosnian Cuisine: For a break from Croatian fare, try the grilled meats and other tasty Bosnian dishes at the misnamed **Taj Mahal.** Though the service can be lacking, the menu offers an enticing taste of the Turkish-flavored land to the east. Choose between the tight interior, which feels like a Bosnian tea house, or tables out on the alley (50-65-kn salads, 60-145-kn main courses, daily 10:00-24:00, Nikole Gučetića 2, tel. 020/323-221).

Sandwiches: **Buffet Škola** is a rare bit of pre-glitz Dubrovnik just a few steps off the Stradun, serving take-away or sit-down sandwiches on homemade bread. Squeeze into the hole-in-the-wall interior, or sit at one of the outdoor tables (25-30 kn, 60-80-kn ham and cheese boards, daily 8:00-22:00 or 23:00, Antuninska 1, tel. 020/321-096).

Ice Cream: Dubrovnik has lots of great *sladoled*, but locals swear by the stuff at **Dolce Vita.** In addition to good ice cream, they have tasty crêpes (daily 9:00-24:00, a half-block off the Stradun at Nalješkovićeva 1A, tel. 020/321-666).

The Old Town's "Restaurant Row," Prijeko Street: The street called Prijeko, a block toward the mainland from the Stradun promenade, is lined with outdoor, tourist-oriented eateries—each one with a huckster out front trying to lure in diners. (Many of them aggressively try to snare passersby down on the Stradun, as well.) Don't be sucked into this vortex of bad food at outlandish prices. The only place worth seeking out here is Nishta (described earlier); the rest are virtually guaranteed to disappoint. Still, it can be fun to take a stroll along here—the atmosphere is lively, and the sales pitches are entertainingly desperate.

Unique Bars

Cold Drinks "Buža" offers, without a doubt, the most scenic spot for a drink. Perched on a cliff above the sea, clinging like a barnacle to the outside of the city walls, this is a peaceful, shaded getaway from the bustle of the Old Town. *Buža* means "hole in the wall"—and that's exactly what you'll have to go through to get to this place. There are actually two different Bužas, with separate owners. My favorite is Buža II (which is actually the older and bigger of the pair). Filled with mellow tourists and bartenders pouring wine from tiny screw-top bottles into plastic cups, Buža II comes with castaway views and Frank Sinatra ambience. This is supposedly where Bill Gates hangs out when he visits Dubrovnik. When the seats fill up—as often happens around sunset—you can order a drink at the bar and walk down the stairs to enjoy it "on the rocks"...literally (26-45-kn drinks, summer daily 9:00-into the wee hours, closed mid-Nov-Jan). Buža I, with a different owner, is more casual, plays hip rather than romantic music, and has concrete stairs leading down to a beach on the rocks below. While lacking a bit of Buža II's panache—and its shade—Buža I is often a bit less crowded, making it a viable alternative (18-45-kn drinks). Both Bužas are high above the bustle of the main drag, along the seaward wall. To reach them from the cathedral area, hike up the grand staircase to St. Ignatius Church, then go left to find the lane that runs along the inside of the wall. To find the classic Buža II, head right along the lane and look for the *Cold Drinks* sign pointing to a literal hole in the wall. For the hipper Buža I, go left along the same lane, and locate the hole in the wall with the *No Toples No Nudist* graffiti.

D'Vino Wine Bar, just a few steps off the main drag, has a relaxed atmosphere and a knowledgeable but unpretentious approach—making it the handiest place in Dalmatia to sample and learn about Croatian wines. Run by gregarious Aussie-Croat Sasha and his capable staff (including Anita), this cozy bar sells more than 60 wines by the glass and lots more by the bottle. The emphasis is on Croatian wines by small-production wineries, but they also have a few international vintages. Each wine is well-described on the menu, and the staff is happy to guide you through your options—just tell them what you like. Sit in the tight interior or linger at the sidewalk tables (20-80-kn glasses—most around 25-35 kn, 50-kn wine flights; light food—70-kn 2-person cheese plate, 90-kn antipasti plate; daily 10:30-late, Palmotićeva 4a, tel. 020/321-130, www.dvino.net).

Picnic Tips

Dubrovnik's lack of great restaurant options makes it a perfect place to picnic. You can shop for fresh fruits and veggies at the open-air produce market (each morning near the cathedral, on the square called Gundulićeva Poljana). Supplement your picnic with grub from the cheap **Konzum grocery store** (one location on the market square near the produce-vendors: Mon-Sat 7:00-20:00, Sun 7:00-13:00; another near the bus stop just outside Pile Gate:

What If I Miss My Boat?

Remember that you can get help from the cruise line's port agent (listed on the destination information sheet distributed on the ship) and the local TI (see page 843). If the port agent suggests a costly solution (such as a private car with a driver), you may want to consider these options instead:

To reach **Split,** the bus is your best option. Dubrovnik's long-distance bus station *(autobusni kolodvor)* is located near Port Gruž.

For both **Italy** and **Greece,** flying is the easiest option. There are a few direct flights to Italy (Rome on Croatia Airlines and easyJet; Venice on Croatia Airlines), but none to Athens—to reach Greece, count on a layover. (An overnight boat sails from Dubrovnik to Bari, Italy, from which it's a several-hour train ride to most Italian cruise ports; there are no direct boats to Greece. Overland connections to both countries are overly long). Dubrovnik's small **airport** (Zračna Luka) is 13 miles south of the city. To get to the airport, you can take a Croatia Airlines bus (ask at the TI), hire a local driver to take you (see recommendations on page 848), or call a taxi at tel. 0800-0970.

For a recommended local **travel agent,** see page 845. For more advice on what to do if you miss the boat, see page 140.

Mon-Sat 7:00-20:00, Sun 8:00-13:00). Good picnic spots include the shaded benches overlooking the Old Port; the Porporela breakwater (beyond the Old Port and fort—comes with a swimming area, sunny no-shade benches, and views of Lokrum Island); and the green, welcoming park in what was the moat just under the Pile Gate entry to the Old Town.

Croatian Survival Phrases

In the phonetics, ī sounds like the long *i* in "light," and bolded syllables are stressed.

English	Croatian	Pronunciation
Hello. (formal)	*Dobar dan.*	**doh**-bahr dahn
Hi. / Bye. (informal)	*Bok.*	bohk
Do you speak English?	*Govorite li engleski?*	goh-voh-ree-teh lee **ehn**-glehs-kee
Yes. / No.	*Da. / Ne.*	dah / neh
I (don't) understand.	*(Ne) razumijem.*	(neh) rah-**zoo**-mee-yehm
Please. / You're welcome.	*Molim.*	**moh**-leem
Thank you (very much).	*Hvala (ljepa).*	**hvah**-lah (**lyeh**-pah)
Excuse me. / I'm sorry.	*Oprostite.*	oh-**proh**-stee-teh
problem	*problem*	proh-**blehm**
No problem.	*Nema problema.*	**neh**-mah proh-**bleh**-mah
Good.	*Dobro.*	**doh**-broh
Goodbye.	*Do viđenija.*	doh veed-**jay**-neeah
one / two	*jedan / dva*	**yeh**-dahn / dvah
three / four	*tri / četiri*	tree / **cheh**-teh-ree
five / six	*pet / šest*	peht / shehst
seven / eight	*sedam / osam*	**seh**-dahm / **oh**-sahm
nine / ten	*devet / deset*	**deh**-veht / **deh**-seht
hundred / thousand	*sto / tisuća*	stoh / **tee**-soo-chah
How much?	*Koliko?*	**koh**-lee-koh
local currency	*kuna*	**koo**-nah
Write it?	*Napišite?*	nah-**peesh**-ee-teh
Is it free?	*Da li je besplatno?*	dah lee yeh **beh**-splaht-noh
Is it included?	*Da li je uključeno?*	dah lee yeh **ook**-lyoo-cheh-noh
Where can I find / buy...?	*Gdje mogu pronaći / kupiti...?*	guh-**dyeh** moh-goo proh-nah-chee / **koo**-pee-tee
I'd like / We'd like...	*Želio bih / Željeli bismo...*	**zheh**-lee-oh beeh / **zheh**-lyeh-lee bees-moh
...a room.	*...sobu.*	**soh**-boo
...a ticket to ___.	*...kartu do ___.*	**kar**-too doh ___
Is it possible?	*Da li je moguće?*	dah lee yeh **moh**-goo-cheh
Where is...?	*Gdje je...?*	guh-**dyeh** yeh
...the train station	*...kolodvor*	**koh**-loh-dvor
...the bus station	*...autobusni kolodvor*	**ow**-toh-boos-nee **koh**-loh-dvor
...the tourist information office	*...turističko informativni centar*	**too**-ree-steech-koh een-for-mah-teev-nee **tsehn**-tahr
...the toilet	*...vece (WC)*	**veht**-seh
men	*muški*	**moosh**-kee
women	*ženski*	**zhehn**-skee
left / right	*lijevo / desno*	**lee**-yeh-voh / **dehs**-noh
straight	*ravno*	**rahv**-noh
At what time...	*U koliko sati...*	oo **koh**-lee-koh **sah**-tee
...does this open / close?	*...otvara / zatvara?*	**oht**-vah-rah / **zaht**-vah-rah
(Just) a moment.	*(Samo) trenutak.*	(**sah**-moh) treh-**noo**-tahk
now / soon / later	*sada / uskoro / kasnije*	**sah**-dah / **oos**-koh-roh / **kahs**-nee-yeh
today / tomorrow	*danas / sutra*	**dah**-nahs / **soo**-trah

In a Croatian Restaurant

English	Croatian	Pronunciation
I'd like to reserve...	Rezervirao bih...	reh-zehr-**veer**-ow beeh
We'd like to reserve...	Rezervirali bismo...	reh-zehr-**vee**-rah-lee bees-moh
...a table for one / two.	...stol za jednog / dva.	stohl zah **yehd**-nog / dvah
Non-smoking.	Za nepušače.	zah **neh**-poo-shah-cheh
Is this table free?	Da li je ovaj stol slobodan?	dah lee yeh **oh**-vī stohl **sloh**-boh-dahn
Can I help you?	Izvolite?	**eez**-voh-lee-teh
The menu (in English), please.	Jelovnik (na engleskom), molim.	yeh-**lohv**-neek (nah **ehn**-glehs-kohm) **moh**-leem
service (not) included	posluga (nije) uključena	**poh**-sloo-gah (**nee**-yeh) **ook**-lyoo-cheh-nah
cover charge	couvert	**koo**-vehr
"to go"	za ponjeti	zah **pohn**-yeh-tee
with / without	sa / bez	sah / behz
and / or	i / ili	ee / **ee**-lee
fixed-price meal (of the day)	(dnevni) meni	(duh-**nehv**-nee) meh-nee
specialty of the house	specijalitet kuće	speht-see-yah-lee-**teht koo**-cheh
half portion	pola porcije	**poh**-lah **port**-see-yeh
daily special	jelo dana	**yeh**-loh **dah**-nah
fixed-price meal for tourists	turistički meni	**too**-ree-steech-kee **meh**-nee
appetizers	predjela	**prehd**-yeh-lah
bread	kruh	krooh
cheese	sir	seer
sandwich	sendvič	**send**-veech
soup	juha	**yoo**-hah
salad	salata	sah-**lah**-tah
meat	meso	**may**-soh
poultry	perad	**peh**-rahd
fish	riba	**ree**-bah
seafood	morska hrana	**mohr**-skah **hrah**-nah
fruit	voće	**voh**-cheh
vegetables	povrće	**poh**-vur-cheh
dessert	desert	deh-**sayrt**
(tap) water	voda (od slavine)	**voh**-dah (ohd **slah**-vee-neh)
mineral water	mineralna voda	**mee**-neh-rahl-nah **voh**-dah
milk	mlijeko	mlee-**yeh**-koh
(orange) juice	sok (od naranče)	sohk (ohd **nah**-rahn-cheh)
coffee	kava	**kah**-vah
tea	čaj	chī
wine	vino	**vee**-noh
red / white	crno / bijelo	**tsehr**-noh / bee-**yeh**-loh
sweet / dry / semi-dry	slatko / suho / polusuho	**slaht**-koh / **soo**-hoh / **poh**-loo-soo-hoh
glass / bottle	čaša / boca	**chah**-shah / **boht**-sah
beer	pivo	**pee**-voh
Cheers!	Živjeli!	**zhee**-vyeh-lee
More. / Another.	Još. / Još jedno.	yohsh / yohsh **yehd**-noh
The same.	Isto.	**ees**-toh
Bill, please.	Račun, molim.	**rah**-choon **moh**-leem
tip	napojnica	**nah**-poy-neet-sah
Delicious!	Izvrsno!	**eez**-vur-snoh

ATHENS
Greece

Greece Practicalities

 Greece *(Hellas)* offers sunshine, seafood, 6,000 islands, whitewashed houses with bright-blue shutters, and a relaxed lifestyle. As the birthplace of Western civilization, it has some of the world's greatest ancient monuments. We have the Greeks to thank for the Olympics; the tall tales of Achilles and Odysseus; the rational philosophies of Socrates, Plato, and Aristotle; democracy, theater, mathematics...and the gyro sandwich.

As a late bloomer in the modern age, Greece retains echoes of a simpler, time-passed world. On the islands, you'll still see men on donkeys and women at the well. Greeks pride themselves on a concept called *filotimo* ("love of honor"), roughly translated as openness, friendliness, and hospitality. It's easy to surrender to the Greek way of living.

Money: Greece uses the euro currency: 1 euro (€) = about $1.30. An ATM, handily, is labeled *ATM* in the Greek alphabet. The local VAT (value-added sales tax) rate is 23 percent; the minimum purchase eligible for a VAT refund is €120 (for details on refunds, see page 135).

Language: For helpful Greek phrases, see page 975.

Emergencies: Dial 100 for police or 171 for English-speaking tourist police; for medical or other emergencies, dial 176 or 199.

Time Zone: Greece is on Eastern European Time (an hour ahead of Italy and seven/ten hours ahead of the East/West Coasts of the US).

Theft Alert: In Athens and any place with crowds, be wary of purse snatchers and pickpockets. For tips on outsmarting thieves, see page 128.

Consular Services in Athens: The US embassy is at Vasilissis Sofias 91 (tel. 210-720-2414, http://athens.usembassy.gov). The Canadian embassy is at Ioannou Ghennadiou 4 (tel. 210-727-3400, www.greece.gc.ca). Call ahead for passport services.

Phoning: Greece has a direct-dial phone system (no area codes). To **call within Greece,** just dial the number. To **call to Greece,** dial the international access code (00 if calling from Europe, or 011 from North America), then 30 (Greece's country code), then the phone number. To **call home from Greece,** dial 00, 1, then your area code and phone number.

Tipping: If you order your food at a counter, don't tip. At sit-down restaurants, service is generally included, although it's common to round up the bill after a good meal, usually 5-10 percent. You'll also round up 5-10 percent to tip a cabbie (give €5 to pay a €4.50 fare).

Tourist Information: www.visitgreece.gr

ATHENS
and the Port of Piraeus

ΑΘΉΝΑ / αθήνα

Democracy and mathematics. Medicine and literature. Theater and astronomy. Mythology and philosophy. All of these, and more, were first thought up by a bunch of tunic-clad Greeks in a small village huddled at the base of the Acropolis. During its Golden Age, Athens dominated ancient Greece, and later conquests by Alexander the Great spread its culture across the known world. The incredible advances in art, architecture, politics, science, and philosophy set the pace for all of Western civilization to follow.

A century and a half ago, Athens was a humble, forgotten city of about 8,000 people. Today it's the teeming home of nearly four million Greeks. The city is famous for its sheer size, noise, and pollution. The best advice to tourists has long been to see the big sights, then get out. But over the last decade plus, the city has made a concerted effort to curb pollution, clean up and pedestrianize the streets, spiff up the museums, and invest in one of Europe's better public transit systems. All of these urban upgrades reached a peak as Athens hosted the 2004 Olympic Games.

And yet, the conventional wisdom still holds true: Athens is a great city to see...but not to linger in. As everything worth a look is gathered around the Acropolis, it's made to order for a quick cruise visit.

Some smaller cruise ships start or end their journey in Athens. If that's the case for you, check the end of this chapter for airport information and recommended hotels.

Planning Your Time

Although Athens is a sprawling city, its main sights can be seen in a busy and well-organized day. Allow up to 1.5 hours to get from

Excursions from Piraeus

Excursion choices from Piraeus swing from the ho-hum to the spectacular. Athens' magnificent **Acropolis** and **world-class museums** easily make for the best excursion from Piraeus. Plenty of other options exist, including those listed below—but think carefully before choosing to miss out on Athens' big sights.

Reconstructed for the 2004 Olympics, a 68,000-seat stadium sits at the center of the **Athens Olympic Sports Complex** (AOSC, better known by its Greek initials, OAKA). Your time is better spent elsewhere. (Note: Don't confuse this with the interesting ancient ruins of the 4th-century B.C. Panathenaic Stadium, which is located just outside the Plaka neighborhood of downtown Athens and also hosted some events in the 2004 Olympiad).

A 45-minute drive south of Piraeus, the Temple of Poseidon perches atop **Cape Sounion** with a knockout view over the Aegean Sea, but it's not worth the drive if you're visiting other ancient sites.

Excursions to **Corinth** (1.25 hours west of Piraeus) focus on its ancient Greek and Roman ruins as well as the **Corinth Canal,** built by Greek engineers in the 19th century to connect the Gulf of Corinth with the Aegean Sea (severing the Peloponnesian Peninsula from the mainland). But Corinth's sights are trumped by those at Delphi.

The mountaintop palace/fortress at **Mycenae** (2 hours southwest of Piraeus) was the hub of a civilization that dominated Greece 1,000 years before its Golden Age. Its archaeological ruins, massive beehive tomb, and iconic Lion Gate are impressive attractions. These impossibly old ruins tickle the imaginations of armchair archaeologists, but are less visually striking than those in Athens or Delphi.

Overlooking the Gulf of Corinth, **Delphi** (2.5 hours northwest of Piraeus) is among the most spectacular of Greece's ancient sites. The Sanctuary of Apollo, home of the legendary fortune-telling oracle, is draped over a craggy mountainside, and next door is the great Archaeological Museum, where statues and treasures found on the site help bring the ruins to life. Though distant from Athens, Delphi's ruins rival those in the capital city; if you've already seen the Acropolis and other ancient biggies in Athens, Delphi is worth the long bus trip.

the port to downtown Athens and back, whether by bus, Metro, or taxi. (The trip can be as quick as 20 minutes one-way by taxi if the traffic doesn't slow you down.)

If your time in Athens is short, head straight for the Acropolis. With more time, I suggest doing the sights in this order:

• Take my self-guided **Athens City Walk** through the heart of town (figure on 2 hours at a speedy pace). When finished, grab a souvlaki lunch near Monastiraki.

• Walk through the **Ancient Agora**. If you're in a rush, just speed through here on your way up to the Acropolis.

• Follow my self-guided tour of the **Acropolis** (allow 2 hours). The Acropolis is less crowded in the afternoon than in the morning, but confirm carefully how late it's open.

• If time allows when you descend from the Acropolis, pay a visit to the nearby **Acropolis Museum** (closed Mon; allow 1.5 hours).

• If you have additional time—or if you skip one or more of the above sights—the **National Archaeological Museum** is well worth a visit, but is far from the other sights listed here (allow at least 2 hours to tour the collection, plus about 20 minutes each way by taxi from downtown).

If shopping interests you more than museums, see page 958.

Arrival at the Port of Piraeus

Arrival at a Glance: To reach central Athens, you can spring for a taxi (€15-20, 20-40 minutes); take public bus #040 (30-60 minutes); or ride the Metro (20 minutes; to reach the Metro station from the cruise terminals can be a 15- to 40-minute walk, or you can take a local bus or taxi).

Port Overview

Piraeus, a city six miles southwest of central Athens, has been the port of Athens since ancient times. Today it's also the main hub for services to the Greek islands, making it the busiest passenger port in the Mediterranean. A staggering 13 million journeys begin or end here each year. While the port is vast, most of it is used for ferry traffic; all of the cruise ships moor at one end.

Piraeus' Great Harbor (Megas Limin) has 12 numbered docks, or "gates," which surround the harbor. Ships dock at **Cruise Terminal A** (at Gate E11) or **Cruise Terminal B** (Gate E12) at the far-south end of the harbor. The two terminals are about a 15-minute walk apart; north of these stretch 10 more "gates" with vessels heading to islands all over Greece and beyond.

As Piraeus is big, grimy, and of no sightseeing value, the best plan is to head straight for Athens. But if you wind up with extra time here, you'll find that the northeast corner of the Great Harbor

Athens Experiences for Cruisers

Athens boasts some of the top sights of the ancient world. But squeezed between the predictable sightseeing biggies are some enticing slices of authentic Athenian life. Here are a few suggestions for fully experiencing Athens.

Eat a souvlaki (shish kebab) or a Greek savory pie (phyllo-dough pastry). Several handy stands around Athens serve one or both of these items, offering a cheap, quick, and filling break from sightseeing.

Learn enough Greek letters to sound out a local sign. For those who pledged a fraternity or sorority in college, this should be a snap. But anyone with a little patience can pretty quickly begin to interpret Greek signs. If you sound them out, you may be surprised by how many words you recognize. Many signs appear in both Greek and English—offering you a built-in cheat sheet. To get started, you'll find the Greek alphabet on page 894.

Stroll all the way around the Acropolis on the "Acropolis Loop." Although this recently pedestrianized, inviting drag feels designed for tourists, and circles Greece's top attraction, it has also been embraced by locals—especially the western end, near the characteristic Thissio district.

Hike high to the Anafiotika district. Clinging to the hillside just below the Acropolis, this castaway neighborhood feels like a Greek island village transplanted to the center of a big city. It's well worth a detour before or after your Acropolis visit to wander its lanes and escape the crowds. (For more on Anafiotika, see page 923.)

has the most activity: the Metro station and suburban train station (connected to the harbor by a modern pedestrian bridge) and—just down the street—Karaiskaki Square, which juts out into the harbor. Cheap eateries, flophouse hotels, and dozens of travel agencies round out the scene.

Tourist Information: Frustratingly, official tourist information is in short supply here, although a TI kiosk is often open just outside Terminal A. The port police (with several offices clearly marked in English) can be helpful. The port authority website is www.olp.gr. For details on the main Athens TI (near the Acropolis Museum), see page 896.

Getting into Athens

By Taxi

Cabbies wait in front of each cruise terminal. The fair metered rate from either terminal into downtown is about €15-20, depending on traffic (includes legitimate €5.20 cruise terminal surcharge—you

Services at the Port of Piraeus

Here are the nearest locations of the following services at the port, though if you can wait until Athens, you'll find everything you need.

ATMs: There are ATMs in each cruise terminal building and at other locations around the port area.

Internet Access: Terminal A has free Wi-Fi. If you walk around the port area, you'll see several Internet cafés.

Pharmacy: Several pharmacies are close to Cruise Terminal A on Sachtouri street. Pharmacy hours in Greece are usually Mon-Fri 8:00-14:30, also Tue and Thu-Fri 17:30-20:00. For 24-hour pharmacies, call 14944.

Baggage Storage: If Piraeus is your first or last stop, and you need a place to store bags, luggage lockers (€3) are at Terminal A and the Metro station. If you're in a pinch, various travel agencies closer to the port might be willing to store your bags for a fee.

can try to avoid this by walking up to the main road and finding a taxi there). The trip can take anywhere from 20-40 minutes or more, depending on traffic. Some drivers offer a three-hour tour around the city center, including basic commentary and waiting time at the Acropolis (about €120). If this appeals to you, find a driver who speaks good English and would be fun to chat with.

By Bus

Bus #040 goes from Piraeus' cruise-terminal area to Athens' main Syntagma Square (€1.20, 6-8/hour, 30-60 minutes depending on traffic). The bus leaves from the stop called Apheteria (ΑΦΕΤΗΡΙΑ, "starting point"), which is on the main road between the two cruise terminals. Several different bus lines stop here, so make sure you get on the right bus. To reach the bus stop from Terminal A, exit the building, bear left, and walk along the road up the low hill. When you reach the main road, turn right and walk along it to reach the Apheteria bus stop. From Terminal B, exit the building, and follow the road to the left of the pretty yellow church. You'll see the row of buses ahead.

By Hop-on, Hop-off Bus: Two companies offer indistinguishable all-day hop-on, hop-off bus tours that include a 70-minute itinerary around Piraeus and link to a separate 1.5-hour bus route around Athens (daily April-Oct 8:30-20:00, Nov-March 9:00-18:30, roughly every 30 minutes; before buying a ticket, carefully check return time and departure point; CitySightseeing-€22, tel. 210-922-0604, www.citysightseeing.gr; Athens City Tour-€20, tel. 210-881-4207, www.athens-citytour.com). The low-pro-

ATHENS

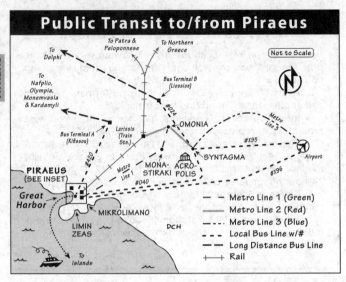

Public Transit to/from Piraeus

[Not to Scale]

To Delphi

To Patra & Peloponnese

To Northern Greece

To Nafplio, Olympia, Monemvasia & Kardamyli

Bus Terminal B (Liossion)

#024

Metro Line 3

Bus Terminal A (Kifissou)

Larissis (Train Stn.)

OMONIA

#X95

Airport

#420

Metro Line 1

MONA-STIRAKI

SYNTAGMA

ACRO-POLIS

#196

PIRAEUS (SEE INSET)

#040

Great Harbor

MIKROLIMANO

DCH

LIMIN ZEAS

To Islands

— — Metro Line 1 (Green)
——— Metro Line 2 (Red)
·—·—· Metro Line 3 (Blue)
– – – Local Bus Line w/#
━━━ Long Distance Bus Line
+—+—+ Rail

file bus stop (a sign on a post) is about 300 yards past Terminal A on the main road, on the port side of the road.

By Metro

The Metro speedily connects Piraeus with downtown Athens' Monastiraki stop. The catch is that the Metro station is between gates E6 and E7, a 15- to 20-minute walk from Terminal A (15-20 minutes more from Terminal B).

The Metro station is a big yellow Neoclassical building with white trim, marked by a pedestrian bridge over the busy street (it's the only such bridge at Piraeus; the bus stop in front is named Stathmos ISAP/ΣΤΑΘΜΟΣ ΗΣΑΠ, and the station is sometimes labeled "Electric Railway Station" on maps). From here, Metro line 1/green links Piraeus with downtown Athens (covered by €1.40 transit ticket, good for 1.5 hours including transfers, train departs about every 10 minutes between 6:00-24:00). In about 20 minutes, the train reaches the city-center Monastiraki stop, near the Plaka and many major sights. (For Syntagma, at the start of my self-guided "Athens City Walk," ride the train one more stop to Omonia to transfer to line 2/red.) Warning: The Metro line between Piraeus and downtown Athens teems with pickpockets—watch your valuables and wear a money belt.

Getting from the Terminals to the Metro Station: You can take a **taxi** there (about €5-7), or catch public **bus #843** from the Apheteria bus stop between the two terminals (6-10/hour Mon-Sat, 3-5/hour Sun, buy €1.40 ticket from kiosk to cover both the bus and the Metro ride, validate your ticket when you board; for di-

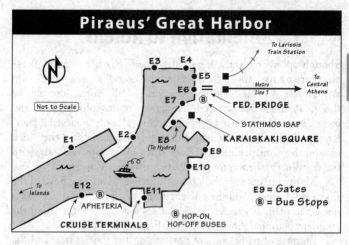

Piraeus' Great Harbor

To Larissis Train Station

E3 E4
E5
Metro Line 1
To Central Athens

E6
E7
Ⓑ PED. BRIDGE

Ⓝ
Not to Scale

STATHMOS ISAP

E1 E2
E8 (To Hydra)
E9
KARAISKAKI SQUARE

E10

To islands

E12 Ⓑ
APHETERIA
E11
Ⓑ HOP-ON, HOP-OFF BUSES

E9 = Gates
Ⓑ = Bus Stops

CRUISE TERMINALS

rections to this stop, see below). To **walk** to the Metro takes 15-20 minutes from Terminal A and 30-40 minutes from Terminal B. From **Terminal A,** exit the terminal building, keep left, and walk up the incline to the main road. Head left onto the main road and simply follow it along the port; turning right takes you to the Apheteria bus stop, where you can ride bus #843 to the Metro. To reach the Metro from **Terminal B,** exit the building and follow the road to the left of the yellow church to reach the Apheteria stop (for bus #843), or continue walking on the same road around the port to the Metro station.

By Tour

For information on bus tours, walking tours, and local guides for hire, see "Tours in Athens" on page 904.

Returning to Your Ship

If you're coming on bus #040 from Syntagma Square, get off at the Apheteria (ΑΦΕΤΗΡΙΑ) stop, right by the cruise terminals.

You can also return to Piraeus by Metro; take line 1/green toward Piraeus (the end of the line). Exit the Piraeus station out the side door, into a chaotic little square filled with vendors slinging knockoff designer bags. Head up the escalator and walk to the far end of the pedestrian bridge, then turn left and take the escalator back down to ground level. At the row of bus stops straight ahead, find the stop for bus #843; hop on and ride it to the Apheteria (ΑΦΕΤΗΡΙΑ) stop, near both cruise terminals (ride covered by Metro ticket).

A taxi from downtown to your ship costs around €15-20.

If you miss your boat, see the sidebar at the end of this chapter.

Orientation to Athens

Though sprawling and congested, Athens has a compact, pleasant tourist zone capped by the famous Acropolis—the world's top ancient site. In this historic town, you'll walk in the footsteps of the great minds that created democracy, philosophy, theater, and more...even when you're dodging motorcycles on "pedestrianized" streets. Romantics can't help but get goose bumps as they kick around the same pebbles that once stuck in Socrates' sandals, with the floodlit Parthenon forever floating ethereally overhead.

Many tourists visit Athens without ever venturing beyond the Plaka (Old Town) and the ancient zone. With limited time, this is not a bad plan, as greater Athens offers few sights (other than the excellent National Archaeological Museum).

Because of its prominent position on the tourist trail and the irrepressible Greek spirit of hospitality, the city is user-friendly. It seems that virtually all Athenians speak English, major landmarks are well-signed, and most street signs are in both Greek and English.

Athens: A Verbal Map

Ninety-five percent of Athens is noisy, polluted modern sprawl, jammed with characterless, poorly planned, and hastily erected concrete suburbs that house the area's rapidly expanding population. The construction of the Metro for the 2004 Olympics was, in many ways, the first time urban planners had ever attempted to tie the city together and treat it as a united entity.

But most visitors never see that part of Athens. In fact, you can pretend that Athens is the same small, charming village at the foot of the Acropolis as it was a century ago. Almost everything of importance to tourists is within a few blocks of the Acropolis. As you explore this city-within-a-city on foot, you'll realize just how small it is.

A good map is a necessity for enjoying Athens on foot. The fine map the TI gives out works great. Get a good map and use it.

Athens by Neighborhood

The Athens you'll be spending your time in includes the following districts:

The Plaka (PLAH-kah, Πλάκα): This neighborhood at the

ATHENS

Athens Neighborhoods

NATIONAL ARCHAEOLOGICAL MUSEUM

OMONIA SQUARE

EXARCHIA

LYKAVITTOS HILL

NAT'L LIBRARY

←To Gazi

KOLONAKI

PSYRRI

SYNTAGMA

THISSIO

MONASTIRAKI

AGORA

SYNTAGMA SQUARE

PARLIAMENT

PLAKA

ACROPOLIS

Nat'l Garden

FILOPAPPOS HILL

ACROPOLIS MUSEUM

TEMPLE OF OLYMPIAN ZEUS

MAKRIGIANNI

KOUKAKI

To Piraeus & Cruise Port

Not to Scale

DCH

ATHINAS, PANEPISTIMIOU/ELEFTHERIOU VENIZELOU, ERMOU, VASILISSIS SOFIAS, APOSTOLOU PAVLOU, ADRIANOU, DIONYSIOU AREOPAGITOU, VASILISSIS AMALIAS, SYNGROU

foot of the Acropolis is the core of the tourist's Athens. One of the only parts of town that's atmospheric and Old World-feeling, it's also the most crassly touristic. Its streets are lined with souvenir shops, tacky tavernas, a smattering of small museums, ancient Greek and Roman ruins, and pooped tourists. The Plaka's narrow, winding streets can be confusing at first, but you can't get too lost with a monument the size of the Acropolis looming overhead to keep you oriented. Think of the Plaka as Athens with training wheels for tourists. While some visitors are mesmerized by the Plaka, others find it obnoxious and enjoy venturing outside it for a change of scenery.

Monastiraki (moh-nah-stee-RAH-kee, Μοναστηράκι): This area ("Little Monastery") borders the Plaka to the northwest, surrounding the square of the same name. It's known for its handy Metro stop (where line 1/green meets line 3/blue), seedy flea market, and souvlaki stands. The Ancient Agora is nearby (roughly between Monastiraki and Thissio).

Psyrri (psee-REE, Ψυρή): Formerly a dumpy ghetto just north of Monastiraki, Psyrri is emerging as a cutting-edge nightlife and dining district.

Syntagma (SEEN-dag-mah, Σύνταγμα): Centered on Athens' main square, Syntagma ("Constitution") Square, this urban-

Greek Words and English Spellings

Any given Greek name—for streets, sights, businesses, and more—can be transliterated many different ways in English. Throughout this chapter, I've used the English spelling you're most likely to see locally, but you will definitely notice variations. If you see a name that looks (or sounds) similar to one in this chapter, it's likely the same place. For example, the Ψυρρή district might appear as Psyrri, Psyrrí, Psyri, Psirri, Psiri, and so on.

Most major streets in Athens are labeled in Greek in signs and on maps, followed by the transliteration in English. The word ΟΔΟΣ (odos) means "street," ΛΕΩΦΌΡΟΣ (leoforos) is "avenue," and ΠΛΑΤΕΙΑ (plateia) is "square."

If a name used in this chapter appears locally only in Greek, I've included that spelling to aid with your navigation.

Greek from A to Ω

Here is the Greek alphabet, with the most common English counterparts for the Greek letters and letter combinations.

Greek		English Name	Common Transliteration	Pronounced
A	α	alpha	a	A as in father
B	β	beta	b or v	V as in volt
Γ	γ	gamma	y or g	Y as in yes or G as in go*
Δ	δ	delta	d or dh	TH as in then
E	ε	epsilon	e	E as in get
Z	ζ	zeta	z	Z as in zoo
H	η	eta	i	I as in ski
Θ	θ	theta	th	TH as in theme

feeling zone melts into the Plaka to the south. While the Plaka is dominated by tourist shops, Syntagma is where local urbanites do their shopping. Syntagma is bounded to the east by the Parliament building and the vast National Garden.

Thissio (thee-SEE-oh, Θησείο): West of the Ancient Agora, Thissio is an upscale, local-feeling residential neighborhood with piles of outdoor cafés and restaurants.

Gazi (GAH-zee, Γκάζι): At the western edge of the tourist's Athens (just beyond Thissio and Psyrri), Gazi is trendy, artsy, and gay-friendly.

Makrigianni (mah-kree-YAH-nee, Μακρυγιάννη) and **Koukaki** (koo-KAH-kee, Κουκάκι): Tucked just behind (south

Greek		English Name	Common Transliteration	Pronounced
Ι	ι	iota	i	I as in ski
Κ	κ	kappa	k	K as in king
Λ	λ	lambda	l	L as in lime
Μ	μ	mu	m	M as in mom
Ν	ν	nu	n	N as in net
Ξ	ξ	xi	x	X as in ox
Ο	ο	omicron	o	O as in ocean
Π	π	pi	p	P as in pie
Ρ	ρ	rho	r	R as in rich (slightly rolled)
Σ	σ,ς	sigma	s or c	S as in sun
Τ	τ	tau	t	T as in tip
Υ	υ	upsilon	y	Y as in happy
Φ	φ	phi	f or ph	F as in file
Χ	χ	chi	ch, h, or kh	CH as in loch (gutturally)
Ψ	ψ	psi	ps	PS as in lapse
Ω	ω	omega	o or w	O as in ocean

*Gamma is pronounced, roughly speaking, like the English "hard" G only when it comes before consonants, or before the letters a, o, and ou.

of) the Acropolis, these overlapping, nondescript urban neighborhoods have a lived-in charm of their own. They're so nondescript that many locals just call Makrigianni the "south Plaka." If you want to escape the crowds of the Plaka, this area—with fine hotels and restaurants within easy walking distance of the ancient sites—makes a good home base.

Kolonaki (koh-loh-NAH-kee, Κολωνάκι): Just north and east of the Parliament/Syntagma Square area, this upscale diplomatic quarter is home to several good museums and a yuppie dining zone.

Exarchia (ex-AR-hee-yah, Εξάρχεια): Just beyond Kolonaki is a rough-and-funky student zone. The home of many protesters grabbing Greek headlines, it's a fascinating but not-for-everyone glimpse into an Athens that few tourists experience.

Major Streets: Various major streets define the tourist's Athens. The base of the Acropolis is partially circled by a broad traffic-free walkway, named **Dionysiou Areopagitou** (Διονυσίου Αρεοπαγίτου) to the south and **Apostolou Pavlou** (Αποστόλου Παύλου) to the west; for simplicity, I call these the **"Acropolis Loop."** Touristy **Adrianou** street (Αδριανού) curves through the Plaka a few blocks away from the Acropolis' base. Partly pedestrianized **Ermou** street (Ερμού) runs west from Syntagma Square, defining the Plaka, Monastiraki, and Thissio to the south and Psyrri to the north. Where Ermou meets Monastiraki, **Athinas** street (Αθηνάς) heads north to Omonia Square. The tourist zone is hemmed in to the east by a series of major highways: The north–south **Vasilissis Amalias** avenue (Βασιλίσσης Αμαλίας) runs between the National Garden and the Plaka/Syntagma area. To the south, it jogs around the Temple of Olympian Zeus and becomes **Syngrou** avenue (Συγγρού). To the north, at the Parliament, it forks: The eastward branch, **Vasilissis Sofias** (Βασιλίσσης Σοφίας), heads past some fine museums to Kolonaki; the north-bound branch, **Panepistimiou** (usually signed by its official name, **Eleftheriou Venizelou**, Ελευθερίου Βενιζέλου), angles north-west past the library and university buildings to Omonia Square.

Tourist Information

The Greek National Tourist Organization (EOT), with its main branch near the Acropolis Museum, covers Athens and the rest of the country. Pick up their handy city map, the helpful *Athens City Guide* booklet, and their slick, glossy book on Athens (all free). Although their advice can be hit-or-miss, they do have stacks of informative handouts on museums, entertainment options, bus and train connections, and much more (April-Oct Mon-Fri 8:00-20:00, Sat-Sun 10:00-16:00; Nov-March Mon-Fri 9:00-19:00, Sat-Sun 10:00-16:00; on pedestrian street leading to Acropolis Museum at Dionysiou Areopagitou 18-20, Metro line 2/red: Akropoli; tel. 210-331-0392, www.visitgreece.gr, info@gnto.gr).

Helpful Websites: Though not officially part of the TI, **Matt Barrett's Athens Survival Guide** (www.athensguide.com) is a great resource for anyone visiting Greece. Matt, who splits his time between North Carolina and Greece, splashes through his adopted hometown like a kid in a wading pool, enthusiastically sharing his discoveries and observations on his generous site. While his practical information isn't always the most up-to-date, his perspectives and advice are top-notch. Matt covers emerging neighborhoods that few visitors venture into, and offers offbeat angles on the city and recommendations for vibrant, untouristy restaurants. He also blogs about his latest impressions on the city.

Other useful websites, some of which you may also see in print form around town, are **Athens in Your Pocket** (www.inyourpocket.com/greece/athens), **Athens Today** (www.athens-today.com), and the online version of the bimonthly Greek lifestyle magazine *Odyssey* (www.odyssey.gr).

Helpful Hints

Theft Alert: Be wary of pickpockets, particularly in crowds, at the Monastiraki flea market, at the changing of the guard at the Tomb of the Unknown Soldier, on major public transit routes (such as the Metro between the city and Piraeus), and at the port. The main streets through the Plaka—such as Adrianou and Pandrossou—attract as many pickpockets as tourists.

Bar Alert: Single male travelers are strongly advised to stay away from bars recommended by strangers encountered on the street. Multilingual con men prowl Syntagma Square and the Plaka looking for likely dupes. They pretend that they, too, are strangers in town who just happen to have stumbled upon a "great little bar." You'll end up at a sleazy bar and be coerced into paying for bottles of overpriced champagne for your new "friend" and the improbably attractive women who inevitably appear.

Traffic Alert: Streets that appear to be "traffic-free" often are shared by motorcycles or moped drivers gingerly easing their machines through crowds. Keep your wits about you, and don't step into a street—even those that feel pedestrian-friendly—without looking both ways.

Slippery Streets Alert: Athens (and other Greek towns) have some marble-like streets and red pavement tiles that become very slick when it rains. Watch your step.

Sunday and Monday Sightseeing: If you're in Athens on a Sunday, consider the Monastiraki flea market, which is at its best today, or the elaborate changing of the guard (including a marching band) that usually takes place at 11:00 in front of the Parliament building. If you're in town on a Monday, note that the Acropolis Museum is closed and several sights open late, including the National Archaeological Museum (13:30) and the Agora Museum (11:00).

Shorter Hours at Major Sights: The hours for sights in Greece are constantly in flux, and with cuts to government spending, many sights have adopted reduced hours (closing in mid-afternoon). Some sights may follow their off-season hours even during peak season. I've listed the posted hours, but be aware

ATHENS

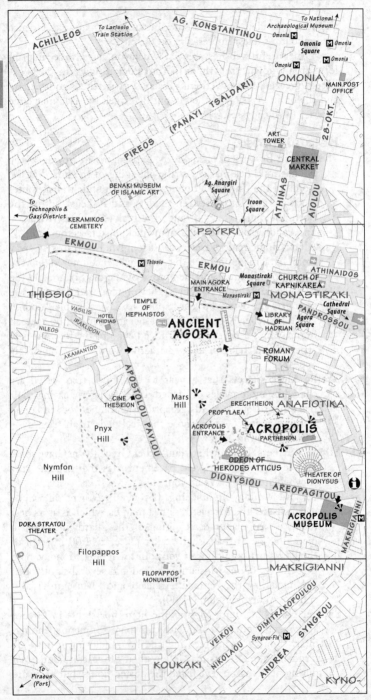

Athens Overview

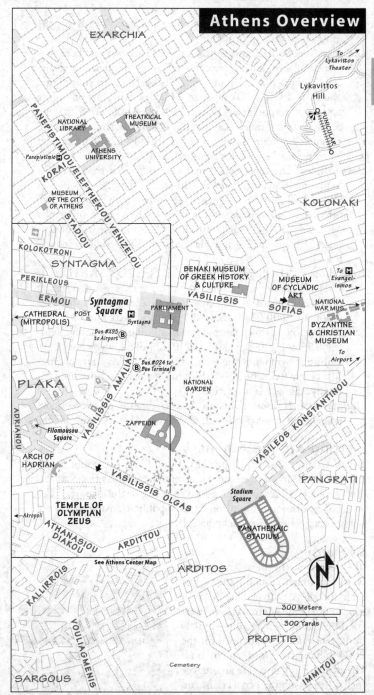

ATHENS

EXARCHIA

PANEPISTIMIOU/ELEFTHERIOU VENIZELOU

NATIONAL LIBRARY

THEATRICAL MUSEUM

Panepistimio Ⓜ

KORAI

ATHENS UNIVERSITY

MUSEUM OF THE CITY OF ATHENS

STADIOU

To Ⓜ Lykavittos Theater

Lykavittos Hill

FUNICULAR

KOLONAKI

KOLOKOTRONI

SYNTAGMA

PERIKLEOUS

ERMOU

CATHEDRAL (MITROPOLIS)

Syntagma Square Ⓜ Syntagma

POST

BENAKI MUSEUM OF GREEK HISTORY & CULTURE

VASILISSIS

PARLIAMENT

MUSEUM OF CYCLADIC ART

SOFIAS

To Ⓜ Evangel-ismos →

NATIONAL WAR MUS.

BYZANTINE & CHRISTIAN MUSEUM

To Airport ↗

Bus #X95 to Airport Ⓑ

VASILISSIS AMALIAS

Ⓑ Bus #024 to Bus Terminal B

PLAKA

ADRIANOU

Filomousou Square

NATIONAL GARDEN

ZAPPEION

ARCH OF HADRIAN

VASILEOS KONSTANTINOU

PANGRATI

← Akropoli

VASILISSIS OLGAS

TEMPLE OF OLYMPIAN ZEUS

ATHANASIOU DIAKOU

ARDITTOU

Stadium Square

PANATHENAIC STADIUM

See Athens Center Map

ARDITOS

KALLIRROIS

VOULIAGMENIS

N

300 Meters
300 Yards

PROFITIS

SARGOUS

Cemetery

IMMITOU

that these hours are likely to change. Check locally for the most up-to-date information.

Internet Access: Bits and Bytes, in the heart of the Plaka, has plenty of terminals, a peaceful folk/jazz ambience, and air-conditioning (€2 minimum, €2.50/hour, can burn your digital photos to a CD or DVD, open 24 hours daily, just off Agora Square at Kapnikareas 19, tel. 210-325-3142). At Syntagma Square, **Ivis Travel** has several Internet terminals (€2/30 minutes, €3/hour, €2 minimum, daily 8:00-22:00, upstairs at Mitropoleos 3—look for signs, tel. 210-324-3365).

Post Offices: The most convenient post office for travelers is at Syntagma Square (Mon-Fri 7:30-20:00, Sat 7:30-14:00, Sun 9:00-13:30, bottom of square, at corner with Mitropoleos). Smaller neighborhood offices with shorter hours (generally Mon-Fri 7:30-14:00 or 14:30, closed Sat-Sun) are in Monastiraki (Mitropoleos 58) and Makrigianni (Dionysiou Areopagitou 7).

Bookshops: Eleftheroudakis (ΕΛΕΥΘΕΡΟΥΔΑΚΗΣ) is Greece's answer to Barnes & Noble, with a great selection of travel guides and maps, along with a lot of English books (Mon-Fri 9:00-21:00, Sat 9:00-18:00, closed Sun, 3 blocks north of Syntagma Square at Panepistimiou/Eleftheriou Venizelou 15, tel. 210-323-3861 or 210-323-3862, www.books.gr). **Public** at Syntagma Square offers a reasonable variety of English books (tel. 210-324-6210, www.public.gr). Both are near the Syntagma Metro station.

Updates to This Book: For news about changes to this book's coverage since it was published, see www.ricksteves.com/update.

Getting Around Athens

Because Athens is such a huge city, you'll likely use public transportation to reach farther-flung destinations (such as the National Archaeological Museum, the port of Piraeus, or the airport).

For information on all of Athens' public transportation, see www.oasa.gr. Beware of pickpockets.

By Metro

The Metro is the most straightforward way to get around Athens. Just look for signs with a blue M in a green circle. The Metro is slick, user-friendly, and new-feeling—mostly built, renovated, or expanded for the 2004 Olympics. Signs are in both Greek and English, as are announcements inside subway cars. Trains run

Athens Transit

— Metro Line 1 (Green)
— Metro Line 2 (Red)
- - - Metro Line 3 (Blue)
- - - Bus Line w/#
⊢—⊢ Rail
— Coastal Tram w/#

• Kifissia
• Irini
Line 1 (Green)
Trains to All Over Greece
Bus Terminal B (Liossion)
Anthoupoli
#024
To Piraeus #X96
Airport
Aghia Marina •
Egaleo
Larissis (Train Stn.)
Attíki
Victoria
NATIONAL ARCHAEO-LOGICAL MUSEUM
Line 3 (Blue)
Omonia
LYKAVITTOS HILL
Keramikos
To Airport
#196
Monastiraki
Evangelismos
#X95
Thissio
ACRO-POLIS
Syntagma
Piraeus
Neo Faliro
Akropoli
Syngrou-Fix
N
#040
Neos Kosmos
CRUISE PORT
1
1 & 2
Line 2 (Red)
NEA SMYRNI
Ferries & Hydrofoils to Islands
Saronic Gulf
2
Helliniko
DCH
To Voula
Not to Scale

about every five minutes on weekdays, and about every 10 minutes on weekends (Sun-Thu 5:00-24:20, Fri-Sat 5:00-2:20 in the morning, www.stasy.gr).

You can buy tickets at machines or from ticket windows. The **basic ticket** (€1.40) is good for 1.5 hours on all public transit, including buses and trams, and covers transfers. Note that you'll need a pricier €8 ticket to go all the way to the airport (€14/two people; see page 970). If planning more than three rides in a day, consider the **24-hour ticket** (€4; does not include airport). Be sure to stamp

your ticket in a validation machine, usually located near the ticket booth, before you board (tickets only need to be stamped the first time). Those riding without a ticket (or with an unstamped ticket) are subject to stiff fines.

The three Metro lines are color-coded and numbered. Use the end-of-the-line stops to figure out which direction you need to go.

Line 1 (green) runs from the

Athens at a Glance

Sights generally are open in the morning but can close earlier than listed in the afternoon. Many closing times depend on the sunset. Check locally.

▲▲▲**Acropolis** The most important ancient site in the Western world, where Athenians built their architectural masterpiece, the Parthenon. **Hours:** Daily June-Aug likely 8:00-20:00, Sept-Oct and April-May 8:00-18:00, Nov-March 8:00-15:00. See page 928.

▲▲▲**Acropolis Museum** Glassy modern temple for ancient art. **Hours:** Tue-Sun 8:00-20:00, Fri until 22:00, closed Mon. See page 933.

▲▲▲**Ancient Agora** Social and commercial center of ancient Athens, with a well-preserved temple and an intimate museum. **Hours:** Daily 8:00-15:00, possibly open later in summer; museum opens at 11:00 on Mon. See page 934.

▲▲▲**National Archaeological Museum** World's best collection of ancient Greek art, displayed chronologically from 7000 B.C. to A.D. 500. **Hours:** Tue-Sun 8:00-15:00, later in summer—until 18:00 or 20:00 depending on sunset; Tue-Sun 9:00-16:00 in winter; Mon 13:30-20:00, may close at 15:00 in winter. See page 935.

▲▲ **"Acropolis Loop"** Traffic-free pedestrian walkways ringing much of the Acropolis with vendors, cafés, and special events. **Hours:** Always open. See page 928.

▲▲**Thissio and Psyrri** Vibrant nightlife neighborhoods near the center, great for eating, exploring, and escaping other tourists. **Hours:** Always open. See page 961.

▲▲**Anafiotika** Delightful, village-like neighborhood draped

port of Piraeus in the southwest to Kifissia in the northern suburbs. Because this is an older line—officially called ISAP or electrical train *(elektrikos)* rather than Metro—it's slower than the other two lines. Key stops include Piraeus (cruise terminals and boats to the islands), Thissio (enjoyable neighborhood with good restaurants and nightlife), Monastiraki (city center), Victoria (10-minute walk from National Archaeological Museum), and Irini (Olympic Stadium). You can transfer to line 2 at Omonia and to line 3 at Monastiraki. (Confusingly, on line 1, the Monastiraki stop is labeled "Monastirion.")

Line 2 (red) runs from Anthoupoli in the northwest to

across the hillside north of the Acropolis. **Hours:** Always open. See page 923.

▲▲**Temple of Olympian Zeus** Remains of the largest temple in ancient Greece. **Hours:** Daily in summer 8:00-20:00, Sept 8:00-19:00, off-season 8:00-15:00. See page 935.

▲**Mars Hill** Historic spot—with a classic view of the Acropolis—where the Apostle Paul preached to the Athenians. **Hours:** Always open. See page 932.

▲**Gazi** Former industrial zone, now the colorful and kinetic heart of Athens' gay community. **Hours:** Always open. See page 962.

▲**Roman Forum and Tower of the Winds** Ancient Roman marketplace with wondrously intact tower. **Hours:** Daily 8:00-14:00, possibly open later in summer. See page 924.

▲**Syntagma Square** Famous public space with a popular changing-of-the-guard ceremony. **Hours:** Always open, guards change five minutes before the top of each hour. See page 908.

▲**Church of Kapnikarea** Small 11th-century Byzantine church with symbols of Greek Orthodox faith. **Hours:** Likely open daily 8:30-13:30; Tue and Thu-Fri also 17:00-19:30. See page 915.

▲**Cathedral (Mitropolis)** Large, underwhelming head church of Greek Orthodox faith. **Hours:** Generally open daily 8:00-13:00 & 16:30-19:00, no afternoon closure in summer. See page 916.

▲**Church of Agios Eleftherios** Tiny Byzantine church decorated with a millennia of Christian bric-a-brac. **Hours:** Likely open daily 8:30-13:30 & 17:00-19:30. See page 917.

Helliniko (Elliniko) in the southeast. Important stops include **Larissis** (train station), **Syntagma** (city center), **Akropoli** (Acropolis and Makrigianni/Koukaki hotel neighborhood), and **Syngrou-Fix** (Makrigianni/Koukaki hotels). Transfer to line 1 at Omonia and to line 3 at Syntagma.

Line 3 (blue) runs from Aghia Marina in the west to the airport in the east. Important stops are **Keramikos** (near Keramikos Cemetery and the lively Gazi district), **Monastiraki** (city center), **Syntagma** (city center), **Evangelismos** (Kolonaki neighborhood), and the **airport** (requires a separate ticket). Transfer to line 1 at Monastiraki and to line 2 at Syntagma.

By Bus

Public **buses** can help connect the dots between Metro stops, though the city center is so walkable that most visitors never ride one. A one-way, bus-only ticket costs €1.20; buy tickets in advance, either from a special ticket kiosk or at a Metro station. Some of the newsstands that dot the streets sell bus tickets as well. Tickets must be validated in the orange machines as you board. In general, I'd avoid buses, which are slow and overcrowded, with a few exceptions. Bus **#035** takes you from Athinas street near Monastiraki to the National Archaeological Museum, and bus **#224** links to the museum from Syntagma Square. Bus **#040** goes from Piraeus' cruise-terminal area to Syntagma Square. Express bus **#X95** zips between the airport and Syntagma Square, and express bus **#X96** connects the airport with Piraeus (airport buses are €5 each).

By Taxi

Despite the vulgar penchant cabbies here have for ripping off tourists, Athens is a great taxi town. Its yellow taxis are cheap and handy (€3.20 minimum charge covers most short rides in town; after that it's €0.68/km, plus surcharges: €1 from Piraeus passenger ports and train and bus stations, €2.30 from the airport, €5.20 from cruise terminal at Piraeus). The €0.68 per kilometer day rate (tariff 1 on the meter) doubles between midnight and 5:00 in the morning (tariff 2). You'll also pay the double rate outside the city limits, and you're responsible for any tolls incurred by the driver (such as on the speedy road to the airport). Baggage costs €0.40 for each item over 10 kilograms (about 22 pounds).

In a semi-legal local custom, Athens' cabbies double up, picking up additional passengers headed the same way. Unfortunately, sharing the cab with strangers doesn't mean sharing the fare. The cabbie makes more and the passengers save nothing. Still, this makes it easier to find an available cab. You can simply hail any taxi, empty or not, and if your destination works for the cabbie, he'll welcome you in.

Hotels and restaurants can order you a cab, but there's a €2 surcharge to call for a taxi ("radio-taxi"). Warning: Cabbies may try to cheat you by saying the surcharge is €5. Hold firm, and they will take the €2.

Tours in Athens

To sightsee on your own, download my series of free audio tours that illuminate some of Athens' top sights and neighborhoods, including the Acropolis, the Agora, the National Archaeological Museum, and my Athens City Walk (see sidebar on page 50).

On Wheels

Bus Tours

Various companies offer half-day, bus-plus-walking tours of Athens for €52-55 (about 4 hours, including a guided visit to the Acropolis). Add a guided tour of the Acropolis Museum, and the price goes up to €68.

Some companies also offer a night city tour that finishes with dinner and folk dancing at a taverna (€63) and a 90-mile round-trip evening drive down the coast to Cape Sounion for the sunset at the Temple of Poseidon (€43, 4 hours—not worth the time if visiting ancient sites elsewhere in Greece). The buses pick up passengers at various points around town and near most hotels.

The most established operations include the well-regarded **Hop In** (modern comfy buses, narration usually English only, tel. 210-428-5500, www.hopin.com), **CHAT Tours** (tel. 210-323-0827, www.chatours.gr), **Key Tours** (tel. 210-923-3166, www.key-tours.gr), and **GO Tours** (tel. 210-921-9555, www.gotours.com.gr).

Beyond Athens: If you're staying in Athens before or after your cruise, note that some of these companies also offer day-long tours to Delphi and to Mycenae, Nafplio, and Epidavros (either tour €101 with lunch, €91 without), two-day tours to the monasteries of Meteora (€162-190), and more. **Olympic Traveller** offers personalized tours to Olympia, Mycenae, or Delphi (reasonable rates, mobile 697-320-1213, www.olympictraveller.com, info@olympictraveller.com; with-it, charming guides Christos and Niki).

Hop-on, Hop-off Bus Tours

Two companies compete for the usual hop-on, hop-off bus tour business, both charging €18 for a 24-hour ticket: **CitySightseeing Athens** (tel. 210-922-0604, www.citysightseeing.gr) and **Athens City Tour** (tel. 210-881-5207, www.athens-citytour.com). The main stop for both buses is on Syntagma Square, though you can hop on and buy your ticket at any stop—look for signs around town. Since most of the major sights in Athens are within easy walking distance of the Plaka, I'd use this only if I wanted an overview of the city or had extra time to get to the outlying sights.

Tourist Trains

Two different trains do a sightseeing circuit through Athens' tourist zone. As these goofy little trains can go where big buses can't, they can be useful for people with limited mobility. The **Sunshine Express** train runs about hourly; catch it on Aiolou street along the Hadrian's Library fence at Agora Square (€5, 40-minute loop, departs hourly; May-Sept Mon-Fri 11:30-14:30 & 17:00-24:00, Sat-

Sun 11:00-24:00; Oct-April Sat-Sun only). The **Athens Happy Train** is similar, but it offers hop-on, hop-off privileges at a few strategic stops (€6, full loop takes 1 hour, 2/hour, daily 9:00-24:00; catch it at the bottom of Syntagma Square, at Monastiraki Square, or just below the Acropolis; www.athenshappytrain.com).

On Foot

Walking Tours

Athens Walking Tours offers two basic walks: the Acropolis and City Tour (€36 plus entry fees, daily at 9:30, 3 hours, departs from Syntagma Metro station, under hanging clock one level down) and Acropolis Museum tour (€29 plus entry fee, Tue-Sun at 13:30, 1.25 hours, meet inside museum, in front of cash desk). Those with energy can sign up for a combo version of these tours (€53, Tue-Sun at 9:30, 5.5 hours, reserve in advance, tel. 210-884-7269, mobile 694-585-9662, www.athenswalkingtours.gr, Despina).

Context Athens' "intellectual by design" walking tours are geared for serious learners and led by "docents" (historians, architects, and academics) rather than by guides. They cover ancient sites and museums and offer themed walks with topics ranging from food to architecture to the Byzantine era. Their Orientation to Athens tour touches on most of these themes while giving you an overview of the city's highlights (€65-70 plus entry fees, generally 3 hours, US tel. 800-691-6036, www.contexttravel.com/city/athens).

Local Guides

A good private guide can bring Athens' sights to life. **Effie Perperi** is a fine choice (€50/hour, tel. 210-951-2566, mobile 697-739-6659, effieperperi@gmail.com). **Faye Georgiou** is another good Athens guide who really knows her archaeology (€50/hour, tel. 210-674-5837, mobile 697-768-5503, fayegeorgiou@yahoo.gr), as does energetic **Anastasia Gaitanou** (€50/hour, mobile 694-446-3109, anastasia2570@yahoo.com).

Athens City Walk

Athens is a bustling metropolis of nearly four million people, home to one out of every three Greeks. Much of the city is unappealing, cheaply built, poorly zoned, 20th-century sprawl. But the heart and soul of Athens is engaging and refreshingly compact.

From Syntagma Square to Monastiraki Square

This self-guided walk takes you through the striking contrasts of the city center—from chaotic, traffic-clogged urban zones, to sleepy streets packed with bearded priests shopping for a new robe or chalice, to peaceful, barely-wide-enough-for-a-donkey back lanes that twist their way up toward the Acropolis. Along the way, we'll learn about Athens' rich history, the intriguing tapestry of Orthodox churches that dot the city, and the way that locals live and shop.

The walk begins at Syntagma Square, meanders through the fascinating old Plaka district, and finishes at lively Monastiraki Square (near the Ancient Agora, markets, good restaurants, and a handy Metro stop). This sightseeing spine will help you get a once-over-lightly look at Athens, which you can use as a springboard for diving into the city's various colorful sights and neighborhoods.

Orientation

Churches: Athens' churches are free but keep irregular hours—generally daily 8:30-13:30 & 17:00-19:30 (evenings hours at the Church of Kapnikarea on Tue and Thu-Fri only). If you want to buy candles at churches (as the locals do), be sure to have a few small coins.

Cathedral: Free, generally open daily 8:00-13:00 & 16:30-19:00, no afternoon closure in summer.

Temple of Olympian Zeus: €2, covered by Acropolis ticket; daily in summer 8:00-20:00 (but may close earlier), Sept 8:00-19:00, off-season 8:00-15:00; Vasilissis Olgas 1, Metro line 2/red: Akropoli, tel. 210-922-6330, www.culture.gr.

Roman Forum: €2, covered by Acropolis ticket, daily 8:00-14:00, possibly open later in summer, corner of Pelopida and Aiolou streets, Metro line 1/green or 3/blue: Monastiraki, tel. 210-324-5220.

When to Go: Do this walk early in your visit, as it can help you get your bearings in this potentially confusing city. Morning is best, since many churches close for an afternoon break, and other sights—such as the Acropolis—are too crowded to enjoy.

Dress Code: Wearing shorts inside churches (especially the cathedral) is frowned upon, though usually tolerated.

Getting There: The walk begins at Syntagma Square, just northeast of the Plaka tourist zone. You can get here by Metro (line 2/red or line 3/blue to Syntagma stop). Conveniently, this is also where bus #040 from the cruise terminals at Piraeus stops.

Audio Tour: You can download this walk as a free Rick Steves audio tour (see page 50).

Length of This Walk: Allow plenty of time. This three-part walk takes two hours without stops or detours. But if you explore and dip into sights here and there—pausing to ponder a dimly lit Orthodox church, or doing some window- (or actual) shopping—it can enjoyably eat up a half-day or more.

ATHENS

Starring: Athens' top squares, churches, and Roman ruins, connected by bustling urban streets that are alternately choked with cars and mopeds, or thronged by pedestrians, vendors... and fellow tourists.

The Walk Begins

This lengthy walk is thematically divided into three parts: The first part focuses on modern Athens, centered on Syntagma Square and the Ermou shopping street. The

second part focuses on Athens' Greek Orthodox faith, with visits to three different but equally interesting churches. And the third part is a wander through the charming old core of Athens, including the touristy Plaka and the mellow Greek-village-on-a-hillside of Anafiotika.

Part 1: Modern Athens

This part of our walk lets you feel the pulse of a European capital.
• *Start at Syntagma Square, worth ▲. From the leafy park at the center of the square, climb to the top of the stairs (in the middle of the square) and stand across the street from the big, Neoclassical Greek Parliament building.*

❶ Syntagma Square (Plateia Syntagmatos)

As you look at posh hotels and major banks, you are standing atop the city's central Metro stop, surrounded by buses, cars, and taxis. Facing the Parliament building (east), get oriented to the square

named for Greece's constitution (*syntagma;* SEEN-dag-mah). From this point, sightseeing options spin off through the city like spokes on a wheel.

Fronting the square on the left (north) side are high-end hotels, including the opulent Hotel Grande Bretagne.

Directly to the left of the

Parliament building is the head of Vasilissis Sofias avenue, lined with embassies and museums, including the Benaki Museum of Greek History and Culture, Museum of Cycladic Art, Byzantine and Christian Museum, and National War Museum. This boulevard leads to the ritzy Kolonaki quarter, with its funicular up to the top of Lykavittos Hill. Extending to the right of the Parliament building is the National Garden, Athens' "Central Park." Here you'll find the Zappeion mansion-turned-conference-hall (with a fine summer outdoor cinema nearby) and, beyond the greenery, the evocative, ancient Panathenaic Stadium.

On your right (south) is one of Athens' prime transit hubs, with stops for bus #X95 to the airport, and bus #024 to Bus Terminal B/Liossion. Beneath your feet is the Syntagma Metro station, the city's busiest.

Behind you, at the west end of the square, stretches the traffic-free shopping street called Ermou, which heads to the Plaka neighborhood and Monastiraki Square. (We'll be heading that way soon.) Nearby is the terminus for one of Athens' two tourist trains (see page 905).

Take a moment to look at the square and modern Athens: People buzz about on their way to work, handing out leaflets, feeding pigeons, or just enjoying a park bench, shaded by a variety of trees. Plane, cypress, and laurel trees make Syntagma a breezy and restful spot. Breathe deeply and ponder the fact that until 1990, Athens was the most polluted city in Europe. People advertising facial creams would put a mannequin outside on the street for three hours and film it turning black. The moral: You need our cream.

But over the last two decades, "green" policies have systematically cleaned up the air. Traffic, though still pretty extreme, is limited: Even- and odd-numbered license plates are prohibited in the center on alternate days. Check the license plates of passing cars (not taxis or motorcycles): The majority end with either an even or an odd number, depending on the day of the week. Wealthy locals get around this restriction by owning two cars—one with even plates, the other with odd. While car traffic is down, motorcycle usage is up (since bikes are exempt). Central-heating fuel is more expensive and much cleaner these days (as required by European Union regulations), more of the city center is pedestrianized, and the city's public transport is top-notch.

• *Using the crosswalk (one on either side of Syntagma Square), cross the busy street. Directly in front of the Parliament you'll see the...*

❷ Tomb of the Unknown Soldier and the Evzone Guards

Standing amid pigeons and tourists in front of the imposing Parliament building, overlooking Syntagma Square, you're at the center of Athens' modern history. Above the simple marble-slab tomb—marked only with a cross—is a carved image of the Unknown Soldier, a heavily armed dying Greek, inspired by statue of a dying nude from the ancient Aphaia temple on the island of Aigina, very close to Athens. Etched into the stone on each side of the tomb are the names of great battles in Greek military history from 1821 for-

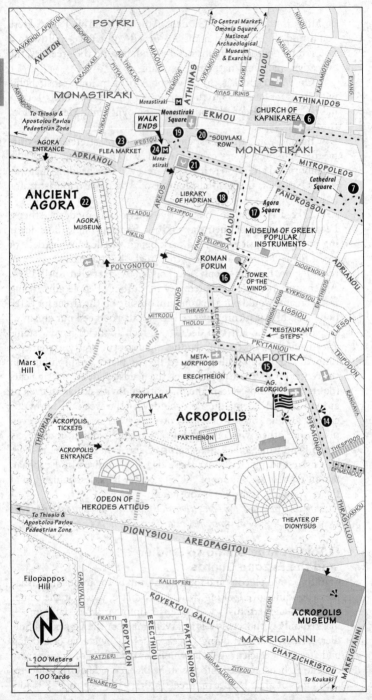

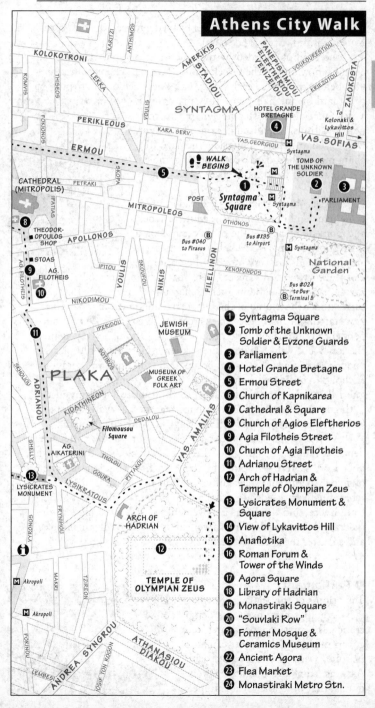

Athens City Walk

KOLOKOTRONI

SYNTAGMA

HOTEL GRANDE BRETAGNE ④

PERIKLEOUS

ERMOU

👣 WALK BEGINS

⑤

Syntagma

Ⓜ

① *Syntagma Square*

Ⓜ Syntagma

TOMB OF THE UNKNOWN SOLDIER ② ③

PARLIAMENT

VAS. SOFIAS

To Kolonaki & Lykavittos Hill →

CATHEDRAL (MITROPOLIS)

⑧

THEODOR- OPOULOS SHOP ■

STOAS ■

⑨

AG. FILOTHEIS ⑩

MITROPOLEOS

POST

OTHONOS

Ⓑ Bus #040 to Piraeus

Ⓑ Bus #195 to Airport

Ⓑ

Ⓜ Syntagma

National Garden

Ⓑ Bus #024 to Bus Terminal B

⑪

PLAKA

JEWISH MUSEUM

MUSEUM OF GREEK FOLK ART

Filomousou Square

AG. AIKATERINI

⑬

LYSICRATES MONUMENT

ARCH OF HADRIAN

⑫

TEMPLE OF OLYMPIAN ZEUS

Ⓜ Akropoli

Ⓜ Akropoli

① Syntagma Square
② Tomb of the Unknown Soldier & Evzone Guards
③ Parliament
④ Hotel Grande Bretagne
⑤ Ermou Street
⑥ Church of Kapnikarea
⑦ Cathedral & Square
⑧ Church of Agios Eleftherios
⑨ Agia Filotheis Street
⑩ Church of Agia Filotheis
⑪ Adrianou Street
⑫ Arch of Hadrian & Temple of Olympian Zeus
⑬ Lysicrates Monument & Square
⑭ View of Lykavittos Hill
⑮ Anafiotika
⑯ Roman Forum & Tower of the Winds
⑰ Agora Square
⑱ Library of Hadrian
⑲ Monastiraki Square
⑳ "Souvlaki Row"
㉑ Former Mosque & Ceramics Museum
㉒ Ancient Agora
㉓ Flea Market
㉔ Monastiraki Metro Stn.

ward (practice your Greek alphabet by trying to read them: Cyprus, Korea, Rimini, Crete, and so on).

The tomb is guarded by the much-photographed evzone, an elite infantry unit of the Greek army. The guard changes five minutes before the top of each hour, with a less elaborate crossing of the guard on the half-hour. They march with a slow-motion, high-stepping march to their new positions, then stand ramrod straight, where you can pose alongside them. A full changing-of-the-guard ceremony, complete with marching band, takes place every Sunday at 11:00.

These colorful characters are clad in traditional pleated kilts *(fustanella)*, white britches, and pom-pom shoes. (The outfits may look a little goofy to a non-Greek, but their mothers and girlfriends are very proud.) The uniforms, worn everywhere in Greece, were made famous by the Klephts, ragtag bands of mountain guerrilla fighters. After nearly four centuries under the thumb of the Ottoman Empire (from today's Turkey, starting in 1453), the Greeks rose up. The Greek War of Independence (1821-1829) pitted the powerful Ottoman army against the lowly but wily Klephts. The soldiers' skirts have 400 pleats... one for each year of Ottoman occupation (and don't you forget it). Although considered heroes today for their courage, outrageous guerrilla tactics, and contribution to the Liberation Army in the 19th century, the Klephts were once regarded as warlike bandits (their name shares a root with the English word "kleptomania").

As the Klephts and other Greeks fought for their independence, a number of farsighted Europeans (including the English poet Lord Byron)—inspired by the French Revolution and their own love of ancient Greek culture—came to their aid. In 1829 the rebels finally succeeded in driving their Ottoman rulers out of central Greece, and there was a movement to establish a modern democracy. However, the Greeks were unprepared to rule themselves, and so, after the Ottomans came...Otto.

• *For the rest of the story, take a step back for a view of the...*

❸ Parliament

The origins of this "palace of democracy" couldn't have been less democratic. The first independent Greek government, which had its capital in Nafplio, was too weak to be viable. As was standard operating procedure at that time, the great European

powers forced Greece to accept a king from established European royalty.

In 1832, Prince Otto of Bavaria became King Otto of Greece. A decade later, after the capital shifted to Athens, this royal palace was built to house King Otto and his wife, Queen Amalia. The atmosphere was tense. After fighting so fiercely for their independence from the Ottomans, the Greeks now chafed under royal rule from a dictatorial Bavarian monarch. The palace's over-the-top luxury only angered impoverished locals.

On September 3, 1843, angry rioters gathered in the square to protest, demanding a democratic constitution. King Otto stepped onto the balcony of this building, quieted the mob, and gave them what they wanted. The square was dubbed Syntagma (Constitution), and modern Athens was born. The former royal palace has been the home of the Greek parliament since 1935. Today this is where 300 Greek parliamentarians (elected to four-year terms) tend to the business of the state—or, as more cynical locals would say, become corrupt and busily get themselves set up for their cushy, post-political lives.

• *Cross back to the heart of Syntagma Square, and focus on the grand building fronting its north side.*

❹ Hotel Grande Bretagne and Neoclassical Syntagma

Imagine the original Syntagma Square (which was on the outskirts of town in the early 19th century): a big front yard for the new royal palace, with the country's influential families building mansions around it. Surviving examples include Hotel Grande Bretagne, the adjacent Hotel King George Palace, the Zappeion in the National Garden (not visible from here), and the stately architecture lining Vasilissis Sofias avenue behind the palace (now embassies and museums).

These grand buildings date from Athens' Otto-driven Neoclassical makeover. Eager to create a worthy capital for Greece, Otto imported teams of Bavarian architects to draft a plan of broad avenues and grand buildings in what they imagined to be the classical style. This "Neoclassical" look is symmetrical and geometrical, with pastel-colored buildings highlighted in white trim. The windows are rectangular, flanked by white Greek half-columns (pilasters), fronted by balconies, and topped with cornices. Many of the buildings are also framed at the top with cornices. When you continue on this walk, notice not only the many Neoclassical buildings, but also the more modern buildings that try to match the same geometric lines.

Syntagma Square is also worth a footnote in American Cold War history. In December of 1944, Greek communists demonstrated here, inducing the US to come to the aid of the Greek government. This became the basis (in 1947) for the Truman Doctrine, which pledged US aid to countries fighting communism and helped shape American foreign policy for the next 50 years.

• *Head down to the bottom of Syntagma (directly across from the Parliament). Stroll down the traffic-free street near the McDonald's.*

❺ Ermou Street

The pedestrian mall called Ermou (AIR-moo) leads from Syntagma down through the Plaka to Monastiraki, then continues westward to the ancient Keramikos Cemetery and the Gazi district. Not long ago, this street epitomized all that was terrible about Athens: lousy building codes, tacky neon signs, double-parked trucks, and noisy traffic. When Ermou was first pedestrianized, in 2000, merchants were upset. Now they love the ambience created as countless locals stroll through what has become a people-friendly shopping zone.

This has traditionally been the street of women's shops. However, these days Ermou is dominated by high-class international chain stores, which appeal to young Athenians but turn off older natives, who lament the lack of local flavor. For authentic, hole-in-the-wall shopping, many Athenians prefer the streets just to the north, such as Perikleous, Lekka, and Kolokotroni.

Even so, this people-crammed boulevard is a pleasant place for a wander. Do just that, proceeding gradually downhill and straight ahead for seven blocks. As you window-shop, notice that many of Ermou's department stores are housed in impressive Neoclassical mansions. Talented street performers (many of them former music professionals from Eastern Europe) provide an entertaining soundtrack. All of Athens walks along here: businesspeople, teenage girls with iPods, Orthodox priests, men twirling worry beads, activists gathering signatures, illegal vendors who sweep up their wares and scurry when they see police, cell-phone-toting shoppers, and, of course, tourists. Keep an eye out for vendors selling various snacks—including pretzel-like sesame rings called *koulouri* and slices of fresh coconut.

After six short blocks, on the right (at the intersection with

Evangelistrias/Ευαγγελιστριασ), look for the little **book wagon** selling cheap lit. You'll likely see colorful, old-fashioned alphabet books (labeled ΑΛΦΑΒΗΤΑΡΙΟ, *Alphabetario*), which have been reprinted for nostalgic older Greeks. The English word "alphabet" comes from the first two Greek letters (alpha, beta).

Part 2: The Greek Orthodox Church

This part of our walk introduces you to the Orthodox faith of Greece, including stops at three different churches. The Greek faith is one denomination of Eastern Orthodox Christianity; for more information, see the sidebar on page 918.

• *Stranded in the middle of both Ermou street and the commercial bustle of the 21st century is a little medieval church.*

❻ Church of Kapnikarea

After the ancient Golden Age, but before Otto and the Ottomans, Athens was part of the Byzantine Empire (A.D. 323-1453). In the 11th and 12th centuries, Athens boomed, and several Eastern Orthodox churches like this one were constructed.

The Church of Kapnikarea—worth ▲—is a classic 11th-century Byzantine church. Notice that it's square and topped with a central dome. Telltale signs of a Byzantine church include tall arches over the windows, stones surrounded by a frame of brick and mortar, and a domed cupola with a cross on top. The large white blocks are scavenged from other, earlier monuments (also typical of Byzantine churches from this era). Over the door is a mosaic of glass and gold leaf, which, though modern, is made in the traditional Byzantine style.

Step inside if the church is open (if it's closed, don't fret—we'll be visiting a couple of similar churches later). The church has no nave, just an entrance hall. Notice the symmetrical Greek-cross floor plan. It's decorated with standing candelabras, hanging lamps, tall arches, a wooden pulpit, and a few chairs. If you wish, you can do as the Greeks do and follow the standard candle-buying, icon-kissing ritual. The icon displayed closest to the door gets changed with the church calendar. You may notice lipstick smudges on the protective glass and a candle-recycling box behind the candelabra.

Look up into the central dome, lit with windows, which symbolizes heaven. Looking back down is the face of Jesus, the omnipotent *Pantocrator* God blessing us on Earth. He holds a Bible in one hand and blesses us with the other. On the walls are iconic murals of saints. Notice the focus on the eyes, which are considered a mirror of the soul and a symbol of its purity.

• *When you leave the church, turn south toward the Acropolis and proceed downhill on Kapnikareas street. Up ahead, catch a glimpse of the Acropolis. Go two blocks to the traffic-free Pandrossou shopping street. Turn left and walk (passing the recommended Restaurant Hermion) up the pedestrian street to the cathedral.*

❼ Cathedral (Mitropolis) and Cathedral Square (Plateia Mitropoleos)

Built from 1842–1862, this "metropolitan church" (as the Greek Orthodox call their cathedrals) is the most important in Athens,

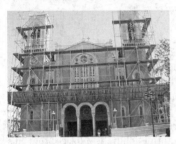

which makes it the head church of the Greek Orthodox faith. Worth ▲, it's unremarkable and oddly ramshackle inside and out...and has been decorated with scaffolding since the earthquake of 1989.

If it's open, head inside. Looking up, you'll notice balconies. Traditionally, women worshipped apart from men in the balconies upstairs. Women got the vote in Greece in 1954, and since about that time, they've been able to worship in the prime, ground-floor real estate alongside the men.

When you're back outside on the square, notice the statue facing the cathedral. This was erected by Athens' Jewish community as thanks to **Archbishop Damaskinos** (1891-1949), the rare Christian leader who stood up to the Nazis during the occupation of Greece. At great personal risk, Damaskinos formally spoke out against the Nazi occupiers on behalf of the Greek Jews he saw being deported to concentration camps. When a Nazi commander threatened to put Damaskinos before a firing squad, the archbishop defiantly countered that he should be hanged instead, in good Orthodox tradition. After the occupation, Damaskinos served as regent and then prime minister of Greece until the king returned from exile.

Here Damaskinos is depicted wearing the distinctive hat of an archbishop (a kind of fez with cloth hanging down the sides). He carries a staff and blesses with his right hand, making a traditional Orthodox sign of the cross, touching his thumb to his ring finger. This gesture forms the letters ICXC, the first and last letters of the Greek name for Jesus Christ (ΙΗΣΟΥΣ ΧΡΙΣΤΟΣ—traditionally C was substituted for Σ). Make the gesture yourself with your right hand. Touch the tip of your thumb to the tip of your ring finger and check it out: Your pinkie forms the I, your slightly crossed index and middle fingers are the X, and your thumb and ring finger make a double-C. Jesus Christ, that's clever. If you were a priest, you'd make the sign of the cross three times, to symbolize the Father, the Son, and the Holy Spirit.

The double-headed eagle that hangs around Damaskinos' neck is an important symbol of the Orthodox faith. It evokes the Byzantine Empire, during which Orthodox Christianity was at its peak as the state religion. Appropriately, the eagle's twin heads have a double meaning: The Byzantine Emperor was both the secular and spiritual leader of his realm, which exerted its influence over both East and West. (Coincidentally, a similar symbol has been used by many other kingdoms and empires, including the Holy Roman Empire and the Austro-Hungarian Empire.)

At the far end of the square from the cathedral is another statue, this one of a warrior holding a sword. This is **Emperor Constantine XI Palaeologus** (1404-1453), the final ruler of the Byzantine Empire. He was killed defending Constantinople from the invading Ottomans, led by Mehmet the Conqueror. Considered the "last Greek king" and an unofficial saint, Constantine XI's death marked the ascension of the Ottomans as overlords of the Greeks for nearly four centuries. On his boots and above his head, you'll see the double-headed eagle again.

• *The small church tucked behind the right side of the cathedral is the...*

❽ Church of Agios Eleftherios

A favorite of local church connoisseurs, the late 12th-century Church of Agios Eleftherios (St. Eleutherius) is also known as Panaghia Ghorghoepikoos ("Virgin Mary, quick to answer prayers") and is sometimes referred to as "the old cathedral." It was used by the archbishops of Athens after the Ottomans evicted them from the church within the Parthenon. Worth ▲, it's a jigsaw-puzzle hodgepodge of B.C. and A.D. adorn-

The Eastern Orthodox Church

In the fourth century A.D., the Roman Empire split in half, dividing Eastern Europe and the Balkan Peninsula down the middle. Seven centuries later, with the Great Schism, the Christian faith diverged along similar lines into two separate branches: Roman Catholicism in the west (based in Rome), and Eastern or Byzantine Orthodoxy in the east (based in Constantinople—today's Istanbul).

The root *orthos* is Greek for "right," and *dogma* is "faith," making orthodoxy the "right belief." And it seems logical that if you've already got it right, you're more conservative and resistant to change. While the Catholic Church has shed some old traditions and developed new ones, the Eastern Orthodox Church has stayed true to the earliest conventions of the Christian faith. Today, rather than having one centralized headquarters (such as the Vatican for Catholicism), the Eastern Orthodox Church is divided into about a dozen regional branches, including the Greek Orthodox Church, which is based at Athens' cathedral.

Orthodox churches look different from their Catholic counterparts. The Orthodox faith tends to use a Greek cross, with four equal arms (like a plus sign, sometimes inside a circle), which focuses on God's perfection (unlike the longer Latin cross, which more literally evokes the Crucifixion). Many Orthodox churches have Greek-cross floor plans rather than the elongated nave-and-transept designs that are common in Western Europe.

Churches also have few (if any) pews. Worshippers stand through the service as a sign of respect (though some older parishioners sit on the seats along the walls). Traditionally, women

ments (and even tombstones) from earlier buildings. For example, the carved marble reliefs above the door were scavenged from the Ancient Agora in the 12th century. They are part of a calendar of ancient Athenian festivals, thought to have been carved in the second century A.D. The frieze running along the top of the building depicts a B.C. procession.

Later, Christians added their own symbols to the same panels, making the church a treasure trove of medieval symbolism. There are different kinds of crosses (Maltese, Latin, double) as well as carved rosettes, stars, flowers, and griffins feeding on plants and snakes. Walk around the entire exterior. Then step inside to sample unadorned 12th-century Orthodox simplicity.

• *Exit the church, go up to the main sidewalk level, and walk around the side of the church, toward the large building at the start of...*

❾ Agia Filotheis Street

This neighborhood is a hive of activity for Orthodox clerics. The priests dress all in black, wear beards, and don those fez-like hats.

stand on the left side, men on the right (equal distance from the altar, to represent that all are equal before God). The altar is hidden by a screen called the iconostasis. Covered with icons, it divides the lay community from the priests—the material world from the spiritual one.

Most Eastern Orthodox churches have at least one mosaic or painting of Christ in a standard pose—as *Pantocrator*, a Greek word meaning "Ruler of All." The image shows Christ as King of the Universe, facing directly out, with penetrating eyes. Behind him is a halo divided by a cross, with the bottom arm of the cross hidden behind Christ—an Orthodox symbol for the Crucifixion, hinting of the Resurrection and salvation that follow. You'll almost never see statues, which are thought to overemphasize the physical world—and, to Orthodox people, feel a little too close to the forbidden worship of graven images.

The doctrine of Catholic and Orthodox churches remains very similar, but many of the rituals differ. As worshippers enter a Greek Orthodox church, they drop a coin in the wooden box, pick up a candle, say a prayer, light the candle, and place it in the candelabra. They then make the sign of the cross and kiss the icon. Services generally involve chanting (a dialogue that goes back and forth between the priest and the congregation), and the church is filled with the evocative aroma of incense, combining to heighten the experience for the worshippers. Each of these elements does its part to help the worshipper transcend the physical world and enter communion with the spiritual one.

Despite their hermetic look, most priests are husbands, fathers, and well-educated pillars of the community, serving as counselors and spiritual guides to Athens' cosmopolitan populace.

Notice the stores. Just behind and facing the little church is the shop of the **Theodoropoulos** family—whose name nearly manages to use every Greek character available (ΘΕΟΔΩΡΟΠΟΥΛΟΣ). They've been tailoring priestly robes since 1907.

This is the first of many **religious objects stores** that line the street (most are open Mon, Wed, and Fri 8:30-15:00; Tue and Thu 8:30-14:00 & 17:30-20:30; closed Sat-Sun). Cross the busy Apollonos street and continue exploring the shops of Agia Filotheis street. The Orthodox religion comes with ample paraphernalia: icons, gold candelabras, hanging lamps, incense burners, oil lamps, chalices, various crosses, and gold objects worked in elaborate repoussé design.

Pop into the **stoa** (arcades) at #17 (on the left) to see workshops of the artisans who make these objects—painters creating or restoring icons in the traditional style, tailors making bishops' hats and robes, carvers making little devotional statuettes.

A few more steps up on the left, the ❿ **Church of Agia Filotheis** (named, like the street, for a patron of Athens—St. Philothei) is adjacent to an office building (at #19) that serves as the headquarters for the Greek Orthodox Church. Athenians come here to file the paperwork to make their marriages (and divorces) official.

Part 3: Athens' "Old Town" (The Plaka and Anafiotika)

This part of our walk explores the atmospheric, twisty lanes of old Athens. Remember, back before Athens became Greece's capital in the early 1800s, the city was a small town consisting of little more than what we'll see here.

• *Continue up Agia Filotheis street until you reach a tight five-way intersection. The street that runs ahead and to your right (labeled* ΑΔΡΙΑΝΟΥ*)—choked with souvenir stands and tourists—is our next destination. Look uphill and downhill along...*

⓫ Adrianou Street

This intersection may be the geographical (if not atmospheric) center of the neighborhood called the Plaka. Touristy Adrianou street is a main pedestrian drag that cuts through the Plaka, running roughly east–west from Monastiraki to here. Adrianou offers the full gauntlet of Greek souvenirs: worry beads, sea sponges, olive products, icons, carpets, jewelry, sandals, faux vases and Greek statues, profane and tacky T-shirts, and on and on. It also offers plenty of cafés for tourists seeking a place to sit and rest their weary feet.

• *Bear left onto Adrianou and walk uphill several blocks. Finally, the street dead-ends at a T-intersection with Lysikratous street. (There's a small square ahead on the left, with palm trees, the Byzantine church of Agia Aikaterini, and an excavated area showing the street level 2,000 years ago.)*

From here you can turn right and take a few steps uphill to the Lysicrates Monument and Square (and skip ahead to the section on the Lysicrates Monument). But if you've got more time and stamina, it's worth a two-block walk to the left down Lysikratous street to reach the remains of the Arch of Hadrian.

⓬ Arch of Hadrian and Temple of Olympian Zeus

After the Romans conquered the Greeks, Roman emperor Hadrian (or Adrianos) became a major benefactor of the city of Athens. He built a triumphal arch, completed a temple beyond it (now ruined), and founded a library we'll see later. He also created a "new Athens" in the area beyond the arch (sometimes known as Hadrianopolis). The grand archway overlooks the bustling, modern Vasilissis Amalias avenue, facing the Plaka and Acropolis. (If you turned left and followed this road for 10 minutes, you'd end up back on Syntagma Square—where we began this walk.)

▲ Arch of Hadrian

The arch's once-brilliant white Pentelic marble is stained by the exhaust fumes from decades of Athens traffic. The arch is topped with

Corinthian columns, the Greek style preferred by the Romans. Hadrian built it in A.D. 132 to celebrate the completion of the Temple of Olympian Zeus (which lies just beyond—described next). Like a big *paifang* gate marking the entrance to a modern Chinatown, this arch is thought by some to represent the dividing line between the ancient city and Hadrian's new "Roman" city. An inscription on the west side informs the reader that "This is Athens, ancient city of Theseus," while the opposite frieze carries the message, "This is the city of Hadrian, and not of Theseus."

• *Look past the arch to see the huge (and I mean huge) Corinthian columns remaining from what was once a temple dedicated to the Olympian Zeus. For a closer look, cross the busy boulevard (crosswalk to the right). You can pretty much get the gist by looking through the fence. But if you want to get close to those giant columns and wander the ruins, enter the site (covered by Acropolis ticket). To reach the entrance (a five-minute walk), curl around the left side of the arch, then turn right (following the fence) up the intersecting street called Vasilissis Olgas. The entrance to the temple is a few minutes' walk up, on the right-hand side.*

▲▲Temple of Olympian Zeus (Olympieion)

This largest ancient temple in mainland Greece took almost 700 years to finish. It was begun late in the sixth century B.C. during

the rule of the tyrant Peisistratos. He died before the temple was completed, and his successors were expelled from Athens. The temple lay abandoned, half-built, for centuries until the Roman emperor Hadrian arrived to finish the job in A.D. 131.

This must have been a big deal for Hadrian, as he came here in person to celebrate its inauguration. When completed, the temple was 360 feet by 145 feet, consisting of two rows of 20 columns on each of the long sides and three rows of eight columns along each end (counting the corners twice). Although only 15 of the original 104 Corinthian columns remain standing, their sheer size (a towering 56 feet high) is enough to create a powerful impression of the temple's scale. The fallen column—which resembles a tipped-over stack of bottle caps—was toppled by a storm in 1852. The temple once housed a suitably oversized statue of Zeus, head of the Greek gods who lived on Mount Olympus, and an equally colossal statue of Hadrian.

• *Return to Lysikratous street and backtrack two blocks, continuing past the small square with the church you passed earlier. After another block, you'll run into another small, leafy square with the Acropolis rising behind it. In the square is an elegant, round, white, columned monument.*

⓮ Lysicrates Monument and Square

This elegant marble monument has Corinthian columns that support a dome with a (damaged) statue on top. A frieze runs along the top, representing Dionysus turning pirates into dolphins. The monument is the sole survivor of many such monuments that once lined this ancient "Street of the Tripods." It was so called because the monuments came with bronze tripods that displayed cauldrons (like those you'll see in the museums) as trophies. These ancient "Oscars" were awarded to winners of choral and theatrical competitions staged at the Theater of Dionysus on the southern side of the Acropolis. This now-lonely monument was erected in 334 B.C. by "Lysicrates of Kykyna, son of Lysitheides"—proud sponsor of the winning choral team

that year. Excavations around the monument have uncovered the foundations of other monuments, which are now reburied under a layer of red sand and awaiting further study.

The square itself, shaded by trees, is a pleasant place to take a break before climbing the hill. Have a frappé or coffee at the café tables, grab a cheap cold drink from the cooler in the hole-in-the-wall grocery store to the left, or just sit for free on the benches under the trees.

• *From here you're only two blocks from the TI—you may want to detour there if you haven't stopped by yet (on pedestrian street leading to Acropolis Museum at Dionysiou Areopagitou 18-20). Otherwise, pass the Lysicrates Monument on its left-hand side, then head uphill toward the Acropolis, climbing the staircase called Epimenidou street. At the top*

ATHENS

of the stairs, turn right onto Stratonos street, which leads around the base of the Acropolis. As you walk along, the Acropolis and a row of olive trees are on your left. The sound of the crickets evokes for Athenians the black-and-white movies that were filmed in this area in the 1950s and '60s. To your right you'll catch glimpses of another hill off in the distance.

⑭ View of Lykavittos Hill

This cone-shaped hill (sometimes spelled "Lycabettus") topped with a tiny white church is the highest in Athens, at just over 900 feet above sea level. The

hill can be reached by a funicular, which leads up from the Kolonaki neighborhood to a restaurant, café, and view terrace at the top. Although it looms high over the cityscape, Lykavittos Hill will always be overshadowed by the hill you're climbing now.

• *At the small Church of St. George of the Rock (Agios Georgios), go uphill, along the left fork. As you immerse yourself in a maze of tiny, whitewashed houses, follow signs that point to the Acropolis (even if the path seems impossibly narrow). This charming "village" is a neighborhood called...*

⑮ Anafiotika

The lanes and homes of Anafiotika, worth ▲▲, were built by people from the tiny Cycladic island of Anafi, who came to Athens looking for work after Greece gained its independence from the Ottomans. In this delightful spot, nestled beneath the walls of the Acropolis, the big city seems miles away. Keep following the *Acropolis* signs as you weave through narrow paths, lined with flowers and dotted with cats dozing peacefully in the sunshine (or slithering luxuriously past your legs). Though descendants of the original islanders still live here, Anafiotika (literally "little Anafi") is slowly becoming a place for wealthy locals to keep an "island cottage" in the city. As you wander through the oleanders, notice the male fig trees— no fruit—that keep away flies and mosquitoes. Smell the chicken-manure fertilizer, peek into delicate little yards, and enjoy the blue doors and maroon shutters...it's a transplanted Cycladic world. Posters of Anafi hang here and there, evoking the sandy beaches of the ancestral home island.

• *You'll know you're on the right track when you see a religious building with the date 1874 on a wall plaque. Follow the narrow walkway a few more steps. Emerging from the maze of houses, you'll hit a wider, cobbled lane. Turn right (downhill) and continue down the steep incline. When you hit a wider road (Theorias), turn left and walk toward the small, Byzantine-style Church of the Metamorphosis. (Note: To walk to the Acropolis entry from here, you would continue along this road as it bends left around the hill. For a self-guided tour of the Acropolis, see the ✪ "Acropolis Tour" on page 937. For now, though, let's continue our walk.) Just before this church, turn right and go down the steep, narrow staircase (a lane called Klepsidras, labeled ΚΛΕΨΥΔΡΑΣ). Cross the street called Tholou and continue down Klepsidras. The lane gets even narrower (yes, keep going between the plants). Eventually you'll run into a railing overlooking some ruins.*

⓰ The Roman Forum and the Tower of the Winds

The rows of columns framing this rectangular former piazza were built by the Romans, who conquered Greece around 150 B.C. and

stayed for centuries. This square (worth ▲)—sometimes called the "Roman Agora"—was the commercial center, or forum, of Roman Athens, with a colonnade providing shade for shoppers browsing the many stores that fronted it. Centuries later, the Ottomans made this their grand bazaar. The mosque, one of the oldest and best-preserved Ottoman structures, survives (although its minaret, like all minarets in town, was torn down by the Greeks when they won their independence from the Ottomans in the 19th century). It now serves as a storeroom for the archaeological finds from area excavations.

Take a few steps to the right to see the octagonal, domed **Tower of the Winds** (a.k.a. "Bath-House of the Winds"). The carved reliefs depict winds as winged humans who fly in, bringing the weather. Built in the first century B.C., this building was an ingenious combination of clock, weathervane, and guide to the planets. The beautifully carved reliefs represent male personifications of the eight winds of Athens, with their names inscribed. As you walk down the hill (curving right, then left around the fence, always going downhill), you'll see reliefs depicting Lips, the southwest wind, holding a ship's steering rud-

der; Zephyros, the mild west wind, holding a basket of flowers; Skiron, scattering glowing coal from an inverted bronze brazier, indicating the warmer winter winds; and Boreas, the howling winter wind from the north, blowing a conch shell. The tower was once capped with a weathervane in the form of a bronze Triton (half-man, half-fish) that spun to indicate which wind was blessing or cursing the city at the moment. Bronze rods (no longer visible) protruded from the walls and acted as sundials to indicate the time. And when the sun wasn't shining, people told time using the tower's sophisticated water clock, powered by water piped in from springs on the Acropolis. Much later, under Ottoman rule, dervishes used the tower as a place for their whirling worship and prayer.

• *It's possible but unnecessary to enter the ruins: You've seen just about everything from this vantage point. If you do decide to enter the ruins, follow the spike-topped fence below the tower down Pelopida street and through an outdoor dining zone (where it curves and becomes Epameinonda) to reach the ticket office and entry gate, near the tallest standing colonnade (tower explained on a plaque inside; entry covered by Acropolis ticket). Don't confuse the Roman Forum with the older, more interesting Ancient Agora, which is near the end of this walk.*

Otherwise, from just below the Tower of the Winds, head to the right down Aiolou street one block to...

⓱ Agora Square (Plateia Agoras)

This leafy, restaurant-filled square is the touristy epicenter of the Plaka. A handy Internet café is nearby (Bits and Bytes, see page 900), as well as a stop for one of the city's tourist trains (see page 905).

On the left side of the square you'll see the second-century A.D. ruins of the ⓲ **Library of Hadrian** (open to the public). The four lone columns that sit atop the apse-like foundations are the remains of a fifth-century church. The ruins around it are all that's left of a big rectangular complex that once boasted 100 marble columns. Destroyed in the third century A.D., it was a cultural center (library, lecture halls, garden, and art gallery), built by the Greek-loving Roman emperor for the Athenian citizens.

• *Continue downhill alongside the ruins to the next block, where Aiolou intersects with the claustrophobic Pandrossou market street (which we walked along earlier). Remember that this crowded lane is worked by expert pickpockets—be careful. Look to the right up Pandrossou: You may see merchants sitting in folding chairs with their backs to one another, competition having soured their personal relationships. Turn left*

on Pandrossou and wade through the knee-deep tacky tourist souvenirs.
Several shops here (including one we just passed on Aiolou, and two more
on Pandrossou) supply fans of the "Round Goddess"—a.k.a. soccer (each
team has its own store). Continue until you spill out into Monastiraki
Square.

⑲ Monastiraki Square Spin-Tour

We've made it from Syntagma Square—the center of urban Athens—to the city's *other* main square, Monastiraki Square, the
gateway to the touristy Old Town. To get oriented to Monastiraki
Square, stand in the center, face the small church with the cross on
top (which is north), and pan clockwise.

The name Monastiraki ("Little Monastery") refers to this
square, the surrounding neighborhood, the flea-market action
nearby...and the cute **Church of the Virgin** in the square's center
(12th-century Byzantine, mostly restored with a much more modern bell tower).

Beyond that (straight ahead from the end of the square),
Athinas street heads north to the Central Market, Omonia
Square, and (after about a mile) the National Archaeological Mu-
seum.

Just to the right (behind the little church) is the head of
Ermou street—the bustling shopping drag we walked down earlier (though no longer traffic-free here). If you turned right and
walked straight up Ermou, you'd be back at Syntagma Square in 10
minutes.

Next (on the right, in front of the little church) comes Mitropoleos street—Athens' ⑳ **"Souvlaki Row."** Clogged with outdoor
tables, this atmospheric lane is home to a string of restaurants that
serve sausage-shaped, skewered meat—grilled up spicy and tasty.
The place on the corner—Bairaktaris (ΜΠΑΪΡΑΚΤΑΡΗΣ)—is
the best known, its walls lined with photos of famous politicians
and artists who come here for souvlaki and pose with the owner.
But the other two joints along here—Thanasis and Savas—have
a better reputation for their souvlaki. You can sit at the tables, or,
for a really cheap meal, order a souvlaki to go for €2. (For details,
see page 964.) A few blocks farther down
Mitropoleos is the cathedral we visited earlier.

Continue spinning clockwise. Just past
Pandrossou street (where you entered the
square), you'll see a ㉑ **former mosque** (look
for the Arabic script under the portico and
over the wooden door). Known as the Tzami
(from the Turkish word for "mosque"), this was
a place of worship from the 15th to 19th century. Today it houses the Museum of Greek Folk

Art's **ceramics collection**. The mosque's front balcony (no ticket required) offers fine views over Monastiraki Square.

To the right of the mosque, behind the fence along Areos street, you might glimpse some huge Corinthian columns. This is the opposite end of the **Library of Hadrian** complex we saw earlier. Areos street stretches up toward the Acropolis. If you were to walk a block up this street, then turn right on Adrianou, you'd reach the ❷ **Ancient Agora**—one of Athens' top ancient attractions (see page 934). Beyond the Agora are the delightful Thissio neighborhood, ancient Keramikos Cemetery, and Gazi district.

As you continue panning clockwise, next comes the pretty yellow building that houses the **Monastiraki Metro station.** This was Athens' original, British-built, 19th-century train station—Neoclassical with a dash of Byzantium. This bustling Metro stop is the intersection of two lines: the old line 1 (green, with connections to the port of Piraeus, the Thissio neighborhood, and Victoria—near the National Archaeological Museum) and the modern line 3 (blue, with connections to Syntagma Square and the airport). The stands in front of the station sell seasonal fruit and are popular with commuters.

Just past the station, Ifestou street leads downhill into the ❷ **flea market** (antiques, jewelry, cheap clothing, and so on—for more details, see page 958). If locals need a screw for an old lamp, they know they'll find it here.

Keep panning clockwise. Just beyond busy Ermou street (to the left of Athinas street) is the happening **Psyrri** district. For years a run-down slum, this zone is being gentrified by twenty-somethings with a grungy sense of style. Packed with cutting-edge bars, restaurants, cafés, and nightclubs, it may seem foreboding and ramshackle, but it is actually fun to explore.

❷ Monastiraki Metro Station

Finish your walk by stepping into the Monastiraki Metro station and riding the escalator down to see an exposed bit of ancient Athens. Excavations for the Metro revealed an ancient aqueduct, which confined Athens' Eridanos River to a canal. The river had been a main axis of the town since the eighth century B.C. In the second century A.D., Hadrian and his engineers put a roof over it, turning it into a more efficient sewer. You're looking at Roman brick and classic Roman engineering. A cool mural shows the treasure trove archaeologists uncovered with the excavations.

This walk has taken us from ancient ruins to the Roman era, from medieval churches and mosques to the guerrilla fighters of Greek Independence, through the bustling bric-a-brac of the modern city, and finally to a place where Athens' infrastructure—both ancient and modern—mingles.

• *Our walk is over. If you're ready for a break, savor a spicy souvlaki on "Souvlaki Row."*

Sights in Athens

While Athens has several interesting museums worth knowing about on a longer visit (including the Benaki Museum of Greek History and Culture, Museum of Cycladic Art, and Byzantine and Christian Museum), for a one-day cruiser visit, I've listed just the main sights in the ancient center. These sights are all within easy walking distance of each other (except for the National Museum of Archaeology).

Don't count on the opening hours printed in this chapter. Though they were accurate at the time of printing, the times are likely to fluctuate wildly at the whims of the government and the Greek economy. Check locally before planning your day. Note that many of Athens' top ancient sites are covered by the Acropolis ticket (see the sidebar).

The Acropolis and Nearby

A broad pedestrian boulevard that I call the "Acropolis Loop" strings together the Acropolis, Mars Hill, Acropolis Museum, and more.

▲▲▲Acropolis

The most important ancient site in the Western world, the Acropolis (which means "high city" in Greek) rises gleaming like a beacon above the gray concrete drudgery of modern Athens. This is where the Greeks built the mighty Parthenon—the most famous temple on the planet and an enduring symbol of ancient Athens' glorious Golden Age from nearly 2,500 years ago.

Cost and Hours: €12 for Acropolis Ticket; free for those 18 and under, on first Sun of month Nov-March, and on all national holidays; open daily June-Aug likely 8:00-20:00, Sept-Oct and April-May 8:00-18:00, Nov-March 8:00-15:00, last entry 30 minutes before closing; free Rick Steves audio tour available—see page 50; main entrance at the western end of the Acropolis—if you're at the Ancient Agora in the Plaka, signs point uphill; tel. 210-321-4172, www.culture.gr.

○ For a self-guided tour, see page 937.

▲▲"Acropolis Loop" (a.k.a. Dionysiou Areopagitou and Apostolou Pavlou)

One of Athens' best attractions, this wide, well-manicured, delightfully traffic-free pedestrian boulevard borders the Acropolis to the south and east. It's composed of two streets with tongue-twisting names—Dionysiou Areopagitou and Apostolou Pavlou (think of them as Dionysus Street and Apostle Paul's Street); for

Acropolis Ticket

Your €12 Acropolis ticket gives you entry to Athens' major ancient sites, including the Acropolis, Ancient Agora, Roman Forum, Keramikos Cemetery, Temple of Olympian Zeus, Library of Hadrian, and Theater of Dionysus. If you see only the Acropolis, you'll still pay €12—so the other sights are effectively free add-ons. (The other attractions do sell cheaper individual tickets—but as you're virtually guaranteed to visit the Acropolis sometime during your visit, these are pointless.) The ticket is technically valid for four days, but there's no date printed on the ticket, so in practice you can use it anytime. You can buy the ticket at any participating sight. Tickets bought at any of the non-Acropolis sights are one long strip; perforated "coupons" are removed and used to enter the smaller sights. If you buy your ticket at the Acropolis, however, you receive a digital printout with a code that gets scanned.

simplicity, I refer to them collectively as the "Acropolis Loop." One of the city's many big improvements made in preparation for its 2004 Olympics-hosting bid, this walkway immediately became a favorite local hangout, with vendors, al fresco cafés, and frequent special events enlivening its cobbles.

Dionysiou Areopagitou, wide and touristy, runs along the southern base of the Acropolis. It was named for Dionysus the

Areopagite, first bishop and patron saint of Athens and a member of the ancient Roman-era senate that met atop Mars Hill (described next). The other section, **Apostolou Pavlou**— quieter, narrower, and tree-lined— curls around the western end of the Acropolis and the Ancient Agora. It feels more local and has the best concentration of outdoor eateries. This section was named for the Apostle Paul, who presented himself before Dionysus the Areopagite at Mars Hill.

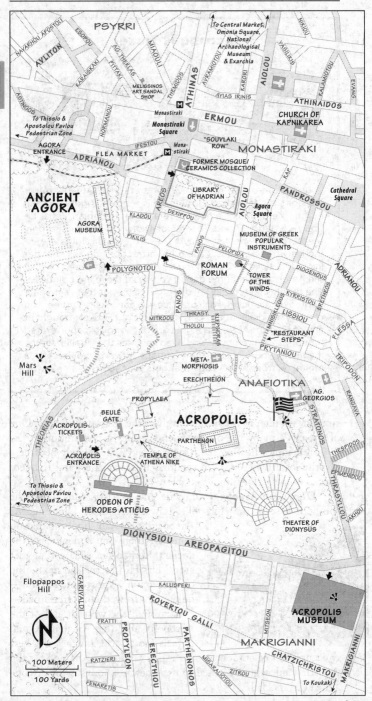

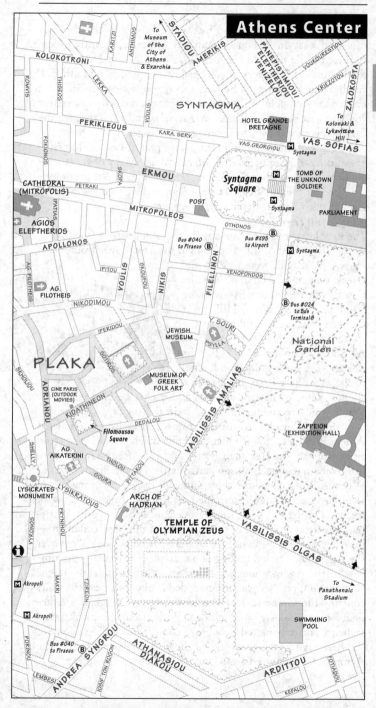

Athens Center

ATHENS

To Museum of the City of Athens & Exarchia

KOLOKOTRONI

KARITZI

ANTHIMOU

STADIOU

AMERIKIS

PANEPISTIMIOU ELEFTHERIOU VENIZELOU

YOUKOUFETSIOU

KRIEZOTOU

ZALOKOSTA

SYNTAGMA

ROMVIS

THISEOS

LEKKA

PERIKLEOUS

VOULIS

KARA. SERV.

HOTEL GRANDE BRETAGNE

VAS. GEORGIOU

M Syntagma

To Kolonaki & Lykavittos Hill

VAS. SOFIAS

FOKONOS

SKOPA

ERMOU

CATHEDRAL (MITROPOLIS)

PETRAKI

IPATIAS

MITROPOLEOS

POST

Syntagma Square

M

TOMB OF THE UNKNOWN SOLDIER

M Syntagma

PARLIAMENT

AGIOS ELEFTHERIOS

APOLLONOS

AG. FILOTHEIS

IPITOU

VOULIS

SKOUFOU

NIKIS

Bus #040 to Piraeus B

FILELLINON

OTHONOS

Bus #X95 to Airport B

XENOFONDOS

M Syntagma

AG. FILOTHEIS

NIKODIMOU

B Bus #024 to Bus Terminal B

IPERIDOU

Y. SOURI

National Garden

PLAKA

SKOLOU

ADRIANOU

SOTIROS

JEWISH MUSEUM

PSYLLA

CINE PARIS (OUTDOOR MOVIES)

KIDATHINEON

MUSEUM OF GREEK FOLK ART

VASILISSIS AMALIAS

SHELLY

Filomousou Square

DEDALOU

ZAPPEION (EXHIBITION HALL)

AG. AIKATERINI

THOLOU

GOURA

PITTAKOU

LYSIKRATES MONUMENT

LYSIKRATOUS

ARCH OF HADRIAN

SONOKLIOUS

FRYNIHOU

VASILISSIS OLGAS

M Akropoli

MAKRI

TZIREON

TEMPLE OF OLYMPIAN ZEUS

To Panathenaic Stadium

M Akropoli

PORINOU

Bus #040 to Piraeus B

ANDREA SYNGROU

ATHANASIOU DIAKOU

SWIMMING POOL

LEMBESI

IOSIF TON ROGON

ARDITTOU

KEFALOU

FOTIADOU

Where Apostolou Pavlou meets the Thissio Metro stop, you can head west on Ermou—a similarly enjoyable, recently pedestrianized boulevard—to reach the Gazi district's Technopolis and the Keramikos Cemetery. If you head east on Ermou (with traffic), you'll come to Syntagma Square. Or, if you want to encircle the base of the Acropolis, head east on Adrianou, the pedestrian street you'll hit just before the Thissio Metro stop, and stroll through the Plaka on your way back to Dionysiou Areopagitou.

Stray cats are common in this warm part of Europe, but Athens also has a huge population of stray dogs. Many of them—including some who hang out along the Dionysiou Areopagitou—are cared for (but not housed) by local animal-rights organizations. Even if a dog has a collar, it might be a stray.

▲Mars Hill (Areopagus)

The knobby, windswept hill crawling with tourists in front of the Acropolis is Mars Hill, also known as Areopagus (from *Areios Pagos*, "Ares Hill," referring to the Greek version of Mars). While the views from the Acropolis are more striking, rugged Mars Hill (near the Acropolis' main entrance, at the western end) makes a pleasant perch. As you're climbing Mars Hill, be warned: The stone stairs (and the top of the rock) have been polished to a slippery shine by history, and can be treacherous even when dry. Watch your step and use the metal staircase.

This hill has an interesting history. After Rome conquered Athens in 86 B.C., the Roman overlords wisely decided to extend citizenship to any free man born here. (The feisty Greeks were less likely to rise up against a state that had made them citizens.) Whereas Rome called the shots on major issues, minor matters of local governance were determined on this hill by a gathering of leaders. During this time, the Apostle Paul—the first great Christian missionary and author of about half of the New Testament—preached to the Athenians here on Mars Hill. Paul looked out over the Agora and started talking about an altar he'd seen—presumably in the Agora (though archaeologists can't confirm)—to the "Unknown God." (A plaque embedded in the rock near the stairs contains the Greek text of Paul's speech.) Although the Athenians were famously open-minded, Paul encountered a skeptical audience and only netted a couple of converts (including Dionysus the Areopagite—the namesake of the pedestrian drag behind the Acropolis). Paul moved on to Corinth and a better reception.

▲▲▲Acropolis Museum

Athens' Acropolis Museum is a custom-built showcase for artifacts from the Acropolis, complemented by modern exhibits about the

site. The state-of-the-art 2009 building—housing the Parthenon sculptures still in Greek hands, the original caryatids from the Erechtheion, and much more—is the boldest symbol yet of today's Athens.

Cost and Hours: €5; open Tue-Sun 8:00-20:00, Fri until 22:00, closed Mon, last entry 30 minutes before closing. The museum faces the south side of the Acropolis from across the broad Dionysiou Areopagitou pedestrian drag, and is right at the Akropoli Metro stop (line 2/red); tel. 210-900-0900, www.theacropolismuseum.gr.

Visiting the Museum: Level 1 of the museum contains relics from the Acropolis, including statues of young men and women, gods and goddesses, and reliefs that once adorned the hilltop temples. It also features five of the six original caryatids (lady-columns) that once held up the roof of the prestigious Erechtheion temple. (The six on the Acropolis today are copies; another original is in London's British Museum.) Despite their graceful appearance, these sculptures were structurally functional. Each has a fluted column for a leg, a capital-like hat, and buttressing locks of hair in the back. The caryatids were modeled on and named after the famously upright women of Karyai, near Sparta.

The highlight of the museum is on level 3 (the top floor): a life-size mock-up of the 525-foot frieze that once wrapped all the way around the outside of the Parthenon. The relief panels depict the Grand Panathenaia, the procession held every four years in which citizens climbed up to the Parthenon to celebrate the birth of the city. Circling the perimeter, you can see the parade unfold.

Men on horseback, gods, chariots, musicians, priests, riders, officers, warriors, and sacrificial animals are all part of the grand parade, all heading in the same direction—uphill. Prance on. At the heart of the procession are maidens dressed in pleated robes. They shuffle along, carrying gifts for the gods, including incense burners, along with jugs of wine and bowls to pour out offerings. The procession culminates in the presentation of a new *peplos* to Athena, as the gods look on.

Look at the details—for example, the muscles and veins in the horses' legs and the intricate folds in the cloaks and dresses. Some panels have holes drilled in them, where accessories such as gleaming bronze reins were fitted to heighten the festive look. Of course, all these panels were originally painted in realistic colors. As you move along, notice that, despite the bustle of figures posed every which way, the frieze has one unifying element—most of the people's heads are at the same level, creating a single ribbon around the Parthenon.

Of the original marble frieze, the museum owns only 32 feet. These panels were already so acid-worn in 1801 that Lord Elgin didn't bother taking them back to Britain. Filling in the gaps in this jigsaw puzzle are white plaster replicas of panels still in London's British Museum (marked BM), in Paris' Louvre, and in Copenhagen. Blank spaces represent panels that are forever lost. Small 17th-century engravings show how the frieze looked before the 1687 explosion that devastated the Parthenon.

▲▲▲Ancient Agora: Athens' Market

If the Acropolis was Golden Age Athens' "uptown," then the Ancient Agora was "downtown." Although literally and figuratively overshadowed by the impressive Acropolis, the Agora was for eight centuries the true meeting place of the city—a hive of commerce, politics, and everyday bustle. Everybody who was anybody in ancient Athens spent time here, from Socrates and Plato to a visiting missionary named Paul. Little survives from the classical Agora. Other than one very well-

preserved temple and a rebuilt stoa, it's a field of humble ruins.

Cost and Hours: €4, covered by Acropolis ticket; daily 8:00-15:00, possibly open later in summer, last entry 15 minutes before closing, Agora Museum opens at 11:00 on Mon; tel. 210-321-0180, www.culture.gr.

Getting There: From Monastiraki (Metro line 1/green or line 3/blue), walk a block south (uphill, toward the Acropolis). Turn right on Adrianou street, and follow the pedestrian-only, café-lined street along the railroad tracks for about 200 yards. The Agora entrance is on your left, across from a small, yellow church. The entrance can be hard to spot: It's where a path crosses over the railroad tracks (look for a small, pale-yellow sign that says *Ministry of Culture—Ancient Agora*).

Audio Tours: You can download a free Rick Steves audio tour of the Agora (see page 50).

Visiting the Agora: The **Stoa of Attalos** likely served as a commercial mall. What you see today is a faithful reconstruction built in the 1950s. Inside, an excellent little museum displays some choice rubble that helps bring the place to life, including a cute baby's commode, a "voting machine" used to choose judges, and bronze ballots from the fourth century.

The hill-capping **Temple of Hephaistos** is one of the best-preserved and most typical of all Greek temples—a textbook example of Golden Age architecture. Like the Parthenon, it's made of Pentelic marble in the Doric style, though it's only about half the size of its grander cousin. You'll also see the **Odeon of Agrippa,** which served as a theater/concert hall and was once fronted by a line of six fierce Triton and Giant statues. Only two Tritons (with fish tails), a Giant (with a snake's tail), and an empty pedestal remain.

Running through the Agora, the **Panathenaic Way** was Athens' main street. It started at the main city gate (the Dipylon Gate, near the Keramikos Cemetery), cut diagonally through the Agora's main square, and wound its way up to the Acropolis—two-thirds of a mile in all. During the Panathenaic Festival held in the summer, this was the main parade route. Today's tourists use the same path to connect the Agora and the Acropolis.

East of the Plaka

These two sights, dating from Athens' Roman period, overlook Vasilissis Amalias, a busy highway at the edge of the tourist zone (just a few steps up Dionysiou Areopagitou from the Acropolis Museum and Metro line 2/red: Akropoli, or a 10-minute walk south of Syntagma Square). Both are described in greater detail in the "Athens City Walk," earlier.

▲Arch of Hadrian

This stoic triumphal arch stands at the edge of the new suburb of ancient Athens built by the Roman Emperor Hadrian in the second century A.D. (always viewable).

▲▲Temple of Olympian Zeus

Started by an overambitious tyrant in the sixth century B.C., this giant temple was not completed until Hadrian took over, seven

centuries later. Now 15 (of the original 104) Corinthian columns stand evocatively over a ruined base in a field. You can get a good view of the temple ruins through the fence by the Arch of Hadrian, but since the sight is included in the Acropolis ticket, you can easily drop in for a closer look.

Cost and Hours: €2, covered by Acropolis ticket; daily in summer 8:00-20:00 (in theory), Sept 8:00-19:00, off-season 8:00-15:00; Vasilissis Olgas 1, Metro line 2/red: Akropoli, tel. 210-922-6330, www.culture.gr.

▲▲▲National Archaeological Museum

This museum is far and away the top ancient Greek art collection anywhere. Ancient Greece set the tone for all Western art that fol-

lowed, and this museum lets you trace its evolution—taking you in air-conditioned comfort from 7000 B.C. to A.D. 500 through beautifully displayed and described exhibits on one floor. You'll see the rise and fall of Greece's various civilizations: the Minoans, the Mycenaeans, those of Archaic Greece, the Classical Age and Alexander the Great, and the Romans who came from the west. You can also watch Greek sculpture evolve, from prehistoric Barbie dolls, to stiff Egyptian-style, to the *David*-like balance of the Golden Age, to wet T-shirt, buckin'-bronco Hellenistic, and finally, to the influence of the Romans. Walk once around fast for a time-lapse effect, then go around again for a closer look.

Cost and Hours: €7; free for those 18 and under, on the first Sun of Nov-Dec, and on the last weekend of Sept; open Tue-Sun 8:00–15:00, later in summer—until 18:00 or 20:00 depending on sunset, Tue-Sun 9:00-16:00 in winter; Mon 13:30-20:00, may close at 15:00 in winter; last entry 30 minutes before closing; tel. 213-214-4800, www.namuseum.gr.

Getting There: The museum is a mile north of the Plaka at 28 Oktovriou (a.k.a. Patission) #44. Your best bet is to take a **taxi,** which costs about €4 from the Plaka. The nearest **Metro** stop is Omonia (as you exit, follow signs to *28 Oktovriou/28 October Street,* and walk seven blocks to the museum). You can also hop a **bus:** The #035 leaves from a stop on Athinas street, just north of Monastiraki, and drops you off around the corner from the museum. Bus #224 leaves from Vasilissis Sofias avenue (next to Syntagma Square) and stops kitty-corner from the museum.

Tours: There are no audioguides, but live **guides** hang out in the lobby waiting to give you a €50, hour-long tour. You can download a free Rick Steves **audio tour** of the National Archaeological Museum; see page 50.

Visiting the Museum: This museum is a great way to either start or finish off your sightseeing through Greece. It's especially worth visiting if you're traveling beyond Athens, because it displays artifacts found all around Greece, including Mycenae, Epidavros, Santorini, and Olympia—and the treasures displayed here are generally better than those remaining at the sites themselves. The sheer beauty of the statues, vases, and paintings helps bring the country's dusty ruins to life.

The collection is delightfully chronological. To sweep through Greek history, simply follow the numbered rooms. Essential stops (in this order) include stylized figurines of the Cycladic Islands, the golden artifacts of the Mycenaeans (including the so-called Mask of Agamemnon), and the stiff, stoic kouros statues of the Archaic age. Then, with the arrival of the Severe style (epitomized by the *Artemision Bronze*), the art loosens up and comes to life. As Greece enters the Classical Period, the *Bronze Statue of a Youth* is balanced and lifelike. The dramatic *Artemision Jockey* hints at the unbridled exuberance of Hellenism, which is taken to its extreme in the *Statue of a Fighting Gaul*. Rounding out the collection are Roman statuary, colorful wall paintings from Thira (today's Santorini), and room upon room of ceramics.

Acropolis Tour

Even in this age of superlatives, it's hard to overstate the historic and artistic importance of the Acropolis (Ακρόπολη). Crowned by the mighty Parthenon, the Acropolis ("high city") rises above the sprawl of modern Athens, a lasting testament to ancient Athens' glorious Golden Age in the fifth century B.C.

The Acropolis has been the heart of Athens since the beginning of recorded time. This limestone plateau, faced with sheer,

100-foot cliffs and fed by permanent springs, was a natural fortress. The Mycenaeans (c. 1400 B.C.) ruled the area from their palace on this hilltop, and Athena—the patron goddess of the city—was worshipped here from around 800 B.C. on.

But everything changed in 480 B.C., when Persia invaded Greece for the second time. As the Persians approached, the Athenians evacuated the city, abandoning it to be looted and vandalized. All the temples atop the Acropolis were burned to the ground. The Athenians fought back at sea, winning an improbable naval victory at the Battle of Salamis. The Persians were driven out of Greece, and Athens found itself suddenly victorious. Cash poured into Athens from the other Greek city-states, which were eager to be allied with the winning side.

By 450 B.C., Athens was at the peak of its power and the treasury was flush with money...but in the city center, the Acropolis still lay empty, a vast blank canvas. Athens' leader at the time, Pericles, was ambitious and farsighted. He funneled Athens' newfound wealth into a massive rebuilding program. Led by the visionary architect/sculptor Pheidias (447-438 B.C.), the Athenians transformed the Acropolis into a complex of supersized, ornate temples worthy of the city's protector, Athena.

The four major monuments—the Parthenon, Erechtheion,

ATHENS

Acropolis Overview

STANDING RUINS
ORIGINAL FOOTPRINT

Propylaea, and Temple of Athena Nike—were built as a coherent ensemble (c. 450-400 B.C.). Unlike most ancient sites, which have layer upon layer of ruins from different periods, the Acropolis we see today was started and finished within two generations—a snapshot of the Golden Age set in stone. Climbing Acropolis Hill and rambling its ruins with my self-guided tour, you'll feel like you've journeyed back in time to the birthplace of Western civilization.

Orientation

Cost: €12 for Acropolis ticket; free for those 18 and under, on first Sun of the month Nov-March, and on national holidays. If you bought your Acropolis ticket at a different sight, you'll need to present your coupon strip at the ticket booth, where you'll receive a separate ticket to be scanned at the entrance.

Hours: Daily June-Aug likely 8:00-20:00, Sept-Oct and April-May 8:00-18:00, Nov-March 8:00-15:00, last entry 30 minutes before closing. *Warning:* Open hours are likely to fluctuate wildly at the whims of the government and the Greek economy. Check locally before planning your day.

When to Go: Arrive early or late to avoid the crowds and midday heat. The place is miserably packed with tour groups from 10:00 to about 12:30 (when you might have to wait up to 45 minutes to get inside). It's not the ticket-buying line that holds you up; instead, the worst lines are caused by the bottleneck of people trying to squeeze into the site through the Propylaea gate (so buying your ticket elsewhere doesn't ensure a speedy entry). Late in the day, as the sun goes down, the white Parthenon stone gleams a creamy golden brown, and what had been a tourist war zone is suddenly peaceful.

Getting There: There's no way to reach the Acropolis without a lot of climbing (though wheelchair users can take an elevator—see below). Figure a 10- to 20-minute hike from the base of the Acropolis up to the hilltop archaeological site. There are multiple paths up, but the only ticket office and site entrance are at the western end of the hill (to the right as you face the Acropolis from the Plaka).

If you're touring the Ancient Agora, you can hike directly up to the Acropolis entrance along the Panathenaic Way. The approach from the Dionysiou Areopagitou pedestrian zone behind (south of) the Acropolis is slightly steeper. From this walkway, various well-marked paths funnel visitors up to the entrance; the least steep one climbs up from the parking lot at the western end of the pedestrian zone. You can reach this path either by taxi or by tourist train (the Athens Happy Train—see page 905), but it still involves quite a bit of uphill hiking.

If you use a **wheelchair,** you can take the elevator that ascends the Acropolis (from the ticket booth, go around the left side of the hilltop). However, once you are up top, the site is not particularly level or well-paved, so you may need help navigating the steep inclines and uneven terrain.

Information: Supplement this tour with the free information brochure (you may have to ask for it when you buy your ticket) and info plaques posted throughout. Tel. 210-321-4172, www.culture.gr.

Tours: If you'd like a live **guide,** consider making advance arrangements with one of my recommended local guides (see page 906). You can hire your own tour guide at the entrance, but I wouldn't—the guides here tend to be rude, overpriced, and under-qualified.

You can download this tour as a free Rick Steves **audio tour** (see page 50). This sight is particularly suited to an audio tour, as it allows your eyes to enjoy the wonders of the Acropolis while your ears learn its story.

Length of This Tour: Figure on two hours. Visitors with more time can easily precede this tour with a visit to the Ancient Agora.

Baggage Check: Backpacks are allowed; baby strollers are not. There's a checkroom just below the ticket booth near Mars Hill.

Services: There are WCs at the Acropolis ticket booth and more WCs and drinking fountains atop the Acropolis, in the former museum building (behind the Parthenon). Picnicking is not allowed on the premises. A juice/snack stand (which sells overpriced sparkling water but not plain bottled water), a drinking fountain, a post office, and a museum shop are near the ticket booth.

Plan Ahead: Wear sensible shoes—Acropolis paths are steep and uneven. In summer, it gets very hot on top, so take a hat, sunscreen, sunglasses, and a bottle of water. Inside the turnstiles, there are no services except WCs and drinking fountains.

Starring: The Parthenon and other monuments from the Golden Age, plus great views of Athens and beyond.

The Tour Begins

• *Climb up to the Acropolis ticket booth and the site entrance, located at the west end of the hill.*

Near this entrance (below and toward the Ancient Agora) is the huge, craggy boulder of **Mars Hill** (a.k.a. Areopagus). Consider climbing this rock for great views of the Acropolis' ancient entry gate, the Propylaea (described later) and the Ancient Agora. Mars Hill's bare, polished rock is extremely slippery—a metal staircase to the left helps somewhat. (For more on Mars Hill and its role in Christian history, see page 932.)

Before you show your ticket and enter the Acropolis site, make sure you have everything you'll need for your visit. Remember, after you enter the site, there are no services except WCs and water fountains.

• *Enter the site, and start climbing the paths that switchback up the hill, following signs on this one-way tourist route (bearing to the right). Before you reach the summit, peel off to the right for a bird's-eye view of the...*

❶ Odeon of Herodes Atticus

The grand Odeon huddles under the majestic Propylaea. Tourists call it a "theater," but Greeks know it's technically an *odeon*, as it was mainly used for musical rather than theatrical performances.

(*Odeon*—like the English word "ode"—comes from the Greek word for "song.")

A large 5,000-seat **amphitheater** built during Roman times, it's still used for performances. From this perch you get a good look at the stage setup: a three-quarter-circle orchestra (where musicians and actors performed in Greek-style theater), the overgrown remnants of a raised stage (for actors in the Roman tradition), and an intact stage wall for the backdrop. Originally it had a wood-and-tile roof as well.

The Odeon is sometimes called the Herodion, after Herodes Atticus, a wealthy landowner who had the building erected in A.D.

161 in memory of his wife. Herodes Atticus was a Greek with Roman citizenship, a legendary orator, and a friend of Emperor Hadrian. This amphitheater is the most famous of the many impressive buildings he financed around the country.

Destroyed by the invading Herulians a century after it was built, the Odeon was reconstructed in the

1950s to the spectacular state it's in today. It's open to the public only during performances, such as the annual Athens & Epidavros Festival, when an international lineup of dance, music, and theater is performed beneath the stars. If there's something on tonight, you may see a rehearsal from here. Athenians shudder when visitors—recalling the famous "Yanni Live at the Acropolis" concert—call this stately place "Yanni's Theater."

• *After climbing a few steps, you'll see two gates: On the right, steps lead down to the Theater of Dionysus; on the left is the actual entry uphill into the Acropolis. Stay left and continue up to reach the grand entrance gate of the Acropolis: the Propylaea. Stand at the foot of the (very) steep marble staircase, facing up toward the big Doric columns.*

As you face the Propylaea, to your left is a tall, gray stone pedestal with nothing on it: the Monument of Agrippa. On your right, atop the wall, is the Temple of Athena Nike. Behind you stands a doorway in a wall, known as the Beulé Gate.

❷ The Propylaea

The entrance to the Acropolis couldn't be through just any old gate; it had to be the grandest gate ever built. Ancient visitors would stand here, catching their breath before the final push to the summit, and admire these gleaming columns and steep steps that almost fill your field of vision. Imagine the psychological impact this awe-inspiring, colonnaded entryway to the sacred rock must have had on ancient Athenians. The odd mix of **stairs** here shows how

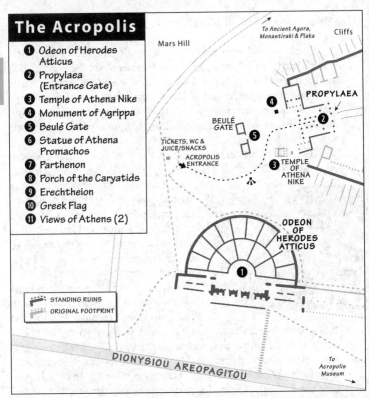

The Acropolis

1. Odeon of Herodes Atticus
2. Propylaea (Entrance Gate)
3. Temple of Athena Nike
4. Monument of Agrippa
5. Beulé Gate
6. Statue of Athena Promachos
7. Parthenon
8. Porch of the Caryatids
9. Erechtheion
10. Greek Flag
11. Views of Athens (2)

STANDING RUINS
ORIGINAL FOOTPRINT

To Ancient Agora, Monastiraki & Plaka
Cliffs
Mars Hill
PROPYLAEA
BEULÉ GATE
TICKETS, WC & JUICE/SNACKS
ACROPOLIS ENTRANCE
TEMPLE OF ATHENA NIKE
ODEON OF HERODES ATTICUS
DIONYSIOU AREOPAGITOU
To Acropolis Museum

the way up looked in different eras. The original ascent, a ramp that allowed sacrificial animals to make the climb, was replaced with a grand marble staircase in Hellenistic times, and then with a zigzag road (partly still intact) in the Middle Ages. (A few original stairs survive under the wooden ramp.)

The Propylaea (pro-PEE-leh-ah) is U-shaped, with a large central hallway (the six Doric columns), flanked by side wings that reach out to embrace the visitor. The central building looked like a mini-Parthenon, with Doric columns topped by a triangular pediment. Originally, the Propylaea was painted bright colors.

The left wing of the Propylaea was the **Pinakotheke,** or "painting gallery." In ancient times this space contained artwork and housed visiting dignitaries and VIPs.

The buildings of the Acropolis were all built to complement one another. The Propylaea was constructed in five short years

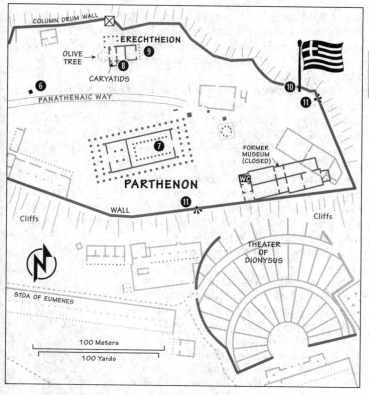

(437-432 B.C.), just after the Parthenon was finished. Its design (by Mnesicles) was meant to give the visitor a hint of the Parthenon to come. Both buildings are Doric (with Ionic touches) and are aligned east-west, with columns of similar width-to-height ratios.

• *Before ascending, notice the monuments flanking the entryway. To the right of the Propylaea, look up high atop the block wall to find the...*

❸ Temple of Athena Nike

The Temple of Athena Nike (Greeks pronounce it "NEEK-ee") was started as the Propylaea was being finished (c. 427-421/415 B.C.). It was designed by Callicrates, one of the architects of the Parthenon. This little temple—nearly square, 11 feet tall, with four columns at both ends—had delightful proportions. Where the Parthenon and Propylaea are sturdy Doric, this temple pioneered the Ionic style in Athens, with elegant scroll-topped columns.

The Acropolis was mainly dedicated to the **goddess Athena,** patron of the city. At this temple, she was worshipped for bringing the Athenians victory ("Nike"). A statue of Athena inside the temple celebrated the turning-point victory over the Persians at the

Battle of Plataea in 479 B.C. It was also meant to help ensure future victory over the Spartans in the ongoing Peloponnesian War. The statue was never given wings because Athenians wanted Athena to stay and protect their city—hence the place became known as the Temple of Wingless Athena.

The Temple of Athena Nike has undergone **extensive restoration.** From 2001 to 2010, it was completely disassembled, then cleaned, shored up, and pieced back together. This was the third time in its 2,500-year history that the temple had been entirely taken apart. The Ottomans pulled it down at the end of the 17th century and used the stone elsewhere, but Greeks reassembled the temple after regaining their independence. In 1935 it was taken apart for renovation and put back together in 1939. Unfortunately, that shoddy work did more harm than good—prompting the most recent restoration. Now it's been done the right way and should hold for another 2,500 years.

• *To the left (as you face the Propylaea) is the...*

❹ Monument of Agrippa

This 25-foot-high pedestal, made of big blocks of gray marble with yellow veins, reaches as high up as the Temple of Athena Nike. The (now-empty) pedestal once held a bronze statue of the **four-horse chariot** owned by Eumenes II, king of Pergamon—the winner of the race at the 178 B.C. Panathenaic Games.

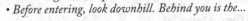

Over the centuries, each ruler of Athens wanted to put his mark on the mighty Acropolis. When Rome occupied the city, Marc Antony placed a statue of himself and his girlfriend Cleopatra atop the pedestal. After their defeat, the Roman general Agrippa (son-in-law of Augustus) replaced it with a statue of himself (in 27 B.C.).

• *Before entering, look downhill. Behind you is the...*

❺ Beulé Gate

This **ceremonial doorway** was built by the Romans, who used the rubble from buildings that had recently been destroyed in the barbarian Herulian invasion of A.D. 267. (The gate's French name comes from the archaeologist who discovered it in 1852.) During Roman times, this gate was the official entrance to the Acropolis, making the Propylaea entry even grander.

• *Climb the steps (or today's switchback ramps for tourists) and go...*

Inside the Propylaea

Imagine being part of the grand parade of the Panathenaic Festival, held every four years. The procession started at Athens' city gate (near the Keramikos Cemetery), passed through the Agora, then went around Mars Hill, through the central hall of the Propylaea, and up to the glorious buildings atop the summit of the Acropolis. Ancient Greeks approached the Propylaea by proceeding straight up a ramp in the middle, which narrowed as they ascended, funneling them into the central passageway. There were five doorways into the Propylaea, one between each of the six columns.

The Propylaea's **central hall** was once a roofed passageway. The marble-tile ceiling, now partially restored, was painted sky blue and studded with stars. Floral

designs decorated other parts of the building. The interior columns are Ionic, a bit thinner than the Doric columns of the exterior. You'll pass by some big column drums with square holes in the center, where iron pins once held the drums in place. (Greek columns were not usually made from a single piece of stone, but from sections—"column drums"—stacked on top of one another.)

• *Pass through the Propylaea. As you emerge out the other end, you're on top of the Acropolis. There it is—the Parthenon! Just like in the books (except for the scaffolding). Stand and take it all in.*

The Acropolis

The "Acropolis rock" is a mostly flat limestone ridge covering seven acres, scattered with ruins. There's the Parthenon ahead to the right. To the left of that, with the six lady pillars (caryatids), is the Erechtheion. The Panathenaic Way ran between them. The processional street and the buildings were aligned east–west, like the hill.

Ancient visitors here would have come face-to-face with a welcoming 30-foot ❻ **Statue of Athena Promachos,** which stood between the Propylaea and the Erechtheion. (Today there's just a field of rubble, the statue's former location marked by three stones forming a low wall.) This was one of three statues of Athena on the

Acropolis. The patron of the city was worshipped for her wisdom, purity, and strength; here she appeared in her role as "Frontline Soldier" *(promachos)*, carrying a shield and spear. The statue was cast by Pheidias, the visionary sculptor/architect most responsible for the design of the Acropolis complex. The bronze statue was so tall that the shining tip of Athena's spear was visible from ships at Cape Sounion, 30 miles south. The statue disappeared in ancient times, and no one knows its fate.

Two important buildings, now entirely gone, flanked this statue and the Panathenaic Way. On the right was the **Chalkotheke,** a practical storage area for the most precious gifts brought to the temple—those made of copper and bronze. On the left stood the **Arrephorion,** a house where young virgins called *ergastinai* worked at looms to weave the *peplos,* the sacred dress given to Athena on her birthday.

• *Move a little closer for the classic view of the...*

❼ Parthenon
West End

The Parthenon is the hill's showstopper—the finest temple in the ancient world, standing on the highest point of the Acropolis, 490 feet above sea level. It's now largely in ruins, partly from the ravages of time, but mostly from a direct mortar-shell hit sustained in 1687 (launched by a Venetian army aiming for the gunpowder stored inside by the Ottomans).

It's impressive enough today, but imagine how awesome the Parthenon must have looked when it was completed nearly 2,500 years ago (much of the west end is behind scaffolding for now—if it's still up during your visit, circle around to the east side). This is Greece's largest **Doric temple:** 228 feet long and 101 feet wide. At each end were 8 outer and 6 inner fluted Doric columns, with 17 columns along each side, plus 23 inner columns in the Doric and 4 in the Ionic style. The outer columns are 34 feet high and 6 feet in diameter. In its heyday, the temple was decorated with statues and

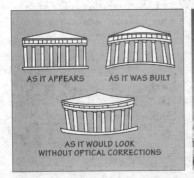

AS IT APPEARS   AS IT WAS BUILT

AS IT WOULD LOOK
WITHOUT OPTICAL CORRECTIONS

carved reliefs, all painted in vivid colors. It's considered Greece's greatest Doric temple—but not its purest example because it incorporates Ionic columns and sculpture.

The Parthenon served the **cult of Virgin Athena.** It functioned as both a temple (with a cult statue inside) and as the treasury of Athens (safeguarding the city's funds, which included the treasury of the Athenian League).

This large temple was completed in less than a decade (447-438 B.C.), though the sculptural decoration took a few years more (finished c. 432). The project's overall look was supervised by the master sculptor-architect Pheidias, built by well-known architects Ictinus and Callicrates, and decorated with carved scenes from Greek mythology by sculptors Agoracritos and Alcamenes.

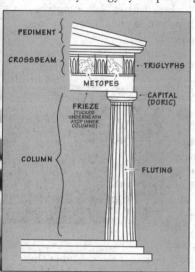

It's big, sure. But what makes the Parthenon truly exceptional is that the architects used a whole bagful of **optical illusions** to give the building an ever-so-subtle feeling of balance, strength, and harmonious beauty. Architects know that a long, flat baseline on a building looks to the human eye like it's sagging, and that parallel columns appear to bend away from each other. To create a building that looked harmonious, the Parthenon's ancient architects calculated bends in the construction. The base of the Parthenon actually arches several inches upward in the middle to counteract the "sagging" illusion. Its columns tilt ever so slightly inward (one of the reasons why the Parthenon has withstood earthquakes so well). If you extended all the columns upward several miles, they'd eventually touch. The corner columns are thicker to make them appear the same size as the rest; they're also spaced more closely. And the columns bulge imperceptibly halfway up (an effect called "entasis"), giving the subconscious impression of stout, barrel-chested men bearing the weight of the roof. For a building that seems at first to be all about right angles, the Parthenon is amazingly short on straight, structural lines.

All these clever refinements form a powerful subconscious impression on the viewer that brings an otherwise boring architectural box to life. It's amazing to think that all this was planned and implemented in stone so long ago.

The statues and carved reliefs that once decorated the outside of the Parthenon are now mostly faded or missing, but a few remain.

Look up at the crossbeam atop the eight columns, decorated with panels of relief carvings called **"metopes,"** depicting Athenians battling Amazons. Originally there were 92 Doric-style metopes in high relief, mostly designed by Pheidias himself.

The crossbeams once supported a triangular pediment (now gone). This area was once filled in with statues, showing Athena with her olive tree competing with Poseidon and his trident to be Athens' patron god. Today just one statue remains (and it's a reconstruction).

Approach closer and look between the eight columns. Inside, there's another row of eight columns, supporting a covered entrance porch. Look up above the inner eight columns. Decorating those crossbeams are more relief carvings—the "frieze." Originally, a 525-foot-long **frieze** of panels circled the entire building. It showed the Panathenaic parade—women, men on horseback, musicians, sacrificial animals being led to the slaughter—while the gods looked on. All of the sculptures—

metopes, pediment, and frieze— were originally painted in bright colors.

Today, most of the originals are in museums across Europe. In the early 1800s, the cream of the crop, the famous Elgin Marbles (you'd better call them the Parthenon Marbles in Greece), were taken by Lord Elgin to England, where they now sit in the British Museum. The Acropolis Museum (which stands at the base of the hill—you'll see it from a distance later on this tour) was built to house the fragments of the Parthenon sculpture that Athens still owns...and to try to entice the rest back from London.

• *Continue along the Panathenaic Way, walking along the long left (north) side of the Parthenon.*

North Side

This view of the Parthenon gives you a glimpse into how the temple was originally constructed, and how it is being reconstructed today by modern archaeologists.

Looking between the columns, you can see remnants of the interior walls, built with thousands of rectangular blocks. The columns formed an **open-air porch** around the main building, which had an entry hall and *cella* (inner sanctum). Large marble roof tiles were fitted together atop wooden beams. These tiles were carved so thin that the interior glowed with the light that shone through it.

The Parthenon's columns are in the Doric style—stout, lightly fluted, with no base. The simple capital on top consists of a convex plate topped with a square slab. The capitals alone weigh eight to nine tons. The crossbeams consist of a lower half ("architrave") and an upper half, its metopes interspersed with a pattern of grooves (called triglyphs).

The Parthenon (along with the other Acropolis buildings) was constructed from the very finest materials, including high-quality, white Pentelic marble from Penteliko Mountain, 16 miles away. Unlike the grand structures of the Egyptians (pyramids) and the Romans (Colosseum), the Parthenon was built not by slaves but by free men who drew a salary (though it's possible that slaves worked at the quarries).

Imagine the engineering problems of quarrying and transporting more than 100,000 tons of marble. Most likely the **column drums** (5-10 tons each) were cut at the quarry and rolled here. To hoist the drums in place, the builders used four-poster cranes (and Greek mathematics), centering the drums with a cedar peg in the middle. The drums were held together by metal pins that were coated in lead to prevent corrosion, then fitted into a square hole cut in the center of the drum. (The Ottomans scavenged much of this lead to make bullets, contributing to the destruction of the temple over the ages.) Because the Parthenon's dimensions are not mathematically precise (intentionally so), each piece had to be individually cut and sized to fit its exact place. The Parthenon's stones are so well-crafted that they fit together within a thousandth of an inch. The total cost to build the Parthenon (in today's dollars) has been estimated at over a billion dollars.

• *Continue on to the...*

East End and Entrance

This end was the original entrance to the temple. Over the doorway, the triangular pediment depicted the central event in Athenian history—the **birth of Athena,** their patron goddess. Today, the pediment barely survives, and the original statues of the gods are partly in the British Museum. Originally, the gods were gathered at a banquet (see a copy of the reclining Dionysus at the far left—looking so drunk he's afraid to come down). Zeus got a headache and asked Hephaistos to relieve it. As the other gods looked on in astonishment, Hephaistos split Zeus' head open, and—at the peak of the pediment—out rose Athena. The now-missing statues were surprisingly realistic and three-dimensional, with perfect anatomy and bulging muscles showing through transparent robes.

Imagine this spot during the age of Pericles and Socrates. Stand back far enough to take it all in, imagine the huge statue of Athena that once stood inside, and picture the place in all its glory on the day of the **Panathenaic parade.** The procession would have traveled through the Agora, ascended the Acropolis, passed through the Propylaea, and arrived here at the altar of Athena in front of the entrance of the Parthenon. People gathered on the surrounding grass (the hard stone you see today was once covered with plants). Musicians played flutes and harps, young women carried gifts, and men on horseback reined in their restless animals. On open-air altars, the priests offered a sacrifice of 100 oxen (a hecatomb—the ultimate sacrificial gift) to the goddess Athena.

Here at the Parthenon entrance, a select few celebrants were chosen to go inside. They proceeded up the steps, passed through the majestic columns into the foyer *(pronaos),* and entered the main hall, the *cella*—100 feet long, 60 feet wide, and 4 stories tall. At the far end of the room stood an enormous, 40-foot-tall statue of **Athena Parthenos** (Athena the Virgin). This was a chryselephantine statue, meaning "of gold and ivory"—from the Greek *chrysos,* "gold," and *elephantinos,* "ivory." Its wooden core was plated with ivory to represent her skin and a ton of pure gold to define her garments (or so say local guides). Dressed as a warrior, she wore a helmet and rested her shield at her side. Her image was reflected in a pool in the center of the room. (The pool also served a practical purpose—the humidity helped preserve the ivory treasures.) In Athena's left hand was a spear propped on the ground. In her upturned right hand was a statuette of Nike—she literally held Victory in the palm of her hand.

The statue—the work of the master Pheidias—was either carried off in A.D. 426 to Constantinople, where it subsequently vanished, or was burned by the Herulians in A.D. 267. (A small-scale Roman copy is on display in Athens' National Archaeological Museum.) Another famous chryselephantine statue by Pheidias—of a seated Zeus—was considered one of the Seven Wonders of the Ancient World.

The culmination of the Grand Panathenaic parade every four years was the presentation of a newly woven *peplos* to Athena. The

Acropolis Now: The Renovation Project

The scaffolding, cranes, and modern construction materials you see here are part of an ongoing renovation project. The challenge is to save what's left of the Parthenon from the modern menaces of acid rain and pollution, which have already caused irreversible damage. Funded by Greece and the EU, the project began in 1976, which means that they've been

at it more than three times as long as it took to build the Parthenon in the first place.

The project first involves cataloging every single stone of the Parthenon—blocks, drums, capitals, bits of rock, and pieces lying on the ground or in museums around the world. Next, archaeologists hope to put it back together, like a giant 70,000-piece jigsaw puzzle. Along the way, they're fixing previous restorations that were either inaccurate or problematic. For example, earlier restorers used uncoated iron and steel rods to hold things together. As weather fluctuations caused the metal to expand, the stone was damaged. This time around, restorers are using titanium rods.

Whenever possible, the restorers use original materials. But you'll also see big blocks of new marble lying on the

ground—freshly cut from the same Pentelic quarries that supplied the original stone. The new marble is being used to replace damaged and missing pieces. Many of the columns have light-colored "patches" where the restorers have installed the new stone, cut to fit exact-

ly. Though it looks much whiter, in time the newly cut marble will age to match the rest of the Parthenon.

When complete, the renovated Parthenon won't look like a fully restored building—just a shored-up version of the ruin we see today. If you want to see what the Parthenon temple looked like in its heyday, there's a full-scale replica open to visitors...in Nashville, Tennessee.

dress was intended for the life-size wooden statue of Athena kept at the Erechtheion (described later).

• *The modern brown-brick building behind you once housed the Acropolis museum—its collection has been painstakingly moved into the modern Acropolis Museum down the hill. The old museum building may reopen someday as a coffee shop, but for now, it just has WCs and a drinking fountain alongside.*

Across the street from the Parthenon stands the Erechtheion, where the Panathenaic parade ended. Start by enjoying its famous...

❽ Porch of the Caryatids

An inspired piece of architecture, this balcony has six beautiful maidens functioning as columns that support the roof. Each of the **lady-columns** has a base beneath her feet, pleated robes as the fluting, and a fruit-basket hat as the capital. Both feminine and functional, they pose gracefully, exposing a hint of leg—a combination of architectural elements and sculpture.

These are faithful copies of the originals, five of which are on display in the Acropolis Museum. The sixth was removed (c. 1805) by the sticky-fingered Lord Elgin, who shipped it to London. The caryatids were supposedly modeled on *Karyatides*—women from Karyai (modern Karyes, near Sparta on the Peloponnese), famous for their upright posture and noble character.

The Erechtheion (c. 421-406 B.C.) is sometimes ascribed to Mnesicles, the man who designed the Propylaea. Whereas the Propylaea and Parthenon are both sturdy Doric, the Erechtheion is elegant Ionic. In its day, it was a stunning white building (of Pentelic marble) with painted capitals and a frieze of white relief on a darker blue-gray background.

Near the porch (below, to the left) is an **olive tree,** a replacement for the one Athena planted here in her face-off with Poseidon (described on next page). Olive trees have been called "the gift of Athena to Athens." Greece has more than 140 million of these trees.

• *Walk around to the right and view the Erechtheion from the east end, with its six Ionic columns in a row.*

❾ Erechtheion

Though overshadowed by the more impressive Parthenon,

the Erechtheion (a.k.a. Erechtheum) was perhaps more prestigious. It stood on one of the oldest sites on the hill, where the Mycenaeans had built their palace. (It lay mainly on the south side, facing the Parthenon, under the huge scattered stones—all that's left of the seventh-century Athena Temple.) Inside the Erechtheion was a life-size, olive-wood statue of Athena in her role of **Athena Polias** ("Protector of the City"). Pericles took the statue with him when the Athenians evacuated their city to avoid the invading Persians. Dating from about 900 B.C., this statue, much older and more venerable than either of Pheidias' colossal statues, supposedly dropped from the sky as a gift from Athena.

This unique, two-story structure fits nicely into the slope of the hill. The east end (with the six Ionic columns) was the upper-level entrance. The lower entrance was on the north side (on the

right), 10 feet lower, where you see six more Ionic columns. (These columns are the "face of the Acropolis" that Athenians see from the Plaka.) The **Porch of the Caryatids** is attached to the south side of the building. Looking inside the temple, you can make out the inner worship hall, the *cella*, divided in two by walls.

This complex layout accommodated the worship of various gods who had been venerated here since the beginning of time. Legend says this was the spot where Athena and Poseidon fought for naming rights to the city. Poseidon threw his trident, which opened a gash in the earth to bring forth water. It left a diagonal crack that you can still see in the pavement of the entrance farthest from the Parthenon (although lightning is a more likely culprit). But Athena won the contest by stabbing a rock with her spear, sprouting an olive tree near the Porch of the Caryatids. The twin *cellas* of the Erechtheion allowed the worship of both gods—Athena and Poseidon—side by side to show that they were still friends.

• *Look to the right (beyond the Plaka-facing porch). The modern **elevator** carries people with limited mobility up to the Acropolis. The north wall of the Acropolis has a retaining wall built from **column drums**. This is about all that remains of an earlier half-finished Parthenon that was destroyed after the Persian invasion of 480 B.C. The Persians razed the entire Acropolis, including an unfinished temple then under construction. The Athenians rebuilt as fast as they could with the scattered material to fortify the city against Sparta.*

Walk to the far end of the Acropolis. There you'll find an observation platform with a giant...

⑩ Greek Flag

The blue-and-white Greek flag's nine stripes symbolize the nine syllables of the Greek phrase for "Freedom or Death." That phrase

took on new meaning when the Nazis entered Athens in April of 1941. According to an oft-repeated (but unverified) story, the evzone (member of a select infantry unit) guarding the flag flying here was ordered by the Nazis to remove it. He calmly took it down, wrapped himself in it...and jumped to his death. About a month later, two heroic teenagers, Manolis Glezos and Apostolis Santas, scaled the wall, took down the Nazi flag and raised the Greek flag. This was one of the first well-known acts of resistance against the Nazis, and the boys' bravery is honored by a plaque near the base of the steps. To this day, Greeks can see this flag from just about anywhere in Athens and think of their hard-won independence.

• *Walk out to the end of the rectangular promontory to see the...*

⑪ View of Athens

The Ancient Agora spreads below the Acropolis, and the sprawl of modern Athens whitewashes the surrounding hills. In 1830, Athens' population was about 5,000. By 1900, it was 600,000, and during the 1920s, with the influx of Greeks from Turkey, the population surged to 1.5 million. The city's expansion could barely keep up with its exploding population. With the boom times in the 1950s and 1980s, the city grew to nearly four million. Pan around. From this perch you're looking at the homes of one out of every three Greeks.

Looking down on the **Plaka,** find (looking left to right) the Ancient Agora, with the Temple of Hephaistos. Next comes the Roman Forum (the four columns and palm trees) with its round,

white, domed Temple of the Winds monument. The **Anafiotika** neighborhood clings to the Acropolis hillside directly below us. Beyond that, find the green-and-red dome of the cathedral.

Lykavittos Hill, Athens' highest point, is crowned with the Chapel of St. George

(and an expensive view restaurant; cable car up the hill). Looking farther in the distance, you'll see lighter-colored bits on the mountains
behind—these are **Pentelic quarries,** the source of the marble used to
build (and now restore) the monuments of the Acropolis.

As you continue panning to the right, you'll spot the beige
Neoclassical **Parliament** building, marking Syntagma Square; the
National Garden is behind and to the right of it. In the garden
is the yellow **Zappeion,** an exhibition hall. The green area in the
far distance contains the 60,000-seat, marble **Panathenaic Stadium**—an ancient venue (on the site where Golden Age Athens held
its games), which was rehabbed in 1896 to help revive the modern
Olympics.

• *Complete your visual tour of Athens at the south edge of the Acropolis.
To reach the viewpoint, walk back toward the Parthenon, then circle
along its left side, by the cliff-top wall. Belly up to that wall for...*

More Views of Athens

Look to the left. In the near distance are the huge columns of
the **Temple of Olympian Zeus.** Begun in the sixth century B.C.,
it wasn't finished until the time of the Roman emperor Hadrian,
700 years later. It was the biggest temple in all of Greece, with
104 Corinthian pillars, housing a 40-foot seated statue of Zeus,
a replica of the famous one created by Pheidias in Olympia. This
area was part of Hadrian's "new Athens," a planned community
in his day, complete with the triumphal **Arch of Hadrian** near
the temple.

The **Theater of Dionysus**—which hosted great productions
(including works by Sophocles) during the Golden Age—lies in
ruins at your feet (a visit to these ruins is covered by your Acropolis
ticket).

Beyond the theater is the wonderful **Acropolis Museum,** a
black-and-gray modern glass building, with three rectangular
floors stacked at irregular angles atop each other. The top floor,
which houses replicas and some originals of the Parthenon's art, is
angled to match the orientation of that great temple.

Looking right, you see **Filopappos Hill**—the green, tree-
dotted hill topped with a marble funerary monument to a popular
Roman senator, Philopappos, who died in the early second century.
This hill is where the Venetians launched the infamous mortar attack of 1687 that destroyed the Parthenon. Today, a theater here
hosts popular folk-dancing performances (described later, under
"Nightlife in Athens").

Farther in the distance, you get a glimpse of the turquoise waters of the **Aegean** (the only island visible is Aegina). While the
Persians were burning the Acropolis to the ground, the Athenians
watched from their ships as they prepared to defeat their foes in

ATHENS

After the Golden Age: The Acropolis Through History

Classical: The Parthenon and the rest of the Acropolis buildings survived through classical times largely intact, despite Herulian looting (A.D. 267). As the Roman Empire declined, precious items were carried off, including the 40-foot Athena statue from the Parthenon.

Christian: The Christian emperor Theodosius II (Theodosius the Great) labored to outlaw pagan worship and to close temples and other religious sites. After near-ly a thousand years as Athena's temple, the Parthenon became a Christian church (fifth century A.D.). It remained Christian for the next thousand years, first as the Byzantine Orthodox Church of Holy Wisdom, then as Mother Mary of Athens (11th century), and at the end a Roman Catholic cathedral of Notre Dame (dedicated to Mary in 1205 by Frankish Crusaders). Throughout medieval times it was an important stop on the pilgrimage circuit.

The Parthenon's exterior was preserved after its conversion to a church, but pagan sculptures and decorations were removed (or renamed), and the interior was decorated with colorful Christian frescoes. The west end of the building became the main entrance, and the interior was reconfigured with an apse at the east end.

Muslim: In 1456, the Turks arrived and converted the Parthenon into a mosque, adding a minaret. The Propylaea gateway was used as a palace for the Turkish ruler of Athens. The Turks had no respect for the sacred history of the Acropolis—they even tore down stones just to get the lead clamps that held them in place in order to make bullets. (The exasperated Greeks even offered

the history-changing Battle of Salamis. In the distance, far to the right, is the port of Piraeus (the main departure point for boats to the islands).

• *Our tour is finished. Enjoy a few final moments with the Acropolis before you leave. If you're not yet ready to return to modern Athens, you can continue your sightseeing at several nearby sights.*

To reach the Theater of Dionysus ruins and the Acropolis Museum: *Head left when you exit the Acropolis site, and walk down to the Dionysiou Areopagitou pedestrian boulevard. Turn left and follow this walkway along the base of the Acropolis. First you'll pass (on the left) the*

them bullets to stop destroying the temple.) The Turks also used the Parthenon to store gunpowder, unfortunately leading to the greatest catastrophe in the Acropolis' long history. It happened in...

1687: A Venetian army laid siege to the Acropolis. The Venetians didn't care about ancient architecture. As far as they were concerned, it was a lucky hit of mortar fire that triggered the massive explosion that ripped the center out of the Parthenon, rattled the Propylaea and the other buildings, and wiped out the Turkish defenders. Pieces of the Parthenon lay scattered on the ground, many of them gathered up as souvenirs by soldiers.

Lord Elgin: In 1801, Lord Elgin, the British ambassador to the Ottomans in Constantinople, got "permission" from the sultan to  gather sculptures from the Parthenon, buy them from locals, and even saw them off the building (Greeks scoff at the idea that "permission" granted by an occupying power should carry any weight). He carted half of them to London, where the "Elgin Marbles" are displayed in the British Museum to this day, despite repeated requests for their return. Although a few original frieze, metope, and pediment carvings still adorn the Parthenon, most of the sculptures are on display in museums, including the Acropolis Museum.

From Independence to the Present: In the 19th century, newly independent Greece tore down the Parthenon's minaret and the other post-Classical buildings atop the Acropolis, turning it into an archaeological zone. Since then the site has been excavated and subjected to several renovations. Today, the Acropolis strikes wonder in the hearts of visitors, just as it has for centuries.

entrance to the Theater of Dionysus ruins, then (on the right) the Acropolis Museum.

To reach the Ancient Agora: Turn right as you exit the Acropolis site, pass Mars Hill, and follow the Panathenaic Way down to the Ancient Agora (possible to enter through the "back door," facing the Acropolis).

Shopping in Athens

Athens may not be a top shopping destination, but it offers plenty of opportunities for visitors who want to pick up some good Greek souvenirs.

Most shops catering to tourists are open long hours daily. Those serving locals generally open Monday through Saturday at 8:30 or 9:00 (closed on Sunday); they close in the early afternoon on Monday, Wednesday, and Saturday (between 14:30 and 16:00), but tend to stay open late on Tuesday, Thursday, and Friday (until 20:00 or 21:00), often with an afternoon break (around 14:00-17:30).

To find out how to get a VAT (Value-Added Tax) refund on your purchases, see page 135.

Shopping Areas

The main streets of the Plaka—especially **Adrianou** and **Pandrossou**—are crammed with crass tourist-trap shops, selling cheap plaster replicas of ancient artifacts, along with calendars, playing cards, postcards, and shockingly profane T-shirts. Competition is fierce between shops, so there's room to bargain, especially if you're buying several items.

For upscale shopping at mostly international chain stores, stroll the pedestrianized **Ermou street** between Syntagma Square and Monastiraki (described in more detail on page 914). While tourists and big-money Athenians strut their stuff on Ermou, many locals prefer the more authentic shops on the streets just to the north, such as Perikleous, Lekka, and Kolokotroni. You can also find upscale, fancy boutiques in the swanky **Kolonaki** area.

The famous **Monastiraki flea market** stretches west of Monastiraki Square, along Ifestou street and its side streets. It's a fun place for tourists and pickpockets to browse, but it's not ideal for buying gifts for friends back home—unless they like junk. You'll see fake designer clothes, antiques, dusty books, and lots of stuff that might raise eyebrows at the airport (something going on every day, but best Sun 8:00-15:00, Metro line 1/green and line 3/blue: Monastiraki or line 1/green: Thissio).

ATHENS

What to Buy

Jewelry

Serious buyers tell me that Athens is the best place in Greece to purchase jewelry, particularly at the shops along Adrianou. The choices are much better than you'll find elsewhere, and—if you know how to haggle—so are the prices. The best advice is to take your time, and don't be afraid to walk away. The sales staff gets paid on commission, and they hate to lose a potential customer. Most stores have similar selections, which they buy from factory wholesalers.

For something a bit more specialized (with very high prices), visit the sister shops of Byzantino and Olympico (both open daily 10:00-21:00, sometimes later in summer, tel. 210-324-6605, www.byzantino.com, run by Kosta). **Byzantino,** which made the jewelry worn by the Greek dancers in the closing ceremonies of the 2000 Sydney Olympics, creates pricey handmade replicas of museum pieces (most cost hundreds of euros; Adrianou 120, plus another location nearby at the corner of Pandrossou and Eolou). **Olympico,** nearly next door, creates modern pieces in the Greek style, including some more affordable options (Adrianou 122).

The gift shop at the **Benaki Museum of Greek History and Culture** in the Kolonaki district is also popular for its jewelry (Wed-Sat 9:00-17:00, Thu until 24:00, Sun 9:00-15:00, closed Mon-Tue; classy rooftop café, across from back corner of National Garden at Koumbari 1, tel. 210-367-1000, www.benaki.gr).

Sandals

The place to buy real leather sandals is **Melissinos Art,** the famous "poet sandal-maker" of Athens. You'll find an assortment of styles for about €30 per pair. Prices depend on size and style: The more leather they use, the more you pay (daily 10:00-20:00, just off Monastiraki Square at the edge of Psyrri, Ag. Theklas 2, for location see map on page 930, tel. 210-321-9247, www.melissinos-art.com). Stavros Melissinos—who's also a poet—ran this shop for decades. Now that he's retired, his son Pantelis (also a painter and playwright) has taken over the family business. When the Beatles came to his shop in 1968, Stavros was asked why he didn't ask for their autographs. He replied, "Why did they not ask for mine? I will be around long after the Beatles." He was right.

Religious Items

For Greek Orthodox items, visit the shops near the cathedral, along Agia Filotheis street (described on page 918).

Worry Beads

You may have noticed Greeks (mostly men) constantly fidgeting with these strings of beads—flipping, spinning, and counting them. Loosely based on prayer beads, but today a secular hobby, worry beads make for a fun Greek souvenir. You'll see them sold all over central Athens.

Chocolate

Genteel **Le Chocolat** sells the good stuff for €29-49/kilo—but it'll only cost you some change to sample a handful of whatever looks good. At the very least, step inside just to take a deep whiff. Notice the case of fancy desserts. Greeks bring these to a home when they're invited for a visit instead of, say, a bottle of wine (daily 8:00-22:00, around the corner from Syntagma Square at 3 Karageorgi Servias; another location a few blocks away at 14 Voulis, on the corner of Karageorgi Servias, www.chocolat.com.gr).

Nightlife in Athens

Athens is a thriving, vibrant city...and the Athenians know how to have a good time after hours. The following tips are intended for travelers who are starting or ending their cruises here.

Athens has a constantly rotating schedule of cultural activities, such as concerts to suit every audience. For local events, look for publications such as the English-language version of the daily newspaper *Kathimerini* (www.ekathimerini.com) and the bimonthly Greek lifestyle magazine *Odyssey* (www.odyssey.gr). Athens' biggest party is the **Athens & Epidavros Festival,** in June and July. Performances at the Odeon of Herodes Atticus are the highlight of the festival, and outdoor performances at other venues enliven an already hopping city.

Nightlife Activities

Strolling

The place to be for people who enjoy an evening stroll is the pedestrian boulevard arcing around the base of the Acropolis—what I call the "Acropolis Loop" (consisting of Dionysiou Areopagitou to the south and Apostolou Pavlou to the west). As the sun goes down, it's busy with locals (lovers, families, seniors, children at play) and visitors alike. For more details about this main drag, see page 928.

Outdoor Cinema

Athens has a wonderful tradition of outdoor movies. Screenings take place most nights in summer (€8, roughly June-Sept, sometimes in May and Oct depending on weather; shows start around 20:00 or 21:00, depending on when the sun sets; many offer a second, later showing). The "theaters" are actually compact open-air courtyards with folding chairs and small tables for your drinks. Movies typically are shown in their original language, with Greek subtitles (though children's movies might be dubbed in Greek). And though Athens has many such venues, the following are particularly well-known, convenient, and atmospheric: **Aigli Village Cinema** (in the National Garden at the Zappeion, tel. 210-336-9369, www.aeglizappiou.gr), **Cine Paris** (in the Plaka overlooking Filomousou Square on the roof of Kidathineon 22, tel. 210-322-2071, www.cineparis.gr), **Cine Psyrri** (in the trendy Psyrri district at Sarri 44, near intersection with Ogigou, tel. 210-324-7234), and **Cine Theseion** (along the Apostolou Pavlou pedestrian drag in the Thissio neighborhood, tel. 210-347-0980 or 210-342-0864, www.cine-thisio.gr).

Folk Dancing

The **Dora Stratou Theater** on Filopappos Hill is the place to go to see authentic folk dancing. The company—the best in Greece—was originally formed to record and preserve the country's many traditional dances. Their repertoire includes such favorites as the graceful *kalamatianos* circle dance, the *syrtaki* (famously immortalized by Anthony Quinn in *Zorba the Greek*), and the dramatic solo *zimbetikos* (€15, June-late Sept Wed-Fri at 21:30, Sat-Sun at 20:15, no show Mon-Tue, 1.5 hours, Dora Stratou Theater, on southern side of Filopappos Hill, tel. 210-324-4395, after 19:30 call 210-921-4650, www.grdance.org).

If you're taking the Metro, get off at Petralona (on line 1/green, plus 10-minute walk) rather than the farther Akropoli stop (on line 2/red, 20-minute walk). To walk to the theater from below the Acropolis, figure at least 20 minutes (entirely around the base of Filopappos Hill, signposted from western end of Dionysiou Areopagitou).

Other Outdoor Venues

The rebuilt ancient theater at the foot of the Acropolis, the **Odeon of Herodes Atticus,** occasionally hosts concerts under the stars. The theater atop **Lykavittos Hill** is another outdoor favorite. Both of these are used in summer for the Athens & Epidavros Festival.

Nightlife Neighborhoods

Just a few minutes' walk from the tourist-clogged Plaka streets, the following neighborhoods feel more local and authentically lively. Travelers of all ages will enjoy all three areas; however, older travelers may feel a bit more comfortable in Thissio, and younger travelers gravitate to Psyrri and Gazi.

Thissio

Thissio is basically composed of three or four streets running into Apostolou Pavlou (part of the "Acropolis Loop"). Iraklidon street is a tight lane with people socializing furiously at café tables squeezed under trees. Akamantos street, while still colorful, is a bit more sedate. Backgammon boards chatter, TVs blare the latest sporting events, and young Athenians sip their iced coffees en masse. As the sun sets and the floodlit temples of the Acropolis ornament the horizon, you understand why this quiet and breezy corner is such a hit with locals. To reach Thissio, walk the pedestrian lane around the Acropolis from either end. It makes a wonderful destination after the more peaceful stretch from the Acropolis Museum (Metro: Akropoli, line 2/red). Or ride the Metro (line 1/green) to Thissio, then follow the crowds uphill along the broad Apostolou Pavlou walkway toward the Acropolis.

Psyrri

The Psyrri district, immediately north of Thissio, is downscale and more cutting-edge...seedy-chic. Until recently it was a grimy area of workshops and cottage industries, famous locally as a onetime hot-bed of poets, musicians, revolution-aries, and troublemakers. The mix of trendy and crusty gives the area a unique charm. The options include slick, touristy tavernas with live tra-ditional music (many are painted in the same Greek saloon style—these places are fresh, formulaic, and part of a chain); highly conceptual café/  bars; and clubs with DJs or live music. The epicenter of the restau-rant area is between two squares, Iroon and Agii Anargiri (with St. Anargiri Church), and along the street that connects them, Agion Anargyron. This is where you'll find the most comfortable, tourist-friendly, all-ages eateries, serving traditional Greek dishes and often featuring live music at dinnertime.

Gazi

Residents here must be dizzy at the rapid change sweeping through what was recently a depressed industrial zone. Towering overhead are the square, brick smokestacks of Technopolis, a complex of warehouses and brick factory buildings that now host galleries and theaters with a world of cutting-edge culture. As a center of Athens' gay scene, the area has a special flamboyance and style. You can't miss the Gazi energy. To get here, ride the Metro to Keramikos. You'll emerge in a delightful park surrounded by streets lined with super-stylish restaurants, clubs, bars, and cafés. The main streets

(Dekeleon, Persefonis, Voutadon, Triptolemou) radiate out from the station.

Eating in Athens

In the Plaka

Traditional Greek Sit-Down Tavernas

Palia Taverna tou Psara ("The Old Tavern of Psaras") is a big, slick, pricey eatery that enjoys bragging about the many illustrious guests they've hosted since opening in 1898. It's the kind of place where a rowdy, rollicking group of a hundred can slam down a dish-'em-up Greek meal. If you don't want a main dish (€10-25), you can order a good selection of their *mezedes* (€3-14). Seating is in two kitty-corner buildings, plus at tables on the atmospheric street between them. The lower building features live folk music and an outdoor terrace with views over Athens' rooftops (daily 11:00-24:00, music nearly daily from 21:00, signposted off Tripodon at Eretheos 16, tel. 210-321-8734, www.psaras-taverna.gr).

Restaurant Hermion is a dressy wicker indulgence in a quiet arcade off traffic-free (and loaded-with-tourists) Pandrossou. Choose between outdoor seating in an inviting courtyard and a cool air-conditioned interior. While dining under a canvas canopy surrounded by potted plants, you forget you're in a big city. The menu offers a wide range of salads and lots of fish (€3-10 starters, €5-7 salads, €9-22 grilled meats, €10-12 fish dishes, daily 12:00-24:00; live music Thu-Sun starting at 19:00; with back to cathedral, leave square downhill to the left, going 50 yards down Pandrossou to *Hermion* sign, then follow arcade passageway to Pandrossou 15; tel. 210-324-7148, www.hermion.gr).

Mezedes

Sholarhio Ouzeri Kouklis, at the intersection of Tripodon and Epicharmou streets, serves only the small plates called *mezedes* (*meh-ZEH-dehs;* known internationally as *mezes*). While you could assemble a meal of these Greek "tapas" at nearly any restaurant, this one makes it their specialty. It's fun, inexpensive, and ideal for small groups wanting to try a variety of traditional *mezedes* and drink good, homemade booze on an airy perch at the top of the Plaka. Since 1935, the Kouklis family has been making ouzo  liquor and running their restaurant—which maintains a 1930s atmosphere to this day. The waiter comes around with a big platter of dishes, and you choose what you like (€3-6/plate). Drinks are cheap, dessert is free, and the stress-free €14 meal deals are worth considering. As the plates are pretty big, this is most fun with a group of four or more. Many people sit on the street, waiting for a spot to open up on their lively front terrace, but you can also climb the spiral staircase to the often-empty upstairs area with its tiny romantic balconies for two. This place is in all the guidebooks—hardly a local scene, but still enjoyable (daily 11:00-2:00 in the morning, Tripodon 14, tel. 210-324-7605, www.sholarhio.gr).

The "Restaurant Steps" at Mnisikleous Street

At the top of the Plaka, the stepped lane called Mnisikleous (stretching up toward the Acropolis) is lined with eateries featuring interchangeable food and delightful outdoor seating. It's enjoyable to climb the stairs and window-shop along this dreamy drag. Note that most of these places have live music and/or rooftop gardens. Don't limit your search to just these two eateries; seek out the music and the setting you like best.

Xenios Zeus (ΞΕΝΙΟΣ ΖΕΥΣ), sitting proudly at the top of the Mnisikleous steps, is in every sense a step above the others. Exuberant Eleni and her husband, Yiannis, offer good, traditional Greek food inside or out on a terrace overlooking Athens' rooftops. Eleni prides herself on using only fresh ingredients...and it shows. Your meal starts with a €1.50 piece of toasted village bread with garlic and olive oil. Consider their "special menu," a €12 *mezedes* sampler plate (€3-8 appetizers, €9-20 main dishes, €15-19 fixed-price meals, daily 12:00-24:00, may close Nov-Feb, Mnisikleous 37, tel. 210-324-9514, www.xenioszeus-plaka.gr).

Geros Toy Moria Tavern is probably the best-regarded of the eateries that line the steps. It has three eating areas: the "oldest tavern in the Plaka"—a group-friendly, powerfully air-conditioned indoor dining hall featuring a more-formal menu and live Greek music and dance (no cover, nightly from 20:15); the more intimate Palio Tetradio ("Old Notebook"), with a terrace, nostalgic/cozy-in-the-winter indoor seating, and more *mezedes;* and, maybe best of all, tables along the steps under grapevines (€4-9 starters and salads, €9-20 main dishes, daily 10:00-3:00 in the morning, Mnisikleous 27, tel. 210-322-1753, www.gerostoumoria-restaurant.com).

In Monastiraki

Eating Cheap on "Souvlaki Row"

Monastiraki Square (where it meets Mitropoleos street) is a popular place to head for fast food. This is souvlaki heaven, with several frantic restaurants—Thanasis, Savas, and Bairaktaris—spilling into the street and keeping hordes of hungry eaters happy. Souvlaki

Tips on Eating in Greece

Greek food is simple...and simply delicious.

A favorite Greek snack is souvlaki pita, a tasty shish kebab wrapped in flat bread. You'll find souvlaki stands everywhere

in Greece. Savory, flaky phyllo-dough pastries called *"pita"* (pies, not to be confused with pita bread) are another staple of Greek cuisine. These can be ordered as a starter in a restaurant or purchased from a bakery for a tasty bite on the run. The most common pies are *spana-kopita* (spinach), *tiropita* (cheese), *kreatopita* (lamb), and *meletzanito-pita* (eggplant).

On the islands, eat fresh seafood. Don't miss the creamy yogurt with honey. Feta cheese salads and flaky, nut-and-honey baklava are two other flavorful treats. Dunk your bread into *tzatziki,* the ubiquitous and refreshing cucumber-and-yogurt dip.

Mezedes are a great way to sample several tasty Greek dishes. This "small plates" approach is common and easy—instead of ordering a starter and a main dish per person, get two or three starters and one main dish to split.

Greece serves up a range of restaurant options: the *es-tiatorio,* a traditional Greek restaurant; the *taverna,* a rustic neighborhood spot with a smaller menu; the *mezedopolio,* specializing in small plates/appetizers; and the *ouzerie,* a bar that makes ouzo (a licorice-flavored liqueur) and often sells basic pub grub to go along with it. Wherever you eat, you are welcome to linger as long as you want—don't feel pressured to eat quickly and turn over the table.

---

is grilled meat on a skewer, served on a plate or wrapped in pita bread to make a sandwich. These places also sell meat shaved from gyros, hearty Greek salads, wine, beer, and ouzo. Souvlaki goes well with *tzatziki,* the thick, garlicky yogurt-and-cucumber sauce. First decide whether you want your meal "to go" or at a table.

Take-Out: Gyros or a single souvlaki sandwich wrapped in a pita "to go" cost about €2—these places can fill and wrap a pita before you can blink. For these cheap carry-out prices, order and pay at the cashier, then take your receipt to the counter to claim your meal. It can be tricky to find a comfortable bench or other suitable perch in this crowded neighborhood—plan to munch as you walk (and watch out for the inevitable dribbles of souvlaki juice).

Table Service: The joints here on "Souvlaki Row" offer a good value if you're getting your food "to go." But you'll pay substantially

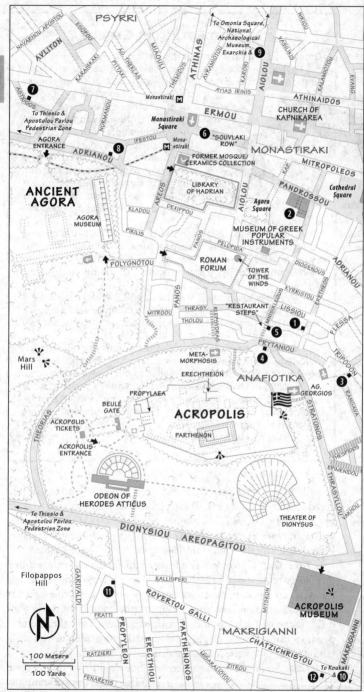

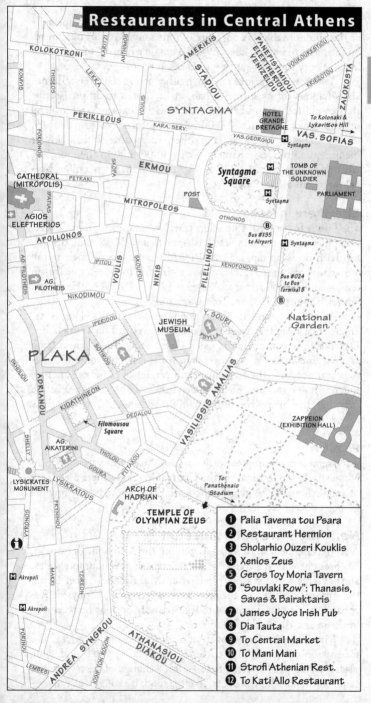

Restaurants in Central Athens

1. Palia Taverna tou Psara
2. Restaurant Hermion
3. Sholarhio Ouzeri Kouklis
4. Xenios Zeus
5. Geros Toy Moria Tavern
6. "Souvlaki Row": Thanasis, Savas & Bairaktaris
7. James Joyce Irish Pub
8. Dia Tauta
9. To Central Market
10. To Mani Mani
11. Strofi Athenian Rest.
12. To Kati Allo Restaurant

more to sit and be waited on. Still, the ambience is lively, especially at the outdoor tables. A big plate of four souvlaki (plus pita bread, onions, and tomatoes) costs €9-10; a smaller helping of two souvlaki—plenty for most eaters—runs about €5-6.

Two popular options face each other across the street: **Thanasis** is famous for its special kebab, made from a traditional recipe that combines ground beef and lamb with Thanasis' secret blend of seasonings (daily 10:00-2:00 in the morning, Mitropoleos 69, tel. 210-324-4705). **Savas** is another old favorite with a similar menu and a little less character (daily 10:00-3:00 in the morning, Mitropoleos 86, tel. 210-324-5048). The dominant operation, **Bairaktaris,** offers lesser value.

Elsewhere in Monastiraki

The **James Joyce Irish Pub** offers travelers an escape from Greece. Stepping inside, the complete Irish-pub menu (€8-12 main dishes), top Irish beers on tap, air-conditioned freshness, and rock 'n' roll ambience combine to transport you to Ireland (between the Thissio temple and Ermou street at Astiggos 12, tel. 210-323-5055, www. jjoyceirishpubathens.com, Tom Cameron).

An enticing stretch of traditional restaurants sits along Adrianou across from the Ancient Agora. I ate well at **Dia Tauta** (a.k.a. Dai Tafta), which offers the usual Greek standards, such as lamb *kleftiko,* and makes a yummy *bougiourdi*—feta cheese with tomatoes and peppers. The free olives and carafes of tap water are nice touches (€4-7 starters, €8-15 main dishes, daily 9:30-1:30 in the morning, live music Tue-Sun at 20:00, Adrianou 37, tel. 210-321-2347).

Picnics

To assemble a cheap meal of your own, head 500 yards north of Monastiraki (on Athinas) to the **Central Market.** There are plenty of small shops in the neighborhood stocking enough to throw together a decent picnic.

Near the Acropolis Museum

New development in this area, including the Akropoli Metro stop, has brought with it a trendy and touristy row of restaurants, cafés, and ice-cream shops along pedestrian Makrigianni street facing the Acropolis Museum. The other pedestrian street, Dionysiou Areopagitou, also has plenty of tourist-friendly options between the museum and the Arch of Hadrian.

Mani Mani offers a touch of class for reasonable prices. The focus is on cuisine from the Mani Peninsula, so you'll find some pleasantly atypical options here—a nice change of pace from the same old standards. The decor, like the food, is thoughtfully updated Greek, with a soothing green-and-white color scheme. As it's all indoor seating, this is an especially good bad-weather option (€6-9 starters, €10-15 main dishes, early-bird special until 18:00 offers half-portions for half the price, Tue-Sun 15:00–24:00 in summer, shorter hours in winter, closed Mon, reservations smart, look for low-profile green MANH MANH banner at Falirou 10 and go upstairs, tel. 210-921-8180, www.manimani.com.gr).

Strofi Athenian Restaurant is my favorite place in town for white-tablecloth, elegantly modern, rooftop-Acropolis-view dining. Because the restaurant is a five-minute walk from the tourist crush, Niko Bletsos and his staff need to be as good as they are. Though they have a fine air-conditioned interior, the breeze makes the rooftop comfortable even on hot evenings (€6-10 starters, €13-17 main dishes, Tue-Sun 12:00-late, closed Mon, about 100 yards down Propyleon street off Dionysiou Areopagitou at Rovertou Galli 25, tel. 210-921-4130, www.strofi.gr).

To Kati Allo Restaurant, under the far side of the Acropolis Museum, lacks tourists and is the quintessential neighborhood hole-in-the-wall. Run by English-speaking Kostas Bakatselos and his family (including an American daughter-in-law), this place offers both sidewalk seating and fan-cooled inside tables. The menu, written on a blackboard, features a short list of cheap, fresh, and tasty local options (€6-8 main dishes, open daily for lunch and dinner, just off Makrigianni street at Chatzichristou 12, tel. 210-922-3071).

Starting or Ending Your Cruise in Athens

If your cruise begins and/or ends in Athens, you'll want some extra time here; with an additional day you can see the National Archaeological Museum or visit the fun, thriving districts of Thissio, Psyrri, and Gazi. For a longer visit here, pick up my *Rick Steves' Pocket Guide: Athens* or *Rick Steves' Greece: Athens & the Peloponnese* guidebook.

Airport Connections

Eleftherios Venizelos International Airport

Athens' airport is at Spata, 17 miles east of downtown (airport code: ATH, tel. 210-353-0000—press 2 for English, www.aia.gr). This impressively slick, user-friendly airport has two sections: B gates (serving European/Schengen countries—no passport control) and A gates (serving other destinations, including the US). Both sections feed into the same main terminal building (with a common baggage claim, ATMs, shops, car-rental counters, information desks, and additional services). Upstairs, on the second floor (above entrance/exit #3), is a mini-museum of Greek artifacts.

Getting from the Airport to Downtown

Your best route into the city depends on where you want to go: If you're headed to Syntagma Square, the bus is generally better (cheapest, very frequent, and scenic). For Monastiraki, Psyrri, or the Makrigianni area south of the Plaka, the Metro is more direct—and isn't susceptible to traffic jams.

By Bus: Buses wait outside exit #5. Express bus #X95 costs €5 and operates 24 hours daily between the airport and Syntagma Square (3-5/hour, roughly 1 hour depending on traffic; tel. 185, www.oasa.gr). The downtown bus stop is on Othonos street, along the side of Syntagma Square; get off after the bus takes a 180-degree turn around a big square filled with palm trees.

By Metro: Line 3/blue zips you downtown in 45 minutes for €8 (2/hour, usually departs at :03 and :33 after the hour, daily 6:00-23:30; €14 for two people, half-price for people under 18 or over 65, ticket good for 1.5 hours on other Athens transit). To catch this train from the airport arrivals hall, go through exit #3, cross the street, escalate to the skybridge, walk to the terminal to buy tickets, and follow *Metro* signs down to the platforms. In downtown Athens, this train stops at Syntagma (where you can transfer to line 2/red) and Monastiraki (where you can transfer to line 1/green).

To return to the airport by Metro, you can catch a train from Syntagma from 5:37-24:00; airport trains depart at :03 and :33 after the hour. Keep in mind that some Metro trains terminate at Doukissis Plakentias. If so, just hop off and wait—another train that continues to the airport will be along within about 10 minutes.

By Taxi: A well-marked taxi stand outside exit #3 offers fixed-price transfers that include all fees (€40 to central Athens). Note that the cabbie will tack on several legitimate fees beyond what's on the meter, including the tolls to take the fast road, per-piece baggage charges, and a special airport fee (for details, see "Getting Around Athens—By Taxi" on page 904).

People on package trips are met at the airport by sign-waving cabbies who take them to their hotel and help get them settled in for about €75. Recently, private English-speaking cabbies have been providing this same service to anyone for about €55—though its value over simply catching a normal cab is questionable.

Getting from Downtown to the Port of Piraeus: When you're ready to head for your cruise ship, you can easily link from downtown to the port by bus, Metro, or taxi. For details, see "Returning to Your Ship" on page 891.

Getting from the Airport to the Port of Piraeus

To reach Piraeus, take bus #X96 outside airport exit #5 (€5, runs 24 hours daily, 2-4/hour, 1-1.5 hours depending on traffic; stops at Piraeus' Karaiskaki Square, then at the Metro station—marked by the pedestrian bridge; tel. 185, www.oasa.gr). A taxi from the airport to the port costs about €40.

Departing from Athens' Airport

From the Piraeus cruise terminals, you can reach the airport by taxi (around €40) or by bus #X96, which connects Piraeus directly to the airport. In Piraeus it stops along the top of Karaiskaki Square (Plateia Karaiskaki/ΠΛ. ΚΑΡΑΪΣΚΑΚΗ stop, between gates E7 and E8), and also in front of the Metro station (Stathmos ISAP/ΣΤΑΘΜΟΣ ΗΣΑΠ stop; €5, runs 24 hours daily, 2-4/hour depending on time of day, 1-1.5 hours depending on traffic).

Hotels in Athens

If you need a hotel in Athens before or after your cruise, here are a few to consider in the Plaka and near the Acropolis.

In the Plaka

$$$ Hotel Plaka has a rooftop bar/terrace and 67 modern rooms (some with Acropolis views) with updated bathrooms. Its classy management adds some nice touches, such as a staff member on hand at breakfast to answer any and all travel questions (Sb-€50-105, Db-€95-135, €5-10 more with balcony, superior Db with Acropolis view-€120-150—request in advance, Tb-€85-145, 10 percent discount if you reserve direct and show this book at check-in, prices are soft—check website for deals, mostly for longer stays—and lower Nov-March, elevator, free Wi-Fi and guest computer, at the corner of Mitropoleos and Kapnikarea, reservation tel. 210-322-2706, reception tel. 210-322-2096, www.plakahotel.gr, plaka@athenshotelsgroup.com).

$$$ Hermes Hotel, professionally run by the folks at Hotel Plaka, is nearly as nice, located on a quiet street closer to Syntagma and a little less convenient to the ancient sites. Many of its 45 rooms have balconies, and guests share a pleasant lounge, a kids' activity room, and a rooftop patio with a peek at the Acropolis (Sb-€75-105, Db-€95-135, Tb-€85-145, 10 percent discount if you reserve direct and show this book at check-in, prices are soft—check website for deals, mostly for longer stays—and lower Nov-March, elevator, free Wi-Fi and guest computer, Apollonos 19, reservation tel. 210-322-2706, reception tel. 210-323-5514, www.hermeshotel.gr, hermes@athenshotelsgroup.com).

$ Hotel Phaedra is simple but wonderfully located, overlook-

What If I Miss My Boat?

Remember that you can get help from the cruise line's port agent (listed on the destination information sheet distributed on the ship) and local TIs (for Athens, see page 896; for Piraeus, see page 888). If the port agent suggests a costly solution (such as a private car with a driver), you may want to consider public transit.

Frequent **ferries** from Piraeus serve most Greek islands, including **Mykonos, Santorini,** and other **Cycladic Islands, Heraklion** (the capital of Crete), and **Rhodes.** Try Blue Star Ferries (tel. 210-891-9800, www.bluestarferries.com), Hellenic Seaways (tel. 210-419-9000, www.hellenicseaways.gr), ANEK Lines (tel. 210-419-7470, www.anek.gr), Aegean Speed (tel. 210-969-0950, www.aegeanspeedlines.gr), SeaJets (tel. 210-412-1001, www.seajets.gr), or Minoan Lines (tel. 210-414-5700, www.minoan.gr).

Buses serving the Peloponnese use the Athens bus station called Kifissou, or "Terminal A." This bus station is about three miles northwest of the city center. Buses leave from Terminal A to **Olympia,** near the port of **Katakolo.**

If you need to catch a **plane** to your next destination, see the information on Athens' airport, earlier.

Any **travel agent** in Athens and Piraeus can help you. For more advice on what to do if you miss the boat, see page 140.

ing a peaceful Plaka square with ancient ruins and a Byzantine church. The very institutional hallways lead to 21 nicely appointed rooms. Rooms without a bath have a private bathroom across the hall (Sb-€60, D-€60, twin Db-€70, Db with balcony-€80, T-€75, Tb-€80-85, 15-20 percent less off-season, breakfast-€5, check website for deals, Acropolis-view rooftop terrace, elevator, free Wi-Fi, 2 blocks from Hadrian's Arch at Herefondos 16, at intersection with Adrianou, tel. 210-323-8461, www.hotelphaedra.com, info@hotelphaedra.com, brothers Kostas and Stamatis).

In Makrigianni and Koukaki, Behind the Acropolis

$$$ **Hotel Acropolis Select** has 72 rooms over a stylish lobby. Well-run by Kyriaki, it features a can-do staff and a generous breakfast. Their service ethic goes way beyond the norm—they've been known to send a guide on a motorbike to lead lost drivers to the hotel (Db-€80-120 depending on size and season, elevator, guest computer in lobby, free Wi-Fi, Falirou 37-39—look for flags out front, tel. 210-921-1611, www.acropoliselect.gr, selective@ath.forthnet.gr).

$$ Art Gallery Hotel is a comfy, cozy, well-run small hotel with 22 rooms near the top of a pleasant, pedestrian stair-step lane. The original artwork in the halls and rooms adds boutique-hotel charm (Sb-€40-70, Db-€50-80, Tb-€70-100, breakfast-€7, credit cards OK, elevator, free Wi-Fi, Erechthiou 5, tel. 210-923-8376 or 210-923-1933, www.artgalleryhotel.gr, artgalleryhotel@gmail. com). Say hello to Nelly and Artie, the hotel's cats.

$ Marble House Pension is a small, family-run place hiding at the end of a little cul-de-sac, a few minutes' walk past my other listings in this area. The 16 cozy rooms are simple but well cared for, and (true to its name) it's decorated with real marble. If you don't mind the dreary urban location, it's an excellent deal (Sb-€35, D-€40, Db-€45, Tb-€55, Qb-€65, cheaper late Oct-mid-March, closed Jan-Feb, breakfast-€5, air-con-€6/day available in Db and Tb, no elevator, pay guest computer, free Wi-Fi, 5-minute walk from Syngrou-Fix Metro at Zini 35a—from Zini street take the alley to the left of the tidy Catholic church, tel. 210-923-4058 or 210-922-8294, www.marblehouse.gr, info@marblehouse.gr).

Greek Survival Phrases

Knowing a few phrases of Greek can help if you're traveling off the beaten path. Just learning the pleasantries (such as please and thank you) will improve your connections with locals, even in the bigger cities.

Because Greek words can be transliterated differently in English, I've also included the Greek spellings. Note that in Greek, a semicolon is used the same way we use a question mark.

English	Greek	Pronunciation
Hello. (formal)	Gia sas. / Γειά σας.	yah sahs
Hi. / Bye. (informal)	Gia. / Γειά.	yah
Good morning.	Kali mera. / Καλή μέρα.	kah-**lee** meh-rah
Good afternoon.	Kali spera. / Καλή σπέρα.	kah-**lee** speh-rah
Do you speak English?	Milate anglika? / Μιλάτε αγγλικά;	mee-**lah**-teh ahn-glee-**kah**
Yes. / No.	Ne. / Ohi. / Ναι. / Όχι.	neh / **oh**-hee
I (don't) understand.	(Den) katalaveno. / (Δεν) καταλαβαίνω.	(dehn) kah-tah-lah-**veh**-noh
Please. (Also: You're welcome.)	Parakalo. / Παρακαλώ.	pah-rah-kah-**loh**
Thank you (very much).	Efharisto (poli). / Ευχαριστώ (πολύ).	ehf-hah-ree-**stoh** (poh-**lee**)
Excuse me. (Also: I'm sorry.)	Sygnomi. / Συγνώμη.	seeg-**noh**-mee
(No) problem.	(Kanena) problima. / (Κανένα) πρόβλημα.	(kah-**neh**-nah) **prohv**-lee-mah
Good.	Orea. / Ωραία.	oh-**reh**-ah
Goodbye.	Antio. / Αντίο.	ahd-**yoh** (think "adieu")
Good night.	Kali nikta. / Καλή νύχτα.	kah-**lee** neek-tah
one / two	ena / dio / ένα / δύο	**eh**-nah / **dee**-oh
three / four	tria / tessera / τρία /τέσσερα	**tree**-ah / **teh**-seh-rah
five / six	pente / exi / πέντε / έξι	**pehn**-deh / **ehk**-see
seven / eight	efta / ohto / εφτά / οχτώ	ehf-**tah** / oh-**toh**
nine / ten	ennia / deka / εννιά / δέκα	ehn-**yah** / **deh**-kah
hundred / thousand	ekato / hilia / εκατό / χίλια	eh-kah-**toh** / **heel**-yah
How much?	Poso kani? / Πόσο κάνει;	**poh**-soh kah-nee
euro	evro / ευρώ	ev-**roh**
toilet	toualeta / τουαλέτα	twah-**leh**-tah
men / women	andres / gynekes / άντρες / γυναικες	**ahn**-drehs / yee-**neh**-kehs

In a Greek Restaurant

English	Greek	Pronunciation
The menu (in English), please.	Ton katalogo (sta anglika) parakalo. Τον κατάλογο (στα αγγλικά) παρακαλώ.	tohn kah-**tah**-loh-goh (stah ahn-glee-**kah**) pah-rah-kah-**loh**
service (not) included	to servis (den) perilamvanete το σέρβις (δεν) περιλαμβάνεται	toh **sehr**-vees (dehn) peh-ree-lahm-**vah**-neh-teh
appetizers	proto piato πρώτο πιάτο	**proh**-toh pee-**ah**-toh
bread	psomi ψωμί	psoh-**mee**
cheese	tiri τυρί	tee-**ree**
sandwich	sandwich or toast σάντουιτς, τόστ	"sandwich," "toast"
soup	soupa σούπα	**soo**-pah
salad	salata σαλάτα	sah-**lah**-tah
meat	kreas κρέας	**kray**-ahs
poultry / chicken	poulerika / kotopoulo πουλερικά / κοτόπουλο	poo-leh-ree-**kah** / koh-**toh**-poo-loh
fish / seafood	psari / psarika ψάρι / ψαρικά	**psah**-ree / psah-ree-**kah**
shellfish	thalassina θαλασσινά	thah-lah-see-**nah**
fruit	frouta φρούτα	**froo**-tah
vegetables	lahanika λαχανικά	lah-hah-nee-**kah**
dessert	gliko γλυκό	lee-**koh**
(tap) water	nero (tis vrisis) νερό (της βρύσης)	neh-**roh** (tees **vree**-sees)
coffee	kafes καφές	kah-**fehs**
tea	tsai τσάι	**chah**-ee
wine	krasi κρασί	krah-**see**
beer	bira μπύρα	**bee**-rah
(To your) health! (like "Cheers!")	(Stin i) gia mas! (Στην υ) γειά μας!	(stee nee) yah mahs
Bill, please.	Ton logariasmo parakalo. Τον λογαριασμό παρακαλώ.	tohn loh-gah-ree-ahs-**moh** pah-rah-kah-**loh**
tip	bourbouar μπουρμπουάρ	boor-boo-**ar**
Delicious!	Poli nostimo! Πολύ νόστιμο!	poh-**lee nohs**-tee-moh

MYKONOS
Greece

Greece Practicalities

Greece *(Hellas)* offers sunshine, seafood, 6,000 islands, whitewashed houses with bright-blue shutters, and a relaxed lifestyle. As the birthplace of Western civilization, it has some of the world's greatest ancient monuments. We have the Greeks to thank for the Olympics; the tall tales of Achilles and Odysseus; the rational philosophies of Socrates, Plato, and Aristotle; democracy, theater, mathematics...and the gyro sandwich.

As a late bloomer in the modern age, Greece retains echoes of a simpler, time-passed world. On the islands, you'll still see men on donkeys and women at the well. Greeks pride themselves on a concept called *filotimo* ("love of honor"), roughly translated as openness, friendliness, and hospitality. It's easy to surrender to the Greek way of living.

Money: Greece uses the euro currency: 1 euro (€) = about $1.30. An ATM, handily, is labeled *ATM* in the Greek alphabet. The local VAT (value-added sales tax) rate is 23 percent; the minimum purchase eligible for a VAT refund is €120 (for details on refunds, see page 135).

Language: For helpful Greek phrases, see page 1001.

Emergencies: Dial 100 for police or 171 for English-speaking tourist police; for medical or other emergencies, dial 176 or 199.

Time Zone: Greece is on Eastern European Time (an hour ahead of Italy and seven/ten hours ahead of the East/West Coasts of the US).

Theft Alert: In Athens and any place with crowds, be wary of purse snatchers and pickpockets. For tips on outsmarting thieves, see page 128.

Consular Services in Athens: The US embassy is at Vassilissis Sofias 91 (tel. 210-720-2414, http://athens.usembassy.gov). The Canadian embassy is at Ioannou Ghennadiou 4 (tel. 210-727-3400, www.greece.gc.ca). Call ahead for passport services.

Phoning: Greece has a direct-dial phone system (no area codes). To **call within Greece,** just dial the number. To **call to Greece,** dial the international access code (00 if calling from Europe, or 011 from North America), then 30 (Greece's country code), then the phone number. To **call home from Greece,** dial 00, 1, then your area code and phone number.

Tipping: If you order your food at a counter, don't tip. At sit-down restaurants, service is generally included, although it's common to round up the bill after a good meal, usually 5-10 percent. You'll also round up 5-10 percent to tip a cabbie (give €5 to pay a €4.50 fare).

Tourist Information: www.visitgreece.gr

MYKONOS

ΜΥΚΟΝΟΣ / Μυκονοσ

Mykonos (MEE-koh-nohs) is the very picture of the perfect Greek island town: a humble seafront village crouched behind a sandy harbor, thickly layered with blinding-white stucco, bright-blue trim, and bursting-purple bougainvilleas. (Thank goodness for all that color, since otherwise this island—one of Greece's driest—would be various shades of dull brown.) On a ridge over town stretches a trademark row of five windmills, overlooking a tidy embankment so pretty they call it "Little Venice."

More recently Mykonos has gained a certain hip cachet as a fashionable, jet-set destination and a mecca for gay holiday-makers. These days, weary fisherfolk and tacky trinket stalls share the lanes with top-end fashion boutiques. Prices are stunningly high here, and the island is crammed full of fellow vacationers, particularly in August (try to come in spring or fall, if you can). But the Mykonians have taken all the changes in stride. Fishermen still hang out on the benches by the harbor—always wearing their traditional caps (Mykonian men are famous among Greeks for their baldness). The natives generally seem appreciative rather than corrupted by all the attention. On my last visit, I overheard a young tourist gushing to her mommy, "Boy, people sure are friendly here!"

While Mykonos has some museums, they are merely an excuse to get out of the sun for a few minutes. The real attraction here is poking around the Old Town streets: shopping, dining, clubbing, or—best of all—simply strolling. The core of town is literally a maze, designed by the Mykonians centuries ago to discourage would-be invaders from finding their way. That tactic also works on today's tourists. But I can think of few places where getting lost is so enjoyable.

Excursions from Mykonos

Most excursions feature one or both of two main attractions: A guided walk around the town of **Mykonos;** and a tour of the ancient site of **Delos,** on a nearby island. Mykonos is beautiful, but there's not much to say about the place—it's simply a delight to wander. Delos, on the other hand, has a fascinating history that's best appreciated with the help of a good guide.

Other excursions may include side-trips to some of Mykonos' **beaches,** which you can easily reach on your own by taxi or bus. And many cruise lines offer an **"island highlights"** itinerary to various villages and countryside churches—but Mykonos town and the beaches are really the only things worth seeing on a short visit.

If you manage to break free, wander up to the windmills for the view, or take a bus (or rent a scooter or ATV) to reach one of the many enticing sandy beaches around the island. Near Mykonos, accessible by an easy boat trip, is the island of Delos—one of the Greek islands' top ancient sites. Delos hosts the remains of what was one of the most important places in the ancient Greek world: the temples honoring the birthplace of the twin gods Apollo and Artemis (it later became a bustling shipping community). Delos was a pilgrimage site for believers who came from all over to worship this "birthplace of light." Judging by the present-day sun worshippers who scramble for the best patch of sand on Mykonos each summer, things haven't changed much around here.

Planning Your Time

Mykonos is a delightful place to be on vacation, even if just for a few hours. Here are some good options for your time:

• Explore the Old Town lanes in Mykonos town. You can dip into the museums, but they're all skippable.

• Beach-lovers will want to head to any one of several fine beaches (described in this chapter, all within a 20-minute ride from Mykonos town). Allow a minimum of two hours, including transportation.

• Archaeologists and historians can take a boat to Delos (easy 30-minute boat trip each way). Figure about three hours total for the round-trip.

Crowd Warning: The island can be painfully crowded in high season, roughly July through mid-September, peaking in August. During this time, the beaches (and everything else) are uncomfortably packed with people.

Arrival in Mykonos

Cruise ships arriving at Mykonos either tender passengers directly to the heart of the Old Town or dock at the big New Port across the bay.

Tendering to the Old Town
If your cruise ship is tendered, you'll disembark at the pier extending out from the heart of town. Just walk down the pier and you're at the harbor (a public pay WC is on the right, along the water).

Docking at the New Port
Cruise ships dock at the New Port, across the bay from the Old Town, about a mile away. Many cruise lines offer a **shuttle bus** (cost varies from free up to $10/day) that zips you right to the Old Port. Or you can reach the Old Port by **taxi** (€5-10) or **public bus** (2/hour, €1.60). From there, it's an easy five-minute walk along the harborfront promenade to the Old Town: Stroll past a stretch of beach, then down a cozy shop-lined lane to "Taxi Square" and the main harborfront.

If the line for the bus is just too long, and you're eager to stretch

Greek Island Experiences for Cruisers

With a few exceptions, sightseeing isn't a Greek island forte; for most travelers, beaches rank above museums. But even on just a brief port visit, you can play "Greek islander" for a day. Consider these suggestions for experiencing the untouristy side of Greek island life.

Sip ouzo at a waterfront perch. The anise-flavored liqueur, ouzo, is worth a try even if you don't like the taste (black licorice). Ouzo turns from clear to milky white when you add ice or water (don't drink it straight). Greeks drink it both as an aperitif and with food. I like to sip it slowly in the early evening while sharing several *mezedes* (appetizers) with my travel partner as we watch the boats come and go.

Go on a photo safari for adorable cats. The predictably warm weather of the Greek islands makes them a haven for stray kittens who seem to be posing for you around every corner. Some travelers enjoy buying a little packet of cat food to offer a snack to their new friends.

Stroll with snacks from a vendor's stall. Some of the best options include souvlaki (shish kebab, often wrapped in pita bread), Greek savory phyllo-dough pastry (such as *spanakopita*—spinach pie, or *tiropita*—cheese pie), or a honey-drenched baklava.

Buy a candle or an icon at a village church. Many small Greek Orthodox churches, filled with atmospheric glittering icons and the heavy fragrance of incense, have humble little counters in the back where a villager sells candles to light and little take-way icons.

your legs, you could do the dreary 25-minute **walk** along the coast into town (turn right, follow the water, and just keep going—you can see the gaggle of white houses across the bay).

Orientation to Mykonos

Mykonos' main town is called Chora (or Hora, Χώρα; roughly "village"), and that's how you'll generally see it signed. For ease, I refer to it as "Mykonos town."

Mykonos town is the main point of entry for the island. The Old Town clusters around the south end of the Old Port (some inter-island boats depart from the north end of the Old Port). Arcing in front of the Old Town is the sandy harbor; at the east end is Taxi Square (a hub for taxis and other services) and, beyond that, the Remezzo bus station and the Old Port; at the west end of the harbor is the pier for Delos ferries and cruise-ship tenders, and beyond that, the Little Venice quarter and the windmill ridge. Squeezed between the harbor and the main road (passing above town on the gentle hill) is a tight maze of whitewashed lanes.

While some streets have names, others don't, and in any case, locals never use those names—they just know where things are. If you can't find something, ask.

Tourist Information

Though there is a TI building (at the corner of the Old Port), the space hasn't been occupied in a while. To fill the void, local hotels, travel agencies, and other friendly locals can answer basic questions. Look for promotional but helpful town maps, or consult www.mykonos.gr, the island's official website.

Getting Around Mykonos

Mykonos is a fun and easy island to explore, with several very different but equally inviting beach coves within a short drive.

By Taxi: The square at the southeast corner of the Old Port, nicknamed Taxi Square, is where you can catch a taxi to points around the island. Fares are reasonable; figure €6-12 one-way to most beaches listed in this chapter (except Super Paradise, which is more like €15). Rather than paying the taxi to wait for you at the beach, hail or call a fresh one when you're ready to leave (tel. 22890-22400). You can also ask a taverna at the beach to call for you.

By Bus: Mykonos' bus network is well-designed for connecting travelers to its many fine beaches. Buses are frequent, though they might leave you a short walk from the beach itself. And because this is a party island, they run late into the night in peak season. Schedules are posted on chalkboards at stops, and many hotels post copies of the schedule near reception. Rides costs €1.60 (may be a little pricier after midnight); buy your ticket from the bus driver.

There are three bus stations in Mykonos town. For tourists, the most useful is the **Fabrika** station, at the south end of town (away from the harbor), where several Old Town streets funnel gradually uphill to the main road that passes above. From the Fabrika station you can catch buses to nearby destinations, including the beaches I've described in this chapter: **Ornos/Agios Ioannis** (1-2/hour), **Paradise** (2/hour), **Platis Gialos** (2/hour), and **Paraga** (hourly in high season, fewer in off-season).

Two other stations are virtually next to each other at the northeast edge of the Old Town (from Taxi Square, head along the port with the water to your left): The **Old Port** station along the water is for buses to the New Port; a block uphill, the **Remezzo** station serves buses to the eastern half of the island (the large town of Ano Mera, plus the smaller towns of Kalafati and Elia).

By Motorized Scooter or All-Terrain Vehicle (ATV): On

MYKONOS

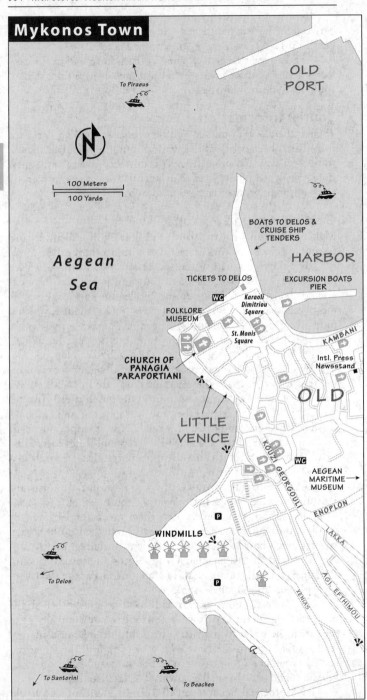

Mykonos Town

OLD PORT

To Piraeus

N

100 Meters
100 Yards

BOATS TO DELOS &
CRUISE SHIP
TENDERS

Aegean
Sea

HARBOR

TICKETS TO DELOS

EXCURSION BOATS
PIER

WC

Karaoli
Dimitriou
Square

FOLKLORE
MUSEUM

St. Monis
Square

KAMBANI

Intl. Press
Newsstand

CHURCH OF
PANAGIA
PARAPORTIANI

OLD

LITTLE
VENICE

KOUZI GEORGOULI

WC

AEGEAN
MARITIME
MUSEUM

P

ENOPLON

WINDMILLS

LAKKA

P

XENAS

AGL. EFTHIMOU

To Delos

To Santorini

To Beaches

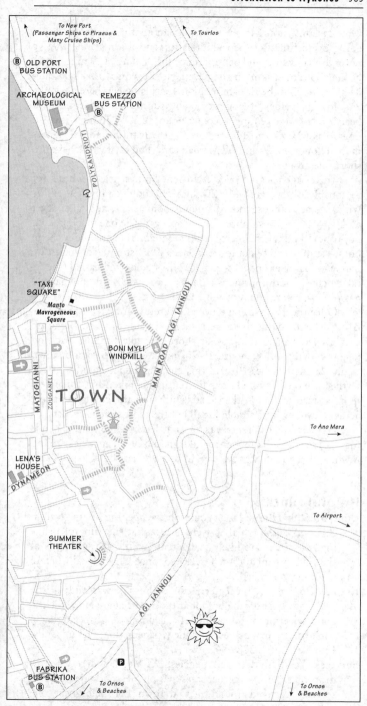

MYKONOS

To New Port
(Passenger Ships to Piraeus &
Many Cruise Ships)

To Tourlos

Ⓑ OLD PORT
BUS STATION

ARCHAEOLOGICAL
MUSEUM

REMEZZO
BUS STATION
Ⓑ

POLYKANDRIOTI

"TAXI
SQUARE"

Manto
Mavrogeneous
Square

BONI MYLI
WINDMILL

MAIN ROAD (AGI. IANNOU)

MATOGIANNI

ZOUGANELI

T O W N

LENA'S
HOUSE

DYNAMEON

To Ano Mera

SUMMER
THEATER

To Airport

AGI. IANNOU

FABRIKA
BUS STATION
Ⓑ

P

To Ornos
& Beaches

To Ornos
& Beaches

Greek islands, tourists are notorious for renting a scooter or an ATV, overestimating their abilities to control a machine they've never driven before, and denting someone's fender or leaving a strip of knee or elbow skin on the pavement...or worse. That said, and keeping in mind the risks inherent in renting wheels here, it can be an affordable, efficient, and memorably fun way to connect distant beaches. If I were renting a scooter or an ATV on a Greek isle, I'd do it here, where the roads are not too heavily trafficked (you'll pass more fellow scooters and ATVs than cars), and idyllic beaches are a short ride away.

Travel agencies all over town rent both types of wheels for reasonable all-day rates (€10-25/day for a scooter or an ATV, ATVs with reverse gear cost about €5 more). Some places add on another €7-10 per day for insurance. Two people can ride one machine, but both should ask for helmets (you'll see many riders without them, but it's stupidly risky not to wear one, and most rental agencies are happy to loan you one). The paperwork is quick and casual (they'll take a credit-card imprint as a deposit, and you'll fill up whatever gas you use before you return it).

Once on the road, be especially careful on turns, where centrifugal forces suddenly make it more difficult to steer. Be aware that even distances that appear short can take time to reach on a slow-moving ATV; figure 15-20 minutes from Mykonos town to any of the beaches I list in this chapter (Super Paradise is the farthest). Note: You'll see ads for renting a "bike," but this refers to motorized scooters—the island is hilly and arid enough to make actual bicycling undesirable for all but the most serious cyclists.

By Car: You can rent a car for as little as €35 per day, depending on demand; look for car-rental signs at several agencies around town, and negotiate a good bargain if you're here outside peak season.

Helpful Hints

Unpredictable Hours: Don't count on the opening hours given in this book. Though they were accurate at the time of printing, the times are likely to fluctuate wildly at the whims of the government and the Greek economy. Check locally before planning your day.

English Bookstore: The **International Press Newsstand,** in the Old Town just off the harbor at the Taxi Square end, stocks a good selection of international (including English-language) paperbacks, magazines, and newspapers (long hours daily, Kampani 5, tel. 22890-78507).

Services: You'll find travel agencies, ATMs, launderettes (€10 drop-off service), Internet cafés, pay phones, and other helpful services scattered around the Old Town. For the highest concentration of services, head for the area around the Fabrika bus station, at the south end of the Old Town (near where it meets the main road; also pay WC, tattoo parlor).

Supermarket: The **Three Wells** supermarket is the oldest in town, with a wider selection than at most of the smaller groceries in the town center (daily 8:30-24:00 in summer, 8:30-14:00 & 17:00-20:00 in winter, just up from maritime museum on Enoplon Dynameon).

Open-Air Cinema: In summer, locals and vacationers sit back and enjoy the movies under the palm trees at **Ciné Manto**, in a lovely garden smack in the middle of town (€8, films shown in original language—usually English, June-Sept only, nearly nightly at 20:30 or 21:00, most nights also at 22:30 or 23:00, café, tel. 22890-26165).

Sights in Mykonos

▲▲Old Town

Mykonos' Old Town seems made for exploring. Each picture-perfect lane is slathered with a thick, bulbous layer of stucco, giving

the place a marshmallow-village vibe. All that white is the perfect contrast to the bright-blue sky and the vivid trim. Sometimes described as "cubist" for its irregular jostle of angular rooflines, Mykonos' townscape is a photographer's delight. Enjoy getting lost, then found again. Try wandering aimlessly for a while—you may be amazed how quickly you find yourself going in circles. To get your bearings, look at a map and notice that three "main" roads (still barely wide enough for a moped) form a U-shaped circuit facing the harbor: Kouzi Georgouli, Enoplon Dynameon, and Matogianni.

Or just relax along the sandy **harbor.** The pier for excursion boats to Delos (described later) sticks straight out; nearby is an impossibly picturesque white chapel with sky-blue trim. Nurse an iced coffee or a beer at a rustic café table and watch the tide of tourists wash over local village life. Glancing offshore, you'll see humble fishing boats bobbing in the foreground, with 2,000-passenger cruise ships looming in the distance. Along the sandy harbor, fisherfolk sort and clean their catch at the marble table (while stray cats

gather below), old-timers toss a fishing line into the water, kids skip rocks and rent ponies for a ride on the sand, and shutterbug tourists flock around the resident pelican, Petros. (Ever since a local fisherman found an ailing pelican and nursed it back to health half a century ago, these odd birds have been the town's mascots.)

The piazza known as **Taxi Square,** at the east end of the sandy harbor, is a hub of activity monitored by a bust of Manto Mavrogenous (1796-1848), a heroine of the Greek War of Independence. A wealthy aristocrat of Mykonian heritage, she spent her fortune supplying Greek forces in a battle against their Turkish rulers. Mavrogenous ended her life destitute on the island of Paros, never regretting the sacrifices she made for Greece's freedom.

▲▲Windmills

Mykonos is infamously windy, and Mykonians have special names for the different winds that blow through: "the bell-ringer," "the chair-thrower," and "the unseater of horsemen." As in many Greek island towns, Mykonos' old-fashioned windmills harnessed this

natural power in order to grind grain to supply its ships. Five of them (plus the bases of two more) stand proudly along a ridge called Kato Myloi at the top of town, overlooking the Little Venice area. While there's nothing to see inside these buildings, they make for a fine photo op and great views over town.

To enter a windmill, head to the opposite (east) end of the Old Town, where the **Boni Myli windmill** is open to visitors (June-Sept daily 16:00-20:00, closed Oct-May, tel. 22890-22591).

▲Little Venice (Mikri Venetia)

Along the bay at the western edge of town, just below the windmills, wealthy local shipping merchants built a row of fine mansions, with brightly painted wooden balconies, that seem to rise from the deep. While "Little Venice" is a bit of a misnomer (where are the canals?), this is a particularly scenic corner of town. At the head of this area, a stately Catholic church (the only one on Mykonos, which boasts some 400 little Orthodox chapels) marks a square filled with restaurant tables.

The embankment here is lined with cocktail bars and cafés (I particularly like **Scarpa, Galleraki,** and **Caprice**), crowded every night with throngs of visitors enjoying the island's best spot to watch the sunset—one of the highlights of visiting Mykonos.

▲Church of Panagia Paraportiani

Huddled at the tip of land between Little Venice and the harbor, this unusual church is a striking architectural oddity—a hodgepodge of five small chapels that gradually merged together, then were draped in a thick layer of whitewashed stucco. While it's a much-touted landmark (and one of the island's most-photographed

spots), there's little to see beyond the initial, otherworldly appearance. One of the chapel interiors is open most days, where a local woman sells votive candles and fills the small space with the rich aroma of incense.

MYKONOS

Archaeological Museum

This small museum, just uphill from the Old Port, displays artifacts found on the nearby island of Rinia, which became the burial isle for Delos when residents of that sacred island's cemeteries were relocated by the Athenians in the sixth century B.C. With limited English labels and almost no descriptions, most of what's here—intricately carved stone grave markers, vases, jewelry, and statue fragments—is pretty dull. One item, however, makes a visit worth considering: a large vase (dead center along the back wall) clearly showing the Trojan Horse filled with Greek soldiers sporting gleeful archaic smiles, and cartoon-like panels telling the story of the massacre that followed when they jumped out. Dating from roughly 670 B.C., it's the oldest depiction of the Trojan Horse ever found. Unlike the museum's other pieces, it wasn't excavated from the Rinia graves, but found right here on Mykonos, discovered in 1961 by a (surely very surprised) farmer who'd set out to dig a well.

Cost and Hours: €2, April-Oct Tue-Sun 9:00-16:00, may close at 15:00 off-season, closed Mon year-round, tel. 22890-22325. Ask for the free brochure when you enter.

Aegean Maritime Museum

This tight but endearing collection traces the story of the local mercantile shipping industry. A desert isle of history in a sea of tourist kitsch, this little place takes its subject very seriously. In its four rooms you'll find amphora jugs, model ships, a collection of stamps celebrating seafaring, and more. Don't miss the tranquil garden, which displays the actual, original lighthouse from the island's Cape Armenistis, as well as replicas of ancient sailors' gravestones. The good English descriptions offer a fine history lesson for those willing to read them.

Cost and Hours: €4, April-Oct daily 10:30-13:00 & 18:30-21:00, closed Nov-March, Enoplon Dynameon 10, tel. 22890-22700.

Lena's House

Adjacent to the Maritime Museum (and part of the Folklore Museum), this is a typical middle-class Mykonian house dating from the late 19th century, complete with original furnishings and artwork.

Cost and Hours: €2, April-Sept Mon-Sat 18:30-21:30, possibly Sun 7:00-21:00, closed Oct-March, tel. 22890-22390.

Mykonos Folklore Museum

Housed in a typically Cycladic former sea captain's residence just up the bluff from the harbor, this museum displays a random mix of traditional folk items from around the island, as well as a typical kitchen and bedroom.

Cost and Hours: Free, April-Sept Mon-Sat 16:30-20:30, closed Sun, closed Oct-March, tel. 22890-22591.

Beaches

Mykonos' array of beaches rivals that of any Greek island. Each beach seems to specialize in a different niche: family-friendly or party; straight, gay, or mixed; nude or clothed; and so on. (Keep in mind that in Greece, even "family-friendly" beaches have topless sunbathers.) Get local advice to find the one that suits your beach-bum preferences, or choose from one of the options listed here (all of my suggestions are within a 15- to 20-minute bus or scooter/ATV ride of town).

To connect the beaches, you'll drive up and down over the steep dusty, dirty, desolate spine of this arid island. You can also connect many of these beaches (including Psarou, Platis Gialos, Paradise, and Super Paradise) by regular shuttle boat.

All of these beaches have comfortable lounge chairs with umbrellas out on the sand. Figure around €10-15 for two chairs that share an umbrella (or half that for one chair). Just take a seat—they'll come by to collect the money. Be warned that in peak season (July and especially Aug), all beaches are very crowded, and it can be difficult to find an available seat.

Mykonos' beaches are lined with cafés and tavernas, with typical Greek-island menus...sometimes functional, sometimes surprisingly good. These can offer a welcome break from the sun.

Agios Ioannis

This remote-feeling patch of sand—my favorite beach on the island—is tucked behind a mountain ridge, and best gives you the feeling of being on a castaway isle. You'll enjoy views across to the important isle of Delos. From Mykonos town go to Ornos, then head toward Kapari; on your way down the hill, turn off on the left at the low-profile beach signs (one directs you to Πύλη, one of the restaurants on the beach). You'll drop down the road to an idyllic Robinson Crusoe spot where a few restaurants share a sandy beach.

For the even more secluded **Kapari** beach, continue down the road past the Agios Ioannis turnoff, then swing right at the white church.

Ornos

Easy to reach since it's in a sizeable town in the middle of the island, this very family-friendly beach is also one of the more functional (and least memorable) of those I list. The whole place has an unpretentious charm.

Psarou and Platis Gialos

These two beaches, along the next cove to the east of Ornos, are much more densely developed. At each one a tight line of hotels arcs along the top of a crowded patch of sand. Psarou is considered a somewhat exclusive, favorite retreat of celebrities, while Platis Gialos feels more geared toward families (the far end from the bus stop/parking is less claustrophobic).

Paradise

This famous "meat-market" beach is a magnet for partiers in the Aegean, and even more of a destination than the other beaches listed here. Located at the southern tip of the island, Paradise (a.k.a. Kalamopodi) is presided over by hotels that run party-oriented bars for young beachgoers—perfect if you want to dance in the sand all night to the throbbing beat with like-minded backpackers from around the world. As you approach, the last stretch is through thick, high grasses, giving the place an air of secrecy; then you'll pass long rows of lockers before popping out at the party.

The next cove over hosts **Super Paradise** (Plintri) beach, which has eclipsed the original as the premier party beach on the island.

Eating in Mykonos

The twisting streets of the Old Town are lined with tourist-oriented restaurants. Don't look for good values here—Mykonos is expensive. With few exceptions, little distinguishes one place from another; simply choose the spot with the menu and ambience that appeal to you: with a sea view, out on a busy pedestrian lane, or in a charming garden courtyard.

The many tavernas and cafés that face the sandy harbor are touristy and overpriced, but it's hard to argue with their appeal. Consider enjoying an iced coffee or frappé—if not a full meal—

from this comfortable perch, which offers the best people-watching (and sometimes cat- and pelican-watching) in town. The harborfront has the workaday action, while the places in Little Venice are more romantic—especially at sunset. A few steps inland, tucked in the town's winding back lanes, are countless charming restaurants filling hidden gardens under trellises of bougainvillea. Take mental notes as you explore, then come back to the place that best suits your fancy.

For yummy desserts, **Komninos Traditional Healthy Flavors** sells baklava, savory pies, and other homemade treats to go (long hours daily, 30 yards off Taxi Square on Polykandrioti).

For general information on eating in Greece, see page 965.

Delos

Popular as Mykonos is today, it was just another island centuries ago, and the main attraction was next door: the island of Delos, worth ▲. In antiquity, Delos lived several lives: as one of the Mediterranean's most important religious sites, as the "Fort Knox" of Greek city-states, and as one of the ancient world's busiest commercial ports. Its importance ranked right up there with Athens, Delphi, or Olympia. Today the island is a ghost town—only ruins and a humble museum remain. Highlights include the much-photographed lion statues, some nice floor mosaics, the view from Mt. Kynthos, and a windswept setting pockmarked with foundations that hint at Delos' rich history—all covered in my self-guided tour.

Orientation to Delos

Cost and Hours: €5 admission, plus cost of the boat trip; open Tue-Sun from the arrival of the first boat to the departure of the last one (roughly 9:30-15:00), closed Mon; tel. 22890-23413.

Warning: Delos is an uninhabited island with virtually no shade

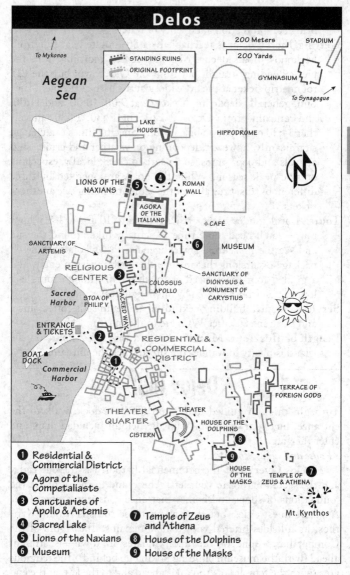

Delos

STANDING RUINS
ORIGINAL FOOTPRINT

200 Meters
200 Yards

Aegean Sea

To Mykonos

STADIUM

GYMNASIUM

To Synagogue

HIPPODROME

LAKE HOUSE

LIONS OF THE NAXIANS

ROMAN WALL

AGORA OF THE ITALIANS

CAFÉ

SANCTUARY OF ARTEMIS

MUSEUM

RELIGIOUS CENTER

Sacred Harbor

STOA OF PHILIP V

COLOSSUS APOLLO

SANCTUARY OF DIONYSUS & MONUMENT OF CARYSTIUS

SACRED WAY

ENTRANCE & TICKETS

BOAT DOCK

Commercial Harbor

RESIDENTIAL & COMMERCIAL DISTRICT

TERRACE OF FOREIGN GODS

THEATER QUARTER

THEATER

HOUSE OF THE DOLPHINS

CISTERN

HOUSE OF THE MASKS

TEMPLE OF ZEUS & ATHENA

Mt. Kynthos

1. Residential & Commercial District
2. Agora of the Competaliasts
3. Sanctuaries of Apollo & Artemis
4. Sacred Lake
5. Lions of the Naxians
6. Museum
7. Temple of Zeus and Athena
8. House of the Dolphins
9. House of the Masks

MYKONOS

and only a small museum and café. Wear good shoes, and bring sun protection and plenty of water.

Getting There: Delos is reachable by a 30-minute boat ride from Mykonos. Boats depart Mykonos in the morning from the pier extending straight out from the Old Town; buy the €17 round-trip ticket at the little kiosk at the base of the pier (Tue-Sun, generally departing Mykonos at 9:00, 10:00, and 11:00, and returning from Delos at 12:15 or 12:30, 13:30, and either 14:30 or 15:00; no boats Mon). Specific times can change significantly, however, depending on weather and cruise-ship arrivals and departures, so be sure to check locally, especially outside peak season. While the boats are operated by three different outfits, they all cost the same and honor one another's tickets.

Tours: Local guides meet arriving boats (€10 for a 1-1.5 hour tour—you'll need more time to actually hike around the site and see the museum). Travel agencies in Mykonos town sell package excursions that include the boat, museum entry, and a guided tour (overpriced at roughly €40, though tours last longer than those offered by on-site guides).

Services: A small building next to the museum sells coffee, juice, and basic snacks. Free WCs are in the museum.

Length of This Tour: Most visitors find that 1.5-2 hours on the island is plenty to wander the site and see the museum.

Delos Tour

To begin this self-guided tour, from the boat dock, walk to the entrance, buy your ticket, pick up the helpful included map, and enter the gate.

• *Pause and survey the site.*

Delos Overview: The commercial harbor was to your right, and the sacred harbor to your left. Ahead and to the right are the foundations of shops and homes that once constituted one of the Aegean's finest cities. Standing above those ruins is Mount Kynthos, its hillsides littered with temple remains. The Agora of the Competaliasts—one of the main squares in town—is straight ahead (with the museum building poking up behind). The religious area (with the temples of Apollo) is ahead and to the left, at the end of the Sacred Way. And far to the left was the Sacred Lake (now a patch of trees), overlooked by the iconic row of lions.

• *Start by wandering through the long rows of foundations on your right. You can circle back to these at the end—after summiting the mountain and winding down past the theater—but it's a good idea to poke around now in case you run out of steam later.*

Residential and Commercial District: Most of these re-

mains were either homes or shops. In the second century B.C. (when Delos was a bustling commercial port), the streets were lined with some 3,000 shops where you could buy just about anything, and the hillsides above were covered with the elaborate homes of wealthy merchants and shippers. Delos was considered to be the most important commercial center in the known world. (One of its major commodities was human beings—it was a major center in the ancient slave trade.) The city was cosmopolitan, with 30,000 residents and distinct ethnic groups, each with its own linguistic and cultural neighborhood (Greeks, Syrians, Beirutis, Italians, and so on). Remains of these same neighborhoods can still be seen today.

Poke into some of the **house foundations.** Homes were generally organized around a central courtyard, above a giant cistern. Look for fragments of elaborate mosaic floors (intact portions are on display inside the museum), as well as marble structures that once decorated the place. The city even had a surprisingly advanced sewer system. Because wood was rare on the arid Cycladic Islands, most buildings were constructed from dry-stone walls; wood was a status symbol, used only by the wealthiest to show off. Delos had some of the biggest homes of ancient Greece, not necessarily because of wealth, but because they could build big here without fear of the devastating earthquakes that plagued other locations. The Greeks attributed this to divine intervention (modern seismologists have found that Delos sits away from major fault lines).

• *Now head toward the agora that's near the ticket building. This is the...*

Agora of the Competaliasts: This was the main market square of the Roman merchants who worshipped the deities called *lares compitales,* who kept watch over the crossroads. This is not *the* agora, but one of many agoras (marketplaces) on Delos—a reminder that several different communities coexisted in this worldly trading city.

• *Just above the upper-left corner of this agora, the Sacred Way leads off to the left. Follow the same path ancient pilgrims walked as they approached the temples of Apollo. Along the left side of the road runs the long ledge of the pediment (with recognizable triglyphs) from the* **Stoa of Philip V** *(what we see here as the "bottom" actually ran along the top of the building). At the end of the Sacred Way is the...*

Religious Center: The **Sanctuary of Apollo** and, beyond

The Rise and Fall of Delos

Delos enters history 3,000 years ago as a sacred place where a number of gods were worshipped. Blessed with a prime location (midway between the mainland of Greece and Asia Minor—today's Turkey—and in the center of the Greek islands), but cursed with no natural resources, the barren island survived as a religious destination for pilgrims bringing offerings to the gods.

According to myth, the philandering Zeus impregnated the mortal Leto. Zeus' furious wife, Hera, banished Leto from the earth, but Zeus implored his brother Poseidon to create a refuge for her by raising up the underwater world of "Invisible" (Greek: *Adelos*) to create an island that was "Visible" *(Delos)*. Here Leto gave birth to twins—Apollo (god of the sun) and Artemis (goddess of the moon). Their human followers built temples in their honor (ninth century B.C.), and pilgrims flocked here with offerings.

As Athens began to assert control over the Aegean (sixth century B.C., it made sure that spiritually influential Delos stayed politically neutral. The Athenians ordered a "catharsis" (purification) of the island, removing bodies from the cemeteries. Later, they also decreed that no one could be born or die there—that is, there were to be no permanent residents. The Delians were relocated to an adjacent, larger island called Rinia. Ostensibly, this was to keep Delos pure for the gods, but in reality it removed any danger of rivals influencing the island's native population.

Because of its neutral status and central location, Delos was chosen in 478 B.C. as the natural meeting place for the powerful Delian League—an alliance of Greek city-states formed to battle the Persians and to promote trade. The combined wealth of the league was stored here in the fabulously rich bank of Delos. But all that changed in 454 B.C., when Pericles moved the treasury to Athens, and Delos reverted to being a pilgrimage site.

Centuries later, under the Romans, Delos' course changed dramatically once more. Thanks to its strategic location, the island was granted the right to operate as a free port (167 B.C.). Almost overnight, it became one of the biggest shipping centers in the known world, complete with a town of 30,000 inhabitants.

Then, in 88 B.C., soldiers from the Kingdom of Pontus, an enemy of Rome, attacked and looted the town, slaughtering 20,000 of its citizens. Delos never really recovered. Plagued by pirate attacks and shifting trade routes, Delos faded into history. Its once-great buildings were left to decay and waste away. In 1872, French archaeologists arrived (so far, scientists have excavated about one-fifth of the site), and Delos' cultural treasures were revealed to the modern world.

that, the **Sanctuary of Artemis,** both consisted of several temples and other ceremonial buildings. Unfortunately, these once-great buildings are in near-total ruin. In its day, Apollo's sanctuary had three large, stern Doric temples lined with columns. The biggest temple was nearly 100 feet long. The nearby Porinos Naos served as the treasury of the Delian League. Other treasuries once held untold riches—offerings to the gods brought by devout pilgrims.

• *Follow the route to the right, then left, then left again around the Sanctuary of Apollo. Before heading off to the right down the main path, pause to find the giant marble pedestal that once held the...*

Colossus Apollo Statue: The 35-foot statue (seventh century B.C.) was a gift from the Naxians and was carved from a single block of marble. It's long gone now, but a few bits of its fingers are on display in the museum.

• *A little way down the path, beyond the Sanctuary, pass the foundations that surround the spacious **Agora of the Italians** (on the right) on the way to the former...*

Sacred Lake: This was supposedly the source of Zeus' seed. When Leto was about to give birth to Zeus' children (according to the "Hymn to Delian Apollo," attributed to Homer), she cried out: "Delos, if you would be willing to be the abode of my son Apollo and make him a rich temple, your people will be well-fed by strangers bringing offerings. For truly your own soil is not rich." The Sacred Lake was drained by French archaeologists to prevent the spread of bacterial disease.

• *Overlooking the lake are the famous...*

Lions of the Naxians: This row of seven sphinx-like lion statues (originally there were 12) is the main, iconic image of this

site. These are replicas, but five of the original statues (seventh century B.C.) are in the museum. One of the originals was stolen by the Venetians, "repaired" with an awkwardly too-big head, and still stands in front of Venice's Arsenal building.

• *Walk through the oval-shaped Sacred Lakebed and hike up toward the museum. Just before the museum, a path detours to the left far into the distance, where you could detour to find the remains of the gymnasium, stadium, and the Jewish synagogue. Olympics-style games were held at Delos' **stadium** every five years. Like the more famous games at Olympia and Delphi, these were essentially religious festivals to the gods, particularly Dionysus. Pilgrims from across the Greek world gathered to celebrate with sports, song contests, theatrical performances, and general merrymaking.*

Make your way to the...

What If I Miss My Boat?

If your ship leaves Mykonos without you, remember that you can get help from the cruise line's port agent (listed on the destination information sheet distributed on the ship). If the port agent suggests a costly solution, you may want to consider public transit instead.

Mykonos has daily flights and ferries to **Athens.** Thanks to its worldwide popularity as a vacation spot, there are flights to many other European cities as well. Mykonos' small airport sits just two miles outside of town, easily connected by a short taxi ride and served by Olympic Air (www.olympicair.com) and Aegean Air (www.aegeanair.com).

Catamarans and ferries run to **Piraeus** (Athens' port); there is likely one fast boat daily, but confirm locally (Hellenic Seaways, tel. 210-419-9000, www.hsw.gr; or Aegean Speed Lines, tel. 210-969-0950, www.aegeanspeedlines.gr). Regular, slower boats (Blue Star Ferries, tel. 210-891-9800, www.bluestarferries.com; or Hellenic Seaways) leave from the New Port, about a mile north of town. If you need to get to another island, try the *Flying Cat* catamaran, which leaves from the Old Port and heads for **Paros, Ios, Santorini,** and **Crete** (operated by Hellenic Seaways, listed above).

Local **travel agents** can also be helpful—there are plenty in Mykonos. For more advice on what to do if you miss the boat, see page 140.

Museum: This scantily described collection includes statuary, vases, and other items. Inside the door is a model of the site in its

heyday. Most of the site's best pieces are in the National Archaeological Museum in Athens, but a few highlights remain, including a beautifully carved stone table, five of the original Lions of the Naxians (in a room of their own), the fingers of Colossus Apollo (in the central hall, on the right), and—perhaps the best part—several bits of striking floor mosaics.

For more body parts of other gods, exit the museum straight out, then go left to the **Monument of Carystius** (once part of the Sanctuary of Dionysus), with its large (broken-off) penis-on-a-pillar statues.

• *If you have time before the boat leaves (allow about 45 minutes), hike up the hill toward more remains of houses and temples. Hardy travelers can huff all the way up to...*

Mount Kynthos: At 370 feet, the island's highest point feels even taller on a hot day. To ancient Greeks, this conical peak looked like the spot from which Poseidon had pulled this mysterious isle up from the deep. Up here are the remains of the **Temple of Zeus and Athena.** As you observe the chain of islands dramatically swirling around Delos, you can understand why most experts believe that the Cycladic Islands got their name from the way they circle (or cycle around) this oh-so-important islet.

• *Head back downhill, toward the theater and harbor. On your way down you'll pass the* **House of the Dolphins,** *with mosaics of cupids riding dolphins, and the* **House of the Masks,** *with a beautiful mosaic of a tambourine-playing Dionysus riding a leopard. As you return to the boat, you'll see the remains of a giant* **cistern** *and the 5,500-seat* **theater***...starring a 360-degree view of the Cycladic Islands.*

MYKONOS

Greek Survival Phrases

Knowing a few phrases of Greek can help if you're traveling off the beaten path. Just learning the pleasantries (such as please and thank you) will improve your connections with locals, even in the bigger cities.

Because Greek words can be transliterated differently in English, I've also included the Greek spellings. Note that in Greek, a semicolon is used the same way we use a question mark.

English	Greek	Pronunciation
Hello. (formal)	Gia sas. / Γειά σας.	yah sahs
Hi. / Bye. (informal)	Gia. / Γειά.	yah
Good morning.	Kali mera. / Καλή μέρα.	kah-lee meh-rah
Good afternoon.	Kali spera. / Καλή σπέρα.	kah-lee speh-rah
Do you speak English?	Milate anglika? / Μιλάτε αγγλικά;	mee-lah-teh ahn-glee-kah
Yes. / No.	Ne. / Ohi. / Ναι. / Όχι.	neh / oh-hee
I (don't) understand.	(Den) katalaveno. / (Δεν) καταλαβαίνω.	(dehn) kah-tah-lah-veh-noh
Please. (Also: You're welcome.)	Parakalo. / Παρακαλώ.	pah-rah-kah-loh
Thank you (very much).	Efharisto (poli). / Ευχαριστώ (πολύ).	ehf-hah-ree-stoh (poh-lee)
Excuse me. (Also: I'm sorry.)	Sygnomi. / Συγνώμη.	seeg-noh-mee
(No) problem.	(Kanena) problima. / (Κανένα) πρόβλημα.	(kah-neh-nah) prohv-lee-mah
Good.	Orea. / Ωραία.	oh-reh-ah
Goodbye.	Antio. / Αντίο.	ahd-yoh (think "adieu")
Good night.	Kali nikta. / Καλή νύχτα.	kah-lee neek-tah
one / two	ena / dio / ένα / δύο	eh-nah / dee-oh
three / four	tria / tessera / τρία / τέσσερα	tree-ah / teh-seh-rah
five / six	pente / exi / πέντε / έξι	pehn-deh / ehk-see
seven / eight	efta / ohto / εφτά / οχτώ	ehf-tah / oh-toh
nine / ten	ennia / deka / εννιά / δέκα	ehn-yah / deh-kah
hundred / thousand	ekato / hilia / εκατό / χίλια	eh-kah-toh / heel-yah
How much?	Poso kani? / Πόσο κάνει;	poh-soh kah-nee
euro	evro / ευρώ	ev-roh
toilet	toualeta / τουαλέτα	twah-leh-tah
men / women	andres / gynekes / άντρες / γυναίκες	ahn-drehs / yee-neh-kehs

In a Greek Restaurant

MYKONOS

English	Greek	Pronunciation
The menu (in English), please.	Ton katalogo (sta anglika) parakalo. Τον κατάλογο (στα αγγλικά) παρακαλώ.	tohn kah-**tah**-loh-goh (stah ahn-glee-**kah**) pah-rah-kah-**loh**
service (not) included	to servis (den) perilamvanete το σέρβις (δεν) περιλαμβάνεται	toh **sehr**-vees (dehn) peh-ree-lahm-**vah**-neh-teh
appetizers	proto piato πρώτο πιάτο	**proh**-toh pee-**ah**-toh
bread	psomi ψωμί	psoh-**mee**
cheese	tiri τυρί	tee-**ree**
sandwich	sandwich or toast σάντουιτς, τόστ	"sandwich," "toast"
soup	soupa σούπα	**soo**-pah
salad	salata σαλάτα	sah-**lah**-tah
meat	kreas κρέας	**kray**-ahs
poultry / chicken	poulerika / kotopoulo πουλερικα / κοτόπουλο	poo-leh-ree-**kah** / koh-**toh**-poo-loh
fish / seafood	psari / psarika ψάρι / ψαρικά	**psah**-ree / psah-ree-**kah**
shellfish	thalassina θαλασσινά	thah-lah-see-**nah**
fruit	frouta φρούτα	**froo**-tah
vegetables	lahanika λαχανικά	lah-hah-nee-**kah**
dessert	gliko γλυκό	lee-**koh**
(tap) water	nero (tis vrisis) νερο (της βρύσης)	neh-**roh** (tees **vree**-sees)
coffee	kafes καφές	kah-**fehs**
tea	tsai τσάι	**chah**-ee
wine	krasi κρασί	krah-**see**
beer	bira μπύρα	**bee**-rah
(To your) health! (like "Cheers!")	(Stin i) gia mas! (Στην υ) γειά μας!	(stee nee) yah mahs
Bill, please.	Ton logariasmo parakalo. Τον λογαριασμό παρακαλώ.	tohn loh-gah-ree-ahs-**moh** pah-rah-kah-**loh**
tip	bourbouar μπουρμπουάρ	boor-boo-**ar**
Delicious!	Poli nostimo! Πολύ νόστιμο!	poh-**lee nohs**-tee-moh

SANTORINI
Greece

Greece Practicalities

Greece *(Hellas)* offers sunshine, seafood, 6,000 islands, whitewashed houses with bright-blue shutters, and a relaxed life-style. As the birthplace of Western civili-zation, it has some of the world's greatest ancient monuments. We have the Greeks to thank for the Olympics; the tall tales of Achilles and Odysseus; the rational phi-losophies of Socrates, Plato, and Aristo-tle; democracy, theater, mathematics...and the gyro sandwich.

As a late bloomer in the modern age, Greece retains echoes of a simpler, time-passed world. On the islands, you'll still see men on donkeys and women at the well. Greeks pride themselves on a concept called *filotimo* ("love of honor"), roughly translated as openness, friendliness, and hospitality. It's easy to surrender to the Greek way of living.

Money: Greece uses the euro currency: 1 euro (€) = about $1.30. An ATM, handily, is labeled *ATM* in the Greek alphabet. The local VAT (value-added sales tax) rate is 23 percent; the minimum purchase eligible for a VAT refund is €120 (for de-tails on refunds, see page 135).

Language: For helpful Greek phrases, see page 1025.

Emergencies: Dial 100 for police or 171 for English-speaking tourist police; for medical or other emergencies, dial 176 or 199.

Time Zone: Greece is on Eastern European Time (an hour ahead of Italy and seven/ten hours ahead of the East/West Coasts of the US).

Theft Alert: In Athens and any place with crowds, be wary of purse snatchers and pickpockets. For tips on outsmarting thieves, see page 128.

Consular Services in Athens: The US embassy is at Vassilissis Sofias 91 (tel. 210-720-2414, http://athens.usembassy.gov). The Canadian embassy is at Ioannou Ghennadiou 4 (tel. 210-727-3400, www.greece.gc.ca). Call ahead for passport services.

Phoning: Greece has a direct-dial phone system (no area codes). To **call within Greece,** just dial the number. To **call to Greece,** dial the international access code (00 if calling from Europe, or 011 from North America), then 30 (Greece's country code), then the phone number. To **call home from Greece,** dial 00, 1, then your area code and phone number.

Tipping: If you order your food at a counter, don't tip. At sit-down restaurants, service is generally included, although it's common to round up the bill after a good meal, usually 5-10 percent. You'll also round up 5-10 percent to tip a cabbie (give €5 to pay a €4.50 fare).

Tourist Information: www.visitgreece.gr

SANTORINI

ΣΑΝΤΟΡ'ΙΝΗ / Σαντορίνη *a.k.a. Thira* (ΘΗΡΑ / Θηρα)

Santorini is one of the Mediterranean's most dramatic islands: a flooded caldera (a collapsed volcanic crater) with a long, steep, multicolored arc of cliffs, thrusting up a thousand feet above sea level. Sometimes called "The Devil's Isle," this unique place has captured visitors' imaginations for millennia and might have inspired the tales of Atlantis. And the otherworldly appeal of Santorini (sahn-toh-REE-nee) doesn't end with its setting. Perched along the ridgeline is a gaggle of perfectly placed whitewashed villages, punctuated with azure domes, that make this, undeniably, one of Greece's most scenic spots.

The island's main town, Fira (Φηρα, FEE-rah)—with Santorini's handiest services and best museum—is both functional and scenic. While Fira is dramatic, the town of Oia (Οια, EE-ah), on the northern tip of the island, with its chalk-white houses and vivid domes, is even more so—it's the place you imagine when you think "Santorini." Strolling through Oia is like spinning a postcard rack—it's tempting to see the town entirely through your camera's viewfinder.

Not surprisingly, Santorini is hugely popular and can be very crowded—and expensive—in high season (roughly July through mid-September, peaking in the first half of August). Tourism—virtually the only surviving industry here—has made the island wealthy. It's one of the few places in Greece where the population isn't aging (as young people don't have to move away to find satisfying work). Fortunately, it's not difficult to break away from the main tourist rut and discover some scenic lanes of your own. In both Fira and Oia, the cliffside streets are strewn with countless

Santorini Island

Excursion/Shuttle Boat ······
Roads ——
Trail - - - -
Beaches ♀

To Mykonos & Piraeus

Oia
Finikia
Riva
THIRASSIA
Manalos
Imerovigli
Firostefani
CABLE CAR
NEA KAMENI
Fira
Aegean Sea
Monolithos
Hot Springs
Old Port
SEA DIAMOND SHIPWRECK
PALEA KAMENI
Athinios (New Port)
AIRPORT
Pirgos
Kamari
Akrotiri Town
ANCIENT THIRA
Emporio
Perissa
AKROTIRI RUINS

3 KM
2 Miles

To Crete

DCH

SANTORINI

cafés, all of them touting "sunset views"...the end of the day is a main attraction here.

For more tips on enjoying an authentic Greek island experience, see the sidebar on page 982.

Planning Your Time

Try to catch the sunset either from Oia (the ultimate) or Fira (nearly as enjoyable and memorable). Here are your top daytime options:

• Go to Oia for classic Santorini views. You can take a bus, taxi, or even a scenic five-mile hike to reach the town. Allow about 30 minutes each way to get there by bus or taxi; plan on at least another hour to stroll and snap photos.

• In Fira, visit the Museum of Prehistoric Thira (allow an hour) and explore town, especially the steep lanes below the Orthodox cathedral (allow an hour or more).

• Sun-worshippers head for the red- and black-sand beaches (accessible by bus or taxi). Allow a half-day to all day.

• Sail from the Old Port out to the middle of the caldera (various options are offered by local travel agencies). Allow a half-day to all day.

Excursions on Santorini

Remember, "Santorini" describes an archipelago of five islands. The official name of the main island is Thira, but travelers know it simply as Santorini. Most excursions are to the main island and feature multiple stops. The prettiest town is **Oia**—be sure your excursion makes a stop there. The main town, **Fira,** while not quite as picture-perfect, is also gorgeous and comes with the island's top museum (the excellent Museum of Prehistoric Thira, but skip the dull Archaeological Museum). Some excursions stop off at **Megalochori,** a traditional village that lacks the dramatic tumbling-down-a-cliff setting of the other two.

If your tour advertises a stop for **wine tasting,** it's likely at the Santo Winery just up the road from the New Port. Santo, a cooperative working with all the island's wineries, is the biggest such operation in the Cyclades. Established in 1947, it produces 500,000 bottles a year, 70 percent of which are consumed in Greece. Most tours stop for about 35 minutes—enough time for a very brief orientation from your guide and a chance to enjoy a few local nibbles and three different island wines. With several buses generally there at the same time, it can be a mob scene. Still, the wine and the views are enjoyable.

Other excursions can include various locations away from the main towns, including Santorini's red- and black-sand **beaches; archaeological sites** (such as Ancient Thira or Akrotiri); the panoramic mountain viewpoint at **Profitis Ilias;** and a countryside winery to learn more about Santorini's unique method of cultivating grapes. For something more volcanic, venture off the main island and head for the smaller, smoldering islets of **Nea Kameni** and **Palea Kameni,** including a dip in the natural hot-spring waters (local agencies sell similar, cheaper tours). Many of these places are described on page 1023.

Arrival in Santorini

Arrival at a Glance: Cruise ships generally anchor in the caldera below the town of Fira. Passengers taking excursions get the first tenders, which go to the New Port at Athinios, about five miles south of Fira (with bus and car access to the rest of the island). Independent day-trippers are then tendered to the Old Port directly below Fira (linked to town by foot, cable-car, or donkey ride).

Getting to the Sights

On Your Own from the Old Port

From the Old Port, there are three ways to reach Fira's town center on the cliff above: Take a cable car, hike up, or ride a donkey. The **cable car** is the easiest option (€4 each way, daily 7:00-21:00, every 20 minutes or more with demand, 3-minute ride to the top). But, because the cable car is small (maximum 36 people per trip), you might be in for a long wait if you arrive on a big ship. **Hiking** up the 587 steep steps is demanding, and you'll share them with fragrant, messy donkeys. You can pay €5 to ride up on a **donkey,** but the stench and the bumpy ride make this far less romantic than it sounds.

Once at the **top** (the cable car and donkey trail converge near the same point), you have several options for exploring the town: If you head straight up the stairs, you'll find (to the left) the Catholic cathedral and nearby folk museum, and (to the right) the less appealing of the town's two archaeological museums. If you turn right onto Gold Street (true to its name, lined with jewelry and tourist-trinket shops), you'll eventually reach the Orthodox cathedral, some recommended eateries, and Santorini's best museum (the Museum of Prehistoric Thira). Or, if you want to escape some of the crowds and browse the scenic veil of cafés that cascade down the cliff, turn downhill toward the water, go left down the stairs just past Kastro Café, turn off onto the road, and explore to your heart's content.

By Excursion from the New Port

From the New Port at Athinios, chartered buses wait to take you to your destination.

From the Athinios port, a serpentine road climbs up the hill. Visible from the road above Athinios, the ringed-off area in the bay just below the switchbacks is the site of the *Sea Diamond* shipwreck—a cruise ship that sank here in 2007; all but two of the 1,195 passengers were rescued. The ship rests in 450 feet of water. Concerned that it might slip deeper and that it's polluting the bay, islanders are hoping to pull it up.

After your excursion, the bus drops you off in Fira. Return tenders leave from the Old Port below.

Returning to Your Ship

At the end of the day, whether you take a bus tour or go on your own, you'll likely find yourself in Fira and will need to get down to the Old Port. From the town, the Old Port is a 20- to 30-minute zigzag downhill walk—hot and stinky by day, poorly lit and dangerous with hidden donkey pies by night. The only way to avoid the smelly path is to ride the cable car, but lines can be long at peak times.

The Old Port is just a concrete pier, but several sleepy tavernas and restaurants add charm, making it a peaceful little spot to kill time before reboarding your tender for the ship.

Orientation to Santorini

The five islands that make up the Santorini archipelago are known to Greeks as Thira (Θηρα, THEE-rah). Most of the settlement is on the 15-mile-long main island, also called Thira. But most travelers call it Santorini (a Venetian bastardization of "Santa Irene," after a local church), and I do too. The west side of Santorini is a sheer drop-off (into the mouth of the former volcano), while the east side tapers more gradually to the water (the former volcano's base).

The primary tourist towns are on the steep, western side of Santorini: The town of Fira is the island's capital and transportation hub, but the main attraction is Oia, a village six miles to the northwest. The relatively level eastern and southern areas have the ancient sites and the best beaches.

Getting Around Santorini

By Bus: Fira is the bus hub for the island. The bus station is a block off the main road, near the south end of town (just downhill from the Orthodox cathedral and Museum of Prehistoric Thira). Buy tickets on the bus and get information at the kiosk at the far end of the lot. In peak season, buses can be extremely crowded.

The most popular destinations from Fira by bus are: **Oia** (2/hour—generally departs at top and bottom of each hour, 25 minutes, €1.60), **Athinios** and the **New Port** (5-7/day, coordinated to meet boats, 20 minutes, €2.20), **Kamari** and its nearby beaches (2/hour, 10 minutes, €1.60), **Akrotiri** with its red-sand beaches and archaeological site (nearly hourly, 30 minutes, €1.80), **Perissa** with its black-sand beaches and access to the Ancient Thira archaeological site (hourly, 30 minutes, €2.20), and the **airport** (roughly every 2 hours, 15 minutes, €1.60). Bus information: tel. 22860-25462, www.ktel-santorini.gr.

By Taxi: Just around the corner from Fira's bus station, along

When Santorini Blew Its Top

Coming to Santorini—by boat or by plane—your eyes can't help but trace the telltale arc of the island, a sure sign that you're about to set foot on what was once a volatile volcano.

Situated atop an edgy stack of tectonic plates, Santorini was created by volcanic activity that lasted more than two million years. The island once had a tidy conical shape, but around 1630 B.C., it exploded in what geologists call the "Minoan eruption"—one of the largest in human history. It blew out 24 cubic miles of volcanic material—at least four times the amount ejected by the huge 1883 explosion of Krakatoa (in today's Indonesia).

It appears that the volcano gave Santorini's inhabitants ample warning before erupting (with a major earthquake and, later, an initial small eruption).

No human skeletons and few valuable items from that time period have been found here, suggesting that islanders had time to pack up and evacuate. Good thing. Soon afterward, large amounts of ash and pumice blasted out of the crater, and superheated pyroclastic flows (à la Mount St. Helens) swept down the island's slopes. Eventually, the emptied-out volcano collapsed under its own weight, forming the flooded caldera (meaning "cauldron") that we see today.

The volcano's collapse displaced enough seawater to send a huge tsunami screaming south toward Crete, less than 70 miles away. Archaeologists speculate that the tsunami (and perhaps

the main road, is a taxi stand (figure €15-20 to Oia, €15 to Athinios port, €15 to Kamari's beaches, €18-20 to Akrotiri, and €18 to Perissa). You can also call for a taxi (tel. 22860-22555 or 22860-23951).

Fira

The island's main town, Fira, is a practical transit hub with an extraordinary setting. Sitting at a cliff-clinging café terrace and sipping an iced coffee gives you the chance to watch thousands of cruise-ship passengers flood into town each morning (on the cable-car and donkey trail), then recede in the afternoon. All of this built-in business has made Fira a bit greedy; its so-called Gold Street, starting at the cable-car station, is lined with aggressive

earthquakes near the same time) caused severe hardship, eventually leading to the downfall of the Minoan civilization.

The volcano isn't done yet. Two little islets in the middle of the caldera emerged from the bay quite recently (by geological standards)—Palea Kameni ("Old Burnt Island") in 197 B.C., and Nea Kameni ("New Burnt Island") in A.D. 1707. To this day, these islets go through periods where they sputter and steam, and earthquakes continue to wrack the entire archipelago (including a devastating one in 1956). The last small eruption (on Nea Kameni) occurred in 1950, and steam and sulfur dioxide are sometimes emitted at the current active crater. Today, the hot springs on Palea Kameni are a popular tourist attraction.

Although the historic eruption devastated the island, it also created its remarkable shape and left behind a unique ecosystem and agricultural tradition. The volcanic soil was also the basis for a local industry. The upper layer of pumice and volcanic ash left by the eruption was quarried, pulverized, and mixed with lime to create a remarkably strong concrete (produced, until recently, in the big, deserted, blocky building on the cliff near Fira—visible from the bay below). Santorini is the country's sole source of this type of material.

Strolling on scenic, seismic Santorini, you're on special ground... carved out more than four millennia ago by one very big bang.

jewelry salespeople and restaurants with great views, high prices, and low quality.

But if you can ignore the tackiness in this part of town, you'll discover that Fira has a charm of its own—particularly in the cozy labyrinth of streets that burrow between its main traffic street and the cliff edge, and on the steeply switchbacked lanes that zigzag down the side of the cliff. Fira also has a pair of cathedrals (Orthodox and Catholic), the island's top museum (the excellent Museum of Prehistoric Thira), and a handy array of services (Internet cafés, launderettes, and so on).

Remember that Fira is not the setting of all those famous Santorini photos—those are taken in Oia.

Orientation to Fira

The core of Fira is squeezed between the cliff and the main road through town, called 25 Martou. This street—with a taxi stand, TI kiosk (sometimes open), various scooter/ATV/car-rental places, Internet cafés, and other services—is busy and fairly dingy. The bus station is a block off this drag (around the corner from the TI and taxi stand). Most places of interest to visitors are in the cluster of narrow streets between the bus station (along the main road near the south end of town) and the cable-car station (along the cliff near the north end of town)—a distance you can easily cover in about a 10-minute walk.

Even where street names exist, locals completely ignore them. Making navigation even more confusing, it's a very vertical town—especially along the cliff. Use a map, and don't be afraid to ask for directions.

Tourist Information

Fira has the island's **TI kiosk,** but hours are sporadic and it's often closed (along the main road, about 50 yards toward the town center from the bus station). If it's not open, try asking at local travel agencies or other businesses for help.

Sights in Fira

▲▲Museum of Prehistoric Thira

While no competition for Greece's top archaeological museums, this little one is Santorini's best, presenting items found in the prehistoric city buried under ash near Akrotiri. (A visit is particularly worthwhile if you plan to see the excavated ruins of that city, at the southern end of the island—see page 1022.) That settlement was the largest city outside Crete in the Minoan-era world, dating back to the earliest documented civilization in the Aegean (third to second millennium B.C.)—impossibly ancient, even to the ancients. The people who lived here fled soon before Santorini blew its top (likely around 1630 B.C.—see sidebar), leaving behind intriguing artifacts of a civilization that disappeared from the earth not long after. Most of those artifacts have been moved off-site, either to this museum or to the biggies in Athens. Everything in this manageable museum is described in English and well-presented in modern, air-conditioned comfort.

Cost and Hours: €3, Tue-Sun 9:00-16:00, closed Mon, tel. 22860-23217, www.culture.gr.

Visiting the Museum: The **model** of the Akrotiri site in Room D puts the items in context. From here, follow the letters coun-

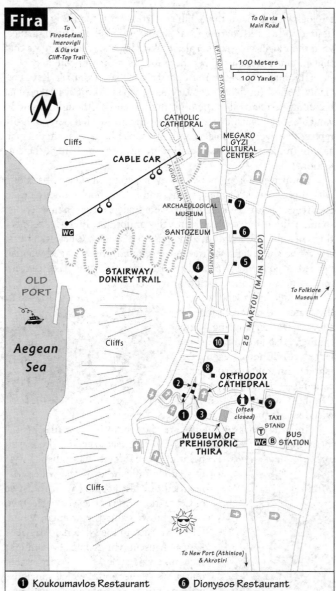

Fira

To Firostefani, Imerovigli & Oia via Cliff-Top Trail

To Oia via Main Road

EFTROU STAVROU

100 Meters
100 Yards

CATHOLIC CATHEDRAL

MEGARO GYZI CULTURAL CENTER

CABLE CAR

AGIOU MINA

WC

ARCHAEOLOGICAL MUSEUM

SANTOZEUM

❼

❻

STAIRWAY/ DONKEY TRAIL

IPAPANTIS

❹

❺

Cliffs

OLD PORT

To Folklore Museum

Aegean Sea

Cliffs

25 MARTIOU (MAIN ROAD)

❿

❽

ORTHODOX CATHEDRAL

❷

❶   ❸

❶
(often closed)

❾

TAXI STAND

MUSEUM OF PREHISTORIC THIRA

WC   BUS STATION

Cliffs

To New Port (Athinios) & Akrotiri

❶ Koukoumavlos Restaurant
❷ Archipelagos Restaurant
❸ Sphinx Restaurant
❹ Argo Restaurant
❺ Nikolas Restaurant
❻ Dionysos Restaurant
❼ Naoussa Restaurant
❽ The Ouzerie
❾ Mama's House Restaurant
❿ Obelix Souvlaki

terclockwise through the exhibit, starting with the Early Cycladic figures and vessels, dating from 2700-2300 B.C. The stiff figurines, with their arms crossed, perplex archaeologists, who speculate that they might represent the Mother Goddess worshipped here.

The majority of the museum's pieces date from the Late Cycladic Period (mid-17th century B.C.), when Akrotiri peaked just before its residents fled the erupting volcano. Although they took valuable items (such as jewelry) with them, they left behind easily replaceable everyday objects and, of course, immovable items such as wall frescoes. These **left-behind items** form the core of the collection.

Primitive cooking pots, clay ovens, and barbecue grills, along with bronze vases, daggers, tongs, and fishing hooks, offer clues to the Aegean lifestyle. The Thirans were traders rather than warriors, so many items reflect their relatively comfortable lifestyle, connection with the wider world, and consumer society. One plaster cast shows the shape left by a (now-deteriorated) three-legged wooden table that could have passed for Baroque from the 17th century A.D.—but it's from the 17th century B.C.

The stack of metal weights illustrates the evolution of standardization during early trading. Also look for the **three large containers,** each one marked differently to suggest its contents—for example, a vessel that held water was decorated with reeds (aquatic plants).

The museum's highlights are the vibrantly colorful, two-dimensional **wall frescoes.** Local artists likely executed these wall

paintings, but their naturalistic style was surely influenced by the wider Minoan culture. In keeping with the style of Crete (the home of the Minoans), men appear brown, and the women, white. (If you've been to the National Archaeological Museum in Athens, you might recognize this style of fresco from that museum's collection, which includes wall paintings of antelopes, swallows, and young men boxing, all from this same Akrotiri site.) The wall frescoes from the House of the Ladies show exquisitely dressed women. In one, an older woman leans over and appears to be touching the arm of another (now-missing) woman and holding a dress in her right hand. Farther along you'll see a fragment of another wall fresco showing blue monkeys. Because monkeys are not indigenous to Greece, these images offer more evidence that the Cycladic and Minoan people traveled far and wide, and interacted with exotic cultures.

Between these frescoes, the **vessels** (such as beautiful vases decorated with dolphins and lilies) give us a glimpse of everyday life back then. Look for the ritual vessel shaped like a boar's head.

In the final display case (near the exit) is an exquisite miniature **golden ibex**—one of the few items of great value that was left behind by fleeing islanders.

▲▲▲Sunset from Fira

While Oia is more famous for its sunsets, Fira's are nothing to sneeze at. If you're on Santorini for just one sunset, ask around about where viewing is best. Or, scout out a bar or restaurant during the day so you'll know where you want to sit well before the magic hour.

Orthodox Cathedral of Candelmas (Panagia Ypapantis)

This modern cathedral, which caps Fira like a white crown, has a grandly painted interior that's worth a look. The cliff-hanging lanes just in front are some of Fira's most enjoyable (and least crowded) to explore.

Archaeological Museum

This museum pales in comparison to the Museum of Prehistoric Thira. Its dusty cases are crammed with sparsely described jugs, statues, and other artifacts from ancient Thira (in contrast to the older Minoan pieces from Akrotiri). Skip it unless you're an archaeologist.

Cost and Hours: €3, Tue-Sun 9:00-16:00, closed Mon, just up the street from the top cable-car station.

Catholic Cathedral

Directly up the stairs from the top cable-car station, this cathedral is the heart of the island's Catholic community—a remnant of the island's past Venetian rule. Compare this rare Catholic cathedral with the giant Orthodox cathedral at the other end of town: Inside this one are pews, few wall paintings, and none of the tall, skinny candles that are a main-

stay of Orthodox worship. Next door is a Dominican monastery and church.

Megaro Gyzi Cultural Center

Hiding in the alleys behind the Catholic cathedral, this modest but endearing local history museum celebrates Santorini life. You'll see photographs of the town from the early to mid–20th century (including scenes before and after the devastating 1956 earthquake), an archive of historic manuscripts and documents, modern paintings of Santorini, and samples of the various types of volcanic rock found on the island. Find the 1870 clipping from a London newspaper article about "Santorin," and, next to it, an engraving of a smoldering islet in the caldera. Linger over the evocative etchings of traditional Santorini lifestyles.

Cost and Hours: €3, May-Oct Mon-Sat 10:00-16:00, closed Sun and Nov-April, tel. 22860-23077, www.megarogyzi.gr.

Santozeum

For a one-stop look at all the most remarkable frescoes excavated at the ancient city near Akrotiri, you could duck into this pleas-antly modern facility...but what it holds is a made-for-tour-groups collection consisting entirely of replicas. If you're already visiting the original versions of these frescoes at the Museum of Prehistoric Thira (5 minutes away) and the National Archaeological Museum in Athens, this collection is a bit pointless.

Cost and Hours: €5, May-Oct daily 10:00-18:00, closed Nov-April, on Gold Street near the cable-car station—look for bright orange lettering, tel. 22860-21722.

Folklore Museum of Santorini

With bits and pieces left over from a bygone era, this museum gives visitors a small sense of how Santorini sustained itself before tourism. See a restored 19th-century cave house, exhibits on winemaking and other traditional crafts, and a small chapel. It's probably not worth the long walk.

Cost and Hours: €3, April-Oct daily 10:00-14:00, closed Nov-March, tel. 22860-22792. It's a 10- to 15-minute walk from the center of Fira, on the northern (Oia) end of town: Find the street one block east of 25 Martou and follow it past several ATV/scooter rental outfits and a launderette or two; after Hotel Horizon, the road bends left—follow it for a few more minutes until you see the *MUSEUM* sign on the right.

Hike to Oia

With a few hours to spare, you can venture out on one of Greece's most scenic hikes. While the main road connecting Fira to Oia

SANTORINI

is drab and dusty, a wonderful cliff-top trail links the two towns, offering fantastic views most of the way. From Fira, head north through the adjoining villages of Firostefani and Imerovigli, then continue along the lip of the crater all the way to Oia. It's long (about 5 miles, plan on at least 3.5 hours one-way), fairly strenuous (with lots of ups and downs), and offers little or no shade in hot weather, so don't attempt it unless you're in good shape and have the right gear (good shoes, water, food, sun protection). Get an early start. You can catch a bus or taxi back to Fira when you're done.

Eating in Fira

SANTORINI

You have three choices: expensive with a view overlooking the caldera, much cheaper at a more typical Greek taverna, or just grabbing a souvlaki to eat on a stool or to go. In general, places that are closest to the cable car lure in cruise passengers with great views, but—because they know cruisers are only in town for a few hours—have little incentive to put out good food. Natives and lingering travelers do better by dining at the places a 5- to 10-minute walk farther from the cable car. For general tips on eating in Greece, see page 965.

With a Caldera View

The streets just under the Orthodox cathedral (the gigantic white-domed building at the south end of town) are lined with several expensive, trendy eateries with good food...you're paying a premium for the high-rent location (€10-15 starters, €20-30 main dishes, all open long hours daily in summer, most close off-season). **Koukoumavlos** is particularly well-regarded (tel. 22860-23807); **Archipelagos** specializes in Greek standards and pasta (tel. 22860-23673); and **Sphinx** has a broader Mediterranean menu that includes a fair bit of Italian (tel. 22860-23823). The steep streets below these restaurants are filled mostly with hotels, but many turn their breakfast terraces into cafés; exploring this area to find your favorite perch for a cup of coffee is a fun activity (I particularly like the Art Café at the Cori Rigas).

Argo, which serves traditional Greek food specializing in fish, is also along the cliffs but a bit closer to the cable car. Reserve ahead for the upper deck, with the best caldera views (€4-12 starters, €10-18 main dishes, open long hours daily, along the donkey path just below Gold Street, tel. 22860-22594).

In the Old Town

Deeper in the Old Town is a pedestrian street lined with several good choices (all open long hours daily). Like most Fira streets, it's nameless, located one block toward the cliff from the main road, a block north of the main square. Along here the following three choices are most enticing: **Nikolas** oozes a family-run taverna vibe, with one big room crammed with tables overseen by the namesake patriarch; the menu consists of stick-to-your-ribs Greek classics (€3-5 starters, €7-14 main dishes, tel. 22860-24550). **Dionysos** has nice energy out on its vast terrace (€4-8 starters, €7-20 main dishes, daily 12:00-23:00, tel. 22860-23845). **Naoussa** is a family-friendly place churning out big plates of sloppy Greek food (€4-9 starters, €8-15 main dishes, tel. 22860-24869).

The Ouzerie (Το Ουζερι) offers sea views from its outside tables, albeit ones looking east, rather than into the caldera. That means it doesn't work well at sunset (unless you're trying to avoid the crowds), but it's great for lunch or after dark. Try some of their local specialties, such as meatballs in an ouzo sauce (€8) and the *tomatokeftedes* starter—fried tomatoes with onions and herbs (€5-7 starters, €7-15 main dishes, daily 11:00-late, near Orthodox cathedral, tel. 22860-21566).

Mama's House, set a few steps down from the main road next to the taxi stand, is a good budget choice with unpretentious Greek fare (€3-7 starters, €8-12 main dishes, daily 8:00-24:00, shorter hours off-season, tel. 22860-21577).

Souvlaki places dot the streets on the eastern ridge of Fira. Of these, locals like **Lucky's** for its quality and **Obelix** for its sizeable menu and long hours.

Oia

Oia (remember, it's EE-ah, not OY-ah; sometimes spelled "Ia" in English) is the classic, too-pretty-to-be-true place you imagine when someone says "Greek  islands." This idyllic ensemble of whitewashed houses and blue domes is delicately draped over a steep slope at the top of a cliff. And in their wisdom, the locals have positioned their town just right for enjoying a sunset over the caldera. On a blue-sky day or at sunset, there's no better place in Greece to go on a photo safari. In fact, if you can't snap a postcard-quality photo here, it's time to retire your camera.

Oia wasn't always this alluring. In fact, half a century ago it was in ruins—devastated by an earthquake on July 9, 1956. When rebuilding, natives seized the opportunity to make their town even more picture-perfect than before—and it paid off. Though far from undiscovered, Oia is the kind of place that you don't mind sharing with boatloads of tourists. And if you break away from its main streets, you can find narrow, winding lanes that take you far from the crowds.

Getting There

To reach Oia from the island's transport hub at Fira, you'll have to take the bus (2/hour, generally departs Fira at top and bottom of each hour, 25 minutes, €1.60) or a taxi (€15-20 one-way).

Orientation to Oia

Oia lines up along its cliff. The main pedestrian drag, which traces the rim of the cliff, is called Nikolaou Nomikou. Oia's steep seaward side is smothered with accommodations and restaurants, while the flat landward side is more functional. The town is effectively traffic-free except for the main road, which sneaks up on Oia from behind, opening onto a parking lot and the town's bus stop. From here, just walk a few short, nondescript blocks toward the cliff and its million-dollar views. Cruise excursions give you nearly an hour here...which seemed like enough for me.

Sights in Oia

▲▲▲Oia Photo Safari

The main sight here is the town itself, and the best advice is to just get lost with your camera ready. Shoot the classic, blue-domed postcard views, but also wander around to find your own angle on the town. At the far tip of Oia, venture down, then up, to reach the old turret-like viewpoint, facing the windmills on the horizon and affording you a breathtaking 360-degree view.

Why all the whitewash? For one thing, white reflects (rather than absorbs) the powerful heat of the sun. White is the color

of lime—the mineral, not the fruit—mixed with water, which makes a good antiseptic (islanders used it to paint their houses, so it would naturally disinfect the rainwater that was collected on rooftops). Later, white evolved into an aesthetic choice...and a patriotic one: During the 400-year Ottoman occupation, Greeks were not allowed to fly their blue-and-white flag. But here in Oia—with its white houses, blue

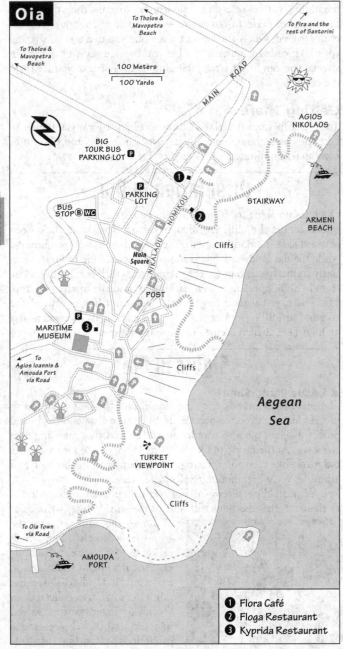

Oia

SANTORINI

To Tholos &
Mavopetra
Beach

To Fira and the
rest of Santorini

To Tholos &
Mavopetra
Beach

100 Meters

100 Yards

MAIN ROAD

AGIOS
NIKOLAOS

BIG
TOUR BUS
PARKING LOT P

PARKING
LOT P

STAIRWAY

BUS
STOP B WC

ARMENI
BEACH

Cliffs

Main
Square

NIKALAOU

NOMIXOU

POST

P

MARITIME
MUSEUM

❸

To
Agios Ioannis &
Amouda Port
via Road

Cliffs

Aegean
Sea

TURRET
VIEWPOINT

Cliffs

To Oia Town
via Road

AMOUDA
PORT

❶ Flora Café
❷ Floga Restaurant
❸ Kyprida Restaurant

domes, and the blue sea and sky—the whole village was one big, defiant banner for Greece.

The most interesting houses are the ones burrowed into the side of the rock wall. These "cliff houses," surrounded by air-filled pumice, are ideally insulated—staying cool in summer and warm in winter. While cliff houses were once the poorest dwellings in town, today only millionaires can afford to own them (and most are rented out as very pricey accommodations).

▲▲▲Oia Sunset

As the best place on Santorini to enjoy the summer sunset, Oia becomes even more crowded when the sun starts to go down. Shutter-

bugs jockey for position on the town's best viewpoints, and all that white captures the swirling colors of the sky for a fleeting moment. Many travelers plan their day around being here at sunset. Before you plant yourself for the evening at a bar or restaurant advertising sunset views, make sure

you really are positioned to see the sun dip down, as the sunset's position on the horizon shifts with the seasons.

Naval Maritime Museum

Every Greek island seems to have its own maritime museum, and Oia hosts Santorini's. With two floors of old nautical objects and basic English labels, the collection includes roomfuls of old ship paintings, letters and documents, model ships, and well-endowed mastheads. It's the only museum in town, but it's nothing to jump ship for, unless you're a sailor or need a place to get out of the sun.

Cost and Hours: €3, Wed-Mon 10:00-14:00 & 17:00-20:00, closed Tue, well-signposted a block off the main clifftop drag, tel. 22860-71156.

Eating in Oia

Dining with a view is a no-brainer here—it's worth the too-high prices to enjoy caldera views with your meal or drink. The cliffside places are pretty interchangeable, but if you can't make up your mind, consider one of these.

Flora Café is an affordable alternative to the budget-busting places along the cliff. Set along the main drag (at the Fira end of town), it's essentially a classy snack bar with a pleasantly casual setting (€4-8 small dishes, €8-10 bigger meals, daily 9:00-late, tel. 22860-71424).

Floga dishes up traditional Greek food with a modern spin. It's a few steps below the main drag at the Fira end of town, with dramatic caldera views—albeit not of the sunset (€8-12 starters,

€11-19 main dishes, daily specials, daily 8:00-late, tel. 22860-71152).

Kyprida Restaurant, serving traditional Cypriot cuisine, is set a couple of blocks back from the cliff edge, but its top terrace still has a fine sunset view (€5-9 starters, €11-20 main dishes, daily 12:00-late, closed off-season, tel. 22860-71979).

More Sights on Santorini

The island of Santorini has several worthwhile side-trips, doable by car, bus, or taxi.

Beaches
The volcanic composition of the island has created some unusual opportunities for beach bums. There are volcanic black-sand beaches near **Kamari** (tidy and more upscale-feeling) and **Perissa** (more popular with backpackers)—both on the east coast, but separated from each other by a mountain. Red-sand beaches are near the town of **Akrotiri** (facing away from the caldera along the southern arc of the island).

▲Akrotiri Archaeological Site
Just before Santorini's massive c. 1630 B.C. eruption, its inhabitants fled the island, leaving behind a city that was soon buried (and preserved) in ash—much like Pompeii was, just 1,700 years earlier. (Consider this: The Minoan-era civilization that lived here was as ancient to the Romans as the Romans are to us; many scholars think this may have been what started the legend of Atlantis.) That city, near the modern-day town of Akrotiri, is still being dug up, with more than 30 buildings now excavated and viewable in a new structure that makes it easy to explore the ruins. Ramps let you climb around and through the streets of the prehistoric city, where careful observers can pick out sidewalks, underground sewage systems, and some ceramic vases left behind. However, the most interesting items discovered here—wonderful wall frescoes, fancy furniture, painted ceramics—are on display elsewhere, mainly at Fira's Museum of Prehistoric Thira (see page 1012) and the National Archaeological Museum in Athens.

Cost and Hours: €5, one-hour guided tour-€10, open Tue-Sun 8:00-17:00, closed Mon, last entry 30 minutes before closing, tel. 22860-81939.

Getting There: Akrotiri is reachable by frequent buses from Fira (roughly hourly, €1.80; from the bus stop, backtrack up the road a minute or two) or taxi (€18-20). Renting a car, a scooter, or an ATV makes sense, as having your own wheels lets you easily combine a visit to the archaeological site with a trip to a winery

What If I Miss My Boat?

Remember that you can get help from the cruise line's port agent (listed on the destination information sheet distributed on the ship) and the local TI (see page 1012). If the port agent suggests a costly solution, you may want to consider public transit instead.

Because Santorini is a popular European getaway, many airlines fly here in the summer. Santorini's airport (a.k.a. Thira International Airport) sits along the flat area on the east (back) side of the island, about four miles from Fira (tel. 22860-28400, www.santoriniairport.com). It's connected to Fira by taxi or bus.

Passenger ferries leave from the New Port at Athinios, a 20-minute bus ride away from Fira. Santorini is connected daily to **Piraeus (Athens)** by catamarans (SeaJets, tel. 210-412-1800, www.seajets.gr; and Aegean Speed Lines, tel. 210-969-0950, www.aegeanspeedlines.gr) and slower ferries (Blue Star Ferries, tel. 210-891-9800, www.bluestarferries.com; and ANEK Lines, tel. 210-419-7470, www.anek.gr). If you need to go to another island, the *Flying Cat* catamaran runs nearly daily in peak season to **Mykonos** and other Cycladic Islands, as well as to **Crete** (Hellenic Seaways, tel. 210-419-9000, www.hsw.gr).

Any **travel agent** in Fira also should be able to help. For more advice on what to do if you miss the boat, see page 140.

and/or one of the beaches that dot the southeastern end of the island.

Ancient Thira

Dramatically situated on a mountaintop between Perissa and Kamari, this site dates from a more recent civilization. It was settled post-volcano by Dorians from Sparta, likely in the ninth century B.C., and continued to thrive through the Hellenistic, Roman, and Byzantine periods. This place is less distinctive than the Akrotiri site and is only worth a visit by archaeology completists. If you've toured other Greek ruins from this era—in Athens, Delphi, Olympia, Epidavros, and so on—you'll see nothing new here. You can reach the Ancient Thira site from Kamari, which has regular bus excursions; hardy hikers could also huff up from Perissa on a very twisty serpentine path.

Cost and Hours: €2, April-Oct Tue-Sun 8:30-15:00, closed Mon and Nov-March, http://odysseus.culture.gr.

Volcanic Islets and Other Caldera Trips

A popular excursion is to sail from the Old Port below Fira out to the active volcanic islets in the middle of the caldera. The quickest trips include only a hike to the crater on **Nea Kameni** (€12); longer tours allow time for a swim in the hot springs on **Palea Kameni** (€15) and a visit to Thirassia, the island across the caldera (€19). The "sunset tour" includes a visit to the volcano and hot springs, followed by a boat trip under the cliffs of Oia for the sunset with a glass of wine (€25, 5 hours). Of these, I'd recommend the volcano-only tour, as the "hot springs" are just a shallow and muddy bay, Thirassia doesn't have much to offer, and Oia isn't hard to reach by land. It is cool, however, to get a volcano's-eye view of the inside of the caldera; and the hike on the crater is exciting if you've never climbed around a lava field before. Various travel agencies around Santorini sell these trips—look for ads locally.

Greek Survival Phrases

Knowing a few phrases of Greek can help if you're traveling off the beaten path. Just learning the pleasantries (such as please and thank you) will improve your connections with locals, even in the bigger cities.

Because Greek words can be transliterated differently in English, I've also included the Greek spellings. Note that in Greek, a semicolon is used the same way we use a question mark.

English	Greek	Pronunciation
Hello. (formal)	Gia sas. Γειά σας.	yah sahs
Hi. / Bye. (informal)	Gia. Γειά.	yah
Good morning.	Kali mera. Καλή μέρα.	kah-**lee meh**-rah
Good afternoon.	Kali spera. Καλή σπέρα.	kah-**lee speh**-rah
Do you speak English?	Milate anglika? Μιλάτε αγγλικά;	mee-**lah**-teh ahn-glee-**kah**
Yes. / No.	Ne. / Ohi. Ναι. / Όχι.	neh / **oh**-hee
I (don't) understand.	(Den) katalaveno. (Δεν) καταλαβαίνω.	(dehn) kah-tah-lah-**veh**-noh
Please. (Also: You're welcome.)	Parakalo. Παρακαλώ.	pah-rah-kah-**loh**
Thank you (very much).	Efharisto (poli). Ευχαριστώ (πολύ).	ehf-hah-ree-**stoh** (poh-**lee**)
Excuse me. (Also: I'm sorry.)	Sygnomi. Συγνώμη.	seeg-**noh**-mee
(No) problem.	(Kanena) problima. (Κανένα) πρόβλημα.	(kah-**neh**-nah) **prohv**-lee-mah
Good.	Orea. Ωραία.	oh-**reh**-ah
Goodbye.	Antio. Αντίο.	ahd-**yoh** (think "adieu")
Good night.	Kali nikta. Καλή νύχτα.	kah-**lee neek**-tah
one / two	ena / dio ένα / δύο	**eh**-nah / **dee**-oh
three / four	tria / tessera τρία / τέσσερα	**tree**-ah / **teh**-seh-rah
five / six	pente / exi πέντε / έξι	**pehn**-deh / **ehk**-see
seven / eight	efta / ohto εφτά / οχτώ	ehf-**tah** / oh-**toh**
nine / ten	ennia / deka εννιά / δέκα	ehn-**yah** / **deh**-kah
hundred / thousand	ekato / hilia εκατό / χίλια	eh-kah-**toh** / **heel**-yah
How much?	Poso kani? Πόσο κάνει;	**poh**-soh **kah**-nee
euro	evro ευρώ	ev-**roh**
toilet	toualeta τουαλέτα	twah-**leh**-tah
men / women	andres / gynekes άντρες / γυναίκες	**ahn**-drehs / yee-**neh**-kehs

In a Greek Restaurant

English	Greek	Pronunciation
The menu (in English), please.	Ton katalogo (sta anglika) parakalo. Τον κατάλογο (στα αγγλικά) παρακαλώ.	tohn kah-**tah**-loh-goh (stah ahn-glee-**kah**) pah-rah-kah-**loh**
service (not) included	to servis (den) perilamvanete το σέρβις (δεν) περιλαμβάνεται	toh **sehr**-vees (dehn) peh-ree-lahm-**vah**-neh-teh
appetizers	proto piato πρώτο πιάτο	**proh**-toh pee-**ah**-toh
bread	psomi ψωμί	psoh-**mee**
cheese	tiri τυρί	tee-**ree**
sandwich	sandwich or toast σάντουιτς, τόστ	"sandwich," "toast"
soup	soupa σούπα	**soo**-pah
salad	salata σαλάτα	sah-**lah**-tah
meat	kreas κρέας	**kray**-ahs
poultry / chicken	poulerika / kotopoulo πουλερικά / κοτόπουλο	poo-leh-ree-**kah** / koh-**toh**-poo-loh
fish / seafood	psari / psarika ψάρι / ψαρικά	**psah**-ree / psah-ree-**kah**
shellfish	thalassina θαλασσινά	thah-lah-see-**nah**
fruit	frouta φρούτα	**froo**-tah
vegetables	lahanika λαχανικά	lah-hah-nee-**kah**
dessert	gliko γλυκό	lee-**koh**
(tap) water	nero (tis vrisis) νερό (της βρύσης)	neh-**roh** (tees **vree**-sees)
coffee	kafes καφές	kah-**fehs**
tea	tsai τσάι	**chah**-ee
wine	krasi κρασί	krah-**see**
beer	bira μπύρα	**bee**-rah
(To your) health! (like "Cheers!")	(Stin i) gia mas! (Στην υ) γειά μας!	(stee nee) yah mahs
Bill, please.	Ton logariasmo parakalo. Τον λογαριασμό παρακαλώ.	tohn loh-gah-ree-ahs-**moh** pah-rah-kah-**loh**
tip	bourbouar μπουρμπουάρ	boor-boo-**ar**
Delicious!	Poli nostimo! Πολύ νόστιμο!	poh-**lee nohs**-tee-moh

SANTORINI

MORE PORTS
Greece

Greece Practicalities

Greece *(Hellas)* offers sunshine, seafood, 6,000 islands, whitewashed houses with bright-blue shutters, and a relaxed life-style. As the birthplace of Western civilization, it has some of the world's greatest ancient monuments. We have the Greeks to thank for the Olympics; the tall tales of Achilles and Odysseus; the rational philosophies of Socrates, Plato, and Aristotle; democracy, theater, mathematics...and the gyro sandwich.

As a late bloomer in the modern age, Greece retains echoes of a simpler, time-passed world. On the islands, you'll still see men on donkeys and women at the well. Greeks pride themselves on a concept called *filotimo* ("love of honor"), roughly translated as openness, friendliness, and hospitality. It's easy to surrender to the Greek way of living.

Money: Greece uses the euro currency: 1 euro (€) = about $1.30. An ATM, handily, is labeled *ATM* in the Greek alphabet. The local VAT (value-added sales tax) rate is 23 percent; the minimum purchase eligible for a VAT refund is €120 (for details on refunds, see page 135).

Language: For helpful Greek phrases, see page 1081.

Emergencies: Dial 100 for police or 171 for English-speaking tourist police; for medical or other emergencies, dial 176 or 199.

Time Zone: Greece is on Eastern European Time (an hour ahead of Italy and seven/ten hours ahead of the East/West Coasts of the US).

Theft Alert: In Athens and any place with crowds, be wary of purse snatchers and pickpockets. For tips on outsmarting thieves, see page 128.

Consular Services in Athens: The US embassy is at Vassilissis Sofias 91 (tel. 210-720-2414, http://athens.usembassy.gov). The Canadian embassy is at Ioannou Ghennadiou 4 (tel. 210-727-3400, www.greece.gc.ca). Call ahead for passport services.

Phoning: Greece has a direct-dial phone system (no area codes). To **call within Greece,** just dial the number. To **call to Greece,** dial the international access code (00 if calling from Europe, or 011 from North America), then 30 (Greece's country code), then the phone number. To **call home from Greece,** dial 00, 1, then your area code and phone number.

Tipping: If you order your food at a counter, don't tip. At sit-down restaurants, service is generally included, although it's common to round up the bill after a good meal, usually 5-10 percent. You'll also round up 5-10 percent to tip a cabbie (give €5 to pay a €4.50 fare).

Tourist Information: www.visitgreece.gr

MORE PORTS IN GREECE

Corfu • Katakolo (Olympia) • Heraklion (Crete) • Rhodes

While your cruise ship can't stop at all of Greece's 6,000 islands—and I couldn't visit them all anyway—here's a brief overview of four other important Greek ports of call. In order from west to east, they are the verdant isle of Corfu; the ancient site of Olympia and its port of Katakolo; the port of Heraklion, on Greece's southernmost island of Crete; and the faraway "crossroads" island of Rhodes, shaped by medieval Crusaders and Ottoman sultans.

For ideas on experiencing Greek culture beyond the sights, see the sidebar on page 982.

Corfu

Less touristy and more real-feeling than its glamour-girl cousins Mykonos and Santorini, Corfu (in Greek: Κερκυρα/Kerkyra) is a

diamond in the rough. One of the Ionian Islands, Corfu island is also one of Greece's northernmost, biggest, and greenest. Rather than an arid, desolate moonscape speckled with whitewashed houses and windmills, Corfu is hilly, thickly forested, and draped with villas that might look more at home in Venice or Croatia. As Europe's gateway to faraway, exotic Greece, Corfu was the likely inspiration for the island in Shakespeare's *The*

Tempest. Its strategic location has made Corfu a bridge between the Greek world and various powers to the north: The Romans, Venetians, French, English, and Germans have all taken turns ruling the Ionian Islands, and only a two-mile-wide channel separates Corfu from Albania. These days Corfu's position attracts not sailors and invaders, but cruise ships seeking a day's rest midway between Venice and Santorini.

The island's main town, also called Corfu, is a fun-to-explore small city that squeezes a maze of Old World lanes between a pair of stout Venetian fortresses. Corfu's architecture is a hodgepodge of its past rulers: The grassy main square, called the Spianada, is lined with Venetian villas, English palaces, and a French colonnade, all of which lend it a certain faded elegance. The town's size (pop. 40,000) makes it feel lived-in—the many churches are alive with devout locals. The Corfiots go about their daily lives seemingly oblivious to the giant cruise ships that release thousands of daily visitors into their streets. Away from a few touristy main drags, shops and cafés outnumber trinket shops. And Corfu's museums—while still modest—are a notch above most islands' offerings.

Out of town are Corfu island's many other enticing, sometimes offbeat stopovers, from the escape-from-it-all villa of a reclusive Austrian empress (the Achilleion) to a series of enticing beaches and rocky coves (most famous is Paleokastritsa). Taken together, Corfu might not knock your socks off, but it'll give you a good picture of a real-world Greek island with a pervasive, gritty charm.

Planning Your Time

With a quick day in port, Corfu offers several options:

• Explore the **Old Town,** dipping into its small but good museums, visiting its busy churches, and hiking up to one or both fortresses. Allow anywhere from an hour (for a quick stroll through town) to all day.

• Tour the **Achilleion** (Austrian palace) and its gardens. Allow an hour or two for the visit, plus another half-hour each way to reach it from Corfu town.

• Hit the beach or climb the hills around **Paleokastritsa.** Allow a half-day to a full day.

You can reach the out-of-town destinations by public bus, but there can be long gaps in the schedule; fill those gaps with taxi rides. If you have a long day in port, you could rent a car or hire a driver to do everything—but it'll be a long and busy day.

Arrival at the Port of Corfu

Arrival at a Glance: Ride a cheap public bus or an overpriced taxi into town, or walk 25 minutes. Everything in Corfu town is walk-able, and you can reach outlying sights by taxi or local bus.

Port Overview

Cruise ships dock at the New Port, about a mile west of the Old Town. It's an easy 300-yard walk from your ship to the terminal building, or you can take the free shuttle bus that zips arriving passengers this short distance.

    Services at the Port of Corfu: Inside the terminal building, you'll find a **TI** kiosk (generally staffed when cruises arrive; pick up the free, excellent town map, with sight hours listed) and a **car-rental** office (varies by season, but in peak season figure roughly €50-60/day including insurance, €10 extra for 4x4 jeeps).

Getting into Town

Exit the terminal building and turn left into a long parking lot with rental cars and taxis, and beyond that, the public bus stop into town. Whether you go by taxi, bus, or foot, you'll wind up at the **Spilia Gate,** which marks the entrance to the Old Town (with an ATM and taxi stand right out front).

By Taxi

Taxi drivers prey on cruise passengers, demanding a no-meter €10 to the Old Town (more than double the fair metered rate; however, since all companies charge this same flat rate, there's little point trying to get them to use the meter). Many cabbies speak good English and will try to talk you into longer excursions to the Achilleion villa (about €20-25 one-way, or €100 round-trip including waiting time) or the picturesque Paleokastritsa bay (€40-45 one-way, €90 round-trip). A three- to four-hour deluxe tour to the island's highlights will run you around €150 (cabbies work on a €45 hourly rate). While this is handy, keep in mind that you can rent your own car for a fraction of the price (see car-rental information above).

By Public Transportation

At the far end of the taxi parking lot is the stop for the **public bus** to the Old Town (bus #2, but other numbers might make the run when a ship arrives—just ask "Old Town?"; buy ticket on board, 2/hour, 5-minute trip to Spilia Gate). If you want to reach some of the outlying sights—such as the Achilleion or Paleokastritsa—ride this bus into town, then walk through the town center to the regional bus station (explained later).

By Foot

To walk from the cruise terminal to the Old Town, simply follow the road with the water on your left, and you'll be there after about 25 minutes.

Returning to Your Ship

From just outside the Spilia Gate, you have the same three options outlined above: Pay for a taxi, ride the bus, or walk.

Orientation to Corfu

Corfu town's Old Town is wedged between the new and old fortresses, facing the Old Port. If you venture to the south, you'll find that the Old Town ends abruptly, depositing you into a workaday New Town with cafés, shops, and offices. At the New Town park/square called Saroko, about a 20-minute walk from the Spilia Gate, is the main TI and the hub for buses to other points on the island (see "Getting Around Corfu Island," below).

Tourist Information

Corfu's helpful TI is in a green kiosk in the middle of Saroko Square (sporadic hours, possibly closed Sat-Sun, tel. 26610-48082, www.corfuvisit.net).

Getting Around Corfu Island

If you'd like to venture to the sights beyond Corfu town, you can ride a bus or take a taxi.

Two different sets of **buses** serve the island from Corfu town: blue local buses and green KTEL long-distance buses (including to the Achilleion and Paleokastritsa). Both leave from near Saroko Square in the New Town. Blue/local buses have a blue ticket office right on the square; bus #10 to the Achilleion departs from two blocks down Methodiou street. Green/long-distance buses to Paleokastritsa depart from four blocks up Ioannou Theotoki street. Specifics for the Achilleion and Paleokastritsa are listed under "Elsewhere on Corfu," later; for an idea of bus schedules, you can check www.terrakerkyra.gr (look for the "Transport Around the Island" link), but it's best to inquire locally. Note that bus routes make it difficult to connect quickly between outlying sights—you'll usually have to go back through Corfu town.

There's a **taxi** stand right in front of the Spilia Gate, and others around town. Corfu's taxi drivers take advantage of cruisers by charging them inflated "flat rates" for popular trips. For example, the fair fare (on the meter) between Corfu town and the Achilleion should be about €15-20, but they'll tell you it's a flat rate of €25. If you feel feisty, you can try to talk them into using the meter, but they might refuse (official rates should be posted somewhere on or inside the taxi; if you can't find them, ask to see them).

Sights on Corfu

In the Old Town

Corfu's mazelike Old Town is enjoyable to explore. It's jammed onto a peninsula between two fortresses—each of which you can

climb for grand views over the rooftops. Nikiforou Theotoki street runs west to east, connecting the Spilia Gate (where buses and taxis from the cruise port arrive) with the Spianada (grassy main square). Along the way, it passes trinket shops and restaurants, as well as Iroon Square (with St. Spyridon Church).

Most visitors to Corfu stick to the souvenir-shop-lined main tourist streets. But if you get out of this rut, you'll discover that the town is big enough to reward those who poke around—especially some of the small neighborhood churches that cluster in the Campielo district, north of Nikiforou Theotoki.

I've listed the sights roughly in the order you'll reach them as you come from the Spilia Gate.

New Fortress (Neo Frourio)

The newer of Corfu's twin fortresses (from the late 16th and early 17th centuries), this is also the less interesting complex—but affords the best view in town. You'll hike up ramps and through tunnels to the imposing British Barracks, where (upstairs) you'll find a sparse ceramics collection and a rusty metal staircase leading up to the top terrace, with excellent views over the Old Town.

Cost and Hours: €3, daily mid-April-early Oct 9:00-21:00, early Oct-Nov 9:00-19:00, closed Dec-mid-April, tel. 26610-27370.

▲St. Spyridon Church

One of Corfu's biggest churches, this sits between two bustling tourist streets. It offers an inviting opportunity to drop into a real, living community church. Stepping inside, you'll see a roughly even mix of tourists and locals. Sit and observe for a while. Worshippers come in to buy candles big and small (the largest are five feet tall and look like fluorescent lightbulbs), which they light when saying a prayer. On the marble counter in front of the iconostasis

(screen with icons), look for the small pads of paper, where locals write out prayer requests, then drop a coin in the box, put the paper in the basket, and light a candle. Step through the door in the right side of the iconostasis into a tiny, evocative chapel. The silver coffin contains the remains of St. Spyridon (A.D. 270-348), the town's patron saint, who fought against heresies in the early church. Stand to one side and watch the procession, as locals enter, cross themselves, and say a prayer. Some kneel at the casket, some kiss it, and others place fresh flowers or other items on it for a blessing. Meanwhile, tourists also step inside to survey the scene. It can be hard to tell who's who. On my last visit, I watched a woman standing for a long time staring intently at the relics, as if communing with the soul of St. Spyridon. Finally she said, in a thick, exasperated English accent, "I don't know who it is!"

If St. Spyridon is crowded, consider exploring the streets of the Campielo district to the north, where several other, smaller, less-touristed churches hide in a maze of streets. In this direction near the water is the Antivouniotissa Church and Byzantine Museum (described below).

Banknote Museum

This little collection, on Iroon Square in front of St. Spyridon, displays Greek banknotes through history.

Cost and Hours: Free, April-late Sept Wed and Fri 9:00-14:00 & 17:30-20:30, Thu and Sat-Sun 9:00-15:00, shorter hours off-season, closed Mon-Tue year-round, tel. 26610-41552, www.alphapolitismos.gr/en/05-Banknote-Museum.

▲Antivouniotissa Church and Byzantine Museum

This late-15th-century Orthodox church has been converted into a fine venue for displaying Corfu's collection of Byzantine artwork, including a marvelous assortment of gilded icons.

Cost and Hours: €2, Tue-Sun 8:30-15:00, possibly later in summer, closed Mon, Arseniou, tel. 26610-38313, www.antivouniotissamuseum.gr.

Theotoki Square

A few short blocks south of the main drag, this square features the Old Town Hall and Corfu's cathedral (with a stark interior and the remains of St. Theodora). There are no museums here, but it's a fine place to sit in the sun (on benches or at an outdoor café) and relax. If you see a commotion in front of the Old Town Hall, it's likely a wedding. After the couple leaves, the custodian sweeps the rice off the steps to the street below, where pigeons gorge themselves.

Spianada

The east end of Corfu's Old Town is filled with a broad expanse of grass, part of which was built by the British occupiers as a crick-

et pitch (and is still periodically used for matches today). This fine square is ringed with monumental buildings, including the Palace of Sts. Michael and George to the north and the Old Fortress to the east (both described below). Running along the western side of the Spianada is a colonnade called the Liston, filled with inviting cafés. Built by a Parisian architect during a time of French occupation, this evokes a northern gentility.

▲Palace of Sts. Michael and George/Asian Art Museum

Holding court at the top of the Spianada, this strange hybrid is two sights in one: a stately, British-built, early-19th-century man-

sion interior, and a well-explained collection of art from all over Asia. While strolling through grand salons and peeking into sumptuously decorated throne rooms and halls with ceilings that drip with stucco, you'll see pieces of art from China, Japan, Cambodia, India, Afghanistan, and Pakistan. Good English descriptions illuminate the small but well-presented exhibits. The main collection is upstairs, while temporary exhibits are on the ground floor.

Cost and Hours: €3, ask for free audioguide that explains the building, Tue-Sun 8:00-15:00, shorter hours in winter, closed Mon year-round, Palea Anatora, tel. 26610-30443, www.matk.gr.

▲Old Fortress (Palaio Frourio)

The peninsula that jabs into the sea just east of the Old Town had already been fortified for many centuries, but in the mid-15th century the Venetians turned it into an even more imposing citadel— cutting it off from the mainland by digging a moat, and capping it with an ensemble of stout buildings. Today it features some underwhelming small museums and offices for local agencies, and fine views across Old Town rooftops to the New Fortress. After buying your ticket and crossing the drawbridge, you'll reach the gatehouse, with a Byzantine Mu-

seum in the right side (featuring some nicely preserved mosaic floor fragments). Heading into the main part of the complex, swing around to the right to the Neoclassical Church of St. George, which looks like it could date from the Golden Age of the Venetian Republic but was actually built during the 19th-century British occupation. Then huff up (past the modern café) to the lighthouse at the very top of the rock, for great views.

Cost and Hours: €4, daily April-Oct 8:00-20:00, Nov-March 8:30-16:00, last entry 30 minutes before closing, tel. 26610-48310.

▲Archaeological Museum

In this collection of Corfu's archaeological artifacts, the prize piece is the gigantic, 55-foot-long Gorgon pediment, which once topped the island's temple to Artemis (Archaic period, c. 590-580 B.C.). The carvings depict the grotesque Gorgon (a.k.a. Medusa), flanked by regal-looking giant cats, moments before she is beheaded by a very-small-in-comparison Perseus. More sculptures, vases, armor, and other ancient bits and pieces round out the collection.

Cost and Hours: €3, Tue-Sun 8:30-15:00, possibly later in summer, closed Mon, a short walk south along the coast to Vralia 1, tel. 26610-30680, www.culture.gr.

Sights South of the Old Town

For about 50 years (from the fall of Napoleon in 1814 until 1864), Corfu was a protectorate of the British Empire. Aside from the Spianada and palace in the heart of town, other remnants of that time still exist. Just west of the Archaeological Museum is a **British cemetery.** Farther to the south (about a mile from the Old Town center) are the manicured grounds of the estate called **Mon Repos,** featuring a Neoclassical mansion (housing both opulent furnishings and an archaeological museum) and the ruins of two ancient temples. This was the birthplace of Britain's Prince Philip (Queen Elizabeth's husband).

Just south of Mon Repos, at the far-south tip of the Kanoni Peninsula, is the picturesque **Mouse Island** (Pontikonisi)—reachable by boat from the little Vlacherena monastery that sits on a spit just offshore.

Shopping

Aside from the typical Greek trinkets (e.g., jewelry and worry beads), Corfu is known for its kumquat brandy; you'll see orange bottles of this everywhere. Ecclesiastical shops, selling small icons and other religious items, cluster around St. Spyridon Church.

Elsewhere on Corfu

Corfu is a huge island (Greece's third largest), but on a brief visit, you'll have to limit your focus. Two nearby places might be worth a look. Cruise excursions generally feature bus tours that include one or both of these stops, then a drop-off (and sometimes a guided tour) in Corfu's Old Town.

▲Achilleion

Tucked into the Greek hillsides six miles south of Corfu town is an unlikely bit of Austrian imperial splendor. While this villa barely

cracks the "Top 10" of Europe's Habsburg sights, it's worth a look for its fine gardens—especially if you're a fan of palaces and Greece is handier than Austria. You can see the entire place in just an hour or so. The gardens are an enjoyable place to kill some time (bring a picnic).

Cost and Hours: €7, €3 for the thorough and good audioguide, daily April-Oct 8:00-19:00, Nov-March 8:45-15:30, near village of Gastouri, tel. 26610-56245, www.achillion-corfu.gr.

Getting There: The palace is near the village of Gastouri, which is served by Corfu's blue bus #10 (departs from the New Town, two blocks down Methodiou street from Saroko Square; 25-minute trip, 6/day, fewer on weekends). Buses make a return trip to Corfu 25-30 minutes after arriving at the Achilleion—leaving you with too little or too much time at the villa. If you're ready to go, you can catch a taxi back to Corfu town (€15-20 is the fair metered rate, though most cabbies try to extort a "fixed rate" of €25; to call for a taxi at the Achilleion, dial 26610-33811, pay phone at café across the street from palace ticket office).

Background: The Austrian Empress Elisabeth (1837-1898)—better known as Sisi—was the troubled and tragic Princess Di-like wife of Habsburg Emperor Franz Josef (who ruled the Austro-Hungarian Empire in the late 19th and early 20th centuries, when its territory covered much of Eastern Europe). Sisi struggled with courtly life and sought escape from the Vienna grind. She built an elegant yellow villa on a forested Corfu hillside, with terraced gardens and sculptures of figures from Greek mythology. After Sisi was assassinated, Germany's Kaiser Wilhelm II bought the place and used it to entertain foreign dignitaries.

Visiting the Palace: Today visitors tour part of the palace, including Sisi's own private chapel, dining room, and grand staircase. Circle around outside the palace to reach the checkerboard terrace behind, lined with Greek statues. Peek into the top of the grand staircase, where you'll see a grandiose painting of Achilles, the great warrior for whom the palace was named. He holds Hector's helmet (and drags his vanquished rival's body behind his chariot) as the terrified people of Troy watch  from their fortified town in the background. In the lower part of the terrace, you'll see how Achilles met his end—a famous sculpture of the fallen warrior pulling an arrow from his vulnerable heel.

▲Paleokastritsa

This picturesque, very touristy resort village sits at a rocky harbor 14 miles northwest of Corfu town. Surrounded by cliffs and enveloped in grand scenery, it's one of the most popular spots on the island. Aside from relaxing on the beach, visitors here enjoy hiking up to the hilltop Theotokos Monastery, with a well-preserved, otherworldly Orthodox interior that hosts a small museum. The garden around the monastery, with views across the sea, is extremely photogenic.

Getting There: Green buses depart from the long-distance bus stop near Ioannou Theotoki street (45-minute trip, roughly 8/day in high season, fewer Sat-Sun and off-season, return bus departs from Paleokastritsa about 45 minutes after arrival). A **taxi** costs around €35 one-way.

Olympia and the Port of Katakolo

A visit to Ancient Olympia (Αρχαία Ολυμπία)—most famous as the site of the original Olympic Games—offers one of your best opportunities for a hands-on antiquity experience. Line up at the original starting blocks in the 2,500-year-old Olympic Stadium. Visit the Temple of Zeus, former site of a gigantic statue of Zeus that was one of the Seven Wonders of the Ancient World. Ponder the temple's once-majestic columns—toppled like towers of checkers by an earthquake—which are as evocative as anything from ancient times. Take a close look at the Archaeological Museum's gold-medal-quality statues and artifacts. And don't forget to step back and enjoy the setting itself. Despite the crowds that pour through here, Olympia remains a magical place, with ruins nestled among lush, shady groves of pine trees.

Planning Your Time

Getting from Katakolo to Olympia takes 30 minutes (for a complete visit, allow about 5 hours total round-trip, including lunch and transit time). Once at Olympia, focus on the two main sights (or, with a bit more time, add the third):

• The **Sanctuary of Olympia** (the archaeological site) takes about 1.5 hours to tour.

• To visit the adjacent **Archaeological Museum,** allow about an hour.

• The modest **Museum of the History of the Olympic Games in Antiquity** is skippable, but gives a good background before touring the site (allow about 30 minutes).

While you can see Olympia's sights in any order, I recommend first quickly touring the Museum of the History of the Olympic Games (to get context), then walking the archaeological site (while your energy is high). Finally, tour the Archaeological Museum to reconstruct what you've seen. If you're passing the Archaeological Museum en route to the site anyway, buy your combo-ticket at the museum and stop in to see the model of the site in the entryway (described on page 1059), which will spark your imagination as you stroll the site.

Unfortunately, Olympia (especially the Archaeological Museum) is most crowded between 10:00 and 13:00—just when you're in town.

MORE PORTS IN GREECE

Arrival at the Port of Katakolo

Arrival at a Glance: When the train is running, it's the easiest way to Ancient Olympia (€10 round-trip, 45 minutes). Otherwise, you'll need to take a private bus (€10 round-trip) or a taxi (€80-100 round-trip), or rent your own car (€40 plus gas, 30-minute drive).

Port Overview

Cruise ships use the port of Katakolo (kah-TAH-koh-loh, spelled Κατάκολο in Greek; sometimes called "Katakolon" in English), about 18 miles from Olympia. It's a tiny fishing village-turned-tourist trap; the closest big city is Pyrgos, which has a TI and bus connections to the rest of Greece.

Katakolo's main street—called Katakoloy Street—begins at the dock. The town has blocks of tacky souvenir shops and waterfront cafés that exist primarily for cruisers.

Tourist Information: A TI is located in a small kiosk as you exit the cruise port, on the right (usually open when ships arrive; Pyrgos TI tel. 26210-37111).

Getting to Olympia

Olympia is east of Katakolo, about a 45-minute train ride or 30-minute drive from the port.

By Train

Your best option into Olympia is most likely the train, though budget cuts sometimes threaten service. Confirm that it's running—and check the current schedule—at the TI at the dock (€10 round-trip; 3-4/day—as of this writing, trains were leaving Katakolo at 9:00, 10:00, 11:00, and 13:15, and returning from Olympia at 12:00, 13:00, 14:00, and 15:45; 45 minutes, tel. 26210-22525, http://tickets.

MORE PORTS IN GREECE

Services near the Port of Katakolo

If you can't wait to get to Olympia for one of the following services, here are the nearest locations for each.

ATM: You'll find one on the main street at the far end of town (away from the dock).

Internet Access: Look for **Internet Service,** on the quiet street uphill and parallel to the main street (Internet terminals and Wi-Fi, tel. 26210-41471, mobile 698-247-0148, kostadinoslagos@yahoo.com). Owner Kostadinos Lagos also rents **bikes.** Some of the waterfront cafés also offer free Wi-Fi.

WCs: They are next to the beach in the public bathhouse.

---

trainose.gr/dromologia). To maximize your time in Olympia, catch the earliest train you can, and double-check the departure time for your return trip. To reach the train, head down Katakolo's tacky tourist street a few blocks until it empties onto a park/parking lot, where you'll find the train platform and nearby ticket booth. (The train-ticket booth also sells entry tickets to the ancient site and archaeological museum in Olympia, but the opening hours posted here aren't necessarily accurate.)

The train brings you to Olympia's station, a five-minute walk from the museum. With your back to the station, turn left at the street and walk until you reach a large parking lot. Look for a brown sign pointing to the museum and archaeological site.

By Private Bus

For the same price as the train, you can take a big bus from one of the two competing agencies on the main street (both charge €10 round-trip); I'd go with **Geo Travel,** which is likely to give you a little more time in Olympia (tel. 26210-30777, www.geo-travel.gr). Both companies understand how much you don't want to miss your boat—and all but guarantee you won't. Unlike the train, however, neither bus leaves Katakolo at a set time—you may have to wait up to 30 minutes until they collect enough passengers to make the trip worthwhile. If there's a train leaving soon after you dock, I'd take that instead.

By Tour

The tour company **Olympic Traveller** offers a package combining round-trip transport to Olympia with a two-hour guided tour of the site and museum, likely with recommended local guide Niki Vlachou (€35/person, 25-person limit, mobile 697-320-1213, info@olympictraveller.com, www.olympictraveller.com). For €15 less, you can skip the guided tour in Olympia, but enjoy a narrated ride and quick pick-up times (they won't dally at the port waiting for the bus to fill up).

You can also make your way to Olympia on your own, and hire a private guide there; for tips, see page 1044.

By Taxi

Taxis descend upon the dock, hoping to pick up passengers; the round-trip fare for a one-hour visit to Olympia runs €80, while a 2.5-hour visit costs €100. For the best prices and service, book in advance (consider friendly George Letsios, mobile 694-457-9917, www.taxikatakolon.gr, georgetaxitours@gmail.com).

By Car

The 30-minute drive from Katakolo to Olympia is easy—you don't even have to go through any towns. But be aware that some car-rental "deals" in Katakolo come with hidden costs. Avoid the sleazy rental agency on the main street as you leave the dock, which tacks on extra fees. Instead, try **Avis** (marked with a big red sign), just uphill from the main street (€40/day plus gas for air-conditioned Fiat with manual transmission, tel. 26210-42200, mobile 694-700-2290, www.katakolo-rentacar.com, helpful Kostas).

Driving to Olympia: It's best to get detailed directions from your rental agent, but here are the basics: Leave Katakolo on its main street and drive about 8 kilometers (5 miles) to the first village, Agios Ioannis. At the first stoplight, turn left onto a country road (following the blue *Ancient Olympia* sign). Follow the road as it winds up a hill and crosses some railroad tracks. At the first stop sign, you meet the main road (E-55) to Olympia. Turn right and follow the modern highway to Ancient Olympia (Αρχαία Ολυμπία, well-marked with brown signs), bypassing the city of Pyrgos. Take the Olympia exit and follow the road, which becomes Olympia's main street and ends at the archaeological site.

Parking is free and easy in Olympia town and at the sights (the main parking lot for cars is near the Archaeological Museum; you can also park in the bus lot near the Museum of the History of the Olympic Games in Antiquity).

Sights in Katakolo

If you find yourself with extra time in Katakolo, you have a few options.

Although it's a small town, Katakolo has two museums—both just a five-minute walk from the dock. However, due to budget cuts, neither may be open (call 694-242-

0157 or ask at the dockside TI). The **Museum of Ancient Greek Technology** is in the town park near the railroad tracks. It holds about 200 reconstructions of ancient Greek machines, covering the period from 2000 B.C. to A.D. 100. The nearby **Museum of Greek Musical Instruments,** which has about 40 instruments on display, is on the left side of the main street at the end of the retail strip.

Renata Beach is just a few steps from the dock on the left. There's a public bathhouse and a café. The water is fine, but this is a pebble beach, so bring beach shoes or flip-flops.

Returning to Your Ship

Drivers leaving Olympia take the highway in the direction of Pyrgos. As you bypass the city, watch carefully for the turnoff to Katakolo, marked in Greek (Κατάκολο) and in English. If you took the train, confirm departure times with the conductor.

Orientation to Olympia

The Sanctuary of Olympia sits in the fertile valley of the Alphios River in the western Peloponnese, nine miles southeast of the regional capital of Pyrgos. The archaeological site curves along the southeastern edge of the tidy modern village of Archaia (Ancient) Olympia. The town's layout is basically a low-lying, easy-to-manage grid, five streets wide by eight streets long. The main road (called Praxitelous Kondyli) runs from Pyrgos in the north and leads right into a parking lot (and bus stop) at the south end of town. From here the museum and site are due east, over the Kladeos River.

Tourist Information

What is technically the town's TI, in the center of town on the main road next to the National Bank of Greece, is unlikely to be of any help...or even open (it does, however, usually post current bus schedules in its windows).

Helpful Websites: For current hours of the main sights, check local guide Niki Vlachou's website (www.olympictours.gr; see listing under "Helpful Hints"). Another good (but unofficial) website is www.olympia-greece.org. It has information on both the sights and the town itself, including a map of the city.

MORE PORTS IN GREECE

Helpful Hints

Uncertain Hours: As at the rest of Greece's ancient sites these days, opening hours for Olympia's sights can change without warning. Staff answering the phone at the sanctuary and museum don't always have the latest info, may not speak much English, and are unlikely to be much help. Recommended local guide Niki Vlachou (listed below) is your best resource for up-to-date hours for the town's sights: Check her website, which she updates regularly with the latest opening times (or contact Niki directly; she happily answers my readers' questions at no cost and no obligation to hire her as a guide).

Services: Olympia's main street has wide sidewalks; countless gift shops; and ample hotels, eateries, ATMs, and other tourist services. You'll also find a small grocery store here.

Taxis: There's a taxi stand in town where the main street meets a shady, angled side street called Georgiou Douma (tel. 26240-22555).

Local Guide: Consider hiring fantastic **Niki Vlachou** to show you around the ruins and museums (reasonable and negotiable rates, contact for exact price; also arranges wine tastings, cooking classes, and meals in local homes; mobile 697-242-6085, www.olympictours.gr, niki@olympictours.gr).

Don't count on finding a local guide to hire once you arrive—unlike at many other popular ancient sites, the Sanctuary of Olympia is not surrounded by hopeful guides-for-hire.

Sanctuary of Olympia Tour

Olympia was the mecca of ancient Greek religion—the location of its greatest sanctuary and one of its most important places of worship. In those times, people didn't live here—the sanctuary was set aside as a monastery and pilgrimage site; the nearest city was 30 miles away. Ancient Greeks came here only every four years, during the religious festival that featured the Games. The heart of the sanctuary was a sacred enclosure called the Altis—a walled-off, rectangular area that housed two big temples, multiple altars, and statues to the gods.

Whereas Delphi served as a pilgrimage destination mostly for groups of wealthy men on a particular mission, every four years Olympia drew 40,000 ordinary dudes (men only) for a Panhellenic party. As the site of the Olympic Games for more than a thousand years (c. 776 B.C.-A.D. 393), it was home to both temples and sports facilities.

Orientation

Cost and Hours: €6, €9 combo-ticket includes Archaeological Museum, free for those 18 and under; mid-April–mid-Sept Mon-Sat 9:00-19:00, Sun 8:00-15:00; may be open one hour later mid-April-Aug; off-season hours generally daily 9:00-15:00—though most likely at least a little longer, especially in early fall and late spring. Last entry generally 45 minutes before closing.

Services: The site itself has WCs just inside the entrance and near the far end of the Sacred Way. An open-air café is located between the site and the Archaeological Museum. No food is allowed inside the site, though you can (and should) bring a water bottle.

Getting There: By **car,** park for free at one of two lots: at the south end of town (closest to the site entrance), or at the east edge of town (closest to the Archaeological Museum). To reach the site from either parking lot, follow the signs, walking several hundred yards and crossing the Kladeos River. It's about a five-minute **walk** from the town center to either the site or the Archaeological Museum.

The Tour Begins

Buy your tickets at the site entrance, then head through the gate. Walk straight ahead, passing WCs on the right, then bear left with the path (passing an orientation board), which leads you down into the ancient world of Olympia.

• *Look to your left (through the trees) to catch glimpses of...*

Kronos Hill

This hill was sacred to the ancient Greeks, who believed it to be the birthplace of Zeus—and the place where as a clever baby he es-

caped his father, Kronos, who'd tried to eat him. Zeus later overthrew Kronos and went on to lead the pantheon of gods. (Other versions of the myth place this event on Mt. Olympus, in northern Greece, where the gods eventually made their home.) The hill was scorched by devastating wildfires in August of 2007—imagine how close the flames came to enveloping this ancient site. Locals replanted the hill, and it's once again green.

• *This main path, called the Sacred Way, leads down into a wide field scattered with ruins. To the left of the path was an enclosed area filled with various temples and altars; to the right were buildings for the ath-*

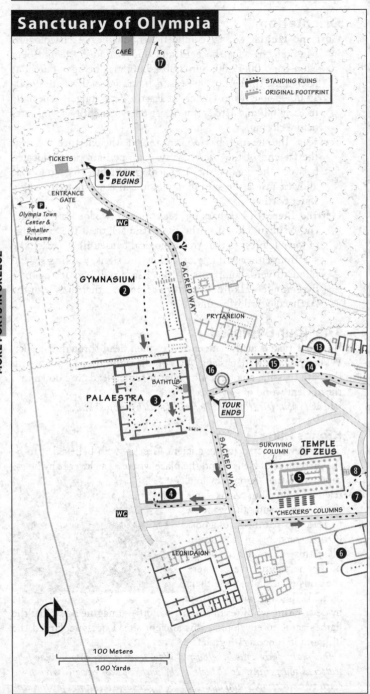

Sanctuary of Olympia

STANDING RUINS
ORIGINAL FOOTPRINT

CAFÉ

To 17

TICKETS

TOUR BEGINS

ENTRANCE GATE

To P Olympia Town Center & Smaller Museums

WC

MORE PORTS IN GREECE

GYMNASIUM 2

SACRED WAY

1

PRYTANEION

13

15 14

16

PALAESTRA 3

BATHTUB

TOUR ENDS

SURVIVING COLUMN

TEMPLE OF ZEUS

5

8

7

4

"CHECKERS" COLUMNS

WC

SACRED WAY

6

LEONIDAION

N

100 Meters
100 Yards

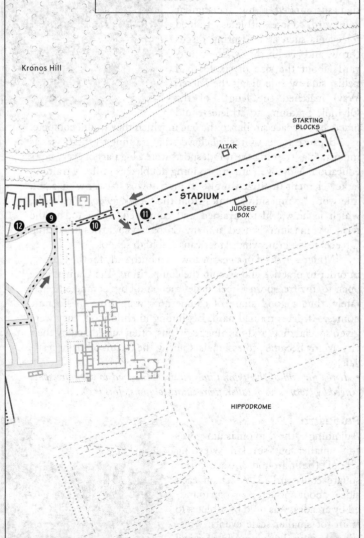

1. View of Kronos Hill
2. Gymnasium
3. Palaestra
4. Workshop of Pheidias
5. Temple of Zeus
6. Bouleuterion
7. Pedestal of Nike
8. Winner's Circle
9. Bases of Zanes & Row of Treasuries
10. Krypti
11. Stadium & Finish Line
12. Metroon
13. Nymphaeum
14. Altar of Hera
15. Temple of Hera
16. Philippeion
17. To Archaeological Museum

Kronos Hill

STARTING BLOCKS

ALTAR

STADIUM

JUDGES' BOX

HIPPODROME

MORE PORTS IN GREECE

letes, who trained and lived in a complex of buildings similar to today's Olympic Village.

Head to the right along the small path just before the two long rows of stubby columns. They mark the eastern edge of what was once the...

Gymnasium

This was the largest building in the whole sanctuary, built in the second century B.C. The truncated Doric columns once supported

a covered arcade, one of four arcades that surrounded a big rectangular courtyard. Here athletes trained for events such as the sprint, discus throw, and javelin throw. The courtyard (about the size of six football fields, side-by-side along the Sacred Way) matched the length of the Olympic Stadium, so athletes could

practice in a space similar to the one in which they would compete.

Because ancient Greeks believed that training the body was as important as training the mind, sports were a big part of every boy's education. Moreover, athletic training doubled as military training (a key element in citizenship)—so most towns had a gymnasium. The word "gymnasium" comes from the Greek *gymnos* ("naked"), which is how athletes trained and competed. Even today, the term "gymnasium" is used in many European countries (including Greece) to describe what Americans call high school.

Athletes arrived in a nearby town a month early for the Games, in order to practice and size up the competition. The Games were open to any free-born Greek male (men and boys competed separately), but a good share of competitors were from aristocratic homes. Athletes trained hard. Beginning in childhood, they were given special diets and training regimens, often subsidized by their city. Many became professionals, touring the circuit of major festivals.

• *At the far end of the gymnasium ruins, stairs lead to a square space ringed by twin rows of taller, more intact columns. This is the...*

Palaestra

Adjoining the gymnasium was this smaller but similar "wrestling school" (built around 300 B.C.). This square courtyard (216 feet on each side—about one acre), also surrounded by arcades, was used by athletes to train for smaller-scale events: wrestling, boxing, long jump (performed

The Ancient Olympic Games

The Olympic Games were athletic contests held every four years as a way of honoring Zeus, the king of the gods. They were the culmination of a pilgrimage, as Greeks gathered to worship Zeus, the Games' patron.

The exact origins of the Games are lost in the mists of time, but they likely grew from a local religious festival first held at the Sanctuary of Olympia in about 1150 B.C. According to one legend, the festival was founded by Pelops, namesake of the Peloponnese; a rival legend credits Hercules. Sporting events became part of the festivities. A harmonious, healthy body was a "temple" that celebrated its creator by performing at its peak.

The first Olympic Games at which results were recorded are traditionally dated at 776 B.C. The Games grew rapidly, attracting athletes from throughout the Greek world to compete in an ever-growing number of events (eventually taking up to five days in all). They reached their height of popularity around 400 B.C. Of the four major Greek games (including those at Delphi, Corinth, and Nemea), Olympia was the first, biggest, and most prestigious.

Besides honoring Zeus and providing entertainment, the Games served a political purpose: to develop a Panhellenic ("all-Greek") identity among scattered city-states and far-flung colonies. Every four years, wars between bickering Greeks were halted with a one-month "sacred truce" so that athletes and fans could travel safely to Olympia. Leading citizens from all corners would assemble here, including many second- and third-generation Greeks who'd grown up in colonies in Italy, France, or Africa. Olympia was geographically central, and for the length of the festivities, it was the symbolic heart of Greece.

This went on for 1,169 years, finally concluding in A.D. 393. Olympia today lives on in the spirit of the modern Olympic Games, revived in Athens in 1896. Every other year, athletes from around the world gather and compete in contests that challenge the human spirit and, it's hoped, foster a sense of common experience. Whether we're cheering on an American swimmer, a Chinese gymnast, or a Jamaican sprinter to go faster, longer, and better than any human has before, the Games bring the world together for a few weeks, much as they united the Greek world in this tranquil pine grove so many centuries ago.

while carrying weights, to build strength), and *pangration,* a kind of ancient "ultimate fighting" with only two rules: no biting and no eye-gouging.

Picture athletes in the courtyard working out. They were always naked, except for a layer of olive oil and dust for a bit of protection against scrapes and the sun. Sometimes they exercised in time with a flute player to coordinate their movements and to keep up the pace. Trainers and spectators could watch from the shade of the colonnades. Notice that the columns are smooth (missing their fluting) on the lower part of the inside face. This way, when it rained, athletes could exercise under the arcade (or take a breather by leaning up against a column) without scraping themselves on the grooves.

In the area nearest the Sacred Way, notice the benches where athletes were taught and people gathered for conversation. You can still see the bathtubs that athletes used to wash off their oil-dust

coating. (They also used a stick-like tool to scrape off the oily grime.)

Besides being training facilities, *palaestrae* (found in almost every city) were also a kind of health club where men gathered to chat.

• *Continue to the right down the Sacred Way, then take the next right. Climb the stairs at the far end, and peek into the ruined brick building that was once the...*

Workshop of Pheidias

In this building, the great sculptor Pheidias (c. 490-430 b.c.) created the 40-foot statue of Zeus (c. 435 b.c.) that once stood in the Temple of Zeus across the street on a huge golden throne. The

workshop was built with the same dimensions as the temple's *cella* (inner room) so that Pheidias could create the statue with the setting in mind. Pheidias arrived here having recently completed his other masterpiece, the colossal *Athena Parthenos* for the Parthenon in Athens (see page 950). According to ancient accounts, his colossal Zeus outdid even that great work.

How do we know this building was Pheidias' place? Because archaeologists found sculptors' tools and molds for pouring metals, as well as a cup with Pheidias' name on it (all now displayed in the museum).

• *Walking back to the Sacred Way, stop to look at the large, open rubble-strewn field (to the right) with dozens of thigh-high Ionic capitals. This was the site of the massive* **Leonidaion,** *a luxury, four-star hotel with 145 rooms (and private baths) built in the fourth century B.C. to house dignitaries and famous athletes during the Games.*

Head back down the Sacred Way, then left up the ramp/stairs toward Olympia's main sight: the ruins of the Temple of Zeus, marked by a single standing column.

Temple of Zeus

The center of ancient Olympia—both physically and symbolically—was the massive temple dedicated to Zeus, king of the gods and patron of the Games. It was the first of the Golden Age temples, and one of the biggest (not much smaller than the Parthenon), and is the purest example of the Doric style.

The temple was built in the fifth century B.C. (470-457 B.C.), stood for a thousand years, and then crumbled into the evocative pile of ruins we see today, still lying where they fell in the sixth century A.D.

Step into the rubble field in front of the temple, walking between big gray blocks, two-ton column drums, and fallen 12-ton capitals. They're made not of marble but of cheaper local limestone. Look closely and you can see the seashell fossils in this porous (and not terribly durable) sedimentary rock. Most of the temple was made of limestone, then covered with a marble-powder stucco to make it glisten as brightly as if it were made of pure marble. The pediments and some other decorations were made of expensive white marble from the isle of Paros.

An olive tree near the temple's southwest corner (to your right) marks the spot of the original tree (planted by Hercules, legends say) from which the winners' wreaths were made. Then as now, olives were vital to Greece, providing food, preservatives, fuel, perfumes...and lubrication for athletes.

You're standing near the back (west) end of the temple, near its most sacred part: The *cella,* where Pheidias' statue of Zeus stood. The interior of the temple is closed indefinitely; to get a good look you'll have to head back to the path that runs along what was once the south porch of the temple—the side facing away from Kronos Hill.

As you walk around the temple, try to reconstruct it in your mind. It was huge—about half an acre—and stood six stories tall. The lone standing column is actually a reconstruction (of original pieces, cleaned and restacked), but it gives you a sense of the scale: It's 34 feet tall, 7 feet thick, and weighs 9 tons. This was one of 34 massive Doric columns that surrounded the temple: 6 on each end and 13 along the sides (making this a typical peripteral/peristyle temple, like Athens' Parthenon and Temple of Hephaistos in the Ancient Agora).

The columns originally supported a triangular pediment at each end (now in the Archaeological Museum), carved with scenes of the battle of the Lapiths and centaurs (west end) and Pelops and the chariot race (east end, which was the main entrance).

To your left, along the south side, you'll see five huge fallen columns, with their drums lined up in a row like dominos. To the right are the ruins of the **Bouleuterion,** the council chamber where, by stepping on castrated bulls' balls, athletes took an oath not to cheat. As this was a religious event, and because physical training was a part of moral education, the oaths and personal honor were held sacred.

Continue down the path to the front (east) end of the temple and duck off the path to the left to find the 29-foot-tall, white-marble, triangular **Pedestal of Nike.** It's missing its top, but it once held a famous statue (now in the museum) of the goddess Nike, the personification of victory.

She looked down upon the **Winner's Circle,** here at the main entrance to the temple, where Olympic victors were announced

and crowned. As thousands gathered in the courtyard below, priests called the name of the winner, who scaled the steps to the cheers of the crowd. The winner was crowned with a wreath of olive (not laurel) branches, awarded a statue in his honor—and nothing more. There were no awards for second and third place and no gold, silver, or bronze medals—those are inventions of the modern Olympics. However, winners were usually showered with gifts and perks from their proud hometowns: free food for life, tax exemptions, theater tickets, naming rights for gymnasiums, statues, pictures on ancient Wheaties boxes, and so on.

In the courtyard you can see pedestals that once held statues of winners, who were considered to be demigods. The inscriptions listed the winner's name, the date, the event won, his hometown, and the names of his proud parents.

The ruined building directly east of here was the Echo Hall, a long gallery where winners were also announced as if into a microphone—the sound echoed seven times.

• *With the main entrance of the Temple of Zeus at your back, walk out to the path, passing several of the inscribed pedestals. Turn left at the tree, then follow the right fork until you bump into the low wall at the base of Kronos Hill. The foot of that hill is lined with a row of pedestals, called the...*

Bases of Zanes (Cheater Statues) and Row of Treasuries

These 16 pedestals once held bronze statues of Zeus (plural "Zanes"). At the ancient Olympic Games, as at the modern ones,

it was an honor just to compete, and there was no shame in not finishing first. Quitters and cheaters were another story. The Zeus statues that once lined this path were paid for with fines levied on cheaters, whose names and ill deeds were inscribed in the bases. As people entered the stadium (straight ahead), they'd spit on the statues. Offenses ranged from doping (using forbidden herbs) or bribing opponents, to failing to train in advance of the Games or quitting out of cowardice. Drinking animal blood—the Red Bull of the day—was forbidden. Official urine tasters tested for this ancient equivalent of steroids.

Just behind the statues (and a few feet higher in elevation) is a terrace that once held a row of treasuries. These small buildings housed expensive offerings to the gods. Many were sponsored by colonies as a way for Greeks living abroad to stay in touch with their cultural roots.

• *Turn right and pass under the arch of the...*

Krypti

As you enter the stadium through this tunnel, imagine

yourself as an athlete who has trained for years and traveled for days, carrying the hopes of your hometown on your shoulders... and now you're finally about to compete. Built around 200 B.C., this tunnel once had a vaulted ceiling; along the walls are niches that functioned as equipment lockers. Just like today's NFL players, Olympia's athletes psyched themselves up for the big contest by shouting as they ran through this tunnel, then emerging into the stadium to the roar of the crowd.

• *On your mark, get set, go. Follow the Krypti as it leads into the...*

Stadium

Line up on that original marble-paved starting line from the ancient Olympic Games and imagine the scene. The place was filled with 45,000 spectators—men, boys, and girls—who sat on the manmade banks on either side of the track. One lone adult woman was allowed in: a priestess of the goddess Demeter Chamyne, whose altar rose above the sea of testosterone from the north (left) bank (still visible today).

The stadium (built in the sixth century B.C.) held no seats except those for the judges, who sat in a special box (visible on the south bank, to your right). These Hellanodikai ("Judges of the Greeks") kept things on track. Elected from local noble families and carefully trained over 10 months for just a few days of Games, these referees were widely respected for their impartiality.

The stadium track is 192 meters (640 feet) from start to finish line. The Greek word *stadion* literally means a course that is 600 traditional Olympic feet long, supposedly first marked out by Hercules. The line at the near (west) end marked the finish, where all races ended. (Some started at this end as well, depending on how many laps in the race, but most started at the far end.) The racers ran straight up and back on a clay surface, not around the track. There were 20 starting blocks (all still visible today), each with two grooves—one for each foot (athletes competed barefoot). Wooden

starting gates (similar to those used in horse races today) made sure no one could jump the gun.

The first Games featured just one event, a sprint race over one length of the stadium, or one *stadion*. Imagine running this distance in 19.3 seconds, as Usain Bolt of Jamaica did at the 2012 Olympic Games. Over time, more events were added. There were races of two *stadia* (that is, up and back, like today's 400-meter event), 24 *stadia* (similar to today's 5K race), and a race in which athletes competed in full armor, including shields.

At the height of the Games (c. 400 B.C.), there were 13 events held over five days (most here in the stadium). Besides footraces, you'd see events such as the discus, javelin, boxing, wrestling, long jump, *pangration* (a wrestling/boxing/martial arts mix), and the pentathlon. (The decathlon is a modern invention.) During the 2004 Games in Athens, the shot-put competition was held in this stadium. South of the stadium was the hippodrome, or horse-racing track, where riding and chariot races took place.

Compare this stadium and the events held here with the gladiatorial contests in ancient Rome several centuries later: In the far more massive Colosseum, the sensationalistic events weren't about honor, athletic glory, or shared humanity, but a bloody fight to the death, staged to remind the citizens of the power of the state. Good thing it's the Greek games we now emulate.

• *Backtrack through the tunnel and continue straight past the pedestals for the Zeus statues. You'll bump into some rectangular foundations, the ruins of the...*

Metroon and the Altar of Zeus

The Metroon (mid-fourth century B.C.) was a temple dedicated to the mother of the gods, Rhea (also known as Cybele). The site also

honored the mother-goddess of the earth, worshipped as "Gaia."

Somewhere near here once stood the Altar of Zeus, though no one knows exactly where—nothing remains today. At this altar the ancient Olympians slaughtered and burned animals in sacrifice to Zeus on a  daily basis. For special festivals, they'd sacrifice 100 cattle (a "hecatomb"), cook them on the altar, throw offerings into the flames, and feast on the flesh, leaving a pile of ashes 25 feet high.

In the middle of the wide path, under an olive tree, is a **sunken apse,** only recently excavated. It's actually the foundation of a 4,000-year-old house—i.e., more than 1,000 years older than the ancient ruins we've seen elsewhere—more evidence that this site was important long before the Olympic Games and the Golden Age of ancient Greece.

• *To the right are the ruins of a semicircular structure built into the hillside, the...*

Nymphaeum

This was once a spectacular curved fountain, lined with two tiers of statues of emperors, some of which are now in the Archaeological Museum. The fountain provided an oasis in the heat and also functioned as an aqueduct, channeling water throughout the sanctuary. It was built toward the end of the sanctuary's life (around A.D. 150) by the wealthy Roman Herodes Atticus (who also financed construction of the famous theater at the base of the Acropolis in Athens—see page 940).

When the Romans conquered Greece, in the second century B.C., they became fans of Greek culture, including the Olympics. The Romans repaired neglected buildings and built new structures, such as this one. But they also changed (some say perverted) the nature of the Games, transforming them from a Greek religious ritual to a secular Roman spectacle. Rome opened up the Games to any citizen of the Empire, broadening their appeal at the cost of their Greekness.

Rome's notorious Emperor Nero—a big fan of the Olympics—attended the Games in the mid–first century A.D. He built a villa nearby, started music contests associated with the Games, and entered the competition as a charioteer. But when he fell off his chariot, Nero ordered the race stopped and proclaimed himself the winner.

• *Directly in front of the Nymphaeum are the rectangular foundations of what was once the...*

Altar of Hera

These humble foundations provide a bridge across millennia, linking the original Olympics to today's modern Games. Since 1936, this is where athletes have lit the ceremonial Olympic torch (for both the summer and winter Games). A few months before the modern Games begin, local women

MORE PORTS IN GREECE

dress up in priestess garb and solemnly proceed here from the Temple of Hera. A curved, cauldron-shaped mirror is used to focus the rays of the sun, igniting a flame. The women then carry the flame into the stadium, where runners light a torch and begin the long relay to the next city to host the Games—a distance of 1,000 miles to Sochi, Russia, for the 2014 Winter Games and more than 6,000 miles to the 2016 Summer Games in Rio.

• *Fifteen yards farther along are the four standing Doric columns that mark the well-preserved...*

Temple of Hera

First built in 650 B.C., this is the oldest structure on the site and one of Greece's first monumental temples. The temple originally honored both Hera and her husband Zeus, before the Temple of Zeus was built.

The temple was long but not tall, giving it an intimate feel. Its length-to-width ratio (and number of columns: 6 on the short sides, 16 on the long ones) is 3:8, which was considered particularly harmonious and aesthetically pleasing, as well as astronomically significant (the ancients synchronized the lunar and solar calendars by making the year three months longer every eight years).

The temple was originally made of wood. Over time, the wooden columns were replaced with stone columns, resulting in a virtual catalog of the various periods of the Doric style. The columns are made from the same shell-bearing limestone as most of the site's buildings, also originally covered in marble stucco.

Inside, a large statue of Hera once sat on a throne with Zeus standing beside her. Hera's priestesses wove a new dress for the statue every four years. The temple also housed a famous statue of Hermes and was topped with the Disk of the Sun (both are now in the museum).

Though women did not compete in the Olympics, girls and maidens competed in the Heraean Games, dedicated to Hera. The Heraean Games were also held here every four years, though not in the same years as the Olympics. They were open only to unmarried virgins—no married women allowed. Wearing dresses that left one shoulder and breast exposed, the girls raced on foot (running five-sixths of a *stadion,* or 160 meters/525 feet) and in chariots. Like the men, the winners received olive wreaths and fame, as well as a painted portrait displayed on a column of the Temple of Hera.

• *Walking out the back of Hera's temple, you'll reach our last stop: a round temple with three Ionic columns still standing, the...*

Philippeion

The construction of the Philippeion marked a new era in Greece: the Hellenistic era. (Compare these gracefully slender Corinthian

columns to the earlier, stouter Doric columns of the Temple of Hera—in the centuries between when they were built, Greek ideals of proportion had shifted away from sturdiness and strength to a preference for elegant beauty.)

Philip of Macedon built this monument to mark his triumph over the Greeks. The Macedonians spoke Greek and had many similar customs, but they were a kingdom (not a democracy), and the Greeks viewed them as foreigners. Philip conquered Greece around 340 B.C., thus uniting the country—by force—while bringing its Classical Age to an end.

The temple—the first major building visitors saw upon entering the sacred site—originally had 18 Ionic columns of limestone and marble stucco (though today it appears dark, as the gleaming stucco is long gone). Inside stood statues of Philip and his family, including his son, the man who would bring Greece to its next phase of glory: Alexander the Great.

Just north of the Philippeion, bordering the Sacred Way and difficult to make out, are the scant remains of the Prytaneion, the building that once housed the eternal Olympic flame.

Olympia's Legacy

After the Classical Age, the Games continued, but not in their original form. First came Alexander and a new era of more secular values. Next came the Romans, who preserved the Games but also commercialized them and opened them up to non-Greeks. The Games went from being a somber celebration of Hellenic culture to being a bombastic spectacle. The lofty ideals for which the games were once known had evaporated—along with their prestige. As Rome/Greece's infrastructure decayed, so did the Games. A series of third-century earthquakes and the turmoil of the Herulian invasion (in A.D. 267) kept the crowds away. As Greece became Christian, the pagan sanctuary became politically incorrect.

The last ancient Games (the 293rd) were held in A.D. 393. A year later, they were abolished by the ultra-Christian emperor

Theodosius I as part of a general purge of pagan festivals. The final blow was delivered in 426, when Theodosius II ordered the temples set ablaze. The remaining buildings were adopted by a small early Christian community, who turned Pheidias' workshop into their church. They were forced to abandon the area after it was hit by a combination of earthquakes (in 522 and 551) and catastrophic floods and mudslides. Over the centuries, two rivers proceeded to bury the area under 25 feet of silt, thus preserving the remaining buildings until archaeologists rediscovered the site in 1766.

• *The Archaeological Museum is 200 yards to the north and well-signed.*

Archaeological Museum Tour

Many of Olympia's greatest works of art and artifacts have been removed from the site and are now displayed, and well-described in English, in this compact and manageable museum.

Orientation

Cost and Hours: €6, €9 combo-ticket includes archaeological site, mid-April-mid-Sept Tue-Sat 8:00-19:00, Sun-Mon 9:00-16:00; may be open one hour later mid-April-Aug; off-season hours generally daily 9:00-15:00—though most likely at least a little longer, especially in early fall and late spring; last entry about 30 minutes before closing, tel. 26240-22742, www.culture.gr.

Getting There: By **car,** park for free at one of two lots: at the south end of town (closest to the site entrance), or at the east edge of town (closest to the Archaeological Museum). To reach the site from either parking lot, follow the signs, walking several hundred yards and crossing the Kladeos River. It's about a five-minute **walk** from the town center to either the site or the Archaeological Museum.

Services: A museum shop, WCs, and a café are to the right of the entrance...but may not be open.

The Tour Begins

This tour takes you past the highlights, but there's much more to see if you have time. As you enter, ask for the free pamphlet that includes a map of the museum (and the site).

• *In the entrance lobby, to the right of the ticket desk, is a...*

Model of the Site, Reconstructed: Looking at Olympia as it appeared in its Golden Age glory, you can see some of the artifacts that once decorated the site (and which now fill this museum). On the Temple of Zeus, notice the pediments, topped with statues and tripods. Southeast of the temple is the Pedestal of Nike, supporting the statue of Nike. Find Pheidias' workshop and the Temple of

Olympia Archaeological Museum

MAIN HALL

BULL

ENTRANCE

1. Site Model
2. Temple of Zeus: West Pediment
3. Temple of Zeus: East Pediment
4. Nike of Paeonius
5. Helmet of Miltiades
6. Workshop of Pheidias
7. Hermes of Praxiteles
8. Nymphaeum Statues
9. Zeus & Ganymede
10. Disk of the Sun
11. Griffins
12. Tripods

Hera, topped with the Disk of the Sun. We'll see all of these items on this tour.

• *Continue straight ahead into the main hall. On the right wall are...*

Statues from the West Pediment of the Temple of Zeus: These statues fit snugly into the 85-foot-long pediment that stood over the back side of the temple (facing the Sacred Way). Study the scene depicting the battle of the Lapiths and centaurs: The centaurs have crashed a human wedding party in order to carry off the women. See one dramatic scene of a woman and her horse-man abductor just left of center. The Lapith men fight back. In the center, a 10-foot-tall Apollo stands calmly looking on. Fresh from their victory in the Persian Wars,

the Greeks were particularly fond of any symbol of their struggle against "barbarians."

The statues from the West Pediment are gorgeous examples

of the height of Golden Age sculpture: Notice the harmony of the poses and how they capture motion at the perfect moment without seeming melodramatic. The bodies, clearly visible under clothing, convey all the action, while the faces (in the statues that still have them) are stoic.

• *On the opposite side of the hall are...*

Statues from the East Pediment of the Temple of Zeus: Olympic victors stood beneath this pediment—the temple's main

entrance—as they received their olive wreaths. The statues tell the story of King Pelops, the legendary founder of the Games. A 10-foot-tall Zeus in the center is flanked by two competing chariot teams. Pelops (at Zeus' left hand, with the fragmented legs)

prepares to race King Oenomaus (at Zeus' right) for the hand of the king's daughter Hippodamia (standing beside Pelops). The king, aware of a prophecy predicting that he would be murdered by his son-in-law, killed 13 previous suitors after defeating them in chariot races. But Pelops wins this race by sabotaging the king's wheels (that may be what the crouching figure is up to behind the king's chariot), causing the king to be dragged to his death by his horses (just like that chariot race in *Ben-Hur*). Pelops becomes king and goes on to unify the Peloponnesian people with a festival: the Olympic Games.

As some of the first sculpture of the Golden Age (made after the Persian invasion of 480 B.C.), these figures show the realism and relaxed poses of the new age (note that they're missing those telltale

Archaic-era smiles). But they are still done in the Severe style—the sculptural counterpart to stoic Doric architecture—with impassive faces and understated emotion, quite different from the exuberant West Pediment, made years later. Still, notice how refined the technique is—the horses, for example, effectively convey depth and movement. But seen from the side, it's striking how flat the sculpture really is.

• *Continue straight ahead, where you'll see a statue rising and floating on her pedestal. She's the...*

Nike of Paeonius: This statue of Victory (c. 421 B.C.) once stood atop the triangular Pedestal of Nike next to the Temple of Zeus. Victory holds her billowing robe in her out-

MORE PORTS IN GREECE

stretched left hand and a palm leaf in her right as she floats down from Mt. Olympus to proclaim the triumph of the Messenians (the Greek-speaking people from southwest Peloponnese) over Sparta.

The statue, made of flawless, pure-white marble from the island of Paros, is the work of the Greek sculptor Paeonius. It was damaged in the earthquakes of A.D. 522 and 551, and today, Nike's wings are completely missing. But they once stretched behind and above her, making the statue 10 feet tall. (She's about seven feet today.) With its triangular base, the whole monument to Victory would have been an imposing 36 feet tall, rising above the courtyard where Olympic winners were crowned.

• *In the glass case to the right as you face Nike are two bronze helmets. The green, battered one (#2) is the...*

Bronze Helmet of Miltiades: In September of 490 B.C., a huge force of invading Persians faced off against the outnum-

bered Greeks on the flat plain of Marathon, north of Athens. Although most of the Athenian generals wanted to wait for reinforcements, Miltiades convinced them to attack. The Greeks sprinted across the plain, into the very heart of the Persians—a bold move that surprised and routed the enemy. According to legend, the good news was carried to Athens by a runner. He raced 26 miles from Marathon to Athens, announced "Hurray, we won!"...and dropped dead on the spot.

The legend inspired the 26-mile race called the marathon—but the marathon was not an Olympic event in ancient times. It was a creation for the first modern Games, revived in Athens in A.D. 1896.

• *Pass the helmet and walk into the room with the Zeus statue painting.*

Workshop of Pheidias Room: The poster shows Pheidias' great statue of Zeus, and a model reconstructs the workshop where he created it. In the display case directly to the

left as you enter, find exhibit #10, the clay cup of Pheidias. The inscription on the bottom (hence the mirror) reads, "I belong to Pheidias." The adjacent case holds clay molds that were likely used for making the folds of Zeus' robe. The case in the opposite corner contains lead and bronze tools used by ancient sculptors to make the statues we've seen all day.

• *The room hiding behind the Zeus poster contains...*

Hermes of Praxiteles: This seven-foot-tall statue (340-330 B.C.), discovered in the Temple of Hera, is possibly a rare original by the great sculptor Praxiteles. Though little is known of this fourth-century sculptor, Praxiteles was recognized in his day as the master of realistic anatomy and the first to sculpt nude women. If this statue looks familiar, that's because his works influenced generations of Greek and Roman sculptors, who made countless copies.

Hermes leans against a tree trunk, relaxed. He carries a baby—the recently orphaned Dionysus—who reaches for a (missing) object that Hermes is distracting him with. Experts guess the child was probably groping for a bunch of grapes, which would have hinted at Dionysus' future role as the debauched god of wine and hedonism.

Circle the statue counterclockwise and watch Hermes' face take on the many shades of thoughtfulness. From the front he appears serene. From the right (toward the baby), there's the hint of a smile, while from the left (toward his outstretched arm), he seems sad. (And, from the back, nice cheeks!)

The statue has some of Praxiteles' textbook features. The body has the distinctive S-curve of Classical sculpture (head tilted one way, torso the other, legs another). Hermes rests his arm on the tree stump, over which his robe is draped. And the figure is interesting from all angles, not just the front. The famous Praxiteles could make hard, white, translucent marble appear as supple, sensual, and sexual as human flesh.

• *Consider detouring left to see more statues, from the Roman Nymphaeum fountain. (If you're in a rush, skip this section and head for the Disk of the Sun.)*

Nymphaeum Statues: The grand, semicircular fountain near the Temple of Hera had two tiers of statues, including Roman

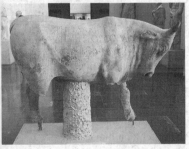

emperors and the family of the statue's benefactor, Herodes Atticus. Here you can see some of the surviving statues, as well as a bull (in the center of the room) that stood in the middle of the fountain. The bull's inscriptions explain the fountain's origins. Compared to the energetic statues we just saw from the west pediment of the Temple of Zeus, these stately statues are static and lackluster.

The next (smaller) room holds more Roman-era statues, from the Metroon and the Temple of Hera.

• *Return to the Workshop of Pheidias Room, then backtrack past the helmets and Nike to find the glass case with the smaller-than-life-size...*

Statue of Zeus Carrying Off Ganymede: See Zeus' sly look as he carries off the beautiful Trojan boy Ganymede to be his cup-bearer and lover. The terra-cotta statue was likely the central roof decoration (called an *akroterion*—see the nearby diagram) atop the Temple of Zeus.

• *Continue into the long hall with the large, decorated terra-cotta pediments, reminding us that these temples were brightly painted, not the plain-white marble we imagine them today.*

Disk of the Sun: This terra-cotta disk—seven and a half feet across and once painted in bright colors—was the *akroterion* that

perched atop the peak of the roof of the Temple of Hera. It stood as a sun- or star-like icon meant to ward off bad juju and symbolize Hera's shining glory.

• *Along the left wall is an assortment of cool-looking...*

Griffins: Because Greeks considered the lion the king of the beasts, and the eagle the top bird, the half-lion-half-eagle griffin was a popular symbol of power for the ancient Greeks, even if no such animal actually existed.

• *The rest of this long room contains several...*

Tripods: These cauldrons-with-legs were used as gifts to the gods and to victorious athletes. For religious rituals, tripods were used to pour liquid libations, to hold sacred objects, or to burn incense or sacrificial offerings. As ceremonial gifts to the gods, tripods were placed atop and around temples. And as gifts to athletes, they were a source of valuable bronze (which could easily be melted down into some other form), making for a nice "cash" prize.

More Sights in Olympia

Perched on a low hill above the southern parking lot are two small museums, one tiny and skippable, the other a bit bigger and worth a visit. They're housed in what used to be Olympia's original ar-

MORE PORTS IN GREECE

chaeological museum and the town's first hotel for antiquity-loving tourists. Today the core of Olympia's collection is displayed at the newer, more modern museum described earlier, but the old hotel building still houses a fine exhibit that nicely complements the other attractions here.

You may see signs pointing to the Museum of the Modern Olympic Games, housed in a low building in the middle of town, but it's currently closed (supposedly for a badly needed renovation), and locals don't expect it to open anytime soon.

▲▲Museum of the History of the Olympic Games in Antiquity

Most people are familiar with the modern-day Olympics, but the games played by those early Olympians were a very different operation. The collection offers a handy "Ancient Olympics 101" lesson that helps bring the events to life. If you can spare the 30-45 minutes it takes to see this museum, stop by here first to get your imagination in gear before seeing the ancient site.

Just inside the entrance are models of the site from three different eras. The rooms around the perimeter of the building tell the story of the original Games—you'll see the awards and honors for the victors, and, in the corner, a beautiful mosaic floor (c. A.D. 200) depicting some of the events. The main central hall focuses on the athletic events themselves, displaying ancient discuses, shots, javelin heads, and large shields that were carried by fully armor-clad runners in some particularly exhausting footraces.

Cost and Hours: €2, Mon-Fri 9:00-16:00, closed Sat-Sun. WCs are just outside the building.

Museum of the History of Excavations

This one-room exhibit, in the small building just outside the Museum of the Olympic Games in Antiquity, explains the various waves of excavations that have taken place since the site of Olympia was re-identified in the mid-18th century. While early investigations were done by archaeologists from France (in the 1820s) and Germany (in the 1870s), most of the site was systematically uncovered to the point you see today by Germans between 1936 and 1966. (When Berlin hosted the 1936 Olympics, Germany took a special interest in the history of the original Games.) You'll see old maps, photos, and archaeologists' tools.

Cost and Hours: Free, same hours as the Museum of the Olympic Games in Antiquity.

Eating in Olympia

As no place in town really has an edge, simply window-shop to find the setting you like best. The shady, angled side-street called Georgiou Douma is lined with touristy places serving mediocre food; but if you're attracted to the area's convenient location and leafy scene, try **Aegean** (Αιγαίο), just across from the taxi stand, where the meals are cooked by the owner (good €9 salads, €8-18 main dishes, open for lunch and dinner, tasty vegetarian options, tel. 26240-22540). **Anesi,** located just outside the tourist zone, has zero atmosphere but is the local favorite for grilled meat (€3 starters, €6-7 main dishes, open daily, one block off main street at corner of Avgerinou and Spiliopoulou, tel. 26240-22644).

For general tips about eating in Greece, see page 965.

Crete and the Port of Heraklion

Heraklion (ee-RAH-klee-oh; also spelled Iraklion or Iraklio; Ηράκλειον in Greek) is the main town of Crete—Greece's biggest, most populous island and the southernmost point in Europe. Crete (Κρήτη) is practically a ministate of its own (in fact, from 1897 to 1913 it was an autonomous state within the Ottoman Empire). Historically, Crete was home to the Minoans—Europe's first advanced civilization, peaking around 1950 B.C., centuries before "the ancient Greeks" of Ath-

ens. The fascinating, colorful Minoan civilization left us with vivid frescoes hinting at a quirky and complicated society, and one of the most beloved myths of the ancient world: the labyrinth, the minotaur, and the brave Athenian warrior Theseus.

Coming to Crete on a quick cruise visit provides, at best, a fleeting glimpse of its charms—but if a few hours is all you have, Crete can easily fill them. The port city of **Heraklion** itself (pop. 137,000) is an urban-feeling, workaday capital, lacking the storied charm of the "Greek isles." Its saving grace is its excellent museum of Minoan artifacts—easily Greece's best on the topic. Most cruisers opt to skip Heraklion entirely and head four miles inland to the ruins of **Knossos,** the palace from which the grand Minoan civilization was ruled.

If you have more time, the rest of Crete offers an engaging diversity of attractions: more Minoan ruins, scenic mountains, enticing beaches, characteristic rustic villages, and dramatic caves and gorges (including the famous Samaria Gorge).

Planning Your Time

Even on a short visit, with a shore excursion or a taxi, you can fit in both of the main sights near the cruise port. If you have more time, you can probably squeeze in both by public transportation.

• The ruins of **Knossos Palace** take you back to Minoan times. Allow two hours.

• The **Heraklion Archaeological Museum** displays artifacts from the Knossos site and other ancient settlements. Allow one to two hours, plus another hour or two if you want to explore downtown Heraklion before returning to your ship.

Arrival at the Port of Heraklion

Cruise ships dock at Heraklion's sprawling main port. Shuttle buses bring you to the terminal building, about a mile east of the city center. From here, you can catch a taxi or bus, or walk into town.

Getting into Town or to Knossos Palace

Taxis charge about €5 into the city center, or €10-15 one-way to Knossos (€50 round-trip to Knossos, including wait time). A taxi between Knossos and downtown Heraklion is about €10-15.

Bus #1 takes you downtown to Eleftherias Square, a crescent-shaped plaza just south of the Heraklion Archaeological Museum (4/hour, 15 minutes). Bus #2 goes to Knossos (2/hour, 30 minutes; tel. 28102-45020, www.bus-service-crete-ktel.com).

Walking into downtown takes about 20-25 minutes (partly uphill).

Orientation to Heraklion

Founded by Saracens, then expanded by crusading Venetians, the city of Heraklion today feels modern and bustling, with a low-rise

Athenian ambience. The city center is a maze of six-story apartment buildings, with cafés, shops, and modern squares. The main part of town focuses on the Venetian-flavored Venizelos Square, whose trademark Morosini Fountain provides its nickname, "Fountain Square." While the streets around here can be fun to explore, from a sightseeing perspective there's just one game in town: the Heraklion Archaeological Museum, a five-minute walk east of Fountain Square.

Tourist Information: The TI is across from the Heraklion Archaeological Museum (Mon-Sat 8:30-17:30, shorter winter

The Minoans
(2000-1400 B.C.)

A safe, isolated location on the island of Crete, combined with impressive business savvy, enabled the so-called Minoans to dominate the pre-Greek world. Unlike most early peoples, they were traders, not fighters. Sailing from their home base on Crete with a large merchant fleet, they exported wine, olive oil, pottery, and well-crafted jewelry. They returned home with the wealth of the Mediterranean and built a lavish palace in Knossos, the capital.

From top to bottom, Minoan society was like one big transnational corporation: ruled by CEO kings, managed by CPA economists, and blessed by bureaucrat priests. The only written records we have of their civilization are meticulous spreadsheets that show the micromanaged details of every business transaction (written in a Cretan script called Linear A). Thanks to their geographical remoteness and strong economy, the Minoans spent virtually nothing on their defense budget, and their cities and palaces had almost no fortifications.

No one knows where the Minoans originated, and their language has never been deciphered (not much literature survives), but they certainly were prosperous. Their palaces (at Knossos, Phaestus, and Akrotiri) were sprawling, serving as both corporate headquarters and centers of cultural life. With tapered columns, airy porticos, and lively frescoes, the palaces exude an atmosphere of intimacy and coziness.

Even the poorest on Crete lived well, in multiroom apartments with indoor plumbing. Blessed with ample leisure time, the Minoans were avid sports fans. Surviving frescoes show athletes staring down a charging bull, then—*shoop*—at the last minute, somersaulting gracefully over the bull's horns, to land upright on their feet again.

Theirs was a delicate, sensual, happy-go-lucky society that apparently worshipped an easygoing Mother Earth and her all-girl pantheon of goddesses. The Snake Goddess was especially popular, shown as a bare-breasted, snake-handling woman. There was relative equality between rich and poor, as well as between the sexes. Though the king was a man, women could be priests and businesswomen, and they competed alongside men in boxing and bull-jumping. Minoan inheritance was probably matrilineal (meaning estates were handed down from mothers to daughters).

The colorful frescoes from Minoan palace walls are unique in the ancient world. Most early cultures painted and sculpted things with a particular function in mind: as propaganda for a king, to commemorate a famous battle, or to represent a god. But the Minoans were among the first to love beauty for its own sake. The frescoes are pure decoration, their creators delighting in everyday Minoans going about everyday life. Tanned, relaxed, good-looking men and women are shown dancing, fishing, or strolling with goddesses through a garden of exotic animals. The Minoans seemed more concerned with the good life than with the afterlife. Their love of beauty became part of the legacy of ancient Greece.

At their peak (c. 1500 B.C.), the Minoans dominated the Greek mainland and neighboring islands, where they built large palaces.

Greek legend has it that "King Minos" demanded a yearly sacrifice of young Greeks to the dreadful Minotaur (half bull, half man), who lived in a labyrinth on the grounds of the palace in Knossos. However, the Minoans' domination was probably more cultural than political. The later Greeks would inherit the Minoans' business skills, social equality, love of art for art's sake, and faith in rational thought over brute military strength. Some scholars hail the Minoans as the first truly "European" civilization.

Precious little survives of this intriguing civilization. The scant remains of the Minoan palace at Knossos are easier to appreciate after visiting the excellent Heraklion Archaeological Museum (both described in this chapter). Perhaps the most interesting Minoan sight is the ruins of the Akrotiri settlement on the island of Santorini; while the site itself is currently closed, some of its best frescoes are in museums on Santorini (page 1012) and in Athens.

In about 1450 B.C., the Minoan civilization suddenly collapsed. Overnight, the great palaces became ghost towns, and no one knows why. Some think the atomic bomb-size eruption of the Santorini volcano (see page 1010) caused earthquakes and a tsunami that swept the Minoans into oblivion. Physically and economically weakened, they were easily overrun and absorbed by the warlike Mycenaeans from the mainland.

Though the Minoans are a very distant memory, their remarkable civilization provided a firm foundation for the Greek civilization that would become so influential worldwide.

MORE PORTS IN GREECE

hours, closed Sun, Xanthoudidou 1, tel. 28102-46298). The city's municipal website has helpful travel information in English: www.heraklion.gr/en.

Sights in Heraklion

Because both of the sights here are tied to Crete's Minoan civilization, it's best to read the Minoans sidebar and both listings before visiting either of them.

▲▲▲Heraklion Archaeological Museum

One of Greece's top museums, this collection of Minoan artifacts is the perfect complement to the site of Knossos Palace. While the palace ruins feature replicas of the Minoans' sumptuous frescoes, here you'll see the originals, and many other artifacts—all well-lit and eloquently described. The full span of the museum covers some 5,500 years, but the prize pieces all relate to the Minoan civilization. The museum is in the midst of a perpetually delayed renovation, with much of its collection in mothballs, but the core of its collection (all that's worth seeing on a quick visit anyway) is on display in an annex down the street. If the museum seems closed, ask around to find the annex.

Cost and Hours: €4 (likely €6 when renovations are complete), €10 combo-ticket with Knossos Palace; late May-Oct Mon 13:00-20:00, Tue-Sat 8:00-20:00, Sun 8:00-15:00; Nov-late May Mon 11:00-17:00, Tue-Sun 8:00-15:00; Xanthoudidou 1, at the corner with Xatzidaki, tel. 28102-79086, www.culture.gr.

Visiting the Museum: Whether the museum has re-opened, or its treasures are still gathered in the annex, look for these highlights as you tour the collection.

The main attraction is the remarkable display of Minoan **frescoes.** The frescoes are vivid, featuring primary colors of red, yellow, and blue, with thick black outlines. These are true frescoes, created by laying a coat of wet plaster on the walls and painting them before the plaster dried. The natural pigments interacted with the plaster, creating a glowing translucent effect. *The Bull-Leaper* (c. 17th-15th centuries B.C.), illustrating the popular pastime of vaulting over a furious bull, demonstrates the grace of the easygoin' Minoan civilization. As in all Minoan frescoes, the women are pale white (the figures flanking the bull), while men have an ochre skin tone (the leaper). Perhaps in Minoan society, women (who were held in high esteem) stayed indoors, while men

toiled under the sun. Take a look at other frescoes. The blue monkeys (from an exotic, faraway land) hint at the Minoans' far-and-wide travel for trade. The woman with the dark hair, doe eyes, and blue shoulder tassels seemed like a chic sophisticate to the early-20th-century archaeologists who discovered her...and nicknamed her *La Parisienne*. Notice her Egyptian-like profile and heavy "eyeliner"—maybe Minoan artists were inspired by their neighbors (Egypt is just 400 miles across the sea). The *Prince of the Lilies*, with his pale hue, is likely actually a woman (he/she wears a headdress similar to the Snake Goddess) who was originally misidentified by archaeologists. Linger over all of these frescoes—the jug-carrying processional, the bluebird—and just bask in the colors.

Exploring the rest of the collection, pause at whatever catches your eye. The figure of the **Snake Goddess** holds a serpent in each hand; perhaps she was a guardian of the home, or maybe the snake (which sheds its skin periodically) symbolizes new life—combined with the ample bosom, an omen of fertility. Nearby, a collection of other clay goddess figurines line up to signal a touchdown.

The drinking vessel (rhyton) shaped like a **bull's head** boasts gorgeous craftsmanship (jeweled eyes, golden horns). The Minoans revered bulls—they'd leap over them but, unlike modern bullfights, would never sacrifice them. (This reverence survived at least until the time of Moses, who came down from Mount Sinai to find his followers worshipping a golden calf—and perhaps even today in India, where cows are sacred.) Nearby, the partial figure of a bull-leaper (c. 1500 B.C.) is a 3-D rendition of the famous fresco.

The **Arkalochori Axe** (2nd millennium B.C.) is a *labrys,* or double-headed axe—a symbol of the Minoan king and origin of the word "labyrinth"; this one is inscribed with iconography. The helmet fortified with pieces of boar tusk made its wearer appear very intimidating indeed.

The **Agia Triada sarcophagus** (c. 1400 B.C.) is covered with intricate frescoes that illustrate Minoan burial rituals—a bonanza for archaeologists struggling to understand that mysterious culture.

The clay **Phaistos Disc** (c. 1600-1450 B.C.) is inscribed with a spiral of hieroglyphic symbols—possibly a

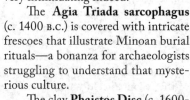

MORE PORTS IN GREECE

very early form of a printing press. (A replica of this disc is a popular Heraklion souvenir.)

▲▲Knossos Palace

Knossos was the main palace of the Minoans, and provided a model for their many other villas around Crete (and on nearby islands). Rather than a "palace" in the monumental Versailles sense, Knossos was a vast (425 feet by 425 feet), mazelike series of interconnected rooms—likely the inspiration for the Minoan tales of the labyrinth. "Labyrinth" comes from the Greek *labrys*, a double-headed axe—you'll see this shape inscribed throughout the ruins.

Cost and Hours: €6, €10 combo-ticket with Archaeological Museum, daily April-Sept 8:00-19:00, Oct 8:00-18:00, Nov-March 8:30-15:00, tel. 28102-31940, www.culture.gr. There are WCs, a snack bar, and a gift shop at the entrance. Guides wait out front, gathering impromptu groups for a one-hour tour (€10/person, departs every 10 minutes or so); hiring your own private guide costs €100.

Visiting the Site: Today's site has sprawling foundations punctuated with some early-20th-century reconstructions that strain to resurrect the majesty of the Minoans. But for the layperson, the site can be as underwhelming as its history is illustrious. Use your imagination (or team up with a good tour guide) to be impressed by the sheer age of this place. You're stepping on stones trod by sandal-clad feet 4,000 years ago.

The black-painted **columns** that taper at the bottom (the opposite of most Greek columns) were made of cypress trees that were felled and turned upside-down. Impressively advanced terra-cotta pipes carried drinking water into Knossos from miles away, and canals carried sewage away from the palace.

But Knossos' defining feature was its colorful **frescoes,** which celebrated life in landscapes and everyday scenes. Poke into some of the reconstructed rooms to see these colorful slices of Minoan life (here you'll see only replicas, but originals are displayed in the Heraklion Archaeological Museum).

At the center of the complex is the **Throne Room,** bathed in red-hued frescoes. The alabaster throne is flanked by fresco depic-

tions of two griffins (mythical animals with a lion's body and an eagle's head and wings).

Long after the peaceful Minoans (who never bothered to erect a wall around their palace) had disappeared, the Venetians felt the need to fortify their settlements on Crete. They scavenged many of the precut stones of Knossos to build a wall around Heraklion. The Knossos ruins were discovered in 1878, and the British archaeologist Arthur Evans began excavating Knossos in 1900. The rebuilt areas that visitors see today are based entirely on Evans' vision.

Present-day archaeologists debate the accuracy of his fanciful reconstructions, pointing out that Evans designed them not for accuracy, but to cheerlead the glories of Minoan civilization. Excavations here coincided with the creation of the modern Greek nation, when other European countries were looking down their noses at Greece. The reconstruction emphasizes how sophisticated this ancient society was (Look: Plumbing! Decoration!). One of its most famous frescoes, nicknamed *La Parisienne*, was embraced partly for how it evoked the elegance of contemporary Europe.

MORE PORTS IN GREECE

Rhodes

Rhodes (in Greek: Ρωδωσ/Rhodos, ROH-dohs), the largest of the Dodecanese Islands, sits at the sunny southeastern extreme of

Greece, just 11 miles from Turkey. Compared to its glamorous Cycladic rivals, Santorini and Mykonos, Rhodes' charms are subtle but substantial—a foot wide and a mile deep. As the longtime bridge between the Aegean islands and Asia Minor, Rhodes is an exotic cultural cocktail of Greek and Turkish, with a dash of Crusaders from all over Europe (see "Rhodes' History" sidebar). The island's main town, also called Rhodes, feels smaller than its population of 80,000. Its walled Old Town—with a bazaar-like atmosphere, a handful of intriguing sights, and very real-feeling back lanes, all lassoed by 3.5 miles of 40-foot-thick medieval walls—is a delight to explore. At the distant end of the island are the ruins of the Lindos Acropolis, with fine views and a scattering of ancient columns.

Planning Your Time

As Greece's fourth-biggest island (pop. 120,000, nearly 50 miles long and 24 miles wide), Rhodes has far more to offer visitors than can be seen in a quick port visit. But even in just a few hours, you can get an enticing feel for its main town.

• In Rhodes' **Old Town,** explore the shopping streets and the back lanes (allow 1-2 hours), and dip into the Palace of the Grand Masters and the Archaeological Museum (allow an hour each).

• Many cruises offer a shore excursion to **Lindos Acropolis** (allow 3-4 hours total). But you'll spend more time getting there (45 minutes each way) than you will at the site (the hilltop acropolis can be seen in just 30-60 minutes, and the town of Lindos below is a quick walk-through).

Arrival at the Port of Rhodes

The cruise-ship harbor is conveniently located in front of the Old Town—you can see the formidable walls and towers from the ship.

Getting into Town

From your ship, you'll either walk or ride a free shuttle bus to the cruise terminal. From the terminal, head out to the main harbor-front road, turn right, and walk for about five minutes (passing a little pebbly beach on your right), then turn left through St. Mary's Gate into the city wall. (Travel agencies in front of this gateway rent cars and provide other tourist services.)

Getting to Lindos Acropolis

With the cruise terminal so close to the town center, there's little need to hire a taxi or ride a bus on Rhodes, unless you're heading to the Lindos Acropolis (see "Getting There" details for Lindos Acropolis, later). Hiring a taxi for a four-hour tour around Rhodes town and the Lindos Acropolis costs about €140 (tel. 22410-69800).

Orientation to Rhodes

Rhodes' Old Town is divided into three sectors: the enjoyably touristy shopping drag, Sokratous street; the sightseeing spine along the northern edge of town, Ippoton, with Rhodes' two main museums (the Palace of the Grand Masters at the top, and the Archaeological Museum at the bottom); and the residential back streets in the southern quadrant of town.

To see it all, follow this route: After entering through St. Mary's Gate, turn right and stroll the narrow streets, passing first through the restaurant-crammed Martyron Square, then the wide Ippokratous Square (with its trademark fountain). From here, you can make a loop through town: Head straight up the main shopping street, Sokratous, then bear right at the minaret to find the Palace of the Grand Masters, and finally head back down Ippoton street (the Avenue of the Knights) to the Archaeological Museum—a few steps from where you began on Ippokratous Square.

Tourist Information: The TI is just outside the city walls, beyond Eleftherias Gate near the New Market (1 Etharhou Makariou, tel. 22410-44330). The city's official website has helpful tourist information in English: www.rhodes.gr/en.

Sights on Rhodes

Rhodes' Old Town

The major sights in the Old Town—including the Palace of the Grand Masters, the Archaeological Museum, and a few others—are covered by a €10 **combo-ticket,** which more than pays for itself even if you're visiting just the palace and the Archaeological Museum (sold at participating museums).

Main Shopping Street (Sokratous)

The closest thing you'll find to a Turkish-style bazaar without setting foot in Turkey, Rhodes' Sokratous street is lined with hole-in-the-wall souvenir shops spilling out into the cobbles. While prices here are inflated, it's a fun place to shop for a Greek and/or Turkish souvenir. You'll find the standard items: jewelry, worry beads, evil eyes, and so on.

This street also gives a glimpse of Rhodes' **Ottoman** past. The highly polished pebbles that pave the streets—typical in Turkish towns—can be slippery even when dry. At the top end of the street stands the bold minaret of the Mosque of Süleyman the Magnificent, built by that powerful sultan to celebrate his conquest of Rhodes in 1552. Nearby are an Ottoman library and baths complex.

▲▲Palace of the Grand Masters

This stout, intimidating palace, perched at the highest point in this hilly town, is—like everything else on Rhodes—layered with history. In the 14th century, the

Knights of St. John added on to an existing Byzantine fortress here to create a residence and political headquarters for their leader, the grand master. The building was destroyed during Ottoman times (in 1856) when artillery stored here accidentally exploded. When the Italians took over in the early 20th century, they elaborately restored it as an island retreat for their king, Victor Emmanuel III, and later for Mussolini. Their rebuild is a fanciful, over-the-top imagining of a medieval fortress that scarcely resembles its original self—but in some ways, that makes it even more interesting to tour.

Cost and Hours: €6, €10 combo-ticket includes Archaeological Museum; April-Oct Tue-Sun 8:00-20:00, Mon 9:00-16:00; Nov-March Tue-Sun 8:00-15:00, closed Mon; Ippoton street, tel. 22410-25500, www.culture.gr.

Visiting the Palace: The exhibit sprawls through imposing stone hallways on two floors, showing off both the building's fine

interiors and a wide-ranging collection of artifacts. Most of the exhibits are corralled into two sections: ancient Rhodes, and Rhodes from the fourth century until the Ottomans. From the ancient Greek period, you'll see a sculpture of the head of Helios, the sun god, with radiating rays. Also from the ancient period come coins, sculptures, vases, and (in the cellar) pointy-based jugs called amphorae. The Byzantine era left behind sumptuous golden icons. But you can thank those Italian restorers for the most striking feature: the grand halls and rooms, fit for a king. Their best flourish—and the highlight of the entire palace—was the addition (mostly upstairs) of fantastically detailed floor mosaics, which they painstakingly transplanted here from their original homes on the isle of Kos.

▲Avenue of the Knights (Ippoton Street)

This atmospheric cobbled lane, leading downhill from the palace (turn left as you exit the palace; street is officially named Ippoton), feels like a microcosm of medieval Europe. That's exactly what it was: The Knights of St. John were divided into seven separate language groups, each one assigned to defending a different section of the town wall. Each group lived in an inn that re-created the home they'd left behind. To this day, the Spanish order's inn still feels like a slice of Spain, the German order's inn resembles a German fort, and so on. While the Italian remodel in the early 20th century made the whole lane more uniform, this is still the best place in town to time-travel to the Middle Ages.

▲Archaeological Museum of Rhodes

Housed in the sprawling former hospital of the Knights of St. John, this collection includes sculptures, vases and other pottery, tomb-

stones, floor mosaics, and other artifacts. Upstairs are a pair of impressive statues of Aphrodite. One small statue shows the goddess looking up, caught in a moment of vulnerable beauty as she washes her hair. Nicknamed the "Rhodes Venus," this is actually a replica of the third-century-B.C. original. Nearby is the life-size *Aphrodite Anadyomene* (literally "rising from the sea," c. 4th century B.C.). The sprawling complex of courtyards and gardens rivals the collection itself. One part of the building was used as a Turkish residence and retains many features of Ottoman dwellings of the era, such as the trademark long sofas for lounging.

Cost and Hours: €6, same hours as palace, Megalou Alexandrou Square, tel. 22410-75674, www.culture.gr.

Other Museums

Various other museums are scattered around the Old Town. The **Decorative Arts Collection,** near the Archaeological Museum, exhibits historical furnishings gathered from homes around the island (€2, closed Mon, Argyrokastrou Square, tel. 22410-25500). Also nearby, the **Byzantine Museum** fills an old cathedral interior with frescoes, icons, and other ecclesiastical art (closed Mon). The **Epigraphical Collection,** sprawling through a different hospital complex, examines the development of inscriptions and writing (closed Mon). The **Modern Greek Art Museum** (formerly the **Municipal Gallery**) collects 20th-century Greek artwork (€3, Tue-Sat 8:00-14:00, closed Sun-Mon, 2 Symis Square, tel. 22410-23766, www.mgamuseum.gr).

Rhodes' History

Rhodes sightseeing is more meaningful to visitors who can tease out its many strands of history. From the ancient Greeks, to a knightly order of Crusaders, to the Ottoman sultans, to a 20th-century tug-of-war among the Italians, Germans, British, and Greeks, Rhodes has long been a crossroads of history.

Because this eastern point is where the sun first shines on the Greek world each morning, the ancient Greeks believed Rhodes to be the home of the sun god, Helios. The local sandstone is embedded with seashells, leading the ancients to surmise that Helios had raised this place from the deep to create a home. In honor of their sun god, they erected here one of the seven wonders of the ancient world: the famous Colossus of Rhodes. Made of bronze and polished to a golden-like sheen, this 100-foot-tall statue of Helios took 12 years to build (in the late third century B.C.) but stood for only 56 years before it was toppled by an earthquake. After the Oracle of Delphi warned Rhodians that they had offended Helios, they decided not to rebuild it. While not a trace of the statue survives (modern bronze deer statues mark one possible location, overlooking the harbor), its legacy does—tales of the statue inspired the creators of the Statue of Liberty, which is of comparable size.

The 304 B.C. defeat of Rhodes' dangerous enemy Demetrius (which the Colossus was erected to celebrate) sparked a golden age for the island. For a time, Rhodes was a trading, naval, and cultural powerhouse. But as the Roman Empire leadership was being reshuffled, Rhodes backed Julius Caesar; after his assassination, its fortunes fell. Rhodes languished through Byzantine times.

Later, in the Middle Ages, Rhodes became a pawn of European power politics in the 14th century. As the nearest Greek is-

Wander the Back Streets

The southern half of the Old Town, while still hemmed in by the walls and within a literal stone's throw of the touristy bazaars, is a remarkably lived-in zone of Greek homes. While you'll find a few tavernas and hotels tucked in this area, workaday Rhodians definitely outnumber tourists here. Perhaps nowhere in Greece can such a short stroll away from the tourist zone reap such great rewards, immersing you immediately in a completely different world than the one you'll find in the main streets. Go for a stroll, peek down lanes and into family living rooms, and be generous with offering a cheery *"Kali mera!"* (Good morning!).

▲Lindos Acropolis

The most popular side-trip from Rhodes is the ruined acropolis over the town of Lindos (Λίνδος, LEEN-dohs), 30 miles south

land to the Holy Land, this became a logical stopping point for passing Crusaders from all over Europe. In 1309, the Knights of St. John—an order of the Knights Hospitaller of Jerusalem—claimed

Rhodes as their headquarters, and transformed it into a bustling European medieval burg, governed by their grand master. Rhodes became a magnet for knights coming from all over Europe, who gave the city a uniquely cosmopolitan appearance.

In 1552, Ottoman Sultan Süleyman the Magnificent kicked the knights off the island, adding it to his empire. (They fled to Malta, where they became the Knights of Malta—an order still in existence.) The Ottomans controlled Rhodes for centuries—erecting pointy minarets, building baths, and imbuing the place with an unmistakably Turkish aura that it retains today. Under the Ottomans, Rhodes remained predominantly ethnic Greek, although a large Jewish population has always existed here.

As the Ottoman Empire floundered in the early 20th century, Rhodes fell under Italian rule (in 1912). The occupying Italians tore down many of the Ottoman structures, rebuilt some of the earlier medieval ones (such as the Palace of the Grand Masters), and added an Italian layer to Rhodes' already eclectic mix. A few decades later, after Italy pulled out of World War II, British and German forces wrangled over who would control Rhodes and the Dodecanese Islands. Only after the dust settled, and Italy signed a 1947 peace treaty, did Rhodes officially become part of Greece for the first time since the Byzantine Empire.

of Rhodes town (about a 45-minute drive or bus ride). The town of Lindos—a whitewashed village huddled at the base of its acropolis-capped hill, with mazelike lanes crammed full of trinket stalls—is extremely touristy, and can be uncomfortably crowded during peak times. And, while the acropolis itself has its share of ruined columns and panoramic views of Rhodes' coastline and hills, it doesn't break into the top 10 of best ancient Greek ruins.

Cost and Hours: €6, April-Oct Tue-Fri 8:00-20:00, Sat-Mon 8:00-15:00, shorter hours and closed Mon off-season, tel. 22410-75674, www.culture.gr.

Getting There: KTEL runs public buses between the Mandraki (MANΔPAKI) stop near the Rhodes TI and Lindos (hourly, 45 minutes, €5, tel. 22410-27706). From the town, you can hike steeply up 278 tourist-clogged steps to the site, or you can pay €5 for a donkey to carry you up. A taxi from the cruise terminal in Rhodes costs about €50-60 one-way, or €115 round-trip including waiting time at the site.

Visiting the Site: Once at the top, you'll wander the remains of various structures. There was an important harbor beneath this

strategic, easy-to-defend pinnacle even before the founding of Rhodes town (which eventually superseded Lindos as the island's main settlement). The neat row of 20 columns at the bottom of the stairway survives from a stoa (covered walkway). The stairway leads up to the partially rebuilt Temple of Athena Lindia (from the fourth century B.C.). Worshippers did not actually enter this small building, which was reserved for priests; instead, they'd gather for worship and sacrifice at an altar out front.

The large granite blocks scattered around the site were bases for statues. Long after the ancient Greeks, Rhodes' rulers modified this hilltop for their own purposes: Also at the site (near the base of the stairway), you'll see a Byzantine church and a fortress erected in the Middle Ages by the Knights of St. John. As you pet an attention-starved kitten, survey the view of the town of Lindos, the surrounding bays and beaches, and the glimmering Aegean. The entirely enclosed bay with the little chapel is the Port of St. Paul, named for the apostle who came here as a missionary in A.D. 54.

Greek Survival Phrases

Knowing a few phrases of Greek can help if you're traveling off the beaten path. Just learning the pleasantries (such as please and thank you) will improve your connections with locals, even in the bigger cities.

Because Greek words can be transliterated differently in English, I've also included the Greek spellings. Note that in Greek, a semicolon is used the same way we use a question mark.

English	Greek	Pronunciation
Hello. (formal)	Gia sas. Γειά σας.	yah sahs
Hi. / Bye. (informal)	Gia. Γειά.	yah
Good morning.	Kali mera. Καλή μέρα.	kah-**lee meh**-rah
Good afternoon.	Kali spera. Καλή σπέρα.	kah-**lee speh**-rah
Do you speak English?	Milate anglika? Μιλάτε αγγλικά;	mee-**lah**-teh ahn-glee-**kah**
Yes. / No.	Ne. / Ohi. Ναι. / Όχι.	neh / **oh**-hee
I (don't) understand.	(Den) katalaveno. (Δεν) καταλαβαίνω.	(dehn) kah-tah-lah-**veh**-noh
Please. (Also: You're welcome.)	Parakalo. Παρακαλώ.	pah-rah-kah-**loh**
Thank you (very much).	Efharisto (poli). Ευχαριστώ (πολύ).	ehf-hah-ree-**stoh** (poh-**lee**)
Excuse me. (Also: I'm sorry.)	Sygnomi. Συγνώμη.	seeg-**noh**-mee
(No) problem.	(Kanena) problima. (Κανένα) πρόβλημα.	(kah-**neh**-nah) **prohv**-lee-mah
Good.	Orea. Ωραία.	oh-**reh**-ah
Goodbye.	Antio. Αντίο.	ahd-**yoh** (think "adieu")
Good night.	Kali nikta. Καλή νύχτα.	kah-**lee neek**-tah
one / two	ena / dio ένα / δύο	**eh**-nah / **dee**-oh
three / four	tria / tessera τρία / τέσσερα	**tree**-ah / **teh**-seh-rah
five / six	pente / exi πέντε / έξι	**pehn**-deh / **ehk**-see
seven / eight	efta / ohto εφτά / οχτώ	ehf-**tah** / oh-**toh**
nine / ten	ennia / deka εννιά / δέκα	ehn-**yah** / **deh**-kah
hundred / thousand	ekato / hilia εκατό / χίλια	eh-kah-**toh** / **heel**-yah
How much?	Poso kani? Πόσο κάνει;	**poh**-soh **kah**-nee
euro	evro ευρώ	ev-**roh**
toilet	toualeta τουαλέτα	twah-**leh**-tah
men / women	andres / gynekes άντρες / γυναικες	**ahn**-drehs / yee-**neh**-kehs

In a Greek Restaurant

English	Greek	Pronunciation
The menu (in English), please.	Ton katalogo (sta anglika) parakalo. Τον κατάλογο (στα αγγλικά) παρακαλώ.	tohn kah-**tah**-loh-goh (stah ahn-glee-**kah**) pah-rah-kah-**loh**
service (not) included	to servis (den) perilamvanete το σέρβις (δεν) περιλαμβάνεται	toh **sehr**-vees (dehn) peh-ree-lahm-**vah**-neh-teh
appetizers	proto piato πρώτο πιάτο	**proh**-toh pee-**ah**-toh
bread	psomi ψωμί	psoh-**mee**
cheese	tiri τυρί	tee-**ree**
sandwich	sandwich or toast σάντουιτς, τόστ	"sandwich," "toast"
soup	soupa σούπα	**soo**-pah
salad	salata σαλάτα	sah-**lah**-tah
meat	kreas κρέας	**kray**-ahs
poultry / chicken	poulerika / kotopoulo πουλερικά / κοτόπουλο	poo-leh-ree-**kah** / koh-**toh**-poo-loh
fish / seafood	psari / psarika ψάρι / ψαρικά	**psah**-ree / psah-ree-**kah**
shellfish	thalassina θαλασσινά	thah-lah-see-**nah**
fruit	frouta φρούτα	**froo**-tah
vegetables	lahanika λαχανικά	lah-hah-nee-**kah**
dessert	gliko γλυκό	lee-**koh**
(tap) water	nero (tis vrisis) νερό (της βρύσης)	neh-**roh** (tees **vree**-sees)
coffee	kafes καφές	kah-**fehs**
tea	tsai τσάι	**chah**-ee
wine	krasi κρασί	krah-**see**
beer	bira μπύρα	**bee**-rah
(To your) health! (like "Cheers!")	(Stin i) gia mas! (Στην υ) γειά μας!	(stee nee) yah mahs
Bill, please.	Ton logariasmo parakalo. Τον λογαριασμό παρακαλώ.	tohn loh-gah-ree-ahs-**moh** pah-rah-kah-**loh**
tip	bourbouar μπουρμπουάρ	boor-boo-**ar**
Delicious!	Poli nostimo! Πολύ νόστιμο!	poh-**lee** nohs-tee-moh

ISTANBUL
Turkey

Turkey Practicalities

Exotic, vibrant Turkey *(Türkiye)* stands at the crossroads of continents. For thousands of years, the fortunes of the greatest empires of East and West have played out on this fertile peninsula. You'll walk in the footsteps of Roman emperors and Ottoman sultans as you explore some of the world's grandest monuments. Today much of Turkey is scrambling into the modern Western world. The empires of the past have given way to a proud parliamentary democracy and a predominantly Muslim population of nearly 81 million. But the traditional way of life is richly dyed and woven into the land like a Turkish carpet.

Visas: If you are starting your cruise in Turkey or getting off the ship to spend the night on land, you will need a visa before you arrive in Turkey (for details, see page 1086).

Money: Turkey uses the Turkish lira: 1 Turkish lira (TL) = about $0.55. One lira is broken down into 100 kuruş. An ATM is called a *bankamatík* or *paramatík.* The local VAT (value-added sales tax) rate is 18 percent; the minimum purchase eligible for a VAT refund is 108 TL (for details on refunds, see page 135).

Language: For useful Turkish phrases, see page 1202.

Emergencies: Dial 155 for police; for medical emergencies, dial 112 (both Turkish-language only).

Time Zone: Turkey is on Eastern European Time (an hour ahead of Italy and seven/ten hours ahead of the East/West Coasts of the US).

Theft Alert: Thieves thrive on fresh-off-the-boat tourists. Leave conspicuous valuables onboard, and be alert in crowds. For more on outsmarting thieves, see page 128.

Consular Services in Istanbul: The US consulate is at Kaplıcalar Mevkii Sokak 2, İstinye Mahallesi (24-hour emergency tel. 0212/335-9000, http://istanbul.usconsulate.gov). The Canadian consulate is at Buyukdere Caddesi 209 (tel. 0212/385-9700, www.turkey.gc.ca). Call ahead for passport services.

Phoning: Turkish phone numbers have seven digits, preceded by a four-digit area code. Within an area code, just dial the local number; otherwise dial both the area code (which starts with 0) and the local number. To **call to Turkey,** dial the international access code (00 from Europe, 011 from North America), then 90 (Turkey's country code), then the area code (without the initial 0) and local number. To **call home from Turkey,** dial 00, 1, then your area code and phone number.

Dress Code: As a sign of respect in mosques, cover your shoulders and knees; women should also wear head scarves.

Water: Don't drink tap water in Turkey. Bottled water is safe, cheap, and plentiful.

Tipping: At cafés and restaurants with table service, tip 10 percent. To tip a cabbie, round up to the next lira (if the fare is 14 TL, pay 15 TL).

Tourist Information: www.goturkey.com

ISTANBUL

Istanbul is the crossroads of civilizations, where Europe meets Asia, and where West meets East. Truly one of the world's great historic cities, Istanbul was once called Constantinople, named for the fourth-century Roman Emperor Constantine the Great. Over the centuries, the city has been the capital of two grand empires. The Byzantine Empire was born here in the fourth century A.D. and lasted until the 15th century, when the Ottoman Empire took over, ruling through the end of World War I. Even though Turkey isn't actually governed from Istanbul (Ankara, in the east, is the official capital), the city remains the historical, cultural, and financial center of the country.

Planning Your Time

This chapter focuses on the compact Sultanahmet district, in the center of the Old Town. From this area, Istanbul's top sights are all within walking distance. Read the list below and choose what appeals. If you'd like to do it all (and have at least 10 hours), here's a good order to follow to minimize backtracking:

• The self-guided **"Golden Horn Walk"** begins near the cruise terminal (and takes 30-45 minutes); if you'd rather get to the major sights ASAP, skip the walk and ride the tram to Sultanahmet.

• The self-guided **"Historic Core of Istanbul Walk"** takes you through Sultanahmet. Allow two hours, which includes visits to the Underground Cistern and Blue Mosque.

• Along the "Historic Core" walk, you'll see the **Hagia Sophia,** a famous domed church-turned-mosque-turned-museum. Allow up to 1.5 hours for my self-guided tour.

Excursions from Istanbul

Most cruise excursions offered in Istanbul are of the city itself, and many ships offer an inexpensive shuttle bus to and from the Grand Bazaar. If you'd prefer to get out of town, consider a mini-cruise on the city's primary waterway. The 19-mile-long **Bosphorus Strait** curves like a snake as it connects the Black Sea in the north with the Sea of Marmara and—eventually—the Mediterranean in the south. Today Istanbul extends pretty much all the way up to the Black Sea, but a few neighborhoods in the north retain a village-like quality, where the men still fish for a living. A boat trip along the waterway (see page 1105) is the best way to appreciate the size and scale of Istanbul, but it's no substitute for experiencing the city itself.

• Behind the Hagia Sophia is **Topkapı Palace,** where the sultans lived. Allow up to two hours here, or skip it if time is tight.

• The sprawling **Grand Bazaar** is a delightful place to wander, shop, and haggle. The Spice Market, a 30-minute walk away, is smaller and also fun. Take the self-guided **"Grand Bazaar and Spice Market Walk,"** allowing at least three hours (or more if you love to shop). Don't miss my shopping tips on page 1178.

If you end your day at the Spice Market, you're just an easy walk (or tram ride) across the Galata Bridge from where you started, near the cruise terminals.

• If you're spending the night in Istanbul, I highly recommend a twilight stroll on thriving **İstiklal Street.** Evening is the most interesting time to experience this classy Istanbul scene (see page 1186).

Visa Requirements

Turkey requires most visitors to get a visa **before** arriving in the country. Cruise ship passengers can make day trips into Turkish ports without a visa, but you can't spend the night on shore without one. Here are some guidelines for various cruise scenarios:

- If you tour Istanbul during the day but spend the night on your ship, **you do not need a visa.**
- If your cruise ends in Turkey and you leave the country without spending the night, **you do not need a visa.**
- If your cruise starts in Turkey, **you must get a visa** prior to your arrival, even if you are going directly from the airport to your ship.
- If your cruise ends in Turkey and you are staying overnight in a hotel or other accommodations, **you must get a visa** prior to your arrival in Turkey.

You can get a visa at a Turkish consulate or embassy, but it is easiest to purchase it online at www.evisa.gov.tr. Simply enter the required information and make your payment by credit card. The e-Visa will be emailed to you within 24 hours. You must print out your e-Visa, show it to airport officials and customs officers when you arrive, and carry it with you at all times during your stay in Turkey. American citizens pay $20, while Canadians pay $60 (also in US currency, Canadian currency not accepted).

Because this is a new requirement, it is smart to get your visa a month in advance. Some provisions may change prior to your trip; check with your cruise line or see www.turkishembassy.org for updates.

Arrival at the Port of Istanbul

Arrival at a Glance: If you're in a hurry to get to the big sights in Sultanahmet, take a taxi (20-25 TL, or about $11-14) or tram (3 TL, walk 5-10 minutes to the nearest tram stop, then ride straight into downtown). If you'd like to stretch your legs and get the lay of the land, consider walking five minutes to the Galata Bridge to do my "Golden Horn Walk;" after that, you can either walk or take a tram to Sultanahmet.

Port Overview

Istanbul is one of the most exciting cities to arrive in by cruise ship, with the minarets and palace towers of the old Ottoman capital growing ever taller as you approach. Ships dock right in the heart of town, near the mouth of the inlet called the Golden Horn, an easy walk or fast tram ride from most of the city's major sights.

The cruise port has a single, very long embankment served by two terminals. The majority of cruises send their passengers through the **Karaköy Terminal,** at the southwest end of the embankment, near the Galata Bridge. Some cruises disembark at the **Salıpazarı Terminal,** at the northeast end of the embankment (next to the Modern Arts Museum).

Tourist Information: The TI at the Karaköy Terminal is rarely open (tel. 0212/249-5776). Unfortunately, you won't get much help from Istanbul's other TIs, either (see page 1096).

Getting to Sultanahmet

Most visitors head directly to the center of the Old Town, Sultanahmet, where the city's top landmarks and sights are concentrated—including Hagia Sophia, Topkapı Palace, and the Blue Mosque. The Grand Bazaar is nearby.

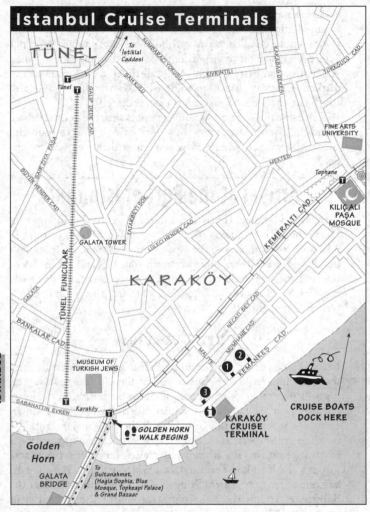

Istanbul Cruise Terminals

By Taxi

Taxi prices are particularly slippery in Istanbul. For tips on taking taxis in Istanbul—and getting a fair fare—see page 1102.

From **Karaköy Terminal,** the fair metered rate to the heart of the Sultanahmet sightseeing zone is about 20 TL (though some cabbies try to charge double or more). Taxis wait in front of the terminal, but if you walk just one or two blocks and find one on the street, you're less likely to be overcharged.

From **Salıpazarı Terminal,** the ride to Sultanahmet should cost about 25 TL. If taxis aren't waiting out front when your ship arrives, just start walking down the street (to the left) and flag one

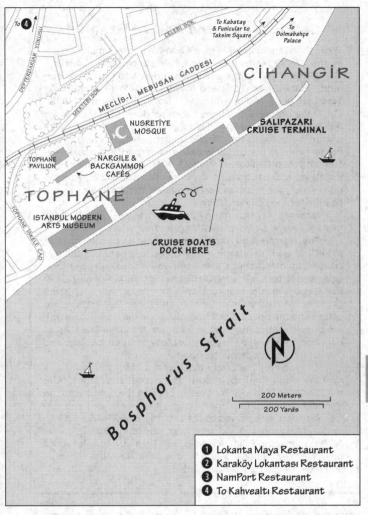

To Kabataş & Funicular to Taksim Square

To Dolmabahçe Palace

CELEBİ SOK.

DEFTERDAR YOKUŞU

To ④

MECLİS-İ MEBUSAN CADDESİ

MEKTEBİSOK.

CİHANGİR

NUSRETİYE MOSQUE

SALIPAZARI CRUISE TERMINAL

TOPHANE PAVILION

NARGILE & BACKGAMMON CAFÉS

TOPHANE

ISTANBUL MODERN ARTS MUSEUM

TOPHANE İSKELE CAD.

CRUISE BOATS DOCK HERE

Bosphorus Strait

N

200 Meters
200 Yards

ISTANBUL

① Lokanta Maya Restaurant
② Karaköy Lokantası Restaurant
③ NamPort Restaurant
④ To Kahvealtı Restaurant

down; taxis also wait near the little park across the street from the mosque and fountain, about 10 minutes' walk from the terminal.

By Foot

From Karaköy Terminal

It takes just five minutes to walk from this terminal to the Galata Bridge: Exit the terminal, turn left, and walk about a block to the small park. Bear left diagonally through the middle of the park and walk along the waterfront (with the water on your left) past two blocks of restaurant and café terraces, and past the fishermen casting into the Horn. My self-guided "Golden Horn Walk" begins

Services near the Port of Istanbul

While both terminal buildings are humble and lack major services, the streets nearby have shops, cafés, and other resources.

ATMs: If you're just arriving in Turkey and need local currency (Turkish lira, TL), head first to an ATM: From **Karaköy Terminal,** you'll find one directly in front of the terminal building, at the Garanti Bank; there's another down the street to the left, at DenizBank, and a cluster of ATMs next to the Galata Bridge. Near **Salıpazarı Terminal,** just on the left as you exit the terminal, at the corner with the main road, is a small, free-standing VakifBank kiosk with an ATM; the TEB bank across the street also has an ATM. If you're taking public transportation, save your coins and small bills—it can be tough to get change for the ticket machines.

Internet Access: Although there are no Internet cafés nearby, several harborside cafés offer free Wi-Fi.

Tea, Nargile, and Backgammon Bars: If you have an hour to kill and want to relax in a very cool scene between the two cruise terminals (about a 10-minute walk from either one), consider a visit to a *nargile* (NAHR-gee-leh, Turkish water pipe) bar. Enjoy a cup of tea, suck on a *nargile,* and/or play backgammon with (or at least among) the locals. Several inviting places line the park a block from the Tophane tram stop along the busy street called Meclis-i Mebusan Caddesi. The strip of bars and cafés is easy to spot: Just look for their awnings and overstuffed, outdoor lounge furniture.

To reach the park from the Tophane tram stop, walk five minutes along the busy road in the opposite direction from the Old Town, and look for the big park on the right. From the Karaköy Terminal, head north along the waterfront and follow the road as it curves to the left; the park (marked by an ornamental fountain) is on the right across from the big Kılıç Ali Paşa Mosque. From the Salıpazarı Terminal, turn left onto busy Meclis-i Mebusan Caddesi, pass the Nusretiye Mosque, and look for the park on your left.

from the small square just next to the bridge. It takes you across the bridge, then left along the embankment to Sirkeci train station. From there, you can catch a tram or keep on hiking up to Sultanahmet (a fascinating 30-minute walk all the way from the cruise terminal to Sultanahmet).

From Salıpazarı Terminal

This terminal is just a 10-minute stroll farther along the embankment. Leaving your ship, turn left and follow the water to the Karaköy Terminal, then exit that terminal and follow the directions described above to the Galata Bridge. If you're not allowed to walk along the embankment, exit the Salıpazarı Terminal and head straight to the busy street called Meclis-i Mebusan Caddesi, then turn left and walk toward the big mosque. Continue on this street past the mosque and the decorative fountain (which looks like a tiny mosque set in a park), and pass the Tophane tram stop, where the street changes names to Kemeraltı Caddesi. Keep following this street all the way to the Galata Bridge (and the start of my "Golden Horn Walk"), or just hop on the tram.

By Tram

Istanbul's handy tram is ideal for connecting most major points in town, including both cruise terminals (explained next). For details on riding Istanbul's user-friendly tram, see page 1103.

From Karaköy Terminal

First, walk to the Galata Bridge, following the instructions above. Once at the Galata Bridge, stand with your back to the water, walk straight ahead up the small staircase, and look for the entrance to the pedestrian underpass marked *tramvay* and *İSKELE GİRİŞİ*. Going down these stairs, you'll find yourself in a confusing maze of hallways lined with shops. You're headed to the tram: At the first intersection, turn left, following signs for *tramvay (tram)*. Before surfacing to street level, you'll need to buy a card for the tram (there may be an automated machine upstairs at the platform itself). Once you buy your card, go up the stairs marked *tramvay*; you'll emerge in the middle of the street. Cross the tracks to the platform for trams headed toward Bağcılar (not toward Kabataş). Hop on the tram and ride it four stops to Sultanahmet, or—if you want to go straight to the Grand Bazaar—five stops to Çemberlitaş.

From Salıpazarı Terminal

It's about a 10-minute walk from the terminal to the nearest tram stop (called Tophane): Exit the terminal to the busy street, then turn left and walk past the mosque and the decorative fountain. You'll find a tram stop in the middle of the street. Catch a tram headed toward Bağcılar (not toward Kabataş). There's likely an automated machine at the platform where you can buy a transit card (takes coins and small bills); if not—or if you need to break big bills to use in the machines—go to a nearby shop or kiosk (cross the street to the small park, which is surrounded by shops).

By Tour

For information on local tour options in Istanbul—including hop-on, hop-off bus tours, Bosphorus cruises, and local guides for hire—see "Tours in Istanbul" on page 1105.

Istanbul Essentials

English	Turkish	Pronounced
Blue Mosque	*Sultanahmet Camii*	sool-tah-nah-meht jah-mee
Bosphorus Strait	*Boğaziçi*	boh-ahz-ee-chee
Burned Column (and major tram stop)	*Çemberlitaş*	chehm-behr-lee-tahsh
Divan Yolu (main street in Old Town)	*Divan Yolu*	dee-vahn yoh-loo
Galata Bridge	*Galata Köprüsü*	gah-lah-tah kohp-rew-sew
Galata Tower	*Galata Kulesi*	gah-lah-tah koo-leh-see
Golden Horn (inlet between Old Town and New District)	*Haliç*	hah-leech
Grand Bazaar	*Kapalı Çarşı*	kah-pah-luh chahr-shuh
Gülhane Park	*Gülhane Parkı*	gewl-hah-neh pahr-kuh
Hagia Sophia (church and mosque museum)-	*Aya Sofya*	eye-ah soh-fee-yah
Hippodrome (ancient chariot racetrack)	*Hipodrom*	hee-poh-drohm

ISTANBUL

Returning to Your Ship

If you're coming on the tram to the Karaköy Terminal, disembark at Karaköy and go down the stairs to the underpass. At the bottom of the stairs, follow signs for *Karaköy İskelesi (Karaköy Pier)*. When you pop out near the waterfront, turn left to walk to the cruise terminal. If you're heading for the Salıpazarı Terminal, continue on the tram to the Tophane stop, and walk 10 minutes from there (follow busy Meclis-i Mebusan Caddesi in the direction the tram was going, and look for the terminal on your right, a few blocks after the mosque).

English	Turkish	Pronounced
Historic Core of the Old Town	*Sultanahmet*	sool-tah-nah-meht
İstiklal Street (main street in New District)	*İstiklal Caddesi*	ees-teek-lahl jahd-deh-see
Mosque of Süleyman the Magnificent	*Süleymaniye Camii*	sew-lay-mah-nee-yeh jah-mee
New District	*Pera, Beyoğlu*	peh-rah, bay-yoh-loo
Rüstem Paşa Mosque	*Rüstem Paşa Camii*	rew-stehm pah-shah jah-mee
Sirkeci Train Station		*Sirkeci Tren Garı*
Spice Market	*Mısır Çarşısı*	muh-suhr chahr-shuh-shuh
Süleymaniye	Neighborhood	*Süleymaniye*
Taksim Square (heart of New District)	*Taksim*	tahk-seem
Topkapı Palace	*Topkapı*	tohp-kah-puh
Tünel (old-fashioned funicular in New District)	*Tünel*	tew-nehl
Underground Cistern	*Yerebatan Sarayı*	yeh-reh-bah-tahn sah-rah-yuh

Orientation to Istanbul

Istanbul: A Verbal Map

Istanbul, with almost 15 million people, sprawls over an enormous area on both banks of the **Bosphorus Strait** (Boğaziçi). The Bosphorus runs north to south (from the Black Sea to the Sea of Marmara) through the middle of Istanbul, splitting the city in half and causing it to straddle two continents: Asia and Europe. Asian Istanbul (east of the Bosphorus) is mostly residential, while European Istanbul (west of the Bosphorus) is densely urban and contains virtually all of the city's main attractions. Two suspension bridges—the Bosphorus Bridge and the Fatih Sultan Mehmet Bridge—span the Bosphorus Strait, connecting the two halves.

Turkish Experiences for Cruisers

While Turkey's grand mosques and ancient ruins are exciting, even on just a short port visit, it's possible to go beyond predictable sightseeing and experience an authentic slice of life. Here are some vivid, fun, and relatively untouristy ideas for dipping your toes into Turkish culture.

Visit a mosque. Stepping into a Muslim house of worship offers Westerners an essential opportunity to better understand Islam. For tips on this, see "Visiting a Mosque" on page 1099. Istanbul's (and Turkey's) top mosques are the Blue Mosque (see page 1150) and the Mosque of Süleyman the Magnificent (page 1158).

Sip Turkish coffee. This is not a type of coffee, but the way the coffee is prepared: The coffee grounds float freely in the brew, leaving behind a layer of "mud" at the bottom of the cup. One good place to sample it is at Şark Kahvesi, inside the Grand Bazaar (page 1139).

Smoke a water pipe *(nargile)*. Even many non-smokers enjoy the Turkish tradition of *nargile* (nahr-ghee-leh)—also known as a "water pipe," "hookah," "hubbly-bubbly," or "shisha." The water pipes you'll see in Istanbul are filled with low-nicotine tobacco leaves mixed with molasses and dried fruit or herbs (apple is the most common, but you'll also see cappuccino, strawberry, and other flavors). Because the fruit-infused tobacco contains zero to very little nicotine, it's not addictive and doesn't give you a buzz—but it's still fun to let the taste and rich aroma linger in your mouth.

Play backgammon *(tavla)*. As with checkers back home,

Public ferries and a rail tunnel also link the banks, carrying millions of commuters each day.

A tapering inlet of the Bosphorus, called the **Golden Horn** (Haliç), runs roughly east to west, slicing through the middle of European Istanbul.

South of the Golden Horn is a peninsula known as the **Old Town**—the 3,000-year-old historical core of the city, surrounded by fragments of the original Byzantine wall. Near the tip of the Old Town peninsula is a compact and welcoming district called Sultanahmet, home to many of the city's most famous sights (Hagia Sophia, Blue Mosque, Topkapı Palace) and its highest concentration of hotels.

North of the Golden Horn is the modern, westward-looking, European-feeling **New District** (called "Pera" or "Beyoğlu" by locals), centered on Taksim Square and bisected by the main pedestrian drag called İstiklal Caddesi (which we'll refer to as İstiklal

most everyone in Turkey knows how to play the ancient game of backgammon. You'll often see people playing the game in coffee shops. If you're outgoing, challenging a local to a game can be a fun icebreaker. As you play, onlookers will gather and give you tips on how to win.

Haggle at the market. At the Grand Bazaar, Spice Market, any carpet shop, and other marketplaces, the first price you're quoted is a highly inflated starting point for a long, back-and-forth negotiation—which, with the right attitude, can turn out to be surprisingly enjoyable. For more on the art of bargaining, see page 1182.

Take a Turkish bath. A visit to a *türk hamamı* (tewrk hah-mah-muh; Turkish bath) is perhaps the best way to rejuvenate your tired body while soaking in Turkish culture. It's not for everyone: Several baths—mostly those that cater to tourists—are mixed-sex, and the bathers are at least partially naked. Attendants touch your bare skin. The air inside is hot and humid, and you won't be able to keep any part of your body dry. Still, for most of those who've tried it, one visit isn't enough. A few handy to the main sightseeing areas of town include Çemberlitaş Hamamı (next to Çemberlitaş tram stop, Vezirhan Caddesi 8, tel. 0212/522-7974, www.cemberlitashamami.com), Süleymaniye Hamamı (next to Mosque of Süleyman the Magnificent, Mimar Sinan Caddesi 20, tel. 0212/519-5569 or 0212/520-3410, www.suleymaniyehamami.com.tr), and Cağaloğlu Hamamı (halfway between Underground Cistern and Grand Bazaar, Prof. Kazım İsmail Gürkan Caddesi 34, tel. 0212/522-2424, www.cagalogluhamami.com.tr).

ISTANBUL

Street). The New District offers some interesting sights, good hotels and restaurants, and a 21st-century contrast to the Old Town.

Unlike many other European cities, Istanbul doesn't branch out from a main Town Hall or central square. In many parts of town, you may get lost if you're searching for a predictable, European-style square. (The Turkish word for "square"—*meydanı*—actually means something more like "area.") Instead, Istanbul is a cobbled-together collection of various landmarks and patches of land, all interconnected by twisty alleys. Sightseeing this decentralized, seemingly disorganized city can be intimidating for first-time visitors. But even though the city is an enormous metropolis, the tourist's Istanbul is compact and walkable, and an impressive public-transportation network efficiently connects the major sightseeing zones (see "Getting Around Istanbul," page 1101).

For a full-color map of Istanbul's Old Town, see the front of this book.

Istanbul Overview

ORTAKÖY

BEŞİKTAŞ

EUROPEAN ISTANBUL

TAKSIM SQUARE

DOLMABAHÇE PALACE

To Bosphorus Bridge, Fatih Sultan Mehmet Bridge, Anadolu Kavaği, & Black Sea

İSTIKLAL STREET

KABATAŞ

Golden Horn

NEW DISTRICT

TOPHANE

GALATA TOWER

Bosphorus Strait

ÜSKÜDAR

GALATA BRIDGE

CRUISE TERMINALS

EMINÖNÜ

MAIDEN'S TOWER

MOSQUE OF SÜLEYMAN THE MAGNIFICENT

SIRKECI STATION

HAREM

OLD TOWN

TOPKAPI PALACE

To Chora Church & Airport

GRAND BAZAAR

HAGIA SOPHIA

ASIAN ISTANBUL

KUMKAPI

BLUE MOSQUE

SULTAN-AHMET

HAYDARPAŞA STATION

2 km
2 mi

Sea of Marmara

KADIKÖY

Tourist Information

Istanbul's state-run TIs, marked with an *i* sign, are often not the best sources of information. They suffer from long lines, offer little or no information, and usually have only colorful promotional booklets, brochures, and maps. The only reason to visit one is to pick up the good, free city map. The TI staff, many of whom are not fluent in English, will try to help you with your requests, but most likely with mixed results.

Tourist Offices

If you must visit a TI, try one of the locations listed below. The first two are in the Old Town, the third and fourth are in the New District, and the last is at the airport (all have sporadic hours; generally daily 9:00-17:00):

• In the **Sultanahmet** neighborhood, in the center of the Old Town (Divan Yolu Caddesi 3, at the bottom of the square called the Hippodrome, next to the tram tracks, tel. 0212/518-8754).

• At the **Sirkeci** train station, near the Golden Horn in the Old Town's Eminönü district (by the station entrance, in the left corner next to a ticket booth, tel. 0212/511-5888).

Daily Reminder

Open Every Day: The Underground Cistern, Bosphorus cruise boats, Galata Tower, and most Turkish baths welcome tourists daily. Mosques are open daily, but close to tourists five times each day, when worshippers come to pray. For tips on visiting a mosque, see page 1099.

Sunday: The Grand Bazaar is closed.

Monday: Most of Istanbul's museums are closed today, including those operated by the Ministry of Culture—such as the Hagia Sophia, Istanbul Archaeological Museum, and Turkish and Islamic Arts Museum. The Dolmabahçe Palace, Galata Dervish Monastery, and Istanbul Modern Arts Museum, are also closed. Topkapı Palace is open (and crowded).

Tuesday: Topkapı Palace is closed. Hagia Sophia is busy today.

Wednesday: Because Topkapı Palace is closed on Tuesday, it may be especially crowded first thing this morning.

Thursday: All sights are open except for Dolmabahçe Palace. The Istanbul Modern Arts Museum is open until 20:00.

Friday: The Blue Mosque is closed until the end of the Friday noon service. All other mosques are closed during this important service, and very crowded before and after.

Saturday: Everything is open except the Quincentennial Museum of Turkish Jews.

Ramadan: During the Muslim holy month (June 28-July 27 in 2014, June 18-July 17 in 2015), a big, convivial, multi-generational festival breaks out each evening at sunset.

Religious Holidays: The Grand Bazaar and the Spice Market are closed on the first day of religious festivals (and often stay closed for the entire holiday). Museum hours are also readjusted for the first day of religious holidays: Most museums are closed in the morning, and a few close the entire day.

• Near **Taksim Square** in the New District (Mete Caddesi 6, a short walk from the square, tel. 0212/233-0592).

• At **Karaköy,** the cruise ship port, located where the Golden Horn and Bosphorus meet—rarely open (Kemankeş Caddesi, inside the passenger terminal, tel. 0212/249-5776).

• At **Atatürk Airport,** Istanbul's main airport, nine miles outside the city center (at the International Arrivals desk inside the terminal, tel. 0212/465-3151).

Helpful Hints

Health Concerns

Pharmacies: Pharmacies (*eczane;* edge-zah-neh) are generally open Monday through Saturday (9:00-19:00) and closed Sunday. In every neighborhood, one pharmacy stays open late and on holidays for emergencies. These *nöbetçi eczane* (noh-bet-chee edge-zah-neh; "pharmacy on duty") are generally within walking distance or a short cab ride from wherever you are. The location of the nearest *nöbetçi eczane* is posted by the entrance to any pharmacy. When interpreting signs, note these translations: *bu gece* (tonight), *Pazar* (Sunday), and *gün/günü* (day). As in the rest of Europe, dates are listed day first, then month (e.g., 06/04 is April 6).

Medical Problems: Istanbul's hospitals *(hastane)* usually have 24-hour emergency care centers (*acil servis;* "emergency service"), but are short on English-speaking personnel. Unless you need to be rushed to the nearest hospital, go to a private facility with English-speaking staff. The **American Hospital** in the New District is a good option (Valikonağı Caddesi, Güzelbahçe Sokak 20, Nişantaşı, tel. 444-3777—dial ext. 9 for English, then 1 for ambulance services). **Med-line** has medical assistance and ambulance service (tel. 444-1212). The **International Hospital** is close to the airport (Istanbul Caddesi 82, Yeşilköy, tel. 0212/468-4444; for an ambulance call 444-9724).

Street Smarts

Advice for Women: Wearing modest attire helps avoid unwelcomed incidents with men. It's best to cover your shoulders and knees, and avoid form-fitting clothes. Buses and trams are very crowded, and some contact is unavoidable. But if someone tries to touch you in a deliberate way, be clear about your disapproval. Push him away and say in a loud voice, "*Çek elini*" (check eh-lee-nee; Take your hands off me).

Street Safety: Be extremely cautious crossing streets that lack traffic lights. Look both ways, since many streets are one-way, and be careful of seemingly quiet bus, tram, or taxi lanes. Don't assume you have the right-of-way, even in a crosswalk. When crossing a street, keep your pace constant and don't stop suddenly. Drivers calculate your speed and won't hit you, provided you don't alter your route and pace. (Don't expect them to stop for you; they probably won't.)

Although it's technically illegal, cars park on sidewalks, especially in the Old Town. These parked cars, as well as freestanding merchandise kiosks or makeshift stands, can make sidewalks difficult to navigate. Try to stay by the side of the road, and pay attention to passing cars.

Public WCs: You'll generally pay 1-2 TL to use a public WC. Carry toilet paper or tissues with you, since some WCs are poorly supplied. Use the WCs in museums (likely free and better than public WCs), or walk into any sidewalk café or

American fast-food joint as if you own the place and find the WC in the back.

In the heart of the Old Town, plumbing isn't always up to modern standards. Rather than flush away soiled toilet paper, locals dispose of it in a designated trash can next to the toilet. It's culturally sensitive—and sometimes essential plumbing-wise—for visitors to do the same (especially if there's a sign requesting this).

Western-style toilets are the norm nowadays, but don't be surprised if you run across an "Oriental toilet," also known as a "Turkish toilet." This squat-and-aim system is basically a porcelain hole in the ground flanked by platforms for your feet. If this seems outrageous to you, spend your squatting time pondering the fact that those of us who need a throne to sit on are in the minority; most humans sit on their haunches and nothing more.

Water: Remember, don't drink the tap water in Turkey. Bottled or canned drinks and water served at better restaurants is fine.

Visiting a Mosque

At the Mosque: Touring some of Istanbul's many mosques (*camii* in Turkish; pronounced jah-mee) offers Westerners an essential opportunity to better understand the Muslim faith. But, just as touring a Christian church comes with a certain protocol, the following guidelines should be observed when visiting a mosque: Both men and women should remove their shoes, and cover their knees and shoulders. Some major mosques (such as the Blue Mosque) loan sheets for this purpose. Women should also cover their head with a scarf, as a sign of respect. Stay behind the cordoned-off area at the front of the mosque, which is reserved for worshippers. Be discreet when taking photos, and ask for permission before photographing worshippers.

When to Go: Specific "opening times" can vary greatly, but figure that most mosques are open to visitors from one hour after sunrise until about an hour before sunset, except during five daily services. The closure lasts from about 30 minutes before the service begins until after it ends (services last 15-30 minutes). If you are already inside when a service begins, you may be asked to leave so as not to disturb the congregation. If

Paying for Public Transportation

Istanbul's public transportation is fairly easy to use, with one caveat: The city is constantly tinkering with the ticketing system, so the following information may change by the time you visit. For the latest, check the Istanbul public transportation website at www.istanbul-ulasim.com.tr/en.

There are three types of tickets: tokens, disposable cards (for one to 10 rides), and a rechargeable pass (best for longer visits). You can buy these at most major bus, tram, light rail, Metro, and ferry stops (if a sign on a ticket machine says *Arızalıdır*, it means it's out of order). You must buy your ticket or pass before you board. Note that none of these options covers Bosphorus cruise boats.

Tokens: The simplest way to go is a 3-TL single-ride token (*jeton*; zheh-tohn). You can buy tokens at ticket booths or at vending machines (*jetonmatik*; zheh-tohn-mah-teek). The machines are easy to use and accept both bills (5-20 TL) and coins (5-50 Kr and 1 TL). To buy one token, insert money into the machine and press the green button on the right. To buy several tokens, insert money, hit the dark-blue button to select the number you want, and press the green button to confirm. Collect your tokens and change from the slot at the bottom.

Note that tokens for rail and ferry services are different and not interchangeable. Tokens are not accepted on buses; to ride a bus you'll need either a card or pass.

Single or Multiple-Ride Cards: These nonrechargeable electronic cards should, in theory, cover all forms of public transit. However, since they're still fairly new to Istanbul, you may find that some forms of transit have switched to electronic cards, while others still use tokens, and some use both. A single-ride card costs 4 TL; multiple-ride cards offer lower fares (2-ride

you're visiting a mosque on Friday, avoid the midday service, which is more heavily attended than others, and longer, because it includes a sermon.

Services

Baggage Storage: Easy-to-use, computerized lockers are available in both terminals at Atatürk Airport and at the Sirkeci train station. Small lockers accommodate two to three backpacks, while larger lockers can fit up to three suitcases (small airport locker-10 TL/3 hours, 30 TL/day; large airport locker-20 TL/3 hours, 60 TL/day; train station lockers about 25 percent less).

English-Language Church: Christian services are held in English every Sunday at the **Dutch Chapel** (Union Church of Istanbul, just off İstiklal Street by the Dutch Consulate at #393,

card-7 TL, 3 rides-10 TL, 5 rides-15 TL, 10 rides-28 TL). You can buy these cards from ticket booths at major bus, tram, light rail, Metro, and ferry stops (not available through vending machines).

İstanbulKart Pass: If you're staying more than a few days and plan to use public transport frequently, consider the İstanbulKart. This credit-card-size pass is embedded with a computer chip and is rechargeable, though there's a nonrefundable 6-TL charge just to buy the card. After that, each ride costs 1.95 TL (compared to the 3-TL token or 4-TL single-ride card), and transfers within a two-hour window are even cheaper, at about 1 TL per ride (up to five transfers; you must wait at least 15 minutes between the start of your first ride and your transfer; no time limit between additional transfers). The pass works on all forms of transit, including double-decker buses that cross the Bosphorus (3.90 TL with pass) and ferries to the islands (3.50 TL with pass).

İstanbulKart passes are available at ticket booths or newsstands; to reload the card you can also use a vending machine or visit a tobacco shop near the central stops. To reload at vending machines, use coins, bills, or credit or debit cards—do not use large bills, as machines do not give change and will load that entire amount onto the card.

To use the İstanbulKart, hold it over the card reader as you go through the turnstile (on the top, just below the LCD screen). The screen will show your remaining balance. For more information about the İstanbulKart, call 0212/444-1871 or visit http://skart.iett.gov.tr/Eng.

If you're traveling outside the main tourist areas, it's a good idea to have a transit pass or extra tokens and cards on hand, in case you find yourself at a stop without a ticket-vending machine (or one that is out of order).

contemporary service at 9:30, traditional worship at 11:00, tel. 0212/244-5212, www.unionchurchofistanbul.org).

Updates to this Book: For news about changes to this book's coverage since it was published, see www.ricksteves.com/update.

Getting Around Istanbul

Even though Istanbul is a huge city, most of its tourist areas are easily walkable. You'll likely need public transportation only to connect sightseeing zones (for example, going from the Old Town to the New District across the Golden Horn). Istanbul has an impressively slick, modern, and user-friendly network of trams, funiculars, and Metro lines. Once you learn the system, it seems custom-made for tourists—the stops are located within a short walking distance of major attractions. Taxis and ferries round out your transportation options.

If possible, try to avoid travel during rush hour, when public transportation is packed with commuters and taxis can be trapped in traffic. On religious festival days—when public transit may be free or discounted—buses and trams can be loaded with locals visiting their families and heading out to parks, fairs, and theaters. Streets are crowded—it's a great time for people-watching. (The city also has a bus system, but it's designed for commuters and useful only for reaching outlying areas not covered by tram—if you're headed anywhere off the city's tram line, it's worth the time savings to take a taxi instead of the bus.)

By Taxi

Taxis are generally an efficient, affordable way to get around town (2.95-TL drop fee, then roughly 1.85 TL/kilometer; no nighttime tariff). Figure about 15-25 TL for a longer trip within the Old Town or New District, or about 35-55 TL between Atatürk Airport and a hotel in European Istanbul.

Taxi Tips: Scams are on the rise in Istanbul. Use only official taxis. These are painted yellow, with their license plate number, name, and home-office phone number displayed on the front doors.

If a taxi's top light is on, it's available—just wave it down. Drivers usually flash their lights when they see you waiting by the side of the road to indicate that they'll pick you up. Taxis can take up to four passengers. If you have difficulty hailing a cab off the street, ask someone where you can find a taxi stand. You can also call a taxi company, usually for no extra charge. Hotels, restaurants, museums, and even shopkeepers almost always have the phone number of a nearby taxi company—just ask.

All cabs have electronic meters and cabbies should use them. As long as the meter is on, the only way you can be cheated is if the driver takes a needlessly long route. Never go for an off-meter deal, because you'll always pay more than if you'd used the meter.

The cabbie may claim you have to pay bogus extra charges; for example, if he claims that you owe him a 5-TL "luggage charge" for a 15-TL ride, politely refuse and pay what's on the meter.

Some cab drivers use a sleight-of-hand trick with bill denominations. For example, they'll take your 50-TL bill, then insist you gave them only a 5-TL bill (while showing you a 5-TL bill they have ready and handy for this scam). If you need to pay your fare with a big bill, announce the bill's denomination as you give it to the cabbie.

Tipping: Although some cabbies are con artists, many are honest and deserve a tip. To tip, simply round up the bill (generally 1-2 TL; for exceptional service, you could add a few liras more). If you need a receipt, ask: *"Fiş, lütfen"* (fish lewt-fehn; receipt, please).

By Public Transportation

Istanbul's transit is convenient and inexpensive. Tram, light rail, funicular, and Metro lines intersect at central locations, and they all use the same cards and passes (in theory at least—see the sidebar on page 1100). Note that some routes may be extended before your visit (see timetables and maps at www. istanbul-ulasim.com.tr/en).

Tram

The seemingly made-for-tourists *tramvay* (trahm-vay) cuts a boomerang-shaped swath through the core of Istanbul's Old Town, then crosses the Golden Horn to the New District, where it continues along the Bosphorus. There's basically one tram line of interest to tourists (aside from the Nostalgic Tram that runs along İstiklal Street): You'll catch a tram marked *Bağcılar* to head for sights in the Old Town, and look for one marked *Kabataş* to return to the cruise terminals. Destinations are posted on the outside of the tram—just hop on the one heading in the direction you want to go. Key tram stops include (from north to south):

- **Kabataş:** End of the line in the New District, next to the funicular up to Taksim Square (described later) and a few blocks from Dolmabahçe Palace.
- **Tophane:** Near the Salıpazarı cruise-ship terminal and the Istanbul Modern Arts Museum.
- **Karaköy:** In the New District (directly across Galata Bridge from the Old Town), near the Karaköy cruise-ship terminal, the Galata Tower, and the Tünel train up to İstiklal Street.
- **Eminönü:** On the Golden Horn in the Old Town, near the Spice Market, Galata Bridge, and several Bosphorus ferry terminals.
- **Sirkeci:** Sirkeci train station, near the Golden Horn and several Bosphorus ferry terminals.

- **Gülhane:** At the side entrance to the Topkapı Palace grounds, near the Istanbul Archaeological Museum.
- **Sultanahmet:** Dead-center in the Old Town, near Hagia Sophia, the Blue Mosque, the Hippodrome, and many recommended restaurants.

• **Beyazıt** and **Çemberlitaş:** Flanking the Grand Bazaar in the Old Town.

There's also the **Nostalgic Tram** that runs up and down İstiklal Street, through the middle of the New District.

Light Rail

West of the Grand Bazaar in the Old Town (at the Yusufpaşa stop), the tram connects to the *hafif raylı sistem* (hah-feef rahy-luh sees-tehm; light-rail system), which stretches west and south. While few sights are on this light-rail line, it's handy for reaching the city's main bus terminal (Otogar) and Atatürk Airport (the stop called Havalimanı, at the end of the line). This tram-and-light-rail connection to the bus terminal or airport—while a hassle with a lot of luggage—is cheap (6 TL to the airport from the Old Town; 9 TL from the New District), costing much less than a cab or airport shuttle. A different commuter rail route, called the **Marmaray Line**, goes under the Bosphorus between Sirkeci train station and Üsküdar on the Asian side.

Funicular

An easy one-stop, two-minute underground *finiküler* connects Taksim Square (and İstiklal Street) in the New District with the Kabataş tram stop along the Bosphorus below. At Kabataş, the tram and funicular stations are side by side; to find the funicular station from Taksim Square, look for the combined funicular/Metro entrance at the center of the square, right across from the Marmara Hotel, and follow *Kabataş-Finiküler* signs.

A second underground funicular, called **Tünel,** connects the Galata Bridge on the Golden Horn with İstiklal Street on the hill above. This late-19th-century funicular is as historic as it is convenient.

Metro

The underground Metro—generally not useful for tourists—begins at Taksim Square and heads north into the business and residential Levent district. However, work is under way to extend the Metro line into the Old Town, and the Metro Bridge over the Golden Horn was recently completed. To find a Metro entrance, look for the big *M* signs.

By Ferry and Seabus

In this city where millions of people sail across the Bosphorus to work each day, the ferry system had better work well...and it does. In fact, locals much prefer ferries to avoid heavy traffic on the bridges over the Bosphorus, especially during rush hour. Ferries are convenient and inexpensive—many cost as little as 3 TL one-way (1.95 TL with an İstanbulKart pass). Note that the Bosphorus cruise boats cost more.

Tours in Istanbul

Hop-on, Hop-off Bus Tours
City Sightseeing's narrated double-decker bus tours enable you to hop off at any stop, tour a sight, and then catch a later bus to your next destination—but departures are so infrequent that this isn't really practical. The tour amounts to a pricey 1.5-hour ride in heavy traffic with useless multilingual commentary (a recorded voice occasionally interrupts the obnoxious loop of music to identify sights and to cross-promote other tours they run). The Old Town's single tram line will take you to any of these sights without the hassle and for a lot less money. The bus does, however, take you along the entire old city wall (quite impressive and hard to see otherwise, unless you catch a glimpse on your way from the airport), and offers views from the top deck, making it a convenient and scenic place to munch a kebab or picnic. (Thanks to a convertible roof, this option still works in rainy or cold weather.) Pick up their brochure at most hotel lobbies or from their booth across from Hagia Sophia. The loop starts on the main street across from Hagia Sophia, but you can hop on at nearly any of the major sights along the route. Buses run year-round, with hourly departures in peak season (roughly mid-April–mid-Oct) and departures every two hours off-season (€20, 10 percent discount with this book, tel. 0212/234-7777, www.plantours.com).

▲▲▲Bosphorus Cruise
To get a feel for the famous Bosphorus Strait, consider a boat tour. You'll pass waterfront palaces, mansions, and mosques, and two continent-straddling suspension bridges. Various companies sell 12-TL cruise tickets on either side of the Galata Bridge (behind bus stops to the west side, and next to Bosphorus cruise pier on the east—look for Bosphorus Tours sign). These boats will take you as far as the second bridge (Fatih Sultan Mehmet Bridge) and back in 1.5 hours, with no stops. **Turyol**—on the west side of the bridge, next to fish-sandwich boats and behind the bus stops—is one of many options (cruises generally run hourly Mon-Fri 12:00-18:00, Sat 12:00-19:00, Sun 11:00-19:30, less frequent mid-Sept-mid-June, tel. 0212/527-9952, ask for Mr. Ihsan). There's no set schedule for these private boats (at least, not one that's strictly adhered to). Boats depart as soon as they have enough people. Just buy your ticket and hop on.

Istanbul at a Glance

▲▲▲**Hagia Sophia** Constantinople's Great Church, later converted to an Ottoman mosque, and now a museum. **Hours:** Tue-Sun 9:00-19:00 in summer, until 17:00 off-season, closed Mon. See page 1150.

▲▲▲**Blue Mosque** Ahmet I's 17th-century "so there!" response to Hagia Sophia, named for its brightly colored tiles. **Hours:** Generally open daily one hour after sunrise until one hour before sunset, closed to visitors five times a day for prayer and Fri morning. See page 1150.

▲▲▲**Topkapı Palace** Storied residence of the sultans, with endless museum exhibits, astonishing artifacts, and the famous Harem. **Hours:** Palace—late March-late Oct Wed-Mon 9:00-19:00, until 17:00 off-season, closed Tue. Harem—Wed-Mon 9:00-17:00, closed Tue. See page 1151.

▲▲▲**Grand Bazaar** World's oldest shopping mall, with more than 4,000 playfully pushy merchants. **Hours:** Mon-Sat 9:00-19:00, shops begin to close at 18:30, closed Sun and on the first day of most religious festivals. See page 1157.

▲▲▲**Mosque of Süleyman the Magnificent** The architect Sinan's 16th-century masterpiece, known for its serene interior and the tombs of Süleyman and his wife, Roxelana. **Hours:** Mosque—generally open daily from one hour after sunrise until one hour before sunset, closed to visitors five times a day for prayer. Mausoleums—daily 9:00-17:00, until 18:00 in summer. See page 1158.

▲▲▲**Bosphorus Cruise** Boat ride on the Bosphorus Strait, offering a glimpse of untouristy Istanbul. **Hours:** Frequent departures all day long. See page 1105.

▲▲▲**İstiklal Street** Cosmopolitan pedestrian-only street in the New District, teeming with shops, eateries, and people. **Hours:** Always open. See page 1159.

▲▲**Underground Cistern** Vast sixth-century subterranean water reservoir built with recycled Roman columns. **Hours:** Daily 9:00-18:30, until 17:30 off-season. See page 1150.

▲▲**Turkish and Islamic Arts Museum** Carpets, calligraphy, ceramics, and other traditional arts on display at the former İbrahim Paşa Palace; closed for renovation but may reopen in mid-2014. **Hours:** Tue-Sun 9:00-19:00, until 17:00 off-season, closed Mon. See page 1151.

▲▲**Istanbul Archaeological Museum** Complex covering Istanbul's ancient civilizations, including sumptuous tiles and highly decorated sarcophagi. **Hours:** Tue-Sun 9:00-19:00, until 17:00 off-season, closed Mon. See page 1156.

▲▲**Spice Market** Fragrant and colorful spices, dried fruit, and roasted nuts inside a 350-year-old market hall. **Hours:** Mon-Sat 8:00-19:30, until 19:00 off-season, Sun 9:30-18:00 year-round. See page 1158.

▲▲**Galata Bridge** Restaurant-lined bridge spanning the Golden Horn, bristling with fishermen's poles and offering sweeping views of the Old Town. **Hours:** Always open. See page 1159.

▲▲**Galata Tower** 14th-century stone Genoese tower with the city's best views. **Hours:** Daily 9:00-19:30. See page 1161.

▲**Hippodrome** Roman chariot racetrack-turned-square, linking Hagia Sophia and the Blue Mosque. **Hours:** Always open. See page 1151.

▲**Gülhane Park** Former imperial rose garden, now a grassy park. **Hours:** Always open. See page 1157.

▲**Rüstem Paşa Mosque** Small 16th-century mosque of Süleyman's Grand Vizier with extravagant tile decor. **Hours:** Generally open daily one hour after sunrise until one hour before sunset, closed to visitors five times a day for prayer. See page 1158.

▲**Taksim Square** Gateway to the pedestrianized İstiklal Street, and heart of Istanbul's New District. **Hours:** Always open. See page 1159.

▲**Galata Dervish Monastery** Meeting place for dervishes, who whirl here once a week. **Hours:** Tue-Sun 9:00-18:00, until 16:00 in winter, closed Mon; dervish services generally held on Sun at 17:00. See page 1160.

▲**Dolmabahçe Palace** Opulent 19th-century European-style home of the sultans, accessible only by guided tour. **Hours:** Tours run late March-late Oct Tue-Wed and Fri-Sun 9:00-16:00, until 15:00 off-season, closed Mon and Thu. See page 1163.

Local Guides

Lale and Tan Aran, the co-authors of this chapter, own **SRM Travel,** which runs city tours, offers private guides, and helps develop custom itineraries for trips to Istanbul and the rest of Turkey. Mention this book to receive free travel consulting when you buy any travel service (tel. 0216/386-7623, www.srmtravel.com).

There are plenty of very good private guides in Istanbul who generally charge from about $225 to $325 for a full-day tour (usually runs 9:00-18:00). The following guides have also served our readers well: **Nilüfer İris** (especially good with senior travelers, mobile 0532-244-1395, tel. 0212/347-3854, niluferiris@hotmail.com), **Attila Kılınç** (mobile 0532-294-7667, www.marmaratours.com, attguide@yahoo.com), **Nilay Çağlı Türkeli** (mobile 0532-720-8679, nilayturkeli@gmail.com), **Kağan Koşağan** of KSG Tours (tel. 0216/343-4215, www.tourguidesinturkey.com, kosagan@yahoo.com), **Dilek Arman** of Backpackers Travel (tel. 0212/638-6343, www.backpackerstravel.net, info@backpackerstravel.net), **Orçun Taran** (mobile 0532-256-9401, www.orcuntaran.com, taranorcun@gmail.com), **Pınar Çağlayan** (mobile 0538-315-5888, guidepinar@hotmail.com), and **Kürşat Taner Ünal** (ktanerunal@yahoo.com).

Golden Horn Walk

From the Galata Bridge to Sirkeci Train Station

The famous Golden Horn—a strategic inlet branching off the Bosphorus Strait—defines Istanbul's Old Town peninsula. The city's fate has always been tied to this stretch of sea: The Golden Horn is Istanbul's highway, food source, and historic harbor all rolled into one. While much of the Old Town area feels dedicated to tourists these days, a visit to the Golden Horn has you rubbing elbows with fishermen and commuters.

This self-guided walk offers a handy orientation to the city, since it affords a sweeping panorama of the Old Town peninsula. The walk is short (about a third of a mile), but allow around 45 minutes if you like to linger.

The walk begins on the New District (north) end of the Galata Bridge, across the bridge from the Old Town. For instructions on getting here from your cruise ship, see page 1087. For tips on linking this walk to my walks through Istanbul's historic core, and the Grand Bazaar and Spice Market, see the sidebar.

Linking My Self-Guided Walks in Istanbul

The self-guided walks in this chapter are designed to help you make the most of one (very busy) day in Istanbul. Each walk picks up more or less where the last one leaves off.

First, the "Golden Horn Walk" takes you from the cruise ship terminal across the Golden Horn to the base of the Old Town. Then, the "Historic Core of Istanbul Walk" (see page 1116) leads you up through the core of the Old Town, covering the Blue Mosque and other sights near the Hippodrome. (You can stop along this walk to tour the Byzantine marvel of Hagia Sophia—easy to see fairly quickly—or splice in a visit to Topkapı Palace, which demands more time.)

A quick tram ride or short walk takes you from Sultanahmet to the Grand Bazaar, where you can follow the "Grand Bazaar and Spice Market Walk" through the bazaar and down to the Spice Market (see page 1129). You'll end up near the Golden Horn waterfront. From there it's a pleasant walk (or short tram or taxi ride) back to your ship.

The Walk Begins

• *Start at the Galata Bridge (at the east side of the north end—see map). If you wind up on the wrong side of the bridge, take the pedestrian underpass (with a WC) connecting the two sides. Position yourself on the riverbank. With the water at your back, you're facing the neighborhood called...*

ISTANBUL

Karaköy

The New District covers the area from Karaköy to Taksim Square, a few blocks up the hill. In Byzantine times, this area was inhabited

by the commercial colonies of Genoese and Venetian settlers. In the late Ottoman era, it was also a residential area for non-Muslims, including Jews, Catholics, and Eastern Orthodox Christians. Today, this part of the city is dominated by the famous Galata Tower (you can just see its cone-shaped top up the hill).

Karaköy is also Istanbul's main passenger port. As you turn and face the Old Town across the Golden Horn, you'll see public ferry and seabus docks along the embankment to your left. The port is the scene of an extensive rebuilding project, as run-down buildings make way for art galleries and convention centers. A deluxe

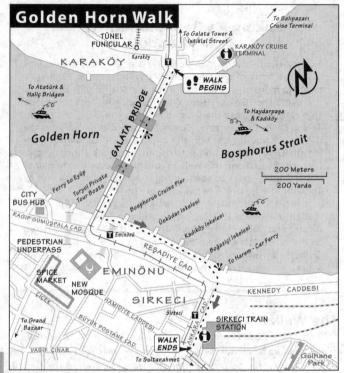

Golden Horn Walk

TÜNEL
FUNICULAR

To Galata Tower &
Istiklal Street

To Salıpazarı
Cruise Terminal

KARAKÖY

KARAKÖY CRUISE
TERMINAL

Karaköy

WALK
BEGINS

To Atatürk &
Haliç Bridges

Golden Horn

To Haydarpaşa
& Kadıköy

Bosphorus Strait

Ferry to Eyüp

Turyol Private
Tour Boats

200 Meters

200 Yards

CITY
BUS HUB

RAGIP GÜMÜŞPALA CAD.

Bosphorus Cruise Pier

Üsküdar İskelesi

PEDESTRIAN
UNDERPASS

Eminönü

Kadıköy İskelesi

Boğaziçi İskelesi

REŞADİYE CAD.

To Harem - Car Ferry

SPICE
MARKET

EMINÖNÜ

KENNEDY CADDESİ

NEW
MOSQUE

SIRKECİ

ÇİÇEK

HAMİDİYE CADDESİ

To Grand
Bazaar

BÜYÜK POSTANE CAD.

Sirkeci

SIRKECİ TRAIN
STATION

ANKARA CAD.

VASIF ÇINAR

WALK
ENDS

To Sultanahmet

Gülhane
Park

hotel is also planned. Locals grumble about political connections
that made the project possible, but it's too late to go back now.
• *Notice that the bridge has two levels. We'll start by walking across the
top level, then duck down to the lower level. Climb the stairs and wander across the bridge—dodging fishing poles as you walk.*

Fishermen

Enjoy the chorus line of fishing rods, dancing their little jig. While
some of these intrepid folks are fishing for fun, others are trying
to land a little extra income. They catch mostly mackerel or anchovies—better than nothing, especially during the commercial

fishing ban (no nets or sonar) that's
in effect from June to September.
During the ban, most of what you
find in the market is the expensive
daily catch, imported frozen fish,
or farm-raised fish.

Approach a fisherman and
wish him well, saying *"Rastgele"*
(pull your lips to your ears and

say "rust-geh-leh"; "May you catch some"). Ask to see his catch of the day: *Bakabilir miyim?* (bah-kah-bee-leer mee-yeem; "May I see?"). Each one has a jar, jug, bucket, or Styrofoam cooler full of wriggling fish he'd love to show off. If you're having fun with the language, try this: Point to someone's bucket of tiny fish and ask playfully, *"Yem mi, yemek mi?"* (yehm mee yeh-mehk mee; "Is that bait or dinner?").

Be careful as you walk among the fishermen—occasionally they get careless as they swing back for a cast.

• *The part of the bridge between its two low-profile towers can be raised to let big ships pass. This is a good place to find a spot out of harm's way and ponder the famous...*

Golden Horn (Haliç)

This four-mile-long horn-shaped inlet glitters like precious metal at sunset. But its strategic value is also worth its weight in gold. Protected from the prevailing north winds, the Golden Horn has served as a natural harbor for centuries—the history of Istanbul is steeped in it.

This was once the main commercial port of Constantinople and a base for the Byzantine fleet. To block enemy fleets sailing into the heart of the city, and to more effectively levy taxes on ships, the Byzantines hung a massive chain across the entrance of the Horn (you can see some of the historic links in the Istanbul Archaeological Museum). The chain was breached only a couple of times, by the Vikings (10th century) and by the Crusaders during the Fourth Crusade (1204).

In 1453, when the young Ottoman sultan Mehmet set out to capture Constantinople, he knew it was crucial to gain control of the Horn. Rather than breaking the chain, he decided to bypass it altogether. His troops pulled their fleet of ships out of the waters of the Bosphorus, slid them on greased logs over the hills through what later became the New District, and launched them back into the Horn—all in just one night.

During Europe's Industrial Revolution, the Ottoman Empire was slow to adapt to the fast-changing new world. It began the industrial race well after the West, then rushed to catch up, often without careful planning. The Horn became more and more polluted as industrial plants and shipyards were built along its banks.

In the 1980s, a clever Istanbul mayor with light blue eyes used a great gimmick to clean things up: He got people on board by saying his project would make the Horn as blue as his eyes. Factories were closed down and moved outside the city. Rotting buildings along the water with no historic significance were torn down, and empty space was converted into public parks. The area's entire infrastructure was renewed—a process that's ongoing.

• Now look inland over the tram tracks and up the Golden Horn (with your back to the Bosphorus), to see the...

Bridges over the Horn

Five bridges over the Golden Horn connect the Old Town to the New District. The first one you see is the brand-new Metro Bridge, completed in 2013 as part of the project to extend the underground Metro line to the Old Town.

Right behind the Metro Bridge is the low-lying Atatürk Bridge, on floating platforms, and beyond that is the taller main highway bridge, called Haliç (hah-leech)—also the local name for the Golden Horn.

The old Galata Bridge was the first and, for decades, the only bridge spanning the Horn. It's the one you see in historic postcards from Istanbul. But the huge platforms it was built on blocked water circulation, worsening the Horn's pollution woes. So, in 1994, this historic bridge was replaced with the new Galata Bridge—the one you're standing on. A public outcry of nostalgia eventually compelled city leaders to reassemble the original bridge farther down the Horn (between the Atatürk and Haliç bridges—not visible from here).

• Now take in the...

Old Town Panorama

Use this sweeping vista of the Old Town to get your bearings. Straight ahead from the end of the bridge, you can see the main entrance to the famous **Spice Market** (stone-and-brick building with three small domes), which sells souvenirs, caviar, dried fruits, Turkish delight, "Turkish Viagra"...and, oh yeah, spices.

The handsome mosque just to the left of the Spice Market (partly obscured by the bridge tower) is the New Mosque of Mother Sultan, or simply **New Mosque.** Dating from the 17th century, it's one of the last examples of classical-style Ottoman mosques. After that time, mosques were built in an eclectic style, heavily influenced by Western architecture.

Behind the Spice Market, twisty streets lined with market stalls wind their way up the hill toward the famous **Grand Bazaar.** While the Spice Market and Grand Bazaar are deluged with tourists, this in-between zone sells more housewares and everyday textiles than souvenirs—meaning that it's packed tight with locals looking for a bargain, particularly on Saturdays. Thanks to these crowds—and a steady stream of delivery trucks and carts blocking the streets—it can take a half-hour to walk just the four blocks between the markets. This is the "real" Istanbul—gritty and authentic.

Farther to the right, past the open space and near the Golden Horn, you see the **Rüstem Paşa Mosque.** This tiny mosque, with its single dome and lone minaret, is dwarfed by the larger mosques around it. But a visit there offers a peek into a more intimate and cozy mosque, with some of the finest 16th-century Ottoman tiles around.

On the hillside just above the Rüstem Paşa Mosque is the 16th-century **Mosque of Süleyman the Magnificent,** with its handsome dome and four tall minarets. Elaborate and impressive, yet tastefully restrained, this mosque offers an insightful contrast to the over-the-top and more famous Blue Mosque.

To the left of Süleyman's mosque is the single, tall **Beyazıt Tower.** Sometimes referred to as the "fire tower," it marks the location of bustling Beyazıt Square and Istanbul University's main campus (next door to the Grand Bazaar).

Now look to your left. At the end of the Historical Peninsula, you can see the lush gardens marking the grounds of **Topkapı Palace.** Most of what you see from here are the palace's lower gardens, called Gülhane, now a public park. You can also see the tower marking the entrance to the Harem complex.

To the right of the palace (up the hill, above the modern buildings), notice the gorgeous dome and minarets of **Hagia Sophia**—once the greatest church in Byzantium, then a mosque, and today one of Istanbul's best museums. The famous Blue Mosque, which faces Hagia Sophia from across Sultanahmet Park, is not quite visible from here.

If you look far to the left, beyond the Topkapı Palace gardens, you can see the Bosphorus Strait and **Asian Istanbul** (the hilltop that bristles with TV towers, like a sea of giant minarets). The Bosphorus Bridge, an impressive suspension bridge, is visible from here (unless it's really hazy).

• *Continue along the bridge to the second tower. Go inside the tower and take the stairs down...*

Under the Bridge

As you descend the stairs, look up for a fun view of dozens of fishing rods twitching along the railing of the bridge. As you walk down here, watch your head—sometimes an amateur fisherman carelessly lets his weight swing under. And keep an eye out for the flicker of a little silvery fish, thrashing through the air as he's reeled in by a happy predator.

Walk along the bridge (toward the Old Town), enjoying this "restaurant row." Passages lead to the other side of the bridge, which is lined with still more restaurants. As you walk, aggres-

sive waiters will try to lure you into
their restaurants. Don't be shy—look
around, get into a conversation, and
compare prices. You may end up here
tonight for a fish dinner or, better yet,
on the other side of the bridge, where
you can watch the sun set over the
Golden Horn. Even if you don't want
a full meal, consider picking up a sandwich or having a drink at a
café. The last restaurant, with dozens of simple brown tables, sells
barbecued fish sandwiches to go—handy to eat as you walk (you'll
smell the outdoor barbecue before you see it). If you cross under,
you'll find a line of trendy teahouses and bars facing up the Golden
Horn—great for backgammon, drinks, and sunsets. At the end of
the bridge on the Old Town side, venerable "fish and bread" boats
sell cheap fish sandwiches literally off the boat.

• *At the end of the bridge, turn right to enjoy the scene around the tippy
fish-sandwich boats. Take a moment to watch the action: families enjoying an affordable meal out, boys deboning filets and tossing bones into
the sea between the boat and the pier, and happy birds scavenging away.
Then cross under the bridge and follow the embankment to the...*

Commuter Ferry Terminals

This embankment bustles with thousands of commuters heading to
and from work (during morning and evening rush hours) and shop-

ping chores (especially Saturdays). Peek into the pedestrian
underpass beneath the bridge
for a taste of the shoulder-to-
shoulder commute that many
locals endure.

This area is also a hub for
intercontinental traffic. Public
ferries carry millions of com-
muters every year between the European and Asian districts of
Istanbul. Until the first bridge over the Bosphorus was built in the
early 1970s, boats were the only way to cross from Europe to Asia.
Locals still prefer the ferries, which are a convenient and cheap way
to avoid the gridlock on the bridges.

Just beyond the first terminal—which serves public ferries
that run up the Bosphorus—are **private tour boats** (look for the
Bosphorus Tours sign). For only 12 TL (hawkers ask more), these
boats take you as far as the second bridge on the Bosphorus and
back again in 1.5 hours (see page 1105).

• *When you spot the Harem ferry, it's time to head inland. For a nice
panorama over the Galata Bridge and the New District, you could climb*

the pedestrian overpass. But for where we're going next, it's better to cross the street at the stoplight in order to stay on the proper side of the tram tracks.

After you cross the street, you're in the Sirkeci neighborhood, and a few steps from the historic train station of the same name.

Sirkeci Train Station

This is a surprisingly low-profile train station for having once been the terminal of the much-vaunted Orient Express. An old loco-

motive decorates the corner of the station, honoring this footnote in history. Pass the locomotive and turn left, finding your way to the station's main entrance (along the modern wall with the white doors, under the sign for *İstanbul Gar*). Once inside the door, a TI and well-signed ticket windows are to your left—and a stat-

ue of Atatürk is staring down at you from the head of the tracks.

Wander deeper into the station, past the ticket windows, and go left to find evidence of a more genteel, earlier age. Consider popping into the humble little **Railway Museum,** with its old photos and equipment (free, Tue-Sat 9:00-12:30 & 13:30-16:00, closed Sun-Mon). To the right of the museum is the old passenger waiting room, with wooden benches and stained-glass windows that recall the station's former glory.

The **Orient Express** train line began in the 1880s. You could board a train in Paris and step off into this very station three days later (after passing through Munich, Vienna, Budapest, and Bucharest). Traversing the mysterious East, and headed for the even more mysterious "Orient," passengers were advised to carry a gun. The train service was rerouted to avoid Germany during the Nazi years, and was temporarily disrupted during both world wars, but otherwise ran until May of 1977. While this is the most famous route, almost any eastbound train from Western Europe could be called an "Orient Express." The train line was immortalized in literature and film—most famously by Agatha Christie, whose *Murder on the Orient Express* takes place on the Simplon Orient Express (Paris' Gare de Lyon station to Milan, Belgrade, Sofia, and Istanbul).

Though the Orient Express is now run by a private company and visits Istanbul only once a year, Sirkeci station still serves trains bound for Europe, and to suburban destinations as well (it can get crowded at rush hour). Most of the travelers are urban workers, but you occasionally spot vagabonds or peasants fresh from the countryside, eyes wide as they first set foot in the big city.

• *Your walk is finished. To head up to Sultanahmet—and the beginning of the next walk—you can take the tram (which departs from directly in front of the station) two stops uphill to the Sultanahmet stop, or follow the tram tracks on foot (10-15 minutes, passing the Grand Portal, described on page 1157).*

Historic Core of Istanbul Walk

Just like Rome, Istanbul's Old Town was built on seven hills. The district called Sultanahmet, on top of the first hill, is the historic core of the city. The Greek city of Byzantium was founded nearby, where Topkapı Palace stands today. Early Greek settlers—weary after their long journey—chose this highly strategic location, which could easily be fortified with walls on all sides. The site gave them control of all three surrounding bodies of water (the Bosphorus Strait, the Golden Horn, and the Sea of Marmara) and was convenient to the Greek colonies on the Black Sea.

This self-guided walk takes you through Sultanahmet—Istanbul's single best sightseeing zone, and host to Istanbul's most important and impressive former church (Hagia Sophia) and mosque (the Blue Mosque), and its most significant Byzantine ruins (the Hippodrome and Underground Cistern).

Orientation

Length of This Walk: Allow about two hours, not including time for visiting Hagia Sophia or Topkapı Palace. To shorten this walk, head straight to the Blue Mosque, then Hagia Sophia (or vice versa, depending on entry lines).

Getting There: If coming by tram, get off at the Sultanahmet stop, then walk to the park between the Blue Mosque and Hagia Sophia.

Hagia Sophia: 25 TL, Tue-Sun 9:00-19:00, until 17:00 off-season, closed Mon, last entry one hour before closing, Sultanahmet Meydanı.

Topkapı Palace: Palace—25 TL, Wed-Mon 9:00-19:00, until 17:00 off-season, closed Tue, last entry one hour before closing, exhibits begin to close one hour earlier; Harem—15 TL, Wed-Mon 9:00-17:00, closed Tue.

Underground Cistern: 10 TL, daily 9:00-18:30, until 17:30 off-season, last entry 30 minutes before closing, Yerebatan Caddesi 1/3.

Blue Mosque: Free, generally open daily one hour after sunrise until one hour before sunset, closed to visitors five times a day for prayer and Friday morning, Sultanahmet Meydanı. To enter the mosque, knees and shoulders must be covered, shoes

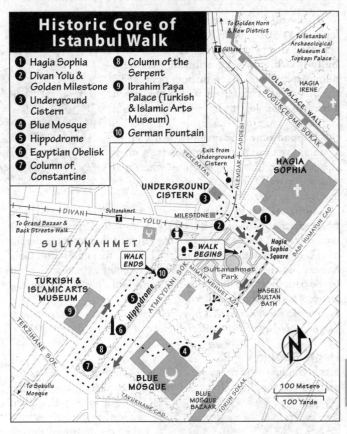

Historic Core of Istanbul Walk

1. Hagia Sophia
2. Divan Yolu & Golden Milestone
3. Underground Cistern
4. Blue Mosque
5. Hippodrome
6. Egyptian Obelisk
7. Column of Constantine
8. Column of the Serpent
9. Ibrahim Paşa Palace (Turkish & Islamic Arts Museum)
10. German Fountain

must be removed, and women should also cover their hair with a scarf (see page 1099 for details).

The Walk Begins

• *Begin at the pond in Sultanahmet Park, sandwiched between Istanbul's two most famous sights: the Blue Mosque and Hagia Sophia.*

Sultanahmet Spin Tour

With your back to the gray-colored Blue Mosque, face the orange Hagia Sophia (eye-ah soh-fee-yah). We'll take a slow spin clockwise to get the lay of the land. Behind Hagia Sophia, not visible from here, are the Topkapı Palace grounds, which also house the Istanbul Archaeological Museum. To reach the main palace entry, you'd walk along the front of Hagia Sophia to the right, then turn left at the first corner and walk along the side of the church until you passed between the old walls through the Imperial Gate (palace described on page 1151).

Now turn 90 degrees to the right. The long terra-cotta-colored building with different-sized domes is the 16th-century **Haseki Sultan Bath,** now a government-owned emporium (see photo). Keep turning right, and at the other end of this lively park is the famous **Blue Mosque.** Just to its right (out of sight) is the long, narrow Byzantine square called the **Hippodrome** (the green-domed German Fountain you can see through the trees marks the near end of the Hippodrome—where we'll finish this walk). Keep turning until you are again facing Hagia Sophia.

Sultanahmet Park is a fine example of a city determined to be people-friendly. In spring it's a festival of tulips. If the fountain is on, notice that the arcs of water are designed to mimic the domes of Hagia Sophia. This is perhaps the best photo op for both Hagia Sophia and the Blue Mosque. The large cobbled street at the end of the park (near the Blue Mosque) turns into a parking lot during festivals and on some weekends.

• *Across the very broad street, two red Turkish flags mark the entrance to Hagia Sophia. Now, let's cross the street and go to church.*

Hagia Sophia

Hagia Sophia—the name means "divine wisdom"—served as the patriarchal church of Constantinople for centuries (similar to the

Vatican in Rome). When an earlier church on this site was destroyed during the sixth-century Nika Revolt, the Byzantine Emperor Justinian seized the opportunity—and this prime real estate—to build the most spectacular church the world had ever seen. He hired a mathematician named Anthemius to engineer a building for the ages, with an enormous central dome unlike anything ever constructed. You could fit Paris' Notre-Dame Cathedral under Hagia Sophia's dome—or the Statue of Liberty, minus her torch. Nearly 1,500 years later, Hagia Sophia still dominates Istanbul's skyline.

When the Ottomans conquered Constantinople in 1453, Hagia Sophia (which they called Aya Sofya) was converted to a mosque, and minarets were added to this otherwise very Byzantine-looking church. Because of its grand scale, grace, and beauty,

Hagia Sophia's design influenced Ottoman architects for generations. That's why many mosques built after the Ottoman invasion—and long after the Byzantines became a distant memory—continued to incorporate many Byzantine elements.

You could tour Hagia Sophia now (✪ using my self-guided "Hagia Sophia Tour," page 1164), or wait until the end of our orientation walk—we'll finish just up the street from here. (If you're visiting in peak season and the line is short, you'd be wise to pop in now—groups can inundate the place at a moment's notice.) Allow up to 1.5 hours to see everything at the church.

• *Leaving Hagia Sophia, you can continue this walk (see next paragraph). But if you have the time and want to see **Topkapı Palace**, this is your best opportunity. Facing the main entrance of Hagia Sophia, turn right and walk to the end of the giant building, then turn left around the corner to reach the palace entry. For more on Topkapı Palace, see page 1151.*

To continue the walk from Hagia Sophia, turn right and walk to the busy street corner. (Hop-on, hop-off tour buses leave near here, at the little red tour kiosk.) Head across the tram tracks to the 30-foot-tall stone-and-brick tower that looks like a large chimney, with a fountain built into it.

Divan Yolu and the Golden Milestone

The busy street with the trams is Divan Yolu (dee-vahn yoh-loo), the main thoroughfare through Sultanahmet. To the left (uphill), it

leads to the Grand Bazaar. To the right (downhill), it heads to the Galata Bridge and New District. Notice the dramatic boomerang-shaped swoop made by the tram tracks as they pass Hagia Sophia. Since Istanbul's Old Town tram has only one line, it's remarkably user-friendly. If Istanbul is a jungle, consider this your vine. It swings to nearly all the places of tourist interest, and it can't get lost (trams run 6-8 times per hour).

Divan Yolu was also Constantinople's main transportation artery in Byzantine times, when it was named Mese ("Middle Way"). The road started right here, where the Golden Milestone (Miliarium Aureum) still stands (in a pit, to the left of the tower). Some 1,500 years ago, the Byzantines considered this point the center of the world. This ancient and once-gilded milestone showed the distances to key locations within the empire. Today it's a mere stub worn down by the centuries. Nothing remains of its decorative arches, or of the statues that once adorned it (of Constantine and his mother, Helen, holding a cross).

• *Go downhill to the first corner and turn left. Across the street from the old yellow police building is the low-profile, red-and-white striped entrance to the...*

Underground Cistern

This vast underground reservoir dates back to Byzantine Emperor Justinian's reign in the sixth century A.D. Because it was built on the site of an earlier basilica, it's often called the "Basilica Cistern." Turks call it *yerebatan sarayı*, which means "sunken palace."

Buy your ticket and descend the stairs into the cistern. The visit is a level, 15-minute, 400-yard underground stroll. (You'll exit up stairs through a different gate, a block down the street.) While your eyes adjust to the dimness, ponder the history of this spectacular site. The Byzantine Empire enjoyed a Golden Age under Emperor Justinian; its currency was so strong that merchants in continental Europe and Asia demanded to be paid in Byzantine imperial coins. This enormous wealth can still be seen in the monuments and even the functional buildings (such as other cisterns) of that era. This massive reservoir—larger by far than any other in Constantinople—was built

to meet the needs of a fast-growing capital city and to provide precious water in case of a shortage. The cistern covers an area about the size of two football fields—big enough to hold 27 million gallons of fresh water.

A forest of 336 columns supports the brick ceiling. Most of these were recycled from earlier Roman ruins in and around the city. Note the variety of capitals (tops of columns). Clay pipes and aqueducts carried water 12 miles to this cistern. (A half-mile-long chunk of the Valens Aqueduct still stands, spanning Atatürk Bulvarı—Atatürk Boulevard—roughly a mile west of here.)

Gradually these pipes became clogged, and the cistern fell out of use. As time passed, neglect became ignorance, and people forgot it was even there. An Ottoman historian wrote that residents of this area were luckier than others, as they could easily drop a bucket into any garden well and collect apparently God-given water. (They didn't realize they were dipping their buckets into a Byzantine masterpiece.)

The platform you're walking on was constructed two decades ago to make the far reaches of the cistern more accessible to visitors. While water once filled this space halfway to the ceiling, today it's just a shallow pond, formed from rainwater that leaks in through cracks and compromised mortar in the ceiling. (Accumulated water is pumped out to prevent damage.) Before the walkway was built, the water was six feet deep, and the only way to see the cistern was to rent a boat and row in the dark—a perfectly evocative setting used for James Bond's adventures in *From Russia with Love*.

Walking toward the far end, notice that part of the cistern (which has suffered structural damage) is separated by a wall.

At the far end of the cistern, find the two recycled Medusa heads lying on the ground—one sideways and one upside-down—squeezed under pillars. The Greeks often carved this fearsome mythological gorgon, with hair made of snakes and a gaze that could turn people to stone, into tombstones or cemetery walls to scare off grave robbers. In Roman times, she became a protector of temples. When Christianity took hold,

Medusa was a reminder of the not-so-distant Roman persecution of Christians—so it may be no coincidence that these pagan fragments were left here in a dark corner of the cistern, never to see daylight again. Another theory proposes that the architect simply needed a proper base to raise the two small columns to ceiling height...and the Medusas were a perfect fit.

On the way out, you'll see huge, blocky concrete columns built more recently to support the structure, which are quite a contrast to the ancient, graceful Roman columns.

• *Leaving the Underground Cistern, turn right and retrace your steps back up to the park where this walk began. Cross the park to find the towering Blue Mosque at the far end. You'll note that we've set out some nice wooden benches from which you can enjoy the view. Read the next page or so while seated here.*

Blue Mosque

This famous and gorgeous mosque is one of the world's finest. It was built in just seven years (1609-1616) by the architect Mehmet

Aga, who also rebuilt Kaaba (the holiest shrine of Islam—the giant black cube at the center of the mosque in the holy city of Mecca). Locals call it the Sultan Ahmet Mosque for the ruler who financed it, but travelers know it as the Blue Mosque because of the rich blue color of the handmade ceramic tiles that dominate the interior.

• *As you face the Blue Mosque, to your right (with the multitude of mini-*

ISTANBUL

*domes and chimneys) is the madrassa, a school of theology. Facing the
mosque, you can see it has...*

Six Minarets

Aside from its impressive scale and opulent interior, the Blue
Mosque is unique because of its six minarets. According to Muslim
tradition, the imam (the prayer leader) or the muezzin (a man chosen for his talent in correctly voicing the call to prayer) would climb
to the top of a minaret five times each day to announce the call to
prayer. On hearing this warbling chant, Muslims are to come to
the mosque to pray. Today, an imam or muezzin still performs the
call to prayer, but now it's amplified by loudspeakers at the top of
the minarets.

A single minaret was adequate for its straightforward function, but mosques financed by sultans often wanted to show off
with more. A story popular with tour guides is that Sultan Ahmet I
asked the architect for a gold *(altın)* minaret—but the man thought
he said "six" *(altı).* In all likelihood, Ahmet probably requested
the six minarets to flaunt his wealth. But at the time, the central
mosque in the holy city of Mecca also had six. The clergy at Mecca
feared that Ahmet's new mosque would upstage theirs—so the sultan built a seventh minaret at Mecca.

• *The walkway by the benches leads to the Blue Mosque. Through the gate
at the end of the walkway, you enter the mosque's...*

Outer Courtyard

Straight ahead, a staircase leads up to the inner courtyard (described next). To the right of the staircase, notice the line of water
taps used for ablution—the ritual cleansing of the body before worshipping, as directed by Islamic law. These are comparatively new,
installed to replace the older fountain in the inner courtyard (which
we'll see soon). To the left, another set of stairs leads to an entrance
into the mosque designated for worshippers (you may exit through
this gate when you leave the mosque).

• *Now take the stairs up into the...*

Inner Courtyard

The courtyard is surrounded by a portico, which provides shade
and shelter. The shutters along the
back wall open in summer for ventilation. In the center of the courtyard
is a fancy fountain, once used for
ablutions but no longer functional.
When the mosque fills up for special
services, worshippers who can't fit inside pray in the large vaulted area in

front of the mosque (on your left) and, if necessary, fill the rest of the courtyard. But today such jam-packed services are rare. Muslims are not required to go to the mosque five times each day; they can pray anywhere. The exception is the midday service on Friday, which the Quran dictates should be a time for all worshippers to come together in congregation—making mosques more crowded on Fridays.

• *Now go into the mosque. (For instructions and etiquette, see page 1099.) The main door on this west end is where visitors generally enter. (If this door is closed, you should be able to go around the corner on the right.) As you enter, take a plastic bag from the container and use it to carry your shoes, which you should remove before you step on the carpet. Entering the mosque is free, but you can make a donation as you exit.*

Interior

Stepping through the heavy leather drape into the interior, you'll understand why this is called the Blue Mosque. Let your eyes adjust to the dim lighting as you breathe in the vast and intensely decorated interior.

Approach the wood railing to take a closer look at the apse (straight ahead from the main gate). The area beyond this barrier is reserved for worshippers, who fill the space at all times of day. The little shin-high wooden shelves are for storing worshippers' shoes.

On the far wall, look for the highly decorated marble niche with large candles on either side. This is the mihrab (meeh-rahb), which points southeast to Mecca, where all Muslims face when they worship. The surrounding wall is decorated with floral-designed stained-glass windows, many of them original.

On the right side of the apse is a staircase leading up to a platform with a cone on top. This is the *mimber* (meem-behr), similar to a pulpit in a Christian church. A *mimber* is symbolic of the growth of Islam—Muhammad had to stand higher and higher to talk to his growing following. It is used by the imam (prayer leader) to deliver a speech on Fridays, similar to a sermon in Christian services. As a sign of respect for Muhammad, the imam stands only halfway up the staircase.

Farther to the right, next to the main pillar, is a fancy marble platform elevated on columns. This is where the choir sings hymns a cappella (mainstream Islam uses no instruments) on important religious days.

Mosque services are segregated: The main hall is reserved for men, while women use the colonnaded area behind the barriers at the back, on both sides of the main entrance. Women can also use the upper galleries on crowded days. While many visitors think it is demeaning to women to make them stay in back, most Muslims feel it's respectful to women and more conducive to prayer. The men are better able to concentrate on God without the distraction of bent-over women in front of them, and the women feel more comfortable not having men behind them.

The huge dome—reaching a height of 141 feet and a diameter of 110 feet—is modeled after the one in Hagia Sophia, which was the first building to use pillars to support a giant central dome. As Turkish engineers improved on this concept over the years, they were able to create vast indoor spaces covered by cascading domes. The same fundamentals are still used today in many contemporary mosques.

Near the corners of the vast room, notice the giant pillars paved with fluted marble panels. These "elephant feet" support the arches, dome, semi-domes, and cupolas. Since the weight is transferred mainly to these four pillars, thick, bulky walls aren't necessary. Like flying buttresses in a Gothic cathedral, this technique allowed the architect to fill the walls with decorative windows. Compare the Blue Mosque (with its 260 windows) with the gloomy interior of the much older (and bulkier) Hagia Sophia.

The low-hanging chandeliers were designed for oil lamps with floating wicks; they were designed to be raised and lowered to tend to the lamps (although now they hold electric bulbs). Years ago, a thick patchwork of handmade rugs covered the floor—these have been removed for preservation and replaced with the current machine-made carpeting. Notice that the carpets have lines to organize the worshippers—just like lined paper organizes words.

Islamic tradition forbids the portrayal of living beings in places of worship, which could distract people from worshipping Allah as the one God. As a result, the Muslim world excelled at nonfigurative art. In this and other mosques, instead of paintings of saints and prophets, you'll see geometric designs and calligraphy.

Along with the painted floral and geometric patterns, more than 20,000 ceramic tiles were used extensively to decorate the mosque. Lower parts of the wall—up to the height of the marble application on the giant pillars—are paved with mostly blue, early-17th-century İznik tiles. İznik (ancient Nicea) was the Ottoman Empire's tile-making center, and its tiles feature prominently in many museums around the world (including the Istanbul Archaeological Museum, nearby).

Artful Arabic calligraphy (*hat* in Turkish; pronounced "hot") is another form of mosque decoration. To make the words appear more beautiful, the *hattat* (hot-taht; calligrapher) takes liberties with grammatical rules and often combines letters irregularly, making it difficult to read. Many of the examples of *hat* around the

mosque are excerpts from the Quran or from the hadith (the collected teachings of the Prophet Muhammad). In a Christian church, you'd have God and Jesus front and center. Here, the two medallions high above the mihrab read *Muhammad* (left) and *Allah* (right).

The Blue Mosque represents the pinnacle of Ottoman architecture—and marks the beginning of the empire's decline. After its construction, the treasury was exhausted, and the Ottoman Empire entered a period of stagnation that eventually led to its collapse. Never again could the empire afford a building of such splendor.

Similarly, the mosque's patron, Sultan Ahmet I, was too young and inexperienced to effectively wield his authority and became mired in bureaucracy and tradition. While a few of his successors (including his son, Murat IV) managed to temporarily revive the dying empire, Ahmet marked the beginning of a long string of incompetent sultans who would eventually rule over an empire known in the early 20th century as the "Sick Man of Europe."

• *Leave the mosque and return to the inner courtyard. With your back to the mosque, walk to the back of the courtyard. Before you exit, consider taking a seat on the marble steps and soaking up the view of the mosque and the people mingling about. The crowd is a fun mix of Turkish tourists, travelers from across the world, wide-eyed cruise groups, and pilgrims. Try out a little Turkish: You can say, "Nasılsınız?" (nah-suhl-suh-nuhz; "How are you?") and "Merhaba" (mehr-hah-bah; "Hello"). Every school kid knows how to say in English, "What is your name?" and "How old are you?"*

As you leave, turn around as you step out of the courtyard for one more glance at the graceful cascading-domes design (go halfway down the stairs and look back for a good photo op, with the domes nicely framed by the portal).

As you step outside the exterior gate, you enter a long, skinny square that was the ancient Hippodrome of Constantinople. The Egyptian Obelisk is directly ahead of you.

Hippodrome

Built in the fourth century A.D., the Hippodrome was Constantinople's primary venue for chariot races. But it became the place where the people of the city gathered, and this racetrack has also been the scene of social and religious disputes, political clashes, and violent uprisings.

Chariot races were the most popular events in Constantinople, appealing to people from all walks of life. Winning teams became celebrities...at least until the next race. Between races, the masses were entertained by dancers, cheerleaders, musicians, acrobats, and performing animals.

The courtyard of the Blue Mosque marks the former site of the Hippodrome's *kathisma* (royal lodge). Supported by gorgeous marble columns, this grandstand was where the emperor and his family watched the races unfold. The lodge was connected to the Great Palace (on the site of today's Blue Mosque) for an easy escape in case the crowd got out of control.

As big as today's gigantic football stadiums, the Hippodrome could seat 100,000 spectators. But when races went out of vogue, the once-proud structure became a makeshift quarry for builders scavenging pre-cut stones.

The last remaining stones of the Hippodrome's "bleachers" were used to build the Blue Mosque. Today, none of the original seating survives, and the ancient racetrack has been replaced by a modern road.

Every year during Ramadan, the Hippodrome attains a festive atmosphere in the evening, when Muslims break their fast at sunset.

• *In its Byzantine glory days, the Hippodrome was decorated with monuments from all over the world. The most famous one is right in the middle of the long square.*

Egyptian Obelisk

This ancient, pointy pillar was carved about 1,500 years before the birth of Christ to honor the Egyptian Pharaoh Thutmose III; its inscribed hieroglyphs commemorate his military achievements. The obelisk was brought here from the Temple of Karnak on the Upper Nile sometime in the fourth century A.D. What you see today is only the upper third of the original massive stone block (take a moment to imagine its original height).

The most interesting part of the obelisk is its Byzantine base, which was cut out of local white marble and stands on four bronze feet. Reliefs on all four sides of the base depict Emperor Theodosius the Great and his family at the royal lodge, watching the Hippodrome races. On the side facing the Blue Mosque, the emperor gives an olive wreath to the winner, while his servant hands out a sack of coins. On the opposite side, envoys bow down before Theodosius in homage. At the bottom of the base (facing Hagia Sophia), find the relief showing the column as it lay horizontal, and how pulleys were used to raise it.

Throughout Asia Minor (the Asian part of today's Turkey), the Latin and Greek languages coexisted during the early stages of the Byzantine Empire. At the obelisk's base, you'll see an inscription eulogizing the emperor, written in both Latin (on the side facing the Blue Mosque) and Greek (on the opposite side). Both inscriptions give basically the same information, but they differ when it comes to how long it took to raise the obelisk: The Latin version says 30 days, the Greek 32. This ancient typo perplexes archaeologists to this day.

• *The tall stone column (that looks like a stone-paved obelisk) at the left end of the Hippodrome (with the Blue Mosque to your back) is the...*

Column of Constantine

Like the Egyptian Obelisk, this column went up in the fourth century A.D. But unlike its Egyptian sister, it was constructed here. In the early 10th century A.D., Emperor Constantine VII Porphyrogenitus sheeted the column with bronze panels. But as the city was looted during the Fourth Crusade (in the early 13th century), the panels were pulled down to make weapons. You can still see the holes where the panels were attached to the column.

• *Between the Column of Constantine and the Egyptian Obelisk is the bronze...*

Column of the Serpent

This was a victory monument dedicated to the gods by 31 Greek city-states to commemorate their victory against the Persians at Plataea (479 B.C.). It stood at the Temple of Apollo in Delphi for 800 years, until—like the Egyptian Obelisk—it was brought to Constantinople from Greece in the fourth century A.D. The names of the sponsoring cities are inscribed at the base (currently underground, buried by earth accumulated over the centuries). Originally, this column showed three serpents twisted together, their heads supporting a golden trophy. The gold was gone even before the reign of Constantine the Great, but the heads survived until just 300 years ago—when they mysteriously vanished. Only the upper jaw of one snake still exists (on display in the Istanbul Archaeological Museum).

Other monuments that once decorated the Hippodrome are long gone, such as four famous cast-bronze horses from ancient Greece. During the Fourth Crusade, these were plundered and taken to Venice...where they're still on display at St. Mark's Basilica.

• *Across the Hippodrome from the Blue Mosque is the Turkish and Islamic Arts Museum, housed in the...*

İbrahim Paşa Palace

The palace—a gift from Sultan Süleyman the Magnificent to İbrahim Paşa in 1520—is one of the best examples of civil architecture in the city. The palace was once much bigger than what you see today, rivaling Topkapı Palace in both its size and opulence. The only surviving bits are the reception hall and areas where guests were hosted, surrounding a small central courtyard. Looking at the facade, notice the Oriental-looking wooden balcony.

Through the years, the İbrahim Paşa Palace has been used as a palace school, a dormitory for single soldiers, and a prison. In 1983, it was restored and became the home of the **Turkish and Islamic Arts Museum,** with its collection of ceramics, glassware, calligraphy, and carpets (described on page 1151).

• *Our walk is nearly finished. Continue down to the north end of the Hippodrome (with the Blue Mosque on your right). You'll run into an octagonal pavilion with a green dome on dark pillars, the...*

German Fountain

This pavilion—which seems a little out of place surrounded by minarets and obelisks—would be more at home in Berlin. The

fountain was a gift from the German government to commemorate Kaiser Wilhelm II's visit to Istanbul in 1898. It was constructed in pieces in Germany, then shipped to Istanbul in 1901 and reassembled on this location.

Kaiser Wilhelm II visited Istanbul three times to schmooze the sultan. By the early 20th century, it was obvious that a war between the great powers of Europe was imminent, and empires were choosing sides. Though the Ottoman Empire was in its waning days, it remained a formidable power in the east and a valuable ally for Germany. Sure enough, when World War I erupted in 1914, the Ottoman Empire joined the fray as Germany's unwilling ally. Less than four years later, the Ottomans had lost the war—and with it, what remained of their ailing empire. The last sultan was sent into exile with the establishment of the Turkish Republic in the 1920s.

• *We've come full circle—you're just up the street from Hagia Sophia (if you haven't yet, you can visit it with the* ✪ *self-guided tour on page 1164).*

At the end of the Hippodrome, just before the street with the tram tracks (Divan Yolu), are a TI and some public WCs. Across the tracks are a pair of recommended local restaurants: Sultanahmet Köftecisi serves just meatballs, and the misnamed Pudding Shop (a.k.a. "Lale Restaurant") offers meat and veggie dishes, döner kebab, and sometimes fish in a cafeteria-style setting where you can see all of the choices (it may look crowded, but there's also seating upstairs). Just uphill from the restaurants on Divan Yolu is the Sultanahmet tram stop.

Beyond that is a bustling commercial zone with more restaurants, a pharmacy, travel agencies, and banks (with ATMs). And farther up is the Grand Bazaar (from the Hippodrome, it's a 15-minute walk, or a quick ride on the tram from the Sultanahmet stop to the Çemberlitaş stop).

Grand Bazaar and Spice Market Walk

This self-guided walk has two parts: In the first, we'll tour the Grand Bazaar, the world's oldest shopping mall, and then we'll walk through the back streets of the Old Town, past the impressive Mosque of Süleyman the Magnificent, to the lively area around the Spice Market and the Eminönü waterfront.

The Grand Bazaar is a labyrinthine warren of shops and pushy merchants—a unique Istanbul experience that shouldn't be missed, even if you're not a shopper. While parts of the bazaar and Spice Market are overrun with international visitors, you'll also find many virtually tourist-free nooks and crannies that offer an insightful glimpse into the "real" Istanbul.

Orientation

Length of This Walk: Allow at least three hours at a fast pace; if you linger in the shops at the Grand Bazaar and Spice Market, it could fill an entire day.

Getting There: From Sultanahmet (in the center of the Old Town), simply hop the tram to the next stop (Çemberlitaş), or walk five gradually uphill blocks along the tram tracks to the Çemberlitaş tram stop. Turn right, cross the parking lot and go behind the Nuruosmaniye Mosque to the Grand Bazaar, where this walk begins.

Pickpocket Alert: The Grand Bazaar probably contains the high-

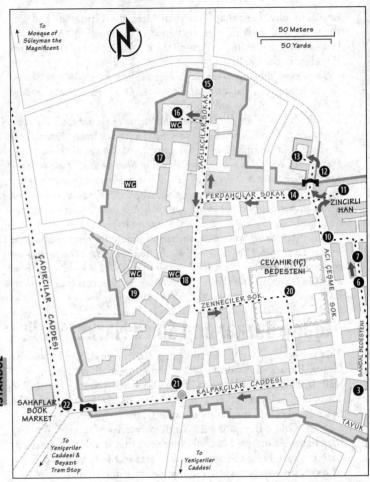

est concentration of pickpockets in Istanbul. Watch your valuables.

Grand Bazaar: Mon-Sat 9:00-19:00, shops begin to close at 18:30, closed Sun and on first day of most religious festivals, www.grandbazaaristanbul.org.

Mosque of Süleyman the Magnificent: Mosque—Free, generally open daily from one hour after sunrise until one hour before sunset, closed to visitors five times a day for prayer. Mausoleums—Free, daily 9:00-17:00, until 18:00 in summer. Located on Sıddık Sami Onar Caddesi, in the Süleymaniye district.

Rüstem Paşa Mosque: Free, generally open daily from one hour after sunrise until one hour before sunset, closed to visitors five times a day for prayer, on Hasırcılar Caddesi, Eminönü.

Grand Bazaar Walk

1 Nuruosmaniye Gate
2 Kalpakçılar Caddesi
3 Jewelry Showcases
4 Sandal Bedesteni
5 Free Exchange Market
6 Ağa Sokak
7 Pawn Shops
8 Mahmutpaşa Gate &
   To Spice Market
9 Kalcılar Han
10 Oriental Kiosk
11 Zincirli Han
12 Mercan Gate
13 Kızlarağası Han
14 Perdahçılar Sokak
15 Eğin Tekstil
16 Astarcı Han &
   Brothers Restaurant
17 Pedaliza Restaurant
18 Şark Kahvesi Coffee Shop
19 Havuzlu Lokanta Rest.
20 Cevahir Bedesten
21 Fountain
22 Beyazıt Gate &
   Sahaflar Book Market

ISTANBUL

Spice Market: Free to enter, Mon-Sat 8:00-19:30 (until 19:00 off-season), Sun 9:30-18:00, shops begin to close 30 minutes earlier, at the Old Town end of the Galata Bridge, near the Eminönü tram stop.

Shopping Tips: This walk goes hand-in-hand with the "Shopping in Istanbul" section (page 1178). Consider reading that section before you shop, perhaps while nursing a cup of Turkish coffee in the bazaar (focus on the bargaining tips if you plan to buy anything).

Navigating the Bazaar: The Grand Bazaar is a giant commercial complex with named "streets" *(caddesi)* and "alleys" *(sokak)*. But few of these streets and alleys are well marked, or the signs are covered by merchandise, so relying on these names isn't always successful. Complicating matters is the bazaar's maze-like floor plan. To make things easier, navigate using the map in this section and by asking people for help. (But be warned that asking a merchant for help may suck you into a lengthy conversation about the wonders of his wares.)

Starring: Some of Istanbul's best markets and mosques...and its people.

Part 1: The Grand Bazaar

Sprawling over a huge area in the city center, Kapalı Çarşı (kah-pah-luh chahr-shuh; "Covered Market") was the first shopping

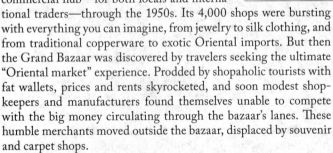

mall ever built. During Byzantine times, this was the site of a bustling market; when the Ottomans arrived, it grew bigger and more diverse. The prime location attracted guilds, manufacturers, and traders, and it grew quickly—its separate chunks were eventually connected and roofed to form a single market hall. Before long, the Grand Bazaar became the center for trade in the entire Ottoman Empire. At its prime, the market was locked down and guarded by more than a hundred soldiers every night, like a fortified castle.

The Grand Bazaar remained Turkey's commercial hub—for both locals and international traders—through the 1950s. Its 4,000 shops were bursting with everything you can imagine, from jewelry to silk clothing, and from traditional copperware to exotic Oriental imports. But then the Grand Bazaar was discovered by travelers seeking the ultimate "Oriental market" experience. Prodded by shopaholic tourists with fat wallets, prices and rents skyrocketed, and soon modest shopkeepers and manufacturers found themselves unable to compete with the big money circulating through the bazaar's lanes. These humble merchants moved outside the bazaar, displaced by souvenir and carpet shops.

Today's Grand Bazaar sells 10 times more jewelry than it used to. And, while tourists find it plenty atmospheric, locals now consider its flavor more Western than Oriental. And yet, even though the bazaar has lost some of its traditional ambience, enough artifacts remain to make it an irreplaceable Istanbul experience. This tour takes you through the schlocky tourist zones...but it also takes you by the hand to the market's outer fringe, still frequented by more Turks than tourists.

• *Enter the Grand Bazaar through the* **Nuruosmaniye Gate** *behind the Nuruosmaniye Mosque. As you walk through the gate, you're at the start of the bazaar's main street, called...*

Kalpakçılar Caddesi

Step through the entryway, past security police and under the Ottoman coat of arms, with its red and green flags (green for the Islamic caliph, and red for the Ottoman dynasty). You'll notice the temperature rise by several degrees—the air inside is heated by thousands of watts of electric bulbs, and by bustling shoppers and merchants. This scene is a little overwhelming at first sight. Welcome to the Grand Bizarre...er, Bazaar.

You're standing on the bazaar's main street, Kalpakçılar Caddesi, which leads straight from the Nuruosmaniye Mosque to the Beyazıt district, where we'll exit, though we'll take a very roundabout route to get there. On this walk, everything of importance is to the right and downhill of this main drag. Kalpakçılar Caddesi (kahl-pahk-chuh-lahr jahd-deh-see) means "Hatmakers' Street." Historically, each street, alley, or corner of the bazaar was dedicated to a particular craft or item, and they still bear those names.

• *All those lightbulbs are illuminating...*

Jewelry Showcases

Today's high-traffic, high-rent Kalpakçılar Caddesi is dominated by these glittering displays, containing bigger-ticket items than the traditional hats. Turks love gold, not because they're vain or greedy, but because they're practical: Since local currency has a tendency to be devalued, people prefer to invest in something more tangible. Traditionally, Turks celebrating special occasions—such as a wedding or a boy's circumcision—receive gold as a gift. In fact, in the most traditional corners of Turkey, the groom's family still must present the bride's family with gold bracelets before the couple can marry.

Because all this gold is used primarily as an investment, and only secondarily as an accessory, it's most commonly sold in the

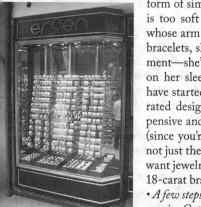

form of simple 22-carat bracelets (24-carat is too soft to wear). If you see a woman whose arm is lined with five or six of these bracelets, she's not making a fashion statement—she's wearing her family's savings on her sleeve, literally. Recently, jewelers have started selling more elaborately decorated designer pieces. These are more expensive and less appealing to thrifty locals (since you're paying for the workmanship, not just the gold itself). Instead, locals who want jewelry for fashion buy cheaper 14- or 18-carat bracelets.

• *A few steps into the bazaar from the Nuruosmaniye Gate (after the fifth shop on the right), look for the entrance marked* Old Bazaar—Sandal Bedesteni *over the doorway, a little off the main street. Duck into the courtyard called...*

Sandal Bedesteni

The Grand Bazaar is made up of a series of *bedestens* (beh-dehs-tehns)—commercial complexes of related shops. The Sandal Bedesteni is one of the oldest, dating from the late 15th century. After the Ottomans arrived and took over a Byzantine marketplace here, the bazaar grew organically—new buildings sporadically sprouted up, each one devoted to a particular trade or item. For the convenience of both the shopkeeper and the customer, shops dealing with similar items clustered together. These distinct units, many of which survive today, are called *bedesten* or *han*. The most traditional *bedestens* (like this one) have a central courtyard surrounded by shops and workshops on two floors. Later, developers roofed these commercial units and connected them with alleys, creating a unified central market hall. But if you pay attention, you'll notice that each part of the bazaar still has its own unique characteristics (and characters).

The Sandal Bedesteni once housed merchants of valuable fabrics (such as silk and velvet), turban makers, and jewelers specializing in precious stones. Today it carries ordinary textile products and assorted tourist knockoffs.

• *Backtrack out to the main drag (Kalpakçılar Caddesi), turn right, and continue to the first intersection, where you'll turn right on Sandal Bedesteni Sokak. Look high above, where signs point to various landmarks. Walk straight downhill on this alley—with a high concentration of souvenir shops, carpets, tiles, leather and kilim bags, and chandeliers—toward the intersecting arches. On the right, you'll pass another entrance to the Sandal Bedesteni we just visited. After that, take the next alley on the right. Walk 50 yards to the...*

Free Exchange Market

You'll hear it before you see it. From about 10:00 until 17:00, the little alleys branching off this strip are squeezed full of hundreds of boisterous men shouting into their mobile phones and waving their arms. These are currency brokers, and this zone of the bazaar is like a poor man's Wall Street. In this humble setting, people are cutting deals involving hundreds of thousands of dollars and euros every minute.

The Turkish lira is (by European standards) an unstable currency. So, in addition to gold, many Turks still invest in euros or dollars to shore up their savings.

• *Backtrack to the alley called Sandal Bedesteni Sokak, turn right, and continue one block to where it intersects with the wider...*

Ağa Sokak

Since the "ğ" is a vowel lengthener, without any sound of its own, the word "ağa" is pronounced "aaa-aah." Looking to the left up Ağa Sokak, you'll see the entrance to Cevahir Bedesteni, where people sell antiques, semiprecious stones, and silver items. We'll pass through that *bedesten* later on the walk.

• *Continue up the narrow alley called Sandal Bedesteni Sokak. Notice that the shops become less colorful and the clientele becomes more local. This section of the bazaar is mostly devoted to...*

Pawn Shops

Many of these shops look empty, with signs on the windows and a few gold items and coins on display. This is where locals can exchange those "investment bracelets" and valuables for some hard cash. When these shops buy jewelry, they deduct whatever the seller paid for workmanship, charge a small commission, and pay for the actual value of the gold.

• *Continue to the end of the alley, where it ends at Aynacılar Sokak (eye-nah-juh-lahr; "Mirror-Makers' Alley"). Looking to your right, you'll see another gate of the bazaar, named after the neighboring district.*

Mahmutpaşa Gate

If you went through this exit and walked about 15 minutes down the hill, you'd reach the Spice Market. If time is short, you could skip the rest of the Grand Bazaar and head to the Spice Market from here (Spice Market described on page 1144). The area between here and there is a huge outdoor textile bazaar, with retail shops, wholesalers, and workshops.

• *Step outside the Mahmutpaşa Gate and continue straight. Walk about 50 yards down to a second gate, which opens onto Mahmutpaşa Yokuşu Sokak. Immediately beyond this second gate, on the left (after a window filled with dandy circumcision outfits), is the entrance to...*

Kalcılar Han

This is also known as the Gümüşçüler ("silversmith") Hanı, because it's a center for the production and sale of all sorts of handcrafted silver objects. The Kalcılar Han, like others of its kind, resembles a factory. In each workshop, an artisan completes a different step of the production process. A single silver object goes from one workshop to another, as in a factory production line, with artisans working together to create a finished piece.

As you walk the long entryway to the open courtyard, you're looking at a typical *han*—built on two floors around a central courtyard. The first (ground) floor contained stables and storage, while travelers stayed in upper-floor rooms. Today, all the rooms on the upper floor are workshops.

Take time to visit a silversmith. Turn to your immediate right as you step into the courtyard, walk in, and take the stairs on the left (mind the low iron bar) to the upper floor. Turn right at the top and find the workshop of **Kapik Usta** at #10. Kapik Usta (kah-

peek oos-tah; "Kapik the Master") is a master *sıvamacı* (suh-vah-mah-juh), a silversmith who uses molds. If he's not too busy, he may show you how he does it. Stay away from the lathe, and watch as Kapik transforms a flat piece of metal into a three-dimensional object.

Head to the opposite side of the *han* (past the stairs). At the workshop at #20, Master Zavel uses sand molds to shape melted silver.

Find **Barocco Silver** at #31. It's owned by Kapik Usta's Armenian business partner, Aruş Usta (ah-roosh oos-tah; "Aruş the Master"). He

is a master *dövücü* (dew-vew-jew), a silversmith who uses a hammer to shape flat metal. Walk into his shop, where he works with his son, Dikran, who is also a master craftsman.

• *Backtrack to the Mahmutpaşa Gate. Step back inside the Grand Bazaar, and walk straight on Aynacılar Sokak until you hit the intersection marked by a charming little...*

Oriental Kiosk

This adorable structure, originally built as a teahouse in the 17th century, sells jewelry today. Notice the fountain next to the kiosk. The alley it's on is Acı Çeşme (ah-juh chesh-meh), which means "Bitter Fountain." Avoid the water here...just in case. (In the thrilling chase scene at the opening of the 2012 James Bond movie *Skyfall*, a motorcycle crashes through the roof here and into this delicate—and now rebuilt—kiosk.)

• *Turn right at the kiosk onto Acı Çeşme, and walk to the end of the alley. On your right, just before the bazaar exit, marked by an arrow hanging from the vaulted ceiling, is the entrance to...*

Zincirli Han

Rough steps take you into Zincirli Han (zeen-jeer-lee hahn; "Chain Han"), which is surrounded mostly by jewelry shops, with some workshops on the upper floor. The shops here are less polished and fancy, and less aggressive, than those in the more touristy zones back in the heart of the bazaar.

At the far end of the courtyard, on the right (unmarked, at #13), is **Merim Kuyumculuk** (koo-yoom-joo-look; "jewelry"). Rather than selling lots of jewelry, this place focuses on production and wholesale—one of the few jewelers in the bazaar with its own workshop nearby.

To the left of Merim, fronting the courtyard, is **Osman's Carpet Shop.** Run by a hard-to-miss "professor of carpets" nicknamed

Şişko (sheesh-koh; "Fatty"), this shop is regarded as *the* place to go to get a high-quality, expensive carpet and expert advice. Şişko—often assisted by son Nurullah or nephew Bilgin—won't hustle you or try to talk you into something, like the cheap carpet hawkers elsewhere in the bazaar. He prefers to equip customers with information to be sure they get the carpet that's right for them. This fifth-generation shop is hardly a secret—notice the celebrity photos, magazine clippings, and guidebook blurbs hanging on the wall.

• *Leave Zincirli Han, return to Acı Çeşme, turn right, and step outside the Grand Bazaar. The jewelry shop to your left immediately outside the* **Mercan Gate**—*with hundreds of 22-karat gold bracelets—will give you an idea of what most jewelry around here looked like a decade or two ago, before fancier bracelets came into fashion.*

Continue a few steps beyond the Mercan Gate, and go through the first building entrance to your left (#94). You're now in...

Kızlarağası Han

The *kızlarağası* was the master of all eunuchs (castrated slaves who looked after the sultan's palace and harem). This humble courtyard is where you'll find middlemen who recycle secondhand gold and silver—or shavings and unwanted fragments from other workshops—and turn them into something usable.

Notice the low-profile teahouse in the center, serving simple glasses of tea to an almost exclusively local crowd.

Ayhan Usta (eye-hahn oostah; "Ayhan the Master") is one of the goldsmiths who works here. His shop is the third one on the left as you enter, across from the teahouse.

ISTANBUL

Ayhan speaks only Turkish, but if you peek into his shop and if he's up for visitors and not too busy, he'll motion you inside to watch him at work. Ayhan belongs to a dying breed. Not much gold production still takes place near the Grand Bazaar, and the few gold-smiths who remain may soon be moved to a plant outside the city.
• *Now go back in the Grand Bazaar, and take the first right as you step in. You'll walk down the big lane called...*

Perdahçılar Sokak

Perdahçılar Sokak (pehr-dah-chuh-lahr soh-kahk) was once the main clothing section of the bazaar; now it's a combination of car-pet stores, souvenir shops, "genuine fake items" stands, and shops selling tourist knockoffs of traditional clothes—like fake pashmi-nas or a tongue-in-cheek "one size fits all" belly-dancing outfit.
• *Continue to the T-junction, and turn right onto Yağlıkçılar Sokak (yaah-luhk-chuh-lahr soh-kahk), with items similar to what you've just seen. Walk all the way to the bazaar exit. To the right, just inside the exit door, notice the textile store called...*

Eğin Tekstil

This unassuming little shop provided many of the costumes for the 2004 movie *Troy* (an adaptation of Homer's *Iliad*). Go inside and say hello to owner Süleyman or his assistants, who'd be happy to tell you all about their shop's history...and, of course, what they're selling. Eğin Tekstil (eh-een tehks-teel) has been in the same fam-ily for five generations, nearly 150 years. In fact, Süleyman—who continues the family tradition even though he's actually a doctor by trade—still has the Ottoman deed to the store. Their specialty is the *peştemal* (pehsh-teh-mahl), the traditional wrap-around sheet for visits to a Turkish bath. I think the quality is reliable, and the prices are marked, fixed, and fair. This is one of the Grand Bazaar's few stores that actually has an annex behind the main shop built during Byzantine times, which is used for storage (the entrance is on the back wall).
• *Stepping outside the store, turn left and head back the way you came on Yağlıkçılar Sokak. After about 50 yards, on the right—marked with a colorful electronic WC—you'll see the entrance to...*

Astarcı Han

Go through the doorway, between shops and stands, into Astarcı Han (ahs-tahr-juh hahn; "Courtyard of the Cloth Lining"). His-torically, this courtyard was home to textile workshops. A few still remain here: As you enter, notice the workshop in the right-hand corner (where workers braid golden trim with a century-old tech-nology). Peek inside with a smile to see the textile makers in action.

On the left as you enter the courtyard is the recommended

Brothers (Kardeşler) Restaurant. This place specializes in southeastern Turkish cuisine and has peaceful outdoor seating upstairs (9-12-TL main courses, 10-15-TL specialty dishes, Mon-Sat 8:00-17:00, closed Sun, Astarcı Han Yağlıkçılar 1/9, tel. 0212/519-3006). Squat WCs are across from the restaurant.

• *Exit Astarcı Han and turn right onto Yağlıkçılar Sokak, continuing in the same direction as before. Within 50 yards look for a sign (on the right) for Cebeci Han. The popular* **Pedaliza Restaurant** *is to your right as you enter this courtyard. (If you'd like a cup of Turkish coffee after your meal, the perfect spot is coming right up.)*

From Cebeci Han, head back out to Yağlıkçılar and go right. After a few blocks, keep an eye out on the right-hand side for the tiny green box-like wooden balcony (attached to the wall above the jewelry store). Used for the call to prayer, like a low-tech minaret, it marks one of the bazaar's mosques (next to it are steps leading up to the mosque).

Go 50 yards past the mosque on the right-hand corner to find a venerable tea and coffee house called...

Şark Kahvesi

The recommended Şark Kahvesi (shark kah-veh-see; "Oriental Coffee Shop") is an Istanbul institution and a good place to sample Turkish coffee if you haven't yet. "Turkish coffee" refers not to a type of coffee, but to the way the coffee is prepared: The coffee grounds float freely in the brew, leaving behind a layer of "mud" at the bottom of the cup.

Traditionally, coffee (*kahve;* kah-veh) is added to cold water in a copper pot. (Some use hot or lukewarm water to speed up the process, but you can taste the difference—Turks call this hasty version "dishwater.") The coffee-and-water mixture is stirred and slowly heated over medium heat. Just before the water boils, the pot is set aside and its contents are allowed to settle. Then the pot is put back on to boil. This time, half is poured into a cup, while the rest is reheated and then used to top off the drink. Turks joke that the last step is to put a horseshoe in it—if the horseshoe floats, you know it's good coffee.

Locals prefer Turkish coffee without sugar, but first-timers—even coffee-loving ones—often prefer to add sugar to make its powerful flavor a bit more palatable. In Turkey, the sugar is added while the coffee is being cooked, so you'll need to ask for it when you place your order: *az şekerli* (ahz sheh-kehr-lee) will get you a little sugar, *orta şekerli* (ohr-tah sheh-kehr-lee) is a medium scoop, and just *şekerli* (sheh-kehr-lee) roughly translates as "tons of sugar—I hate the taste of real coffee."

Because it's unfiltered, the coffee never completely dissolves. When drinking Turkish coffee, the trick is to gently agitate your cup time and time again to remix the grounds with the water. Otherwise you'll drink weak coffee, and wind up with a thick layer of grounds at the bottom when you're done.

• *Just past Şark Kahvesi on Yağlıkçılar Sokak, a lane on the right leads to the* **Havuzlu Lokanta** *restaurant, which serves a sped-up version of traditional Ottoman cuisine (7-TL salads, 12-TL vegetarian dishes, 18-28-TL grilled meats, 14-18-TL main courses, 1 TL extra for water and bread, Mon-Sat 12:00-17:30, closed Sun, look for sign near Şark Kahvesi café, Gani Çelebi Sokak 3, tel. 0212/527-3346). Unless you're stopping for lunch, head left, going downhill on Zenneciler Sokak (zehn-neh-jee-lehr soh-kahk). After about 100 yards, you'll emerge into a courtyard we saw earlier from the other side...*

Cevahir Bedesten

Cevahir Bedesten (jeh-vah-heer beh-dehs-tehn) was built as a freestanding warehouse for merchants in the 15th century. It has been used for many purposes since, but the basic structure—with domed bays supported by eight massive pillars—is still intact. Entering the courtyard, you may notice it's taller than the rest of the bazaar, and, since it's devoted to big-ticket items, it's a bit quieter. Most merchants here are antique dealers, selling icons, metal objects, miniatures, coins, cameras, daggers, and so on; others here sell semiprecious stones, either by the piece or on chains. There are also a few silver shops and places where you can buy worry beads with semiprecious stones.

• *From the center of Cevahir Bedesten, turn 90 degrees to the right and leave through the door into the bustling alleys of the bazaar—this zone is packed with shops selling souvenirs, as well as carpets and traditional metal items. Soon you'll run into the main street, Kalpakçılar Caddesi. Turn right on Kalpakçılar Caddesi and walk about 200 yards to the gate leading to the Beyazıt (beh-yah-zuht) district. Halfway to the Beyazıt exit, keep an eye on your right, behind the* **fountain,** *for a stretch of shops selling leather, denim, and other textiles.*

At the end of Kalpakçılar Caddesi, you'll exit through the **Beyazıt Gate,** *where our bazaar tour ends. Spend some time exploring and shopping—you've only seen a few of the 4,000 shops that sprawl through the market.*

When you're ready, continue on the second part of this walk, which takes you through the back streets of Istanbul's Old Town to the Spice Market (near the waterfront and a short walk or tram ride back to the cruise terminals)—giving you a taste of the authentic city.

If you'd prefer to skip the rest of this walk, head to Beyazıt Square, where you can catch a tram back to the Sultanahmet stop (for the center of the Old Town), or to the Karaköy or Tophane stop for your ship (see "Returning to Your Ship" on page 1092).

Part 2: Back Streets Walk to Spice Market

This next stretch—through the Beyazıt district, connecting the Grand Bazaar to the Spice Market, by way of the Mosque of Süleyman the Magnificent, Rüstem Paşa Mosque, and oodles of fascinating slice-of-life shops—involves about a half-mile of walking, with relatively little to see in between...but it's worth the trek.

• *Exiting the bazaar (through the Beyazıt Gate), go right and walk a couple hundred yards through the outdoor textile market. At the end of the textile alley, you'll be facing the wall of **Istanbul University**'s main campus (across the street). Continue straight down the busy street (Fuat Paşa Caddesi) with the university wall across the street on your left. We'll continue about a quarter-mile straight downhill along this road; keep going until the end of the wall. Then you'll need to decide if you'll visit the massive Mosque of Süleyman the Magnificent (following the wall 300 yards uphill to your left) or turn right steeply downhill toward the Rüstem Paşa Mosque. Both options are explained below.*

Mosque of Süleyman the Magnificent

Perched high on a hill overlooking Istanbul, this stately mosque befits the most "Magnificent" sultan of the Ottoman Empire. De-

signed by the empire's greatest architect (Sinan) and dedicated to one of its greatest sultans, the Mosque of Süleyman the Magnificent gives the Blue Mosque a run for its money. Its pastel interior is a serene counterpoint to the Blue Mosque's vivid colors. The mosque complex holds the mausoleums of Süleyman and his wife, Roxelana, and its "backyard" offers sweeping views of the city below. The surrounding Süleymaniye neighborhood includes a former madrassa (seminary) that now hosts restaurants and tea gardens.

• *To skip the mosque (or if you're rejoining this walk after touring the mosque), head downhill about 150 yards to the second street on your left (Uzun Çarşı Caddesi—look for a sycamore tree on the corner and a fast-food kiosk across the street). Turning downhill and left onto this street, you'll see the brick minaret of a 15th-century mosque straight ahead and, behind it, the minaret of our next stop...*

Rüstem Paşa Mosque

Built by Sinan in the 16th century, this mosque stands on an ele-

ISTANBUL

Back Streets & Spice Market Walk

1. Beyazıt District
2. Istanbul University
3. Mosque of Süleyman the Magnificent
4. Uzun Çarşı Caddesi
5. Rüstem Paşa Mosque
6. Hasırcılar Caddesi
7. Food Vendors
8. Eminönü Square
9. New Mosque of Mother Sultan
10. Spice Market

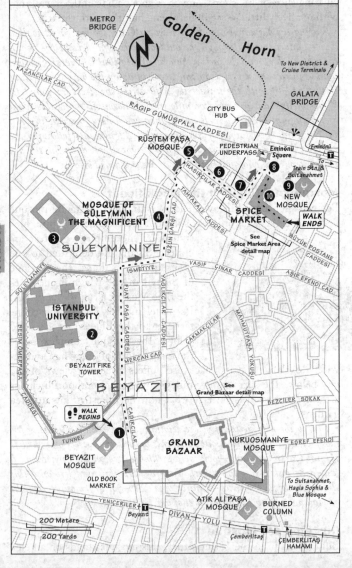

vated platform, supported by vaults that house shops (which once provided income for the mosque's upkeep). Its namesake, Rüstem Paşa (ruhs-tehm pah-shah), was a Grand Vizier of Süleyman the Magnificent. He found great success in this role, not just because he was Süleyman's son-in-law (he married Süleyman and Roxelana's daughter Mihrimah, whose tomb is next to Süleyman's), but also because he was clever and efficient. Like King Midas, Rüstem Paşa could turn anything into revenue, and he filled the sultan's treasury. But the public hated him because he taxed everything in sight, and he was frequently accused of embezzling funds.

The mosque's facade is slathered in gorgeous 16th-century İznik tiles, but the interior is even more impressive. To enter, go around the left side to find the visitors' entrance. Inside, virtually every surface is covered with floral-designed tile panels. (Locals say that if the Blue Mosque is Istanbul's Notre-Dame, this tiny gem is its Sainte-Chapelle.)

• *Because the next alley we'll be using is always packed with people—especially on Saturdays—consider reading the following section before you start walking. Leave the mosque complex through the door you entered, passing some enticing tile souvenirs. Turn left and walk down...*

ISTANBUL

Hasırcılar Caddesi

Hasırcılar (hah-sur-juh-lahr) Caddesi ("Mat-Weavers' Alley") is a real-life market street—part of the commercial sprawl surrounding our next sight, the Spice Market.

As you walk, notice the porters and the carts squeezing their heavy, wide loads through the alley. You'll pass old *bedestens* (traditional commercial buildings) and stores, many of them family-owned for generations. If you had strolled this street a century ago, only the shoppers' clothes would have been different.

One block before the Spice Market entrance, you'll smell the aroma of fresh-roasted coffee and spices. If you're in the market for spices, dried fruits, sweets, and nuts, start checking the prices along here—they're cheaper than in the high-rent Spice Market. Ask for a sample, and don't feel obligated to buy. While bargaining has become common in the Grand Bazaar, around here you'll generally pay what's on the price tag for food and spices—though souvenirs and exotic items (such as saffron and imported caviar) may be haggled over.

Half a block before the arched entry to the Spice Market (the big brick-and-stone building at the end of the alley), you'll be immersed in a lively bazaar of **food vendors**. On your left, look for the thriving, century-old deli, **Namlı Şarküteri,** with the large containers of olives, pickled peppers, and hanging pastramis out front (get a sample inside). A little farther ahead on the right, just before the Spice Market entrance, is one of the best coffee vendors in town: the venerable **Kurukahveci Mehmet Efendi Mahdumları** (say it three times fast).

• *Just after the coffee shop is the Spice Market's Hasırcılar Gate. Rather than entering the market here, let's walk around the side of the L-shaped building to the main entrance, facing the Golden Horn. Turn left and continue along the street (following the Spice Market wall).*

Along this alley you'll spot several more shops displaying spices, dried fruits, and sweets, alongside butcher, fishmonger, and dairy shops. The alley opens into the large **Eminönü Square,** with the Golden Horn (not quite visible from here) on the other side of the busy street.

Continue around the corner of the Spice Market to the right to reach the main entrance. The square in front of the Spice Market is dominated by the **New Mosque of Mother Sultan** (or simply "New Mosque")—one of the latest examples of classical, traditional-style Ottoman mosques. With the mosque on your left, you're facing the front of the Spice Market. Notice the outdoor plant and pet market to the left. A WC is just around this corner, in the inner corner of the "L" formed by the Spice Market.

• *Now go through the main entrance into the...*

Spice Market

Built in the mid-17th century, this market hall was gradually taken over by merchants dealing in spices, herbs, medicinal plants, and pharmaceuticals. While it's quite a touristy scene today, most stalls still sell many of the same products, and the air is heavy with the aroma of exotic spices. Locals call it the Mısır Carşışı (Egyptian Bazaar) because it was once funded by taxes collected from Egypt.

While smaller and less imposing than the Grand Bazaar, the Spice Market is more colorful, with the ambience of a true Oriental market. On either side of the long, vaulted central hall are a wide range of merchant stalls, most of them with sacks and barrels out front showing off their wares. While merchants once sat

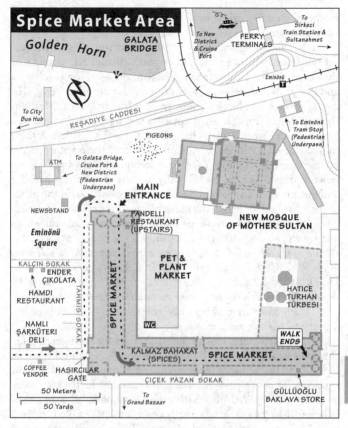

quietly, cross-legged, next to their shops, today they engage in a never-ending game of one-upmanship, competing for the attention of passersby. If you're offered a sample of something (such as Turkish delight), feel free to accept—but be warned that it can be difficult to pry yourself away from the sales pitch that's sure to ensue.

Aside from the spice shops, you'll also see stores slinging natural sponges, lentils and beans, dried vegetables, dried fruits (especially figs and apricots), pistachios

and hazelnuts, and sweets of several different kinds—including, of course, Turkish delight. While most Westerners think of Turkish delight as being colored and fruit-flavored, locals prefer more adventurous varieties: with double-roasted pistachios, or the kind with walnuts in grape or mulberry molasses called *sucuk* (soo-jook; also the name of a spicy veal sausage).

Look for the granddaddy of spices, **saffron.** Locals still use saffron (mostly in rice pilaf and dessert), though not as much as they used to. The best saffron is Spanish; the local kind—cheaper and not as dark-red—usually comes mixed with other herbs. The **caviar** you see isn't local; it's mostly from Iran or Russia. More authentic are the Turkish dried **apricots** and **figs.** Dried vegetables, eggplant, and green peppers hang from the walls. Cooks use these to make *dolma* (dohl-mah; "to stuff"), stuffing them with rice and raisins, or rice and meat. You'll also see lots of sacks full of green powder. This is **henna,** traditionally used by women as a hair dye and for skin care. In the countryside, young women stain the palms of their hands with henna the night before they get married. Lately all of these old-fashioned shops are being joined by souvenir shops and jewelry stores, making this a mini-Grand Bazaar of sorts.

• *Walk to the far end of the hall, at the intersection with the side wing of the Spice Market (to the left). Straight ahead is a gate leading to an always-busy street that heads five blocks up to the Grand Bazaar; to the right is the Hasırcılar Gate, leading to the alley we just came down.*

Go left and start walking down the side wing—less crowded and less colorful than the main concourse.

After a few steps, look for a tiny shop on the left (second from the corner) called **Kalmaz Baharat.** *Baharat* (bah-hah-raht) means "spice," and this is one of the few remaining shops that still sells the exotic spices of the past. Adnan, the owner, has herbal teas, thick aromatic oils, natural-fiber bath gloves, and olive-oil soap (white is better than green). He also sells the aphrodisiac called "sultan's paste" (more recently dubbed "Turkish Viagra"). This mix of several kinds of herbs and exotic spices supposedly gave the sultan the oomph to enjoy his huge harem, and is still used as an all-purpose energy booster today.

Browse your way to the end of this side wing (notice the great **Güllüoğlu Baklava** store on the right, the third shop before the exit), then head back the way you came.

• *When you're ready to finish this walk, retrace your steps and leave the Spice Market through the main entrance. You'll be facing the Galata Bridge over the Golden Horn, with your cruise ship just past the far side of the bridge.*

*To head back across the bridge **on foot,** walk to the pedestrian underpass ahead of you (a little to the left, with an ATM kiosk nearby) that will take you under the busy street to the Galata Bridge. (Notice the many restaurants on the lower level of the bridge; this area is described in the "Golden Horn Walk," earlier.)*

*To reach the Eminönü **tram** stop—where you can catch the tram either to your ship or back up to the center of the Old Town (Sultanahmet* *stop)—walk to the right between the New Mosque and the busy street. Where the mosque ends, you'll see the entrance to another pedestrian underpass. Halfway through the underpass, steps lead up to separate platforms: The first one is for the Old Town. The second platform—a little farther on—is for trams across the Galata Bridge to the cruise port and the New District. Ride the tram one stop to reach the Karaköy cruise terminal or two stops for the Salıpazarı terminal.*

*Alternatively, you can generally wave down a **cab** along the main street right in front of the Spice Market.*

Sights in Istanbul

While Istanbul has many interesting sights well-worth knowing about on a longer visit, for a one-day cruiser visit, I've listed just the most important and central sights.

The sights listed in this section are arranged by neighborhood for handy sightseeing. Don't let the length of these descriptions determine your sightseeing priorities. In this section, some of Istanbul's most important sights have the shortest listings. These sights are covered in much more detail in one of the walks or tours elsewhere in this chapter.

Renovations: Istanbul is one of the fastest-changing cities in Europe. Add to this the fluctuating agenda of the government and the wait-until-the-last-minute attitude of its officials, and even locals have a hard time keeping up. Renovation projects are announced late, and the information often is inaccurate. Expect changes during your visit—ask the TI for the latest news about the sights you're planning to visit.

Opening Hours: The ticket offices of the city's museums are in the process of being privatized. It's unclear what changes that could bring, but it may mean that opening times will differ from what we've listed here. If a sight is a must-see for you, check its hours in advance (on its website or at a TI), and visit well before the closing times listed here.

In the Old Town

Istanbul's highest concentration of sights is in its Old Town, mostly in the Sultanahmet neighborhood.

In the Sultanahmet Area

Some of the following sights are linked by the ✪ "Historic Core of Istanbul Walk," which describes the Blue Mosque, the Hippodrome, and the Underground Cistern (Basilica Cistern) in greater detail (see page 1116).

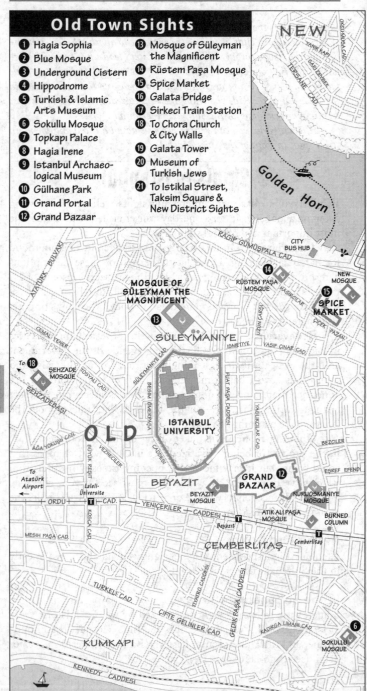

Old Town Sights

1. Hagia Sophia
2. Blue Mosque
3. Underground Cistern
4. Hippodrome
5. Turkish & Islamic Arts Museum
6. Sokullu Mosque
7. Topkapı Palace
8. Hagia Irene
9. Istanbul Archaeological Museum
10. Gülhane Park
11. Grand Portal
12. Grand Bazaar
13. Mosque of Süleyman the Magnificent
14. Rüstem Paşa Mosque
15. Spice Market
16. Galata Bridge
17. Sirkeci Train Station
18. To Chora Church & City Walls
19. Galata Tower
20. Museum of Turkish Jews
21. To Istiklal Street, Taksim Square & New District Sights

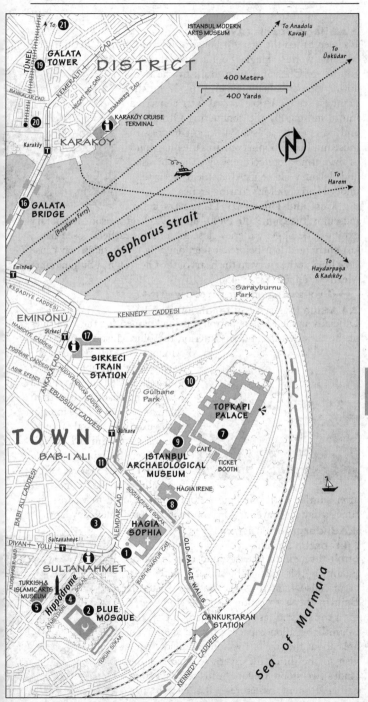

▲▲▲Hagia Sophia (Aya Sofya)

It's been called the greatest house of worship in the Christian and Muslim worlds: Hagia Sophia (eye-ah soh-fee-yah), the Great Church of Constantinople. Built by the Byzantine Emperor Justinian in A.D. 537 on the grandest scale possible, it was later converted into a mosque by the conquering Ottomans, and now serves as Istanbul's most impressive museum. Hagia Sophia remains the high point of Byzantine architecture. Enjoy the Christian and Islamic elements that meld peacefully under Hagia Sophia's soaring arches.

Cost and Hours: 25 TL, covers entire museum; Tue-Sun 9:00-19:00, until 17:00 off-season, temporary exhibits and upper galleries close 30 minutes earlier, closed Mon, last entry one hour before closing; ongoing renovations may cause slow lines at the entry, in the heart of the Old Town at Sultanahmet Meydanı, tel. 0212/528-4500.

✪ For a self-guided tour, see page 1164.

▲▲▲Blue Mosque (Sultanahmet Camii)

Officially named for its patron, but nicknamed for the cool hues of the tiles that decorate its interior, the Blue Mosque was Sultan

Ahmet I's 17th-century answer to Hagia Sophia. Its six minarets rivaled the mosque in Mecca, and beautiful tiles from the İznik school fill the interior with exquisite floral motifs. The tombs of Ahmet I and his wife Kösem Sultan are nearby.

Cost and Hours: Free, generally open daily one hour after sunrise until one hour before sunset, closed to visitors five times a day for prayer and Fri morning, Sultanahmet Meydanı.

▲▲Underground Cistern (Yerebatan Sarayı)

Stroll through an underground rain forest of pillars in this vast, subterranean water reservoir (also known as the Basilica Cistern). Built in the sixth century A.D. to store water for a thirsty and fast-growing capital city, the 27-million-gallon-capacity cistern covers an area about the size of two football fields. Your visit to the dimly lit, cavernous chamber includes two stone Medusa heads recycled from earlier Roman structures. The cistern also

hosts occasional concerts of traditional Turkish and classical Western music.

Cost and Hours: 10 TL, daily 9:00-18:30, until 17:30 off-season, last entry 30 minutes before closing, Yerebatan Caddesi 1/3, Sultanahmet, tel. 0212/512-1570.

▲Hippodrome (Sultanahmet Meydanı)

This long, narrow park-like square in the center of Istanbul's Old Town was once a Roman chariot racetrack. Today it's the front yard for many of Istanbul's most famous sights, including Hagia Sophia, the Blue Mosque, and the İbrahim Paşa Palace (home to the Turkish and Islamic Arts Museum). Strolling the Hippodrome's length, you'll admire monuments that span the ages, including the Egyptian Obelisk, Column of Constantine, and German Fountain.

▲▲Turkish and Islamic Arts Museum (Türk-İslam Eserleri Müzesi)

Housed in the former İbrahim Paşa Palace across from the Hippodrome, this museum's 40,000-piece collection covers the breadth of Islamic art over the centuries (may be closed for renovation during your visit; scheduled to reopen in mid-2014). The compact exhibit displays carefully selected, easy-to-appreciate works from the Selçuks to the Ottomans, including carpets, calligraphy, ceramics, glass, and art represented in wood, stone, and metal.

Cost and Hours: 10 TL, Tue-Sun 9:00-19:00, until 17:00 off-season, closed Mon, last entry one hour before closing, no photography, Sultanahmet Meydanı—across from the Hippodrome's Egyptian Obelisk, Sultanahmet, tel. 0212/518-1805, www.muze. gov.tr/turkishislamic.

Topkapı Palace and Nearby

This walled zone, at the tip of the Old Town Peninsula, is a five-minute walk from the heart of the Sultanahmet district. On the sprawling grounds of the Topkapı Palace complex, you'll find the former residence of the sultans, one of Istanbul's top museums, and all the historical trappings of a once-thriving empire.

▲▲▲Topkapı Palace (Topkapı Sarayı)

For centuries, this was the palace where the great sultans hung their turbans. Built on the remains of ancient Byzantium, established by Mehmet the Conqueror as an administrative headquarters, and turned into a home by Süleyman the Magnificent, Topkapı Palace's history reads like a who's who of Istanbul. Your wander through the many pavilions and courtyards includes a 16th-century

Topkapı Palace

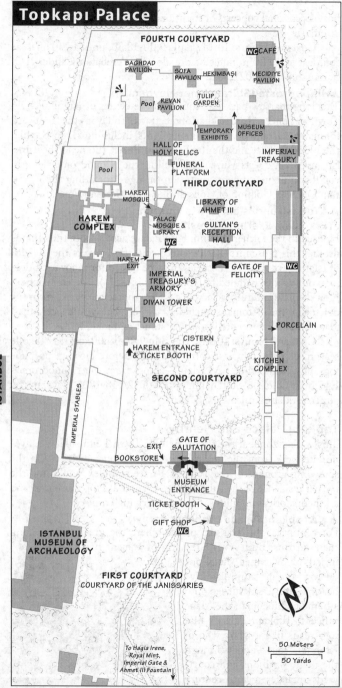

FOURTH COURTYARD

WC CAFÉ

BAGHDAD PAVILION

SOFA PAVILION

HEKIMBAŞI

MECIDIYE PAVILION

Pool

REVAN PAVILION

TULIP GARDEN

TEMPORARY EXHIBITS

MUSEUM OFFICES

HALL OF HOLY RELICS

IMPERIAL TREASURY

Pool

FUNERAL PLATFORM

THIRD COURTYARD

HAREM MOSQUE

LIBRARY OF AHMET III

HAREM COMPLEX

PALACE MOSQUE & LIBRARY

SULTAN'S RECEPTION HALL

WC

HAREM EXIT

GATE OF FELICITY

WC

IMPERIAL TREASURY'S ARMORY

DIVAN TOWER

DIVAN

PORCELAIN

CISTERN

HAREM ENTRANCE & TICKET BOOTH

KITCHEN COMPLEX

SECOND COURTYARD

IMPERIAL STABLES

EXIT

BOOKSTORE

GATE OF SALUTATION

MUSEUM ENTRANCE

TICKET BOOTH

GIFT SHOP

WC

ISTANBUL MUSEUM OF ARCHAEOLOGY

FIRST COURTYARD
COURTYARD OF THE JANISSARIES

To Hagia Irene,
Royal Mint,
Imperial Gate &
Ahmet III Fountain

N

50 Meters

50 Yards

ISTANBUL

kitchen (closed into 2014 for renovation), 10,000 pieces of fine Chinese porcelain, traditional weapons, royal robes, ceremonial thrones, and Sultan Ahmet III's tulip garden. The Imperial Treasury is home to the famous jewel-encrusted Topkapı Dagger and the stunning 86-carat Spoonmaker's Diamond. Its Holy Relics exhibit—with some of the most important fragments of Islamic history anywhere—sends chills down even non-Muslims' spines. A separate ticket covers the cloistered rooms of the famous Harem, where the sultan's wives and concubines lived (note that parts of the Harem will likely be under renovation during your visit).

Cost and Hours: Palace—25 TL, Wed-Mon 9:00-19:00, until 17:00 off-season, closed Tue, last entry one hour before closing, exhibits begin to close one hour earlier; Harem—15 TL, Wed-Mon 9:00-17:00, closed Tue; audioguide-15 TL for whole palace complex except the Harem, 10 TL for Harem; between the Golden Horn and Sea of Marmara in the Sultanahmet district, a short walk from Hagia Sophia and the Sultanahmet tram stop. You can also take the tram to the Gülhane stop, go in the gate on the side wall of the Topkapı complex, and bear right up the hill. Tel. 0212/512-0480, www.topkapisarayi.gov.tr.

➋ Self-Guided Tour: Allow up to two hours for this tour. The palace complex's main entry is near the back of Hagia Sophia, through the **Imperial Gate** in the outer wall. Going through the Imperial Gate, you find yourself in Topkapı's **First**

Courtyard. This wide-open space was reserved for public officials and civil servants. It was also called the "Courtyard of Janissaries," for the royal soldiers who assembled here.

As you walk from the Imperial Gate toward the palace through the First Courtyard, notice the terra-cotta church on your

left (not generally open to the public). **Hagia Irene** dates back to the reign of Justinian in the sixth century. Soon after Constantine split the Roman Empire between West and East—with the Eastern capital here, in Byzantium (renamed Constantinople)—Hagia Irene hosted the Second Ecumenical Council to set the course for the new church (in A.D. 381).

Past the Imperial Gate are the palace's ticket office and gift shop, and a WC. As you pass through security and ticket control, look up to see the ornate decorations on the underside of the large eave. Once through the gate, you're now in the palace complex's

Second Courtyard. This was not a private garden, but a ceremonial courtyard—host to centuries of coronations, successions, and other major benchmarks.

Along the right side of the Second Courtyard, marked by the domes and tall chimneys, are the palace workshops and **imperial kitchens,** which now house a porcelain and silver collection. To the left of the tall Divan Tower (at the far-left corner of the courtyard) is the **Divan**—the council chamber where the viziers (ministers) of the imperial council governed the Otto- man Empire for almost 400 years. Inside the council chamber (the larger room), the viziers would sit on the sofa according to their rank in the hierarchy. (This is why some people call sofas "divans.")

To the left of the Divan, just around the corner, is the ticket booth and entrance to the **Harem** (hah-rehm). (If there's a line at the Harem entrance, you'd be wise to skip it now and return after you've seen the rest of the palace—keeping in mind the Harem's early closing time—and proceed now to the Gate of Felicity, described later.) The one-way route through the Harem includes about 20 rooms, including stun- ning tile work, the mother sultan's private apartments, wives' and concubines' courts, the sultan's own living quarters, and the grand reception hall, all well-described by audioguide.

The word "harem" refers to two things: the wives, favorites, and concubines of the sultan; and the part of the palace where they lived.

Contrary to Western fantasy, the Harem was not the site of a round-the-clock orgy, but a carefully administered social insti- tution that ensured the longevity of the Ottoman Empire. Its primary role was to provide future heirs to the Ottoman throne, an essential responsibility that was too important to be left to coinci- dence. Thanks largely to the Harem, the Ottoman Empire was ruled by a single dynasty from start to finish, avoiding many of the squabbles and battles for suc- cession that tainted other great empires.

The sultan was the head of the household, which he shared with his mother. The only men who could enter the Harem—other than the sultan and young princes—were the sultan's close relatives, the "black eunuchs" (enslaved and castrated North Africans who served the Harem) and, when necessary, doctors. The sultan could have up to four wives, with the first one being considered the senior, most influential wife. Also living in the Harem was a collection of several hundred concubines—female slaves who kept house.

Leaving the Harem, you'll find yourself in the Third Courtyard of the palace complex. To go back where you started, turn right and follow the wall to pass through the striking **Gate of Felicity.**

The gate leads to the **Third Courtyard** and, in it, the sultans' **Reception Hall,** a throne room designed to impress visitors. Go right into the throne room—admiring the gorgeous 16th-century throne—and out the other side. The gray-white marble building straight ahead is the 18th-century **Library of Ahmet III.**

On your right, at the edge of the courtyard, is the impressive **Imperial Treasury.** Its four chambers display a sumptuous collection of the sultans' riches: imperial thrones, jewels, and more. The fourth room is the most spectacular, holding the famous Topkapı Dagger and the 86-carat pearl-shaped Spoonmaker's Diamond—one of the biggest diamonds in the world (they say a poor man found this diamond in the dirt in the 17th century and bartered it to a spoonmaker for wooden spoons).

Back outside, follow the portico to the right (notice the stairs, to your immediate right, leading down into the Fourth Courtyard and its Mecidiye Pavilion, with a restaurant, cafeteria, and WC). In front of the large hall at the end of the portico, look for the marble slab to the left of the door, next to the columns—the **Sultan's Funeral Platform.** According to Muslim tradition, after a dead body is washed and wrapped in a white shroud, it's laid on a slab for a final religious service—to honor and pray for the deceased.

Step into the **Hall of Holy Relics,** which shows off some of the most significant holy items of the Muslim faith. (Note that women may need to cover their heads, knees, and shoulders in this area due to the importance of these items to Muslim worshippers.) These relics were brought to Istanbul in the early 16th century, when their original locations—Egypt, Mecca, and Medina—were conquered by the Ottomans. As this is a very holy site for Muslims, you'll see many people praying with their hands open. Read the rules on the sign next to the entrance, and be respectful as

ISTANBUL

you visit this exhibit. You'll see items related to the Kabaa (the big black cube in the center of the mosque at Mecca, the holiest of Muslim shrines), strangely well-preserved everyday items from the lives of religious figures (the footprint of Muhammad, Muhammad's sandals, bone fragments of John the Baptist, Moses' staff, Abraham's granite cooking pot, David's sword, Joseph's turban), and relics from Muhammad, including hair from his beard, a piece of his tooth, and his sword and bow. In the tiled Fountain Room, an imam (cleric) reads verses from the Quran 24 hours a day—as imams have nonstop since the 16th century.

The last section of the palace, just through the portico described earlier, is the **Fourth Courtyard.** The most intimate and

cozy of Topkapı's zones, it enjoys fine views over the Golden Horn and Bosphorus, and is dotted with several decorative pavilions.

At the far end of the courtyard is the **Mecidiye Pavilion.** In addition to spectacular views, the pavilion hosts a restaurant (with self-service and sit-down sections) offering a convenient and scenic finish to your tour.

▲▲Istanbul Archaeological Museum (İstanbul Arkeoloji Müzesi)

In a city as richly layered with the remains of fallen civilizations as Istanbul, this museum is a worthwhile stop. Although not as

extensive as its more-established European counterparts (such as London's British Museum), the variety and quality of the Istanbul Archaeological Museum's collection rival any. The complex consists of three separate museums (all covered by the same ticket). The Museum of Archaeology houses a vast exhibit on the Greeks, Romans, and other early civilizations of the Near East. The star attraction here is the world-class collection of ancient sarcophagi, including the elaborately decorated and remarkably well-preserved Alexander Sarcophagus. The Museum of the Ancient Orient shows off striking fragments from the even-more-ancient civilizations of Mesopotamia and Anatolia (the Asian portion of modern-day Turkey, east of the Bosphorus Strait), such as the 13th-century B.C. Kadesh Treaty—the first written peace agreement in world history. And the Tiled Kiosk sparkles with a staggering array of sumptuous ceramics and tiles.

Cost and Hours: 10 TL includes all three sections; Tue-Sun 9:00-19:00, until 17:00 off-season, closed Mon, last entry one hour before closing; Osman Hamdi Bey Yokuşu, Gülhane, Eminönü, tel. 0212/520-7740, www.istanbularkeoloji.gov.tr.

▲Gülhane Park

Originally Topkapı Palace's imperial garden, today it's Istanbul's oldest park and a welcoming swath of open green space within the bustling city. Located on the hillside below the palace, with terraces stretching to the shore below, Gülhane is a favorite weekend spot for locals. Come here to commune with Turks as they picnic with their families and enjoy a meander along the park's shady paths. On some summer weekends, the park hosts free concerts.

Grand Portal (Bab-ı Ali)

In the 19th century, this grand gate with its wavy roof and twin fountains was the entrance to the office of the Grand Vizier. The gate was called Bab-ı Ali because, historically, the word *bab* (door) was also used to refer to the authority of the state. Each Wednesday and Friday, commoners could enter here and tell their problems to public officials. It was here that all domestic and foreign affairs were discussed and presented to the sultan for a final decision. The surrounding neighborhood (also known as Bab-ı Ali) was the center of the Turkish news media for about 50 years (until the 1990s). Now it's a dull administrative district. But you can still find the historic gate just outside the old palace walls, near the Gülhane tram stop (see map on page 1148).

West of Sultanahmet: From the Grand Bazaar to the Golden Horn

Heading west from Sultanahmet, you enter an area that's more residential and less touristy, offering an opportunity to delve into the "real" Istanbul—rubbing elbows with locals at some of the city's best mosques and markets. While some attractions here—such as the Grand Bazaar—are tourist magnets, the lanes connecting them are filled mostly with residents.

✪ The following sights are linked by—and more thoroughly described in—the "Grand Bazaar and Spice Market Walk," on page 1129.

▲▲▲Grand Bazaar (Kapalı Çarşı)

Shop till you drop at the world's oldest market venue. Although many of its stalls have been over-

ISTANBUL

taken by souvenir shops, in many ways Istanbul's unique Grand Bazaar remains much as it was centuries ago: enchanting and perplexing visitors with its mazelike network of more than 4,000 colorful shops, fragrant eateries, and insistent shopkeepers. Despite the tourists and the knickknacks, the heart of the Grand Bazaar still beats, giving the observant visitor a glimpse of the living Istanbul.

Cost and Hours: Free, Mon-Sat 9:00-19:00, shops begin to close at 18:30, closed Sun and on the first day of most religious festivals, www.grandbazaaristanbul.org. It's across the parking lot from the Çemberlitaş tram stop, behind the Nuruosmaniye Mosque.

▲▲▲Mosque of Süleyman the Magnificent (Süleymaniye Camii)

This soothing and restrained—but suitably magnificent—house of worship was built by the great 16th-century architect Sinan for his sultan Süleyman. Although less colorful than the Blue Mosque, this mosque rivals it in size, scope, and beauty. Enjoy the numerous courtyards and tranquil interior, decorated in pastel hues and stained glass. Completed in 1557, the whole thing took just one decade to finish. Today the mosque is almost as clean and shiny as it was the day it opened, thanks to a three-year renovation completed in 2010. Out back are the elaborate tombs of Süleyman the Magnificent and his wife, Roxelana, as well as sweeping views of the city below.

Cost and Hours: Mosque—free, generally open daily from one hour after sunrise until one hour before sunset, closed to visitors five times a day for prayer; mausoleums—free, daily 9:00-17:00, until 18:00 in summer. It's on Sıddık Sami Onar Caddesi, in the Süleymaniye district.

▲Rüstem Paşa Mosque (Rüstem Paşa Camii)

This small 16th-century mosque, designed by the prolific and talented architect Sinan, was built to honor Süleyman the Magnificent's Grand Vizier, Rüstem Paşa. Elevated one story above street level in a bustling market zone, it has a facade studded with impressive İznik tiles—but the wall-to-wall decorations inside are even more breathtaking.

Cost and Hours: Free, generally open daily from one hour after sunrise until one hour before sunset, closed to visitors five times a day for prayer, on Hasırcılar Caddesi, Eminönü.

▲▲Spice Market (Mısır Carşısı)

This market was built about 350 years ago to promote the spice trade in Istanbul...and, aside from a few souvenir stands that have wriggled their way in, it still serves essentially the same purpose. Today the halls of the Spice Market are filled with equal numbers of locals and tourists. In addition to mounds of colorful spices (such as green henna and deep-red saffron), you can also get dried fruits (including apricots and figs), fresh roasted nuts, Turkish delight, supposed aphrodisiacs (Sultan's paste, or "Turkish Viagra"), imported caviar, and lots more.

Cost and Hours: Free to enter; Mon-Sat 8:00-19:30, until 19:00 off-season, Sun 9:30-18:00 year-round; shops begin to close 30 minutes earlier. It's right on Cami Meydanı Sokak along the Golden Horn, at the Old Town end of the Galata Bridge, near the Eminönü tram stop.

▲▲Galata Bridge (Galata Köprüsü)

Lined with hundreds of fishermen dipping their hooks into the water below, the new Galata Bridge is an Istanbul fixture. A stroll across the Galata Bridge offers panoramic views of Istanbul's Old Town.

In the New District

The New District, across the Golden Horn from the Old Town, offers a modern, urban, and very European-flavored contrast to the historic creaks and quirks of the Old Town. These sights are listed roughly in the order you'll reach them going from Taksim Square toward the Golden Horn.

Taksim Square and İstiklal Street

▲Taksim Square (Taksim Meydanı)

At the center of the New District is busy, vibrant Taksim Square. Taksim is the gateway to Istanbul's main pedestrian thoroughfare, İstiklal Street, with its historic buildings and colorful shops. This enormous square is also the New District's "Grand Central Station," connecting to the rest of the city by bus, Metro, funicular, and Nostalgic Tram.

Getting There: From the Old Town or from the cruise ship terminals, ride the tram to Kabataş (the end of the line) and follow the crowds directly into the funicular station. Take the handy little one-stop funicular up to Taksim Square, and exit following signs for *İstiklal Caddesi*.

▲▲▲İstiklal Street (İstiklal Caddesi)

Linking Taksim Square with the Tünel district (and, below that, the Galata district), İstiklal Street is urban Istanbul's main pedestrian drag, passing through the most sophisticated part of town. The vibrant thoroughfare, whose name translates as "Independence Street," is lined with a lively mix of restaurants, cafés, shops, theaters, and art galleries. Visitors are enchanted by İstiklal Street's beautiful Art Nouveau facades and intrigued by the multicultural

ISTANBUL

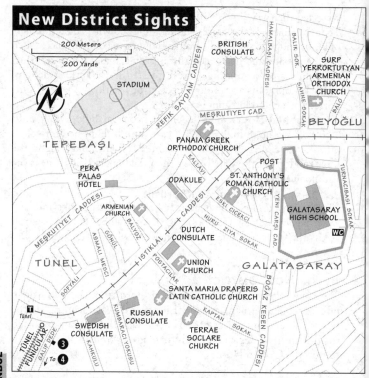

New District Sights

mix of tourists, international businesspeople, and locals who throng its elegant sidewalks.

▲Galata Dervish Monastery (Galata Mevlevihanesi)

Recently reopened following a multiyear renovation, this *mev-levihane* (mehv-leh-vee-hah-neh) serves as one of the few meeting places left for dervishes in Istanbul. Poke into the modest courtyard and the surrounding religious buildings. The museum is dull, but the monastery is worth visiting on Sundays for the once-a-week dervish services conducted here.

Cost and Hours: Monastery museum—5 TL, Tue-Sun 9:00-18:00, until 16:00 in winter, closed Mon; dervish services—40-50 TL, generally held on Sun at 17:00 (possibly on some Sat), Galip Dede Caddesi 15, tel. 0212/245-4141. Dervish service tickets are available at the monastery on the day of the performance; show up no later than 16:00 to be sure you get a ticket. For advance tickets, try contacting Tebit Çakmut (mobile 0536-607-4163).

In the Galata District

The old-feeling neighborhood climbing up a hill from the Golden Horn into the New District, called Galata, has a seedier, less

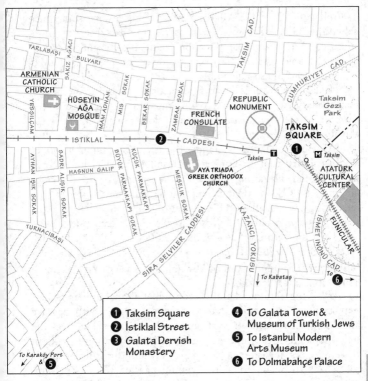

① Taksim Square
② İstiklal Street
③ Galata Dervish Monastery
④ To Galata Tower & Museum of Turkish Jews
⑤ To Istanbul Modern Arts Museum
⑥ To Dolmabahçe Palace

modern-European ambience than Taksim Square or İstiklal Street. Running up and down the hill under Galata is the old-fashioned subterranean funicular called Tünel (the entrance at the top of the hill is at the end of İstiklal Street; down below, it's near the Karaköy tram stop and Galata Bridge). The following sights are listed in order from the top of the hill down to the waterfront.

▲▲Galata Tower (Galata Kulesi)

The most prominent feature of the New District skyline, the 205-foot-tall stone Galata Tower was built by the Genoese in the mid-14th century and has been used over the centuries as a fire tower, a barracks, a dungeon, and even as a launch pad to test the possibility of human-powered flight.

In the Middle Ages, when Byzantines controlled the historic core of the city, this was the territory of Genoa (the Italian city once controlled much of the Mediterranean). This tower—sometimes called the "Genoese Tower"—was part of a mid-14th-century fortification. But, with a key location facing the Byzantine capital across the Golden Horn, the dramatic tower's purpose was likely as much to show off as to defend.

Today, the tower is a tourist attraction—offering visitors perhaps the best view of Istanbul. Climb the little staircase behind the tower, take the elevator to the seventh-floor restaurant, and go to the observation terrace.

As you enjoy the view, ponder the attention-grabbing story of a 17th-century aviation pioneer, Hezarfen Ahmet Çelebi. According to legend, Hezarfen Ahmet was so inspired by the drawings and models of Leonardo da Vinci that he built his own set of artificial wings, which allowed him to hang-glide a few miles from the top of this tower, across the Bosphorus, to Asian Istanbul.

Cost and Hours: 13 TL, daily 9:00-19:30, Büyük Hendek Sokak, tel. 0212/293-8180.

Quincentennial Museum of Turkish Jews (500 Yıl Vakfı Türk Musevileri Müzesi)

In 1492, King Ferdinand and Queen Isabel of Spain ordered their Sephardic Jewish population to accept the Christian faith, or leave and "dare not return." The Ottoman sultan Beyazıt Han was the only monarch of the time who extended an invitation to take in these refugees. Jewish people—many of whom can still trace their roots back to Spain—remain a vibrant part of Turkey's cultural mosaic. This museum, founded 500 years after the Spanish expulsion (hence the "quincentennial"), commemorates those first Sephardic Jews who found a new home here. Housed in an inactive early-19th-century synagogue built on the remains of a much-older synagogue, the small museum displays items donated by the local Jewish community. Particularly interesting are the ethnographic section, showing scenes from daily life, and a chair used in the Jewish circumcision rite.

Cost and Hours: 10 TL, Mon-Thu 10:00-16:00, Sun and Fri 10:00-14:00, closed Sat and on Jewish holidays, Karaköy Meydanı, Perçemli Sokak, tel. 0212/292-6333, www.muze500.com.

Getting There: The museum is conveniently located in Karaköy, close to the New District end of the Galata Bridge. It's on a dead-end alley, Perçemli Sokak, near your cruise ship and a few hundred yards from the Karaköy tram stop. If you're coming across the Galata Bridge by tram from the Old Town, get off at Karaköy, then take the pedestrian underpass as if you're heading for Tünel; once you're up the steps, back on the street level, Perçemli Sokak is the alley on your right.

Along the Bosphorus, Between Galata and Beşiktaş

This area, stretching north along the Bosphorus from the Galata Bridge, has been enjoying a wave of renovation, yet still retains the charm of its genteel past. We've listed these sights in the order you'll reach them coming from Galata.

Istanbul Modern Arts Museum
(İstanbul Modern Sanat Müzesi)

The main museum in Istanbul dedicated to the works of contemporary Turkish artists, "Istanbul Modern" offers a look at Istanbul's current art scene and the upper crust of local society that it attracts. Located in a huge warehouse in the port area (often dwarfed by cruise ships moored at the adjacent wharf), the museum is a bright and user-friendly space. Here you can see the well-described art of a hundred Turkish painters from the 20th century on one floor, with temporary exhibits downstairs. The good but expensive museum cafeteria has an outdoor terrace with fine Old Town views (or a claustrophobic peek at the hull of a giant cruise ship, if one happens to be in port).

Cost and Hours: 15 TL, open Tue-Sun 10:00-18:00, Thu until 20:00, closed Mon, last entry 30 minutes before closing, closed on January 1 and on the first day of religious festivals, near your cruise ship at Meclis-i Mebusan Caddesi, Liman İşletmeleri Sahası, Antrepo 4, tram stop: Tophane, tel. 0212/334-7300, www.istanbulmodern.org.

▲Dolmabahçe Palace (Dolmabahçe Sarayı)

This palace was the last hurrah of the Ottoman Empire. By the late 19th century, the empire was called the "Sick Man of Europe," and other Euro-

pean emperors and kings derided its ineffective and backward-seeming sultan. In a last-ditch attempt to rejuvenate the declining image of his empire, Sultan Abdülmecit I built the ostentatious Dolmabahçe (dohl-mah-bah-cheh) Palace—with all the trappings of a European monarch's showpiece abode—to replace the unmistakably Oriental-feeling Topkapı Palace as the official residence of the sultan. It didn't work—instead, Dolmabahçe was the final residence of the long line of Ottoman sultans, falling empty when the royal family was sent into exile in 1922. Built over a decade by an Ottoman-Armenian father-and-son team of architects, and completed in 1853, the palace is a fusion of styles—from Turkish-Ottoman elements to Neo-Baroque flourishes that were all the rage in Europe at the time. Its construction drained the already dwindling treasury, and the empire actually had to take a foreign loan to complete Dolmabahçe. Today the building belongs to the Turkish Parliament, which uses it only for important occasions, such as the 2004 NATO summit.

Two parts of the palace can be visited, and only with a tour—the Selamlık and the Harem. Visit the Harem only if you have time to spare—it's nothing compared to the Selamlık.

Cost and Hours: With limited time, the palace is best enjoyed from the water, as its interior, while certainly impressive, doesn't stack up against the city's major sights. The palace is accessible only with a guided tour, which is available in English; 30 TL for Selamlık, 20 TL for Harem, 40 TL for both sections; 2-4/hour, one hour, late March-late Oct Tue-Wed and Fri-Sun 9:00-16:00, until 15:00 off-season, closed Mon and Thu; best to reserve ahead by calling 0212/327-2626 (ask to be connected to an English-speaking agent). If you hear a recording in Turkish, just wait to be connected; reservation office hours Mon-Sat 9:00-17:45, closed Sun. Palace tel. 0212/236-9000, www.dolmabahcepalace.com.

Hagia Sophia Tour

This self-guided tour takes you through the Hagia Sophia—first a church, then a mosque, now a museum—and still one of the most important and impressive structures on the planet. For centuries, it was known as Megalo Ekklesia, the "Great Church" of Constantinople. The Greeks called it Hagia Sophia (eye-ah soh-fee-yah), meaning "Divine Wisdom," an attribute of God. The Turkish version is Aya Sofya.

Emperor Justinian built Hagia Sophia between A.D. 532 and 537. For 900 years, it served as the seat of the Orthodox Patriarch of Constantinople—the "eastern Vatican." Replete with shimmering mosaics and fine marble, Hagia Sophia was the single greatest architectural achievement of the Byzantine Empire.

When the Ottomans took Constantinople in 1453, Sultan Mehmet the Conqueror—impressed with the Great Church's beauty—converted it into an imperial mosque. Hagia Sophia remained Istanbul's most important mosque for five centuries. In the early years of the Turkish Republic (1930s), Hagia Sophia was converted again, this time into a museum. It retains unique elements of both the Byzantine and Ottoman empires and their respective religions, Orthodox Christianity and Islam. In a sense, Hagia Sophia is Istanbul in architectural form: ancient, grand, gigantic, with some rough edges, but on the whole remarkably preserved—a fascinating, still-vigorous blend of East and West.

Orientation

Cost: 25 TL covers the entire museum, including the upper galleries. Unless the other windows are closed, avoid the right-hand ticket window, which is reserved for tour guides with groups.

Hours: Tue-Sun 9:00-19:00, until 17:00 off-season, temporary exhibits and upper galleries close 30 minutes earlier, closed Mon, last entry one hour before closing.

When to Go: Try to avoid Tuesdays in peak season, when Topkapı Palace is closed, and Hagia Sophia gets even more crowded.

Getting There: Hagia Sophia is in the Sultanahmet neighborhood in the heart of the Old Town, facing the Blue Mosque. The main entrance is at the southwest corner of the giant building, across the busy street with the tram tracks (Divan Yolu). If you arrive by tram, get off at the Sultanahmet stop, and walk a couple hundred yards downhill along Divan Yolu. Cross the wide street at the traffic light.

Getting In: A crowd generally gathers just before 9:00 outside the ticket office and rushes the doors when they open, so arrive at 9:15 to miss the mob. If you're early and also have the Underground Cistern in your plans, go there first (the cistern is across the street with the tram tracks—described in the "Historic Core of Istanbul Walk"). Note that ongoing museum-entrance renovations may cause slow-moving lines. Guided tours often bunch up at Hagia Sophia's security checkpoint and ticket taker. Be patient—the logjam usually clears quickly.

Information: As you approach Hagia Sophia, loitering tour guides may offer to guide you around for a fee (generally 70 TL). Thanks to this self-guided tour, you won't need their help. And once inside, you'll find that most museum descriptions are in English. Tel. 0212/528-4500.

Length of This Tour: Allow at least an hour for the main floor and 30 minutes or more for the upper galleries.

Security and Baggage: After buying your ticket, but before entering, you'll go through an airport-type security checkpoint. There is no bag check.

Services: The cafeteria is across from the main building entrance, to the left of the walkway that leads past ticket control. The WC is at the end of the walkway, past the cafeteria. The bookshop is in the interior narthex.

Photography: Photography is allowed, but don't use your flash when taking pictures of icons, mosaic panels, or frescoes. English-language signs indicate where you should turn off your flash.

Nearby: Five *türbes* (sultans' tombs) along the south side of Hagia
  Sophia are open to the public and worth a look if you have
  extra time (daily 9:00-19:00).

Starring: The finest house of worship in the Christian and Muslim
  worlds.

Background

Hagia Sophia was built over the remains of at least two earlier
churches. After the second of these churches was destroyed in

the Nika riots in A.D. 532,
Emperor Justinian I (r.
527-565) wasted no time,
immediately putting his
plan for Hagia Sophia into
action. He asked for the
near-impossible: a church
with unbelievably grand
proportions, a monument
that would last for centu-
ries and keep his name alive for future generations.

Justinian appointed two geometricians to do the job: Anthemius, from the Aegean town of Tralles, and his assistant, Isidore
of Miletus. Both knew from the start that this would be a risky
project. Making Justinian's vision a reality would involve enormous
challenges. But they courageously went forward, creating a masterpiece unlike anything seen before.

More than 5,000 architects, stonemasons, bricklayers, plas-
terers, sculptors, painters, and mosaic artists worked around the
clock for five years to complete Hagia Sophia—and drain the treasury—faster than even the emperor had anticipated. In December
of 537, the Great Church of Constantinople held its first service in
the presence of Emperor Justinian and the Patriarch of Constantinople.

The church was a huge success story for Justinian, who was
understandably satisfied with his achievement. As the story goes,
when he stepped inside the church, he exclaimed, "Solomon, I have
surpassed you!" In the long history of the empire, the Byzantines
would never again construct such a grand edifice, but its design
would influence architects for centuries.

Hagia Sophia was a legend even before it was completed. People came from all over to watch the great dome slowly rise above
the landscape of the city. It was the first thing that merchants saw
from approaching ships and caravans. Hagia Sophia soon became
a landmark, and it continues to hold a special place in the mystical
skyline of Istanbul.

The structure served as a church for nearly a millennium. For

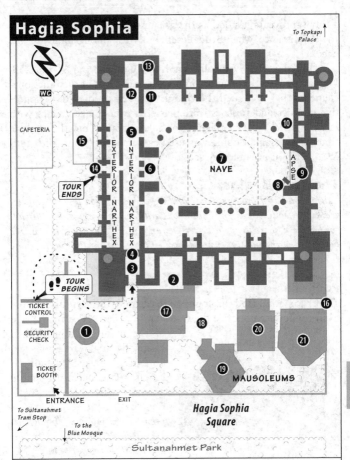

Hagia Sophia

To Topkapı Palace

WC

CAFETERIA

EXTERIOR NARTHEX

INTERIOR NARTHEX

TOUR ENDS

NAVE

APSE

TOUR BEGINS

TICKET CONTROL

SECURITY CHECK

TICKET BOOTH

ENTRANCE

EXIT

To Sultanahmet Tram Stop

To the Blue Mosque

Hagia Sophia Square

Sultanahmet Park

MAUSOLEUMS

ISTANBUL

1 Fountain
2 Baptismal Pool
3 Vestibule of Guards
4 Donation Mosaic
5 Interior Narthex
6 Imperial Gate & Mosaic of Christ with Emperor Leo VI
7 Great Dome
8 Mimber
9 Apse & Mosaic of Mary and the Christ Child
10 Sultan's Loge & Exit from Upper Galleries

11 Column of St. Gregory
12 Doorway to Upper Galleries
13 Ramp to Upper Galleries
14 Main Entrance/Exit
15 Ruins of Theodosian Church
16 Entrance to Sultans' Türbes
17 Türbe of Sultan Mustafa I
18 Türbe of Crown Princes
19 Türbe of Sultan Murad III
20 Türbe of Sultan Selim II
21 Türbe of Sultan Mehmet III

a thousand years it stood as the greatest dome in the world, until the Renaissance, when Brunelleschi built his famous dome in Florence.

The day the Ottomans captured Constantinople in 1453, Hagia Sophia was converted into a mosque. Most of the functional elements that decorated the church were removed, and its figurative mosaics and frescoes were plastered over in accordance with Islamic custom. Today the interior holds elements mostly from the time when Hagia Sophia was used as a mosque (from 1453 until 1934, when it became a museum).

The Tour Begins
• *After you pass through security and ticket control, you'll see the official walkway leading straight ahead, toward the main entrance. Instead, we'll take a shortcut for a better entrance route: Turn right, cross the big paved path, and slip past the wooden kiosk toward the giant, ornate Rococo...*

Fountain
The Ottomans added this fountain in the mid-18th century. Across from the fountain, notice the water taps in the portico by the side

of the main building. When Hagia Sophia was a mosque, both of these were used for ablution (ritual cleansing before prayer) as part of Islamic tradition.

• *Enter the museum through its exit door at the far end of this courtyard (to the left). On the pillar before the door (to your right as you face the door, at the corner of the small museum bookstore), notice the Arabic translated into Turkish. According to Islamic tradition, in the seventh century, Muhammad himself predicted that Constantinople (which was Christian and ruled the Western world at that time) would be conquered, and he praised the commander and soldiers as "güzel" (elite or distinguished). Eight centuries later, his prediction came to pass.*

Just past this pillar, before you enter the building, walk to the open chamber to your right, and take a few minutes to see the massive, pre-sixth-century...

Baptismal Pool
This immense baptismal pool was hewn out of a massive piece of marble, and amazingly is still in one piece despite spending centuries buried amid construction debris in a corner of Hagia Sophia's courtyard. It was finally unearthed in 2010. More than ten feet

long and nearly four feet deep, the pool likely was used for communal baptisms common in early Christianity. Urns found nearby held olive oil, which—in the Byzantine Orthodox tradition—was added to water during baptism.

The pool sits in what was once the baptistery courtyard. The baptistery itself, next door, was converted into the tomb of Sultan Mustafa I in the 17th century (to the right as you enter the chamber, look through the glass to see the interior of the tomb). The pool and other items from the baptistery were moved here to make way for Mustafa's tomb.

• *Now backtrack and step into this historic place of worship through the...*

Vestibule of Guards

This entry is named for the imperial guards who waited here for the emperor while he was attending church services. Byzantine emperors used this entryway because of its proximity to the royal palace, which stood where the Blue Mosque is today.

Scholars believe that the entrance's imposing **bronze doors** were brought here from an ancient temple in Antioch sometime after Justinian's reign. At the top of the flat panel (about eye-level on the first door), you can see traces of the silver imperial monograms that were once affixed to the bronze sheeting. Notice that these doors can't open or close—they became stuck in place when the marble floor was renovated and raised.

Stepping inside the vestibule, look up: The vaulted ceiling is covered with original mosaics, dating back nearly 1,500 years to Justinian's time. The mosaics in his church—such as these—depicted geometric patterns rather than people, as was the fashion at the time. Later, figurative mosaics were also added.

• *Above the doorway into the church, notice the gorgeous...*

Donation Mosaic

The mosaic dates from the 11th-century reign of Basil II. Scenes such as this became common in later Orthodox churches, and they usually depict the patron who funded the church's construction and to whom the church is dedicated. In the mosaic, you see Mary and the Christ child enthroned. Jesus holds the Gospels in his left hand and makes the three-fingered sign of the Trinity with his right hand. Two mighty Roman emperors flank the Holy Family: On the right, Constantine presents Mary and Christ with a model of his city, Constantinople (symbolized by city walls). On the left is Justinian, presenting a model of his greatest achievement, Hagia Sophia. Note the differences between this model and today's Hagia Sophia: Justinian's version had no minarets and no retaining or garden walls, and its dome was topped with a cross. It's fortunate that this mosaic has survived so beautifully intact, because many such mosaics were destroyed during the Iconoclast Era. If your neck is sore, or just for fun, turn 180 degrees, block the light with this book, and see the same mosaic more comfortably.

• *Now walk under the donation mosaic and straight into the…*

Interior Narthex

Hagia Sophia's interior narthex is an attractive space, with nine vaulted bays richly decorated with mosaics. The walls on either side

are lined with inch-thick **marble panels,** which were glued to the wall with stucco and pinned with iron rods. In some parts of the building, such as the Vestibule of Guards, the iron rusted, and over time the marble pieces began to fall off (the Vestibule of Guards' walls are painted to replicate the original marble covering). But here in the interior narthex, which is more protected from the elements, after 15 centuries, the panels hang on.

On the narthex ceiling are original **Justinian mosaics** that survived the Iconoclast Era because they were nonfigurative. The church's designer, Anthemius, sought to give the impression of movement. These mosaic pieces—interspersed with randomly placed bits of semiprecious stones—change from muted shades to brilliant reflection, depending on the direction of the light. Since services generally took place after sunset, the mosaic artists designed their work to be vivid even in flickering candlelight: simple polychrome crosses and starry shapes on a golden background.

Five doors on the left wall lead into the narrow, unadorned **exterior narthex.** Less splendid than the interior narthex, it holds a few uninteresting relics and the occasional temporary exhibit, along with the main visitors' entrance. We'll skip this for now.

At the far end of the interior narthex, notice the huge doorway leading to the ramp to the upper galleries. We'll go up this ramp later, after visiting the nave.

• *Just ahead of you, the central (and biggest) door to the nave is called the…*

Imperial Gate

This majestic doorway was reserved for the emperor—it was opened only for him. Notice the **metal hooks** attached to the top of the doorway. The Ottomans added these to hold leather curtains—similar to those used in today's mosques—to protect worshippers from dust and to reduce the interruption of a giant door opening and closing.

Look at the panel glittering above the gate, the **Mosaic of Christ with Emperor Leo VI.** The emperor known as "Leo the

Wise" is remembered more for his multiple marriages than for his intellect. His first three wives died without giving him a child, so he married Zoe Carbonospina (meaning "Black Eyes")—his mistress and the mother of his son. This sparked a scandal: The emperor was excommunicated by the patriarch and barred from attending the Christmas service in A.D. 906. In this scene, Leo seems to be asking for forgiveness—prostrating himself before Jesus, who blesses the emperor. The Greek reads, "May peace be with you. I am the light of the earth." Mary and the Archangel Gabriel are portrayed in the roundels on either side of Jesus. Whitewashed over by the Ottomans, the mosaic was only rediscovered in 1933.

• *Now step through the Imperial Gate and into Hagia Sophia's...*

Nave

Overwhelming, unbelievable, fantastic: These are the words that fall from the open mouths of visitors to Hagia Sophia. Take a few

steps into the grand space, close this book, shut your ears to the rumble of excited visitors, and just absorb the experience: You are in Hagia Sophia, the crowning achievement of the Byzantine Empire.

Paris' Notre-Dame would fit within Hagia Sophia's great dome, and New York City's Statue of Liberty could do jumping jacks in here.

• *Take a few minutes to appreciate the feat of engineering that is Hagia Sophia. First, tune into the...*

Architecture

Hagia Sophia was designed as a classical basilica covered by a vast central dome. By definition, a "basilica" is characterized by a large, central open space, called a nave, flanked by rows of columns and narrow side aisles. It sounds simple, but even the two geometricians Justinian chose to build Hagia Sophia had doubts about whether the plan would work. Every so often, Anthemius would go to the emperor to tell him about potential risks. And every time, he got the same response: "Have faith in God." Anthemius was right to have worried. Despite his mastery of geometry, he made some miscalculations: A few decades after Hagia Sophia was completed, part of the gigantic dome collapsed. The dome was repaired using steeper angles than the original; even so, it would collapse and be rebuilt again in the sixth and tenth centuries.

The main dome—185 feet high and roughly 105 feet in diameter—appears to float on four great arches. The secret is the clear glass windows at the base of the dome. The triangular pendentives in the corners gracefully connect the round dome to the rectangular building below, and the arches pass the dome's weight on to the massive piers at the corners. Semi-domes at the ends extend the open space. Over 100 columns provide further support

to the upper parts of the building. Many of these columns were brought here from other, even more ancient monuments and temples.

Hagia Sophia was a worthy attempt to create a vast indoor space, independent of the walls. But in practice, quite a bit of the dome's great weight is held up by the walls, which is why there aren't very many windows. The Byzantines built additional arches inside the walls to further help distribute the weight. These "hidden arches" are visible here and there, where the stucco layers have worn away.

As you look around, note the basic principle of Byzantine architecture: symmetry. All the architectural elements, including

decorative pieces, are placed in a symmetrical fashion. If symmetry demanded a window or door that would weaken a wall, then a false, painted-on one would be created in its place.

The artful use of light creates the interior's stunning effect. The windows at the base of the dome used clear glass, while other windows throughout the building used thin alabaster to further diffuse the light and create a more dramatic effect.

• With the Imperial Gate directly behind you, face the apse and look up into the massive dome to see the...

Dome Decorations

During the centuries that Hagia Sophia was used as a mosque, many of its original decorations—especially mosaics or frescoes depicting people—were covered over with whitewash and plaster. Ironically, in some cases, the plaster actually helped to preserve the artwork. For others, damage was inevitable, as the stucco absorbed the whitewash. In the 19th century, the sultan invited the Swiss-born Fossati brothers to complete an extensive restoration of Hagia Sophia. They cleaned and catalogued many of the Byzantine

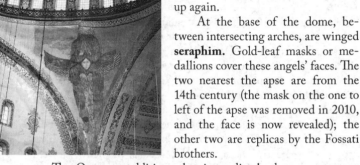

figural mosaics before covering them up again.

At the base of the dome, between intersecting arches, are winged **seraphim.** Gold-leaf masks or medallions cover these angels' faces. The two nearest the apse are from the 14th century (the mask on the one to left of the apse was removed in 2010, and the face is now revealed); the other two are replicas by the Fossati brothers.

The Ottoman additions that immediately draw your attention are Arabic calligraphy, especially the eight 24-foot-wide **me-**

dallions suspended at the bases of the arches supporting the central and side domes. These huge, leather-wrapped wooden medallions were added in the 19th century and decorated by master Islamic calligraphers. In a church, you'd see paintings of Biblical figures and saints; however, in a mosque (which allows no depictions of people), you'll see ornately written names of leading Muslim figures. The two medallions on the arches flanking the apse are painted with the names of Allah (on the right)

and Muhammad (on the left). The four at the center name the four caliphs, Muslim religious and social leaders who succeeded the Prophet Muhammad: Abu Bakr, Umar, Uthman, and Ali. The two medallions on the arches above the Imperial Gate bear the names of Muhammad's grandchildren and Ali's sons, who were assassinated.

• Walk toward the front of the church. The heavy chandeliers hanging from the dome, additions from Ottoman times, held candlesticks or glass oil lamps with floating wicks. The highly decorated staircase before you, set diagonally away from the wall, is the...

Mimber

The *mimber* (meem-behr) is the pulpit in a mosque, used by the imam (cleric, like a priest or rabbi) to deliver his sermon on Fridays, or to talk to the public on special occasions. The imam stands halfway up the stairs as a sign of respect, reserving the uppermost step for the Prophet Muhammad.

• *Go beyond the* mimber *and face the...*

Apse

When Hagia Sophia (the original church, facing Jerusalem) was converted into a mosque, a small off-center niche was added in the apse's circular wall. Called the mihrab, this niche shows the precise direction to face during prayers (toward the holy city of Mecca, which is south of Jerusalem). The stately columns flanking the mihrab are actually huge candles—standard fixtures in royal mosques.

High above the mihrab, on the underside of the semi-dome, is a colorful **Mosaic of Mary and the Christ Child** on a gold background (to see better, raise this book to block the light). Christ is also dressed in gold. Part of the background is missing, but most of the scene is intact. This mosaic, the oldest one in Hagia Sophia, dates from the ninth century. It may have been the first figurative mosaic added after the Iconoclast Era, replacing a cross-design mosaic from the earlier period. The gold "clubs" on Mary's forehead and both shoulders stand for the Trinity. Notice also the red "spades" among the "clubs" on the pillows.

On the right end of the arch, just before the semi-dome (behind the large medallion), find the **Mosaic of Archangel Gabriel** with his wings sweeping down to the ground. On the opposite end of the arch, there was once a similar mosaic of the Archangel Michael.

To your left, by the side of the apse (the frilly gilded room under the big medallion), is the elevated prayer section for the sultans, or the **sultan's loge** (behind the gold-glazed metalwork). This area was added in the 19th century.

• *With your back to the apse, wander to the*

far right-hand corner of the nave. As you walk, notice the golden mosaics on the ceiling from Justinian's age. Past the large buttresses, separating the aisles from the nave, are rows of...

Green Marble Columns

These columns carry the upper galleries and also provide support to the domes, easing the burden on the buttresses and the exterior walls. Notice the richly decorated white-marble capitals of these columns (with the joint monograms of Justinian and Theodora).

• In the far corner (to your right, still facing the entry) is what looks like a five-foot-tall alabaster egg, but is actually an...

Alabaster Urn

This is one of two Hellenistic-era **urns** (second century B.C., one on each side of the nave) that the sultan brought to Istanbul from Per-

gamon—the formidable ancient acropolis of north Aegean Turkey. Find the tap mounted in the side. Traditionally, Ottoman mosques had functional fountains inside, to provide drinking water for worshippers.

The two purple **porphyry columns** behind each urn are older than Hagia Sophia. Two columns stand at each corner—eight in all. Long ago, iron girdles were placed around the columns to prevent further damage (they already had cracks in them).

• In the rear right-hand corner, about 10 yards beyond the alabaster urn, is the quirky and purportedly miraculous...

Column of St. Gregory

This is the legendary "perspiring column"—the Column of St. Gregory, the miracle worker. For centuries, people believed this column "wept" holy water that could cure afflictions such as eye diseases and infertility.

How does it work? Put your thumb in the hole, and if it comes out feeling damp, your prayer will be answered. No? Try this. Put your thumb in the hole again, and this time, make a complete 360-degree circle with your hand, with your thumb still in the hole. The metal surrounding the hole has been polished by millions of hands over the years.

• Walk through the door to the left of this column, leaving the nave and re-entering the interior narthex. The huge door to your right leads to the...

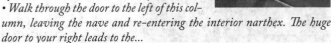

Upper Galleries

The upper level of the church holds Hagia Sophia's best-known mosaics—but if you have limited time and are hoping to visit Topkapı Palace or linger in the Grand Bazaar, you may want to skip them.

To access the upper galleries, go through this door and follow the long, stone-paved ramp up (watch your step, as the stones are smooth and uneven). Why a ramp, and not stairs? Because those of exalted rank were either carried by their servants, or rode up on horseback. As you step off the ramp, keep to the right and enter the well-lit...

West Gallery

This gallery provides a direct view of the apse. Walk to the center of the gallery and look for a **green marble circle** in the floor right before the balustrade, with an ensemble of matching green columns on either side. This was the spot reserved for the empress' throne, directly across from the apse.

• *Turning left at the end of this gallery, you'll pass through the marble half wall—known as the Gate of Heaven and Hell—into the...*

South Gallery

This area originally was used for church council meetings. The frescoes on the ceiling are copies of ancient designs, redone by the Fossati brothers during their 19th-century restoration work.

Go to the first window on your right. To the right of the window is the ***Deesis* Mosaic,** one of the finest of Hagia Sophia's Byzantine mosaics—though certainly not its best preserved. It dates from the 13th or 14th century, and its theme—the Virgin Mary and John the Baptist asking Jesus for the salvation of souls—is common in Eastern Orthodox churches. Notice how Mary's and John's heads tilt slightly toward Christ. The workmanship is fascinating, especially the expression and detail in the faces. Get up close to  examine how minuscule and finely cut the pieces are.

• *Walk to the far end of this gallery to see two more Byzantine mosaic panels, placed side by side.*

As you approach the end of the gallery, look for the 12th-century **Mosaic of the Virgin and Child with Emperor John Comnenus and Empress Irene.** Mary stands in the center, holding the Christ Child in her arms. Christ's right hand extends in blessing, and he holds a scroll in his left hand. As in many such mosaics, the emperor offers Christ a bag of money (representing his patronage), and the empress presents a scroll. Their son Prince Alexius is portrayed to his mom's left on the adjoining pier—added to the scene only after he became co-emperor at age 17.

To the left is the 11th-century **Mosaic of Christ with Emperor Constantine IX Monomachus and Empress Zoe.** Constantine and Zoe are portrayed in ceremonial garments, flanking Christ on his throne. The inscription above the emperor's head reads, "Sovereign of Romans, Constantine Monomachus," while the empress is identified as "Zoe, the most pious Augusta."

Standard fare so far, but if we dig deeper, this mosaic gets quite interesting. If you look carefully, you can see that critical sections of text were erased and then restored (in what looks like a different font). Here's the story: Empress Zoe—the daughter of an emperor who had no male heirs—married Romanus Argyrus, but he was killed in his bath a few years later. Zoe then married her young lover, Michael IV, and, within a few years, he was dead, too. His nephew, Michael V, was named co-emperor and sent Zoe into exile. But the well-connected Zoe found a way back, had Michael V deposed, and at the age of 65 married a third time, to Constantine Monomachus.

That's three husbands in all—and a lot of extra work for the mosaic artists. So, instead of changing the image of Zoe's husband each time, they simply changed the title over his head. And Zoe's face, which was erased by Michael V, was restored to its youthful appearance after she resumed her reign and married Constantine Monomachus.

• *Retrace your steps back to the northwest corner (where you entered the galleries). This time walk along the North Gallery to the exit at the far end.*

North Gallery

As you walk, take a moment to look at the graffiti carved into the walls by bored, non-Byzantine church attendants during the long evening services. Graffiti is visible on the walls in the bays overlooking the nave, usually at upper body height. Graffiti in the form of sailing ships makes you wonder whether these servants wished they could just sail away.

• *The exit ramp takes you down to the north aisle (you'll emerge by the Sultan's Loge). Head for the narthexes straight ahead, and exit the way others are entering. Just outside in a hole on your right are the remains of the earlier Theodosian Church.*

Previous Churches

At least two earlier churches have stood on this spot. No trace remains of the first church, which was probably built in the fourth century A.D. as Constantine moved to strengthen his hold on the fledgling Byzantine Empire.

The next church, believed to have been built by Theodosius II, was grander in scale and more elaborate. But as fate would have it, this second church was also destroyed during a religious uprising—the Nika riots of 532 that caused the death of more than 30,000 people. Half of the city was reduced to ashes, including the church.

Some remains of the Theodosian Church are visible in the pit just outside the main entrance to Hagia Sophia. You can see part of the steps that led to the entrance portico, the bases of the columns that supported the entry porch, and fragments of marble blocks with carved designs of sheep. Other Theodosian Church artifacts, columns, and capitals are scattered nearby throughout Hagia Sophia's outdoor garden.

• *Your tour is finished. You're close to several other major sights, including the Blue Mosque, Hippodrome, and Underground Cistern (all described in the "Historic Core of Istanbul Walk," earlier). And directly behind Hagia Sophia is the wall of Topkapı Palace (described on page 1151).*

If you have a few minutes, it's worth a quick walk to see the Sultans' Türbes (mausoleums), which can only be accessed from outside the Hagia Sophia complex. To get there, exit the museum grounds through the turnstiles, head left along Hagia Sophia's garden wall, and find the entrance just around the southeast corner.

Shopping in Istanbul

Shopping can provide a good break from Istanbul's mosques, museums, and monuments. And diving into the city's bustling, colorful marketplaces can be a culturally enlightening experience. For information on VAT refunds and customs, see page 135.

Where to Shop

Shopping in the Grand Bazaar and at other Old Town merchants (such as the craft market tucked behind the Blue Mosque) is lively, memorable, and fun, and prices can be low—but the quality is often questionable. Istanbul's residents prefer shopping at the more expensive but reliably good-quality stores.

Dealing with Aggressive Merchants

Throughout the Grand Bazaar—and just about everywhere in the Old Town—you'll constantly be barraged by people selling everything you can imagine. This can be intimidating, but it's fun if you loosen up and approach it with a sense of humor. The main rule of thumb: Don't feel compelled to look at or buy anything you don't want. These salesmen prey on Americans' gregariousness and tendency to respond politely to anyone who offers a friendly greeting. They often use surprising or attention-grabbing openers:

"Hello, Americans! Where are you from? Chicago?! I have a cousin there!"

"Are you lost? Can I help you find something?"

"Nice shoes! Are those Turkish shoes?"

"Would you like a cup of tea?"

The list is endless—collect your favorites.

If you're not interested, simply say a firm, "No, thanks!" and brush past them, ignoring any additional comments. This may seem cold, but it's the only way to get around without constantly getting tied up in unwanted conversations.

If, on the other hand, you're looking to chat, merchants are often very talkative—but be warned that a lengthy conversation may give them false hopes that you're looking to buy, and could make it even more difficult to extract yourself gracefully from the interaction.

ISTANBUL

What to Buy
Textiles

The cotton T-shirts you'll see around the Old Town and in the Grand Bazaar make decent souvenirs or gifts, but are usually low-quality—they'll likely fade and shrink after a few washes.

Many people associate Turkey with **pashminas**—high-quality shawls traditionally made with Himalayan goat wool. And, in fact, the Old Town is a pashmina paradise, with every color of the rainbow. But Turkey doesn't produce pashmina wool, so the ones you see here are imports. Still, they're practical and fun, and cheaper than the fakes sold in the US.

A *peştemal* (pehsh-teh-mahl) is a large, thin, cotton **bath towel** that Turks wrap around themselves at the baths; nowadays they're also used as curtains or tablecloths. Bathing Turks scrub away dead skin and dirt with *kese* (keh-seh)—simple rectangular **mittens** made out of raw silk or synthetic fabric. Look for these two authentically Turkish items at the **Eğin Tekstil** shop on Yağlıkçılar Caddesi in the Grand Bazaar (see page 1138).

The **Sivaslı Yazmacı** shop carries a wide collection of handmade textiles, including the traditional gauzy cotton *yazma* (yahzmah), the head-covering worn by rural Turkish women (on the same street as Eğin Tekstil, Yağlıkçılar Caddesi 57, Grand Bazaar).

Jennifer's Hamam, run by a Canadian expat, sells bath towels, bathrobes, *keses,* and tablecloths at set prices. They're made by a small group of **fine weavers** from throughout Turkey, using organic fibers on old-style shuttle looms (Arasta Bazaar 135 & 43, by the Blue Mosque, tel. 0212/518-0548).

Turkey produces wonderful **silk,** but be careful: In the Grand Bazaar and other Old Town shops, scarves and other items billed as silk are often made of polyester or, at best, low-grade silk.

Carpets and Kilims

If you want to buy a Turkish carpet, it's worth knowing a bit about what you're looking for—if only to avoid advertising your inexperience. For example, folding a carpet to check the knots will not only give you away as a novice, but can actually ruin the carpet if it's silk. Rubbing a carpet with a piece of wet tissue to test its colorfastness is akin to licking a shirt before you buy it. And beware of shopkeepers who stress "authenticity" over quality. Authenticity is an important consideration when shopping for traditional wool-on-wool carpets. But for wool-on-cotton or silk-on-silk, it can actually be better to get a piece made with newer techniques, which produce tighter weaves, brighter and more durable colors, and more intricate patterns.

Carpets can range in price from several hundred dollars to several thousand or more, depending on the age, size, quality, and uniqueness. Merchants will ship them home for you, though many tourists find it cheaper and more foolproof to carry them back (the carpets can be folded and tied tightly into a squarish bundle).

Wool-on-wool carpets are the most traditional kind of Turkish carpet. Although becoming less common, these are still woven in countryside villages. Each region has its own distinctive, centuries-old design-and-color combination. In general, wool-on-wool carpets cost less than other Turkish rugs. The best way to gauge the authenticity of a wool-on-wool carpet is to look for the natural, less-vibrant colors that come from vegetable dyes made from local plants.

Newer carpet styles, such as **wool-on-cotton** (wool pile on a cotton skeleton) and **silk-on-silk,** first appeared in the 19th century. The new materials allowed weavers to create more intricate floral and geometric patterns than those found in traditional designs. Wool-on-cotton and silk-on-silk carpets are colored with chemical dyes, which can be as good, or even better, than natural dyes. Unlike wool-on-wool carpets, density is important in assessing quality for wool-on-cotton and silk-on-silk carpets.

Kilims (kee-leem) feature a flat weave without the pile, similar to a Navajo rug. These also have traditional designs and natural colors. Used in the past as blankets and bedspreads, they're mainly popular now as decorative items (and can be used as wall hangings). Kilims are generally inexpensive, but old and rare pieces can cost several thousand dollars. For a wearable, affordable kilim, consider a vest made out of the material; you'll see these at the Grand Bazaar and elsewhere.

Osman's Carpet Shop, in Zincirli Han in the Grand Bazaar, is regarded as *the* place to go for expert advice—and high-quality (expensive) carpets. Osman, who's often assisted by son Nurullah or nephew Bilgin, won't hustle you. Instead, he educates customers so they can select just the right carpet for them.

Punto of Istanbul, a couple of blocks away from the Grand Bazaar's Nuruosmaniye Gate, carries a wide variety of carpets—from simple kilims to fancy silk carpets—and has down-to-earth prices compared to most. Shop anonymously as you haggle, then, before you pay, show this book for an additional 10 percent discount from manager Metin (Nuru Osmaniye, Gazi Sinan Paşa Sokak, Vezirhan 17, tel. 0212/511-0854).

Tiles and Ceramics

A Turkish ceramic specialty is *çini* (chee-nee), which is usually translated in English as **"tile"** (or "quartz tile"). The word *çini* can

describe flat tiles used for architectural decoration or functional items such as bowls, vases, and cups. The clay in *çini* products has a high quartz content and technically is difficult to work with. High-quality glazed *çini* tiles were at their peak in the 16th and 17th centuries, and the style is considered very traditional in Turkey. Other ceramics (*seramik;* seh-rah-meek) don't have much of a history here—though you will find them sold in markets. You'll also see **pottery** (*çömlek;*

How to Get the Best Bargain

Many visitors to Istanbul are surprised to find that bargaining for a lower price is no longer common in much of the city. At modern stores or shopping malls, the posted prices are final. But in the tourist zones—such as the Grand Bazaar, Spice Market, and other shops around the Old Town—merchants know you're expecting to haggle...and they're happy to play along. (Local shoppers have less patience for this game. Notice that even in the Grand Bazaar, locals don't often haggle—if they think something is overpriced, they either ask for a discount or simply walk away.)

In the Old Town market areas where bargaining is common, you'll constantly be bombarded by sales pitches. If you aren't interested in what they're selling, try not to establish eye contact. Although this may feel rude, it's the best way to avoid unnecessary conversations and save your time and energy for the items you do want. One great line for hustlers: "*Yok*," which means, simply, "No."

If you are interested in an item, don't make it obvious. Take

chom-lehk): simple, fired earthenware objects shaped on a wheel, usually without any design or glaze.

High-quality items are often too costly for regular stores to carry. If you are seriously interested in the best ceramics and tile, try the **İznik Foundation,** which carries on Turkey's long-established tile tradition. Their main store is in the Kuruçeşme neighborhood, north of the New District, by the Bosphorus Bridge at Öksüz Çocuk Sokak.

If you're looking for something simple, you'll find plenty of inexpensive, pretty pieces at souvenir stores all around the Old Town and Grand Bazaar.

Traditional Arts: *Hat* and *Tezhip*

Hat (pronounced "hot") is artful Arabic calligraphy. To make written words appear more beautiful, the calligrapher (*hattat;* hot-taht) bends grammatical rules and often combines letters irregularly. Over the centuries, this decorative art has reached a very sophisticated level of expression, almost like a painting. *Tezhip* (tehz-heep) is the illumination and embellishment of manuscripts, scrolls, and books with geometric or floral patterns.

If you're just curious, the **Turkish Handicrafts Center** is a

your time, browse around, and pretend you might just wander off at any moment—feigned disinterest is part of the game. You're better off keeping a low profile—this isn't the time to show off your nicest clothes, jewelry, and wads of cash.

Merchandise often doesn't have price tags, because shop owners want you to ask—giving them an opening to launch into a sales pitch. Don't suggest a number; let them be the first to mention a price. When they do, assume it's elevated. Even if you counter with only half their original offer, you may find your price easily accepted—meaning you've already offered too much.

More likely, a spirited haggling war will ensue. If you don't like to bargain, you'll pay more than you should. Play along to get a lower price and a fun cultural interaction. These haggling sessions can drag on for some time, as you sip tea (usually apple-flavored) offered by shopkeepers who want to keep you around. When you start to walk away, that last price they call out is often the best price you'll get.

There's room for bargaining even on fixed-price commodities, such as gold and silver, where you're being charged not only for the precious metal but also for the workmanship.

If you're haggling over something unique, be prepared to pay a premium. Shopkeepers already know that you won't be able to find it elsewhere.

good place to visit. You're welcome to watch amateur artists learning the techniques of *tezhip* and *hat*, and musicians practicing classical music on the *ney* (reed flute), *kanun* (zither), and *ud* (lute). The center is in the historic and lovely Caferağa Medresesi. Each room around the madrassa's peaceful courtyard is assigned to a particular art form (Tue-Sun 8:30-19:00, closed Mon; kitchen serves basic meals, snacks, tea, and coffee; Caferiye Sokak, Soğukkuyu Çıkmazı 1, next door to Yeşil Ev Hotel on a dead-end along Hagia Sophia's outer wall in Sultanahmet, tel. 0212/513-3601).

For traditional dolls, visit the **doll shop** in the handicrafts center by the Blue Mosque at Kabasakal Caddesi 5. The folk dolls made by Lütfiye Bakutan and Selma Yurtlu are masterpieces you can't find anywhere else (daily April-Oct 9:00-18:00, until 17:00 in winter, Sultanahmet).

Gold Jewelry

Gold is a good buy in Turkey. Prices change with the daily rate of gold; when you ask the price of a piece, the shopkeeper will weigh it for you. Simple bangles often cost little more than the gold itself.

Most mass-produced jewelry is made from molds with 14-carat gold, as it is harder and cheaper. Handmade items are the most expensive; in some pieces, the fine workmanship is more valuable than the gold itself. While the cheaper items (14-18 carat) cost around $25-40 per gram, the price can go as high as $50-75 per gram for finely crafted pieces. Precious and semiprecious stones are generally paired with 18-carat gold.

Silver Objects and Jewelry

Silver jewelry, with or without semiprecious stones, is a good and affordable alternative to fancy gold pieces. As with gold, silver items usually are sold by weight and won't have a price tag. Look around a bit in the Grand Bazaar to get an idea of what's available and the range of prices. **Kalcılar Han** in the Grand Bazaar (see page 1135) is a production center for silver items, with shops on its lower and upper levels. Most of the silver you see in the Grand Bazaar shops is handcrafted on site.

You can also find **beads** to make your own jewelry. A few shops in the Grand Bazaar (in and near **Cevahir Bedesten,** see page 1140) carry silver jewelry and semiprecious stone beads.

Souvenirs and Trinkets

The Grand Bazaar is filled with stalls hawking endless mountains of junk, most of it imported. This stuff sells well, as it's cheap and looks "Oriental." Those hats with tiny  circular mirrors are common not because they're crafted by local artisans (they're made outside of Turkey), but because the merchants know tourists will buy them. Fortunately, the bazaar is also filled with plenty of affordable, authentically Turkish trinkets that make wonderful gifts.

You can't miss the **"evil eyes"** (*nazarlık;* nah-zahr-luhk)—blue-and-white glass beads that look like eyes. Traditionally thought to ward off negative energy from jealous eyes, these are a kind of good-luck charm popular among Turks. You'll see them on doorways, hanging down from rearview mirrors, or anywhere else people want protection. Babies wear them, adults wear them, and teenage girls braid them in their hair. *Nazarlık*s are authentically and uniquely Turkish, which makes them good gifts. They come in various sizes—some with a metal frame, others on a hooked pin, still others embedded in tiles.

Small Turkish **tea glasses,** made of clear glass and shaped like a tulip blossom, are easy to find.

Machine-made textiles with traditional designs make good tablecloths, pillowcases, bedspreads, and sofa throws. Some are velvet, with silky-looking, colorful embroideries.

Coffee and pepper grinders don't break easily, since they're made of brass or wood.

The same goes for **backgammon sets** and **inlaid wooden boxes.** The best are inlaid with mother-of-pearl, while the cheapest are inlaid with plastic.

If you decide to buy a glass **water pipe** (*nargile;* nahr-gee-leh), get the kind that separates into parts and is easily reassembled.

Mined in central Turkey, **onyx** is plentiful, affordable, and popular in decorative objects such as vases and bowls, as well as chess sets (but not so common in jewelry).

Gifts for children are more limited. Consider Halloween **costumes.** You'll find tiny, colorful Turkish princess outfits for girls, with coins adorning the sleeves and trousers. Cheap knockoffs of **soccer jerseys** also abound.

Nightlife in Istanbul

If you'll be staying in Istanbul before or after your cruise, here are a few ways to experience the city after dark.

Low-Key Evenings on the Golden Horn and the Bosphorus

Warm, clear evenings in Istanbul are perhaps best enjoyed with a short walk across the **Galata Bridge** to watch the sun go down. Take in the Old Town's magnificent skyline, dominated by floodlit domes and minarets. After sunset, head to the lower level of the Galata Bridge, where you'll find several moderately priced tavern-style eateries (*meyhane;* mehy-hah-neh) and seafood restaurants.

Restaurants, bars, and clubs along the Bosphorus tend to be expensive, but some areas are more affordable than others. For instance, the **Ortaköy neighborhood,** by the European side of the Bosphorus Bridge, is a pedestrian area with many bars, teahouses, and restaurants. In nice weather, especially on weekends, the area is packed with hundreds of people strolling its streets and alleys. But even on the warmest evenings, you'll want to bring along a sweater or shawl, as a cool breeze blows along the Bosphorus at night (in bad weather, the area is often empty). If you're on a tight budget, get a baked potato or a sandwich from one of the numerous summertime food stalls. Grab a drink from a grocery store, and enjoy your evening picnic on a bench by the Bosphorus, watching the boats pass by, with the bridge lit up like a pearl necklace and the Ortaköy Mosque as its backdrop. A couple of teahouses with good views of the Bosphorus are usually packed with Turks playing backgammon or a tile game called OK. To get to Ortaköy from Taksim Square in the New District, catch bus #40 or #40T.

Partying on İstiklal Street, in the New District

In the evenings, the neighborhood surrounding İstiklal Street is transformed into a vast entertainment center. The street itself has several bars, jazz clubs, and *meyhanes* (taverns), all popular among the locals. From the Karaköy cruise terminal, take the Tünel funicular (find it near the end of the Galata Bridge) up to İstiklal Street. Starting near the Galata Tower, walk down the street to Taksim Square; from there, it's easy to catch a taxi back to your cruise ship.

Fasıl Music

Many visitors enjoy *fasıl* (fah-suhl) music, often performed in the inviting ambience of a *meyhane*. *Fasıl* is live, old-time Istanbul songs or classical Turkish tunes, performed by a trio of musicians. Locals sing along as they drink *rakı* (firewater) and nibble on *mezes* (appetizers; see the "Eating in Istanbul" section). You won't have to pay a cover charge for the music, but it's customary to tip the musicians—watch locals and imitate.

One good venue is **Şahika** (shah-hee-kah), in a narrow townhouse on Nevizade Sokak (find the Flower Passage/Çiçek Pasajı at 80 İstiklal Street, enter the fish market from the Flower Passage, then take the first right, tel. 212-249-6196, www.sahika.com.tr). A different style of music, including *fasıl* and contemporary, is played on each of its five floors. If you're a solo male, they may not let you in, so find a fellow traveler to bring along.

Note that some of the restaurants in the Flower Passage and others on İstiklal Street feature "Gypsy music," which is louder, faster, and more danceable than *fasıl*.

Clubs and Nightspots

If you're serious about nightlife, dip into one of the many nightspots on or near İstiklal Street. These generally get rolling late in the evening, around 23:00 or later, and hit their peak around 1:00 to 2:00 in the morning. Quite a few clubs stay open until 4:00.

Babylon, near Tünel, is a popular club featuring international bands and performers. It usually has jazz and ethnic music, but it's not unusual to see reggae or percussion bands. Its box office opens at noon, although for more popular performances, you might want to buy tickets in advance (Seyhbender Sokak 3, tel. 0212/292-7368, www.babylon.com.tr).

Hayal Kahvesi is a bar and rock-music venue with daily live performances. It's an institution on the Turkish rock scene; almost all of Turkey's famous rock bands and singers have taken the Hayal Kahvesi stage at least once (just off İstiklal Street at Meşelik Sokak 10, tel. 0212/245-1048, www.hayalkahvesibeyoglu.com).

Nardis Jazz Club, hosting both local and international performers, has been called Istanbul's best live-music club. There's live jazz daily except Sunday, with programs starting at 21:30 on weekdays and 22:30 at weekends (15-TL drinks, 35-70-TL cover charge based on who's performing, Kuledibi Sokak 14, Galata, tel. 0212/244-6327, www.nardisjazz.com).

Ghetto Istanbul offers the full spectrum of live music—everything from electro swing to Gypsy. Reservations are a must for dinner. Doors open at 21:30; performances usually start at 23:00 and go until 2:00 or so in the morning (generally closed Sun-Mon and Sept; 20-50-TL cover charge, Kamer Hatun Caddesi 10, Beyoğlu, tel. 0212/251-7501, www.ghettoist.com).

The prestigious **IKSV Salon** hosts quality jazz and classical music performances. Schedules are irregular, so check their website for the latest (50-90-TL seats, 25-50-TL standing tickets, 25-50 percent student discount on standing tickets, Sadi Konuralp Caddesi 5, Şişhane, tel. 0212/334-0752, www.saloniksv.com).

Love Dance Point is a classy, predominantly gay dance club with popular DJs, special events, and occasional theme parties. Doors open on weekends at 23:30, and they party until 4:00 or 5:00 in the morning (20-25-TL cover charge, open Fri-Sat only but check website for additional days, across from Military Museum at Cumhuriyet Caddesi 349/1, Harbiye, tel. 0212/296-3358, www. lovedp.net).

Eating in Istanbul

In the Old Town's Sultanahmet Area

These restaurants—along with much of Istanbul's best sightseeing—are concentrated in the Sultanahmet area.

Matbah Restaurant—where the manager and chef share their nearly two decades of research into imperial Ottoman cuisine—has a seasonal menu using fresh ingredients. Try the lamb neck with apricots and plums served alongside saffron rice with grape molasses, lamb shanks served with smoked eggplant puree, or *nergis kalyesi*, a vegetarian stew with mixed vegetables, walnuts, dill, and sour grapes (12-TL soups and salads, 15–20-TL starters, 35–40-TL main courses, 15-TL desserts, show this book for 10 percent discount, daily 11:30-23:30, next to Hagia Sophia in Ottoman Imperial Hotel, Caferiye Sokak 6/1, Sultanahmet, tel. 0212/514-6151).

Yıldız Restaurant started as a coffee shop run by Erol Taş, a popular 1970s Turkish actor who always played the bad guy. Lo-

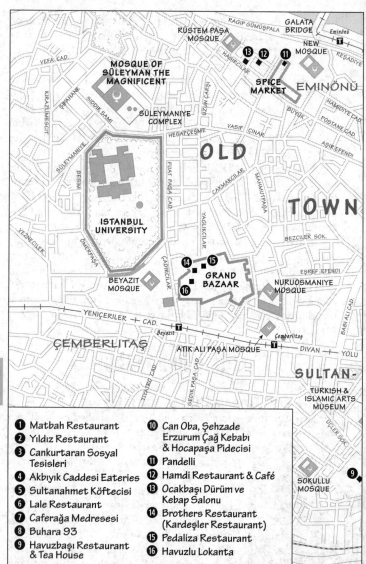

1 Matbah Restaurant
2 Yıldız Restaurant
3 Cankurtaran Sosyal Tesisleri
4 Akbıyık Caddesi Eateries
5 Sultanahmet Köftecisi
6 Lale Restaurant
7 Caferağa Medresesi
8 Buhara 93
9 Havuzbaşı Restaurant & Tea House
10 Can Oba, Şehzade Erzurum Çağ Kebabı & Hocapaşa Pidecisi
11 Pandelli
12 Hamdi Restaurant & Café
13 Ocakbaşı Dürüm ve Kebap Salonu
14 Brothers Restaurant (Kardeşler Restaurant)
15 Pedaliza Restaurant
16 Havuzlu Lokanta

cals often call it by its old name, "Erol Taş Kıraathanesi" (Erol Taş coffee shop). Today, hardworking İsmet Yıldız runs the place as a simple restaurant and neighborhood café. Inside, the walls are covered with photos of famous Turkish actors and actresses; many were personal friends and clients of the iconic villain. There's a real neighborhood vibe here, with people reading newspapers, playing backgammon, and occasionally smoking water pipes. The staff,

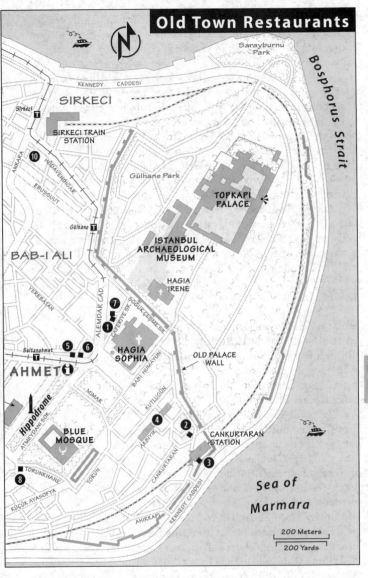

Old Town Restaurants

accustomed to serving local regulars, provide mediocre service by American standards—it's not intentional. From time to time, famous Turkish actors drop in, and sometimes extras gather here for film-industry gossip (5-6-TL vegetable *mezes*, 10-15-TL seafood *mezes*, 5-10-TL salads, 12-20-TL main courses, daily 9:00-24:00, Cankurtaran Meydanı 25, Sultanahmet, a few blocks toward the Sea of Marmara by the train tracks, tel. 0212/518-1334).

Cankurtaran Sosyal Tesisleri is a spacious, family-friendly restaurant, located within the Byzantine city walls south of Cankurtaran Meydanı. You can eat inside or out. The tables outdoors have a great view of the Bosphorus, Sea of Marmara, and Asian side of Istanbul (the downside is the noise from the four-lane road on the other side of the wall). The food is remarkably good and inexpensive. Their specialty, Topkapı Kebab, is a mix of chicken, veal, mushrooms, and tomatoes topped with cheese. They also serve delicious *künefe* (4-5-TL soups and starters, 5-10-TL hot starters, 9-20-TL kebabs, 12-18-TL seafood, 5-8-TL desserts, 10-TL breakfast plate, daily 8:30-23:00, no alcohol, Ahırkapı İskele Sokak 1, Cankurtaran, tel. 0212/458-5414). Their simple cafeteria in the garden serves only beverages.

On the Backpackers' Strip: **Akbıyık Caddesi** ("White Moustache Street") is lined with casual restaurants serving simple food and beer to a United Nations of gregarious young travelers. Eateries usually open early in the morning to offer breakfast to youth hostelers. You'll find several small grocery stores selling basic food items and fruit on the same street (one block below the Blue Mosque, toward the Sea of Marmara).

Budget Eateries on Divan Yolu, in the Heart of Sultanahmet

The first two famous and very convenient restaurants stand side by side along the busy street called Divan Yolu, across the tram tracks from Hagia Sophia and the Hippodrome (just downhill from the Sultanahmet tram stop).

Sultanahmet Köftecisi ("Sultanahmet Meatballs") is so famous for its meatballs that it's inspired an epidemic of imitation joints, rolling out knockoff *köfte* throughout Turkey. The very limited menu includes just two main courses (12-TL *köfte* and 18-TL *şiş kebab*), four sides (including a tomato-and-onion salad and the local favorite, *piyaz*—a white-bean salad in olive oil for 5 TL), and two desserts. You can't come to Istanbul without sampling these *köfte* (daily 11:00-23:30, Divan Yolu 12, tel. 0212/520-0566).

Lale Restaurant is the **"Pudding Shop,"** where a generation of vagabond hippies started their long journey east on the "Freak Road" to Kathmandu in the 1960s. (Enjoy the hippie history shared on its wall full of clippings.) Today, this much tamer but still tourist-friendly self-service cafeteria cranks out a selection of freshly cooked, seasonal Turkish food and chicken and beef kebabs. It's a well-oiled machine, but don't expect personal attention when it's crowded. Show this book to the cashier before you pay and receive a 10 percent discount (6-TL soups and salads, 9-TL cold starters, 8-10-TL vegetarian dishes, 15-17-TL main courses, 7-TL desserts, daily 7:00-22:30, Divan Yolu 6, tel. 0212/522-2970).

Tips on Eating in Turkey

Turkey's multiethnic cuisine reflects the rich cultural interaction of its ancestry: Turkish, Arab, Persian, and Greek. You'll find many similar foods in the countries that neighbor Turkey.

Restaurants in Turkey generally have a single menu and price list for both lunch and dinner. For the most part, once a restaurant is open, it serves meals nonstop until closing time.

"*Self-servis*" restaurants function like cafeterias. These are some of the best-value and most atmospheric places to eat. As you move through the line, point to what you'd like. Prices are set for full portions. Even if you ask for smaller portions, you'll still pay the full price per item. If you're with a com-

panion and want to sample several items, it's cheapest and simplest if you both order full portions at the counter and then split your order later when you sit down at your table.

For the traditional Turkish meat dish, look for a kebab restaurant (*kebab lokantası* or *kebabçı*). The meat is traditionally veal or a mix of lamb and veal, but more recently chicken (*tavuk*) and even fish have become popular. Kebabs have different names based on how they're cooked. A *şiş kebab* is any type of meat grilled on a skewer. A *döner kebab* is grilled, thinly sliced meat wrapped in pita or sandwich bread.

Seafood restaurants (*balık lokantası* or *balıkçı*) often offer a variety of small plates (*mezes*) and salads.

Dolma refers to stuffed vegetables such as bell peppers, tomatoes, eggplants, zucchinis, or grape leaves. *Börek* is a savory pastry made of phyllo dough. *Pide*, a Turkish-style pita bread, is topped with vegetables and cheese. Take a thin, flat *pide*, top it with meat, onions, and parsley, and you have *lahmacun.*

Cheap and filling, Turkish street food is easy to find. Common fare includes kebabs, sandwiches, *simit* (like sesame-covered bagels), and mussels (*midye tava*). For a cheap picnic, buy a crunchy, freshly baked *simit*, and top it with tomatoes, cucumbers, and some *beyaz peynir*—white cheese made from cow's or sheep's milk—from a grocery.

Caferağa Medresesi, in an old madrassa (seminary) next to Hagia Sophia, serves basic food (mostly grilled meat and chicken) to students, amateur artists, and a handful of in-the-know locals. Drop in for a look, or stay for a cup of traditional Turkish coffee or a meal. The setting is casual and friendly, with tables in the atrium, which is filled with hundreds of tulips in the spring (7-10-TL soups, salads, sandwiches, and side dishes; 15-20-TL main courses; madrassa open 8:30-19:00, lunch served 11:00-16:00, drinks served until 19:00, Sogukkuyu Çıkmazı 5, entrance on dead end off Caferiye Sokak—the alley that runs along Hagia Sophia's outer wall, tel. 0212/513-3601). The madrassa trains students in traditional Turkish arts and crafts, including tile painting, calligraphy, gold gilding, miniature painting, and the reed flute.

Budget Eateries Behind the Blue Mosque, near the Top of the Hippodrome

These two popular budget options—friendly rivals facing each other across the street—are a few steps off the top of the Hippodrome and tucked behind the Blue Mosque. They distinguish themselves by remaining humble, affordable, and local-feeling, despite their prime locations. To get here from the Hippodrome, face the Column of Constantine with the Blue Mosque on your left, then leave the Hippodrome on the street to the left, and hook downhill to the right...following the sounds of happy al fresco diners.

Buhara 93's affordable, down-to-earth food tastes like Grandma just cooked it: simple and tasty. Their *lavaş* (flat bread) is baked after you order and served right out of the wood-fired oven. This is also a fine place to sample *pide* (8-12-TL main dishes, daily 8:00-22:30, can be crowded at lunch and early dinner but no reservations needed, no alcohol, Nakilbend Caddesi 15, tel. 0212/516-9657).

Havuzbaşı Restaurant and Tea House, situated on a relaxed, idyllic outdoor patio just beyond the tourist crush below the Hippodrome, is a fine place to enjoy a late evening. Stop by after dinner for dessert or coffee accompanied by live music, hookahs (15 TL per group, free extra mouthpieces), backgammon, and non-alcoholic drinks—it's near a mosque (Küçük Ayasofya Mahallesi, Nakilbent Sokak 2, tel. 0212/638-8819).

Sirkeci Area, near the Train Station

Can Oba looks and feels like any other restaurant in the Old Town, but its owner, Chef Can Oba, was trained by a Michelin-star chef in Germany. The regular menu is also similar to other area restaurants, so ask for the special seasonal menu, revised weekly (5-TL regular salads and soups, 15-20-TL special salads and soups, 10–15-TL kebabs, 25–30-TL main courses, daily 11:00–22:00, a few blocks south of the train station at Hocapaşa Sokak 10, tel. 0212/522-1215).

Şehzade Erzurum Çağ Kebabı, a carnivores' fantasy, specializes in *yatık döner,* meat rotated over an Eastern-style horizontal coal or wood-fire grill until tender but crisp, then finely cut and served on skewers with *lavaş* bread (7-TL/skewer, Mon-Sat 11:30–21:30, closed Sun, Hocapaşa Sokak 4/6, tel. 0212/520-3361).

Hocapaşa Pidecisi is a unpretentious little eatery, with communal tables filled with locals, plus a few tourists who seem to have dropped in accidentally. Third-generation owner Yusuf Bey seems to do all the work, including preparing and baking the *pide*. Try the excellent *kavurmalı pide*, topped with dried meat—an uncommon menu item (10-12 TL for most *pides*, no alcohol, daily 11:00–20:00—or until food is gone, Hocapaşa Sokak 19, tel. 0212/512-0990).

In or near the Spice Market

Pandelli, on the Spice Market's second floor, is open for lunch only. Started by Chef Pandelli in the 1930s, it still serves a mouthwatering traditional Turkish-Ottoman menu, including an especially good eggplant *börek*. Although the restaurant always appears to be overcrowded with businesspeople, they eat quickly, so you won't wait long for a table (14-45-TL starters, 18-50-TL main dishes, daily 11:30-19:00, go up tiled staircase just inside Spice Market's main entrance at Eminönü Mısır Çarşısı 1, tel. 0212/527-3909).

Hamdi Restaurant is a dressy, white-tablecloth place with vested waiters, a bright glassed-in roof terrace, and great views of the city and over the water—push for third-floor seating. Be warned that the service is slow. They serve a variety of traditional kebabs from southeast Turkey (upper Mesopotamia). Consider the various kebabs: pistachio lamb, grilled eggplant, plum lamb, or grilled garlic lamb. The delicious *beyti* (behy-tee) kebab—a mix of barbecued beef and lamb wrapped in thin filo bread—takes longer to make. The wheat pilaf, called *firik* (fee-reek), is also good. For dessert, try the pistachio *katmer* or the baklava (22-32-TL kebabs, 8-15-TL desserts, daily 11:30-23:30, next to Spice Market, Kalçın Sokak 11, tel. 0212/528-0390). Take the elevator to the crowded third-floor terrace—the views are best from the narrow balcony (if there's an empty table here, grab it).

Hamdi Café, next door to the Hamdi Restaurant, offers simpler meals (meatballs, *döner kebab*, and grilled meat) in a casual, less-crowded setting. The first floor is a pastry shop with a few tables for a quick bite, while the upper floor has a large seating area overlooking the Galata Bridge and the square. Try the *kahke* cookies, made with St. Lucie cherries (14-TL meatballs, 12-TL *döner kebab*, 14-25-TL grilled meat dishes, 6-8-TL desserts, daily 7:30-20:00).

Ocakbaşı Dürüm ve Kebap Salonu is exactly what its name suggests: *Ocakbaşı* means "by the grill." Grab a chair by the grill, or join a communal table indoors or out. Specialties include the Adana kebab (spicy hot ground beef on skewer), Urfa kebab (similar to Adana but less spicy), and chicken *şiş*—all are succulent and juicy (most kebabs-9 TL, Mon-Sat 11:00–19:00, closed Sun, Hasırcılar Caddesi 61, tel. 0212/526-3229).

In Karaköy, by the Cruise Port

For locations of these restaurants, see the map on page 1088.

Lokanta Maya is owned and operated by chef Didem Şenol, who was educated at the French Culinary Institute in New York and uses the finest Turkish ingredients. Located right across from the Karaköy cruise terminal, the restaurant's decor is casual-chic (20-TL starters, 20–30-TL main courses, 15-TL desserts, Mon-Sat 12:00–17:00 & 19:00–23:00, closed Sun, Kemankaş Caddesi 35A, tel. 0212/252-6884).

Karaköy Lokantası, with a down-to-earth ambiance and flashy blue tiles, is a well-known landmark famous for its *mezes* and main courses such as sea bass baked in foil. Rushed service hasn't hurt its popularity (8–10-TL vegetarian *mezes*, 15–20-TL seafood *mezes*; Mon-Sat lunch served 12:00–16:00, tavern-style dinner served 18:00–24:00; Sun dinner only; Kemankeş Caddesi 37A, tel. 0212/292-4455).

NamPort (Namlı Şarküteri) is a deli with a huge selection of cheeses, sausages, and *mezes* from all over Turkey—all so delicious you'll "eat your fingers," as the Turkish saying goes. Dine at a full-service table, or get it to go. On weekends, they serve an all-day buffet brunch for 44 TL per person (15.50 TL/pound vegetarian *mezes*, 9–12-TL grilled meat and chicken dishes, daily 7:00–22:00, Rıhtım Caddesi 7, tel. 0212/251-1541).

Between Karaköy and the New District: **Kahvealtı,** near the Firuzağa Mosque in Cihangir, is a popular, gay-friendly restaurant and café serving tasty organic and natural food (5-TL tea/coffee, 14-18-TL salads, 10-TL sandwiches, 13-24-TL main courses, daily 9:00-23:00, Akarsu Caddesi, Anahtar Sokak 13/A, tel. 0212/293-0849).

Starting or Ending Your Cruise in Istanbul

If your cruise begins and/or ends in Istanbul, you'll want some extra time here; for most travelers, two days is a minimum to see the highlights of this gigantic, historical layer-cake of a city. Remember, if you are starting your cruise in Istanbul or planning to spend one or more nights on land after your cruise, you must have a Turkish visa **before** you arrive in Turkey (see page 1086).

For a longer visit here, pick up the *Rick Steves' Istanbul* guidebook.

Flying in Turkey

Atatürk Airport is the hub for Turkish Airlines (www.turkishair-lines.com), the country's major airline. Smaller, private carriers—which fly from Atatürk Airport to other major Turkish cities, such as Ankara, İzmir, and Trabzon—include Atlasjet Airlines (www.atlasjet.com), Pegasus Airlines (www.flypgs.com), and Onur Air (www.onurair.com.tr).

Istanbul's other airport, Sabiha Gökçen Airport, is on the Asian side. It's served mainly by budget airlines such as EasyJet and Wizzair. The ticket prices may seem reasonable if bought ahead of time, but the added expense of getting across the Bosphorus Bridge to a hotel or the cruise port might negate your savings. Bus connections and transfer services are available or figure 85-100 TL for a taxi; it takes at least an hour—depending on traffic (airport code: SAW, tel. 0216/588-8888, www.sabihagokcen.aero).

For a domestic economy flight within Turkey, estimate 75-250 TL one-way (about $45-150). You can buy your ticket in Turkey from a travel agent, or book online through the airline's website. Flights book up more quickly in high season (May-Sept).

Airport Connections

Atatürk Airport

Istanbul's main airport, Atatürk, is used for most international flights (except some flights from Europe, which use Sabiha Gökçen Airport—described in the sidebar). Located to the west of the city center on the European side, Atatürk Airport is a 30- to 60-minute taxi ride (depending on traffic) to either the Old Town or the New District (airport code: IST, airport info tel. 0212/463-3000, www.ataturkairport.com).

Atatürk Airport's international and domestic terminals are located across from each other and connected by an indoor corridor on the upper level. Both terminals occupy two floors, with arrivals on the ground level and departures on the upper level. The arrivals level of the international terminal has a TI desk, where you can pick up a free map and brochures. Each terminal also has an airport information desk, a pharmacy, car-rental agencies, exchange offices, and ATMs (located mainly on the arrivals level).

Arriving at Atatürk Airport

When you arrive at the international terminal, signs and airport staff direct you to passport control, then baggage claim, then customs and into the arrivals lounge.

From here, you have several options for getting to the Old

Town or the cruise port and New District: cheap public transportation (via light rail and tram, easiest for the Old Town), the airport shuttle bus (most convenient for the New District), a private transfer service, or a taxi. The last two options are the priciest, but provide door-to-door service to a hotel or the cruise port. The following website has good information about transportation within and from Istanbul: www.turkeytravelplanner.com/go/Istanbul/Transport.

By Light Rail and Tram: Public transportation from the airport into Istanbul is inexpensive (6 TL to the Old Town, 9 TL to the cruise port or New District) but involves at least one transfer. From the international terminal's arrivals level, take the escalator (located midway along the terminal) to the light-rail platform; trains leave from the airport station (called Havalimanı) every 5-15 minutes (6:00-24:00, www.istanbul-ulasim.com.tr/en). Take the light rail to Zeytinburnu, where you can catch the tram (look for signs to the tram, or ask). To reach the Old Town, take the tram to the Sultanahmet stop. To go all the way to the cruise port or New District, stay on the tram and take it across the Golden Horn; after crossing the bridge, you can get off at the Karaköy stop (near Karaköy cruise terminal and the Tünel funicular up to the New District) or the Tophane stop (for the Salıpazarı cruise terminal). The terminals are within easy walking distance of the tram line—see the map on page 1088. Remember that any time you change between the light rail, tram, Metro, or funicular, you'll need to pay for a new ride (for ticket details, see sidebar on page 1100).

By Airport Shuttle Bus: Airport shuttle buses are usually white and marked with *Havaş* (hah-vahsh) signs. As you exit the arrivals level, go past the taxi stand to the Havaş stop. Shuttles leave the airport every 30 minutes around the clock—except from 1:00 to 4:00 in the morning (10 TL, www.havatas.com). If you're heading to the Old Town, get off at Aksaray (ahk-sah-ray), and then take a taxi or tram to the core of the Old Town or to the cruise port.

By Private Transfer Service: Several private companies offer transportation between your hotel and your arrival/departure point: either of the two airports or the cruise-ship port. Prices are slightly above what you would pay for a taxi, but it's money well spent, as they usually have a set fee between the Old Town and the airport (about $30-35, not affected by traffic or route).

One of these companies, **Ataturk Airports Transfer Services,** has a large fleet and a staff that works around the clock (book online, pay driver, fees for each destination shown on website, http://ataturkairporttransfer.com). The company is run by Backpackers Travel, so if you are arriving at the airport, look for a driver holding their sign. Your cruise line may also offer a transfer service (for a fee).

By Taxi: The taxi stand is right outside the arrivals (ground) level of the terminal. Airport cabs are yellow; as long as they're in the line, you know they work for the official airport-taxi service. It's a 30-60-minute ride to a hotel in the Old Town or to the cruise port; expect to pay roughly 35-55 TL ($20-30). Up to four people can fit into a cab—share to save money. For taxi tips, see page 1102.

Departing from Atatürk Airport

The easiest way to get from the cruise port/downtown to the airport is by taxi (around 35-55 TL, depending on where you are in town). Or you can pay for a shuttle service through your cruise line. If you're heading from the Old Town to the airport, you'll probably notice that local travel agencies advertise shuttle-bus services for as little as €5 per person (get details at each agency). If you go this route, note that you may need to catch the bus at the travel agency; some buses don't pick up at hotels. The public-transportation connection from downtown to the airport is time-consuming, but doable: Ride the tram to Zeytinburnu, and switch to the light-rail line to the airport (explained above).

To leave Turkey by air, enter the airport's international terminal after first going through a security checkpoint. Once inside, scan the screens for the check-in desk for your flight. After checking in, you'll go through passport control and a second security checkpoint to reach the gate area. If you want a VAT tax refund, the tax-free approval desks are at check-in counters A14 and C32—before security. However, these locations can change—be prepared to ask airport staff for help. For more about VAT tax refunds, see page 135.

Hotels in Istanbul

If you need a hotel in Istanbul before or after your cruise, here are a few to consider.

In the Old Town

$$$ Hotel Sultanhan SC is an elegant hotel just off Divan Yolu, close to the Grand Bazaar and within walking distance of the Blue Mosque and Hagia Sophia. Its 40 rooms—larger than the norm for most Old Town hotels—have been restored with considerable care, and the staff is especially attentive (Sb-€240, Db-€280, Tb-€330, room rates can vary—check website for specials, 10 percent off best Internet rate if you mention this book when you reserve and show it at check-in, air-con, elevator, free Wi-Fi, Piyer Loti Caddesi 7, tel.

ISTANBUL

0212/516-3232, www.hotelsultanhan.com, info@hotelsultanhan.com, manager Enis Akça).

$$ Aya Sofya Pensions SC is beautifully located on a quiet, traffic-free lane squeezed between Hagia Sophia and the Topkapı Palace wall. The pension consists of a whole street's worth of 19th-century Ottoman row houses, converted into 67 rooms for rent. Higher prices are for rooms with a view of Hagia Sophia. The pension may be under renovation in 2014 (Sb-€85-140, Db-€110-160, Tb-€150-260, lower rates off-season, 5 percent off best Internet rate if you mention this book when you reserve and show it at check-in, request room with air-con in summer, lots of stairs but no elevator, all along Soğukçeşme Sokak, tel. 0212/513-3660, www.ayasofyakonaklari.com, info@ayasofyakonaklari.com).

$$ Uyan Hotel SC is family-run and convenient—it's a very short walk to the Blue Mosque, Hagia Sophia, and Topkapı Palace—and offers sweet views from its terrace. The 29 tidy rooms are as advertised: Single rooms are true singles, and "small doubles" are minimal with no views (Sb/Db-€99-119, deluxe Db-€115-130, 5 percent off best Internet rate if you mention this book when you reserve and show it at check-in, free airport pickup with 3-night stay, air-con, elevator, Utangaç Sokak 25, tel. 0212/516-4892 or 0212/518-9255, www.uyanhotel.com, info@uyanhotel.com, manager Humeyra Masanovic).

$$ Hippodrome Hotel SC is owned by the nearby Azade Hotel. Its recently renovated rooms, while small, are comfortably decorated with new furniture (S-€99-139, Db-€109-149, Tb-€135-175, family room for four-€200, 10 percent off best Internet rate if you mention this book when you reserve and show it at check-in, check website for specials and free airport pickup, breakfast at Azade Hotel, air-con, elevator in main building only, free Wi-Fi, Mimar Mehmet Ağa 22, tel. 0212/517-6889, www.hippodrome-hotel.com, hippodrome@hippodromehotel.com).

$ Romantic Hotel SC's nine smallish rooms are warm and woodsy, tucked inside a converted old mansion only three blocks down from the Blue Mosque. Some rooms have great views and balconies, and breakfast is served on a teeny terrace with a magnificent view of the Sea of Marmara (Sb-€65-85, Db-€85-105, Tb-€95-125, 8 percent off best Internet rate if you mention this book when you reserve and show it at check-in; free airport pickup with 3-night stay, plus free airport drop-off with 5-night stay; air-con, Wi-Fi, Amiral Tafdil Sokak 17, tel. 0212/638-9635, www.romantichotelistanbul.com, info@romantichotelistanbul.com, friendly Atilla and Erdal).

What If I Miss My Boat?

Remember that you can get help from the cruise line's **port agent** (listed on the destination information sheet distributed on the ship) and the local TI (see page 1096). If the port agent suggests a costly solution (such as a private car with a driver), you may want to consider other options. Any local **travel agent** also should be able to help.

One daily night **train** connects Istanbul's Sirkeci Station with Sofia and Bucharest (and points west in Europe), but there are no trains between Turkey and Greece. Istanbul's Asian-side train station—Haydarpaşa Garı—is closed for renovation, possibly into 2015. If you need to travel in Asian Turkey by train, you'll have to take a bus across the Bosphorus Bridge or a ferry across the Sea of Marmara to a city with rail connections. See a travel agent or the Turkish Railways website (www.tcdd.gov.tr) for more information.

Long-distance **buses,** which leave from the city's main bus terminal (*otogar*; oh-toh-gar), located in the Esenler (eh-sehn-lehr) district on the European side, are quite comfortable, and may also be helpful in a pinch.

If you need to catch a **plane** to your next destination, see "Airport Connections" for information on Istanbul's two airports.

For more advice on what to do if you miss the boat, see page 140.

In the New District: Near İstiklal Street

$$ Pera Tulip Hotel** is large and modern, with 85 clean and spacious rooms on seven floors (some windows open onto a ventilation shaft). Top-floor "executive balcony" rooms have Golden Horn views. Renowned Turkish jazz musicians sometimes perform in their lounge (Sb/Db-€99-119, Tb-€129-139, rates vary by season, 10 percent off best Internet rate if you mention this book when you reserve and show it at check-in, air-con, elevator, Wi-Fi, in-room safes, Meşrutiyet Caddesi 103, Tepebaşı, tel. 0212/243-8500, www.peratulip.com, sales@peratulip.com).

$$ Hotel Troya SC is a newly renovated hotel just a short walk from İstiklal Street. Ask for a room with a real window—some of its 77 rooms face a ventilation shaft (Sb-€99, Db-€109, Tb-€119, rates vary by season, 10 percent off best Internet rate if you mention this book when you reserve and show it at check-in, free airport pickup with 5-night stay, air-con, elevator, Wi-Fi, Meşrutiyet Caddesi 45, tel. 0212/251-8206, www.hoteltroya.com, troya@hoteltroya.com).

In Karaköy, Close to the Port

$$$ Karaköy Rooms, in an elaborate early-20th-century building, offers nine simple, designer-decorated rooms with hardwood floors, plain white walls, and striking copper pipes. Some rooms have Bosphorus views (Sb-€130, Db-€160, breakfast-€10, discounted nonrefundable rates available, Necatibey Caddesi, Galata Şarap İskelesi Sokak 10, Karaköy, tel. 0212/252-5422, www.karakoyrooms.com, info@karakoyrooms.com).

$$ Hettie Hotel is small and homey, and most rooms have amazing views of the Bosphorus, Golden Horn, and Old Town. Its peninsula location is convenient to diverse eateries and the ferry terminal, but can be noisy (standard Sb/Db-€109, view Db-€144–154, view family room-€180, discounted nonrefundable rates available, free Wi-Fi, Kemankeş Mahallesi, Rıhtım Caddesi 8, Karaköy, tel. 0212/244-6874, www.hotelhettie.com, info@hotel-hettie.com).

$$ Karaköy Port Hotel is a little tacky, with inexpensive, gold-gilded furniture, but the gasp-inducing terrace view—including the Bosphorus, Old Town, and Golden Horn—makes up for it. Its location, with many nearby eateries, comes with noise (Sb-€99, partial-view Db-€139, Tophane İskele Caddesi 10, Beyoğlu, tel. 0212/243-9868, www.karakoyporthotel.com).

Turkish Survival Phrases

When using the phonetics, pronounce "ī" as the long "i" sound in "light"; "ew" as "oo" (with your lips pursed); and "g" as the hard "g" in "go."

English	Turkish	Pronunciation
Hello.	Merhaba.	mehr-hah-bah
Good day.	İyi günler.	ee-yee gewn-lehr
Good morning.	Günaydın.	gew-nī-duhn
Good evening.	İyi akşamlar.	ee-yee ahk-shahm-lahr
How are you?*	Nasılsınız?	nah-suhl-suh-nuhz
Do you speak English?	İngilizce biliyormusunuz?	een-gee-leez-jeh bee-lee-yohr-moo-soo-nooz
Yes. / No.	Evet. / Hayır.	eh-veht / hah-yur
I understand.	Anlıyorum.	ahn-luh-yoh-room
I don't understand.	Anlamıyorum.	ahn-lah-muh-yoh-room
Please.	Lütfen.	lewt-fehn
Thank you (very much).	Teşekkür (ederim).	teh-shehk-kewr (eh-deh-reem)
I'm sorry.	Üzgünüm.	ewz-gew-newm
Excuse me. (to pass)	Afedersiniz. / Pardon.	ah-feh-dehr-see-neez / pahr-dohn
No problem.	Sorun yok.	soh-roon yohk
There is a problem.	Sorun var.	soh-roon vahr
Good.	İyi.	ee-yee
Goodbye. (said by person leaving)	Hoşçakal.	hohsh-chah-kahl
Goodbye. (said by person staying)	Güle güle.	gew-leh gew-leh
one / two	bir / iki	beer / ee-kee
three / four	üç / dört	ewch / dirt
five / six	beş / altı	behsh / ahl-tuh
seven / eight	yedi / sekiz	yeh-dee / seh-keez
nine / ten	dokuz / on	doh-kooz / ohn
How much is it?	Ne kadar?	neh kah-dahr
Write it?	Yazarmısınız?	yah-zahr-muh-suh-nuhz
Is it free?	Ücretsizmi?	ewj-reht-seez-mee
Is it included?	Dahilmi?	dah-heel-mee
Where can I find...?	Nerede bulurum...?	neh-reh-deh boo-loo-room
Where can I buy...?	Nereden alabilirim...?	neh-reh-dehn ah-lah-bee-lee-reem
I'd like / We'd like...	İstiyorum / İstiyoruz...	ees-tee-yoh-room / ees-tee-yoh-rooz
...a room.	...oda.	oh-dah
...a ticket to ___.	...___'ya bilet.	___ yah bee-leht
Is it possible?	Olasımı?	oh-lah-suh-muh
Where is...?	...nerede?	neh-reh-deh
...the train station	Tren istasyonu...	trehn ees-tahs-yoh-noo
...the bus station	Otobüs durağı...	oh-toh-bews doo-rah-uh
...the tourist information office	Turizm enformasyon bürosu...	too-reezm ehn-fohr-mahs-yohn bew-roh-soo
...the toilet	Tuvalet...	too-vah-leht
men / women	bay / bayan	bī / bah-yahn
left / right	sol / sağ	sohl / saah
straight	doğru	doh-roo
What time does this open / close?	Ne zaman açılıyor / kapanıyor?	neh zah-mahn ah-chuh-luh-yohr / kah-pah-nuh-yohr
At what time?	Ne zaman?	neh zah-mahn
Just a moment.	Bir saniye.	beer sah-nee-yeh
now / soon / later	şimdi / birazdan / sonra	sheem-dee / bee-rahz-dahn / sohn-rah
today / tomorrow	bugün / yarın	boo-gewn / yah-ruhn

*People will answer you by saying, *"Teşekkür ederim"* (Thank you very much).

In a Turkish Restaurant

English	Turkish	Pronunciation
restaurant	lokanta / restaurant	loh-kahn-tah / rehs-toh-rahnt
I'd like / We'd like to make a reservation.	Rezervasyon yapmak istiyorum / istiyoruz.	reh-zehr-vahs-yohn yahp-mahk ee-stee-yoh-room / ees-tee-yoh-rooz
One / Two persons.	Bir / İki kişilik.	beer / ee-kee kee-shee-leek
Non-smoking.	Sigarasız.	see-gah-rah-suhz
Is this table free?	Bu masa boşmu?	boo mah-sah bohsh-moo
The menu (in English), please.	(İngilizce) menü lütfen.	een-ghee-leez-jeh meh-new lewt-fehn
tax included	KDV hariç	kah-deh-veh hah-reech
tax not included	KDV değil	kah-deh-veh deh-eel
service included	servis hariç	sehr-vees hah-reech
service not included	servis değil	sehr-vees deh-eel
"to go"	Paket	pah-keht
and / or	ve / veya	veh / veh-yah
menu	menü	meh-new
daily menu / meal of the day	günün menüsü / günün yemeği	gew-newn meh-new-sew / gew-newn yeh-meh-ee
portion / half-portion	porsiyon / yarım porsiyon	pohr-see-yohn / yah-ruhm pohr-see-yohn
daily special	günün spesyali	gew-newn spehs-yah-lee
appetizers	meze	meh-zeh
bread	ekmek	ehk-mehk
cheese	peynir	peh-neer
sandwich	sandöviç	sahn-doh-veech
soup	çorba	chohr-bah
salad	salata	sah-lah-tah
meat	et	eht
poultry	tavuk	tah-vook
fish	balık	bah-luhk
seafood	deniz ürünleri	deh-neez ew-rewn-leh-ree
fruit	meyve	mey-veh
vegetables	sebze	sehb-zeh
dessert	tatlı	taht-luh
water	su	soo
milk	süt	sewt
orange juice	portakal suyu	pohr-tah-kahl soo-yoo
coffee	kahve	kahh-veh
tea	çay	chī
wine	şarap	shah-rahp
red / white	kırmızı / beyaz	kuhr-muh-zuh / beh-yahz
beer	bira	bee-rah
glass / bottle	bardak / şişe	bahr-dahk / shee-sheh
big / small	büyük / küçük	bew-yewk / kew-chewk
Cheers!	Şerefe!	sheh-reh-feh
more / another	biraz daha / bir tane daha	bee-rahz dah-hah / beer tah-neh dah-hah
The same.	Aynısından.	ī-nuh-suhn-dahn
Bill, please.	Hesap, lütfen.	heh-sahp lewt-fehn
tip	bahşiş	bah-sheesh
Delicious!	Nefis!	neh-fees

ISTANBUL

EPHESUS
Turkey

Turkey Practicalities

Exotic, vibrant Turkey *(Türkiye)* stands at the crossroads of continents. For thousands of years, the fortunes of the greatest empires of East and West have played out on this fertile peninsula. You'll walk in the footsteps of Roman emperors and Ottoman sultans as you explore some of the world's grandest monuments. Today much of Turkey is scrambling into the modern Western world. The empires of the past have given way to a proud parliamentary democracy and a predominantly Muslim population of nearly 81 million. But the traditional way of life is richly dyed and woven into the land like a Turkish carpet.

Visas: If you are starting your cruise in Turkey or getting off the ship to spend the night on land, you will need a visa before you arrive in Turkey (for details, see page 1206).

Money: Turkey uses the Turkish lira: 1 Turkish lira (TL) = about $0.55. One lira is broken down into 100 kuruş. An ATM is called a *bankamatík* or *paramatík*. The local VAT (value-added sales tax) rate is 18 percent; the minimum purchase eligible for a VAT refund is 108 TL (for details on refunds, see page 135).

Language: For useful Turkish phrases, see page 1239.

Emergencies: Dial 155 for police; for medical emergencies, dial 112 (both Turkish-language only).

Time Zone: Turkey is on Eastern European Time (an hour ahead of Italy and seven/ten hours ahead of the East/West Coasts of the US).

Theft Alert: Thieves thrive on fresh-off-the-boat tourists. Leave conspicuous valuables onboard, and be alert in crowds. For more on outsmarting thieves, see page 128.

Consular Services in Istanbul: The US consulate is at Kaplıcalar Mevkii Sokak 2, İstinye Mahallesi (24-hour emergency tel. 0212/335-9000, http://istanbul.usconsulate.gov). The Canadian consulate is at Buyukdere Caddesi 209 (tel. 0212/385-9700, www.turkey.gc.ca). Call ahead for passport services.

Phoning: Turkish phone numbers have seven digits, preceded by a four-digit area code. Within an area code, just dial the local number; otherwise dial both the area code (which starts with 0) and the local number. To **call to Turkey,** dial the international access code (00 from Europe, 011 from North America), then 90 (Turkey's country code), then the area code (without the initial 0) and local number. To **call home from Turkey,** dial 00, 1, then your area code and phone number.

Dress Code: As a sign of respect in mosques, cover your shoulders and knees; women should also wear head scarves.

Water: Don't drink tap water in Turkey. Bottled water is safe, cheap, and plentiful.

Tipping: At cafés and restaurants with table service, tip 10 percent. To tip a cabbie, round up to the next lira (if the fare is 14 TK, pay 15 TL).

Tourist Information: www.goturkey.com.

EPHESUS
and the Port of Kuşadası

Efes

The port city of Kuşadası, Turkey's second-busiest cruise destination (after Istanbul), is at the heart of a seaside resort region. Virtually every visitor here does one of two things: Tour the remarkable ancient Roman ruins at nearby Ephesus (EFF-eh-suhs), or shop for a Turkish carpet and other souvenirs in Kuşadası (koo-shah-DAH-suh) itself.

With extra time, there are other options: The House of the Virgin Mary, in the hills above Ephesus, is where Mary supposedly spent the last several years of her life. The town of Selçuk (SELL-chuck) features the Ephesus Museum, with some of the best artifacts from the site, plus the ruined Basilica of St. John, where the apostle and evangelist is said to be entombed. (Due to ongoing renovations, the Ephesus Museum may be closed in 2014.)

But the ancient city of Ephesus is truly the only must-see. The ruins of that grand metropolis rank among the top archaeological sites anywhere. Even those who don't like ruins are turned on by Ephesus' ancient landscape and visible history. While the shopping in Kuşadası is good, don't do it at the expense of missing Ephesus.

For ideas on experiencing Turkish culture beyond the sights, see the sidebar on page 1094.

Planning Your Time

Even on a short visit (7-8 hours), you can fit in any or all of these options:

• Tour ancient **Ephesus;** allow 2-3 hours for a good look at the site, plus about 30-45 minutes each way to get there from the Kuşadası cruise port.

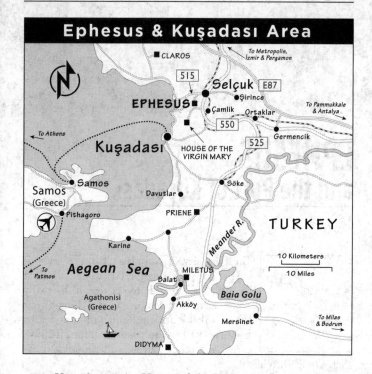

Ephesus & Kuşadası Area

• Visit the nearby **House of the Virgin Mary;** allow 1 hour total round-trip from Ephesus.

• Visit the town of **Selçuk** (next to Ephesus), with three attractions: the Ephesus Museum (may be closed in 2014; allow 1 hour), the Basilica of St. John (allow 30 minutes), and—for shoppers—the Carpetium carpet shop (allow as much time as you like).

• Kuşadası itself offers little in the way of sightseeing, but its **bazaar** of shops and cafés is enjoyable to explore (an hour or more)—particularly if this is your only stop in Turkey.

While cruise lines (hungry for commissions) try to steer you into Kuşadası and its shops, it's more satisfying to linger at the outlying sights than to kill time back at the port. With a long enough stop at Kuşadası and your own taxi or driver, you can squeeze in all of the above and make it back to port for your ship's departure.

Visa Requirements

Turkey requires most visitors to get a visa **before** arriving in the country. Cruise ship passengers can make day trips into Turkish ports without a visa, but you can't spend the night on shore without one. Here are some guidelines for various cruise scenarios:

• If you tour Ephesus, Selçuk, or Kuşadası during the day but spend the night on your ship, **you do not need a visa.**

- If your cruise ends in Turkey and you leave the country without spending the night, **you do not need a visa.**
- If your cruise starts in Turkey, **you must get a visa** prior to your arrival, even if you are going directly from the airport to your ship.
- If your cruise ends in Turkey and you are staying overnight in a hotel or other accommodations, **you must get a visa** prior to your arrival in Turkey.

You can get a visa at a Turkish consulate or embassy, but it is easiest to purchase it online at www.evisa.gov.tr. Simply enter the required information and make your payment by credit card. The e-Visa will be emailed to you within 24 hours. You must print out your e-Visa, show it to airport officials and customs officers when you arrive, and carry it with you at all times during your stay in Turkey. American citizens pay $20, while Canadians pay $60 (also in US currency, Canadian currency not accepted).

Because this is a new requirement, it is smart to get your visa a month in advance. Some provisions may change prior to your trip; check with your cruise line or see www.turkishembassy.org for updates.

Arrival at the Port of Kuşadası

Arrival at a Glance: To reach Ephesus on your own, you can either take a taxi (efficient but expensive—120 TL/about $75 round-trip, 30 minutes each way) or ride in a shared minibus, called a *dolmuş* (dirt-cheap at 6.50 TL, or about $3.90, per person—but it requires a transfer plus a 15-minute walk).

Port Overview

Kuşadası, a city of about 65,000, is the primary port for accessing the ancient site of Ephesus. Cruise ships arrive at a pier right in the heart of town. Leaving the ship, you will be directed left (to the tour buses) or right (to the awaiting local guides and the town). As you walk toward town, you'll funnel into a gauntlet of local trinket and carpet shops and international chains (Starbucks, Burger  King, and so on). As you exit the other end, the busy bazaar of more tourist-oriented shops is ahead and uphill. You'll find plenty of tours, guides, and taxis—eager to take arriving passengers to Ephesus—clustered near the cruise terminal.

Tourist Information: The TI is straight ahead as you exit the terminal complex, on the right-hand corner of the first intersection (Mon-Fri 8:00-12:00 & 13:30-17:30, closed Sat-Sun except on busy days mid-May-Sept).

Price Warning: The prices for just about everything in Kuşadası (not just big-ticket carpets, but also restaurants, taxis, and more) increase dramatically when the first cruise ship docks in the morning, then drop again when the last one pulls out in the evening. In general, you can expect to pay a premium for the privilege of arriving by cruise ship. The farther you walk into town, the lower the prices.

Heat Warning: In the height of summer, Ephesus can be scorchingly hot, with little shade. Wear light colors and comfortable shoes. Bring water, a hat, sunscreen, and sunglasses.

Getting to Ephesus and Other Sights

The rich and complicated story of Ephesus is best explained by a local guide, and getting to the site by public transportation is time-consuming. For these reasons, taking a shore excursion to Ephesus or hiring your own local guide is worth considering. If you want to go to Ephesus on your own, follow this chapter's self-guided tour.

With a Private Guide

Hiring your own private guide for Ephesus is a great way to have an informative, well-organized visit. Local guides routinely wait for their clients at the port (just outside the terminal door). And you can hire guides at a moment's notice at either entrance to Ephesus. Because demand is high when cruisers hit town, the top guides book up early; to get the best-quality guides, make arrangements well in advance. The price for a guided tour varies based on demand, duration, specific destinations, the guide's level of expertise, and whether transportation is included; for a full-day tour, a couple will likely pay around €300-400. The companies and individuals listed below will charge fairly.

Two companies can help you find a guide for Ephesus: İzmir-based **Melitour,** run by Mehlika Seval and Asli Kumari (mobile 0533-368-3113, www.melitour.com, melitour@yahoo.com); and Istanbul-based **SRM Travel,** run by Lale and Tankut Aran (tel. 0216/386-7623, www.srmtravel.com).

Guides who can sometimes be booked independently include **Mert Taner** (mobile 0532-263-6430, merttaner@hotmail.com), **Secil Gündoğdular** (mobile 0533-571-9148, secilgundogdular@hotmail.com), **Can Yiğit** (mobile 0532-426-6335, guidecan68@yahoo.com), **Gökhan Alataş** (gokhanalatas@yahoo.co.uk, tel. 0533-722-7180), and **Mesut Yilmaz** (mesutephesus@yahoo.com).

Services near the Port of Kuşadası

You'll find everything you need in town, but if you want it now, here are the nearest locations:

ATMs: Cash machines are in the mall-like shopping zone right at the cruise terminal complex.

Internet Access: You can get online in the terminal complex: Exit the terminal building, turn left, and look for the **Kuşadası Calling Station** (Internet terminals with English keyboards, Wi-Fi, cheap international calling cards). You can also get online inside the **Liman Hotel** (exit straight ahead, turn right at the TI; three lonely terminals in the lobby, €2/hour, also Wi-Fi, Kıbrıs Street, Buyral Road 4).

Pharmacy: Two pharmacies are within a few blocks of the cruise terminal. Head to Barbaros Boulevard (see "Shopping in Kuşadası," later); you'll find one pharmacy near the top of this boulevard (just before the intersection with Sağlık Caddesi) and another down Bahar Sokak (the second narrow street leading to the left as you head up Barbaros Boulevard—roughly across the street from the upper corner of the old caravanserai).

Guides are required to have a registered car or minibus, so it can be tough to get a guide other than through an agency.

By Taxi

A taxi stand is in front of the cruise terminal complex. If going to Ephesus, ask to be dropped off at the upper gate (the trip takes about 30 minutes each way). Here are the approximate fares:

- One-way to Ephesus: 80 TL
- Round-trip to Ephesus (with 2-3 hours of waiting time): 120 TL
- Round-trip to Ephesus (2-3 hours) plus the House of the Virgin Mary (30 minutes): 160 TL
- Round-trip to Ephesus (2-3 hours) plus the House of the Virgin Mary (30 minutes) and Selçuk (one hour): 180 TL

The 180-TL fare (about $110) for a do-it-all day is reasonable, especially if you split the cost with other travelers (taxis fit up to four people).

Cabbies will quote prices in Turkish lira (TL) or in euros, and will generally accept either form of payment. If the cabbie's initial estimate is much higher than the prices given above, negotiate him down or ask the next guy. Also, be aware that cabbies tend to give better prices for package deals. (Taking different taxis for each segment of the Ephesus/Virgin Mary/Selçuk/port trip, for example, will likely total more than the round-trip fares listed above.) Sharing a cab with friends makes the price a far better value. While you

EPHESUS

can arrange for a cabbie to drop you at the upper gate to Ephesus and wait for you at the bottom, rather than hang around, he will likely arrange for a different cab to meet you at the lower gate. While this is an accepted practice, I'd wait to pay until you're back at the cruise port, knowing that everything has gone smoothly.

Remember that cabbies, unlike private guides, provide only transportation and no information.

By Public Transportation

To reach Ephesus from Kuşadası, you'll take a short ride within town on one *dolmuş* minibus, then switch to a different *dolmuş* for the longer ride to Ephesus (figure about 30-40 minutes total one-way), followed by a 15-minute walk to the site's lower entrance gate. If you want to connect to the House of the Virgin Mary or the sights in Selçuk, you'll need to fill in the gaps with shorter taxi rides.

The ride on the *dolmuş* (which means "stuffed"—named for the way riders are packed in) can be a great experience in itself. Confirm that the minibus is going where you think it is, grab a seat, and observe. Follow the other passengers' example: Pass your fare (just ask those around you how much) up to the front. Let locals on board take you into their care. Get to know the *dolmuş* boy who helps people on and off. It's a fun scene, and the ride itself could well be a highlight of your day.

Step 1: From the Ship to Downtown Kuşadası

Exit the cruise terminal complex and go straight ahead. Bear left past the TI, and just beyond the taxi stand, wait along the street for a *dolmuş*—look for a boxed "D" on the sign at the curb. Take any minibus marked *Kadınlar Denizi* ("Ladies' Beach")—they come by every 10 minutes or so. When you get in, tell the driver you're going to Selçuk (SELL-chuck) and pay him 1.50 TL per person; after just a few minutes, he'll tell you where to change to the next *dolmuş*. (Your stop is after the yellow "taxi office" sign.)

Step 2: From Downtown Kuşadası to Ephesus' Lower Gate

When you leave the first *dolmuş*, cross the street to the stand at the corner, and look for the Kuşadası-Selçuk *dolmuş*. A minibus leaves from here about every 20 minutes; don't be surprised if the driver waits to fill his *dolmuş* before taking off. Pay the driver 5 TL per person (rates are posted inside), and tell him you want to go to Efes (EH-fehs). The trip, passing resort beaches and water parks, takes about 25-30 minutes. The driver will let you off at a road branching to the right with an *Efes (Ephesus)* sign—listen for him to announce "Efes." This stop is also called "Efes Yolu," the road to Ephesus.

Excursions from Kuşadası

The main destination from Kuşadası—and easily the best option—is the ancient city of **Ephesus.** When comparing excursions, look for one that gives you plenty of time at Ephesus and includes a visit to the excellent Terrace Houses. Cruise-line excursions typically bundle some combination of three nearby sights with Ephesus: the **House of the Virgin Mary,** the **Ephesus Museum** of archaeological finds in Selçuk (may be closed in 2014), and the **Basilica of St. John** just above Selçuk. Read the detailed descriptions in this chapter to see which sights most appeal to you.

If you've already seen Ephesus on a previous trip, consider an excursion to one or more of the other ancient sites near Kuşadası, including **Metropolis, Claros, Priene, Didyma,** and **Miletus.** (If you're arriving at İzmir, you may be offered an excursion to the famous ancient site of **Pergamon.**) If you're not interested in ancient sites, your best options are the traditional Turkish-Greek village of **Şirince,** or Turkey's third-largest city, **İzmir.**

Every cruise excursion includes an engaging presentation at a **carpet shop,** and leaves you plenty of time afterward to linger, get your hopes up, and try haggling with the vendor. The carpet presentation can be fun, but don't let it hijack your day

You'll catch the return *dolmuş* to Kuşadası at the same spot, but across the street—wave one down for a ride back to town. If going to Selçuk sights first, just stay on the *dolmuş* into the town center (about five minutes beyond Ephesus, and—for most minibuses—the end of the line).

To get from the Ephesus *dolmuş* stop along the main road up to the ruins, walk up the slightly uphill road (branching off the main road) for about a half-mile (15 minutes). When the road forks to the right, keep going straight (even though the right fork is signed for Ephesus—that's for drivers). You'll pass (on your left) the ruins of the ancient stadium, which once held 20,000 spectators. Walk through the big bus parking lot to the ticket office.

Note: The *dolmuş* leaves you closer to the lower entrance gate of Ephesus, from where it's a 20-minute hike to the upper gate. Most package excursions begin at the upper gate and work their way downhill through the site. If you want to begin at the upper gate without the extra walking, ride the *dolmuş* all the way into Selçuk, then take a taxi to the upper gate (15 TL).

EPHESUS

Returning to Your Ship

If you're hiring a taxi or private guide, they'll get you back to the port.

If you're taking public transportation back from Ephesus, remember that the return *dolmuş* departs across the street from where you were first dropped off (opposite the road leading to Ephesus' lower gate). Wait by the roadside turnout and flag down any passing *dolmuş* marked *Selçuk-Kuşadası* (with Ephesus behind you, take a *dolmuş* going toward your left). Pay 5 TL per person and ride into Kuşadası, where you can walk, taxi, or ride another *dolmuş* to your ship. If you're in a rush, hire a taxi back to Kuşadası (there are taxi stands at both Ephesus gates); to split the cost, team up with other travelers returning to your ship.

If you have extra time to spend in Kuşadası, you can linger in the bustling **shopping** zone that sprawls in front of the cruise terminal. For pointers, see the next section.

If you want to hit the **beach,** just walk along the coastal road (with the sea on your left) for about 10 minutes from the cruise terminal. Better yet, if you have enough time, join the locals for a sunset **stroll** along the waterfront promenade, which eventually meets with the marina.

Shopping in Kuşadası

While there's not much sightseeing in Kuşadası, it's an entertaining place to buy some souvenirs.

The fun (if touristy) Kuşadası **bazaar** is pleasant to explore even if you're not shopping. From the cruise terminal, go straight ahead past the TI and taxi stand, then turn left and pass the old stone caravanserai (inn) on the right (now a carpet shop, hotel, and restaurant—peek inside to see the courtyard, with pointed arches). The bazaar is just beyond the caravanserai on the right, along the pedestrianized Barbaros Boulevard and its intersecting alleys. Many of the same items sold in Istanbul are available here, at similar prices—carpets, leather, tiles, silver and gold jewelry, and so on (for more on these items, see page 1179). Salespeople can be extremely aggressive, especially toward single women. Avoid eye contact, and ignore attention-grabbing sales pitches; even saying "No, thanks" elicits a lengthy conversation. If buying anything, it's expected that you'll try to haggle down the price (for bargaining tips, see page 1182). The prices are more down-to-earth the farther you get from the main drag.

Buying a Turkish Carpet in Kuşadası

People back home—not to mention your cruise director—will rave to you that shopping for a carpet is a "quintessential Turk-

ish experience." There's no doubt that high-quality Turkish carpets are impressive works of art created by master craftspeople, and many are museum-worthy. But buying a good carpet for a good price is next to impossible on a short port visit. The carpet industry in Kuşadası is a finely tuned machine, calibrated expressly

for the tourist trade—and the cruise lines are their eager partner. Wrapped up in the $3,000 price of your carpet is several hundred dollars in kickbacks for your cruise line.

First, realize that an authentic, high-quality carpet will cost you many thousands of dollars (though smaller ones can be more affordable). As with any big purchase, do some homework before you get serious about buying. Research from home, and visit Turkish carpet importers in your area to educate yourself about how much various carpets are worth. (For starters, see the carpet explanation on page 1180.) Ideally, once in Turkey, you'd shop for your carpet at a small-town cooperative, the best place to buy as directly as possible from the person who made it. To get the best deal, you'd select a rug, already knowing roughly what it's worth, and confidently haggle to an agreeable price without middlemen and markups getting in the way. Unfortunately, this isn't feasible on a short visit, especially by cruise ship.

When you arrive at Kuşadası, your cruise line will hand out a list of "authorized" or "recommended" carpet shops. This list offers peace of mind and some measure of consumer protection. But it also creates the false impression that the cruise line has already done the hard work of comparison-shopping and quality control for you. In fact, the list primarily consists of carpet shops willing to pay commissions to the cruise line. At the beginning of each season, some carpet shops pay cruise companies a small fortune for the privilege of being "recommended."

Most excursions from Kuşadası include a stop for a carpet-weaving demonstration. The best of these are enjoyable and truly educational cultural experiences. You'll be invited into a comfortable carpet sales hall, and offered tea and snacks. Your charming, articulate host will poetically describe both the art and technique of carpet-weaving, stressing the painstaking work involved ("A poor village woman toiled for two years at her loom to create this masterpiece..."). After a demonstration of how silk is teased from silkworms and a good look at the weaving process, you'll be taken into the showroom and educated on the various types and qualities of carpets. You'll take off your shoes and walk across a carpet to feel the pile under your toes. Shop assistants will unroll carpet after carpet, dizzying you with gorgeous patterns unlike any seen at big-box furniture stores back home. And then it's time for the hard sell, when the carpet you fall in love with drops 20 percent in price after the first bargaining exchange, and you think: Maybe I can get a good deal here. Don't count on getting unbiased advice from your shore excursion's local guide, who likely gets a cut of your purchase price.

Back on the ship, the cruise line encourages you to "register" your carpet with them to activate the "shopper's guarantee," or to drop a copy of your carpet receipt into a raffle for a prize. The real motive is to discover which carpet shops made sales, and for how much, generating further commissions for the cruise line.

Ultimately the carpet shop may hand over as much as 60 or 70 percent of the sales price to the cruise line. The shop passes on this huge expense—in the form of dramatic markups—to cruise passengers. I wish I could tell you that there's one spunky carpet shop in Kuşadası that sidesteps this whole mess and sells its wares directly to the cruise passenger without the huge markup. But, in truth, there's effectively no way to avoid this racket at the port.

But there is an alternative in the small town of Selçuk, near the site at Ephesus. **Carpetium** is across the street from the road leading up to Ephesus' lower gate, on the main highway that connects Kuşadası to Selçuk (you can stop off here if you're going to the site by taxi or *dolmuş*, or with a private guide/driver). This shop carries a wide variety of carpets—from simple kilims to fancy silk carpets—and has down-to-earth prices compared to places around the cruise port. Shop anonymously as you haggle; then, before you pay, show this book for an additional 10 percent discount from manager Varol. If you make any purchase, they'll cover your ride back to the cruise port (Kuşadası 1. km Caddesi, Selçuk, tel. 0232/892-4316).

Ultimately, locals explain, it's a toss-up whether you pay less for a carpet in Turkey or at a good importer back home. But for many travelers, buying a Turkish carpet in Turkey is worth the premium. If that's your preference, be a smart consumer and equip yourself with good information.

Arrival at the Port of İzmir

While Kuşadası is the primary port of entry for this part of Turkey, some cruises call instead at the large city of İzmir, about an hour north of Ephesus (and 1.5 hours north of Kuşadası).

Because of the greater distance and complexity of reaching Ephesus by public transportation, if you are arriving in İzmir, the cruise line's shore excursion to Ephesus is probably your best option (or hire your own guide and driver, through the companies described on page 1208). Cabbies charge about 300 TL for the round-trip taxi ride from İzmir to Ephesus, including wait time.

If you'd rather take public transportation to Ephesus, here's the complicated scoop: From İzmir's cruise port, take a taxi to the main bus station, or *otogar* (25 TL, 30-minute ride). Then catch a public bus toward Kuşadası (15 TL, 4/hour). Rather than riding the bus all the way to Kuşadası, hop off after about an hour—just after you leave the town of Selçuk, at the road to Ephesus (ask the driver to let you off at "Efes" or "Efes Yolu"). You'll get off along a country road, about a 15 minute-walk from Ephesus' lower gate (see directions on page 1210).

Ephesus

Ephesus—one of the most important cities of the Roman Empire—is among the world's best ancient sites. Whether you're strolling its broad boulevards, appreciating the pillared facade of the famous Library of Celsus, peeling back the layers of dust to understand the everyday lifestyles of the rich and Roman at the Terrace Houses, or testing the acoustics in the theater where the Apostle Paul once spoke, Ephesus is a perfect place to time-travel back to the grandeur of Rome.

Background

At its peak in the first and second centuries A.D., Ephesus was one of the grandest cities of the ancient world, ranking among the four leading centers of the Roman Empire (along with Alexandria, Antioch, and Rome itself). With a staggering quarter of a million residents, Ephesus was the second-biggest city in the empire (after Rome). The Ephesus we see today reflects the many civilizations—Greek, Persian, Roman, and Christian—that passed through Asia Minor (today's Turkey) in the days before the Ottomans. Julius Caesar, Anthony and Cleopatra, St. Paul, and possibly St. John and even the Virgin Mary have all walked these same marble roads.

The area was first settled around 1000 B.C. According to legend, the Oracle of Delphi prophesied that the Greek prince Androklos would found a city at a place revealed to him by "a wild boar and a fish." Androklos set sail to the west, and eventually found his way to the beach where the Cayster (a.k.a. Meander) River met the

Aegean Sea. While Androklos grilled his dinner at a campfire, a fish fell into the fire, knocked some embers into a bush, and ignited it—flushing out a boar. Androklos tracked the boar into the valley where he would found Ephesus. (You'll see a carving of this story later, in the Temple of Hadrian.)

The city grew as a seaport and the worship center of the goddess Artemis. By 500 B.C., it was a bustling cultural capital on the Mediterranean. It sported the enormous Temple of Artemis, famous in its day and now in ruins.

Ephesus was part of the sophisticated Ionian world of western Asia Minor that inspired the rise of Golden Age Greece across the pond. The Ephesians spoke Greek (but with an Ionian dialect), produced "Greek" philosophers such as Heraclitus (who said the only constant is change), and popularized the style of Greek columns called Ionic (topped with scroll-like capitals). From time to time over the centuries, more warlike people—Lydians, Persians, Athenians, Alexander the Great, and Romans—overran Ephesus, but everyday life went on unchanged in this cosmopolitan city.

Oddly, the physical location of ancient Ephesus has moved over time. The sandy composition of the valley's soil and the constant movement of alluvial sands have made this an ever-changing landscape. The Meander River (whose circuitous course gave us the word) had a tendency to shift its path over time. When the river's access to the sea silted up in the third century B.C., the Ephesians relocated their city to the valley where the ruins now sit.

It was under Roman rule that Ephesus reached its peak. In A.D. 27, Emperor Augustus made the city the capital of the Roman province of Asia (roughly corresponding to today's Turkish west coast). The harbor at Ephesus bustled with trade (including the slave trade) throughout the vast Roman Empire. By A.D. 100, it had become a city of marble buildings and grand monuments, with an infrastructure that  could support hundreds of thousands of toga-ed citizens. The ruins you'll see today date largely from the city's Roman heyday in those first two centuries after Christ.

Ephesus' prominence attracted some of the earliest followers of Christ. St. Paul came to Ephesus (about A.D. 52), where he conducted missionary work and wrote his First Epistle to the Corinthians ("Love is patient, love is kind. It does not envy, it does not boast, it is not proud"). St. John also may have come to Ephesus (about A.D. 90), having been charged with spreading Christianity in the Roman province of Asia. And even the Virgin Mary supposedly retired to Ephesus (brought by John).

The Ephesian Artemis

Throughout its history, the area around Ephesus has had a deep connection to various incarnations of a life-giving female deity: first a Hittite mother-goddess called Kubaba, then an Anatolian one named Cybele. During the Greek period, the cult of the goddess Artemis (daughter of Zeus, twin sister of Apollo) caught on here. This Greek virgin-goddess was associated with childbirth and chastity, the moon and the wilderness, and the hunt and wild animals. The Romans later worshipped her as Diana.

The Ephesian version of Artemis took on characteristics of previous local mother-goddesses. According to tradition, Artemis was born in May, when Ephesians celebrated a festival of roses (and the month when we celebrate Mother's Day). They'd sacrifice bulls at the Temple of Artemis, cut off the testicles, and drape them over the statue of Artemis to celebrate her fertility. Many depictions of Artemis (including the famous statue in the Ephesus Museum in Selçuk) show her covered with these bulbous shapes. Another interpretation: These are not bulls' balls, but the many breasts of a life-sustaining mother-goddess. Or perhaps they are eggs, signifying her potent fertility.

In the sixth century B.C., locals built a spectacular Temple of Artemis, one of the Seven Wonders of the Ancient World. Only a single pillar of that temple survives today, on the other side of the hill from the archaeological site at Ephesus (see page 1237). Through Roman times, devotees of Artemis worshipped her using small carved statues.

Some historians believe that it's no coincidence that this ancient site so connected with the cult of a mother-goddess was later believed to be the final earthly home of the Virgin Mary (see "House of the Virgin Mary," page 1231).

As the Roman Empire fell, so fell Ephesus. In A.D. 263, invading barbarians looted the city, and it never really recovered. Ephesus limped along under the wing of the Byzantine Empire—the Christian empire ruled from Constantinople (today's Istanbul). By the seventh century A.D., that same old problem—the silting up of the harbor inlet—finally closed Ephesus' port for good. The city was relocated once again, this time to the area around today's town of Selçuk. The marshy ground bred mosquito-borne malaria that decimated the population. The impressive buildings were scavenged for their conveniently precut stones. Earthquakes further leveled the monuments. Buried over the centuries, Ephesus was forgotten until the 1860s, when a series of British, German, and Austrian archaeologists rediscovered and excavated the site (many of its treasures are now on display in Vienna's Ephesus Museum, and others are in the British Museum in London). Although only 15 percent of the site has been unearthed, it is still one of the largest excavated areas in the world.

Ephesus Tour

Orientation

Cost: 25 TL site entry, plus 15 TL for the Terrace Houses.

Hours: Daily April-late Oct 8:00-19:00, off-season until 17:00. The ticket office closes an hour before the site does. Ideally (if your ship's arrival and departure schedule allows it), visit Ephesus late in the day—when it's cool, the tour mobs are gone, and the stone is bathed in rich warm light.

Getting There: There are two entrance gates to the site, about 1.5 miles apart. I've oriented this tour the way most visitors see Ephesus, beginning at the upper gate and working down to the lower gate. Cruise-line excursions take this approach, and it's how you'll likely do it if you're riding a taxi to Ephesus. But if you are relying on a *dolmuş* minivan to reach Ephesus, you'll begin at the lower gate. In that case, you can hike or hire a taxi (15 TL) to bring you around to the upper gate, or simply see the site uphill...and hold this book upside-down.

Tours: To sightsee on your own, download my free **audio tour** of Ancient Ephesus (see sidebar on page 50 for details). At the site, it costs 10 TL to rent a decent audioguide, with 1.5 hours of commentary on the main site, plus 20 minutes on the Terrace Houses. The 20-TL (or €10) deposit will be refunded when you return the audioguide at the other end of the site.

> **Local guides,** hoping you'll hire them for a tour, hang out at each entrance. These guides charge about €35-50 per hour; a typical tour of the site takes about two hours and costs 120 TL. Negotiate a good price, and don't be afraid to talk to a few different guides to decide who you like best.

Services: You'll find WCs and basic snack stands at each entrance gate.

Be Prepared: If it's hot, remember to wear light clothes and bring sunglasses and water (but remember not to drink Turkish tap water). Even with a hat, sunscreen is essential, as sunlight reflects off the marble. Wear durable shoes to traverse the uneven, sometimes steep terrain.

❶	State Agora	❿	Baths
❷	Stoa Basilica	⓫	Temple of Hadrian
❸	Odeon	⓬	Public Toilets
❹	Prytaneion	⓭	Terrace Houses
❺	Sacred Way	⓮	Library of Celsus
❻	Domitian Square	⓯	Commercial Agora
❼	Hercules Gate	⓰	Great Theater
❽	Curetes Road	⓱	Harbor Road
❾	Trajan's Fountain		

The Tour Begins

The excavated area of Ephesus basically represents the city center—the "downtown" of the ancient metropolis. Beginning at the upper gate and working downhill, this self-guided tour passes through the government center, residential neighborhood, shopping area, and theater and nightlife district. Along the way, you'll walk parts of three different roads: the Curetes (Priests') Road, connecting the upper gate to the Library of Celsus; the Marble Road, between the library and the Great Theater; and the Harbor Road, connecting the theater to the harbor (and, along the way, today's modern lower gate).

• *Just inside the upper gate is a large, rectangular space ringed with the ruins of various buildings. Survey the scene from the stack of terra-cotta pipes about 50 yards below the ticket turnstile.*

❶ The State Agora

Standing here, at the top of the site with your back to the modern upper gate, survey what's been excavated of the ancient city. Residential zones sprawled up the ridges high above you on the right and the left. Between these neighborhoods was this vast upper square, which was an agora (marketplace).

The State Agora (or Upper Agora) was an open-air courtyard surrounded by covered arcades. Here shoppers could get out of the sun and rain, catch up with their neighbors, and talk politics. This agora—about 500 feet long and 240 feet wide—originally had a temple to the goddess Isis in the center.

While there's little left of the buildings, you can see evidence of extensive plumbing in the dirt near the stack of pipes. Ephesus had one of the ancient world's most sophisticated public waterworks systems. Runoff from the surround-ing hills streamed into a network of four major aqueducts before being funneled into the city. Logically, the main reservoir was here, at the high end of the city. From here, with the help of clay pipes (like those piled here) and gravity, water flowed to the city's fountains and the homes of the wealthy.

• *Walking beyond the pipes, you'll find what was a ceremonial road lined with columns and the remains of the...*

❷ Stoa Basilica

The northern side of the agora was a colonnaded, covered walkway (called a stoa), which was eventually remodeled into a basilica-like structure. The double row of pillars in the middle of the field marks the footprint of a typical basilica floor plan: a large central hall flanked by two narrower side aisles. The columns are Ionic—slender, fluted, and topped with (mostly missing) scroll-like capitals. While today the word "basilica" signifies a church, back then—centuries before the first basilica-style church—it meant a hall, like this, where merchants met and traded goods.

• *Beyond the Stoa Basilica, cut into the hillside, the largest structure you see (with semicircular rows of seats) is the...*

❸ Odeon

Dating from around A.D. 150, this indoor theater—once topped with a wooden roof—seated 1,500. Compared with the huge

open-air theater we'll see later, this was an intimate venue for plays and concerts. Its primary function was as the meeting place *(bouleuterion)* for the city council. According to records, every Thursday morning, 450 aristocrats would hash out the civic business of Ephesus. While some of the lower marble seats are original, with elegant lion-feet armrests surviving, the upper seats were restored on the cheap in the 1950s. (By the way, to get a sense of how deeply this site was excavated, note that the theater was once buried up to its top seats.)

• *At the end of the colonnaded stoa, on the right, two big Doric columns mark the...*

❹ Prytaneion

The Prytaneion was a kind of town hall. It was from here that a committee of six officer-type priests (or *curetes*) made decisions

about city administration. One of the city's most important sites, this was where the "eternal flame" was kept (in the rectangular pit). Just as Rome had its eternal flame tended by Vestal Virgins, honored citizens of Ephesus made sure this fire always flickered, to guarantee the city's continued prosperity. The eternal flame of Ephesus was finally snuffed out when paganism was outlawed in A.D. 395.

• *Just next to the Prytaneion, enjoy the viewpoint at the top of the...*

❺ Sacred Way

From here, looking far beyond the city stretching below, you might catch a glimpse of the Aegean Sea. While the sea once lapped at the gates of the city, 1,500 years of silt and big-city drainage left Ephesus high and dry. Beyond the State Agora, to your left, is the site of the Domitian Temple (currently being excavated). Ahead of you is the path called the Sacred Way (a procession honoring Artemis proceeded here annually). This short road leads downhill from the State Agora to Domitian Square.

Strolling down, notice hints of Roman engineering: Drainage pipes under the road kept sewage flowing. (However, the runoff from the water used by a million Ephesians contributed to the silting up of the harbor, which eventually spelled the end of the city.) Look also for metal rings in the road, which some believe were attachment points for guy-lines that held up poles for street lamps, which were set up at night. Crosshatching on the street stones gave ancient sandals a better grip when wet.

After a long block, you'll come to two stone pillars with carved reliefs. These were directional aids: One, facing the market, is a statue of Hermes (god of merchants); the other, facing a pharmacy, is a carving of Asklepios (symbolizing medicine). Cosmopolitan Ephesus was filled with traders and merchants who spoke a Babel of languages, so these pictograms helped arriving sailors find their way.

• *Just past these carved stones, enter Domitian Square and turn left.*

❻ Domitian Square

The square was ringed by important buildings and monuments. The highest surviving arch (on the left) marks what was a public

water fountain. The centerpiece of this quarter (straight ahead) was the **Temple of Domitian,** dedicated to the notorious first century A.D. Roman emperor. Though little remains today, the temple was large—two stories tall (as the ruin suggests) and covering the area of a football field. A bit of the temple facade still stands with statues capping a couple of columns. Domitian was the cruel, lunatic emperor who, it is believed, sent John the Prophet into exile to the nearby island of Patmos, where he worked in a rock quarry and wrote the Book of Revelation. Opposite the Temple of Domitian stood a monument with carved reliefs describing the great deeds of the Roman tribune Gaius Memmius.

Resting on the ground across from the temple site, look for an impressively carved piece of stone—the **Nike frieze,** which once topped a gate. This depicts the Greek goddess Nike giving the wreath of victory to the Romans.

• *Walk 30 yards farther down to the...*

❼ Hercules Gate

This gate—intentionally too narrow to let chariots pass—marks the transition from pedestrian-only upper Ephesus to the commercial Curetes Road. Just before the gate, notice the remains of a road branching off to the left that provided the ancient equivalent of a "truck bypass route" detour leading around to the harbor. Also, look around to see pieces of the original arch that once welcomed pedestrians (and which archaeologists will soon put back together). There's a little perch a couple of steps up, just to the right of the gate, that provides a great photo op. Pass through the gate and look back at its pillars to see its namesake draped with lion skins.

• *Now begin your stroll down...*

❽ Curetes Road

This lane gives you a small glimpse of the epic scale of Ephesus at its peak. Mentally replace the tourists with toga-clad ancients to imagine the Roman metropolis in its heyday. Statues, bubbling fountains, arches, and shops lined the street. Columns supported a covered sidewalk for pedestrians, while chariots, wagons, and men on horseback traveled the road. In the shade of the arcades, people could hang out and play games such as backgammon. The buildings on either side of the street had shops below, and homes above.

• *About 50 yards down from the Hercules Gate, on your right is...*

❾ Trajan's Fountain

This public fountain, a huge reservoir basin (66 by 33 feet), is topped by a pediment on stilts. Beneath the pediment once stood a statue of the powerful Emperor Trajan proudly gazing over the pond. While the wealthy had indoor plumbing, fountains like this were the sole source of water for everyone else. The carving of Trajan with his foot on an orb and the phrase "Trajan ruled the world with his right foot" provide clear evidence that ancient Romans assumed the world was round. Little holes on the lower left of the fountain are a re- minder that to let loose a stream of water to cool and clean their town, Ephesians would just uncork the fountain.

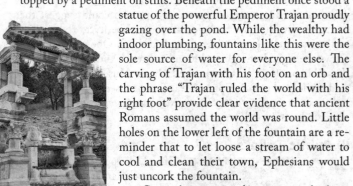

Cross the street and step up to the ban- nister to survey the fine mosaic sidewalk of a colonnade once lined with shops that likely catered to the fancier aristocracy.

• *Back across the street (about 30 yards below Trajan's Fountain), take a little detour through...*

❿ The Baths

Like all Roman baths, the bath complex at Ephesus was divided into rooms with special purposes: a changing room, a cooling-off room *(frigidarium)*, a warm room *(tepidarium)*, a hot steam room *(caldarium)*, and so on. The tradition of large public baths in Mediterranean lands has continued through the centuries—from Romans to Byzantines to Ottomans to today's Turks. Back in Kuşadası, contemporary locals are enjoying the steamy descendants of bath complexes just like this. (You could, too...if you didn't have a cruise ship to catch.)

• *Pop back out onto the main street and notice the next building down, one of the most photographed in all of Ephesus. The Corinthian columns and lone surviving curved arch mark the ruined vestibule of the...*

⓫ Temple of Hadrian

Symbolism abounds on this structure. The central relief over the arch is popularly thought to depict Hadrian's lover, a boy named

Antinous (with a captivating beauty considered the most ravishing in all the realm), whom the heartbroken Hadrian had deified after his early death. The figure in the lunette over the entrance to the temple proper likely represents the snake-haired **Medusa.** The eggs on the portal frame and the little flowers carved into the stone are symbols of fertility.

The swastika-like repeating geometric pattern could suggest the Meander River (which brought life and prosperity to the people) or the rising sun (a promise of good fortune). One of the friezes shows the legend of Ephesus' founding, with **Androklos** stalking the wild boar (originals are in the Ephesus Museum in Selçuk; to read the legend of how Ephesus was founded, see page 1215).

• *A few steps farther down Curetes Road, go in the little doorway by audioguide marker #143 to find...*

⓬ Public Toilets

The U-shaped **latrine** room features marble seating surrounding an open-air courtyard with a fountain. Few Ephesians could afford private bathrooms, so most people took care of business at a public latrine like this one. Visiting the loo evolved into a social event, and

EPHESUS

this room had seats for a rollicking party of 40. A wooden roof once topped the seating area. A constantly flushing stream of water ran beneath the seats, whisking waste immediately to a sewer. Along the floor was a second stream with clean water for washing.

• *Across the street is a separate sight, which requires its own ticket. It's well worth the extra 15 TL to visit the...*

⑬ Terrace Houses

This modern complex protects seven three-story **homes,** each with its own courtyard and elaborate decorations. They present

a vivid picture of the lifestyle of upper-class Ephesians. Excavated in 1999, and opened to visitors in 2006, the Terrace Houses offer an unparalleled opportunity to see how the ancients lived and to watch ongoing excavations. Visitors follow a one-way route through the complex, appreciating carefully restored mosaic floors and frescoed walls. I've mentioned several things to watch for, but because excavations are ongoing, your route may differ from the description below, and certain sites or rooms may be inaccessible. To get oriented, consult the handy floor plans and room descriptions displayed throughout the complex.

The buildings and decor you'll see date from the early Roman Imperial period—from roughly the first two centuries after Christ. The basic architectural unit was an open courtyard, lined by columns, with main rooms and utility rooms arranged around it.

Dwelling Unit 6 shows features typical of all upper-class **Roman homes:** living and dining rooms on the ground floor, bedrooms upstairs, and an open-air courtyard in the center. This allowed air to circulate, while the lack of windows on the outer walls kept out dust, noise, and sun—a system still used in homes of both the wealthy and the poor in hot climates around the world. Beneath the courtyard floor is a cistern that collected rainwater to supply the house. Although most of the walls today are rough brick (stripped of their original decoration), they once were covered with marble or frescoes, generally depicting mythological scenes.

Keep an eye out for surviving **water pipes** in the passages. While ordinary Roman citizens used shared bathing and latrine facilities (like the complex you saw across the street), the wealthy enjoyed private plumbing. There were two systems of pipes in these homes: one for water, and one (under floors and between walls) to carry hot air for heating.

The **Marble Hall** was the dining room, where homeowners entertained casual guests. This one had all marble floors and walls;

archaeologists have identified some 120,000 fragments, which they are trying to piece back together (you may see workers actually sorting the marble like a huge jigsaw puzzle). In the middle of the room, a gurgling pool provided both decoration and a soothing soundtrack.

The huge vaulted hall of the **Basilica,** with its restored ceiling, was used as a formal reception room. It housed a decorative pool. Remnants of frescoes can still be seen along the walls.

Continuing upstairs to the bedrooms, you'll have a good view down into the courtyard of Dwelling Unit 7. But keep heading up toward Units 5 and 3. You may see a small **storage room** that held amphorae (pointy-bottomed clay jugs) containing household supplies such as wine or olive oil. The amphorae were partially buried in soil or sand to keep their contents cool. On the walls, overlapping layers of several frescoes are faintly visible (successive waves of earthquakes and fires over the generations forced homeowners to periodically redecorate).

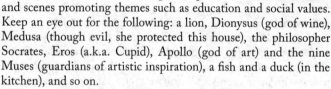

You'll see **frescoes**, **drawings**, and **mosaics** of gladiators and animals, graffiti poems, and scenes promoting themes such as education and social values. Keep an eye out for the following: a lion, Dionysus (god of wine), Medusa (though evil, she protected this house), the philosopher Socrates, Eros (a.k.a. Cupid), Apollo (god of art) and the nine Muses (guardians of artistic inspiration), a fish and a duck (in the kitchen), and so on.

In Dwelling Unit 2, look for the small **bathroom.** Like the large latrine across the street, this one was communal, with two side-by-side seats (even in a wealthy household, pooping was a social event) and a constantly flowing channel of clean water at one's feet for washing.

From the very top of the complex, look down through the glass walkway to a particularly well-preserved **mosaic floor,** with the sea god Triton on the right, and a Nereid (protector of sailors), riding a seahorse, on the left.

• *Leaving the Terrace Houses, a lane leads back to the main road. From there, turn left to face the commanding facade of the Library of Celsus. Before approaching the library, look to your right, down the Marble Road. Little survives along this road (which is generally open to visitors only on weekends). It ran along the side of the commercial agora (which you'll walk through momentarily) to the theater and the road leading to the harbor.*

Now set your sights on one of the most iconic Roman-ruin images in the world, the...

⑭ Library of Celsus

This breathtaking structure epitomizes Ephesus at its peak. It was the third-largest library of the ancient world (behind the collections in Alexandria and Pergamon), with some 12,000 volumes. Its namesake was a well-read governor of this province, whose son built the library as a mausoleum in his honor in A.D. 123. The ruined library was restored to its current appearance in the 1970s.

The library's facade—two monumental stories tall—features a distinctive grid of columns and recessed niches. Those **Corinthian columns** (topped with leafy capitals) on the ground floor are 40 feet tall. There were three grand doorways, each matched by windows above. The four statues in the niches represent the traits of Celsus: wisdom, knowledge, intelligence, and valor. An optical illusion causes this grand facade to seem even bigger—the outer columns are actually shorter than the central ones, making the facade appear to bulge in the middle.

Begin climbing the steps to the library. On the second step from the top, on the right side, look for the metal box that protects an image of a **menorah** lightly carved into the step. Ephesus had a large Jewish population that was on relatively good terms with the Romans (since, unlike Christians, the Jews never attempted to convert pagans to their own faith).

Step into the small interior, and picture it in its prime. The walls and floors were once gleaming **marble** (which covered the restored brick understructure we see today). Light poured in through the big east-facing windows, which caught the morning sun. The niches that you see once held scrolls. A three-foot-wide gap between the inner and outer walls helped to circulate air to preserve the delicate documents.

The earliest **scrolls** were made of Egyptian papyrus (a plant material). But as the collection at the Pergamon library grew, rivaling that of Alexandria, the Egyptians jealously refused to export any papyrus. As always limited only by their ingenuity, the Romans simply invented a different material: parchment, made of dried-out animal skin. (This library's collection included both types of scrolls.) Eventually the sheets of parchment, rather than being rolled, were stacked and bound at one end—creating the book format that you're holding right now.

Back outside, notice the triple-arched **gate** next to the library. This area was part of another library complex that included a lecture hall (now destroyed). The gate (rebuilt in 1989) is inscribed

in bronze letters with two names: Mazaeus and Mithridates. These were slaves who, freed by their master Emperor Augustus, became wealthy enough to build this gate in appreciation of their liberty.

• *Step through the gate into a huge empty square that was once the...*

⓯ Commercial Agora

This large marketplace was the main supermarket and shopping mall of Ephesus. Like standard agoras throughout the ancient Mediterranean, this was an open

courtyard (360 feet square) surrounded by columns that supported a portico to shade businesses. From the array of shops stocked with goods brought in from the nearby harbor, Ephesians could buy anything they wanted. Engraved marble slabs out front pictured what each shop sold: a cleaver for the butcher, an olive branch for the oil vendor, a fish for the fishmonger, and so on. The raised island of pine trees in the center of this area—nearly seven feet overhead—illustrates how much dirt archaeologists removed when they excavated this part of Ephesus.

• *Walk across the agora (keep parallel to the Marble Road, above you to the right), and follow the crowds up a ramp to the top end of Harbor Road. Fanning out across the hill to your right is the...*

⓰ Great Theater

Before climbing the steps and entering the theater, notice the stones lined up, identified, and awaiting reconstruction. And swing by

the lovely Greek **fountain** (just to the right of the steps leading into the theater), with two graceful, fluted Ionic columns, once an elegant place for theatergoers to stop for water. Dating from Hellenistic Greece, at least a century before Christ, this is one of the oldest structures you'll see at Ephesus. (Its elegant design was obscured when Romans expanded it centuries later.)

Now, climb halfway up the stairs and follow a tunnel-like gallery (perhaps the actors' entry) to your right, which deposits you right on the stage floor.

It's huge. The theater held about 25,000 spectators (possibly the largest anywhere). Since a Roman theater was typically designed to accommodate 10 percent of its city's population, experts guess that ancient Ephesus had 250,000 residents.

Although the theater is partly ruined, the **acoustics** are still so good that performers don't need microphones to be heard (as tour guides and would-be divas love to demonstrate to the delight of sightseers).

Check out the 66 rows, divided into the classes of Roman society. The lower level was reserved for VIPs and the emperor's box. Many seats here were covered in marble, with comfy seatbacks. The middle level held Roman citizens (most middle-class Ephesians). The upper level was bleacher seating for the lower classes—free men and women, and foreigners.

The ancient Greeks built the theater in the third century B.C. When the Romans came, they enlarged and modified it for their particular brand of entertainment, raising the stage and adding a backdrop. They enlarged the stage wall (to 60 feet high) to improve acoustics and framed the stage area with pillars, creating a proscenium. Notice the wall around the orchestra (in front of the stage). When the theater hosted gladiator fights, this wall protected spectators from the action.

In modern times, the theater became a popular venue, presenting concerts by everyone from Sting to Pavarotti (who sang with no microphone in a performance that people still talk about) to Diana Ross. (Concerts have been suspended in recent years, while the theater is retrofitted to prevent vibrations from damaging the structure.)

This theater played a role in the dramatic story of the **Apostle Paul,** who lived in Ephesus about A.D. 52-54. While Christianity's message that all are created equal in God's eyes resonated with "the 99 percent," it threatened and offended that society's elites. Paul also ruffled feathers by strongly denouncing the worship of false idols. Remember that the cult of the goddess Artemis was big business in Ephesus. Artemis idol-carvers didn't like Paul's interference one bit. According to the Bible (Acts 19), they stirred up an angry mob and snatched some of Paul's Christian companions. Shouting "Artemis is great," the rabble-rousers dragged the captured Christians to this theater. Paul wanted to save them, but cooler-headed colleagues held him back. Fortunately, the enraged crowd inside calmed down and spared the Christians from harm.

• *Step back outside the theater. Standing at the top of the steps, look down the big road that once led to the sea (now over three miles away).*

⑰ Harbor Road

In ancient times, most visitors entered Ephesus on this road, which links the city and the harbor. It made a powerful first impression: marble-paved, 35 feet wide, lined with covered sidewalks, and lit with 50 street lamps (a luxury rare in the ancient world). Like the Strip in today's Las Vegas, this was the city's glitzy main drag. The shops along the way sold a dazzling array of goods from around the known world. While the functional Marble Road is rutted with tracks from cart wheels, this showcase boulevard (also known as the Arcadian Way) is in great condition. Ceremonial processions traveled this route, and it was also *the* place in town to promenade—just as families around the Mediterranean still enjoy an evening stroll.

The original **harbor** sat at the far end of this road, a third of a mile away, on an inlet of the distant sea. This was the west end of the Royal Road—the chief thoroughfare of the Roman East—making Ephesus an important port in its day. The harbor gradually silted up over the centuries—first becoming marshland, and then solid ground—leaving today's waterfront miles away. Trade dried up with the harbor, and the city declined. Eventually Ephesus was literally buried and forgotten. Fortunately for us, archaeologists reopened this cultural time capsule and brought the treasures of Ephesus back to life.

• *Your visit to ancient Ephesus is over. To exit, walk down the Harbor Road a short distance, and look for the row of trees on your right. This marks the path (with great photo ops through the trees to the theater) leading to the lower gate, where* **taxis** *await to take you back to* **Kuşadası** *(about 60 TL), to the* **House of the Virgin Mary** *(70 TL round-trip from the lower gate, including 30 minutes of waiting time; from the upper gate, the same trip is about 60 TL), or to the nearby town of* **Selçuk** *(15 TL one-way). The taxi trip between the upper and lower gates is about 15 TL.* **Tour buses** *also wait at the lower gate.*

Remember, if you're taking the **dolmuş** *back to* **Kuşadası***, you can catch it either in Selçuk (if you're going there to see the Ephesus Museum) or along the main road below the lower gate (a 15-minute walk from the lower gate). There is no dolmuş from the upper gate (to Kuşadası, Selçuk, or anywhere else). Note also that there is no public transportation from Ephesus to the House of the Virgin Mary—only taxis.*

EPHESUS

House of the Virgin Mary

According to many observant Christians, the hillside of Mount Koressos above the ancient city of Ephesus is where the Virgin Mary, mother of Jesus Christ, spent the last 11 years of her life. (For the whole story, see the sidebar on the next page.) While the House of the Virgin Mary is a major Catholic pilgrimage site, Muslims also consider this a special place and appreciate Mary as the mother  of a great prophet. They refer to her as "Mother Mary" and to the site as Meryemana (Mother Mary's House).

The experience of visiting the house is powerful to some, underwhelming to others. After twisting up a high road above Ephesus, you'll pay 12.50 TL per person to enter the parking lot (same hours as the Ephesus site). Leave your taxi and walk through the beautiful **garden,** on a path lined with olive trees. You'll pass a large hole in the ground, which may have been a cistern (see the water pipes buried in the ground) or a baptistery. Then you reach an outdoor amphitheater, where priests celebrate outdoor Mass.

The stone **house** itself—a rebuilt shrine on the original foundations—is small and humble. The earlier structure was likely a typical Roman house—two stories, made of stone, and with four or five rooms. The red line on the outside wall marks the house's first foundation. Inside, devoted visitors shuffle through and say a prayer. The house has two rooms open to sightseers: the large living room and the small bedroom.

Down the hill in front is a wall of spouting **fountains.** The natural spring water is blessed as holy water, which the faithful believe has healing powers. The wishing wall nearby is full of tissues and notes with requests for the Virgin Mary.

Mary in Ephesus?

When Jesus saw his mother and the disciple whom he loved standing nearby, he said to his mother, "Woman, behold, your son!" Then he said to the disciple, "Behold, your mother!" And from that hour the disciple took her to his own home.
John 19:26-27

Christian belief is split on where Mary lived late in life: Jerusalem or Ephesus? Adherents of the Ephesus tradition think she may have come here with the Apostle John, to whom Jesus had entrusted his mother (see biblical passage above). Believers offer these details: After Jesus' death, the Apostle John was sent to convert the pagans of Rome's province of Asia. He came to its capital, Ephesus—and, because of Jesus' commission, he likely would have brought Mary. To avoid antagonizing the local population of pagan Artemis-worshippers, Mary lived in a house on Mount Koressos, high above the city. After 11 years, Mary was taken up into heaven (the Assumption).

Another piece of evidence that Mary lived here, say the faithful, is the existence of the Church of the Virgin Mary in the city of Ephesus (now in ruins). During the early years of Christianity, such churches were only dedicated to people who lived or died in the immediate area.

During Byzantine times (fifth and sixth centuries), "Mary's house" was converted into a chapel but sustained damage in various earthquakes. The house—and the specifics of the story surrounding it—gradually crumbled over the centuries. And yet, a ragtag band of local Christians still venerated this place. For reasons that even they were unsure of, every 10 years they would

Selçuk

The sleepy town of Selçuk is the modern-day descendant of Ephesus. It's an unexceptional but pleasant small Turkish town with a pair of important sights: the Ephesus Museum (collecting artifacts from the ancient site nearby; possibly closed for renovation in 2014), in the center of town; and the foundations of the Basilica of St. John, on a hilltop a five-minute walk beyond the museum.

Selçuk's **TI** is in front of the museum (Mon-Fri 8:30-12:00 & 13:00-17:30, closed Sat-Sun, shorter hours off-season, tel. 232/892-6328). **Taxis** wait nearby (the ride between Selçuk and Kuşadası should be about 50 TL—if your cabbie says it's more, try talking him down). The bus station (where *dolmuş* minibuses arrive and depart constantly, and with plenty of cheap eateries nearby) is a couple of blocks from the museum.

visit the site on August 15—the feast day of the Assumption of Mary.

In the early 1800s, a nun named Anne Catherine Emmerich—who lived halfway across Europe, in Germany, and never set foot in Turkey—had a vision of Mary's house on the slopes of this distant mountain. Decades later, the remains of the house were discovered by priests familiar with Emmerich's visions and the tradition of local reverence for the site. Catholic officials eventually determined that this was the final residence of the Virgin Mary and, in the late 19th century, declared it a place of pilgrimage. The house was restored and opened to visitors in 1951; since then, three sitting popes (Paul VI, John Paul II, and Benedict XVI) have visited here.

Doubters question this entire account. For one thing, biblical scholars believe that John the Apostle, John the Evangelist (who wrote the gospel), and John the Prophet (a.k.a. John of Patmos, who wrote the Book of Revelation) were most likely three different people, whom early church fathers mistakenly amalgamated into a single person. Based on hard historical evidence, only John the Prophet is certain to have spent time in Ephesus. And even if the various Johns were one and the same, the Bible isn't entirely explicit about precisely who became Mary's caretaker—that person is identified only as "the disciple whom [Jesus] loved." And the only gospel to relate this story at all was the one attributed to—guess who?—John. Is the story possible? Yes. Probable? No.

But if you do believe that this really was Mary's final home, it's comforting to imagine that, after a tumultuous life, she was able to retire in such a tranquil setting.

Sights in Selçuk

Ephesus Museum

There's no actual museum at the ancient site of Ephesus, so if you want to see some of the artifacts found there, this is your best opportunity. Unfortunately, this museum may be closed for renovation in 2014. While not critical, a visit here can round out your understanding of Ephesus.

Cost and Hours: 5 TL, daily April-late Oct 8:00-19:30, off-season until 17:30.

◉ Self-Guided Tour: The U-shaped museum has six rooms.

Room 1 displays findings from the **Terrace Houses**, including some original frescoes and mosaics, as well as medical tools, cosmetics, and jewelry. In the middle of the room is an ivory frieze, reassembled from tiny fragments, showing war preparations under Emperor Trajan (second century A.D.). The statue in the niche (far corner of room) depicts Artemis as a hunter. While Roman-era iconography depicts "Diana" (as they called her) this way, we'll see the local interpretation of her later.

In Room 2, you'll see various **statues** that filled the niches at some of the fountains at Ephesus, including the Fountain of Trajan. The backgammon boards carved into the marble show that this game, invented by the Persians and still popular among Turks today, was adopted and enjoyed by Romans.

Room 3 is the **Eros** (Cupid) Room—many items here (frescoes, statues, and so on) are decorated with the lovesick little cher-

ub. From here you pass along the end of an outdoor courtyard and follow arrows into Room 4. But first browse through the courtyard to see a sundial that once sat in Ephesus' marketplace and some sarcophagi from excavated cemeteries.

Room 4 collects **tomb findings** from different historical periods. Look for the diagram explaining nine different historical burial methods. This collection of tomb pottery, weapons, and glass dates from a time when you *could* take it with you—which made these graves a big target for looters and tomb raiders. To the left of the stairs, notice the display with five pre-Greek/pre-Roman depictions of the **mother-goddess** (the prototype for Artemis-Diana, and arguably even Mary); for more on this evolution, see page 1217.

Speaking of the mother-goddess, Room 5 shows off the collection's highlight (on the left)—a larger-than-life, first-century A.D. statue of **Artemis** (from the Prytaneion, the "eternal flame" temple at Ephesus). Whether the bulbous orbs hanging from her torso are eggs, breasts, or bull testicles, they certainly represent fertility. Notice how she is surrounded by the wild animals she's thought to rule over. Her headdress resembles the Temple of Artemis (a model of that temple is in the middle of the room). Looking down into the model and seeing where the statue once stood,

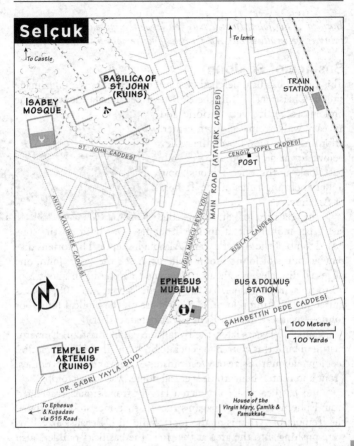

you can imagine the wonder of the place. Across the room is a smaller, later (second century A.D.) statue of Artemis, which has similar themes (many breasts, wild animals)—but adds a new one, the signs of the zodiac around her neck.

Finally, in Room 6, you'll see exhibits about the **emperors,** who

were venerated as gods. Immediately left of the entry, see the original frieze from the Temple of Hadrian, with Androklos chasing the boar of the Ephesian founding legend, along with the head and forearm of a 23-foot-tall statue of Domitian (from his namesake temple near the upper gate), and busts of various other emperors.

• *To get from the museum to the*

Basilica of St. John, turn left as you leave the museum and hike five minutes, generally uphill. Ask for help if you're not sure of the way.

Basilica of St. John

This ruined basilica, perched on a hill over Selçuk, is a pilgrimage site for Christians. While there's little to see here (aside from some broken walls), it's very historic and an easy walk from the town center, affording fine views over the valley below. From here, you also get your best look at the once famous, now underwhelming ruins of the Temple of Artemis.

The Basilica of St. John—the last great monument of ancient Ephesus—was built on the supposed tomb of the Apostle John. Although skeptical historians dispute accounts of John's life in Ephesus, here's the story: John, one of Jesus' disciples, is said to have come to Ephesus in about A.D. 90 to preach the gospel. When John died about A.D. 100, he was buried at this hilltop location. (For more on the biblical John—or Johns—see the "Mary in Ephesus?" sidebar, earlier.)

Some 400 years later, the Byzantine (and Christian) Emperor Justinian built this church to venerate St. John. The church was 360 feet long (about the size of Westminster Abbey) and had six domes. Front and center, beneath the central dome, was John's tomb.

The basilica was constructed largely from stones scavenged from Ephesus and from a pagan structure that once stood nearby—the Temple of Artemis at the foot of the hill. Because Muslims were pushing into the area at the time, the basilica's builders also erected a castle nearby, with walls extending down to encompass the basilica. Ultimately the walls failed to protect the hilltop; the Muslims took over and converted the basilica into a mosque (you can just make out the top of its minaret, without its pointy cap), before it was damaged by an earthquake and fell into disrepair.

Today visitors can pay 5 TL to walk through the rubble (daily mid-March-late Oct 8:00-19:30, off-season until 17:30). The supposed site of St. John's tomb is marked by a marble slab and four pillars, representing the four Evangelists. You'll also see the baptistery's plunge pool and (in the little chapel in the left transept—protected in a brown wooden hut labeled *treasury*) some frescoes of Jesus, Mary, and St. John.

From the viewpoint terrace in front of the basilica ruins, in one glimpse, you can take in the full 3,000-year sweep of this region's spiritual history: the Christian basilica ruins; the more recent Muslim **İsabey Mosque** complex at the foot of the hill ("İsabey"

What If I Miss My Boat?

Remember that you can get help from the cruise line's port agent (listed on the destination information sheet distributed on the ship) and the local TI (see page 1207). If the port agent suggests a costly solution (such as a private car with a driver), you may want to consider public transit.

If your next stop is **Istanbul,** all connections are through the city of İzmir, about an hour and a half north of Kuşadası; a train runs several times daily from Selçuk to İzmir's airport (station name: A. Menderes) and to İzmir (station name: Basmane). From İzmir, you can continue by train (there's an overnight connection from İzmir to Istanbul, with a change in Eskişehir) or plane (İzmir and Istanbul are connected by frequent flights).

If you're heading for the **Greek islands,** your gateway will be the island of Samos, which is connected to Kuşadası by a daily ferry. From Samos, boats go to Piraeus (Athens) as well as various Greek islands.

If you're in a hurry to reach **Athens,** consider flying instead (via İzmir).

Any **travel agent** can help you. For more advice on what to do if you miss the boat, see page 140.

means Jesus, who is considered by Muslims to be a prophet); and the pagan temple ruins in the distance.

Those ruins—the **Temple of Artemis**—first put Ephesus on the tourist map. Today the site is marked by a lone rebuilt pillar, one of the 127 that once supported a huge structure that was completed in Greek times (about 550 B.C.). The ancients considered the fabled temple one of the Seven Wonders of the World. Financed by the famously wealthy King Croesus, the marble temple rose five stories high and was about three times as big as Athens' Parthenon—making it the ancient Greeks' all-around largest building. A giant statue of Artemis presided over an opulent interior adorned with marble, paintings, gold, and silver, which drew pilgrims and tourists from throughout the ancient world. In 356 B.C., the temple was burned by a man named Herostratus, who was desperate to become famous at any cost (a motive still called "Herostratic fame" today). The Ephesians rebuilt and enlarged it, then had to rebuild it once more after the Goths trashed it. When the first Christian missionaries (including St. John) came here in the first century A.D., they met resistance from locals who were still worshipping Artemis.

But soon Christians had the upper hand in Ephesus. In A.D. 401, the temple was destroyed for good by order of Christian authorities intent on stamping out paganism. The structure lay buried

EPHESUS

for 17 centuries, until archaeologists came prospecting. Their goal was not so much the city of Ephesus as it was this legendary structure—the place where, for centuries, the faithful worshipped the goddess Artemis.

At the Basilica of St. John, a plaque commemorates the 1967 visit of Pope Paul VI. That was a big year for tourism for this region. With the papal acceptance of the legitimacy of the "House of the Virgin Mary," Ephesus was suddenly a major destination. The next year, Kuşadası built the pier your ship is tied to...and today, this is a major cruise port.

Turkish Survival Phrases

When using the phonetics, pronounce "ı" as the long "i" sound in "light";
"ew" as "oo" (with your lips pursed); and "g" as the hard "g" in "go."

English	Turkish	Pronunciation
Hello.	Merhaba.	mehr-hah-bah
Good day.	İyi günler.	ee-yee gewn-lehr
Good morning.	Günaydın.	gew-nī-duhn
Good evening.	İyi akşamlar.	ee-yee ahk-shahm-lahr
How are you?*	Nasılsınız?	nah-suhl-suh-nuhz
Do you speak English?	İngilizce biliyormusunuz?	een-gee-leez-jeh bee-lee-yohr-moo-soo-nooz
Yes. / No.	Evet. / Hayır.	eh-veht / hah-yur
I understand.	Anlıyorum.	ahn-luh-yoh-room
I don't understand.	Anlamıyorum.	ahn-lah-muh-yoh-room
Please.	Lütfen.	lewt-fehn
Thank you (very much).	Teşekkür (ederim).	teh-shehk-kewr (eh-deh-reem)
I'm sorry.	Üzgünüm.	ewz-gew-newm
Excuse me. (to pass)	Afedersiniz. / Pardon.	ah-feh-dehr-see-neez / pahr-dohn
No problem.	Sorun yok.	soh-roon yohk
There is a problem.	Sorun var.	soh-roon vahr
Good.	İyi.	ee-yee
Goodbye. (said by person leaving)	Hoşçakal.	hohsh-chah-kahl
Goodbye. (said by person staying)	Güle güle.	gew-leh gew-leh
one / two	bir / iki	beer / ee-kee
three / four	üç / dört	ewch / dirt
five / six	beş / altı	behsh / ahl-tuh
seven / eight	yedi / sekiz	yeh-dee / seh-keez
nine / ten	dokuz / on	doh-kooz / ohn
How much is it?	Ne kadar?	neh kah-dahr
Write it?	Yazarmısınız?	yah-zahr-muh-suh-nuhz
Is it free?	Ücretsizmi?	ewj-reht-seez-mee
Is it included?	Dahilmi?	dah-heel-mee
Where can I find...?	Nerede bulurum...?	neh-reh-deh boo-loo-room
Where can I buy...?	Nereden alabilirim...?	neh-reh-dehn ah-lah-bee-lee-reem
I'd like / We'd like...	İstiyorum / İstiyoruz...	ees-tee-yoh-room / ees-tee-yoh-rooz
...a room.	...oda.	oh-dah
...a ticket to ___.	...___'ya bilet.	___ yah bee-leht
Is it possible?	Olasımı?	oh-lah-suh-muh
Where is...?	...nerede?	neh-reh-deh
...the train station	Tren istasyonu...	trehn ees-tahs-yoh-noo
...the bus station	Otobüs durağı...	oh-toh-bews doo-rah-uh
...the tourist information office	Turizm enformasyon bürosu...	too-reezm ehn-fohr-mahs-yohn bew-roh-soo
...the toilet	Tuvalet...	too-vah-leht
men / women	bay / bayan	bī / bah-yahn
left / right	sol / sağ	sohl / saah
straight	doğru	doh-roo
What time does this open / close?	Ne zaman açılıyor / kapanıyor?	neh zah-mahn ah-chuh-luh-yohr / kah-pah-nuh-yohr
At what time?	Ne zaman?	neh zah-mahn
Just a moment.	Bir saniye.	beer sah-nee-yeh
now / soon / later	şimdi / birazdan / sonra	sheem-dee / bee-rahz-dahn / sohn-rah
today / tomorrow	bugün / yarın	boo-gewn / yah-ruhn

*People will answer you by saying, "Teşekkür ederim" (Thank you very much).

In a Turkish Restaurant

English	Turkish	Pronunciation
restaurant	*lokanta / restaurant*	loh-kahn-tah / rehs-toh-rahnt
I'd like / We'd like to make a reservation.	*Rezervasyon yapmak istiyorum / istiyoruz.*	reh-zehr-vahs-yohn yahp-mahk ee-stee-yoh-room / ees-tee-yoh-rooz
One / Two persons.	*Bir / İki kişilik.*	beer / ee-kee kee-shee-leek
Non-smoking.	*Sigarasız.*	see-gah-rah-suhz
Is this table free?	*Bu masa boşmu?*	boo mah-sah bohsh-moo
The menu (in English), please.	*(İngilizce) menü lütfen.*	een-ghee-leez-jeh meh-new lewt-fehn
tax included	*KDV hariç*	kah-deh-veh hah-reech
tax not included	*KDV değil*	kah-deh-veh deh-eel
service included	*servis hariç*	sehr-vees hah-reech
service not included	*servis değil*	sehr-vees deh-eel
"to go"	*Paket*	pah-keht
and / or	*ve / veya*	veh / veh-yah
menu	*menü*	meh-new
daily menu / meal of the day	*günün menüsü / günün yemeği*	gew-newn meh-new-sew / gew-newn yeh-meh-ee
portion / half-portion	*porsiyon / yarım porsiyon*	pohr-see-yohn / yah-ruhm pohr-see-yohn
daily special	*günün spesyali*	gew-newn spehs-yah-lee
appetizers	*meze*	meh-zeh
bread	*ekmek*	ehk-mehk
cheese	*peynir*	peh-neer
sandwich	*sandöviç*	sahn-doh-veech
soup	*çorba*	chohr-bah
salad	*salata*	sah-lah-tah
meat	*et*	eht
poultry	*tavuk*	tah-vook
fish	*balık*	bah-luhk
seafood	*deniz ürünleri*	deh-neez ew-rewn-leh-ree
fruit	*meyve*	mey-veh
vegetables	*sebze*	sehb-zeh
dessert	*tatlı*	taht-luh
water	*su*	soo
milk	*süt*	sewt
orange juice	*portakal suyu*	pohr-tah-kahl soo-yoo
coffee	*kahve*	kahh-veh
tea	*çay*	chī
wine	*şarap*	shah-rahp
red / white	*kırmızı / beyaz*	kuhr-muh-zuh / beh-yahz
beer	*bira*	bee-rah
glass / bottle	*bardak / şişe*	bahr-dahk / shee-sheh
big / small	*büyük / küçük*	bew-yewk / kew-chewk
Cheers!	*Şerefe!*	sheh-reh-feh
more / another	*biraz daha / bir tane daha*	bee-rahz dah-hah / beer tah-neh dah-hah
The same.	*Aynısından.*	ī-nuh-suhn-dahn
Bill, please.	*Hesap, lütfen.*	heh-sahp lewt-fehn
tip	*bahşiş*	bah-sheesh
Delicious!	*Nefis!*	neh-fees

APPENDIX

Contents

Tourist Information

Tourist Information Offices

Before your trip, scan the websites of national tourist offices for the countries you'll be visiting, or contact them to briefly describe your trip and request information. Some will mail you a general-interest brochure, and you can often download many other brochures free of charge.

Spain: www.spain.info
France: www.franceguide.com
Italy: www.italia.it
Croatia: http://us.croatia.hr
Greece: www.visitgreece.gr
Turkey: www.goturkey.com

In Europe, a good first stop in a new town is the official tourist information office (abbreviated **TI** in this book). TIs are usually good places to get a city map and information on public transit (including bus and train schedules), walking tours, and special events. But be wary of the travel agencies or special information services that masquerade as TIs but serve fancy hotels and tour companies. They're in the business of selling things you don't need.

Travel Advisories

For up-to-date information on health and security abroad, check these helpful resources before leaving on your cruise.

US Department of State: Tel. 888-407-4747, from outside US tel. 1-202-501-4444, www.travel.state.gov

Canadian Department of Foreign Affairs: Canadian tel. 800-387-3124, from outside Canada tel. 1-613-996-8885, www.travel.gc.ca

US Centers for Disease Control and Prevention: Tel. 800-CDC-INFO (800-232-4636), www.cdc.gov/travel

Telephoning

Smart travelers use the telephone to get tourist information, reserve restaurants, confirm tour times, and phone home. For details on your options for making calls—both from a cruise ship and from mobile phones—see page 87. For more in-depth information, see www.ricksteves.com/phoning.

For emergency telephone numbers, see the Practicalities sidebar at the beginning of each destination's chapter.

How to Dial

Calling from the US to Europe, or vice versa, is simple—once you break the code. The European calling chart on the next pages will walk you through it.

No matter where you're calling from, to dial internationally you must first dial the international access code of the place you're calling from (to "get out" of the domestic phone system), and then the country code of the place you're trying to reach.

The US and Canada have the same international access code: 011. Virtually all of Europe, including Turkey, has its own shared international access code: 00. You might see a + in front of a European number; that's a reminder to dial the access code of the place you're calling from. If you're calling from a mobile phone, you can simply insert a "+" before the number—no additional access code required.

Each country has its own country code; you'll see those listed in the European calling chart. Specific dialing instructions for each country are also included in the Practicalities sidebar at the beginning of each destination's chapter.

APPENDIX

Transportation

While in port, you're likely to use public transportation to get around (and, in some cases, to get to) the cities you're here to see.

Taxis

Taxis are underrated, scenic time-savers that zip you effortlessly from the cruise terminal to any sight in town, or between sights. Especially for couples and small groups who value their time, a taxi ride can be a good investment. Unfortunately, many predatory taxi drivers prey on cruisers who are in town just for the day by charging them inflated fares for short rides. Prepare yourself by reading the "Taxi Tips" on page 124.

City Transit

Shrink and tame big cities by mastering their subway, bus, and tram systems. Europe's public-transit systems are so good that many Europeans go through life never learning to drive. With a map, anyone can decipher the code to cheap and easy urban transportation.

Subway Basics

Most of Europe's big cities are blessed with an excellent subway system, often linked effortlessly with suburban trains. Learning a city's network of underground trains is a key to efficient sightseeing. European subways go by many names, but "Metro" is the most common term.

Plan your route. Figure out your route before you enter the station so you can march confidently to the correct train. Get a good subway map (often included on free city maps, or ask for one at the station) and consult it often. In the stations, maps are usually posted prominently. A typical subway map is a spaghetti-like tangle of intersecting, colorful lines. Some cities, like Rome, have just two lines, while Barcelona has eight. Individual lines are color-coded, numbered, and/or lettered; their end points are also indicated. These end points—while probably places you will never go—are important, since they tell you which direction the train is moving and appear (usually) as the name listed on the front of the train. Figure out the line you need, the end point of the direction you want to go, and (if necessary) where to transfer to another line.

Validate your ticket. You may need to insert your ticket into a slot in the turnstile (then retrieve it) in order to validate it. If you have an all-day or multi-day ticket, you may only need to validate it the first time you use it, or not at all (ask when you buy it).

Get off at the right place. Once on the train, follow along with each stop on your map (some people count stops). Sometimes the driver or an automated voice announces the upcoming stop—

European Calling Chart

Just smile and dial, using this key:
AC = Area Code, LN = Local Number.

European Country	Calling long distance within ...	Calling from the US or Canada to ...	Calling from a European country to ...
Austria	AC + LN	011 + 43 + AC (without initial zero) + LN	00 + 43 + AC (without initial zero) + LN
Belgium	LN	011 + 32 + LN (without initial zero)	00 + 32 + LN (without initial zero)
Bosnia-Herzegovina	AC + LN	011 + 387 + AC (without initial zero) + LN	00 + 387 + AC (without initial zero) + LN
Croatia	AC + LN	011 + 385 + AC (without initial zero) + LN	00 + 385 + AC (without initial zero) + LN
Czech Republic	LN	011 + 420 + LN	00 + 420 + LN
Denmark	LN	011 + 45 + LN	00 + 45 + LN
Estonia	LN	011 + 372 + LN	00 + 372 + LN
Finland	AC + LN	011 + 358 + AC (without initial zero) + LN	999 (or other 900 number) + 358 + AC (without initial zero) + LN
France	LN	011 + 33 + LN (without initial zero)	00 + 33 + LN (without initial zero)
Germany	AC + LN	011 + 49 + AC (without initial zero) + LN	00 + 49 + AC (without initial zero) + LN
Gibraltar	LN	011 + 350 + LN	00 + 350 + LN
Great Britain & N. Ireland	AC + LN	011 + 44 + AC (without initial zero) + LN	00 + 44 + AC (without initial zero) + LN
Greece	LN	011 + 30 + LN	00 + 30 + LN
Hungary	06 + AC + LN	011 + 36 + AC + LN	00 + 36 + AC + LN
Ireland	AC + LN	011 + 353 + AC (without initial zero) + LN	00 + 353 + AC (without initial zero) + LN
Italy	LN	011 + 39 + LN	00 + 39 + LN

European Country	Calling long distance within ...	Calling from the US or Canada to ...	Calling from a European country to ...
Latvia	LN	011 + 371 + LN	00 + 371 + LN
Montenegro	AC + LN	011 + 382 + AC (without initial zero) + LN	00 + 382 + AC (without initial zero) + LN
Morocco	LN	011 + 212 + LN (without initial zero)	00 + 212 + LN (without initial zero)
Netherlands	AC + LN	011 + 31 + AC (without initial zero) + LN	00 + 31 + AC (without initial zero) + LN
Norway	LN	011 + 47 + LN	00 + 47 + LN
Poland	LN	011 + 48 + LN	00 + 48 + LN
Portugal	LN	011 + 351 + LN	00 + 351 + LN
Russia	8 + AC + LN	011 + 7 + AC + LN	00 + 7 + AC + LN
Slovakia	AC + LN	011 + 421 + AC (without initial zero) + LN	00 + 421 + AC (without initial zero) + LN
Slovenia	AC + LN	011 + 386 + AC (without initial zero) + LN	00 + 386 + AC (without initial zero) + LN
Spain	LN	011 + 34 + LN	00 + 34 + LN
Sweden	AC + LN	011 + 46 + AC (without initial zero) + LN	00 + 46 + AC (without initial zero) + LN
Switzerland	LN	011 + 41 + LN (without initial zero)	00 + 41 + LN (without initial zero)
Turkey	AC (if there's no initial zero, add one) + LN	011 + 90 + AC (without initial zero) + LN	00 + 90 + AC (without initial zero) + LN

- The instructions above apply whether you're calling to or from a European landline or mobile phone.
- If calling from any mobile phone, you can replace the international access code with "+" (press and hold 0 to insert it).
- The international access code is 011 if you're calling from the US or Canada.
- To call the US or Canada from Europe, dial 00, then 1 (country code for US and Canada), then the area code and number. In short, 00 + 1 + AC + LN = Hi, Mom!

but don't count on this cue, as a foreign name spoken by a native speaker over a crackly loudspeaker can be difficult to understand. As you pull into each station, its name will be posted prominently on the platform or along the wall.

Transfer. Changing from one subway line to another can be as easy as walking a few steps away to an adjacent platform—or a bewildering wander via a labyrinth of stairs and long passageways. Fortunately, most subway systems are clearly signed—just follow along (or ask a local for help).

Exit the station. When you arrive at your destination station, follow exit signs up to the main ticketing area, where you'll usually find a posted map of the surrounding neighborhood to help you get your bearings. Individual exits are signposted by street name or nearby landmarks. Bigger stations have multiple exits. Choosing the right exit will help you avoid extra walking and crossing busy streets.

Bus and Tram Basics

Getting around town on the city bus or tram system has some advantages over subways. Buses or trams are often a better bet for shorter distances. Some buses go where the subway can't. Since you're not underground, it's easier to stay oriented and get the lay of the land. In fact, some public bus routes are downright scenic—Rome's cute *elettrico* minibus #116 winds you through the medieval core of the city for €1.50. The obvious disadvantage of buses and trams is that they're affected by traffic, so avoid them during rush hour.

Plan your route. Tourist maps often indicate bus and tram lines and stops. If yours doesn't, ask for a specific map at the TI. Many bus and tram stops have timetables and route maps posted, and some have electronic signs noting how many minutes until the next bus or tram arrives.

Validate your ticket. Tickets are checked on European buses and trams in a variety of ways. Usually you enter at the front of the bus or tram and show your ticket to the driver, or validate it by sticking it in an automated time-stamp box. In some cases, you buy your ticket directly from the driver; other times, you'll buy your ticket at a kiosk or automated machine near the bus stop. Observe and imitate what the locals do.

Trains

If you venture beyond your port city, European trains generally go where you need them to go and are fast, frequent, and affordable. "Point-to-point" or buy-as-you-go tickets can be your best bet for short travel distances anywhere. (If you're doing a substantial amount of pre- or post-cruise travel on your own, a railpass can be a good value.) You can buy train tickets either from home, or once you get to Europe. If your travel plans are set, and you don't want to risk a specific train journey selling out, it can be smart to get your tickets before your trip. For details on buying tickets on European websites and complete railpass information, see www.ricksteves.com/rail. To study ahead on the Web, check www.bahn.com (Germany's excellent Europe-wide timetable).

If you want to be more flexible, you can keep your options open by buying tickets in Europe. Nearly every station has old-fashioned ticket windows staffed by human beings, usually marked by long lines. Bridge any communication gap by writing out your plan: destination city, date (European-style: day/month/year), time (if you want to reserve a specific train), number of people, and first or second class.

To get tickets faster, savvy travelers figure out how to use automated ticket machines: Choose English, follow the step-by-step instructions, and swipe your credit card (though you may need to know your PIN, and some machines don't accept American cards unless they have an electronic chip—see page 131). Some machines accept cash. It's often possible to buy tickets on board the train, but expect to pay an additional fee for the convenience.

Seat reservations guarantee you a place to sit on the train, and can be optional or required depending on the route and train. Reservations are required for any train marked with an "R" in the schedule. Note that seat reservations are already included with many tickets, especially for the fastest trains (such as France's TGV, Le Frecce in Italy, or AVE in Spain). But for many trains (local, regional, interregional, and many EuroCity and InterCity trains), reservations are not necessary and not worth the trouble and expense unless you're traveling during a busy holiday period.

Be aware that many cities have more than one train station. Ask for help and pay attention. Making your way through stations and onto trains is largely a matter of asking questions, letting people help you, and assuming things are logical. I always ask someone on the platform if the train is going where I think it is (point to the train or track and ask, *"Roma?"*).

Buses

In most countries, trains are faster, more comfortable, and have more extensive schedules than buses. But in some countries—especially Greece, Turkey, and parts of Croatia and Spain—buses are often the better (or only) option. Use buses mainly to pick up where Europe's great train system leaves off.

Resources

Resources from Rick Steves

Rick Steves' Mediterranean Cruise Ports is one of many books in my series on European travel, which includes country guidebooks, city guidebooks (including Rome, Venice, Florence, Istanbul, Athens, and more), Snapshot Guides (excerpted chapters from my country guides), Pocket Guides (full-color little books on big cities such as Barcelona, Rome, Florence, Venice, and Athens), and my budget-travel skills handbook, *Rick Steves' Europe Through the Back Door*. Most of my titles are available as ebooks. My phrase books—for Spanish, French, Italian, German, and Portuguese—are practical and budget-oriented. My other books include *Europe 101* (a crash course on art and history designed for travelers); *Northern European Cruise Ports* (how to make the most of your time in port); and *Travel as a Political Act* (a travelogue sprinkled with tips for bringing home a global perspective). A more complete list of my titles appears near the end of this book.

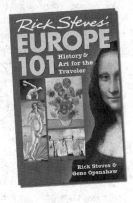

Video: My public television series, *Rick Steves' Europe*, covers European destinations in 100 shows. To watch episodes, see www.ricksteves.com/tv.

Audio: My weekly public radio show, *Travel with Rick Steves*, features interviews with travel experts from around the world. I've

also produced free, self-guided audio tours of the top sights in Florence, Rome, Venice, Athens, and Ephesus—and other great cities. All of this audio content is available for free at Rick Steves Audio Europe, an extensive online library organized by destination. Choose whatever interests you, and download it for free via the Rick Steves Audio Europe smartphone app, www.ricksteves.com/audioeurope, iTunes, or Google Play.

Maps

The black-and-white maps in this book are concise and simple, designed to help you locate recommended places and get to local TIs, where you can pick up more in-depth maps of cities and regions (usually free). Better maps are sold at newsstands and bookstores, though you likely won't need them for a brief port visit. Before you buy a map, look at it to be sure it has the level of detail you want.

Begin Your Trip at ricksteves.com

At our travel website, you'll find a wealth of free information on European destinations, including fresh monthly news and helpful tips from thousands of fellow travelers. You'll also find my latest guidebook updates (www.ricksteves.com/update), a monthly travel enewsletter, my personal travel blog, and my free Rick Steves Audio Europe app (if you don't have a smartphone, you can access the same content via podcasts). You can also follow me on Facebook and Twitter.

Our **online Travel Store** offers travel bags and accessories specially designed by me to help you travel smarter and lighter. These include my popular bags (rolling carry-on and backpack versions), money belts, totes, toiletries kits, adapters, other accessories, and a wide selection of guidebooks, planning maps, and DVDs.

Want to travel with greater efficiency and less stress? We organize free-spirited, small-group **tours** to dozens of Europe's top destinations. Many of our tours begin or end at the major ports of embarkation (Barcelona, Rome, Venice, and Istanbul). Tours such as Venice-Florence-Rome, Rome in Seven Days, Istanbul in Seven Days, Best of Turkey, Barcelona-Madrid, and Spain in 14 Days are great ways to extend your European adventure before or after a cruise. For all the details, and to get our Tour Catalog and a free Rick Steves Tour Experience DVD (filmed on location during an actual tour), visit www.ricksteves.com or call us at 425/608-4217.

Other Resources

If you're like most travelers, this book is all you need. But if you're heading beyond my recommended destinations, $40 for extra maps and books can be money well-spent. There's a staggering array of websites, guidebooks, and other useful resources for people interested in cruising. Every avid cruiser has their favorite go-to site for tips and information, but my list below will help you get started with some of the best-regarded.

Books

For reviews of various cruise lines and ships, refer to my list on page 18. For more destination-specific information, the following books are worthwhile, though are not updated annually; check the publication date before you buy. The Rough Guide and Lonely Planet series, which individually cover various countries and cities included in this book, are both quite good. If choosing between these two titles, I'd buy the one that was published most recently. Lonely Planet's fat, far-ranging *Mediterranean Europe* overview book gives you little to go on for each destination, but their country- and city-specific guides are more thorough.

The colorful Eyewitness series, which focuses mainly on sights, is fun for their great graphics and photos, but relatively skimpy on content, and they weigh a ton. You can buy them in Europe (no more expensive than in the US), or simply borrow a book for a minute from other travelers at certain sights to make sure you're aware of that place's highlights. The tall, green Michelin guides include great maps and lots of solid, encyclopedic coverage of sights, customs, and culture (sold in English in some parts of Europe). The Cadogan guides offer a thoughtful look at the rich and confusing local culture, as does the Culture Shock series.

Beyond the guidebook format, look for the well-written history of the cruise industry, *Devils on the Deep Blue Sea* (by Kristoffer Garin). There's also a variety of tell-all type books offering behind-the-scenes intrigue from a life working on cruise ships. More titillating than well-written, these are good vacation reads to enjoy poolside. They include *Cruise Confidential* (by Brian David Bruns) and *The Truth about Cruise Ships* (by Jay Herring).

Holidays and Festivals

Europe celebrates many holidays that close sights and bring crowds.

Note that the following list isn't complete. Your best source for general information is the TI in each town. Before your trip, you can check with the national tourist offices of the countries you'll be visiting, listed at the beginning of this appendix. It's worth a quick look at websites of your must-see sights to turn up possible holiday closures.

Jan 1	New Year's Day
Jan 6	Epiphany
April 3, 2015	Good Friday
April 5-6, 2015	Easter Sunday and Monday
May 1	Labor Day
May 14, 2015	Ascension
May 24, 2015	Pentecost
May 25, 2015	Whitmonday
June 4, 2015	Corpus Christi
Aug 15	Assumption
Nov 1	All Saint's Day
Nov 11	Armistice Day/St. Martin's Day
Dec 25	Christmas Day
Dec 31	New Year's Eve

Note that many of the above holidays are Catholic and Protestant dates; in Orthodox countries (such as Greece and certain communities in Croatia and Turkey), the dates for these holidays can differ.

Conversions and Climate

Numbers and Stumblers

- Europeans write a few of their numbers differently than we do. 1 = 1, 4 = 4, 7 = 7.
- In Europe, dates appear as day/month/year, so Christmas 2015 is 25/12/15.
- Commas are decimal points and decimals commas. A dollar and a half is $1,50, one thousand is 1.000, and there are 5.280 feet in a mile.
- When counting with fingers, start with your thumb. If you hold up your first finger to request one item, you'll probably get two.
- What Americans call the second floor of a building is the first floor in Europe.
- On escalators and moving sidewalks, Europeans keep the left "lane" open for passing. Keep to the right.

Metric Conversions (approximate)

A kilogram is 2.2 pounds, and 1 liter is about a quart, or almost four to a gallon. A kilometer is six-tenths of a mile. I figure kilometers to miles by cutting them in half and adding back 10 percent of the original (120 km: 60 + 12 = 72 miles, 300 km: 150 + 30 = 180 miles).

1 foot = 0.3 meter	1 square yard = 0.8 square meter
1 yard = 0.9 meter	1 square mile = 2.6 square kilometers
1 mile = 1.6 kilometers	1 ounce = 28 grams
1 centimeter = 0.4 inch	1 quart = 0.95 liter
1 meter = 39.4 inches	1 kilogram = 2.2 pounds
1 kilometer = 0.62 mile	32°F = 0°C

Clothing Sizes

For US-to-European clothing size conversions, see page 135.

APPENDIX

Climate

First line, average daily high; second line, average daily low; third line, average days without rain. For more detailed weather statistics for European destinations (as well as the rest of the world), check www.wunderground.com.

J	F	M	A	M	J	J	A	S	O	N	D

SPAIN
Barcelona

55°	57°	60°	65°	71°	78°	82°	82°	77°	69°	62°	56°
43°	45°	48°	52°	57°	65°	69°	69°	66°	58°	51°	46°
26	23	23	21	23	24	27	25	23	22	24	25

FRANCE
Nice

50°	53°	59°	64°	71°	79°	84°	83°	77°	68°	58°	52°
35°	36°	41°	46°	52°	58°	63°	63°	58°	51°	43°	37°
23	22	24	23	23	26	29	26	24	23	21	21

ITALY
Florence

40°	46°	56°	65°	74°	80°	84°	82°	75°	63°	51°	43°
32°	35°	43°	49°	57°	63°	67°	66°	61°	52°	43°	35°
25	21	24	22	23	21	25	24	25	23	20	24

Rome

52°	55°	59°	66°	74°	82°	87°	86°	79°	71°	61°	55°
40°	42°	45°	50°	56°	63°	67°	67°	62°	55°	49°	44°
13	19	23	24	26	26	30	29	25	23	19	21

Naples

54°	55°	60°	64°	72°	79°	85°	85°	80°	71°	62°	56°
40°	41°	44°	48°	55°	62°	66°	66°	61°	55°	47°	42°
20	19	22	18	25	27	29	28	23	23	17	20

Venice

42°	46°	53°	62°	70°	76°	81°	80°	75°	65°	53°	46°
33°	35°	41°	49°	56°	63°	66°	65°	61°	53°	44°	37°
25	21	24	21	23	22	24	24	25	24	21	23

CROATIA
Dubrovnik

53°	55°	58°	63°	70°	78°	83°	82°	77°	69°	62°	56°
42°	43°	57°	52°	58°	65°	69°	69°	64°	57°	51°	46°
18	15	20	20	20	24	27	28	23	20	14	16

| | J | F | M | A | M | J | J | A | S | O | N | D |

GREECE
Athens

56°	57°	60°	66°	75°	83°	88°	88°	82°	73°	66°	59°
44°	45°	47°	53°	60°	68°	73°	72°	67°	59°	53°	48°
24	22	26	27	28	28	30	30	28	27	24	24

TURKEY
Istanbul

48°	49°	53°	63°	70°	79°	82°	82°	77°	68°	60°	52°
35°	36°	39°	45°	53°	60°	65°	66°	60°	53°	45°	39°
13	14	17	21	23	24	27	27	23	20	16	13

Temperature Conversion: Fahrenheit and Celsius

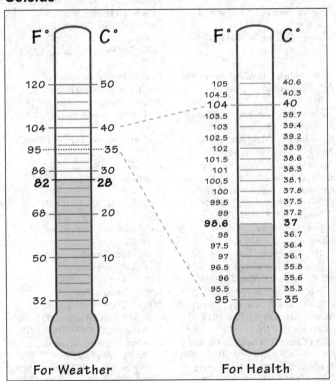

Europe takes its temperature using the Celsius scale, while we opt for Fahrenheit. For a rough conversion from Celsius to Fahrenheit, double the number and add 30. For weather, remember that 28°C is 82°F—perfect. For health, 37°C is just right.

APPENDIX

INDEX

MAP INDEX

Our website enhances this book and turns

Explore Europe

At ricksteves.com you can browse through thousands of articles, videos, photos and radio interviews, plus find a wealth of money-saving travel tips for planning your dream trip. And with our mobile-friendly website, you can easily access all this great travel information anywhere you go.

TV Shows

Preview the places you'll visit by watching entire half-hour episodes of Rick Steves' Europe (choose from all 100 shows) on-demand, for free.

your travel dreams into affordable reality

Radio Interviews

Enjoy ready access to Rick's vast library of radio interviews covering travel

tips and cultural insights that relate specifically to your Europe travel plans.

Travel Forums

Learn, ask, share! Our online community of savvy travelers is a great resource for first-time travelers to Europe, as well as seasoned pros. You'll find forums on each country, plus travel tips and restaurant/hotel reviews. You can even ask one of our well-traveled staff to chime in with an opinion.

Travel News

Subscribe to our free Travel News e-newsletter, and get monthly updates from Rick on what's happening in Europe.

Rick's Free Travel App

Get your FREE **Rick Steves Audio Europe**™ app to enjoy...

- Dozens of self-guided tours of Europe's top museums, sights and historic walks
- Hundreds of tracks filled with cultural insights and sightseeing tips from Rick's radio interviews
- All organized into handy geographic playlists
- For iPhone, iPad, iPod Touch, Android

With Rick whispering in your ear, Europe gets even better.

Find out more at ricksteves.com

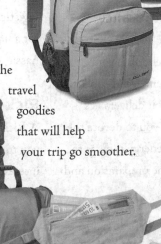

Save time and energy

This guidebook is your independent-travel toolkit. But for all it delivers, it's still up to you to devote the time and energy it takes to manage the preparation and logistics that are essential for a happy trip. If that's a hassle, there's a solution.

Rick Steves Tours

A Rick Steves tour takes you to Europe's most interesting places with great

with minimum stress

guides and small groups of 28 or less. We follow Rick's favorite itineraries, ride in comfy buses, stay in family-run hotels, and bring you intimately close to the Europe you've traveled so far to see. Most importantly, we take away the logistical headaches so you can focus on the fun.

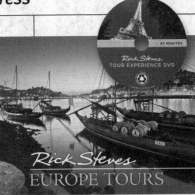

customers—along with us on 40 different itineraries, from Ireland to Italy to Istanbul. Is a Rick Steves tour the right fit for your travel dreams? Find out at ricksteves.com, where you can also get Rick's latest tour catalog and free Tour Experience DVD.

Join the fun

This year we'll take 18,000 free-spirited travelers—nearly half of them repeat

Europe is best experienced with happy travel partners. We hope you can join us.

See our itineraries at ricksteves.com

EUROPE GUIDES

Best of Europe
Eastern Europe
Europe Through the Back Door
Mediterranean Cruise Ports
Northern European Cruise Ports

COUNTRY GUIDES

Croatia & Slovenia
England
France
Germany
Great Britain
Ireland
Italy
Portugal
Scandinavia
Spain
Switzerland

CITY & REGIONAL GUIDES

Amsterdam, Bruges & Brussels
Barcelona
Budapest
Florence & Tuscany
Greece: Athens & the Peloponnese
Istanbul
London
Paris
Prague & the Czech Republic
Provence & the French Riviera
Rome
Venice
Vienna, Salzburg & Tirol

SNAPSHOT GUIDES

Berlin
Bruges & Brussels
Copenhagen & the Best of
  Denmark
Dublin
Dubrovnik
Hill Towns of Central Italy
Italy's Cinque Terre
Krakow, Warsaw & Gdansk
Lisbon
Madrid & Toledo
Milan & the Italian Lakes District
Munich, Bavaria & Salzburg
Naples & the Amalfi Coast
Northern Ireland
Norway
Scotland
Sevilla, Granada & Southern Spain
Stockholm

POCKET GUIDES

Amsterdam
Athens
Barcelona
Florence
London
Paris
Rome
Venice

Rick Steves guidebooks are published by Avalon Travel,
a member of the Perseus Books Group.

NOW AVAILABLE: eBOOKS, DVD & BLU-RAY

TRAVEL CULTURE

Europe 101
European Christmas
Postcards from Europe
Travel as a Political Act

eBOOKS

Nearly all Rick Steves guides are available as eBooks. Check with your favorite bookseller.

RICK STEVES' EUROPE DVDs

11 New Shows 2013–2014
Austria & the Alps
Eastern Europe
England & Wales
European Christmas
European Travel Skills & Specials
France
Germany, BeNeLux & More
Greece, Turkey & Portugal
Iran
Ireland & Scotland
Italy's Cities
Italy's Countryside
Scandinavia
Spain
Travel Extras

BLU-RAY

Celtic Charms
Eastern Europe Favorites
European Christmas
Italy Through the Back Door
Mediterranean Mosaic
Surprising Cities of Europe

PHRASE BOOKS & DICTIONARIES

French
French, Italian & German
German
Italian
Portuguese
Spanish

JOURNALS

Rick Steves Pocket Travel Journal
Rick Steves Travel Journal

PLANNING MAPS

Britain, Ireland & London
Europe
France & Paris
Germany, Austria & Switzerland
Ireland
Italy
Spain & Portugal

RickSteves.com 🅵 🅣 **@RickSteves**

Rick Steves books and DVDs are available at bookstores and through online booksellers.

Photo © Patricia Feaster.

Credits

Contributors

Steve Smith

Steve manages tour planning for Rick Steves' Europe and co-authors the France guidebooks with Rick (as well as this book's coverage of Provence and the French Riviera). Fluent in French, he's lived in France on several occasions starting when he was seven, and has traveled there annually since 1986.

Lale Surmen Aran & Tankut Aran

Istanbul-based Lale and Tankut are co-authors of *Rick Steves' Istanbul* (and this book's Istanbul chapter) and lead tours for Turkish and American groups, including Rick Steves' Europe. They have a passion for unusual travel destinations, and with each trip, they say they become new souls, enriched and enlightened.

Gene Openshaw

Gene is a writer, composer, and lecturer on art and history. Specializing in writing walking tours of Europe's cultural sights (including many featured in this book), Gene has co-authored a dozen of Rick's books. Gene lives near Seattle with his daughter, and roots for the Mariners in good times and bad.

Acknowledgments

This book would not have been possible without the help of our cruising friends. Special thanks to Todd and Carla Hoover, cruisers extraordinaire, and to Sheri Smith at Elizabeth Holmes Travel (www.elizabethholmes.com). Applause for Vanessa Bloy at Windstar Cruises, Paul Allen and John Primeau at Holland America Line, Courtney Recht at Norwegian Cruise Line, and Melissa Rubin at Oceania Cruises. And high fives for Ben Curtis, Sheryl Harris, Paul and Bev Hoerlein, Jenn Schutte, Lisa Friend, and Noelle Kenney.

Images

Full-page image (Mykonos):
Mykonos harbor   Cameron Hewitt
Mykonos   Cameron Hewitt
Full-page image (Santorini):
View of Santorini caldera   Cameron Hewitt
Santorini   Cameron Hewitt
Full-page image (More Greece Ports):
Rhodes market street   Cameron Hewitt
Corfu   Cameron Hewitt
Full-page image (Istanbul):
Hagia Sofia   Carol Ries
Istanbul Docks   Cameron Hewitt
Full-page image (Ephesus):
Library of Celsus   Dominic Bonuccelli
Library of Celsus, Ephesus   Cameron Hewitt